zallaudet Univ Press
4-18-04
15.00

WITHDRAWN

WITHDRAWN

LEARNING RESOURCES CENTER
SANTA FE COMMUNITY COLLEGE

P9-DUA-482

THE
DEAF
WAY

THE DEAF WAY

Perspectives from the International Conference on Deaf Culture

Carol J. Erting
Robert C. Johnson
Dorothy L. Smith
Bruce D. Snider

Editors

Gallaudet University Press ❖ Washington, D.C.

The editors wish to thank AT&T and Ronald McDonald Children's Charities for their generous support of The Deaf Way.

Gallaudet University Press
Washington, DC 20002

© 1994 by Gallaudet University. All rights reserved
Published 1994
Printed in the United States of America

Library of Congress Cataloging-in-Publication Data
International Conference on Deaf Culture (1989 : Washington, D.C.)
The deaf way : perspectives from the International Conference on Deaf Culture / Carol J. Erting . . . [et al.] editors.
p.   cm.
Selected papers from the conference held in Washington, D.C., July 9–14, 1989.
Includes bibliographical references and index.
ISBN 1-56368-026-2 (alk. paper)
1. Deaf—Social conditions—Congresses.   I. Erting, Carol.   II. Title.
III. Title: Deaf culture.
HV2359.I487   1989
305.9'08162—dc20   94-17860
                          CIP

Cover and interior design by Kathy Klingaman

The paper used in this publication meets the minimum requirements of American National Standard for Information Sciences—Permanence of Paper for Printed Library Materials, ANSI Z39.48-1984. ∞

In Memoriam

This book is dedicated to these friends of The Deaf Way whose work was devoted to improving the lives of deaf people around the world:

Ildi Batory (*Hungary/Denmark*)
Jean-François Mercurio (*France*)
Dorothy Miles (*England*)
Laura Rampelli (*Italy*)
Eli Savanick (*United States*)
Manfa Suwanarat (*Thailand*)

Contents

Contents

PART FOUR: *Diversity in the Deaf Community*

PART FIVE: *Deaf Clubs and Sports*

PART SIX: *The Deaf Child in the Family*

PART SEVEN: *Education*

PART EIGHT: *Deaf/Hearing Interaction*

Foreword

MERV GARRETSON

How does one capture on the pages of a book the magic and excitement of The Deaf Way International Conference and Festival? Nearly five years have passed since over 6,000 people from practically every corner of the world converged upon Washington, D.C. the week of July 9–14, 1989, at Gallaudet University and the Omni Shoreham Hotel. And still today, in 1994, the memories linger on.

The Silent News, a leading national monthly publication for deaf people, devoted their entire September 1989 issue to The Deaf Way, replete with pictures and stories and a three-inch headline on the front page: **A W E S O M E**. Immediately below was another huge subhead: **OVER 6,000 JAMMED 1ST WORLD 'CONFEST.'** In providing tremendous and comprehensive coverage of the extraordinary week, the publication's Deaf culture editor, Ann Silver, described the conference as a passport to the international deaf world.

A crowning celebration of the success, skill, and artistry of deaf people, The Deaf Way accentuated the cohesion and sense of identity of deaf people regardless of which part of the world they might be from. Browsing through the papers that will appear in this book reminds me that the events of that week in July continue even at this time to live with crystal clarity in the minds and hearts of the participants and those with whom they have shared this unique experience. It was a time of intense communication and interaction at the Omni Shoreham, at Gallaudet University, and in the huge, colorful, fun-filled international festival tent on the Gallaudet campus. With a total disregard for nationality, religion, and ethnicity, everyone melded into a magic celebration of joy, self-identity, togetherness, and love.

In going through my files to prepare for this Foreword, I could not help recalling the overwhelming detail and logistics that went on backstage during the planning and implementation period. All of this would not have been possible without the 350 people who worked to bring The Deaf Way to fruition over a span of more than two years. The original planning committee began its work in 1987 with the blessing of Gallaudet's President Jerry C. Lee and Provost Catherine Ingold. The first chairman, Ed Corbett, initiated the actual nitty gritty of launching the program, developing a logo and laying the essential groundwork. An important step was setting up an exhibit in Helsinki, Finland, in July 1987, during the tenth conference of the World Federation of the Deaf (WFD). This early publicity helped to alert the 3,000 international WFD participants about the coming Deaf Way spectacle. Later, Corbett was to be succeeded by Michael Karchmer [see Afterword], who continued the momentum until March 1988, when newly appointed President I. King Jordan asked me to take over for the next sixteen months.

Heavy responsibilities fell on a number of Gallaudet staff people, certainly on program cochairpersons Carol J. Erting and Rachel Stone, who carried the charge of identifying and contacting many of the widely diverse key people whose presentations appear in this book. Jane Norman spearheaded the festival portion, assisted by Bob Hiltermann, Paul Singleton, Harvey Goodstein, and many other capable volunteers. Paul Kelly and Chuck Mann of Gallaudet's administration and business division provided outstanding service with campus coordination, made available needed funding, facilitated transportation arrangements, including provision of regularly scheduled shuttlebuses between the Omni Shoreham and Gallaudet, set up campus tents, and took care of many other on-campus necessities.

Annemarie Pittman of Courtesy Associates covered scheduling, registrations, hotel reservations, and the complicated meeting room logistics at the Omni Shoreham Hotel. Eli Savanick and Ethel Pacheco tended to the sticky and endless communications for protocol, embassy clearance, translating of letters, and the always necessary diplomatic contacts. Muriel Strassler assisted with publicity and the daily newsletter during the conference. Extensive TV, captioning, and satellite support were provided through the leadership of Marin Allen, chairperson of the Gallaudet TV Department, and her staff. Roz Rosen, Jo Linder Crow, and others on the staff of Continuing Education assumed responsibility for provision of nursing, medical, infirmary, and housing arrangements for the artistic and theatrical performers arriving from the many participating countries. The intricacies of interpreting and translating fell under the province of Susan Karchmer.

All of this required enormous expenditures. At times, the escalating costs placed severe strains on President Jordan's nervous system. The slow rate of registrations during the early months was also a constant cause of concern and worry, but through it all, President Jordan remained completely supportive and fully sensitive to the importance, impact, and magnitude of this endeavor. Regan Quinn met head-on the challenge of finding funds to help meet expenses. Technical support was coordinated by Mal Grossinger and his aides. Sue Mather worked on the host family program and, with Al Couthen, looked after the children's theater and other activities. And through all the weeks and months of preparation, assistant coordinator Jean Lindquist manned the Deaf Way office on two floors of the Gate House on the campus, keeping track of expenditures, setting up appointments, arranging committee and other special meetings, and meticulously following up on all detail work, frequently working far into the night.

To recall once more the magnitude of The Deaf Way and to share some of the minutiae—eighty-one countries were represented; some 5,000 individuals were officially registered, plus a couple of thousand additional "walk-ons" who mingled with participants in the lobby of the Omni Shoreham Hotel and on the Gallaudet campus; there were 1,000 visual arts performers, 350 interpreters and translators, 16 plenary speeches, 100 artistic performances, 75 film/video shows, 500 scholarly presentations, and an additional 37 poster talks. In the Omni Shoreham's main conference hall (the Regency Ballroom) were three gigantic live video screens, one for instant captioning and the others to make the signs of the interpreters more visible for people in the back of the huge conference hall. Screens were also available in some of the larger meeting rooms. Not to be overlooked was the unforgettable, glittering, starstudded, opening night performance at the Lisner Auditorium, available through satellite TV for simultaneous viewing at Gallaudet by an overflow crowd.

In addition to interested deaf and hearing participants, present at the conference/festival were parents of deaf children, students, deaf and hearing scholars, researchers, linguists, scientists, sociologists, psychologists, and educators. Major funding sponsors were AT&T and Ronald McDonald Children's Charities. Funding also came from many other sources, including government agencies such as the National Endowment for the Arts, foundations, individuals, and corporations like Coca Cola, and from Gallaudet University itself. The conference carried official endorsements from the United States National Association of the Deaf and from the World Federation of the Deaf. International signs were used everywhere, complemented by native signs used by personal interpreters brought by participants from their own countries. Voice translators in French, Spanish, and English were available for those using headsets. Program highlights were broadcast via satellite to Europe and Scandinavia, South America, Canada, and Central America.

The Deaf Way had become a veritable deaf Mecca, a most appropriate follow-up to the Deaf President Now protest that had happened a year earlier, although the DPN had not exactly been planned for! The moving spectacle of Senator Tom Harkin signing his presentation during the opening ceremony brought tears to the eyes of many deaf people from other nations who had never seen a top-ranking politician using their sign language! The positive cultural, linguistic, and artistic talents of deaf people from every corner of the world had come together to create a significant milestone in history.

To give a random sampling of some of the individual and group entertainers from the festival side of The Deaf Way—Phyllis Frelich, Linda Bove, Lydece Campbell, Ed Waterstreet, Yola Rozynek, Marlee Matlin, Terrylene, Gunilla Wagström-Lundqvist, Howie Seago, Julianna Fjeld, Peter Wolf, Amnon Damti, Guy Wonder, Chuck Baird, Tony McKnight, Bob Daniels . . . at campus theaters and the Omni Shoreham Hotel, the multifaceted festival of national theaters of the deaf, the erotic Norwegian production "Mirandolina's Inn," the National Theatre of the Deaf and its "King of Hearts," Bernard Bragg and Eugene Bergmann's "Tales from a Clubroom" . . . comedians Charlie McKinney, Alan Barwiolek, Ricky Smith, the London deaf comedians . . . a mind-boggling panorama of exhibits and fashion, slide, TV, and video shows . . . murals, sculptures, stained-glass creations . . . mime performers, magicians, jugglers, artists, sculptors, folk and professional dancers from the Philippines, Hawaii, Bulgaria, India, Spain, Ecuador, SriLanka, Thailand, and other countries . . . children's theaters—all of these pervaded the campus, the Omni Shoreham, and the Smithsonian Museum Discovery Theatre.

Today, the momentum continues. Mini-Deaf Way conferences have been held in many parts of the United States and in other countries around the world across this time span, especially during the month of September, designated as "deaf awareness month" by the World Federation of the Deaf. Perceptions of deaf people and sign language have become increasingly positive. The number of deaf administrators in education, industry, and government has risen dramatically. Research and experimentation in a variety of areas have gone into high gear. As another small instance of the continuing impact after nearly five years, this year's holiday cards from Dr. Dilip Deshmukh of India were designed with a quotation from the opening ceremonies of The Deaf Way!

The week of July 9–14 in Washington was no tower of Babel. Deaf people have an uncanny knack for communicating with each other, and they did so perfectly at The Deaf Way, in spite of their diverse backgrounds. Most important of all, perhaps, was the sense of peopleness that was everywhere prevalent. This book will provide, in some measure, an enduring documentation of many of the formal presentations. But above and beyond these serious overtones on the reality and vitality of deaf people, on empowerment, advancement, pride, and self-identity, the week was a deaf Woodstock, an exhilarating and unbelievable extravaganza brimming with the wonder of self-fulfillment and realization.

Acknowledgments

So many people contributed to the success of The Deaf Way and, therefore, to the possibility of this volume that it is impossible to name them all. However, the first word of thanks must go to all of the people at Gallaudet University who caught the vision and worked so hard to make it a reality. We also thank all of the presenters who shared their stories at The Deaf Way and then agreed to allow us to include them in this book. Many of the presenters overcame great obstacles to make their contribution.

Putting the conference together was an expensive undertaking and we could not have accomplished it without the financial assistance of a number of organizations. The major sponsors, in addition to Gallaudet University, were AT&T and Ronald McDonald Children's Charities. Without their generosity, The Deaf Way would have been impossible. In addition, we are grateful to the following foundations and organizations for contributions that enabled presenters to travel to the conference: the Wenner-Gren Foundation for Anthropological Research, the Inter-American Foundation, the Voluntary Fund for the United Nations Decade of Disabled Persons, the Mason Perkins Fund, the German Marshall Fund, and Pan American World Airways. Many presenters obtained funding from sources unknown to us, and we wish also to express our gratitude to these unnamed benefactors.

A special word of thanks goes to Dr. Michael Karchmer, Dean of Graduate Studies and Research at Gallaudet University, who made the production of this book possible. His support and encouragement during the years following The Deaf Way kept us going; he was unswerving in his resolve that these papers would be made available to a larger audience. Gallaudet University Press, under the leadership of Dr. Elaine Costello, saw the importance of this undertaking and provided us with invaluable moral support, as well as financial assistance. We thank Dr. Costello and Ivey Pittle Wallace at the Press for their patience during the seemingly interminable process required to develop this document into its present form.

Because papers presented at The Deaf Way could be written in English, Spanish, or French, many papers selected for inclusion in this English volume had to be translated before they could be edited. Staff at *Consultores Asociados S.A.*, Inc. (C.A.S.A.) of Bensalem, Pennsylvania proved invaluable for their many reliable translations of Spanish papers. Carol Macomber of The French Connection (in Media, Pennsylvania) is to be commended for her many rapid, accurate translations of French papers and correspondence into English. On numerous occasions, C.A.S.A. and Ms. Macomber also translated correspondence from the editors to the authors. Silvia Golocovsky of Gallaudet's International Center on Deafness not only translated Spanish correspondence into English, but also provided information vital for contacting foreign authors, particularly Latin American authors, when missing information or permissions were needed. Harry Markowicz from Gallaudet's English Department, helped contact French authors and also translated French correspondence into English. Bernard Mottez, from France, contacted French authors for needed biographical information, and Michel LaMothe provided materials needed for the completion of French papers and helped secure needed permission forms.

Many of the papers in this volume are based partially or entirely on videotapes of signed presentations, for which either no paper or only a synopsis was provided. We wish to thank Jean Lindquist (who was an assistant coordinator of The Deaf Way) for applying her interpreting skills to the task of transcribing American Sign Language presentations into written English. In those cases where images from videotaped presentations were needed to illustrate papers, the technical assistance of Ron Reed of Gallaudet's Television Department and Chun Louie of Gallaudet's Department of Art and Photography were indispensable. Chun Louie also deserves credit for the majority of the photographs that appear in this book. Thanks are also due to Johnston Grindstaff, Barbara Gerner de Garcia, Susan Karchmer, Renato Sindicic, Abdulaziz Al-Obaid and the Saudi Arabian Embassy (in Washington, D.C.), and the Fray Luis Ponce de Leon Society of Ecuador for photos and slides that we have included.

We wish to express particular thanks to Gallaudet University Press for the generous use of its endowment fund to support the editorial work needed for this volume. Among those editors who assisted in the editorial process (including Todd Byrd, Janice Bouck, Donna Chitwood, Deborah Weiner, and Ivey Pittle Wallace), Vickie Walter deserves special recognition for the sheer amount of work she completed. Eileen Mengers is to be commended for her skill and persistence in the enormous task of carefully copyediting the entire manuscript. The editors also wish to thank Jean Stambach and Carlene Thumann-Prezioso for helping them search through the voluminous Deaf Way files for the missing pieces of information needed in the last phase of editing. Thanks also go to Hank Young and Sheryl Johnson for their work in securing revisions and permissions from the many contributors to this volume.

Finally, the editors wish again to thank the hundreds of presenters and thousands of participants whose various, often difficult journeys to The Deaf Way Conference and Festival in 1989 provided the materials and inspiration for this book.

Carol J. Erting
Robert C. Johnson
Dorothy L. Smith
Bruce D. Snider

Introduction

CAROL J. ERTING

What is the Deaf Way? For as long as Deaf[1] people have formed communities, a Deaf way of life has been recognized by Deaf people themselves. These patterns of behavior, attitudes, beliefs, and values have been referred to in American Sign Language as "DEAF TEND (THEIRS)"[2] and in English as the "Deaf world," the "Deaf community," or, more recently "Deaf culture." It has taken much longer for those who do not interact with Deaf people on a regular basis to see and to begin to understand that there are, indeed, vibrant, intricately structured, and richly elaborated Deaf cultures around the world. Perhaps they have been hidden from view because of the traditional labels applied to Deaf people—*handicapped, disabled, hearing impaired*—labels originating from a pathological, medical model rather than a cultural one (Woodward, 1989). This book and the event during which these papers were first presented are evidence that, after centuries of ignorance and oppression, things are changing for Deaf and hearing people alike. Progress is not uniform across the globe, and it is not always steady, but the Deaf Way—the language, culture, history, and art of Deaf people—is beginning to be recognized as the valuable resource that it is. Deaf people are eager to learn about their own heritage and take pride in their accomplishments, and ever-increasing numbers of hearing people are excited about entering into partnerships with them to work toward common goals.

Over a century ago, following the infamous Congress of Milan in 1880 (Lane, 1984; Van Cleve and Crouch, 1989), the assault began in earnest against Deaf communities and their sign languages. Oralism was proclaimed the only acceptable method for educating deaf children since, it was argued, deaf people could only participate in society, develop morally and intellectually, and hold employment if they developed speech. Furthermore, spoken language was promoted as more precise, more abstract, and the only means by which equality with hearing people and communion with God could be achieved. Sign language was viewed as limited to concrete references, too imprecise to convey subtleties and nuances of thought, and incapable of promoting the development of the soul. It was seen as an inferior language in evolutionary terms, unfit for civilized human beings (Baynton, 1993). In addition, proponents of the oral method argued that

---

1 In the introductory portions of this volume, the editors have used "deaf" with a lower case *d* as an adjective referring primarily to the audiological condition of hearing loss and "Deaf" with an upper case *D* as an adjective referring to social groupings and cultural identifications arising from interactions among people with hearing losses. This distinction was explained in greater detail by Erting and Woodward (1979). Use of this convention in the papers in this volume occurs only when explicitly adopted by the authors.

2 This is an English gloss of signs from American Sign Language (ASL). Glosses are words from the written form of a spoken language, written entirely in capital letters to indicate that they are to be regarded as approximate translations of signs.

signing served to set Deaf people apart from society and could not help them learn the written language. These were but a few of the arguments used against the languages and cultures of Deaf people during the Congress that, sadly, continue to be used today by some members of the medical and educational establishment.

After the Congress of Milan deaf teachers were removed from the schools, and sign language was banned in the majority of schools for deaf children. In the United States, where Edward Miner Gallaudet, as President of Gallaudet College, was and continued to be an influential opponent of pure oralism and where the National Association of the Deaf had been established in the same year—1880—the effects of the resolutions passed in Milan were somewhat attenuated. Deaf teachers were not totally eliminated from schools; they were, however, usually assigned to teach older children who were labeled "oral failures," no longer pursuing academic subjects. Gallaudet College, then known as the National Deaf-Mute College, continued to endorse sign language as the appropriate way to teach deaf college students, although E. M. Gallaudet's compromise with the oralists earlier had resulted in his promotion of "the combined method"—oral education for those deaf students for whom it was possible, education through sign language for the rest. Gallaudet's formidable opponent, Alexander Graham Bell, campaigned vigorously for oralism and assimilation and against sign language, intermarriage among deaf people, and residential schools. Deaf leaders organized international congresses to protest oralism and argue in favor of the combined system of instruction, wherein manual language was used as the primary means for educating deaf children. Hearing educators in favor of the oral method prevailed, however, and Deaf people were systematically denied access to their linguistic and cultural heritage and prevented from determining their own destiny. By the 1960s in the United States, Deaf teachers who had once comprised half of all teachers of deaf children were reduced to one-eighth of the total, and most of them were teaching manual trades in a few schools (Lane, 1984; Moores, 1987). In Europe, there were virtually no Deaf teachers in the schools.

Despite the suppression of the sign languages of Deaf communities by means of the educational establishment after 1880, and in spite of efforts to prevent deaf people from associating with one another, Deaf people around the world maintained their languages and their communities. Sign languages were passed on from Deaf parents to their own Deaf children and to other Deaf children at residential schools largely through interaction with their peers and the few Deaf adult employees of the schools. While sign language was banned from the classroom, it was used freely in the dormitories and on the playgrounds of residential schools the world over. Furthermore, Deaf people continued to socialize at their clubs, compete in deaf sports events, publish newspapers and magazines, and work through associations to improve their lives (Van Cleve and Crouch, 1989). Oralism, however, had taken its toll. Academic achievement of deaf children was far from satisfactory, and Deaf people, by and large, thought of their language and themselves as inferior and inadequate, as they had so often been told by those in control of their education.

Then, in 1960, William Stokoe, a professor of English at Gallaudet College, published his monograph entitled *Sign Language Structure*, claiming that the sign language of Deaf Americans was indeed a language with a structure analogous in complexity and richness to the structure of spoken languages yet essentially independent of them (Stokoe, 1960). Stokoe was ridiculed for his position by deaf and hearing colleagues alike, but he persisted in his work. In 1965, with support from the National Science Foundation, the American Council of Learned Societies, and Gallaudet College, and with the collaboration of two Deaf colleagues, he published *A Dictionary of American*

Sign Language, the first dictionary of any sign language based on linguistic principles (Stokoe, Casterline, and Croneberg, 1976). Stokoe's work laid the foundation for a new generation of linguistic studies of sign languages and Deaf communities as well as for a new movement within the educational establishment to bring signing back into the classroom. Deaf and hearing educators referred to this educational strategy as Total Communication—an approach to educating deaf children that, in theory, incorporated any and every means of communication available in order to teach the child (Denton, 1972; Holcomb, 1970). Sign systems, such as Signing Essential English (Anthony, 1971), Signing Exact English (Gustason, Pfetzing, and Zawolkow, 1972), and Signed English (Bornstein, 1975), were developed for use as tools for making English visible to deaf children. In practice, American Sign Language, the language of the Deaf community, was rarely used in the classroom, unless the teacher happened to be Deaf. More commonly, spoken English accompanied by signs for support, continued to be the language of classroom instruction during the two decades that followed the publication of the dictionary. A similar progression of events was occurring in European countries with the advent of Signed Swedish (see Bergman, this volume; see Wallin, this volume), Signed French, Signed Danish (see Hansen, this volume), and so on.

In 1974, Stokoe and his colleagues organized the first symposium on sign language and the deaf community for the annual meeting of the American Anthropological Association. Although it was given a place on the program, only a handful of people attended the symposium. The idea that Deaf people constituted a cultural and linguistic group was still too new to attract the interest of social scientists. During the 1970s, while Total Communication programs were gaining in popularity, a few Deaf and hearing linguists and educators in the United States, Sweden, France, and Denmark began to argue for models of bilingual education to be applied to the education of deaf children (Erting, 1978; Kannapell, 1974; Woodward, 1978; see Bergman, this volume; see Wallin, this volume; see Smith, this volume; see Hansen, this volume). They argued that the natural sign languages of Deaf communities, rather than contrived sign systems designed for the purpose of representing the spoken language, should be used in schools for deaf children. Furthermore, they argued, Deaf teachers should be hired in much greater numbers, not only to teach, but also to be positive role models for young deaf children. A milestone was achieved in 1981 when Sweden became the first country to recognize Swedish Sign Language as the first language of Deaf people in Sweden, and therefore the language to be used as the primary language in the schools for deaf children. Swedish, declared the first foreign language of Deaf Swedes, was to be taught through reading and writing (see Bergman, this volume; see Wallin, this volume).

At the same time that a handful of people were calling for use of the natural sign languages of Deaf people in the classroom, a powerful movement for mainstreaming "handicapped" children—including deaf children—into public school classrooms was occurring. In 1975, the United States Congress enacted Public Law 94–142. This legislation guaranteed all handicapped children the right to free and appropriate education within "the least restrictive environment." For deaf children, the latter was usually interpreted to mean that their education should take place within the local school for normally hearing children with such assistance as was deemed necessary through a process that resulted in an Individualized Education Plan (IEP). One result of this legislation and the ideology behind it was a decrease in enrollment of deaf children in residential and special day schools. For many deaf children for whom sign language is the preferred and only fully accessible language, the mainstreaming movement has not provided "the least restrictive environment." Instead, it has isolated deaf children from their peers, deprived them of adult Deaf role models, and prevented them from acquiring American Sign Language during their formative years. Furthermore, educational achievement has not significantly improved (see Johnson, Liddell, and Erting, this volume). A similar movement for integration of deaf children with their hearing peers occurred in several countries of Western Europe during the late 1970s and 1980s with similar results (e.g., see Corazza, this volume).

In 1987, a commission was established in the United States—and charged by the United States Congress—with evaluating the current status of education for deaf children nationwide. The conclusion of the Commission on Education of the Deaf (COED) (1988) was that the educational system, in all of its forms, had failed to provide appropriate and acceptable levels of achievement for deaf children. They explicitly criticized the system for failing to recognize and utilize American Sign Language and the Deaf community as a resource for education:

> Almost unrecognized is the legitimate status of American Sign Language (ASL) as a full-fledged native minority language to which all of the provisions of the Bilingual Education Act should apply. Also too seldom recognized is the need for a deaf child to have other deaf children as part of his or her peer group, and to be exposed to deaf adults. (1988, p. 9)

During the same year as the release of the COED report, an event occurred at Gallaudet University, the effects of which reverberated around the world. In March 1988, Gallaudet students, supported by deaf and hearing faculty and staff and the deaf community, protested the selection of a hearing woman to become the president of their university (see Malzkuhn et al., this volume). They closed down the campus and insisted upon a reversal of the Board of Trustees' decision, demanding that one of the two deaf candidates for the presidency be selected and that the Board of Trustees be reconstituted with a deaf majority. The Deaf President Now (DPN) movement was successful, and Dr. I. King Jordan was installed as Gallaudet University's first deaf president. President Jordan's message—"Deaf people can do anything except hear"—was heard by the American people and their representatives in Congress, contributing to the enactment of the Americans with Disabilities Act of 1990, legislation designed to ensure full participation of disabled people in American society. DPN was widely covered by the media during the week-long protest and, as numerous papers in this volume demonstrate, the protest and President Jordan's message inspired deaf people around the globe to work for equality and access with renewed hope and an invigorated vision of themselves.

The eighties was a decade of empowerment for deaf people in the United States and other countries such as Sweden and Denmark. It was also a period during which the academic study of sign languages and Deaf communities spread from the few centers of scholarly activity that existed in the 1970s to numerous universities worldwide. The idea for an international meeting to discuss and celebrate the accomplishments and creativity of Deaf communities grew out of this context. Support from the Organization of American States, a NATO postdoctoral fellowship, and Gallaudet had enabled me to travel extensively in Latin America and Western Europe from 1982 to 1986, and during those years I met countless Deaf people who—often against great odds—created political, educational, social, and artistic programs to respond to the needs of their own communities. I also met linguists, psychologists, sociologists, and other scholars who were working with Deaf people to learn more about their languages and ways of life. My wish was that deaf students and colleagues at Gallaudet could all share these enlightening international experiences. When I took the idea of a conference and festival built around the positive achievements of Deaf people back to Gallaudet, Dr. Michael Karchmer, then assistant Dean of the Gallaudet Research Institute, immediately saw the value and importance of such an endeavor. At the same time, the president of Gallaudet, Dr. Jerry Lee, was looking for a theme for an international meeting to be hosted by the university. In the spring of 1987, the first meetings were held to begin planning for this event.

At first, it was difficult to communicate our vision to others. We could see that we were not conveying to them just how pioneering this international meeting had the potential to be. We would build the event around a linguistic and cultural view of Deaf people rather than a pathological view. Furthermore, we would create a state-of-the-art event in terms of its accessibility to an international Deaf, hard of hearing, and hearing audience. It would be planned by Deaf and hearing people working as partners: Deaf people would assume the majority of leadership roles and would comprise the majority of all committees. There would be both a conference and a festival so that participants could experience the Deaf perspective through the arts and discuss and analyze their experiences during conference sessions. For me as a cultural anthropologist, both ways of knowing were essential, since participant-observation is the hallmark of anthropological fieldwork. The goal was for participants to come to know more about what it means to be Deaf and what The Deaf Way is, and participants would include hearing and deaf professionals, families with deaf family members, and grass-roots deaf people. In addition, there would be a commitment to substantial international participation, ensuring that cross-cultural comparison of sign languages and Deaf communities would be on-going. For the planners, that meant an early and continuing commitment to interpretation in American Sign Language and International Sign as well as three official spoken languages (English, Spanish, and French). It also meant accessibility for all through technological advances such as video enhancement of presenters and interpreters by projection of their images onto large screens, the use of real-time captioning, audio loops, and vibrating beepers for conference and festival staff.

What would we call this event? We struggled to find a name for it that would capture the spirit and convey the sense of the event in American Sign Language and English, French, and Spanish. I thought of a class I taught several years before when I had asked the Deaf members of the group to tell us how the concept of Deaf culture or Deaf way of life was expressed in American Sign Language, prior to influence from the English words "culture" or "world." They agreed that the signs glossed as DEAF TEND (THEIRS) and translated into English as "the way Deaf people tend to be, think, or do things" expressed the concept of Deaf culture or Deaf way of life in American Sign Language. "The Deaf Way," signed as DEAF TEND (THEIRS) or simply DEAF (THEIRS), seemed to be the perfect name, one that worked in both ASL and English.

It was an ambitious dream, and we would have to meet many challenges to make the dream a reality. Perhaps the most difficult task was to find a way to pass our vision to others. In the beginning, only a handful of people grasped the idea. One of the difficulties was that the Deaf people who comprised the majority of the planning committees had never experienced this kind of power or control before at Gallaudet. I began to realize, after months had gone by with few, if any program decisions, that no one believed the planning would actually lead to results. Deaf people who had agreed to serve on the program committees were excited about the idea but didn't really believe the event would materialize, not if *they* were the ones being asked to plan it.

Fortunately, the success of the Deaf President Now protest in March of 1988 changed everything. Almost overnight, there was a new confidence and enthusiasm, a new vision of what was possible. Planning proceeded, major donations from AT&T and

Ronald McDonald's Children's Charities were received, and the mind-boggling logistics of The Deaf Way were put in place. When we began, we were planning for an attendance of five hundred; in the end, over 6,000 people from more than eighty countries attended. Over 350 interpreters worked to provide access to conference and festival activities, including 16 plenary sessions, 45 symposia, and over 200 smaller workshops, panel discussions, demonstrations, and individual paper sessions. The Deaf Way began on July 9, 1989 with an opening performance created especially for the event under the direction of Jane Norman. The performance, a sculpture by Guy Wonder, and a mural by Chuck Baird were commissioned for the Festival with support from the National Endowment for the Arts. The conference took place during the mornings and early afternoons, followed by Festival activities throughout the late afternoons and evenings, where hundreds of Deaf actors, poets, mimes, dancers, magicians, storytellers, and other deaf artists performed and exhibited their works on seven different stages. Conference papers, films, videos, performances, and more than 100 exhibits continued through July 14th, and at the end of every evening, the International Deaf Club, an enormous tent accommodating up to 1500 people, was the site of entertainment, reunions, and new friendships in the making. A children and teen program, made possible by a donation from Ronald McDonald's Children's Charities, ran concurrently with the conference so that young people could experience The Deaf Way, too.

The papers included in this volume were originally prepared for The Deaf Way Conference. They represent approximately half of the total number of conference papers (more than 300) and include the sixteen invited plenary addresses. Forty-one countries are represented, with 34 percent of the papers written by authors from the United States and 37 percent by authors from Western Europe, Canada, Australia, and New Zealand. The remaining 29 percent come from Asia, Africa, South America, Eastern Europe, and the Middle East. The majority of the authors are deaf (over 60 percent), distributed across all of the regions of the world represented in the volume.

In selecting the papers for the book, the editors confronted a number of challenges. First, not all presenters provided us with written papers. Those who did had written them in a variety of formats ranging from completed, scholarly texts to one-page outlines of main points. Some of the conference presentations we considered essential to include were not in written form at all but, because they were recorded on videotape during The Deaf Way Conference, we were able to create a paper from this visual and/ or auditory record. Secondly, we considered how well each paper represented the main themes of the conference: culture, language, history, and the arts of deaf communities. While our goal was to be inclusive, it was logistically impossible to publish all of the papers. Therefore, we decided that papers focused more narrowly and those related to curriculum design, for example, even though they might have been excellent papers, would not be candidates for inclusion.

Third, there is the translation issue—and that deserves special attention. We received written papers in English, French, and Spanish. If the author were deaf, it is likely that the paper was first formulated in sign language and then translated, perhaps more than once, so that it could appear in one of the three conference languages. Papers in French and Spanish were then translated to English. If the presentation were transcribed from a videotape and the presenter were deaf, the camera was usually focused on the international sign interpreter with an audio track of one of the spoken language interpreters. For example, Jean-François Mercurio, a Deaf Frenchman, made his presentation in French Sign Language. The audio track of the videotape picked up the Spanish translator's voice and the camera was focused, most of the time, on the international sign interpreter. In addition, he was referring to a videotape of his daughter that was not visible on our videotape of his presentation. In order to reconstruct his presentation—one we knew to be of great interest to many Deaf Way participants—a Spanish interpreter's words were transcribed, translated into English, compared with the international sign version for clarification and verification, and edited. Then we sent for the videotape Mercurio had presented at the conference so that we could make sense of his references to it and selected illustrative frames for accompanying photographs. Finally, we sent the paper we had produced to France for approval.[3]

While this case is an especially complicated one, it illustrates the complexities involved in this editing project. It also serves to remind the reader that errors have probably occurred along the way, even though we have taken a number of precautions to prevent mistranslations and misinterpretations. Most of the papers went through several rounds of editing by different persons. To ensure that we had not drifted from the intended meaning of the presenter, we compared the original version of the paper, realizing that the "original" was often a translation itself, with the edited version. After those changes were made (each paper usually needed a few adjustments), papers were sent out to authors for approval. Unfortunately, we were unable to translate our English versions into any other languages so the authors either had to trust our judgment or find an English speaker to help them review the paper.

Our intent throughout this process was to preserve the "voice" of the author to the extent possible while rendering the ideas in standard written English. Readers may be struck by the lack of consistency in terminology and style and the lack of documentation in the scientific sense in many of these papers. Some authors are academics—historians, anthropologists, linguists, psychologists, sociologists, psychiatrists; others are professional educators, interpreters, actors, counselors, artists, librarians; and many are members of local Deaf communities whose message is derived from the lived experience of the Deaf Way in their everyday lives. It is important to remember the linguistically and culturally varied experiences these papers represent. In other words, they are presented by particular persons from specific cultures expressing themselves in a variety of specific languages at a particular point in time. We, as editors, had relatively little access to this contextual information for each paper, making the interpretation of meaning difficult at times. Nevertheless, we decided that it was more valuable to provide access to the diversity of "voices" represented through these papers and risk some error than to leave the task undone and the papers unpublished.

One editorial decision deserves special mention. In recent years in the United States and subsequently elsewhere, it has become customary to refer to Deaf people as members of a socially constructed visual culture by using an upper case letter "D" and to the audiological condition of hearing impairment with the lower case letter "d" (Erting and Woodward, 1979; Woodward, 1972). Some of the authors in this volume used this convention in their papers; others did not, even though they were clearly distinguishing between culturally and audiologically deaf individuals. We chose to allow the authors' usage to remain rather than impose one standard on all papers. Our feeling was that use or the nonuse of the "D/d" distinction carried meaning and was a part of the particularity of each paper that we did not wish to destroy.

We realize that these papers will only be accessible to readers of English and, therefore, many deaf individuals as well as large sections of the potential international audience will not be able to read them. Ideally, we would have made this volume as accessible as The Deaf Way itself was, through video as well as print, and in several

---

3 This is one of several papers in this volume—including, notably, those by Guy Bouchauveau and Alberto Paliza Farfan—that reached their final edited form primarily as a result of the efforts of Robert Clover Johnson.

different spoken and signed languages. Financial constraints made translations and videotaped versions impossible; in addition, video footage from The Deaf Way Conference was technically uneven and only exists for plenary presenters and symposia. Recognizing the limitations inherent in an English-only print version of the papers, we nevertheless felt it was important to disseminate the material, even in this monolingual, single-channel format, in hopes that it will be useful to Deaf people, hearing and deaf professionals, students of Deaf culture, and families of deaf individuals.

The Deaf Way was an event whose time had come. The statement it made, reflected in the papers in this book, was long overdue—Deaf people are able, creative, and productive citizens of the world who long for equal treatment and equal access to society's institutions. All too often they are discriminated against out of ignorance and prejudice, and they live as an oppressed people. The Deaf Way was liberating for many. It was common for Deaf attendees to comment that they hadn't realized that Deaf people could achieve so much and that they would go back to their own countries inspired and determined to accomplish their goals. From what we have learned, that is exactly what happened and continues to happen today. As several colleagues around the world have noted, The Deaf Way has become a reference point, even for Deaf people who did not attend. It set a standard for accessibility, respect, pride, and perhaps most of all, celebration of a rich heritage and the determination to improve life for Deaf people around the world.

References

Anthony, David. 1971. *Seeing Essential English*. Vols. 1 and 2. Anaheim, California: Educational Services Division, Anaheim Union School District.

Baynton, Douglas C. 1993. " 'Savages and Deaf-Mutes': Evolutionary Theory and the Campaign against Sign Language in the Nineteenth Century." In *Deaf History Unveiled*, ed. John Vickrey Van Cleve. Washington, DC: Gallaudet University Press, pp. 92–112.

Bornstein, Harry. 1975. *The Signed English Dictionary for Preschool and Elementary Levels*. Washington, DC: Gallaudet College Press.

Commission on Education of the Deaf. 1988. *Toward Equality. A Report to the President and the Congress of the United States*. Washington, DC: United States Government Printing Office.

Denton, David. 1972. "Rationale for Total Communication." In *Psycholinguistics and Total Communication: The State of the Art*, ed. Terrence J. O'Rourke. Washington, DC: American Annals of the Deaf, pp. 53–61.

Erting, Carol. 1978. "Language Policy and Deaf Ethnicity." *Sign Language Studies* 19: 139–152.

Erting, Carol, and James Woodward. 1979. "Sign Language and the Deaf Community." *Discourse Processes* 2: 183–300.

Gustason, Gerilee, D. Pfetzing, and E. Zawolkow. Eds. 1972. *Signing Exact English*. Rossmoor, CA: Modern Signs Press.

Holcomb, Roy. 1970. "The Total Approach." *Proceedings of the International Congress of Education of the Deaf*. Stockholm. pp. 104–107.

Kannapell, Barbara. 1974. "Bilingual Education: A New Direction in the Education of the Deaf." *The Deaf American* 26 (10): 9–15.

Lane, Harlan. 1984. *When the Mind Hears: A History of the Deaf.* New York: Random House.

Moores, Donald. 1987. *Educating the Deaf: Psychology, Principles, and Practices.* 3d ed. Boston: Houghton Mifflin.

Stokoe, William C. 1960. "Sign Language Structure: An Outline of the Visual Communication System of the American Deaf." *Studies in Linguistics: Occasional Papers 8.* Buffalo: University of Buffalo. Reprinted 1976, Silver Spring, MD: Linstok Press.

Stokoe, William C., Dorothy Casterline, and Carl Croneberg. 1976. *A Dictionary of American Sign Language on Linguistic Principles.* New ed. Silver Spring, MD: Linstok Press.

Van Cleve, John Vickrey, and Barry A. Crouch. 1989. *A Place of Their Own.* Washington, DC: Gallaudet Unversity Press.

Woodward, James. 1972. "Implications for Sociolinguistic Research Among the Deaf." *Sign Language Studies* 1: 1–7.

———— 1978. "Some Sociolinguistic Problems in the Implementation of Bilingual Education for Deaf Students." In *American Sign Language in a Bilingual, Bicultural Context. The Proceedings of the Second National Symposium on Sign Language Research and Teaching,* ed. Frank Caccamise and Doin Hicks. Silver Spring, MD: National Association of the Deaf. pp. 183–203.

———— 1989. "How You Gonna Get to Heaven if You Can't Talk with Jesus? The Educational Establishment vs. the Deaf Community." In *American Deaf Culture,* ed. Sherman Wilcox. Silver Spring, MD: Linstok Press.

The Deaf Way: Touchstone 1989!

I. KING JORDAN

Welcome to all of you assembled today for this extraordinary meeting of deaf people and others who want to share in our community. Welcome, also, to the satellite audience who will be sharing our discussions and our festival activities throughout the week.

We are making history together. We are adding to the rich heritage of Deaf culture throughout the world. Last night we began our celebration of deaf talent, and today we will look at ourselves carefully to see how far we have come. We will set agendas for future research and inquiry, and we will present an Artistic Manifesto from deaf artists. We will be proudly displaying the talents, insights, and creativity of deaf performers and artists of all media and all ages. More than 300 performers will demonstrate how the alert eyes and experienced souls of deaf people create art.

We are building signposts to help the world know us, to mark where we are today and the distance we have come. We are building signposts as points of reference for where we are going as a world community of deaf and hard of hearing people.

We have a rich and complex history. Many times people interested in deafness have convened. Some of these conferences have become very important to us. One such conference took place in 1880 in Milan, Italy, an infamous conference in which deaf people's points of view were willfully excluded. Thank heavens, we are no longer at the Congress of Milan! This is 1989, and this is The Deaf Way! When the Milan Congress met, there were 164 members present, representing eight countries. This morning, we have more than 5,000 people, and we represent more than seventy-five countries. Highlights of this week will be seen daily in Europe and Scandinavia by satellite, and specials will be aired in South America and Central America to all of the Gallaudet Regional Centers, and in parts of Canada.

It is interesting to compare our meeting here with meetings that happened before. Look, for example, at the congress that took place in Paris September 23–30, 1878. A total of twentyseven people attended.

I believe that one of those twenty-seven, the representative from Sweden, would have marveled at the Swedish television crew here to take images back to show on programs designed for deaf viewers. I know that he would have been astonished at the satellite images of our meetings that will be shown back home in Sweden. Today, we are a community, a community of people who reach out to people of any age, with any degree of hearing loss: people who sign, people who speak, and people who both sign

---

Note: This address was the opening presentation at The Deaf Way Conference and Festival, presented on Monday morning, July 10, 1989, to an immediate audience of more than 5,000 people and an even larger satellite audience.

and speak; people who were born deaf and people who became deaf later in life; and people who are not deaf but who still share in the lives of deaf people.

As I was looking back over the proceedings of the famous Milan Congress, I noted that the meeting included questions to be deliberated that were divided into four major topics: Building and Furniture, Instruction, Methods, and Special Questions. Some of the special questions were "What are the professions generally followed by the deaf and dumb? What do they follow most advantageously? May new careers be offered to them?" To those who wrote those questions, I answer more than 100 years later with a reverberating *"Deaf people can do anything! Deaf people can do anything!"*

As I thumb through this week's extensive program—with more than 500 papers and performances—I know that this week will become a touchstone, a place that deaf people will look back on and use as a standard of comparison. All of the congresses are part of our history, part of the process we have shared as deaf people in the world community. Each international event has been a signpost.

The Deaf Way is one more signpost. It is also a good touchstone because The Deaf Way is inclusive. We are using every possible technology and every known language strategy to make this week fully accessible to every person who comes. The logistics of this undertaking were extremely challenging. The sign language interpreting will involve more than 300 interpreters. The voice interpreting for Spanish, French, and English requires another fifty interpreters. To train these interpreters, we conducted a special workshop and retreat. Arrangements for housing and the construction of sets has kept us very busy. Performers began to arrive in mid-June. Imagine, if you will, the detailed planning necessary to arrange for things such as loop systems, vibrating beepers, large screens, and captioning and standards-conversion for satellite broadcast.

Along with the technological planning has been planning for the best way to present, light, and place art objects of great beauty and importance and the best ways to schedule all of the challenging scholarly papers and encourage international dialogue.

We are extremely grateful for the wonderful support of our major corporate sponsors, Ronald McDonald Children's Charities (RMCC) and AT&T. Not only did RMCC and AT&T give us significant financial support, they have given us constant advice and counsel in all the areas in which they have so many years of experience and knowledge. Professionals from their staffs were able to guide us and to anticipate solutions to problems. AT&T and RMCC have also added to the visual effectiveness of every area of the hotel and campus and to the accessibility of many of our events.

We are also indebted to the National Endowment for the Arts, The Coca-Cola Foundation, the Smithsonian Institution, The National Gallery of Art, the Corcoran Gallery of Art, the Capital Children's Museum, the Voluntary Fund for the United Nations Decade of Disabled Persons, the Organization of American States, the United States Department of State, The Discovery Channel, and many other individuals and group sponsors. I hope you will take a few minutes to read through pages 64 and 65 of the program book to see how many contributors have made this week possible through their gifts of money, time, and imagination to The Deaf Way.

We are especially proud that we received the endorsement of the World Federation of the Deaf and the National Association of the Deaf for the conference and festival celebrating deaf talent and knowledge.

The Deaf Way is the work product of almost every person on the Gallaudet University campus. The motivation, enthusiasm, and commitment of our Gallaudet University students, faculty, and staff have been inspiring. Over the past year we have talked about excellence at Gallaudet and how to make it accessible and visible. The Deaf Way is a tangible, accessible, and visible demonstration of the excellence that is within the Deaf community.

For many years, we at Gallaudet have discussed the notion of hosting a large, international conference in Washington, D.C. We envisioned this as an opportunity for deaf people to know what was happening in our communities in every corner of the world. Researchers, scholars, and performers from Gallaudet visited with their colleagues in other countries, and as they learned more, the vision of a major conference grew larger. The concept became a large, international, academic conference. It became clear to us, however, that to share truly in the international deaf experience, all of the elements of Deaf culture needed to be present, and the idea of a festival was born.

Rather than excluding controversy, this conference will invite it. Rather than excluding variety, this festival will nurture it. Rather than excluding differing philosophies within the community, this conference will examine them. The Deaf Way is about accessibility, inclusion, and advocacy. The Deaf Way is about celebration. The Deaf Way is about freedom of expression. The Deaf Way will be a touchstone for future meetings of deaf people around the globe.

This week, we are placing science and art side by side. We are observing and discussing our observations. We are presenting research, and we are sharing insights and aspirations. We will look at what is universal and what is not. Deaf, hard of hearing, and hearing people have traveled here from more than seventy-five nations around the world, and each has brought a unique definition of what is meant by The Deaf Way.

When your registrations began to arrive, we started to color a map of the world indicating which countries were represented. I am delighted to say that on that map not much is left uncolored. It is our sincere hope that at the end of the week, the world will have been deeply touched by the experiences we have had together here.

All of us have known the experience of walking in an unfamiliar city signing and having a stranger approach and ask, "Are you deaf?" "Yes," we answer, "I am." We are then given the time and place the deaf club meets because we are not really strangers to one another.

On the Gallaudet campus we will create an International Deaf Club. The International Deaf Club tent will hold 1,500 people and will be an excellent place to share our cultures, to laugh, and to enjoy the company of old friends and new ones. With people from more than seventy-five countries here, the club will be a good place to practice and improve our international signs.

Last night, more than 100 actors and dancers from around the world gave us a spectacular opening for our events of the week. Today, the scholars will have an opportunity for exchange.

The Deaf Way is more than a conference, more than a festival. More than captions or gestures, more than signs vs. voice, deaf vs. hearing, more than metaphors for sound or for silence. The Deaf Way brings us a new confidence rooted in a week-long demonstration of renewed spirit, common experience, and the abilities and the aspirations of deaf people. The Deaf Way is a touchstone and a signpost for where we are in 1989. *Enjoy! Argue! Deliberate! Appreciate The Deaf Way!*

PART ONE

Deaf Cultures Around the World

Editor's Introduction

This section contains contributions by twenty-eight deaf and eight hearing authors representing deaf communities in twenty different nations. It is primarily a view from the inside—in anthropological terms, an emic perspective—created to inform others, both deaf and hearing, about Deaf life as these authors experienced it in their own countries, in 1989. The papers derive their meaning not only from within, but also from the juxtaposition of each with the others, just as lives lived in communities are made richer and more meaningful through relationship with the whole. Insiders' views are presented alongside etic, or outside, perspectives from anthropologists, sociologists, and other hearing supporters of the Deaf community. The major themes of the section are discernible in the first four papers, while the remaining papers flesh out those themes with details of place, circumstance, and specific culture.

Paddy Ladd (England), begins this section by defining Deaf culture as a way of life, a shared perspective, based on knowing the world primarily through vision and suffering oppression at the hands of the hearing majority. Sign language, inextricably linked with Deaf culture, is the most visible and important manifestation of this visual life, and it is still largely unrecognized as a viable language by deaf and hearing people alike. Furthermore, since over 90 percent of all deaf children are born to hearing parents, transmission of the culture from one generation to the next does not occur in the usual way, within the family, but instead primarily through the peer group. Ladd argues that deaf people have the right to be bicultural, but oralism, the prevailing educational philosophy since 1880, has denied them this right by suppressing the recognition of Deaf culture. He calls upon deaf people self-consciously to work to rebuild, enhance and preserve their weakened culture, especially within the schools, which they should develop into deliberate models of Deaf culture. Recognizing the diversity within deaf communities and the differences among Deaf cultures around the world, Ladd calls for a comparative approach to research. He also challenges deaf people worldwide to build on the embryo of the international Deaf culture, demonstrating for the rest of the world the effects of a spirit of cooperation, rather than the prevailing international tone of ethnic and national strife.

In the next two papers, M. J. Bienvenu (United States) and Guy Bouchauveau (France) discuss the ways in which the culture of deaf people is revealed in their humor. Perhaps most striking is the way in which the study of this domain reveals the central role played by vision in the lives of deaf people. Deaf humor, Bouchauveau points out, is based on visual logic, inspired by visual images, and it is often capable of transcending national cultural boundaries when deaf people from different countries come together. It does not translate well into spoken language, however, since its foundation is in shared Deaf experience, and, most critically, expression through sign language. That experience, Bienvenu points out, is shaped by seeing, the inability to hear, sign language, and oppression by hearing people.

Edward T. Hall (United States), an anthropologist specializing in the study of nonverbal communication, argues that since the nonverbal component of culture is 80 to 90 percent of human communication, deaf people have developed a culture that is more in tune with their organism than are the cultures of hearing people. He describes Deaf culture as a mood-sensitive, high-context culture, one whose members share a deep and rich information base. Along this dimension, it stands in sharp contrast to the dominant American culture, which is an analytical, low-context culture—one that implicitly denies the existence of the Deaf culture and tends to view sign language as a degraded form of the spoken language. Hearing culture, in other words, is essentially blind to Deaf culture, just as all cultures are blind to other cultures, especially the tacit dimension that operates outside of awareness. Hall argues that only an increase in self-awareness will solve the problem. However, he suggests that studying Deaf culture will provide new insights into problems faced by other ethnic and minority groups as they interact with each other globally and promises to contribute to improved ethnic relations worldwide.

The next four papers address the topic of Deaf identity. Breda Carty (Australia) calls for research on how deaf people learn what it means to be Deaf, comparing and contrasting the experiences of Deaf children from Deaf families with those of deaf children from hearing families. She presents a six-stage working model of the process of identity formation and suggests it be used as a framework to elicit stories from deaf people about their experiences. Barbara Kannapell (United States) emphasizes the complexity of the topic and contrasts the views of educators and other hearing professionals with those of the Deaf community. She proposes researchers ask how Deaf people see themselves in terms of language identity, personal identity and social identity, in order to understand better what constitutes cultural identity among Deaf people. Rachel Stone and Lynn Stirling (United States) conducted interviews with deaf children of Deaf and hearing parents. Their results suggest that deaf children with hearing parents and Deaf children with Deaf parents are learning different values related to their identity as Deaf people in their families. These authors suggest that deaf children with hearing parents are more ambivalent and have a more difficult time accepting their identity as Deaf people than Deaf children who have Deaf parents. In the fourth paper, Larry Coleman and Kathy Jankowski (United States) describe the role of folklore and Deaf storytellers in Deaf culture, particularly in building positive attitudes toward Deaf identity and pride in the heritage of Deaf people.

Following these eight papers from Western Europe and the United States, the focus shifts to descriptions of deaf communities in Asia, Africa, Latin America, Eastern Europe, Ireland, Quebec, and Australia. Repeatedly these authors point to the negative attitudes of the larger societies in which they live as being more handicapping to deaf people than the physical difference of not hearing. Because of these attitudes, arising from ignorance or indifference, deaf people are excluded from full participation in the majority culture and denied access to appropriate education, a full range of employment opportunities, and other benefits society has to offer. These circumstances have led to widespread discrimination against deaf people as well as oppression of their sign languages and cultures. Isolated in hearing families where there is usually little communication with parents or siblings, deaf people turn to each other for support, community, and full access to communication through sign language. It is with other deaf people that they share a common bond and have a vision of the future, and it is not only their own Deaf community they identify with and look to for support. They also call upon what Anwar Shamshudin (Pakistan) refers to as the "deaf nation" around the world to come to the aid of deaf people everywhere, and in doing so, as Simmons suggests, become a model of cross-cultural cooperation for all peoples.

Clearly the papers reveal diversity both within and among Deaf cultures. As Kampol Suwanarat (Thailand), Michiko Tsuchiya (Japan), Patrick Devlieger (Kenya), Robert Simmons (South Africa), and others illustrate, it is important to understand the sociocultural context within which each Deaf culture exists, including the national culture, since the Deaf culture of a particular nation and the attitudes of its hearing people toward deaf individuals will be influenced by the cultural values and social institutions of the larger society. Robert E. Johnson's (United States) description of a traditional Yucatec-Mayan village where hearing people know and use the sign language of the deaf villagers is the most striking illustration of this principle. In sharp contrast to the rest of this section, we see deaf individuals who have nearly full access to the economic and social life of the community. With this exception, however, the most striking thing about these papers are the similarities in what deaf people have suffered at the hands of the majority, in their resourcefulness in combating prejudice and oppression, and in the solutions called for by these authors. Antonio Campos de Abreu (Brazil), Miguel Santillán (Ecuador), and Trude Dimmel (Austria), among others, emphasize that it has been the Deaf clubs and associations as well as the residential schools that have preserved Deaf culture and sign language, and they call for these institutions, under Deaf leadership, to lead the way into the future. Papers throughout this section proclaim that deaf people must take responsibility for educating each other about their language and culture, and they must organize in their struggle to gain recognition of their sign language, their rights, and their abilities, including their ability to teach in schools using their own language.

Deaf Culture: Finding It and Nurturing It

PADDY LADD

My subject, deaf culture, is enormous, and space is limited, so I won't be able to qualify my examples as carefully as I would like and will therefore be overgeneralizing. Most of my illustrations will be from the Western World (especially Britain), so I hope you will think of your own examples and make notes of where your experiences differ. In my view, it is ultimately by comparing our various experiences that we will begin to build a clear picture of what deaf culture is. Third World countries especially will have a big role to play in the development of a composite picture of deaf culture in future years.

In England, many hearing people think that culture is the special province of members of the upper class: their way of life, their houses, their artistic interests (opera, theater, and so on). These people even try to distinguish themselves from other groups and other classes by calling themselves "cultured." But this definition of culture is both narrow and false. In the largest and truest sense, culture means the way of life of a group of people: their way of looking at the world, their beliefs, the things they create, the stories they tell. The way the upper class in England lives is only one example of one form of culture. It is certainly not the only way of living, nor is it necessarily a better way than those ways by which other groups of people live.

One of the most difficult things about studying culture is that most of the time people are not aware that they have it. Culture, in other words, tends to be an implicit rather than an explicit part of their lives. People regard the way they do things as "just the way we live." If you say to many deaf people, for instance, that "storytelling is a big part of your culture," they will look at you very strangely. Often, they are not even aware that they tell stories. But at the deaf club, they do it every night.

One unfortunate consequence of culture's implicit nature is that people come to believe that their way of life is the only way to live. Thinking this way leads to efforts to impose a dominant group's way of life on other groups. The white man has been especially guilty of this in the last 300 years, a well-known example being the concept of "the white man's burden," now generally regarded as extremely suspect, but once widely accepted in England as a justificaiton for the imposition of British rule and British ways on the natives of India and other nations.

Today, clever politicians use widely accepted cultural values to manipulate people when they know rational arguments will fail. Margaret Thatcher and Ronald Reagan, for instance, have done this superbly in the 1980s. It is done by presenting a political agenda as a cultural necessity. For example, capitalism tries to deny its political goal of benefiting the rich and mighty by promoting the idea that everyone must struggle to improve his or her "standard of living," which really means that people should buy or aspire to buy lots of consumer goods they may not genuinely need.

Again, because culture is implicit, people who do not have power in their societies are vulnerable to having their way of life threatened by those who do. They may be viewed as less than complete human beings if they keep to their own ways. In my opinion, those in power tend to resist the idea of studying cultures for fear that those not in power will begin to realize that things don't have to be done in one particular way, and this realization might encourage them to rebel. The powerful are aided in this tendency to resist understanding the true nature of culture by the unwillingness of humans to believe that they behave in predictable ways, like animals, with mating rituals and so on. People often prefer to think that they have no choice: "It is just the way things are," they say. This belief allows these people to carry on with a quiet life, as if nothing can be done to change things.

All of the above are relevant when we look at deaf culture, a way of life that has been suppressed or discredited in every country in the world. And yet, we do not have to look very far to find proof of our culture. When we get together, for instance, we use our language, a language as fine as any that comes from the mouth. When you first see deaf people, you see them signing. That's how you know they are deaf. The two cannot be separated. A group doesn't have to have its own language to have a culture, but if it does have one, then it definitely has got its own culture too!

Sign languages have been suppressed, yet many of us deaf people lead happy lives, with some pride. How have we done that? Through our language and culture. If you look at people who are deafened later in life, you see how miserable their lives are. They may be no more or less deaf than we, audiologically, yet while we are connected through our language and culture, they are cut off from the society with which they identify. What keeps us from their fate is our togetherness, our way of life built around our language. Each of us knows the feeling of coming out of darkness into a place of warmth and light. That is the feeling I associate with each deaf person's discovery of sign language and the deaf community. Once we and others recognize the value of our language, then we are on the road toward the discovery and appreciation of our culture.

One of the reasons deaf culture tends to be unrecognized is that societies generally think about deafness in terms of the inability to hear sounds. In Britain, for example, deafness is constantly described as "not hearing the birds sing." The view of most hearing cultures, in fact, is that deafness means something is missing. This view tends to be so strongly held that the obvious is overlooked: Sound is not the barrier. It is only when sound is used for spoken language that barriers go up. What prevents our being integrated into hearing cultures is our not being fully able to use the spoken form of their language. Even if we can write it, we can't follow spoken conversation with our parents, workmates, or anyone. Nor can we follow speech on telephones, television, radio, the cinema, theater, or public meetings. Obviously, these are more important things than birds singing. Until we are recognized as a minority group with our own distinct language, the importance of our abilities—as opposed to our inabilities—will remain hidden, along with the concept of deaf culture.

Social attitudes are made much worse by the power of the medical profession. Doctors tend to see deaf people as defective hearing people and to resist accepting the concept that we have a language and culture. We all have experienced the power exerted by the medical profession on deaf people; for example, the medical perspective has—to varying degrees in different countries—drastically affected our ability to get jobs as teachers, to become drivers, or to be understood as having our own rights of access to the telephone. It is hard to remember that medical people were once valuable in establishing that deaf people were not, by definition, insane!

Of course, deaf people have been identified as "disabled," and that is at least technically correct. In fact, there are some important reasons for us to accept this view of deafness. If we totally reject this concept, we can be viewed as collaborating with nondisabled people in oppressing those with disabilities. But we are also significantly different from most disabled groups because of our language and culture. We are able to walk and find our way around the world and to emerge from our villages and tribes to become what truly appears to be a worldwide society.

Although many disabled groups dream of a physical cure for their disability, such a dream is inconceivable to most people who have grown up deaf. If we could hear tomorrow, we wouldn't want to. We wouldn't want to become hearing people, because inside we are deaf. Our minds are deaf. This sense of identity has come from seeing the world in a different way, shaped by our language and culture. A simple example of how deaf people as a group differ from other disabled groups can be seen when we look at the heart of deaf culture: deaf parents with deaf children. The positive value we deaf people give to having deaf children of our own marks us as different.

Unfortunately, however, because 90 percent of deaf people have hearing families, it is difficult to "prove" that deaf culture exists. After all, if the very people who gave birth to us are not of us, nor are we of them, this threatens the whole concept of family. The family is generally where we absorb the main culture, and as long as deaf culture is not fully recognized, we are subconsciously torn: We believe that the family, somehow, is the norm. The truth, of course, is that we are *bi*cultural. Our parents, too, have the chance to become part of our community. Thanks to oralism, however, this basic right is nothing more than a pipedream for all too many of us.

The British National Union of the Deaf (NUD), by the way, found under Article 27 of the United Nations (U.N.) Charter of Civil and Political Rights a statement that people who belong to linguistic minorities should not be denied the right to use their own language or enjoy their own culture. If this principle were generally accepted and implemented, the NUD observed, oralism would be wiped out immediately! However, when the NUD examined the U.N. Charter of Rights of the Child for references to children with disabilities, it found merely the following: "The child who is physically . . . handicapped shall be given the special treatment, education, and care required by his particular condition." There is nothing in this statement to help stop oralism or protect sign language and deaf culture.

So, if we look carefully, we can see both the culture that we have and the reasons for its not being recognized. That culture is simply not so strong as we would like it to be, because of the oppression it has suffered. It is not so strong as it was 100 years ago, for example. Before we can strengthen it, we have to become conscious of it. The more we talk about the Deaf Way, and the more we think about it, the more we can change it, improve it, build on it.

One of the hardest things to explain is the concept of the *deaf mind*. Something happens when we are very small. Cut off from meaningful sound or language, our brains compensate. They make sense of the world in a different way, a visual way. When we meet a deaf child or a foreign deaf person in the street, something happens deep inside. We can understand the person, not just because we can communicate, or because "we know how it feels to be deaf, poor thing." It is something deeper inside, a place where we switch to understand how deaf people see the world.

If we need to prove the existence of a shared deaf perspective, the answer may lie in the fact that most sign languages seem to have similar grammatical structures. This is not so for spoken languages at all! These similarities suggest that the visual medium has neurolinguistic determinates. More work needs to be done on this subject, particularly by deaf people, who can describe the phenomenon from experience. We need to make the remarkable fit between deaf people and sign language more clearly evident and visible. The results of such work will have immense implications for education, for instance.

Deaf culture has been kept alive by the deaf offspring of deaf parents. Who knows where we would be without that 10 percent? The fact that deaf culture is formed in the schools and learned from other children is highly unusual. It makes me wonder how much stronger deaf culture would be if deaf adults were allowed to shape it more fully. Some deaf families are known to go back as many as seven generations, as far back as the time of the French Revolution, to a time when deaf education itself was new. We could learn so much more if we were better able to see the progression of deaf culture from generation to generation.

But deaf history has to a great extent been denied existence, largely because deaf people have been regarded as medically impaired individuals rather than as members of a cultural group. Characteristics of the deaf community itself have been a factor also, in that sign language can't be written down and that too little use has been made of film. It is regrettable that the deaf community's historical record is so incomplete, particularly in light of the fact that without history, a culture is severely weakened. We need to do much work in finding and preserving our history. History is culture, after all, as I found out for sure when a group of us saw Harlan Lane talk in Rome five years ago, describing French deaf history. Some of us, including the interpreter who had deaf parents, found ourselves crying! While we need to figure out what made us cry, I know that much of it had to do with our sense of the importance for deaf people of learning about our collective past.

Luckily, you can find out a lot about our history from deaf magazines, which in many countries go back as far as 150 years. Reading these magazines can give you a sense of how deaf people thought and felt in the past, especially if the magazines had deaf editors.

One reason some people have difficulty seeing the deaf community as a cultural group is that we don't have our own religion, cook special foods, or build special buildings. But it is hardly necessary for us to be special in those areas for us to call ourselves a culture. Through sign language, for instance, our culture has created its own art. It has even created new art forms like sign poetry, sign song, and deaf theater. It has been heavily damaged by oralism, but it exists still. Our culture will only be as healthy as its deaf art is healthy, for art helps to focus change and growth in societies.

The importance of sign language has already been discussed, and the more deaf researchers there are, the more likely it will be that deaf culture can be described from the perspective of those who know and use this language. It seems ridiculous to note that in 1823, the major British *oralist,* Watson, fully accepted that British Sign Language (BSL) *is* a language, and yet in 1989 we are still struggling to convince the British deaf people who use it of that fact!

As for buildings, we may not have special buildings, but we have built and kept alive clubs, schools, associations, sports organizations, and even political structures. All that is deaf culture; that's the roof of the deaf world we live in. The more we compare these elements of the deaf world to mainstream culture, the clearer our different cultural identity becomes. In fact, one example of the uniqueness of deaf culture is being made apparent here at The Deaf Way. In spite of our international origins, we seem to be more of a united cultural group than could ever be said of a comparable international assembly of hearing people.

How we behave—the moral and social codes of our society—also is culture. People find it hard to believe we have such behavioral codes, but of course we do. Often these codes differ from those of hearing people. Deaf and hearing people, for instance, have quite different behavioral patterns regarding physical contact. In our culture, we are aware of things like sitting opposite rather than next to people, and of our use of peripheral vision. But how many of us are aware that we hug and touch each other more than hearing people?

Another behavioral difference I have noticed is that British deaf women appear to be "stronger," on average, than hearing women in one way or another. I also notice that they swear more. This may be partly because they do not receive the same intense brainwashing hearing women do about "femininity." These differences are worthy of study because British deaf women are still discriminated against by British deaf men for reasons that need to be better understood.

We need to describe and become aware of these and other behavioral differences if we are to grow. If we don't become aware of our own cultural identity, we become vulnerable to others imposing theirs on us. Here is a small example:

A social worker went to a deaf man's house, to find him in the living room doing his football pools coupon. "Where's your wife?" the social worker asked. "Upstairs in bed," replied the deaf man. The social worker went upstairs and found the deaf woman there, dead. He came down and told the man this, and the man replied, "Yes, I know."

This story has been told to other social workers all over Britain as an example of how hardhearted deaf people are. Yet what was left out of the story was the fact that the woman had been ill for a long time, and that the deaf man had nursed her patiently. So it was not a case of a deaf person being uncaring—and therefore subhuman—but of his having a different attitude toward death. Who knows? Perhaps that man's attitude could even demonstrate a lesson to hearing people!

Instead, of course, examples like this often lead to horrible results: Deaf parents have their children taken away, or deaf adults are placed in institutions. And yet the deaf people involved may simply have been behaving according to deaf cultural norms hard for hearing people to understand. The reverse can also happen: Deaf people who violate social norms can be perceived sympathetically by hearing people. For instance, there was recently a court case involving a deaf man who had raped deaf girls from the club. It took a lot of courage and pain to take the case to court, but then the man was found not guilty by a hearing jury. This happened because the court felt that the man was being victimized by the club, rather than the other way around. The defense counsel also concentrated on evoking sympathy for the man because he was unable to hear. If he had been tried by a deaf jury, however, I'm sure they would have read the cultural signals and information easily and found him guilty.

The same subtle cultural processes apply when the *wrong* deaf person is given a job. If a deaf person were conducting the interview, he or she would have seen the deaf person's weaknesses more clearly.

Partly because the deaf community is now in a state of cultural change and growth, we tend not to bring our social and moral codes to the level of conscious formulation and widespread discussion. But such formulation and discussion are the foundation on which other cultures have developed philosophies of life. Ironically, our relative lack of self-consciousness may be partly to our advantage when one considers that many of the cultures with highly formulated ways of life have become rigid and resist change. It would be true to say that none of the world's major cultures is changing as fast as the planet requires if human life is to survive.

We deaf, in other words, are in an interesting position. Our culture has been weakened by oralism, but as we rebuild it now, we have more flexibility to change it and shape it for the twenty-first century. In Britain, for example, we have accepted that deaf people never praise others, only criticize them. This happens in hearing society too, but I think we do it more. If you talk about changing this pattern, you often get the reply, "It's the deaf way." Perhaps so, but it doesn't have to stay that way! I'd guess this negativity is the result of oralism—the oralists wanting to divide us, never praising us, but instead putting us in a position of always being at the brunt of negative evaluations in a system in which we can't succeed! We mustn't become so tied to our negative attitude toward oralism, however, that we lose the flexibility necessary to accommodate changing attitudes among many hearing people.

Language and culture cannot easily be separated; in fact, they are intricately linked. Some would even suggest that language shapes how people see the world. An old example is that the Eskimo has several words for snow, and desert people have several for sand. We have one for each. If we go to their lands, we therefore only see one type. Yet once we are taught words for them, we can learn to see them. It's like a form of magic! Words have a magical power: They transform what our eyes see! We need to look at our own language and cultural connections. Can we express all the deepest things we need to discuss, or has our culture been attacked so much that we have to use signed English to attempt it? Are we using the full visual power of sign language?

There are numerous small examples that show the connections between language and deaf culture. In Britain "deaf" is signed "deaf and dumb." But we don't allow hearing people to call us that, for the same reason that black Americans can call each other "nigger" but woe betide a white person who tries it, and rightly so. In each case, the respective culture is rejecting what has been done to it by people of other cultures who have used these words. One also finds that written deaf English shows our cultural ideas. If hearing people write "the deaf," we feel as if we are like animals in a zoo. Yet *we* can write "the deaf" and feel a sense of pride in who we are, almost as a race of people would. It's a great example: Just two little words can show our cultural differences!

So far, we have been talking about one undivided thing, deaf culture. Yet, in fact, deaf culture can be broken down into national, regional, local, and situational components, to name just a few. Although we feel that all deaf people in the world are one, we have to be careful not to over-romanticize this perception of interconnectedness and homogeneity. We are all islands in a hearing sea because we don't all live near each other, unfortunately.

Few would deny that the hearing cultures in the North and South of England have major differences. There are subcultures where people with different views get together, like hippies, or Rastafarians, for example. This is also true for deaf culture, and we need to be aware of diversity within the deaf community. In Britain people say that British Sign Language (BSL) is much stronger in the North than in London, and this matches oralism's path across Britain; it reached the North last of all. Also, deaf women have their own differences, as do gay deaf people and black deaf people, for example.

The deaf middle class, for instance, can be looked at as a distinct group within the deaf community. This population is not marked by birth so much as by educational attainment. As with other cultures, we find that this class takes on more of the values of mainstream society and looks down on ordinary deaf life. This can cause friction in many areas of deaf life, but I will give only a couple of examples. The deaf middle class may look down on BSL as something used by the "stupid deaf." Thus, the rise of BSL is threatening to them, as their superiority is endangered. And grass roots deaf people may reject useful aspects of middle class culture along with the middle class attitude of superiority.

A similar process occurs among partially deaf people. Many have been educated in hearing schools, and their minds are not often 100 percent deaf. Again, each group may reject useful cultural values in the other. There is often tension between deaf people and another special group that could be a valuable part of the deaf community, the hearing children of deaf parents. This tension has its roots in history, and until we look at it consciously, much potential growth resulting from openness to that group's perspective goes to waste.

If we use deaf history, we can identify ways in which these attitudes are shaped. For example, until oralism and hearing aids grew stronger thirty years ago, there was much less division. We can also see that oralism made deaf children compete against each other, becoming individualistic and not working as a group.

The more we become aware of the causes of these divisions, the more we can remedy them. For example, in Britain, if you formed a deaf pressure group like the NUD, hearing welfare officers would try to squash you by putting it about that you weren't "proper deaf people," that is, you didn't just accept what you were given.

It is important to remedy these divisions because more and more deaf youth are mainstreamed and separated from the deaf community. If we do not adjust to include them, our whole future is threatened. As it is, such fragmentation has already held us back from making progress in fighting for our rights.

In spite of these internal distinctions and tensions, however, the larger conflict for deaf culture has always been and will continue to be between deaf culture as a whole and the hearing culture around it. As a rule, when two cultures clash, the stronger wins and imposes itself on the other. One tactic is to try to make the losers believe that they have no culture or at best only an inferior one. Such is colonization. Well, we deaf people too have been colonized!

It would be of great use to us in our studies to look across the world and compare the attitudes of other societies to those of us deaf people. We might learn much from that, especially from societies where there are more positive attitudes, as in some South American or Mayan villages [Editor's note: See R. Johnson, this volume], or even as among the Anglo-Saxons of Martha's Vineyard 100 years ago! There, so many used sign language that often there wouldn't even be a deaf person present but the hearing people—signing anyway—wouldn't necessarily notice it.

The logical goal is to be members of two cultures, the deaf culture and one of the hearing cultures. There are several studies that show the benefit of having a bicultural upbringing, and deaf people would benefit from being seen in the same class as other bicultural people. But a bicultural perspective cannot be fully developed as long as we are unclear about the nature of deaf culture. If we are unclear about our culture, promoting a bicultural educational agenda would lead to the same results that came from the so-called integrated deaf education and theater groups: no deaf cultural content and a lot of hearing liberals making themselves look good.

It is within the educational system from which the majority culture imposes its beliefs on future generations that the cultural battle is fought. Examples can be found the whole world over. In Britain, the Welsh and Gaelic languages were suppressed in the schools, for example. This process touches even the smallest details. The best way to change over to the metric system, for instance, is to teach it to the children, so that they will grow up with it and pass it on to their children after we all have gone.

In deaf education, this process is even more crucial, as most deaf children do not experience deaf culture until they go to school: They learn it primarily from each other, not from deaf adults.

And, as we all know, deaf education has been run by a bunch of criminals for the last 100 years. It is not surprising that they have damaged deaf culture, since they set out to destroy it. The wonder is that they have not succeeded. We all know about deaf illiteracy, the banning of deaf teachers and deaf marriages, mainstreaming, etc.

If we are to strengthen deaf culture, there are several things we need to do. For instance, we have to examine our culture to see which values have been placed there by oralists, and which by ourselves. Do we have to accept, for example, that Protestants should fight Catholics, Christians fight Muslims, whites fight blacks? Whose culture would have given us such notions? Is it really ours?

Further examples might include the concept of success and failure. Much of deaf education is measured by the idea that to be like a grass roots deaf person is to be a failure. The more one behaves like a hearing person, the more one is deemed successful. This view takes away from deaf culture many of its potential leaders, who set up their own groups and societies, leaving the clubs to fend for themselves.

We need to start over, regarding ourselves as rebuilding a country after a devastating war. In this effort, we can find parallels with the work being done in African countries after independence was won. If we continue—as we have been doing for the last fifteen years—trying to change things bit by bit, we lose sight of what we are aiming for. That is what has been happening with Total Communication, for example. It hasn't worked because it ignores the idea of the *deaf mind*, which the deaf child embodies, which is the core of deaf culture. We have to start from the inside and work outward to society, not vice versa.

We need to record examples of deaf culture found in the schools—not just the habits and traditions, but the ways we behaved when we have been in conflict with oralism. These should be regarded as a source of pride. Here are a few British examples:

At one school, deaf children rigged up an electrical system so that when the dormitory door opened, the lights went out. Thus, they could sign away happily until someone came. When that person closed the door, the lights went on again, and the signing continued.

Another school had a tradition that on the last day of school, those about to leave marched down to the railway line at the bottom of the field and placed their hearing aids on the line. When the train came and crushed the aids, the students shook hands, and school was out, forever. Similarly, another school had a thick bush on its grounds. Deaf children were able to throw their aids into the middle of the bush, which was far too thick for any teacher to penetrate.

It is my opinion that schools must be developed into strong, aware, deliberate models of deaf culture. Deaf people must run the whole system and must become responsible in particular for the cultural atmosphere within it. Once these prerequisites are met—and only then—it will be appropriate for hearing people, partially deaf people, and middle class deaf people to work in the system, in support of those models.

I recall a few years ago, *begging* the few deaf teachers in Britain to take the time to write down every tiny example they could recall of something they did with the kids that they knew was right that the other teachers couldn't understand or disagreed with. Of course, it would be pointless to try to argue for the benefits of one such example at a time. Hundreds of examples gathered together, however, could collectively build a dossier that would make deaf culture and the deaf mind clear to those in power.

It is essential to study biculturalism, to collaborate with other groups fighting for their own political rights, and to achieve linguistic minority recognition. Many of us were delighted and even relieved when Gallaudet finally rebelled through its Deaf President Now movement. But proof that we have a strong deaf culture will only come when we march and fight for the educational rights of deaf children, not just for ourselves.

As we move ahead in the process of rebuilding deaf culture, it will be critical for us to know as much as possible about what the culture is, so I want to list some more examples of what I believe that culture consists of. Art's role in deaf culture, for instance, is vital. It can first of all show us our culture, then it can dramatize conflicts within it. Such drama can lead people to think about how to change and grow. Often the artist is seen as a bit of an outsider—even in his or her own culture—but that can mean that the artist is able to stand back and see it better than people who just get on with their everyday life. In addition, forms like science fiction can show us possible worlds different from our own that can lead us to question our own way of life.

At present, there is still too little of deaf culture in our art forms and too much copying of hearing models. There is also too little use of BSL and other sign languages. A few positive examples exist: The sign poetry of Dorothy Miles, the American National Theatre of the Deaf, and so on. But we have a long way to go yet.

Sign song is an interesting example. Many deaf people still rebel at the idea of using sound. We have to remember that this is connected to rejecting oralism, that sound in itself is not bad. Most sign song is not based on BSL and is largely unintelligible. Yet we have a golden opportunity, by writing our own songs, really to convey our messages and our pride to mainstream society.

Many of us are aware that storytelling is a major deaf talent, yet most deaf people are not even aware that they themselves use it. To them, storytelling is just "deaf talk." Western society has recently begun to accept storytelling as an art form that also contains and transmits history. Film and video technology present a challenge to us to develop our natural storytelling tendencies into an art form and legacy of great value to present and future generations.

So far, we have made far too little use of film and video to record our culture. And yet, this technology is so perfect for our deaf needs that it almost could have been designed especially for us. There is no better way to set about developing and recording deaf culture than by using video.

The power of TV to link us all as an international nation has been sadly underestimated. Hearing people watch so many different TV programs that it is only things like the moonshot that bring them together. We, of course, have so few TV programs that we would benefit greatly from the production of something everyone could watch once a week to promote deaf culture and deaf progress. Yet we don't.

So why don't we? Partly, I suspect, because we have not yet the technical skills to take charge of programs, and partly because we cannot wrest control from those who are in charge. Another factor, however, is that we have not yet examined deaf culture and therefore are unable to give clear examples of how we would like such programs to look. As a result, we have programs that seem like hearing programs, except that they are signed instead of spoken. We are not alone in this. Black programs often seem just like white ones, except with black presenters. TV culture has not yet been fully pulled away from the white, hearing man's model.

A healthy culture is one that understands and uses political power to defend and promote itself, and here we still have a long way to go. Our isolation from hearing culture often means that we adopt only the parts of it that are most visible. This means, in effect, that we are strongly influenced by those in power and are often regrettably unaware of the existence of groups who disagree with the establishment. As a result, deaf culture is often cut off from potentially valuable ideas related to political change and influence. In Britain, for instance, we would benefit greatly from more aware-ness of the reformist thinking of trade union movements, socialism, feminism, or black consciousness.

Furthermore, deaf culture will not have strong roots until we fight for and gain recognition of our language and culture, through laws and policies. Sweden has led the way for us all, but we as a united deaf force can save ourselves much time if we fight for language recognition, not only in our own countries, but through the United Nations. The more success we have in this human rights struggle, the less power the medical profession will have over us.

It is often useful in presenting new ideas to try to wrap them into an easily under-stood package. All of the above suggestions, as well as subjects like deaf history, could be incorporated into Deaf Studies courses. Deaf culture would then have a foothold in schools and colleges for both deaf and hearing people, and funding would be available to support research into the subject.

Most work surrounding deafness and disability in general is done on an *ad hoc* basis, to our detriment. If we fully grasp our minority language and cultural status, however, we can centralize our development around concepts of language planning used by other linguistic minorities. Indeed, joining this field opens up a whole new arena of political allies with impressive expertise from which to draw.

In Britain, we need to shift our culture's center of gravity by accepting that the BSL-using community and its grass roots members are the heart of our deaf culture. Partially deaf, educated deaf, and hearing members of the culture need to move back from the front row and bring grass roots deaf people forward. Similarly, grass roots people need to accept that deaf culture is wide enough to embrace the other deaf who do not spend 100 percent of their time in the culture. What is needed is a balancing act, each section of the community supporting the other, using its particular skills to enable the culture to grow.

There is another group of deaf people whose behavior needs to be respected. There are many grassroots individuals who seem a bit strange—often a little isolated from the center of the club scene. I could describe them better in BSL than in written English. These people often spend a lot of time in hearing society, often in rough-and-ready pub life where they pick up all kinds of useful knowledge. Some of them may be passionate about a particular subject and pursue it diligently even when they have great difficulty reading English. We may frown upon their rough-and-ready ways at the moment, but to continue ignoring this group is a loss we cannot afford.

People like this embody something of what we might call "the deaf archetype": the primitive, aboriginal deaf person struggling in a village or a tribe, trying to make sense of all that is going on around him or her. That primitive person is inside all of us. We have been doing our best to get as far away from that person as possible, which is no surprise, since we are trying to forget how we were seen as animals or savages.

But there is a great strength to be had from facing up to the fact that this primi-tive person has *not* gone away. There are still millions of people out there who see our gestures and grimaces as worthy of mocking. Our task is to turn that concept of primi-tiveness into something *positive,* to be proud of the fact that our minds are different, and to revel in the status of being freaks. Our difference is the source of our power: Our culture has to be nourished on it.

The stronger we feel about our own culture, the sooner we can develop another major attribute of deaf people—the fact that we can be found in every country in the world and we can communicate with each other internationally. Our chances of building a genuine world culture are growing. But we must beware of making the same mistake as hearing people, imposing the language and culture of one country onto another. Each country's sign language must be developed from within, not forced on its deaf people from outside.

In the last twenty years, hearing people have started to realize that we all have to live together on this one planet and keep it healthy. Unfortunately, this realization has arisen in an already badly damaged environment. For the last 100 years, Western culture has developed industries, armaments, and poisons that now threaten the survival of the whole planet. Our only way forward is to accept the fact that we must become world citizens and take care of the planet as a whole. To belong only to a tribe or a nation is no longer enough.

But the world needs to see an example of such thinking and behavior in order to know what to copy. We have such an example right here. We have in our combined deaf cultures the embryo of a world culture—the potential to love other deaf people deeply whom we have never seen or met. We are the Fourth World, with the potential to unify the other three. This view may seem far-fetched, but culture is nourished by vision. And we do have inside us the seeds that can make this vision grow.

It is highly appropriate that this conference takes place exactly 200 years after the French Revolution. That revolution's particular vision not only changed France, but half the world. And, of course, it was the French Revolution that finally established the deaf community, when for the first time in the history of the world a government began to pay for deaf children to receive an education and hence enabled deaf people to develop their culture. [Editor's note: See Quartararo and Karacostas, this volume.] Most of Europe and America followed and—despite the damage of Milan—that path led right across the world to where we stand today!

Reflections of Deaf Culture in Deaf Humor

M. J. BIENVENU

It is a pleasure to be given the opportunity to share my research on humor in the American Deaf community and to work with my favorite Frenchman, Guy Bouchauveau. It has been eleven years since I first met Guy. At that time, neither of us was fluent in the other's language, so working together for six weeks gave us the opportunity to share and learn from each other. I picked up some LSF (French Sign Language) from him; he learned some ASL from me. But, most importantly, we exchanged the wit and sarcasm unique to both our cultures.

Humor and Culture

People often pity Deaf people, because their culture has taught them that we are born with five senses: hearing, sight, smell, taste, and touch. And of course, with Deaf people, the first sense is absent, leaving only four. Many people see that as deprivation. This is really a fallacy, because Deaf people have an added sense—a sense of humor—and therefore all five senses are intact.

This paper is drawn from several sources: from the work of Dr. Susan Rutherford, from my knowledge of American Deaf culture, and from my personal observations. At first glance, the study of humor may appear to be insignificant, yet upon further analysis it is apparent that what people respond to is very revealing. Humor is a difficult aspect of culture to study. One needs to have deep knowledge of the culture, with a full understanding of the people and the situations that the humor represents. You see, humor is integrally related to culture. Humor is based on people's perceptions of the world, and it is shared between groups of people who share similar values and belief systems.

Humor is almost a necessity. Like air, water, or fire, we need humor to survive our daily existence. Without it, life would be intolerable at times. One example of how humor is used to balance our lives can be seen in the entertainment industry. Movie directors have closely studied the need to mix fear and humor in films. Often comic relief is provided at the most suspenseful moments, to relieve the physical and mental pressure of the cinematic action. Similarly, people in very stressful situations often find that humor is one way to relieve some of the pressure and to help them cope with their problems.

Of course, humor is essential at social gatherings where people cluster in groups and exchange stories, jokes, and experiences. Humor is one way people share their perceptions of the world, express different levels of intimacy, and find comfort in knowing that others share their beliefs and their sense of humor.

Often, at conferences, the presenter will begin a lecture with a joke. It is usually a silly joke, and everyone laughs. This may seem frivolous on the surface, but it really serves two purposes. It helps everyone relax, and it also creates a bond between the audience and the presenter.

Humor is an integral part of our lives. It can be found in our homes, at our work place, in every form of media and entertainment. Can you imagine what life would be like if there were absolutely no humor?

There are many cultures throughout the world, and each one has developed its own unique brand of humor. For example, in America, different minority cultures each have their own sense of humor, but there is also a larger humor that we all share—American humor—which consists of ethnic jokes, political jokes, and even jokes related to America. Europeans have developed jokes about America, just as we have developed similar ethnic jokes that target other nationalities. This is one way cultures identify their members and create solidarity—by excluding or making fun of outsiders.

It is interesting that American jokes that seem very funny to insiders may be misunderstood or even seen as insulting if shared with cultural outsiders from another country. Likewise an American traveling abroad may not always be able to appreciate that culture's unique humor. This is because humor cannot be learned. It must be acquired through an understanding of the people's shared experiences and world view.

This article will not focus on cultural humor in general. I have simply laid the groundwork for a basic understanding of how humor is culturally dependent. I would now like to focus specifically on humor in the American Deaf community and how it reflects our culture.

American Deaf culture has flourished for hundreds of years, and through our language, ASL, our history and heritage have survived. This rich folklore has been handed down through generations and continues to be an essential method for transmitting cultural norms, values, and belief systems. Humor is an important way these messages are conveyed. I have been investigating the way humor reflects Deaf culture for quite a few years and have determined four major categories on which the humor is based: the visual nature of humor; humor based on deafness as an inability to hear; humor from a linguistic perspective; and humor as a response to oppression. Each of these four categories reflects the values, norms, and belief systems in our American Deaf culture.

The Visual Nature of Deaf Humor

As most of you know, Deaf people perceive most things through their eyes. Naturally, we acquire language visually. It is worth noting that sign languages throughout the world adapt to meet the physical needs and comfort of the people who use them. We also acquire world knowledge visually. Everything we value and everything we experience are acquired visually. American Sign Language was developed over a period of time in America, just as other countries developed their own sign languages naturally to express themselves and to interpret the world around them.

Because this visual communication is so critical in Deaf languages, it comes as no surprise that Deaf humor also has a strong visual base. In short, we depend on our eyes for most things, and humor is no exception. ASL jokes that are visually funny often do not have the same wit when spoken. Likewise, people who are not deaf often find things funny in the aural mode that Deaf people cannot relate to.

To many Deaf people, the world is filled with comical sights. But this humor is not always shared with the larger American culture. There have been many stories recounting the experiences of Deaf people who go to the movies and are unable to relate to the culture around them. At times, the hearing audience is in stitches, laughing uncontrollably at a conversation that is visually dull: The humor is English/sound dependent. Of course, this humor isn't a part of Deaf culture.

Likewise, the Deaf couple may laugh hysterically at an inappropriate place in the movie, because their cues are all visually dependent. The screen may have an image of people in terror. With the sound effects booming, and people screaming, the hearing audience is frightened. But for Deaf people, the funny reactions and overly dramatic expressions of the actors are enough to send us into unrestrained laughter.

One experience I had several years ago may clarify this point. I coordinated an intensive ASL retreat for a group of people who are not deaf. They were not allowed to use voice or depend on their hearing, which meant they could not depend on their alarm clocks, for example. One night we gathered to watch a movie on TV, *King Kong*. Of course, the volume was off, and for the first time, they realized what Deaf audiences have known all along: The actors' expressions are hysterically funny. On the screen, the New Yorkers were running for their lives, with the shadow of the monster ape looming over their heads, yet the people experiencing this spectacle *visually* for the first time were laughing. I asked them what they found so funny. They said, "Their faces!" The same people would have felt scared if they had heard the people screaming in terror with threatening music in the background. So they got a glimpse of how funny visual humor can be.

Deaf people find many things visually humorous that others, particularly from auditory-based cultures, do not. Many Deaf people are quite creative in their descriptions of life around them. This talent is fostered in residential schools, where most children learn the art of storytelling and most importantly, how to imitate different people. No one was safe from our stories: neither the strict teacher reprimanding (in speech) another student nor the behavior of other friends. Every identifying characteristic of the person would be imitated, right down to the way he or she walked. It is this intimate detail that remains such a crucial part of the humor of Deaf people.

Often people who are not members of the culture will respond negatively to this form of humor, a common misunderstanding with outsiders who do not understand the goal. We are not insulting the people we describe; we are merely delighting in the precision of our language to convey these characteristics accurately. It is not meant to harm or ridicule; it is simply a form of entertainment.

Other related humor is reflected through the media. Even before captions on TV were invented, Deaf people watched television. Deaf children in residential schools were often sent to the recreation room on Saturday mornings and would watch, primarily, cartoons. The older forms of cartoons were much easier to understand and visually funny; thus many jokes were developed from the characters and events we had just seen on the screen. One of my childhood favorites was this one:

> **Question:** A train is roaring down the tracks, black clouds of smoke puffing from the smokestack. All of a sudden it screeches to a halt, and all the cars topple and crash into one another, until there is nothing left but a smoking charred pile of demolished cars. What happened?
> **Answer:** There was a tiny ant standing on the tracks with its arm outstretched to stop the train.

Many people may not find this funny, and in a sound-based language such as English, it loses much of its humor. But for Deaf children, and even adults, the visual irony of a wee, insignificant ant causing so much damage to something as powerful as the locomotive is an image rich with humor.

Visual perception is a strong component of Deaf humor, which can include characteristics of different people, world events, and basically everything we perceive through our eyes. One way our culture is passed on and reinforced is the shared experience of how we as a culture see the world and translate it into humor.

Humor Based on Deafness as the Inability to Hear

As we all know, being Deaf is much more than the inability to hear. Deafness is a complete culture, where one's decibel loss is much less important than one's allegiance to the Deaf community. Yet a significant amount of Deaf folklore contains jokes and stories that deal with the inability to hear. It all depends on one's perspective. While the majority culture may perceive a Deaf person as an object of pity and despair, most Deaf people feel healthy and satisfied with the richness of their culture and heritage. This attitude is particularly clear in this category of humor, which always portrays the Deaf person as victorious.

Interestingly, in Roy Holcomb's book, *Hazards of Deafness*, it is evident that his humor does not follow the lead of the culturally Deaf tradition, but rather focuses on stories in which Deaf people lament their "condition." Not surprisingly, it isn't exactly a popular book among the Deaf community. This humor is typical of an outsider's view of deafness and does not accurately reflect the values and traditions inherent in authentic Deaf folklore.

Let me describe one of the scenes in the book to clarify my point: A Deaf person is having a difficult time vacuuming the carpet. He goes over the same spot of dirt repeatedly, to no avail. In a fit of frustration, he turns around and notices that the machine is unplugged.

This is a perfect example of humor that is not a part of Deaf culture. Of course, this would never happen in the first place, because a Deaf person would naturally feel the inactive motor and immediately respond appropriately. What is more disturbing is the emphasis on hearing and the dependency on sound the book portrays. Culturally Deaf people are quite articulate in defining the world in terms other than sound and have adapted to technology as swiftly as people who are not deaf. The fact that the author does not address Deaf people's keenly developed sense of sight and touch is rather significant.

Many stories have been handed down for generations in Deaf folklore, and the most treasured are those that delight in our inability to hear as an advantage. The following tale is one of the most popular:

> A Deaf couple has just arrived at the motel for their honeymoon. They start unpacking for the night, and then the nervous husband goes out to get a drink. When he returns to the motel, he realizes that he has forgotten his room number. Because it is dark outside and all the rooms look alike, he walks out to his car and continues to honk the horn until the rooms start lighting up with angry hearing boarders who were awakened by the noise—all but one room, where his Deaf wife is waiting for him!

This story shows how Deaf people can solve a problem creatively and humorously.

Humor from a Linguistic Perspective

A third component of Deaf humor can be categorized as linguistic. There are several ways to manipulate American Sign Language in humorous ways: by using puns, humor related to use of words, and unique syntactic structures. Many Deaf people are quite prolific in their use of language to convey wit.

Production/misproduction of signs is one common way to elicit laughs in ASL. As stated in Bellugi and Klima's book, *The Signs of Language*, one example of this is how we have changed the root-sign UNDERSTAND to LITTLE-UNDERSTAND by using the pinkie finger in the production, rather than the larger index finger.

Much of this linguistic humor is lexically based, and the punch lines to many ASL jokes are related to the production of the words. One of my favorite examples is the "Giant" joke that many Deaf people have also seen and enjoyed. It is funny both culturally and linguistically:

> A huge giant is stalking through a small village of wee people, who are scattering throughout the streets, trying to escape the ugly creature. The giant notices one particularly beautiful blonde-haired girl scampering down the cobblestone street. He stretches out his clumsy arm and sweeps up the girl, then stares in wonder at the slight shivering figure in his palm. "You are so beautiful!" he exclaims. The young woman looks up in fear. "I would never hurt you," he signs. "I love you. I think we should get MARRIED." With the production of the sign MARRY, of course, the beautiful mistress is crushed. The giant then laments, "See, ORALISM is better."

Several components make this joke successful in American Sign Language. First, it is visually active, because the expressions of the townspeople, the beautiful girl, and the giant can be dramatized to perfection. Second, it is linguistically funny because of the sign production MARRY, which causes the girl of his affection to splat in his palm. Third, it is funny in its irony, because culturally Deaf people hate oralism, having been oppressed by that method. Therefore, the giant's conclusion that oralism would have saved his beloved girl is funny. That's just one of many examples of how linguistic-based humor can be expressed through ASL.

Humor as a Response to Oppression

It is no secret that Deaf people are an oppressed minority, and one way that cultures often deal with this oppression is through humor. For many years Deaf people have experienced oppression from the majority culture, so naturally our humor has incorporated the dynamic spirit of our people. This category of humor, sometimes called zap stories, usually features Deaf people getting even.

Often when Deaf people are naturally conversing in public, hearing people will stare at them in curiosity or disbelief. When they finally gain the courage to initiate a conversation with Deaf people, they will inevitably start flapping their lips, and for the millionth time, the Deaf person will be asked, "Can you read my lips?" Well, of course, Deaf people are keenly aware of the configuration of this one sentence and will always answer "No!" which is pretty funny, indeed. If they couldn't read lips, how could they understand what the person asked in the first place? But it would be interesting if the tables were turned. Suppose a Deaf couple were conversing, and suddenly one of them turned around to the nosy person and signed, "Can you read my hands?" That would serve them right. People who are not deaf are always forcing Deaf people to try to make sense out of the odd mouth movements and over-exaggerated facial expressions. Just once, it would be nice to reverse the trend.

Another way Deaf humor fights back at this oppression is to show hearing people in a stupor, shocked at being outsmarted by a Deaf person. One famous example, which is a true story, provides the required ending:

> A group of Deaf people are at a restaurant, chatting away. At the table next to them is a group of hearing people who are rudely mimicking their signs and behaviors. One particularly bright Deaf woman decides she's had enough of this abuse. She leaves the table, walks to a nearby phone booth, picks up the receiver, and puts the coins in the machine, making sure that she is being observed by the hearing group. After a short pause, she starts signing into the receiver, using natural expression and pausing for the person on the other end to respond. When she has completed her call, she hangs up and strolls back to the table to resume her conversation. Needless to say, the hearing people are dumbfounded and unable to move, much less ridicule the Deaf crowd. When the Deaf group leaves the restaurant, they watch as the hearing people run over to inspect the phone.

Deaf people love this one, because we finally have the last laugh. There are many stories in this category, and most of them target people who have the nerve to ridicule Deaf culture. For example, a group of Deaf people may be conversing in public and perhaps a person in the group is the hearing daughter or son of Deaf parents, or maybe a Deaf person with excellent speech. It is common for a group of hearing people to rudely mimic the signs, making fun of our language.

Imagine what would happen if a member of the Deaf group turned around and said, "Do you know what you just said?" Of course, the hearing "signer" would have no idea what he or she might have said. "No, what?" With a straight face, the person from the Deaf group says, "You just said your mother looks like a monkey!" Of course, that would leave the hearing delinquents flabbergasted, and probably afraid to lift their hands again. These kinds of tales are rich with justice, because the rude offender is always put in his or her place. Another good example of this type of humor is typified in the famous "Hitchhiker" story:

> A Deaf man is driving along and stops to pick up a hitchhiker, who cannot understand his signs but welcomes the ride. The Deaf man, anxious to reach his destination, is speeding and eventually is pulled over by a cop. Of course, the policeman begins talking with pursed lips to the driver. When it is clear that the driver is deaf, the officer, who cannot sign, decides to gesture a simple warning to slow down. The hitchhiker observes this with interest. Later on that night, the weary Deaf man pulls over and trades places with his passenger. The hitchhiker, also in a hurry, does exactly what the Deaf man did—he speeds. He too sees the flashing police lights behind him and pulls over. Again, an officer starts speaking to the driver. The hitchhiker, expecting to take advantage of his new-found trick, shakes his head and points to his ears. However, this time, the police officer begins to sign, "My parents were deaf. I know sign language. You were speeding . . . ."

This is a significant joke because it underlies the unanimous fear that hearing people, if given the opportunity, would find ways to benefit from the language and culture of the Deaf community. This joke serves as a warning to those who would dare to profit from our Deaf heritage.

In the same way that American Deaf culture, as well as European Deaf culture, is oppressed by the majority community, so our language is oppressed. From oralism, to Signed English systems, to other ludicrous forms of English/sound coding, Deaf people have suffered under the thumb of hearing educators for many years.

From the signs these so-called experts invent, it is obvious they have no knowledge of Deaf culture or ASL. In fact, some of their signs are so vulgar that it would really be best to send young children to another room when using them. Of course, the vulgarity is unintentional, but it's humorous just the same. Often the signs they invent already have an established meaning. Many of them look sexual and are really inappropriate for young children to see, which is ironic, because often school systems will teach them. It's even worse when they are printed in sign language books, which often look as if they were purchased at porno shops. Deaf children leaf through the pages of these sign-coded manuals with delight, snickering at all the "dirty" signs pictured in the textbook.

As one response to these oppressive attempts at linguistic isolation, Deaf people have chosen to incorporate into their discourse some of the artificial codes created from the oral/Cued Speech/Signed English systems. One sign of Deaf empowerment is the freedom we have to take back control of the signs that were so oppressive in the past. Coded English signs for IS, AM, ARE, WERE, BEING, -ING, -ED, and so on, have all been reclaimed by Deaf speakers and are used with sarcasm directed toward those who created them. Of course, the humor is most pronounced when a contorted face accompanies the deviant signs—an editorial on the ineffectiveness of these codes.

Conclusion

Humor is an essential part of all our lives. I am sure you have all heard the expression, "Laughter is the best medicine." Well, there is much truth to that, particularly when you analyze minority cultures and realize that they all inevitably incorporate the mechanisms of majority oppression into their humor. It is a common response to the frustration and tedium of our everyday lives. It is also one way people have found to cope with their problems, for in humor, the storyteller determines who will "win"! The following story is an apt illustration of the principle and a fitting way to end this paper:

> Three people are on a train—one Russian, one Cuban, and one Deaf person. The Russian is drinking from a bottle of vodka. She drinks about half the bottle, then throws it out the window. The Deaf person looks at her, surprised. "Why did you throw out a bottle of vodka that was only half-empty?" The Russian replies, "Oh, in my country we have plenty of vodka!" Meanwhile, the Cuban, who is smoking a rich, aromatic cigar, abruptly tosses it out the window. The Deaf person is again surprised and asks, "Why did you throw out the cigar?" The Cuban replies, "Oh, in my country we have plenty of cigars!" The Deaf person nods with interest. A little while later, a hearing person walks down the aisle. The deaf person grabs the hearing person and throws *him* out the window. The Russian and Cuban look up in amazement. The Deaf person shrugs, "In my country we have plenty of hearing people!"

References

Holcomb, Roy. 1977. *Hazards of Deafness*. Northridge, CA: Joyce Media.

Bellugi, U., and E. S. Klima. 1979. *The Signs of Language*. Cambridge: Harvard University Press.

Deaf Humor and Culture

GUY BOUCHAUVEAU

The subject of this paper is the humor unique to sign language and the deaf community and how this form of humor develops within deaf culture.

First, let us consider where evidence of humor among deaf people can be found. In France, it is quite unusual to see deaf children spontaneously sharing humor in school. It is only when there are adult deaf people in these schools that small deaf children can start using sign language, communicating effectively, and thus learning to use humor. When adult deaf people laugh, a deaf child can understand the joke and laugh in turn, but if the adult is a hearing person, the deaf child is excluded from the understanding and the laughter.

On the other hand, deaf culture and its humor resurface in places where deaf people tend to gather: associations, banquets, dances, and the like. We usually meet to help one another quench our thirst for communication. It's like the desire of hearing people who, deprived of music, feel they must listen to a record.

Hearing people can read a funny story and laugh at it. I have noticed that deaf people never laugh at these stories, regardless of whether or not they are oralists. Hearing and deaf people don't find the same things funny. For example, I can understand plays on words in French, but that's not what it takes to make me laugh. When a joke in French is translated into sign language, deaf people respond, "Yes, that's interesting," but never actually laugh—for them it's not really funny because the two cultures are too far apart.

I have referred to meetings of deaf people. This is where they laugh, and it's sign language that makes it possible.

If we consider what happens to mainstreamed deaf people who, as adults, end up as members of deaf associations, they can't impart humor because of their lack of competence in sign language. If I compare these deaf people, whom I will call oralists, with deaf people fluent in French Sign Language (LSF), I find the latter's humor to be more creative.

About twenty years ago, this was the situation in France: Humor existed wherever deaf people got together. Comic art emerged spontaneously in the context of communication among deaf individuals. But artistic productions or theatrical performances of comedies did not yet exist. There was an extremely rich gestural comic art everywhere, but because it was not publicly performed, there was little awareness of it.

The deaf community has progressed over the last ten years with the creation in Paris of the International Visual Theatre (IVT). Theatrical plays in sign language appeared at the same time as the first courses in LSF. It was then that thoughtful evaluation of sign language began that the deaf community became conscious of the beauty of its language and of its artistic and comic dimensions. I think some very interesting plays already existed in the deaf community well before I was born, but they were never shown in public. It's a shame, though, that deaf humor never leaves the deaf community and that hearing people are being deprived of it.

Let's consider now who is using humor and what kinds they are using. The kind of humor differs according to age level. Deaf adolescents like to crack jokes based on mockery. They poke fun at physical changes, teasing with a sexual connotation. For twenty-year-olds entering their professional lives, humor is more diversified: There are elements of ridicule but also visual word games. Deaf people around the age of forty who have mastered their language and can distance themselves from it are the best at comedy. They incorporate political themes into their funny stories and take jabs at hearing individuals. They have become conscious of their oppression by hearing people and, through mockery, take their revenge upon the hearing world. This is where sign language is being used to its fullest creative potential.

As an example of the last category, I will use a story from the world of soccer, the national sport of France that is played all over the world. The photographs in figure 1 are taken from a videotape of me telling a story of a soccer match between a team of hearing players and a team of deaf players. Stories of this kind serve an important purpose. Often, it is only when different kinds of people—deaf and hearing in this case—are placed side by side in a story that we are able to see their defining characteristics.

In the story, the two teams arrive at the big stadium. Players from each team sign autographs for their respective fans. The teams look each other over, then go to their separate locker rooms to prepare for the match.

Deaf people practice this comic art among themselves and unfortunately, even hearing people who know sign language may have trouble appreciating the humor. These individuals—sometimes parents with one deaf child—can't seem to participate in the visual logic and therefore don't fully share the deaf culture, unlike their deaf children who are immediately in tune with it. Perhaps these parents are too timid to take it on or they can't understand it—it's hard to say. There is a parting of the ways between hearing parents and their deaf children in this area: They don't laugh at the same things. The same situation occurs among deaf parents with hearing children. I hope that in the future there will be an exchange and a meeting of the two worlds. It is important that we be able to share humor.

Conversely, some comical elements from the hearing world can amuse deaf people. For example, I—for one—adore Charlie Chaplin and Laurel and Hardy films.

I remember going to Seville a few years ago to participate in a colloquium on the theme of culture and the handicapped. The conference lasted until noon, or rather a little later, as is Spanish custom, and all of us went to lunch together. Of course, the deaf individuals all sat together. There were some French, Spanish, German, and Belgian people in this group. As the meal progressed, exchanges became more and more meaningful and we very quickly got to the point of telling funny stories about various countries.

The atmosphere at the deaf group's table was very warm and cheerful, unlike the very cold and stiff aspect of the hearing group's tables. We were nearly embarassed over the difference. The hearing group probably thought we had had too much to drink, but that wasn't the case. Communication—on a very happy note—quickly started among members of our group, despite our different nationalities. I think that here we have touched upon what is unique to our culture. We can meet deaf people from anywhere in the world and find ourselves immediately on the same wavelength. There is no boundary between us. This is not the case with hearing individuals.

Three different forms of humor can be distinguished in sign language. The first form is a funny story whose punch line inspires laughter, as in the story above about a

The deaf players plan their strategy in their locker room.

The hearing players are worried about the strategies of the world champion deaf soccer players.

The hearing players put their ears to the wall to hear the deaf strategy, but hear nothing.

In the stadium galleries, the deaf fans are signing excitedly.

The hearing fans are not moving much—only their mouths move.

The stiff, hearing referee speaks the rules without signing, forgetting the deaf players can't hear him.

A female interpreter is brought onto the field. When the referee blows his whistle, she signs "WHISTLE!"

This was a table soccer match—only table soccer.

FIGURE 1: An example of adult humor.

A woman walks along in
high heels.

A man pursues the woman
with apparent interest.

The woman nervously
observes the man walking too
closely beside her.

The woman threatens to kick
the man in his shins.

FIGURE 2: An example of caricaturization with people.

soccer match. It is revealed only in the punch line that the tournament being described
is *table soccer*, not *real* soccer.

Another form is the imitation of animals or people, various roles being played to
the point of caricaturization (see figures 2 and 3 for some examples). The third form of
humor is the invention of images through signing that don't actually exist in life—the
creation of absurd images (see figure 4). This form is akin to cartoons, always featuring
an original, imaginative element. The second form amounts to imitation, and the first is
comparable to a funny story. But note that it's never a matter of word games as hearing
people play them. It's not a question of reversing syllables or using slang or hip words.
That doesn't work for us. Our humor or poetry is always inspired by an image—the
potential, or the redundancy, of an image—by a visual logic, a description.

Now I'm not making a value judgment here. Deaf people's humor is neither better
nor worse than hearing people's, but I think it has to be analyzed differently.

Humor exists for deaf people. It's undeniable. But note that it is nearly untranslatable: Words that should represent the translation of an image communicate nothing,
and the comic aspect totally disappears; the reverse is also true, and it is useless to try
to inspire laughter using interpretation—it would be meaningless. What is unique to
sign language has nothing to do with words and thus is untranslatable.

German Shepherd walking

German Shepherd growling at intruder

Bulldog walking

Bulldog eating

FIGURE 3: An example of caricaturization with animals.

So take care when using the word "culture." Deaf culture is inseparable from the sign language naturally used by deaf people, and it is sign language that permits access to the comic mode. On the subject of bilingual education for deaf students, I would like to make it clear to all that the basic language is sign language. Very often people confuse everything, and we end up with a kind of "tossed salad." What I consider important is that sign language is the primary language for a deaf person and the deaf children who, little by little, appropriate it. With it, deaf children can be themselves and can acquire a clear sense of identity. For me, real mainstreaming occurs when two people feel good about themselves and respect their differences.

Now I'll give you another kind of example. This one, however, is about a very serious subject, DEATH, so you must not laugh. The top five photographs in figure 5 show a person's death, the bottom five photographs show an animal's death. You see, this is difficult to translate and is even untranslatable.

To conclude, humor exists among deaf people of all generations, and what I have just shown is a number of funny things communicated nonverbally so as to be accessible to all.

Biplane wings in their normal position

One wing prods the other to suggest going north.

That wing goes north, but the other insists on going south, with disastrous results.

FIGURE 4: Creating an absurd image.

A man is walking.

He is stricken.

He falls on back.

One foot falls.

The other foot falls.

Bird with top-knot.

The bird is walking.

It is stricken.

It falls on its side.

Its toes curl into fists.

FIGURE 5: Examples of how sign language can be untranslatable.

Deaf Culture, Tacit Culture, and Ethnic Relations

EDWARD T. HALL

When I was invited to address The Deaf Way Conference, I was more than happy to oblige. While I could not in any way be considered knowledgeable in the subtleties and innuendos of Deaf culture, I have a long familiarity with being different and struggling to make myself understood in a low context word culture in which verbal symbols are more important than the more subtle language of behavior and context.

However, I accepted for other reasons. My specialty for more than forty years has been the field of nonverbal communication, and Deaf culture is a classic case of the strength of nonverbal culture. Viewed from the perspective of those who are not deaf, everything except the elimination of the auditory channel seems quite the same. On the surface, only the language is different. Yet the *culture*, as Carol Padden and Tom Humphries (1989) so elegantly state, *is significantly different.*

When examined by a specialist in nonverbal cultures, these differences become blatant. Focusing on Deaf culture will shed new light on the problems faced by members of other minorities as they interact with each other on a global scale. With each passing year, the need for the ethnic and minority groups of the world to evolve effective means of communication without tearing each other to bits becomes more pressing.

Imprinting

There is much to be thankful for in this world, including the insights of individuals such as the great and perceptive ethologist Konrad Lorenz (1952). Among his many contributions to the understanding of animal life is the concept of *imprinting*. Imprinting is an innate process that causes some birds, such as geese, to follow not only their mother when young, but *any* moving object, including a human being, that they see at birth. The imprinted image becomes embedded in a pre-existing set of responses. As the young male goose matures, he will choose whomever and whatever he was imprinted with as a gosling as an object of his affections. This does not mean that the maturing goose cannot learn and adapt to changing conditions—only that the imprinted part of his "personality" continues to play a prominent role in his life.

A slightly different version of this paper appeared under the same title in *Sign Language Studies*, volume 65 (Winter 1989), pp. 291–304.

Clearly we humans are not geese, or mice, or Sika deer, who die off from over-crowding. But there is an important aspect of human culture that, in its manifestations, is similar to—if not a direct spinoff of—a process like imprinting in animals. And the gap between the imprinted part and the consciously manifested part is causing no end of mischief.

States of Culture

What I am talking about are two states of culture: *manifest-prescriptive* and *personal-tacit* (MP and PT).[1] At present, the gap separating the two might well be likened to the distance between the earth and the moon.

Manifest-prescriptive culture is what people talk about and use in the course of every-day life—their "designs for living," including myths, beliefs, values, dogmas, ideologies, and religious beliefs. It includes all the things people think of as external to themselves that they can verbalize. These things are used for prescriptive purposes (that is, they are laid down as rules).

Within the culture, where the rules are known and shared, stereotypes about out-siders are common, hence the judgmental character of individuals in the prescriptive mode. Manifest-prescriptive culture also includes imposed or "received" culture, such as what the upper-class English receive at Eaton and Harrow. The disingenuous use of the racist label to achieve political ends also fits into this category.

Personal or tacit culture is the antithesis of prescribed culture. It contains the paradox that although it is shared, each person is also unique. Tacit culture is not experienced as *culture*, but simply as *being!* This may be why people have so much trouble acknowl-edging that they, too, in the most personal part of themselves, are not only products of culture, but *are* culture. It includes the programming of the perceptual systems, includ-ing the senses, and the tacit aspects of the Primary Message Systems,[2] all of which have significant components that are out of our awareness.

We are all imprinted by personal (or tacit) culture, which is why it *is* so personal. It is this highly personalized experience, the "me" quality, that makes it so difficult for people to come to grips with the reality of tacit culture. When different ethnic groups interact en masse, tacit cultural differences can be devastating. A proper understand-ing of nonverbal culture—augmented by what can be learned from the study of Deaf culture—can contribute to improved ethnic relations worldwide.

My basic premise is this: Behind the power of culture lies the power of the self in the membership in a group. But the self can only be formed around symbols that are shared with others. The symbols and how they are used determine how people orga-nize their worlds—how they think, how they communicate, and the feeling and tone of the communication.

---

1 The "tacit" dimension of culture is very close to my use of the term "informal culture" first introduced in the context of *formal, informal,* and *technical* culture in my book *The Silent Language* (1959) and in Michael Polanyi's small volume, *The Tacit Dimension* (1966). Polanyi was a physical chemist at the University of Manchester, England, so that while the overall patterns he describes are quite similar to mine, his approach is that of a hard scientist. The term *tacit* is, however, somewhat more precise and is used here for that reason.

2 The ten Primary Message Systems (PMS) are paired: (0) communication and (9) material systems; (1) social structure and (8) perpetuation systems; (2) labor and (7) play; (3) the sexes and (6) enculturation; (4) territoriality and (5) temporality. Rooted in biology and the history of the species, they represent culture's core systems. See *The Silent Language* (Hall, 1959).

Language and Culture

Any discourse on language and culture faces the problem of separating the language from the culture and vice versa. While the majority of descriptive linguists and cultural anthropologists have known for a long time that language and culture are embedded in each other, there are teachers of language who see language as completely separate from culture and really do teach it that way. Their counterparts can be found among those who teach Deaf people.

Language is an extension of various expressive systems, both vocal and nonvocal, springing from practically every part of the body (Hall, 1959). And there was a time when language and culture were indistinguishable.

The verbal-nonverbal dichotomy is a false product of manifest culture that overlaps both the tacit and the manifest aspect of culture. Users of the dominant verbal culture project characteristics of their own system onto Deaf people, frequently with tragic consequences (Padden and Humphries, 1989). In the process, they manage to misinterpret and underrate the speed, subtlety, and richness of what, for want of a better name, may be termed the "languages of the body."[3] We see this in a particularly poignant way in Padden and Humphries' book, *Deaf in America: Voices from a Culture* (1989).

A feature of all highly *contexted* (Hall, 1976) cultures such as that of Deaf people, the Native Americans, and the Japanese (as well as Mediterranean, Eastern European, Latino, and a large proportion of third world countries, which seem to belong in this category)—whose members share a deep and rich information base—is the importance attached to *mood*. This quality, plus a strong emotional link to the culture, emphasizes the limbic functions of the central nervous system over the more linear, less emotional expression of the highly articulate, left brain cultures, in which the emotions are apt to be either repressed or suppressed.

Those who speak and write about Deaf culture reveal that there is this added gap between the high sensitivity to mood on the part of Deaf people and the relative insensitivity to mood in the culture of the dominant society. I have encountered this same dichotomy frequently in my research with the Germans, the French, the Japanese, white Americans, Hispanic Americans, and Native Americans living in New Mexico. With the exception of the Germans and white Americans, all of the above are acutely aware of mood shifts and often will respond to such shifts within seconds. A similar point of tension must exist between Deaf people and the hearing peoples whose world they inhabit. This is because *the language of the body, like the pupillary reflex, does not have to be translated from concept into words. There are fewer steps in the neurological chain.*

More should be said concerning tacit culture, and what better place to begin than with language. All languages ride on a tacit axiomatic base, which can be illustrated by the work of one of our country's top linguists, Charles Ferguson. In the 1950s, while working as a linguistic scientist at the United States Department of State's Foreign Service Institute, Ferguson tackled the task of creating an orthography for colloquial Arabic, which did not have a written form. To linguists who had been previously asked to create orthographies for American Indian languages such as Navajo, there was nothing new about what he was doing. What was new was that Ferguson had been asked to analyze *colloquial* Arabic, a language within a language, which was considered profane.

Because of the nature of this language, Ferguson encountered an extraordinary array of theories, not just on the part of lay people but even from well qualified, highly

---

3 While there will be points in my paper that are applicable, I did not make use of Birdwhistell's term *kinesics* because it is not in any way applicable to the problems of Deaf people when using American Sign Language (ASL), nor does it apply as currently used to such basic matters as *gait* as it is read by others.

intelligent academicians with advanced degrees. They said that colloquial Arabic was not a language: that it had no structure; that there was no syntax, and therefore there could be no such thing as improper usage—none of which was true. If people speak and understand, then there are rules and regularities that will be revealed under the proper system of analysis.

The misconceptions that Ferguson encountered appear to be applicable to any behavior—including language—not reduced to letters or numbers. But when did all this start? How did it happen? While it is doubtful that we will ever know the real or whole truth, some inklings can be gleaned from history.

In Western culture the enshrinement of words originated in the seventh and sixth centuries B.C. with Solon and his legal codes, and roughly 150 years later with Socrates and Plato. Since Solon's time, Western civilization has had as one of its cornerstones the belief in words as an instrument of laws, and an accompanying belief that democracy without laws is unthinkable. Implicit in Solon's thinking was that words be used systematically. Socrates, and later his pupil Plato, advanced these ideas several steps further. While important to philosophers and those gifted with their tongues, the belief that words used by laypersons—as in Ferguson's colloquial Arabic—are not lawful has proved to be a mixed blessing: Socrates and his intellectual heirs were apparently the first to get really technical about how to use words systematically to craft, test, and inspect ideas and concepts. The defect, which was not shared with the Sophists, was that they confused *talking* (and later writing) with *knowing,* a serious flaw and one that has been with us ever since.

The issue that impinges on the entire arena of tacit culture revolves around Socrates' belief "that the shoemaker should stick to his last"—that what the shoemaker says is not worth listening to, and that "the opinions of ordinary men are only *doxa*— beliefs without substance, pale shadows of reality, not to be taken seriously, and only likely to lead a city astray" (Stone, 1989). Socrates meant that there is neither wisdom nor pattern in what the anthropologists think of as culture, but only in the constructed ideas in philosophers' heads. That is, words are real, while common people and what they do are not worth noticing.

Culture as a Manifestation of Nature

Another facet to the complex story of intercultural relations has to do with culture as a natural system that evolved on its own without conscious direction. Culture at this level should be considered as simply another manifestation of nature. It is one thing to conduct a Socratic dialogue dealing with ideas rooted in unstated assumptions, and something else to look at nature with an open mind in the search for patterns inherent in the data.

It is axiomatic that nature does not send messages to humans. It just *is*. It is important, therefore, to keep one's eye on whatever nature, in its unanalyzed cultural form, serves up to us. There is a fundamental difference between language as nature—language spoken without conscious awareness, such as colloquial Arabic—and language in its extended[4] and altered self-conscious state—after it has been *reduced* to writing.

---

4 The term *extension* applies to a process that occurs when some aspect or feature becomes detached from the organism or a previously extended function, while continuing to serve its original purpose. Writing is an extension of language, while printing is an extension of writing. See my books *The Hidden Dimension* and *The Silent Language* (1966, 1959).

Why are all "natural" (nonextended, nontechnically described) systems of behavior treated so inappropriately? Why are the language and culture of Deaf people denied as legitimate systems of communication and being in their own right? Why can time be accepted as an astronomical and philosophical event, but rejected as a culture-specific, highly elaborated code for ordering behavior and for classifying relationships? And, last but not least, why did Socrates and Plato classify all natural cultural events—many of which required well developed skills, wisdom, and knowledge—as *doxa?*

There is a 2,500-year-old pattern here that distorts perceptions and obstructs the road to understanding. This is particularly applicable in considering that part of nature closest to all of us—the hidden rules of culture that not only guide our everyday lives, but also are projected onto others.

An image that never leaves me regarding this tacit side of culture is that of the yet unformulated algorithms—a vast sea that cannot be explored by philosophic means but only through observation. Linguists and anthropologists learned years ago that all languages and cultures should be approached with a mind open to what can be learned about how that system works, without theories or preconceived ideas and without reference to what is known about one's own linguistic or cultural system. This is precisely what William Stokoe (1960) did when he studied the language and culture of Deaf people using modified techniques borrowed from the descriptive linguists.

Nonverbal Communication

While Deaf people share practically all nonlanguage components of the dominant culture, they have put their own stamp on everything. Differences are a matter of shifting emphasis. However, Deaf people have their own language and their own culture, which that language generates. All cultures are blind to other cultures, especially so toward those in their own midst. Insofar as the dominant culture is concerned, the issues that are real to the Deaf culture are far from assured. In much of North America, even some hearing people who teach sign language are apt to choose a deficit model[5] and, consistent with that model, deny the very existence of Deaf culture. To make matters worse, they look on sign language as a degraded and imperfect form of the spoken language (Mykelbust, 1957). This is a view that is also projected onto all other nonlanguage cultural systems.

Given the insights generated by human and mammalian paleontology, ethology, MacLean's brain studies, and descriptive linguistics, it is clear that communication with the body not only *predates* language but differs radically from its spoken and written forms. The various forms of body communication are, as a rule, more direct, faster, less ambiguous, and therefore more reliable than words. The reasons are complex, but there is evidence to support this hypothesis even among high context peoples such as the Japanese, who distrust words and look for the underlying meaning in the expressions of the body and in the situation.

Body communication falls into several classes:[6] kinesics (gesture), which is a close

---

5 Rooted in Social Darwinism, the deficit model is one that Western countries used to apply to Third World peoples, Black peoples, and Native Americans, which held that they were all exactly like "Americans" except that they lacked certain crucial skills and habits. All that one had to do was to make them over in the white man's image and then they would be "just like us," and there would be no problem. It would appear that the deficit model has gone underground or into the closet (whichever metaphor you prefer), but it is still present and most certainly is a factor in relations between Deaf and hearing people.

6 In the context of this paper, I am restricting my analysis literally to the physiological and chemical responses of the body in transactions with others, including the physical environment.

accompaniment to and is normally in sync with spoken language; proxemics[7] (the language of spatial relations), chronemics (the language of temporal relations), and other forms that, while in and of the body, do not quite fit the category of kinesics.

My own research demonstrates that gait, for example, is one of the most widely relied upon of all body systems, because it is not only less likely to be faked, but is also very difficult to copy. Gait is an indicator of age, gender, mood, status, state of health, strength, energy level, and ethnicity.

One might say that what follow are the basic substrata in which American Sign Language (ASL) is embedded. They constitute major elements in the structure of Deaf culture and are commonly used as a means for reading mood and even relative status.

The eyes are powerful communicators. Among the Navajo as well as ethnic blacks, a look can be as assertive and forceful a message as a slap in the face. Dominance and submission are often signalled by the eyes. Both genders can use the eye in courting and wooing ("Drink to me only with thine eyes and I will pledge with mine"). The eyes become metaphors, as in "Yon Cassius has a lean and hungry look" and are used extensively by writers to describe relationships and character: "As he entered the room, his eyes darted about, missing nothing, penetrating every nook and cranny" and "His look was so commanding that women and men alike all came under his spell."

The pupillary reflex is not under control of the conscious mind. The size of the pupil accurately reflects interest or desire and has been used for millennia as a means of discerning the deepest feelings of the customer during bargaining in the Arab market place. This fact was also discovered independently by psychologist Ekhard Hess while teaching at the University of Chicago (Hess, 1960).

Synchrony of body rhythms is a fundamental component in body communication and one of a number of chronemic-kinesic features exerting a powerful, though subtle, influence on interpersonal and group processes. An individual who is "out of sync" with a group can have a devastating effect on the business of the group, without that person's conscious knowledge. Individuals in perfect synchrony with each other are matched sympathetically in more than a few ways, an important feature of which is that such people usually work well together. The photographs I have seen of Deaf students at Gallaudet University reveal an unusual degree of symbiotic synchrony. Culture in the international and inter-ethnic sense also is a factor in interpersonal synchrony (Hall, 1983).

Galvanic skin response was originally measured by Jung, along with heart and breathing rates, in conjunction with his word association tests. Galvanic skin response refers to electrical impulses produced by the body, which are measured through electrodes attached to the hands. Sweaty palms communicate volumes. Whether Deaf people are more or less sensitive to such signs, I do not know.

Radiant heat: My own work (1966) on the radiation of heat from various parts of the body shows that radiant heat is also an indicator of emotional state. The skin is one of the best emitters and receivers of radiant heat in the world. Clues indicate that it is a residual manifestation of what was once a piloerector display system, dating back to the earliest differentiation of mammals and birds. One of my students who was particularly sensitive to radiation in the infrared range of the spectrum could distinguish between her spouse's anger and lust in the dark at distances of up to two meters.

---

[7] Within the corpus of proxemic analysis, there are eighteen sensory scales employed by interlocutors in reading as well as setting: intimate, personal, social, and public distances.

Blushing, like the pupillary reflex, is beyond conscious control. People "blush" with their torso and abdomen, but because these areas of the body are normally covered by clothes, the message of the blood coming to the surface of the body is picked up by the radiant heat that is generated. Metaphors such as "He's a cold fish," "She's a hot number," "He was overcome by a burning, all-consuming passion," and the like indicate general recognition of body heat as a marker of emotional state.

Olfaction: Although we do our best to disguise and deny it, olfaction—the sense of smell—is a sensitive receptor of information regarding another person's health and physical condition, emotional state, sex, phase of menstrual cycle, familial relationship, success or failure ("the sweet smell of success"), and disposition (one has a sour or sweet disposition). A Washington psychoanalyst friend could smell the difference between anger and anxiety in her patients at one and one-half to two meters. Schizophrenics have a characteristic odor (Smith and Sines, 1960). Olfaction is a precursor, as well as a powerful stimulant, in sexual activity in animals and humans alike. The smell of the urine of another male can even suppress pregnancy in a female mouse (Parkes and Bruce, 1961).

In addition to body synchrony, proxemics has always played a strong role in the communication process. For northern European cultures and their offshoots in the new world, the four distances—intimate, personal, social/consultative, and public—must be used appropriately. Otherwise some form of a double bind or parataxic communication occurs. All of this has been amply documented in my own work (1966).

Time as a nonverbal system is as much a part of Deaf culture as it is of the culture of those who hear. Being late sends a message; *how late* signals the "volume" of the message. To be very late under certain conditions is an insult. Much of my early work as well as my most recent book (1983) was devoted to time. *Cultural* differences in time systems are as manifest and dramatic as any I know.

The preceding forms of communication are a rich and fertile resource of nonverbal information. And because Deaf people have their own versions of these forms—equivalent to "dialects"—they must be included in the content of Deaf culture. Furthermore, all the primary systems listed in *The Silent Language* (Hall, 1959) also would qualify. The nonverbal component of culture has been estimated at anywhere from 80 to 90 percent of the entire communication process. So it would appear that, in many ways, Deaf people not only do not have to struggle with the relationship of words to the rest of culture because they are equipped with a system that is infinitely more in sync with their organism than is that of hearing people. It is no wonder that many of you are willing to fight for the right to your own language and culture, which is so correct and so true, that you cannot abide outsiders messing with the very system that gives life its meaning.

What is remarkable is the blindness of hearing people to your needs. But then, they are blind to the tacit side of most other cultures as well. Only an increase in self-awareness can fix that. And self-awareness is a personal matter, not a political one.

Summary

In considering the above discussion of tacit culture, it is important to remember that we are looking through the microscope of the mind's eye at what amounts to 80–90 percent of all human communication. The rules and laws applicable to this percentage are outside of our awareness, and like Ferguson's speakers of colloquial Arabic and Socrates'

THE
DEAF
WAY
⤴

doxa, they are thought by most people to have no substance and to be hardly worthy of attention!

To recapitulate, we find a formidable array of armamentarium pointed in our direction: (a) the historical philosophies, dating back to Socrates and Plato, separating word constructs from nature; (b) the awareness gap separating manifest-prescriptive culture from tacit-personal culture; and (c) the cultural-channel blindness gap separating Deaf culture from the cultures of those who can hear.

It is axiomatic that the logic of science is rooted in the language used and that language must be rooted in the events in nature under observation (e.g., Newton's need to develop a new language—calculus—in order to carry on his work). Each new set of events can generate a need for a new language.

Words are the language of ideas (beginning with Solon, Socrates, and Plato), but not necessarily of events. That function is served by the language of the body or of the senses. The language of perception is different from the language of ideas, and the difference is a function of "channels" (visual vs. auditory, for example).

In order to understand another person, it is essential to understand their logic. This means understanding their symbol system, and that symbol system is not restricted to words. Like Einstein's clock, a symbol can be anything that releases a response.

Except for minor details, all of the above are matters that most people take for granted because they imbibed them "with their mother's milk," and as you know, mother's milk is sacred. All minorities suffer from some aspect of this paradigm. The gap between manifest-prescriptive culture and tacit-personal culture has so far been the most difficult to bridge. Why? Because, unlike the others, this one calls for basic changes in the deeper layers of the personality, changes that make it possible for people to accept each other *as they are* instead of as one would wish them to be. And this means that they must confront anxiety in the self as a consequence of shattering the projected images we all have of the worlds we create.

References

Hall, Edward T. 1959. *The Silent Language.* New York: Anchor Press/Doubleday.

———. 1966. *The Hidden Dimension.* New York: Anchor Press/Doubleday.

———. 1976. *Beyond Culture.* New York: Anchor Press/Doubleday. Chapters 6, 7, and 8.

———. 1983. *The Dance of Life: The Other Dimension of Time.* New York: Anchor Press/ Doubleday.

Hess, Eckhart H. 1960. "Pupil Size as Related to Interest Value of Visual Stimuli." *Science* 132: 349–350.

Lorenz, Konrad. 1952. *King Solomon's Ring.* New York: Crowell.

Mykelbust, E. 1957. *Psychology of Deafness.* New York: Grune and Straton.

Padden, Carol, and Thomas Humphries. 1989. *Deaf in America: Voices from a Culture.* Cambridge: Harvard University Press.

Parkes, A. S., and H. M. Bruce. 1961. "Olfactory Stimuli in Mammalian Reproduction." *Science* 134 (October 13): 1049–1054.

Polanyi, Michael. 1966. *The Tacit Dimension.* New York: Doubleday & Company, Inc.

Smith, Kathleen, and Jacob O. Sines. 1960. "Demonstration of a Peculiar Odor in the

Sweat of Schizophrenic Patients." *AMA Archives of General Psychiatry* 2 (February): 184–188.

Stokoe, W. 1960. "Sign Language Structure: An Outline of Visual Communication Systems of the American Deaf." *Studies in Linguistics, Occasional Papers* 8. New York: University of Buffalo.

Stone, I. F. 1989. *The Trial of Socrates*. Boston: Little, Brown. p. 212.

The Development of Deaf Identity

B R E D A   C A R T Y

hat is *identity?* How do we, as Deaf people, define *identity?* Australian Sign Language does not have a single sign that corresponds to this English word. Identity is a very complicated concept, and most sign languages have signs for different aspects of it. For example, the sign for "identifying with a group" is often an emphasized form of JOIN. Many of the terms Deaf people in Australia use to describe themselves and others are about identity rather than about hearing level. Examples include DEAF, STRONG-DEAF, ORAL, THINK-HEARING, HEARING, etc.

For the purposes of this paper, identity will be defined as "the condition of being oneself . . . and not another" (*The Macquarie Dictionary*, 1985) and as "the subjective sense of his own situation and his own continuity and character that an individual comes to obtain as a result of his various social experiences" (Goffman, 1963, p. 129). The search for identity is the search for answers to the questions "Who am I?" and "Where do I belong?"

According to Erikson (1968), a sense of identity develops as a person learns to resolve internal conflicts. These conflicts must be resolved in order for one to develop fully. One of the major conflicts to be resolved during adolescence is that of identity versus confusion, and the resolution of this conflict results in a sense of one's own identity. The sense of identity is considered crucial for the satisfactory resolution of further crises in a person's life, such as the ability to form relationships and to become a mature, productive, self-accepting adult.

Some social scientists (e.g., Goffman, 1963) have proposed two types of identity—personal identity and social identity. In their view, one realizes personal identity within a sometimes restrictive social milieu. Other researchers, such as Laing (1965), and existentialist philosophers also propose dual identities—the true self and the false self—and they warn of a danger of alienation if there is too much discrepancy between the two. So it seems the central question of "Who am I?" almost always involves some conflict between the individual and society. Lack of resolution of the conflict is generally agreed to have serious consequences in a person's life.

We Deaf people, like everyone else, must develop a sense of identity that enables us to function effectively as whole persons throughout our lives. If asked, "How important is deafness in this identity development?" any Deaf person will answer that it is crucial. Both as individuals and as members of a community, Deaf people have developed an identity based on their deafness. Some of the characteristics of Deaf identity include:

1. embracing deafness as an essential, positive part of oneself,
2. recognizing and participating in Deaf culture, particularly through Sign Language, and
3. interpreting the surrounding world in a way that is compatible with one's experience as a deaf person.

Studying how Deaf identity develops is especially challenging because 90 percent of Deaf people do not learn the essential characteristics of this identity from their families, and because the development of this identity is actively discouraged by the educational system most Deaf people grow up in. A further difficulty in exploring the development of this identity is that many Deaf people have effectively blocked out some of the painful experiences that have shaped their identities. Recalling these experiences may be seen as risking loss of acceptance by the larger Deaf community.

The following description of Deaf identity from an Australian perspective is based on discussions at Deaf studies workshops around Australia. These groups consisted of Deaf people from both Deaf and hearing families, as well as children of Deaf adults (CODAs), hearing professionals, and hearing people with no connection with the Deaf community.

Two starting points for discussing Deaf identity emerged from these workshops:

1. "I thought everyone in the world was deaf."
2. "I thought I was the only deaf person in the world."

The first statement is obviously from Deaf people with Deaf parents and/or siblings. Essentially, what these people are saying is, "I thought I was normal; I thought everyone was like me because those closest to me were like me. I was not aware of being 'deaf' in any sense."

The experiences of these Deaf people are of great importance in studying the development of Deaf identity, because they are the only Deaf people who learn language, culture, and the beginnings of identity from their parents. They become the bearers or carriers of this information. Their subsequent role in the Deaf community is closely scrutinized. Padden and Humphries (1988) point out that "on the one hand they are respected and on the other stigmatized" (Padden and Humphries, 1988, p. 48). These Deaf people are respected by other Deaf people for their fluency in Sign Language, for their extensive knowledge of the Deaf community, and for their automatic acceptance as members of this community. At the same time, Deaf families may be stigmatized by the wider hearing community, and other Deaf people may unconsciously absorb this negative value, resulting in an ambivalent attitude toward Deaf people from Deaf families.

As one Deaf woman put it succinctly, "We are like royalty in the Deaf community!" (Jean St. Clair, personal communication, 1988). In other words, they are widely known and admired, but also viewed with jealousy and curiosity and subjected to more criticism and gossip than other members of the Deaf community. How these people come to learn that not everyone in the world is deaf, that, in fact, they are members of a cultural/linguistic minority, should be the subject of further study.

The second statement comes from deaf children of hearing parents who, because of mainstreaming or late onset of deafness, do not meet other deaf people during their early years. What they are saying is essentially, "I felt abnormal, different; even though I may have known that there were other deaf people in the world, I always seemed one of a kind, a freak."

The experiences of these people are also of great importance in the study of Deaf identity development because they can offer conclusive evidence for the strength of the attraction of Deaf culture. These people often travel great psychological distances to explore and embrace Deaf identity. They may abandon or devalue their connections with the hearing world in order to do so. The fact that these Deaf people *learn* the Deaf language and culture and consciously develop a Deaf identity provides an opportunity to analyze this learning process. In addition, because often they are not totally accepted as members of the Deaf community, it is possible for us to isolate the characteristics that make one Deaf and those that detract from being Deaf.

As indicated earlier, the two statements represent the extremes of the range of experiences. Most Deaf people fall somewhere in between. The experiences of CODAs can also be illuminating—their process of learning that they are *not* Deaf may parallel the experiences of Deaf people from hearing families.

So how is it that so many of us end up in the Deaf community, sharing its language and culture, and having what is loosely termed a "Deaf identity"? Considering the long journeys that some of us make, can we identify any common stages on this journey to Deaf identity? The following description of the stages of Deaf identity development comes from discussions with groups of Deaf adults in Australia. At this stage, it is a framework for discussion only.

Confusion. Confusion arises from the realization that one is not the same as everyone else in the family. The early closeness to parents and family that most children experience helps, but is not always sufficient to understand one's place in the world. Deaf children from hearing families are more likely to experience confusion over this difference than are deaf children from Deaf families, although even this group may experience some confusion too.

Frustration/Anger/Blame. The emotional reactions of frustration, anger, and blame are natural responses to a lack of acceptance or understanding by the people in one's immediate environment. The deaf person may internalize these emotions, developing a type of self-hate, or may express them in explosions of temper or periods of noncooperation.

Exploration. At some point, a deaf person will begin to explore self-identity options more closely, by choosing to associate with Deaf people or with hearing people, for example, or by learning sign language or practicing speech skills. Access to these groups and availability of information are crucial at this stage. One of the difficulties of this stage is the general lack of information about Deaf people, Deaf history, and Deaf culture. It is difficult to develop an identity as a Deaf person when this information is not easily accessible.

Identification/Rejection. Identification with one or more groups may be tentative for a time and is subject to early experiences with the group. For example, a deaf person with hearing parents, who attends a mainstream school, may identify with the Deaf community in a rush of enthusiasm at finally having found a place to belong, only to experience difficulty being accepted by members of the Deaf community. The person may then have to reconsider, or perhaps even reject, identification with this group. A Deaf person from a Deaf family may be convinced that he or she can get along fine in the hearing world, and so reject the Deaf community. However, after experiencing rejection by hearing people, this person may see the Deaf community with newly appreciative eyes.

Ambivalence. Feelings of ambivalence may occur after an initial sense of identification when one experiences negative aspects of the group. Such feelings arise especially when one sees members of the group behaving in a way that seems to confirm the negative stereotypes others hold about the group, for example, that deaf people are passive or behave foolishly (Goffman, 1963).

Acceptance. Acceptance of one's personal and social identity comes when people have sufficient information and experience to know who they are and where they belong. Acceptance implies being comfortable with oneself and with the reactions one may get from both the in-group and others. Acceptance enables one to proceed with one's life, develop personal relationships, and function effectively in the chosen social setting.

These six stages are guidelines only. The value of formulating the development of Deaf identity in this way is that it provides a framework within which to elicit personal stories from Deaf people about their experiences, which eventually helps us all to clarify the process of developing the Deaf identity.

Understanding the process of identity development may be made easier if we compare the Deaf experience with the experiences of some other minority groups. In the Australian context, there are valuable parallels to be drawn with the experiences of Aborigines. Although aboriginality is passed on from parent to child, many generations of Aboriginal children were removed from their biological parents by white authorities and placed with white foster families. They were encouraged to become as much like white people as possible by officials who assumed that this was best. Even those Aboriginal families that stayed intact often tried to adopt the white people's values, out of fear and because of effective brainwashing.

The Aboriginal community has been decimated—much of its culture and many of its languages have been lost—but a strong Aboriginal identity still prevails and has gathered momentum during the last few decades. Those Aborigines who were brought up with white people are returning to search for their identities, and the process has many parallels with that of Deaf people.

In a time when many Deaf people feel that educational practices such as mainstreaming are threatening the chances for deaf children to develop their identities as Deaf people, it is essential for us to understand the process of identity development. We must be able to make it easier for those deaf people who may be struggling with identity crises.

References and Recommended Reading

Baker, C., and R. Battison, eds. 1980. *Sign Language and the Deaf Community: Essays in Honor of William C. Stokoe.* Silver Spring, MD: National Association of the Deaf.

Erikson, E. 1968. *Identity, Youth and Crisis.* New York: W.W. Norton.

Goffman, E. 1963. *Stigma: Notes on the Management of Spoiled Identity.* Harmondsworth: Penguin.

Laing, R. D. 1965. *The Divided Self.* Baltimore, MD: Penguin.

Padden, C., and T. Humphries. 1988. *Deaf in America: Voices from a Culture.* Cambridge: Harvard University Press.

Deaf Identity: An American Perspective

BARBARA KANNAPELL

O f the various factors generally associated with membership in the American Deaf community, which ones should be considered essential? A certain degree of hearing loss is generally one, but it has been recognized for at least twenty years that linguistic competence in American Sign Language (ASL) is an equally important factor in the Deaf communities of the United States. More recently, cultural competence in Deaf culture has been added to this list of critical elements. Before a definitive list can be created, however, much more research is needed on certain other important aspects of membership in the Deaf community, such as Deaf identity, common knowledge, and shared rules of behavior and values. Here we will focus on Deaf identity.

I know of only a few American studies focusing extensively on the concept of identity among Deaf people (Kannapell, 1985; Stone-Harris and Stirling, 1987; Erting, 1982). My own research explored the relationship between identity choice and language choice among deaf college students. The study by Stone-Harris and Stirling compared Deaf children of Deaf parents with those of hearing parents, examining in particular their opinions of themselves as "deaf," "hard of hearing," or "hearing impaired" and the beliefs held by many of these students that they would change their identity, that is, become hearing, when they grew up [Editor's note: See Stone and Stirling, this volume]. Erting's research focused on the interaction of deaf preschool-age children with their parents, teachers, and with Deaf adults.

In spite of the value of these completed studies, there is clearly a great need for more research on the identity of Deaf people. Thus, a theoretical framework is proposed here. The following are a few of the many questions that still need to be answered:

❖ Are Deaf people ambivalent about their personal identity?

❖ Are there more Deaf people who are marginal members of the Deaf community now than before because more and more deaf children go to mainstream schools?

❖ Is group identity more important in the Deaf community than individual identity?

A revised and expanded version of this paper appears as "The Role of Deaf Identity in Deaf Studies," 1992, in *Deaf Studies for Educators* (Proceedings of Deaf Studies for Educators Conference, Dallas, Texas, March 7–10, 1991), edited by J. Cebe, Washington, DC: Gallaudet University College of Continuing Education, pp. 105–116.

❖ What is the role of education in the identity development of deaf children?

❖ Do Deaf people change their identities for political reasons?

Of course, the subject of identity is complex among hearing people as well as among Deaf people, depending on such factors as how they think they are seen by others, and in terms of gender, race, family membership, or occupation. The subtleties of identity are such that hearing, white male Americans, for example, rarely think of identifying themselves as hearing, white males. As members of a dominant group in the United States, they are far more likely to view their identities in terms of occupation. In fact, hearing people—except at such exceptional places as Gallaudet University—seldom identify themselves as "hearing." Similarly, white people usually don't identify themselves as "white." More and more women, on the other hand, are now consciously identifying themselves as women or feminists. Black people generally see themselves as "black" first, with other characteristics, though important, being secondary. Similarly, people who have grown up Deaf generally see themselves as "Deaf" first. As they become aware of being oppressed by the hearing majority, their experience of being oppressed strengthens their Deaf identity.

The issue of Deaf identity is extremely complicated. Professionals in the field of the education of deaf students and the community of Deaf people have different views on the identity of deaf children and adults. For example, educators usually identify deaf children by their degree of hearing loss:

| Normal Hearing | Slightly Hard of Hearing | Mildly Hard of Hearing | Moderately Deaf/ Hard of Hearing | Severely Deaf | Profoundly Deaf |

In spite of educators' heavy reliance on data about degrees of hearing loss to categorize deaf children, these distinctions mean nothing to the American Deaf community. A Deaf person does not bring an audiogram as a proof of his hearing loss in order to be recognized and accepted as a member of the Deaf community. A person who is identified by educators as audiologically hard of hearing may identify him or herself as culturally Deaf and a member of the Deaf community. Such apparent paradoxes commonly occur, in fact, among hard of hearing children of Deaf parents.

The key question, I believe, is how do Deaf people identify themselves as members of the Deaf community? Based on my observations, I propose that the definition of cultural identity among Deaf people should be based on how Deaf people view themselves in terms of language identity, personal identity, and social identity (see table 1). These three major types of identities are strongly interrelated.

TABLE 1: Aspects of Deaf Identity

Language Identity	Personal Identity	Social Identity
American Sign Language	Deaf	Deaf People
ASL/English (contact language)	Hard of Hearing	Mixed, Deaf and Hearing
English	Oralist	Hearing People
	Hearing Impaired	
	Deafened	

Language Identity

Language identity refers to the language in which a person is most at home or, in some cases, the language in which a person *chooses* to be most at home. Many Deaf people in the United States feel strongly identified with other Deaf people through the use of American Sign Language. In fact, the use of ASL is a crucial requirement of membership in the American Deaf community. Does this mean that English is excluded? How do Deaf people feel if other Deaf people use English with them in signing or voice? Many deafened or hard of hearing people, for example, tend to use English in their interactions with other Deaf people. Do Deaf people reject these or other people who use English with members of the Deaf community? It depends on the attitude of the Deaf people using English in these situations. If their attitude is holier than thou, Deaf people who generally use ASL with each other will reject these individuals immediately.

As we move from the situation in the Deaf community to the realm of deaf education, however, there is much more question as to whether Deaf people really have a choice of using either ASL or English to reinforce their identity. In my research, deaf college students were clearly ambivalent toward ASL and English. Also, National Technical Institute for the Deaf researchers (Meath-Lang et al., 1984) showed that many deaf college students see English as an external object they must study—a thing they are supposed to learn but with which they cannot personally identify.

In my research, however, I found that some students saw a combination of ASL and English, that is, a contact variety language, as their basic language identity. In essence, they believed that if they used a mixture of ASL and English, they were better off than those who used ASL alone. Upon interviewing these students, I found that they had acquired this attitude largely as a result of their having gained greater teacher approval for using a mixture of ASL and English than for using ASL alone. They usually use ASL/English, or contact language, with hearing people.

Personal Identity

In the context of this paper, personal identity refers to how deaf people see themselves or how they are aware of who they are. Depending on many factors that shape their personal identities, people who grow up deaf usually identify themselves as Deaf, by which they mean culturally Deaf. In recent years, however, more and more young deaf people have been identifying themselves as hearing impaired. Deaf people did not use this term ten years ago. Why is it accepted and used today? Even though the term has been imposed on deaf people by hearing people who apparently wish to define them by a characteristic they lack—hearing—rather than by one they have—deafness—many young deaf people seem to regard it as an acceptable term to describe their identity.

One unfortunate result of this creation of a new identity is an unnecessary division between people who see themselves as Deaf and people who see themselves as hearing impaired. Although the term "hearing impaired" was originally intended to include people with all different kinds of hearing losses and ages at onset, ranging from birth to old age, in practice it has become a label to be applied to deaf children from mainstreamed schools, deaf people who can speak, or deaf people who are not culturally Deaf. The term "Deaf" has come to be applied only to people who are culturally Deaf, do not speak, cannot hear at all, or are from deaf schools.[1] I suggest that the term "hearing

---

1 These labels were described to the author by deaf and hard of hearing people who attended mainstream schools.

impaired" should be rejected because it is a new definition created by individuals wittingly or unwittingly imposing "hearing" values on Deaf people. This term has served only to create confusion among Deaf people to the point that they now obligingly identify themselves as hearing impaired on their job applications in order to please hearing employers.

Deafened people were born hearing but lost their hearing sometime after the age of three. In the past, they usually identified themselves to Deaf people they would meet as individuals who had been hearing but had become deaf at a given age. A deaf person who defines him or herself as an oralist is a person who was trained in the oral method. Usually they do not know sign language and prefer to communicate via voice and gestures. I have noticed that the terms, "deafened" and "oralist" are being used less and less and are being replaced with the term "hearing impaired." People who identify themselves as "hard of hearing" can mean they are audiologically hard of hearing or can use the term to indicate their status of passing almost as a hearing person.

Social Identity

Social identity is a powerful tool in the Deaf community. Often a deaf person claims that he or she is Deaf and should be identified as belonging to a group of Deaf people, but the Deaf people in that group may reject him or her for various reasons. These may include unacceptable attitudes, inappropriate behavior, or violations of group norms. Members of the Deaf community may conclude that this person is a "heafie." A heafie is someone who grew up culturally Deaf who now appears to reject Deaf culture and act like a hearing person. If existing groups don't accept a person, however, it is possible to form a new group of deaf people who have similar backgrounds or experiences, such as deafened people or oralists, who prefer to use English with each other.

Group identity is very important in the Deaf community—even more important than individual identity. Deaf people seem to feel, "I am nothing until I belong to a group." Group identity grows from a special bonding that happens among Deaf people, especially those who were together in deaf schools. Paradoxically, deaf schools want deaf children to fit into the hearing world, but these schools tend more than anything to strengthen the group identity of Deaf people. Deaf people will go everywhere in a group and will support each other when in need of help. If a Deaf person does not belong to a group, Deaf people consider him or her to be a loner. That person will feel lost because he or she has neither group nor individual identity. The interrelatedness of Deaf people's social and individual identities is such that I think it will be important for research purposes to look into *both* the group and individual identities of Deaf people.

In conclusion, we need to examine the role of education in identity development among deaf children. Again, Deaf community members and educators have different views of the identity of Deaf people. Educators impose a hearing identity on deaf children and want to mainstream them into a larger community of hearing people. There are four possible ways that deaf children can define their identity:

1. harmonious identification with both Deaf and hearing cultures;
2. identification with hearing culture, rejection of Deaf culture;
3. identification with Deaf culture, rejection of hearing culture; and
4. failure to form identification with either culture.

One of the goals of educating deaf children should be harmonious identification with both Deaf and hearing cultures, but educators should strengthen the Deaf identity among deaf children first. In the same way, deaf children should master ASL first, before they learn English. Deaf people will continue feeling ambivalent toward both languages and cultures as long as educators feel ambivalent toward deaf people. It is important for deaf people, educators, and parents to work for a bilingual, bicultural education system where the identity and reality of deaf persons are fully accepted.

References

Erting, Carol J. 1982. "Deafness, Communication, and Social Identity: An Anthropological Analysis of Interaction among Parents, Teachers, and Deaf Children in a Preschool." Ph.D. diss., The American University, Washington, DC.

Kannapell, Barbara. 1985. "Language Choice Reflects Identity Choice: A Sociolinguistic Study of Deaf College Students." Ph.D. diss., Georgetown University, Washington, DC.

Meath-Lang, B., F. Caccamise, and J. Albertini. 1984. "Deaf Persons' Views on English Language Learning: Educational and Sex Implications." In *Interpersonal Communication and Deaf People. Working Paper No. 5,* ed. H. Hoeman and R. Wilbur. Washington, DC: Gallaudet College.

Stone-Harris, R., and L. Stirling. 1986. "Developing and Defining an Identity: Deaf Children of Deaf and Hearing Parents." *Proceedings of Social Change and the Deaf: Second Conference on the Social Aspects of Deafness.* Washington, DC: Gallaudet College.

Developing and Defining an Identity: Deaf Children of Deaf and Hearing Parents

RACHEL STONE AND LYNN O. STIRLING

This study compares the impressions that deaf children of deaf parents and deaf children of hearing parents have about their identities as deaf[1] individuals. Previous studies have shown that deaf children are often ambivalent about their own identities, perhaps because they have received inadequate or conflicting information from their families or other caregivers about deafness and the deaf community and its cultural values (Benderly, 1980; Erting, 1982; Washabaugh, 1981). Today, however, it is more likely that deaf children of deaf parents will identify themselves without as much ambivalence, because some of the values and attitudes of the deaf awareness movement that began in the 1970s[2] may have been shared with the children by their deaf parents. Furthermore, deaf children of deaf parents, who are a part of the deaf community from birth, experience less conflict about their deafness than do deaf children of hearing parents, who may not receive positive information, values, and attitudes toward deafness during their early years (Becker, 1980).

In this study, we sought answers to such questions as (1) How aware are individual children about themselves as deaf persons? (2) Are they confident and accepting of their own identities? and (3) How do they define and interpret the terms "deaf," "hard of hearing," "hearing impaired," and "hearing?"

We expected that most of the deaf children of deaf parents in our study would express less ambivalence about their identity as deaf people than would the deaf children of hearing parents. It seemed possible to us that, because of their interaction with deaf adults and exposure to deaf culture, the deaf children of deaf parents would accept their deafness more readily than would the deaf children of hearing parents. The deaf children of hearing parents often live exclusively in the "hearing" culture and have minimal contact with deaf role models, a situation that may lead to more identity confusion and less acceptance among members of this group. To test this theory, we devised questions that would show whether deaf children of deaf parents expected to maintain their childhood identity when they became adults and conversely, whether deaf children with hearing parents expected to become hearing themselves as they grew older.

---

[1] The term "deaf" is used in this paper to identify the general population of deaf and hard of hearing children at the Kendall Demonstration Elementary School. These children have a wide range of hearing loss from mild to profound.

[2] This movement resulted partly from the Civil Rights movement of the 1960s, as well as from such technological advances as TDDs and closed captioning of television programs.

To summarize, we hoped to explore the world views and the perceptions of both groups of children, to determine how they viewed themselves as individuals and as deaf people.

Background

A structured interview consisting of thirty-six questions was designed to elicit open-ended responses from the children using their own communication modes. We video-taped and later analyzed each fifteen-minute interview. This paper will focus only on the students' responses to the questions of self-identification and their definitions of the terms "deaf," "hard of hearing," "hearing impaired," and "hearing."

We interviewed a total of forty-three students from the Kendall Demonstration Elementary School in Washington, D.C.—fourteen children with deaf parents and twenty-nine with hearing parents. The children's ages ranged from seven to fifteen years. We included academic classification, age, hearing status of parents, gender, and degree of hearing loss as some of the variables in the study. The breakdown for age, gender, and parental hearing status is shown in Table 1.

The Interview: Self-Identification

The first interview question asked whether and why the children labelled themselves as "deaf," "hard of hearing," "hearing impaired," or "hearing." Fifty percent of the children with deaf parents and 64 percent of those with hearing parents identified themselves as deaf. Forty-three percent of the children with deaf parents and 28 percent of those with hearing parents claimed that they were hard of hearing. One student chose the category "hearing impaired," but none of the children identified himself/herself as "hearing." One child from each group claimed to be both deaf and hard of hearing. Regardless of parents' hearing status, 60 percent of all the children identified themselves as "deaf," while 33 percent said they were "hard of hearing." It is interesting to note that children from both groups described their own degrees of hearing, indicating, for example, that they could "hear a little," "hear some," or "could not hear" instead of using the terms "deaf," "hard of hearing," or "hearing" when they introduced themselves at the beginning of the interviews.

The same question was repeated at the end of the interview at which point the children were also asked to predict their identities as adults (i.e., would they remain the same or would they be different when they grew up).

Although little difference was found between the earlier responses and the responses at the end of the interview, more deaf children of hearing parents (29 percent)

TABLE 1: Distribution of the Variables of Age, Gender, and Parental Hearing Status by Academic Classification

Academic Classification	Age	Male	Female	Deaf Parents	Hearing Parents
Primary Grades	7–9 years	4	9	8	5
Intermediate Grades	10–12 years	11	10	6	15
Middle Grades	13–15 years	6	3	0	9
Totals:		21	22	14	29

predicted changes in their future identity than did those with deaf parents (8 percent). Deaf children of deaf parents seemed to be more concerned about losing residual hearing, but few in this group expressed the possibility of improving their hearing. Deaf children of hearing parents, on the other hand, tended to focus on hopes or expectations of becoming hard of hearing or hearing. Examples of this are shown by the deaf children who thought that they might "move up one level," going from "profoundly deaf" to "hard of hearing," for example. "Hard of hearing" seemed to be a more appealing and possibly more prestigious designation to them than "deaf." It should be noted, however, that while most of these children expected to improve their hearing slightly, very few aspired to a "two-level" change.

Some of the children elaborated on their answers to this question, as shown in the examples below.

Responses from children with deaf parents:

❖ I will stay the same. I have never heard of anyone growing up and changing with claims that he/she can hear (child with profound hearing loss).

❖ Sometimes hearing can be improved or decreased depending on the nerve system (child with moderate hearing loss).

❖ I may lose some more hearing; it is difficult to say. My mom lost some hearing (child with moderate hearing loss).

Responses from children with hearing parents:

❖ I hope to become hard of hearing if I use a hearing aid, just like my deaf teacher (child with severe hearing loss).

❖ I may become hard of hearing, because one boy I know became hard of hearing (child with profound hearing loss).

❖ I have a friend who is hard of hearing, and we both will become hearing when we grow up (child with profound hearing loss).

After the second time we asked the self-identification question, we also asked the children if they were satisfied with their identity. Eighty-six percent of the children of deaf parents and 56 percent of those with hearing parents said that they were. The difference between the percentages could be interpreted to mean that deaf children of deaf parents see themselves as being like their parents, while deaf children of hearing parents see themselves as being different from their parents. Two typical responses to this question are shown below.

❖ Yes, I'm satisfied because I think I'm someone special. I know many hearing people who have never met deaf people and they couldn't tell if I was deaf until I tell them (child with deaf parents).

❖ Me, happy? No. My mommy cried because she wanted me to be hearing. I don't like to be hard of hearing. I prefer to be hearing and go to public school with hearing children (child with hearing parents).

When we compared the responses between the two groups, we found that most deaf children of deaf parents appeared to accept their identities, while many of the children with hearing parents seemed to hope or expect their identities to change when they became adults, when they might become more similar to the hearing members of their families.

The Interview: Defining Terms

Several investigators (Benderly, 1980; Erting, 1982; Washabaugh, 1981) have pointed out that deaf people form a sociocultural group in which members share similar interests and needs regardless of their degree of hearing loss. Thus, deaf people may define deafness in a different way from those outside of the sociocultural group, who tend to define deafness in aural/oral terms. We expected that, as a result of their home and school experiences, the distinctions between deaf, hard of hearing, hearing impaired, and hearing might be viewed differently by deaf children of deaf parents and deaf children of hearing parents.

Accordingly, some of the interview questions were designed to elicit definitions from the children. The children were first asked to define the word "deaf." Sixty-eight percent of the deaf children of deaf parents and 44 percent of those with hearing parents responded that "deaf" meant "cannot hear." Almost all of the children with deaf parents (thirteen of fourteen) were able to define the term, but six of the twenty-nine children with hearing parents could not.

Nine children of hearing parents emphasized that deaf people cannot speak, but none of the children with deaf parents mentioned speech in their definitions. It is our experience that most deaf people do use speech or mouth movements either at home or in public places. This may have led the deaf children of deaf parents to believe that any individual could speak regardless of hearing status. In contrast, deaf children of hearing parents may have never seen deaf adults communicate by speech. Deaf children in a hearing family are constantly confronted with a speaking environment. It is possible that hearing parents may emphasize speech and point out that the child must work hard to learn how to speak because he or she is deaf.

There was almost no difference between the two groups in the number of children who mentioned the use of sign language. However, it is interesting to note that only two children (both with deaf parents) mentioned the use of eyes in their definition of "deaf."

Most of the children were able to distinguish between hard of hearing and deaf. For example, 88 percent of the children with deaf parents and 53 percent of those with hearing parents defined the term "hard of hearing" as having some degree of hearing. Only 22 percent of the children with hearing parents commented on the speaking ability of hard of hearing people, while none of the children with deaf parents mentioned speech in their definitions. There was more emphasis on audiological aspects of hearing loss among the children with hearing parents than among those with deaf parents.

Most of the children were unfamiliar with the term "hearing impaired." Overall, 50 percent of those with deaf parents and 64 percent of those with hearing parents stated that they did not know what the term meant.

Eighty percent of the children of deaf parents defined the term "hearing" by focusing on the sense of hearing, e.g., "hear well/not deaf," while only 26 percent of the children of hearing parents defined it that way. On the other hand, 59 percent of deaf children with hearing parents defined "hearing" as being able to speak, while only 20 percent of the children with deaf parents used that distinction. A few deaf children with hearing parents believed that hearing people in the general population could not use sign language, while a large number of those with deaf parents thought hearing people could learn sign language to some extent. Further analysis of the definitions of the term "hearing" might provide more evidence of the different values and cultures surrounding hearing and deafness that the two groups of children are learning from society.

Summary

As we have shown, more deaf children of deaf parents expressed certainty about their own identity without showing the ambivalent feelings that the deaf children of hearing parents revealed. The responses to questions of self-identification remained almost constant from the beginning to the end of the interview among the deaf children of deaf parents. But among those with hearing parents, eight out of twenty-nine children had changed the way they would classify themselves by the end of the interview.

Of those with hearing parents, 52 percent of the children were unable to explain their reasons for choosing the classifications deaf, hard of hearing, hearing impaired, or hearing when describing themselves. Fifty percent of the deaf children of deaf parents mentioned degree of hearing as the basis for their choice of identity label. Eighty-six percent of the deaf children of deaf parents were satisfied with their identity, while 56 percent of those with hearing parents said they were satisfied.

Deaf children of hearing parents appeared to have less understanding of the terms "deaf," "hard of hearing," "hearing impaired," and "hearing" than those with deaf parents. Neither group was really familiar with the term "hearing impaired," however. Both groups mentioned the inability to hear and the use of sign language as part of the definition of the term "deaf." Deaf children of hearing parents said deaf people cannot speak, but none of the children with deaf parents made such a claim.

The deaf children with deaf parents interpreted the terms "deaf," "hard of hearing," "hearing impaired," and "hearing" more from an audiological perspective than the deaf children with hearing parents, who tended to emphasize speech ability in their definitions. These responses may indicate the perspectives of the parents as well.

To the degree that children are influenced in their attitudes and perceptions by their parents, the responses of the children in this study demonstrate the effects parental hearing status and resultant parental attitudes may have on how deaf children identify themselves. We believe that more emphasis should be placed on family communication and parents' involvement in building the child's self-concept. However, input from the school and from deaf adults will be critical in helping deaf children and their parents become more familiar with the values and culture of the deaf community, which in turn will lead to a more positive self-concept among these children.

References and Recommended Reading

Becker, G. 1980. *Growing Old in Silence.* Berkeley: University of California Press.

Benderly, B. L. 1980. *Dancing Without Music.* Garden City, NY: Doubleday.

Chough, S. 1983. "The Deaf Community: Our Sociological Perspective." *Deaf American* 35 (8).

Erting, C. J. 1982. "Deafness, Communication, and Social Identity: An Anthropological Analysis of Interaction Among Parents, Teachers, and Deaf Children in a Preschool." Ph.D. diss., The American University, Washington, DC.

Jacobs, L. 1980. *A Deaf Adult Speaks Out.* (2nd ed.). Washington, DC: Gallaudet College Press.

Meadow, K. P. 1980. *Deafness and Child Development*. Berkeley: University of California Press.

Padden, C., and H. Markowicz. 1975. "Cultural Conflicts Between Hearing and Deaf Communities." In *Proceedings of the Seventh World Congress of the World Federation of the Deaf*. Silver Spring, MD: National Association of the Deaf.

Stirling, L, and R. Stone-Harris. 1986. "Developing and Defining an Identity: Deaf Children of Deaf and Hearing Parents." In *Proceedings of Social Change and the Deaf*. Washington, DC: Gallaudet College.

Washabaugh, W. 1981. "Sign Language in Its Social Context." *Annual Review of Anthropology*. Palo Alto, CA: Annual Reviews, Inc. pp. 237–252.

Empowering Deaf People Through Folklore and Storytelling

LARRY COLEMAN AND KATHY JANKOWSKI

It is important to explain at the outset of this paper the differences we perceive between the terms "deaf community" and "Deaf culture." As we see it, the deaf community includes a wide range of people, including not only people who grow up deaf, but also late deafened people, hard of hearing people, hearing children of deaf parents, and other groups. When defined in this broad way, the deaf community includes many people who do not share the characteristics of the small cultural group we are focusing on in this paper. We are looking primarily at Deaf people who grow up using sign language, who identify themselves as members of the Deaf culture, who are seen by other members of the Deaf culture as Deaf, and who have been oppressed by hearing cultures because they are Deaf.

Some Deaf people have no difficulty seeing themselves as an oppressed minority, but others may not have thought about it on a conscious level, so before we begin our exploration of the role played by storytelling and folklore in combating oppression we will briefly suggest who oppresses Deaf people, how the oppression of Deaf people manifests itself, and how Deaf people can—at least theoretically—liberate themselves from this oppression. Historically, Deaf people have been oppressed by various groups of people, including hearing teachers and administrators who play a major role in their education, hearing family members, deaf leaders who do not identify with and support sign language and Deaf culture, deaf people who talk, deaf people who THINK-LIKE-HEARING and demonstrate a negative attitude toward Deaf culture and other deaf people, and both deaf and hearing people who have paternalistic attitudes toward members of the Deaf culture.

The notion of empowerment—of central importance in this paper—is critical to the well-being and continued prosperity of both individual people and society. It refers to a process by which we gain greater control over our life experiences, our social and intellectual development, our career paths, and our social relations. In addition, for Deaf people, empowerment means liberating ourselves from ideas and behaviors that have oppressed us in the past in areas such as education, careers, and social relations.

One way oppression happens is that Deaf people are encouraged to stay dependent on hearing people throughout their lives. The obvious solution for Deaf people fed up with this form of oppression is to stop always depending on hearing people and to look inside themselves for the strength and resources needed to be self-reliant.

Some of the worst forms of oppression have to do with attitudes transmitted from hearing to Deaf people concerning who Deaf people are and what they can be expected to do. One subtle form of this sort of oppression is the assumption that Deaf people can't compete with hearing people for jobs or in other arenas without extensive help from hearing people. To combat this, Deaf people must insist on working relations with hearing people characterized by a spirit of cooperation on an equal footing. On a more damaging level, hearing people who always regard Deaf people with pity and conde-scension—as if Deaf people were completely helpless—are in fact inflicting a terrible form of oppression on Deaf people. Most of us who are Deaf share a feeling of anger toward this attitude, which shows up in one way or another in practically every country.

One certain indication that the hearing people running institutions intended to serve Deaf people have this pitying, condescending attitude is that they assume it to be their right to make critical decisions concerning Deaf people's lives without even consulting Deaf people to see what their opinion is. To liberate ourselves from such oppression, it is necessary for Deaf people to insist on either making those decisions for ourselves or at least being properly consulted before such decisions are made. Deaf people must make it clear that although hearing people with positive attitudes are wel-come to cooperate with us on an equal basis in planning the future of Deaf people's institutions, they are emphatically *not* invited to plan and decide Deaf people's futures *for* them.

Although it is possible to describe what needs to be done to change oppressive conditions for Deaf people, such change does not come easily. Much of the time, Deaf people must turn to Deaf culture and draw upon the resources available in storytell-ing and folklore in order to gain the inner strength we need to continue our struggle. Consider, for example, the following transcription of a story entitled "Dreams," told by Charles "C. J." Jones, a Deaf storyteller and comedian from California:

> Two Deaf men who had been shipwrecked and stranded on an island in the middle of the Atlantic Ocean for several weeks were beginning to believe they would never be found. Ships would pass in the distance beyond a coral reef that encircled the island, but none came close enough to discover these men.
>
> One of the men became tired of waiting to be seen, so he told his friend he was going to swim out beyond the coral reef and wait for a ship or plane to come along and discover him. He was determined not to die on the island. The other man, however, was frightened by this plan. "No! No! No!" the second man said to his courageous buddy. "Sharks and jellyfish may kill you. The coral reef over there will cut you to pieces. Please don't go and kill yourself out there. I'll be left alone."
>
> But the first man was determined to go. He waded out into the ocean, and as he swam away the second man could only see a tiny head bobbing up and down in the water.
>
> As he stood on the island watching and weeping, the second man began to fantasize. His mind traveled back to the days of his youth, when he had once been given a rare opportunity to play quarterback for his high school football team. It was the fourth quarter. Forty-five seconds remained on the clock, and his team was losing. The ball was in his hands, and there was a small hole in the defensive line. Frightened, he started running and running. The man re-membered that back in those days he was a thin, frail kid, but he ran and ran and ran past 250-pound linemen who seemed like giants. He kept running and

running until, when he looked back, no one was close to him. He was home free, and he scored a touchdown that won the game.

Now, when his mind returned to the present situation from his dream, the man decided to take the risk needed to escape from the island. Yes, he would swim out beyond the coral reef to join his friend. It would be better than remaining alone on the island. So he swam out and joined his friend. Within hours a ship came by and took them aboard. They were safe.

So remember, never stop dreaming. Never give up hope. Take the risk to achieve your dreams.

The above story is an example of an empowering tale. Deaf people watching the story learn that Deaf people will find less comfort in isolating themselves from the dangers of the world than in venturing bravely together into the world of risks, making their way toward success by virtue of sheer pluck and determination. Stories such as this one are often shared among members of the Deaf culture. Such empowering tales join the large body of stories, jokes, proverbs, and other witty sayings that make up the body of folklore of a culture. This body contains stories and expressions about heroic characters, some of them invented to represent Deaf people's typical situations in life, and others drawn from recorded data and real experiences.

Walter Fisher's theory of human communication as narration or story postulates that people are essentially storytellers who use symbolic interpretations of aspects of the world tempered by history, culture, and character (1987). Fisher argues that this use of symbols or signs is designed to help humans manage their environment and control their growth and development, and that, in essence, folklore and storytelling play an important role in shaping reality. This theory suggests that stories such as the one above by C. J. Jones have the power to affect Deaf people's actions, urging them to venture forth and accept risks rather than to shrink from challenges.

William Bascom (1965) discusses storytelling and folklore as having purposes that may or may not pertain to the realm of action, that may have their most important effects on the development of cultural awareness among members of a particular cultural group. In an essay concerning the functions of folklore, Bascom argues that folklore provides release from repression or feelings of oppression by allowing escape into fantasy. These fantasies, Bascom says, reinforce traditions, educate members of a cultural group concerning the culture itself, and help maintain behavioral norms.

Bascom also points out that the expression and performance of folklore occur within a social and a cultural context. In the social context, the audience takes into account who is telling the story, where it is being told, how gestures and sounds are used, how the audience participates, and what people recognize and feel about the kind of story or folklore performed. The cultural context of the story or piece of folk expression indicates how it is related to other aspects of culture, such as language, dance, dress, or religion.

In more general terms, our research shows how stories have been used to affirm the culture and identity of Deaf individuals. Such stories often teach Deaf people how to resist obstacles in the environment; how to take risks that may be beneficial to their intellectual, cultural, and psychological growth; and how to develop their imaginations and creativity.

Although the purposes of storytelling can justifiably be discussed in such serious terms, it is important to remember that the experience of hearing or seeing a story is usually enjoyable and often quite humorous. In fact, the presence of humor in a story is often an enhancement to the storyteller's artful way of communicating serious themes.

The following story about Deaf newlyweds, which has become part of Deaf America's folklore, may serve as a good example:

> Deaf newlyweds checked into a motel. Late at night, the husband left his bride to get a bucket of ice, but forgot to take the room key and number with him. Although he could not remember which of the dark motel rooms his bride was in, he had an idea. He went to his car and pressed the car horn until lights in all of the motel rooms but one were turned on. He left his car, knowing his bride was in the room that was still dark.

The newlyweds story is essentially a joke, but the significance of its humor is that it presents a situation in which the common perception of deafness as a handicap is reversed. The husband finds a way to make hearing a disadvantage for most of the motel guests and take advantage of his wife's not being able to hear.

In America, one of the central sources of Deaf culture during the last 150 years or so has been the residential school for Deaf students. One story that has been passed down through generations of Deaf people concerns how a certain group of Deaf residential students dealt victoriously with an oppressive school situation. This empowering story is taken from the book *Deaf in America* by Padden and Humphries (1988).

The story is told by a Deaf female student. It begins when the girls in her residential dormitory learn that they will have a new counselor at school—a woman who has transferred to the job from a women's prison. The woman turns out to be huge and humorless. She maintains her prison-warden mentality, complete with the drab uniform of a warden, a thick leather belt, and a heavy key ring with a whistle, which she will find useless at this new setting. Her treatment of the girls is unduly rough. Each morning, instead of gently waking them, she flashes the ceiling lights of their bedrooms, tears the covers off them, and—for those who linger a bit too long—pulls pillows from under their heads. Worse, she carries her prison-warden role into the shower, where she insists on watching their every move.

The female student continues the story, roughly as follows:

> Now, there was this one girl this counselor picked on mercilessly. She [the girl] was one of those types who unconsciously used her voice when she signed. You know, she'd do little squeals and grunts and other kinds of noises. This counselor couldn't stand her, thought she was mad. She would yell at her to stop, but of course the poor girl couldn't. It was just the way she talked. (Lots of Deaf people do this; you know the type.) Anyway, the counselor made life miserable for her, to the point where all she wanted was to run away. We told her she oughtn't, that we'd find a way. Well, we did; we decided we'd get back at her [the counselor], and we began making plans.
>
> We came up with this plan. We'd set out bait. We'd put this poor girl in the bathroom, get her started on her squealing and stuff, and once we got the counselor after her, into the bathroom, we could trap her and put our plan into action. We were in the bathroom, and we got her to start squealing and making all kinds of noises, and exactly according to plan, the counselor came running down the hall after her. We could even feel her coming; the floors shook at every heavy step. She came into the room and didn't even bother to look at us, but looked directly at the poor girl, who then panicked and escaped from the bathroom behind us into the sleeping quarters where she'd be protected.

> The next part of the plan was to force the counselor to go through us to catch the girl. She began chasing after her into the large sleeping room, where a group of us were lined up on either side. She came running, only one thing on her mind—to catch the poor girl. Then, one of us extended a leg, and the counselor flew through the air and landed on the floor with a heavy thud.

The retaliation is complete; the girls have tricked the counselor into humiliation. But the story is not yet completed and takes an unexpected turn:

> At long last, we had made up for what she had done to us. We cheered and cheered until we realized she wasn't moving. We very carefully approached her. Maybe she had fainted? We came closer. Then she lifted her head and tried talking to us. (What a useless thing to do! Now, this woman never bothered to learn to sign. Here she was trying to talk to us, and we couldn't understand her.) She kept mouthing something to us, and we sensed her desperation. Finally, she lifted her arm and her hand hung limply on the floor, dangling from her arm. "She broke her arm!" we signed.
>
> The girls run to get another adult, and the counselor is taken away. Three weeks later she returns to the dormitory, her arm in a cast, and they anxiously wait to see what will happen next.
>
> We waited for her old self, but it was gone. Instead, this was one of the most loving people. She was sweet, affectionate. And the most surprising thing of all: She loved that girl, the one she had hated so much before. Loved her more than anything. We couldn't figure it out.

The story leads to an ideal ending. The malevolent character has received a suitable punishment—if a bit too harsh—and the punishment leads to redemption.

> Another counselor said this woman told her she had been under the mistaken impression that Deaf children were like prisoners: bad, insane, and mean. Instead, she found we were all good people, better organized and more intelligent than those prisoners she worked with. After her carefully planned and instructive punishment, she respected us and loved us. And I guess we loved her too. She threw away her leather belt, her heavy key ring, and her whistle. She became what she should have been—a mother to us.

Although the counselor exerts oppressive control over the girls, it is not until she mistreats one of them on the grounds of unacceptable noises that they decide to strike back. This supposedly informal story is a powerful one, for it shows how Deaf people can imagine regaining, however briefly, ownership of sound.

Another story not explicitly related to Deaf people has become popular among Deaf people because of the clear relationship between its moral of resilience triumphing over oppression and the strength against adversity needed by any member of the Deaf culture. Every Deaf person watching this story will identify strongly with farmer Johnson's mule:

> Farmer Wilson was a jealous and evil man, and he was jealous of everything farmer Johnson, his neighbor, owned. He was jealous of farmer Johnson's trac-

tor, his barn, his cows, even his wife; but most of all farmer Wilson was jealous of farmer Johnson's prizewinning mule. In fact, he was so envious he plotted to kill that prize mule

One dark night, Wilson dug a hole seven feet long, four feet wide, and six feet deep, and he led that mule to that hole with a trail of oats and trail mix. He was going to bury that mule alive. Well, the mule fell into the hole and Wilson commenced to shovel in dirt to bury that mule alive. But every time that mule started to feel some dirt on his back, he'd start shakin' it off and stompin' it down—as mules do cuz they don't want anything on their backs.

The more dirt Wilson shoveled, the more that mule would shake it off and stomp it down. And by doing this, the mule started to rise by shakin' it off and stompin' it down. Well, the mule rose clean level with the ground, turned himself around, and while farmer Wilson was bent over, the mule kicked him clean into the next week.

The moral: If people throw dirt, garbage, insults, prejudice, suffering into your life, just shake it off and stomp it down and use it to rise to the highest level you can.

As you can see from the samples we have presented, the subjects used by Deaf storytellers are as diverse as storytelling itself. Similarly, the moods conveyed may cover the full range of human emotion, from fear to sadness, or from anger to hilarity. Deaf storytellers differ from hearing storytellers, of course, in that they present their cultural lore in ways that are entirely accessible visually. Although Deaf storytellers from different nations may differ to the extent that their stories tend to reflect the conditions affecting Deaf people in the different countries, they also tend to have much in common. In general, Deaf storytellers tend to use their art to help instill a positive attitude within Deaf individuals toward themselves and toward their identities as members of the Deaf culture. Deaf people's sense of having a proud cultural heritage tends to grow as they watch and assimilate the tales recounted by other members of the Deaf culture. This growing sense of Deaf identity and Deaf pride—communicated in large measure through storytelling and folklore—is what empowers Deaf people to resist the oppression that also constantly affects them.

References

Bascom, W. 1965. "Four Functions of Folklore." In *The Study of Folklore*, ed. A. Dundes. Englewood Cliffs, NJ: Prentice Hall. pp. 279–298.

Fisher, W. R. 1987. *Human Communication as Narration: Toward a Philosophy of Reason, Value and Action*. Columbia, SC: University of South Carolina Press.

Padden, C., and T. Humphries. 1988. *Deaf in America: Voices from a Culture*. Cambridge: Harvard University Press.

Deaf Thai Culture in Siam: The Land of Smiles

KAMPOL SUWANARAT

The sign for Thailand is derived from the sign movement meaning elephant trunk. In the old days, Thailand had thousands of elephants, and the elephant was so revered that even our national flag showed the figure of a white elephant on a background of red. The appearance of the flag has changed over the years, however. The first change was to a flag with five stripes of three colors—red for the nation, white for religion, and royal blue for the monarchy—but still with the elephant in the center. Now, however, the flag has only the five stripes of color and no elephant.

Thailand, a country that is more than 700 years old, is the only country in southeast Asia that has never been colonized by western nations. Our culture is very old.

The deaf Thai community is very small compared to the nation as a whole. There are only 100,000 deaf Thai in a country of 55 million people. Thus, deaf Thai undoubtedly constitute a minority group. We who are deaf live among hearing people and are unavoidably influenced by the majority culture, but we still have our own culture, too.

When we were born, we automatically became part of the Thai nationality. We live in an environment filled with the hearing Thai culture and have adopted many of its customs. For example, the hearing Thai greet each other with a movement called a "wai," which is a salutation with varieties and degrees of movement to indicate respect for different levels of rank or seniority. We, the deaf Thai, also practice this custom. So, undoubtedly, the deaf culture in Thailand is actually part of the Thai national culture. This does not mean that all other cultural aspects are the same, however. Some of our own deaf Thai culture is quite different from the hearing culture. Some of the differences and similarities between the two cultures will be illustrated by my presentation.

You may already know that Thailand, or Siam as it was called in the old days, is known as the land of a thousand smiles. The Thai, whether rich or poor, whether experiencing difficulties or not, smile often. We, the deaf Thai, smile often too. But we have less to smile about, because we are oppressed by ignorance—the ignorance of not knowing about our surroundings as well as do hearing Thai. We often have fewer friends and are often lonely.

Whereas the hearing Thai have a spoken and written language and sometimes also use gestures, we, the deaf Thai, have only sign language. Very few of us can read and write, either newspapers or personal letters.

Generally the hearing Thai often assume that we deaf Thai are terribly strange, especially when we are seen talking through sign language. Some say that we behave like monkeys. This shows their ignorance of sign language. Hearing people do not understand the significance of sign language.

It is well known that before deaf people can communicate their stories, such as where they went last weekend, with whom, and what exciting events they experienced, they need both hands and mouth movements to communicate. And for more and clearer information, they have to add facial expressions and other body movements. Hearing people are astonished and sometimes frightened upon seeing a deaf person talk about some health problem, for example a sore throat, headache, or stomachache. The facial expressions are so precise they look frightening. In reality, the deaf person may not be experiencing any pain at all, but the hearing onlooker may think he or she is in extreme pain, judging from facial expressions.

As I mentioned a moment ago, one distinct custom we take from the majority culture is the *wai*. This is a sign of both formal greeting and politeness. There are varieties of *wai* that show different degrees of respect, depending on the age, status, or position of the person greeted. For example, if the first person is much younger than the second, the younger one will give a respectful wai with his palms raised up to the middle point between the eyebrows. The older one, or the one of higher status, responds to this sign of respect with a lower positioned wai, which indicates less formality. The highest rank of *wai* for the Thai is used to show respect to the Buddha image and to monks. For this kind of *wai*, the joined palms are raised with the thumbs touching the middle point between the eyebrows.

The deaf Thai accept this cultural act of showing respect in formal situations. However, we have our own greetings, such as one that involves touching one's own forehead with the fingertips, then moving the hand outward in the backhand direction, with a bow at the same time. To deaf Thai this means "good day" or "hello." The degree of politeness in this case depends solely on the bow. A lower bow shows more politeness. We use this sign with familiar persons and friends, but with unfamiliar people and with older persons we usually wai instead.

These two ways of greeting can also be used to say goodbye. Other practices that are used by the majority of Thai to show good manners include lowering the head and shoulders when passing an older person, showing gratefulness with a wai, and paying great attention when in conversation with an older person or with those in a high position. We deaf Thai also accept these practices as indications of good manners.

When talking about good manners, it is also necessary to talk about what should be done and not done in the presence of a deaf Thai. Politeness and impoliteness may be measured by the following behaviors:

❖ To greet a deaf Thai, you should approach him or her face to face, and you should never touch any part of his or her clothing or hair, or pat or stroke the person's head or back, except with close friends. You should wait for him or her to turn. Only when absolutely necessary should you gently touch the person's arm or shoulder. You should not communicate with a deaf Thai by stroking his or her cheek, body, head, buttocks, or other body parts, and you should not use your foot to call or point at anything. In the Thai culture, the head is considered to be the most important and highest part of a person, and the foot to be the lowest. Thai people, both deaf and hearing, are very sensitive regarding this distinction.

❖ When trying to attract the attention of a deaf Thai from a distance, you should not beckon, clap your hands, shout, or throw things at the person.

❖ You should not call a deaf person "dumb" or "mute," because this conveys negative meaning. It may indicate that you feel that person is stupid, brainless, or unable to communicate. Actually we deaf Thai have brains and *can* communicate, only we do it with our hands instead of our voices. We should be called deaf rather than deaf-mute. We have no impairment other than our deafness.

❖ Knocking on a door to summon a deaf person is useless. Instead, you should slide a piece of paper under the closed door or press electric light buttons or other light signals to attract the deaf person's attention.

❖ Other ways of behaving properly around deaf people can be easily understood with common sense. For example, you should not walk between or interfere with people who are signing or walking, unless it is an emergency.

In hearing families, the social group that gives a person warm feelings, knowledge, and positive experiences is the family—parents, siblings, and close relatives. But the family of the deaf Thai gives only frustration and bitterness. That is, in each family, most of the members are hearing and do not understand the nature of deafness. This causes communication problems as the deaf child grows up. Communicating their feelings and needs to their parents is difficult at best for the deaf child. There is little or no understanding between parent and child because most parents of deaf Thai do not know the Thai Sign Language. Further, they do not let their deaf children be independent, fearful that the child will get into difficulties or danger. Consequently, most deaf Thai lack self-confidence.

Even relationships with brothers and sisters can be affected by deafness. If family members don't understand the deaf child, then who else will?

The only social group that provides a deaf Thai with feelings of security are other deaf Thai, because they communicate in the same language, share the same experiences, and feel the same way. If there is a deaf parent or deaf relative in the family, the deaf child can learn more and be provided with their own culture more successfully than those deaf children with hearing parents. The deaf child of deaf parents will also be more confident about learning new things.

It is well known among educators of deaf people in Thailand that learning by deaf children occurs at a slower pace than that of hearing children. The reason this is so in my country is because our schools are of poor quality and low standards. The result is the slower development of the deaf society. The deaf adult is left with problems in spelling, reading comprehension, vocabulary, mathematics, science, social science, and many other areas.

These problems are hard to eliminate because deaf people are not allowed to use their sign language fully in the schools or to be taught in sign language. Adult deaf Thai signs are not used in the classrooms, and deaf adults are rarely allowed to teach. So the experiences and knowledge of deaf Thai children are limited.

We deaf Thai love to gather in our deaf groups. We can learn more from friends than from schools. Deaf Thai gather in various vocational groups, such as groups of carpenters, artists, painters, vendors, dressmakers, and so on. We teach each other our work, and by this process we now have many skilled workers. For example, long ago there was only one deaf vendor working in an arts and crafts business on a busy Bangkok street, near Silom and Suriwong Roads. He could communicate with foreign customers quite well by writing the price he wanted for his goods. Other deaf people were then persuaded to follow the same career. Now almost all the street vendors selling arts and crafts are deaf.

Some of the carpenters and painters have also established a vocational training center named Silent World Crafts. This center provides deaf members with work skills and a way to earn a living. The center produces a large quantity of toys and wood crafts of such good quality that most are purchased for export to other countries. Many members of the center thus work and earn their living freely.

In 1984 deaf Thai established the National Association of the Deaf in Thailand (NADT) and vowed to make it strong. Presently the NADT has 400 members in four regional clubs scattered over the country. The NADT acts as the center for the Thai deaf community and provides services to all members, including employment counseling, vocational training, interpreter services, education, and sign language training.

We, the deaf Thai, have developed to a stage where we can smile more now. We know more about appropriate work systems, about ways to help ourselves, and about how to help others understand us. While our lives are not so successful as we want, progress has been made.

We each hope that someday we will no longer be under the oppression of the hearing society and will be able to smile more widely and more beautifully. Our deaf Thai culture will then be something we can all smile about.

The Deaf Japanese and Their Self-Identity

MICHIKO TSUCHIYA

The focus of this paper is on the problems of self-identity facing the deaf Japanese who live their daily lives in a country that does not readily accept any disabled person as a member of the society. Oralism has been the main instructional method used with deaf students for almost sixty years, and as a result, deaf Japanese usually feel uneasy about presenting themselves to society as deaf persons. The deaf culture fostered by older deaf adults who were educated using sign language is not being shared with the younger deaf people, whose language preferences and values more closely resemble those of the hearing majority.

Japan's isolation throughout its history has contributed greatly to its becoming a homogeneous country. Surrounded by the sea, Japan saw few successful foreign invasions in its early history and was in seclusion for almost 250 years (until 1858) under the Shogunate rule. To assure national unification, the Shogunate strengthened the feudal system by classifying those it ruled into four categories: warriors, peasants, manufacturers, and traders.

On the local level, the daily activities of the villagers were under the constant surveillance of a community leader. If any member of the group disobeyed a rule or did not cooperate with the others, he or she could be expelled from the group. It was difficult for a person so expelled to continue living in the community, so people tried to conform to the rules. Although this system no longer exists, its influence can be seen in the lifestyle of the group-oriented Japanese who continue to value conformity. Today, for example, if one is different in appearance or behavior (such as evidenced by those Japanese who were brought up or educated abroad), he or she is likely to be unwelcome in Japanese society. In other words, the Japanese are anxious to belong to the group-conscious majority, and the self-identity of the deaf Japanese has been strongly influenced by this socio-cultural background.

In ancient Japan, deaf people were feared and pitied, and their lives were made miserable by hearing people. When a deaf child was born, the birth was considered a sign of misfortune for the family, and the child was treated harshly or abandoned. The ancient Japanese believed so strongly in reincarnation that deafness was sometimes considered to be a person's punishment for past sins; however, by the 1850s, a few deaf children of affluent or noble families were permitted to attend temple schools to be taught along with their hearing peers. Monks or other cultivated men provided instruction in reading, brush-writing, and counting on an abacus, but, because they believed that deaf children were really uneducable, the teachers ignored their deaf charges most of the time, and the children learned only to read and write their own name.

In 1858, Commodore Matthew C. Perry arrived in Japan with his armed warships. His arrival resulted in the overthrow of the Shogunate-ruled system and the opening of Japan to the outside world. To modernize Japan, the new government dispatched delegations to both Europe and the United States to study current international relations and to investigate various institutions and cultures. The government also used education as a tool for modernization, issuing a school law in 1872 that required every child to attend official primary schools. Although the delegations reported on the education of deaf students abroad, Japanese deaf children did not become full participants in the educational system until the early 1950s, almost eighty years after the law went into effect.

Yozo Yamao, a government official who had traveled to England in 1863 to study ship manufacturing, saw deaf workers at a shipyard in Glasgow. Thus he learned that deaf people could become productive members of society if they were educated. In 1871, after his return to Japan, Yamao proposed that the government establish a school for deaf and blind children, stressing the necessity of education for disabled people. Unfortunately, his efforts to start a school were in vain.

It was not until 1875, when a primary school teacher in Kyoto named Taishiro Furukawa began teaching two deaf children in his classroom, that education for deaf people began to become a reality in Japan. As the number of deaf and blind pupils who wished to be enrolled increased, parents began to support the idea of a special school. Thus, the first official school for deaf and blind students was founded in 1878, strongly supported by the Governor of Kyoto who had been impressed with the Yamao proposal. Furukawa, the first instructor at the new school, taught reading, writing, geography, and counting on an abacus. He used a manual method that he had originated, as well as writing in the air or on the palm of a deaf/blind student's hand. He also attempted to teach his deaf students to speak. Furukawa believed that muteness was a result of the lack of auditory input, not a necessary consequence of deafness; thus he believed that deaf-mutes could be taught to speak through training. Unfortunately, there is no further information available about his methods and how successful they were.

The second school for the deaf and blind in Japan was founded in Tokyo in 1880. Because of financial problems, the Tokyo School was taken over by the Ministry of Education five years later. Presently known as the School for the Deaf, the school is affiliated with the University of Tsukuba. It is the only national school for deaf students in Japan, although other local schools for deaf and blind children were later founded throughout the country. Despite the insistence of one of the founders of the Tokyo School, who quoted the resolution of the International Congress on Education for the Deaf held in Milan, Italy in 1880, the manual approach was preferred over the oral approach, and all of the Japanese schools adopted the manual teaching method used at the Kyoto School.

During the early years of deaf education in Japan, and indeed throughout its 110-year history, reading and writing skills have been considered a critical part of the curriculum. As one old deaf man explained, the teacher always carried paper and pen. Any deaf student who signed to him had to write down what had been signed, and the teacher instantly corrected the student's grammar. This is why so many elderly deaf people are very skilled writers today.

Most of the early schools were residential, thus providing a place for the deaf students from various parts of Japan to share their local signs with each other. This naturally enriched manual communication and contributed to the solidification of Japanese Sign Language (JSL). The deaf students who were educated through manual communication had a clear picture of themselves as deaf persons, and were fully aware of the social prejudice against them. They also knew where they were expected to stand in the family and in society in general, something that the young deaf Japanese students of today do not experience.

The period between 1910 and 1920 saw many heated arguments about the most desirable teaching method. Ultimately, there was a transition from the manual method to oralism. Reports on oral educational methods used abroad, success stories of oralism, and a visit to Japan by Alexander Graham Bell all affected the course of education for the deaf in Japan. Shuji Izawa, who had studied under the father of A. G. Bell in the United States, introduced "visual speech" to Japan. He later interpreted during Bell's 1898 lecture tour to promote the necessity of an appropriate educational program for deaf students.

Bell's advocacy for speech training had a profound impact on many teachers in Tokyo. For example, a school for deaf children in Nagoya encouraged the teachers to study ways of teaching speech to deaf children, and its principal wrote articles on speech training. The father of a deaf girl who had learned to speak devoted himself to the spread of oralism and founded an oral school for deaf students in the Shiga district in 1919. Later, A. K. Reischauer, who had come to Japan as a missionary, asked the Clarke School for the Deaf in Massachusetts to send a teacher to Tokyo for his deaf daughter. This led to the establishment of a private oral school for deaf students there in 1929.

Although the manual method was still being used in the early 1930s, many teachers felt that it was too difficult to teach deaf children written and spoken Japanese through sign language. The Tokyo School became very interested in introducing the oral method into its curriculum. When the administrators expressed their intentions to the alumni, however, they met with much resistance and resentment. Emphasizing the importance of meeting the needs of each deaf child, the Osaka City School for the Deaf used all means of communication in teaching, but divided the deaf children into three groups according to their capabilities: oral, manual, and total communication. Gradually, however, more and more schools began to adopt the oral method in the belief that speech training would promise happiness in the future for the deaf. Oral successes gave teachers confidence and, in due course, the manual method dramatically declined.

Oralism reached its peak in Japan in the 1930s. At school, all deaf children had to undergo a strict series of speech training and were told to abstain from using JSL. If they were found signing among themselves, they were punished. The parents, happy to see that their deaf children could speak, cooperated with the teachers in support of oralism. These attitudes caused deaf children to feel guilty about signing, and today deaf adults who attended school during that time have bitter memories of their school days.

After World War II, aural training was introduced and welcomed as a supplement to oralism. With improved hearing aids, speech training and mainstreaming programs became the norm. Enforcement of oralism, however, not only resulted in the decline of the deaf culture that the manual deaf had built, but also fostered the biased feelings that young deaf Japanese now have against older deaf adults.

Spoken and written Japanese is considered to be the only language used in Japan, and JSL has been assumed to be an inferior form of communication for the deaf. That is, JSL is not considered to be a language. Teachers strongly believe that the use of JSL distorts the language development of deaf children and do not allow them to sign. Asked for evidence of this distortion in language development caused by the use of JSL, the teachers usually point out that the older deaf people rarely speak because of their education through manual communication and are unable to integrate into society despite their good writing abilities.

Thus, for nearly sixty years the deaf people of Japan have been taught to identify themselves with hearing people by mastering speech and striving to behave as normally as possibly in the group-conscious majority. Many younger deaf Japanese feel ashamed of their deafness and try to prevent hearing people from noticing it. Thus, they avoid the old manual deaf adults and their way of communicating. However, some oral deaf do sign while speaking, with or without voice, using what is called Pidgin Japanese Sign Language. The more they use this method, the more they become frustrated with their inability to convey their message fully, and occasionally they invent a new sign for a Japanese word that has no definite sign. This tendency to create artificial signs can also be found among hearing people who are interested in using JSL. It may well imply their insensitivity to the uniqueness of the two languages—Japanese and JSL.

The older, manual deaf people, needless to say, become irritated or confused when trying to communicate with the younger, oral deaf, and are no longer eager to share their experiences with them. Because of their past experiences with oralism, many of the older deaf people may feel inferior to the oral deaf, and may have given up their efforts voluntarily to impart their culture to the younger deaf people. Thus, the young deaf Japanese are quite unfamiliar with the deaf culture of their country. Oralism has caused a generation gap that seems almost insurmountable.

The oral deaf in Japan are not so able to deal with problems, including those of self-identity, as are the older, manual deaf people. At school the young are taught the necessity of speech training for access to social integration, but once they leave the school, they are discriminated against as deaf persons. The promises of the school do not come true in the outside world. Recently, some of the congenitally deaf adults who have not acquired spoken language despite years of training have begun to question the educational philosophy and methods the schools have adopted.

Inspired by the International Congress on the Education of the Deaf held in Tokyo in 1975, a project was set up to establish an institute of higher education for deaf Japanese, but more than a decade passed before the proposal became reality. The newly created Tsukuba College of Technology will admit its first deaf students in the spring of 1990. The school will offer a three-year career program, using all modes of communication. This institution is expected a play an important role in the education of deaf students in Japan and in the affirmation of a more positive self-image for deaf Japanese.

In ancient times, the Japanese were exposed to ideas from China that arrived in Japan through Korea. Today these influences come from Europe and the United States. Yet Japan remains a country where public consensus is paramount. The harder the deaf Japanese strive to reestablish their self-respect and re-awaken awareness of their deaf culture and language—necessary processes for self-identity—the more they are confronted with discrimination by the homogeneous Japanese society. Thus, to perpetuate their unique deaf culture and to continue the development of self-identity there—especially among the young—deaf people in Japan must face the objections of a society that values conformity over individual differences.

Nepal: A Paradise for the Deaf?

RAGHAV BIR JOSHI

epal, a country about the size of Tennessee with a population of eighteen million people, is located between Tibet and India. Nepal is divided into three distinct geographical areas. The mountainous region in the north, called the Himalayas, contains eight of the ten tallest mountains in the world. The middle region is called the Middle Hills and the Valleys, and the southern part, which is mainly agricultural, is called the Terai.

Background

In the beginning of the country's history, Nepal was carved up into many small kingdoms. King Prithvi Narayan Shah, an ancestor of the present King Birendra, unified Nepal around the sixteenth century. In 1846, a military general named Jung Bahadur Rana usurped the throne and established his family as the rulers for the next 104 years. In 1951, the Nepalese people backed King Tribhuvan, the grandfather of the present king, in his overthrow of the Rana family rule and the establishment of a democracy, with the monarchy as the source of power. In 1963, King Mahendra, the father of the present king, started the Panchayat partyless democracy, which continues to be the political system of the nation today.

Nepal's population is 90 percent Hindu, 8 percent Buddhist, and 2 percent Islamic. The three religions differ in several ways. For example, Hinduism recognizes a great number of deities, while Buddhism emphasizes the "Middle Way," rejecting excess and fanaticism. Although other religions can be practiced in Nepal, proselytizing is forbidden by law. The religious beliefs of the country have deeply influenced all aspects of the life, culture, and history of Nepal.

The people of Nepal are mostly Tibeto-Burmans, who came from the north, and Indo-Aryans, who came from the south. Nepalese culture follows the caste system, in which the population is classified into four general groups: (1) the Brahmins ("Head Class") are the priests—the highest caste, (2) the Chhetris ("Arm Class") are the rulers and warriors, (3) the Vaisyas ("Leg Class") are artisans and traders, and (4) the Sudras ("Feet Class") are the serfs. In addition, there are sub-castes and many ethnic tribes in the country. Marriage and other contact between castes is strongly discouraged.

A slightly different version of this paper has appeared in *Sign Language Studies*, volume 71 (Summer, 1991), pp. 161–168.

The Educational System

The general educational system in Nepal consists of ten classes divided into three levels: (1) Class 1–5 = Primary level; (2) Class 6–7 = Lower Secondary level; and (3) Class 8–10 = Higher Secondary level. Some postsecondary education is also available. Primary education is compulsory, and the textbooks for these classes are provided by the government. As of 1988, the national literacy rate was 30 percent.

Deaf education in Nepal did not begin until 1966. There are now four government schools in the country serving approximately 300 students.

1. The School for the Deaf, Bal Mindir, Naxal, Kathmandu, was founded in 1966 and currently enrolls 160 students. The grade levels offered include Kindergarten 1–4, Class 1–7 (Primary and Lower Secondary Levels), Vocational Class 8–10 (where tailoring, knitting, carpentry, and electrical work are taught), and a remedial class called Bridge Class.
2. The second school was founded in 1974. The Deaf Children School, Dishartha Nagar, Bhairahawa, currently has sixty students taking courses on three levels— Kindergarten 1–2, Class 1–5, and Vocational Class (tailoring and knitting).
3. Sidha Deaf Children School, Birenda Nagar, Surkhet, was founded in 1985 and presently serves about thirty students. The school offers courses in Kindergarten 1–2 and Class 1–3, in addition to Vocational Class (tailoring, knitting, jewelry-making, and purse-making).
4. The fourth school, the Deaf Children School, Rajbiraj, Saptari, opened in 1985 and now enrolls about thirty students. The class levels include Kindergarten 1–2, Class 1–3, and Vocational Class (tailoring and knitting).

There are an estimated 500,000 deaf people in Nepal, about 3 percent of the total population. Many deaf children are prevented from attending the schools because of financial restraints, long travel distances between home and school, or lack of awareness of the educational opportunities available. However, quite a few deaf students attend schools for the mentally retarded or other disabled groups.

There is currently only one deaf teacher in the entire country, who usually works as a substitute teacher or art teacher at the school for the deaf in Kathmandu. There are no deaf teachers or deaf staff members at any other government schools for deaf children in the country.

There are two nongovernment schools for deaf students in the town of Pokhara, west of Kathmandu. The first, sponsored by a local youth support organization, has about twenty students taught by two deaf teachers. The other is a private school with fifteen students operated by a Japanese priest who receives financial support from the Society of Jesuits.

The Welfare Society for the Hearing Impaired (WSHI), the agency responsible for the four government schools for deaf students, was established in 1984 under the direction of the Health Services Coordination Committee (HSCC). Unfortunately, there has been no deaf participation or input in this organization since its creation.

Oralism has been the prevalent mode of instruction since deaf education began in Nepal. However, since 1988 the Total Communication approach has become more accepted and will become the country's educational approach after the HSCC officially recognizes the new *Nepali Sign Language Dictionary*, which is nearing completion.

There are very few extracurricular activities for deaf students in Nepal. Occasionally some participate in public contests in the arts (primarily drawing and painting) and in crafts (clothesmaking and knitting). Although there are no competitive athletic games with other schools, each individual deaf school holds sports days from time to time.

The parents of deaf students are not adequately included in the education of their children. The only service available to the parents is auditory evaluations of the children. Parents have no opportunity to provide input or receive feedback from the schools about their child's educational development. However, the schools are beginning to develop plans to provide sign language classes for the parents, which may help increase their opportunities to participate in their children's education in the future.

In general, the education of deaf children in Nepal succeeds in only about 15 percent of the cases. The causes for this low success rate include the lack of resources, low motivation of teachers, poor teacher training and skills, and weak administration and/ or government support. Although many teachers have college degrees, very few have received any formal training in deaf education. A few teachers have traveled abroad to attend special programs in deafness, and some have enrolled in a new, six-month training program in deafness provided by the WSHI. Many deaf adults who have now completed school are angry and bitter about the quality of the education they received. Some of them have tried to express their concerns to the school administration, but to date there has been no working relationship established between the schools and the deaf community.

Employment

Services of any kind for deaf adults are virtually nonexistent in Nepal. There are very few vocational training classes beyond the school levels, no interpreting services, and no personal counseling available. It is difficult for deaf adults to obtain employment because they do not have a "School Leaving Certificate," which is equivalent to a high school diploma. Most older deaf adults are unemployed and usually have very minimal communication skills. They often stay with their families and work on farms or as servants. Very few of these adults marry.

The adults who are under thirty years of age and who were educated at the deaf schools received vocational training there in tailoring and knitting only. A few deaf individuals who wanted other types of vocational training have attended a special training program for deaf people in India to study such things as photography and printing. Some have taken short courses in typing, printing, or carpentry offered in Kathmandu. Currently many deaf adults work as tailors; however, they know only how to sew, not how to measure and cut the fabric.

About half of the educated deaf adults are unemployed. While some continue to seek jobs, others stay at home and help with chores. Many of them cannot afford or are unaware of the vocational training opportunities offered by foreign organizations.

Deaf people who do work usually secure their jobs through the efforts of their families. It is rare for deaf individuals to find employment by themselves. Examples of positions held by deaf employees include those of accountant, photo lab technician, carpenter, office worker (such as typist, layout artist, printer), and owner of such small businesses as a video rental shop. One deaf person who attended school but did not graduate taught himself to make metal models of Hindu and Buddhist temples. In Pokhara, several deaf men established their own tailoring business. In the beginning, the public was wary of the enterprise, but now the business is thriving.

Deaf women who work are employed only in the area of tailoring. Most deaf women stay with their families and help with home chores.

The entire population of Nepal—not only disabled groups—is affected by the fact that more than 70 percent of the national economy depends on foreign aid and tourism. In a country where the per capita income is $160.00 in United States money (4,160 rupees), it is difficult for the general public to accept the fact that deaf people (as well as other disabled individuals) are able to do many types of jobs. In general, deaf people have both limited opportunities for vocational training and limited choices of work. However, the situation is neither impossible nor hopeless. There is now an increase in the number of vocational training programs for the disabled and disadvantaged groups in the nation as the general population becomes more aware of the needs of these people.

Discrimination

Deaf people in Nepal do not receive a School Leaving Certificate (SLC), primarily because they are not encouraged to take the required examinations. The Nepali government has claimed that they have not yet developed an academic program and tests appropriate for the Class 8–10 levels at the deaf school in Kathmandu and for the Class 4–10 levels at the other schools. Although it is possible for a deaf person to receive special tutoring on the Class 8–10 level and then take the examinations for an SLC, no deaf person has yet done this.

Deaf people are not allowed to apply for a driver's license in Nepal. However, through personal contacts with government officials, a few deaf adults have been able to obtain licenses to operate motorcycles.

Deaf people, as well as other disabled groups in Nepal, are often subjected to public ridicule. Many Nepalese, especially the uneducated, consider people with disabilities to have "bad karma." Bad karma means that the deaf person must have done something bad in a previous life and must now work hard to rectify the misdeed in this life. Many parents are ashamed of their disabled children, and a few parents have even committed suicide. These misconceptions are slowly being overcome by increased public education. People who work with deaf individuals or with other disabled groups are considered virtuous and courageous.

Most of the movies that the Nepalese people watch are made in India. In these films, deaf and disabled persons are portrayed as helpless or pitiful. Misconceptions about deaf people are evident in the use of such terms as "deaf-mute" and "deaf and dumb" in newspaper articles. There are virtually no public awareness programs on deafness or other disabilities presented by the government.

Very few deaf persons marry deaf persons, both because of the various religious beliefs and because of the restrictions imposed by the caste system. Many parents fear that if a deaf person marries another deaf person, the couple would be unable to take care of themselves or their children. Further, some believe that a deaf couple may continue the bad karma by producing more deaf children. A few deaf individuals have overcome these obstacles and married. One deaf couple, from different castes, dared to elope, and now they have two healthy children and good jobs.

The United States Peace Corps Volunteer Service in Nepal

The United States Peace Corps is the organization that provides manpower and technical skills in agriculture, forestry, health care, education, and other essential areas to the nations of the Third World. Currently, there are 150 Peace Corps volunteers in Nepal.

Sometimes they work with UNICEF, United States AID, or other foreign volunteer organizations in providing services to the country.

When the first school for the deaf was founded in 1966, one of the Peace Corp volunteers provided auditory and speech training to the children. In 1987, another volunteer assisted in the development of the first-ever *Nepali Sign Language Dictionary*, working with two deaf Nepali artists who compiled the handsigns from the deaf community in Nepal. She also assisted in developing the first Nepali fingerspelling system. In 1988 and 1989, the Peace Corps volunteers provided five teachers and speech/language therapists to the four government-supported deaf schools. It is hoped that the Peace Corps will provide manpower for the teacher training program at Tribhuvan University and for other services for deaf adults in Nepal in the future.

Besides their work roles, the Peace Corps volunteers participate in community activities and can use secondary project funds such as the Peace Corp Partnership fund and the Small Project Assistance fund to help at their work sites or communities. Those funds are available only because of the presence of the Peace Corps volunteers. The Peace Corps is able to provide its services only when a host government requests or agrees to the volunteer services; however, the schools and deaf organizations can also request other foreign organizations to provide financial assistance, donations of equipment and supplies, or volunteer manpower.

Social and Community Activities

After the first group of deaf students completed their schooling in Kathmandu, they established the Deaf Development Club (DDC). Their main activity was sports, primarily soccer and volleyball.

In 1980, when the DDC decided to apply for a register from the government, they changed the name of the organization to the Deaf Welfare Association (DWA). Their request was denied, however, because of the planned establishment of the Welfare Society for the Hearing Impaired, which came into being in 1984. Although the government insisted there should be no more than one organization serving the deaf population of Nepal, the DWA continued their activities on an unofficial basis.

In 1988, the DWA reapplied for a register after again changing its name, this time to the Kathmandu Association of the Deaf (KAD). In their application they emphasized the difference in the missions of the KAD and the WHSI. The main purpose of the KAD was to provide rehabilitation and recreational services to deaf adults and deaf awareness classes to the public, while the WHSI would be responsible for the education of deaf people. The application papers are still at the office of the Health Services Coordination Committee awaiting a decision.

In addition to the KAD, there are two informal clubs for the deaf, located in Pokhara and Bhairahawa. Their main focus is on social activities.

Until 1979, deaf people in Nepal had contact with no other deaf community outside their country except for those in India. Then a deaf couple from Italy visited Nepal. This was an enormous surprise to the deaf community, who learned that there were indeed many deaf people living outside Nepal, that there were many types of organizations and services for deaf communities in other countries, and that deaf people in other countries were permitted to marry each other without restrictions. Since then, deaf Nepalese have met deaf persons from many other countries as well.

In 1987 a deaf representative from Nepal was invited to participate in the World Federation of the Deaf Conference in Finland and in the Stockholm Association of the Deaf

Conference in Sweden. He shared with the audience and with his fellow deaf Nepalese his experiences, especially as they related to human rights for deaf individuals.

To promote deaf awareness among the general public, KAD members have participated in several national activities, including donating blood to the Red Cross Society, raising earthquake relief funds, preparing mountaineering trips to India, arranging the annual New Year picnics, participating in governmental marches for festivals, and helping with fundraising projects.

Some of the deaf men in the KAD have become involved in competitive sports, especially in such individual activities as gymnastics, track, karate, and yoga. Deaf adults have not yet formed teams to play against hearing players, however, because there is no hearing person available in Nepal who can use sign language and interpret for them.

The KAD, which relies heavily on donations from other groups, has recently received the following contributions: a donation from the Stockholm Association of the Deaf for travel expenses to the conferences in Finland and Sweden, funding from the American Women of Nepal for furniture, a donation from the Norwegian Association of the Deaf, and two typewriters (in Nepali and English) from UNICEF. Currently the KAD is trying to obtain assistance from the United States Peace Corps and UNICEF for printing sign language calendars and Nepali fingerspelling cards.

The KAD currently has about fifty-six active members, including a few hearing advocates. As previously stated, there are about 300 students at the schools for the deaf and thousands of deaf people who never went to school or obtained any vocational training. Thus, some of the future goals of the deaf community in Nepal include vocational training classes and other short-term educational classes for deaf adults; interpreting services; social and recreational activities for deaf adults; sign language classes and deaf awareness training for the public; support groups for parents of deaf children; support of deaf youth in their endeavors; a networking system both within the country and with other foreign countries; a newsletter for the members of the KAD, for the Nepal public and for people around the world; and office space and classrooms for the KAD.

Many of these goals will be accomplished when more deaf people become better educated, when the government becomes more aware of and better understands the needs of the deaf community, and when there are more resources and financial support available to alleviate some of the problems. It is obvious from this brief overview that the deaf community of Nepal faces an enormous challenge in overcoming these obstacles, many of which are based on fear and ignorance; nevertheless, the members of the Kathmandu Association of the Deaf are ready to undertake these enormous responsibilities with hope, persistence, and diligence.

Deaf Culture in Pakistan

ANWAR SHAMSHUDIN

*I*n Pakistan, a Muslim country, religion plays a very significant role in our general culture and thus in our deaf culture as well. Respect for elders is essential, and the younger generation does not have as many rights or as much freedom as they do in Western countries. The masses, in general, experience feelings of inferiority, and deaf people, especially, are considered outsiders with very few opportunities to prove their abilities or establish their identity.

The majority of people in our country—nearly 80 percent—dwell in villages, where they are born into poverty and die in distress. They live a life that does not permit them to go beyond these meager means, primarily out of respect for the elders in their family, because to achieve beyond the family's status is considered disrespectful. They live in limited space with no ventilation, sanitation, cleanliness, or facilities for health care. Schools do not exist, even in areas where there are thousands of people. In such a culture it is not hard to imagine the plight of deaf people, who live in helplessness and are neglected most of the time.

In a culture such as this—where even the common people with hearing children can ill afford education—it would be a dream come true for deaf children to have a right to an education or an educational facility to attend. Their level of illiteracy and lack of ability to communicate with hearing people drives deaf people to a state of despondency, so that some lead a caged life, forever dependent on their families for their daily needs.

Members of the older generation in our country are orthodox in their views and consider deafness a taboo and a curse from heaven. They therefore tend to hide deaf children from others. When a deaf child reaches an age at which he or she can no longer be kept indoors, the elders then go in search of a so-called cure from the leader of one of the religious cults. Sometimes they even resort to witchcraft.

Parents who are a little more educated often seek out the village doctor, who typically is not qualified to diagnose or treat deafness. The well-qualified doctors, who can correctly diagnose "muteness," do not want to practice in the rural areas. This frustrates the parents as well as the child. Unfortunately, it is the child who has to bear the brunt of the parent's rage as the illiterate parents lose not only their time but also their money to the village doctor.

There are also some parents who pamper and overprotect their young deaf children, with the result that these children never develop any self-confidence. Such overattention is more of a curse than a blessing for a deaf child. It is true, of course, that there is no cure for deafness, but understanding, care, and love during the early years, followed by a proper education, can change the deaf child's life. Deaf people, although they cannot hear or speak, possess a sharp mind that is full of know-how and, if given direction, will often prove to be more worthy than a "normal" person.

Owing to financial difficulties, Pakistani parents often force their children—both hearing and deaf—to join the labor force as soon as they are old enough. In the larger cities, however, this is not so prevalent because people there have sufficient financial resources to provide a good education for their hearing children.

For hearing children whose parents can afford it, there are scattered educational facilities, such as the Mosque schools in some villages, but the doors of education are closed to deaf children. Their right to an education is denied because they cannot speak, and they grow up feeling they do not belong to society. If a deaf child has some skill or ability that can be self-developed, he may, however, strive for achievement in his own humble way.

All children love to go to school, and it is the prime duty of all parents not to deny this right to their child. But most deaf children do not get even an opportunity to know what education is. To them, the print on paper is merely a black mark. Special schools for these children are very few. Even where there *are* schools, there are no qualified teachers to teach deaf students. In Karachi, where there are schools for deaf children, the students go only to the tenth grade—which barely compares with the fifth grade in America or in other Western countries. Higher education for deaf students is a far-distant dream in Pakistan.

As we look deeper into the situation for deaf people of Pakistan, we observe that girls are even further behind, again owing primarily to our religious customs. Girls—both deaf and hearing—are confined within the four walls and safety of the home, which eliminates any chance for a formal education. Deaf people are always at the mercy of hearing people, and deaf girls have no rights at all. For example, if a girl is molested, she cannot point out the culprit for fear of humiliation. She would be cursed for the rest of her life if she even opened her mouth to make the accusation.

Even if a deaf girl were fortunate enough to obtain some formal education, there is little or no possibility that she would be able to use that education to work outside the home; her education is beneficial neither to her nor to others. Deaf girls lead a very depressed life, not having the confidence even to go alone to meet friends or relatives. In the cities, some of these situations have improved and, after attending school, deaf girls are more confident and can work in the sewing or tailoring trades to earn a little pocket money. But this situation is new and still does not exist for deaf women living in the villages.

Recently Ms. Donna Platt, a deaf woman from America, visited Pakistan while on a world tour and was my guest for a couple of days. Our organization introduced her to deaf members of our community and to other deaf people residing in Karachi. All who met her were amazed to learn that she had travelled alone from one side of the world to the other.

In most cases, our culture does not permit boys and girls to choose their own life partner. Marriages are permitted only by arrangements of the elders—the dowry system still exists and must be agreed upon ahead of time. Marriages for deaf people are all the more difficult.

A deaf boy can marry a hearing girl, but the reverse is practically impossible and is not acceptable within the orthodox society. Even when an arranged marriage takes place for a deaf girl, she is usually ignored and neglected by the families. If a deaf child (God forbid) is born to a deaf couple, the deaf woman is considered an outcast. Such is the situation for deaf people, not only in Pakistan but in neighboring countries as well.

However, to achieve through struggle has been the most popular and celebrated maxim in the lives of great men. In recent years, young deaf people struggled to form an organization that we hope will improve the plight of deaf people in our society. Our central focus, despite all hardships, is achieving the best in all our endeavors. One of our goals is to enlighten people about our sign language. With the help of other nations, we are beginning to do that. Recently Munizeh T. Hussain, a hearing woman who runs the Anjuman Behbood-e-Samat-e-Atfal (ABSA) School for the Deaf, arranged a Language Research Project with the help of the Norwegian Association of the Deaf and the Norwegian Church Aid. Fifteen Pakistani deaf members collaborated with two Norwegians—Mr. Odd-Inge Schroeder and Mr. Patrick Coppock—to develop a dictionary of Pakistan Sign Language. This project will benefit deaf and hearing people alike in our country.

The aim of our struggles in Pakistan can be summed up in the following plea: "Deaf people have a right to live, so let them live with honor, dignity, and pride." We hope and trust that the worldwide deaf nation will be with us in this effort.

The Role of Educational Systems and Deaf Culture in the Development of Sign Language in South Africa

ROBERT M. T. SIMMONS

The situation for deaf people in South Africa is complex. It is linked to the country's political and social views regarding different ethnic groups as well as the history of education for deaf people in South Africa.

There is no uniform sign language in South Africa like that found in the United States, Great Britain, or Australia. Instead, there are many different sign language systems that have developed among South African ethnic groups during the past 100 years. For example, there are two groups of White people, two groups of Colored, and one group of Indian South African, each of which may use English and/ or Afrikaans language as their medium of education and means of communication. In addition, there are ten to twelve different tribes of Black Africans, each possessing its own distinctive language, e.g., Zulu, Tswana, Sotho, etc. Thus the diversity of "mother tongues" (spoken languages) and cultures has influenced the formation of different sign languages in South Africa. These sign languages originated in places that were demographically and geographically isolated from one another, and their development was not greatly encouraged by the domination of oral education in schools for deaf Africans, especially during the past forty years. For these reasons, Deaf culture has not developed as strongly in South Africa as it has in other countries, and sign language researchers are confronted with the great problem of studying various sign languages and finding their common meeting ground.

Characteristics of Deaf Communities in South Africa

As with most other disabilities, exact statistics on deafness in South Africa are not readily available; however, table 1 contains approximate figures.

I would like to express my gratitude to Mrs. Henna Opperman, National Director of the South African National Council for the Deaf, and to Professor Claire Penn for their encouragement and interest in this paper. Thanks must also go to Ms. Dale Ogilvy and Sister Gemma for their valuable information on Black deaf education, and to Mrs. Susan Weil-Venter for her patience and diligence in typing and proofreading the original manuscript of this paper.

TABLE 1: The Population of Deaf People in South Africa

Population Group	Total Population	Totally Deaf (1%)	Meaningfully Hearing Impaired (3%)	Measurably Hearing Impaired (6%)
Blacks	18,238,000	182,380	547,140	1,094,280
Whites (includes Afrikaans)	4,807,000	48,070	144,210	288,420
Coloreds	2,817,000	28,170	84,510	169,020
Indians and Other Asians	887,000	8,870	26,610	53,220
Totals	26,749,000	267,490	802,470	1,604,940

A hearing community in Johannesburg or Cape Town may be composed of different ethnic and cultural groups; the same is the case for deaf communities. Each deaf community in South Africa is uniquely affected by its location. For example, the Johannesburg deaf community is shaped by the fact that it is located in one of the largest urban areas in South Africa. A large number of deaf people are employed in this area, and thus they make up a very large and powerful community. Likewise, the identity of the Pretoria community is undeniably influenced by the political and educational institutions in that city.

Deaf people can move from one geographical location to another and enter into new communities with ease, e.g., the Wittebome deaf people can easily visit the deaf community of Natal. They carry with them the knowledge of their specific cultures, which helps them establish new community ties and learn the specific issues and operations of the new community. Unlike in the United States, where there is a single Deaf culture whose members live in different communities, there are many different deaf communities across South Africa, each with its own Deaf culture.

Language Use

The deaf communities in South Africa are composed of people from different cultural groups, and thus language use within the *community* is different from language use within the particular *cultural group*. This is primarily a result of the South African educational system, which will be discussed later in this paper. Unlike the situation in the United States, where all members of the deaf community use American Sign Language (ASL), the sign languages of the various deaf communities in South Africa differ from one community to the next. If there could be one uniform and national sign language (South African Sign Language or SASL) developed by searching for a common ground among the various cultural groups, then all Deaf South Africans would use the same sign language.

Deaf people who prefer to use their own sign language in public speaking situations must obtain the services of sign-to-voice interpreters. When Deaf people are involved in community activities that include hearing people who use English, they may prefer to use Signed English. Language use at the community level is rather flexible, but within the culture group, language use is more restricted.

The distinction between *community* and *culture* allows us to explain how some Deaf people may accept, respect, and even use the language of the majority group—

English—but at the same time prefer the language of their own cultural group. Deaf people feel a strong identification with their own particular variety of sign language because it is a part of their cultural background. But when they are involved in community activities, the use of another language allows them to interact with other people who are not Deaf. The same situation applies to hearing South Africans, who may use one spoken language in the home but the language of the majority in social settings.

Education for White Deaf Children

The Europeans who settled in South Africa brought with them the idea that deaf people were uneducable. This notion combined with the native African belief that deafness was a divine visitation and should be accepted as such. Such attitudes toward deaf people prevailed in South Africa through three centuries of white rule. These beliefs may still exist in some rural areas, particularly in the Black homelands, e.g., Transkei, Bophuthatswana, and Venda. However, many of the notions that were prevalent in those dark years are now being swept away by the enlightened conviction that all deaf people are educable and capable of doing everything as well and as efficiently as hearing people.

Included in the political and social situations found in South Africa is the distinction between White, Afrikaaner, non-White (Colored and Indian), and Black. The history of the educational system for deaf children in South Africa reflects these distinctions as well.

The first public school for White hearing children of Dutch origin was founded in the Cape of Good Hope colony as early as 1663, but the first school for white deaf children did not appear until 200 years later, when the Roman Catholic Church established a school in Cape Town in 1863. This school—first called the Dominican School and later renamed the Grimley School for the Deaf—was opened by Bishop Grimley, who brought nuns to Cape Town from Ireland. These nuns introduced the Irish Sign Language (ISL) and its variety of one-handed fingerspelling. Thus, Cape Town became the first site for an English-medium education for deaf children in Southern Africa.

In the beginning of the educational system in South Africa, many deaf citizens of all ethnic groups attended school for only short periods of time or not at all. Hospitals, clinics, and treatment and assessment facilities were very limited until the mid-1950s. In rural areas, children often were not diagnosed as deaf until their teens or young adulthood. Today, there is a large group of deaf adults who lack language skills, all of whom come from population groups that have had limited or no educational opportunities.

Before 1937, when South Africa introduced compulsory education for all disabled children of European descent (including deaf children), both White and non-White (Colored and Indian) students were accommodated in the Grimley School. After the law went into effect, however, the numbers of deaf children attending the school increased, and the Non-White children were transferred to Wittebome, a suburb south of Cape Town. They brought with them the Irish Sign Language used at the Grimley School, and ISL has been maintained in Wittebome to this day. This Wittebome Sign Language has become the hallmark of the Cape Town Colored deaf community (mainly those of Malay descent) and, to a lesser extent, of the White deaf community of the Cape Peninsula.

In 1881, Rev. G. de la Bat of the Dutch Reformed Church opened the first school for Afrikaans-speaking White deaf children in Worcester, a town in the wine-farming area east of Cape Town. The language of instruction at that school was Afrikaans, although English was taught as a second language. The British two-handed alphabet was adapted for use with their signs, which became known as the Worcester Sign System. It was not until 1954 that another Afrikaans-medium school was established, this time in Pretoria. The goal of this school (the Transoranje School for the Deaf) was to serve children who lived in the northern provinces of South Africa, such as Transvaal, Orange Free State, and the northern part of Natal.

In 1884, a group of German Dominican nuns in King William's Town began teaching deaf children who lived in Eastern Cape Province. The language of instruction was English rather than German, and the method of instruction was mainly oral, although the sign language that was permitted was based more or less on British Sign Language and its two-handed alphabet.

During the 1920s, a small private school in Johannesburg was begun by Miss Jessica Davis, a British-born teacher trained to work with deaf students. Later, Dominican Sisters established a convent in Johannesburg and built a school for deaf children whose parents found the distance to King William's Town too great to travel. The convent school was called St. Vincent's School for the Deaf, and it later joined with Miss Davis' school. This amalgamated institution officially opened in 1934. The St. Vincent Sign System, an offshoot of BSL, became the hallmark of the English-medium schools for deaf children.

Several schools were established between 1933 and 1988 for the Colored, Indian, and Black deaf communities. These have been supported both by the Department of Education and by various religious organizations. Today, the trend in education is toward new programs, such as mainstreaming, not only for various ethnic groups but also for moderately to severely hearing impaired students.

Education for Indian Deaf Students

Until 1968, Indian and other Asian deaf children had attended the schools with White deaf children in Worcester and Wittebome in the Cape Province. By 1968, the need for a school for deaf Indian children had become pressing, mainly because of the long distances these children were forced to travel. Furthermore, the non-White deaf students came from an ethnic group with its own cultural, social, and religious values that were different from those of the White deaf students. Therefore, in 1969, the first school for the more than 200 Indian deaf children opened in Durban, and was soon filled to capacity. A second school (the V.N. Naik School for the Deaf) was established north of Durban in 1984.

At about the same time, a third school for deaf Indian students was established in the Transvaal. This school (the Lenasia School for the Hearing Impaired) also serves deaf Indian children from the independent states of Bophuthatswana, Swaziland, and Lesotho. The method of signing used there is loosely based on the St. Vincent and the Wittebome sign languages as well as on American Sign Language.

Education for Black Deaf Students

The history of education for deaf Black students goes back to 1937, when education became compulsory for all deaf children in South Africa. At present, there are eighteen well-established schools for deaf African children, each serving a different ethnic group or area. These schools include the Kutluwanong School near Rustenburg, Transvaal (serving the Tswana); the Dominican School in Hammanskraal near Pretoria (Tswana); St. Thomas School in King William's Town (Xhosa); the Vuleka School in Zululand (Zulu); and Sizwile School for the Deaf in Soweto near Johannesburg (Sotho, Tswana,

Zulu). These schools have developed their own sign language systems independently of one another. These systems have yet to be linguistically analyzed or compared with the sign language systems used by the White, Indian, and Colored deaf communities. All of these schools use American fingerspelling, but most of these seem to have based their in-class sign language on the Nieder-Hartman sign language book, *Talking to the Deaf* (1980).

All of these schools are under the control of the Department of Education and Training (Special), which has developed an internal system of in-service teacher training. Research on and application of the different African sign languages is beginning to receive a lot of attention within the Black education system. At present, a more or less uniform system of instruction is used in the African deaf schools. The schools have also recently adopted English as an educational medium: The native spoken languages of various groups (with their respective regional and employment limitations) had previously been used.

Although Signed English is the teaching method used in these schools, there exists the possibility that regional variations occur both inside and outside the classroom. Of major concern is the fact that the signs used in the classroom do not appear to be the same as the signs children use on the playground. Further research on South African sign languages, particularly those of Black deaf communities, was attempted once, but this effort was rejected owing to its unscientific approach. Hearing people have made the final decision on what signs would be used in the classroom.

There are no high schools for Black deaf children. The highest level they can attain in school is Standard 5, which is equivalent to approximately the eighth grade in the United States. The teachers use Signed English and speech in the Black schools, with the home languages (e.g., Zulu or Sotho) taught as a second language. However, teachers are aware that they are not using Signed English but rather Pidgin Sign English (PSE).

The Department of Education and Training provides guidelines for education and administration of schools in the homelands. Black deaf children start school at an average age of two to three years in urban areas. In the rural areas, where schools have limited facilities and long waiting lists, most Black deaf children do not enter school until the age of seven to eight.

Oral education for deaf students was favored in Europe and the United States between 1940 and 1980, and South Africa followed suit. Thus, sign language was frowned upon and was so severely suppressed by the educational authorities that its natural development among White deaf children was stunted. However, the opposite was true in the African deaf schools. Because at that time, schools for the Black deaf students were few and far removed from one another, and because their education barely reached the high school level, the development of their sign language was not encumbered by the restrictions placed upon the White deaf community. Thus the African deaf children were first taught their local sign language at home and in their preprimary classes (from ages two to six). They were also encouraged to develop spoken language skills so that they could learn and assimilate their spoken "mother tongue" with comparative ease.

Once every three months, the schools for Black deaf children now hold meetings and workshops in various locations throughout South Africa to discuss methods of teaching oral and manual languages and to search for a common ground for all Black sign languages. This may eventually lead to the formation of one common sign language system not only adaptable to all different African Deaf cultures but also able to bridge the gap of communication between deaf school children and deaf adults. Black deaf children have English as their third language, because this language is essential for communication with other people and for employment in towns and cities. With the acquisition of "White" languages—English and Afrikaans—Black deaf people will be able to establish contact with White and other ethnic deaf communities.

At present, the White school system discriminates against deaf teachers, and there are no certified deaf teachers in these schools. The Black deaf education system employs two deaf teachers, but they had been qualified as teachers prior to becoming totally deaf. These facts should be viewed in light of the fact that there are only about forty deaf college graduates in South Africa within a total population of 27 million people. All forty of these graduates have been forced to acquire their degrees either by being mainstreamed into the universities and technicons, or through correspondence courses with the University of South Africa. No special tuition assistance is available for deaf students attending any of the sixteen South African universities or at the technicons in large cities.

Social Relations

Deaf people in South Africa, in spite of their different racial groups, educational backgrounds, sign languages, and second languages, are drawn to each other. After establishing some sort of understanding of each other's sign language, they feel a sense of comradeship and identification of status in the Deaf world. This does not seem to be the case with hearing people. When hearing people stay in foreign countries for a length of time, they must take a crash course in speaking and reading the language of the country in order to obtain some mastery of the foreign language. But when deaf people come into contact with other deaf communities in foreign countries, they seem to be able to enter into conversation with each other with greater ease.

I was recently involved in a sign language research study with nine other deaf people from different cultural/linguistic groups. We communicated with each other in such a relaxed and unself-conscious manner that it seemed our racial, linguistic, and social differences were thrown out the window. We became one fraternity of deaf people. Hearing people should pay attention to this—it teaches a valuable lesson about showing respect for and cooperating harmoniously with other cultural groups. The existence of political and social conflicts seems to bring out the best in those aspects of Deaf culture that are unique and separate from other cultural groups. The reactions of deaf people in such situations also points out that a group of deaf people is not merely a group of like-minded people, e.g., a sports club or bridge club, but is also a group of people who share a code of behaviors and values that is learned and passed on from one generation of Deaf people to the next. Entering into Deaf culture and becoming Deaf mean learning all the appropriate ways of behaving like a Deaf person.

In 1989, the South African National Council for the Deaf and the Human Sciences Research Council initiated an extensive research program on South African sign languages and their variants. Under the directorship of Professor Claire Penn, a team of hearing and deaf researchers (including myself) negotiated with different deaf ethnic communities to collect signs for the first South African Sign Language dictionary. This research program, still in progress, has compiled about 420 signs [as of March, 1989]. In the next three years, we hope to compile over 3,500 signs by holding further sign language board meetings every three months with the goal of videotaping 500 signs per meeting. We are standing on the threshold of an exciting era of advancement in education and sign language development for all groups of deaf people in South Africa. We appeal to you, our comrades in the Deaf world, to give us encouragement and advice, and share our interest in developing our South African Sign Language, which is unique among all other sign languages in the world.

References

Nieder-Hartman. 1980. *Talking to the Deaf: A Visual Manual of Standardized Signs for the Deaf.* Pretoria: Government Printer.

Culture-Based Concepts and Social Life of Disabled Persons in Sub-Saharan Africa: The Case of the Deaf

PATRICK DEVLIEGER

For the purposes of this discussion, "culture" must be understood in a holistic sense, as the relation of human beings to their environment in its widest sense. It is only within this wider perspective that the development of deaf culture as a genuine expression of the deaf community is a realistic possibility. To consider deaf culture within the framework of a holistic concept of culture will prevent the isolation and self-marginalization of the deaf community from its wider social environment. Such a view will also prevent the stereotyping of deaf culture, and will instead account for the variety of its development.

This paper focuses on understanding disability in the sociocultural context of sub-Saharan Africa. Knowledge about African concepts of disability, which has always been available, has been ignored in the planning and implementation of services for disabled people. However, before service institutions were imposed on the African people, disability was approached solely in a community-oriented way. Recently there has been a shift back from the institution-based services to community-based and integrated services for disabled people as a way to adapt services to the realities of African countries. New interest in sociocultural aspects of disability is beginning to develop (Momm and Konig, 1989). The application of such knowledge to the development of services for disabled people is a challenge for the future.

The shift to community-based services that take into account the African view of disability, however, has been based primarily on economic realities, i.e., the motive has been to reach more people in a more cost-effective way. As a result, the social-cultural elements of disability have not received enough consideration (Ingstad, 1989). What has developed instead is an individual-centered approach to the disabled person. A truly community-based approach, in which the community is the center of attention, is still lacking. One explanation for this could be that the information on sociocultural aspects of disability is available only to a limited extent. Thus, there is a need for additional sociocultural research on disability that can be used in the implementation of programs

I am indebted to Mr. J. Kisanji and Dr. M. Ndurumo for fruitful discussions on this paper. The ideas expressed remain, however, my sole responsibility as the author. I am also grateful to the organizers of The Deaf Way and to the Wenner Gren Foundation for Anthropological Research for facilitating my participation in this conference.

for disabled people. Such work supposes that organizations will include qualitative elements in their conception of development. Such an attitude will help the development of African self-reliance in rehabilitation.

The Disabled Person in the African Social-Cultural Environment

The term "marginal" has been used to describe the status of disabled children in African communities. However, I will argue that the disabled person's status in the community is not marginal, but *ambiguous.*

In the African context, disability is thought of in a holistic way. The most significant question is *"Why?—why is the person disabled?"* The entire sociocultural system of a community comes into play in thinking about the cause of a disability. The discourse about disability is in terms of *relations* and differs from scientific discourse. In this holistic scheme, disability is the starting point from which one reflects on relations of a deeper nature. The levels of relations will be discussed in this paper. To illustrate these statements, I will refer to the culture of the Songye, a tribe living in East-Kasai, Zaire.

Abnormality—any deviance from an established norm—is known in every culture, and the criteria that are used to define normal and abnormal are culture-specific. Thus, to define the abnormality of a child, the Songye use specific criteria that do not necessarily apply to other societies. There are three categories of abnormal children in the Songye society: "ceremonial children" (*baana mishinga*); "miserable children" (*baana ba malwa*); and "faulty children" (*baana ba bilema*). Each of these types of children has a different status in the community.

"Ceremonial children" are those who are born under special circumstances, or who exhibit special bodily characteristics at birth. Examples of ceremonial children include twins, children born with teeth, children born with the umbilical cord around the neck, or children born with feet or hands first. These children are surrounded with ceremonies to secure their integration into the society. Given a specific name according to the situation of their birth, they are said to have special powers. Because of these characteristics, the Songye regard these ceremonial children as being of higher status than other children, and display an attitude of respect toward them. Thus it becomes obvious that, within the Songye culture, abnormality does not necessarily lead to a marginal status.

In contrast, "miserable children" are not considered to be human beings at all, because they do not possess certain essential human attributes. Miserable children include those affected by albinism, dwarfism, and hydrocephaly. They are considered supernatural beings, because they are thought to have been in contact with the anti-world of sorcerers. The Songye believe miserable children have come to this world to stay only a short time and will soon return to their world. Thus, their relations with other people are indeed marginal, because social contact with miserable children is limited and often rule-governed.

The third category is that of "faulty" or disabled children. These children do not have a special, higher status as do the ceremonial children, but they *are* considered to be human beings, unlike the miserable children. The label "faulty" indicates that the disabled person's body is characterized by a fault, the cause of which lies either with God or with the relations of a family member with the environment, family members of the same or different lineages, or ancestors. Because the removal of the fault is impossible, the disabled person is accepted in the world as a "normal abnormality."

Disabled people are integrated into society, but in an indifferent way. Their status is, therefore, ambiguous. Murphy et al. (1988) have labeled this status "liminal"—betwixt and between—referring to the transitory nature of the *rites de passage*. In the liminal stage of such rites, the person involved is neither a child nor an adult. It is characteristic of this stage for the subject to be under the strong authority of a supervisor and to experience a strong sense of solidarity with the other participants (Turner, 1967). The liminal stage is a temporary condition that is resolved by completing the rites. For disabled people, however, this liminal status is not temporary, but fixed, thus making their status in the community one of permanent potentiality. With sufficient stimulation from the environment, this potential can be exploited, but, in the same way, it can become marginal owing to societal constraints.

The attitude of nondisabled people follows the perception of the status of disabled people, and is one of tolerance and acceptance, not of normalization. The disabled person is not stimulated by his community to be active. Rather, the initiative must come from the individual him or herself.

The view of disability as ambiguous becomes an urgent social and human problem when disabled persons find themselves rejected by a society on its way to urbanization. Disability then becomes part of the major problem of poverty. At the age of adulthood, disabled people may be forced into begging. However, isolation—a problem that is common to Western societies—is alien to African societies. Although a disabled person may find him or herself marginalized as a street beggar, this does not mean the disabled person is isolated from friends and family members. (It should be noted here that begging is not a common practice among deaf people, who are known to be hard-working and sometimes possessing special skills.)

African Concepts of Disability—The Holistic View of Relations

As stated earlier, traditional African thinking about disability is holistic in nature. As opposed to scientific thinking, it takes into account relations between human beings and their environment at various levels. Although scientific thinking is accepted by African people, it is not viewed as sufficient to explain phenomena such as disability. Accordingly, the Songye explain disability in terms of relationships. They take into account the interaction between human beings and their environment, although, in biomedical thinking, most of these relationships would be considered irrelevant. In that sense, the African concepts offer elements that might help to complete Western thinking about disability.

The Songye believe that the appearance of a disability can be explained by problems that have occurred at different levels of relationships, from the most basic level of a person's relationship with the physical environment, to relationships with family members through sorcery, to relationships with ancestors, and finally to relationships with God.

Relations with the Environment

The relationship of the family to the physical environment finds expression in certain dietary prescriptions and taboos that a pregnant woman must observe in order to deliver a child who is physically normal and characterized by normal behavior. The appearance of certain "faults" (*bilema*), therefore, can sometimes be attributed to the mother's negligence or nonobservance of prescriptions or taboos. If the mother eats a forbidden animal, for example, it is believed that the child will take on some of the animal's characteristics. Thus, the meat of a sheep must not be eaten, as this will cause bodily weakness in the child; the meat of a serpent will prevent the child from walking upright, and so on.

Relations between Family Members of the Same Lineage through Sorcery[1]

Sorcery is a belief system in sub-Saharan Africa that is used to explain evil in terms of relationships between family members of the same lineage. Therefore, if a disability appears either at birth or later, the relationships between the parents of the disabled child and other family members will be examined. If it is discovered that there were bad relations prior to the occurrence of the disability, the cause of the disability will be attributed to sorcery, because the Songye believe that opportunistic evil forces intervene at times when a link in the lineage system is weak.

Relations between Two Lineages

The relationship between two lineages is thoroughly regulated through the dowry system. Among the Songye, the dowry is given by the husband to his father-in-law, and usually has its final arrangements at the birth of the first child. If a child is born disabled, the father of the child might consider whether the dowry was well presented to the family of his wife. In addition, he might ask his father-in-law about the distribution of goods within the family. The father-in-law has certain responsibilities concerning the dowry as well. Although he may keep a good part of the dowry for himself, he is supposed to distribute some to his brothers and to his wife. If the dowry had not been handled properly, the cause of the child's disability might be attributed to relationships involved in the dowry system.

Relations with Ancestors

When disability appears at the moment of birth, as in the case of a clubfoot, the relationship between the family and its ancestors will be examined. The focal point of this relationship occurs at the moment of the ancestor's burial. The Songye believe that if an ancestor is not buried with owing respect, he or she may manifest anger by being reborn with a fault. Ancestors can also punish their descendants if the descendants do not observe the rules of the society, as in the case of theft, adultery, or the violation of the postpartum taboo.

Relations with God

In many cases, the appearance of a disability is explained as something caused by God. In such instances, the disability could not be explained in sociofamilial terms, and God, as the absolute and unknown force, remains the only possible cause. The former practice of killing disabled children at birth is related to the belief that disabled children were sent by God. The logical solution, then, was to send the child back to God so that he

---

1 The relation between sorcery and disability is more extensively described in my paper, "The Cultural Significance of Physical Disability in Africa," presented at the Annual Meeting of the Society of Applied Anthropology, Santa Fe, New Mexico, April 5–9, 1989.

would send well formed children. Community leaders were involved in this practice, which became ritualized and therefore was not viewed by society as murder.

Thus, it can be seen that, in sub-Saharan Africa, a thorough understanding of the disabled person's social status goes beyond individual characteristics and places the person in the framework of a wider sociocultural system. This view answers the existential question, *"Why* is this person disabled?"—a question that is ignored and unanswered in the Western context, but whose therapeutic and social effects are undeniable.

To understand the African societal attitude toward a disabled person, one must understand the level at which a weakness in relations was detected. In African thinking, the disabled person is not the primary focus of solutions. Instead, focal points in the broader environment, such as the family, ancestors, and God, are the center of attention. Programs for disabled people in Africa should take this information into account. For example, programs for family members—especially parents—should examine focal points in the parents' relationships with the environment, with other family members, with ancestors, and with God. A restoration of the weak relationships believed to have caused the disability should be included in the service program. The attitude that African thinking cannot be incorporated in service delivery, because it is unscientific, primitive, and so on, should be revised. Belief systems such as sorcery can be effectively and positively used in service delivery systems, as has been shown by De Mahieu (1984).

As was mentioned earlier, the disabled person in Africa is considered a "normal abnormality." Disabled people's ambiguous status is one of potential; they are part of life and are integrated into society. The primary focus of service delivery in Africa cannot, therefore, be "integration"—for this already occurs—but rather must be on preventing services from having disintegrative effects on society. Thus, the challenge to service developers in Africa is to safeguard and build on the already existing situation of integration, and to develop the potential of disabled people inherent in their ambiguous social status.

Programs for disabled people tend to concentrate on giving answers to the question *"how"*: how to provide disabled people with medical, social, vocational, and educational assistance. This has led to the invention of special equipment, appropriate technology, and programs adapted to the environment of disabled persons. These rehabilitation programs have had a significant impact on the quality of life, making the lives of disabled people more comfortable and useful. Many times, however, these programs do not incorporate the more significant question of *why*: why the person is disabled. This question is left out because the answer varies according to the culture and personality of the disabled person. It is, however, a very important question, as it deals with the very existence of the disabled person and his or her relations with nondisabled people. To answer this question, many disabled people rely on elements within their cultures affecting their attitudes towards themselves and toward other people. Anthropology, as a human science, has the task of bringing these elements to the surface so they can be used by professionals in their work.

Communication of Deaf People in Eastern and Southern Africa: The Rise of Deaf Culture

The major problem for the deaf community is *communication*. In Eastern and Southern Africa, this problem results from the early adoption and continued use of the oral/aural system of education for deaf children. However, in a few West African countries, such as Ghana and Nigeria, sign language was introduced as the first formal communication system for deaf people.

In an oral system, the deaf person is taught to speak as a hearing person and to understand spoken language through speechreading. The system is difficult to implement for a number of reasons, most obviously because this communication mode is alien to deaf persons, very tiring to learn, and inefficient—it is estimated that very little oral communication can be understood through speechreading.

Furthermore, the success of oral programs has been weakened in Africa because the oral system depends on a lavish supply of hearing aids, which must be used throughout the school day. In Africa, hearing aids are in short supply, and their maintenance and repair is problematic owing to lack of skilled personnel.

The acquisition of concepts through the oral system is very difficult and slow, because too much time and attention are devoted to speech. A lack of materials prevents African deaf children from being exposed to different contexts in and outside the classroom.

The oral system is very demanding on the teacher. It is also very demanding on the deaf children. The system requires a great deal of concentration but results in only partial understanding (to the extent that communication with signs or gestures is not allowed in the classroom).

The limited success of students in the oral system has led to the general belief that deaf people can not advance beyond primary education. Most deaf Africans who have gone beyond the primary level have received their higher education outside their own countries, primarily in the United States, where sign language is permitted in educational environments. Thus, it has been shown that the use of sign language helps to expand educational opportunities for deaf people (Ndurumo, 1988).

There has been a long, hard struggle between advocates of oralism and those who advocate the use of sign language as a communication mode for deaf people. The oralists argue that deaf people must adapt themselves to the conversational modes of hearing people, while advocates of sign language are convinced that deaf people have their own mode of conversation and should have the right to use it. Both oralism and sign language have their disadvantages: The first does not respect a specific mode of communication for deaf people, and the second does not take into account a way for hearing and deaf people to converse together. One thing becomes clear: All of the discussions about the appropriate language for deaf people have been led by hearing people and reflect their relations with deaf people. In short, the question "Who must adapt to whom?" is central. Although hearing people might know that signing is an easy medium for deaf people to learn, and that it is a natural medium for them, they retain the oral method because signing "is not an easy exercise for the hearing," as mentioned by Msengi (1987, p. 9). The need is great for deaf people to argue for themselves and to strive for a communication mode that is appropriate.

The introduction of formal sign language in the subregion began during the first half of this decade, when a standardized sign language was developed in Zambia and Ethiopia. To accomplish this, surveys were conducted on local signs, which were complemented with American signs. Kenya is now in the process of formalizing its own sign language as well.

There is still a long way to go in the implementation of total communication as an acceptable tool of communication in educational settings for deaf persons in the subregion. In English-using Eastern and Southern Africa, the most important difficulties to overcome include

1. the historical aspects of communication as it applies to deaf people and the attitudes of hearing people towards change. It is amazing to see that Tanzania still advocates the oral system as the only viable system in the country (see Hokororo, 1987),
2. the need to formalize sign language based on an inventory of local signs,
3. the need to invent or borrow certain signs not available locally, and
4. the need to train teachers of deaf students in the techniques and use of total communication.

Recreational and Social Activities for Deaf People

One of the big challenges facing national associations of the deaf in such countries as Ethiopia, Kenya, and Tanzania is to organize recreational and leisure activities for their members. Another challenge is to develop the talents of deaf people, which have gone untapped. The development of artistic expression could provide many opportunities for deaf people to express their experiences of the world. Drama has been used in the schools to teach concepts, but it has not been exploited enough as a leisure activity. The organization of such activities will help deaf people defend themselves against "a force which is ever present and permeates the society. This force is called attitudes. It is a strong force, and depending on the degree of impairment, more handicapping than the handicap itself" (Ndurumo, 1984, p. 2).

Societal attitudes about disability have been encoded in the language. In Kiswahili, nouns in the "ki-vi" category are mainly used to refer to things or, when used to refer to persons, to indicate a lack of wholeness. Such nouns have been used to designate people with disabilities. Kalugula et al. (1984) have noted some changes that are occurring in Tanzania in the use of such terminology. Blind people, for instance, have rejected the Kiswahili term "vipofu" and replaced it with the term "wasioona," which means "those who cannot see." A similar move can now be observed among deaf people, who want to replace the term "viziwi" with "wasiosikia," which means "those who cannot hear" (Ndurumo, personal communication, 1989).

Needed Research Activities

The United Nations' World Programme of Action Concerning Disabled Persons (1983) indicated that, in view of the little knowledge available regarding the place of disabled people within certain countries (which in turn determines attitudes and behavior patterns), there is a need to undertake studies focusing on the sociocultural aspects of disability.

The reasons why so little has been done in this area are many. One is related to the priorities set by organizations. Organizations tend to work toward the fulfillment of urgent needs in delivery of services. In focusing on the urgent, however, one tends to forget the important; thus the development of African self-reliance is being postponed. Furthermore, there is the danger and the fear among service organizations that research might question the premises on which their work is based. One such premise in the field of disability is the belief in negative attitudes towards disability.

Another reason for the lack of research in this area is that African sociocultural values have been seen as barriers, rather than aids, to development. Only very recently has it been discovered that development has a cultural dimension. The African intelligentsia will play a crucial role in either the further destruction of African values, or in the reevaluation and growth of those values in the development of new programs. It has been believed that traditional values would disappear as a result of economic development. An active and dynamic incorporation of these values, however, would result in a genuine development.

Research on African sociocultural values and their accommodation into the establishment of services is a challenge for the future and should form a basis for international cooperation. Examples of possible developments are numerous: Concepts such as "integration" and "community-based services" should be rethought in view of this exercise; other notions such as "sorcery" should be dealt with and positively incorporated into service delivery.

As far as the rise of deaf culture in Sub-Saharan Africa is concerned, there are four specific items that need to be examined:

1. Most urgent is the need for more surveys of local signs so that a sign language that is culturally appropriate can be developed.
2. In terms of communication, Africa is predominantly an oral world. The urban centers are the exception, as life there is organized in a more visual way, and people there depend more on written communication. Rural and urban environments present completely different conditions for communication. It would be interesting to analyze these conditions, and in view of this, to observe how deaf persons manage communication and, consequently, their lives.
3. The rise of deaf culture in Africa will require better educational conditions in which deaf people can acquire higher concepts and develop their potential. Organizing such activities in a recreational and enjoyable way will be one of the greatest tasks for the deaf associations. Activities in the area of drama and the visual arts are highly recommended.
4. There is a need for a semantic analysis of terminology designating disabled people, in particular deaf people. The awareness and use of appropriate terminology will support the rise of a culture of deaf people.

References

Devlieger, Patrick. 1989. "The Cultural Significance of Physical Disability in Africa." Paper presented at the Annual Meeting of the Society of Applied Anthropology, April 5–9, at Santa Fe, New Mexico.

De Mahieu, W. 1984. "La Sorcellerie Comme Systeme de Pensee." *Telema* 10 (1): 37–43.

Hokororo, T. 1987. "The Communication Controversy. Is There a Need for an Alternative to Oralism in Tanzanian Schools for Hearing Impaired Children?" *Special Education Bulletin for Eastern and Southern Africa* 5 (3): 2–5.

Ingstad, B. 1989. *Disabled and the Community. Social and Cultural Aspects.* Norway: Institute of Social Medicine, University of Oslo.

Kalugula. 1984. *The Development of Special Education in Tanzania.* Dar es Salaam: Institute of Education.

Momm, W., and A. Konig. 1989. *From Community-Based to Community-Integrated Programmes: Experiences and Reflections of a New Concept of Service Provision for Disabled People.* Geneva: International Labour Organisation.

Msengi, Z. M. 1987. "Opting for a Medium of Communication for Deaf Children in Tanzania." *Special Education Bulletin for Eastern and Southern Africa* 5 (3): 6–11.

Murphy, R. F., J. Scheer, Y. Murphy, and R. Mack. 1988. "Physical Disability and Social Liminality: A Study on the Rituals of Adversity." *Soc. Sci. Med.* 26 (2): 235–242.

Ndurumo, M. 1984. "Self Advocacy Among Deaf Persons in Africa." Paper presented at the UNESCO Subregional Seminar for Special Education Administration and Teacher Trainers, Limuru Conference and Training Centre, Nairobi, Kenya, 10–21 September.

———. 1988. "The Significance of Sign Language to the Deaf." Paper presented at the First Eastern and Southern Africa Sign Language Seminar, Arusha, Tanzania, August.

Turner, V. 1967. *The Forest of Symbols: Aspects of Ndembu Ritual.* Ithaca, NY: Cornell University Press.

United Nations. 1983. *World Programme of Action Concerning Disabled Persons.* New York.

Transmitting Cultural Values within the Burundi Deaf Community

ADOLPHE SURURU

In Burundi society—as is the case in many other cultures within the Third World with a high rate of illiteracy—education in its broadest sense is still basically informal, unstructured, and passed orally from parent to child.

Within the family circle, the child is exposed to and can imitate a variety of roles as demonstrated by his parents, by other adults in his community, and by the peers with whom he associates. Various cultural norms exist that enable this informal, family-oriented education to prepare children for their future life as adults. In hearing families, parents use tales, songs, and poetry to instruct their children. Thus, while he is still very young, a male child learns about grazing cows and breeding stock—as well as about an entire pastoral tradition—from his father. The father teaches the son the songs and stories associated with an animal breeder's life. If the father is a farmer or craftsman, the son learns—also through songs and stories—the secrets of farming or craftsmanship.

From her earliest youth, a little girl learns the repertoire of lullabies used to console a tearful child and is taught the social graces of her people by her mother. For example, through dance the girl is taught certain realities of her life and given a means of expressing certain emotions. These skills help her acquire a definite image of her role as a woman and as a mother in her country. This education occurs outside the context of any formal academic training.

This transmission of values is possible because Burundi's primarily speech-oriented culture is well developed, complex, and pertinent to its people. However, one question that has long intrigued me centers around the ways deaf people in Burundi society deal with this oral transmission of culture and training. In a speech-oriented culture, how do deaf individuals manage to pass on their experiences to their children? How can parents explain to their deaf children the wisdom behind these tales, poems, and dances that the hearing community uses to prepare its young people for adult life?

To answer these questions, my colleagues and I sought out the deaf population in the context of their daily social and work lives. During our research, we observed that the transmission of cultural values is very rudimentary in the deaf community.

A culture develops within the framework of a given community, and three criteria are necessary to constitute this community: a group of people, common goals, and social activities designed to discover, as a group, how to reach these goals. The Burundi deaf population meets the first requirement, but lacks the other two. Communication between members of the deaf population is very difficult because of the infrequent contact between the various deaf communities inside the country. Families isolate deaf adults and, because of certain preconceptions, prohibit them from realizing their potential and fulfilling their roles as fathers, mothers, and responsible, autonomous adults. Because of this isolation, deaf children who attend the few classes available to them often cannot communicate in signs with deaf adults living in the same village.

The following stories epitomize the situation for Burundi's deaf population. The first story is about Pierre, who is 58 years old and totally deaf. He washes clothes in town, a trade he learned while working as a youth in the home of a doctor who had befriended him. For the moment, he lives with his brother, who has set aside a work area for him so Pierre can wash the clothes his clients bring him. He spends all his time working and lives in a country where clubs or any official school for deaf children does not exist, so it would be futile to ask if he meets other deaf people socially. The training centers that do exist are open only to deaf children, not adults. In fact, when we arranged a meeting between Pierre and a young deaf child who attends the training center, the two could not communicate at all because their signs were so different.

Pierre has never married—no one in the village was willing to live with this deaf man, even though he is a hard worker. Yet this man—so wealthy in experience—could be a virtual library of information for young deaf people—if the communication barrier could be overcome. Unlike his hearing counterparts, who can share their knowledge, experience, and insight with the hearing community, Pierre is cut off from the rest of the deaf population.

The second case involves a woman who sells flour at the village market. Because this woman does not know how to read or write, she is always accompanied by a family member who verifies the buyer's payments. The deaf woman sees her own role in these transactions as limited.

This woman, too, has never married, although she has five hearing children. Because of the interference of her hearing family members, the children have grown up without respect for their mother. Although hearing mothers have the responsibility and opportunity to teach moral standards to their children, we have observed that, in the case of deaf parents with hearing children, other hearing family members undermine the mother's influence over the children. They do this believing that they are helping the mother, but the children learn to respect the hearing members of the family and disrespect the deaf parents. Thus, this mother is being deprived of the chance to pass on her experiences to her children because of societal attitudes, which encourage over-protectiveness of deaf people. This woman will probably remain husbandless and her social status will continue to be tenuous.

The last story is about those deaf people who are less isolated from each other, either because they have been fortunate enough to have other deaf individuals within the same family—as is the case of four deaf brothers and sisters in one village born to hearing parents—or because they are young and thus can attend the centers for deaf students where they can meet other deaf people. Because these deaf people are in contact with each other, they can exchange their experiences and teach each other, if only by expressing their joy or sadness at living as deaf people. Thus, it is from each other that they learn what it means to be deaf and to exist as a deaf person in Burundi.

In conclusion, we hope that this last category—the less isolated deaf individuals—will represent the cornerstone for the transmission of cultural values within the Burundi deaf community. This may happen, provided the younger deaf generation is not cut off from the experiences of deaf adults. And the best way to avoid this separation between the two generations is to involve, consult, and integrate the adult deaf people into every educational, socio-cultural, and political program intended for the Burundi deaf community. We hope this involvement will become a reality in Burundi in the near future.

Deaf Culture in Ghana

ALEXANDER DANIEL OKYERE
AND MARY JOYCELYN ADDO

I
t is not easy to explain to non-natives about the culture of a group of people whose very identity within their own country is difficult to portray. Until formal education for deaf children was introduced in Ghana, deaf people were scattered all over the country, without any possibility of meeting each other and thus establishing their own culture and community.

In Ghana, culture is transmitted orally from the elders to the children, especially among those who cannot read and write. Unfortunately, deaf people in Ghana lack this opportunity to learn about the Ghanaian culture in general, and so they become simply passive observers of whatever happens in their society, making their own interpretations of social events and activities. For example, a seventeen-year-old deaf student said that her family made preparations for a "party" when her grandfather died. This is how she understood the preparation for the funeral rites.

It is also difficult to write about the true culture of a country that has experienced foreign rule for 113 years and frequent political upheaval with different ideologies imposed by each government. Despite these outside influences, however, Ghanaians do have some cultural practices that identify them as a unique group of people.

This paper will identify some aspects of the general Ghanaian culture that illustrate the customs, beliefs, skills, institutions, and socially transmitted behavior patterns of Ghana. Further, the paper will explore how the Ghanaian deaf culture conforms to or deviates from the general Ghanaian culture. The "deaf people" referred to in the paper are those who have little or no hearing and who identify themselves as deaf.

Languages

Ghana, like many other African countries, has many languages and several dialects. In fact, there are more than forty languages used in Ghana. Even within a small geographical area, a major language may have several dialects. For example, in Accra, the capital, there are slight differences in the Ga language spoken by the people of Labadi, Osu, Jamestown, and other areas within the city. Similarly, among the Guans in the Akwapim hills, there are variations in the Kyerepong language spoken by those living at Larteh, Abiriw, and Adukrom.

We would like to acknowledge the following people for their assistance in writing this paper: E.K. Ansah—Abiriw, A. M. Oppong—Sec/tech-Deaf, Norkor Qauye—Osu-Accra, Asokwahene Nawa Ntifo—Adamorobe, Beatrice Okyere—Abiriw, Hanna Adwoa Oye—Abiriw, Martha Odeibea—Abiriw, Elizabeth Agyakwa—Akropong, and Kofi Paul—Dzode.

Deaf people's problem with communication starts from this multilanguage system. Our educational institutions for hearing students teach whichever language is commonly spoken in the area where the institutions are located. At school, the child is forced to learn the language of the area. Back home, however, he or she may use the parents' language. To complicate the matter further, English is added later in the educational system.

Because of the oral policy in Ghana, some deaf schools follow the same pattern as the hearing schools. This causes deaf children to become even more confused, especially when they have to change from the second Ghanaian language to English.

Social customs can sometimes hinder communication with a deaf person. For example, in Ghanaian culture, it is not considered good manners to stare into a person's face, especially if the one staring is younger. However, one way a deaf person acquires information is by looking at the face and lips of the speaker. When the speaker is from a different linguistic area, the deaf person often ends up staring in an effort to understand, but this kind of staring is considered an offense.

Ancestor Worship

We Ghanaians worship our ancestors because it is believed that their spirits still live with us, protecting us from evil spirits and gods. We also believe that they bless our land, our community, and our families with all the things we need in life. For example, we may ask them to help barren women have children or we may ask them to intercede on our behalf to stop some evil that repeatedly occurs in the family, such as the constant dying of young children. One significant benefit of this worship is the strong tie that it brings to the members of a family. Because of the fear of ancestors, members within a household behave well and live peacefully with each other.

Ancestor worship also makes Ghanaians appreciate the value of the extended family system. The unity that exists in the family helps to protect such family property as farm land, family plots for buildings, and so on.

Deaf people in Ghana may not take direct and active part in the frequent ceremonies to remember ancestors, but they may be involved in the annual ceremonies. For example, a family may decide to have a final funeral ceremony for a deaf relative when the year ends. On such an occasion, all members of the family would be required to gather in the family house. During such meetings, deaf females might be involved in preparing and serving the food, while deaf males may help erect sheds, arrange seats, and serve drinks.

Both deaf and hearing people in Ghana believe that deafness is caused by the displeasure the parents might have caused living or dead relatives—witches. Thus, deaf Ghanaians do not oppose any rituals their parents perform in order to restore hearing. Over 90 percent of the parents take their deaf children to fetish or witch doctors for consultation.

Naming Ceremonies

Custom demands that every individual who is born into this life be given a unique identity, which is a name. "God abhors evil; that is why each person is given a name," is a saying among many communities in Ghana.

The ceremony of naming a baby is universally accepted in Ghana, and deaf children go through the same naming ceremony used with hearing children. Different tribes may use different methods for naming a baby, but the central idea involves pouring a libation to evoke the ancestral spirits so they can be thanked for the gift of life and the baby the family has been given. Further, the spirits are asked to protect the newborn baby, its mother, the family it has come to stay with, and the entire community; to endow the child with wisdom, courage, and strength to enable it to subdue the enemies of the community; and to ensure that the child is not barren.

Naming ceremonies must occur within a prescribed time period. If a child is born on Saturday, July 1, for example, he or she must be named on Saturday, July 8. The baby's father selects the name by which he wishes the child to be known. Usually it is the name of one of the baby's grandparents, living or dead.

The naming ceremony takes place at the residence of the baby's father. The head of the family and other relatives and friends are invited. Early in the morning of the ceremony, the elders in the family assemble and the baby's father informs them formally that he has a new baby and that he wants to name the baby after his own father or mother. He gives the elders a small amount of money and a bottle of "white man's drink," usually Schnapps, and then reveals the name he has selected. The oldest among the elders accepts these items and performs the rest of the ceremony.

Following the ceremony, gifts are presented to the baby and the baby's mother, and all invited guests and family members gather for a meal provided by the father. In the old days, the young people's orchestra would be invited to play from the morning until late at night. Nowadays, the baby's father may rent or use his own sound system to provide music to entertain the guests.

In Ghana, when a couple delivers twins, the couple is required to perform special rites for the babies. It was believed that if the rites were not performed, the twins might become ill, the mother might not fare well, and the family into which they had been born might experience a series of mishaps. Twin rites are still performed in many communities, and deaf twins receive these rites without any modifications.

It is interesting to note that from infancy twins are dressed alike and are named after the same person. Further, family members, especially the mother, are required to avoid certain types of food crops each year until a yearly "twin fee" has been paid to the fetish or witch doctor.

Puberty Rites

In Ghana, persons who have reached manhood or womanhood are subjected to puberty rites. If any male or female fails to receive their rites before the male makes the female pregnant, they both are subjected to public ridicule and often banished from the community because of the taboo.

Different communities have different names for puberty rites. Many communities do not normally perform puberty rites for the males, but they may be sent to live with relatives and friends to lead a hard life, which later prepares them to be good husbands. The main significance of the puberty rite is to announce to the community that a girl has reached womanhood (somewhere between the ages of twelve and fifteen) and is ready for marriage. As a prospect for marriage, she is exposed to as many suitors as possible.

Although the naming ceremonies are the same for deaf and hearing children, puberty rites are not extended to deaf adolescents. Most are neglected or shunned by the community, and the parents of deaf daughters may even be grateful for any attention paid to their deaf daughters, whether taboo or not.

Marriage Rites

Traditionally, parents arrange marriages for their children. However, if a young man of the proper age meets a young woman he wants to marry, he discusses the matter with her first. If she agrees, they then inform their parents, usually the mothers first. The mothers pass the news on to their husbands. The parents then investigate the backgrounds of each family involved, because it is taboo to marry into a family in which any of the following conditions are known to exist: witchcraft, insanity, leprosy, tuberculosis, drunkenness, and any handicapping condition such as deafness, blindness, mobility impairments, and mental retardation. If the parents approve of the marriage, they give their blessing. If the parents do not approve, they do not give their consent, and if the children marry anyway it is without the blessing of the family. On the other hand, if the parents of two families want their children to marry but the children themselves did not like the relationship, in most cases they have to obey their parents and enter into the marriage anyway.

Handicapped women are sometimes impregnated and later abandoned by their lovers. When a father is identified, he may deny responsibility, or he may accept the child but not the mother because the handicapped are believed to have been visited by the gods. In rare cases, a pretty deaf woman will be accepted by a hearing man and married in the traditional way, but most such marriages soon end owing to communication problems.

Despite the gloomy picture of the past, things are beginning to change for deaf people in Ghana. Education of the handicapped has improved their lot so much that most of them are becoming accepted into society. Now, because of this new view of deaf people, hearing people have been approaching the relatives of deaf people and marrying in the same way as among hearing families. When two deaf people are in love with each other, the families encourage them to follow the normal procedures for marriage; however, as in the past, lack of communication between deaf and hearing partners often ends the marriage in a short time.

There is one village in Ghana, Adamorobe, where 15 percent of the inhabitants are deaf. In the past, the practice was that deaf people in this village married other deaf people, but not hearing people. A recent chief, in an attempt to eradicate deafness from the village, made a law that deaf males could not marry deaf females, only hearing females. It was found, however, that some hearing couples produced deaf offspring and some deaf couples produced hearing offspring. In the past fourteen years, however, no deaf child has been born at Adamorobe.

One interesting note about Adamorobe: Even though the hearing and deaf villagers have co-existed in this community since 1733, only a few hearing villagers can properly communicate with the deaf people in the deaf villagers' sign language.

Clothing and Food

Clothing is not a problem for deaf Ghanaians: Deaf and hearing villagers dress in the same manner. However, dietary preferences can cause some problems. Food eaten by Ghanaians may vary from community to community, and deaf people are highly influenced in their choice of food by their tribal background. If their family members do not like pork or crab or snails, for example, deaf people will not eat these also. As a result, when deaf Ghanaians gather for camping, anniversaries, or sporting activities, food has to be carefully selected in order not to offend anyone.

Recreation

To an observer, it may seem that a Ghanaian's life is not exciting. Because Gahnaians spend most of their time on their farms or on the sea, one rarely sees people in the towns or villages playing or watching games. Nevertheless, in addition to soccer and video games, Ghanaians play several indoor and outdoor games both during the day and, more often, at night.

"Oware" is an indoor game that is normally played by two people. It is played by filling grooves in a wooden object with marbles. Another common game for boys and men, also played using marbles, is commonly played by Akans and Ashantis, especially after the cocoa season. Small children can just sit, stretch their legs, and start counting the number of legs with a song in a game called "Pemprann." Little girls love "Ampe," a sort of exercise they perform by jumping, kicking their legs alternately and clapping their hands. Women may organize moonlight games of "Aso" and "Search For Your Loved One." "Anto-Wakyiri" is played by putting an object behind one person in a group that forms a circle. Deaf people can play Oware, Ampe, Anto-Wakyiri, and even Aso, which could be played without the songs that accompany it.

"Ananse" and other animal stories not only teach children to be brave and act courteously, but also help adults through the morals, wisdom, and other lessons they contain. Deaf children miss these stories at home because of the communication barrier. However, when they are told these stories at school, they seem to love them very much.

Music, Dancing, and Drumming

Ghana is famous for its music. In fact, music is indispensable to a Ghanaian as well as to his society. From infancy, children are educated through songs. Politicians sing patriotic songs and chiefs are praised for their brave deeds in songs and drumming. Farmers sing while weeding their farms, and fishermen row their canoes and pull their nets while singing. Men learned the musical language of drums before they went to war. Woman sang dirges in towns and villages when their men were at the battlefront. Even the dead are mourned with touching songs. Singing, drumming, and dancing are performed during funerals, festival celebrations, and church services. Singing is also used to enhance storytelling and to play games.

The first school for deaf people in Ghana was founded by a missionary who taught religious songs in English. Deaf people who have attended these missionary schools enjoy signed hymns and choruses. But most deaf people in Ghana miss the significant cultural activities that involve singing. Sadly, most deaf people cannot sing any of the Ghanaian cultural and patriotic songs, like "Yen Ara Asase Ni" ("This is Our Land"), which is broadcast daily at dawn and evening. Nevertheless, deaf people have managed to learn how to play the drums and dance most of the dances performed by different tribes. Like hearing Ghanaians, they also enjoy dancing to pop music. In fact, recently educated deaf adults have come together to organize cultural troupes. This may imply that the Ghanaian spirit and love for music, drumming, and dancing has caught up with deaf Ghanaians. However, we have yet to see deaf people dance side by side with hearing people.

Sign Language and the Concept of Deafness in a Traditional Yucatec Mayan Village

ROBERT E. JOHNSON

I t has been observed for nearly a century and a half that deafness creates unique social groupings and identities. Both deaf authors (Flournoy, 1856; Veditz, 1913; Jacobs, 1974) and researchers (Becker, 1986; Carmel, 1976; Erting, 1978; Croneberg, 1976; Groce, 1980; Higgins, 1980; Johnson and Erting, 1989; Lane, 1984; Lou, 1988; Markowicz and Woodward, 1978; Meadow, 1972; Padden and Markowicz, 1975; Padden and Humphries, 1988; Padden, 1980; Schein, 1968; Stokoe, 1970; Vernon and Makowsky, 1969) have demonstrated that deaf people create communities based on the fact of deafness, on modes of communication, and on the necessity to achieve access to the economic benefits of the society at large.

These observations have led to three major claims about the structure of deaf communities that relate to communication, ethnic identity, and solidarity.

Communities of Communication

The unique communication modes of deaf people and the general difficulty they find in communicating with hearing people lead to the construction of communities of interaction based on language use. Interactional choice among deaf people tends to be made on the basis of the mode and type of language they prefer. Thus, a large proportion of the interaction of deaf people who sign is with other deaf people who sign.

In addition, in the United States interaction may be structured by preferred use of American Sign Language (ASL) as opposed to English signing. Similarly, in some societies, the preferred interaction among oral deaf people is with other oral deaf people.

It is common for these informal interactional communities to be mirrored in the membership of deaf associations, which are also often structured along lines of language choice. Interaction across the boundaries of such formal and informal groups tends to be comparatively less frequent than interaction within the groups, and tends to occur in situations involving access to the benefits of mainstream society.

Ethnic Identity

Within many such communities, there have developed patterns of behavior and identity that may best be described as "ethnicity" (Markowicz and Woodward, 1978; Erting, 1978; Padden, 1980; Johnson and Erting, 1989). Ethnic identity involves two essential features. The first, called paternity, defines members of the groups in biological terms. For deaf ethnicity, the essential biological trait is to have some degree of diminished hearing. Some deaf individuals have the added characteristic of having been born into a deaf family. Deafness itself, not degree of deafness, then, has become the defining characteristic necessary for membership in deaf ethnic groups.

The second feature of ethnicity, called patrimony, recognizes the fact that, within the groupings created by deaf people, customary patterns of behavior and shared sets of values develop. In order to be considered a member of the deaf ethnic group, a person, in addition to meeting the requirement of having diminished hearing, must also accept to some extent the values of the community and act according to the norms of behavior for the group.

Among the details of patrimony of the North American deaf ethnic group are the identification of oneself as deaf, regardless of degree of hearing loss; the appropriate use of sign language in appropriate situations; and a core identification with the group's values and behaviors—that is, with the "culture" of the group. Among these values is the notion that deafness itself is not necessarily seen as a negative trait. Rather, it is the trait that defines people's acceptability to the group and, in fact, is the trait that defines that group.

Thus, ethnicity is a social force, created from within the community, that both results from and in interaction and identity with the group. In this sense, it is possible to speak of a "boundary" around the deaf ethnic group—a boundary created and reinforced by attitudes, values, and interactions that occur within the group.

Of course, because deaf ethnic groups are embedded within larger mainstream societies, many of the values and behavior patterns of the mainstream are incorporated into the culture of the deaf ethnic group. Thus, the deaf ethnic group in the United States shares many core aspects of culture with other ethnic groups and with mainstream Americans. Among these are values such as religion, a work ethic, economic values, attitudes about family structure, and ethical principles. Nevertheless, the fact must be recognized that deaf Americans differ from other Americans in their core identification with deafness and the communities that emerge around deafness.

Communities of Solidarity

Mainstream attitudes tend to associate deafness with negative values. From the perspective of society at large, deafness is seen as a lack of something, rather than as the presence of something. From this point of view, degree of hearing loss becomes important because the less a person hears—and therefore the less he or she can communicate effectively with hearing people—the more difficult it becomes for that person to fill the range of social, education, and economic roles expected of citizens in an industrial society. For this reason, deaf people in general, and those with the least hearing in particular, experience difficulties in gaining access to the economic and social benefits of mainstream society.

These attitudes and practices cause deaf individuals in the society to have similar experiences in attempting to achieve access to social and economic benefits, and to organize activities on the basis of deafness that enhance access. Thus, although these attitudes have their source outside the deaf ethnic group, they function to reinforce the boundaries of the group.

From this perspective, the social boundary between deaf and hearing people is maintained by a dynamic tension between the social forces within the group and those outside the group. In this sense, then, deafness also becomes a political force.

Restricted economic and social access creates "solidarity" among the members of the group. Solidarity refers to an enhanced identification among deaf people, who share similar experiences in their attempts to achieve success, as defined by the core values of their society at large. Accordingly, deaf people often identify more closely with other deaf people than with people outside the group.

These patterns seem to be relatively consistent among deaf people in industrialized societies. In addition, the solidarity among deaf people often maintains itself across national boundaries. Deaf people from different countries often see themselves as more like each other and as having more in common with one another than with the hearing members of either society. The Deaf Way and other international deaf events are testimony to this pattern.

After experiencing this phenomenon repeatedly in personal interactions in many countries and after seeing it in action at international conferences, it is tempting to assume that it is a universal characteristic of deaf society.

But this model of deaf society is built almost exclusively from observations in industrial societies. It is verifiable only by observing the lives of deaf people in situations different from those societies. By examining the communities deaf people create under different conditions, we can determine whether the patterns of interaction, ethnicity, and solidarity are truly created for the reasons we propose—and are therefore a universal condition of deaf communities—or if, when social and economic conditions are different, the patterns of interaction and identification differ as well.

A Yucatec Mayan Deaf Community

With this in mind, we have been studying a small deaf community in a traditional Yucatec Mayan village in the state of Yucatan in Mexico. The first observations were made by Hubert Smith, who spent a number of years in the village making ethnographic films about adaptations to economic and social changes in Mexican society. He discovered, quite accidentally, that in the village of about 400 inhabitants, there were twelve (now thirteen with a recent birth) deaf people, a very high proportion, owing to marriage patterns.

In 1987, Smith, Carol Erting, and I made a brief visit to the village, and in 1988 we returned with Jane Norman for a week. I remained for a month and attempted to learn something of the sign language and to observe the life of the deaf and hearing people who live there.

Patterns of Life in Traditional Yucatec Society

In order to understand the lives of the deaf people, it is necessary to understand the social context in which they live. The village is located in the north central part of the Yucatan peninsula of eastern Mexico.

The land surrounding the village is hilly, rocky, and dry, densely covered by sub-tropical scrub forest. It is divided into political divisions, each belonging to a small village. Each of these areas is available to the residents of the village for agricultural use. The village is composed of family compounds surrounded by a stone wall. Inside the compounds are several one-room, palm-thatched dwellings built of adobe, small poles, and woven sticks.

Each house tends to be occupied by one of the nuclear families that make up the extended family of the compound. In general, the members of the extended family share one cooking house, in which food is prepared and eaten. Many marriages take place among residents of the village; when marriages occur between people of different villages, it is common—although not universal—that the wife moves to the village of the husband.

The men of an extended family tend to work together in the production of food by slash and burn agriculture, a process that involves chopping down all the trees of a large square of forest (a "milpa"), burning the slash, and then planting corn, beans, and squash among the ashes. Each milpa created in this way is planted in the same year it is burned and then left to fallow for fifteen to twenty years before it is cut, burned, and planted again.

Most of the vegetable food of the village is produced in the milpas, although each compound also has fruit trees, and, depending on the success of the crops, some food and certain staples must be bought through the central Mexican economy. In addition, clothing, household products, medicine, and fertilizer must be purchased through the central economy in a nearby market town.

Virtually all men in the society are farmers, although most supplement their income through other pursuits, such as cottage industry, small stores, or day labor in the towns and cities.

Women also have relatively narrowly defined economic roles, involving primarily food preparation, the maintenance of domestic animals, and child rearing. Many women supplement the family income through cottage industries such as embroidery, hammock weaving, and piecework sewing.

In the village there are few packaged products, no cars, and possibly three television sets (used mostly to watch baseball and boxing). Although each compound has electricity, it is used primarily for lighting and pumping water. Thus, for the most part, the society remains very traditional, accepting only what it needs to maintain its life rather than blindly adopting all technological innovations.

The values of the Mayans appear to have remained fairly traditional as well, focusing on maintenance of the family and self-reliance of the village.

Relations with the Outside World

Life in the village stands in contrast to that of the towns and cities of the region, which have fully adopted the urban, industrial lifestyle of central Mexico. Interaction with the towns is primarily economic, involving periodic visits to the market to buy and sell merchandise and to obtain access to social and medical services. Interaction with the cities is primarily in the form of day labor by the men, who go for a week at a time to earn supplemental cash, particularly in years when the crops have not been good.

Interaction with other villages is generally through sports competition, especially baseball, and social events such as dances and fiestas. Although such outside interaction is not unusual for both men and women, the primary focus remains on the village and the family. The Mayan villagers do not strongly identify with life outside the village.

The Deaf Villagers

Mayan Sign Language

In the context of this pattern of life, the thirteen deaf villagers interact and communicate exclusively in sign language. Upon examination, the sign language has revealed itself to be a true sign language which, although somewhat less elaborate than sign languages of industrial societies, shares structural features present in all sign languages.

As with all natural sign languages, Mayan Sign Language is not a manual representation of either of the spoken languages of the village—Yucatec Mayan and Spanish. It is independent in structure although, as always, the structure of the lexicon reflects the interests and necessities of the society in which the deaf community is embedded.

The language contains most of the structural features we have come to expect in natural sign languages. It has a syntactic organization, verbs of motion with classifier hand configurations, verbs that show agreement with subject and object, a bit of numeral classification, non-manual morphemes with syntactic and adverbial functions, and temporal and distributional aspect inflections on predicates.

Although the sign language of the village was originally assumed to be an isolate— the deafness gene was thought to be localized in the village—we found evidence of a widespread use of Mayan Sign Language throughout the Yucatan and possibly reaching into the Mayan populations of Guatemala. We found small populations of deaf people in most villages, and we were told of at least one other village 100 kilometers away with an equally large proportion of deaf inhabitants—some of whom were cousins of the families of the village in which we stayed.

Through visits, we found the sign language of the village to be mutually intelligible with the sign language of deaf Mayans in other villages, although it is different from and mutually unintelligible with the sign language of the towns and cities—the Mexican Sign Language associated with the educational institutions of the country.

Mayan Sign Language appears to have been maintained through infrequent interaction among deaf people from different villages. For example, the oldest deaf man in the village was drafted into the army at about the age of twenty. There were a number of other deaf men there as well, and all were placed in the same unit for several months until discharged. In addition, deaf people see each other occasionally at inter-village social events. This interaction, however limited, appears to have maintained a core sign language throughout the area, in a manner possibly quite similar to that said to have been present in France and the United States prior to the establishment of deaf educational institutions (Lane, 1984; Woodward, 1978).

The situation in the village, however, is unlike any other we know of, with the exception of the historic Martha's Vineyard situation reported by Groce (1980). All hearing adults we met could sign well, and some could sign very well. It appears that all people in the village, both hearing and deaf, have acquired sign language naturally, through interaction. This fact alone creates a condition in which both social and economic benefits are more readily accessible to deaf people and in which the formation of a strong ethnic group and the politicization of deafness are unnecessary.

The Deaf Community

Some of the patterns we observed are reminiscent of those in other deaf communities; others are quite different. As in most deaf communities, language creates a community of communication among the deaf inhabitants of the village. Chatting is a common pastime during the evenings for all men in the village. Deaf men typically seek each other out for conversation and, although the chatting groups are typically formed of a mixture of deaf and hearing men, if there is one deaf man present there will generally also be several others. Ease of communication seems to draw them together.

The deaf women also appear to interact with each other frequently, and also with deaf male relatives. Although women tend to get out of the compounds less frequently than men, the deaf women appear to prefer to interact with one another at public events.

However, even with the existence of this pattern, we did not observe any activities that could be labeled as exclusively, or even mostly, "deaf." Near the end of our visit, we gave a lunch party for all the deaf people and their extended families. To our knowledge, it was the first event in the village that was defined solely on the basis of deafness.

In addition, we observed surprisingly little solidarity with deaf people from outside the village. We discovered that in recent history there have been seven deaf residents in the next village, which is seven kilometers away, and through which the deaf villagers pass frequently, often on foot, on their way to the market town. Two of the remaining deaf people live almost next to the road, and yet when we visited them together with several deaf people from the village, we found that it had been several years since they had seen each other.

These deaf people in the next village, and the deaf people living in other villages, were not mentioned to Hubert Smith during the course of the twelve years of visits to the village, even though, upon questioning, the deaf people were found to know of their existence. It is clear from these observations that the deaf villagers do not seek out other deaf people in other places with nearly the vigor we have observed in industrial societies.

Similarly, the deaf member of our team was welcomed and treated nicely, but not with the same degree of commonality and solidarity as she has experienced in her visits to deaf communities in industrial societies.

It appears, then, that identity for the deaf people of the village is first with the family and the village, then Mayan society. Thus, although they all recognize themselves as deaf and often prefer to interact with each other, deafness itself does not appear to have coalesced a strong ethnic group within the society of the village nor to have become politicized in the form of solidarity.

Differences Between Mayan Deaf Society and Industrial Deaf Societies

It appears that these differences stem in part from the differences in the core values of the Mayan society to which the villagers belong and in part from a striking difference in the social and economic circumstances they experience in their lives. We have already indicated that deaf people generally reflect the central values of the society at large. In Mayan society hearing people also tend to identify with family and village, and by comparison with many other traditional groups in nations such as Mexico, the Mayans tend to be resistant to and relatively disinterested in outside forces.

Their society is noticeably self-contained. There has been no serious migration out of the village to the towns and cities, in spite of day labor patterns, and both deaf and hearing men tend to return from their work on weekends. (A notable exception is one deaf woman who is a domestic worker in the city and returns only rarely.) Given this context, it is not surprising that the identity of the deaf villagers is also focused on the village. That is the appropriate way to be in the society.

Probably of equal importance is the fact that the deaf people of the village have full access to the economic benefits of the society. The men perform the same roles as hearing men. All the deaf men are farmers, and they excel at it. All the deaf men and women participate in the cottage industries with success equal to that of hearing people. It is true that deaf children do not go to school like hearing children, but school is only a few hours a day, and education is not essential to success in the society, and therefore is not so highly valued or so critical as it is in industrial societies. Thus, being deaf in Mayan society does not restrict access to ordinary economic success, and thus has not become an issue for political solidarity.

The most crucial difference, in our view, is the fact that the deaf people of the village have nearly full access to the social community. They are fully participating members of families, around which most important activities are centered. Access to family life is governed by access to communication.

To be sure, however, deaf people remain different from hearing people. The deaf people of the village have a lower marriage rate than the general population, among whom almost everyone gets married. Only three of the seven eligible deaf men are married, all to hearing women, and all have had only hearing children, a fact that reinforces the belief that the deafness trait is passed on by women. It is difficult for a deaf man to find a wife. None of the deaf women is married, and they all say it would be impossible to find a husband.

In addition, although everyone can sign, deaf people do not have access to the majority of discourse, which is conducted in Mayan. This probably accounts for the presence of their community of communicating.

Conclusion

The comparison of deafness in this traditional society serves to verify our notions about the structure of deaf communities in industrial societies.

First, the influence of linguistic factors such as ease of communicating on the creation of interactional choices is clearly present: The deaf villagers tend to choose to interact with each other. But the presence of a large population of hearing people who also sign tempers this community of communication so that it is not so evident as those of industrial societies.

Second, the comparison verifies the notion of the influence of economic and social access on the emergence of political deafness in the form of solidarity. In the case of the deaf Mayan villagers, where social access is extensive and where economic access is complete for deaf people, deafness as a political phenomenon is apparently lacking.

References

Becker, Gaylene, and Regina Arnold. 1986. "Stigma as a Social and Cultural Construct." In *The Dilemma of Difference: A Multidisciplinary View of Stigma*, ed. Stephen Ainlay, Gaylene Becker, and Lerita Coleman. New York: Plenum. pp. 39–57.

Carmel, Simon. 1976. "Ethnic Identity and Solidarity in the Deaf Community in the United States." Unpublished manuscript.

Croneberg, Carl. 1976. "The Linguistic Community." In *A Dictionary of American Sign Language on Linguistic Principles*. (New Edition), ed. W. C. Stokoe, D. Casterline, and C. Croneberg. Silver Spring, MD: Linstok Press. pp. 297–311.

Erting, Carol. 1978. "Language Policy and Deaf Ethnicity in the United States." *Sign Language Studies* 19: 139–152.

Flournoy, J. A. 1856. "A Deaf Mute Commonwealth." *American Annals of the Deaf* 8: 120–125.

Groce, Nora Ellen. 1980. "Everyone Here Spoke Sign Language." *Natural History* 89: 10–16.

Higgins, Paul C. 1980. *Outsiders in a Hearing World: A Sociology of Deafness.* Beverly Hills, CA: Sage.

Jacobs, Leo. 1974. *A Deaf Adult Speaks Out.* Washington, DC: Gallaudet College Press.

Johnson, Robert E., and Carol Erting. 1989. "Ethnicity and Socialization in a Classroom for Deaf Children." In *The Sociolinguistics of the Deaf Community*, ed. Ceil Lucas. San Diego, CA: Academic Press. pp. 41–83.

Lane, Harlan. 1984. *When the Mind Hears: A History of the Deaf.* New York: Random House.

Lou, Mimi WheiPing. 1988. "The History of the Education of the Deaf in the United States." In *Language Learning and Deafness*, ed. Michael Strong. New York: Cambridge University Press.

Markowicz, Harry, and James C. Woodward. 1978. "Language and the Maintenance of Ethnic Boundaries in the Deaf Community." *Communication and Cognition* 11: 29–38.

Meadow, Kathryn P. 1972. "Sociolinguistics, Sign Language and the Deaf Sub-Culture." In *Psycholinguistics and Total Communication: The State of the Art*, ed. T. J. O'Rourke. Washington, DC: American Annals of the Deaf. pp. 19–33.

Padden, Carol. 1980. "The Deaf Community and the Culture of Deaf People." In *Sign Language and the Deaf Community*, ed. Charlotte Baker and Robbin Battison. Silver Spring, MD: National Association of the Deaf.

Padden, Carol, and Tom Humphries. 1988. *Deaf in America: Voices from a Culture.* Cambridge: Harvard University Press.

Padden, Carol, and Harry Markowicz. 1975. "Cultural Conflicts Between Hearing and Deaf Communities." In *Proceedings of the Seventh World Congress of the World Federation of the Deaf.* Silver Spring, MD: National Association of the Deaf. pp. 407–411.

Schein, Jerome D. 1968. *The Deaf Community: Studies in the Social Psychology of Deafness.* Washington, DC: Gallaudet College.

Stokoe, William C., Jr. 1970. "Sign Language Diglossia." *Studies in Linguistics* 21: 21–41.

Veditz, G. W. 1913. *The Preservation of the Sign Language.* [film] Silver Spring, MD: National Association of the Deaf.

Vernon, McKay, and K. Makowsky. 1969. "Deafness and Minority Group Dynamics." *The Deaf American* 21: 3–6.

Woodward, James C. 1978. "Historical Bases of American Sign Language." In *Understanding Language Through Sign Language Research*, ed. Patricia Siple. New York: Academic Press. pp. 333–348.

The Developing Deaf Community in the Dominican Republic

BARBARA GERNER DE GARCIA

The Dominican Republic is a Spanish-speaking country that shares the island of Hispaniola with Haiti. It is located between the other two Spanish-speaking Caribbean islands—Puerto Rico to the east and Cuba to the west. In this country of over 6,000,000 there are no statistics on the deaf population.

In the Dominican Republic there was no national system of deaf education until 1967, when the first national school was established. Since then, education has varied in quality as governments and the internal politics of the school itself have changed. There are now about 800 students in the national school and its thirteen satellite classes around the country.

About seven years after the founding of the national school, a group of American missionaries who came to the Dominican Republic from Puerto Rico to run a summer bible camp introduced a manually coded Spanish that used the American Sign Language (ASL) lexicon. Although deaf Dominicans report that there was no sign language on the island before the missionaries' arrival in the mid-1970s (sign language seems to be looked upon as a gift from the outside, brought by the missionaries), it is likely that there was some kind of indigenous sign language in the Dominican Republic at that time. The result of the introduction of the missionaries' sign language somewhat parallels what occurred in the United States when Laurent Clerc brought French Sign Language (LSF) to America. LSF creolized with the existing signed languages used in America at the time.

Indigenous signs still exist in the Dominican Republic, but how and when they originated is a matter of conjecture. There are reportedly no deaf children of deaf parents in the country. Marriages between deaf people have occurred only in the past six years or so, as young deaf people have been brought into contact with one another through the school. There are two families, one in Santo Domingo and one in the second largest city, Santiago, that each have four adult deaf children and a number of hearing children. The family in Santo Domingo uses home signs, and its youngest member is also fluent in Dominican Sign Language and interprets for his older brother and two sisters. This family likely makes up what Washabaugh (1979) calls a "linguistically critical mass." That is, it has enough deaf people to evolve a code for communication. Such families, and other linguistically critical masses, are a means by which indigenous signs may evolve. It is likely that in the Dominican Republic, before the arrival of the missionaries, deaf children at school were communicating with each other, ignoring the prohibition on signing, and that their signs became part of the indigenous sign language.

The sign language these deaf Dominicans used as children in school was most likely immature (they probably did not think of it as their language) and did not have the chance to mature because deaf children were together for only seven or eight years before the ASL-based system—which was more complete than the evolving indigenous system—was introduced. Their perception that sign language came to them from Puerto Rico is probably owing to the lack of an identity for the indigenous sign language.

The Deaf Community in the Dominican Republic

The Dominican deaf community has been in formation only since the founding of the national school. The group of deaf students first brought together in the national school twenty years ago now forms the base for an emerging deaf community. In 1982 this group set up a deaf club, and although the club is still controlled by the organization that runs the national school, its members are struggling for autonomy.

There has been little research on the deaf communities of the Spanish-speaking Caribbean, but Washabaugh and Woodward (1979, 1980, 1981, and 1986) have each done research on the deaf people of the English-speaking Caribbean. Washabaugh (1981) describes three kinds of deaf communities:

1. *diglossic* deaf communities, such as the United States deaf community, where there is a majority language to be learned and the minority language is disdained;
2. *isolated* deaf communities, like Providence Island, where formal education is not necessary in order to contribute to the life of the community, and deaf people are accepted, though they are not part of the real life of the community and do not feel a sense of unity with other deaf people; and
3. *developing* deaf communities, as found on the Caribbean island of Grand Cayman. Communities of this type have an "inconsistent educational tradition" and do not show contempt for their vernacular sign language.

The status of indigenous signs is related to the second characteristic of developing deaf communities: They lack the contempt for vernacular signing that is found in diglossic communities. Washabaugh (1981) declares that political diglossia requires a "uniformity of proscription" that drives people to learn the language of the dominant community at the expense of their own language.

The deaf community of the Dominican Republic may be in the process of transition from a developing deaf community to a diglossic deaf community. Deaf Dominicans appear to value sign language highly, even in the face of hearing people's disdain, and express concern for the preservation of indigenous signs. However, there appears to be a diglossic situation developing in their use of sign language. ASL signs have higher status than indigenous signs, which are often referred to as the "wrong" signs. The dominant language of the country, Spanish, influences communication between deaf and hearing people. When conversing with the few hearing people who sign, deaf people use a variety that is more like a manually coded Spanish, and there is some conscious code switching done around outsiders.

An additional factor in the development of sign language diglossia in the Dominican Republic may be the existence of a colonial mentality, or what Fanon (1963) calls the internalization of the mentality of the oppressor. Consider the relationship of the

Third World to the developed world, and specifically the relationship of the Dominican Republic to the United States, which has dominated it for over 120 years. (Many of us recall the 1965 invasion of the island by United States marines.) Deaf Dominicans are not immune to the colonial mentality transmitted through the American influence, which is pervasive in their country.

Researchers generally find indigenous signs difficult to collect, largely because users of these signs have been taught to regard their own signs as of lower status than one language normally used by outsiders. Deaf communities also tend to try to maintain their ethnic boundaries. One missionary couple—a hearing American woman and her deaf Bolivian husband—collected only a few dozen signs in two years of constant interaction with the Dominican deaf community. This couple reported that they always gave preference to indigenous signs. The missionaries now working in the Dominican Republic do not accept indigenous signs. They correct the Dominicans' use of indigenous signs, offering the ASL sign as the "right" one. Deaf Dominican informants estimate that there are between 100 and 200 indigenous signs, but they do not use these signs with outsiders because such signs would not be understood.

Some indigenous signs seem to remain in use. These signs appear to be linked to strongly culturally bound notions or perceptions of the world. There are at least three subcategories of such signs: signs that represent objects according to their function or their treatment in the culture; signs for Spanish words not directly translatable into the ASL lexicon; and signs that encode cultural perceptions of reality and the world.

Some examples of the first category—those denoting a culturally bound treatment or function—are the sign for "orange," which mimics the way the fruit is typically consumed, and the sign for "coconut," which represents the cutting off of the top of the coconut and drinking the coconut milk.

The second category—untranslatable words—is represented by the sign corresponding to the Spanish verb "faltar," which means "to lack something needed." This may be a Puerto Rican sign—an example of the influence of Spanish on the sign language used in the Dominican Republic. In ASL, we could sign NOT HAVE, but this would not satisfy all the meanings of the Spanish verb.

The third category—signs that encode cultural perceptions—is represented by signs reflecting the cultural notion of skin color. In the Dominican Republic, the majority of people are mulato or what they call "cafe con leche" (coffee with milk). There is a minority of black people and a smaller minority of whites. Deaf informants produced indigenous signs for black and white skin colors, but no signs at all for the mulato skin color that predominates. They did not use ASL color signs to refer to skin color.

Conclusion

The situation of the deaf community in the Dominican Republic raises a number of questions. Have other developing deaf communities made the transition from developing community to diglossic community so quickly? Do deaf communities inevitably become diglossic? If the primary transmitters of ASL in a situation are hearing, do they also transmit the devaluing of the vernacular that results in diglossia? What effect does the promotion of a foreign sign language such as ASL have on deaf people in developing countries?

Contact with the United States and Puerto Rico has had the positive influence of giving deaf Dominicans a better sense of their own identity and a realization of their potential power. They are now fighting for the right to hold driver's licenses and to eradicate the use of the term "sordomudo"—deaf-mute. They also hope to increase the number of deaf people receiving postsecondary education. At present, only three deaf Dominicans have had a postsecondary education.

On the other hand, contact with the United States and Puerto Rico has led to a low status for indigenous signs, and there is danger of a paternalistic relationship developing between deaf people of the developed world and deaf people of the Third World. Moreover, in the United States, control by hearing people of institutions that serve deaf people, such as schools, has resulted in a legacy of paternalistic treatment of deaf people, which hearing "do-gooders" might perpetuate by extending it to underdeveloped countries. Deaf people might become accessories in this process as they internalize the mentality of the oppressor (Fanon, 1963). Mexico—and it is surely not the only such case—was the scene of a struggle between the use of ASL signs (advocated by deaf Mexicans educated at Gallaudet University) and the use of indigenous signs. It is ironic that the deaf culture of one country can contribute to the oppression of deaf people in another country.

It is important that we recognize the value of cultural differences. American deaf culture and ASL should not be exported to developing countries in the belief that they are filling a vacuum. If we are not sensitive to the status and power they represent, they may stifle or annihilate existing cultures and languages.

References

Fanon, F. 1963. *The Wretched of the Earth.* New York: Grove Press.

Washabaugh, W. 1979. "Hearing and Deaf Signers on Providence Island." *Sign Language Studies* 24: 191–214.

———. 1980. "The Manu-facturing of a Language." *Sign Language Studies* 29: 291–330.

———. 1981. "The Deaf of Grand Cayman, British West Indies." *Sign Language Studies* 31: 117–133.

———. 1986. *Five Fingers for Survival.* Ann Arbor, MI: Karoma Press.

Woodward, J. 1982. "Beliefs About and Attitudes Toward Deaf People and Sign Language on Providence Island." In *How You Gonna Get to Heaven if You Can't Talk to Jesus?* ed. J. Woodward. Silver Spring, MD: T.J. Publishers. pp. 51–74.

The Deaf Social Life in Brazil

ANTONIO CAMPOS DE ABREU

There are no historical statistics about deafness in Brazil from the age of its discovery by Europeans in the sixteenth century to the year 1855, when a deaf Frenchman, Hernest Huet, arrived in the country. With the help of the Brazilian government, he founded the National Institute for the Deaf and Dumb in Rio de Janeiro, with the aim of developing cultural and educational activities. The Institute opened on September 26, 1857.

Many deaf people attended the school, and the use of sign language increased in the country. Yet the problems of the deaf Brazilians using that language also increased because of discrimination and prejudice that continue today. In contrast, it is said that the situation is easier for the deaf Brazilian Indians. In their tribes, deaf and hard of hearing people are respected, and sign language is used for communication.

Today, Brazilian cities are experiencing a decay in the education and social integration of deaf people. Specialized institutions for deaf people are weak and inactive, which causes feelings of anger and mistrust within the deaf community. In the area of special education, the government lacks such fundamental statistics as the number of disabled people in the country. As a result, there is only one school for deaf-blind youngsters in Brazil. The population must be made aware of the problems that deaf-blind people face. Society discriminates against them, and many do not have the right to attend school.

At present, deaf people in Brazil are struggling to develop themselves in spite of education-related problems. The Ministry of Education has established an educational policy which, from the point of view of deaf people, is inadequate; thus the crisis continues. Discrimination occurs frequently. Deaf people now compare their plight to that of the black people upon whom slavery was imposed, or the Brazilian Indians who are about to lose their lands for political and economic reasons.

Brazilian deaf people continue to demand an educational program to accomplish their social integration, but they receive almost nothing. The government and the professionals in deaf education seem to have become more and more distant from and unconcerned about issues of communication. As in the past, the majority advocate only oral communication, using teaching methods from France, Germany, Italy, and Yugoslavia. Brazilian professionals imitate these methods without respect for the deaf community and without listening to their grievances.

For these reasons, we feel that the deaf associations are critical, as they provide a place where deaf people can gather to discuss these issues and develop strategies to combat them. The first deaf association in Brazil was founded in 1913, and today there are about forty associations all over the country. They keep in touch with each other through sports competitions and correspondence.

The National Federation for the Education and Integration of the Deaf (Federação Nacional de Educação e Integração dos Surdos or FENEIS) was founded in 1987. This organization has begun a program to expose the discriminatory behavior of the professional community and the government toward the deaf community. FENEIS aims to secure the rights of deaf people to social integration and to persuade professionals and the schools to adopt the Total Communication philosophy.

By espousing the oral methods of Europe, professionals have become biased against the use of sign language. A few years ago, some Brazilian professionals visited the United States to observe the educational methods used at Gallaudet University. Despite what they said, they did not accept the Total Communication philosophy, not even trying to obtain the materials necessary for its use in this country. Oralism continued to dominate the field of deaf education in Brazil until very recently.

Many teachers reject the use of sign language, believing that intelligent deaf people must be taught speech in order to achieve high school graduation. In the opinion of these teachers, the use of sign language interferes with the deaf person's learning to speak.

During the International Year of the Disabled (1981), a warning cry was issued about the situation for deaf people, and as a result the government began to change its policies regarding deaf education. This change grew out of a series of disclosures about the state of social integration of deaf people in Brazil. In 1984 and again in 1988, I travelled around Brazil, visiting almost the entire country and standing face to face with deaf people who worked within deaf communities. The power of the deaf community has grown, but there are still many difficulties and problems that remain owing to the communication gap between deaf and hearing people. Deaf people must push the professionals in the field toward courageous and thoughtful change.

At present, the professionals in deaf education are beginning to accept and understand some of the concerns of the deaf community. This understanding and acceptance, in turn, is beginning to diminish the dominance of the oral method. Total Communication is now accepted in a few institutions, and although small, this acceptance is growing.

The lack of educational opportunity at the secondary and university levels remains a problem for the deaf people of Brazil. The only secondary school for deaf people in Brazil is Escola Especial Concórdia, located in Rio Grande do Sul. (This school used the oral method for thirteen years, adopting the Total Communication philosophy after visiting and observing schools in Europe and the United States.) A few deaf people have succeeded under oralism in learning to speak and have attained positions as lawyers, engineers, librarians, dentists, architects, computer analysts, psychologists, and mathematicians. But these people have had the economic support of their families, and they are very few.

I would like to make one last point on the subject of education. Families usually receive no orientation about how to deal with a deaf child. Thus, they often lack patience with their deaf children and may neglect them. As a result, deaf youngsters look to the deaf association as a place to communicate with each other and to develop socially. The association is a place for them to gather together, to share information, and to enjoy parties. So the association serves a vital role for deaf youth as well as deaf adults.

The major focus of many of the associations for deaf people in Brazil is on sports. To provide opportunities for these athletes to compete with each other, the National Confederation of Sports for the Deaf (an organization recognized by the Brazilian federal government) was formed in 1982. Here deaf athletes can associate and remain united in the struggle against prejudice and social discrimination. Despite the efforts of the associations, however, difficulties in social integration continue to exist.

Brazil is a very large country formed by twenty-seven states. In the north, deaf people have established none of the formal activities necessary for social integration. Their lives are very difficult. They are without deaf associations and cultural activities and must gather together in the streets to converse. In the northeastern region, deaf people do have limited cultural and social activities. However, in the south, they have begun to develop more cultural activities on a simple level, and in some cities matters are improving. In the southeastern region, the variety of activities is larger. The movement for deaf community rights is stronger in this region than in any other.

Brazil is not a poor country, but it is a difficult place for deaf people to live well because there is not enough consciousness of their needs and concerns on the part of the government agencies, the schools, the professionals, and the poorly instructed and uninterested families. Generally, deaf people live well within their immediate community. The greater problem is the communication gap between deaf and hearing Brazilians. The smaller this difficulty becomes, the greater will be deaf people's social and cultural integration, knowledge of the world, and participation in deaf associations in society in general.

The Origin of the Deaf Community in Brazil

ANA REGINA E SOUZA CAMPELLO

The first school for deaf Brazilians, the National Institute for the Deaf and Dumb in Rio de Janeiro, was founded—with the support of Emperor Don Pedro II of Brazil—in 1855 by a deaf Frenchman, M. Hernest Huet. The first seven students were deaf orphans who boarded at the school. Over time deaf people from other states were accepted, and the student body began to grow. The founding of the National Institute marked the beginning of the Brazilian deaf community and eventually led to the creation of deaf associations.

The first deaf clubs in Brazil were established after some deaf people from the city of São Paulo visited Argentina and observed the activities of the deaf association there. (It had been founded in 1912 by a wealthy deaf man who had experienced similar deaf clubs in Europe. He may well have been the first person to organize within the deaf community in Latin America.) Soon after the founding of the first Brazilian deaf association in São Paulo, deaf clubs in Rio de Janeiro and Minas Gerais were also created, primarily by ex-students of the National Institute for the Education of the Deaf (INES), who, upon completion of their education, returned to their homes and established regional deaf associations. It is easy to see that sign language and the contacts between deaf people it made possible greatly eased this process.

In order to have a representative national deaf organization, the Association of Deaf People of Brazil was later formed. This organization was administered by deaf people and teachers at INES. The association published *Deaf's Magazine*, a periodical written for deaf people living in other Brazilian states as well as outside the country. The publication included social, educational, sports, and cultural news. The Association of Deaf People in Brazil also became interested in obtaining special electronic devices for deaf people like those available in Japan, the United States of America, and Europe, such as keyboard telephones, illuminated bells, and televisions with captions. A project designed to obtain keyboard telephones from the Telephone Companies of Minas Gerais (TELEMIG) began in 1987, but no equipment has yet been made available.

Unfortunately, the Association of Deaf People of Brazil was dissolved because of divergent political views between the deaf members and the teachers who insisted on continuing the oral approach in the special education curriculum. The policy adopted by another organization, the National Federation for the Education and Integration of the Auditorially Handicapped (FENEIDA), reinforced the segregation of deaf people instead of working to integrate deaf and hearing worlds.

On May 16, 1987, after FENEIDA had been dissolved, the National Federation for the Education and Integration of the Deaf (FENEIS) was created, in large part through the goodwill and cooperation of deaf people themselves. Deaf FENEIS members were included in a commission on the new Brazilian constitution. They supported and won the classification of deaf people as disabled people and as citizens under the constitution—another victory for the struggling deaf community.

More recently, regional deaf associations joined in a struggle for captioned programs on television. Their work resulted in the passage of Law 6.606, which requires Brazilian broadcast companies to provide captioning for the films they air. However, owing to the inefficiency of the government's National Movie Counsel (CONCINE) and its inability to regulate the industry, captioned films are shown only at inappropriate times, such as late at night. This creates difficulties for deaf viewers.

In 1986, through the efforts of the Commission to Fight for the Rights of Deaf People, it was decided that interpreted programs would be shown on Bandeirantes TV in Rio de Janeiro, but for political reasons this service was never instituted. Later, the Deaf Association of Minas Gerais (ASMG) managed to get interpreted programs on TV Minas Gerais. One show, *Visual Journal,* has been transmitted throughout Brazil on educational television since November 1988 as a result of backing from FENEIS.

Improving communication for deaf people is one of the main subjects of The Deaf Way Conference. Few hearing people know sign language, the natural language of all deaf people. That we, members of a minority group, are classified as "deaf and dumb" reflects a widespread ignorance of deafness and deaf people. Because our communication is conveyed manually, we are segregated by society. As a result, society does not understand us, and we don't understand society.

Because of the difficulty deaf people have in obtaining information, our distant relationships with the authorities, the lack of sign language interpreters, and the generally low levels of education in the deaf community, deaf people seek out leaders who are able to overcome these obstacles to communication and who can act as a link to the hearing society.

We have a few such leaders in Brazil, and they are looking to the international deaf community for support and help in acquiring information. Only by meeting face to face, however, can they form the ties they seek with deaf people from other countries, for only through sign language will they be able to communicate fully. Written languages are not compatible with our way of thinking, and without direct contact, we are limited to communicating through drawings, photos, slides, and video cassettes.

I believe that the deaf communities of other Latin American countries are experiencing the same problems as we are in regard to communication, and that these problems demand immediate attention. Interpreter training programs must be strengthened, and legislation in support of communication rights must be passed. There also is a need for further innovation in specialized technology for deaf people and public education to raise popular awareness of deaf people and the difficulties we face.

Efforts in these areas will move us toward the time when deaf people will be able to exercise all the rights of citizenship and participate fully and equally in the life and work of society.

The Ecuadorian Deaf Community

History of the Deaf in Ecuador and the Moment of Awareness

MIGUEL SANTILLÁN

One of the problems inherent in describing the history of the deaf community in Ecuador is that there are no official historical records about deaf people in the country. Aside from a few references in school records and in the records of the adult deaf associations, resources for developing the history of Ecuadorian deaf people are limited to surveys and interviews with deaf individuals.

In fact, this paper represents the first attempt at a written history of deaf people in Ecuador. The majority of information contained here has been extracted from deaf people's memories.

In the past, deaf people in Ecuador were ridiculed by society. They were believed to be sick individuals who were unable to learn anything, and they were primarily used as laborers for difficult physical work. Not a single institution was concerned about their welfare at that time.

This situation began to change in 1940, when Enriqueta Santillán, the pioneer of special education for deaf people in Ecuador, began a special institution for the education of deaf children in the city of Quito. At the beginning, deaf students were mixed in classes with other disabled children, but later they were placed into their own classes.

The institute did not have a permanent location until the ladies of the Kiwanis Club persuaded Mayor Jaime del Castillo to donate a large parcel of land for the school. The building itself was erected thanks to the efforts of the ladies of the Engineers of Pichincha. In 1977, the school was given the name "Enriqueta Santillán Cepeda."

Twelve years after Santillán's school opened, the wives of ambassadors to Ecuador began an institute called Mariana de Jesus. This institute, which was dedicated to providing free education to deaf and blind children, opened in Quito in November 1952. The ambassadors' wives later also formed the Friends of the Blind Foundation.

In 1964, again in Quito, the Aida Penafiel de Dobronsky Institute was created as a branch of the municipal Espejo School. Its founder, Magdalena Guevara, worked with both deaf and mentally retarded children. The two groups were later separated, and the school's name was changed to the National Institute of Hearing and Language.

The Early Influence of the Deaf Sports Clubs

In 1966, Guillermo Zurita, a Mariana de Jesus graduate, began organizing meetings for deaf people in Quito so they could participate in sporting events. This small group, originally composed of only four or five members, communicated through the sign language the members had learned in school. The group later became known as the Ecuador Sporting Club.

During the early 1970s, several deaf people associated with the Municipal Institute of Hearing and Language in the city of Guayaquil organized a soccer team. This team had its first friendship match with the group in Quito in 1973.

In 1975, the deaf adults from Quito and Guayaquil traveled to Maracaibo, Venezuela, to play a friendship sports match. Later, a group of deaf people from the Quito Society traveled to Colombia. Those trips resulted in signs from Venezuela and Colombia being incorporated into the Ecuadorian language, just as Ecuadorian signs were shared with those countries.

Once contact had been made with other countries, the Quito sports club became more sophisticated as an organization and, as a consequence, new deaf members started to join. The organization began to develop new goals and objectives, geared toward other activities in addition to sports. Thus, this large group gave birth to a smaller group with the same objectives but with different activities.

The groups that began to be formed were in many ways a continuation of the school environment, because alumni tended to join the associations. The work of the associations was very difficult, because they had to fight against people who neither understood nor respected them. At first, the Quito club received the support of a religious group that let them use a room in the church building on certain days. This arrangement did not last long, however, and the deaf members decided to collect membership fees so they could finance their own meeting place.

Finally, on December 5, 1975, the first Deaf Assembly met in the city of Quito. The fifty people who attended elected a provisional board and agreed upon several basic goals:

❖ To create a society called the Fray Luis Ponce de León Society, a name suggested by Mrs. Teresa Santillán in honor of the first educator of deaf students in the world.

❖ To organize teams in a variety of sports.

❖ To maintain contact with other similar societies throughout the world.

❖ To commit themselves to cooperation with each other and with similar organizations.

❖ To encourage society to be responsible for training deaf people in different occupations.

In 1976, Antonio Chacón, one of the founders of the soccer team in Guayaquil, traveled to Quito and met with Oswaldo Racines, president of the provisional board, who instructed him to create an association in Guayaquil that would go beyond the objective of sports.

In 1978, the Ministry of Education and Culture approved the statutes of the Fray Luis Ponce de León Society for Deaf Adults in Quito. With this act, the Quito group became the first deaf association legally formed in Ecuador. In the same year, the organization began several new activities, including a literacy program.

The Mano a Mano (Hand to Hand) Project, which helped develop activities such as audiovisual shows, and photography and serigraphy exhibits, was born in 1983. This project also began much-needed research into Ecuadorian Sign Language. As a result of this linguistic research, the first book of signs, sponsored by the Interamerican Foundation, was published in 1988. This was the first document on Ecuadorian Sign Language.

Meanwhile, in other cities of Ecuador, other associations were being formed. In 1984 the Ministry of Social Welfare approved the statutes of the Association of the Deaf of Guayas. In 1986, the same Ministry approved the statutes of the Silent Association of Ecuador. The Association of Hearing Deficiencies of Marabi also had its statutes approved.

Associations for deaf people in both Tungurahua and Chimborazo were created, although they have not yet had their statutes approved. In other provinces of the country, deaf people are beginning to meet as well.

On April 26, 1986, representatives from all of these groups met with the hope of forming the National Federation of the Deaf in Ecuador. Because some associations do not yet have statutes, the federation cannot be recognized legally, although it continues working.

Discrimination and Oppression of Deaf People

Before the formation of the organizations noted above, deaf people were the object of jokes, rejection, and criticism. Society did not respect them or their way of communicating and gave them derogatory names such as "dumb" and "fools." Their families simply ignored them because they could not communicate.

After special schools were established (most of which were oral), deaf students were deprived of using their natural sign language. The nuns in the schools allowed them no choice in the way they communicated. There were no opportunities for higher education for the deaf students. When they were older, they were forced to leave the schools, marry, or take jobs not related to their abilities. Some were committed to psychiatric institutions as patients for life.

Deaf heritage was passed on through the schools. The children of the higher grades were responsible for passing on their experiences to the youngest children. The older students also explained things from the classes that their schoolmates did not understand—generally for a reward, of course! Formal classes in the history and culture of deaf people have never been taught in the schools, because of the teachers' misconceptions about deaf people.

Only when they began to form groups did the situation really begin to change for deaf Ecuadorians. They began to participate in social activities, counsel each other about living in the world, and share their experiences.

The creation of deaf associations did not solve all of the problems, however. One of the things that deaf people still suffer from today is a lack of respect from hearing people, who still believe that deaf individuals are unable to perform any job, even when they have been properly trained. The labels of "little dummy," "dumb," or "deaf-dumb" are particularly sad, because deaf people's level of achievement is much higher than it was forty years ago. Still, deaf Ecuadorians have yet to take their rightful place as fully participating members of society.

Business people still believe that all deaf people are alike and are limited to manual labor. An interrupted and poorly planned education is partly responsible for keeping deaf people in the same limiting situation. Relatives and others members of the community, particularly those from higher social classes, still lack respect for the communication system of deaf people.

In the face of these difficulties, deaf people are creating even stronger associations, so that together they can fight in defense of their rights.

A change can be noted among some hearing people, who are beginning to respect deaf people, their language, and their culture. Deaf people can sometimes choose to join in events and activities with hearing people. Also, some deaf and hearing people are falling in love and establishing relationships with each other. Before, this did not occur because deaf people could only identify with other deaf people.

Ecuadorian Deaf People in Other Countries

As part of this project, we interviewed two deaf people, Mrs. Geoconda Vivar and Mr. Antonio Lucio Paredes, both of whom have had the opportunity to live outside Ecuador in more developed countries. These two individuals moved to other countries to study, because the educational opportunities for deaf people in Ecuador were so limited. They both said that their stays in Europe were strange in the beginning, but that later they became accustomed to the European way of life.

Vivar spent her childhood and part of her teenage years in Spain and learned sign language there. She developed positive relationships with and received support from the other deaf people at her school, and returned to Ecuador when she was twenty years old.

Paredes, an oral deaf person, did not establish contact with other deaf people until he was fifteen years old. These people taught him about the deaf way of life and about the solidarity found in the deaf community. These experiences were very important for him, and he says he has never forgotten them. He studied art in different European countries and returned to Ecuador when he was thirty-three years old.

Both experienced similar situations when they came back to Ecuador. At first they both felt different from the other Ecuadorians and had problems adapting. This situation soon ended for Vivar when she contacted deaf people and joined their group. For Paredes, who did not have contact with other deaf people until four years after his return, integration was more difficult because life in Ecuador is so very different from the life he had experienced in Europe.

Ecuador's Oldest Deaf Person

Mr. Oswaldo Racines, the oldest deaf person we have found in Ecuador, was born in 1923. When he was seven years old, he realized that he was different from his parents: He was deaf. He began to develop his own sign language and to identify people by their most characteristic features.

Racines was an individual who paid a lot of attention to the activities that surrounded him. He watched his grandmother knitting, and started to knit himself, because he did not have anything else to do. He had no friends, because people were afraid of him and called him dumb. Because of these situations, when he was nine years old he thought about committing suicide, although he never acted on this impulse.

Eventually Racines enrolled at the National School of Fine Arts. Enrolled at the same time was the now-famous painter Oswaldo Guayasamin. But Racines did not understand any of the spoken instruction. He watched what his classmates were doing and imagined what was going on. He studied painting, pottery, carving, and technical drawing, but he could not understand the lectures. (In a chance encounter with his instructor two years after graduation, Racines learned that the teacher had considered him the best in the class and had tried to contact him for a painting assignment. However, unable to get in touch with Racines, the instructor chose Guayasamin for the job instead.)

When his brother was born, Racines was the first to realize that his brother was also deaf, and later he became the one who helped his brother the most. When Racines was fourteen years old, his father died, and the young boy had to go to work selling advertising signs to be able to buy the materials needed for his artistic studies. In 1941 he graduated from the National School of Fine Arts and began selling drawings for monographs. Later his grandfather took him to work on his farm, where Racines tried to paint scenery in his spare time. Although he sold these first paintings, his uncle and grandfather did not allow him to continue to paint. Later, when he tried to purchase a house, he was turned down by the attorneys because of his deafness.

In 1958, a friend took him to work at an iron factory called Ser Ben. The factory was about to go bankrupt, but thanks to Racines' ideas, the owners changed the type of production and began to make furniture, a move that made the factory viable again. In 1959, Racines began to look for other deaf people to work with him at the factory, and a friend from school, Juan Borja, put him in contact with deaf people who were beginning to organize a group. Racines became involved in the newly formed deaf organization.

In 1975, this group got together in the first Deaf Assembly, and Racines was named provisional president. He still works at the Ser Ben furniture factory, but does not paint any more.

The Birth of Ecuadorian Sign Language

CARMEN VELÁSQUEZ GARCIÁ

L anguage has a great deal of influence in the life of a human being. We communicate with each other through our senses—sight, hearing, smell, taste, and touch—which receive information from the external world. Once received in the brain, this information acquires a meaning and, consequently, a response. This is the most important skill we learn through communication, but because it is natural and easy for the majority of people, we do not give it much importance.

The ability to use language efficiently also allows children to develop a sense of their world. Language development influences children's emotions, academic development, and social maturity; it is the base from which they learn.

From birth, the child learns to communicate. In the beginning, the baby's communication is in the form of crying, vocalizations, body movements, sighs, and sounds of pleasure. The need to communicate desires to one's family in one's own and natural language is felt by every child. This is the foundation of what is today our Ecuadorian Sign Language.

Communication within the Family

It is important to note that the starting point for sign language development is the family. To communicate with the family, the deaf child invents natural gestures that are sometimes shared with members of the family. For example, the child will often "name" a member of the family with a sign referring to some characteristic of that person. These gestures, however, are often limited as a communication method owing to the lack of participation of all the relatives.

This is how the natural language of deaf people begins to take shape within the family. This was the beginning of Ecuadorian Sign Language.

Communication at School

Once they were within the school environment and had contact with deaf peers, individual deaf children were highly motivated to communicate with each other. Though the deaf children were unable to understand each other fully in the beginning, their desire to communicate was such that they attempted to reinforce their messages by elaborating, expanding, and rephrasing. This natural process of elaboration became another step toward the formation of Ecuadorian Sign Language.

But our own natural language has been affected primarily through influences from the United States, Spain, and other South American countries.

Influence from the United States

The education of deaf children in Ecuador and the development of Ecuadorian Sign Language have both been influenced by people from the United States.

In 1940, a school was founded in the city of Quito by two sisters, Enriqueta and Teresa Santillán. This school, which followed the oral tradition, was visited by North American professionals in the area of deaf education.

Because Ecuadorian Sign Language had a limited vocabulary, American Sign Language (ASL) became a strong influence. Many signs were incorporated into our language from ASL, resulting in greater exchange of information and improved communication.

In addition, less than five years ago, a group of Jehovah's Witnesses who knew ASL arrived in our country from the United States and started to teach the Christian word in some Ecuadorian deaf groups. In order to establish better communication, these deaf groups incorporated some ASL signs into Ecuadorian Sign Language as well.

Influence from Spain

Around 1952, again in the city of Quito, another school for deaf children was created. This school, Mariana de Jesus, was administered by nuns, who brought from Spain two teachers with some experience dealing with deafness and who communicated in Spanish Sign Language. Within this educational institution, the foundations of what was later called Total Communication could be seen, because these teachers allowed each student to use whatever was the most convenient means of communication.

The United States and Spain were the first outside influences on the communication of deaf people in Ecuador. Under their influence, the vocabulary of Ecuadorian Sign Language was increased, and the first steps were taken to teach deaf children.

Influence from Other South American Countries

The students who graduated from different schools for deaf students formed deaf organizations for the purpose of playing sports and, in 1975, received an invitation to participate in an international sporting event held in Venezuela. This was the first contact that Ecuadorian deaf adults had with deaf people from other countries. For the first time, deaf participants observed the different kinds of sign language used by deaf people from other areas. However, they found the vocabulary of Ecuadorian Sign Language lacking.

Because of the need to communicate and better understand the language of sister countries, the trip to Venezuela provided another opportunity to incorporate signs from other languages into Ecuadorian Sign Language. In the same way, organizations for deaf people in our country were visited by representatives of foreign deaf associations, who also strongly influenced the communication system used in Ecuador at that time. Those have been the main sources of influence on our own natural language.

Sign Language versus Oralism in the Schools

Although, as stated previously, the doors to Total Communication began to open in one of the early schools in Ecuador, unfortunately those who professed that philosophy later left the country. As a result, the oral teaching methodology, which strictly banned the use of sign language, again prevailed. Students were required to use voice and articulate clearly when communicating and were punished for using sign language during class to try to explain or reinforce concepts. However, those in authority failed to notice that, besides wasting time trying to achieve "perfect" articulation, the children were developing many gaps in their knowledge, and the teacher-student relationship was deteriorating to the point where both were rejecting the classes.

Despite (or because of) these conditions, student leaders, generally those in the higher grade levels, developed in these schools. They became responsible for rescuing their sign language—the natural instrument for their communication—and spreading it to the other children. An example of the importance of this battle can be seen in what was a common occurrence in the schools: A student from a lower grade would give up his supper to an older student in exchange for an explanation about the class he had attended but not understood.

Education in these schools continued for some years following the oral tradition, and sign language experienced a setback owing to limitations on its use and development.

During this time, new schools were established and slowly began to accept and incorporate sign language into their curriculum; however, the battle between the oral approach and sign language continued.

The Mano a Mano Project

In 1982, the deaf adults society in Quito—the Fray Luis Ponce de León Society—developed the Mano a Mano (Hand to Hand) Project with the assistance of the Interamerican Foundation and the collaboration of a young American, Candice Bannerman. One of the objectives of this project was the creation of a book of Ecuadorian Sign Language.

To implement this important project for our community, work groups conducted much research on the use of sign language in different regions of Ecuador, so that the most commonly used signs could be collected and described. Work groups were organized and charged with studying the sign language of the different regions of the country.

While this work was difficult, the compilation of all this information created awareness among deaf people of the importance of establishing, keeping, and developing Ecuadorian Sign Language. There was a willingness on the part of all deaf people to reach this goal. Furthermore, this work turned the attention of schools toward the language used by deaf people. Deaf adults again began to teach deaf children the importance of acquiring one's own language, and in the same way, this importance was spread to the rest of the deaf community.

The success of this project can be summarized by looking at the following accomplishments. The project led to

❖ The active participation of deaf people in researching their own language

❖ A greater understanding of the importance of Ecuadorian Sign Language for education and communication

❖ A recognition of the need to broaden the vocabulary of Ecuadorian Sign Language without the influence of other languages

❖ The compilation of signs into a book on Ecuadorian Sign Language.

On February 22, 1988, there was a public ceremony during which the book, *Sign Language—Basic Guidelines about a Special Form of Communication*, was unveiled. This manuscript was the first published document about sign language in our country. It provides a wealth of reference material for teachers, parents, students, and professionals who wish to learn, know, and use Ecuadorian Sign Language.

We reiterate that one of the benefits of doing this work was our developing awareness of the importance of having our own language. We Ecuadorian deaf people have committed ourselves to continue with this great task—researching new areas and broadening the vocabulary so that, in the not too distant future, we can develop new materials about Ecuadorian Sign Language.

We deaf people have also decided to try to lay aside those influences of the oral method that have held back the development of our sign language. We know about the importance of developing our language now and its important role as part of our culture.

One can already see certain differences between the sign language used by a deaf person who graduated fifteen or more years ago and that used by a graduate of the last five years. But the work has only begun, and we still have many things to do.

Principles, Changes, and Current Guidelines in the Education of the Deaf

ORLANDO BENALCÁZAR

Educational trends from Spain greatly influenced the established institutions for deaf people in Ecuador. The arrival of two Spanish nuns brought to one Ecuadorian institution a communication philosophy that could be identified with what is now called Total Communication, although this terminology was not used in Ecuador at that time. The nuns allowed the children to use all available resources to communicate. Unfortunately, the departure of these nuns marked the demise of their work.

For many years before and afterwards, the oral method was dominant in all of the schools for deaf children in South America, including those in Ecuador, Mexico, Argentina, and Venezuela. Only 20 percent of the students were able to attain any degree of academic success with this teaching method, and those were mostly hard of hearing students. The deaf person's feelings or preferred ways of communicating were never taken into account.

Consequently, an extraordinary sense of responsibility developed among students in the higher grades, who took on the task of teaching sign language to the students who were in the lower grades. Sometimes the older students benefitted in practical ways from this experience. For example, the younger students could be persuaded to give their meals to the older students in exchange for an explanation of what they could not understand in class. All of this was hidden from the teachers for fear of being punished for signing.

In the early 1980s, the philosophy of Total Communication as developed in the United States began to be used to teach deaf students. This new trend caused an impact at the level of governmental institutions as well as in educational institutions. It was broadly welcomed, but it has not really been properly applied. Many people think that Total Communication refers to the use of sign language only, but this is erroneous; the Total Communication philosophy is one that respects the use of *all* the resources that are available to each individual. Some institutions have preferred to continue with oralism.

For deaf people, the Total Communication philosophy, as suggested by Gallaudet University, inspired hope. It not only encouraged respect for and freedom to use any and all resources available, but it helped eliminate old misconceptions held by hearing people about deaf people by demonstrating that all deaf people have the capacity and ability to do productive work.

However, while the educational situations and conditions of deaf people have improved since the introduction of this philosophy in Ecuador, we cannot say that we have achieved complete success. This is owing to the fact that the few Total Communication seminars that have been offered present too much information on too many topics to be assimilated at one time. A better approach would be to offer in-depth training to only those educators who are really motivated and willing to work. By organizing ourselves, both deaf and hearing, we can create a plan of action that would define roles for both deaf and hearing people, taking advantage of the resources of both groups.

The majority of hearing teachers of deaf students have worked hard to obtain all the knowledge that they now possess. Many of them work hard and with motivation and are concerned about the future of their students. But at this moment of truth, that is not enough: The majority of deaf people, once they have finished their elementary education, still must struggle in their further studies, work, and social life. The battle over what educational methods to use with deaf children has created gaps in the education they receive, with powerful repercussions on their lives. Focusing on "perfect articulation" in the classroom results in a loss of time spent on academic subjects in school when they are children; this, in turn, limits the possibilities for deaf individuals when they reach young adulthood, because their education has not adequately prepared them for the future.

To date, the authorities in charge of special education for deaf students have not included deaf adults in any educational planning. The work meetings organized with representatives of different institutions have most frequently focused on the area of mental retardation, and the outcomes of these meetings have then been modified to apply to deaf students as well.

Although Ecuador does not offer professional careers aimed at working with deaf people, now, for the first time, deaf people and hearing professionals are combining their experiences to build a better future and eliminate the abyss in which we deaf people find ourselves.

Approximately ten years ago, two deaf teachers joined the faculty in one of the Ecuadorian educational institutions and caused a revolution in the education circuit. Many teachers welcomed the opportunity to have deaf individuals teaching deaf students, but equally as many hearing teachers disagreed with their participation and undervalued their capabilities. However, these two deaf teachers remained in the system in spite of the pressures that surrounded them.

The training they received was very similar to that received by the hearing teachers, but because they were deaf themselves, they could understand the needs of the deaf students and their desire to learn. Most of all, they could communicate easily with their students. These combined abilities made it possible for the deaf teachers to help their students in a way that the hearing teachers could not.

In view of the problems that education for the deaf community has faced so far, we reiterate that now is the time for deaf and hearing people to join efforts and experiences so that future generations of deaf people do not continue along the same paths walked until now.

The Art and Culture of the Deaf

NELSON GARCIÁ

Members of the deaf community in our country have been motivated to pursue different artistic activities, including mime, dance, and painting. These activities are not just "busy work;" rather, they have become the way in which deaf people can communicate with others, both deaf and hearing. Through these activities, for which many deaf people seem to have a natural predisposition, we can express our most personal feelings.

Deaf people relate to art in different ways. Generally, we are afraid to show our abilities to others. Once this fear is overcome, however, and we feel the support of others, our self-confidence grows, and our creativity emerges. Then we are able to view our art as something positive, as an area that allows us to become ordinary people.

The development of artistic activities can reveal some basic problems we have with other people, such as the lack of understanding by the hearing community, which tends to undervalue the activities of deaf people, whether these be artistic, educational, or physical labor. Another problem is the lack of permanent collaboration of specialized people in the training of deaf people.

Deaf individuals feel a great attraction toward mime and dance, particularly because these give us the opportunity to express graphically and bodily what we cannot say with a spoken language. Mime is an intrinsic activity for us, because our communication in this domain is based on a rich array of total bodily expression and gives much less prominence to oral communication with the hearing audience.

We Ecuadorian deaf people participate in different associations that have very important and diverse objectives. Among them are mutual support and the defense of our rights within society—including equality with the rest of society and the right to a better education. Our artistic endeavors allow us to make known everything we have learned in these areas. For example, in offering artistic performances that show our skills, we are guided by the desire to motivate other members of the different associations, plus the desire for enjoyment, recreation, and the sense of being active members of the society to which we belong.

The various artistic groups are organized under the direction of the different associations, and our main objective is to get in touch with more and more deaf people. This is done in a very natural way, although we are somewhat limited regarding the activities of deaf women, because there are activities in which women cannot participate because of societal restrictions.

Our performances at the national and international levels have given us great satisfaction. Through these performances, we have gained experience that has enriched our work, allowing us to do better day by day. We have been able to reach the difficult goal of pleasing both a deaf and a hearing public that demands the best we can give from our work.

Our public performances have been successful, but we have been faced with some obstacles as well, which we overcame thanks to the help of people who have collaborated with us. There have been humorous situations as well. For example, at one presentation one of the artists had to lift his dance partner, who was heavier than he was, onto his shoulders. It required great effort for the dancer both to lift the woman and keep his balance at the same time. It looked as if at any moment he would drop her. This struggle was reflected on his face, along with his desire to put an end to that part of the presentation.

We have set a number of goals for the future, including establishing and continuing permanent workshops in artistic areas, training new generations in these fields, and, above all, using deaf instructors to do the training. We have worked hard and with tenacity to reach these goals. One accomplishment was establishing an internal set of rules for the mime and dance workshops that has allowed us to develop these activities better.

In addition to artistic activities, I believe it is important to refer to the legal rights of deaf people and their development in the work force in my country. The legal rights that we deaf people in Ecuador have are still not sufficiently beneficial for us. It is true that we have some privileges, such as the exemption from any taxes in the country, because we are covered by the Handicapped Law. However, it is important to clarify that we do not consider ourselves handicapped, because we can depend on ourselves.

Although we need help in some areas, we are not dependent in terms of carrying out our own lives. This law benefits us, but we are fighting to achieve better prospects for development in our country. It is a constant battle, and we hope that in the future we can attain better legal benefits for ourselves.

Deaf people in Ecuador are still marginal workers in the job market. Business managers prefer to give jobs to hearing people. Deaf people always have blue-collar jobs. Unfortunately, in Ecuador there are no professional training centers for deaf people and, in most cases, deaf people have only completed elementary school. Many deaf people do not like being limited to blue-collar jobs. They also have to cope with the fact that their coworkers make fun of them, as well as the fact that deaf people are often on the fringes of society.

We hope that in the not-so-distant future we can reach new horizons so that we can better develop ourselves and, in this way, help the progress of the deaf community in our country.

The Social Situation of the Deaf in Austria as Seen by a Deaf Woman

TRUDE DIMMEL

I t is generally estimated that one person per thousand in Austria is deaf, and the tendency toward hearing loss is increasing. According to a detailed census in 1986, 6 percent of the population is born deaf or hard of hearing, or experiences some significant hearing loss during their lives. In spite of these figures, it is very hard to find accurate information on Austria's deaf people.

As general secretary of the Austrian Society for the Deaf for more than four years, I know from personal experience that the Federation of Societies for the Deaf has had great difficulty in obtaining information on hearing disability. It is said that deaf people cannot read, that they write and speak poorly and, therefore, that they lack knowledge of the world. But better information than this would be desirable. Also desirable would be greater cooperation among educated deaf people in the interest of bettering the lives of others in the deaf community.

The field of deafness has been flogged to death by people who make their money from deaf people, but there are very few hearing people who are genuinely interested in deaf people, who really talk with them. For deaf people, obtaining information is always connected to money, and deaf people have little of that because they speak poorly, read poorly, and write poorly. Hearing people usually act according to the motto, "Don't give them money; just give them a little something."

The deaf person who cannot speak well is a bit of an awkward presence in the workplace, especially when it comes to taking instructions. It takes a great deal of time to explain a new rule to a deaf employee, and if the person explaining the rule speaks poorly or has an accent and cannot communicate manually (even with the manual alphabet), then the best intentions in the world will not overcome the communication barrier. The hundred-year-old battle against teaching deaf people to use sign language has made communication more difficult than it was before oralism became the dominant method in deaf education.

We should examine the legal basis for this form of education in Austria. Some ethnic and linguistic minorities such as the Turks and Yugoslavs in Austria and other German-speaking countries have demanded and have often received their own schools and kindergartens—and sometimes even their own television programs—in their own languages. Why isn't this possible for deaf people? Sign language in education would make it easier for deaf students to absorb information and would aid in their understanding of problems. We can only assume that those people who are involved in the field of education do not understand sign language or its value.

A dissertation on employment socialization of teachers of deaf students entitled "Silencing the Contradiction" (Migsch, 1986) includes the following remarks by two young teachers of deaf children:

> I can see what force—real brute force, that is—is needed to carry out language training; if you want to do it really intensively, then you half kill the child in the process.
>
> It's quite easy really. If a child doesn't make the noise you want him to make, because he's so tense, then you can make him collapse in about 20 minutes, and when he collapses, well, then he relaxes. I just have to torment him enough until he breaks down into tears, and falls down on his knees, and then he's totally relaxed. Then he does anything I want him to . . . .

During childhood, thanks to treatment such as that described above, the foundations are laid in the deaf child for aggression, behavioral disturbances, and aversion to language. The child has no time for literature; any feeling for the spoken language is lost. Only the regulations of salaried officials are adhered to. (The children of deaf parents also often experience problems. The prejudice of teachers in the state schools toward deaf parents is a chapter in itself.)

The abuse does not end when the deaf student leaves the educational system. According to research commissioned by the University of Salzburg (Schindler, 1980), 66 percent of deaf people are forced by parents and teachers into jobs they don't really want. Forty-four percent of all trained tailors, 26 percent of all skilled carpenters, and 66 percent of all shoemakers change careers at some point in their lives. Clearly, deaf people first get jobs that require few qualifications. As a rule, they are not satisfied with their education and realize later, when bringing up their own children, what they have missed.

Today deaf children are increasingly being placed in state schools, which are all oral. Generally, this experience fails to prepare them for higher education, because the amount of information they can obtain orally is not sufficient. For example, the principles of physics and chemistry cannot be explained in short sentences, and not everyone can spend hours reading these principles, either in fingerspelling or on the printed page.

Whenever and wherever deaf people are confronted with people who insist on using an oral approach rather than sign language, they turn to their fellow deaf people for social and emotional support, because they cannot cope with the isolation they experience in the "normal hearing" environment.

In Austria, only a small proportion of deaf or hard of hearing people are able to get a higher education. There is only one college that they can attend, and the principal himself has said that he suspects the deaf people at his college are in the wrong place. The more extensive the curriculum, the more impossible it is to cover without the use of sign language.

With the exception of one person, there are no deaf people employed as teachers or educators in Austria. The schools generally prefer to hire hearing educators with no knowledge of sign language through newspaper advertisements.

In Austria, there are a number of group homes for deaf people, funds for which are provided by various societies. Vienna, Linz/Kirschlag, Salzburg, Innsbruck, Vorarlberg, Graz, and Klagenfurt all have group homes for deaf people. Problems connected with these homes include their administration by hearing people and the small number of deaf people who find employment in these institutions. Legal regulations need to be enacted so that the number of deaf people involved in operating these homes becomes equal to the number of hearing people involved.

Without wishing to insult anyone, I must say that we need more deaf people who can represent our situation, rather than hearing psychologists who give long speeches about the problems of deaf people. Deaf people also should be able to study law, so that they can better interpret the legal situation of deaf people: Only a white elephant knows what it's like to be a white elephant.

Only within the past few years, through cooperation with the societies for deaf people, have deaf people received better information on legal matters. I would say that much progress has been made by those in official positions toward becoming more understanding of the concerns of deaf citizens. Nevertheless, problems often arise. As an example, one government ministry recently published a brochure about self-help groups that failed to list the Austrian Society for the Deaf, even though that organization returned a completed questionnaire. It appears that only the societies in the federal provinces were listed in the directory.

Technology is increasingly helping deaf people, but many deaf people have difficulty using this technology because they have not been properly introduced to it. This is all the more distressing because technology could provide a means of improving the social situation of deaf people.

At present, five hundred people in Austria have text telephones. The post office is planning to place a special notice in telephone directories publicizing these devices. But although a deaf person with a 70 percent "degree of disability"—which used to be known as "reduction in employment ability"—receives a supplement (based on income) from the Office for the Disabled, deaf people must meet the cost of the telephones themselves. Fax machines may be a better possibility.

Other benefits provided to deaf people include half-price train fares for any deaf person carrying a special identity card. The various federal provinces also offer fare reductions for deaf people using their public transportation systems.

Approximately 1,000 deaf people in Austria have driver's licenses. No exact figures have been published; however, the organizations and agencies that could supply such information hide behind data-protection laws. Mandatory car inspections are conducted in groups with sign language interpreters for deaf car-owners.

In Austria we have about twenty-seven approved interpreters who, for the most part, are women who have deaf parents. These interpreters generally have other full-time jobs, and do not earn their living as interpreters, which means that it is often difficult for a deaf student to engage a full-time interpreter. On the other hand, a sign language interpreter who may be employed as a housekeeper, for example, probably cannot explain a mathematical problem to a student. Thus, the necessity exists to recognize sign language as a means of conveying knowledge and to train interpreters who can use that language to convey a variety of information of differing degrees of difficulty.

Financial assistance for services for deaf people has been more than modest and has not been revised in more than ten years. There are no means at our disposal for any kind of social activities. The film *Children of a Lesser God* inspired some people to try to form a jazz dance group for deaf pupils at a school for deaf students. The school had a suitably equipped gymnasium and acoustic equipment, and a trained gymnastics teacher (who had no experience working with deaf children) expressed much interest in the project. But the project directors got no further than receiving the key to the gymnasium.

Aside from a few scattered broadcasts, we have no programs of our own on television where sign language is used. However, many programs are subtitled, and some teletext pages are reserved for deaf people wishing to write. Deaf people are exempt from the television license fee.

For a year now, Austria has had its own small amateur deaf theater group, consisting entirely of deaf actors. Because the deaf performers lack knowledge of literature, however, the performances are modest. The group could be better organized and better funded to teach young deaf people more about acting. Hearing people enjoy much greater opportunities in this area than deaf people, who are generally left to their own devices.

Every year we in the deaf community organize a holiday project for deaf senior citizens, and we have started a similar project for young people. The costs are approved by the Federal Social Ministry.

It is not yet possible to offer regular courses or seminars in living skills either for deaf parents or for parents of deaf children. But this situation is gradually changing, thanks to an American woman living here in Linz who has a deaf child and who teaches English to deaf adults. Parent societies and adult deaf people are beginning to work with one another, and we hope that from these beginnings, better cooperation for the good of deaf people will be achieved.

No financial assistance is available for members of societies for the deaf to attend meetings, seminars, and courses. While such requests to the appropriate official bodies are almost always refused when made by a deaf person, hearing teachers, social workers, educators, and interpreters can travel to such events with no trouble at all. This state of affairs keeps deaf people from gaining further knowledge and is a source of anger at those who are in a better situation because of their hearing status.

Personally, I would like to work more in the direction of establishing an increased number of workshops or businesses where deaf people could work, share in administration and decision-making, and also take on part of the financial risk. Because of communication problems, deaf workers would need a hearing colleague who knew sign language to be employed as an intermediary. These businesses could work together with other businesses operating on the same basis, even in other countries. With hard work—deaf people are hard workers—and with better information provided in their own language, deaf people could achieve a better image. I hope I can help achieve this goal.

In Austria, the public writes off sign language as a curiosity. In former times, small children had their hands tied behind their chairs when they wanted to explain something to their hearing parents. People constantly emphasize the hearing disability and forget the human factor. Much more public relations work is needed on the part of educated deaf people and on the part of hearing people who are on deaf people's side. Let us hope that in this way we shall be successful in overcoming some of the obstacles faced by the deaf people of Austria.

References

Migsch. 1986. *Silencing the Contradiction.* Ph.D. diss., University of Salzburg.

Schindler, S. 1980. *Die Sozialisation Gehörloser.* Unpublished manuscript.

The Deaf Community in Czechoslovakia

JAROSLAV PAUR

Czechoslovakia has a long-standing heritage involving the culture and education of deaf people. In 1786, the first school for deaf students was established in Prague, with sign language as the language of instruction. During the first half of the nineteenth century, other schools for deaf children were established, also with a preference for sign language.

After the Milan Congress in 1880, however, a significant change occurred in our country. As happened all over the world, hearing teachers spread the oral method through the schools for deaf students. Although the deaf teachers fought this trend, they were slowly but surely removed from the schools. As a result, the oral method became the only method used in Czech schools after 1930: It was said that the use of sign language was the main reason for deaf people's being backward in their education.

This situation began to change in the 1960s, partly because of the good results that other countries had with total communication methods, and partly because of increased self-esteem and recognition of their own language among deaf people in Czechoslovakia. Young teachers are no longer afraid to use sign language in the classroom, but it is still difficult to overcome the old prejudices. Although sign language has been used in some classrooms for more than fifteen years, some people still do not appreciate its use for teaching deaf students. Sign language training is offered to teachers-in-training in Czechoslovakia, but only through the department of special pedagogy of Charles University and only for two terms. There are some prepared videotaped programs for schools using sign language.

What are the goals in the upbringing and education of deaf children? One, of course, is to offer all deaf people professional training at the same level as that received by the hearing population. At present, however, only 6.5 percent of deaf Czechs are university graduates—this is only one-half of the average for the hearing population. Thirteen percent have finished secondary school, which is only one-third of the average for the hearing population. This situation is not acceptable, and we hope that it will change with the increased use of total communication. At present, because job choices are limited, many deaf people take additional evening classes to improve their qualifications for employment.

The Union of the Disabled

The Union of the Disabled is a social organization that organizes special classes, publishes a dictionary of sign language, and at present is the primary group concerned with the issue of total communication. The Union cooperates with special workplaces and schools for deaf students to organize sign language lessons for the parents and teachers of deaf children.

In addition to the goals of equal education and professional preparation, we at the Union emphasize the importance of deaf people participating in society. To accomplish this, we presuppose that the deaf person needs good speechreading ability and oral skills in addition to knowledge of sign language. It is important to be able to communicate without any "middleman," such as a sign language interpreter, and without the uncomfortable and slow use of paper and pen. These skills are necessary for independence and freedom, although every deaf person has an interpreter at his disposal if one is needed. To summarize, we consider bilingual ability an important aim in the education of deaf students.

What about the social position of deaf people in Czechoslovakia? Sign language is a reputable means of communication among deaf people, and according to the Civil Law, deaf individuals have the right to use their language. Authorities also have a duty to use sign language. If an interpreter is not present during an exchange between a deaf person and a government official, any negotiations that result from this exchange are considered invalid.

In Czechoslovakia there is no discrimination against deaf people, and no unemployment; in fact, their interests and needs are protected by law. For example, they cannot be fired from a job without agreement by the State authority. They also enjoy such advantages as free public transportation in the city and a 50 percent discount on intercity transport.

Deaf people who are employed receive a stipend from the government equal to one-third of their monthly income. This income is included in the calculation of retirement income as well. Parents of hard of hearing children receive financial benefits provided by the State. The Union is also economically powerful and provides deaf people with such support as vocational training, various technological aids, interest-free loans, and the financial support of sports clubs and various interest groups. These funds are provided from the profits of our own factories.

In cooperation with the Czechoslovakian Academy of Sciences, the Union has also established the Research Laboratory of Aids for Hearing Impaired. For example, at present they are preparing the "writing phone" for production. This device meets high Czechoslovakian standards and is compatible with "writing phones" in neighboring countries.

There are two regularly scheduled television programs for deaf viewers, interpreted in sign language, that provide news and cultural information. Beginning in 1990, one live evening news broadcast will be interpreted. In addition, the Union bought a complete professional TV studio for use by individuals and deaf clubs for videotaping programs.

A special part of the life of deaf people in our country includes cultural activities found in the deaf community. Many of the best graphics in the country are produced by deaf people. In addition, the deaf theatrical troop Pantomima S.I. is a prominent Czechoslovakian ensemble often sent by the Ministry of Culture to represent Czechoslovakia at festivals abroad. In 1985 this group represented not only our country but also our deaf citizens at the World Festival of Youth Theater in Toyama, Japan. This year it will participate in the most important festival of amateur theaters in Monte Carlo, the first time ever that deaf people have participated in this festival.

It is my opinion that these achievements I have described represent our common theme here—The Deaf Way.

The Deaf Community in Soviet Estonia

VALDEKO PAAVEL

stonia, the smallest republic in the Soviet Union, has a population of 1.5 million people and a territory of 45,000 square kilometers (17,400 square miles). For centuries, Estonia has been in the sphere of interest of greater neighboring powers, primarily owing to its geographical position on the south coast of the Baltic Sea. At different times, Estonia has been ruled by German, Swedish, Danish, Polish, and Russian kingdoms, and was an independent state from 1918 to 1940. In 1940, Estonia was incorporated into and for the last fifty years has been a part of the Soviet Union, formally regarded as a sovereign republic but essentially treated as a province with limited rights. It has been almost impossible for Estonia to conduct an internal policy not dependent on Moscow. Therefore, before we proceed with a discussion of the problems of the deaf community in Estonia, some background explanation is necessary.

In essence, the Soviet Union is a unitarian state developed to the extreme. It has never tolerated anything that deviates from an abstract "average model," both on individual and group levels. Different means have been used to fight digressions from the norm, with force in its different manifestations the prevailing method. Until the 1950s, an open physical reign of terror existed. At the end of the 1960s, a new wave of violence started, which began to subside only in the mid-1980s. This oppression was less overt, characterized by suppression, secrecy, and unequal conditions. Such an approach was quite characteristic until very recent times, and was evidenced in the attitude towards physically and mentally handicapped persons and particularly towards deaf people.

The situation is made more complicated by the fact that the state allocates substantial funds for this group of people. On the other hand, these expenditures have a certain fixed orientation that does not foster to the necessary degree genuine and equivalent inclusion of deaf people into social life.

In the Soviet Union, and also in Estonia, there are three degrees of disability. The highest degree of disability, the first, is given to persons unable to take care of themselves whose condition demands continuous supervision and guardianship. The second group consists of persons who have lost their working capacity either permanently or for an extended period of time. Deafness is considered a disability, and, as a rule, deaf individuals are viewed as disabled people of the third group, which is the lowest degree of disability.[1]

---

[1] In this paper, the terms "hard of hearing" and "deaf" are used to designate hearing disabled persons. In some places a distinction is made between "deaf" persons (those deaf at birth) and "hearing impaired" (those who became deaf during their lifetime).

This disability classification is useful for deaf people because it brings some material advantages, e.g., subsidies amounting to 10 to15 percent of the average wage, price concessions in public transportation, and so on. On the other hand, deaf people are considered "invalids," and the word "invalid" has a clearly derogatory meaning in Soviet cultural context, i.e., imbecile, insane, etc.

So in everyday life, deaf people are not treated as members of a sociocultural group with its own specific interests and requirements, but rather as disabled, somewhat imbecilic people. Such an attitude can also be felt on an official level. The conditions of the deaf population can serve as an example of how it is possible to prevent smaller groups with specific interests and demands from participating in the sociopolitical and cultural life of the larger society. Fortunately, the situation has started to improve.

Focusing on the Estonian deaf community, I must mention, first of all, that the very first thorough investigation of deaf people and their social problems in Estonia was undertaken jointly in 1985 by Tartu University and the Estonian Union of the Deaf (EUD), who financed the study. There had been a few earlier studies of Estonian deaf people, but these focused only on certain narrow aspects of their lives and were quite informal. Thus, a comprehensive survey was needed. Three to four investigators were continuously engaged in this joint study, which resulted in a more complete picture of deaf people and their problems in Estonian society. Some of these problems are being solved, but the number of unsolved problems is huge.

According to our data, there were over 1,400 deaf persons in Estonia in 1988, a little less than one percent of the total population. With the exception of infants (all those under the age of five) and the elderly population, these data can be considered quite reliable. The lack of data about infants can be explained by the fact that Estonia does not possess a reliable system of infant deafness diagnosis.

At least 22 percent of the total deaf population, both males and females, were reported to be deaf at birth; the rest were deafened. The number of people in the "deaf at birth" category increases annually by four to five persons; that of people deafened after birth increases annually by fifteen persons, with half of these becoming deaf before their tenth birthday. The main cause of deafness is reported to be inflammation of the middle ear (tympanitis), followed by infectious diseases and various traumas.

The number of deaf people in Estonia rose sharply during the period of World War II and, for reasons unknown to us, again in the second half of the 1960s. At that time, the number of both deaf and hearing impaired individuals increased twofold in only a few years.

When compared to their hearing peers, deaf students fall below the average level of education. Almost 41 percent of those deaf at birth and 53 percent of those deafened in childhood fail to achieve more than eight years of schooling, while only 18.6 percent of hearing children leave school in less than eight years. Only 25 percent of the people deaf at birth and 16 percent of those who were deafened have over eight years of formal education, compared to 27.8 percent of the hearing population. There is also a considerable lack of deaf students in higher or vocational education. No person deaf at birth has received a higher education in Estonia. Only 2.6 percent of deafened Estonians have completed higher education courses, and most of them became deaf during or after their studies. The situation in vocational education is no better.

Nevertheless, almost all men and women in the Estonian deaf population are employed. Nearly half of them work in some form of industry, such as sewing, woodworking, or metal working. An almost equal percentage of deaf people are employed as farm laborers, construction workers, lower level service personnel, and public service staff

(10 percent for each category). Very few deaf people (2 percent) work as white collar employees or as engineering and technical staff, and those who do are deafened rather than deaf at birth. Almost no deaf people are engaged in the science, culture, and education fields, and very few are heads of organizations, including at times the Estonian Union of the Deaf (EUD), the organization of deaf people.

The EUD, which will celebrate its seventieth anniversary in 1992, is the central Estonian body concerned with deaf people and their problems. At present about 1,600 people belong to this union; two-thirds of them are deaf, and the rest are hard of hearing and hearing people. (The hard of hearing do not have their own organization in Estonia.) The present chairman of the EUD is deaf.

The organizational structure of the EUD consists of elective local organizations, territorial organizations, a central government, and the presidium. The executive power rests with the Central Board, three clubs, and three training and production workshops located in three towns.

According to its statutes, the EUD deals with the problems and changing demands of deaf people in Estonia, because there are no governmental organizations to deal with these issues. Clubs that were originally organized for amateur art activities, sports, and recreation have gradually begun to approach the problems of rehabilitation of adult deaf Estonians, for example. Regretably, this is not an easy task—as Estonia lacks specialists trained in rehabilitation services—although there is a very real demand for vocational rehabilitation throughout Estonia. The situation is complicated by the fact that Estonia also lacks staff who could train such specialists. So the programs through the EUD are the only vocational rehabilitation services available to the deaf population in that republic.

Although the EUD financed the first thorough, scientific study of the Estonian deaf population, as mentioned above, it seems that the EUD has focused too much of its attention on economic activities and too little on such areas as social policy. If science and education are neglected, it could mean that deaf people will never reach leadership roles in these fields.

EUD's funds come mainly from the activities of its workshops. These workshops focus primarily on production of consumer goods (clothing, leather goods, custom-designed furniture, woodpacking crates, and so on). The net income of these workshops in 1987 amounted to 1.5 million rubles, 65 percent of which remained at the disposal of the EUD. Unfortunately, no deaf people head these workshops. In fact, the number of deaf people among the workshop workers is decreasing. For example, of a workforce of 350 people employed in these workshops, the deaf make up only a little more than half. This is less than 20 percent of the able-bodied deaf population.

The emphasis on professional training in these workshops has also decreased. The practice teaching courses provided by the workshops have been dissolved, and no new teaching courses have been organized. Therefore, the professional training of deaf people has become a serious problem in Estonia.

One of the most serious problems for deaf people in Estonia is obtaining a good education. This has been confirmed by a public opinion poll conducted by the researchers at Tartu University in addition to data gathered during a joint EUD/Tartu University study. Nearly half of those polled expressed dissatisfaction with the possibility of obtaining an education. At first glance this may seem strange, because the state invests quite a large sum of money in educational programs for deaf students.

There are two schools in Estonia for hearing disabled children, one for hard of hearing students and the other for deaf students. Both schools are specialized boarding schools, i.e., children spend five days at school and go home to their parents on weekends. Tuition, food, and school equipment are provided free of charge by the government.

The school for the deaf is situated in a comparatively remote countryside. An average of 125 students are enrolled annually, beginning as early as age four. Staff number about forty to fifty. Children study there for twelve years and as a rule get an education corresponding to about nine years of schooling received by hearing children. Many children leave school before graduation.

Secondary education can be achieved by correspondence study through a special secondary school. The schools do not provide any vocational training for deaf students. Deaf students can study at higher education institutions but are subject to some restrictions. At the moment there is only one deaf female student attending a higher education institution. She has reached the junior level.

The oral method has dominated in Estonian deaf schools for decades. Only a few staff people have mastered Estonian Sign Language (ESL). Since last year, however, there has been an increase of interest in sign language and the philosophy of total communication. Unfortunately, effective use of ESL is hindered by the fact that there are very few specialists in the domain of sign language in Estonia, and the investigation and description of the language leaves much to be desired. As for total communication, there are neither specialists nor clear ideas about its theoretical implications at the present moment.

Some words about the language policy in effect in Estonia are in order here. The language policy of the Soviet Union is notable in that, for many years, as little as possible has been done to develop and encourage national minority groups and minority languages. The primary attention and preference have been devoted to the Russian language. Unfortunately, such policy has been carried out overzealously in Estonia. And it remains a fact that the purposeful study of Estonian Sign Language was not started until 1988, although some preliminary preparations were made a bit earlier.

At the end of 1988, the first Estonian sign language vocabulary text was published. This volume contained about 400 signs. It is, of course, an elementary vocabulary in its essence and describes an insignificant share of the sign language and its possibilities. There are no exact data regarding the size of the Estonian sign language community, but indirect estimates place the number at approximately 2,000. Estonia has only six interpreters, employed by the EUD, only one of whom has higher education. None of the six interpreters has received any special training either in Estonian Sign Language or in the problems of investigating it.

Until the beginning of last year, one very serious problem for the deaf community in Estonia concerned the distribution and availability of information through mass media, specifically television. Beginning in May of 1988, however, Estonian TV began broadcasting a 45-minute program about and for deaf people once a month. This program is shown in sign language with Estonian subtitles. In 1989, the possibilities of text TV for providing captioned information to deaf viewers began to be explored.

Until May of 1988, the Estonian deaf population lacked their own regular publication. Since that month, however, the EUD has begun publishing a one-page newsletter, reaching 2,000 persons. The newsletter discusses the problems of Estonian deaf people, informs its readers about the life of deaf people in other countries, and publishes information that might be of interest to its readers.

The year 1988 was in many senses a remarkable year for Estonian deaf people. This can be attributed partly to the change of general policy in the Soviet Union that began in 1985 and to the cooperation between the EUD and Tartu University in the field of scientific research. The socalled "initiative from below," i.e., the activities of the deaf people themselves, is of great importance. Estonian deaf people have achieved outstanding results in many fields. There are now masters in their professions who have won top places in competitions with hearing people and who are highly esteemed for their craftsmanship. Estonian deaf sportsmen have won medals in international competitions for the deaf, are world champions among deaf people, and in many events compete on an equal level with hearing people. Some Estonian deaf artists are also well known beyond our republic, as are several amateur artists and photographers.

I would like to conclude on an optimistic note and express my conviction that if Estonian deaf people and their friends have sufficient energy and purposefulness to successfully solve the above-mentioned problems, we can then apply to them the words of Dr. I. King Jordan, who said that deaf people can do anything—except hear.

where the Deaf in Ireland Stand Today

JOSEPHINE O'LEARY

For centuries, deaf people have been deprived of their rightful place in Irish society, as was common in most countries of the world. Today, the 18,000 deaf and hard of hearing people in Ireland are awakening to their needs and making great progress. This awakening began in 1981 as a result of the United Nations-sponsored Year of the Disabled. Many deaf groups have since been formed, and they are working to improve life for all Irish deaf people. Through our connections with the European Community Regional Secretariat (ECRS) of the World Federation of the Deaf and the Irish Deaf Society, our voices are being heard by the public. However, we have approached national and local governments with various requests, but nothing much has been forthcoming from them. We are not discouraged, however; we know what we want to achieve, and we will continue to pursue our goals.

The standard of living for deaf people has improved in Ireland. However, we are still working to improve the following areas that affect all members of the deaf community.

Education

There are five major schools for deaf students in Ireland. The oldest school, a small Protestant institution, opened in 1816. The Catholic school for girls opened in 1846, followed by the Catholic school for boys in 1857. These three schools remained the only educational choices for deaf students for many years. The two largest ones—the Catholic girls' and boys' schools—were separate from each other, and each had its own teaching methods. The girls' school was run by the Dominican nuns, while the boys' school was operated by the Christian Brothers. This situation remains the same today. Both schools used sign language until 1946, when they became oral schools, and they remain oral. Since the 1970s, two more schools for deaf children have opened, and many mainstream units for deaf students have been established in local schools. The school for deaf children in Cork adopted the total communication method last year [1988]. Much controversy still rages over total communication versus the oral method, however.

The education of deaf students is financed by the Irish government. Most deaf children start school at the age of four or five, and they remain in school until they are eighteen or older. All the children go home on the weekends, and those who live near the schools go home every day. Their traveling expenses are paid for by the government.

In addition to the primary and secondary departments, most schools have a vocational program. Schools for deaf students teach the same subjects as do schools for hearing children, and the educational systems are very good. However, many deaf children leave school with poor reading skills.

Ireland does not have any preschools for deaf children, although many parents see a need for such programs because they realize they must learn to communicate with their deaf children.

Postsecondary Education

Ireland does not have a college for deaf students, so many do not consider further education after completing the secondary program. Some students do attend hearing colleges, but they face severe communication barriers there. Some may need extra years to complete the program, while others leave in frustration. A few deaf people go abroad to study, but the financial strain is great.

Many deaf students get good marks on the school exams that could qualify them for college, but they are discouraged by the communication barriers in hearing colleges, as well as by the lack of interpreters. The Rehabilitation Training Centres are becoming very popular because students are comfortable with the communication/teaching methods, and they feel they receive a good education at these sites. Others receive training through FAS, a government agency, but students often report communication barriers in the FAS programs. Still, they put up with these barriers because they receive government financial assistance while in training, and that is preferable to being on the dole.

Because most students are taught through the oral method, they leave school without knowing how to sign. They have their own local signs, which have been created at the individual schools, and when they meet someone from another school they experience communication problems. They are really lost in the deaf community until they learn the "right" signs. The Irish Deaf Youth Association is doing a lot for young deaf people by organizing social activities that help young deaf adults meet older deaf adults.

Unemployment and emigration rates are high among young deaf adults. Many return home to their parents after school, and that often leads to isolation in the smaller towns. A great deal needs to be done for this segment of the deaf population. Going into the hearing world can be a marathon task for these young people.

Employment

We have come a long way from the days when deaf people did only manual work (for example, coppersmithing, harnessmaking, tailoring, and lacemaking). In the past, no one would employ deaf adults in office or skilled jobs. Thankfully, times have changed. While employers in Ireland may still be afraid to hire deaf people, they are less reluctant to do so now. Many deaf workers are hired for trial periods and are kept on afterwards. Today, deaf people are employed as government workers, draughtspersons, architects, opticians, shopkeepers, teachers, artists, scientists, performers, secretaries, and computer programmers, to name a few career areas. Some deaf people even operate their own businesses. We still do not have deaf doctors, lawyers, dentists, psychiatrists, members of government, and so on, but we hope that the day is not far off when we do see deaf people achieving these goals.

Discrimination, in both employment and in other areas of life, is not very widespread in Ireland. Deaf people are able to stick up for themselves, and, if things become bad, they turn to the deaf associations for help. However, the unemployment rate in

Ireland is so high today, it is very hard for a deaf person to get a job here, and so we see many people emigrating.

Many deaf people who are unemployed become depressed and often do not know what to do. Some struggle to get into job training programs. Ireland has a great need for an organization that deals solely with the employment needs of the deaf population and could help them cope when they are out of work. One of the tragic side effects of unemployment is that people have no money to spare for a social life, which isolates them further.

The Social Life of Irish Deaf People

Irish deaf people have been highly successful in organizing clubs for social activities. There are clubs catering to the needs of deaf people of all ages, as well as clubs that focus on sports and theatrical events. Many clubs have activities scheduled throughout the week, so at times it is difficult to choose among them.

Activities include sports, dinner dances after sporting events, and seasonal parties. The various clubs plan their own events for their members. The largest deaf club in Ireland is the Dublin Deaf Association, which has a membership of almost 1,000. Many deaf people from other areas of Ireland have moved to the capital city of Dublin. In the past, most of the activities were held in that city, but now it is possible to hold them in other towns as well because of the improved transportation services in the country.

Deaf people are permitted to drive cars in Ireland. While the accident rate is low, insurance rates are often very high. Yet, this ability to drive allows deaf people who would otherwise be isolated to participate in the many social events for deaf people around the country. There are no special concessions for deaf people, such as half-price tickets for movies or plays, so many deaf people do not frequent these events. Some of the deaf youth team up with European deaf youth in activities, which broadens their horizons and enables them to learn about the different cultures of other countries.

Almost all these clubs are run on a volunteer basis, and many people give their time to the cause of their friends. All of the activities are designed for the well-being of the deaf community and are organized by the deaf people themselves. Some deaf adults join hearing clubs as well, but they report that they do not feel "at home" because of the communication problems.

Sports

Although many deaf people participate in deaf sporting events, there is a need to reach deaf people from all parts of Ireland. Because of lack of funds to cover training and/or transportation costs, many are not able to keep playing the sports they love. The Irish Deaf Sports Association is a member of the Comité International des Sports des Sourds, and participates in games at home and abroad. Club sports include soccer, basketball, table tennis, snooker, swimming, and bowling. Our football team placed second in the World Games for the Deaf in New Zealand. All these activities are planned by deaf people for deaf people. It is very expensive to take up a sport in hearing clubs.

The Deaf-Blind Population

There are quite a number of deaf-blind people in Ireland. Until recently, there were no services available for them. Many were kept at home and were uneducated. Today, there is one home for deaf-blind people, and a section in one of the deaf schools caters to their educational needs.

At present, one deaf-blind woman is trying to set up an Irish organization for deaf-blind people. She travels widely to all the deaf-blind activities organized throughout Europe and is learning all she can. We hope she will receive full support for her work. Deaf-blind people can be very isolated, and much needs to be done for them, including public awareness.

Sex Education

The Catholic Church has a very strong influence in Ireland. Consequently, sex was rarely talked about openly in the past; in fact, for many years, it was considered a sin to talk about sex. This resulted in deaf students leaving school ignorant or badly instructed on the facts of life. Fortunately, those days are behind us now.

Sex education is very important. Such training should begin when deaf children are very young so that they will grow up with a healthy outlook. We don't know how much sex education is being taught in the deaf schools at the present time, but we often see young girls who are pregnant. So much of what deaf teenagers learn is through visual means, and we feel that media coverage and videos with sexual themes can be misleading for these young people.

Family planning clinics were recently set up in Ireland, despite public outcry. Contraception is still forbidden by the Catholic Church; nevertheless, contraceptive devices became available in Ireland in 1987. We need to develop more materials to teach sex education to our deaf youth. The need for seminars, videos, and books on this topic is especially great, but nothing has been developed yet in this area. Because of the spread of AIDS, it is especially important that these materials be developed and used now.

Deaf people in Ireland are now more openminded than they used to be, but there still may be a stigma attached to talking about sex. I think there is too much media coverage of the subject, and it can be confusing for deaf viewers. Sex is an important part of human dignity, and we should teach it with dignity.

Religion and Marriage

Most deaf people in Ireland are Catholic and have received a Catholic upbringing. They first learn about the religion in school, but once they leave school and go out into the world, they lose access to the Church. They may still go to Mass, but cannot understand what the priest is saying. They can read the leaflets in the church, but they cannot hear the sermons.

Ireland now has a national chaplaincy for the deaf population. Pastoral groups travel around the country giving one-day retreats for deaf people in rural areas. This helps in some ways, but it is not enough. Recently, a group of priests from all over Ireland met to learn sign language and to learn about deaf people. This may improve the situation.

We know that some deaf people have lapsed in their religion, but who can blame them? Some try hard to keep it up, while others continue to attend on a regular basis. One chaplain is now beginning to hold a few masses in sign language, and there is a deaf choir to sign-sing the hymns.

Many Irish deaf people marry other deaf people, although some do have hearing partners, and these marriages often work out well. Most deaf couples marry in the Catholic Church and then move into homes they purchased prior to the wedding.

Most deaf people cope very well in their marriages, but couples whose marriages do not succeed may either stay together or separate. However, they cannot divorce in Ireland. Counseling services are not available for deaf people who are in troubled marriages. There are no specially trained marriage counselors to help them, and only two social workers in the entire country work with the deaf population.

Interpreter Services

Formal interpreter services for deaf people are nonexistent in Ireland. Most of the interpreters we have are volunteers. Very few hearing people have learned sign language and even fewer are fluent in it. It is obvious that there is a crying need for interpreters in Ireland.

So far, there are no interpreter training programs in the country. Although some groups have tried to set up interpreter services, the Irish government has not given any support to these endeavors. Financial assistance in this area is desperately needed. The ECRS is working on this service, so we hope something can be set up soon.

Sign Language

We have a great need for books and videos to help teach sign language. Research needs to be done on effective teaching techniques, and we must standardize our teaching methods. Many hearing people are now beginning to join sign language classes, so the teachers of these classes need to be trained in the right way to teach. Last year, a group of twelve deaf persons completed a tutorial course, and we are hopeful that this is the beginning of more standardized instruction.

Our official language should be Irish Sign Language, but as yet no books are printed on this subject. One of the problems in Ireland is that different signs are being used. This goes back to the time when deaf boys and deaf girls attended separate schools and used different signs. Also, the change to oralism caused an influx of alien signs. A field study on the subject is now being conducted.

Television for Deaf Viewers

Until last year, there were no programs for deaf people on Irish television. In October 1988, a program called "Sign of the Times" began being aired once a month. This program, aimed at the deaf community, is presented in sign language by myself and another deaf person. This program not only benefits the deaf community, but also increases public awareness of the deaf world. So far, "Sign of the Times" has been very well received by the viewing public.

Conclusion

On the whole, deaf people in Ireland look after themselves well. What is lacking is government support, acceptance of sign language as the language of deaf people, more employment prospects for deaf people, and more pamphlets and videos for the education of deaf children. We also need to have captioned television programs.

On behalf of the Irish deaf, I send greetings to all our friends here in America and worldwide. Let us unite and fight together for the rights of deaf people everywhere.

The Deaf Community of Quebec

The Deaf Way of Life in Quebec

ARTHUR LEBLANC

We are delighted to have this opportunity to discuss the existence of what might be called a marginal group of deaf people in North America. In Canada, which is an immense country, two official languages are used: English and French. French is used by only 25 percent of the Canadian population, and the majority of this group is concentrated in a single province, Quebec. This situation inevitably influences the minority we represent—the deaf population.

Like all deaf people in the world, we have a right to exist. We know that our sign language is not an impediment. We would like people to know about our unique sign language, Langue des Signes Québécoise (LSQ), and the ways in which we assure its survival and development, awash as we are in a sea of English.

Because our language is different, we do not participate in the same academic system used by deaf people in other Canadian provinces and in the United States. For this reason, once their collegiate studies (the intermediary step between secondary school and the university level) are completed, our most promising young people do not always know where to go to complete their studies. Some deaf people who use LSQ have succeeded in surmounting obstacles and have been able to attend Gallaudet University. But for the majority, options are simply unavailable at the present time, as one of my colleagues will explain shortly.

During the last decade, the academic system for deaf people in Quebec has undergone vast changes, similar to those of other Canadian provinces and certain American states. The purpose of these changes is to integrate deaf students within the hearing academic system. As we know, this too often operates in a one-way manner, producing more failures than successes.

During the International Year of Disabled Persons in 1981, we began to develop our platform. Two years earlier, our provincial government had voted in support of a law guaranteeing enforcement of the rights of disabled people, a law that created the Agency for the Handicapped of Quebec. At first it was the parents of deaf children who were most involved in this campaign, but in time we deaf people have succeeded in occupying our proper place as well. We did this so effectively that the Agency for the Handicapped of Quebec is most probably the only organization on a government level in Canada—and perhaps even in the entire world—in which a representative of every category of people with disabilities is serving on the Board of Directors. We serve there as the authentic ombudsmen of our own rights and needs.

Although our accomplishments are very modest when we consider all that remains to be done to ensure our own future, we have, however, obtained financial exemption, through government subsidies, from the cost of certain technological devices deaf people use to compensate for communication handicaps. We are continuing to exert what political pressure we can so that a system of interpreting services can be made available at every level of need and in every region of the province. Interpreting services are already functioning in some of the main regions, and we are making progress in extending them to all of Quebec province.

In addition, Quebec has a private, nonprofit organization called the Quebec Center for the Hearing Impaired, whose membership consists of deaf and hard of hearing people, parents of deaf children, and suppliers of services to deaf people. In 1986, this organization prepared the first Provincial Summit on Hearing Impairment, which was a big first in the lives of many deaf people, both because of its scale and because of the number and pertinence of the recommendations proposed. The organization held a symposium earlier this year on the subject of the deaf community.

We French-speaking deaf people have our own journal, perpetuating a decades-old tradition of publishing our own informational organ. Over the years its name and owners have changed, but we have always been able to reactivate it through our own resources. The journal reflects the opinions and concerns of the French-speaking deaf community of Quebec.

The Secretary of State of Canada includes a Consultative Committee whose purpose is to respond more effectively to the needs of deaf people in areas within its jurisdiction. Both English- and French-speaking deaf representatives are members of this committee. Communication between English- and French-speaking deaf people in Canada does not produce any problems or barriers, and we have many contacts and exchanges on social, cultural, political, and sports-related levels.

Nevertheless, we French-speaking deaf people remain very proud of our own identity and intend to develop our language and culture without attempting to distance ourselves from the rest of the deaf population. This will help to preserve and expand the rich cultural diversity of Canada.

Quebec Education of the Deaf

HÉLÈNE HÉBERT

The problem of educating deaf people is as old as the world. I do not think any country has come out of it unscathed. Several efforts are underway, however, to improve the educational level of deaf people in Quebec.

The Milan Congress of 1880 had vast repercussions for education. Bonds between deaf generations were severed, and deaf culture was not easily transmitted under the oral system. For Quebec, Total Communication was officially re-established in 1971 through the use of signed French as a communication tool with deaf clients. I said "officially re-established" because at schools for deaf students in both Montreal and Quebec, sign language had been used clandestinely to communicate for many years.

During the 1970s, a movement toward deinstitutionalization of deaf people began in the United States. Several academic establishments in Quebec were influenced by this trend. Services were decentralized, and the government took over various cases concerning deaf clients. For example, academic commissions were charged with the task of teaching deaf people and integrating them into the public school network. The Center of Social Services for Metropolitan Montreal was responsible for social service activities. Deaf children who had boarded at institutions for deaf students found themselves living with host families and in group hostels for elderly people. Rehabilitation centers were charged with speech therapy and psychology for the infant-to-four-year-old group.

This philosophy was not popular with the leaders of the deaf community because they foresaw the eventual degeneration of deaf culture over the long term. Previously, when services were centralized, younger and older deaf individuals could mix. Members of religious communities had been charged with educating the young. There were doubtlessly high and low periods during that time, but one can appreciate the services they rendered. Clergymen, who taught the deaf boys, adopted French Sign Language, while the nuns, who were responsible for the education of deaf girls, used American Sign Language in their school. That is one reason why gestural language is highly developed in Quebec. During the early 1980s, the name "Quebec Sign Language" was applied to the signs being used in the province among the French-using deaf people.

As deinstitutionalization began, the number of clergymen and women decreased considerably. They were replaced by laymen less devoted to the deaf cause. Academic circles became totally controlled by hearing people. Today, it is difficult for deaf individuals to integrate themselves into this academic environment because of the shortage of jobs and the union system, which favors staff seniority. Deaf people's competence, language, and culture are still not recognized. This is an injustice that is far from being corrected. So far, people who use LSQ have not been encouraged to become teachers. Currently, most teachers use sign language as a second language and thus have not mastered it as well as deaf people. Therefore, an inequality exists from the start for deaf children as they begin school.

For several years, it has been known that the conventional French language of hearing people is very difficult for most deaf people to master. Several teaching methods to improve reading and writing ability in French are being tried. Up to now they have been a failure. It is important first to master the native language, LSQ, and to know it well in order to be capable of learning a second language. Imagine a house without a foundation—it can't remain standing for long. The same principle holds true for a language.

Deaf people in Quebec also face problems obtaining the secondary study program diploma. The educational objectives determined by the Minister of Education do not reflect the reality of deaf individuals and their difficulty in using French. Without a diploma, no door in the job market will open. However, an opposition movement is now underway at the collegiate level, with the help of the people and resources operating in this area.

On an educational level, the province of Quebec is split into two camps over the use of signed French. The cities of Montreal and Quebec do not share the same school of thought. Montreal is moving closer to LSQ, while the city of Quebec is emphasizing a single meaning per word without variation, regardless of the sentence spoken.

Because of these complex problems, the idea of a private school that would be a model for bilingual education is beginning to germinate in the minds of several deaf directors. It remains to be seen if it can be realized. The project may see the light of day if parents and the various representatives are willing to adopt a new point of view, by respecting deaf culture and by agreeing to collaborate.

This plan would represent the first use in Quebec of the French-originated system called 2LPE (deux langues pour une éducation—two languages for one education). Through such an educational endeavor, deaf people would no longer be bound to a hearing world and would have a more viable language model available. Deaf people would manage the enterprise, and deaf culture would be preserved.

Postsecondary Education for the Deaf in Quebec

MIREILLE CAISSY

The deaf population of Quebec is too small in number to permit us to establish a postsecondary school only for ourselves. At the present time, only one percent of the entire deaf population takes advantage of services being offered at the college level, which have been available for less than ten years.

Seven years ago, the first deaf individuals gained access to college education and to such support services as interpreters and notetakers. Before that, no such help existed, and only a few deaf students pursued college studies, supported by family and friends. After young deaf individuals petitioned the government for access to the college level, the Quebec government launched a three-year experimental pilot project in two large cities of the province: Montreal and Quebec. This pilot project proved to be successful, and five years later the project became a permanent service that permitted access to colleges.

At the same time the project was starting at the college level, I was taking steps to receive financial aid in order to pay for university interpreter services. Hélène Hébert joined my efforts, and we received grants from the Quebec government that made us responsible for managing the services. It was very challenging to organize all the services: We had to locate interpreters and notetakers, pay them, and allocate the money properly. It was a lot of work for two young women who were also university students. Our combined energy was devoted to the organization of the services. We found people to assist us and managed to survive the three years required to obtain our diplomas.

The year following graduation, I worked in student services at the university in order to help deaf students. I did not remain there, however, because the university wanted me to work for all students with disabilities, but I wanted to continue working only with the deaf students.

Today, four years later, I have returned to my psychology studies. Sadly, the university services have not evolved very much during my absence. With the help of the Centre Québécois de la Déficience Auditive, we organized a committee to pressure the government. We want a clear policy, not necessarily laws, guaranteeing our right to a higher education with support services, so that we might succeed as others do. Our work is progressing slowly, but it is moving forward.

Deaf Community Life

JEAN DAVIA

Early in 1978, the Association for Hearing Impaired Adults (Association des Adultes avec Problemes Auditifs or AAPA) was founded by a group of English-speaking individuals. Gradually, the number of English-speaking members diminished, while the French-speaking group replaced them, eventually becoming the majority.

In 1985, French-using deaf leaders developed and promoted their objectives and requirements related to education, employment, and welfare. More and more French-speaking members joined them. When those leaders left the association, the activities within the deaf community came to a standstill for a year, but today new growth has begun in the AAPA. The members have confidence in the new team of directors and have increased contacts with other associations and resource people.

The AAPA offers services to deaf adults, although we are also vitally concerned with the educational opportunities for deaf children as well. We try to determine and evaluate the needs and concerns of our members with respect to welfare, education, leisure, and employment. Our services are bilingual, offered in both French Sign Language (LSQ) and American Sign Language (ASL).

Concrete Actions of the AAPA

In 1987, I began to prepare activities and information for deaf people. Our association is esteemed by the deaf community because we listen to their opinions and criticisms and strive to improve our services in order to meet the needs that are being expressed. We keep the deaf community informed about our various activities on a monthly basis.

Our association also has produced several reports on the subjects of communication, leisure, and welfare. One of the statements, addressed to the Health and Occupational Safety Commission (CSST), endeavored to increase the compensation rate paid for communication-related personal injury. Another report concerned reducing the admission price for deaf people at Quebec movie theaters.

Finally, the AAPA has carried out studies to encourage the reduction of the master/pupil ratio at the adult education, secondary school level. Other subjects also have been tackled: the proposition for Law 107 concerning public instruction, treatment of deaf prisoners, and the necessity for captioning audiovisual documents in colleges. We have had some encouraging successes, but a lot remains to be done.

Problems and Accomplishments

In the course of their development, deaf individuals find themselves constantly facing new problems and also experiencing some successes. The deaf population has a lot to say about education, communication, and the job market, and their concerns need to be noted.

I have walked through many cities in Quebec and noticed that most of the deaf people seem unaware of their language, culture, and history. This ignorance inhibits the development of a legitimate pride and a healthy self-esteem among members of the deaf community. In the spirit of a beneficial integration of deaf people within a hearing world, we plan to initiate activities to rectify these identified weak areas and to increase awareness of the value of deaf individuals in Quebec society.

On the plus side, there are some services already in existence for deaf people, including interpreting services, French captioning of televised broadcasts, and the telephone relay service. These are useful, but there is still a lot left to do, particularly with respect to deaf education.

The Importance of Deaf Education

In the past, we have been cruelly aware of the lack of any communication between Quebec deaf and hearing people, evident in the educational guidelines for deaf individuals. This absence of communication explains why there is a problem in the quality of deaf education and why the situation worsens from year to year.

If the academic representatives of Quebec were to accept collaboration with deaf people, an immense energy would be released to create original deaf-directed programs. The involvement of deaf people in deaf education would go a long way toward solving the problem.

Hearing parents with deaf children do not know what type of communication to choose with their children: oralism, signed French, or Quebec Sign Language (LSQ). It has been falsely claimed that the use of Signed French was growing, but hearing people are the ones who invented the rumor and who believe it. This is not the opinion of the deaf community.

Our policy is clear: *We wish to work toward the recognition of LSQ as the official French language equivalent of ASL, which English-speaking people in both Canada and the United States use, and for the adoption of LSQ as the instructional language of schools for deaf children, adolescents, and adults.* We stand ready to take any steps necessary to achieve this, so that once and for all deaf education may develop according to the beliefs and desires of deaf people.

During the last few months, deaf and hearing people have been collaborating on a research project concerning the problem of deaf education. This collaboration must be extended to allow the formation of a solidarity movement that could be fruitful for the future of the deaf people of Quebec. We are presently experiencing a slowdown of the educational project because we lack the required financial resources to move forward.

Moreover, there are many problems involved in the activities of deaf associations. Our association, the AAPA, is trying to change the structures of the other associations so that they will adopt common objectives, and so that effective collaboration can be established among them. I polled the members and Board of Directors of various associations and discovered that the majority of them favored the propositions I had fostered. Next fall, in collaboration with others, I plan to begin a tour of several Quebec cities to offer special courses on the five essentials of deaf life. We hope in this way to be able to restore purpose to deaf people's lives and encourage the growth of Deaf culture, so that deaf people throughout Quebec can develop the sense of belonging to a single linguistic and cultural community.

The interests of our association are not limited to education. We wish to continue to intervene in all matters concerning the welfare, education, leisure, and employment of deaf people so that peace, love, and justice may be encouraged in all those areas.

We have often thought of establishing a private school, but will not be able to finalize this project for five years. We feel, however, that this project will be realized, considering the excellence of our collaborators.

We do not believe that we should adopt a negative attitude as we confront the lack of existing services for deaf people in Quebec and the incompetence in services that exist. We wish to act in a positive manner to improve the living conditions of all deaf people in Quebec, regardless of their age, and to help the hearing population understand us better. Success is always possible when we are firmly committed. Our accomplishments will be our legacy to the new generation.

The Development of Australia's Deaf Community in the Twentieth Century

CAROL O'REILLY

I remember that as a young deaf girl, I was keen to meet other deaf people. I attended a school for hearing students, but I thirsted for knowledge about how other deaf people led their lives, especially teachers, doctors, lawyers, and other professionals. After I was introduced to deaf people in my city, I was inspired to meet other members of the deaf community across Australia and abroad.

Imagine, then, the frustration experienced by deaf people living in Australia before the twentieth century, when there was no formal deaf community. The fragmentation of the deaf community at that time thwarted many attempts made by deaf people to form friendships and enjoy social activities with other deaf Australians.

Some fortunate individuals in Australia's deaf community who knew how to communicate in sign language would dress up and meet their deaf neighbors socially, usually on a street corner near the local school for the deaf, or at a tennis court, another popular gathering place. However, formal meeting places for deaf people were nonexistent at that time.

Deaf Clubs

Deaf clubs in Australia were established at different times in the various states. Although available records indicate that deaf people have met at a number of places for social contact and religious worship since 1883, the first club—or Deaf Society—on record was formed in Sydney in 1913 with fifty pounds in borrowed currency. The club met in different locations until 1947, when property was purchased in Stanmore (a suburb of Sydney) and a clubhouse was built.

In Melbourne, the city's Deaf Society purchased a large lot and buildings in 1924 in the area called Jolimont Square. The original club building is still standing today.

In Adelaide, the Deaf Society building was constructed in 1928 for the sum of 10,447 pounds and continues to serve the city's deaf community to this day. In Perth, a large club building and an adjoining hostel were built on a sizeable tract of land to replace

My special thanks go to my daughter Karin; Dorothy Shaw, president of the Australian Association of the Deaf; the Adult Deaf Societies of New South Wales, Victoria, South Australia, West Australia, Tasmania, and Queensland; the Department of Health (Cairns); and the National Acoustic Laboratory (Cairns).

the old club, which was built in 1921. (The new facility, which opened in 1983, is a magnificent structure with a spacious lounge and a glassed-in upper landing affording spectacular views of sporting activities on the playing fields below. The building also houses administration offices for welfare and counseling.)

In Hobart, where the deaf population is relatively small compared with Australia's other major cities, deaf people gathered in a variety of places over the decades until 1962, when a clubhouse was eventually constructed for the deaf and blind communities.

Finally, Brisbane's deaf community formed a club in a church hall and later purchased land at Newmarket, a suburb of Brisbane, where a round community hall and an adjacent office building were built.

Public Services

In each Australian state, the state government supports nursing homes for elderly, low-income deaf people and hostels for underprivileged deaf youth. However, the economic recession that has plagued Australia and the rest of the world in the early 1980s has put the future of many of these public services in jeopardy.

Employment

Until late in the twentieth century, deaf people did not have jobs that paid well, and educational and vocational training opportunities to give them the skills for better employment were scarce. Most deaf people worked at manual labor on farms and in factories, and a few secured jobs as clerical workers. However, when World War I broke out, there was a call for deaf people and others who were not enlisted in the war effort to keep the wheels of industry turning. This turned out to be a positive step for deaf people because it gave them the chance to prove that they were dependable and industrious workers. By the second World War, when the call for military service came, deaf men were not exempt from enlisting.

Postwar Climate

By the end of World War II, deaf immigrants who wanted to settle in Australia ran into resistance from the country's government. For example, restrictions applied to the following groups of people: those with "cancer or other malignant condition, extensive paralysis, blindness, deaf mutism, organic disease of the nervous system, leukemia, primary anemia," and "people who would produce offspring falling into the above categories." Restrictions on entering the country were also levied on "people suffering from defects which cannot be cured by medical treatment and which prevent employment."

Native deaf Australians who tried to improve their lives also ran into obstacles, and many were thwarted in their efforts to enter college, to perform community work, to work in public service positions in the federal or state governments, or to start their own businesses.

However, the situation had changed for the better by the time the International Year of Disabled People arrived in 1981. By this time, deaf people were allowed to take the public service examination to qualify for employment with the government, and deaf people were opening businesses and entering business partnerships with other entrepreneurs.

Opportunities for higher education also improved in the 1980s. Until recently, deaf people who entered a university did not have interpreters available to communicate spoken course material to them. Usually, deaf students relied on their hearing colleagues to help them with their note taking. But through their determination, deaf students have been able to overcome these obstacles and graduate. (One deaf man has received his Ph.D. from Cambridge University and gone on to become chief librarian for the British Deaf Society in London.)

Today, more opportunities for deaf people have opened at the Brisbane College of Advanced Education, where deaf students can now enroll in a program to become teachers of deaf and hard of hearing students. Other deaf students are taking course work in sports studies at the college. Courses are also offered for deaf students who wish to take advantage of higher education in other areas as well, with the help of full time interpreters and support groups.

Outreach Services

Many of the remote regions of Australia, such as the coastal towns of Queensland and the Northern Territories up to Thursday Island at the top of Cape York, have hearing impaired Aboriginal children. It is estimated that as many as 70 percent have hearing loss, mainly owing to poor health resulting from unsanitary living conditions. These children are given educational opportunities by visiting teachers who are supported by the Department of Education. They are also assisted by the Department of Aboriginal Affairs and the National Acoustic Laboratory, which provides hearing aids to school-age children.

Unfortunately, there is a scarcity of written history about deaf people as a society in Australia, and most of the history can only be traced through conversations with deaf people representing different generations. Despite this lack of historical resources, a picture emerges of the efforts deaf Australians have made to develop and maintain their deaf communities. As a deaf citizen of Australia, I am proud of our accomplishments.

PART TWO

Deaf History

Editor's Introduction

The study of the history of Deaf communities is a recent phenomenon. Until deaf people were first brought together in significant numbers for the purpose of education, there was little note taken of their groups and no means for Deaf people themselves to preserve knowledge of their daily lives. Some literate cultures left a record of the legal status of and popular attitudes toward deaf individuals, but only with the advent of large-scale education of deaf students was information about Deaf communities and the perspectives of Deaf people saved for future generations.

This section contains papers that take a variety of approaches to the history of Deaf communities. Some present the views of majority cultures toward the deaf people in their midst. Venetta Lampropoulou draws on historical sources from ancient Greece, finding attitudes ranging from Athenian acceptance of deaf people and sign language to Spartan disdain for deaf people. (Whatever the conditions of deaf people's lives, large-scale education of deaf students would not appear in Greece until the twentieth century.) Abraham Zwiebel describes the status of deaf people under Jewish law, citing ancient texts to support his view of Judaism as a system of laws with a long tradition of respect for deaf people. According to Zwiebel, deaf people as early as the first century A.D. had achieved high social and economic status in Jewish society, and there is evidence of education of deaf students throughout Jewish history.

In many countries, the source of significant historical information about deaf people begins with the founding of large schools for deaf students. Among the earliest of these were the state-run institutions founded in France after the French Revolution. Papers by Alexis Karacostas and Anne T. Quartararo describe Revolutionary French efforts to provide aid and education to deaf people, and the effect of these efforts on the acceptance of Deaf culture in French society. Bernard Truffaut examines the French Deaf community of the late nineteenth and early twentieth centuries, finding progress in many areas but also a damaging divisiveness over the issue of educational method.

While the history of Deaf communities and the history of deaf education are two separate topics, at times they are so intertwined as to be inseparable. The gathering of large numbers of deaf students in residential schools is often noted as a critical early step in the formation of Deaf linguistic and cultural communities. In countries where such schools were founded relatively recently, a study of educational institutions and methods may hold important keys to understanding Deaf communities in their early stages of development. Several papers in this section are concerned with the history of education of deaf students in Italy (Serena Corazza, Paola Pinna, et al.), Spain (Susan Plann), Puerto Rico (Yolanda Rodríguez Fraticelli), Nigeria (Emmanuel Ojile), and Saudi Arabia (Zaid Abdulla Al-Muslat).

In countries with a longer history of educating deaf students, too, exploration of school records and analyses of competing educational theories can yield benefits for those seeking to understand both Deaf communities and the mainstream cultures in which they reside. Barry Crouch finds in the records of the American School for the Deaf a rich, and largely unexplored, source of information on the education of deaf students in the early years of the United States and insight into the emergence of the United States Deaf community. Günther List examines the tradition of oralism in the German-speaking countries, explaining not only its devastating effect on Deaf communities, but also the social and economic conditions that led to its century-long dominance and the changes that have led to its decline.

Where Deaf communities have flourished, they have often left records of their activities that benefit both historians and subsequent generations of Deaf people. Based on the records of associations of Deaf people in Denmark, Jonna Widell constructs a theory of the development of the Danish Deaf community comprising three phases: Opening (in which Deaf people form associations and are accepted by hearing society); Isolation (in which oralism leads to societal rejection of Deaf culture and sign language); and the current stage, Manifestation (in which Deaf people emerge from isolation to exert an influence on educational policy and the political process). Robert Buchanan and John B. Christiansen describe in their papers two Deaf vocational communities: the Deaf industrial workforce of Akron, Ohio and Deaf printers, respectively. They draw on a rich store of information on Deaf people in the twentieth-century United States, including Deaf newspapers and the work of Deaf historians as well as mainstream scholarly works.

James J. Fernandes and Jane F. Kelleher recount the landmark achievements of Laurent Clerc, Agatha Tiegel Hanson, and George Veditz, whose influence was exercised largely through their powers as American Sign Language orators.

One of Veditz's causes was the preservation of sign language. Three papers in this section are addressed to the topic of preserving the language, literature, history, and folkways of the Deaf communities. Ulf Hedberg of the Gallaudet University Archive stresses the necessity of archives to the preservation of Deaf history from a Deaf perspective. Ted Supalla describes a pilot project designed to make accessible to researchers and educators an archive of films that contain images of Deaf folklife; Karen Lloyd, a project to solicit and collect the stories and personal histories of Deaf people in Australia as a contribution to Deaf history.

Personal history is a theme also of the two final papers in this section. Both are concerned with genealogy and the generational links between Deaf people. For those people who are hereditarily deaf, knowledge of one's family history can serve as a tie to the history of Deaf people as a whole.

The Deaf Population During the French Revolution

ALEXIS KARACOSTAS

The French Revolution of 1789 marked a very special time in the history of the French deaf population for at least three reasons.

First, the Revolution fostered a heady brew of ideas and opinions. From the heart of the common folk, to genteel drawing rooms, to the National Assembly, diverse questions were raised, particularly the question of power: Who has retained power? On what basis can we evaluate his legitimacy? These ideas could not help influencing deaf people, who also were caught up in the furor and excitement of the times.

Second, reforms inspired by this swell of ideas and debate affected economic policy as well as politics. It is fairly obvious that deaf people were not the only group finding it hard to make ends meet. The privileged nobility and high clergy, representing only 2 percent of the French population, jealously guarded the reins of power. The majority of the population—consisting of peasants—faced severe trials: famine, insufficient harvests, disastrous weather. Deaf people did not escape these difficulties; their situation was closely linked to the general hardships of the period and to those limited rights society granted them.

Third, institutional reforms, including the creation of national institutions for deaf people and the proliferation of private establishments, drastically altered deaf people's place in society and their future potential.

These changes were not spontaneous; they had been simmering a long time before the revolution exploded. Much of the foundation for change can be attributed to the work of the Abbé de l'Epée, a man who earned his reputation through his works and to whom deaf people worldwide pay tribute.

The Abbé de l'Epée created his own school for deaf students in 1760. For twenty-nine years, he tirelessly instructed up to seventy pupils at a time. He did not hesitate to invest his own personal fortune in his school, which remained solvent thanks also to gifts from individuals and grants provided by King Louis XVI. De l'Epée died on December 23, 1789 at the age of seventy-seven, shortly following the storming of the Bastille and the Declaration of the Rights of Man and the Citizenry.

De l'Epée was an innovator in several ways. First, he united deaf people by directing his instruction toward a group, rather than isolated individuals. Unlike most of the teachers of deaf students that preceded him, such as J. R. Pereire, de l'Epée did everything he could to bring large numbers of deaf students together. He expected noteworthy improvement in his students' comprehension levels because of their ability to discuss with each other the information he provided. He also expected students to feel less isolated in an environment that enhanced their communication and interaction.

Second, de l'Epée supported the idea that public education must be made available to all children, regardless of social status. He courageously defended public education against the elitist education of the clergy and nobility. De l'Epée was a Jansenist Catholic whose ideas were controversial and who was destined to suffer for his ideological commitment. However, by the middle of the eighteenth century, the idea of popular education had begun to make headway in France, not only with the Encyclopaedists, but also in practical application. By establishing the Committee of Public Education, the French Revolution gave support to the realization of these ideas.

Lastly, de l'Epée emphasized the importance of using sign language to instruct his students. His attempts to "reform" natural sign language, however, were controversial. Trained as a grammarian, de l'Epée had as his goal to systematize and formalize this unwritten language. He was convinced he could apply the basic structures of grammatical French to sign language by means of methodical signs, which he invented. But that is irrelevant in my opinion: The essential point is that he recognized the existence of sign language and the key role it had to play in teaching deaf children.

At the time de l'Epée died, the French Revolution was well under way. The Revolution took up his three causes—the deaf community, public education, and sign language—and tried to implement them.

With respect to the deaf community, the revolutionaries supported the idea that deaf people were an authentic social group in their own right and should not be treated as isolated individuals. National representatives often used the term "disadvantaged class" or "so singular a disinherited class" to designate the deaf population. Reforms were aimed at these "orphans of nature" as a social group, not just as individuals.

Deaf people also began expressing themselves and recognizing their cultural identity. For example, a deaf man named Desloges, of whom I will speak again later, considered his peers to be members of a foreign nation whose language it was useful to know.

Simultaneously, the idea of deaf citizenship was gaining ground. A memorable speech was presented by a deputy at the deathbed of de l'Epée: "Die in peace—your fatherland will adopt your children." These children, of course, were the deaf members of the population, who like all citizens, are "sons and daughters" of their fatherland. De l'Epée was the foster father of these "orphans of nature." It was now up to the nation, with its patriarchal power, to substitute for him after his death. Deaf people, like hearing people, became children/citizens of the great family/nation.

The first public institution to specialize in serving deaf individuals was founded in Paris on July 21, 1791. A second opened in Bordeaux two years later. Operation of these institutions gradually came under government control. The Abbé Sicard was named head schoolmaster (director) of the Parisian establishment after review by a tribunal of academicians and prominent citizens. A tribunal procedure was also used for the nomination of the staff, financial administration, student admissions, and determination of initial administrative policy, all of which were under the jurisdiction of the Ministry of the Interior.

But the creation of these institutions was accompanied by obstacles that had to be overcome. The first challenge was to define the primary purpose of the institutions. Most of the deaf students were destitute. Should they receive money to help them survive? Should they receive temporary shelter? Or should they be provided with sufficient education to enable them to acquire a profitable trade? In other words, which was it to be, charity or instruction?

Deputy Raffron supported the position of providing financial assistance. Speaking before the National Convention on February 1, 1794, after the institutions had been in operation for more than two years (but voicing an opinion that predated even the revolution), Raffron claimed, "Deaf people are born speechless; they will die speechless. That is how Nature wanted it." Instructing deaf people was useless, he said, particularly because the nation was not lacking in educated people. He added that living conditions were very difficult in the new boarding schools (which was true) and that the purpose of these institutions was to assist the poor but not to flatter national pride. Consequently, it made more sense to offer deaf pupils financial support and then send them back to their homes.

As you may suspect, this viewpoint was not adopted, and the idea of instructing deaf students developed in progressive stages. But the charitable idea did not totally evaporate, as evidenced today by the National Institute of Paris for Young Deaf Persons, which is a branch of the Ministry of Solidarity, not of the Ministry of National Education.

The second problem was the one observed by Raffron: Living conditions in the two schools were harsh. Sometimes the students had nothing to eat or wear. They lacked heat during harsh winters, were assailed by epidemics, and sometimes died at the institution. Moreover, as boarders, they were totally cut off from their relatives. The young deaf students had to put their courage to the test to survive revolutionary times.

Last, the institution in Paris was originally associated with the National Institute of Blind Workers. The two schools shared the same premises—the former Célestins convent near the Bastille. It was only in 1794 that the two groups were geographically separated and the deaf students were perceived as a separate group.

At the time of the French Revolution, cultural perceptions of deaf people ran the gamut from savages, to children, to animals, to soulless machines. Numerous references to deaf people can be found in the minutes of the National Assembly, whose deputies expressed popular cultural perceptions of that period:

❖ The deaf individual was perceived as a savage—that is to say, as a radically different and singular being, as strange as the "savages" met by Bougainville or Cook in their far-off expeditions.

❖ Deaf people were perceived as children because civilization supposedly could not influence their nature. For example, Lanjuinais, a member of the Council of Five Hundred ("Conseil des Cinq-Cents"), in 1796 suggested that deaf people be included in the legal category of minors.

❖ Deaf individuals were compared to animals because they did not possess speech (oral language), which would legitimize their relationship with humanity.

❖ Finally, deaf people were perceived to be machine-like. The theories of the philosophers Locke and Condillac accorded an essential role to the physical senses. From this viewpoint, deaf people would be comparable to soulless machines because they had been deprived of one of their senses.

These perceptions also involved sign language, a living image of thought (according to Talleyrand) and a direct expression of nature (according to Abbot Grégoire) that supposedly appeared on earth before the advent of oral language. This idea pleased some, who imagined that they could use sign language as a model for the reform of the French language. Others were distressed and wanted, in the name of French culture, to suppress the animality that this idea appeared to suggest. The conflicting perceptions of sign language deserve more detailed study. For two centuries, they have continued to influence successive policies governing the role to be played by sign language in everyday life and education.

Before concluding, I would like to share some overall thoughts on the status of the deaf population at the time of the French Revolution.

Originally, the founding of deaf schools was not of primary importance to deaf individuals, who had long been struggling to survive, to unite, to instruct themselves, and to learn a trade—all without the official intervention of hearing people. Several testimonies concur on this point. In March 1794, in the National Assembly, Deputy Thibaudeau reviewed the situation of deaf people working in print shops. Deputy Roger-Ducos cited cases of deaf people working as painters, silk-winders, hat-sellers, gardeners, fabric manufacturers, designers, sculptors, dressmakers, and embroiderers.

Before and during the revolution, there were two paths open to deaf people. Some, the smaller number, went through the schools that were set up for them. The others, the majority by far, did not have any formal education, although this did not always prevent them from practicing a trade. Two deaf men illustrate clearly these two paths: Deseine and Desloges.

Deseine, educated by l'Abbé de l'Epée, was a sculptor who enjoyed a certain notoriety. In contrast to his brother (also a sculptor, but hearing and a royalist), Deseine embraced the ideals of the revolution. Among other subjects, Deseine sculpted busts of Mirabeau and Robespierre, which he presented to the National Assembly. For Danton, he sculpted a bust of Mrs. Danton, who had just died.

Desloges, on the other hand, was never a student of l'Abbé de l'Epée. He was a bookbinder and furniture-paper decorator. He left behind a beautiful volume, published in 1779 (and which I recommend that you read), in which he describes the situation of his peers, their way of life, and their trades. It is interesting to note that deaf people of this time preferred to live in the city rather than in the country, where they felt isolated from the deaf community.

The life of Deseine and the work of Desloges are evidence that deaf people were struggling for meaningful integration into society and against the marginalization that menaced them.

If deaf people did not wait for the hearing society to concern itself with their fate and transform it into a national cause, it was also because the newly created schools could not meet their needs. Academic structures and vocational learning workshops were not immediately operational, and they did not provide effective training.

During the French Revolution, deaf individuals in these schools were in an unusual position. Because they were children or adolescents relating to adults, and because they were governed by hearing people, they had practically no power to make their own decisions. They were dependent upon the good will of hearing people. Outside of the institutions, however, deaf people were struggling and going on strike in the print shops. Major political policies on deafness, of course, were still determined by the nation's representatives, all hearing people.

Deaf people also suffered in the numerous conflicts between the two schools in Paris and Bordeaux, which marked the first ten years of their existence. Manipulated like pawns in a mysterious strategy, young deaf people were often exploited. Public performances depicting Sicard's efforts from Paris to undermine the authority of the Bordeaux school director (by inciting his best pupils to leave) serve as evidence that deaf people were oppressed.

But there is a reverse side to the story: Deaf students strove to protect their schools—even to expand them. Jean Massieu, the best-known deaf instructor at the time of the French Revolution, led deaf student delegations to demand the release of Sicard, who had been imprisoned several times for his Royalist opinions. Deaf people banded together to defend not only themselves but their institutions. These pupils, the triumphant generation of the revolutionary period, included some of the future stars of the deaf movement: Laurent Clerc, Ferdinand Berthier, Claudius Forestier, and Pelissier, among numerous others.

It was the French Revolution that galvanized this movement toward acceptance of deaf education and culture. Today, the national institutes are still extraordinary schools: They are the privileged (but nonexclusive) sites of deaf association meetings and of the cultural and political expressions of the deaf community.

The Revolutionary Ideal and the Deaf Community in France, 1792–1795

ANNE T. QUARTARARO

The purpose of this paper is to analyze a very small part of deaf history in the context of the French Revolution. As France celebrates the bicentennial of the French Revolution, and historians assess its impact on the lives of French citizens at the end of the eighteenth century, this paper will focus on the popular phase of the Revolution, 1792–1795, and use selected archival documents to evaluate what benefits, if any, deaf people drew from the revolutionary period.

Hidden from "traditional" history because of social stereotyping and economic misery, deaf people do not often play a direct role in the political debates so often studied among Revisionist historians, who view the Revolution as a power struggle, a battle of "rhetoric and ideology" devoid of class conflict. This view is in opposition to the Marxist school of thought, which sees class conflict as the driving force behind social change.

While a Marxist interpretation, with its categories of social class, may no longer be useful, the interplay of economic development and social status could significantly broaden the Revisionist approach to the Revolution (Furet, 1981). The socioeconomic condition of deaf people during this time can be a measure of how "rhetoric and ideology" affected the lives of this outsider group in a revolutionary society. (The plea for more socioeconomic study in the Revisionist school came recently from Colin Jones in his paper entitled, "Was the French Revolution a Social Revolution?")

One of the many goals of the revolution that broke out in France during the summer of 1789 was the "improvement of humanity," as historian R. R. Palmer has written (1985). Although Palmer uses this concept to study the progress of education between 1789 and 1799, I would like to use this idea of "improvement of humanity" to focus on another aspect of the revolution that affected the lives of ordinary citizens and, in particular, deaf citizens.

The Revolution of 1789 marks the first time in modern history that a nation made a public commitment to help relieve the economic misery of its citizens. While the revolutionaries certainly did not invent the notion of social welfare, they made it a central part of their plan for a revolutionary state.

Alan Forrest, in his study entitled *The French Revolution and the Poor*, points out that the men who made public policy in the Revolution were a product of the mid-eighteenth century Enlightenment (1981). They grew up with the writings of philosophers who believed in the perfectibility of humankind. It is not surprising that, once in power, these men would try to alleviate the misery that they believed was sapping the moral strength of the nation.

Poverty, seen as a national humiliation, would be contrary to the goals of a new and improved society. As one observer put it, "The first debt of society and its first commitment . . . is to give to all its members . . . the happiness that they can enjoy. Society must, if it is well-organized, protect the weak [and] . . . support the indigent" (Archives Nationales (AN), 1790).

For deaf citizens, this attitude meant that the national government would theoretically intervene on their behalf to improve their lot in life. In the hearing community, people began to acknowledge that deaf people lived in a society that rejected them and that they "only [seemed] to live for suffering" (AN, 1790). As we shall see, however, this government intervention was not comprehensive enough to affect the lives of the majority of deaf people, who continued to live in poverty.

During the early years of the Revolution, the Constituent and Legislative Assemblies created special committees to study the problem of poverty and coordinate requests for financial assistance. The Comité de Mendicité concentrated on defining the extent of poverty and was responsible for developing solutions. By 1791, this committee had compiled data from a survey of more than half the departments (departments are geographical and administrative divisions) in France. By its overall estimates, one in eight people in France was living in poverty (Forrest, 1981).

These figures no doubt put pressure on another committee, the Comité des Secours Publics, which was in charge of allocating national funds for the poor and answering complaints directed to the representatives in Paris. Through the Comité des Secours Publics, citizens could directly petition their national government for public assistance, and many families with deaf children did just that during the era of the National Convention. After the monarchy was abolished in 1792 and the Jacobins rose to power, these two committees wielded even greater authority in the interest of social welfare, and their actions had the potential to improve the lives of deaf people.

During the height of the popular phase of the Revolution, in the summer of 1793, members of the Comité des Secours Publics sent a letter to all departments requesting information about the number of deaf people in each of their districts (AN, 1793). From their responses, it is clear that local officials took this charge quite seriously: Responses began to arrive at the Committee as early as August 1793. They noted the age and occupation of each deaf person and sometimes made additional comments about physical ailments, family problems, or personal character.

In one response from the district of Grenoble in the department of Isère, authorities listed fifty-five deaf people. Only thirty-two were reported with any sort of occupation (AN, 1793), and six of these thirty-two were listed as "beggars." Only five of these thirty-two were listed as skilled or semiskilled laborers, such as carpenters or wigmakers. Most, both male and female, were laborers of one kind or another, and almost all of the six children in the group from Grenoble had parents who were day laborers. The one exception was the daughter of a policeman.

Despite limited data, we can still try to place the socioeconomic condition of deaf people in 1793 in a broader perspective. The promise of "the improvement of humanity" still seemed illusory for deaf citizens. More than 90 percent of deaf adults listed from the Grenoble region were surviving at the lowest level of the economic ladder and most likely did not have the financial or educational resources to change their lives in any significant way. Even if local authorities inflated these numbers to make the case for more national funding, the percentage of the deaf population hovering near the poverty level would still have been very high.

From the list of occupations, it is clear that gainful employment was a serious problem for deaf adults. The narrow range of professions given on the list from Grenoble suggests that there were few job prospects for deaf people in this community, and those who did have a trade were the exception rather than the rule. Jean Baptiste Cartin, thirty-two, a cobbler singled out by local authorities for his intelligence, may have been the best, if practically the only, example of a local success story.

It was much more typical for authorities to stress the hardships faced by deaf people, as they did with the Combe family, poverty-stricken and supporting a fifteen-year-old deaf daughter. The list from Grenoble was replete with such families, who lived on the margin of subsistence. We also can assume that the deaf people listed as "beggars" were indigent and living from public or private charity. On this list, they were all men ranging in age from nineteen to forty-three, in the prime of their laboring years and yet unable to find employment.

The men sitting on the Comité des Secours Publics were aware that in order to improve deaf people's social and economic prospects, they would have to reach this population at an early age and give them a stake in the new revolutionary society (Palmer, 1985). One limited method of social welfare was to have the national government pay room and board stipends for deaf children to attend special schools. This would relieve the economic burden on families who had limited resources to care for children who could not contribute to the family economy. Education was one concrete way to offer the promise of a better life to deaf people.

By the last days of the National Convention, the Comité des Secours Publics formally organized two schools, one in Paris and the other in Bordeaux, for deaf children up to age sixteen (AN). Each department would be responsible for recommending which indigent deaf children would attend the five-year, state-funded school program.

The large pool of available deaf children for these two national schools underscores the fragile socioeconomic condition of many families with deaf children. Moreover, some families seemed desperate to have their children admitted to the government schools.

It is difficult for us today to understand the precarious economic condition of the lower-class family in late eighteenth-century Europe. In order for the family to survive as a unit, each member, whether adult or child, had to contribute financially to the group. As Louise Tilly and Joan Scott point out, "The demands of the family enterprise or the need to earn wages for the unskilled could not be postponed or put aside to care for children who, in their earliest years, represented only a drain on family resources" (1978).

Children became an important resource for the family economy when they could be put to work for a useful wage. This transformation usually took place about the age of seven or eight. Children were treated no differently than adults in the burden of labor they were expected to undertake (Tilly and Scott, 1978).

This condition of the lower-class family is even more significant in the context of deaf history. Because children must be employed to help maintain the family unit, families with deaf children probably felt even greater economic pressure. Parents would have extra mouths to feed, but no prospect of additional labor to balance the noticeable deficit (Schwartz, 1988). Unlike hearing children, who could eventually become laborers, deaf children would grow to adulthood dependent on parents and later on brothers and sisters.

It is therefore not surprising that many lower-class families eagerly anticipated placing their deaf children in the new schools for deaf students in Paris and Bordeaux. The national government afforded them perhaps the only chance to improve their eco-

Deaf History

DEAF
WAY
🙢

nomic condition. The rest of the family might survive by sending a deaf child away to boarding school. In turn, the child would learn a useful skill and could become a productive member of society. The family unit, society-at-large, and deaf children would all benefit. Or so these revolutionaries logically might have reasoned.

In one request for schooling, from the department of the Somme, we can glimpse the misery and limited opportunities for deaf children and their families. The mayor and municipal officials of the town of Montdidier asked the Comité des Secours Publics in Paris to consider the case of Felix-François Lainé, who had become deaf at the age of four after an illness (AN). His father, Pierre Lainé, was a window-glass maker and could scarcely support his eight children. The local officials expressed the hope that this young boy could learn some basic skills at school that might, in turn, help his brothers and sisters.

It was difficult for young deaf children to be admitted to the Paris and Bordeaux schools, although the law stipulated that indigent deaf children under age sixteen would automatically be qualified to attend either the Paris or the Bordeaux school (AN). But a father would first have to certify that his child was unable to hear *or* speak, that the child was not mentally handicapped, and that the family could be classified as indigent (AN). Any child younger than age ten could not be accepted for the five-year program (AN). (Department of the Indre-et-Loire to the Minister of the Interior, 26 messidor an IV. The report requests the admission of two girls, ages five and seven, to the Paris school, but they are still too young for consideration.)

From the department of the Marne, we have lists of deaf children being considered for the government schools. Twenty young people between the ages of nine and fourteen are listed. In 75 percent of these cases, authorities described the families as indigent, with no resources to support their deaf or hearing children. Only one child from this list, however, would eventually enter the Paris school. Pierre Jean-Baptiste Ory came from a family of six children and at age 11 began his schooling. The other eligible children could reapply for admission, but the shortage of available slots made their chances of admission slim (AN).

Another list from the department of the Vosges in eastern France, drawn up in 1794 as was the list from the Marne, indicates the breadth of the socioeconomic problems facing officials. These officials seemed compelled to list every deaf citizen within their jurisdiction on school application lists, including a three-year-old child and men well past the age of 60 (AN).

In total, the Vosges officials notified the Comité des Secours Publics in Paris that there were fifty-three deaf people in their area, more than 90 percent of whom were described as indigent. Rare was the reference to a person who was self-supporting, even through unskilled labor. Two children would be chosen from this particular list to attend the Paris school: Jean-Baptiste Frayard, an orphan, and François Tanneur, a child from a very poor family (AN). (This listing even makes a distinction between indigent and very indigent. Officials were forced to make rankings of the poverty level.)

What do all these lists mean to historians of the French Revolution and of deaf society? We can conclude that the concept of "the improvement of humanity" did affect deaf people during the popular phase of the Revolution, but to a limited degree. Authorities did try to get some perspective on the situation of deaf citizens. Never before had the national government tried to determine the size of the deaf population and its economic make-up through official surveys.

The few results of the data we have considered here indicate that deaf people suffered from deep-seated economic and social misery. Their jobs were largely unskilled, and deaf men had few prospects for economic advancement.

Revolutionaries did seem to recognize that only educational opportunity would break this cycle of poverty and isolation. However, if the creation of schools for deaf students in Paris and Bordeaux was the epitome of the revolutionary ideal, then that ideal fell far short of meeting the needs of deaf people. The limited recruitment and the large number of deaf children who were unable to obtain help underscore the continuing tension between the high-minded goals of the Revolution and the practical needs of its deaf citizens.

References

Archives Nationales. F^{15} 2584, untitled document, 1790–1795?

————. F^{15} 2584, Responses from various departments about number of deaf people in their areas, July 30, 1793–August 1793.

————. F^{15} 2584, Condition of deaf people from birth in the district of Grenoble, department of the Isère, 4 nivôse an II.

————. F^{15} 2459, Comité des Secours Publis, an III.

————. F^{15} 2586–2587, Petition to the Comité des Secours Publics, department of the Somme, 4 nivôse an III.

————. F^{15} 2459, Comité des Secours Publics, an III.

————. F^{15} 2586–2587, Response to Citizen Bourgeois about his son entering the deaf institution, 24 Thermidor an IV.

————. F^{15} 2586–2587, Department of the Indre-et-Loire to the Minister of the Interior, 26 messidor an IV.

————. F^{15} 2586–2587, General list of deaf from the department of the Marne, 25 prairial an III.

————. F^{15} 2586–2587, General list of deaf from the department of the Vosges, 28 floréal an III.

Forrest, Alan. 1981. *The French Revolution and the Poor.* New York: St. Martin's Press. p. 23.

Furet, Francois. 1981. *Interpreting the Revolution,* trans. Elborg Forster. New York: Cambridge University Press.

Jones, Colin. May 5, 1989. "Was the French Revolution a Social Revolution?" Paper delivered at the International Congress on the History of the French Revolution. Place unknown.

Palmer, R. R. 1985. *The Improvement of Humanity: Education and the French Revolution.* Princeton: Princeton University Press. pp. 80–85.

Schwartz, Robert. 1988. *Policing the Poor in Eighteenth-Century France.* Chapel Hill: University of North Carolina Press. pp. 107–112.

Tilly, Louise, and Joan Scott. 1978. *Women, Work, and Family.* New York: Holt, Rinehart, & Winston. pp. 58–59.

The French Deaf Movement After the Milan Congress

BERNARD TRUFFAUT

The 1889 International Deaf-Mute Congress of Paris—intended to evaluate the progress made over the previous one hundred years in the status of deaf people worldwide—was undoubtedly the first event of its kind ever convened. I wish I could follow the example of the 1889 Congress and review the succeeding one hundred years (1889–1989), but there is such a vast, dispersed, and incomplete literature on this last century that I have chosen to limit my presentation to the thirty years in France from 1889 to 1919. This proves, in fact, to have been a very interesting period for deaf people in France, and one abounding with activity. The following are some of what I consider its most noteworthy aspects.

Associations

Before 1880, only one formal deaf association existed in France, the "Société Centrale," which was founded in 1836. This association's diverse aims included mutual assistance, retirement, leisure, sports, and so on. In 1892, the first of a number of associations specifically called a Mutual Aid Society was established in Rouen. The most successful of these groups was formed in Reims in 1895. The Reims society opened the first hostel for deaf people in France in 1896. Another association, "Le Sou du Cercle" (The Penny Circle), founded around 1896, sought to acquire—by saving pennies—the sum necessary to establish the Deaf-Mute Hostel of Paris. Members of this group saved pennies for this purpose for nearly thirty-five years. The popularity of bicycling inspired the formation in 1898 of the first deaf "Association Cycliste."

The Silent Press

Between 1880 and 1919, twenty new journals by and for deaf people appeared in France. But there were problems: The small numbers of subscribers resulted in budgetary restrictions on format, number of pages, and frequency of publication. Many of these journals did not survive.

Social Advancement

Apart from one serious setback—the near-disappearance of deaf people from teaching positions that resulted from the influence of decisions reached at the Milan Congress—

deaf people's overall social status improved a little. There were many individual success stories. For example, a deaf decorator-architect named Cochefer designed the doors of the City Hall of Paris. Many deaf people achieved success in press-related trades. A "Press Shop for Deaf-Mute Workers" was even created in Paris in 1894; the owner and most of the staff were deaf individuals. But this experiment was short-lived. At the beginning of the century, deaf automobile owners were not rare. There were four in the region of Champagne; one of them, a talented mechanic, built his own small car.

Sports

The Deaf-Mute Sports Club of Paris was founded in 1911. In 1918 came the Sports Federation of French Deaf-Mutes. Shortly thereafter, in 1924, France played a pioneering role in the initiation of the first International Silent Games. We have already noted the growth in the sport of cycling.

The Arts

There were dozens of deaf artists during this period, most of whom participated in the Annual Exhibits of French Artists, side-by-side with hearing peers. There was a remarkable abundance of talented deaf sculptors: Martin, Choppin, Hamar, Hennequin, and Morice, to name a few. Hamar created the statue of Marshall de Rochambeau that was erected in Washington, D.C. in 1902. The silent press owed most of its illustrations to gifted deaf designers and engravers. Simultaneously, theater arts were expanding, especially in mime and pantomime, with performances for the hearing public. There were also a number of reputable deaf writers and poets.

Politics

Militant deaf people of the time did not hesitate to become involved in any affair affecting their cause, rectifying errors in the press, responding to attacks (like those by Vibert, who wrote some strong criticisms of the Abbé de l'Epée), protesting abusive statements made by lawyers (as in 1889, in Orléans), and interceding to demand recognition of deaf people's civil rights (as in cases where marriage witnesses were rejected by authorities because they were deaf). In the area of education, they made remarkably persistent—though often unsuccessful—demands for the obligatory education of deaf-mutes, the creation of regional schools, the transformation of the oral method by the adoption of a combined system of communication (signs plus speech plus writing), and the transfer of the schools from the Ministry of the Interior (or Public Assistance) to the Ministry of Public Education. They challenged everything, fighting on every front—at formal assemblies (to which legislators, civic leaders, and journalists were invited), at banquets, and in the press.

International Exchanges

The deaf people of France were very active in the international arena during this period. Three international congresses were held in Paris: one in 1899, another in 1900, and a third in 1912. Yet another international congress was held in Liège in 1905. French participation was high at the international congresses held abroad, at Chicago in 1893, and at Saint Louis in 1904. The "Entente Cordiale" between France and Britain was celebrated with Franco-British exchanges. In 1917, despite the War and the threat presented by German submarines, a French delegation attended the centennial celebration of the founding of the American School for the Deaf by Laurent Clerc and T. H. Gallaudet, the French and American pioneers of deaf education in the United States. Associations like the Mutual Aid Society of Reims sent delegates to remote exhibitions to describe the nature of their work.

The silent press also provided occasions for exchanges: French newspapers reported news events about deaf people worldwide (for example, the 1906 earthquake in San Francisco, where the deaf sculptor Douglas Tilden resided). As evidence of the reciprocal nature of the international spirit at work in that period, during the serious floods of 1910 in France, deaf Americans took up a relief collection for French deaf people affected by that situation. Also, during his various visits to France, E. M. Gallaudet was always warmly welcomed, with parties given in his honor.

The Continuation of Traditions

Three things remained unchanged: tributes to the Abbé de l'Epée in November, with banquets throughout France and pilgrimages to Versailles, where de l'Epée was born; July banquets commemorating the Laws of the Revolution Favoring Deaf Individuals; and the use of sign language, despite the emergence of an ever-larger contingency of speaking deaf persons. While sign language was not being researched or (with the exception of fingerspelling) explicitly promoted, it was nevertheless esteemed for the scope of its expressiveness, particularly in the hands of such virtuosos as Dusuzeau, dubbed the "Gambetta of Deaf-Mutes."

Conclusion

In spite of the many pervasive and negative effects of the Milan Congress, the period between 1889 and 1919 in France was a truly fertile and positive one. One can only be grateful for the often thankless work of deaf militants of that time, considering the conditions under which they acted: professional obligations tougher than today's, modest incomes, limited leisure time, the frequent need to do night work by oil lamp, interminable trips, and so on. Such circumstances did not stop deaf people of that period.

But two serious difficulties did handicap deaf French people during those three decades. One of these, the dissension and disagreement within the deaf population itself, was somewhat attributable to what has been called the "Mal Francais," a term descriptive of a controversy-ridden time for the French in general. This generally divisive mindset was aggravated for deaf people by numerous personal troubles: grudges, jealousies, suspicions, ideological differences (including religious differences), and a lack of tolerance. Deaf people urged unity on all sides, but this did not occur, except once—miraculously—in 1912, during the Bicentennial celebration of the birth of the Abbé de l'Epée. Later, unfortunately, the old rivalries resumed, worse than ever. The divisiveness of this period regrettably cost deaf people a considerable loss of time, energy, and progress.

Another unfortunate development of this period was the polarization of the "specialized community" in France. By "specialized community," I mean all of the groups concerned with deafness: deaf people, parents, professionals (teachers, medical personnel, and so on)—that is, both the consumers and the providers of services. Before

1880, this community was relatively homogeneous. Sign language was acceptable to the hearing group, and there was no major conflict between hearing and deaf people. After 1880, the divorce began. Views concerning deaf education diverged and became more intransigent. From that moment on, there were two pressure groups: one consisting of deaf persons and friends adopting their cause, the other consisting of professionals—closely echoed by parents—who had adopted an oralist stance.

This separation was not yet complete at the beginning of the twentieth century. At that time, when deaf individuals intervened in a situation, the partisans of the other group often intervened too. At the Congress of 1900, the two camps were present but separated because of linguistic incompatibility. At the 1912 Congress, the two camps were reunited, like two adversarial debate teams. After that, the separation became more radical. On the one hand, deaf people ended up "talking in the air" without a hearing audience; on the other, hearing people decided to work autocratically, without feeling any necessity for deaf people even to be present. Each pressure group tried to influence the civil and legislative authorities capable of wielding power over deaf people's lives. This divorce, doubtless particularly dramatic in France, was most regrettable: In such a stalemate, no advance can be made. On one side are the better ideas, on the other, the more forceful means, but the two must be united for real success to occur.

These problems still exist and impede progress in France today. I personally believe that an internationalization of the deaf community—throughout Europe and the world—would be the most effective way to eliminate obstacles of this kind.

Signs of Eloquence: Selections from Deaf American Public Addresses

JAMES J. FERNANDES AND JANE F. KELLEHER

I f I have seen far, it is because I have stood on the shoulders of giants." In 1959, George McClure, a ninety-seven-year-old Deaf educator, writer, and champion of the rights of Deaf Americans, addressed these words of Isaac Newton to an audience in Indianapolis (McClure, 1960). McClure was reflecting on the progress Deaf people had made since the founding of the first school for Deaf students in the United States.

Deaf Americans have not always had schools or been able to hold jobs or own property, and in many ways the lives of Deaf people in our country used to be bleak. Today, however, almost every state has schools for Deaf students; Deaf people are employed in nearly every occupation and profession; Deaf people drive their own cars, own homes, and have the freedoms of life, liberty, and the pursuit of happiness. Deaf people in the United States even have their own university, now headed by a Deaf President. They got these things because they have been able to "stand on the shoulders of giants." Who were these giants? What did they do? How did they grow so tall?

This paper looks at three such giants among Deaf Americans. Although no more than ordinary folk, these "giants," like the heroes and heroines in fairy tales, overcame life's difficulties and challenges through their wit and persistence. They are revealed here through their "speeches"—sign language addresses presented before varied audiences. The history of achievement of Deaf Americans has been influenced in no small part by the public addresses of Deaf leaders such as these.

The purpose of this examination of a small sampling of Deaf public addresses is to point out the value of the contributions to American history made by Deaf public speakers and to encourage the documentation of orations presented by Deaf people, not only through published manuscripts or written translations of their speeches but, more importantly, through film and videotape recordings of the actual presentations in sign language. The preservation and study of the art of public speaking as practiced by Deaf men and women can open a valuable window through which to view and understand the Deaf Way.

The three orators included in this paper represent the first hundred years of Deaf American public address. Laurent Clerc, the first Deaf person on record to address an American audience, was instrumental in achieving educational rights for Deaf people in the United States early in the nineteenth century. Agatha Tiegel Hanson, the second woman to graduate from Gallaudet University, presented a valedictory address in 1893 that established her as a champion of equal rights for women. Finally, George Veditz, the feisty president of the National Association of the Deaf, was the earliest to use film to record visually and preserve signed oration by Deaf Americans, including his own 1913 address.

Laurent Clerc's Mission to America

"Teach Deaf people to read and write? Impossible! A waste of time and effort." While American ministers were delivering messages like these from their pulpits in 1816, Thomas Hopkins Gallaudet was returning from France to begin an American school for Deaf students.

Despite the opposition to Deaf education in the United States at that time, a group of citizens in Hartford, Connecticut had sent Gallaudet to Europe to learn the methods used there to teach Deaf people. Gallaudet, eager to start an American school, brought back from France a bright young Frenchman—Laurent Clerc—who had been Instructor at the Royal Institution for the Deaf in Paris. Clerc had the knowledge and skills to teach Deaf students and also to train American teachers. Even more important, Clerc himself was Deaf, and was uniquely qualified to convince United States citizens that an American school for Deaf students would surely succeed.

When they stepped off the gangplank of the *Mary Augusta* onto a New York dock on August 9, 1816, Clerc and Gallaudet faced a huge task. Not only did they need to locate students, prepare a curriculum, and find facilities for a school in Hartford, they also had to overcome misconceptions about deafness and Deaf people, convince the American people of the need for and value of Deaf education, and collect the funds necessary to establish their school.

To accomplish these goals, the two men set out on a tour of the eastern states. Handbills and newspaper articles announced their arrival in each capital city. Gallaudet and Clerc visited small groups of influential citizens who would then arrange for larger public meetings.

At these public gatherings, Clerc presented speeches he had written, which Gallaudet would read aloud. Then the audience would ask questions—in writing or interpreted in sign language by Gallaudet—and Clerc would respond by writing on a blackboard. After nine months of travel, the two men judged their efforts a success: They had collected a total of $12,000 and received an additional $5,000 from the Connecticut General Assembly.

Thus the performance of Laurent Clerc as a Deaf public speaker was instrumental in creating a significant piece of American history—the establishment of Deaf education in the United States.

There are a number of reasons for Clerc's success as a persuasive orator. Perhaps most significant was his credibility. Clerc himself was living proof of the effectiveness of the French method of educating Deaf students. Deaf from birth or infancy, he had been educated at the Paris school, where he later taught the most advanced classes. Although he had only recently taken up the study of English, he displayed an excellent command of the language through his written addresses and responses to questions from the public. The novelty of an educated Deaf man from France who understood and expressed abstract concepts through sign language and writing aroused curiosity and attracted people to the public meetings. Clerc also exhibited refined French manners and a warm personality, qualities that set his audiences at ease.

As a public speaker, Clerc was a master of matching his persuasive goals to the beliefs and values of his listeners. His audiences consisted of the American elite—successful merchants, doctors, lawyers, government officials, wealthy landowners. They were religious people who believed that charitable works would be rewarded in heaven and that Christians had the responsibility to aid less fortunate people and spread the word of God. They were proud of their young nation, which had recently proved itself a match for Great Britain in the War of 1812. And they were practical people, having achieved their success through diligence and hard work. In writing his speeches, Clerc appealed to these characteristics in his American audiences.

For example, in Boston during September, he appealed to the religious convictions of his audience by using himself as an example of the kind of growth education could produce in a Deaf person:

> I had, it is true, a mind; but it did not think; I had a heart; but it did not feel . . .
> I believed that God was a tall, big and strong man and that Jesus Christ having come to kill us, had been killed by us and placed upon the cross as one of our triumphs.
>
> I believed many other droll and ridiculous things . . . . I am sure that the Deaf . . . who are in your Country, think as I once did. You must be so kind as to undeceive them. We shall cultivate their minds and form their hearts. (Clerc, 1816a)

In the same speech Clerc also appealed to American nationalism:

> In Europe, each nation, however small, has an Institution for the Deaf . . . and most of these Institutions are at the expense of the Government. Will America remain the only nation which is insensible to the cry of humanity?

For Americans, eager to prove their new country deserved a place of prominence among the nations of the world, this was an effective appeal to national vanity.

In his November address in Albany, New York, Clerc linked nationalism with the missionary zeal in America at that time:

> The United States of America, which are in the number of civilized nations, are yet in arrears! What a wonder! They send missionaries to Africa and Asia to convert the Idolatrous to the true religion, and they forget there are among them persons who have no idea of God, of Jesus Christ and the immortality of our Soul and of the conditions we must perform here below to obtain a better happiness in the other world! What a contrast! Do foreigners merit your preference rather than your own countrymen? (1816b)

In this appeal to both national pride and evangelism, Clerc reminded his audiences that charity begins at home.

His December address in Philadelphia emphasized the practicality of educating Deaf people and of preparing them for a profession or trade. He described the Deaf citizens of Europe who had achieved independence through education:

> Many are married and have children . . . . Many others are employed in the offices of the government, and other publick administrations. Many others are

good painters, sculptors, engravers, workers in mosaick, and printers. Some others . . . are merchants, and rule their affairs perfectly well. (1816c)

The practical New Englanders who heard Clerc's addresses or read the printed versions in the newspapers readily understood the benefit to society of preparing young citizens for respectable trades and professions. Clerc showed them that they would get value back for money contributed to establish a school for Deaf students.

Laurent Clerc, France's gift to the Deaf people of America, is best remembered as a teacher. But his accomplishments as a public speaker, his credibility as a well-educated Deaf person, and his mastery of persuasive oratory may be even more important to his place in history. Through clever use of appeals to nationalism, religious beliefs, missionary zeal, and New England practicality, his public addresses helped bring a new era for Deaf Americans. If Clerc had not been such a successful public speaker, the securing of Deaf Americans' right to education might have been long delayed.

Agatha Tiegel Hanson: An Early Advocate of Women's Rights

In the years following the opening of the school in Connecticut, educational institutions for Deaf people spread across the country. Most schools followed the model established by Clerc and Gallaudet.

In 1864 the institution now known as Gallaudet University opened its doors to Deaf people who wanted to pursue a college education. Four young women were among the first students, but none of them advanced beyond the introductory class. Twenty years passed before the college decided once again to admit females—on an experimental basis. In 1887, six young women enrolled, and in 1888, fifteen-year-old Agatha Tiegel entered the college.

The few colleges in the nation accepting female students in those years were combatting prevalent beliefs that higher education for women was without value and that women were intellectually inferior to men. In 1893, Tiegel became the first woman to complete the full college program at Gallaudet and graduate with a B.A. All of her fellow seniors were men, yet she was awarded the honor of a valedictory address. She used the occasion to deliver a fiery refutation of the myth of women's inferiority and predicted that eventually all the barriers of discrimination against women would fall.

Like Laurent Clerc, Tiegel had unique credentials to help her challenge false beliefs. Just as Clerc had appeared on the shores of America as living proof that Deaf people could become well educated if given the chance, Tiegel's academic success helped prove that women were the intellectual equals of men.

Born in Pittsburgh in 1873, Tiegel contracted spinal meningitis at age seven. The illness left her deaf and blind in one eye. She entered a private Catholic school at the age of nine and began attending the Western Pennsylvania School for the Deaf when she was thirteen years old. Two years later she entered the preparatory class at Gallaudet. As an elderly woman, Tiegel remembered how it felt to be a guinea pig in this experiment in coeducation: "Barely fifteen at the time, conscious of youth and energy, of ability to think, to feel, to act, I resented this being on trial, both at Gallaudet and in the world at large" (Hanson, 1937).

The freedom of women students at that time was strictly curtailed. The female undergraduates were not allowed to leave campus alone and had no clubs or societies of their own. They were allowed to attend the males' literary society meetings, if chaperoned, and could watch lectures, debates, and declamations. Women were aware of being under constant scrutiny in whatever they did. As a result of these restrictions, in her junior year Tiegel organized and served as the first president of the OWLS, a literary society for women students that later became the Phi Kappa Zeta sorority.

Despite the restrictions placed upon her, she found the college environment stimulating. Professor E. A. Fay, head of the languages department, made the biggest impression on her. A voracious reader, Tiegel loved poetry and later published several of her own works. An independent thinker, she turned from her Catholic upbringing to oriental philosophy while in college. She later became Episcopalian.

Following her graduation, she became a teacher at the Minnesota School for the Deaf. In 1899 she married the architect Olof Hanson, and the two moved to Seattle. Through their lifetimes, both Agatha Tiegel Hanson and Olof Hanson served as influential leaders of the American Deaf community.

But in 1893 Tiegel had felt oppressed. As she described it many years later:

> I was a very young girl at the time, and I resented that there might be any question of the right, the God given right, of my sisters and myself to take our places in the sun. An expression of this vague resentment is shown in the subject of my graduating oration, "The Intellect of Woman." I closed the oration with . . .words, which in those days burned my heart, and who shall say that I was not an unconscious prophet? (Hanson, 1937)

As one of the first women to graduate from Gallaudet, Tiegel's topic for her commencement oration, "The Intellect of Woman," was fitting. The audience of parents, faculty, alumni, and dignitaries must have been curious to see how this early product of the coeducation experiment had turned out.

While there is no filmed recording of her valedictory address, some reasonable assumptions can be drawn about Tiegel's delivery. It is likely that she emulated the signing style of her favorite professors, Fay and E. M. Gallaudet (who was then the college president). The earliest films of presentations in American Sign Language, dating back to 1913, include Fay and Gallaudet, who were considered masters of sign language. The films show a deliberate, formal, broad-gestured manner of signing, with sedate facial expression, no lip movement, and frequent alternating of signing or fingerspelling from one hand to the other.

Surely something of Tiegel's personality was also conveyed in her valedictory presentation. She was described as possessing "a sparkling vivacity and boundless enthusiasm that made her the 'life of the party,' never at a loss for conversation or a witty remark" (*The Intellect of Women*, anonymous, 1975). Skilled at lipreading and having retained easily understandable speech, she described herself as a "semimute" and sometimes felt trapped between the Deaf and hearing worlds. In 1893, she also felt trapped as a woman in a world controlled by men. Even President E. M. Gallaudet was apprehensive about the wisdom of admitting young women to the college program (Gallaudet, 1983).

In the first words of her valedictory speech, Tiegel confronted head-on society's doubts and oppressive beliefs about women, labelling them "evil." She anticipated by several decades the work of developmental psychologists in declaring that the subservient role of women was not biologically determined but rather learned from infancy:

> The apparent inferiority of woman's intellect is to be attributed to many restrictive circumstances. We are so accustomed to behold her in a stage of develop-

ment so far below her powers that we do not apprehend the full evil of these circumstances. The error begins before she leaves the cradle. Her sex is ever a chain and a restraint. Many liberties, healthy and helpful in themselves, are denied her. . . . In childhood she is tutored in the idea that her role on the great stage of life is secondary to that of the brother who plays by her side; and all meek and docile graces are carefully cultivated in her. She is not expected to reflect for herself. (Hanson, 1893)

She blamed society for falling into a rut of laziness in maintaining stifling traditions, such as excluding women from university education: "Popular opinion exerts a powerful influence to hold her in this condition; a rut has been made on the highway, and the wheel slips into it easily and glides along smoothly" (Hanson, 1893).

She noted that women who broke with tradition to pursue higher education or careers risked ridicule and faced unfair restraints. But, despite these risks and barriers, the myth of intellectual inferiority had been disproved throughout history by the singular achievements of individual women. Imagine, suggested Tiegel, what women could do if they were given opportunities equal to those enjoyed by men:

That such repression and restraint upon mental action are artificial has been demonstrated in all ages by women whose independence has burst every fetter and won them recognition in the fields of science, theology, literature, politics, and art. It is impossible to estimate the immensity of the influence that woman's mind has exerted on the history of the world . . . . If, during these ages of wrong custom, of false sentiment, she has often retained much of her greatness of intellect and soul, she will better do justice to her inborn powers when she has room and light in which to grow. (Hanson, 1893)

In allowing women to attend Gallaudet, the college community had considered establishing a separate curriculum for women students. Tiegel, who graduated at the top of her class of male students, resented such a notion and minced no words in objecting to it:

The idea is absurd that a special course of study should be selected different from the one pursued in the average college under the impression that such a selection would be better adapted to women's needs and sphere in life. The agitation of this topic is merely the old current of prejudice against women turning up in a new channel . . . . No one has the right to say to a woman: "In this path of knowledge shalt thou walk, and in no other." Knowledge, like religion, admits of no trammels and no narrowing boundaries . . . . (Hanson, 1893)

Tiegel refuted arguments that women were lacking in logic and reason by pointing out that they had been denied the opportunity to develop such skills. To argue that women are inferior, she stated, "is to copy the fallacies of the opponents of emancipation, who used as arguments those very faults in slaves that slavery had produced" (Hanson, 1893). Tiegel's point is interesting, for it alludes to one source of motivation for the women's rights movement that surfaced in America in the latter nineteenth century. Women who had worked diligently against slavery came to realize that they were similarly deprived of rights, and they began to agitate for their own freedom and equality.

182

THE
DEAF
WAY
₫

Deaf History

To be a black woman meant facing a double dose of oppression, something that Tiegel experienced also as a Deaf person and a female during a time when both women and Deaf people were greatly under-represented on college campuses.

Tiegel closed her address on an optimistic note, prescient of the stirring words of Martin Luther King, Jr.'s "We Shall Overcome" speech. She recognized progress, symbolized by her own graduation from Gallaudet, and predicted a promising future:

> It is true that we have made a start in the right direction. But that start has been made very recently, and it is still too early to pass sentence on the results. There yet remains a large fund of prejudice to overcome, of false sentiment to combat, of narrowminded opposition to triumph over. But there is no uncertainty as to the final outcome. Civilization is too far advanced not to acknowledge the justice of woman's cause. She herself is too strongly impelled by a noble hunger for something better than she has known, too highly inspired by the vista of the glorious future, not to rise with determination and might and move on till all barriers crumble and fall. (Hanson, 1893)

In her later years, Tiegel exerted a quiet leadership within the American Deaf community as she balanced raising a family with service to organizations of Deaf people. But her accomplishment as the first woman to graduate from Gallaudet University, and her outspoken defense of women's rights in her valedictory address, firmly establish her place in the history of the struggle for equal rights for all Americans.

George W. Veditz on "Preservation of the Sign Language"

A contemporary of Agatha Tiegel Hanson's, and equally a champion of human rights, was George W. Veditz. The son of German immigrants, Veditz became deaf from scarlet fever when he was eight years old. As a student at the Maryland School for the Deaf in Frederick, he added American Sign Language to his command of English and German, becoming trilingual. After graduating from Gallaudet in 1884 with record-setting high grades, he became an outspoken advocate for the rights of Deaf people.

In 1889, Veditz established the Gallaudet College Alumni Association; in 1892, the Maryland School for the Deaf Alumni Association; and in 1904, the Colorado Association of the Deaf. Also in 1904, he was elected president of the National Association of the Deaf (NAD), a position to which he was reelected in 1907.

As president of the NAD, Veditz was a militant firebrand for the rights of Deaf people. One writer described his tenure at the helm of the NAD as "a vigorous, active, if somewhat turbulent reign" (Garretson, 1951).

Veditz is chiefly responsible for two accomplishments of lasting benefit to the American Deaf community. The first was his success in waging a campaign to repeal civil service regulations that blocked the hiring of Deaf people for jobs within the Federal government. The second lasting legacy of the Veditz presidency was the NAD Moving Picture Fund, which was used to film addresses in American Sign Language made by prominent educators and leaders of the Deaf community. The purpose of the films was to record, preserve, and promote the use of Sign Language during a period when the domination of a strictly oralist approach to instruction threatened the use of sign language in schools for Deaf students.

The words of Veditz's final address as NAD president, given at the Colorado Springs convention on August 6, 1910, echo Agatha Tiegel's speech about the educational rights of women:

> And right here let me say that the organized deaf do not understand their own rights. It is their power, if united, to dictate to the schools what methods of education should be pursued therein. Their cause is so palpably just that the public, legislators, and parents must in the end side with them. (Veditz, 1910)

In 1913, Veditz himself became the subject of one of the NAD films, delivering a powerfully moving, almost poetic appeal for the preservation of sign language. Fortunately, this historically valuable film and others produced with the NAD Moving Picture Fund are now preserved on videotape as part of the George W. Veditz Film Collection of the Gallaudet University Archives.

The creation of the NAD Moving Picture Fund was first announced in the Deaf press near the close of Veditz's second term as president. The *Northwest Silent Observer* (1909) described plans to raise money for the fund through a chain letter. The recipient of a letter would be asked to send ten cents to the fund and pass the letter on to three friends. The stated goal was to have "motion pictures made of addresses and lectures delivered in the sign language by such persons as Dr. E.M. Gallaudet and others." By March 1910, the chain letter idea had been abandoned in favor of collectors who were offered prizes for gathering donations.

By 1913, the fund amounted to over $5,000, with several films of prominent educators already completed and more in production. The films found their way to different parts of the country and were shown to gatherings of Deaf people as a means of enlightenment, entertainment, and fund-raising. Some of the films were brought for a showing at the 1913 NAD convention in Cleveland. Movie equipment was also brought to the meeting, and a film was made of Veditz delivering an appeal for the preservation of Sign Language.

Veditz's address is a persuasive message aimed at winning appreciation for and financial contributions to the NAD film collection. One can imagine Veditz's speech being shown along with other films at gatherings of Deaf people. Perhaps a Deaf club would sponsor a viewing of entertaining films such as E. M. Gallaudet's *Lorna Doone County of Devonshire, England* or Robert McGregor's *The Irishman's Flea*. These might have been followed by Veditz's address, thus encouraging the audience to contribute to the film fund.

As an historical record, Veditz's film helps preserve sign language, just as he said it would. Linguists have found it and other examples from the NAD film collection invaluable in their recent research on American Sign Language and the historical changes it has undergone. But Veditz's address can also be appreciated as an example of impassioned oratory.

The speech reveals a style that is near poetic in its impact and reminiscent of Lincoln's Gettysburg Address. From the simple opening sentence, the speech builds, increasing in complexity and emotional pitch as Veditz uses evocative language and images—"cruel-hearted demands," "eyes of jealousy," "a jailed man chained at the legs"—to portray the threat to American Sign Language. He employs a three-part repetitive cycle throughout the speech and uses parallel language for dramatic effect, as exemplified in the sentence: "But we American Deaf know, the French Deaf know, the German Deaf know that, in truth, the oral method is poorest" (Veditz, 1913).

The organization of ideas in the speech is based on a classic problem-solution or need-satisfaction model often used in persuasive messages. Using forceful signs, Veditz describes the threat to American Sign Language. After vividly establishing this threat as a problem or need, he proposes a solution: the NAD moving picture collection of "masters of sign language," which can be used to preserve and pass on signs.

The persuasive effect of the style and organization of the speech is enhanced by his masterful delivery. Using a tight-lipped, straight-faced, broad-gestured, formal method of presentation, he conveys a sense of the seriousness and dignity of his topic. Despite the old-fashioned appearance of some of Veditz's signs, the present-day viewer of the address is still impressed by their forcefulness. In an unpublished paper Richard Zimmer (1982) describes his own reaction to Veditz's manner of delivery: "When he said 'Their teachers have cast them aside and refused to listen to their pleas,' his expressions and careful posturing portrayed the gulf between the teachers and pupils with such clarity that it was like seeing the actual conflict being acted out in front of me."

Certainly conflict was a major theme of Veditz's public life as a leader of the American Deaf community. But he often employed conflict strategically in his efforts to win civil service jobs for Deaf people and to create interest in the NAD. In his speech "The Preservation of the Sign Language," Veditz showed that as an orator he also could make skillful use of conflict to create a sense of drama and to involve his audience emotionally in his message.

Conclusion

The three Deaf orators discussed in this paper represent the barest tip of the iceberg of Deaf American public address. Yet the significance of their roles in the history of the American Deaf community and the struggle for human rights is clear. Laurent Clerc, Agatha Tiegel Hanson, and George Veditz are just a few of the giants of the history of the American Deaf community. Many others—John Carlin, Robert McGregor, Amos Draper, and Olof Hanson—were also important early Deaf orators, but the written, film, or videotape records of their speeches are scant and incomplete.

The value of preserving and studying the language and literature of different cultures is now fairly widely recognized. With respect to Deaf culture, research and classes on American Sign Language linguistics flourish, and American Sign Language literature is now beginning to be studied and taught.

Rhetoric may be broadly defined as the use of communication to influence the behavior of others. Perhaps one effect of the Deaf President Now movement of March 1988 will be to turn scholarly attention to the rhetoric of the Deaf community. We hope this paper begins to illustrate the value of studying and coming to understand the role that the rhetoric of the Deaf community has played in American history.

References

Anonymous. 1909. "Moving Picture Chain Letter Scheme." *Northwest Silent Observer*, December 9.

Clerc, L. 1816a. "Asylum for the Deaf and Dumb." *Boston Intelligencer*, September 14.

———. 1816b. "The Deaf and Dumb." *Albany Daily Advertiser*, November 12.

———. 1816c. "Publick Meeting." *Poulson's American Daily Advertiser*, December 12.

Gallaudet, E. M. 1983. *History of the College for the Deaf, 1857–1907*, ed. L. Fischer and D. de Lorenzo. Washington, DC: Gallaudet College Press.

Garretson, M. D. 1951. "The Veditz Genius." Parts I and II. *Silent Worker*, May and July, pp. 15 and 18.

Hanson, A. T. 1937. "The Victorian Era at Gallaudet." *Buff and Blue*, pp. 5–8.

Hanson, A. T. 1893. *The Intellect of Woman*. Agatha Tiegel Hanson Papers. Gallaudet University Archives, Gallaudet University, Washington, DC.

"The Intellect of Women." 1975. *The Lamp of Delta Zeta*, pp. 12–15.

McClure, G. M. 1960. "There Were Giants in Those Days." *Kentucky Standard*, January 14, pp. 1–4.

Veditz, G. W. 1912. "The President's Message." *Proceedings of the Ninth Convention of the National Association and the Third World's Congress of the Deaf, Colorado Springs, 6–13 August 1910*. Los Angeles: Philocophus Press.

———. 1913. *Preservation of the Sign Language*. Sixteen millimeter film produced by National Association of the Deaf. Videotaped version available through Gallaudet University Media Distribution Service, Washington, DC.

Zimmer, R. 1982. "Critical Analysis of George Veditz as a Persuasive Communicator." Unpublished paper. Gallaudet University, Washington, DC.

The History of Sign Language in Italian Education of the Deaf

SERENA CORAZZA

*I*taly is not immune to the controversy surrounding sign language and the education of deaf students. Sign language is both accepted and rejected by Italian society. Today, many deaf people affirm that sign language should be used in schools because it plays a vital role in permitting young people to pursue their academic programs. This stance is widely discussed in Italian circles, even though a great many deaf individuals retain the conviction that school should teach students to learn how to speak.

In seeking to understand the reasons behind these differing opinions, I have gathered information on the education of deaf students in Italy from the late 1700s to the present.

1780–1880

While consulting texts from this time period (e.g., Ferreri, 1883) I discovered two types of information:

❖ data concerning the special schools for deaf people—their location, organization, and financing; and

❖ explanations of the educational methods they adopted.

The oldest institute for deaf students was established in Rome in 1784, followed by a second school in Napoli in 1786. Table 1 lists the place and year of the establishment of institutes for deaf people (see also Facchini, 1985).

Toward the end of the nineteenth century a total of forty-nine institutes for deaf people existed, twenty-seven coeducational and the remainder either all male or all female. At Modena, for example, there was one institute for boys and another for girls. The number of pupils at each institute ranged from fifteen to 107.

The institutes were financed by state taxes and the provincial and communal governments, or by funds from nonprofit or charitable organizations. All were organized as private boarding schools, and only a few children could return to their homes in the evening. Together, all of the institutes were able to accommodate approximately 2,000 deaf students. In his 1883 publication about deaf people in Italy, Ferreri asked the gov-

This paper, originally presented at The Deaf Way, has been published in a slightly different form in *Looking Back: A Reader on the History of Deaf Communities and Their Sign Languages,* edited by Harlan Lane and Renate Fischer, 1993, Hamburg: SIGNUM-Press.

**TABLE 1: Founding Dates of Italian
Institutes for Deaf People**

City	Year of Establishment
1. Rome	1784
2. Napoli	1786
3. Genova	1802
4. Milano	1806
5. Torino	1816
6. Modena	1821
7. Parma	1826
8. Siena	1828
9. Cremona	1829
10. Verona	1829
11. Ferrara	1829
12. Palermo	1834
13. Rento	1842
14. Bologna	1850

ernment to construct other institutes so that the remainder of the 4,000 deaf children identified by the census could be served.

As for educational methods used, there is no written testimony from deaf people themselves, only from their educators. Lane (1984) notes that in the nineteenth century, French deaf people participated actively in the debate over educational methods and the use of sign language, while in Italy these discussions were nonexistent.

Although Ferreri's book lists works by deaf people toward the mid-nineteenth century—Paolo Basso, Giacomo Carbonieri, and Giuseppe Minoja—I have been unable to find them despite intensive efforts. Because the opinions of deaf people from that time period are important, I intend to continue my research.

Reviewing the available materials, it is obvious that from the end of the eighteenth century to around 1860, the method developed by the Abbé de l'Epée in France was highly respected by Italian educators (Lane, 1984; Facchini, 1981). For example, we have rediscovered, thanks to Facchini, an 1857 grammar book for deaf students by Ciro Marzullo (1857) that illustrates signs created intentionally to teach certain parts of speech (Figure 1).

Figure 1 indicates that so-called methodical signs were used as much by the Italian schools as by the French. It is not known whether this form of signing—comparable to the present "signed Italian" used in bimodal education—was used exclusively for the teaching of Italian grammar or for general class instruction of the various subjects. It would appear that the objective of educators was above all to teach the Italian language and, thereby teach other subjects. I am inclined to call this system a kind of "expanded Italian." The "Marzullo signs" appear to be designed to teach the rules of Italian grammar. These were not signs that could be used in general communication.

The author himself indicates the "fairest" method to be followed by the young teachers: "The teacher must know his pupil: study his gestures, his jokes, his mimicries, in short, the 'chironomia' (deaf hand language) used by the Student himself, and which will blend with the other through the aid of continual practice" (Marzullo, 1857).

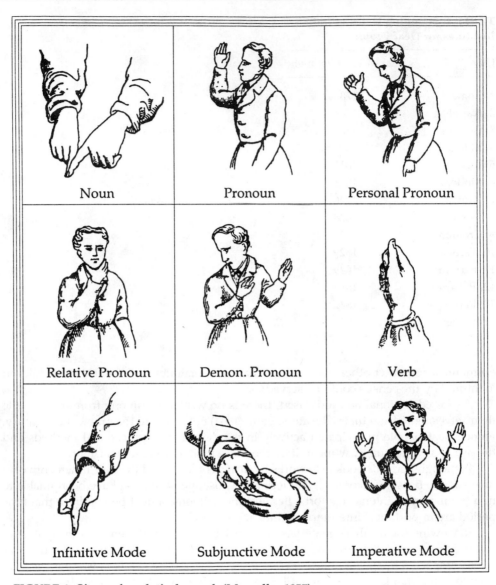

FIGURE 1: Signs of analytical speech (Marzullo, 1857).

In these limited words, it is difficult to understand what kind of sign language the pupil should have received. Remember, the student was attending the institute specifically to receive an education. How did the educators learn or understand the visual-gestural method? What kind of language could they learn from deaf students that would enable them to accomplish their instructional goals?

Today, we would expect the instructional methods used in the nineteenth century to yield limited results, because we are aware that systems of methodical signs are not conducive to successful language development (Supalla, 1989). But, on the other hand, these methods might have been successful because deaf Italians—very intelligent as they are—easily learn the rudiments of the Italian language and are capable of receiving effective instruction with the aid of speechreading and writing.

We should remember that the illiteracy level of the hearing population was very high at that time, so much so that deaf people who received any education at all were privileged. At any rate, the failure or success of their methods might have influenced educators to change their system. We know that after 1860, the influence of the German school became more and more pronounced, culminating in the triumph of oralism at the Milan Congress in 1880. Facchini (1985) very effectively describes the political, religious, and educational reasons that resulted in this choice.

I will not elaborate upon these reasons because in this paper I have chosen to authenticate the presence of sign language in education without expressing a personal judgment upon the methodologies used. I believe that research on sign language—its existence, its potential, the people who adopt it and in what contexts—is essential because, in my opinion, deaf people can develop verbal as well as gestural language, provided that they have the possibility of early and continuous "input" in their own language.

Linguistic ability can develop effectively in the areas of both comprehension and expression when one is spontaneously interested in one's native language. By native language I mean, for example, the Italian language (auditory-oral modality) or the Italian Sign Language (visual-gestural modality).

I do not consider signed Italian, which follows the grammatical order of the Italian language, as a native language. Because it is important that this point be clarified, I recommend the account by Sam Supalla (1989), who confronts much better than I this problem of a "false language."

1880–1960

The period of "pure oralism" began in Italy with the Milan Congress in 1880 and has continued to the present. I feel it is advisable to subdivide this period into two parts: from 1880 to 1960 and from 1960 to today. Regarding the first period, I have already stated that many educators who previously supported the use of sign language later adopted the idea of "giving first priority to the spoken word and to labial reading . . ." (Ferreri, 1893, p. 24).

During this same period, educators struggled to obtain from the Italian state recognition of the right of deaf people to receive education, a right that had already been granted in other countries. Ferreri claimed that "passing the buck," which is what the ministries were doing, was destined to continue for a long time because of financial difficulties in the area of education.

Although the Italian government deemed it had accomplished enough by establishing a school for deaf students in Milan, a government survey in 1887 affirmed that in certain areas of southern Italy only 4 percent of deaf people were educated, while in other areas, no deaf individual received any kind of formal instruction. At that time the census counted 15,300 deaf people, and the 2,300 attending the institutes were considered lucky to receive any instruction, even by the oral method.

It is not known if the visual-gestural communication used among the deaf students in the institutes during the late 1800s or early 1900s was permitted or prohibited. According to the oldest deaf people, the ban on sign language began to grow more strict after 1920. This ban could vary from one school to another. In some schools, signs were outlawed only during lesson hours, but the children could communicate with each other by signs outside class. In other institutes signs were totally forbidden either in class or during recreation time. Rules for boys and girls could vary in the same institute. Sometimes the Sisters enforced a stronger ban for the young girls, while the boys enjoyed a greater liberty in gestural communication.

Outside the academic classes, students trained to be apprentices in various trades: shoemaking, carpentry, or tailoring for the boys; sewing and embroidering for the girls. Sometimes the instructors were deaf adults who used signs. Even hearing instructors often used gestures during manual activities. Thus, within the fortress of oralism, sign communication retained its importance, even if limited to manual activities. But students were not permitted to bypass the "temple" of the spoken word by which they received their "true" instruction.

Instruction for deaf students became obligatory during the period from 1923 to 1928 with the reform instigated by Minister Gentile, who developed a kindergarten program for six- to eight-year-olds, and an obligatory elementary school for eight- to sixteen-year-olds. During those years, in addition to the three state and eighty private and religious institutes, special classes for deaf students were created within the public schools (Pizzuto, 1986).

It is important to mention that in the early 1900s secular and religious associations for deaf people in Italy had just begun to be established. These groups were united in 1932, clearly showing the need of deaf people to band together. It is thought that the birth of these associations is linked to deaf people's need to express in sign language all kinds of disciplines and cultures, a need that had long been frustrated in the institutes, as well as to their need for autonomy and independence.

It should be emphasized that the more literate deaf people made efforts to assist those deaf individuals who had just left school with a very modest education. It is a duty of the leaders of the associations to know spoken and written language well and to play a "mentor" role with respect to other deaf members.

The better-educated "speaking" deaf people were usually not born deaf. The time when one becomes deaf is closely linked to one's development of linguistic competence: Children who become deaf after age four or five have already acquired a language base. The later one becomes deaf, the easier re-education will be. The task of the educators, then, consists of "re-education," a term inappropriate if used with respect to children born deaf or having become deaf before age two. If they have not received linguistic input by that time, it will not be a question of re-education, but only of education, to provide them with the linguistic competence they do not yet possess. Unfortunately, this modern information was not well known until recently. As a result, many deaf children living in the country, far from urban centers, only began their "re-education" at the age of six or later.

The unification of deaf associations in the 1930s marked the birth of the E.N.S. (National Institute for the Deaf). After the Second World War, thanks to the determination of Mr. A. Magarotto, the E.N.S. began to organize, among other programs, professional courses in areas such as bookbinding and printing. Because some activities related to printing required a good knowledge of the written language, such programs demonstrated that deaf people were capable of learning professions requiring a higher level of education. To qualify for these professional courses, the students often had to take supplementary studies, also organized by the E.N.S., because their educational level did not always correspond to that needed for the elementary school diploma.

Because the objective was to combine professional competence with manual skills, sign language was not prohibited. Moreover, there were deaf teachers, such as Magarotto himself. These courses were recognized by the state and were taken by boys who had attended the institutes and other special classes where apprenticeships for manual trades were nearly nonexistent.

Beginning around 1957, the E.N.S. organized a number of secondary schools for deaf students. In so doing, the association wished to show that, contrary to the opinion of educators, deaf students could pursue studies beyond the basic academic level offered in the institutes or special classes. Deaf people could not only just survive, but could pursue further education and training.

The structures established by the E.N.S. also provided the possibility of using sign language in teaching, a form of communication that, despite the efforts of oralist educators, seems impossible to deny to deaf people.

1960–1988

Deaf students' attendance at secondary schools only became obligatory with the academic reform of 1962, which forced the institutes to form special classes.

Statistics around that time showed that the academic situation of deaf people was not the best. A national census carried out in 1955 indicated an illiteracy rate among the deaf population of 53 percent, compared with 8.4 percent of the Italian population in general (ISTAT, 1965; Pigliacampo, 1982; Pizzuto, 1986). Doubtless, we should question by what method the data were determined and the definition of the term "illiterate."

In any case, during the period 1950–1970, while new schools were established for deaf students and the world of specialized medicine was becoming interested in deaf students, educational methods still tended to change slowly. Teachers had no special education to prepare them to work with deaf people, and often they did not manage to adapt to new teaching methods or technologies.

Overall, schools for deaf students were not capable of adapting to the changes that were occurring in Italian society during that time. Deaf children received a very low level of education compared with their potential and abilities.

My personal involvement dates back to these years and concerns every kind of school. I attended kindergarten with hearing children and later with deaf students. I spent two years in an elementary school in an institute for deaf students and then attended a special class for deaf students within a school for hearing children. Finally, I went to a secondary school and an art high school for hearing students. I still feel very unhappy with respect to my stay at the institute: The programs there were restricted in comparison with those developed in the special classes, although the methods and preparation of the teachers were nearly identical. However, I could speak in sign language inside the classroom at the institute, whereas in the special class, sign language was prohibited, and people there dubbed me "monkey." As for the elementary and high schools with the hearing students, I never encountered any difficulties except in written Italian; my oral grades were good. Although I was the only deaf student in the class, I encountered no problems at all with my fellow students; on the contrary, I tutored them in geometric design, for pay!

In 1977, Law 517 declared that every disabled child, including deaf children, could attend the same schools as hearing children. Through this resolution, Italian society wished to acknowledge the right of disabled people to an education and to socialization by granting them complete equality with all other citizens. What did this law signify for deaf children? Families of deaf children, both then and today, can choose between the institutes and the schools for hearing students. The special classes have been abolished.

At the age of three, a deaf child can attend kindergarten, which is optional. Elementary school (six to ten years) and secondary school (eleven to thirteen years) are obligatory and equal for all. Once secondary school is completed, deaf children can enroll, if they wish, in high school and later in a university. The state guarantees deaf children a teacher's aide for several hours a week for the duration of the obligatory academic period. People are beginning to discuss the benefits of having this support in the high school as well. There are now fewer elementary and secondary schools—both public and private—for deaf students because families prefer to send their children to regular schools. But, there are three professional schools of higher education for deaf students located in Torino, Padova, and Rome. These schools were established by E.N.S. and are now state-owned.

Sign language is used only in the schools for deaf students, both private and state-owned. Deaf students who attend hearing schools are given no opportunity to learn sign language or to know other deaf people.

It is not my intention to discuss the results of this educational system; they have already been analyzed by teachers, doctors, audiologists, parents, and recently, by deaf people themselves.

Because both deaf children and teaching personnel are intelligent, Law 517 should realize its full potential. I am in favor of children attending a local school, because that will give them an opportunity to remain at home. But it must be remembered that the family circle requires communication. In a hearing environment, this communication will always be verbal, which represents a true penalty for the deaf person who must communicate with hearing people through speech alone.

Linguistic, psychological, and sociological research in various countries and recently in Italy has demonstrated that sign language is very important for deaf people in developing linguistic competence and acquiring a true identity. Research at the C.N.R. (National Research Center) over the past several years (Rampelli, 1986; Casselli and Rampelli, 1988) shows that the linguistic competence (in Italian and sign language) of deaf children, at both residential schools and schools with hearing students, is inferior to the linguistic competence of their hearing schoolmates. This shortcoming, which could have serious consequences for the intellect and the personality, was completely foreseeable. There was and always will be among deaf people a need to challenge their own abilities and competence, a need that cannot be satisfied today at their present level of socialization.

Conclusion

What I have related is the product of my personal experience and research on historical documents, and testimonies gathered from Italian deaf people. Because of the importance of the education of deaf people, I should hope that the debate and exchange of information will continue. There must be a close collaboration between family and teachers in order for deaf children to receive a good education.

As I noted earlier, even among deaf people there are totally divergent opinions. One may affirm that sign language usage in school is indispensable for the optimum development of potential and intelligence in the deaf child. Another may believe that the school should teach the child to speak well in order to know written and spoken Italian perfectly. In spite of these differences, it seems to me that all are pursuing the same goal: to provide deaf children with a very high level of education, sometimes through sign language, at other times by teaching them spoken language as a second language.

References

Caselli, M. C., and L. Pagliari Rampelli. 1989. "Il Bambino Sordo Nella Scuola Materna: Interazione e Competenza Linguistica." *Età Evolutiva* 34: 51–62.

Facchini, G. M. 1981. "Riflessioni Storiche sul Metodo Orale e il Linguaggio dei Segni in Italia." In *I Segni come Parole*, ed. V. Volterra. Torino: Boringhieri.

Facchini, G. M. 1985. "An Historical Reconstruction of Events Leading to the Congress of Milan in 1880." In *Proceedings of the Third International Symposium on Signed Language Research*, ed. W. Stokoe and V. Volterra. SLR 1983. Silver Spring: Linstok Press and Rome: I.P. CNR. pp. 356–362.

Ferreri, G. 1883. *L'Educazione dei Sordomuti in Italia.* Siena: Tip. Edit. S. Bernardino.

Ferreri, G. 1898. "I Sordomuti e l'Istruzione Obbligatoria." In *Estratto dagli atti del Primo Congresso di Beneficenza dei Sordomuti.* Milano: Typografia Pulzato & Giani. pp.1–23.

I.S.T.A.T. (Istituto Centrale di Statistica). 1965. Annuario Statistico dell'Istruzione Italiana. Vols. 15 and 16.

Lane, H. 1984. *When the Mind Hears. A History of the Deaf.* New York: Random House.

Marzullo, C. 1857. La Grammatica dei les Sordo-Muti. Palermo: Tipografia di Michele Amenta.

Pagliari Rampelli, L. 1986. "Il Bambino Sordo a Scuola: Interazione e Didattica." Rapporto Tecnico, Roma: Istituto di Psicologia—CNR.

Pigliacampo, R. 1962. *Indagine Medico-Socio-Culturale su Soggetti Affetti da Sordomutismo e Sitazione dell'Inserimento dei Sordi Gravi Nella Scuola Ordinaria.* Recanati: USL 14.

Pizzuto, E. 1986. *Gallaudet Encyclopedia of Deaf People and Deafness,* ed. J. Van Cleve. New York: McGraw-Hill Books. pp. 105–109.

Supalla, Sam. 1989. "Equality in Educational Opportunities: The Deaf Version." Paper presented at The Deaf Way, Gallaudet University, Washington, DC, 9–14 July 1989.

Written and Unwritten History of a Residential School for the Deaf in Rome, Italy

PAOLA PINNA, LAURA PAGLIARI RAMPELLI, PAOLO ROSSINI, AND VIRGINIA VOLTERRA

In 1988, when we received the first announcement of The Deaf Way, we decided to provide a contribution on the history and culture of the deaf people of Rome—a reconstruction of the history of a residential school for deaf students there. Residential schools are places where deaf people, especially in the past, spent many years of their childhood and adolescence, far away from their families; where many of them had their first opportunity to meet other deaf people; where they learned sign language and received an education; and where they began friendships and relationships that would last their entire lives.

In Rome there were, and still are, many schools for deaf students, each with different traditions and each located in a different part of the city. For this paper, we chose the oldest school—the State Residential School of the Deaf of Via Nomentana. The school, which has occupied its present location in Via Nomentana since 1889, was founded in 1784 by the Abbé Tommaso Silvestri, a disciple of the Abbé de l'Epée.

This paper draws on both "official" sources (mostly documents located in the library and archives of the school) and interviews with deaf people who attended the school at different periods. Using the written documents found in the school's archives, it was possible to reconstruct the history of the school with regard to its founder and his successors and to the administrative, organizational, and educational methods used at the school. The written records, in such forms as books, papers, and journal articles, covered the time period from the end of the eighteenth century to the present. As expected, the history of the school was closely related to and influenced by the historical events of this period.

The written references for this paper consist of works by Silvestri (1785), Donnino

The authors wish to thank Serena Corazza for her suggestions and criticism, Elizabeth Bates and Elena Pizzuto for their great help with the English version of this paper, and all the people we interviewed for their patience and collaboration. We also thank the director of the State Residential School of the Deaf of Via Nomentana for making available the school's written records.

Versions of this paper were published in *Sign Language Studies*, volume 67 (summer, 1990) and in *Looking Back: A Reader on the History of Deaf Communities and Their Sign Languages*, edited by Harlan Lane and Renate Fischer, 1993, Hamburg: SIGNUM-Press.

**TABLE 1: Time Period Covered by
Biographical Research**

Initials of Person Interviewed	Year Entered School	Year Left School
I.R.*	1897	1915
E.V.	1900	1916
A.P.	1911	1917
M.M.	1916	1926
C.V.	1927	1932
M.R.*	1927	1936
G.F.	1937	1943
L.C.	1944	1953
P.P.	1953	1958
P.R.*	1953	1964
R.B.	1953	1962
G.B.	1960	1970

*These people were from the same family.

(1889), Ferreri (1893), Lazzarotti (1927), Boggi-Bosi (1939), Leproux (1941), Scala (1965), Facchini (1981, 1983), and Lane (1984). Some of these are writers on the history of deaf education; others (Silvestri, Donnino, Lazzarotti, and Scala) were teachers or directors at the school.

The written records of the school are often very detailed, but they were always written by hearing people for official purposes and with a formal style, and provide no information about the everyday life, thoughts, or feelings of deaf children attending the school. To collect this second type of information, we conducted interviews with deaf people who had attended the school at various times from the early 1900s to the present.

To obtain the oral history, a list of questions was prepared to be used with each person interviewed. Our goal was to obtain comparable information from deaf people who attended the school at different times, covering the entire period from 1900 to the present. To date, twelve biographies have been collected using this method, covering the period 1897–1970 (see Table 1).

Three of the interviews were conducted with the children (one who is deaf and two who are hearing and work as Italian Sign Language interpreters) of former students who are now dead. All of the interviews were conducted in Italian Sign Language (LIS). Half were videotaped and then transcribed into Italian, while the other half were written down through detailed notes taken during the interviews. The original transcripts are available in Italian for anyone interested in reading them. The existence of these interviews will ensure that the memories of deaf people from this century are not lost, as those of previous generations have been.

Finally, the people being interviewed were asked for any family records they could find (diaries, school albums, photographs). Interestingly, although many did bring photographs, none of the families kept diaries or written material from their school.

The Written History of the Via Nomentana School

Around the year 1782, Pasquale Di Pietro, a wealthy Roman lawyer well known for his charitable acts, decided that he wanted to help the deaf people of his city. At that time Roman deaf children received no public education. To remedy this situation, Di Pietro sent the Abbé Tommaso Silvestri to Paris to learn from the Abbé de l'Epée his method for instructing deaf students. Six months later Silvestri returned to Rome, and early in 1784 he started his school, with eight deaf students, in the home of his patron, Di Pietro. The school met with great success, and various disciples came from Napoli, Malta, Modena, and other cities to learn Silvestri's method. Silvestri continued teaching for five years, until his death in 1789.

Silvestri described his teaching method in a work entitled *Maniera di far Parlare e di Istruire Speditamente i Sordi e Muti di Nascita* ("A quick method for teaching speech and instructing those who are deaf and mute from birth"). Only part of this manuscript has been found.

In one of the pages, Silvestri clearly states that he has adopted the method he learned from de l'Epée: teaching deaf people through the use of "methodical signs." From his writings it appears that he also taught his pupils articulation and lipreading with remarkable success, but he always kept signs as the main form of communication. As he states:

> Our aim in Rome is not only to give back speech to these poor people, but also to improve their most interesting part, that is, their intelligence. Toward this end I use very simple natural means that do not violate the natural strength of the deaf-mute, but rather favor that very same manner of communication with which he is well acquainted, derived from the very nature of this terrible infirmity, rendering him agile and at ease. By the means of signs every deaf-mute fully expresses his wishes and needs; these signs have thus been adopted by the school for his education, with certain systematic corrections. They are systematically subjected to grammatical ordering, giving verbs their correct tenses, moods, persons, numbers, etc. To nouns in turn, we add cases and genders where convenient. Signs are distinguished according to their qualities as substantives, adjectives, and other aspects of their character, energy and meaning; in short, to clarify the activity and use of each part of speech, exposing its spirit and feeling, arriving step by step at the ability to compose. And in order, finally, to restore him completely to society, the school does not neglect to instruct him also in the understanding of movements of the lips and the thoughts behind them, permitting him to give the right answers immediately, with no help other than the living voice. (Silvestri, 1785)

After Silvestri died, Pasquale Di Pietro entrusted the Abbé Mariani with the direction of the school. Mariani had no experience in instructing deaf students and learned the method used by his predecessor by reading Silvestri's writings and asking the deaf pupils themselves about the way they had been taught. He taught in the school for forty-two years (until 1832), an indication that he must have learned the method quite well. All of Mariani's successors continued to use the same teaching method until approximately the time of the Milan Congress (1880), when the official educational policy of the school changed and a strict oral method was adopted. Interestingly, it seems that the school was not very actively involved in spreading the oralist philosophy: The school teachers from Rome are not mentioned in the proceedings of the oralist meetings before and after Milan. However, from the time of the Milan Congress on, all people writing about the school tend to present Silvestri as a pioneer of the oral method, stressing his inclination toward teaching deaf people to speak and forgetting that he did so through the use of methodical signs.

At the beginning of the twentieth century the school, which had been managed by a religious order, passed into secular hands, with only the girls' section remaining under the control of nuns. In its history, the school has had seventeen directors (eleven of whom, indicated in the following list by *, belonged to religious orders): Silvestri* (1784–1789), Mariani* (1789–1832), Gioazzini* (1832–1849), Ralli* (temporary), Morani* (1849–1865), Muti* (1865–1879), Sironi* (1879–date unknown), Procida* (dates unknown), Donnino* (date unknown–1901), Tamburrini* (1901–1904), Maggioni (1904–1905), Fabbri* (1905–1910), Lazzerotti (1910–1936), Scala (1936–1939), Gaddi (1939–1952), Scuri (1952–1970), and Cifariello (1971–present). That one of the most recent directors, Decio Scuri, was a phoniatrician, is an indication of the progressive "medicalization" of deaf education. Scuri was also one of the directors who more strongly advocated the primacy of the oral method. What this really means in terms of educational policy and sign language status inside the school can be seen more clearly in the biographical interviews.

The Di Pietro family continued to provide most of the school's funding until 1827, when it became an "opera pia," or charitable institution, under the administrative control of the Papal States. Pope Gregorio XVI transformed the school into a residential institution (boarding school) in 1838. For special occasions, following the example of other institutions, the school presented public demonstrations, which were highly acclaimed. Many cardinals and important prelates, including Popes, attended these demonstrations.

Apart from a brief period during the Roman Republic (1849), the school continued to be financed by the Papal State until 1870, when the various states were unified and Rome became capital of the kingdom of Italy. As a royal institution, the school fell under the control of the Ministry of Public Instruction, and student boarding was financed by the local administration (provincia). From this period on, the protection of the school was undertaken by the royal family of Savoia, and on various occasions the Queen herself and other dignitaries visited the school. After World War II, all royal institutions became state institutions, but their administrative organization remained more or less the same.

Over the past 200 years, the number of students has varied considerably, from the eight pupils of Silvestri to more than 200 enrolled in 1965. Today there are only seventeen children attending the school. This decrease in enrollment is owing to a 1977 law that allows deaf children to be mainstreamed in normal classes with hearing peers. Figure 1 shows the number of male and female students enrolled at various times during the school's history.

The school's location has also changed many times, from the home of its patron, Di Pietro in 1784 to the present building in Via Nomentana in 1889.

The Unwritten History

Our biographical interviews with deaf former students provided a great deal of information about life at the school. After some initial hesitation, the people interviewed were very happy to answer questions, and they provided many useful anecdotes. Only a direct viewing of the videotapes or close reading of the interview transcripts can give

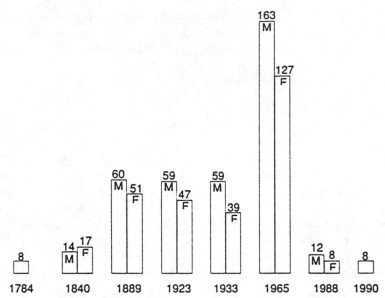

FIGURE 1: A sampling of the number of male (M) and female (F) students enrolled at Via Nomentana.

a faithful and complete report of all the information gathered, but the following pages summarize some of the stories about the life children led inside the institution, the type of communication they used with other children and adults, and their personal feelings and memories about the school.

From 1900 until 1950, children entered the institution at six to eight years of age and remained there for about ten years. Thus, when they left they were seventeen to twenty years old. The students went home only during summer holidays, and some never returned home, attending summer camps instead. Relatives could visit the school at Christmas and Easter and on Sunday mornings if they lived in Rome or its surrounding areas. Only a few children, whose families lived near the school, were able to go home on Sundays. Children at the boarding school were supervised by assistants—laymen for boys and nuns for girls. All of these caretakers were hearing people.

Life was strictly regimented: Up at 7:00; breakfast and classes from 8:30 to noon; lunch until 1:00, followed by play time. In the afternoon from 3:00 to 6:00, the younger children played and did homework, while the older children learned a trade in one of the workshops. Dinner was served at 7:00 p.m., and then the children had about an hour for visiting with each other before going to bed (in large dormitories) at 9:00.

Girls, who were strictly separated from the boys, attended Mass every morning and said the Rosary every evening. On Sunday everyone went to church, and some students received visits from their relatives. Everyone took a walk on Sunday afternoon.

These rules changed somewhat after 1950, when the nursery school was opened and children were admitted at the age of four. Still, only a very few pupils were allowed to attend the school as day-boarders, staying from 8:00 a.m. to 7:00 p.m. After 1950, children could go to the cinema on Sunday, and many more began to return home during holidays, unless prohibited by distance.

Classes began at 8:30 a.m. for boys and at 9:00 a.m. for girls. The boys had lay teachers, both men and women, while the girls received their education entirely from nuns. After 1950, when the nursery school was founded, nuns cared for the smaller boys and girls together.

Although the pupils remained at the school for many years, they went no further than the fourth elementary grade, and at most they were able to obtain only an elementary school diploma upon "graduation." After 1970, the school experimented with secondary education for a short period of time.

All of the former students interviewed remember being given exercises in articulation, followed by the teaching of such subjects as writing, mathematics, and history. Many of those interviewed commented that "they forced us to study verbs a lot." Reeducation with earphones had been tried with some of the pupils, but only for a short time. With very few exceptions, these efforts apparently had negative results. When the pupils made mistakes, some of the stricter teachers spanked their hands with a stick or pulled their ears. We must remember, though, that such forms of discipline were once quite common.

Even after fifty years, the former students could easily remember their teachers' names (both Italian and sign-names), along with their temperaments (strict or patient). The deaf students remembered whether their teachers were bad or good, and above all, whether they were lazy or attentive in their work. In every case, classroom teachers were hearing.

In the afternoon, the students went to workshops taught by expert craftsmen to learn trades. The boys studied to become shoemakers, tailors, bookbinders, carpenters, and during certain periods, printers and upholsterers. The girls learned dressmaking, embroidery, mending, and knitting. The teachers of these manual trades included both hearing and deaf people. There were at least three deaf teachers, one of whom taught drawing, one shoemaking, and one knitting. Two of these deaf teachers (the shoemaker and the knitting instructor) had been students at the school years before. All of the people interviewed expressed pleasure and pride in having learned a profession, but they were much less sure of their academic education.

Means of Communication

All the children communicated among themselves with signs, a form of communication they usually learned after entering the institute. Even the children with deaf parents who already signed in their families learned to use the particular signs of the Via Nomentana school, signs that were different in many cases from those they used at home. For example, one interviewee, P.R., and his brother attended two different deaf schools in Rome (Via Nomentana and Gualandi). P.R. remembers very clearly the different signs that he and his brother used, signs that in turn differed from the ones they both used at home with their parents. Examples include the signs for numbers and the signs PAPA (daddy), DONNA (woman), LAVORO (work), VECCHIO (old man), BAMBINA (girl), and COME-SI-CHIAMA (what is your name?).

Some school signs are still used by the deaf children attending the school today, although they are no longer used outside the institution because they look "old fashioned." Examples include the signs MILANO (Milan), ZIO (uncle), ESAME (exam), and UOMO (man).

All of the children had sign-names, usually created at the school. For example, A.P. had the sign-name "monkey" because he was extraordinarily quick at climbing. Even when a child (coming from a deaf family) arrived with a sign-name, he or she was often given another at the school. P.R., for example, received the sign-name of a cousin who was just leaving the school when he entered. The teachers, assistants, nuns, and the director each had a sign-name that always remained the same, passing from one generation of students to another.

In the classroom, students were forced to communicate orally, but when something was not clear, they were permitted to switch to signs. The students could sign freely outside the classroom, during playtime, in the workshops, and in the dormitory. The adults all knew some form of gestural communication, and some assistants and nuns were particularly good at it. It is clear that the instructors in the manual activities, some of whom were deaf, used sign a great deal.

Sign communication was accepted and tolerated at Via Nomentana much more than at other institutions, according to several people who compared their situation at Via Nomentana with that of friends or relatives attending other schools. In particular, P.P., who transferred to Via Nomentana from the Tarra school in Milan, confirmed that signs were used much less there. Of all the directors, only the phoniatrician Scuri is remembered as being openly hostile to sign ("He was very strict, he wanted everyone to speak . . . .").

During playtime or in the evening before going to bed, the older children told the younger ones about events they had seen or learned about from others. Usually the assistants studied while the children played dominoes, draughts, or chess. Sometimes a schoolmate told them about a movie, e.g., *Tom the Cowboy or Tex*) they had seen, while others invented stories. One man, a former day-boarder and the child of deaf parents, remembered school friends asking about news "from the outside," information he may have gathered from his father or his friends outside of school. One woman interviewed told about "a nun who told us what the radio was saying about the story of San Francisco—she spoke and signed together."

Anecdotes

It is difficult to choose among the various anecdotes provided by the deaf informants. Some are amusing and others rather sad, but all are still vivid in the former students' minds. Here are few of those memories:

❖ The long wait for King Victor Emmanuel, who never did arrive, but sent in his place a representative who gave every child a box of chocolates.

❖ The first student protest, for better food and heat, which had good results.

❖ The screening of a film on loan to the school by the House of Savoia, with boys and girls trying to arrange dates and exchange tickets despite a barrier between the sexes consisting of a curtain and a long line of nuns.

❖ The first theatrical recital, with comic scenes, presented to the entire school and guests invited from outside the school.

❖ Long walks toward Montesacro, a busy quarter that was still countryside in the early 1900s.

❖ Fistfights with schoolmates and arguments with the director, who called in a deaf adult to serve as referee.

❖ Tales, part reality and part imagination, of escapes from the dormitory and pirate raids into a giant attic.

❖ In general, a great sense of liberation when school was finally over, accompanied by profound sadness at the loss of deaf schoolmates.

Conclusion

We do not consider this historical research concluded—more work still needs to be done. But some interesting points have emerged from both the written and oral records, and above all, from a comparison between the two.

In many respects, the two sources concur, illustrating, for instance, the rigid separation between males and females, the opportunity to learn a manual skill, and so on. But there are other respects in which the two sources are complementary. Above all, we hear about signs. Signs were officially accepted and used continuously throughout the nineteenth century in the education of deaf students in reading, writing, and lipreading. Obviously, for those students who were predisposed to it, articulation was taught as well. But it was only after the Congress of Milan that the oral method was imposed by various directors of the institution.

Despite the use of the oral method, gestures (or—better—sign language) continued to play an important, even crucial, role in the students' lives and education. In contrast with other institutions, signs were never really banned at Via Nomentana. Children signed in the courtyards, dormitories, workshops, and even in the classroom, although there students were permitted recourse to sign only to clarify something presented orally they did not understand. Everyone—the students, the teachers, the assistants—knew sign; some knew more, some less. Furthermore, the signs of Via Nomentana have a character of their own that has been passed on from one generation of student to another. None of this is mentioned in the written records, however. The "official" account does not correspond in this case to the facts as remembered by the students.

These facts force us to confront the current situation: Even though the teaching methods have remained virtually unchanged in the last forty years, the number of students has decreased sharply, and their scholastic level has decreased notably as well. The present teachers and educators are discouraged, attributing this decline to the fact that the great majority of deaf children are now mainstreamed with hearing children, leaving the institute with only those children who are "most difficult" or "less gifted."

Now, with fewer than twenty students attending the school, we think that something else is missing: the system of communication and transmission of culture that former students benefitted from through signing within a much larger deaf community. The rich stimulation provided by the deaf community fostered their cognitive and linguistic development and facilitated the academic process, even though these contributions were never recognized explicitly after the Congress of Milan.

It is no accident that in the last few years one hears of the need for a "gestural method," "bilingual education," or a "bimodal method." At Via Nomentana, as at other institutions for deaf children, a bilingual community once existed in full force, albeit without official recognition. Given all that we know today, there is, of course, no way to justify a return to practices that separated children for many years from their families and from the rest of society. But the institute at Via Nomentana is now moving in new directions that may remedy the loss of community suffered by deaf students in the past ten years. On the one hand, the school is experimenting with a project that brings mainstreamed deaf children back to Via Nomentana for special training in the use of new computer technologies. On the other hand, small groups of deaf adults have begun to organize activities within the school, using the institute as a meeting place for theater groups and a chess association. These efforts may result in the re-creation of a bilingual community that can maintain and transmit the language, culture, and traditions of deaf people and facilitate the educational process for which the school was founded more than 200 years ago.

References

Boggi-Bosi, G. 1939. *Il Regio Istituto de Sordomuti: Dall-ospizio di Termini all Sede di Via Nomentana (1838–1939)*. Roma: Tipografia del Giannicolo.

Donnino, C. 1889. *L'Arte di far Parlare i Sordomuti dalla Nascita & l'Abate Tommaso Silvestri-Memorie*. Roma: Tipi di Mario Armani.

Facchini, M. 1981. "Riflessioni Storiche sul Metodo Orale eil Linguaggio dei Segni in Italia." In *I Segni come Parole*, ed. V. Volterra. Torino: Boringhieri.

Facchini, M. 1983. *Commenti al Congresso di Milano del 1880*. Unpublished manuscript.

Ferreri. 1893. *L'Educazione dei Sordomuti in Italia*. Siena: Tipi Edit. S. Bernardino.

Lane, H. 1984. *When the Mind Hears*. New York: Random House.

Leproux, O. 1941. *Studio sulla Vita Onirica dei Sordomuti*. Rapporto dell'Istituto di Psicologia del CNR.

Lazzerotti, C. 1927. *Disegno Storico del Regio Istituto de Sordomuti in Roma*. Roma: Tipografia nel R. Ist. Sordomuti.

Scala, M. 1965–66. "L'Evoluzione Storica dell'Istituto Statale de Sordomuti in Roma." Estratto da *Udito—Voce—Parola*. Fasc. 1, 2e, 3, 4e. Padova.

Silvestri, T. 1785. *Maniera di far Parlare e di Istruire Speditamente i Sordi e Muti di Nascita*. Unpublished manuscript.

Three Nineteenth-Century Spanish Teachers of the Deaf

SUSAN PLANN

The year 1805 marked the opening in Madrid of the Royal School for Deaf-Mutes, the first official school for deaf students in Spain. In this enterprise, three teachers of deaf students were brought together: José Miguel Alea, Tiburcio Hernández, and Roberto Prádez.

Spain was no stranger to the teaching of deaf children, for it was there that such teaching originated. In antiquity and during the Middle Ages, it had been "common knowledge" that deaf people were uneducable, and this belief went largely unchallenged until the mid-sixteenth century, when Pedro Ponce de León, a Benedictine monk, first taught the deaf sons and daughters of the Spanish nobility. During the first decades of the seventeenth century, Manuel Ramírez de Carrión also taught the deaf children of the Spanish nobility, and another Spaniard, Pedro de Castro, carried the teaching of deaf students to Italy. In 1620 Juan Pablo Bonet published the first book on how to teach deaf people.

The teaching of deaf students was gradually extended throughout Europe, and in the 1760s France's Abbé de l'Epée founded the first public school for deaf children. But in Spain, the land of its birth, education of deaf students languished until nearly the nineteenth century, when the first official school was established.

Three pivotal figures of this era are José Miguel Alea, Tiburcio Hernández, and Roberto Prádez.

The Abbot José Miguel Alea was born in Asturias in 1758 and spent his boyhood at the side of the bishop of Orense. In Santiago de Compostela he studied literature and was ordained a member of the clergy. In 1788 Alea went to Madrid, where he became a librarian in the royal libraries. During this period, Alea translated works on a wide range of topics, including philosophy, history, religion, and literature. His personal predilection, however, was for the philosophy of language and, in particular, philosophical grammar (a forerunner of today's transformational grammar).

In 1795 Alea chanced to meet Gregorio Santa Fe, a deaf youth from Aragón who had been educated by a mysterious Jesuit, Diego Vidal. This fortuitous encounter sparked Alea's interest in deaf people and moved him to write a letter to the newspaper, arguing for public education of deaf people in Spain. "The art of teaching the deaf and mute to speak," Alea concluded, "is a matter worthy of occupying the pen of an honest man." Although at this point his interest was purely intellectual, in the coming years, the education of deaf people came to occupy much more than just Alea's pen.

In 1803 Alea became a member of Madrid's Royal Economic Society of Friends of the Country. (The Economic Society, whose motto was "Socorre enseñando" (Help by teaching"), had numerous objectives, foremost of which was Spain's industrial and scientific progress.) The Society was in the process of establishing Spain's first official school for deaf students. Alea was appointed to the governing board and put in charge of the theoretical aspects of the education of deaf students and of overseeing their teaching. He also was responsible for writing the necessary books for their instruction and translating into Spanish those books published abroad that were deemed useful to the school.

At about this same time, Tiburcio Hernández also joined the Economic Society and was appointed to the governing board of the school for deaf students. Hernández was born in Alcalá de Henares in 1772 and attended the university there before becoming a lawyer to the Royal Council and reporter of the Sala de Alcaldes.

Alea and Hernández contrasted sharply in both intellectual orientation and personal style. Alea was a man of the Church, a scholar of the classics and the European Enlightenment. Tiburcio Hernández was a lawyer, a married man, the father of two children, and a patriot who would come to reject the French method of educating deaf students in favor of the Spanish tradition. Alea's writings revealed an overriding concern for reason, fairness, and diplomacy. Indeed, he once suggested the desirability of establishing "the laws, circumstances, and manner with which criticism should be used . . . in each science and art" (1800). Hernández, who cared more for straight talk than for diplomacy, boasted that his "never prostituted pen will tell the truth in energetic tones" (Archives). As we shall see, the two men also differed markedly in their views about deaf people.

In 1805 Roberto Prádez also approached the Economic Society. Prádez was born in Zaragoza in 1772. His father, Pedro Prádez, had been born in France. His mother, María Gautier, was most likely also of French origin, judging from her name.

Deaf from birth, Prádez was educated by his mother, who taught him to read and write. Prádez communicated easily with hearing people by writing or using the manual alphabet. Although his speech was unintelligible, he was highly skilled at lipreading.

We can only guess how Prádez's mother learned the art of teaching her deaf son and what method she used. If, however, it is fair to judge a teacher by her student's achievements, María Gautier was surely one of the most successful teachers of deaf children, because her son went on to become an award-winning artist and a teacher who educated many, many deaf students over a period of more than thirty years.

Although born to a distinguished family, Prádez was orphaned and left destitute at an early age. At sixteen, he enrolled at the Royal Academy of Fine Arts of San Carlos in Valencia, where he studied engraving for seven years. In 1797 he went to Madrid, where he enrolled at the Royal Academy of Fine Arts of San Fernando and received a pension from the king. In 1798 Prádez entered a contest sponsored by the Academy of Fine Arts. For his engraving he was awarded first prize, a gold coin that he accepted on bended knee from the crown prince himself.

Prádez's life's work, however, was not as an engraver but, rather, as a teacher of deaf students. In 1805 he applied to teach reading, writing, and drawing at the newly established school for deaf students in Madrid. Reading and writing were already being taught, but the governing board agreed to hire him to teach drawing. That Prádez himself was deaf was recognized as a distinct advantage. When the Economic Society was unable to obtain funds to pay the new art teacher, Prádez was undaunted. His offer to teach the children for free was gratefully accepted, and the Economic Society celebrated the collaboration of this remarkable deaf man. And so began the career of Spain's first deaf teacher of deaf people.

Thus the three teachers—José Miguel Alea, Tiburcio Hernández and Roberto Prádez —were brought together during the early years of the nineteenth century at Madrid's

Royal School for Deaf-mutes, Alea and Hernández as members of the governing board and Prádez as an instructor.

At about this same time, Alea undertook the teaching of four deaf children, whom he lodged at his home. His motives were not solely philanthropic: This was an experiment designed to advance knowledge of the philosophy of language. For fifteen months Alea taught his charges. Then he published the conclusions of his experiment: Deaf children are as capable of generalizing and forming abstract ideas as are their hearing counterparts (1803).

Although Alea's point seems obvious to us now, it was not at all clear to many philosophers of his day. Centuries earlier, it had also not been clear to Aristotle, who believed deaf people incapable of thought. Ever an advocate of empirical observation, Alea chided Aristotle for this assertion, calling it "a hasty judgment he doubtlessly would not have made had he lived just three days with any deaf person" (1803). "Philosophy," admonished Alea, "is nothing without facts" (1803).

In a subsequent article (1805), Alea methodically refuted the claims of Ramón Campos' book *El Don de la Palabra (The Gift of Speech)*. Alea argued that deaf people could be instructed through sign language; moreover, even before receiving formal instruction, deaf people are not without language, for they have their signs, and with them "express grandly a multitude of ideas of various kinds" (1805). The "organization of man" (the innate language capacity), according to Alea, is as suited to the sign language of deaf people as it is to spoken language. Given time and appropriate circumstances, sign language could become as subtle and complex as any spoken language. Experience, and the principles of metaphysics, refuted Campos' claim that deaf people are incapable of abstract thought.

Clearly, Alea held deaf people in high regard: They were capable of abstract thought even before receiving formal instruction; they could be taught just as hearing children could; and their sign language was as appropriate for the expression of thought as was oral language.

In 1807 Alea published his translation of l'Abbé Sicard's manual for teaching deaf students through signs, for use in the Madrid schools. By now Alea had first-hand knowledge of Sicard's method, having personally tested it on a deaf child. During these years, the French manual approach held sway at the school for the deaf in Madrid. Although some speech was taught, it was not emphasized: Speech, to Alea, was "an embellishment, more appropriate for surprising and fascinating the crowd, than useful to the deaf" (Archives).

The French occupation of Spain (1808–1814) spelled the end of business as usual at the Royal School for Deafmutes. During the years of the War of Independence, José Miguel Alea collaborated openly with the French and was appointed royal archivist. Alea was named headmaster of the school, and the instruction of the deaf students there was officially in his hands. Records suggest, however, that Roberto Prádez may in fact have been doing much of the teaching. (In addition to art, Prádez on occasion taught reading, writing, and arithmetic.)

During the French occupation, Tiburcio Hernández consolidated his power at the Economic Society. Because the political situation precluded attending public gatherings or going out at night, Hernández turned to ruminating about deaf education. The result was his *Plan de enseñar a los sordo-mudos el idioma español* ("Plan to teach deaf-mutes the Spanish language"). Although Alea opposed Hernández's plan, the Society eventually adopted it (in 1814).

While Alea was busy collaborating and Hernández was busy theorizing, it was Prádez who cared for the deaf students, accompanying them when they were moved first to a municipal school and then to the poorhouse, sharing their misery, and pleading for the betterment of their situation. In these wretched conditions, the question of the education of deaf students was reconsidered. Academics were a luxury in the poorhouse. Prádez and the children were set to weaving. The children were turned out on the streets to beg. Naked and starving, three of the seven died before the French occupation ended and the school reopened once again, under the auspices of the Economic Society.

At the close of the War of Independence, Alea, like many other *afrancesados*, left Spain for France, where he taught languages and literature in Marseilles. His interest in deaf people continued, and in 1824 he published a eulogy to l'Abbé de l'Epée. Alea died in Bordeaux without ever returning to the country of his birth.

When the school for deaf students reopened in 1814, Hernández was appointed headmaster. Scorning manualism as the exchange of one type of muteness for another, he rejected the French method employed by Alea in favor of the Spanish oralism of Bonet. Under the influence of Bonet's doctrine, Hernández stressed the importance of speech and lipreading and forbade any use of sign language. A few years of practical experience sufficed, however, to convince Hernández that sign language was essential for teaching deaf students.

Hernández subscribed to the "medical model" of deafness—deafness as pathology. He bragged that his medical experiments in search of a "cure" predated those of the French doctor Jean-Marc Itard. For a time, Hernández actually convinced himself that the experiments, which consisted of directing steam into the children's ears at bedtime, were successful.

Initially, Hernández professed a favorable view of deaf people. They possessed an innate capacity for learning, he said: "Within them Divine Providence has placed all they need in order to learn" (1814). With time, however, he modified this opinion: "Working a great deal, it is possible to teach these unfortunate ones very little" (1821). I suspect that Hernández's apparent lack of success at teaching deaf students may be owing to his rigid methodology, with its emphasis on speech over sign language and rote memorization over comprehension. He was openly cynical about the purpose of teaching deaf people to speak. He felt that deaf people were taught to speak not so that they could understand each other, but, rather for the sake of the hearing, and the experience was not particularly pleasant: "Not so that they might understand each other, but rather in order that we might understand them, we make [them] suffer great anguish" (1821). Thus did this hearing teacher handicap his deaf students by forbidding them the use of their "mother tongue" and imposing speech on them, not for their own benefit, but for that of hearing people.

Hernández continued at the head of the school until 1823, when he was forced to flee to Gibraltar, persecuted for his liberal political ideas. Like Alea, Hernández died in exile.

Roberto Prádez taught at the school for deaf students until 1837. He participated fully in the life of the school, presiding over examinations of the students alongside his hearing colleagues, attending meetings, collaborating on curriculum design, and developing teaching materials. After a career of more than thirty years of teaching at the Royal School for the Deaf-Mutes, Prádez died in abject poverty in 1838.

In Spain today, José Miguel Alea and Tiburcio Hernández have secured their place in deaf history, but Roberto Prádez has been completely forgotten. I hope this paper may be a first step toward restoring Prádez, Spain's first deaf teacher of deaf people, to his rightful place in history.

References

Alea, José Miguel. 1795. "Carta Dirigida al Editor del *Diario de Madrid*." Republished in *La Academia Calasancia*. Nov. 1906 to Nov. 1907. Vol. 16: pp. 256–263, 286–290, 322–326, 353–361.

————. 1800. Reply to a letter from P. de C. Republished in *Colección Española de las Obras Gramaticales de Cesar du Marsais: Ordenada para la Instruccion Pública, con Aplicaciones y Exemplos Correspondientes a la Elocucion Castellana*, ed. Cesar du Marsais, trans. José Miguel Alea. Madrid: Imprenta de Aznar.

————. 1803. "De la Necesidad de Estudiar los Principios del Lenguage, Expuestos en una Gramática General, y Aplicados a la Lengua Materna." In *Variedades de Ciencias, Literatura y Artes. Obra Periódica*. Toma primero. Madrid: en la Oficina de Don Benito García, y Compañia. pp. 101–117.

————. 1804 and 1805. Review of Ramón Campos. *El Don del la Palabra en Orden a las Lenguas y al Exercicio del Pensamiento, ó Teórica de los Principios y Efectos de Todos los Idiomas Posibles*. In *Variedades de Ciencias, Literatura y Artes. Obra Periodica*. first year: Vol. 3: pp. 340–355; Vol. 4: pp. 36–49, 95–108, 219–235; second year: Vol. 1: pp. 278–294.

————. 1824. *Éloge de l'Abee de l'Epée, ou Essai sur les Avantages du Système des Signes Méthodiques, Appliqué a l'Instruction Générale Elémentaire*. Paris: Chez Rosa, Libraire, au Palais-Royal.

Archives of the Real Sociedad Económica Madritense de Amigos del País, leg. 213, doc. 34.

Archives of the Real Sociedad Economica Matritense de Amigos del País, leg. 175, doc. 10.

Bonet, Juan Pablo. 1620. *Reduction de las Letras y Arte para Enseñar a Ablar los Mudos*. Madrid: Francisco Abarca de Angulo.

Hernández, Tiburcio. 1814. *Discurso Pronunciado en la Apertura del Real Colegio de Sordo-Mudos, la Tarde del 16 de Octubre de 1814*. Madrid: en la Imprenta de Sancha. pp. 9–10 and 21.

————. 1815. *Plan de Enseñar a los Sordo-mudos el Idioma Español*. Madrid: en la Imprenta Real.

————. 1821. *Discurso Pronunciado en el Exámen Público de los Sordo-mudos del Colegio de Madrid, la Tarde del 14 de Noviembre del Año de 1820*. Madrid: en la Imprenta de la Minerva Española. p. 10.

Sicard, Roch-Ambroise. 1807. *Lecciones Analíticas para Conducir a los Sordomudos al Conocimiento de las Facultades Intelectuales, al del ser Supremo y al de la Moral: Obra Igualmente Útil para los que Oyen y Hablan*, trans. Jose Miguel Alea. Madrid: en la Real Imprenta.

Events in the History of Deaf Education in Puerto Rico

YOLANDA RODRÍGUEZ FRATICELLI

The objective of this paper is to highlight the most important events contributing to the development of education for deaf people in Puerto Rico. The events have been grouped by decades, starting at the beginning of the twentieth century. A gap in available information seems to indicate that little work was done in educating deaf people in Puerto Rico prior to this time.

It is not possible to determine precisely when widespread deafness first showed up on the island of Puerto Rico. However, based on historical records, it can best be traced to the first quarter of the sixteenth century, when the island was besieged by a chicken pox epidemic. One-third of the Taino Indian tribe that populated the Caribbean region died from the disease. Of the many natives who were seriously ill from chicken pox but who survived, it is likely that many became deafened. Other factors that are also believed to have contributed to deafness among the inhabitants of Puerto Rico during that period were the plagues brought to the island by Spaniards and Africans.

1900–1909

After the Spanish-American War, Bishop Monsignor James F. Blenk invited the Sacred Heart missionaries to Puerto Rico to educate the deaf population. Prior to that time, no efforts had been made to educate deaf people on the island, and there was no school for deaf children in Puerto Rico or any other region of the West Indies.

In 1902, four Catholic missionaries came to the island from Maryland to teach deaf children. Evidence has been found that at least one of the missionaries had received training from the renowned educator of the deaf, Dr. Thomas Gallaudet. Another missionary was deaf. Even though they were limited in their knowledge of deaf education, had few financial resources at their disposal, and knew little of the Spanish language, these missionaries started a school for deaf children in a residence located in the northwest coastal town of Aguadilla.

The school, which opened in 1903, used signed English as the official method of communication. The school quickly grew, and later that same year the missionaries had to find larger facilities. The boys were sent to a new school in the town of Cayey, and the girls attended a school in San Juan.

1910–1919

The Sacred Heart missionaries built two wooden school buildings on land they purchased in Santurce, but a hurricane destroyed both structures. This caused additional financial woes for the missionaries, who were already in a desperate situation owing to lack of economic support. In 1910, the Cayey School had to be closed, and the boys were integrated with the girls at the Santurce school.

Since the school was not sufficient to meet the needs of the deaf students, in 1913 the missionaries began planning another educational center, which they called the Saint Gabriel School for the Deaf-Mute. This residential facility was located in a metropolitan area of San Juan, and the missionaries found it easier to obtain funding for this school. When it opened in 1915, the Saint Gabriel School accepted students up to the age of thirteen. Most of the students who completed their education there obtained work, or—if they came from wealthy families—went to the United States to continue their education.

1920–1939

There is a lack of evidence in historical documents during these two decades regarding the education of deaf students in Puerto Rico. Apparently, the use of the signed English method continued. Students who could afford to do so moved to the United States to continue their education, usually at schools for deaf students in Baltimore, Maryland or in Ohio.

1940–1949

The first and only census related to the deaf population was initiated by Puerto Rico's Labor Department in 1944. The department estimated the number of deaf people on the island by consulting physicians, nurses, teachers, social workers, religious groups, and the general population. At the time of the study, deaf people in Puerto Rico had little formal education, and the rate of unemployment among this population was very high. The census gave the Labor Department concrete facts about the dire situation facing the country's deaf population and groups with other disabilities. In 1947 the Puerto Rico Vocational Rehabilitation Law was signed, and in 1948 the Department released the results of its census.

1950–1959

In 1955, after working for more than forty years with the deaf population, the Sacred Heart missionaries requested permission to leave the island and return to the United States. To fill the gap, Bishop Monsignor James Davis spoke with the Franciscan Sisters of Spain and arranged for them to take over as educators at the school for deaf children.

The four new teachers were Franciscan nuns who came from Spain, Chile, Peru, and Venezuela and were trained in the oral/aural method. When they arrived in 1956, they changed the method of communication at the school from signed English to oralism in the Spanish language. In 1957, the Rotary Club donated an amplification system to the Saint Gabriel School.

Another group of missionaries (American Evangelical) came to the island in 1957 from Jamaica, where they had already established a school for deaf children. This group opened a school at Luquillo called the Evangelical School for the Deaf, and incorporated the Total Communication method into the classrooms. This school also received teachers and financial support from the Canadian Evangelical community.

1960–1969

A group of deaf students and the Franciscan Sisters came to Washington, D.C. to attend a conference and to help celebrate the Golden Anniversary of the White House. This event brought awareness to the general public about the deaf people of Puerto Rico.

Puerto Rico's governor, Luiz Muñoz Marin, signed a law that allowed the Department of Public Works to sell an area of land to the Franciscan Sisters for a new school. In 1965, the facility, called the New Saint Gabriel School for the Deaf, was built in the Puerto Nuevo section of San Juan. The school became known locally as "The City of Silence."

Owing to the increasing number of deaf students, the Public Instruction Department proposed a special education program for deaf and auditorially impaired children. At that time, no public schools offered special classes for deaf students. About the same time, the Evangelical School for the Deaf at Luquillo was forced to close owing to the lack of teachers prepared to educate deaf students. In 1969 the Governor's Commission for the Study of Rehabilitation for the Handicapped released a study (Comisión de Gobernador, 1969) that outlined the problems of the deaf community.

1970–1979

A new school was opened in Ponce in 1970. Called the Fray Pedro Ponce de León School, it was initiated by a deaf woman, Emilia Dasta. The school followed the oral method.

This decade also saw the visit of a Catholic priest who was concerned with the problems of the deaf community. Father Patrick McCahill published an article (McCahill, 1971) that described the situation of the deaf population in Puerto Rico. He stated that there was great disinterest among the hearing population in the problems being experienced by deaf people, and that the deaf population was a forgotten minority.

Meanwhile, the Public Instruction Department established special classes for deaf students within regular school programs. The Rafael Hernandez School in Rio Piedras became the first public school in Puerto Rico to have a program in deaf education. Other schools in Arecibo, Mayaquez, and Ponce also started special programs for deaf children.

Because of the need for interpreters in a variety of situations, the Vocational Rehabilitation Program opened the Auxiliary Services Unit for the Deaf in 1977. It provides services in San Juan, Ponce, and Arecibo.

The growing concern for the deaf community created a need to provide the public with information related to deafness. A new movement was initiated—the International Organization of Orientation of Deafness, Inc. (Organización International de Orientación de las Sordera, or OIDOS, which means "ears" in Spanish). This group addresses deafness issues such as prevention, rehabilitation, education, and orientation. The organization also provides sign language classes to the public.

During this decade, a parents' association was also founded in Guayama (1973) that led to the establishment of the Regional School for Deaf and Multiply-Handicapped Children (1978). This facility provides services to deaf children in the southeast region of the island.

Also in 1978, Antonio Rivera became the first deaf man to graduate from a private university in Puerto Rico, earning an undergraduate degree in business administration from the Interamerican University of San German.

1980–1989

The past decade has seen great strides in the development of the educational system for deaf people in Puerto Rico. For example, the University of Puerto Rico in Rio Piedras graduated its first female deaf student (Yolanda Rodríguez), who received her undergraduate degree in special education. The university also accepted her into the Deaf Education program in its graduate school.

Special courses were taught by Gallaudet University for members of the state's Education Department and the Public Instruction Department. In 1986, the Caribbean Center of Educational Resources for the Deaf was inaugurated at the University of Puerto Rico, with Gallaudet's sponsorship. This center provides assistance to Caribbean countries and develops workshops, seminars, and conferences about deaf education. In 1986, the first teacher preparation program in deaf education began at the graduate school of the University of Puerto Rico. In 1987, the first preschool laboratory facilities for deaf children were established at the University of Puerto Rico.

A state law was proposed that would create a public school for deaf students, which, it is hoped, will provide Puerto Rico with a Spanish-language high school for its deaf students. At present, this is still an unresolved issue and one that needs more work in order to be approved by the United States Senate and House of Representatives.

In 1987 the Puerto Rico Interpreters Association, Inc. was founded. Other services such as recreation and leisure activities have also been made available to the deaf community. Sporting events, summer camps, and folklore activities have been set up to enrich the quality of life for all deaf people. The First National Conference on Puerto Rican Deaf Education was held in 1988, as well as the first Deaf Sports Encounter, which was sponsored by the Department of Recreation and Sports.

References

Comisión de Gobernador para el Estudio sobre Rehabilitatión de Lisiados. 1969. *Informe sobre el Comité a Cargo las Personas del Habla y en Audición*. Rio Piedros, PR: Departamento de Servicios Sociales, División de Rehabilitatión Vocacional.

McCahill, P. August, 1971. A Case of Disinterest: The Deaf in Puerto Rico. *American Annals of the Deaf* pp. 413–414.

Historical Phases of Deaf Culture in Denmark

JONNA WIDELL

"C ulture" refers to the ways in which a given group of people solves its problems of existence. When such solutions are organized and practiced for a long time, social habits develop, and these allow us to identify a culture. It is important to see culture from a practical viewpoint; only then can a given culture be understood and accepted.

When a culture—and in the case of the deaf community, a subculture or minority culture—is not understood by the majority of society, the majority's attitude will continually fluctuate between tolerance and intolerance. The minority culture will then always have to fight for respect, understanding, and equality. If a culture is constantly forced to fight for matters that are regarded and defined as basic and necessary, the group will then have difficulty finding the strength needed to express its potential cultural richness. From this, it follows that when society prevents minority cultures from expressing themselves, it is depriving itself of considerable enrichment.

The Opening Phase of Deaf Culture in Denmark: 1866–1893

In 1866, after a deaf Norwegian traveler had enthusiastically told deaf people in Denmark about an association for the deaf community in Berlin, a group of deaf Danish artisans established the Deaf-Mute Association of 1866.

During that period, the city of Copenhagen was experiencing a boom in new associations—primarily of skilled workers, or journeymen—whose purposes were primarily social and service oriented. Because of the low standard of living in the eighteenth century, associations were established to provide support to their members in such emergencies as unemployment, disease, and death.

The majority of the deaf community also consisted of skilled workers. United under the leadership of Ole Jørgensen, founder and workshop leader of the Deaf and Dumb Institute, the new Deaf-Mute Association also began to provide services for its members. Within a few years, the deaf community had established an emergency fund, an insurance fund, and a burial club. In addition, the association helped unemployed skilled workers find jobs.

This article is excerpted from the book *Den Danske Døvekultur (The Danish Deaf Culture)* published in November 1988 and available from Danske Døves Landsforbund, Bryggervangen 19, 2100 Copenhagen 0, Denmark.

This article has also appeared in *Looking Back: A Reader on the History of Deaf Communities and Their Sign Languages*, edited by Harlan Lane and Renate Fischer, 1993, Hamburg: SIGNUM-Press.

Members of the Deaf-Mute Association of 1866 were among the first deaf people in Denmark to receive an education through sign language and the manual alphabet. Only half a century earlier, deaf people had been at the bottom of the social ladder, without status and often without language. Now they were educated and often could read and write the Danish language.

Sign language and the manual alphabet were used both in deaf clubs and families. Most deaf men married deaf women whom they had met at school. Most of their children could hear, and these children helped by interpreting for their parents and providing a link to the hearing society. The members of the deaf community lived their lives as best they could, and in the association they were fortunate enough to have friends to console and encourage them through the ups and downs of life.

Outside the deaf community, workers from the countryside had migrated by the thousands to Copenhagen, where they constituted a poorly educated and highly exploited segment of the labor force for growing industry. These families most often lived in poverty under miserable conditions. Compared to them, the skilled workers of the deaf community lived a considerably better, albeit modest, life. Furthermore, the attitude of middle-class society to the deaf community and "the deserving poor" was positive and open.

According to the standards of the time, teachers at the Deaf and Dumb Institute were well educated, and some of them had connections to the leaders of society, who encouraged deaf adults to become teachers at the school. In those early years of the developing deaf community, the school also stayed in touch with former students by holding association meetings on its premises. Several of the teachers participated in these meetings, and they often served as lecturers in the association. Moreover, the school contributed extensively to the integration of the deaf community into the labor market.

On the basis of these activities, a positive relationship was formed between the deaf community and the general Danish society. The Deaf and Dumb Institute was even favored by the royal family, and at the school's twenty-fifth anniversary in 1891, the founder, Ole Jørgensen, was honored with the Silver Cross of the Order of the Dannebrog. Members of the deaf community also were given royal authority to work as independent skilled workers and to employ hearing journeymen.

But times were changing. In the Opening Phase of the deaf community in Denmark, society was in transition between the feudal system and the new, industrial capitalistic system. This transition allowed more freedom of thought and action, which also applied to education. It is no coincidence that sign language first saw the light in France in the period just before the French Revolution. But with the establishment of the industrial society around 1880, societal thinking began to be bounded by new and more rigid forms, and these extended into the educational realm as well, in the form of new approaches and methods.

The thoughts we accept as our own without hesitation or question and our views of right and wrong are bounded by the framework of society. As human beings, we must rid ourselves of these thought images through reflection. For the deaf community, the new thought images at the end of the eighteenth century took the form of oralism—that is, the oral method began to be seen throughout the Western world as the only proper training method for deaf people.

Some might wonder why I talk about educational methods in a discussion of deaf culture. The educational system functions as the arm of society and reflects society's attitudes. This is a very important factor if we are to understand the development and nature of deaf culture.

In 1880 it was decided at the Congress of Milan that the oral method should be the only proper training method for deaf people. At the same time, sign language was rejected because it was claimed that signs destroyed children's ability to speak. The rationale for this decision was that deaf children are lazy and, therefore, whenever possible they will use sign language instead of oral communication because signing is easier. On this questionable basis, the oral method spread as an ideology. Some deaf teachers were fired immediately, while others were gradually forced to leave the schools for deaf people.

From a sociological perspective, it is clear that the oral method did not become dominant because of its superiority. It became the dominant ideology because it was especially suited to the new historical period.

How did it fit in? First, the influence of Darwin's theory of evolution had already spread to other branches of science. In much the same way that monkeys were considered to be at a low evolutionary stage and human beings at a higher stage, other cultures were considered lower than Western civilization. In the same vein, sign language was considered to be at a lower stage and had to be abandoned for the benefit of the higher stage—the oral language.

The new period involved another type of social control. In all societies, common rules and sanctions must exist in order to ensure the unity of the society. Religion and show trials were important features of the old feudal system, but from the eighteenth century onward, the *power of the norm* applied.

The power of the norm was evident in the strict discipline of large institutions, including the schools for deaf students, and in the attitude that it was normal to be able to hear. According to this principle, we can all hear *something*, although a hard of hearing person does not hear so well and a deaf person hears very poorly. Therefore, "deaf" was equivalent to a poorly functioning hearing person, which is the same thing as "deviant." Moreover, this power of the norm was manifested in bodily limitations that favored work routines: Gesture and animation were replaced by immobility, and signs were replaced by speech.

In the transitional society, an individual was perceived to be a mobile, contributing citizen in relation to society. Thus the creators of the sign method observed deaf people and the language they had created and formed teaching methods accordingly. At a later stage in society, however, industrial production was given priority at the expense of the individual. Psychologically, humans were considered empty vessels to be filled. Within deaf education, the needs of the deaf child were not considered. For the benefit of society, children were taught only the most common standard pronunciations. This level of language was considered acceptable because industry's requirements for oral communication were limited to a few short messages and technical instructions.

The Isolation Phase: 1893–1980

Oralism was thus well suited for this new society. But how did the attitudes hidden in this teaching method affect deaf culture? Did the deaf community one-sidedly adapt to the requirements of society? The answer to this is no. But although the Milan Congress and the opening of the first State Speech Training School for the Deaf in Fredericia had already taken place by 1880–1881, the deaf community's first real serious break with the norms of society did not take place until 1893. From that time on, a new attitude was to prevail in the deaf community.

Society's attitude toward the deaf community was slowly changing. In some circles changes happened fast; in others, more slowly. Society was still open to deaf people as shown in the concrete support from leading citizens for the building of the Deaf-Mute Association's own house in Brohusgade, Nørrebro, in 1898. The house was the setting for association activities and also provided accommodations for elderly deaf people.

But where schools were concerned, new, strict demands were soon to be made. The deaf community was required to adapt to "a higher development" and therefore give up sign language and learn to speak. Georg Jørgensen was a capable signer and the leading hearing person in the deaf community's association work. From 1881 he was also principal of the Speech Training School in Fredericia, where he firmly supported these new demands. Although he was still a member of the board of the Deaf-Mute Association, he prevented two deaf sisters from having contact with each other. One of the sisters had been trained in sign language in Copenhagen, and the other educated in an oral environment in Fredericia. The signing sister was not to be allowed to destroy her sister's ability to speak. Later, Jørgensen even succeeded in stopping a traveling church service for the deaf community. Through the ministry, he had an injunction issued against Reverend Heilberg as "a hand alphabet preacher for the deaf who have learned to speak" (Smaablade for Døvstumme, 1891–1895).

An event of vital importance contributing to the breach marking the Isolation Phase of 1893–1980 was the situation around the establishment of the association called "Effata." On July 25, 1893, the newspaper *Berlingske Tidende* reported that the teachers for the speaking deaf community at the schools in Fredericia and Nyborg had formed an association for the students of these schools. The objective was to remove the deaf community from its isolation and create a link with the surrounding world—without sign language. At the same time, the association applied for public support for this work!

This was too much for the deaf community! Attempts were now being made to split the deaf group by turning deaf people in Denmark against each other. Furthermore, the old association was prevented from receiving gifts and contributions for the deaf community.

The split between the deaf community and the leading groups of society took place that year at the general meeting of the Deaf-Mute Association. Georg Jørgensen was made an honorary member, primarily because polite older members of the deaf community wanted to show their gratitude for his service. At the same meeting, however, the association decided on a new goal: The main task of the future would be the preservation of sign language.

Society *did* set limits, but this does not mean that deaf culture was not allowed to develop. The self-confidence and strength acquired during the Opening Phase of 1866–1893 were preserved in the deaf culture and passed on through contact between the generations. The selfconfidence and strength of the deaf community were now used for expansion and stabilization. Branches of the Deaf-Mute Association were established across the country. The association in Copenhagen got its own house, and the deaf congregation, its own church. Participants were sent to international meetings and congresses and worked actively on the new task of developing a sign language dictionary. The deaf community also participated in the public debate on schools, signs, and speech—usually through its magazine, *Papers for the Deaf-Mute Community*.

The Isolation Phase lasted for almost a century, which is a long time to live under pressure and lack of acceptance. Hearing professionals working with the deaf community would say, "Deaf people want to isolate themselves; they do not want to learn to speak, so they do not want to become integrated!" In this way the members of the deaf group went from being "physical deviants" to being "social deviants," with resulting sanctions against them. It was considered legitimate to make fun of the deaf community and to tell spiteful jokes. Unfortunately, many of these distortions and negative stereotypes have been allowed to survive for too long.

The fact is that the deaf group had been isolated because it insisted on maintaining sign language to facilitate communication. That the deaf community had insisted so strongly on maintaining its language could be owing to a deep respect for an inner creative force of a human and social nature. This creative force had made it possible for the deaf community to discover a positive and practical language—sign language—that facilitated deaf people's development despite all odds against them.

The issue here involves uniting with and making friends with nature. The deaf community's maintenance of sign language can be seen as an example of such a friendship. It was the environment that, in conformity with the spirit of the time, alienated itself from the deaf community's natural ability to create the language best suited to its situation.

This rejection of the lifeblood of the deaf culture, and the demand that deaf children learn to speak the Danish language in a manner unnatural and unreasonably difficult, eventually began to leave its mark on the personalities of deaf individuals. Especially at school, deaf children experienced a feeling of "I cannot; I am no good. Hearing is good; deaf is bad," and this often-repeated experience left deep marks.

Fortunately, the deaf community had united during the favorable period, the Opening Phase. The strength and confidence deaf people developed in this period—through, among other things the comprehensibility, and therefore humaneness, of sign language—were still built into the deaf culture and passed as a gift from one generation to the next.

The Isolation Phase weakened the deaf group, but the rich experience and the strength of the Opening Phase allowed the Danish deaf culture to close itself off without the degrading submissiveness seen in the deaf people of some other countries. This reaction provided the deaf community with the strength to build an internal organization capable of meeting its needs. The deaf community's many associations and self-initiated institutions testify to this. Here social life was often lively, but it was also serious.

"Socialization" means learning about social life in the family, at school, at work, among friends, in a shop, in a cinema, and so on. It could be said that within the association, a tertiary—or third-level—socialization had taken place. This socialization process had literally protected the life of the deaf community from failure, as life must be a meaningful interplay with the rest of society.

This tertiary socialization through associations was particularly important because primary socialization in the family was difficult in a society where the parents of deaf children were not given any assistance. In addition, the secondary socialization in the school was alarmingly incomplete—both psychologically and academically—and, on certain points, even damaging.

The school had provided deaf children with a simple level of speech and the discipline necessary to enter the workforce. But it was owing to tertiary socialization in the deaf association that deaf people learned how to succeed socially in a job. It was in the association that solutions to issues ranging from on-the-job teasing to trade unions were discussed.

On the basis of these mechanisms for adapting and understanding, the concept of "deaf workplaces" was created. Deaf workplaces were companies that had good experiences with deaf workers and therefore wished to continue hiring deaf workers and deaf apprentices.

The End of the Isolation Phase: 1960–1980

In the 1960s conditions changed, first and foremost in the workforce, and consequently in education and the deaf community as well. The deaf community was still in its Isolation Phase, but now there were changes enabling the community to emerge from isolation.

The growing economy of the 1960s, which formed the basis of the welfare society, demanded more manpower. Marginal groups, particularly women but also people who had been excluded because of disease or disability, now joined the workforce. New laws ensured rehabilitation for these groups and made it possible for deaf people to receive interpreting assistance. This was the beginning of educational interpreting.

Education became more important for the broader community also. Young people from working class families now had the opportunity to sit for the General Certificate of Education examination and to obtain higher education. Deaf people began graduating from comprehensive schools, senior schools, and technical schools. They became draftsmen, social workers, teachers, educators, accountants, and so on. At the same time, vocational schools were established.

The prerequisite for the success of oralism thus began to disintegrate. A workforce—and society, for that matter—where brief routine messages and discussion of concrete matters were adequate no longer existed. Abilities such as reading, writing, abstract thinking, and understanding complex matters were now required.

In 1979, Dr. R. Conrad in Oxford, England published an analysis of the results of oralism that documented that British oralism had been able to live up to its own objectives only in a few exceptional cases. On the whole, it fell far short of its goal. Such an evaluation could, of course, have been made fifty years earlier, but the labor market and society would not support such an exposure of oralism's weaknesses at that time.

Because young deaf people wished to use sign language interpreters in their education, their parents began to support the attempts of the deaf community to introduce sign language in primary schools. When both parents and the deaf community began to exert heavy pressure in this direction, the oral method lost favor, and Total Communication projects gained a footing in the schools. Today, the philosophy of Total Communication has spread to those countries where oralism has not been able to maintain its status, and the concept is becoming more and more popular.

Total Communication, a concept used by the anthropologist Margaret Mead, suggests that when encountering another culture, people should use any means available to exchange ideas and understand each other. Total Communication is a humane philosophy, but it is not a teaching method and is not suitable for teaching deaf students. Nevertheless, it has been used as such. In the resulting projects, Total Communication could be characterized as an *ad hoc* method: "Perhaps this time we shall succeed!" It was only because people with disabilities still had a low priority in Danish society that a teaching method based on chance was accepted.

But the workforce continued to change. The shortage of labor, increased competition from other countries, and the wish for higher productivity paved the way for the introduction of new, advanced technology and automation. One of the first areas to be affected was the textile industry, where new technology made the ordinary tailor unnecessary. Tailoring had been one of the common occupations of the deaf community (others included shoemaking and joinery). Now deaf tailors, facing the disintegration of their craft, were given jobs as semiskilled workers. Such was the fate of several other crafts as well.

This trend, along with new educational opportunities, meant that deaf people were introduced to a variety of new jobs. At the same time, the old boarding school system disappeared, and deaf children were sent to different types of schools—schools for deaf students, integrated schools, and public schools where the deaf student functions as an integrated individual. The deaf community thus changed from a homogeneous group of people with highly similar backgrounds to a heterogeneous group of people with different backgrounds, types of education, and working environments.

The new mobility, especially within higher education, provided the impetus needed for minority groups. In the deaf group, there was a renewed effort aimed at gaining acceptance for the attitudes and wishes of deaf people. The deaf community entered a new phase when, in 1980 in Fredericia, the Danish National Association of Deaf People held a school conference. On that occasion, the association made it very clear to the educators invited that from then on deaf adults would assume responsibility for the schooling and future of deaf children—not just as children but as *deaf* children.

The Manifestation Phase: 1980–?

The present phase is characterized by changes. The negative images carried over from the Isolation Phase are being replaced with deaf awareness; "deaf people cannot" has been reworded "deaf people can." An inner dynamic has begun to make things happen. In addition, in the transition from an industrial economy to an information economy, society has begun to change drastically. Society is opening to minority opinions. Still, nothing comes easy; every step forward takes a struggle.

With renewed self-confidence, the deaf community has begun fighting political battles—regarding videotaped programs, text telephones, high schools for deaf people, and sign language as a subject in school—and the first three items are a reality today. Further advances are outlined in the action plan of the National Association, and there is still plenty of work to be done.

A bilingual teaching method for deaf people has been given top priority. Teaching of this kind requires the introduction of sign language as an independent subject in school. Sign language, which is suited for *all* deaf children, must be the basic language. After the children have learned sign language, Danish will be taught as a foreign language. In order to develop an actual teaching method, the following steps will be necessary: training teachers of deaf students in sign language; ensuring that approximately half the teachers of deaf students are deaf; and the development of a new series of curricula.

The "twin school" will be the best approach for children who need both sign language and Danish—that is, for deaf children and many hard of hearing children. This type of school will offer the best two-culture teaching, because deaf culture as well as hearing culture will be emphasized. The children need both.

Furthermore, it is important to discern how the deaf community can use the new technology that will play a critical role in the information society of the future. Information technology will touch many areas of society, so a wide spectrum of complex knowledge will be required to master it.

A major area of focus in the future will be the activities of deaf associations. The deaf community today consists of people from a variety of backgrounds, and this raises many questions: Do they understand each other? Are some isolated because they lack the ability to analyze a situation? Is there a lack of tolerance toward the individual? When is a person considered "arrogant and clever" rather than merely having a different line of thought? And what about multihandicapped people—where do they fit in? And young unemployed people? Are nonworking members of society given sufficient opportunities for daytime activities? If we have deaf centers instead of the old-fashioned deaf houses, how are they to be managed? How do we enhance members' participation? Do management and members have sufficient knowledge of recent developments in society? Do they realize that every deaf individual will have to change his or her thoughts and attitudes before the deaf community can change and improve? And how is it possible to change from being an onlooker to being a participant in one's own life?

The new association-manager training courses of the Danish National Association of Deaf People held at Castberggård try to shed light on these questions. This is not a traditional management training course: Everyone can participate, and the main issue is group cooperation. Common initiative and joint responsibility result in goal-oriented management and joint action. These group-based structures will play an important part in the society of the future.

It is of the utmost importance that deaf people obtain knowledge in areas that today are referred to as "alternative." Much of that which is alternative today will be the mainstream of tomorrow, and this is especially true of a society in transition.

Finally, it should be stressed that a deaf person in Denmark belongs to two cultures: the deaf culture and the Danish culture. Many deaf people think that the Danish culture is simply a hearing culture and therefore is not suitable for them. This is an unfortunate fallacy. Deaf people can participate in all but a small part of Danish culture.

Deaf people are in a double situation in another way: They are both a disability group and a cultural minority as regards language. The latter identity is expressed only to the extent that the members of the group know how to manage their own lives. The cultural identity of the Danish deaf community will become even more pronounced in the Manifestation Phase—if deaf people want it to. The reward is an equal and open interplay with the hearing community—if deaf people dare!

References

Conrad, R. 1979. *The Deaf School Child*. London: publisher unknown.

Smaablade for Døvstumme. 1891–1895. København: publisher unknown.

The Oralistic Tradition and Written History: Deaf People in German-Speaking Countries

GÜNTHER LIST

The history of deaf people in Germany does not readily lend itself to thrilling historical narrative, such as that found, for example, in Harlan Lane's *When the Mind Hears* (1984), in which he describes the French and American roots of the deaf community.

Every plausible history needs a subject with which the reader can identify. In Lane's book, this role is filled by the deaf community itself. His narrative gains excitement from the dramatic fight of the deaf minority in France and the United States for linguistic, cultural, and social autonomy during the nineteenth century.

Even after the Milan Congress of 1880 halted—for a time—the growth of deaf culture, the reality of the past hundred years remained through the legacy of the Abbé de l'Epée, who founded an educational model based on sign language in Paris during the 1770s. Fresh historical strength could be gained from evoking this memory.

In Germany, by contrast, there were no such dramatic beginnings for the education of deaf children. In fact, the history of deaf people in Germany can more appropriately be termed a history of modernization—one that must be viewed within the context of an increasingly industrialized society—rather than a history of educational method or linguistic theory.

After 1880, the educational strategy that triumphed over sign language throughout Europe was called the "German method," also known as oralism. Samuel Heinicke, the German contemporary of de l'Epée, founded a school in Leipzig that became a counter-model to de l'Epée's school. Heinicke's educational system became known as the "German method" because of its absolute opposition to the French sign language method advocated by de l'Epée. Although German-speaking Switzerland and Austria first followed the French tradition, they soon turned to the German method. It is, therefore, legitimate to say that this method arose from a unity of German-speaking countries.

Following Heinicke's institutionalization of oralism, the history of the deaf community worldwide became one of collective submission to the languages of hearing majorities, a history of systematic oppression of natural signing in schools. Prometheus-like educators claimed to breathe into deaf people, through oralism, a sort of divine breath that would finally make them human beings. To quote an oralistic scholar of our times, "Signing must be inhibited if the student is to acquire oral language and grow into human society" (Kröhnert, 1966, p. 173). Oralism has its longest history in German-speaking countries, a tradition that has lasted for 200 years.

Is the German method typically German? In view of the almost worldwide recognition and practice of oralism today, it is hardly worthwhile to attribute its development to German cultural characteristics. Neither could Heinicke nor his successors be considered less moral than de l'Epée, in view of their engagement in religious and educational activities. Reactionism—a movement toward a less advanced condition—also is not a plausible explanation for the development of oralism. On the contrary, I am afraid we have to accept the fact that in the society of the nineteenth and early twentieth centuries, oralism was considered more up-to-date than de l'Epée's model. This modern character, in fact, helps explain the attractiveness of the German method at that time.

From today's perspective, it was a dubious and threadbare modernity, based not on teaching methods or linguistic theory, but on the idea of assimilating a particular minority group—deaf people—into society. But that is the material from which the history of the suppression of the deaf community is made. For this ideal of social assimilation to become realized, the framework of industrialization was needed. The appropriate conditions for oralism occurred first and most conducively in Germany.

The Confirmation Model

De l'Epée and Heinicke had very different views about how deaf people could be assimilated into society—based, in part, on their religious beliefs. In de l'Epée's school, the souls of deaf people were rescued by integrating them into French civilization, with the help of their own language. Heinicke advocated a similar spirit of bourgeois enlightenment, although his educational model was based on the necessity of private education for deaf children of the aristocracy. This education was inevitably oralistic because speech was legally required for one to claim one's inheritance. From the Protestant perspective also, education must inevitably be oral, because in no other way could children be granted "confirmation," the ritual entrance into Christian and bourgeois society.

By using the idea of confirmation in a secularized context and making confirmation a goal of oral public education, Heinicke created an attractive formula for integrating deaf individuals into society. Confirmation at oralist schools, occurring normally at graduation, initiated deaf students into society. Because school was separated from daily life, students were able to concentrate all their energy on working toward this confirmation of their oral competence, while the academic content of their education became relatively insignificant.

This concentration on the ritual of initiation relieved teachers from taking into account everyday abilities as criteria of success. Deaf individuals themselves became responsible for the result of the educational process; lack of achievement after leaving school was judged to be their own fault.

The oral education system thus tended to produce isolated individuals and to destroy the deaf community. This divisive process actually completed the integration of deaf people required by modern industrial society. This kind of society required serviceable and unobtrusive individuals who did not attract attention through any threatening and subversive differences.

The Framework for Oralism

Let us now look at the framework necessary for oralism to become successful. Even in German-speaking countries, the success of oralism was one of long-term development. Until the middle of the nineteenth century, most institutions for deaf students in Switzerland, Austria, and southern Germany were under Vienna's influence, and followed a policy inspired by de l'Epée to produce a more or less mixed sign language. Even in places where oralism had already been established, such as Leipzig, it was not yet firmly entrenched at the time of Heinicke's death. Indeed, the organizational model that arose in most German territories during the first decades of the nineteenth century did not promote oralism. Following an idealistic concept of integration, general teacher training programs continued to include methods for teaching deaf children.

This led to a situation where a second generation of educators followed the first, in that they, too, did not yet blindly adhere to the oralistic model. The school in Berlin, founded by Heinicke's son-in-law Eschke, especially represents the relative open-mindedness of the first half of the century. It is also during this period that one finds the only renowned deaf teachers of deaf students: Schütz, who founded and directed Camberg; Habermaß, whom Kruse called the "German Massieu"; Senß and Wilke in Berlin; and Kruse himself at Schleswig.

Heinicke's oralism proceeded step-by-step until it finally became entrenched in the educational world in 1880. Historians of education for deaf students tend to mistakenly attribute this fact to the progress of methodology. From a sociohistorical perspective, however, the so-called "Taubstummenbildungswesen" (education system for deaf students) was a subsystem that was extremely dependent on the organization of the education system in general. This organization was exemplified by the classification policy of the schools, which on the one hand promoted social differentiation, and on the other hand, social homogenization. This classification mechanism, I think, provided the framework for assimilating deaf students.

The mechanism of classification existed even within the schools for deaf students. It was the separation of schools for blind students from those for deaf students that marked the beginning of special education. Two decades after 1880, the principle of oralism excluded from classes those deaf students who did not seem to be qualified for oralistic education. On the other hand, postlingually deafened and hard of hearing students were rarely excluded; these students were needed to demonstrate publicly the success of oral education.

This leads us to consider oralistic education of deaf students as a model of the history of modernization. In spite of initial difficulties, the oralistic method found favorable conditions in Germany because special education was subject to the unitarian organization of the educational system as a whole. As early as the 1830s, observers such as Berthier and Degérando recognized the advantage of government influence on schools in Germany (as well as in Scandinavia and Eastern European countries), as opposed to the random conditions of private foundations that prevailed in other parts of Europe.

Based on governmental organization, the decisive factor for expanding education for deaf students became the training of teachers as professionals. This training started at the beginning of the century with the founding of the Royal Prussian Teachers' Training Seminar in Berlin. In nearly all German territories after 1840, teachers were no longer qualified to teach deaf students merely by taking supplementary courses. Lane is correct in holding responsible for the new era of oralism a disproportionate increase in the number of teachers who did not know sign language, but whose role was not called into question by this fact. Germany became an early model of this development, where a group of professionals, trained by the government, were in harmony with an ideology that had developed in their own country.

For other countries, oralism, as it was established in Germany, must have been a very appealing product of a modernized nation-state, especially after 1870–1871 and especially in countries where special education was still predominantly carried out by clerics. Gradually, oralism invaded newly unified Italy and moved into France at the time of the Third Republic. These countries also began to train teachers, who adopted the principles of individualization and achievement. If we disregard for a moment developments in North America, where the acceptance of a variety of religious beliefs lessened the pressure for total assimilation, then we can see a clearcut picture in Europe: Heinicke's ideal of assimilating deaf students into society through oralism was in accordance with secular trends.

For the time being, the liberal practice of de l'Epée's sign-based educational model was bound to fail in the era of organized capitalism. On the one hand, sign-based education reflected certain characteristics of the time period prior to 1789. On the other hand, it anticipated greater acceptance of linguistic, cultural, and social minorities beyond the history of modernization of nation-states in the nineteenth and twentieth centuries, a position that really is definable only today.

Mother Language/Fatherland

I have tried to sketch the framework of conditions that historians of deaf people encounter when looking at our oralistic countries. Let me now make a few remarks on the situation of actually working and writing history in this field.

With the exception of a few recent presentations on specific areas or extreme historical situations, a critical history of deaf people in German-speaking countries has not yet been written. Caramore wrote on the change toward oralism in Switzerland around 1840; Biesold on the fate of deaf people under the National Socialist law for prevention of "genetic deviation." The time is now ripe for a general history of deaf people, a history that will show how educational processes for deaf people are connected with psychological and institutional themes in society in general.

Today in Germany, consciousness is growing in academic and public discourse, as well as in the media. It is becoming clear that the oralistic method has prevented deaf people from gaining, through the use of their own natural language, qualifications needed to function in society. The recognition of deaf people's resulting low economic position and role in society has become a huge scandal within the educational system.

Although this change of consciousness, which sheds light on a 200-year history of oppression, was originally initiated by linguists, the concern is, in fact, much broader. After the experience of the National Socialist regime, sensitivity in our country to various subgroups began to grow. In this sense, Biesold's study on sterilization of deaf and disabled people marks that point at which the history of deaf people became a part of general history—transcending by far the status of a pure language problem.

Let me reduce this interlacing of general historical interest with the interest in sign language communities to a formula that I would like to use as a working title for my investigations: mother language-fatherland. The interdisciplinary theme of the history of deaf people results from the tension between these two poles: the lack of acceptance of deaf people's primary language and the system as a whole, which promises identity and demands submission.

Education is not the core of this interdisciplinary theme, but becomes a central concern when linguistic, psychological, and anthropological aspects intersect with historical, sociological, and political ones.

Mother language vs. fatherland—a claim for self-determination vs. the reality of the system—is the terminology that logically applies to this "theory of history." In

German-speaking countries, a theory of history is necessary to compensate for the lack of historical narrative, because models of native language integration do not exist. In our countries, the history of the deaf community has always been latent. If we had been confronted only with an oralistic disaster coming from *outside*, as may have been the case in France and the United States, narration would be an adequate way to reanimate history. However, because this isn't the case for us, our theory of history will first have to explore the conditions for a possible future that does not yet have a past.

Aspects of Participation and Cooperation

The categories of majority and minority seem to be inevitable in this discussion, and not only as academic concepts. In the future, historical research projects can make a fresh start by involving deaf people and making obvious a history of oppression. The principle of inclusion must govern research, even in light of the results of a 200-year scandal in the education of deaf people. We can not presuppose that deaf people will be immediately qualified for professional historical work; such qualification constitutes an essential aim and result of the research process itself—learning history by doing history.

Through a shared learning process, deaf and hearing people will have to reconstruct their social relationship, a subject eliminated by oralistic history. By ignoring the primary language of its students, as well as the historical background of its own role, special education of deaf students reduced deaf people's real history to a matter of methodology. It organized the written history of deaf people as simply a mirror of the course of education. German oralistic historiography, established after 1880, confirms this in a rather depressing way: The role of historical subjects is taken by those who care for people with disabilities, while deaf people themselves remain mute. History is virtually confined to being a report of 200 years of achievement in methods and measures of educational institutions.

Today, we must pick up the thread at those few points where the history of the deaf community presents itself in its own right. During the first half of the nineteenth century, there is some evidence of an experimental liberality within the education of deaf students. One may recall the utopia of a deaf colony formulated by Graßhoff in 1820. Around the same time, Kruse's collection of personal biographies and successful careers of deaf individuals appeared (1832), one of the rare documentations of its kind. Kruse, one of the few deaf teachers of deaf students, also wrote an autobiography (1877), an exceptional achievement for a deaf German living under oralist conditions.

These isolated examples show that the prevailing circumstances turned the history of the deaf community into a private event, concentrating more or less on family and club life. The collective activity of deaf signers was barely recognized in the written history of society in general. Where it was recorded—for example, at the occasion of anti-oralist protests around 1890 (during the time of cancellation of the laws against the Socialists) and around 1918 (the date of the German Revolution)—there are interesting and thus far uninvestigated constellations to be explored.

Likewise, the history of deaf people's daily lives, which can be investigated through historical linguistics, sociolinguistics, and social history, no doubt contains a wealth of material. Handwritten chronicles of associations of deaf people exist, at least up to the World War II period. Finally, in the context of sign language, an oral history remains to be discovered. In any case, the more this research is connected with deaf awareness and deaf consciousness, the more deaf people themselves will have to become involved with historical research and in revising written history.

Hearing investigators, approaching the subject from the outside—in my case, from the perspective of general history—can contribute in two ways: They can provide methodological support, and they can offer the general framework for interpretation in a social structural context.

At present in Germany, some deaf people reject the term "minority," which in the eyes of hearing people is an indispensable category of critical history. Hearing people must respect deaf people's preference. However, I think that the rejection of this term could itself be a symptom of the history I have tried to sketch.

Above all, members of the majority—hearing people—should not feel themselves excused from studying, for the sake of self-clarification, a predominantly negative history essentially made by us. It is my hope that deaf and hearing people—both in Germany and across the Atlantic—can work together productively.

References

Lane, H. 1984. *When the Mind Hears: A History of the Deaf.* New York: Random House.

Kröhnert, O. 1966. *Die Sprachliche Bildung des Gehörlosen: Geschichtliche Entwicklung und gegenwärtige Problematik.* Weinheim.

Kruse, O. F. 1832. *Der Taubstumme im uncultivirten Zustande nebst Blicken in das Leben merkwürdiger Taubstummen.* Bremen.

Kruse, O. F. 1877. *Bilder aus dem Leben eines Taubstummen: Eine Autobiographie.* Altona.

Lessons Learned from the Connecticut Asylum

BARRY A. CROUCH

On April 15, 1817, the Connecticut Asylum for the Education and Instruction of Deaf and Dumb Persons opened its doors in Hartford, Connecticut. Known today as the American School for the Deaf (ASD), it was the first permanent residential school for deaf students established in the western world. Earlier efforts had been made to educate deaf people, but they were private endeavors, restricted to a select group of deaf children and adults. In contrast, the Connecticut state school, founded as part of the reform movement that pervaded American thinking in the early decades of the nineteenth century, was organized to educate deaf children from all classes of society.

There was nothing inevitable about the form that deaf education assumed in the early years of the nineteenth century, although by the 1810s it seemed clear that some kind of school for deaf pupils would exist in the United States. Schools were becoming more popular as many people began to believe that an educated citizenry was a necessary prerequisite to economic growth and a stable democratic government. In the words of David Rothman (1971), American reformers discovered the asylum. But the asylum in the form of a deaf residential school did not take the shape or form that Rothman suggests characterized other social institutions.

The records of the American School for the Deaf encompass almost all aspects of deaf history and culture in the early years of our nation. A study of ASD records and the information they contain about deaf people and deaf education in these early years is important for many reasons. The Connecticut school's background and influence, the founders of the institution, and the actual education available there raise important questions about the environment within which education of deaf students in the United States emerged. The records preserved by ASD can assist historians in answering some of these questions.

A brief examination of the archival materials at ASD will allow us to determine what kinds of questions can be asked. Although they are not catalogued, the papers in the ASD archives are a treasure for any historian researching the early years of the rise of a deaf community in the United States. Most of the important documents related to the early background, development, establishment, and supervision of ASD have been preserved in the school's archives. There must be 5,000 to 6,000 manuscript pages that pertain only to deaf history, culture, and education before 1830, the year that Thomas Hopkins Gallaudet resigned the principalship of ASD. The records suggest he resigned owing to internal conflicts and disagreements with the Board of Trustees.

Who were the individuals who initially thought of educating deaf students, what was their background, and how did they perceive such an undertaking? Three men,

Mason Fitch Cogswell, Thomas Hopkins Gallaudet, and Laurent Clerc, share the major responsibility for founding the Connecticut Asylum, establishing its characteristics, and making their own contributions to educating deaf students. Their efforts add another dimension to nineteenth century historical reform. Cogswell was a Yale graduate and prominent Hartford physician who had a deaf daughter, Alice. It was his organizational and fiscal prowess that ensured the school's continuing success. T. H. Gallaudet, also a Yale graduate, was a frustrated minister, champion of the socially dispossessed, and neighbor of Cogswell. He became ASD's first principal and guided the institution through its rocky early years.

Clerc, a deaf Frenchman who was a teacher at the Royal Institution for the Deaf and Dumb in Paris, emigrated to the United States with Gallaudet in 1816 and assisted him in establishing the school. Clerc was responsible for introducing sign language as the sole method of instruction. The precise role Clerc played in developing the educational system at ASD and the larger contribution he made to the American deaf community are questions that still need to be answered.

Cogswell, Gallaudet, and Clerc came together almost accidentally, yet they shaped the contours of deaf education for years to come. Much of this story is well known, but no historian, to my knowledge, has really mined the papers at ASD. These significant archives flesh out the background and details of the coming together of these three individuals who, perhaps inadvertently, provided an institutional setting around which deaf people could coalesce. At ASD we see simultaneously the emergence of a community and the beginnings of American Sign Language. A complete account of this process cannot be gleaned from the ASD records alone: They have to be supplemented with other manuscripts from the libraries at Yale University and other local archives in the Hartford area.

How was such an enterprise conceived, and what steps did the individuals involved take to bring it to fruition? Cogswell's daughter, Alice, as is well known, was the immediate cause for his efforts on behalf of educating deaf children. His correspondence, contained in the ASD collection, suggests a man with considerable organizational skills, attention to detail, and fiscal responsibility. He was precisely the type of individual needed to secure the financial backing for the establishment of a school for deaf students.

Cogswell knew that he could not do it alone. As the ASD administrative board files suggest, he drew on a wide variety of assistance from a prominent group of individuals and established a large base of subscribers for the intended institution. Student records reveal that some of the major subscribers had deaf children themselves. They knew and trusted Cogswell's abilities.

Numerous letters between Cogswell family members, beginning in the 1790s, provide insight into the background and character of the family. Much of the correspondence that led to the foundation of the school is part of the ASD collection. Interesting memorabilia and significant documents are displayed, perhaps the most important being the handbill of an exhibition of some French deaf students, including Laurent Clerc, which Gallaudet saw in London; he subsequently attended the demonstration. The rest of the story is well known. Additionally, there is wonderful background information on the students. Not only are their financial records detailed in numerous account books, but there is also important material on how they became deaf and whether or not any other family members were deaf.

What method of instruction was employed in teaching the children—a question that still has ramifications today—and what were the consequences? We know that children at ASD were taught in sign language. Gallaudet would have it no other way. But what kind of sign language? The recent Deaf President Now movement at Gallaudet University has stirred a new debate in relation to American Sign Language and its use. In much of this new debate, and even in past conflicts, few discussions about ASL are grounded upon historical research. What better place to begin than in the ASD archives?

To be sure, deaf people had a communication system before attending ASD, as Nora Groce (1985) argues, for Martha's Vineyard, but it was not ASL. The nuances of sign language are not easily articulated in the written or printed page, but the papers at ASD contain some hints.

As early as 1819, three different methods of sign communication were used in educating children at ASD. According to Gallaudet, the first method, upon which the other two were based, was

> the natural language of signs, originally employed by the deaf and dumb in all their intercourse with their friends and each other, singularly adapted to their necessities, and so significant and copious in its various expressions, that it furnished them with a medium of conversation on all common topics the very moment that they meet, although, before, entire strangers to each other. (p. 6)

The students could even "denote the invisible operations of their minds and emotions of their hearts" (p. 6). Clearly, from Gallaudet's description, this was the beginning of ASL.

ASL, however, was not the only method of communication at ASD. A second mode of communication, the principal wrote, "is the *same* natural language of signs, divested of certain peculiarities of dialect which have grown out of the various circumstances of life under which different individuals have been placed, reduced to one general standard, and methodized and enlarged by the admirable genius" of l'Epée and the "still more ingenious improvements of his venerable successor," Sicard. The second method was necessary "so as to accommodate it to the structure and idioms of written language, and thus to render it in itself a perspicuous, complete and copious medium of thought" (pp. 6–7).

Comparing the second sign system used at ASD to the Chinese written language, Gallaudet wrote that the "latter forms its symbols with the pencil, while the other portrays them by gesture, the attitudes of the body and the variations of the countenance" (p. 7). This system was probably signed English.

The third method of communication used at ASD during these early years of instruction was the manual alphabet. This enabled the students, "after they have been taught the meaning and use of words, to converse with their friends with all the precision and accuracy of written language," Gallaudet concluded, and "with four times the rapidity with which ideas can be expressed by writing." Through these methods, the teachers at ASD labored to "convey important intellectual and religious knowledge," following the institution's philosophy of not confusing "the gift of speech with the gift of reason." Considerable progress also was made in providing a pool of teachers upon which newly established deaf institutions could draw.

Where did the students that attended this institution come from, and what were their family backgrounds? Quite naturally, when ASD first began, a majority of the students came from the New England area. The comprehensive financial accounts of the pupils provide information on what state was paying for their attendance at ASD. By 1819, only two years after it opened, ASD had an enrollment of fifty students from eleven states.

Other personal information can be gleaned from these files, related to students' hearing loss and whether other family members were deaf. In some instances, more detailed background characteristics can be obtained from the correspondence of the parents. Overall, the information obtained through the ASD archives may not be as in-depth as we would wish, but nevertheless, it reveals something about the extent of deafness among the population in the first three decades of the nineteenth century.

Before the rise of the Connecticut Asylum, there had been one earlier attempt to establish a school in the United States for deaf children. It was a private school, with few pupils, and emphasized teaching the students how to speak through a combination of speech training and lipreading. By contrast, the Connecticut school pioneered a pattern of deaf education that has remained dominant in the United States until the present day. This pattern and its dominating influence on the education of deaf students has only begun to be explored.

What Cogswell, Gallaudet, and Clerc created has endured. First, the American School was a residential institution, drawing students from a broad geographical area and becoming in effect their surrogate parents. (Oralists later charged this was a major failing of deaf education because it disrupted family life.) Second, after its establishment the school received substantial financial support from the state and federal governments. This freed the Connecticut school from the uncertainty of charitable or private contributions. Third, from its very inception the school's usual method of communication for both instruction and everyday interaction was sign language. Articulation (oralism) was not taught because Gallaudet refused to waste his instructors' "labor and that of their pupils upon this comparatively useless branch of the education for the deaf and dumb. In no case is it the source of any original knowledge to the mind of the pupil" (Gallaudet, 1817, p. 7). Fourth, deaf teachers were always prominent among the faculty, beginning with Clerc. Later, the school actively recruited its best students to become instructors after they graduated.

Too often, the major focus of deaf history has been upon the oralism vs. sign language debate. Only minor attention has been paid to the historical context and background in which educational ideas and methods for teaching deaf students developed. In fact, there are still so many misconceptions about the entire process of teaching deaf students that it is difficult to sort out historical truth from distortions of the material and vague ideas that are largely unsubstantiated.

Further work on the rise of deaf education in the United States and the subsequent formation of an American deaf community should be grounded in a cultural perspective rather than a medical (or pathological) model of deaf people. The ASD archives hold exciting material and possibilities for research into many facets of the history of deaf people in the United States. This extensive collection has never been used comprehensively by any researcher. As a result, we still do not know many of the subtleties that characterized the emergence of the deaf community in America.

Cogswell, Gallaudet, and Clerc catalyzed the emergence of deaf Americans from marginality, isolation, and ignorance to community solidarity, organizational strength, and substantial intellectual achievement. This struggle needs to be chronicled.

References

Gallaudet, T. H. 1817. *Report of the Committee of the Connecticut Asylum for the Education and Instruction of Deaf and Dumb Persons.* Hartford: Hudson and Company.

Groce, N. 1985. *Everybody Here Spoke Sign Language: Hereditary Deafness on Martha's Vine-yard*. Cambridge: Harvard University Press.

Rothman, D. J. 1971. *The Discovery of the Asylum: Social Order and Disorder in the New Republic*. Boston: Little, Brown, & Company.

Judaism and Deafness: A Humanistic Heritage

ABRAHAM ZWIEBEL

The purpose of this paper is to shed light on the legal status of deaf people throughout Jewish history and to illustrate the humane attitude toward deaf people found in Jewish sources. In addition, this paper will present evidence—both direct and circumstantial—of the existence of education for deaf people in Jewish society throughout the ages. Research for this paper involved examining such sources as the Bible, the Talmud, the Mishnah, the Responsa, and literature containing judicial rulings, including the Halacha and the Psika. These sources will be described in further detail throughout the paper.

Traditional Jewish attitudes toward deafness have been ambivalent (Dicarlo, 1960; Mann, 1983). Mann has described the predominant attitude as being characterized by a sense of charity. The Book of Leviticus in the Bible contains an admonition against cursing deaf people, and the Mishnah, which has been further explicated by the Talmud, states that "the deaf, the retarded,[1] and minors cannot be held responsible." This statement has led Mann, among others, to maintain that in terms of legal rights, deaf people were originally treated as helpless and retarded individuals. One purpose of this paper is to define better the phrase "the deaf, the retarded, and minors," which has been interpreted as proof of the inferior status of deaf people. Laws against harassing, abusing, and robbing deaf people have been interpreted by researchers as historical evidence that such actions were actually taking place. Moores (1987) states that although the Talmud, written in later times, modified some of the more negative beliefs about the inability of deaf people to reason, there is no evidence of any attempt to educate them. Other scholars disagree.

Conducting research into Jewish sources regarding attitudes toward deaf people is important for a number of reasons. First, Jewish culture is an ancient culture, one that has existed from the dawn of history to the present. Secondly, it must be remembered that Jewish society is considered a scholarly society, one that has spread throughout the world, both influencing and being influenced by other cultures. The Jewish religion has influenced the religions and cultures of large parts of the world (mainly the Christian

This paper was supported by the Professor Eliezer Stern Institute for Research and Furthering of Religious Education of the Bar Ilan University School of Education.

A version if this paper was published as "The Status of the Deaf in the Light of Jewish Sources" in *Looking Back: A Reader on the History of Deaf Communities and Their Sign Languages*, edited by Harlan Lane and Renate Fischer, 1993, Hamburg: SIGNUM-Press.

1 A literal translation of the word used would be "fool," which is interpreted to mean "emotionally disturbed." However, most sources use the translation "retarded" and this paper will do likewise.

world and the Moslem world). Information about the status of deaf people in different periods of Jewish history might, therefore, teach us about the status of deaf people in general in various countries.

Thirdly, the laws that defined the legal status of deaf people were valid in Eretz Yisrael (the land of Israel) and the Diaspora throughout Jewish history, both at the time of Jewish independence in ancient times (up to 70 A.D.) and in subsequent generations (the periods of the Talmud, the Geonim, the Middle Ages, and the modern world). Even in the modern State of Israel, Jewish laws still form the only legal system as far as family laws are concerned, and serve as an important source of legislation on other matters. These legal points are important because legal definitions have influenced the general attitudes of people towards deaf individuals—and continue to do so.

It is appropriate first to present a short summary of the Jewish legislative system and its development. Juridical rulings in Jewish sources—the Psika and Halacha—are characterized by continuity. That is, a later source does not contradict or cancel an earlier one, but explicates and interprets it according to the traditions of the oral interpretation of the scriptures, i.e., the Bible.

Until the first century A.D., the Bible was explicated by the sages, and these interpretations were compiled and written down by the Tanaim in the first and second centuries A.D. This compilation is known as the Mishnah. During the third to fifth centuries A.D., the Mishnah was interpreted by the Talmudic scholars in the two main centers of Jewish life at that time—Babylon and Israel. The Talmud includes legal arguments as well as descriptions of everyday life of the Jewish community.

In the sixth century A.D., Biblical scholarship spread to both Moslem and Christian Europe as well, and such sages as Maimonides and Rabbi Yoseph Caro wrote legal books that summarized the sources existing before their time. A large part of this scholarly work is included in the Responsa, books published in various locations that contained the answers of great rabbis to questions posed to them. These questions dealt with various legal problems and religious laws. The rabbis also corresponded and argued with one another, and the books include a compilation of all these opinions. The Middle Ages were an extremely prolific period as far as this Halachic literature is concerned.

Recent technological advances have enabled the establishment of computerized data centers that concentrate many Jewish sources, including Responsa and Halachic literature from the tenth century A.D. to the present. The renewal of Jewish sovereignty in the last forty years has resulted in growth in the number of Jewish scholars, which has in turn borne fruit for deaf people, as research into the legal definitions of deafness as a basis for legislation and daily jurisdiction has increased.

The Legal Status of Deaf and Hard of Hearing People

"The deaf" are included in the legal category of "the deaf, the retarded, and minors" in the Mishnah and the Talmud and, as a result, throughout Halachic (legislative) literature. This category includes people who are not considered fully competent cognitively. Therefore, their legal responsibility concerning money and possessions is invalidated, they are not obligated to observe religious commands, and their responsibility for any action requiring sense, thought, purpose, or hearing and speech is negated. On the other hand, they have full one-sided protection. That is, any person who hurts them is culpable, whereas if they harm anyone else, they are considered blameless.

Those sources that define a "deaf person" restrict the definition to those persons who do not speak at all, that is, deaf-mute persons (Mishnah, Trumot, A,2). This means that deaf people who speak are considered to have rights and responsibilities equal to those of anyone else. "Speech" includes both perfect speech and partial speech. As far as nonspeaking deaf people are concerned, the ruling is that marriage and divorce are legally binding for them (in contrast to retarded people and minors, for whom these actions are not binding). In addition, a system was arranged for determining the existence of a minimal non-oral communicative ability, enabling deaf people to receive full equality in legal categories where property (except for real estate) is concerned.

Three schools of thought are discernible in the Mishnah as far as this group of deaf-mutes is concerned. The first school of thought—the one that has set the custom—states that deaf-mutes do not possess full cognitive competence and need all the laws passed for them in order to maintain personal and possessory status. This is the position taken by some of the Tanaim (Mishnah, Trumot, A,1).

A second position held by the Tanaim is that taken by Rabbi Yehudah, who claims that even deaf-mutes possess full cognitive competence (Tosefta, Trumot, A,1). A third opinion is that of Rabbi Eliezer (Tosefta, Trumot, A,1), who does not totally negate the cognitive abilities of deaf people, and whose opinion is interpreted as meaning that there are areas or times at which the deaf person might be functioning at a normal cognitive level.

The large number of opinions and the debates in Jewish sources regarding the cognitive level attainable by deaf people concentrate on the small group of deaf people who do not speak at all and who have no other communicative ability. These arguments are fairly advanced in comparison to other civilizations in antiquity, for example the Hellenistic and Roman civilizations, as described by Moores (1987). The Justinian Code, which parallels the harsher opinion in Judaism, was legislated only in the sixth century A.D., and even this position was greatly eroded in large areas of Europe. Deaf people were denied the right to participate in Christian religious rituals throughout the Middle Ages, for example, and even their right to marry was limited.

The various subgroups of deaf and hard of hearing individuals are treated differently by Jewish sources. The first group is composed of people deafened at a later period in life rather than being deaf from birth, but who nevertheless do not speak at all. Here too, three opinions are discernible. The first one excludes this group of deaf-mutes from the group of people who have no cognitive competence and states that, although they may not be communicating at present, they are considered normal individuals (Raban Shimon ben Gamliel in Talmud Yerushalmi, Trumot, 1,A and Gittin 7,A). The second view claims that persons who have lost their hearing and who have in addition lost their communicative ability are considered the same as deaf people who are not fully competent cognitively and cannot be held responsible for their actions (Mishnah, Yevamot 14,A; Talmud Yevamot 14,A; Rabbi Meir in Talmud Yerushalmi, Trumot 1,A and Gittin 7,A; Maimonides as interpreted by *Melechet Cheresh*, 1864). The third view claims that these individuals are questionably competent cognitively (*Peri Megadim*, 1954).

The second subgroup of deaf-mutes are hard of hearing people who have no language and no communication with their surroundings. All opinions indicate that hard of hearing people who do not speak are considered to be normal human beings as far as legal rights are concerned (Maimonides, Mechira 29,2; *Peri Megadim*, 1954; *Rosh*, Responsa, 1959; *Halakhot Ketanot*, 1897; *Ginat Veradim*, 1970; *Maharsham*, 1962; *Shevut Yaakov*, 1972; Feinstein, 1981). With the recent development of hearing aids, deaf and hard of hearing persons who were previously considered deaf and whose receptive abilities can now be improved, are now considered to be normal, even if they do not speak. They are, however, free from observing those commandments requiring speech and hearing, according to a number of rabbis (*Igrot Moshe*, 1964).

The third subgroup of deaf-mutes consists of learned persons, those who have acquired knowledge and skills requiring a high level of cognitive function. Discussions concerning this group have occurred mainly in the last few centuries, with the development of educational institutions in society, and reflect divergent opinions as well. Some include such people in the normal juridical category (*Heichal Yitzchak*, 1960; *Halakhot Ketanot*, 1897; *Maharsham*, 1962; *Shevet Sofer*, 1899) and some classify them as deaf people, claiming that it is impossible to take exceptions into account and preferring to see deaf people as a homogenous group (Talmud, Gittin 71,B; Rabbi Chayim Halberstein in *Melechet Cheresh*, 1864). In addition, there are a number of scholars who do not reach any conclusion regarding this question (*Minchat Yitzchak*, 1955).

The Philosophy and Basic Attitude toward Deafness Underlying Legal Decisions

A study of the reasoning and argumentation between the supporters of various views reveals their beliefs concerning the emotional and cognitive levels of different groups of deaf people.

As far as emotional level is concerned, no source casts doubt on the emotional maturity of even deaf-mute people who lack communicative ability. In any case, emotional immaturity cannot be a reason for their being included in the category of "non-reasoning persons" (those who exhibit signs of insanity)—among whom we also find the emotionally disturbed. Rabbi Moshe Sofer (*Chatam Sofer*, 1972) explicitly states that deaf people are not included in the category of "emotionally disturbed" found in the Mishnah and the Talmud.

There *are* doubts expressed throughout Jewish history, however, regarding the cognitive level of deaf-mute people. All concerned state that it is clear that a deaf person who has communicative abilities (however partial or imperfect they might be) must have a normal cognitive level. Maimonides, who presents a minority view, does not attribute any retardation to deaf people either (Maimonides, Mechira 29,2). There are, however, doubts about deaf persons who do not have this communicative ability, and who therefore lack the channels for cognitive development and environmental enrichment. The school of thought that accords a restricted legal status to deaf-mute individuals claims that they cannot understand things in depth.

The second opinion, which maintains that deaf-mute people are cognitively competent, bases its stand on objective facts. In the Mishnah, in the first century A.D., Rabbi Yehuda points to a number of well-known people of his time who were deaf-mutes but who nevertheless held highly responsible positions in the Temple in Jerusalem, positions that demanded great learning and understanding. These were the sons of Rabbi Yochanan ben Gudgeda, who were in charge of purification. The reasons given for seeing deaf people as possessing normal cognitive level are also based on cases of deaf professionals who proved through their deeds that they possessed high reasoning powers.

Those holding to the school of thought that regards deaf-mute people as mentally handicapped do not generalize from these examples, however, stating that even in cases where it is clear that deaf persons are intelligent in spite of their total deafness and inability to speak, they should still be included in the legal category of "deaf." This is done so that no mistakes should be made concerning those deaf people who have no reasoning powers, to ensure that they are not accorded normal status as far as rights are concerned and are thus not required to fulfill duties they are unable to. As stated above, the rabbis holding this opinion wrote laws that actually enable these people to receive an almost normal legal status while still receiving legal protection.

The fact that these four subgroups of deaf-mute people—hard of hearing persons, people who have partial hearing with a hearing aid, deaf people who speak, and deaf people who can communicate with signs (meaning minimal pantomime, not proper sign language)—are all treated as normal persons indicates that Jewish sources (including the most ancient) do not see deafness in itself as a cause of a low cognitive level in deaf people who cannot speak. Rather, the key element is the fact that they cannot communicate. The doubts arising about educated deaf people who speak do not contradict this view. The opinions that regard such persons as belonging to a legally restricted category are based on a legal rule that does not recognize differences, distinctions, or exceptions. Today, because there are very few deaf people who are not educated, there is a great deal of debate on this point. Legal rulings, even today, are divided on this subject, but the majority opinion is to regard the legal status of deaf people as normal.

The view taken by Jewish sources on the cognitive level of deaf people shows that doubts, deliberations, and debates existed during certain periods in the past, in which researchers claimed that deaf people possessed an inferior cognitive ability because of their inferiority in spoken language (see reviews in Moores, 1987; Myklebust, 1964). The theory, as expressed in Jewish sources, always referred to environmental deprivation and not to deafness as such. The importance of the aural/oral element lies not in any parallel between language and thought, but in connection to environmental deprivation. This is in accordance with views commonly held today (Furth, 1964, 1971; Rosenstein, 1961), as well as with studies proving equality between deaf individuals and hearing individuals (Conard and Weisenkrantz, 1981; Karchmer et al., 1978; Kusche et al., 1983; Sisco and Anderson, 1981). Recent scientific developments, however, postulate a different cognitive structure for deaf people and present evidence that their cognitive development is not totally identical to that of hearing individuals (Zwiebel and Mertens, 1985). These developments indicate that there are still some strong doubts as to the cognitive development of deaf people, and that this complex subject has not yet been answered in a fully satisfactory way.

Assessing Communicative and Cognitive Development

A number of Jewish sources refer to the way in which evaluations were carried out to determine whether a deaf-mute individual was able to understand the procedures of property purchase, marriage, and divorce. It has been mentioned that the rabbis found various ways to ensure that these people could lead normal lives. However, doubts did sometimes arise about those deaf people who were mute and lacked communicative abilities. Thus, rabbis were required to validate a will, a property deed, or the parting of a family when a deaf-mute person was involved.

In the Mishnah and the Talmud, a number of ways are mentioned for checking the cognitive level of even deaf people who lack any way of communicating (Mishnah, Gittin 5,7; Mishnah, Yevamot 14,1; Talmud, Gittin 59,A; Maimonides, Mechira 29,2). The rabbis used pantomime to ensure that the deaf person did indeed understand the legal action that was to be made valid. Such procedures are described in a divorce proceeding found in *Melechet Cheresh* (1864). The understanding of the deaf person must be checked three times. Through pantomime, he is asked "Should we write a divorce bill for your wife?" and he is to answer in the affirmative. Then he is asked, "And for your sister?" to which he should answer in the negative. Then he is asked again, "And your wife?" In addition, he is to be asked questions that are not connected with the divorce bill, to make sure that he is indeed capable of understanding what is being communicated to him.

The Status of Deaf People in Jewish Society

A study of historical sources shows that some deaf-mute people were able to attain high social status in Jewish society. Throughout the literature, one finds that deaf individuals who do speak, as well as individuals who are hard of hearing, are not even referred to as "deaf." As far as deaf-mute people are concerned, there are lively discussions of their legal status (fifty-four sources in the Mishnah and 333 sources in the Talmud). The plurality of the different schools of thought and their debates helped form a social view of deaf individuals that was not automatically a negative one. The Mishnah mentions cases where deaf individuals married hearing individuals (Mishnah, Yevamot, 14,4). The Mishnah also mentions the deaf sons of Rabbi Yochanon ben Gudgeda, a Levite who was considered a righteous person with special status in the Temple. His deaf sons received positions that demanded studying and theoretical knowledge. The Talmud mentions the case of Rabbi Malchio, who lived in the fourth century A.D. and was one of the prominent personages of his age, who looked after a deaf person who lived nearby, married him to a wise and praiseworthy wife, supported him financially so that the match would work, and helped him to become self-supporting (Talmud, Yevamot, 113,A). This is an example of how to help those deaf individuals who cannot attain normal status on their own.

There is evidence of deaf people in seventeenth century Moravia writing Torah scrolls, phylacteries, and mezuzot (*Shivat Zion*, 1966), work that demands practical training as well as theoretical understanding. There is also evidence of deaf tailors who were considered learned in Israel in the seventeenth century (*Halakhot Ketanot*, 1897) and three cases of well-educated Polish Jewish merchants in the seventeenth century, who conducted business negotiations in mime and signs and were financially well off (*Maharsham*, 1962; *Tzemach Tzedek*, 1769).

The cases above indicate that individual education for deaf people existed in the first century A.D., as well as in later periods. There is an interesting story dating from seventeenth century Israel about an associative teaching method (*Halakhot Ketanot*, 1897). Rabbi Yaakov Hagiz tells about a deaf man who was well educated and literate. He would be shown all the letters of the alphabet and would have to spell out the words for objects, such as bread, that were brought to him. In this way he learned to read and write.

There is also evidence of Jewish deaf children studying in general schools in eighteenth-century Hungary (*Chatam Sofer*, 1972). As far as schools specifically for deaf students are concerned, the first known reference is found in the Responsa and concerns nineteenth-century Vienna (*Shevet Sofer*, 1899). The writer says he was invited to visit the Jewish deaf school and to examine its educational policies and methods closely. He was pleasantly surprised by the students' knowledge, and instructed the school to buy the deaf students ritual objects and treat them as hearing individuals. In 1864, all rulings concerning deaf people were collected in a single book. The author claimed that he wrote this book after seeing how a Jewish school in Vienna had succeeded in making deaf students as cognitively competent as their hearing colleagues (*Melechet Cheresh*, 1864).

In summary, there is evidence pointing to deaf individuals with high socioeconomic status in Jewish society from as early as the first century A.D. There is also evidence of educational opportunities for deaf people, both individually and within Jewish frameworks. Jewish legal thought regarding deaf people has been advanced for its time. Finally, with recent advances in technology, it seems that the legal status of scholarly deaf-mute persons in Jewish society has now become equal to that of hearing individuals. Thus, it seems that, in spite of all the complexity and deliberation in Jewish sources regarding the legal status of deaf people, the facts indicate an overall attitude of respect towards deaf individuals in Jewish society.

References

Chatam Sofer (Rabbi Moshe Sofer) (Hungary, 18th and 19th centuries). 1972. Jerusalem: Machon Chatam Sofer.

Conard, R., and B. C.Weisenkrantz. 1981. "On the Cognitive Ability of Deaf Children with Deaf Parents." *American Annals of the Deaf* 126. 995–1003.

Dicarlo, L. M. 1964. *The Deaf.* New Jersey: Prentice Hall.

Furth, H. G. 1962. "Research with the Deaf: Implications for Language and Cognition." *Psychological Bulletin* 64: 145–164.

Furth, H. G. 1971. "Linguistic Deficiency and Thinking: Research with Deaf Children, 1964–1969." *Psychological Bulletin* 76. 58–72.

Ginat Veradim (Rabbi Avraham ben Mordechai Halevi) (Egypt, 17th and 18th centuries). 1970. Jerusalem: Planographic printing, Constantinople, 1716.

Halakhot Ketanot (Rabbi Yaakov Yisrael Hagiz) (Israel, 17th century). 1897. Krakow, Poland: Horowitz.

Heichal Yitzhak (Rabbi Yitchak Izik Halevi Herzog) (Ireland and Israel, 20th century). 1967. Jerusalem: Mosad Harav Kuk.

Holy Scriptures (2 vols.). 1917. Philadelphia: Jewish Publication Society.

Igrot Moshe (Rabbi Moshe Feinstein) (Lithuania and the United States, 20th century). 1964. New York: Balshan.

Karchmer, M. A., R. J. Trybus, and M. M. Paquin. 1978. "Early Manual Communication, Parental Hearing Status, and the Academic Achievement of Deaf Students." Paper presented at the Convention of the American Education Research Association, Toronto, Canada.

Kusche, C.A., M. T. Greenberg, and T. S. Garfield. 1983. "Non-verbal Intelligence and Verbal Achievement in Deaf Adolescents: An Examination of Heredity and Environment." *American Annals of the Deaf* 127: 458–466.

Maharsham (Rabbi Shalom Shvadron) (Poland, 19th and 20th centuries). 1962. New York: Grossman.

Maimonides, M. (12th century). 1962. *Mishneh Torah* (6 vols.). New York: M.P. Press.

Melechet Cheresh (Rabbi Yehudah Leibush ben Rabbi Chayim). 1864. Vienna: Verlag des Verfassers.

Minchat Yitzhak (Rabbi Yitzchak Yaakov Weiss) (England and Israel, 20th century). 1962. London: Hachinuch.

Mishnah, 1964. Jerusalem: Mif'al Lehotzaat Mishnaiot.

Moores, D. F. 1987. *Educating the Deaf*. 3d ed. Boston: Houghton Mifflin.

Myklebust, H. R. 1964. *The Psychology of Deafness*. New York: Grune and Stratton.

Peri Chadash (Hezkiah ben David da Silva) (Israel, 17th and 18th centuries). 1954. In *Shulchan Aruch*. New York: Grossman.

Peri Megadim (Rabbi Yoseph ben Meir Teomim) (Galicia, 18th century). 1954. In *Shulchan Aruch*. New York: Grossman.

Rosenstein, J. 1961. "Perception, Cognition, and Language in Deaf Children." *Exceptional Children* 27: 276–284.

Rosh (Rabbi Asher ben Yechiel) (Germany and Spain, 13th century). 1954. New York.

Shevet Sofer (Rabbi Simcha Bunim Sofer) (Hungary, 19th century). 1899. Budapest–Vienna: Presburg Printing.

Shevut Yaakov (Rabbi Yaakov Reisha) (Poland and Germany, 17th and 18th centuries). 1972. Jerusalem.

Shivat Zion (Rabbi Shmuel ben Yechezkel Landa) (Moravia, 18th and 19th centuries). 1966. New York: Planographic printing, Warsaw, 1881.

Sisco, F. H., and R. J. Anderson. 1980. "Deaf Children's Performance on the WISC-R Relative to Hearing Status of Parents and Child-rearing Experiences." *American Annals of the Deaf* 125: 923–930.

Talmud (18 vols.), ed. I. Epstein. 1961. London: Soncino Press.

Talmud Yerushalmi. 1899. Jerusalem: Lunz.

Tosefta, ed. Zukermandel. 1938. Jerusalem: Baberger and Wahrmann.

Tzemah Tzedek (Rabbi Menachem of Mikolshberg). 1769. Poland.

Vernon, M. 1968. "Fifty Years of Research on the Intelligence of the Deaf and Hard of Hearing Children." *Journal of Rehabilitation of the Deaf* 113: 1–12.

Zwiebel, A. 1981. "More on the Effects of Early Manual Communication on the Cognitive Development of Deaf Children." *American Annals of the Deaf* 133: 16–20.

Zwiebel, A., and N. Milgram. 1982. "Cognitive and Communicative Development in Deaf Children." *Israel Journal of Behavior Sciences* 26: 115–130 (Hebrew).

Zwiebel, A., and D. M. Mertens. 1985. "A Comparison of Intellectual Structure in Deaf and Hearing Children." *American Annals of the Deaf* 130: 27–32.

The History of Deaf Education in Greece

VENETTA LAMPROPOULOU

To trace the history of deaf education in Greece and to examine the parameters that played an important role in it are rather difficult jobs, though my task may be easier than that of my colleagues from Spain, France, England, and Germany, where education of deaf children started earlier. But the history of deaf education must be examined, in a broader sense, through the whole history of deaf people. The existence of deaf people in ancient Greece and society's attitudes toward deafness are known mainly through the works of the Greek philosophers and writers of that period. Around 385 B.C. Plato was writing about the sign language of deaf Athenians ("Cratylus" from *Dialogues*). The general belief of that time appears to have been that children who were born deaf could not be educated.

The conditions of deaf people in ancient Greek society, with the exception perhaps of the Spartan society, was not so bad as has been assumed by some educators (Moores, 1978). According to some reports, people with disabilities in classical Greece received an allowance, though this was not the case for slaves who were disabled (Lazanas, 1984).

Aristotle is one of the most well-known, and often misinterpreted, philosophers to have dealt with the subject. He considered hearing the most important of all the senses because it contributes, he believed, to the mental development of man. He thought that hearing was the main organ of instruction. Aristotle also believed that deafness was organically connected with speechlessness. According to this idea, he assumed that damage to the hearing organs also causes damage to the speech organs (Aristotle, *Problems*). In another book, Aristotle states that blind people are more mentally advanced than deaf people because blind people can communicate with their environment (*The Senses*).

Aristotle's statements might have influenced some doctors and educators who, misinterpreting his ideas, assumed that deaf people could not be educated. Some writers and educators have condemned Aristotle for his ideas and held him responsible for keeping deaf people in ignorance for more than 2,000 years (Deland, 1931).

The truth is that Aristotle never refers to the education of deaf children in his works. He only places a high importance on the sense of hearing for instruction, which generally speaking, is valid even today. He also states that a child deaf from birth will not learn to speak, which is also very often true today.

In Plato's *Dialogues*, we also get some useful information about the status of deaf people in Athenian society. Socrates expresses the idea that thought is expressed by people through speech, except if someone is deaf or speechless. In these writings, the philosopher shows an awareness that deaf people don't speak, and he also makes a distinction between deafness and speechlessness ("Theatetus").

The first written statement about sign language is by Plato. Noting that sign language is a spontaneous tool, he states that even hearing people will use signs if they suddenly lose their speech ("Cratylus").

In another of Plato's *Dialogues*, Socrates, Hermogenus, and Cratylus talk about word-object correspondence and the arbitrary or natural symbols of this relationship. Here, Socrates is talking about sign language as a communication system used by deaf people ("Cratylus").

From Plato's *Dialogues*, we can assume that deaf people and sign language were very much accepted by Athenian society. This might not have been true for the Spartan society. In Sparta, according to Plutarch, all babies were inspected soon after birth, and the ones with disabilities were thrown in a gully of the mountain Tavgetus, known as Kaiadas or Apothetas (Plutarch, *Lykurgus*). Some writers had doubted Plutarch's description, but given the militaristic ideology of Lykurgus' Sparta, the position of people with disabilities could not be so good as in other Greek cities of the same period.

During the Byzantine epoch, asylums and orphanages were established, and children in need were cared for and protected. Some deaf children benefitted from these social and welfare programs, but education had not yet been provided for them (Lazanas, 1984).

Development of the First Schools

The education of deaf children in Greece began relatively late in comparison with other European countries, and its development has been slow. This delay can be attributed to a number of factors. One may have been the 400 years of Turkish occupation of Greece; others included the political, social, and economic priorities of the newly independent Greek nation after Turkey's occupation.

In 1907, a rich landowner named Charalambos Spiliopoulos took the initiative to try to establish a school for deaf children in Athens. He went to the notary public to get all the legal papers for this purpose, and on May 14, 1907, he got permission to establish a philanthropic asylum (Government Paper, 1907). But, for primarily bureaucratic reasons, such a school did not become a reality until 1937, after his death. Spiliopoulos left a great amount of money and property for the establishment of the new school.

In the meantime, in 1922, after the defeat of the Greek army by Turkey and the destruction of the Greek civilization on the east coast of Turkey and in Constantinople (Istanbul), a ship carrying Greek refugee orphans from Turkey approached the port of Athens. Among these orphans were ten deaf children. The American Philanthropic Organization for Near East Relief, which was helping Greek refugees from the east coast of Turkey, established an orphanage for the refugee children in Athens and later established another on the island of Syros. This organization also undertook the responsibility of educating the ten deaf orphans. To this aim, a teacher named Helen Palatidou was sent to the Clarke School for the Deaf in the United States to receive training (Epetiris, 1950).

Helen Palatidou was a refugee from Turkey, with a good education and a great interest in working with deaf children. She studied at the Clarke School from 1922 to 1923. Upon her return to Greece she began teaching the deaf orphans. As the results of her teaching became known in Greece, the number of her deaf students increased. More teachers also were recruited for this residential school, and some were sent for training to the Clarke School, which became an important influence on deaf education in Greece.

According to Palatidou's students, the oral method was used in the school. Palatidou taught speech sounds to her students, followed by reading and writing. She also trained the new teachers with her method.

In 1932, the Organization for Near East Relief met with the Ministry of Welfare, and it was decided that the school would come under the auspices and support of this ministry (Government Paper, 1932). In 1937, the property of Spiliopoulos was transferred over to this school and became what is known today as The National Institute for the Protection of Deaf-Mutes (Government Paper, 1937). The school moved to a new, larger building and extended its services to more deaf children. In the period between 1956 and 1970, the National Institute established residential schools in five more cities.

Today the National Institute provides free education, residence, and diagnostic and related services to deaf children from birth to fourteen years of age. It is supervised by the Ministry of Health and Welfare through a board of trustees appointed by the ministry. Over the past years, the National Institute has developed in-service training programs for teachers and has organized seminars and activities on the education of deaf children.

Some teachers have played a leading role in the development of the National Institute. Besides Palatidou, one of the most important figures, according to deaf people and the Institute's records, was Helen Varitimidou. She went to the United States in 1945–1946 to receive her training. When she returned to Greece, she taught deaf students with the oral method and trained new teachers for a number of years. She soon became a director of the National Institute. She helped the deaf graduates from her school establish the first deaf club in Greece in 1948. Helen Varitimidou was dedicated to her job and to her deaf students.

Another influential figure at the National Institute was Vasilis Lazanas. He was not a teacher, but a scholar who had a great interest in deaf people. He was the administrative director of the Institute from 1955 to 1979. Lazanas was the first person in Greece who studied the literature extensively and wrote many articles about the education, vocational rehabilitation, and status of deaf people in different societies.

Most of Lazanas' works were included in the first volume of his book, *The Problems of the Deaf* (Lazanas, 1984). Lazanas had been influenced by the oral method of the institute, and he tried to convince his readers that deaf people can learn to talk.

Although the National Institute used the oral method of communication and emphasized the articulation of sounds and the development of speech, some teachers knew how to sign and, according to deaf graduates, used signs unofficially in the classroom. In their dormitories and in the school yard, deaf students communicated among themselves with sign language.

During World War II the Institute had to give its building to a hospital and move to a small building near the Acropolis. This period was very difficult for the Institute, as it was for all Greek people. It took years to recover from the setbacks resulting from the war, and only in about 1960 did the Institute return to its large building and begin to develop again.

Meanwhile, another development in Greece influenced deaf education to a large extent. Andreas Kokkevis, a member of Parliament, had a deaf daughter. He became very interested in deaf education. From his position in Parliament and later as Minister of Health and Welfare from 1964 to 1974, he supported legislative and other actions favorable to deaf children.

In August 1956, Kokkevis proposed an amendment to a law that was under discussion in Parliament. The amendment was passed and the law became the first supporting deaf education. According to this law, the public insurance organizations were to pay the tuition of deaf children attending special schools (Parliament Records, 1956).

In September of the same year, Hro Kokkevis, Andreas Kokkevis' wife, obtained a license and established the first private school for deaf children in Glyfada, near Athens (Government Paper, 1956). This school was recognized by law as equal to all other public schools (Government Paper, 1956).

Amalia Martinou, a teacher at the National Institute, became the life director and owner of this private school until 1986, when she transferred the school to the state. Martinou was influenced by the methods of the British oral schools she often visited. She and her teachers used the pure oral method and did not allow the students to sign at all. According to graduates from Martinou's school, the students had to speak all the time and learn to lipread. Most of the morning hours in school were spent in articulation and lipreading exercises. Later, in 1966, with the help of parents and Andreas Kokkevis, the school was extended to include junior high school. It is now a public school, the Public School for Deaf and Hard of Hearing of Argiroupolis.

Another private, nonprofit school was officially established in 1973 by an organization called the Institution for the Welfare and Education of Deaf and Hard of Hearing Children. The President of this organization, Sofia Starogianni, was the mother of two deaf sons. Hro Kokkevis was the honorary president of this organization (Government Paper, 1973).

This school was an oral residential school and included preschool, elementary, and high school departments. The director was Victoria Daousi, a Greek language teacher who was very skillful and dedicated to deaf children. In 1982, this school was given to the state (Government Paper, 1982).

Recent Developments

In the beginning, the government had little to do with the development of deaf education in Greece (Special Education Office, 1988). But from 1976 to the present, the lobbying and the pressure of parents and people with disabilities have provided the impetus for the government to address some of the problems and to take some responsibility for educating disabled children, including those who are deaf.

Some very influential organizations played a leading role in this development. The Greek Union of Deaf-Mutes, the first organization of deaf people in Greece, founded in 1948, began to publish its newspaper in 1956. The problems of deaf education were constantly discussed in this paper (*Newspaper of the Deaf-Mutes*). As more organizations of deaf people were established in Athens and in other cities, the "voice" of deaf people grew louder.

In 1968, the Greek Federation of the Deaf was established as an umbrella organization to represent the deaf people of Greece. One of its main objectives was to improve the educational status of deaf children, and an educational committee was formed for this purpose. In 1986, a representative of the Federation became a member of the Board of Trustees of the National Institute for the Deaf (*The World of Silence*, 1986).

Parallel with deaf people, parents began to organize themselves. In 1954, the previously mentioned two mothers of deaf children, Hro Kokkevis and Sofia Starogianni, formed the Organization for the Welfare of the Deaf. This organization took a number of actions and organized activities to improve both education and the lives of deaf people. It helped organize the other organizations for deaf people and held meetings on different subjects.

In 1965, the Association of Parents of the National Institute for the Deaf was founded, followed in 1980 by the Organization of the Parents of the Private School of Martinou. These parents' organizations, together with the other organizations of deaf people, composed a very powerful body that put pressure on the government to improve the education of deaf children in Greece.

As a result, in 1975 a two-year course in special education was established at one of the teachers' academies (Government Paper, 1975). Unfortunately this course, even as it exists today, provides only general information to teachers about children with special needs. It does not offer any kind of specialization.

In 1976, an office for special education was established in the Ministry of Education (Government Paper, 1976). Soon after, a law for the vocational rehabilitation of people with disabilities was passed (Government Paper, 1979).

The first law for the education and vocational training of special children was passed in 1981. It was replaced in 1985 by Law 1566 (Government Papers, 1981, 1985).

In the decade of the 1980s, some rapid developments took place. The parents' organizations held a conference in 1982 and invited specialists from abroad to talk about the education of deaf children. The issue of sign language and other current issues were discussed by some professors from Gallaudet University in the United States. It was the first time that Greek people involved in the education of deaf children had met deaf professors and listened to their speeches. Interpretation for deaf people was also something new to be seen in the conference. The impact of that conference, according to deaf people and some parents and teachers, was great.

In 1984, a study was done on the educational needs of deaf children (Lampropoulou, 1985). It was the first systematic study to be done in the area of deafness in Greece. In this study, five different groups—educators, parents, deaf adults, administrators, and government officials—assessed the educational needs of deaf children. The major findings indicated that there was a great need for development in the areas of teacher training, curricula, diagnostic services, infant programs, and vocational training programs.

According to the same study, parents' perceptions of the educational needs of deaf children were very different from those of the deaf group. Parents considered it very important that students learn oral skills at school, while deaf adults thought that literacy skills, appropriate teaching methods, and the use of sign language were the most important areas to be developed.

The results of this study were used by the National Institute for the Deaf in order to improve its services. In 1986, an infant program, the first of its kind, was developed by the institute in three major cities: Athens, Thessaloniki, and Patras. It is presently serving forty-two families with infants (Table 1).

Two programs for vocational training of deaf youth were also developed for the first time. One of these programs, developed by the Institute for the Deaf, offers courses in hairdressing. The other program, developed by the local authority of Argiroupolis, a suburb of Athens, offers courses in computers and in graphic art.

A number of seminars for teachers were organized in the last few years by the Institute for the Deaf and the Ministry of Education. A committee is presently working to develop curricula for language and other subject areas for deaf children.

TABLE 1: Characteristics of Deaf Students Attending Programs for Deaf Students

Schools	Students	Age	Sex		Resident
			Male	Female	
Elem. NID Athens	65	5–16	29	36	34
Elem. NID Athens II	39	5–16	20	19	20
Elem. NID Thessaloniki	108	7–18	56	52	58
Elem. NID Patras	53	5–17	26	27	30
Elem. NID Kriti	11	7–16	5	6	9
Elem. NID Serres	20	5–16	10	10	13
Elem. NID Volos	7	7–15	4	3	7
Elem. PS Argiroupolis	67	5–16	39	28	
Elem. PS Philothei	26	6–16	20	6	13
Elem. SU Chalkis	7	4–16	3	4	
Elem. SU Thessaloniki	13	9–15	4	9	
Elem. SU Thessaloniki II	4	6–7	4		
Elem. SU Ioannina	12	6–17	5	7	
Elem. SU Volos	4	7–14	2	2	
JH-HS Ag. Paraskevi	103	14–25	66	37	58
JH-HS Argiroupolis	78	13–25	36	42	
JH-HS Thessaloniki	50	13–22	30	20	19
JH-HS Patras	20	14–18	6	14	14
Pre-PS Argiroupolis	12	3–5	9	3	
Pre-PS Ampelokipi	21	3–5	10	11	6
Pre-PS Philothei	9	3–5	6	3	
Pre-PS Thessaloniki	12	3–5	8	4	1
Pre-PS Patras	9	3–5	6	3	
Infant Programs NID	42	0–4	19	23	
TOTAL	792		423	369	282

Schools for Deaf Children Today

Implementing the existing Public Law 1655/85, the Ministry of Education has recently established some new schools and classes for deaf students.

According to data collected for this study, the total number of deaf students attending the different school programs is 792 (Table 1). These special schools belong to two systems: the schools of the National Institute for the Deaf (NID), which belong to the Ministry of Health and Welfare but have educational programs supervised by the Ministry of Education; and the schools of the Ministry of Education itself (see Table 1).

As seen in Table 1, there are seven Institute schools throughout Greece; two of these are in Athens. All these schools are elementary and residential schools. There are two more elementary schools in Athens (Argiroupolis and Philothei), one of which is residential. There are also two junior high and high schools in Athens; one is resi-

TABLE 2: Methods of Communication for Professionals Working in Schools for Deaf Students

Schools	Students	Sex of Teachers		Teacher		Method of Communication	Other Specialists
		Total	Deaf	Male	Female		
Elem. NID Athens	65	12			12	T.C.	8
Elem. NID Athens II	39	8	1		8	T.C.	4
Elem. NID Thessaloniki	108	22		3	19	T.C.	4
Elem. NID Patras	53	10			10	T.C.	2
Elem. NID Kriti	11	2		1	1	T.C.	1
Elem. NID Serres	20	2		1	1	T.C.	
Elem. NID Volos	7	1	1		1	T.C.	
Elem. PS Argiroupolis	67	15		4	11	Oral	2
Elem. PS Philothei	26	6		3	3	Oral*	1
Elem. SU Chalkis	7	1		1		Oral	
Elem. SU Thessaloniki	13	2			2	Oral	
Elem. SU Thessaloniki II	4	1			1	Oral	
Elem. SU Ioannina	12	2		2		Oral	
Elem. SU Volos	4	1			1	Oral	
JH-HS Ag. Paraskevi	103	22	1	5	17	Oral*	
JH-HS Argiroupolis	78	13		5	8	Oral	
JH-HS Thessaloniki	50	16		10	6	Oral*	
JH-HS Patras	20	5	1	2	3	Oral*	
Pre-PS Argiroupolis	12	2			2	Oral	
Pre-PS Ampelokipi	21	3			3	Oral*	
Pre-PS Philothei	9	1			1	Oral	

continued on next page

TABLE 2: Continued

Schools	Students	Sex of Teachers		Teacher		Method of Communication	Other Specialists
		Total	Deaf	Male	Female		
Pre-PS							
Thessaloniki	12	2			2	Oral*	
Pre-PS Patras	9	1			1		
Infant							
Programs-NID	42	5			5	T.C.	3
TOTAL	792	155	4	37	118		25

Some teachers in these schools use total communication in their classrooms.

dential. There are five preschool programs—three in Athens, one in Patras, and one in Thessaloniki. Smaller cities do not have early intervention programs.

There are five classes with deaf children within the public schools for hearing children throughout Greece. Finally, there are schools of all grades including infant programs in Patras and Thessaloniki.

As seen in Table 1, of the 792 students attending programs for deaf students, 423 are boys and 369 are girls. The students' ages range from birth through twenty-five, while the age range of hearing students is three through eighteen.

According to Table 2, 155 teachers work in the above schools: Thirty-seven are men and 118 are women, indicating that tradition is still strong in Greece. Teaching deaf students was a woman's job, and this probably explains why the majority of teachers in the National Institute for the Deaf, which is the oldest establishment, are still women. According to these data, the teacher-student ratio is one teacher per six students.

As seen in Table 2, there are four deaf teachers working in the different schools. The teaching profession is rather new for deaf people in Greece. Another interesting figure is the age level of teachers. The majority of them are between thirty and forty years old (Table 3).

As of 1984, The National Institute for the Deaf has adopted the Total Communication method, while most of the other schools in Greece use the oral method. There are a few exceptions where some teachers in one school will use Total Communication in their classroom, while other teachers of the same school use the oral method (Table 2).

The methodology of teaching is still a hot issue in Greece, and parents of students in the Ministry of Education schools are not much in favor of sign language.

The training of teachers is a big problem in Greece. There has not yet been any university training program for teachers of deaf children. The National Institute for the Deaf offers a one-year in-service course for its new teachers.

Another two-year course is offered in one of the teacher academies, as mentioned above. It is a general course in special education and does not provide specific training for teachers of deaf children. Table 4 illustrates this problem. Very few teachers (six of 154) hold bachelor's or master's degrees in deaf education. Some teachers (thirteen) have taken courses in deaf education abroad, and most of the rest have taken some seminars related to their content areas.

Many of the teachers working in programs for deaf students (especially those working in the newly established schools of the Ministry of Education) have had very little experience.

TABLE 3: Age Level of Teachers Working in Schools for Deaf Students

Schools	Number of Teachers	Ages of Teachers			
		20–30	30–40	40–50	>50
Elem. NID Athens	12	4	1	3	4
Elem. NID Athens II	8	2	3	1	2
Elem. NID Thessaloniki	22	7	7	6	2
Elem. NID Patras	10	2	5	1	2
Elem. NID Kriti	2		2		
Elem. NID Serres	2	1		1	
Elem. NID Volos	1	1			
Elem. PS Argiroupolis	15		11	3	1
Elem. PS Philothei	6	1	3	1	1
Elem. SU Chalkis	1			1	
Elem. SU Thessaloniki	1	1	1		
Elem. SU Thessaloniki II	1	1			
Elem. SU Ioannina	2		2		
Elem. SU Volos	1			1	
JH-HS Ag. Paraskevi	22	3	10	8	1
JH-HS Argiroupoli	13	5	5	2	1
JH-HS Thessaloniki	16	2	8	4	2
JH-HS Patras	5	3	1	1	
Pre-PS Argiroupolis	2	1	1		
Pre-PS Ampelokipi	3	1	1	1	
Pre-PS Philothei	1		1		
Pre-PS Thessaloniki	2	2			
Infant Programs-NID	5	3	1	1	
TOTAL	154	40	63	35	16

TABLE 4: Educational Background of Teachers

Schools	Degree[a]							
	MA	BA	CA	NID	GSE	NT	Sem	Tch
Elem. NID Athens	1	2	2	12			12	12
Elem. NID Athens II			3	8			8	8
Elem. NID Thessaloniki			2	22			22	22
Elem. NID Patras				10			10	10
Elem. NID Kriti				2			2	2
Elem. NID Serres				2			2	2
Elem. NID Volos								1
Elem. PS Argiroupolis			2		8		10	15
Elem. PS Philothei			2	3	3		3	6

continued on next page

TABLE 4: Continued

Schools	MA	BA	CA	NID	GSE	NT	Sem	Tch
Elem. SU Chalkis					1			1
Elem. SU Thessaloniki								2
Elem. SU Thessaloniki II				1				1
Elem. SU Ioannina					2			2
Elem. SU Volos			1		1			1
JH-HS Ag. Paraskevi	1						10	22
JH-HS Argiroupolis							10	13
JH-HS Thessaloniki			1				6	16
JH-HS Patras							1	5
Pre-PS Argiroupolis					2			2
Pre-PS Ampelokipi					2		1	3
Pre-PS Philothei					1			1
Pre-PS Thessaloniki							2	2
Infant Programs-ND		2		4			5	5
Total	2	4	13	64	20		104	

[a]MA = Master's; BA = Bachelor's; CA = Courses Abroad; NID = Courses of N.I.D.; GSE = General Special Education; NT = No Training; Sem = Seminar; Tch = Teachers (total).

Finally, there is a relatively small number of multihandicapped deaf students in the schools for deaf students (fifty-five out of 792). Most of these students have mild physical problems and mental retardation. According to a recent study, most of the multihandicapped deaf children in Greece stay home because there is no appropriate program available for them (Lampropoulou, 1988).

Many problems still exist in the education of deaf children in Greece, and further efforts must be made by the government in order to solve these problems. But parents, deaf people, and teachers are determined to see that deaf children receive the kind of education they deserve.

References

Aristotle. *Problems*. Athens: I. Zaharopoulos.

Aristotle. *The Senses*. Athens: I. Zaharopoulos.

Deland, F. 1931. *The Story of Lipreading*. Washington, DC: Volta Bureau.

Epitiris. 1950. Athens: National Institute for the Deaf.

Greek Union of Deaf-Mutes. 1988. *Forty Years Union Booklet*. Athens.

Government Paper 68/15.3.1932.

Government Paper A.N. 1726/16-6.1937.

Government Paper 96/17-5.1907.

Government Paper 41/4-2.1907.

Government Paper 185/6.9.1956.

Government Paper 243/12.12.1956.

Government Paper 281/16.11.1956.

Government Paper D. 53/19.1.1973.

Government Paper 273/4.12.1975.

Government Paper T.A. 202/1979

Government Paper 80/31.3.1981.

Government Paper G. 287/20.1.1982.

Government Paper A.T. 167/30.9.85

Lampropoulou, V. 1985. *A Needs Assessment Study for the Education of the Deaf Children in Greece*. Unpublished Ph.D. diss., New York University.

Lampropoulou, V. 1988. *Etiological Distribution and Characteristics of Deaf Children in Greece*. Unpublished document.

Lazanas, V. 1984. *The Problems of the Deaf*. Athens: publisher's name unavailable.

Moores, D. 1978. *Educating the Deaf: Psychology, Principles, and Practices*. Boston: Houghton Mifflin Company.

Parliament Records of the Discussion of the Act to Support Schools for the Deaf. August, 1956.

"The Problems of Education." 1956. *Newspaper of the Deaf-Mutes*, August.

The World of Silence. February 1985. (newspaper).

Special Education Office. 1988. *Booklet of Information*. Athens: Ministry of Education.

Building a Silent Colony: Life and Work in the Deaf Community of Akron, Ohio from 1910 Through 1950

ROBERT BUCHANAN

As participants at The Deaf Way Conference, we come together to celebrate the contributions of this nation's deaf citizens within both the deaf and hearing communities. This paper traces the development of a factory-based work force and deaf community in Akron, Ohio from 1910 through 1950. In that period, deaf men and women migrated to Akron, where they built what local observers described as the nation's largest "silent colony."

In 1916, officials in the Firestone and Goodyear Corporations, encouraged by a general economic upturn, decided to recruit deaf workers, and by 1920, a national campaign had brought nearly one thousand workers into the company's factories. But the World War I-driven boom soon went bust, and officials slashed the ranks of their workers.

Twenty years later, international conflict once again brought new possibilities for deaf citizens, and in the early 1940s, another six hundred men and women joined the two hundred deaf workers remaining from the earlier era. A local wit in Akron had been nearly correct: It *had* taken another world war for deaf workers to enjoy greater job opportunities.

I will review these developments from three perspectives. First, this unprecedented assembly of deaf workers capped what may have been the first large-scale effort to hire deaf workers ever undertaken by a major employer. This endeavor suggests that workers would find in Akron a diverse and equitable range of work opportunities. Second, I will highlight some of the activities and organizations of Akron's deaf community. Finally, I will consider the national implications of these local developments. Many leaders within the national deaf community argued that these advances in Akron would help persuade other employers to hire deaf workers.

This paper would not have been possible without support from the professional staff and resources of the Gallaudet University Archives, where the papers of Benjamin M. Schowe, Sr. are located. Shortly after graduation from Gallaudet College, Dr. Schowe joined Firestone. In the course of his career, he wrote extensively on employment issues relating to deaf workers. Dr. Schowe worked at the Firestone Corporation for more than four decades and dedicated his energies and life to securing broadened job opportunities for deaf workers.

Akron: Pre–World War I

Prior to World War I, a small number of deaf workers were hired by Akron's expanding rubber companies. The Diamond Rubber Company was the first firm to employ deaf workers, but a dispute of unknown origin developed between management and one or more of these workers, and all were fired (Schowe, 1943). The problems at Diamond apparently did not carry over into the other firms, as both the Firestone and Goodyear Corporations hired deaf workmen soon thereafter. Harry Ware joined Firestone in 1910, for example, and Park Meyers began working for Goodyear the following year (Schowe, 1943). During this same period, officials at the Ohio State Labor Bureau encouraged Goodyear's management to hire deaf workers as a matter of policy (Long, 1919).[1] Other workers joined Meyers there, and in the following months a small number of workers were taken on at Firestone as well (Long, 1919).[2] This pattern of small-scale employment of deaf workers continued until World War I.

World War I and the Recruitment of Deaf Workers

Conflict in Europe and the outbreak of World War I spurred production in the rubber industry, and men and women soon migrated to Akron in search of work. Rubber company recruitment drives drew workers from throughout the region. Between 1914 and early 1917, some 30,000 workers, including native-born men and women as well as immigrants and a small number of blacks, arrived in Akron. "Rubber City" may have been one of the fastest growing locales in the United States (Nichols, 1976).[3] Despite this tremendous increase, however, even more workers were needed to meet wartime needs.[4]

Officials at both Goodyear and Firestone, troubled by this shortfall, actively recruited deaf laborers in 1916. This unprecedented decision was fostered by the positive work record established during the previous six years by Ware, Meyers, and their counterparts. This experience provided management with a favorable perspective from which to contemplate a more encompassing recruitment drive. Charles Sieberling at Goodyear and Harvey Firestone at the Firestone Corporation had experience (Schowe, no date) with deaf workers and supported this initiative (Nelson, 1988).[5] Benjamin

---

1 The timing and efficacy of the activities of the state Labor Bureau is unclear. Long outlines an influential role for the Bureau, basing his conclusions upon the testimony of Goodyear Manager Paul Litchfield, who explained that state officials had encouraged Goodyear to hire deaf workers. On the other hand, J. F. Meagher, an Akronite and columnist for the *Silent Worker*, argued that the Labor Bureau did not influence Goodyear's decision to hire deaf workers (10/1919). Meagher considered the argument that the Ohio Labor Bureau had been instrumental to be "tommy rot."

2 Goodyear's Paul Litchfield was initially concerned that deaf workers might have a disproportionate number of accidents, but this concern was unfounded. In the first two years at Goodyear, not a single deaf worker was involved in an accident.

3 Nichols notes that between 1910 and 1920 Akron's population increased by some two hundred percent. Common lore had it that Akron was an "easy place to find a job, but an impossible city in which to find a place to sleep."

4 For works that review the migration of rural residents into the industrial centers of Ohio and the midwest, see Bodnar, 1962; Eller, 1982; and Kirby, 1983.

5 For a general treatment of these internal shifts, see Nelson, 1975. The establishment of these personnel departments raised crucial issues for deaf workers. On the one hand, acting as gatekeepers, these offices could influence

Schowe later observed that "deaf workers had already proven themselves to be fully competent on the production line" (Schowe, 1943).

In addition, this decision may have complemented the industrial relations initiatives then being developed by Firestone and Sieberling. Both companies, strained by recent labor conflicts and spurred by the introduction of routinized production systems, had advanced extensive social engineering efforts designed to solidify the allegiance of their labor forces. This new "industrial order" would be broadened to include deaf workers (Schowe, no date).[6]

Growth of the "Silent Colony"

It did not take long for the news of this initiative to spread, and in the following months, deaf men and women from across the United States migrated to Akron. Advertisements in deaf newspapers and notices at deaf clubs and schools made official what many already knew—applicants were wanted in Akron, and for steady work! One local observer, noticing the arrival of these newcomers in Akron, exclaimed, "[y]ou can scarcely land in the Rubber City without seeing a few Silents" (Silent Worker, 2/1920). Migrants found in Akron a city bustling with activity, where finding a job seemed easier than securing a place to sleep. Attics, even chicken coops, held newcomers, as homeowners created makeshift boarding houses where they rented out spare rooms and beds, sometimes for three separate shifts a day (Grismer, no date).[7]

Who were these newcomers? Company records, although incomplete, suggest that many of the initial newcomers were males in their twenties and thirties who had attended residential schools—some had studied at Gallaudet College—and who had varied work experiences, skills, and backgrounds. Initial recruiting efforts had been directed toward men, as the piecework production system then being advanced demanded "machine gun speed and accuracy" (Schowe, 1922), and management believed these physical requirements made men the more attractive candidates for production lines. As the war progressed, however, increasing numbers of women came to Akron, where they labored on the production lines and in the offices (Lief, 1951; see also O'Reilly and Keating, 1972).[8]

The majority of deaf workers, as was the case with rubber company workers in general, labored at semiskilled piecework. At Firestone, for example, over one hundred and fifty deaf workers, supervised by a hearing supervisor knowledgeable in sign language, worked in the tire finishing department (Long, 1919). Other deaf applicants, especially those with advanced training from either residential schools or Gallaudet College, found employment in technical and professional positions, including some within the department of chemical research (Farquhar, 3/1920). At Goodyear, nearly fifty men, including veteran teachers from residential facilities, worked as printers, many in linotyping, a

---

hiring policies. In Akron, this meant that the decision to recruit and train deaf workers could be protected against any informal resistance that might arise. At the same time, this centralization of power within the personnel offices, if misused, could be an effective barrier to either informal or union-sponsored hiring of deaf workers.

6 Schowe's comments are illuminating: "It is no strain on the imagination to believe that management was gratified with the opportunity to demonstrate its resourcefulness in the utilization of what so many other managements considered waste material. That the accommodation of deaf workers was related to the 'social responsibility' of industrial management was well recognized and management no doubt was pleased that the discharge of such responsibility went hand in hand with sound business practice."

7 Chapter 14. For descriptions of housing, see p. 379; for descriptions of transportation, p. 381.

8 Over 500 women worked at Firestone, while some 3,000 were employed at Goodyear.

trade long-favored in many schools (*Ohio Chronicle*, 5/31/1919). A few deaf individuals, including Dr. Schowe at Firestone and Kreigh B. Ayers at Goodyear, worked within management, where their responsibilities included oversight of and consultation with the expanding "silent colony." All available evidence underscores the successful integration and safe operating record of these workers, whether in the rubber, steel, or mechanical departments (Long, 2/1919).[9]

The advances of deaf workers in Akron's factories may have been surpassed only by their accomplishments in constructing an active and diverse community outside the workplace. Company-supported activities[10] and services (*Ohio Chronicle*, 5/10/1919)[11] for both hearing and deaf workers were diverse and included a clubhouse with reception and reading rooms, as well as sports facilities and teams (*Ohio Chronicle*, 2/15/1920).[12] Organized sports between the deaf and hearing communities were common, and both company and neighborhood teams competed in many activities.

The efforts of the Goodyear Silent football team are illustrative of the pride and spirit shared by deaf spectator and participant alike (Farquhar, 2/1920). From 1917 through 1922, the Silents won fifty-four games, lost only six, and tied three (Dietrich, no date). And what they lacked in size and experience, they made up in skill and spirit.

Silents manager and Goodyear worker K. B. Ayers recounted one discussion with the coach of the formidable Camp Sherman team, which included several All-American athletes. Upon witnessing the arrival of the Silents, the opposing manager scribbled on a pad, "When will your first team arrive?" Ayers explained to his surprised counterpart that this *was* the first team! Apparently, the conscience of the opposing manager was troubled by this seeming mismatch because the next day, when the Silents arrived at the field, three ambulances sat ready—presumably to carry away the Silent casualties (Dietrich, no date). While the Silents were unable to defeat their opponents that day, they nonetheless held them to a tie (and the ambulances were never used!).

In addition to these company-sponsored teams and events, deaf citizens built numerous organizations that offered a broad range of business, social, and philanthropic activities and sustained a vibrant community. These efforts centered on local, regional, and national concerns, as they encompassed both deaf and hearing worlds. Deaf Akronites worshiped in church, acted in dramas, danced at masquerade balls, viewed silent movies, held charity drives for needy elders (*Ohio Cronicle*, 9/28/1918, 10/12/1918, 5/13/1919)[13] debated in local literary clubs (Meagher, 1918), and reminisced at reunions. The Akron branches of the Gallaudet College Alumni Association and the National Fraternal Society of the Deaf were among the largest and most active in the country. And social activities were joined by business ventures. Deaf businessmen launched "The

---

9 In the first two years at Goodyear, no deaf workers were involved in any accidents.

10 The company welfare initiatives at Goodyear and Firestone have received much scholarly attention. Daniel Nelson's study, *Managers and Workers: Origins of the New Factory System*, 1975), pp. 55–60, is a good place to begin. For a less balanced and more favorable treatment, see Alfred Lief, *The Firestone Story: A History of the Firestone Tire and Rubber Company*, pp. 75–87. Lief points to a wide range of company-sponsored efforts including parks, social clubs, life insurance, and stock options.

11 Options available to workers included housing and stock.

12 Deaf workers, with help from Fred Fuller at Goodyear, established the Goodyear Silent Athletic Club at 1233 East Market Street, on a self-sustaining basis.

13 *Ohio Chronicle*, 9/28/1918, see the discussion of the activities of the knitting club; *Ohio Chronicle*, 10/12/1918—this article mentions a range of activities, including fund-raising drives for the Home for Elders and picnics to raise money for the Ladies Aid Society, Advance Society, National Association of the Deaf, and National Fraternal Society of the Deaf. See also *Ohio Chronicle*, 5/13/1919, for descriptions of these events. For an overview of activities, see Ralph Busby, "A woman who is doing wonderful work," *Silent Worker*, 6/1920, p. 277.

Silent Cooperative Company," which offered groceries and hardware supplies to deaf and hearing citizens alike (*Ohio Chronicle*, 3/6/1920).[14]

By 1920, then, Akron had acted as a "strong industrial magnet" (*Ohio Chronicle*, 9/28/1918) as one observer noted, drawing workers away from old jobs and pulling them into new ones. Within four years, from 1916 to 1920, one thousand men and women had secured employment and built a diverse community in Akron. In an age of limited employment opportunities, these jobs[15] had brought economic independence to single workers, home ownership for many family-minded couples, and the prospects of long-term stability to all (*Ohio Chronicle*, 11/29/1919). For those so inclined, advancement through company-supported preparatory classes, endorsed by Gallaudet College, seemed to promise a bright future (*Ohio Chronicle*, 3/20/1920).[16]

Post World War I: The "Downturn"

These employment-related advances depended upon an unparalleled expansion in the rubber industry, but by 1920 this war-driven boom had collapsed (O'Reilly, 1972).[17] Management at Goodyear and Firestone scaled back production and laid off thousands of workers. For those who remained, wages were cut and work hours increased. Both hearing and deaf laborers suffered. The *Silent Worker* newspaper advised readers to "keep away from Akron" (11/1920), and the *Ohio Chronicle* mourned the passing of the "Era of Great Prosperity" (12/25/1920). Cutbacks had been so severe that by Christmas only some 30 workers remained at Firestone and another 120 at Goodyear (*Ohio Chronicle*, 2/14/1920, 10/20/1920, 12/25/1920).[18] Firestone's Schowe urged patience. "Give Akron time," he reasoned, "but don't count it out, don't count it out" (Schowe, 1/1922).

Between 1920 and 1939, the large-scale rehiring of either deaf or hearing workers, desired by Schowe and others, did not occur. Indeed, the inter-war years were noted for an opposite trend. Management at both Goodyear and Firestone increasingly relied on labor-reducing technology. Although some workers were rehired, these new methods eliminated many jobs, especially for the more vulnerable semiskilled workers (Grismer, no date).[19]

By 1940, international conflict in Europe had begun to revive the Depression-weakened economy. In the coming months, factories ran seven days a week, three shifts a day to supply goods for the Allied war effort. The number of rubber workers leaped from 30,000 in 1939, to over 75,000 by 1944. A new aircraft division created another 30,000 jobs (Grismer, no date).

---

14 On the fifteenth of January the following year, the *Chronicle* explained that completion of the store had been delayed. Apparently the contractor suffered setbacks during the recession. The original proponents of the enterprise remained interested, but it is not known if the venture ever came to fruition.

15 Labor historian Daniel Nelson suggests that the real value of wages for Akron's rubber worker increased as much as 30 percent between 1917 and 1920. See, e.g., Nelson, 1988, p. 73.

16 A. D. Martin, one of the first and most prominent of Goodyear's deaf workers, was placed in charge of these classes. Information on the number of students is not available. For further reference see also *Silent Worker*, 10/1917, p. 45.

17 Goodyear's sales in 1920 of $192 million led to profits of $51 million. With the business downturn in 1921, sales dropped to $105 million. A net loss of $5 million contributed to changes within the top management.

18 See the following issues for a sketch of work conditions after the downturn: 1/5/1921; 12/21/1921; and 12/22/1921.

19 Grismer points out that from 1919 through 1929, production in Akron's rubber factories increased three hundred percent. At the same time, management reduced the number of workers from 70,000 to 52,000. At Goodyear, for example, 33,000 workers were employed in 1919, but by 1929, management had reduced the workforce to 20,000 workers.

World War II

This massive employment upturn, in Akron and throughout the nation, brought new opportunities to the nation's deaf citizens. As early as 1940, one year before the United States' entry into the war, management at Goodyear and Firestone recruited hearing workers, first in local employment drives and then in national sweeps. Concurrent with these efforts, deaf citizens were also recruited once again. During the war years, approximately 800 deaf men and women worked within the factories of Goodyear and Firestone. Men and women held over two dozen different positions, from unskilled to highly advanced, with the majority at semiskilled stations ("Duplicates," Schowe Papers, no date).[20] Contemporary observers speculated that the size of the deaf workforce fell slightly below that of World War I, because, in part, deaf citizens enjoyed more numerous employment possibilities nationwide.

For deaf citizens, Akron remained an appealing city in which to work and live. Increasing numbers of firms nationwide brought deaf workers into their workforce, yet evidence suggests that some newcomers favored Akron over alternate locations. Working conditions in Akron, while generally favorable, were not exceptional; regular work was available elsewhere. However, Akron's deaf citizens had developed a broad array of community organizations and events including social, charitable, athletic, intellectual, and patriotic activities (Lief, 1951). These community-based opportunities, collectively constructed, gave Akron a distinctive character and attractiveness. National organizations such as the National Fraternal Society of the Deaf and the National Association of the Deaf flourished, as did such local organizations such as the Akron Club of the Deaf, which had over 300 members by 1943 (Hammersley, 12/1948).

In addition to their work and community activities, deaf citizens supported the war effort through a wide range of initiatives. Editorials in the *Ohio Chronicle*, published at the Ohio School for the Deaf, urged residents to assist the Allied drive. Enlistment in the service, *Chronicle* writers explained, was preferred but not possible. Instead, deaf citizens had a special obligation to help on the homefront through "self-sacrifice and unending effort." Factory workers were reminded that the "country needs the work we are doing no matter how humble" (*Ohio Chronicle*, 12/13/1941).[21] And Akron's citizens rallied to back the war. At the factories, deaf workers purchased bonds and attended rallies. After work, men and women donated blood and canned food, made bandages, knitted sweaters and blankets, and held scrap drives (Lief, 1951).

How did Akron's residents themselves interpret these war-time challenges and opportunities? Unfortunately, available records are incomplete. Nonetheless, certain patterns emerge from existing records. The steady work available within the factories nourished in Akron's citizens a strong sense of independence and pride. War-time activities, especially, seemed to strengthen an already keen sense of responsibility and citizenship. These work-based openings, in turn, enabled Akronites to develop a diverse and active community, one which spanned four decades and withstood the Depression and severe shifts in population.

---

[20] This report indicates that men were employed at twenty-eight different positions. Women, on the other hand, were stationed at only eight stations. The majority of positions for women seemed to have entailed challenging physical activity and included such classifications as rubber worker, riveter, assembler of aircraft, and job press feeder.

[21] R. M. G. "Our Post in the Fight for Freedom," *Ohio Chronicle*, December 13, 1941; "The Time Is Now," *Ohio Chronicle*, January 10, 1942. (Reprint from the "Fanwood Journal").

National Implications

Many observers within the deaf community held great hopes that deaf workers would enjoy increased employment opportunities in the years following the war. This wish rested on the premise that ignorance—not overt discrimination—on the part of hearing employers had been the major obstacle blocking deaf workers. Advocates hoped that deaf workers would establish favorable work records during the war, thus illustrating their varied talents and skills. These records would then be used to educate employers (Elstad, 1943).[22] Indeed, the positive work records compiled by deaf workers affirmed their abilities. By 1943, evidence suggests that all able-bodied deaf workers were employed in war-related industries. One study, completed by the Department of Labor, surveyed the work records of some 600 deaf and hard of hearing men and women employed nationwide. Stationed at positions requiring a wide range of skills, these workers were as productive and reliable as their hearing counterparts (GPO, 1948). Overall, more than two dozen companies in twelve major war industries employed productive deaf workers during World War II. This evidence suggests that employers recognized the abilities of their deaf workers.

The most effective strategy to broaden opportunities for deaf workers, advocates reasoned, would be to educate unknowing or reluctant employers about this record of success. Some proponents argued that alternative approaches such as legal action or governmental intervention—techniques used by other minorities, including African Americans and Native Americans—while well-intentioned, could be counterproductive and should be avoided (Howard, 1941).[23] Benjamin Schowe, Sr., argued that the examples of hard-working men and women, shown first by Ware and Meyers and in the following decades by hundreds of deaf workers, had removed employment obstacles in Akron and would therefore work elsewhere as well. "Each deaf workman of this sort," Schowe later argued, "is like a man with a lantern on a moonless night. He dispels the gloom of prejudice all around him, and others can see the gleam of his light from afar. These are the unsung heroes we must depend on" (7/16/1959). And Schowe's arguments seemed to have worked in Akron, where some officials at Goodyear and Firestone had contended that the best deaf workers had been more effective than their hearing counterparts.

The Challenge Ahead

Historical evidence, however, indicates that two additional points merit consideration in this portrait of deaf workers' success. First, for those admitted to the workforce, access must be backed up by the opportunity for advancement. Recent historical trends illustrate that deaf workers have been admitted into the workforce, but have found their upward mobility impeded (Schein and Delk, 1974). The power of employers to regulate and reward workers is particularly important for the many deaf workers laboring in the manufacturing industry. While these workers may be without formal training or advanced degrees, many have developed substantial skills and experience that would enable them to advance within their fields. As a consequence, deaf laborers in the manu-

---

22 At the time, Elstad was with the Minnesota School for the Deaf.

23 Howard explained that "in Minnesota we thought we were smart by having a clause put in a compensation law that specified that handicapped people should *not* be discriminated against. The result was to call attention to handicaps, and handicapped people were adversely affected by this noble experiment to protect them. They were simply *not* employed."

facturing sector and elsewhere may be underemployed, working in positions below their backgrounds and abilities.

A second factor that has limited the upward mobility of deaf workers is the position adopted by employers in regard to this hearing impairment. In Akron, for example, the majority of jobs held by deaf workers entailed neither special training at the outset nor exceptional oversight once the workers had completed their break-in period. Some advocates, including Schowe, regularly pointed out that deaf workers were "just like other employees." But deaf workers can ably perform at an even wider array of positions if their employers provide additional support services, such as a TDD or an interpreter, when appropriate. Securing adequate support services within an unrestricted work environment remains a challenge facing deaf and other minority citizens.

Following the Second World War, deaf and hearing workers alike were laid off *en masse* in Akron, as the local economy was converted to peace-time production (Grismer, no date).[24] Many citizens tried to remain in the community, but were forced to leave in search of work. Even as conditions within Akron grew more difficult, the example built there endured, as a letter sent to Ben Schowe by Elmer Ashley suggests. Employed for ten years in Mississippi as a mill hand, Elmer Ashley had recently been laid off when he wrote to Schowe in 1952. Somehow, Ashley knew of Schowe and of the traditions within Akron's deaf community. "I am a mute. And here where I live there aren't any jobs for a deaf person," Ashley explained. "I have tried at the shipyards, paper mill, rubber plant, cat food plant, and several places. They all say the insurance don't allow them to hire deafs. Write and let me know and I will be there as soon as possible" (Ashley, 12/10/1952).[25]

As we consider the obstacles facing deaf people and the accomplishments of deaf citizens worldwide, let us remember, as Ashley did, the thousands who built within Akron a "Silent Colony." Their contributions are part of The Deaf Way.

References

Ashley, Elmer to Benjamin Schowe. 10 December 1952. Benjamin Schowe Papers, Gallaudet University Archives, Box 14/Folder 13.

Bodnar, John. 1982. *Workers' World: Kinship, Community and Protest in an Industrial Society, 1900–1940*. Baltimore: Johns Hopkins University Press.

Busby, Ralph. 1920. "A Woman Who Is Doing Wonderful Work." *Silent Worker*, June, p. 277.

"Cooperative Grocery of Deaf Men Soon to Open Store in Akron." 1920. *Ohio Chronicle*, 6 March.

Dietrich, Phillip J. n.d. *The Silent Men*. Akron: Goodyear Tire and Rubber Company. Foreword and p. 9.

"Duplicates." n.d. Benjamin Schowe Papers, Gallaudet University Archives, Box 13/Folder 3.

---

[24] In August 1945, 103,000 men and women labored in manufacturing in Akron. By December 1947, nearly 10,000 workers had been released. Many deaf workers labored within Goodyear Aircraft during the war but were released at the end of the conflict. Management reduced the number of workers from 22,500 to under 4,000. See also Hammersley, 12/1948, p. 9. Hammersley describes the factory-based employment downturn and highlights the efforts of deaf residents to remain in Akron.

[25] This is but one of more than twenty letters forwarded to Schowe between 1950 and 1953.

Eller, Ronald. 1982. *Miners, Millhands and Mountaineers: Industries of the Appalachian South, 1880–1930*. Knoxville: University of Tennessee Press.

Elstad, Leonard to Benjamin Schowe. 21 January 1943. Benjamin Schowe Papers, Gallaudet University Archives, Box 13/Folder 19.

Farquhar, G. C. 1920. "The Deaf in Industrial Rubber Chemistry," *Silent Worker*, March, p. 151.

———. 1920. "A Winter's Tale." *Silent Worker*, February, p. 123.

"Goodyear Company Has School for Deaf-Mute Employees." 1920. *Ohio Chronicle*, 20 March.

Grismer, Karl. n.d. "Akron—America's Boom Town." In *Akron and Summit County*. Akron: Summit County Historical Society. Chapter 14. pp. 379–381.

———. n.d. *Akron and Summit County*. Akron: Summit County Historical Society. pp. 413 and 518.

Hammersley, J. O. 1948. "Akron: NAD Stronghold." *Silent Worker*, December, p. 9.

Howard, Jay Cooke to Benjamin Schowe. 30 June 1941. Benjamin Schowe Papers, Gallaudet University Archives, Box 3/Folder 21.

Kirby, Jack Temple. 1983. "The Southern Exodus, 1910–1960: A Primer for Historians." *Journal of Southern History* 49: 594.

Lief, Alfred. 1951. *The Firestone Story: A History of the Firestone Tire and Rubber Company*. New York: McGraw Hill. p. 93.

Long, J. S. 1919. "What The Goodyear Tire and Rubber Company of Akron, Ohio Is Doing for the Deaf." *Silent Worker*, February, p. 181.

Meagher, J. F. 1919. "NadFratities." *Silent Worker*, October, p. 25.

———. 1918. "Last to Fight." *Silent Worker*, October, p. 45.

Nelson, Daniel. 1988. *American Rubber Workers and Organized Labor, 1900–1941*. Princeton: Princeton University Press. p. 54.

———. 1975. *Managers and Workers: Origins of the New Factory System*. Madison: University of Wisconsin Press.

Nichols, Kenneth. 1976. *Yesterday's Akron: The First One Hundred Years*. New York: Seaman Publishing Co. p. 40.

Ohio Chronicle, 28 September 1918, 12 October 1918, 13 May 1919, 15 May 1919, 31 May 1919, 29 November 1919, 14 February 1920, 20 October 1920, 25 December 1920, 15 January 1921, 21 December 1921, 22 December 1921.

O' Reilly, Maurice, and James T. Keating, eds. 1972. *The Goodyear Story*. Elmsford, New York: Benjamin Company. p. 43.

The Performance of Physically Impaired Workers in Manufacturing Industries. 1948. Washington: United States Government Printing Office. pp. 74–83.

R. M. G. 1941. "Our Post in the Fight for Freedom." *Ohio Chronicle*, 13 December.

Schein, Jerome, and Marcus Delk, Jr. 1974. "Occupations." *The Deaf Population of the United States*. Silver Spring: National Association of the Deaf. Chapter V. pp. 73–99.

Schowe, Benjamin M., Sr. 1922. "Akron, City of Opportunity?" *Silent Worker*, January.

Schowe, Benjamin M., Sr. n.d. Rough draft for "Deaf Workers on the Home Front."
Benjamin Schowe Papers, Gallaudet University Archives, Box 13/Folder 4. p. 34.

Schowe, Benjamin M., Sr. to Marcus Miller. 16 July 1943. Benjamin Schowe Papers,
Gallaudet University Archives, Box 13/Folder 5.

Silent Worker. 1917. October, p. 45.

———. 1920. November, p. 54.

Text of speech before National Fraternal Society of the Deaf in Akron, Ohio, 16 July
1959, Benjamin Schowe Papers, Gallaudet University Archives, Box 9/Folder 4, p. 9.

"The Time Is Now." 1942. *Ohio Chronicle*, 10 January, Reprint from the *Fanwood Journal*.

"Those Who Hear Not—in Akron." 1920. *Silent Worker*, February, p. 119. Reprinted from
the *Firestone Non-Skid*.

Deaf People and the World of Work: A Case Study of Deaf Printers in Washington, D.C.

JOHN B. CHRISTIANSEN

A number of studies have shown that, at least throughout this century in the United States, hearing workers have enjoyed proportionately more white collar jobs than have deaf workers. Deaf workers have more frequently been found in jobs emphasizing skilled, semiskilled, or unskilled manual labor—blue collar jobs (see, e.g., Martens, 1937; Best, 1943; Lunde and Bigman, 1959; Schein and Delk, 1974; Schein and Delk, 1978; Christiansen, 1982; Barnartt and Christiansen, 1985; Christiansen and Barnartt, 1987; Schein, 1989). Among the hundreds of different blue collar jobs deaf people have held in the United States, one occupation has occupied a special place in the history of deaf people and the deaf community. That profession is printing.

The major purposes of this paper are (1) to describe briefly some of the experiences of deaf printers working at the *Washington Post* and the Government Printing Office (GPO) in Washington, D.C., (2) to examine some recent changes in the world of work and some of the potential consequences of these changes for deaf people, and (3) to offer some suggestions about how the experiences of deaf printers in Washington might help deaf workers in the future succeed in an increasingly complex global economy.

Before discussing these issues, however, a few comments about the importance of printing and printers in the development of the deaf community are in order.

Deaf People and Printing: An Historical Overview

Printing has been an important part of the deaf community in the United States for more than a hundred years. During the second half of the nineteenth century, for example, dozens of residential schools established periodicals that collectively became known as the "little paper family" (Gannon, 1981; Van Cleve, 1987; Van Cleve and Crouch, 1989). Since these papers were written, edited, and printed on the campuses of residential schools, vocational training programs in the field of printing were established on many campuses. These programs instructed some of the very best deaf students in the various skills required in the printing industry. In addition to giving students an opportunity to develop new skills, the "little papers" helped shape the deaf community in the United States during this period since "they served as the cultural connections that established and maintained group cohesion" (Van Cleve and Crouch, 1989, p. 98).

Throughout the first half of the twentieth century the little papers continued to be important, both in terms of providing vocational training for young deaf students and in terms of maintaining close ties among those who considered themselves part of the deaf community. In addition, the "silent" press, which included newspapers and magazines published by and about deaf people, thrived during this time. The *Silent Worker*, which included articles about deaf leaders as well as travelogues, news, and other items, was perhaps the best known, but certainly not the only, "silent" publication (Gannon, 1981, pp. 238–247).

In addition to occupational opportunities in the silent press and the little papers, deaf printers have, over the years, frequently found employment in newspaper composing rooms. Deaf people have also worked as editors, writers, and even owners in the newspaper industry (Gannon, 1981, pp. 251–254).

Throughout the late nineteenth century and continuing until at least the mid-1970s, printing was one of the most popular occupational goals for young deaf persons. While jobs in printing paid well, this was probably not the only reason why printing attracted many bright deaf people, including many college graduates. Since both the little papers and the silent press were important in the development of the deaf community in the United States, deaf printers (especially those working in white collar positions as writers and editors) became quite influential, enjoying a considerable amount of status and prestige. Also, since printing has long been a highly unionized profession and because printers achieving journeyman status enjoyed considerable opportunities for mobility (both geographical and occupational) and collegiality, deaf printers were able to move to new locations, if necessary, in order to work with others with whom they could easily communicate (Lipset, Trow, and Coleman, 1956; Van Cleve and Crouch, 1989).

During the past fifteen years, however, the printing industry has changed dramatically. As the industry has moved from "hot metal" to "cold type,"[1] good-paying, skilled jobs in printing, especially those in large printing houses or in newspaper composing rooms, have been increasingly difficult to find. While space precludes an in-depth analysis of these changes here, many observers have described the job simplification and de-skilling that has occurred in the printing industry (see, e.g., Williams, 1979; Friedman, 1980; Rogers and Freiberg, 1981; Wallace and Kalleberg, 1982; Marshall, 1983). While there are still a number of deaf printers in the composing rooms in some large metropolitan newspapers such as the *Washington Post* and the *Detroit Free Press*, as well as at the Government Printing Office, few printers, deaf or hearing, are now being hired by these organizations. Within the next ten or fifteen years, as deaf printers working in many newspaper composing rooms retire or accept lucrative "buy out" arrangements (large lump-sum payments offered in lieu of future employment), printing is likely to lose its unique status as a special occupation within the deaf community.

Deaf Printers at the *Washington Post* and the Government Printing Office

At the Government Printing Office and the *Washington Post*, deaf printers are involved in a variety of jobs.[2] While some of the positions, especially at GPO, are quite demand-

---

1 The term "hot metal" refers to printing processes in which hot lead is involved. "Cold type" basically refers to those printing processes in which hot metal is absent. According to Rogers and Friedman (1980), the basis of cold type is photocomposition. In this process, type is "set" on film or specially treated paper instead of casting metal slugs. Work done with cold type is generally much cleaner and safer than work that involves hot lead.

2 Comments on the experiences of deaf printers at the *Washington Post* and GPO are based on more than fifty interviews I conducted with these workers in 1987. While each interview lasted about an hour-and-a-half and

ing and challenging, many if not most of the jobs at both places are somewhat repetitive and do not vary much from one day to the next. Even though most of the jobs are less dangerous and certainly cleaner than they used to be, the experiences of deaf printers reflect the de-skilling which has taken place generally in the industry. Moreover, especially at the *Post* but also at GPO, this de-skilling has resulted in a great deal of free time; there is simply not always enough work for many of the printers, deaf or hearing, to do. While the number of hours varies considerably depending on the type of job, printers at the *Post* generally work only about twenty hours a week (or even less in some cases), even though they are physically present at their workplace at least thirty-five hours each week.

In the past, deaf printers held skilled jobs such as handman (composition), stereo-typer (platemaking), and linotype operator (typesetting). Now, with the advent of cold type, most of these jobs have been eliminated, and deaf printers are now involved in such things as paste up, text entry, and text modification (at a computer terminal), proofreading, platemaking, advertisement control (controlling the flow of printed advertisements in the composing room at the *Post*), and, occasionally, supervision.

Many of the deaf printers I talked with lament the passing of the hot metal era, feeling they are no longer "real" printers and thinking they are not using all the skills they have. In addition, while most are more or less satisfied with their jobs, primarily because they are paid quite well and enjoy reasonably comfortable working conditions and good benefits (better at GPO than at the *Post*, however), fewer feel a sense of accomplishment at the end of the day. Many, in fact, said they found the work somewhat more boring now than it used to be.

In the past, at both the *Post* and GPO, there was considerable discrimination against deaf printers. And, in some ways, discrimination continues in both places. Discrimination has ranged from subtle "communication discrimination," where deaf printers have problems getting proper, detailed instructions from supervisors who can't communicate with them, to more overt forms of exclusion. For example, especially at GPO but also at the *Post*, until recently there was an outright refusal to place deaf workers in some positions they were thought to be unable to handle solely because of their deafness. For a long time, deaf printers at GPO were not allowed to be proofreaders (or offset printers either, for that matter) because of the way the work was structured. Two proof-readers were always required, one to read the manuscript being proofed, and the other to listen and follow along on a duplicate copy. Since this structure precluded the use of deaf printers, they were simply excluded from this job. After considerable efforts, the structure was changed. Now only one person is required, and deaf printers do work as proofreaders. As far as is known, this modification has not led to any increase in the number of errors that occur in finished manuscripts printed by GPO.

In the eyes of most of the printers I talked with, discrimination is not so bad now as it used to be, but it still exists. There is still a widespread perception, for example, that some of the hearing workers who are promoted are not so qualified as some of the deaf printers who are left behind. Further, a deaf person's inability to use the telephone (without a TDD) has frequently been used as an excuse for excluding deaf printers from all but the lowest level supervisory positions. While some of the deaf printers I talked with think this arrangement is reasonable, many do not, and see it as yet another form of discrimination.

covered a variety of topics ranging from job satisfaction and discrimination to interaction patterns and communication problems, only a brief summary of some of my findings appears here.

Other forms of discrimination have existed, and continue to exist, at both the *Post* and GPO. For example, deaf printers at GPO were required to take what were perceived to be inappropriate examinations for new positions until the National Center for Law and the Deaf intervened to get the examinations modified and eventually eliminated. Also, many printers mentioned that in the past, deaf workers were given the "dirty work," and, not infrequently, the most physically demanding work.

Deaf printers continue to face discrimination in terms of promotion and training opportunities, and, at least at GPO, are still excluded from some positions (such as pressman). At the *Post* many deaf printers mentioned that conversations among deaf workers are broken up more frequently than are discussions among hearing workers. Further, when their work at one job is finished, deaf printers at the *Post* feel they are more likely to be sent to other jobs than are their hearing peers. In addition, some supervisors apparently have a difficult time believing that deaf printers can work and sign at the same time.

Deaf People and the Future of Work

In a recently published article, economist Robert Reich (1989) identifies three broad types of work that are becoming apparent in the United States. The first, "symbolic-analytic services," is based on the manipulation of information and ideas and includes much of the creative work done by lawyers, investment bankers, academics, and the like. This type of work, according to Reich, now accounts for about 20 percent of the jobs in America. The second, "routine production services," includes tasks done repetitively, as one step in a sequence that produces a finished product. Jobs reflecting this type of work are not limited to manufacturing, but occur in the banking and insurance industries, health care, and elsewhere. Repetitively entering data into a computer, retrieving it, perhaps modifying it, and re-entering it would be an example of this type of work. In the past, many workers in repetitive, monotonous jobs, especially in the automobile and steel industries, received fairly good pay. Now, however, because multinational companies are often able to turn to inexpensive foreign labor for routine production services, wages are not nearly so good as they once were. While forty years ago this type of work made up over half of the jobs in the United States, such services now make up only about a quarter of the jobs in America.

The third type of work, "routine personal services," is similar to routine production services in that it involves relatively simple, repetitive tasks that are closely supervised. Unlike routine production services, however, these tasks are provided in person (checking out groceries at the supermarket or serving hamburgers in fast food restaurants, for example). Workers who provide these services are almost all paid comparatively low wages. These services make up about 30 percent of the jobs in America at this time, according to Reich.

Altogether, about 75 percent of the jobs in America are covered by the three categories. (Reich argues that many government employees, including public school teachers, utility workers, and others sheltered from the vicissitudes of the global economy are not included.) And, in an increasingly global labor market, only those engaged in symbolic analysis are likely to prosper in the future.

In a recently published book, Shoshana Zuboff (1988) shows that some large organizations have responded more creatively and effectively than others to recent technological changes. She suggests that while job simplification and de-skilling often occur as a result of automation, these are by no means the only possible outcomes; new technology can also "informate." By this she means that new, computer-based technology can create opportunities that allow workers to develop new and complex skills based on abstract reasoning and logical thinking.

Unfortunately, while the potential for developing intellectual skills among workers has grown with computerization, managerial and organizational imperatives frequently make it difficult to actualize this potential. Large organizations are characterized by, among other things, a fairly rigid hierarchy of authority, explicit rules and regulations, and a clear-cut division of labor. Not surprisingly, any technological changes that threaten those who enjoy privilege and power in such a bureaucracy are not likely to be looked upon favorably by those so threatened. In the final analysis, it is only in those organizations where managers make conscious efforts to tap the potential of the new technology that automation actually leads to something other than de-skilling and/or job simplification. In addition to giving workers an opportunity to develop intellectual skills, such efforts can also lead to a modification of traditional superior-subordinate authority relationships in a large organization.

Zuboff suggests that to take advantage of the possibilities offered by recent computer-based technological changes, workers must be given more responsibility and more opportunities to make important decisions. Further, she suggests that since appropriate actions in different situations are not always clear-cut, small work groups will be necessary. In such groups, workers can collectively develop and test hypotheses in a collaborative search for solutions to a variety of problems. Thus, workers will need to communicate clearly with one another, whether in person or via computer-based communication networks, to participate effectively in what she calls the "age of the smart machine."

Since jobs based on symbolic-analytic services in the age of the smart machine are becoming more numerous, are usually more interesting, and pay better wages than other types of work, we might ask ourselves how deaf people can take advantage of these developing opportunities. What can be done to ensure that deaf workers in the future are prepared to become high-paid symbolic analysts and not low-paid repetitive workers? Is there anything we can learn from the experiences of deaf printers in Washington, D.C. that can, perhaps, make it more likely that deaf workers in the future will be successful symbolic analysts?

While I certainly don't have all the answers to these questions, it seems reasonably clear that education, including a college education, is very important.[3] A college degree, though, while perhaps necessary in our degree-inflated world, is probably not sufficient; symbolic-analytic work demands well developed critical thinking skills, the ability to read well and communicate clearly, and at least above-average skills in mathematics. For deaf people to succeed in the emerging global economy, it seems to me that we not only have to work to break down various barriers in the workplace (including barriers in the hiring process) that stand in our way, but we also have to do what is necessary to make sure deaf children have every opportunity to develop their intellectual skills in the first place. It is simply unconscionable in this day and age that, because of the absence of adequate communication between a deaf child and his hearing parents or

---

3 A recent Brookings Institution study documented the monetary value of a college education. It was discovered that, as of 1986, the average annual income of college graduates was almost 50 percent higher than it was for high school graduates. This represents a distinct change from the early 1970s, when the income of college graduates was only about 40 percent higher than for high school graduates. Further, this change was particularly apparent among younger (twenty-five to thirty-four years of age) workers. Thus, it appears that well educated individuals, many of whom are presumably engaged in symbolic analytic work, are likely to be relatively well compensated for their efforts compared to their less educated peers (Levy, 1988, p. 124).

siblings or because of years wasted in a mainstream classroom trying to lipread a poorly trained teacher and learning little, or for any number of other reasons, so many deaf adolescents leave school without any hope of getting the kinds of symbolic-analytic jobs that, with a more positive socialization experience, they might be capable of securing.[4]

In addition to emphasizing these skills, what other things could be emphasized so deaf workers in the future might be able to participate successfully in an increasingly complex, global economy? What can we learn from the experiences of deaf printers in Washington, D.C. that might be useful to the increasing number of well educated deaf people who will be seeking jobs that utilize their skills in the future? If, as Zuboff argues, workgroups emphasizing clear communication and frequent interaction are likely to become more important in the future, particularly among those involved in symbolic analysis, how will deaf people be able to take advantage of these changes?

While exceptions exist, the deaf-hearing communication milieu at the *Post* and GPO is generally characterized by pointing, home signs, one word summaries, and gestures. While this "system," such as it is, seems to be good enough for skilled workers familiar with their jobs (jobs that, for the most part, are quite routine), it would clearly not be satisfactory in a complex workplace where meaningful communication is essential. While it is likely that some communication among deaf and hearing colleagues in such an environment could occur via computer terminals, it seems unrealistic to expect that this can substitute for frequent face-to-face interaction. So what can be done?

In large organizations where a number of deaf people work, one alternative I do not think will help much is to provide sign language classes or interpreters to facilitate communication. Interpreters are provided at the *Post* and, to a lesser extent, at GPO for important meetings and conferences, but this seems somewhat impractical for the type of day-to-day interaction that must occur if deaf people are to participate fully in symbolic-analytic work. As far as sign language classes are concerned, at both the *Post* and GPO the training is far too brief to teach anything more than very rudimentary signs, and once the initial enthusiasm of trying something new and different wears off, few hearing people seem to care much about developing their manual communication skills. It seems somewhat unrealistic to expect that many hearing coworkers or supervisors will learn to sign well enough to interact comfortably with their deaf colleagues.

Another alternative, which I think holds more promise for large organizations where a significant number of deaf people work, is to build workgroups composed primarily of deaf people and those able to communicate manually. Most workplaces that involve more than a few dozen employees are made up of various "informal structures" anyway. These structures are based on such things as location, friendship patterns, people who are frequently in contact with one another in order to get a job done, and so on. If companies are willing to emphasize the informating potential of automation, such informating will require frequent communication and interaction among workers, and if well-trained deaf workers are to participate meaningfully in the type of symbolic analysis likely to take place in this setting, then I see no alternative other than to emphasize the need for deaf people, and those able to communicate easily with deaf people, to work together as much as possible.

It could be argued that such workgroups would tend to create an isolated deaf work force, cut off from the rest of the workers in a given organization. From my interviews with printers at the *Post* and GPO, however, it seems to me that the opposite is more

---

4 For an interesting and, to some, controversial discussion of these and other related issues, see Johnson, Liddell, and Erting (1989).

likely to be true: To the extent they are separated from those with whom they can easily communicate, deaf workers tend to be kept "in the dark." In any event, even if deaf people working together in a large organization were to become somewhat isolated, partial isolation from the rest of the organization is the norm for virtually everyone in such complex structures.

Since there are more occupational opportunities available for well-trained and well-educated deaf people now than there were in the past, it is inevitable that there will be times when a deaf worker, in whatever capacity, will be the only deaf person working in the organization. Deaf dentists, accountants, stockbrokers, and attorneys, for example, may often be working with few other deaf people, at least for a while. In the future, as more and more deaf people enter occupations such as these, I hope we won't lose sight of the importance of maintaining a sense of community in the workplace, a community that emphasizes ease of communication and interaction as a means of promoting productivity and efficiency, and ensuring that the job itself remains enjoyable.

As noted earlier, deaf people were drawn to the printing industry in the nineteenth century because jobs in this field offered relatively good pay and because newspaper composing rooms and other places where printers practice their trade became known as areas where one could enjoy working with deaf colleagues. Given the enormous number of new, specialized occupations today, it is not realistic to suggest that deaf workers might find an occupational niche that would replace printing. However, the interaction and ease of communication characteristic of the printing industry for at least a hundred years are still important. Carving a similar niche today may still be possible.

It seems to me that a new niche should not be so much occupation-specific as organization-specific. That is, we should be looking for those organizations that are, first of all, engaged in creatively meeting the challenge of automation by establishing the type of interactive workgroups described by Zuboff rather than using new technology as a new, improved form of scientific management. These occupational environments would seem to provide an excellent milieu in which well-educated deaf people could interact with one another, as well as with hearing people able to communicate comfortably with them. Again, many well-educated deaf people will probably not find jobs in large organizations. However, given the nature of recent economic changes, at least in the United States, many will. And if some large organizations were to get a reputation for not only using new technology in a creative way, but also for being places where highly motivated, well-trained deaf workers were able to work and communicate in a supportive environment, then they, along with the workers themselves, would surely benefit from this arrangement.

References

Barnartt, S. N., and J. B. Christiansen. "The Socioeconomic Status of Deaf Workers: A Minority Group Approach." *Social Science Journal* 22: 19–32.

Best, H. 1943. *Deafness and the Deaf in the United States.* New York: Macmillan.

Christiansen, J. B. 1982. "The Socioeconomic Status of the Deaf Population: A Review of the Literature." In *Socioeconomic Status of the Deaf Population,* ed. J. Christiansen and J. Egelston-Dodd. Washington, DC: Gallaudet College.

Christiansen, J. B., and S. N. Barnartt. 1987. "The Silent Minority: The Socioeconomic Status of the Deaf Population." In *Understanding Deafness Socially,* ed. P. Higgins and J. Nash. Springfield, IL: Charles C. Thomas, Publisher.

Freiberg, J. W. 1981. "Defensive Strikes of a Doomed Labor Aristocracy: The Case of the Printers in France." In *Research in Social Movements, Conflict, and Change,* ed. L. Kriesberg. Vol. 4. Greenwich, CT: JAI Press, Inc.

Gannon, J. 1981. *Deaf Heritage: A Narrative History of Deaf America.* Silver Spring, MD: National Association of the Deaf. pp. 251–254.

Johnson, R., S. Liddell, and C. Erting. 1989. "Unlocking the Curriculum: Principles for Achieving Access in Deaf Education." Washington, DC: Gallaudet Research Institute.

Levy, F. 1988. "Incomes, Families, and Living Standards." In *American Living Standards: Threats and Challenges,* ed. R. Litan, R. Lawrence, and C. Schultze, Washington, DC: Brookings Institution. p. 124.

Lipset, S. M., M. Trow, and J. Coleman. 1956. *Union Democracy.* Glencoe, IL: The Free Press.

Lunde, A., and S. Bigman. 1959. *Occupational Conditions Among the Deaf.* Washington, DC: Gallaudet College.

Marshall, A. 1983. *Changing the Word: The Printing Industry in Transition.* London: Comedia Publishing Group.

Martens, E. 1937. *The Deaf and Hard-of-Hearing in the Occupational World.* Washington, DC: United States Government Printing Office.

Reich, R. 1989. "As the World Turns." *The New Republic,* 1 May, 23–28.

Rogers, T. S., and N. S. Friedman. 1980. *Printers Face Automation.* Lexington, MA: Lexington Books, D.C. Heath and Company.

Schein, J. D. 1989. *At Home Among Strangers.* Washington, DC: Gallaudet University Press.

Schein, J. D., and M. Delk. 1974. *The Deaf Population of the United States.* Silver Spring, MD: National Association of the Deaf.

Schein, J. D., and M. Delk. 1978. "Economic Status of Deaf Adults: 1972–1977." In *Progress Report #12,* ed. J. Schein. New York: New York University.

Van Cleve, J. V. 1987. "Little Paper Family." In *Gallaudet Encyclopedia of Deaf People and Deafness,* ed. J. V. Van Cleve. New York: McGraw-Hill.

Van Cleve, J. V., and B. A. Crouch. 1989. *A Place of Their Own: Creating the Deaf Community in America.* Washington, DC: Gallaudet University Press.

Wallace, M., and A. Kalleberg. June, 1982. "Industrial Transformation and the Decline of Craft." *American Sociological Review* 47: 307–324.

Williams, M. June 14, 1979. "The New Print Technology." *New Society* 48: 638–640.

Zuboff, S. 1988. *The Age of the Smart Machine.* New York: Basic Books.

Education of the Deaf in Nigeria: An Historical Perspective

EMMANUEL OJILE

L ess than a third of a century ago, deaf people in Nigeria had almost no opportunities for advancement. Schools for deaf students did not exist, and no services were available for deaf people.

But today, thanks to both missionary and government efforts, Nigeria has forty-three schools with deaf students enrolled. All use sign language and share the philosophy of Total Communication. Postsecondary educational opportunities also are beginning to open up to deaf individuals.

The earliest efforts to establish schools for deaf students—beginning in 1958 and continuing until 1975—were made primarily by various missionaries and humanitarians. It was not until after 1975 that the various state governments in Nigeria recognized the necessity of establishing schools for deaf students and others with disabilities.

Deaf Schools in Nigeria: 1958–1975

The oldest school for deaf students in Nigeria, the Wesley School for the Deaf in Surulere, Lagos, was established in 1958 by the Lagos Society for the Care of the Deaf. The school, which is still in operation, is run by a board of management sponsored by the Wesley Methodist mission with support from the state government of Lagos and the federal government of Nigeria. In 1968, a nursery school for deaf children, which serves as a feeder for the Wesley School, was started in Lagos by the same group.

In 1958, the Anglican mission opened the Oji River School for disabled students at its rehabilitation center in the state of Anambra. The school had an initial enrollment of eleven children and was used as a practice teaching site by teachers who were being trained at the mission. It was closed on a temporary basis in 1967 in the wake of the Nigerian civil war, during which the school facilities were damaged. When the school re-opened after the war, it admitted children from seven to ten years of age and was under the firm hand of the east central state government of Nigeria. Students who passed the primary school exit examinations, conducted by the state government, were admitted to vocational training. As of 1985, 125 deaf pupils were enrolled, with several on the waiting list.

During the 1960s, the work of the late Rev. Andrew Foster—the first black graduate of Gallaudet University—was instrumental in expanding deaf education in Nigeria. Before the 1960s, Dr. Foster was based in Ghana, West Africa, and had established a school for deaf students there. From Ghana, Foster traveled extensively in Nigeria, where he identified deaf individuals and sent them to complete a certificate course at his school for deaf students in Ghana. When these men returned to Nigeria, they were often sent to one of the schools opened there by Foster, where they served as administrators, teachers, and office workers. Foster opened missionary schools for deaf students in Kaduna in northern Nigeria, Enugu in eastern Nigeria, and Ibadan in western Nigeria.

The school in Kaduna no longer exists. The Ibadan school, opened in 1960, was originally housed in a rented building and later moved to its permanent quarters. This school grew from an enrollment of about eighty deaf pupils in 1972 to about 300 students. Most of its graduates went on to learn trades at nearby vocational training centers. The Ibadan school was later merged with what is now the Ibadan School for the Deaf.

The Enugu missionary school, established in 1962, was merged with classes for deaf students begun by the Enugu municipal council in 1964. The school was closed in 1967 because of the Nigerian civil war. In 1976 it was taken over by the state, and various organizations, including Foster's mission, helped restore the losses the school suffered during the war. In 1977, it became a residential site, with an enrollment of thirty children and a waiting list of forty-five others. After 1977, little was heard about the school. It is speculated that its students may have been merged with two other state-run schools in Anambra, a state in east-central Nigeria.

Even though Foster did not succeed in establishing a permanent school for deaf students in Nigeria, he must be remembered for his early efforts in starting such schools. Moreover, he was instrumental in the education of deaf Nigerian pioneers who have either started state deaf schools or have been involved in helping others start schools for deaf students.

The Ibadan School for the Deaf was founded in 1964 through the efforts of Mrs. Oyesola, an active member of the Girls Brigade of Ibadan. Through one of the brigade's activities, she met a homeless deaf girl named Seliatu. The child was scorned by the other girls, but Oyesola had compassion for her and later adopted her. An American women's group in Ibadan, recognizing her concern for Seliatu but at the same time noting the continuous communication barriers between Oyesola's children and Seliatu, made it possible for Oyesola to get an American scholarship and study at Gallaudet University. She returned from Gallaudet and began teaching Seliatu and three deaf boys in her home. In September 1963, she applied to the state government to establish a private school, and permission was granted for the opening of the Ibadan School for the Deaf. As of 1985, the total enrollment stood at 240.

The Kwara State School for the Deaf and Blind in Ilorin was established in 1974 by Gabriel Adepoju, one of the deaf pupils trained by Foster. After receiving his B.A. and M.Ed. in Deaf Education from Gallaudet University, Adepoju returned to his home state and fought for his state government to provide a school for deaf students. Through his influence and commitment, the school has expanded greatly.

In 1975, the Catholic mission, under the leadership of Rev. Sister Gwen Legault, made a breakthrough by establishing what is now the St. Francis School for the Deaf and Blind in Vandekiya, in the state of Benue. By 1987, the school had seventy-six pupils. Since its beginning, the school has changed hands administratively, first coming under the control of the Benue state ministry of education when Legault left Nigeria, and returning to Catholic control in 1984, when the Benue government decided to hand schools back to their former missionary owners.

1975–1985

The year 1975 was the turning point in the education of deaf students and others with disabilities. The Nigerian federal government's third national development plan (1975–1980) contained the following statement:

> The problem for providing for children who are handicapped as a result of disabilities such as blindness, deafness and dumbness has become more complex with growing awareness of need in this area. The current level of effort has proved inadequate in meeting its needs and argues for a change in improving the situation both qualitatively and quantitatively (Federal Ministry of Information, Republic of Nigeria, 1977).

Accordingly, the national policy assumed full responsibility for special education in Nigeria for the first time. It recognized the importance of integrating disabled people and the need to educate them, provide trained teachers, and make available free education for all people with disabilities. Federal and state coordinators of special education were appointed to monitor the progress of the established schools. Between 1976 and 1977 alone, twelve schools that admitted deaf students were established.

Further efforts by the government to establish schools for deaf or disabled students were made between 1978 and 1985 (see Table 1 for a list of schools). Out of the twenty-four schools for deaf students established during this period, only four were established by missionaries. For the first time, the Church Missions in Many Lands (CMML) ventured to establish a school in Iyale, Benue. The other three mission schools, all in the state of Cross River, were opened by Catholic missionaries.

By 1985, several states in Nigeria had established special schools enrolling deaf students. Oyo continues to lead the other states in the number of deaf schools or units established.

Categories of Deaf Schools

Throughout the 1970s and 1980s, state governments did not focus on opening schools solely for deaf students; rather, most preferred to open special schools where all kinds of students with physical, mental, and learning disabilities—including deafness and blindness—could be educated together.

Four broad categories of educational facilities for deaf students exist in Nigeria:

❖ Schools for deaf students: All students admitted to such programs are deaf. Emphasis is on academic training.

❖ Deaf units: Located adjacent to normal schools, deaf units have deaf students who are either mainstreamed or taught in self-contained classrooms. The units also emphasize academic training.

❖ Schools for disabled students: Students with all kinds of disabilities—physically handicapped, deaf, blind, mentally retarded, and learning disabled—are educated in the same school, with emphasis on academic training.

❖ Special Education Centers: These centers admit students with all kinds of disabilities, but here students learn vocational skills in addition to regular academic work.

TABLE 1: Schools for the Handicapped, Including the Deaf, in Nigeria (1958–1985)

Name of School	State	Date Opened	Founding Organization
Wesley School for the Deaf, Surulere	Lagos	1958	Humanitarians/ Missionaries/ Government
Special Education Center Oji River, Enugu	Anambra	1958	Missionaries/ Government
Ibadan School for the Deaf, Ibadan	Oyo	1963	Individual
Special Education Center, Ogbunike	Anambra	1964	Missionaries/ Government
Kwara State School for the Deaf, Ilorin	Kwara	1974	Government
St. Francis School for the Handicapped, Vandekiya	Benue	1975	Individual/ Missions
UMC Deaf Unit, Oke-Ado, Ibadan	Oyo	1976	Government
Oniyanrin Special Unit, Ibadan	Oyo	1976	Government
Eruwa School for the Deaf, Eruwa	Oyo	1976	Government
School for the Handicapped, Tudin, Maliki	Kano	1977	Government
Plateau School for the Deaf, Jos	Plateau	1977	Government
Ondo School for the Deaf, Akure	Ondo	1977	Government
The Community School for the Handicapped, Ogbomoso	Oyo	1977	Government
Special Education Unit, Ayegbaju-Ile-Ife	Osun	1977	Government
Handicapped School, Iwo	Osun	1977	Government
Special Education Unit, St. Philip's Anglican School, Ilaro, Ife	Osun	1977	Missionaries/ Government
School for the Handicapped Children, Ibereokodo, Abeokuta	Ogun	1977	Government
Special Education Center, Orlu	Imo	1977	Government
Special School, Ikoyi	Osun	1978	Government
H L A Special Education Unit, Agodi	Oyo	1978	Government
Kaduna State School for the Deaf	Kaduna	1979	Government
Special School for the Handicapped, Ilesa	Oyo	1979	Individual/ Government
Deaf Unit, Methodist Grammar School, Bodiga Ibadan	Oyo	1979	Missionaries/ Government
Lagelu Special Education Unit, Lalupon	Oyo	1980	Government
Ijokodo High School, Deaf Unit, Ibadan	Oyo	1980	Government
Omoyemi Special Unit, Apevin, Ibadan	Oyo	1980	Government
Special Education Center, Jada	Gongola	1981	Government
School for the Handicapped Children, Benin City	Bendel	1981	Government
School for the Handicapped, Roni, Kano	Kano	1982	Government
CMML Special School, Iyale	Benue	1982	Missionaries

continued on next page

TABLE 1: Continued

Name of School	State	Date Opened	Founding Organization
Niger State School for the Deaf, Minna	Niger	1983	Government
St. Louise Centre, Ifuho, Ikot Ekpene	Cross River	1983	Catholic Missionary
The Child Special School, Ikot Ekpene	Cross River	1983	Catholic Missionaries
Sokoto State School for Handicapped	Sokoto	1984	Government
Ogbomoso Grammar School, Deaf Unit	Oyo	1984	Government
Seventh Day Adventist Grammar School, Deaf Unit, Iwo	Oyo	1984	Missionaries/ Government
Imo State Secondary School for the Deaf, Ofa-Kala, Orodo	Imo	1984	Government
School for the Handicapped, Bauchi	Bauchi	1984	Government
Good Shepherd Special Education Centre, Ogoja	Cross River	1985	Catholic Missionaries
All Saints Special School, Osogbo	Osun	1985	Missionaries/ Government
School for the Deaf, Ijebu-Ode	Ogun	not sure	Government
School for Handicapped Children, Ilaro, Ogun	Ogun	not sure	Government
School for Handicapped Children, Sagamu-Remo	Ogun	not sure	Government

Method of Communication

Because it imported formal systems of educating deaf students from other countries, Nigeria also adopted the communication methods of these countries. The Wesley School for the Deaf in Surulere, Lagos—the first deaf school in Nigeria—was opened with the assistance of British Methodist missionaries, who introduced the oral method of communication in the school. The arrival of the Rev. Andrew Foster from America introduced the American manual method of communication in schools in Ibadan, Enugu, and Kaduna. Initially, it appeared that a manual-oral method controversy would develop in Nigeria as it did in the United States. But the arrival of deaf education pioneers such as Mrs. Oyesola, Dr. Peter Mba, Gabriel Adepoju, and Ezekiel Sambo, all of whom had acquired their training in America, strengthened the use of Total Communication, which includes American Sign Language.

A 1984–1985 survey on methods of communication used in existing educational facilities for deaf students indicates that all forty-three Nigerian schools that have deaf students enrolled—including the formerly oral Wesley School—now use Total Communication, which includes American Sign Language, reading, and amplification. It is likely that some deaf units that mainstream deaf students in regular classes may rely on speechreading and writing because of the relative absence of interpreters. Outside the mainstream environment, however, deaf students are educated through Total Communication.

Potential Threats to Schools for the Deaf

Two potential threats to the continued existence of deaf schools in Nigeria are the absence of qualified teachers and the lack of related services.

In a comparison of deaf education in Nigeria and Canada, Ojile (1986, cited in Ojile and Carver, 1987) reported the following educational levels of teachers of deaf students: master's degree, 6 percent; bachelor's degree, 11 percent; Nigerian Certificate of Education (NCE), 19 percent; certificate or diploma, 31 percent; grade I or II certification (traditionally the minimum teaching qualification at the elementary level in Nigeria), 24 percent. At least 37 percent of the teachers working with deaf students were reported to lack specialized training and knowledge in their field. There is an urgent need for more trained teachers of deaf students in Nigeria.

Provision of Related Services

Two categories of related services lacking in Nigerian schools for deaf students have been identified (Ojile, 1986). The first is services that are remedial in nature (e.g., periodical audiological/hearing-aid evaluations and speech/auditory training). The second is related to services aimed at successful adjustment, both academically and socially (e.g., psychological evaluations and counseling services). Two factors contribute to the lack of services. One is the expense of purchasing the needed tools, such as audiometers, visa-pitch and speech spectrographic displays, otoscopes, monofonotors, auditory and visa-pitch trainers, oscilloscopes, and hearing aids. The other is inadequate funds to hire qualified personnel such as audiologists, speech clinicians, counselors, and psychologists.

Negative consequences of the lack of these needed services include the following:

❖ Many deaf children have never been evaluated to find the cause and extent of their hearing loss. Consequently, the school is not certain whether a child's hearing loss can be improved or not.

❖ Some children who experience moderate hearing loss could benefit from auditory or speech training through custom-fitted aids and cultivation of residual hearing but cannot get such services.

❖ Some deaf students with serious academic difficulties have never been evaluated to diagnose problem areas, while others have been wrongly placed in classes in which they do not belong.

These issues urgently need to be addressed through the joint efforts of missionaries, private individuals, and federal and state ministries of education.

Postsecondary Educational Facilities

Postsecondary education for deaf Nigerians could be discussed as a separate topic, but it is significant to mention here that future career prospects for deaf Nigerians look bright. In the past, Gallaudet University was the only place where deaf students from Nigeria could obtain a higher education. Today, deaf students are currently enrolled at the University of Ibadan, the University of Jos, the Federal Advanced Special Teacher's College in Oyo, and the Department of Special and Rehabilitative Education at the Kaduna Polytechnic.

Steps taken by the various institutions of higher learning in Nigeria to provide higher education to qualified deaf people are laudable, especially as the country's poor economic situation makes it difficult at the moment to send qualified deaf Nigerians abroad for training. The only obstacle for deaf students in institutions of higher learning in Nigeria is obtaining interpreter services in the classroom—a necessity because the majority of teachers are not trained in the use of sign language. Perhaps now is the right time for these institutions of higher learning to turn abroad to deaf organizations and educational facilities for possible assistance.

References

Federal Ministry of Information. 1977, 1981. *Federal Republic of Nigeria National Policy on Education*. Lagos: Federal Ministry of Information.

Ojile, O. E. 1986. *Teacher's Qualification, Method of Instruction and Provision of Related Services in Nigerian Deaf Schools*. List of faculty research. Jos, Nigeria: University of Jos.

Ojile, O. E. 1985. *An Updated List of Educational Programs for the Hearing Impaired in Nigeria*. University of Jos. Unpublished research, Special Education Department.

Ojile, O. E., and E. Carver. 1987. "Education of the Deaf in Nigeria and Canada: A Comparison." *The ACEHI Journal/LA Revue ACEDA* 13: 96–103.

The History of Deaf Education in the Kingdom of Saudi Arabia

ZAID ABDULLA AL-MUSLAT

Formal education in Saudi Arabia, for both deaf and hearing children, is a product of the twentieth century. Not until King Abdulaziz unified the Kingdom of Saudi Arabia in 1932 did education for any of its citizens become a reality. King Abdulaziz entrusted the responsibility of education to one of his sons, the present King Fahd, who established schools all over the country and offered scholarships for study abroad.

Organized special education in Saudi Arabia began in 1960, when the Ministry of Education established the Light Institute for Teaching and Training Blind Persons. In 1964, the first two specialized institutes for the education and training of deaf children were opened. In 1971–1972, two institutes for educating, training, and caring for mentally retarded boys and girls were opened in Riyadh.

Educational Philosophy in Saudi Arabia

The philosophy of education in Saudi Arabia was set forth in the Educational Policy of 1970. This philosophy springs from the religion of Islam in which the nation believes, which provides the basis for its system of government, laws, morals, and its people's way of life. The Educational Policy is a basic component of the general policy of the state. The state is the main body responsible for providing free education of all types and at all levels to all citizens and residents. The state establishes schools, providing the necessary facilities, textbooks, and instructional materials, and grants financial aid to students. The state also trains and qualifies teachers, pays their salaries, promotes them to higher educational posts, grants them internal and external scholarships for cultural exchange with other countries, and pays their pensions.

Several articles in the Educational Policy are devoted to the education of handicapped students. For example, the policy states that "[t]he state is concerned about the education of sensorially, physically, and mentally retarded individuals. Special and diversified educational and training programs are set up to suit their needs."

Several governmental agencies are responsible for providing services to handicapped citizens in Saudi Arabia. The Ministry of Education provides educational programs to different types of educable, school-age handicapped children and youth. Within the Ministry of Education, the secretariat-general of special education supervises educational, social, technical, and welfare services for these populations. The Ministry of Labor and Social Affairs provides training and rehabilitation programs for handicapped individuals beyond school age, and the Ministry of Health provides physical re-habilitation programs, including medical, psychological, and counseling services. Many hospitals have clinics for audiology, speech, and hearing therapies. The Coordination Committee of Handicapped Services organizes the work of these three ministries.

The General Presidency for Youth Welfare provides sports and recreational services for handicapped youth, especially for deaf people. A special club was established in 1980 for deaf youth to meet for different types of cultural, social, and physical activities. This club, which competes with hearing clubs, is furnished and supported by the government. The Presidency of Youth Welfare also supports an annual olympic sports week for handicapped individuals.

Two new professional-level programs began at King Saud University a few years ago. One, in the College of Education, trains special education teachers; the other, in the College of Applied Medical Science, prepares people to work as audiologists and speech and hearing specialists.

Education in Saudi Arabia is free for all citizens and residents, and education for deaf children is no exception. The budget for education is increased by the state in accordance with the growing educational needs of the country.

In general, the goal of special education, as stated by the Ministry of Education, is to give the children of the Kingdom of Saudi Arabia every possible chance for learning according to their abilities.

The Al-Amal (Hope) Institutes

The idea of teaching deaf students became a reality in Saudi Arabia in 1964, when two special institutes were established in Riyadh, one for boys and another for girls. There were only a few students enrolled in the first school year—sixteen boys and twenty-five girls. However, it did not take very long to increase this number many times over. Government efforts to raise public awareness regarding the desirability of education for deaf people have succeeded, and parents of deaf children have responded positively toward education.

Current data show that the number of deaf and hard of hearing students in the Riyadh Education District alone now includes 727 students in the following schools: 299 students in the Al-Amal Institute for Deaf Boys, 325 students in the Al-Amal Institute for Deaf Girls, and 103 boys in the Al-Amal Intermediate Institute for the Deaf.

In addition, other institutes for deaf students have been established in different educational districts. At present, there are twelve elementary institutes and six inter-mediate vocational institutes distributed in seven educational districts. The total number of students enrolled in these institutes in the 1989 school year was 2,129.

The school for visually handicapped students began four years before the schools for deaf students. In 1964, when the deaf schools were first established, there were already 600 blind students enrolled in four schools, compared to only forty-one deaf students. Between the 1969–1970 and 1971–1972 school years, the number of visually handicapped students exceeded 1,000 in eight schools, while the number of deaf students was only 362 in four schools. Two schools for mentally retarded students were opened in 1971–1972, with a combined enrollment of 100 students.

In the 1970s, the number of blind students began to decline, although more schools were established in new locations. In 1983, blind students numbered about 300 in ten schools, while at the same time the number of deaf students rose sharply to a total of 1,263 in eleven schools. In 1983, the number of mentally retarded students numbered 757 in eight schools. The number of deaf students in the 1988–1989 school year exceeded

2,000 in fourteen institutes, while the blind students numbered 514, and the mentally retarded numbered about 1,500. Currently, the Ministry of Education sponsors a total of thirty-three institutes, serving 4,071 special students.

To be admitted to the Al-Amal Institutes, a child must meet the following conditions: The child must be completely deaf or hard of hearing with an average hearing loss of 50dB, have an intelligence quotient no less than seventy, have no other handicap that may prevent him or her from using the educational services at the Al-Amal Institutes, be no younger than four years of age, and be a Saudi citizen or a legal resident of the Kingdom. More than one-fifth of the total number of deaf students enrolled in 1989 were not Saudi citizens.

In 1972, an Educational Administration of the Deaf was established to prepare and administer educational programs, evaluate the programs' progress, and ensure their effectiveness. This unit is also responsible for educating deaf and hard of hearing children and their families about the educational programs available to them.

The Administration supervises the Al-Amal Institutes; evaluates and selects special curricula and textbooks suitable for use with deaf students; participates in educational research and encourages studies related to the field of deafness; seeks new methodologies for teaching hearing impaired students; studies the need for additional teachers and personnel, equipment, and materials for each school; plans sports, recreation, and social activities in each institute; participates in public awareness activities about the abilities of deaf people to study and work successfully; and suggests new programs and new institutes for each Five-Year Plan prepared by the Ministry of Planning.

The Physical Facilities of the Al-Amal Institutes

The government's concern for educating hearing impaired students was accompanied by a concern to provide specialized school facilities and buildings that would meet their needs and circumstances. To achieve this goal, large tracts of land (about 50,000 square meters) were reserved for each institute.

The buildings at each institute are divided into different units. The academic unit has soundproof classrooms furnished with overhead loop systems. Other rooms are designed for individualized speech therapy, audiological testing, arts, storage of instructional materials, and library functions. The administration unit provides office space for the principal, student affairs officer, social worker, and educational supervisor. The auditorium is designed for multipurpose uses such as exhibits, theater productions, and sports activities.

Each school has an olympic-size swimming pool and an open sports field and provides facilities for football, basketball, and other activities. The health clinic located at each institute has a physician, a nurse, a hall for inpatients, and a pharmacy. The dormitories are divided into several ten-bed halls with a room between each two halls for direct observation and supervision. The kitchen-dining hall and all utilities needed for storage and domestic work are located on the ground floor of the dormitory units.

These buildings are centrally air-conditioned and are designed to accommodate 300 residential students. The first institute was completed in 1980 in Jeddah. The total cost of building that institute was more than $16 million in United States currency. The newest of these buildings is Al-Amal Elementary Institute in Riyadh. The total cost of all special education institutes built to date comes to about $207 million.

Other building projects are underway. Special designs for the intermediate institutes for deaf students are being developed to accommodate the vocational education programs that will be housed there.

Provisions for the Different Educational Stages

Educational Stages

There are four educational stages for the deaf students in Saudi Arabia: preparatory, elementary, intermediate vocational, and vocational training for adults.

1. The preparatory (kindergarten) stage lasts for two years. Most children in this stage go to the Al-Amal Institute for Girls where boys and girls between four and six years of age receive special instruction to prepare them for the elementary stage. The curriculum concentrates on the child's language development and the use of residual hearing with continuous speech training. In addition, a simple academic program includes Islamic education, reading, writing, science, math, physical education, and art. Play therapy is the most common methodology used in teaching.

2. The elementary educational stage lasts for six years. Every student studies a special curriculum adapted from the regular education curriculum to suit the needs and conditions of the deaf child. Such subjects as speech therapy, stimulation of residual hearing, proper use of earphones, and training in lipreading are given special attention. Lipreading is considered the most important means of communication between deaf and hearing children.

3. The intermediate vocational education stage continues for three years. In this stage, boys and girls study theoretical and vocational subjects that include Islamic education, Arabic language, science, math, physical education, and social science. Vocational subjects make up almost one-third of the weekly educational plan. Boys study typing on the Arabic typewriter, photocopying and printing, and electrical technology, with a concentration in one profession. Girls study typing on the Arabic typewriter, tailoring, manual and machine knitting, in addition to other vocational and cultural subjects. By the end of the 1988 school year, a total of 749 students had graduated from the intermediate program.

4. Vocational training for deaf adults is a two-year program during which training and rehabilitation prepare deaf adults to enter the job market. This is the main responsibility of the Ministry of Labor and Social Affairs, which provides programs for individuals over fifteen years of age. Although the Ministry of Education initiated special education for adults at the Al-Amal institutes, these sections were later transferred to the Ministry of Labor and Social Affairs, which opened five vocational rehabilitation centers for the handicapped in Riyadh, Damman, and Taif. About 300 deaf adults have graduated from these centers after being trained in one of the following areas: electrical work, typewriting, reading water or electricity meters, tailoring, carpentry, or manual and machine knitting. The vocational training section located at the Al-Amal Institutes is limited now to deaf students between twelve and fifteen years of age who have not received formal education from the elementary stage. These students learn carpentry, bookbinding, or furniture repair in addition to educational subjects. About eighty-five adult deaf persons have completed this special three-year program.

Class Schedules

There is not much difference between schools for students who are deaf or hard of hearing and those for students who are not deaf in terms of the number of days of attendance and length of lessons in the weekly plans. In general, schools are open five days a week, Saturday to Wednesday. The daily plan includes six lessons for classes below the intermediate level. Each lesson lasts forty-five minutes, with a five-minute break between one lesson and the next. A thirty-minute snack break is offered after the third lesson. The number of students in each class is limited to ten.

Textbooks

The Ministry of Education has tried to make special textbooks available for each subject. Most of the prescribed textbooks for each level have been prepared, adjusted, and written in accordance with the weekly plans. These books are given to the students free of charge. The Ministry of Education also provides the children in these institutes with other supplies such as pens, pencils, notebooks, and so on.

Auditory Aids and Equipment

The Ministry of Education provides auditory aids and equipment to all Al-Amal institute students. This equipment is used to help the deaf and hard of hearing children use their residual hearing to the maximum degree possible, as well as to train them in the correct pronunciation of letters and words. Among the important hearing aids and equipment available at Al-Amal Institutes for the deaf are individual hearing aids given to each student who has sufficient residual hearing to make use of such technology. The individual aids are either body aids, behind-the-ear units, or eyeglass units.

Equipment for the classrooms is provided to amplify sound and enhance speech with a high degree of clarity. The teacher controls this equipment from his or her table and the students can control it from their desks. This equipment can transmit speech between the teacher and student or between the student and his peers. Loop systems are used for amplification inside the classroom. Equipment used specifically for speech training is also provided.

Teacher Training

When the first two institutes for teaching deaf students were established in Riyadh, the teachers to staff them were hired primarily from other Arab countries. In 1968 a six-month training course was organized in Riyadh for male and female teachers to expand the teaching pool. Two separate groups of thirty teachers each enrolled in the course. The United Nations Educational, Scientific, and Cultural Organization also contributed to the course, which included the following subjects: methodology of teaching deaf students; tools, equipment, and audiovisual aids prescribed in teaching deaf students; personality of deaf children and their psychological, social, and physical education; welfare of deaf students in residential programs; and vocational rehabilitation and training for deaf people.

In 1982, a one-month course was organized to educate teachers of deaf students further. The first course took place in Jeddah under the supervision of the Directorate-General of Education in the Western Region in cooperation with the Secretariat-General of Special Education. Twentyfive teachers from the elementary and intermediate levels of the regular schools and professional staff of the Al-Amal Institutes in the region enrolled. A similar course was organized in Al-Ahsa in the Eastern Region in 1985. At the same time, the Department of Special Education at the College of Education, King Saud University, established a new program to prepare teachers in deaf education and other types of special education. The government encourages teachers to enter these fields by providing financial incentives.

The Ministry has also sent a number of teachers abroad for academic studies and in-service training. Seven teachers were sent to England for three years to specialize in deaf education and welfare. Another group of male and female teachers were given grants for master's degrees, and were sent to the United States for three years. The Ministry has also participated in several international conferences in the field of special education and in conferences that deal with the education and training of hearing impaired people. The Kingdom is one of the founders and an active member of the Arab Federation for Deaf Welfare in Damascus.

Special Services for Deaf Students

Residential Programs

The programs at the Al-Amal Institutes are residential. Students in the boys institutes are supervised by adult males and students at the girls institutes are supervised by adult females. Residential services include leisure time activities, health care, social events, household services, beds, and free meals. The residential program is not an educational aim by itself, but is a place for pupils whose families do not live in the same city where the institute is located. A total of 866 male and female students are enrolled in the residential programs.

Social Services

Social guidance in the Al-Amal Institutes plays a major role in the students' adaptation to life both inside and outside the institutes. The relationship between the social worker and the student is a very close one. The social worker's understanding of the conditions, problems, and needs of the students plays an important role in coordinating services in the areas of religion, education, culture, and sports to help the student make the maximum use of the services available in the institute.

Financial Stipends

Students at Al-Amal Institutes are provided with a monthly allowance so that they can devote all their attention to education rather than having to work. These allowances are determined as follows for both male and female students:

❖ At the preparatory and elementary levels, day students receive S.R. 300.00 monthly, residential students receive S.R. 90.00 monthly, while

❖ At the intermediate levels, day students receive S.R. 375.00 monthly, while residential students receive S.R. 135.00 monthly.

❖ At the vocational training level, day students receive S.R. 450.00 monthly, while residential students receive S.R. 180.00 monthly.

Physical Education

Physical education receives much attention at the Al-Amal Institutes. Students practice various sports, such as football, volleyball, basketball, handball, track and field sports, weightlifting, table tennis, swimming, and gymnastics. Students in these institutes can compete with regular-education students in athletic activities and in the boy scouts. Deaf students from Saudi Arabia also have participated in activities in Turkey and the United Arab Emirates.

Art Activities

In most of the Kingdom's districts, Al-Amal Institutes arrange student art exhibitions to give the public the opportunity to see the students' art work and theatrical performances.

Special Considerations After Graduation

By 1988, more than one thousand deaf and hard of hearing persons had graduated from the vocational intermediate institutes and the handicapped rehabilitation centers. They have been offered jobs in both public and private sectors. The government's care of deaf students after graduation includes

❖ Missions abroad: The Ministry of Education, represented by the Secretariat-General of Special Education, has established a program to send gifted and talented graduates from Al-Amal Intermediate Institutes to the United Kingdom to receive training courses in such areas as typing, English, secretarial work, and computers.

❖ Deaf Welfare Committee: A committee has been formed under the auspices of H. R. H. Prince Faisal Bin Fahd Bin Abdulaziz, the General President of Youth Welfare. The task of this committee is to attend to the needs and desires of the deaf citizens of Saudi Arabia.

❖ Special transportation fares: This service provides deaf people, whether students or not, a 50 percent reduction on all types of public transportation, including airplane tickets.

New Programs and Institutes

There are several new projects that have been carried out in recent years or that will be implemented in the near future. Among these are a center for speech and hearing at the Al-Amal Institute in Riyadh, designed to provide special services to children who are having difficulties in hearing and/or speech and who need diagnostic and evaluation services to diagnose and treat such problems. Treatment is provided in small groups (no more than ten students in each classroom). Students are referred—most by public schools, though some are referred by special education schools—when an auditory problem is evident but not severe enough to justify transfer to a deaf school. The program lasts for one academic year, after which time the students return to their regular schools.

A new elementary institute for the deaf will be opened in the 1990 school year in the eastern region in the city of Al-Qatif. A technical secondary school for the deaf will also open in 1990 in Riyadh. Approval for the secondary school has been signed by the Minister of Education, and a committee is working at present to prepare curricula in the areas of business administration, computer science, and library science.

Thus, one can see that the Kingdom of Saudi Arabia has provided facilities and methods to disseminate knowledge to each citizen, including deaf citizens. Based on the Government's belief that education is for everyone, in a relatively short time the Kingdom of Saudi Arabia has made available to its deaf citizens learning and training opportunities in a form suited to their circumstances and consistent with their capabilities.

The Deaf Archive: Our History, Our Future

ULF HEDBERG

I t is very important for Deaf people to acquire an awareness and understanding of Deaf history. Education about our history can help us to understand what struggles and ordeals our Deaf forefathers went through and to appreciate all they did to improve our lives. It is also important to understand the lives of those people and their perspectives to gain a better understanding of the society we live in today and the present situation for Deaf people.

Schools for Deaf students should offer not only the opportunity to study sign language, as hearing students study their mother tongue, but also to study Deaf history. Deaf children must be given the opportunity to learn about their past and to identify with the Deaf people who lived before them in order to respect Deaf people and our achievements. I once met a Deaf man from Milan, Italy who had never heard about the 1880 Congress of Milan, even though he was from that same area where it took place.

Deaf people must nourish and take responsibility for Deaf culture. Deaf history is an important part of Deaf culture. We cannot let the development of a Deaf heritage be left to hearing people. It is very important for Deaf people to take an active role in the decisionmaking processes in every area that concerns Deaf people, and to be active in the leadership of our own cultural identity. We must save all the material we leave behind us to develop a strong bond with our Deaf heritage.

Hearing people have oppressed Deaf people in the past, both purposefully and out of ignorance. This still occurs in all countries worldwide and in every area of life important to Deaf people. This does not mean, however, that we cannot work with hearing people, but it does mean that they must be hearing people who are very sensitive and respectful of our history and culture.

Deaf history should be included in the curriculum of Deaf schools and in regular universities as well (not only in universities for Deaf students, like Gallaudet University). In Sweden during the late 1800s, Deaf heritage was included in the training of teachers of Deaf people. Deaf history and Deaf heritage should be mandatory for all students in interpreter training programs and in those designed to produce educators of Deaf students so these professionals can function appropriately in a crosscultural situation. Offering these classes to hearing people will help us spread knowledge of and respect for Deaf people as well as our heritage.

The Archive

An archive is a place where documents such as correspondence, minutes of meetings, records, diaries, verifications, and photos are preserved and stored. A general misconception is that an archive keeps only old documents, but they can also store present-day documents.

What are some of the reasons for collecting and keeping documents in this place called an archive? First, it offers a safe place to prevent documents from being destroyed by fire, air pollution, water, or temperature fluctuations. Archives are also useful for research and for keeping materials systematized and classified.

In general, the work done in an archive includes the receiving and collecting of materials, filing and storing them in systematic order, and protecting them in acid-free boxes. All documents are processed, and a historical background and classification are developed.

A well-established and well-maintained archive is valuable for research because the researcher can go to one place to find sources for an investigation. An archive and the research it generates can also provide publications and material for use in education about Deaf heritage. The Gallaudet University Archives, for example, are where well-known authors like Harlan Lane (*When the Mind Hears*) and Jack Gannon (*Deaf Heritage*) have done some of the research for their publications.

Our Future

Those countries that have education and organizations for Deaf individuals should locate funding and develop interest in establishing a Deaf archive. My hope is that, in the future, Deaf people in every country can establish their own Deaf archives. This may take many years. Some countries—especially those in the Third World—don't even have education for Deaf children or organized associations for Deaf adults. Some might say it is irrelevant to even think of establishing a Deaf archive in those countries, but it is important for all Deaf people to be aware of the need to save all material for the future.

Even though materials about Deaf people might be available in the national archives of a country, there could be problems finding the records, because the people well known to the Deaf community might be unknown among hearing people. Another problem is that records about Deaf heritage are, for the most part, spread out in different places and institutions.

Deaf archives in different countries could cooperate to make research on Deaf subjects easier. If, for instance, one were doing research on Per Aron Borg, the founder of the first Deaf school in Sweden, Deaf archives in the various European countries Borg visited during his life could cooperate to make documents and records accessible.

Because there is only one Deaf archive in the world at present—at Gallaudet University—I would like to see a program developed to give Deaf people who are archivists an opportunity to specialize in Deaf archives. As more Deaf archives are established, they could offer internships and cooperate to make documents and records more accessible for research. It is important for Deaf people to receive education in managing archives so they know how to keep and care for their Deaf heritage materials for future generations.

Deaf Folklife Film Collection Project

TED SUPALLA

*D*eaf filmmakers in the United States have been making films for deaf audiences at various times from the 1920s to the present (Gannon, 1981; Schuchman, 1984). I believe that such film materials are uniquely valuable to the scientific investigation of minority group lifestyles and useful in the genesis, development, and demonstration of ideas promoting greater general interest and understanding of deaf folklife and literature. However, the uses noted above would require a systematic organization, such as a film library with a nationwide base, to locate such films and preserve them in film archives. In addition, the contents of the films would need to be cataloged to make it possible for researchers, educators, and other users to access the appropriate films for their needs.

This paper describes a demonstration project involving a collection of local deaf folklife films. It first presents background on the importance of deaf folklife films and then describes our pilot version of the film library. One critical tool in such a facility is a film indexing system designed to help locate specific film segments. A primary goal of our project was to develop appropriate modifications of indexing and cataloging procedures so that the new indexing system would incorporate relevant information on cultural and linguistic aspects of the Deaf community. The rest of the paper explains how our film-indexing system works and shows how a film index can be used for gaining access to deaf folklife films.

Background

The cinema has played a significant role in American society. The early 1900s saw the build-up of the cinema as an entertainment industry. But it was not until 1923 that 16mm film, smaller portable equipment, and flameproof celluloid acetate film stock became available. And it was later still, in the 1940s, that the 8mm format became available to individuals for making their own motion pictures (Happé, 1971; Lipton, 1972). This started the popular hobby of home movies as well as the production of films by members of minority groups for distribution within their communities.

This project is made possible with the help of my colleagues Rosemary Martin, Sam Supalla, Jenny Singleton, Roger Strouse, Julie Ann McNeilly Zamora, Jayne Kercheval, and Carol Padden, and is supported by a Research Board grant from the University of Illinois to Ted Supalla, a grant from the Laurent Clerc Fund of the Gallaudet University Alumni Association to Ted Supalla, and an NIH grant to Elissa Newport and Ted Supalla.

A version of this paper was published in 1991 in *Sign Language Studies*, volume 70, pp. 73–82.

What impact has motion picture technology had on deaf people? Those people with hearing losses that prevent them from participating in the mainstream of society tend to associate with others who share their background and social values (Schein and Delk, 1974; Gannon, 1981). This community functions as a minority group within the hearing society, in the sense that its members have an active social life and maintain their own system of values through which they define what it means to be a hard-working, independent deaf citizen (Higgins, 1980; Benderly, 1980).

Benderly, a cultural anthropologist, assesses the roots of this community as follows: "We know little about the true history of deaf people. What has come down to us is the history of their treatment at the hands of the hearing" (1980, p. 106). We may know little of how deaf people lived in the past, but I feel we have overlooked the potential value of films made by deaf people themselves in this century.

My own investigation of such films has revealed a rich heritage of how deaf people lived during this period. Deaf filmmakers have gone beyond making home movies to recording Deaf community events such as conventions, games, and drama; making profiles of individual success models, such as deaf business owners; documenting vocational skills and performing arts among deaf people; and even making feature films of their fantasies, such as cowboys vs. deaf Indians, and Deafula, a hybrid monster who is a cross between a deaf person and Dracula. They also have made promotional films for organization membership drives and in support of civil rights, such as the right to drive a car. Several even got involved in the Hollywood film industry, especially during the silent movie era of the early 1900s (Ballin, 1930; Schuchman, 1982).

From my observations of their work and through my personal acquaintance with present-day deaf filmmakers, I have found that these deaf individuals share similar motives and a similar attraction to film. They have found the medium suitable for recording the visual communication of deaf people using sign language and for projecting their deaf image in a form other than spoken or written English.

Films made by such deaf individuals can be a means of access to the history, lifestyle, values, and literature of deaf Americans. Some have already made efforts to raise awareness of this resource. John Schuchman of Gallaudet University, in his article in *The Deaf American* (1982), urges the Deaf community to recognize the value of and need for a program to preserve films made by deaf individuals. Another example is Beyond Sound (the visual-media company that produced the film *The Story of L.A.C.D.*), which promotes the use of such films in Deaf Studies as well as by the general public.

There are also several archives around the nation that preserve historical film materials related to the Deaf community. Two examples are the Gallaudet University Archives and the National Fraternal Society of the Deaf Archives. The primary purpose of archives, however, is the accumulation and storage of historical materials, rather than the distribution of information about these materials. Furthermore, access to the historical film materials in an archive is difficult for people living outside the area where the archive is located.

Meanwhile, there are few media distribution centers that provide materials relating to the Deaf community. (One is the Gallaudet University Media Library, which distributes some historical films made by the National Association of the Deaf and some videotapes of stage performances by the National Theatre of the Deaf.) Those involved in developing curriculum and instructional materials for Deaf Studies programs have often found limited choices of films projecting a realistic image of the Deaf community. Better access to genuine deaf folklife films would require nationwide coordination of resources and a strong commitment to support a national film library program.

A Deaf Folklife Film Library

The national film library program I have in mind would work as follows: The library would make an inventory of the old films already acquired by different archives and contact various organizations and individuals for the location of more films. The library would provide technical advice so that these films would be properly preserved at the archives through the restoration and storage procedures suggested by the International Federation of Film Archives (Volkmann, 1965). The film library also would include facilities permitting review, selection, and preparation of data from the films.

To solve the problem of making all the footage and the vast data contained in the film library accessible to researchers, the cataloger must record items found in each segment of the films. The basic cataloging of films would be organized in accordance with the Anglo-American cataloging rules (Gorman and Winkler, 1978), while the shot-listing and indexing of film segments would be done using the film library techniques suggested by Harrison (1973). A shot list is a descriptive list of shots, including camera positions and footage, in the order in which they appear in a film. It is useful for both reference and cataloging processes in a film library. Such indexes would later be published and distributed to other libraries and archives so that outside researchers would have access to the materials. Arrangements could then be made to duplicate segments or whole films from film and videotape masters for use in research or as instructional materials.

Demonstration Project

Our demonstration project began in 1982 at the University of Illinois, where I worked as a researcher. I first learned from my assistant, Rosemarie Martin, about Charles Krauel and Chaos Yanzito of Chicago, who filmed deaf people performing a variety of activities in the Midwest during the period from 1925 to 1940. We obtained access to fifteen 400-foot reels of their 16mm films and organized the project in two parts: transferring the original 16mm films onto videotape and cataloging them with an indexing system we developed, and making a documentary film on the work of these filmmakers.

The first part of the project is aimed primarily at the educational and research community, for whom we plan to demonstrate a pilot version of the film research library. This library facility, when operated on a full scale, would locate films on deaf folklife, preserve them, and catalog their contents so that they are accessible to researchers in various disciplines.

The first step in the pilot film library project was to identify and restore each reel in our collection of Krauel and Yanzito's films. The films were identified with the filmmaker's name, date of filming, and title. We then previewed the films by hand with a viewer and recorded a general description of the contents. We examined the footage for physical damage, such as worn splices and torn perforations, and repaired whatever was necessary. Then the films were lubricated and prepared for shipment to a commercial laboratory in Chicago for transfer to videotape.

First, a three-quarter-inch videotape master was made from the film; then a half-inch VHS videocassette was duplicated from this master for our use in cataloging in detail the contents of each film. We located each shot of a film on the videocassette and listed items found in this segment in terms of cinematographic details, subject or activity filmed, and names of places and people. The content items were then organized into an index.

Deaf Folklife Film Indexing System

This index can be used to find particular events, individuals, etc. on the videotaped copies of the films. But in order to locate particular items in the index, one must understand how they are entered. The index user must know what terminology was used in setting up the index and how various concepts have been indexed.

We put the film index into computer format by using the Cornerstone™ data-management software program, which operates on the IBM personal computer. This program organizes the index as a listing of records, with each record including several attributes associated with a particular film shot. Most of these attributes can be used in a computer search during the selection process outlined later. Below is a list of common attributes we used, with an explanation of each.

❖ *Filmmaker name:* The name of the filmmaker is one of the attributes included in the record.

❖ *Videotape time:* This attribute gives the location of the shot on the videotape. It is designed to provide quick access to specific scenes.

❖ *Film date:* When known, the date of filming has been included.

❖ *Cinematographic information:* This includes information regarding the specific camera angle and whether the filming was indoors or outdoors.

❖ *Film location:* When known, the location of the scene has been listed. It may be a geographic location (city, state, country) or a relative location (in front of school building, on a boat, on stage, etc.).

❖ *Message content:* The message content tells exactly what information appears in the title or signpost. This attribute indicates that the filmmaker inserted a brief description of what follows, often giving dates and/or locations.

❖ *Subject type:* The subject type can be one of the following: Vehicle, People, Place, Building, Tree, etc. Generic subject types may be included as needed, but they should be kept very general and should remain consistent throughout the index.

❖ *Subject name:* If the subject type is People or Place and any or all of the names are known, they are included here.

❖ *Activity type:* If the film subject is involved in an activity, the type of activity is recorded here.

❖ *Signing:* If there is a signed dialogue in a shot—for example, when people sign to the camera or to each other—the dialogue is recorded here.

The computer database expands whenever a record is entered for one of the attributes listed above. Each record is automatically associated with a certain shot. The way the data are organized in the computer is comparable to how the information would be recorded onto the shot lists by hand. But the computer can be used to search for a specific shot that includes the desired features.

The procedure for searching with the computer can be described as follows: First choose the "search" mode in the database program and then enter the criteria by which you wish to select records. Select an attribute (e.g., subject name) and fill in the particular word(s) you wish to match (e.g., Illinois School for the Deaf). You may fill in one or more attributes; the more you fill in, the more precise your search becomes. The search will be initiated, and then you will see a list of shot records that meet your criteria. You may either browse through each individual record or narrow the search by entering more attributes by which the program will edit the selection forms you created earlier. This procedure can lead you to the target record whose information may help you find the desired film shot or segment in the film collection.

To improve the effectiveness of this data-management system, we plan to expand the computer program to provide an overall index of relevant cultural items that are documented in the films. This film index may be modeled after the index used in the book *Deaf Heritage* (Gannon, 1981). This book gives an intensive review of historical events, places, and people in Deaf America, and its index would provide an excellent reference framework for our film index.

Moreover, we will try to link the film index to the book index so that one can match a particular shot in deaf folklife film to related information in the book. This would make the film index more useful to people interested in the area of Deaf Studies.

When this project is completed, we will be able to distribute the index of this film collection to researchers and provide videotape duplicates to people who may need such materials for research or instructional purposes.

Use of the Library Materials

As mentioned above, the demonstration project has two parts. The second part of the project involves the production of a documentary film on the work of the two Chicago filmmakers, Krauel and Yanzito. Segments of their films were interspersed with segments of a one-hour filmed interview I conducted with Charles Krauel when he was ninety-two years old regarding his work and the events he and his now-deceased collaborator had recorded on film.

I also want to point out how the index of the Krauel films helped with the production of a documentary film on their work. To keep the original films intact, I made arrangements with a professional film laboratory to duplicate certain segments of footage. To select and locate this footage in the film reels, I used the index we made, which provides a shot list with descriptive information as well as the location of the individual shot in the film.

The film index also helped with content analysis and interpretation. For example, when Carol Padden and I were working on a viewer's guide for the film, we were able to check on our information by using the index to access details in the shot lists.

This production, now completed, is a twenty-minute silent 16mm color/black and white documentary film entitled "Charles Krauel: A Profile of a Deaf Filmmaker." This film and the accompanying viewer's guide can be distributed to deaf education and vocational rehabilitation training centers, school and college programs for deaf students, and programs for students of American Sign Language or Deaf Studies. I am hopeful that this part of the project will help encourage the preservation and use of materials illustrating Deaf culture and folklife.

Conclusion

It is my intention to use this project as a demonstration model to encourage the preservation, cataloging, and use of film materials illustrating deaf heritage, literature, and folklife. I also see this project as having the potential to attract support for the establishment of a nationwide deaf folklife film library, with a systematic procedure for preserving and making accessible the film record of deaf heritage. This project, with the work of Krauel and Yanzito as models, may inspire present and future deaf individuals to continue producing and preserving records of our culture.

References

Ballin, A. 1930. *The Deaf Mute Howls.* Los Angeles, CA: Grafton Publishing Co.

Benderly, B. L. 1980. *Dancing Without Music.* Garden City, NY: Anchor Press.

Gannon, J. R. 1981. *Deaf Heritage: A Narrative History of Deaf America.* Silver Spring, MD: National Association of the Deaf.

Gorman, M., and P. W. Winkler, eds. 1978. *Anglo-American Cataloguing Rules.* Chicago: American Library Association.

Happé, L. B. 1971. *Basic Motion Picture Technology.* New York: Hastings House.

Harrison, H. P. 1973. *Film Library Techniques: Principles of Administration.* New York: Hastings House.

Higgins, P. C. 1980. *Outsiders in a Hearing World.* Beverly Hills, CA: Sage Publications.

Lipton, L. 1972. *Independent Filmmaking.* San Francisco: Straight Arrow Books.

Schein, J. D., and M. T. Delk. 1974. *The Deaf Population in the United States.* Silver Spring, MD: National Association of the Deaf.

Schuchman, J. 1982. "Granville Redmond Lives!" *Deaf American* 36. 1: 2–4.

Schuchman, J. 1984. "Silent Movies and the Deaf Culture." *Journal of Popular Culture* 17 (4): 58–78.

Volkmann, H. 1965. *Film Preservation: A Report of the Preservation Committee of the International Federation of Film Archives.* London: National Film Archive.

Reaching the Deaf Community for Literacy

KAREN LLOYD

When I was asked to speak about literacy and the Deaf community, I thought, "I can't talk about literacy: I don't know anything about it!"

I felt intimidated by the fact that I didn't know anything about teaching people to read and write—as a librarian I'd never been involved in programs addressing literacy. That word, "literacy," bothered me. It seemed like a word that only people such as teachers of remedial reading could discuss with any authority.

Then I realized that in the course of my involvement with the Deaf community, I had actually been talking about and working around the problems of literacy for years. What was giving me a mental block regarding this paper was that we never called it "literacy"! What we talked about was the difficulty that many Deaf people have with English.

Australia is a multicultural society: A large proportion of its population comes from non-English-speaking backgrounds. Whether or not these people are literate in their own language, is it appropriate to say that, because they are now living in a country whose official language is English, they must be able to read and write fluently in English in order to be considered "literate"? Is it appropriate to say that their skills and proficiencies in their own language are no longer of value? How insulting! And what a waste!

Deaf people who are fluent in Australian Sign Language (Auslan) are part of that multicultural population. Auslan is officially recognized as a language in its own right, and for many deaf Australians, English is a second language. How appropriate is it to say that Deaf people who are fluent in Auslan but have trouble with English are illiterate?

Most of us, when we think of literacy, think of the printed page. The problem with talking about sign language and literacy is that sign language cannot be written down. "Literacy" seems an inappropriate word when we are talking about nonwritten languages. But Deaf people do have a means of recording information in their own language: Film and video are to sign language what the printed page is to English.

Another reason I panicked at the idea of talking about literacy was that literacy, both in English and in sign language, can be a sensitive issue in the Deaf community. I'll tell you two stories to illustrate this point.

The first one is about me. When I first got involved with the Deaf community, I didn't know anything about it. I was born hearing. I became deaf when I was eight and grew up in a hearing environment in a small country town, so I never really met other

Deaf people until I moved to Sydney when I was in my early twenties. The first thing I had to do was learn the language. Eight years later, I am embarrassed to admit that I am still not fluent enough to be able to present this paper in Auslan.

The second story is about an organization of Deaf people with which I am involved. Last year another organization working with Deaf people sent our organization a draft policy paper and asked for our comments. In their cover letter, they said that if we preferred, we could send our comments in sign on video and they would arrange to have the video transcribed into English.

There were two very different reactions to this offer. One group of people said, "That's nice of them, but how can we comment on this paper when we can't understand it in the first place? If it's okay to send our response on video, why didn't they send us the paper on video?" The second group said, "We're insulted! Do they think our English is so bad we can't write our response?"

The point, of course, is that deafness alone does not tell us anything about a person's literacy skills. Some Deaf people are fluent in English and some are not; some are fluent in sign language and some are not; some are bilingual and some are not; and many of us are sensitive about the area in which we feel our skills are lacking. Anyone who makes assumptions or generalizations is liable to hurt somebody's feelings or get jumped on, so I feel rather like a sitting duck.

However, I am not going to talk about solving Deaf people's literacy problems. I don't know how to solve them anyway, except to say that if people *want* material that will help them develop their English literacy skills, then the library is there for them to use and will give them this sort of material. The State Library of New South Wales also has a limited collection of materials for people who want to develop their sign language skills. I do not see it as my role to convince Deaf people that they should improve their English literacy skills. If they want to, fine; if they don't, then let's work with the skills they already have.

As I got more involved with the Deaf community, and as my signing improved, I began to realize that the Deaf community was a mine of information and marvelous stories. But where was this information being recorded? I looked around me, and what I saw in each Australian state was a plethora of newsletters and local gossip rags describing what the different organizations were doing, who got married, who won the local squash championships, and so on. These newsletters had their role. I read them myself. I even wrote some of them. But as a librarian, I knew there was almost nothing about Deaf history or Deaf culture in our libraries. How could libraries collect Deaf history if Deaf people weren't writing it? Organizations such as state Deaf societies and schools for Deaf students had historical records, but they were composed mostly of documents such as annual reports, and they were written for the most part by hearing people about hearing people who had worked with Deaf people. Where were all those wonderful, rich stories about Deaf people's lives that I kept seeing told in the Deaf community? Who was writing this important part of Australia's Deaf history? Why weren't Deaf people writing their stories down? So many stories, so much history—lost!

About this time I was beginning to develop as a writer. In an effort both to help myself—because I felt a need to talk about my writing with other Deaf writers—and to encourage other Deaf people to write, I decided to form a Deaf writers' group. At our first meeting I hit the English literacy minefield! Three and a half years later, I am still trying to navigate my way through it.

So many people who have come to our meetings have said, "I'd love to write, but my English isn't good enough." And I have said, over and over, "If you're worried about your English, some of us will help you, but the important thing is not so much *how* you write but *what* you write, the stories you tell. Just tell them your own way; don't worry about your English."

I've used the example of Aboriginal stories written in English. Aboriginal stories are fascinating because of what they tell, but often much of their feeling, their appeal, lies in their use of "imperfect" English—English used in an idiosyncratic way. And so it is with many Deaf stories. Much depends on the story itself. A boring story is a boring story whether it is written in perfect or imperfect English. But if a story is worth telling, then imperfect English often can enhance it.

Unfortunately it is very difficult to convince Deaf people that this is true. So many Deaf people went through school continually being told their English was bad and having it corrected. They don't want to read and write English anymore, or else they *want* to be literate in English but are convinced they'll never get it right. Those who do try to write are often haunted by vocabulary. They have so often been told not to use so many "little" words, that they must learn to use "big" words. They don't believe me when I tell them that some of the best writing uses little words.

Eighteen months after I set up the writers' group, we started to publish our own magazine, *Sound Off*. More minefields to navigate! Some people felt that it was time the Deaf community had a magazine that showed that not all Deaf people had trouble with English. They felt we should correct "bad" English. Others felt we should leave the English alone. They felt a Deaf magazine should reflect Deaf people's use of English. As editor, I trod a very fine line between these two points of view.

I set a policy that any Deaf person, regardless of English literacy skills, was welcome to write for us, but we would not publish anything unless it was worth publishing. By "worth publishing," I meant that it had to be interesting, topical; it had to say something of value. Some stories have been rejected, but we have not rejected anything because of its English. We have received very few stories written in bad English, because people who don't have good English skills just won't write for us, no matter what I've said.

Almost all of the comments we have received have been favorable, but all of the criticisms have concerned the language level. Readers feel it is too high. Deaf people who find English hard to read seem to feel we are neglecting them. I have asked them many times, "How can we print the sort of stories you want to read if you won't write them for us?" There has been a great deal of discussion about how to be fair to everyone. For example, if we do not require people to write "up" to a level they are not comfortable with, is it fair to ask other people to write "down" to a level they aren't comfortable with? The magazine is supposed to be for all Deaf people, but today, two years after it began, I am still trying to persuade people that their English is good enough. I hope that one day the magazine will contain stories that reflect all levels of English language skills in the Deaf community. Only then will I feel it is truly a Deaf magazine.

Soon after we started *Sound Off*, a series of workshops on Deaf studies began in Australia. Originally developed in Melbourne for high school students, the series was adapted for the Deaf community and first tried out in Sydney, where it was an immediate success. Since then, Deaf studies workshops have been held in most states, and the Deaf community is becoming more aware of the importance of recording its history. Appealing to this emerging awareness has become part of my strategy in trying to encourage people to record their stories.

Another important development in New South Wales was a project—for the bicentennial year, 1988—to make a series of videotapes of oral history interviews with older Deaf people, communicating in Auslan, of course. These videos are among our most valuable records of Deaf history and culture, both in terms of the information they contain and as a record of Auslan as it is used today. Auslan, like any other language, changes over time, and these videos will, in the future, show how it has changed.

Australian Deaf people have two languages with which to record their history. They can work in Auslan on film or video, and they can work in English on paper. Libraries collect all types of media, so there is really no excuse now for the Australian Deaf community not to have a Deaf history collection in our libraries.

As part of our continuing efforts to persuade Deaf people to contribute to such a collection, we have planned a workshop at the State Library as part of Deafness Awareness Week in September of this year [1989]. We are also endeavoring to make writers' festivals and workshops accessible to Deaf people. Many people feel intimidated by writers, and part of the value of these activities is that they allow people to see that writers are really just ordinary people telling stories.

When I first started working in libraries, I was a cataloger in a large university library. Part of my job was to catalog Ph.D. theses. Many of these theses were written by students from overseas, and their English was often very poor. People with poor English could get a Ph.D. in Australia, so obviously it wasn't the language that was on trial, but the content of their papers. I often wish Australian Deaf people had the same confidence as these students.

And I wish they had the confidence and courage of the emerging Aboriginal community. This year a few other Deaf writers and I attended two writers' festivals, one in Sydney at the State Library and the other in Canberra. At both festivals we had interpreters, and interpreters are still such a novelty—especially at writers' festivals—that we attracted a great deal of attention. In Sydney, one session was about oral history, and during question time, one member of our group stood up and discussed the oral history video project. She received a large round of applause. The historian convening the session said that it had never occurred to him to look at Deaf history and thanked her for telling him it was there! In Canberra the most interesting and moving session was on Aboriginal writing. Afterwards, one of the Aboriginal speakers came up to us and asked if we had a session on Deaf writing at the festival. He wanted to come and hear our stories.

Last year was the bicentennial of the European settlement of Australia. It has taken Deaf Australians 200 years to begin to think seriously about recording their stories. Two hundred years of Deaf history have been, for the most part, completely lost. So I say to Deaf people everywhere: You have stories to tell; tell them now—on film or video in sign, or on paper in your country's written language. They are valuable, and people want to see them. And I say to librarians: It's important to have literacy material for people who want it, but there's a lot more to literacy than the perfect printed page. Are we all prepared to meet the challenge?

A Cultural and Historical Perspective on Genetics and Deafness

KATHLEEN SHAVER ARNOS AND KATY DOWNS

hat causes deafness? Why are people in both the deaf and hearing communities interested in the causes of deafness? We know today that in the United States the majority of individuals who are deaf at birth or shortly thereafter have a genetic cause of deafness. Genetics is the study of how physical traits or characteristics are passed from parents to children.

An understanding of how genetic traits are inherited in families has existed only since the early 1900s. At that time, the work of an Austrian monk, Gregor Mendel, was rediscovered and led to significant progress in understanding the principles of inheritance in humans. Unfortunately, even today, a lack of knowledge concerning cultural and linguistic aspects of deafness is widespread in the genetics community, as are misunderstandings in the Deaf community concerning the purpose and goals of genetic counseling. The goal of this paper is to narrow the gap of misunderstanding between those who view deafness as a pathological state and those who view Deaf people as a separate cultural and linguistic group.

The major topics in this paper—which will focus on events and data from the United States—include

- ❖ A brief review of historical information, beginning in the late 1800s, that has had a profound influence on both the field of genetics and the Deaf community's perception of that field

- ❖ A review of the facts related to genetic causes of deafness as they are known today, the goals of genetic counseling, and the importance of cultural and linguistic considerations in the provision of appropriate genetic counseling to Deaf individuals and their families

- ❖ A discussion of what the future may bring: new technology that may have an impact on genetics and deafness.

An Historical Perspective

During the late 1800s, a number of individuals became interested in investigating the possible causes of deafness. This interest was perhaps related to the growing debate about the best ways to educate deaf children and the use of sign language. At the same time, the eugenics movement was also very strong in the United States. Eugenics was a movement concerned with the improvement of hereditary qualities of the human race. Eugenicists wanted to apply Darwin's theory of "survival of the fittest" to improving society as a whole. They advocated selective breeding to keep America free of "inferior" people.

One of the proponents of this way of thinking was Alexander Graham Bell, who also had a lifelong interest in the education of deaf children and the integration of deaf children into the larger, hearing society. In order to benefit society as a whole, Bell naively proposed an end to the segregation of deaf children in special schools, an end to the employment of deaf teachers for deaf children, and the end to the use of sign language. All of these measures were designed to discourage deaf people from marrying one another. Bell firmly believed that if deaf people were discouraged from marrying one another, the number of deaf children born in this country could be greatly reduced. He wrote about this extensively in his *Memoir upon the Formation of a Deaf Variety of the Human Race* (Bell, 1883).

Bell considered the rights of individuals to be less important than the well-being of society as a whole and certainly failed to understand that deaf people were satisfied with their lives, considered themselves normal, and many times preferred to have deaf children. Although Bell suspected that many instances of deafness were influenced by heredity, his assumptions about how deafness was inherited were incorrect.

Another very important historical figure who had an influence on the field of deafness during the late 1800s was Edward Allen Fay. Dr. Fay served at Gallaudet College for more than fifty years, as a professor and later as vice president. One of his most important contributions was a study of marriage among deaf people in the United States, published in his book *Marriages of the Deaf in America* (Fay, 1898). In this study, Dr. Fay set out to investigate and, he hoped, refute Alexander Graham Bell's assertion that as more deaf people married one another, they produced more deaf children.

Fay accomplished this by collecting information on marriages between American deaf people. He collected extensive family-history information on close to 4,500 marriages of deaf people that had occurred in the United States between 1801 and 1894. This information included names and birth dates of more than 30,000 deaf and hearing family members of these deaf individuals.

One of the conclusions of this study was that fewer than ten percent of the children of deaf parents were themselves deaf, which disproved Bell's theory that deaf people were producing a deaf race. Dr. Fay's study remains of monumental importance, and his results have been confirmed by recent studies of deafness performed using modern genetic statistical techniques. As did Dr. Fay, geneticists today respect the right of all people, whether deaf or hearing, to have children.

The data Dr. Fay collected have also been available to assist deaf individuals in understanding more about the causes of their own deafness and the possible existence of deaf relatives living in the United States in the nineteenth century. In the 1970s, family history information on 100 deaf individuals who were students at Gallaudet University was collected as part of their participation in a study of genetic factors in deafness (Nance, Rose, Conneally, and Miller, 1977). For fifteen of those 100 individuals, a link to the family names in the Fay data files was identified. These fifteen individuals had deaf relatives living before 1900 who had participated in Fay's study. Most of the individuals had been unaware of these relatives. This information in some cases helped explain more about the cause of deafness in those families. It is hoped that the Fay data will become available on a more widespread basis so that other deaf families can find information on any deaf relatives living in the United States in the nineteenth century.

Genetic Causes of Deafness

Medical knowledge about the causes of deafness has increased tremendously since the early 1900s. It is now known that about 50 percent of deafness present at birth or in early childhood has a genetic cause. These types of deafness are hereditary—they are passed from parents to their children. A person may have a genetic type of deafness even when no one else in the family is deaf. There are approximately 200 different types of genetic deafness. The most common types cause only deafness, with no other associated medical or intellectual problems. With most types of genetic deafness, one or more children in the family may be deaf, while the parents are hearing.

Sometimes, genetic deafness is associated with other physical or medical characteristics; this combination is called a *syndrome*. Some examples of genetic syndromes involving deafness and other physical or medical conditions are Usher syndrome and Waardenburg syndrome.

Usher syndrome involves deafness, which is most commonly present at birth, along with a visual problem called Retinitis Pigmentosa (RP). RP is a slowly progressive visual disorder involving loss of night vision and loss of peripheral (or side) vision. Deaf people with Usher syndrome can be found in every ethnic group and in countries around the world.

Waardenburg syndrome is another very common type of genetic deafness that involves other physical features. Waardenburg syndrome also occurs in members of deaf communities in every country of the world. The features of this syndrome are extremely variable and can involve white patches of hair or early graying of the hair, different colored eyes or different colors in the same eye, the appearance of widely spaced eyes, and deafness. Not all individuals who have Waardenburg syndrome are deaf or hard of hearing; in fact, most people with Waardenburg syndrome are hearing. Usher syndrome and Waardenburg syndrome are inherited in very specific ways in families. These patterns of inheritance will not be described here, but more information can be found in many of the references listed.

What Is Genetic Counseling?

It is apparent that the information presented above is very medically oriented and does not consider the deaf person as an individual or in the context of culture. However, explanations such as those above can be very helpful for deaf individuals who want to learn about the causes of deafness in general, their own cause of deafness, or the possibility that their own future children and grandchildren would be deaf. In these situations, genetic counseling can be helpful.

Genetic counseling is a nondirective process of providing information to individuals about a particular hereditary trait or characteristic. It does *not* involve telling people if they should or should not have children. Genetic counseling should incorporate medical information, such as that found above, in the context of the cultural and linguistic background of the person who is seeking that information.

More and more deaf people are seeking genetic counseling. For example, since genetic counseling became available at Gallaudet University in 1984, an increasing number of deaf people (more than 100 every year) have requested genetic counseling to learn the cause of their own deafness and their chances of having deaf children. Because of this, it is even more important that genetic counselors learn more about Deaf culture and sign language, and that Deaf people learn more about the purpose of genetic counseling and the role of the genetic counselor.

Part of the genetic counseling process is the genetics evaluation, which involves seeing a genetics physician (a doctor who has special training in genetics). The genetics physician often works with a genetic counselor, who is not a physician but has an advanced degree in genetics. This genetics team looks for clues or a pattern that can explain the cause of a person's deafness. Unfortunately, there is no simple test—such as a blood test or an audiological test—that can determine the cause of deafness. The genetic evaluation process is the same for any person, deaf or hearing, seeking genetic counseling for any reason.

Hearing and deaf individuals also seek genetic counseling to get information about other genetic traits in their families that may be unrelated to deafness, such as diabetes, kidney problems, and heart problems. The basic steps that the genetics physician and the genetic counselor use to determine the cause of deafness or other genetic traits include

❖ Family history information. The genetics team will ask questions about both sides of the family, including: Are there any other deaf individuals, any history of genetic conditions, or any medical, physical, or intellectual disabilities?

❖ A brief physical examination. This examination will include measuring the size of the head, measuring the distance between the eyes, and searching for other physical clues that may be associated with the deafness.

❖ Medical records. Sometimes the geneticist needs to review other medical records, such as audiograms and other special tests that may have been done.

❖ Other tests. Occasionally the geneticist may order X-rays, an EKG, or other tests.

After these steps are completed, the genetics team will meet with the family to answer questions and address concerns they may have. In some cases, the geneticists can determine exactly what caused the deafness and whether it is genetic or nongenetic. If the cause of the deafness is genetic, the counselor can explain the pattern of inheritance and the chance that future children will be deaf. Sometimes the cause of deafness is not clear. In this situation, the genetic counselor will explain the possible causes of the deafness and what this may mean for future children.

During the process of genetic counseling and evaluation, good communication between the client and the genetics team members is essential. It is certainly true that many genetic counselors have never met a deaf person. Most genetic counselors have very little understanding of Deaf culture or sign language, because this information is not included as part of their training. Genetic counseling is a nondirective process, meaning that the counselor's job is to answer the client's questions by providing factual information. A genetic counselor does not tell a client what to do or what decisions to make based on this information.

Many Deaf clients perceive some genetic counseling to be culturally biased because the genetic counselor may not understand that Deaf people often do not consider themselves handicapped and may actually prefer to have deaf children. A genetic counselor may unintentionally display cultural bias by talking to a Deaf person about the "risk" of having a deaf child. This inappropriate wording reflects a cultural bias that is present because the counselor may not be informed about the value systems of Deaf people. A genetic counselor may be surprised to learn that a Deaf person or couple may prefer to have deaf children. However, a good genetic counselor will always respect the right of individuals to make informed choices regarding having children.

Successful interaction between geneticists and Deaf people is possible when both groups have had the opportunity to learn about each other. Many Deaf people are now requesting and receiving information that incorporates cultural and linguistic sensitivity. This has been facilitated in a number of ways, including

❖ The availability of a few genetic counselors who are fluent in sign language, training genetic counselors in the use of sign language, and training genetic counselors and physicians in the proper use of sign language interpreters

❖ Education of genetic counselors regarding Deaf culture and value systems and informing counselors that many Deaf couples prefer to have deaf children

❖ Changes in culturally biased terminology traditionally used in genetic counseling that can be offensive to Deaf people. For example, genetic counselors are being informed about the importance of using the terms "deaf and hearing" instead of "normal and affected," or "chance" instead of "risk" of having deaf children.

❖ Availability of information to the Deaf community regarding the purpose and process of genetic counseling through seminars and workshops held throughout the country and through conversations with other members of the Deaf community who have already participated in genetic counseling. This allows more opportunities for geneticists and Deaf people to interact with one another and learn more about each other.

The Future of Genetics and Deafness

Many deaf and hearing people in the general population have learned about new technology in the field of genetics through newspapers and magazines. This new technology includes ways to test for some genetic traits, discovery of the ways that genes work, and the development of therapies for some genetic conditions. For example, new technology in genetics has helped to develop better treatment for diabetes and safer ways to treat children who lack the hormone that is essential for growth. It has allowed some families with specific genetic conditions to make their own choices about preventing genetic problems in their children. Advances in knowledge about genetic traits and conditions are occurring every day. In the future, new technology will make significant contributions to knowledge of the various types of genetic deafness.

So far, however, this technology has not contributed much to knowledge regarding the different types of genetic deafness. Some members of the Deaf community fear that geneticists and some members of the medical community will use new technology to try to eliminate deafness. Members of the Deaf community can be reassured that this will never be possible. There are a number of reasons why deafness will never be eliminated, even if society wished that to happen.

1. Ways to test for most types of genetic deafness are not now available. There are so many types of genetic deafness that it will be many years before scientists have the capability to test for many genes for deafness.

2. Therapy or treatment for most types of genetic deafness is not available now and is not expected to be widely available in the near future. Many years of research are required to learn about ways to treat genetic conditions. For example, for many years scientists have been doing research on the cause of the visual problem that occurs in Usher syndrome; however, a treatment for this visual condition has not yet been found.

3. Most deaf people will continue to be born into hearing families and may be the only deaf individuals in their families. Hearing couples who are carriers for a genetic type of deafness, and who therefore have a higher chance than the general population (and some deaf couples) to have deaf children, have no way of gaining that information before one or more deaf children are born to them. Even if the couples want to determine if their children are deaf before they are born, there is no way that this can be done for most types of genetic deafness. In the future, deaf children will continue to be born into hearing families, and genetic technology will not have a significant effect on the number of deaf children born into these families. It will likewise continue to be true that most deaf couples have hearing children.

4. The most important point related to the future effect of genetics technology is that families will *always* have the right to choose and make decisions for their own families. It has been shown, for genetic traits other than deafness, that even when genetics technology has allowed families to determine if their children will have a specific genetic condition before they are born, many families are not interested in using that technology. When the tests for some genetic types of deafness are developed, allowing people to decide whether or not to have deaf or hearing children, those individuals, deaf or hearing, would still have the right to choose whether or not to use that technology.

Conclusions

Both deaf and hearing people have been interested in the hereditary nature of deafness for many decades. As geneticists and members of the Deaf community have come to know more about each other, they have begun to interact with each other and learn still more. However, only a beginning has been made, and much more education is required of both communities so that they can work together in better ways. The three main points that were emphasized in this paper can be summarized as follows:

1. The perception of the Deaf community about genetics and genetic counseling has been influenced by past events related to the desire of some hearing people to eliminate "undesirable" traits, including deafness, from the population. Fortunately, the field of genetics and genetic counseling is now nondirective. The goal of genetic counseling is to provide information so that individuals and families can make their own decisions based on accurate information.

2. Many deaf people are interested in getting information about the causes of their own deafness and their chances of having deaf children. Also, deaf people may have questions about other genetic conditions that have nothing to do with deafness. This type of information can be provided to the Deaf community through genetic counseling that is sensitive to the cultural and linguistic differences of Deaf people. However, more geneticists need to be educated about Deaf culture and sign language.

3. Future technology in human genetics may have a big impact on genetic deafness. However, deaf and hearing families will *always* have the right to choose to use technology and information in ways they consider appropriate.

References

Bell, A. G. 1883. *Memoir upon the Formation of a Deaf Variety of the Human Race.* Washington, DC: National Academy of Science.

Fay, E. 1898. *Marriages of the Deaf in America.* Washington, DC: Gibson Brothers.

Moores, D. 1987. *Educating the Deaf: Psychology, Principles and Practices.* 3d ed. Boston: Houghton Mifflin Co.

Nance, W. E., S. P. Rose, P. M. Conneally, and J. Z. Miller. 1977. "Opportunities for Genetic Counseling through Institutional Ascertainment of Affected Probands." In *Genetic Counseling,* ed. H. A. Lubs and F. delaCruz. New York: Raven Press.

Shaver, K. 1988. "Genetic Causes of Childhood Deafness." In *Hearing Impairment in Children,* ed. F. H. Bess. Parkton, MD: York Press.

Van Cleve, J. V. 1987. Edward Allen Fay. In *Gallaudet Encyclopedia of Deaf People and Deafness,* ed. J. V. Van Cleve. New York: McGraw-Hill.

Winefield, R. 1987. Alexander Graham Bell. In *Gallaudet Encyclopedia of Deaf People and Deafness,* ed. J. V. Van Cleve. New York: McGraw-Hill.

Addendum

Since the time of The Deaf Way, much progress has been made in understanding hereditary deafness. Several genes for different types of genetic deafness have been located on the chromosomes, and their functions have been determined. Further information about these scientific advances can be obtained by writing to Kathleen Arnos at The Genetic Services Center, Gallaudet University.

Were Your Ancestors Deaf?

CATHERINE FISCHER

ho are you? Who were your ancestors? Was anyone among them deaf? Were the causes identified? Do you have that type of deafness? Will your offspring carry this same gene? What should you and your family expect? Questions such as these can sometimes be answered through genealogy. Genealogy is one of the most popular hobbies in America. Searching for one's past is a basic urge because it can answer our primal need for identification.

Why Do People Do Genealogical Research?

Some people want to reconstruct their family history out of curiosity, or so that they can pass this information on to future generations. Others do it for special reasons, such as to confirm medical histories. For example, an individual who has a hereditary illness may want to do genetic research to trace the source of the illness.

Two families with deafness on both sides could be merging without knowing about their backgrounds. Someone may be deaf or suffering from disabilities such as Usher syndrome and not know how to deal with it. Or someone may suddenly become deaf in a family without a prior history of deafness (deafness can skip several generations). In all these examples, the identification of deafness in the family through a genealogical investigation can be an invaluable tool for a genetic counselor trying to help the families involved.

For the deaf individual, knowledge of one's family history can become a survival tool. One of the most motivating questions for a genealogical study is, "When or how did deafness appear in the family bloodline?" Although I will not go into how to do extensive research, I will try to provide leads and sources that will help answer this question.

Conducting genealogical research can be both exciting and challenging. Of course, you will face some frustrations and detours. It can take a lot of time. It can be costly if, for example, you want to buy archival copies and/or reprints of publications that might answer some of your questions. You also may uncover family secrets forbidden even to be mentioned because of prejudices or pride—criminal activities, for example, or handicaps. Years ago deafness was considered a curse or a punishment. Deaf family members were often abandoned or misdiagnosed as mentally retarded and locked away in insane asylums.

Begin with Yourself and Your Family

In starting your genealogical study, you should get as much vital information as you can about your parents, grandparents, great-grandparents, and other close family members. You will need to focus on five key items: names, dates, places, relationships, and disabilities, if any. Keep written notes.

First, find information about yourself, such as the date and place of your birth. If you are deaf, do you know if your deafness is hereditary? Next, find out about your parents, including the dates and places of birth and death. If they are or were deaf, find out if their deafness is hereditary. As you go farther into your family line, you may not be able to find the dates of birth and death of your ancestors or if they were deaf.

You might find out that a great-grandparent lost his or her hearing in old age. In this case, you will want to look into possibilities of the deafness being one of the hereditary types that show up only late in life. You may want to examine the possible impact of this information on you and your offspring.

Some of the sources of information are described below:

Home sources: Some excellent sources of information can be found in your own home. These include birth, baptismal, marriage, and death certificates; picture albums, diaries, newspaper clippings, letters, the family bible, and other memorabilia; school records, fraternity memberships, diplomas, and military discharge papers; and legal records such as deeds, wills, tax records, and voter registrations.

Relatives: Visit other members of your family, however remote a relative they might be. Make special efforts to talk with the older members, who will probably know relatives who died before you were born. If you write letters to your relatives, don't list too many questions; if you do, they may feel overwhelmed or that their privacy is being invaded. Start by saying that you are interested in the history of the family, and work up to more specific questions.

School and library sources: If you suspect that a certain relative may have attended a school for the deaf, find out how far back records are kept in that institution. Good sources of information are application forms, school yearbooks, newsletters, report cards, sports records, and annual reports. Annual reports are important because they usually include a list of the graduates. However, some schools turn over their records, especially the annual reports, to state archives or historical societies, which means that you will need to knock on more doors.

Deaf organizations: Publications of organizations for deaf people will mention names of their members and other people who might have been involved in events related to the organization. Attend their parties, meetings, and other events if you can. Seek out old members who might have some information about the family member you are researching.

The Gallaudet Archives: The Gallaudet University Archives has many resources that might be helpful if your ancestors attended Gallaudet University, Kendall Demonstration Elementary School, or the Model Secondary School for the Deaf. Some of the Archives resources include

❖ Index cards with names of students who attended Gallaudet University. Usually, the cards document the person the student married and his or her career after graduation. Information is available for the years between 1857 and 1970.

❖ Student records of pupils who attended Kendall School and Gallaudet University (1857–1940). The Registrar's Office keeps Gallaudet student records from 1941 to the present.

❖ Gallaudet Yearbooks (1941–present) and Senior Issues of *The Buff and Blue,* the Gallaudet student newspaper (1911–1940).

❖ Student records from Pennsylvania School for the Deaf, Philadelphia (1820–1935).

❖ Biographical files on many well known deaf people (in conjunction with the Gallaudet University Alumni Association).

In addition, the Gallaudet University Library has books that may be helpful. They include

❖ *Memoir Upon the Formation of a Deaf Variety of the Human Race* by Alexander Graham Bell (Bell, 1883). He presents data on deaf offspring of deaf marriages and lists many names of people who intermarried (1811–1877).

❖ *Marriages of the Deaf in America* by Edward Allen Fay (1898). This book lists all Kendall and Gallaudet students, their families, and siblings. It also lists many names of deaf people and whom they married (1857–1897).

❖ *The Gallaudet Almanac* (1974) lists names of all people who attended Gallaudet from 1866–1972.

❖ *Deaf Heritage* by Jack Gannon (Gannon, 1981) mentions the names of many deaf people.

The National Archives: The National Archives in Washington, D.C. has many records useful in genealogical research. A very good source is the United States Census, conducted every ten years since 1790. From 1830 until 1920, except for 1900, the censuses provide information on whether any person in the household is deaf, mute, or blind. Unfortunately, more than 99 percent of the 1890 census was destroyed in a fire in 1921, and most of the institutions that supplied information have also permanently closed. The 1880 and 1900 censuses include a special count taken of individuals staying in institutions, such as homes for the aged, disabled veterans, and "insane"; schools for deaf or blind persons, or for girls; and hospitals and sanatoriums. The censuses from 1920 to the present are withheld from the public out of respect for the privacy of individuals who may still be living.

You can also check naturalization records, immigration records, passenger lists, military records, discharge records, and registrations for the military draft.

I hope this information will spur your interest in looking into your past, understanding more about deafness, and—most important—discovering heretofore unknown facets of your identity.

References

Bell, A. G. 1883. *Memoir Upon the Formation of a Deaf Variety of the Human Race.* Washington, DC: National Academy of Science.

Fay, E. 1893. *Marriages of the Deaf in America.* Washington, DC: Gibson Brothers.

The Gallaudet Almanac. 1974. Washington, DC: Gallaudet College Alumni Association.

Gannon, J. 1981. *Deaf Heritage: A Narrative History of Deaf America.* Silver Spring, MD: National Association of the Deaf.

The Deaf Way Conference and Festival opened with a performance funded by the National Endowment for the Arts, celebrating the common bonds uniting deaf people around the world.

Actress Phyllis Frelich (U.S.) during the opening performance.

Gallaudet University's President I. King Jordan uses the Gestuno (international) sign for STRONG FRIENDSHIP to emphasize the importance to deaf people of international solidarity.

Deaf Way coordinator Merv Garretson sees a future of global cooperation among deaf people.

U.S. Senator John McCain, chief cosponsor of the Telecommunications Accessibility Enhancement Act of 1988, addresses Deaf Way participants. Dr. Zaid Abdullah Al-Moslat (Ministry of Education, Saudi Arabia-far left) also participated in this symposium, moderated by World Federation of the Deaf President Yerker Andersson (Sweden/U.S.-center). American Sign Language (ASL) and Gestuno interpreters provide translations.

President I. King Jordan greets Prince Bandar bin Sultan Al-Saud, Saudia Arabia's ambassador to the U.S. and member of the Deaf Way Honorary Board. Abdul Aziz Al-obaid (back, right) arranged this historic meeting heralding Saudi Arabia's commitment to quality deaf education.

The enormous space in the Omni Shoreham Hotel's Regency Ballroom made videoscreen enlargement of presentations and interpretations a vital part of communication accessibility.

Applause was made visible—the Deaf way.

Greg Hlibok (U.S.) describes the Deaf President Now movement in ASL while real-time captions in English and Gestuno interpreting appear on the large screens. Spoken interpretations in English, Spanish, and French were available to hearing participants through headsets, and deaf groups that brought their own interpreters had access to the presentations in their own national sign languages.

Many participants had never seen or used telecommunications devices for deaf people (also known as TTYs) until The Deaf Way.

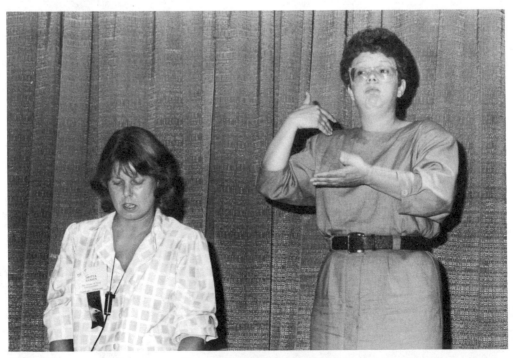

Britta Hansen (Denmark) presented her paper in spoken English, which was translated into ASL for deaf Gustuno interpreter Marie Philip (U.S.). An unprecedented number of deaf interpreters worked alongside hearing interpreters at The Deaf Way.

I. King Jordan poses with winners of the deaf students' history contest. The theme of this Deaf Way contest was "Deaf Heritage."

The Society of Deaf Adults in Quito, Ecuador (Fray Luis Ponce de Leon) sent a delegation to The Deaf Way.

A Brazilian group gathers around I. King Jordan, inspired by his declaration that "Deaf people can do anything!"

A hearing participant learning to sign, "Nice to meet you!"

Deaf-blind participants experienced The Deaf Way through their sense of touch. In this photograph, actress Marlee Matlin (U.S.) communicated with Art Roehrig (U.S.), while Phyllis Frelich (U.S.) waits her turn.

Reflecting the role of deaf clubs in deaf communities worldwide, the International Deaf Club tent became the social hub of the Deaf Way experience for many participants.

Socialization at the International Deaf Club tent included family members of all ages, as is common in most deaf clubs.

Deaf Way participants renewed their energies and spirits in the International Deaf Club tent.

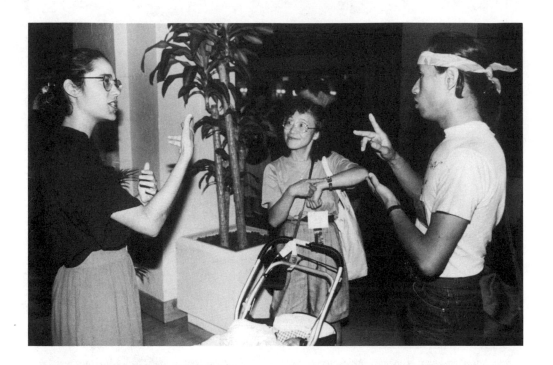

Cross-cultural communication was an essential element of the Deaf Way experience. Participants enjoyed comparing signs from different sign languages and learning about other cultural traditions (see facing page).

Even T-shirts played a role in promoting cultural and linguistic awareness.

*Deaf participants proudly showed many attributes of their homelands'
national cultures through traditional costumes and dance.*

Nipaporn (Jum) Reilly performed a traditional Thai dance at the international dance night.

PART THREE

The Study of Sign Language in Society

Editor's Introduction

The papers in this section describe the work of many individuals and groups around the world to increase knowledge of specific sign languages and their patterns of use in Deaf people's lives. The papers show how greater knowledge of sign languages challenges the prejudices that still prevail in many countries against sign languages and the people who use them. Several authors describe how basic research into the properties of sign languages has led to a range of efforts to promote increased acceptance and use of sign languages in society.

The first two papers, by Brita Bergman and Lars Wallin (Sweden) describe the history and significance of Sweden's establishment of an enlightened national policy concerning sign language and the rights of Deaf individuals. Linguistic research clearly led the way in that country as educational policy departed from earlier efforts to "normalize" deaf children, eventually embracing the view that Swedish Sign Language should be considered deaf children's first language and the preferred language for communication at home and face-to-face instruction in the classroom.

The original context of William Stokoe's (United States) paper at The Deaf Way Conference was as an introduction to several presentations describing the creation of "serious" sign language dictionaries. (Stokoe considers a dictionary serious if it emphasizes how signs are used by Deaf people: not as substitutions for spoken words but as parts of signed languages that generally thrive independently of spoken languages.) The three papers immediately following Stokoe's in this volume—concerning sign languages in New Zealand, Namibia, and the Republic of China—demonstrate that such dictionaries can be developed either by an outsider (provided the outsider understands and adheres to the appropriate linguistic and sociolinguistic considerations) or by Deaf people themselves, working with and becoming linguists in order to increase awareness of the status and potential of sign language in their own countries.

The following three papers collectively suggest both that linguistic studies in the United States have attained a high degree of subtlety and that there is a gap in the United States between linguistic knowledge and educational practices. The first paper, by Dolores Oglia, Marilyn Mitchell, and Frank Caccamise (United States), explores the critical issue of finding a "natural" process whereby sign languages can be enlarged to accommodate new technical subject matter. The second, by Ceil Lucas and Clayton Valli (United States), searches for principles underlying codeswitching behavior among Deaf signers. The third, by James Tucker (United States), discusses the relationship between linguistic and political issues as they affect the use or neglect of American Sign Language in schools.

The complexity of using signed television broadcasts to increase awareness and appreciation of sign languages is explored in the next two papers—one from France (by MarieThérèse Abbou), the other from England (by Bencie Woll, Lorna Allsop, and Rachel Spence). It is clear that the rarity of such broadcasts adds weight to the importance placed on them, and that efforts to maintain a balance between pleasing Deaf and pleasing hearing viewers are often perilously difficult.

Several papers follow that provide overviews of progress in sign language linguistics in various nations. From behind the former "iron curtain," an Estonian investigator (Regina Toom) reports that in spite of the general oppression of all minority languages in the Soviet Union, the need for greater knowledge of Estonian Sign Language was clear, and studies were underway. A paper by Penny Boyes Braem (Switzerland) concerning sign languages in Switzerland points out that linguistic boundaries cannot always be expected to adhere to national boundaries.

Three papers from Germany describe efforts to examine and promote the use of German Sign Language in a nation with a long and formidable oralistic tradition. The work described by Gudula List had not, by the time of The Deaf Way, had a great impact on Germany's educational system. Nevertheless, the computer system called "Ham-NoSys" (described by Heiko Zienert) has the potential of influencing many people in Germany and other nations to use computers to bridge gaps in knowledge between users of spoken and users of signed languages. One of these papers, by Horst Ebbinghaus and Jens Hessmann, explores the interesting topic of the role of mouthed words in a signed language.

A paper by Anna Folchi (Italy) discusses the complexity of sign language variations in a nation where oral and gestural traditions are both quite strong and religious, and town-based histories play powerful roles. In the paper by Tomas Hedberg (Sweden) that follows, principles underlying the assignment of name signs are given, some of which apply to the process of acquiring name signs in other countries as well.

Once the existence and nature of a sign language reaches a certain level of recognition, a demand for sign language instruction often follows. The sources of this demand generally include parents, teachers, and individuals interested in becoming interpreters. The remaining papers in this section address various concerns related to this demand. Two English papers (by Clark Denmark and Frances Elton) describe the development of university-sponsored programs in England designed to prepare Deaf tutors for the task of teaching British Sign Language (BSL) to hearing people. The papers emphasize that by the time of The Deaf Way, students learning from these tutors were expected to focus on BSL exclusively during classes and to spend as much time as possible mixing with members of the Deaf community to learn the language naturally.

Asger Bergmann (Denmark) then illustrates the degree of sophistication attained by the interpreting field in that country. Interpreters in Denmark study ethics and psychology, as well as sign language, in an effort to determine their optimal role in a Deaf and hearing society.

At the time of The Deaf Way, France had not yet officially accepted a bilingual philosophy toward the education of Deaf children. (A law has since been passed, allowing parents to choose bilingual programs for their deaf child.) Nevertheless, French Sign Language (LSF) had by 1989 attained some prominence through television, sign language dictionaries, theatrical productions, and the existence of a few bilingual education programs. Interest in sign language classes among parents and others was high. The first of the French papers, by Josette Bouchauveau, provides advice to Deaf sign language teachers concerning ways to put hearing people at ease and establish a productive teacher-learner rapport in a signing-only environment.

The following four papers discuss the principles and functions of the French interpreter training program, SERAC. Giles Verlet emphasizes that communication is a basic human right and that the interpreting field is based on that premise. Agnes Vourc'h points out that although Deaf native signers are the best teachers of LSF, Deaf people need to learn the linguistic principles of LSF in order to teach these principles effectively. The paper by Dominique Hof discusses the need for greater understanding among Deaf as well as hearing people concerning the nature of the interpreting process and areas in which consumer demands may at times be unreasonable. The final French paper on this topic, by Victor Abbou, nevertheless describes the qualities Deaf consumers justifiably wish to find in interpreters.

The last paper in this section, by Jeffrey Davis and Kathy Jankowski (United States), discusses how interpreters' roles are complicated by the fact that signs tend to have multiple possible interpretations in spoken languages and that the same is true when interpreting from spoken to signed language. The authors imply that the more interpreters know about the nuances of meaning associated with signs and words, the more likely they are to make wise choices while interpreting.

The Study of Sign Language in Society: Part One

BRITA BERGMAN

I n Sweden, linguistic research on sign language has contributed to improving the status of Swedish Sign Language, and thereby the situation of deaf people. To our knowledge, Sweden leads the world in official recognition of the sign language used by the deaf community. We are proud to have been invited to The Deaf Way Conference and to have the opportunity to inform you about recent developments in Sweden.

The paper that follows this one, written by Mr. Lars Wallin, will present a description of the successful fight for full recognition of Swedish Sign Language led by the Swedish National Organization of the Deaf and the changes that victory has brought to both the Deaf community and to hearing Swedish society. In my paper, I will give some background information to explain this development. Then I will introduce you to the concept of language in general, after which I will focus on sign language. In so doing, I will deal with some of the misconceptions about sign language that I encountered in the early 1970s, when the study of sign language in our country began, and I will give examples of what is now known about sign language.

Sweden, one of the Scandinavian countries, is about the size of California. The population is approximately 8 million, with about 8,000 deaf people (one per thousand). There are five schools for deaf students.

We can still see an increasing interest in sign language in Sweden, both from hearing people in general and from deaf and hearing signers in particular. I do not think that users of other languages are as eager to learn about their respective languages as signers are. After all, it could be argued that there is nothing very special about sign language. Swedish Sign Language is a language like any other—one that has evolved naturally through the need of human beings to communicate with each other. It is linked to the lives of its users, and it is a reflection of the culture in which it is used. It has a vocabulary and grammar of its own. It is as complicated and richly structured as any other human language.

It is true that sign language lacks a written form, but so do many spoken languages in the world. It is also true that sign language is not an official language of any nation, but there are many languages that are not. And yet, there is one aspect of sign language

A revised version of this paper, which was originally presented at The Deaf Way, was later presented at the International Congress on Sign Language Research and Application, March 23–25, 1990 in Hamburg. That version has been printed in Sign Language Research and Application, edited by Siegmund Prillwitz and Tomas Vollhaber, 1990, Hamburg, Germany: SIGNUM-Press.

The signs shown in this article are demonstrated by Inga-Lena Adolfsson, the photographs are by Yngre Fransson.

that *is* special: It is a signed language, not spoken. So there are two types of human natural languages that differ with respect to how they are produced and perceived: Sign language can be characterized as a gestural-visual type of language, and spoken language as a vocal-auditory type.

Because hearing people are in the majority and in power, spoken language has been regarded as the only true form of language. The language of the deaf minority has been thought of as an insufficient system of communication, not a real, full-fledged language, and this is still the case in many countries. Ignorance and prejudice have led to oppression of signed languages by those in power. You all know that the oppression has gone so far that sign language has been excluded from the schools of deaf students, not only as a subject in its own right, but also as a means of communication. The exclusion of sign language from education also has made deaf people themselves think that signed language is inferior to spoken language. Nothing could be more wrong. Languages may be different, but they have the same value and fulfill the same communicative tasks.

It is generally agreed that it is necessary to study officially accepted languages, both to learn more about a specific language and to gain more knowledge about human language in general. As for oppressed languages, I can also see another impetus to study them: Knowledge about languages is a powerful weapon in the fight against the demeaning attitude toward sign language. The results of research are useful in the work for attaining full recognition of sign language and, as a consequence, deaf people and deaf culture. This is what we have been actively working for since the beginning of sign language study in Sweden and what sign language research has contributed to accomplishing.

Language

One way of characterizing language is to describe it as a tool for communication. Such a characterization emphasizes what language is used for and may contain statements such as, "Language is used for expressing thoughts and feelings," and "Language is used for conveying culture and history to other generations." Another way of characterizing language is to describe what it looks like—to describe its structure. And that is what I will focus on.

Broadly speaking, language can be said to consist of two parts: a lexicon and a grammar. Let us imagine individuals who are about to learn a new language. The task they have undertaken is twofold: They must learn the symbols of the language—parts of the vocabulary, or lexicon, as it is called. But even if they managed to learn every sign or word of the language, that would not suffice, because they still would not know how to use these words or signs. They also must learn the rules for their combination into phrases and sentences—the grammar of the language. And this is what the child does in acquiring his or her first language. Growing up in an environment where sign language is used, a deaf child will acquire a signed language, and a hearing child will learn a spoken and/or a signed language. This still amazes linguists—the fact that the young child is able to figure out the complicated rules of a language and gradually use them more like the adult version. Because the child is not taught this, but makes it up, as it were, all alone, it has been suggested that human beings have an innate capacity for acquiring language, that we are pre-programmed for language acquisition, so to speak.

The task of the linguist is similar to that of the child, although the main purpose of the researcher is not to learn the language but, rather, to analyze and describe it. A sad thing from the linguist's point of view is that, whereas the child will master a first language within a couple of years, the researcher will not be able to come up with a complete description of one single language within a lifetime. Compared with the child, the adult researcher seems to have a very limited capacity for understanding human language, since no language is yet fully understood and described. If we did have a satisfactory description of some languages, we would be very close to having translation machines. We would then be able to tell a computer to interpret, for example, spoken English into spoken French. At present we are not able to do it, because we do not know what instructions to give to the computer.

The reason I dwell on these general issues is that I would like you to be as impressed by the complexity of language, and by our capacity to acquire it, as linguists are. Anyone who has learned a language, be it spoken or signed, has performed an extremely complex and abstract act, and has the right to be proud of this accomplishment.

Knowing a language implies knowing its grammar, because you must follow its rules whenever you communicate in that language. Sometimes in watching a signer, you deaf people may unconsciously observe that the person does not sign like a deaf person. In so doing, it is your inner grammar that is reacting against the ungrammatical signing. This shows that you know the grammar of your own language, whether or not you can describe the rules.

Lexicon

When acquiring or studying signs, two facets of the sign must be taken into account: form and meaning. The form is what you see, and the thing to which a certain content is associated—in other words, the meaning of the sign. In looking at a person using a foreign sign language, you may be able to see the forms, the movements, but you do not understand them, because you do not know which meanings are associated with them.

The most obvious fact about the *form* is that signs consist of movements performed by one or two hands on the signer's body or in space in front of the signer. For those sign languages that have been studied up until now, it has been observed that the signs can be analyzed into a small set of building blocks, such as a limited number of handshapes, movements, and positions. It also has been noticed that the building blocks may differ from one language to another. British Sign Language and Danish Sign Language have a handshape in which the index and the little finger are extended from a fist, a configuration not found in Swedish Sign Language.

Another perhaps less obvious characteristic of the form of signs is that many require a facial component in addition to the manual component. Two such signs are those that mean "to exist or to have" (Figure 1) and "to be irritated." The examples used in this paper are from Swedish Sign Language and are chosen to be as general as possible (general in the sense that it should be easy to find equivalents in your own sign languages).

The mouth movements of these signs are not borrowed from spoken Swedish; they are genuine sign language movements constituting a necessary part of the sign. The mouth movements in such signs do not have any meaning of their own, but there are other facial movements that *do* have meaning. In the following examples, the manual parts of the signs are very similar, two of them almost identical, but the facial components differ in form and in meaning. The first two signs mean "big or much" and "small or little" (Figures 2a and 2b). The last sign means "about this much," and there the eye gaze directed toward the hand (Figure 2c) is also a necessary part of the sign.

These signs illustrate that sign language is not only a language of the hands. Other

FIGURE 1: EXIST

FIGURE 2a: BIG   **FIGURE 2b: SMALL**   **FIGURE 2c: THIS MUCH**

bodily parts participate in the production of the language. Later we will see how facial components are a necessary part of the grammar of sign language.

The *meaning* of a sign is far more complicated to describe than the form. Meaning is not something that you can pick up and examine; it is an abstract phenomenon. I would like to stress, though, that signs have meanings of their own. Signs are symbols in their own right; they are *not* symbols for words, nor are they tied to or dependent on the words of a spoken language.

Swedish Sign Language and Swedish are two different languages, and it is therefore quite natural that signs and words do not have identical meanings. A sign may require several words for its translation into Swedish, and, likewise, a word may require several signs for its translation into sign language. An example of such a "mismatch" between signs and words is the following: Swedish Sign Language has two signs, both of which are normally translated into the word "deaf" (Figures 3a and 3b). The first sign actually means "deaf, without hearing" (a physiological term) and is not seen as frequently as the second sign, which means something like "(nonhearing) member of the Deaf commmunity, a person using sign language" (a linguistic, sociocultural term).

The fact that signs and words are different types of symbols and that they do not have identical meanings has been misinterpreted to mean that sign language is deficient when compared to spoken language. In many countries, committees have been set up to "improve" sign language—to change it to become more like spoken language. This happened in Sweden in the early 1970s. To my knowledge, however, no one has suggested that there is something wrong with the spoken language and that the spoken language needs improvement.

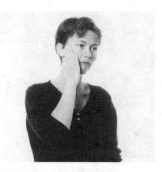

FIGURE 3a: DEAF   **FIGURE 3b: DEAF-MUTE**

FIGURE 4: DEAF; VERY DEAF

Morphology

One may think that signs always appear in the same form, but that is not so. Signs change their form for various reasons. Some changes are merely accidental and do not affect the meaning of the sign as, for example, when one hand is occupied and the signer signs with only one hand. This, of course, radically changes the form of many signs, but they are still perceived as the "same" signs as if both hands were used.

There are, however, other formational changes that do affect the meaning of the sign. The study of such recurring patterns of sign formation is called morphology and is one of the rule systems in the grammar of a language.

The signs meaning "deaf" and "angry/mad at" may undergo the same formational change, in which the hand changes its orientation in the beginning of the sign, is held there for a while, and then the movement is rapidly completed. There is also movement of the head involved in the signs. The change in meaning is the same in both signs; the changes add emphasis to the basic meaning (Figure 4).

The form of some signs may undergo directional modification. The following two verbs, which mean "to influence" (Figure 5a) and "to be influenced/to catch" (Figure 5b) illustrate this point. In "to influence," the hands normally move away from the signer's body (Figure 5a). When directionally modified into a movement toward the signer's body, the sign means "be influenced" (Figure 5b) and "to be caught."

There are also signs of an altogether different morphological type, signs with a very complex structure. In such signs, each building block seems to have a meaning of its own, and by exchanging some part of the form for another, the signer may alter the

**FIGURE 5a: TO INFLUENCE—
outward movement**

**FIGURE 5b: TO BE INFLUENCED/
TO CATCH—inward movement**

**FIGURE 6a: TWO-LEGGED BEING
STANDING NEAR TWO-
DIMENSIONAL OBJECT**

**FIGURE 6b: TWO PEOPLE
SITTING NEXT TO EACH OTHER
FACING THIRD PERSON**

meaning in systematic and rule-governed ways. The first example of this (shown in Figure 6a) means something like "twolegged being standing near a two-dimensional object" and can be used to express that a person is standing by a car.[1] The second sign means "two people are sitting next to each other facing a third person" (Figure 6b).

---

1 Editor's note: Swedish Sign Language uses the same classifier for car as it does for book, paper, and other flat or two-dimensional objects.

q
FIGURE 7: DEAF-MUTE INDEX-left

rel.
FIGURE 8: TWO BOYS HERE, DEAF-MUTE BOTH

Syntax

In a language, you also find rules for sentence formation, the study of which is called syntax. Just as all languages have a lexicon of their own, so they all have syntactic rules of their own. In this respect, Swedish Sign Language used to be compared with Swedish, which led to statements such as, "Sign language is ungrammatical;" "Sign language is telegraphic;" "Sign language is shortened Swedish." But German is also different from Swedish. Should we therefore draw the conclusion that German is nothing but bad Swedish? No. This is as absurd as the suggestion that a signed language is a shortened and ungrammatical form of a spoken language.

When talking about sign language syntax, I would like to draw your attention to the use of facial expressions, one of the most misunderstood aspects of sign language communication and one of the keys to sign language grammar.

Not very long ago, the curriculum found in the schools for deaf students in Sweden stated that students should be taught to use more careful and neat facial expressions. This emanated from the observation that when signing to each other, deaf children use facial expressions to a greater extent than do hearing people. This was interpreted by observers as "making faces;" it was believed that deaf children, lacking an otherwise fully expressive language, overused facial expressions.

However, the use of different facial expressions is crucial to sign language grammar. Compare the facial expression accompanying the sign meaning "deaf" in Figure 7 with the facial expression in Figure 3b. The neutral expression in Figure 3b would be used in a declarative sentence, such as, "He is deaf." The expression used in Figure 7, however, indicates a yes-no question is being asked, such as, "Is he deaf?" If the eyebrows are not raised, then the signer has not produced a well-formed yes-no question. Also, the duration of the last sign in a yes-no question is longer than it is in a declarative sentence. It should be noted that there are other types of questions using other kinds of facial signals such as lowering of brows.

Another, more complicated, example of the use of specific signals in the face is the relative clause (Figure 8). In the sentence, "The two boys who were here are both deaf," the first four signs are accompanied by the following facial signals: raised eyebrows and raised cheeks with the chin drawn back. Together, they mark this part of the sentence as a relative clause in Swedish Sign Language. It is necessary to use this particular facial expression for the sentence to be acceptable.

In view of what I have just said, it is obvious that signers must use their faces in order to produce grammatical sentences. It is not up to the individual signer to decide which expressions to use; their use is prescribed by the syntactic rules of the language. Thus, when attempts were made to teach deaf children not to use facial expressions, one actually was teaching them not to use grammatical sign language but to use a broken, less intelligible language instead.

Another task involved in the study of sign language syntax is to find the rules that govern the order of the signs in sign language sentences—in other words, to describe the order of subject, object, and verb. Only some combinations are acceptable grammatical utterances in sign language. For example, if you use a spoken language and support the speech with signs, you violate the rules of sign language and, as a result, produce ungrammatical sign language sentences. Not only may the order of the signs be wrong, but the grammatical facial signals also tend to disappear. This is the reason why it is difficult—if not impossible—to understand such use of signs, even for a bilingual person.

In the early 1970s, the Swedish National Association of the Deaf (SDR) strongly advocated such a system under the name of Signed Swedish. The system was spread through a rapidly increasing number of sign language programs, and it was the only way of signing that was taught to hearing people. Interpreter training was initiated in Sweden during the same period, and interpreters were trained to use only Signed Swedish. Some of you may have experienced that such a system can be extremely tiring to read and very hard to follow for long periods of time. But during the 1970s, most deaf people who used interpreters would not admit openly that it was difficult to understand Signed Swedish. Because it was a system intended to mirror Swedish, it had high status, and interpreters kept on using it.

So, during the 1970s, even the association of deaf people took an active part in oppressing the language of the Swedish deaf community. Most deaf people never changed their own way of signing, however. It was mainly hearing people learning sign language who were cheated into using this new system, because they were not informed that there was another way of signing—a true sign language. During this period, many deaf signers had a feeling that they did not know their own language and apologized for their signing. It was a time of great confusion.

I regard it as one of the main achievements of sign language research in Sweden that SDR finally took notice of the research results and stopped advocating Signed Swedish. I admire the leaders of the organization for having the courage to admit that they had been on the wrong track and to change direction. SDR no longer advocates Signed Swedish, but only Swedish Sign Language, and the organization is supported in this policy by the parents' association.

One of the most respected deaf people in Sweden, Dr. Lars Kruth, who is an honorary doctor of Stockholm University, once said that thanks to sign language research, deaf people in Sweden now realize how much they love their language. I can think of no better result of the study of sign language than contributing to changing the attitude of deaf people toward their language, changing the attitude from a feeling of inferiority into one of pride.

Before I conclude, I would like to mention just one very concrete result of sign language research. Stockholm University now has a department of sign language within the Institute of Linguistics. So far, the staff at the Department of Sign Language consists of eight people—five deaf and three hearing. Sign language is established as an academic subject of its own, on a par with languages such as Swedish, German, English, and Russian, and deaf people can study it both at the undergraduate and graduate level; there is also a Ph.D. available in sign language.

To make the situation as favorable as possible for the deaf students in our program, lectures in these courses are delivered in Swedish Sign Language and are not interpreted. Only deaf students are accepted in these groups, and all communication is in sign language; speech or Signed Swedish are not accepted. Last year we started programs in sign language for hearing students, as well as an advanced course for sign language interpreters.

In addition to the programs for which we are responsible, we also continue the study of sign language. This is of vital importance, because research is the foundation on which our work rests and is necessary for a continued development in the future.

My paper has been presented primarily from a linguist's point of view. In the next paper, Mr. Lars Wallin will discuss recent developments in Sweden from the point of view of the deaf community.

The Study of Sign Language in Society: Part Two

LARS WALLIN

Sign language studies, and some other factors that I will mention later, have had a positive impact on deaf people in Sweden during the past twenty years. Life as a deaf person has become very good there, and I do not exaggerate if I say that Sweden has become a model society for deaf people in many countries all over the world. The decision as to whether this is true or not is yours to make after I have told you about our deaf community—what we have achieved, and how we got there.

Sweden Today

I would first like to enumerate what we in the deaf community have achieved for ourselves, and what we now have access to in Swedish society.

❖ 1969—Free interpreter services are recognized as a right of deaf people.

❖ 1969—Deaf people's own "folk high school," where the interpreter training program is located, becomes a reality.

❖ 1981—The first official recognition of Swedish Sign Language is stated in Government Bill 1980/81: 100, Supplement 12. A declaration by Parliament on its decision states: "The commission on integration points out that the profoundly deaf, to function among themselves and in society, have to be bilingual. Bilingualism for their part, according to the commission, means that they have to be fluent in their visual/gestural Sign Language and be fluent in the language that society surrounds them with: Swedish."

❖ 1983—A new Special School Curriculum for schools for deaf and hard of hearing students is issued. It states that deaf pupils will study not only (written)

A revised version of this paper, which was originally presented at The Deaf Way, was later presented at the International Congress on Sign Language Research and Application, March 23–25, 1990 in Hamburg. That version has been printed in *Sign Language Research and Application*, edited by Siegmund Prillwitz and Tomas Vollhaber, 1990, Hamburg, Germany: SIGNUM-Press.

Translated into English by Anna-Lena Nilsson.

Swedish but also Swedish Sign Language, and that both languages will be used as languages of instruction in schools for deaf and hard of hearing students. It also states that pupils should be ensured an opportunity to develop as bilingual individuals.

❖ 1989—A decision is made requiring that applicants to the School of Education for training teachers of deaf and hard of hearing students have previous knowledge of Swedish Sign Language.

There are now deaf board members at all schools for deaf students, deaf representatives within various public institutions, free TTYs and sign language interpreter services, sign language courses for hearing people, sign language as an academic subject—both at basic and graduate levels, our own video production unit, newscasts and other programs in sign language on national television, production of materials for sign language instruction, and a professional theater group of deaf actors.

Many institutions require that their staff know Swedish Sign Language. These include blocks of housing for deaf senior citizens, nursery schools for deaf children, various institutions that care for deaf people with psychological or other problems, and, of course, schools for deaf students.

Looking at some areas that specifically concern deaf people and sign language, deaf people now work as teachers in schools for deaf students, in nursery schools, and in universities; sign language teachers; principals; psychologists; social workers; TV producers; actors; advisors on questions relating to deaf clubs and their study programs; youth recreation leaders; nursing assistants for the care of mentally retarded individuals, the elderly population, and deaf people with various types of other problems; consultants in matters regarding deaf and blind people; researchers; and development assistance workers.

The Swedish National Association of the Deaf (SDR) initiates and takes an active role in discussions on topics that concern deaf children and their families, schools for deaf and hard of hearing students (on subjects related both to compulsory schooling as well as further studies at all levels), training of teachers for deaf students, audiological centers and their staffs, psychological and social issues concerning deaf people, the development of media and technology; and questions concerning developing countries. The SDR now receives committee reports for consideration, and the group can no longer be ignored by society.

Many local deaf clubs not only arrange the traditional kind of meetings and cultural activities for their members, but work politically as well.

The Three Cornerstones of Our Work

The deaf community would never have come as far as it has if it had not been for the following three cornerstones of our work:

❖ Sign language research

❖ Deaf people's own organization, SDR

❖ Cooperation with many organizations, especially the organization for parents of deaf and hard of hearing children.

Sign Language Research

Sign language research has provided us with the facts and arguments necessary to prove that Swedish Sign Language *is* a language, equally as good as any other language. Many of us felt that was the case all along, but maybe we did not realize that our language is quite as rich and complex as we now know it to be.

During the years before sign language was re-introduced (in the form of Signed Swedish) in schools for deaf students during the late 1960s and early 1970s, it was not considered a language at all. The prevalent oralistic view defined "language" as a vocal system for human communication, based on speech and sound. Oralists connected language and thinking, meaning that thinking required a language—the spoken language. Sign language did not fit their definition of language: The oralist view was that the use of sign language would be hazardous for the deaf child, because it would not provide the child a means of thinking or would be a considerable impairment to the child's thinking capacity. Sign language was viewed as a natural system of gestures with no structure of its own and limited areas of use. These gestures were seen as iconic and therefore not suitable for conveying abstract concepts. These views resulted in sign language being kept outside education of deaf students and limited to use in deaf families, deaf clubs, and on the school yard.

Sign language research has shown that sign language *is* a language, on par with any other. In the previous paper, Dr. Bergman described sign language as a language with its own structure, symbols, and grammar. Sign language can fill every need of communication for a human being, including that of acquiring knowledge. Sign language research also has shown that the use of sign language is of crucial importance for the deaf child's normal development.

Fortunately, sign language survived the long period of oralist oppression and now, supported by research, is alive and well in Sweden, spreading joy in many ways. Today, sign language has taken its natural, central place in the lives of many deaf children. Through it they can get answers to all their many questions about what is going on around them. Through the use of sign language, parents can now raise their deaf children the same as any other child. When parents—90 to 95 percent of whom are hearing—use sign language in their communication with their deaf or hard of hearing children, the children will come to the first grade with a language, concepts, and knowledge of the world around them. It is not the quality of the parents' skills in sign language that is crucial to the development of the deaf child, but the fact that they sign willingly and understand the signing of their child. This parental attitude toward deaf children and sign language is vital to the language development of their children. Sign language gives them a stable foundation for their further development and self-reliance. Through sign language, the lives of deaf people can become more and more like the lives of hearing people.

Contact and communication between deaf and hearing people has been greatly facilitated. Through sign language interpreters, we can make our opinions known to society much more easily than before, and we also can make use of everything that society has to offer. Many more avenues of education are now accessible to deaf people.

Another positive occurrence is the fact that many parents of deaf adults who attended school during the oral period are now learning sign language. My parents, for example, have attended sign language classes in their old age. It really warms my heart that I can finally share my language with them.

From having lived on the outskirts of society—in deaf clubs that were always our safe havens—we are now stepping out into society, prouder than ever and with increased self-confidence. *Our* sign language has achieved higher status, and it is something to be proud of.

Sign language research has been invaluable to the development of our situation. Researchers have not limited themselves to research alone, but have taken an active part in issues concerning deaf people, assisting us and our national association with their knowledge. They have worked with us politically for our cause, and this has been of great importance to us. They have shared their knowledge in various conferences and meetings. This work was crucial to the re-introduction of sign language in the education of deaf and hard of hearing students, and the establishment of bilingualism for deaf people. They also helped change the attitudes of parents, teachers, and others through their many lectures all over Sweden, resulting in an increased respect for sign language. The fact that they take part in what is going on in the deaf community has given us, and continues to give us, great pleasure.

The Swedish National Association of the Deaf and Deaf Awareness Activities

Although it can be said that sign language research was the factor that finally opened the doors of Swedish society to full participation of deaf people, the process of opening doors was begun by our national association. Untiring efforts to improve deaf people's situation and to reestablish sign language created the foundation from which we now continue our work.

The oldest deaf club in Sweden was founded in 1868. In 1922, the various clubs joined together to form the national association, today's Swedish Association of the Deaf (SDR). The local deaf clubs are the foundation on which SDR rests. Individual members can make their opinions known to the association through the strong channels of communication established between the clubs and the SDR. Every three years, representatives of the forty-seven local deaf clubs elect representatives to the committee of the national association. These elections take place at a congress where decisions are made regarding which issues should receive the SDR's attention during the three years until the next congress.

SDR works according to ten-year action programs that contain such areas of concern as culture, work in the deaf clubs, child care, health care, and employment. The action plans are sanctioned by the deaf clubs. To help promote the work, SDR has a number of commissions that focus on important issues such as preschools, schools, culture, and social issues. The Swedish Deaf Youth Association and the Council of Deaf Pensioners are also affiliated with the SDR.

SDR is a strong and forceful organization that society can no longer ignore without strong reactions from its members. It also serves as security for many of the smaller clubs, which, working alone, do not have the resources necessary to pursue deaf issues effectively. There are SDR representatives in many public institutions, including the National Board of Education, the Swedish Institute for the Handicapped, and the School of Education for training teachers of deaf students. SDR also is a member of the General Committee of Organizations for the Handicapped, a cooperative committee for various organizations of people with disabilities. Additionally, SDR has useful contacts with some members of the government—a few of whom have deaf children—and with some members of Parliament. The local deaf clubs are represented in their communities in various public institutions as well. This local and national network makes it possible for us to influence matters concerning deaf people in the best way possible. Sometimes we have problems coming up with enough representatives for all the positions where they are needed, but that is a pleasant problem.

Deaf people in Sweden and within our national association would never have become so strong if it had not been for the period of "deaf awareness," when we increased our belief in ourselves and began to view Swedish Sign Language as a true language, on a par with any other. We declared our right to exist as deaf people and, as such, to be treated with respect.

Before the movement toward deaf awareness, many of us had not realized the importance of our language. As described in the previous paper, we had lived with language oppression for a long time, and, as a result, had viewed our own language as inadequate. Our negative view of the Swedish language and our lack of knowledge about it also contributed to the oppression. Knowledge of Swedish was seen as the only path to "being someone"—without it, we deaf people would not get very far.

It was not unusual that deaf people with a good command of Swedish were elected to various positions on the committee of the local deaf club, because they were considered most capable of conveying the members' opinions to society. Command of the Swedish language became a kind of "merit" for being elected to the committee. This, of course, meant that deaf people who did not have a good knowledge of Swedish felt even more restricted. Added to this were the daily experiences of students in oral schools, which tended to praise only knowledge of Swedish. Many deaf people thus ended up feeling completely worthless.

It was also very common to measure the cognitive capacity of deaf people by their knowledge of Swedish; if your knowledge of Swedish was poor, then your mental capacity was assumed to be poor as well; if your knowledge of Swedish was good, then your mental capacity was assumed to be good as well. This view was reflected in the deaf community, where, even among ourselves, the notion that there was a link between knowledge of Swedish and talent was present.

The situation was such that many deaf people limited themselves to working within the deaf clubs, and very few worked politically. For a long time, a mere handful of people spoke out for deaf people and SDR. One of them was our former president, Dr. Lars Kruth, whom Dr. Bergman mentioned in her paper. He has been a spokesman and representative of SDR since 1951, and had held various offices in the organization. In November, 1989, he will finally retire and devote himself to working with issues concerning senior citizens. Had it not been for Dr. Kruth, SDR would never have risen to the position it has today.

Let us return to language oppression. As I mentioned earlier, this oppression resulted in the view that command of the Swedish language was superior to knowledge of Swedish Sign Language and was an indication of the talents of a person. When Signed Swedish entered the picture, the situation became even worse. Many people felt ashamed that they only knew the "old sign language," as Swedish Sign Language was then called. Signed Swedish was called the "new sign language," and many deaf people practically apologized for not knowing it. The oppression was so strong that they even attended classes to learn the new language.

But Signed Swedish was the last straw for some people, and from it deaf awareness developed. A few deaf people realized that the situation was intolerable and started campaigning for a changed view of our language and of ourselves. New notions began to spread all over Sweden, notions such as: Our sign language is okay; the schools for deaf students are wrong; Knowledge of Swedish is not everything that matters; We can make it if we want to; Knowledge of life is more important than knowledge of Swedish; Deaf people are also worthy of respect; We have a culture of our own, and it is fantastic.

Swedish Sign Language was not considered good enough any longer. Sign language research also helped give us a more positive view of Swedish Sign Language. More and more deaf people started to believe in themselves and in their ability to speak for themselves in society. As more of us began to work politically, SDR grew stronger. One advancement followed another. More deaf people started to work both in various commissions within the national association and as representatives in various public institutions. Today deaf people lead very good lives in Sweden. We have our own identity and know who we are, and Swedish Sign Language is accepted.

Cooperation with Other Organizations and the Fight against Mainstreaming

I will now discuss the third cornerstone of the deaf community: cooperation. As I mentioned earlier, the cooperation between SDR and sign language researchers is very important. But we also have established cooperation with another partner that has been of equal importance to deaf people: the organization for parents of deaf children. Together, we have managed to get some of our ideas accepted. One example of this cooperation is the fight against mainstreaming deaf children in schools for hearing children.

Without this cooperation with the parents of deaf children, there would probably be no schools for deaf students in Sweden today. The early 1950s saw the beginning of the notion that deaf children should be placed in schools for hearing children. Audiological equipment had been greatly improved, and deaf children were now being diagnosed as having "residual hearing." It was considered possible to communicate with them via speech with the use of technical aids, and it was felt that the best environment for doing this was in schools for hearing children.

These new ideas were implemented during the 1950s, 1960s, and a good deal of the 1970s, when more and more deaf children were placed in schools for hearing children. In the beginning they were placed there in groups, but later on it became more common that one deaf child was placed in a group of hearing children.

At first the process was called "normalization." Deaf people were to be normalized, as if being deaf meant *not* being normal. Deaf children were to be taught to behave just like hearing people, not as deaf people who, with their signing, were regarded as different from the norm. Later normalization was renamed "mainstreaming," because it was felt that deaf people should not isolate themselves and form groups of their own. Instead, they must become a part of society. It was believed that this aim would be achieved more easily by starting the education of deaf children in schools for hearing children.

People with disabilities were no longer to be viewed as different and put away in special institutions, but treated as "normal" people, who attend ordinary schools and lead normal lives in the community, just like everyone else. Special segregated schools for people with disabilities should now be abolished. All groups—except for us deaf people—supported this ambition, which was seen as something noble. Because deaf people did not support the new idea, it was said that we did not know what as best for us. Nobody could understand why we wanted to keep segregated schools for deaf people. Mainstreaming became prestigious; segregation, something ugly. Many special schools for disabled people were closed, and the schools for deaf students just barely remained open.

Of course, parents did not oppose the idea of mainstreaming. It meant that their child could live with them, instead of being sent away to the nearest city with a school for deaf students. Because deaf children would grow up to live in a hearing society, it was considered best if they could start getting used to it as early as possible. Promises were made that the children would get all the assistance they needed and not miss out on too much of the instruction. No wonder parents were pleased with this generous offer from society. Nobody really considered how the children would feel—until it was too late.

But *we* thought about the well-being of deaf children. We realized the disastrous consequences of mainstreaming at an early stage in the process. We deaf people differ from other groups of people with disabilities when it comes to one thing, something that is crucial to the success of mainstreaming: We cannot communicate by way of hearing; they all can. Our communication has to build on sign language, and that is why we are opposed to mainstreaming. If mainstreaming is to succeed, all communication has to take place in sign. There are no shortcuts, something the supporters of mainstreaming had not acknowledged.

Our view was that if deaf children are to develop as other children, only using another language—sign language—they must be allowed to attend a school for deaf students, which would be just like any other school but with a signing environment. There would be no difference in instruction and relations, apart from the fact that everything would be based on sight instead of hearing.

In a signing environment, deaf children can develop together. In such a school, there would be deaf children of all ages, as well as deaf adults who work there. The presence of deaf adults is important if the child is to find role models and an identity in an otherwise hearing society. In a group of other deaf people, deaf children can feel that they are just like everyone else, with their own advantages and their shortcomings. Not being able to hear becomes something peripheral and of minor importance. They get to see and use sign language in various situations with their peers and adults. They will develop as deaf people and find their own identities that correspond to their own needs.

If deaf children were placed in schools for hearing children, they would not have access to everything described above. The signing environment would be watered down or nonexistent. Deaf children would be surrounded by hearing children only or, if they were lucky, be in classes with a few deaf peers. There would be no deaf adults for them to meet, and they would have to live with the feeling of being different. Constantly faced with hearing children and what they can do with their hearing, deaf children would see being deaf as a burden. Finding role models and a suitable identity to live with would be difficult. The search for deaf role models would have to continue long after they finished school.

It was not a simple task to convince parents that deaf children need a school of their own with a signing environment. Faced with the choice of sending their child away to such a school or keeping their child at home, they naturally chose the latter. When we tried to argue for schools for deaf students, people said that we were trying to separate deaf children from their parents. It was said that we denied deaf children a chance to get accustomed to life in a hearing society: By not living among hearing people from an early age, it was said that these children would also be denied the opportunity to learn to speak and write Swedish. We were regarded as conservative, and it was said that we wanted to keep the schools for deaf students for nostalgic reasons. In short, we were accused of denying deaf children their right to live in a hearing society.

But it was the other way around. The schools for deaf students, with their signing environment, would give deaf children a place where they could build their mental and spiritual resources without undue stress, just like any other child. This would give them the strength to live satisfactory lives as deaf adults in a hearing society, with the inherent security of having found their identity and their role in society.

After a while we began to convince parents that schools for deaf students were important and worth fighting for. Today, more and more parents send their children to such schools, and many parents move with their children to a city that has one. In this way we managed to stop the advancing mainstreaming, and schools for deaf students were allowed to continue their existence.

Today, SDR and parents of deaf children cooperate on a number of issues concerning deaf children, and we complement each other in positive ways. We are a strong force that is very hard for society to ignore.

This cooperation with parents of deaf children, together with research efforts, has helped make our political work easier and less lonely. Results of our work came in quick succession, highlighted by the above-mentioned parliamentary decision and new curriculum for schools for deaf students. Cooperation has now expanded to include the organization of hard of hearing people. An increasing number of people who are hard of hearing are beginning to question their own schooling, being mainstreamed individually or in groups. They are demanding the right to learn to communicate in sign language—something that has not been offered previously—and to be taught in sign language. Together, we (the SDR, hard of hearing people, researchers, and parents) are now discussing a model for future schools for deaf and hard of hearing people. Sign language will be the main form of communication; bilingualism, the prevailing ideology. In this particular project, as well as on other issues, we also cooperate with the organization of teachers of deaf students.

The three national associations also have appointed their own commission to look into the area of cochlear implants. We need knowledge about this subject to be able to take an active part in this discussion.

Bilingualism: Swedish Sign Language and Swedish

I will now discuss the best thing that ever happened to deaf people in Sweden, something I am very happy to share with you: the bilingualism of deaf people. With bilingualism we feel we are finally beginning to reach our goal of becoming equal citizens and taking an active part in every facet of society.

What does "being ensured a development toward bilingualism" mean? It means that—as stated in the parliamentary decision—deaf people will be fluent in both sign language and Swedish to function both among themselves and in society. The bilingualism of deaf people as such is nothing new. The deaf community has always been bilingual with regard to using Swedish as well as Swedish Sign Language. This is most apparent in looking at the work in the deaf clubs: newsletters, minutes, letters to authorities, the use of TTYs, and so on. The bill was a confirmation of our language situation: The deaf community is bilingual.

According to the Special School Curriculum, 1983, "ensuring deaf children a development toward bilingualism" means that they are to be given the opportunity to learn both Swedish Sign Language and Swedish. This is what the curriculum states regarding bilingualism and the two languages:

Sign language and Swedish are separate languages. The bilingualism aimed at deaf and many hearing impaired pupils is not absolutely comparable with other bilingualism. The bilingualism of the deaf is monocultural since both languages convey essentially the same culture.

Bilingualism does not occur spontaneously. Sign language is learned naturally and spontaneously, as part of the child's general development, in the environment where it is used, while acquisition of the second language—Swedish—is more dependent on instruction.

The two languages—sign language and Swedish—perform different functions for the pupil. Sign language is the deaf pupil's primary means of acquiring knowledge and is the language used by him in direct communication with others. It is by way of sign language and in his contacts with parents and others that the pupil develops socially and emotionally. Swedish has primarily the function of a written language, but lipreading and speech, of course, are also important elements of this subject.

In the course of teaching, names and contexts that are important in order for the pupil to assimilate the content of reading passages must be given both in sign language and in Swedish. Information about the Swedish language, however, must not be given such prominence as to relegate the content of subject teaching to second place.

The pupil's language learning must be supported by comparisons between the various linguistic expressions of sign language and Swedish and must be based on language being an implement used in handling perceptions, experiences, and knowledge, etc. (pp. 6–7)

I would like to point out that the contents of this text, as well as the rest of the Special School Curriculum, was arrived at after discussions in a commission where deaf people were represented. That is part of the reason why the description of deaf people's bilingualism, and how to achieve it, corresponds with our view of the issue.

The Special School Curriculum also states that the instruction in sign language and Swedish should be based on what the pupils have already acquired:

A person's language is closely connected with his personality and situation in life. If that connection is severed, the development of both language and personality is blocked. An important objective in the teaching of sign language and Swedish, therefore, is to strengthen the pupils' self-confidence so that they will have the courage to express themselves and stand up for their opinions. Work should therefore be based on the language and the experience that the pupils have already acquired. (pp. 7–8)

For deaf pupils, this implies starting from sign language, but also making the most of any knowledge of Swedish they may have acquired.

The aim for the teaching of sign language and Swedish, according to the Special School Curriculum, is stated below:

By the time they leave compulsory school, pupils must have achieved the confidence to express themselves in the linguistic situations confronting them in the family, together with their friends, in voluntary associations, at work, and in subsequent education. They must have had the opportunity of meeting and using official written language. They must be given preparation to read well enough to have a solid foundation on which to acquire knowledge, information, and experience for themselves through the medium of newspapers and periodicals, reference works, and works of fiction and non-fiction. (p. 8)

The objective is to give deaf children a wider base of knowledge, concepts, and language than ever before. They will have a more solid foundation on which to build their lives after school, and stronger self-confidence. The life of a deaf person will be more equal to that of a hearing person.

Studying Sign Language

In school, pupils should receive instruction in the subject Sign Language. According to the Special School Curriculum, the instruction should cover the following aspects of the language:

> The pupils must develop their ability to penetrate other people's conditions, understand their purposes, and adapt their own language and behavior to the requirements of different contexts. They must learn to study other people's opinions and values, to stand up for their own, and to subject their own arguments and other people's to critical scrutiny. The pupils must also acquire a knowledge of the structure and grammar of sign language. They must learn the rules applying to different conversational situations, and they must also learn that these [rules can] be influenced and improved.
>
> By making video recordings, the pupils must learn to document and convey information and cultural activities. The pupils must be given practice in using interpreters in various situations.
>
> They should also acquire knowledge of the international sign alphabet and sign language in other countries, especially within the Nordic area. General information on national and international organizations of the deaf should be included. (pp. 9–10)

Studying Swedish

The main aim of instruction in Swedish is for students to learn to read and write Swedish via instruction in sign language. When it comes to reading, the Special School Curriculum states the following:

> Reading is one of the most important ways of giving the pupils a knowledge of the Swedish language and making them aware of the written language as a means of augmenting their knowledge. (p. 11)

How is it possible to learn to read and write Swedish through instruction in sign language?

The approach to be used includes the following. Students will receive in sign language the explanations and descriptions of how the Swedish language is structured, as well as its grammatical rules. After reading Swedish texts, they will retell the content in sign language, thereby showing the teacher they have understood it. If they are able to do this, it could be argued that they have learned to understand and interpret the texts well, including all the formulations and nuances. If the students experience problems, the teacher is there to help with explanations and translations in sign language.

It is not a question of a mechanical reading of the texts, which is often the case within the oral school system. The bilingual approach allows pupils the opportunity to try to interpret a text they have read, then retell it in sign language. When the teacher is convinced the pupils have understood the context of the text, he or she will work through it, using sign language to discuss its linguistic structures. Reading can be seen as a tool for the pupils to organize the knowledge of Swedish they have gradually acquired, a tool which at the same time displays the various forms of expression available in Swedish.

Writing is also discussed in the Special School Curriculum:

> The pupils must learn to use writing as a means of coming into contact with other people. They must relate, inform, and describe, through the medium of letters, notice boards, and posters, convey news or debate conditions and problems with the aim of exerting influence and bringing about improvements. They must reflect and speculate about personal experiences by writing poetry, diaries, letters, narratives, short stories, etc. (p. 14)

Writing gives pupils the chance to put their knowledge into practice. They practice expressing themselves, applying the grammatical rules they have learned—rules for spelling, inflection, sentence structure, choice of vocabulary, and so on. If something is not correct, they will receive explanations in sign language regarding what is wrong and why. Pupils can write about their own observations, experiences, and fantasies. Their writing should be based on their own experiences; they should feel that they have created the texts themselves, with the teacher only assisting them, correcting grammatical errors, and explaining other linguistic problems. This is not a mechanical drill, as opposed to the common oral method of letting pupils copy the teacher's ready-made sentences. With the bilingual approach, pupils make up the sentences, and the teacher assists with the grammatical knowledge.

Studying Speech

Speech constitutes a complementary aspect of the bilingualism of deaf people, and speech instruction should be in the form of teaching pronunciation built on the knowledge of Swedish that pupils have acquired. The Special School Curriculum states the following:

> The pupils must acquire a basic knowledge of the workings of speech, lipreading, and the organs of speech.
>
> Pronunciation teaching forms part of the teaching of Swedish and must be based on each individual pupil's aptitudes, must have individualized objectives, and must emanate from the concept and the language that the pupil has mastered.

> It is important that other teaching items, e.g., the reading of texts for the sake of their content, should not be combined with pronunciation practice. (pp. 16–17)

Pronunciation practice should aim at teaching pupils to pronounce Swedish words and sentences they have learned during language lessons. It is easier to master the pronunciation of words and sentences where the content is understood than it is to mimic words that have no meaning. The students should be allowed to work with the rhythmical units of speech. Speech instruction, just like any other instruction, should be carried out in sign language. A reasonable aim for speech training, possible for all pupils to attain, is that the pupils should be capable of communicating their basic needs: asking for items such as a newspaper or an airline ticket, telling someone they are not feeling well, and so on. Developing this skill further has to be based on individual aptitude.

Concluding Remarks on Bilingualism

Deaf children's development toward bilingualism can be seen as a model consisting of many steps, with each new step built on the previous one. The first step is sign language. It is acquired naturally and spontaneously in a signing environment. Deaf children's cognitive, social, and emotional development will be enhanced through the use of Swedish Sign Language in direct communication with parents and other people in their surroundings. Sign language will be the primary tool for acquiring knowledge.

The next step is to learn the Swedish language. This learning should be based on the language the child has already acquired—sign language. The two steps together will form the foundation on which the child will be ensured a development toward bilingualism.

Speech, the third step, will give the child an extra opportunity to communicate with his or her surroundings in situations where sign language cannot be used. Speech should be regarded as a complementary aspect of bilingualism, and speech instruction should be based on the knowledge of Swedish the child has acquired. This is the order in which the various aspects of the deaf child's bilingualism must develop.

With bilingualism we will finally be able to reach our goal of becoming equal citizens and taking an active part in the development of society. With a command of both Swedish and Swedish Sign Language, deaf people will have the ability to influence and take control of their own lives. With adequate services from society, such as the necessary number of sign language interpreters, deaf people will be absolutely equal to hearing people in society, able to rise higher in society in new ways, politically as well as in other careers. It may still be a while away. The many different jobs and professions I enumerated at the beginning of my paper are an example of this development, which has just started. Life on the outskirts of society, where we have been for centuries, will become a fading memory.

When we look at deaf children today, we get a taste of what the future will be. They are like any other children, only they use a different language. You can discuss all kinds of things with them today—the danger of riding a motorcycle, pollution, pop stars, whether Austrian and Swedish eggs taste the same, what comic books they read, and many other things. They express their opinions on most issues at an early age, something that used to be inconceivable. What we managed to learn during ten years in the oral school system, they already know when they start school. In the first grade, some children can already write their own sentences—maybe not with correct grammar, but with content. An increasing number of pupils are using ordinary educational materials instead of materials adapted for schools for deaf students. They are more confident in their use of Swedish. What will happen when they finish school is something about which we can only fantasize. But there are great changes ahead, of that I am sure.

Even though what they have learned is not really extraordinary—they are ordinary children using a different language—it almost makes me feel like crying when I meet them and witness all the things they know and can do. At the same time, I feel rage toward the oralists for what they did to us, all the things that they ruined for us. Denying us sign language is one of the worst acts that could be committed. But seeing the correctness of what Sweden has done in acknowledging Swedish Sign Language as deaf people's language—*our* language—also makes the joy in seeing deaf children of today much greater.

What Remains To Be Done

We have come a long way on the road toward our goals, but this is not utopia. There is still a lot to do before we can feel completely satisfied. In November 1989, we will decide on our new ten-year action program, which starts with 1990. This will be a revised version of our current action plan, decided on in 1979. A draft is currently being discussed among deaf people. It contains suggestions for demands regarding measures to be taken in the areas of sign language, the labor market, education, child care, deaf clubs, international issues, culture, social services, family issues, interpreting services and technical aids, media issues, and informational techniques. For example, in addition to the continuing work for bilingual schools for deaf students—with sign language as the first language—and continued expansion of the number of preschools using sign language, we also suggest that deaf people should be acknowledged as a cultural and linguistic minority. Further, we feel the history and culture of deaf people should be included in the curriculum in schools for deaf students.

The draft of the new action plan includes our demand for regional sign language centers, a cultural center, and a professorship in Swedish Sign Language. Hearing children of deaf parents and hearing children with deaf brothers or sisters should have the right to study Swedish Sign Language in school. Hearing parents of deaf children should have the right to attend courses regarding their child, with full payment from their social insurance. These are a few of the areas our new action plan will address.

In this paper, I have tried to describe the "Swedish model" to you and to convey what our situation is like today and how we got there. Our achievements are based on the three cornerstones I mentioned: our national association, which fought against society for the sake of deaf people; sign language research, which showed that sign language *is* a language and led to an official acknowledgment of Swedish Sign Language; and, finally, cooperation, mainly with parents of deaf children, which has ensured the future of schools for deaf students and the future of deaf children. I would like to end my paper with a motto that I feel expresses what we have done: United we stand, divided we fall.

A Sign Language Dictionary

WILLIAM C. STOKOE

About three months ago publication of a new edition of a dictionary was a major news story. Editors and reviewers had their moments on talk shows. Someone even managed to set up an interview with the granddaughter of the scholar who edited the original *Oxford English Dictionary*. Yes, a dictionary made headline news. With all that is going on in the world these days, you may wonder why all that fuss about a word book? Why spend expensive broadcasting time on something that sits on a shelf in the reference room of libraries?

One answer to that question is that a serious dictionary is a lot more than a word book. It is not just another reference work collecting dust in a corner of the library. A serious dictionary is an important matter, and the *Oxford English Dictionary* is surely the most serious—as well as the largest—dictionary in the world. By defining hundreds of thousands of English words in phrases and sentences of English, it describes this language more completely than any other single book can do. By quoting the passage in which a word was first used and by quoting other examples of its use as the meaning has changed, the *Oxford English Dictionary* also presents a rich history of the language and a history of the users' thought. That is why publication of a serious dictionary makes news. Between the covers of a serious dictionary we find, all ready for use, the tools of thought.

Any language is shaped and formed—in a sense, created—by the thinking of the people who use it. And this works both ways. Language, as a serious dictionary sums it up, is what its users must have with which to do their thinking. And certainly a serious dictionary, or a new edition of one, makes news because it records advances in thinking: New words equal new ideas; new ideas equal new words. The words and the ideas are inseparable, and a serious dictionary is the place where they are arranged for our convenience in looking them up. Without serious dictionaries we would be at a tremendous disadvantage. When we want to point to the foolishness of some activity, we say that those doing it are "reinventing the wheel." Without serious dictionaries of our languages, all of us would have to reinvent the wheel, and just about everything else, over and over again.

You may have noticed that I keep qualifying the word "dictionary." I'm talking here about *serious* dictionaries, the kind of dictionaries that lists the words of a language and tries to define them by using other words of that language. A serious dictionary is about language and not just words. Sure, you can buy pocket calculators now that have keyboards and displays like a TDD. These toys let you key in a word of English and then display a word to translate it in the language of the country you are visiting, e.g., plug in the German language chip and key in "railroad station" and up comes "Bahnhof."

Too many sign language books have been ink and paper versions of these cute little pocket toys. The Gallaudet library is full of books that list English words and after each word tell you in words or photographs or drawings how to make a sign with your hands that is supposed to translate the word. This kind of thing is not a serious dictionary. The pocket translator or the word-sign book may have some limited uses, but they are really just toys. My three-year-old grandson had a toy lawn mower that he used to enjoy pushing around while his father was mowing the lawn, but you and I know one thing for sure, and now he knows it, too: That toy never cut any grass.

What I hope you will remember from the following papers is that a serious dictionary of a *sign language* can do as much as other serious dictionaries do. It can describe and arrange the tools of thought that signers of that sign language use and need. But a serious dictionary of a sign language can do something more. It can show the world that deaf signers can think in their sign languages, with logic and precision and even elegance. It can wipe out, as nothing else can so well, the false ideas that ignorant people have about deaf people and deaf society and sign languages.

The word-to-sign toys of signing let ignorant people keep on supposing that sign language is nothing but a way other than print to make the words of a spoken language visible. A serious sign language dictionary flattens that false idea as surely as a pin flattens a balloon. What we want to do in these papers, then, is look at serious sign language dictionaries and how they are made.

Making a serious dictionary of a sign language is serious work. Some of you here know that firsthand. My own task is to talk about the first serious dictionary of a sign language, the *Dictionary of American Sign Language on Linguistic Principles* (DASL), compiled over a nine-year period and published twenty-four years ago this November. That gives me about thirty-three years of perspective to see what might have been done better, what seems to have stood the test of time, and what some of the consequences of the project have been.

If I were starting the project again or preparing a new edition, I would start with the face and head and body, and then go on to the hands. You who may be starting now are lucky; a book just out by Gilbert Eastman, *From Mime to Sign,* will give you a good idea of how sign language begins from inside a person and shows on the face and body first, before the hands get involved. I am afraid that many readers of DASL think that ASL is a language of the hands only.

Another of my decisions back then was not so good. Starting over, I would not call the action of a sign the signation or *sig* and the place of action the tabula or *tab* and the active element the designator or *dez.* Those terms told a reader that the editor had studied Latin, but so what? The important thing is to be clear and clearly understood. What I would do now—beginning, as I said, with the face—is refer to the face, eyes, or arms in a sign as the active part. If the *active part* was one hand or both hands, I would describe *handshape* so that it would include the position of the arm, especially the forearm. The *action* needs simple but accurate description, too: If the active part of the sign is the face, I would use a simplified version of the Ekman and Friesen *Facial Action Coding System* to describe what the face "does." If the action of a sign involves movement between shoulder and fingertips, I would indicate which muscle or muscle groups produced the action.

In addition to avoiding tricky terms and trying harder to be simple and clear, I would certainly try to learn the language better. Like other hearing people newly brought in to teach at Gallaudet College in the 1950s, I was shown first how to fingerspell, then how to make certain signs (and also to avoid using other signs that our teacher called "slang"). We were expected to make ourselves models of good English presented in speech with signs and fingerspelling, and to model good language manners as well—to sign as nearly as possible like E.M. Gallaudet as recorded in 1913 on film. No time was given to learning to read fingerspelling or to understanding the signing others might direct to us. Therefore, it was about two years before I knew for sure that we had two languages to deal with: on the one hand, English in signs and fingerspelling, and on the other hand, the language students used, the language that I later decided to call American Sign Language (ASL). (Sad to say, the knowledge that these two are different languages has still not trickled down to the general public.)

Like anyone who has finished some serious work, I would like to have had more time to check and recheck before publication. One thing the maker of a serious sign language dictionary faces is pressure—pressure to get it out. When an institution and faculty salaries are involved, the deadline is built in—finish it on time or run out of money before it's done. That is one consequence of outside funding; and certainly today no group of dictionary makers will be able to function without outside funding. I was extremely fortunate to have generous funding (with extensions of time) from the National Science Foundation and to have also the encouragement of Dean George Detmold, who suspected before I did that ASL was its own language.

Something else would be useful for one starting over or for anyone who wants to make a sign language dictionary that seriously goes into the nature of signs. Starting again, I would take time out to study physiology, anatomy, and kinesiology—how the limbs are put together, how the muscles operate on them, what actions are possible, and what the limits are. That would make a good foundation for a semester in Gil Eastman's course or, failing that, long sessions of practice with his book.

But looking back, it does not seem too bad a piece of work. Some things don't need changing. I picked a good team: Dorothy Casterline and Carl Croneberg, coeditors, were full bilinguals—writing English as expertly as they signed ASL. As luck would have it, they also brought together the two essentials of vision. Dot has the microscopic eye and attention to detail and patient keyboard fingers that enabled her to produce camera-ready copy on a Vari-Typer machine with a unique character set. Carl has the imagination to see analogies between hearing and deaf cultures and to make the necessary re-calibration of linguistics and ethnography to sign language and deaf people. Whatever you do, if you do decide to make a dictionary, pick a good team.

It was a good thing, too, that we had a theory based on real data to guide us in making the dictionary. Linguistics today, or much of it, concentrates so closely on the theory that everything important about language is built into the brain at birth, that actual language in use can be forgotten. The problem is that whatever is or isn't in the brain is not easy to put on a dictionary page.

My own guides to linguistic theory in 1957, when my serious study of sign language began, were George Trager and Henry Lee Smith, members of a department of anthropology. They insisted that language could not be studied by itself, in isolation, but must be looked at in direct connection to the people who used it, the things they used it to talk about, and the view of the world that using it imposed on them. With a theory like that—connecting words to what people use them for—a dictionary can last, has lasted.

I am afraid that if one were to look into the linguistic and psycholinguistic theories fashionable right now, and more closely into the phonological theories of how signs are made and distinguished, one would stand a good chance of picking a theory that would go out of date before the dictionary project was finished. But take note that this caution is only about theories. Genuine discoveries about sign language grammar, e.g., Ted Supalla's discovery of how ASL nouns and verb forms differ, of course need to be built into a revised dictionary.

A final good choice was listening for advice only to those who had done the job better. I had no lack of advice in the five or six years the dictionary was in the works. Some said it should tell readers which signs were proper to use and which were not. Some said its most important function would be to standardize the language. (They didn't know that people, not dictionaries, do that, and then never successfully.) The majority close at hand, however, said a dictionary shouldn't be made at all, that sign language needed to be suppressed and English elevated. None of these advisors, of course, had ever done anything like a serious dictionary; some, not even much serious work of any kind. Fortunately I did not listen to them.

I would like to finish by looking at some of the things the first serious dictionary of sign language helped to happen. First, public attitudes toward deafness and deaf people and their sign languages have changed. Along with the main listing of some 2,000 to 3,000 signs, the first dictionary contained an appendix by Carl Croneberg that showed how language and culture as well as deafness formed a special community. I would like to think anyway—when the student leaders stood in front of TV cameras in March of 1988 and said the University needed a deaf president now because the language and culture of deaf people must be respected—that the germ of that idea was presented in the dictionary twenty-three years earlier.

I know for sure, from talking with them, that social scientists with no previous acquaintance with deaf people learned from the dictionary that there was a special language and culture well worth their attention. I also remember meeting the first of the deaf associates, former students of mine, who worked in San Diego with Ursula Bellugi, and hearing their complaints that they had to spend too much time studying the dictionary. "Why," they asked me, "do we have to learn all those funny symbols? We know the language already." But that was almost twenty years ago. Some of them who asked that at first have since made discoveries that will need to be included in any future edition.

And perhaps that is the best consequence of all. Owing in part, at least, to the existence of *A Dictionary of American Sign Language,* there now are deaf men and women engaged in studying sign language and the culture of deaf communities. A world this far advanced can't be turned around even by the Supreme Court of the United States.

Issues in Preparing and Presenting a Dictionary of New Zealand Signs

MARIANNE COLLINS-AHLGREN

Having had experience with deaf communities in several countries, I went to New Zealand in 1981 with two goals in mind: learning the sign language of the New Zealand deaf community and having fellowship with the deaf community in Wellington. To that end, I searched for a dictionary of New Zealand signs, or a class where I could learn New Zealand Sign Language (NZSL), or an interpreter who could tutor me in sign language.

My quest was initially unsuccessful on all three accounts. I was advised that there was no New Zealand Sign Language. After some probing, however, I obtained photocopies of fifty illustrated signs used by deaf children and adults in Auckland, prepared by a teacher of deaf students there. This same teacher was the representative to the Australian Sign Language Development Committee, and that group's dictionary of Australian Total Communication signs, *Aid to Communicating with the Deaf* (1979), was also available.

The single piece of analytical research into NZSL at that time was a 1972 unpublished research paper by Peter Ballingall, a teacher of deaf students. Ballingall analyzed his deaf pupils' signs and included in the paper descriptions of a list of signs he had observed.

In New Zealand, there were individuals who mistakenly believed that Total Communication was a natural language, and that the deaf community needed to communicate through English because they did not have a native language of their own. These individuals were trying to impose Australasian Total Communication on the adult deaf community. It was clear to me that a proper description of the language of the deaf community in Wellington was necessary if people were to become interpreters for deaf people or to communicate comfortably with members of the deaf community. Thus, it was necessary to establish the authenticity of NZSL as a language.

That description of NZSL was eventually prepared by me as a dissertation. Volume 1 attempts to demonstrate that NZSL has the properties of arbitrariness, duality, productivity, cultural transmission, and consistent grammar. The data in the dictionary that follows this analysis were used for phonological and morphological analysis and in discussing cultural transmission. Volume 2 contains hundreds of photographs of the NZSL signs referred to in the text. Because a lexicon was not available at the outset of my research, signs were recorded in volumes 3 and 4 as a "dictionary" or glossary of NZSL lexicon, which I will describe in this paper.

Brief History of Sign in New Zealand

A brief history of sign used in New Zealand should be helpful in understanding why hearing individuals were attempting to introduce Australasian Total Communication in the 1980s, and why a considerable variation in sign forms is recorded in the dictionary.

Because British Sign Language (BSL) was widely used to educate deaf children in Britain during the mid-nineteenth century, it was the language brought by deaf British immigrants when they came to New Zealand. British tutors in New Zealand also used BSL, as did the teachers in schools for deaf students in Australia and England, where some deaf children from New Zealand attended school.

In 1880, van Asch, who was active in reviving the oralist philosophy of educating deaf students in Europe, was selected to direct Sumner School, the first New Zealand School for deaf students. Van Asch refused to allow the use of sign in Sumner School or to admit children who knew sign. Evidence indicates, however, that from its founding in 1880 onward, deaf students surreptitiously used sign for communication. It appears that owing to the absence of a BSL model or adult sign model, combinations of home signs, dependent on context, changed into a more abstract system of school signs over time in the school dormitories. As children were segregated by age and sex in the dormitories, variations in school signs grew.

In 1942, the New Zealand army needed the school's dormitories, and the children were split up. Pupils from the South Island moved to temporary quarters, where they remained until 1944. Children from the North Island were moved to a temporary school near Auckland, where a permanent school was established. After 1942, sign variations between geographically separated schools grew. Variations also arose from a school with Irish influences, established on the North Island after World War II, and from day classes for deaf students established in Wellington and other cities.

In communities of deaf adults in New Zealand, BSL and various school signs were fused through continuous use over succeeding generations. Through consensual validation within area deaf clubs, lexical variations were, and are, established among geographical and generational groups.

Preparing a New Zealand Sign Dictionary

I proceeded through the following stages in preparing a "dictionary" or glossary of New Zealand signs.

Data Collection

The research population was the deaf community in Wellington, which is located in the extreme south of the North Island. It was, and is, within the district of the Sumner School on the South Island and is also near St. Dominic School (the one with Irish influence) on the North Island. In particular, the community was represented by members of the Wellington Deaf Society, the Wellington Deaf club, and fifteen consultants. These people ranged in age from young adults to seniors. Some had deaf parents and/or older siblings; others had hearing parents but demonstrated native signing competence. They included representative former students from three schools: Sumner School, St. Dominic School, and day classes in Wellington.

Collection of signs proceeded both from sign to gloss and gloss to sign. During a two-year period, I observed and recorded signs used by deaf individuals at parties, social functions, meetings, and small gatherings where few or no hearing people besides myself were present. Because I am a hearing, non-native NZSL signer, initially there was a strong tendency for native signers to shift to an English accommodation style when communicating directly with me. An approach of unobtrusive observation tended to minimize this. These informal observations were helpful in learning new signs and, later, in confirming meanings and uses of signs learned in more formal sessions. On the other hand, the formal elicitations helped me confirm or disconfirm the meanings of signs observed informally.

When possible, two or more consultants contributed during elicitation sessions. When they did not communicate directly with me, they tended to communicate with each other in a more informal "club" style of sign. For almost two years, I held weekly elicitation sessions in the homes of some of the consultants.

Visual materials were helpful during formal elicitation sessions to attempt to minimize English influence. The most useful materials were newspapers, magazines, and photographs. Books for children with pictures but few or no words were helpful. When introducing pictorial materials, it was important that the consultants understood that they were to use the pictures as suggestions, but not to feel bound to identify only the item or action shown. For example, if a picture showed someone fishing with a pole and line, the consultant should tell me not only about that type of fishing, but also about rods and reels and so forth.

Published 3 × 5 picture cards in decks with various themes for preschool or young children were useful, particularly those showing a series of events or things of different sizes. Sketches drawn by a local artist to illustrate themes I suggested also were helpful. After I had learned some vocabulary, signed stimuli situations were fun and useful in eliciting many words within a semantic field or in eliciting a target word or concept. A variety of elicitation methods within a session helped in preventing boredom and fatigue.

Data Recording

Data were recorded primarily through notetaking; new signs were recorded in a sign notation system. I used the sign notation system of Stokoe (1965), adapted by Brennan, Colville, and Lawson in *Words in Hand* (1980). The handshapes were represented by English alphabet letters that were described in the phonology section of my dissertation text. I made adaptations as I proceeded, such as inventing a symbol to show if a prominent thumb was opposed or unopposed to the four fingers, and putting an "X" in the movement slot to show a hold segment in contact or an "O" to show a hold segment not in contact.

Because any interruption of visual contact between the consultant(s) and me interrupted the communication or resulted in a loss of ongoing information, a rapid system of recording that required a minimum of visual attention was needed. Consultants and deaf people at the club soon became accustomed to my frequent notetaking, and it became a relatively unobtrusive means of recording data. I checked the accuracy of my notes by signing the recorded data back to a consultant at an appropriate time or by clarifying questions the notes raised when the discussion would not interrupt the communication of the consultant(s).

Data also were recorded with a video camera. This was clearly a more obtrusive means of collecting data than was notetaking, but it was essential to use video recordings to be able to examine signs closely. Because use of a video camera potentially created a "performer/audience" situation, two deaf consultants were present during taping whenever possible so one could communicate, with the other as audience.

Sign forms noted during formal or informal direct observations and from watching videotaped materials were recorded at the time of observation and then re-recorded onto looseleaf notebook pages headed with the English gloss. Thirty-five looseleaf notebooks were labeled with categories from the Council of Europe framework, which will be described below. Notebook pages were placed in the appropriate notebook, and additional entries, if any, were later included on the same page.

One of the tasks of collecting and reporting signs in a gloss-to-sign order is to determine the most common meaning of the English gloss and then to find a sign that best represents that meaning. The *General Service List of English Words* (West, 1953) was used for determining the most frequent meanings of English words, and these meanings were written onto the looseleaf notebook paper page under the gloss.

An alphabetical index was made of all the target glosses from the lists described below. When a sign form translating a gloss was recorded and entered into a notebook, that gloss was checked off in the index. A list of target signs for each division of the word list was glued to a notebook divider and placed in front of each notebook. When a sign translating a gloss listed there was entered into the notebook, that gloss was checked off, or the gloss not previously listed was added to the list.

Framework for Collecting

The *Systematic Vocabulary List* printed by the Council of Europe (1973) was the primary framework for reporting signs in the glossary. This list is widely used by teachers of modern languages to teach vocabulary systematically in major word classes. In addition to those in the word list, I added the following categories: sports/recreation, occupations/agent nominalizers, animals, nationalities, superordinates, compounds, fixed expressions, and signs not easily translated into English gloss.

Words from a Stokoe and Kuschel elicitation list (1978) and from a Ballingal list of signs (1972) were integrated into the Council of Europe word list.

Using the Council of Europe word list to report the NZSL lexicon was potentially problematic because of the use of English words to represent signs and to report signs grouped as parts of English speech. In recording the signs, it was important to justify labeling a sign as a given part of speech on the basis of properties intrinsic to the sign, rather than by association with an English gloss. For example, signs listed under the heading of "adjectives" on the Council of Europe word list are glossed by an English adjective, but the signs do not function syntactically and morphologically as adjectives in NZSL. Therefore, it must not be assumed that signs listed under the heading of a given part of speech in English function as that part of speech in NZSL. Additionally, because of the word formation process of conversion, some signs may change word class without changing form in NZSL. For instance, some signs that translate an English transitive verb also translate an English noun.

Sign translation for English adverbs, prepositions, and conjunctions are signs used in an English accommodation style of NZSL. Concepts such as amount, degree, direction, distance, time, and aspect, and connections between ideas are expressed through nonmanual behaviors and productive signs rather than through established lexicalized signs in the strong NZSL style. Similarly, while the council of Europe verb groupings into punctual or durative—with or without interpersonal contacts—perceptual, and attitudinal apply to NZSL verbs, the aspect of volitionality appears to be indicated by nonmanual behaviors rather than by fixed list.

If the reader is mindful of not classifying the lexical items into the English part of speech, and if he or she understands the inadequacies of using English word glosses to translate signs, then the Council of Europe's Systematic Vocabulary list appears to be a good framework for collecting and reporting the NZSL lexicon. Verbs might be better reported if productive verbs are not included in the dictionary.

Lexicalization of NZSL verbs results in two different types of morphological outcome. The first type is lexicalized with cells that must be filled by a morphological feature in the articulatory tier. This first type should be divided into those where the locative morpheme refers to a location and secondly into those where the locative morpheme refers to a grammatical person. The second type of verb is fully specified, and classes suggested by the Council of Europe, where applicable, may be subclasses.

Data Presentation

The symbols that were used to report signs in the dictionary were printed on a WANG computer. The Prestige Pica, 10 Pitch (# 719-6072) and the Scientific, 10 Pitch (719-8068) daisy wheels were used to report the lexical data. Because it was not possible to have selected characters from the two wheels combined into a single daisy wheel, it was necessary to enter symbols from each wheel on separate documents. Thus, the coded representation of each lexical entry was recorded on two documents. After one document was printed, the wheel was changed, and after the paper was carefully aligned, the second document was printed onto the page. Because the data were stored on two sets of documents, it was too difficult to add new lexical entries into a page that had been printed. It also was too difficult to "reshuffle" entries after the pages were entered and printed. Bits of information for some signs that are not included in the code are noted in parentheses to the right of the coded sign.

The WANG printout provided a uniform presentation of the NZSL signs that were collected in the initial phase of my research. However, in the future, I would use a computer format that recorded each sign on a single document, allowing the addition of additional entries under a gloss and the shifting of signs within the dictionary until the final printout.

Regarding the Sign Notation System format, while it was an excellent means of recording signs, it may be less "user friendly" as a means of reporting signs in a dictionary. Although it is an easy system to learn, it is not attractive to the general public. On the other hand, as a linguist, I found it an incomplete report. Perhaps a system such as that suggested by Liddell and Johnson (1985) is more suitable for a linguistic dictionary, whereas the general public may prefer a picture dictionary.

Having presented hundreds of pictures to describe signs in this dissertation, I found that they are not without problems. Frequently, even if the first and final segments of a sign are shown and arrows are drawn to indicate motion, a description is needed to indicate the exact relationship of the hands or the simultaneity of internal hand movement with lateral motion. Time-lapse photographs are better, but they are expensive and time-consuming. While the Sign Notation System allows several variations of a gloss to be printed, use of pictures to show variations is not an efficient use of space; therefore, it, too, is an expensive method. Perhaps the answer for the future is to present a dictionary of signs on videotape or even compact videodisc.

Issues of Homony, Polysemy, and Synonomy

Homophonous NZSL signs—those which can have different meanings for the same sign—were observed. A note reporting other meanings of the form was annotated, along with facial expressions or manner of articulation that might distinguish between meanings. Polysemous signs are those with several distinguishable related meanings. Some polysemous noun signs share form and appearance, and others share form and process. Synonomy of NZSL signs is observed when two or more sign forms have the same or nearly the same essential meaning in some of their senses. Different forms are used by signers of different areas or generations. Different lexicalizations result from focus on process or form. Some glosses are translated by both compound and simple signs. Some are translated by both single and two-handed signs, one or both of which may be the "citation form" rather than an emphatic, extensional, casual, or formal variation. Forms with lexicalized width or instrumental handshape morphemes vary, as noted in HOSE, PIPE, CUT, DRINK, SHUT, CLOSE, OPEN, and PICK UP.

There are many examples of interlanguage synonomy between English words and NZSL signs. However, homophonous and polysemous English words must be translated by different sign forms, such as those for THINK, FOLLOW, GRAVE, MISS, and FINE.

Issues of Validation

Lexicalization is a diachronic process and, as Pawley (1982) writes, it is a more-or-less thing. How does the dictionary writer determine if a sign offered by a consultant is an established sign in the community? How large a percentage of the community or of an age group or geographical group within the community must use and recognize the sign in order for it to be validated?

Although the preparer of a sign dictionary declares that it is descriptive rather than prescriptive, the general public almost surely reads it as standardized, and, therefore, prescriptive. Consequently, unless the preparer presents sign variations as he or she finds them, the preparer must decide which of the variations is "correct," because the general public will perceive that form as standard.

More importantly, unless the preparer gains the consensus of the nationwide deaf community, those deaf people in regions or age groups not consulted will view the dictionary as standardized but "wrong." They will feel that someone or some other nation's signs are being imposed upon them. This reaction was widespread in Wellington in 1983 when the National Association of the Deaf published the *Handbook of Basic Signs* and when Levitt (1986) published the *Introduction to New Zealand Sign Language.* Although Levitt deftly represented variations by photographing a person representative of a school background, those photographed were all from the Auckland area.

Issues of Grammatical and Morphological Influence

Should notes or separate entries be included in the dictionary to show signs that form plurals by reduplication or that show greater distance in time by greater length of movement, for example? Should examples of modified form to show aspect be indicated in signs that are frequently so modified? To call a presentation of signs a "dictionary," what elements must it contain in addition to the sign form translating English (or other spoken language) glosses? These and other questions remain to be answered.

References

ASLDP. 1979. *Aid to Communication with the Deaf.* Kelston School for the Deaf, Auckland, NZ.

Ballingall, Peter. 1971. *The Sign Language of Deaf Children in New Zealand.* Unpublished manuscript. University of Auckland, NZ.

Brennan, Mar, Martin D. Colville, and Lilian K. Lawson. 1980. *Words in Hand: A Structural Analysis of the Signs of British Sign Language.* Moray House, Edinburgh: BSL Research Project.

Council of Europe. 1973. *Systems Development in Adult Language Learning: A European Unit/ Credit System for Modern Language Learning by Adults.* Strasbourg: Council for Cultural Co-operation.

Levitt, Dan. 1986. *Introduction to New Zealand Sign Language.* Auckland, New Zealand: NZAD.

Liddell, Scott K., and Robert E. Johnson. 1985. *American Sign Language: The Phonological Base.* Unpublished manuscript.

Pawley, Andrew. 1982. *Lexicalization.* Unpublished manuscript presented at the Fourth New Zealand Linguistic Conference Christchurch.

Stokoe, William C. Jr., Dorothy C. Casterline, and Carl G. Croneberg. 1965 rev. 1976. *A Dictionary of American Sign Language on Linguistic Principles.* Maryland: Linstok Press.

———. and Rolf Kuschel. 1978. *A Field Guide for Sign Language Research.* Maryland: Linstok Press.

West, Michael P., ed. 1953. *A General Service List of English Words with Semantic Frequencies and a Supplementary Word List for the Writing of Popular Sciences and Technology.* London: Longman.

The Development of a Dictionary of Namibian Sign Language

SACKEUS P. ASHIPALA, PROFELIUS DANIEL,
MARIUS N. HAIKALI, NANGOLO ISRAEL,
FESTUS T. LINUS, HENOCK H. NIILENGE,
TIMONY F. HAIDUWAH, AND RAUNA N.
HASHIYANAH IN COLLABORATION WITH RUTH MORGAN

We are a group of six Deaf and two hearing Namibians who have come to Gallaudet University for fifteen months. The United Nations Commission on Namibia is funding our program. Our aim is to learn how to analyze our own sign language, to improve our English, and to receive leadership training. Later we will discuss how and why we are analyzing our sign language. To do this, we are working with Ruth Morgan, a linguist at Gallaudet.

The situation we come from is unique and complex. Therefore, we need first to give you some background information before we discuss how we are making a dictionary of our sign language, so you will understand how special circumstances have influenced our Deaf culture and the development of our sign language.

We were living in Northern Namibia until the late 1970s and early 1980s, when we left our country because we felt we could not receive the education we wanted. Our education system was under the South African government, which has controlled Namibia since 1915. We went to live in Angola, where we stayed until we came to Gallaudet University in 1988. We expect Namibia to be independent by December. When our country is independent, we will go home and begin to improve Deaf education there. We will first describe our life in Namibia and then describe our life in Angola.

Life in Namibia

Our families are all hearing and live in traditional villages, where they farm. Namibia is a country that has many different cultural groups, so many different languages are used in our country. We are all Ovawambos, which is the largest cultural group in Northern Namibia. Our families all speak Oshiwambo, one of many Bantu languages spoken in Namibia. Oshiwambo has many different dialects. Some of the other languages spoken by different cultural groups are Nama, Herero, Damara, English, Afrikaans, Oshikwangali, and Oshirozi. Most hearing Namibians know several languages, and communication among different groups is common.

Even though Namibia is home to numerous hearing cultural groups who speak many different languages, we don't know yet what the situation is for most deaf people in Namibia; sign language in our country has never been researched before. There may be many sign languages in Namibia, or there may be only one sign language. We will know this after we do our own work in Namibia.

The South African government's apartheid policy has influenced our sign language situation; we do not know the sign language used by white Deaf Namibians or by San Deaf Namibians. We grew up in a country where apartheid forced members of these different groups (whether hearing or Deaf) to live separately. In Namibia there are separate living areas and separate schools for blacks and whites. Schools for Deaf students are segregated as well, with different schools for black and white deaf children.

Our sign language comes from that used outside the classroom by black deaf students in schools in Northern Namibia. While we were living in Namibia, there were two schools for black deaf students—Engela and Eluwa. Engela was the first school for deaf students. It was started by the Evangelical Lutheran Church in Namibia around 1970. This church was originally founded by Finnish missionaries in the late 1800s and later was given over to the Namibian people themselves.

The teachers in the school used Simultaneous Communication, with signs that followed Oshiwambo word order. One of the deaf members of our group attended Engela as a student from 1972 to 1974. He told us that the first two teachers in this school were black Namibians who had been sent to Pretoria, South Africa, for training. The sign system used in some of the schools for black deaf children in South Africa at that time was the Paget-Gorman system. This system, invented in England by a hearing person to teach English to deaf children, is not a natural sign language. It had been used in South African black schools since the 1960s. At Engela, the children used the same sign vocabulary as the teachers who had been trained in Pretoria, but the children's signs did not follow Oshiwambo word order.

Our colleague who attended Engela told us that he also spent a lot of time with a group of deaf adults who worked in Engela. He often sat and watched them tell stories. They, too, used the same sign vocabulary as was used in the school. However, they did not sign in Oshiwambo word order either. We think that the sign language used by these adults was the true beginning of Namibian Sign Language.

In 1975, the South African government started a school named Eluwa, the second school for deaf students in Namibia. All students under the age of seventeen (a total of twelve children), together with their teachers, were moved from Engela to this new school, leaving behind about five deaf adults, who continued to work at Engela. Our colleague who attended the Engela school was the only member of our group who had learned the sign language used by the adult deaf people at Engela. The students who were moved to Eluwa were able to take the adult sign language with them. Three other members of our group started attending this new school between 1975 and 1978. All four of us left Namibia in 1980 and went into exile.

Our Years in Angola

Before we came to the United States in 1988, we had been living in Southern Angola for nine years. Because there were thousands of Namibians living there, the different

Namibian cultures could be maintained. We are all Deaf Ovawambos, and none of us met Deaf people from other cultural groups.

When we arrived in Angola, the deaf people were not organized into any real community. They did not live near each other, and there was no school for deaf students. Therefore, we were not greatly influenced by the Angolan Deaf culture because we did not come into contact with many Deaf Angolans. The few Deaf Angolans we later met used different signs, and we taught them our sign language. Of the students who had attended Eluwa, only one was mainstreamed while in Angola; the other three did not attend school, because there was no school for deaf students.

The three of us who were not mainstreamed would often get together; we continued to use our old sign language, which we had learned at Eluwa School for the Deaf in Namibia. For convenience, we will call this language Namibian Sign Language (NSL), although we know that there are probably other varieties of Namibian Sign Language or other sign languages in Namibia.

Later, we were joined by the fourth member of our group. He had never been to school in Namibia, and he used home signs only. We taught him our signs. We used to spend most of our time together, playing soccer and volleyball with hearing people every day. The four of us would practice art on a daily basis, because we were not in school. After some hearing people saw our artwork, we were then employed as illustrators. But we could not read the English texts of the books we were illustrating. We wanted to learn how to read English, so we decided we needed a school for deaf students and requested one.

At first, two of us were mainstreamed, in separate schools, so we did not have much contact with each other, apart from an occasional visit. We socialized mainly with hearing people. We knew of only a few other deaf people who were mainstreamed and whom we saw occasionally. These mainstreamed students used different signs and gestures, although one had been to a school for deaf students in Namibia and therefore knew Eluwa signs. We picked up his Namibian signs.

In 1982, a school for deaf students was started, and all the deaf students in the area started to go to the same school. The students who had not been attending school were joined by the students who had been mainstreamed. The start of our deaf school was important because it gave us a place to meet other deaf people in the area every day. There were nine students in our school when it started. The sign language we continued to use was the variety we had brought with us from Namibia, which we taught to the other four pupils.

In 1983, an important thing happened that influenced the deaf people in our school. Three Namibian Deaf people who had never attended a deaf school before were sent to Sweden in 1980 to further their education. When they came back from Sweden in 1983, they taught in our school. They taught us Swedish Sign Language as well as the history of Deaf people in Sweden. They also taught us math and English. This was the first time we had ever heard about the theory of Deaf culture. The three teachers did not know our sign language because our school had been established after they had left for Sweden. We taught them our sign language. Only a few Swedish signs remained in our NSL, such as the signs for "thank you" and the names of some countries: Africa, Russia, and Finland, for example.

The Deaf Namibians in exile in Angola used to socialize together after school, when we could play volleyball and perform plays. In the afternoons, and evenings when the moon shone, we frequently told stories under a big tree.

In summary, a Deaf culture was initially formed in Namibia at the first school for black deaf students at Engela. This was carried to Eluwa in 1974 and then brought into

Angola when we left Namibia. Once the school for deaf students was formed in Angola, there was a place where many Deaf people could become enculturated.

By 1988, there were about thirty deaf students in the school. At this time, the present group was selected to go to Gallaudet to receive further training so we could be better prepared to set up future services for Deaf Namibians in Angola and in Namibia itself after independence.

Why a Dictionary of NSL?

We are developing this NSL dictionary because we want to have a book of our own natural sign language used by Namibian deaf people in Southern Angola. We want people to know that NSL is a real language like Oshiwambo or English. We want deaf Namibians to be proud of their Deaf culture and sign language, and we want hearing people to respect our culture and our sign language. We want people to know the history of our sign language—that it was developed in Namibia in the school for deaf students and taken with us to Angola, where others started to learn it. We want people to know that NSL has its own vocabulary and structure.

We also want to learn how to make a sign language dictionary so that when Namibia is independent, we can go home and compare the sign languages used by the different cultural groups still in the country to our particular sign language. We will need to do a lot more research in the future to see if other Ovawambo deaf people who stayed inside the country have the same sign language as we do, or whether their language is different. It may be that there is not one but, rather, there are many different Deaf cultures and sign languages inside Namibia. With independence there will be an end to separate schools for each racial group; we want to research what happens to NSL when deaf people from different groups are brought together in a single school and a single adult Deaf culture.

Procedures for Making the NSL Dictionary

The signs in this manual were taken from videotapes of Namibian Sign Language. Each person in the group was videotaped the same week we arrived in the United States. Each person told his life story on the videotape. Then the artists in the group drew many pictures of everyday life in Namibia: village scenes of people plowing their fields with oxen, planting seeds, growing and harvesting vegetables, killing animals for food, storing grain, and eating. The group was again videotaped as we discussed these pictures and told stories about our lives in Namibia before we went into exile.

After making these videotapes, we started to transcribe them, using a slow-motion playback control to slow down the videotape. We discussed each sign in depth before writing down its meaning in English. We also wrote down information about the sign's structure—handshape, location, orientation, segmental structure, and non-manual signals or facial expressions. We discussed whether there were other signs that could be used to mean the same thing. If there were differences in the production of a sign, such as different handshapes or movements, we discussed these and wrote them down. We decided which sign was used by most people and which signs were accepted as variants by most people.

We are still busy transcribing the signs. By August, 1989, we will have collected 1,000 signs for our dictionary. This method of getting NSL data for the dictionary takes a long time, but it is really the only way to understand the structure of the language.

We want to explain the structure of NSL in our dictionary, as well as the vocabulary. We want to explain how verbs work in NSL, how negatives and questions are formed, and how facial expression and space are used in the grammar of NSL. We need this information before we can teach NSL to others.

We then need to draw each sign in the most accurate and clear way for people to learn. In August 1989, two of us will be trained in the latest technical methods of sign language drawing. From August to December, we will organize the signs for our manual. Each sign will be glossed in English onto an index card. We will group together signs that have the same handshape, such as animal signs or people signs.

Each sign will be illustrated in the dictionary using line drawings and arrows to indicate movement. The meaning of the sign will then be explained in both Oshiwambo and English. We will not use single word glosses. Notes on each sign explaining its meaning, and structural information—such as a sign's grammatical function or what part of speech it belongs to—will be included.

Educating People about NSL

It is obvious that we will have a lot to do when we go home. First, we will need to do more sign language research. Once schools for deaf students in an independent Namibia become integrated for all cultures, it will be necessary to research what happens to NSL. We will use our dictionary to compare our vocabulary and sign language structure to that used by deaf people from different cultural groups who remained inside the country. We will then have to create a second dictionary with our findings. We want to start teaching deaf students using NSL when we go back home. With our sign language dictionary, we will be able to teach NSL to teachers and interpreters who work with deaf people, as well as to the parents of deaf children.

Hearing people in Namibia and Angola do not know that deaf Namibians have their own sign language—NSL—and their own Deaf culture. We want to go back and teach hearing people in independent Namibia about our sign language and culture. It is important for people to understand that NSL has its own vocabulary, which is different from the vocabulary of sign languages in other countries. Our dictionary will contain information about the vocabulary and grammar of NSL, as well as information about how our Deaf culture was formed. We will explain how the first school for deaf students was started in Namibia and how it was moved to Eluwa and then to Angola, where we became part of a free society. We will educate others about our Deaf culture so they understand that we have our own cultural identity as well as our own language.

Taiwan Natural Sign Language Research Work

JAMES CHIEN-MIN CHAO

The educational system for deaf people in Taiwan is extremely backward, and deaf people face many problems in society. Therefore, on September 18, 1977, the Deaf College Student and Alumni Association was organized in Taipei, Taiwan. I was elected first president of the association. Together with a few other deaf people, I began to devote my time to an effort that would change the lives of many deaf people in Taiwan. Through the association, we began to unite deaf people. Our confidence grew as we tried, for the first time, to communicate as a group to a society that is mostly hearing. Our efforts resulted in the establishment of sign language classes, research, and a book, *Taiwan Natural Sign Language.*

In October 1977, Dr. Wayne H. Smith, assisted by myself and several other deaf people, established the first introductory classes in Taiwan Natural Sign Language. In May of 1978, I established the first advanced class and began the job of training sign language instructors. In July 1978, five large introductory sign language classes were started in Taiwan. Deaf members of the Deaf College Student and Alumni Association, as well as hearing members of the Sign Language Club, helped in research to develop class materials and sometimes served as instructors in the classes.

In September 1978, I passed up the opportunity to serve a second term as president of the association in order to more actively pursue sign language research and instruction. Because there were no data on Taiwan Natural Sign Language, my first step was to collect a lot of signs. I thought about signs when I walked, slept, and ate; I watched deaf people communicate in sign language and recorded their signs. Many deaf people and I met every Thursday evening to pursue Taiwan Sign Language research and discuss how to translate signs into written Chinese. Several hearing people also joined our meetings to assist us in recording each sign with a detailed explanation of facial expression and how the sign should be produced.

In 1979, I organized the data and wrote the manuscript for the book. Another deaf member of the association helped me draw more than 500 pictures of signs, and a third deaf member helped me photograph appropriate facial expressions. Then I reviewed and corrected the graphic representations of facial expressions, handshapes, movements, and locations of signs. To provide a way to look up a sign in my book, I compiled a Taiwan Sign Language index that set apart such areas as nose, eyes, mouth, maxilla, head, ears, cheeks, face, neck, shoulders, one hand, two hands, chest, abdomen, and the outside of the body. I also wrote a Chinese and English index. Several deaf members and I compiled the pages of the book, which I then carefully proofread.

In March 1980, the Deaf Sign Language Association of the Republic of China was formally instituted in Taipei. On September 11, 1980, I came to the United States and

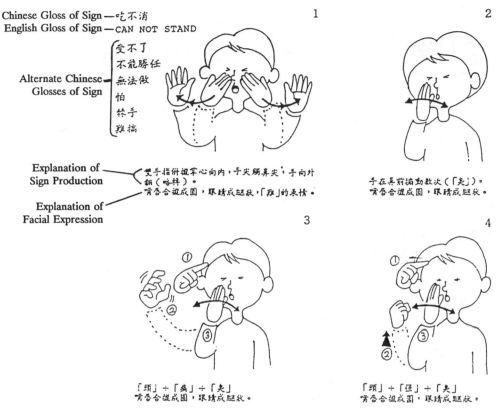

FIGURE 1. Four signs with essentially the same meaning in Taiwan Sign Language, glossed in English as "CANNOT STAND."

enrolled at Ohlone College. Because the Taipei association was conducting an advanced class in Taiwan Sign Language and needed to use my book as a textbook, I published a photocopy edition of *Taiwan Natural Sign Language* in September 1981. But I was not very satisfied with it.

Since then, I have continued conducting research on the natural sign language of Taiwan and adding other sign data, adaptations, and revisions. Dr. Smith helped me translate the book into English. I added an article about the history of Chinese Sign Language and a preface, "Comparison of the Structure of Spoken Language and Sign Language."

The sign systems of Taipei and Tainan are approximately the same. But the Taipei system has gradually adopted some traditional Chinese Sign Language and has created new signs, making it a complicated dialect.

Virtually all the previous research on the linguistic and structural characteristics of Taiwan Sign Language has been carried out by hearing people who, in spite of their prior training and experience with the language, still lack a native feel for it. My book, *Taiwan Natural Sign Language*, is, I hope, the first of many books that will reflect the insights of native users of Taiwan Sign Language.

The book has several noteworthy features. The emphasis throughout is on facial expression, and this is dealt with in two ways. The first chapter of the book describes in detail—with accompanying photos—more than fifty-eight distinct facial expressions commonly used by deaf people in Taiwan during their signed utterances. In addition, each illustration of a sign in the book is carefully drawn to include a facial expression, which adds to the meaning of the sign it accompanies. Also, individual signs and strings of signs that have essentially the same meaning are listed together and glossed by appropriate Chinese written translations (Figure 1). Each sign or sign sequence also is accompanied by an approximate English translation for the benefit of foreign scholars who are interested in Taiwan Sign Language, but who are not fluent in Chinese.

Each lesson in the book is followed by sample sentences in both Mandarin Chinese and Taiwan Sign Language, with glosses used to indicate the exact signs for the Taiwan Sign Language version. Although this method of encoding signed utterances may lack some of the detail needed for actual production, such as indications of appropriate facial expression, pauses, and emphasis, it is certainly a start in the direction of a deeper understanding of the structure and use of the language.

A second edition of *Taiwan Natural Sign Language* was published by the Deaf Sign Language Association of the Republic of China in January 1988 (Chao, Chu, and Liu, 1988). I feel the book is greatly improved, and I have applied for a copyright to the United States Library of Congress. Meanwhile, I am continuing to conduct research on traditional Chinese Sign Language.

References

Chao, C., H. Chu, and C. Liu. 1988. *Taiwan Natural Sign Language*. Taipei, Taiwan: Deaf Sign Language Association of the Republic of China.

A Dictionary Process for Documenting and Sharing Signs Used by Skilled Signers

DOLORES OGLIA, MARILYN MITCHELL, AND FRANK CACCAMISE

Increased academic and career opportunities and achievements of deaf people in the United States have led skilled sign users *naturally* to develop signs for technical and other specialized vocabulary. This paper describes the Technical Signs Project (TSP), a "dictionary" type project that occurred at the National Technical Institute for the Deaf in the United States for documenting and sharing these naturally developed signs. This description includes an overview of the natural sign development process (NSDP) and the relationship of this natural process to the TSP, as well as information about TSP materials and guidelines/suggestions for users of sign dictionaries.

The Natural Sign Development Process and the Technical Signs Project

In the natural sign development process (NSDP), skilled sign language users naturally develop and refine signs to meet their communication needs, leading to standard sign usage. It was at this point that the Technical Signs Project (TSP) began. The five steps of TSP include sign collection, evaluation, selection, recording, and sharing. The TSP is a dictionary project that documents signs used by skilled signers. As illustrated in Figure 1, the TSP process must be ongoing to include both new signs and modifications of existing signs that occur through natural sign language development and usage. Ten principles guided the TSP process:

1. The project respects all language and communication users.
2. Identification of important vocabulary precedes sign collection.
3. The project collects, but does not invent, signs.
4. Dialectical and contextual variations in signs are acceptable.
5. Fingerspelling is the preferred alternative to "artificial" sign invention.
6. Signs selected are recommended, not required.
7. Ongoing evaluation is a necessity.
8. Cooperation is important, both internal/local and external/national.
9. Continued research on sign language, including observation of sign language use in natural communication situations, is important.

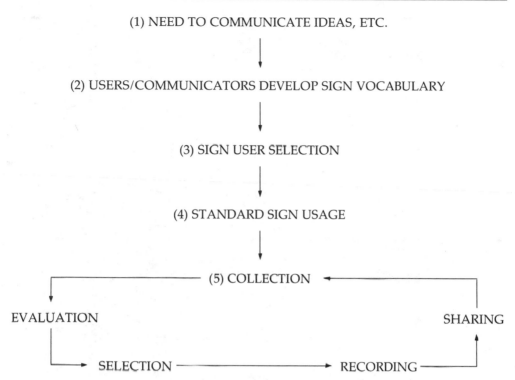

(1) NEED TO COMMUNICATE IDEAS, ETC.

(2) USERS/COMMUNICATORS DEVELOP SIGN VOCABULARY

(3) SIGN USER SELECTION

(4) STANDARD SIGN USAGE

(5) COLLECTION

EVALUATION

SHARING

SELECTION — RECORDING

FIGURE 1: Relationship between the natural sign development process (#1–#4) and the technical signs project process (#5).

10. The following are guidelines for sign collection, evaluation, selection, recording, and sharing:
    a. Consistency of use by native signers who know content area is the first major guideline.
    b. Consistency of use by "content" experts who are skilled signers is the second major guideline.
    c. Consistency with the structural characteristics of naturally developed signs in the United States is necessary.

The following items further elaborate the steps in the TSP process. The terms *internal* and *external* are included in order to indicate the importance of cooperation among programs and geographical regions throughout the process.

1. Identification of important vocabulary: Internal and External (I & E).
2. Collection of existing signs (I & E).
3. Evaluation of collected signs (I & E).
4. Selection of currently used signs.
5. Recording and storage of signs.
6. Dissemination/sharing (I & E).
7. Evaluation (I & E).
8. Development and evaluation of new and modified signs (I & E).

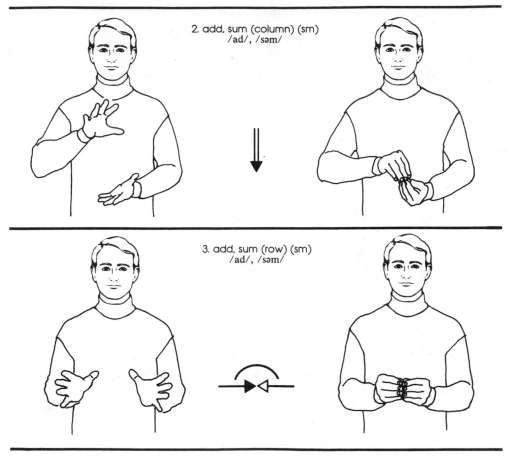

FIGURE 2: Sample sign diagrams from technical signs project mathematics manual (Caccamise, Pocobello, Outermans, Mitchell, Peterson, Newell, and Sutton, 1982b).

Technical Signs Project Materials

As shown in Figure 1, the TSP records signs for sharing. Because media such as films and videotapes can show all four basic sign parameters—handshape, position, orientation, and movement—and because videotape equipment is readily available to potential users of TSP materials in the United States, we decided to use videotapes as the major means for documenting signs selected for TSP dictionary materials.

Following production of videotapes for a technical or specialized area—for example, mathematics—a manual that illustrates signs in the same order as they are recorded on videotape may be produced. These manuals are intended to be used for review of signs that are either viewed on videotape or demonstrated live.

In TSP manuals, signs are illustrated by line drawings and movement symbols. Generally, for each sign there are two line drawings, the first showing the initial position of the sign and the second showing the final position of the sign. Movement symbols are placed between line drawings. Thus, sign illustrations are read in the manuals from left to right. In addition, print information for both Technical Signs Project videotapes and manuals includes key words in parentheses to clarify meaning when appropriate. Examples are *add* (column) and *add* (row), as shown in Figure 2.

Since 1975, the Technical Signs Project has produced fifty-seven videotapes in twenty-five technical or specialized areas and published nine manuals, using the principles and process discussed above. Two other manuals are currently in preparation. Additional information about these materials is provided in the appendix to this paper. (For additional information about recording methods for TSP videotapes and manuals, see Caccamise, Newell, Mitchell, Naiman, Outermans, Pocobello, Smith, and Liebman, 1982a, and Sutton, Caccamise, Mitchell, Newell, Merchant, Pocobello, and Outermans, 1982.)

Guidelines/Suggestions for Users of Sign Dictionaries

As previously discussed and documented by Technical Signs Project materials, sign language users have a natural process for developing sign vocabulary important for meeting their communication needs. Mechanisms used by signers in this process, as documented by Battison (1978), Bellugi and Newkirk (1981), Frishberg (1975), and Rimor, Kegl, Lane, and Schermer (1984), include compounding (e.g., MALE SAME for BROTHER and MEASURE LONG-THIN-RECTANGULAR for RULER); derivational processes (e.g., noun-verb pairs such as AIRPLANE and FLY, and adjectival-adverbial pairs such as WRONG and UNEXPECTEDLY); mimetic devices (e.g., JET-LAG and SATELLITE); and modifications of fingerspelling (e.g., JOB, ALL, and GO-BACK-TOGETHER).

Unfortunately, some authors of sign language materials have chosen to include artificially developed/invented signs, rather than document signs used by skilled signers. Users of sign dictionaries, therefore, are encouraged to evaluate critically the principles and processes used by authors in selecting signs for their sign materials. Materials that include artificially developed signs should be used with caution. Preferably, all signs in such materials should be evaluated by skilled signers, with signs unacceptable to them being rejected.

In addition, academic programs that establish policies for sign selection and use are encouraged to include input from skilled signers to assist in identifying signs used by skilled signers in their program and in the local community. Dialectical sign variations are acceptable and should be respected.

In brief, sign communicators, and not authors, inventors, or committees, *should* and *do* determine what is and is not acceptable in sign communication. As Stokoe (1976) has stressed:

> Standard is of course not a matter of legislation but of currency. When leaders of the national deaf organizations discuss standardization of Sign as part of their work, e.g., the National Association of the Deaf, the Communicative Skills Programs (of the NAD) or the Jewish Deaf Association, they are not trying to halt the tides of natural language change but only to recognize that there are local, provincial, standard, conservative, and puristic kinds of Sign, and to indicate that one who studies, practices, and uses standard Sign is on the surest ground (p. 21).

Summary and Conclusions

We have given a brief description of the natural sign development process and the Technical Signs Project that builds upon that process. We wish to stress that it is the process used by the TSP, and not the sign materials produced, that we most wish to share with our colleagues in other countries. Vocabulary, regardless of communication modality (speech, writing, sign), develops in a natural manner in accordance with the communication needs, values, ideas, and materials of the cultural groups that use the vocabulary. Therefore, we encourage our colleagues in other countries to undertake sign dictionary projects based on the natural sign development process in their countries. As Battison (1978) stressed, "Just as we cannot divorce a language from the way it is physically expressed, we cannot separate it from the culture or cultures in which it is used" (p. vii).

The publication of sign dictionaries that document standard signs can contribute to effective communication among signers by sharing signs *currently used* by skilled signers. Further, such documentation can serve to demonstrate the richness and expansiveness of natural sign lexicons/vocabularies, thus helping more people understand why artificial sign development or invention is unnecessary. There is no need for artificial sign development or invention; rather, there is a need for observing, documenting, and sharing what skilled sign users do.

Overview of Technical Signs Project Materials

To date [1989], fifty-seven videotapes have been produced in the following twenty-five technical/specialized areas:

Anthropology	English	Science/Biology
Business	Fine and Applied Arts	Science/General
Career Education	Human Sexuality	Science/Physics
Communication: Audiology	Legal	Secretarial
and Speech Pathology	Mathematics	Social Work
Computer Terminology	Photography	Sports
Economics	Printing	Television/Media
Employment	Psychology	Theater
Engineering	Religion/Catholic	

Videotapes are currently in preparation for several other areas, including vocational rehabilitation, legal, printing, and linguistics.

All TSP videotapes, except Computer Terminology, are available for purchase and on a free loan basis from Modern Talking Picture Service (MTPS), 5000 Park St. North, St. Petersburg, Florida 33709, (800) 237-6213 (V/TDD). The Computer Terminology videotapes are available for free loan from MTPS and for purchase from the National Association of the Deaf (NAD), 814 Thayer Ave., Silver Spring, Maryland 20910, (301) 587-1788 (V/TDD). Also, a manual that includes the signs on these videotapes is available from the NAD. TSP manuals produced to date include:

❖ *Manual 1: Project Overview,* which provides an overview of the TSP principles and process, suggestions for use of TSP materials, and a list of vocabulary on TSP videotapes.

❖ *Manual 2: Reading Technical Sign Diagrams,* which provides information on how to read sign diagrams in subsequent TSP manuals accurately.

❖ *Manual 3: Mathematics.*

❖ *Manual 4: Communication: Audiology and Speech Pathology.*

❖ *Manual 5: Career Education.*

❖ *Manual 6: English.*

❖ *Manual 7: Religion/Catholic.*

❖ *Manual 8: Theater.*

❖ *Manual 9: Social Work.*

❖ *Manual 10: Science and Manual 11: Legal* are currently in production.

Signs in each TSP manual are presented in the same order as the signs on the videotapes for each technical area. TSP manuals are available for purchase from Modern Talking Picture Service; Rochester Institute of Technology (RIT) Bookstore (P.O. Box 9887, Rochester, New York 14623-0887), and the Gallaudet University Bookstore (Gallaudet University, 800 Florida Avenue N.E., Washington, DC 20002-3695).

For further information about the Technical Signs Project, please contact Dolores Oglia, (716) 475-6836 (V/TDD) or Frank Caccamise, Ph.D., (716) 475-6420 (V/TDD). The address for both is P.O. Box 9887, NTID/RIT, Rochester, New York 14623-0887.

References

Battison, R. 1978. *Lexical Borrowing in American Sign Language.* Silver Spring, MD: Linstok Press.

Bellugi, U., and D. Newkirk. 1981. "Formal Devices for Creating New Signs in American Sign Language." *Sign Language Studies* 30: 1–35.

Caccamise, F., W. Newell, M. Mitchell, P. Naiman, L. Outermans, D. Pocobello, N. Smith, and Aron Liebman. 1982a. *Technical Signs Manual #1: Project Overview: Videotape and Print Materials for Sign Words Used in Academic and Career Environments.* St. Petersburg, FL: Modern Talking Picture Service.

Caccamise, F., D. Pocobello, L. Outermans, M. Mitchell, P. Peterson, W. Newell, and V. Sutton. 1982b. *Technical Signs Manual #3: Mathematics.* St. Petersburg, FL: Modern Talking Picture Service.

Frishberg, N. 1975. "Arbitrariness and Iconicity: Historical Change in American Sign Language." *Language* 51: 696–719.

Rimor, M., J. Kegl, H. Lane, and T. Schermer. 1984. "Natural Phonetic Processes Underlie Historical Change and Register Variation in American Sign Language." *Sign Language Studies* 43: 97–119.

Stokoe, W. 1976. "The Study and Use of Sign Language." *Sign Language Studies* 10: 1–36.

Sutton, V., F. Caccamise, M. Mitchell, W. Newell, K. Merchant, D. Pocobello, and L. Outermans. 1982. *Technical Signs Manual #2: Reading Technical Sign Diagrams.* St. Petersburg, FL: Modern Talking Picture Service.

When Is ASL?

CEIL LUCAS AND CLAYTON VALLI

Q uestions that have arisen with increasing frequency in the study of American Sign Language (ASL) are, "What is ASL and what is not? What criteria do we use to determine whether a given language sample constitutes ASL or not?" In this paper, we will describe one aspect of an ongoing study of the linguistic outcome of contact between people in the American deaf community who are bilingual.

The ultimate goal of the project is to provide a linguistic description of the signing that results from the contact between ASL and English and that exhibits features of both languages. It has been claimed (Woodward, 1973; Woodward and Markowicz, 1975) that this kind of "contact signing" is a pidgin—often known as Pidgin Sign English (PSE)—and is the result of deaf-hearing interaction. The goal of the study is to re-examine this claim, based on a structural description of contact signing resulting from natural interaction. (Based on a preliminary examination of the linguistic and sociolinguistic data, we are reluctant at this point to call the contact signing that we have observed a *variety* or a *dialect,* and the absence of such labels in the present study is conscious. Further study may reveal the need for such a label.)

An extensive discussion of the linguistic and sociolinguistic features of contact signing can be found in Lucas and Valli (1989). The focus of this paper is on one part of the data collection methodology, that is, the judgments made by native signers regarding portions of videotaped interviews.

The Interviews

First, we will describe the interviews that yielded our videotaped data. Six dyads of signers were formed. Eleven of the twelve signers rated themselves as very skilled in ASL, and all twelve rated themselves as skilled in English. Nine were born deaf, one was born hard of hearing and is now deaf, and two were born hearing and became deaf at fifteen months and three years of age, respectively. Five of the twelve came from deaf families; of the remaining seven, five attended residential schools for deaf students and learned ASL at an early age. One signer learned ASL from other deaf students in a mainstream program.

Considering the family and educational backgrounds of all but one of the signers, their self-evaluations of personal language skills are accurate: They are bilingual individuals who learned ASL either natively from their parents or at a very early age from peers—all but one in a residential school setting. They have had exposure to and con-

TABLE 1: Composition of Dyads

Dyad	Participant A	Participant B
1	Deaf family, born deaf, residential school	Deaf family, deaf at 15 months, public school
2	Deaf family, born deaf, deaf day school	Deaf family, born hard of hearing, now profoundly deaf, deaf day school
3	Deaf family, born deaf, residential school	Hearing family, born deaf, residential school
4	Hearing family, born deaf, residential school	Hearing family, deaf at age 3, residential school
5	Hearing family, born deaf, residential school	Hearing family, born deaf, mainstream program
6	Hearing family, deaf at age 3, residential school	Hearing family, born deaf, learned ASL at age 21, public school

tact with English all of their lives. The data from one signer who did not learn ASL until age twenty-one (born deaf, hearing family) are excluded from the analysis and, in fact, the videotapes for this signer reveal minimal use of ASL. (The database will eventually consist of the signing production of twenty individuals: twelve white and eight black. The sign production of the black signers reflects their interaction with both black and white, and hearing and deaf interviewers.)

The composition of each of the six dyads is shown in Table 1. The participants in dyads 1 and 2 share similar backgrounds, as do the participants in dyads 4, 5, and 6. Dyad 3 was deliberately "mixed," with one individual born deaf in a deaf family and one individual born deaf in a hearing family, but both attended residential school. In dyads 1, 3, and 6, the participants did not know each other; in dyads 2, 4, and 5, they did.

In the first part of the data collection, the video cameras were present, but at no point were the technicians visible. The signing of the subjects in the six dyads was videotaped during several types of interaction: first with a deaf interviewer who signed ASL, then with the dyad alone; next with a hearing interviewer who produced English-like signing and used her voice while she signed, then with the dyad alone again; and finally with the deaf interviewer again. The whole interview experience began with exclusive contact with the deaf interviewer.

Each interview consisted of a discussion of several broad topics of interest to members of the deaf community. Four statements were presented, and participants were asked if they agreed or disagreed, and why. The four statements were: "(1) Someone in a public place (airport, restaurant) discovers that you are deaf and wants to help you. That is acceptable. Agree or disagree?; (2) The hearing children of deaf people are members of deaf culture. Agree or disagree?; (3) Gallaudet University should have a deaf president. Agree or disagree?; (4) Mainstreaming is better than residential schools. Agree or disagree?"

It was predicted that (a) the situation with the deaf researcher would induce ASL, but the relative formality of the situation and the presence of a stranger could preclude it; (b) the situation with the hearing researcher would induce a shift away from ASL to contact signing; and (3) the signers alone with each other would elicit ASL.

TABLE 2: Distribution of Language Choice by Interview Situation and Participant

Situation	Dyad 1 Participants		Dyad 2 Participants		Dyad 3 Participants		Dyad 4 Participants		Dyad 5 Participants		Dyad 6 Participants	
Situation	A	B	A	B	A	B	A	B	A	B	A	B
With deaf interviewer	ASL	CS/SE[a]	ASL	ASL/CS	ASL/CS	CS	ASL	SE	ASL	CS	ASL	CS
Dyad alone	ASL	CS	ASL	ASL	ASL/CS	ASL/CS	ASL	CS	ASL	ASL	CS	CS
With hearing interviewer	ASL	SE	ASL/CS	CS	CS	SE	ASL	CS	CS	CS	CS	CS
Dyad alone	ASL	CS	ASL	ASL	ASL/CS	ASL/CS	ASL	CS	CS/ASL	CS/ASL	CS/ASL	CS/ASL
With deaf interviewer	ASL	CS	ASL	ASL/CS	ASL/CS	ASL/CS	ASL	CS	ASL	ASL	ASL	CS

CS = contact signing; SE = signed English

Overall Language Use

Table 2 provides an overview of language use during the interviews, based on the judgments of the researchers. First we will discuss the overall pattern of use, and then return to the judgment issue. The information in Table 2 should be read as follows: In the first dyad, participant A used ASL in all interactions; A's language use contrasted with B, who used no ASL. B used contact signing and Signed English with the deaf interviewer, and so on.

As Table 2 reveals, some participants started out with one kind of signing in a particular situation and later changed to another kind of signing in the same situation. Participant B in dyad 5, for example, first produced contact signing with the deaf interviewer. When alone with A, B produced ASL and then produced contact signing again when the hearing interviewer appeared. When the hearing interviewer left, and A and B were alone again, B continued to produce contact signing for a while and then produced ASL. B continued to produce ASL when the deaf interviewer returned and did so until the end of the interview.

In keeping with our prediction, ten of the twelve signers produced a form of signing that was other-than-ASL with the hearing interviewer—either contact signing or Signed English with voice. In some cases, the signers produced ASL with the deaf interviewer and while alone with each other, as was expected. In other cases, however, some unexpected results emerged. For example, three signers used ASL with the hearing interviewer, contrary to a widely held belief that deaf native signers automatically switch away from ASL in the presence of a non-native signer.

Furthermore, two of the signers (1A and 4A) used ASL consistently across all of the situations. One might predict that both of these signers come from deaf families; however, 4A is from a hearing family. Another unexpected result is the production of contact signing both with the deaf interviewer and when the signers were left alone. The deaf interviewer consistently signed ASL, and it was predicted that the signers would produce ASL in this situation and when left alone. But this was not the actual outcome. Indeed, in one case, a signer produced Signed English with the deaf interviewer.

These results are particularly noteworthy given another widely held belief—that deaf native signers will consistently sign ASL with each other if no hearing people are present. The observations on the overall pattern of language use during the interviews can be summarized as follows:

❖ Some signers used contact signing or signed English with the hearing interviewer, as expected; others used ASL throughout.

❖ ASL was used with the hearing interviewer by some signers but not others.

❖ Contact signing sometimes was produced with the deaf interviewer and when the signers were alone.

❖ ASL was used not only by deaf signers from deaf families, but also by deaf signers from hearing families.

These observations appear to challenge the traditional perspective on language contact in the American deaf community. For example, it is traditionally assumed that contact signing appears in deaf-hearing interaction primarily for the obvious reason that the hearing person might not understand ASL. On the extreme is the position that the very purpose of contact signing is to prevent hearing people from learning ASL (Woodward and Markowicz, 1975, p. 12). More measured approaches simply describe contact signing as the product of deaf-hearing interaction. Little is said, however, about the use of contact signing in exclusively deaf settings.

Although the need for comprehension might explain why contact signing is used in deaf-hearing interaction, it is clearly not an issue in portions of the interviews described here; all of the participants are native or near-native signers and, in some instances, sign ASL with each other. The choice to use contact signing with other deaf ASL natives, then, appears to be motivated by sociolinguistic factors. Two applicable factors identified in the present study are the formality of the interview situation (including the presence of videotape equipment) and the participant's lack of familiarity, in some cases, with both the interviewer and the other signer.

The videotaped data also clearly present counterevidence to the claim that deaf people never or rarely sign ASL in the presence of hearing people, because two of the signers chose to sign ASL throughout their respective interviews. This choice may be motivated by other sociolinguistic factors, such as the desire to establish one's social identity as a *bona fide* member of the deaf community or cultural group, a desire that may supersede considerations of formality and lack of familiarity.

Different sociolinguistic factors motivated the language choices of different individuals. This is further illustrated by the differences in language choice among signers within a given interview situation.

The Judgment Issue

As we stated earlier, these observations on the overall pattern of language use during the interviews are based on the judgment of the researchers. ASL and other-than-ASL (contact signing) were judged by a deaf native signer. Input from the hearing researcher was needed to judge the use of Signed English, because it consistently included the voice.

The ultimate goal of the study is an analysis of contact signing, and the initial judgment by the researchers indeed attests to the occurrence of contact signing during the interviews. The final analysis, however, certainly cannot be limited to the judgment of the researchers. The second part of the data collection will consist of having thirty or more native signers view a selection of clips from the data base. These clips will include segments that have been judged to be ASL and other-than-ASL by the deaf researcher and two additional native signers. Segments consistently judged as other-than-ASL by all judges will form the data base for the eventual description of contact signing. (This methodology was first designed and employed by Robert E. Johnson, Scott Liddell, Carol Erting, and Dave Knight in a pilot project entitled "Sign Language and Variation in Context," sponsored by the Gallaudet Research Institute.)

Judgments of language use have been a central component of numerous research studies. Language attitude studies—for example, Bouchard, 1973; Rosenthal, 1974; Hoover, 1978; and Light et al., 1978—have investigated users' attitudes toward languages or varieties of language by requiring them to respond to audio tapes or fill out questionnaires. Other studies—for example, Anisfeld and Lambert, 1964; Shuy, Baratz, and Wolfram, 1969; and Williams, 1970, 1971b—have required native users to judge the demographic or personality characteristics of speakers whose language use was recorded on audio-tape. Finally, other studies similar to ours have required native users to rate the relative fluency and degree of accent of tape-recorded speakers, in attempts to isolate the specific linguistic variables that shape judgments. (See, for example, Grebler et al., 1970; Chiasson-Lavoie and Laberge, 1971; Muench, 1971; Williams et al., 1971b; Palmer, 1973; Brennan et al., 1975; and Thompson, 1975.)

Our study has in common with the latter group of studies the fact that it requires the raters to focus strictly on linguistic events, as opposed to providing evaluations of attitude based on linguistic events. In all other studies, however, the basic structural nature of the linguistic events being judged was not at issue. The focus may have been on the relative accentedness or fluency of a code, but the very status of the code as English or Spanish or French was not at issue. In our study, the structural nature of the contact signing *is* the central issue, and the native raters' judgments will play a key role in defining and describing its features. In addition to their judgments of the selected clips, some of the judges will also be asked to describe the structural criteria they used for making judgments.

When Is ASL?—The Pilot Study

While the focus of our study is on the structural features of contact signing, a judgment issue that emerged in Williams' studies also has relevance to our work. That issue, simply stated, is: Does information that the judge has about the language user being judged influence the judgment of the language used?

In one study of teacher's attitudes about children's speech, Williams hypothesized that "to varying degrees, persons have a stereotyped set of attitudes about social dialects and their speakers and these attitudes play a role in how a person perceives the cues in another person's speech" (1973, p. 113). In another study, he demonstrated that ratings of children's speech could be obtained simply by presenting a teacher with an ethnic label of a child and asking her to rate her experiences with, and anticipations of, children of that type (Williams, 1971a).

In yet another study, Williams (1971b) describes an experiment in which audio tracks of a standard English passage were dubbed onto the videotapes of children from three ethnic groups—black, white, and Mexican-American. Teachers rated the speech sample quite differently, depending on the "ethnic guise" under which it was presented. That is, the black child with a standard English sound track was rated as more "ethnic—non-standard" than was the white child with the identical sound track. As Williams states, the "implication is that the visual image of the children on the tape served as an immediate cue of a type of child. This elicited a stereotype, and the presentation was judged relative to that stereotype" (1973, p. 126).

These studies have direct relevance for studies of language contact in the American deaf community. There is ample anecdotal evidence, for example, that a deaf native ASL user may initiate an interaction with another individual whom he believes to be deaf or whose audiological status has not been clarified. The latter participant may well be a near-native user of ASL. If the latter is hearing, however, and his or her hearing ability becomes apparent, it is not at all unusual for the deaf participant to switch automatically from ASL to a more English-based form of signing.

What one participant knows or thinks he knows about another clearly influences choice of code in language use. The related question that arose in our study was whether what the judges knew about the signers influenced their judgments. We decided to explore this question with a small pilot test.

The pilot test proceeded as follows: Two judges had previously viewed a portion of dyad 5's interaction with the deaf interviewer. As can be seen from Table 1, Participant A in dyad 5 was born deaf in a hearing family and attended a residential school. Participant B in dyad 5 was born deaf in a hearing family and attended a mainstream program. The deaf researcher, born deaf in a hearing family and educated in a residen-

TABLE 3: First Viewing Judgments, without Demographic Data

Dyad 5 Participants	Judge 1	Judge 2	Deaf Researcher
Participant A	ASL, 3 instances of "ASL stops"	"most ASL"	ASL
Participant B	A lot of "ASL stops"	"most ASL"	ASL

TABLE 4: Second Viewing Judgments, with Demographic Data

Dyad 5 Participants	Judge 1	Judge 2
Participant A	ASL	"ASL mostly"
Participant B	A lot of "ASL stops"	A lot of "ASL stops"

tial school, had judged the production of both participants to be ASL. The judgments of the other two judges can be seen in Table 3.

Judge 1 is deaf from a deaf family and attended residential school; Judge 2 is deaf from a hearing family, was mainstreamed until age eleven, and then enrolled in a residential school. All of the data videotapes have counter numbers indicating time elapsed in the lower left-hand corner of the monitor. Judges were asked to view the tapes and stop the tape when they perceived that a shift away from ASL had occurred. They were asked to make note of the shift point using the counter numbers, and also to note when ASL resumed again.

As can be seen in Table 3, in the first viewing, Judge 1 found that Participant A's production was ASL with the instances of "ASL stops," while Participant B's production was "a lot of ASL stops" and not ASL. Judge 2, on the other hand, found that both participants used mostly ASL.

After ascertaining that neither judge knew either participant, the judges were given some demographic information. Judge 1 was told that the participants were from deaf families but had attended mainstream programs; Judge 2 was told that the same participants were from hearing families but had attended residential schools. As can be seen from Table 4, Judge 1's assessments were basically consistent across viewings. Judge 2 was consistent for Participant A, but changed judgment from "mostly ASL" to "a lot of ASL stops" for Participant B.

The immediate question that arises from the findings in Table 4 is to what extent the demographic information provided about the participants affected Judge 2's change in judgment of Participant B's production. It is interesting to note that the judgments of the judge who is deaf from a deaf family remained consistent when demographic information was provided, but it is equally interesting that Judge 1 thought the participants were from deaf families.

This is a very preliminary pilot study, and more questions emerge from it than do answers: What is the relationship between the judge's demographic characteristics and those of the participants being judged? That is, if the judge is from a deaf family, is he more apt to judge someone whom he thinks is also from a deaf family as using ASL? Furthermore, what does being from a deaf family, as opposed to being from a hearing family, mean to judges in terms of judging language usage? What does having attended a residential school mean, as opposed to having attended a mainstream program? Finally, are the judgments of native signers such as Judge 1 apt to focus more on linguistic form than on demographic characteristics, as opposed to signers like Judge 2, who learned ASL not at home but from peers in a residential school setting?

This pilot study merely shows some discrepancies in judgments when demographic information about signers was provided. It is our hope that further research in this area will begin to provide answers to the questions raised. Given further research, it may be that the question, "What is ASL?"—that is, what are the linguistic features of the language—should sometimes be accompanied by the question, "When is ASL?"—that is, is ASL said to be occurring in part as a function of *when* it is being used and *who* is using it.

References

Anisfeld, M., and W. Lambert. 1964. "Evaluation Reactions of Bilingual and Monolingual Children to Spoken Languages." *Journal of Abnormal and Social Psychology* 69: 89–97.

Bouchard, Ryan E. 1973. "Subjective Reactions Toward Accented Speech." In *Language Attitudes: Current Trends and Prospects*, ed. R. Shuy and R. Fasold. Washington, DC: Georgetown University Press.

Brennan, E. M., E. B. Dawson, and W. E. Dawson. 1975. "Scaling of Apparent Accentedness by Magnitude Estimation and Sensory Modality Matching." *Journal of Psycholinguistic Research* 4.

Chiasson-Lavoie, M., and S. Laberge. 1971. "Attitudes Face au Francais Parle a Montreal et de Re de Conscience de Variable Linguistiques." Unpublished research paper, McGill University.

Grebler, L., J. W. Moore, and R. C. Guzman, eds. 1970. *The Mexican American People*. New York: The Free Press.

Hoover, M. 1978. "Community Attitudes Toward Black English." *Language in Society* 7.

Light, R. Y., D. P. Richard, and P. Bell. 1978. "Development of Children's Attitudes Toward Speakers of Standard and Non-standard English." *Child Study Journal* 8.

Lucas, C., and C. Valli. 1989. "Language Contact in the American Deaf Community." In *The Sociolinguistics of the Deaf Community*, ed. C. Lucas. San Diego: Academic Press.

Muench, E. 1971. "Preliminary Report: Scaling of Accentedness by Magnitude Estimation." Unpublished manuscript, University of Notre Dame.

Palmer, L. A. 1973. "A Preliminary Report on a Study of the Linguistic Correlates of Raters' Subjective Judgements of Non-native English Speech." In *Language Attitudes: Current Trends and Prospects*, ed. R. Shuy and R. Fasold. Washington, DC: Georgetown University Press.

Rosenthal, M. 1974. "The Magic Boxes: Pre-school Children's Attitudes Toward Black and Standard English." *The Florida FL Reporter* 12.

Shuy, R. W., J. Baratz, and W. Wolfram. 1969. "Sociolinguistic Factors in Speech Identification." Project Report No. MH15048-01. National Institute of Mental Health.

Thompson, R. M. 1975. "Mexican-American English: Social Correlations of Regional Pronunciation." *American Speech* 50.

Williams, F. 1973. "Some Research Notes on Dialect Attitudes and Stereotypes." In *Language Attitudes: Current Trends and Prospects*, ed. R. Shuy and R. Fasold. Washington, DC: Georgetown University Press. pp. 113–128.

Williams, F., J. L. Whitehead, and L. M. Miller. 1971a. "Ethnic Stereotyping and Judgments of Children's Speech." *Speech Monographs* 38: 166–170.

Williams, F., J. L. Whitehead, and Traupmann. 1971b. "Teachers' Evaluations of Children's Speech." *Speech Teacher* 20: 247–254.

Williams, F. 1970. "Psychological Correlates of Speech Characteristics on Sounding 'Disadvantaged.'" *Journal of Speech and Hearing Research* 13: 472–488.

Woodward, J. 1973. "Some Characteristics of Pidgin Sign English." *Sign Language Studies* 3: 39–46.

Woodward, J., and H. Markowicz. 1975. "Some Handy New Ideas on Pidgins and Creoles: Pidgin Sign Languages." Paper presented at the Conference on Pidgin and Creole Languages, Honolulu, Hawaii.

The Impact of ASL Research on the American Deaf Community

JAMES TUCKER

This article explores the observed and potential effects of American Sign Language (ASL) research on the American Deaf community. The new and ever-expanding body of knowledge demonstrating that ASL is a separate language with its own grammatical rules—rules not derived from English—has changed how Deaf people, both as individuals and as members of a group, perceive themselves and their social environment. ASL is now a driving force behind the emergence of the Deaf community as a visible and vibrant minority group.

In the 1800s, many residential schools for Deaf children and young Deaf adults were established across the country. These schools were the bedrock and the wellspring of the Deaf community. In their years at the residential schools, young students solidified relationships that lasted throughout their lifetimes.

Their language, ASL, with its origins in old French Sign Language and old American Sign Language, evolved and endured over the generations. ASL was passed on by Deaf parents to their Deaf children and, in the residential schools, from Deaf children of Deaf parents to Deaf children of hearing parents. Educators, primarily those who advocated oral education, attempted to eradicate ASL from Deaf children, but this attempt was—and continues to be—futile.

The resiliency of ASL is not surprising. Deaf people communicate *with* their hands, face, and body and *for* their eyes. ASL is simply a language that meets the needs of Deaf people to communicate visually with one another using their bodies. More recent attempts by educators to teach Deaf students various forms of Manually Coded English (MCE)—sign systems using ASL signs in English word order—also have been unsuccessful. Researchers now see MCE signs being ASL-ized—the children are imposing ASL grammatical rules on MCE signs.

Today, ASL is signed in the Deaf community across the country. Deaf people gather locally, regionally, and nationally for social, political, religious, and athletic functions. The Deaf community is not homogeneous, and its leadership is fragmented. But the increasingly powerful Deaf consumer group is making demands on industry, education, and the law. The rallying force behind this is, of course, the Deaf experience and the language of Deaf people, ASL.

In the 1960s, the Civil Rights movement, the recognition of language minority groups, and new psycholinguistic theories of language that allowed formulation of questions about sign languages together paved the way for the emergence of metalinguistic awareness in the Deaf community. This awareness enabled Deaf people not only to sign ASL and to think in ASL, but to think and sign *about* ASL. Linguistic research gave

ASL credibility and brought attention to ASL users, Deaf people, and then to the Deaf community.

Deaf people, branded for centuries as deaf and dumb, capable only of expressing concrete concepts through crude gestures, now are being recognized as a linguistic minority group using ASL, a visual-gestural language possessing the same kinds of grammatical properties as any other language. Many Deaf people have become self-conscious about their language use, and a few Deaf ASL researchers have set up their own ASL research labs. Deaf people now esteem the elegant signing of highly articulate members of the Deaf community.

Moreover, Deaf people are able to recognize the continuum of sign systems: ASL, Pidgin Sign English (a rudimentary sign system used for communication between Deaf and hearing people), and MCE. In Deaf theater, new forms of experimentation with signs and storytelling reflect awareness of ASL structure.

Most significantly, ASL research has for the first time enabled Deaf people to talk about ASL as an object. This metalinguistic awareness is the new vehicle for members of the Deaf community to understand their social environment and to facilitate changes in their everyday lives to meet their cultural, social, economic, religious, educational, employment, and political needs.

The sum of all these needs may be translated into communication needs. Using ASL/English interpreters has bridged the gulf between the Deaf community and the hearing community. As a result, Deaf people are making advances in areas that were once uncharted.

The research on ASL has influenced Deaf people in various ways. The majority of Deaf people are still ignorant or ambivalent about ASL. In 1984, the National Association of the Deaf, the largest Deaf advocacy group, passed a resolution recognizing ASL as the language of Deaf people. This act was long overdue, and it sparked no celebrations. There are Deaf people who still believe that ASL is a form of broken English, used only by low verbal Deaf people, which, if used in excess, will ruin English skills. Other Deaf people remain suspicious of hearing people who are interested in ASL, for they believe that a hearing person learning ASL may be out to exploit them.

Many Deaf people, however, have been positively influenced by ASL research. ASL has become their source of pride and confidence. These people have emerged as leaders and role models, often as ASL instructors, in promoting awareness of ASL and Deaf culture among Deaf and hearing people alike.

Probably the greatest achievement of the Deaf community was the creation of the interpreter industry. During the last twenty years, Deaf people increasingly demanded interpreters in many activities in their lives. Interpreter training programs were established across the country, and the graduates were evaluated by Deaf professionals and were awarded credentials on the basis of their ASL and interpreting skills. Laws were passed requiring courts to provide interpreters to Deaf people and ordering educational and medical institutions to provide "accessibility," that is, interpreters in classrooms and hospital rooms.

Deaf students in record numbers, with the aid of interpreters, now earn more advanced degrees in many disciplines. Larger corporations are seeing the value of Deaf employees and are becoming more sensitive to their interpreting needs in departmental meetings. Many places of worship have interpreters, and cultural events such as plays, museum tours, and travel tours are now frequently being interpreted.

In demanding interpreters, the Deaf community has transformed itself into a Deaf consumer group. Businesses now cater to this new market; doctors, psychologists, dentists, bank tellers, waiters, and people from the service sector now take ASL classes. ASL courses are proliferating in universities, colleges, continuing education centers, and now in high schools across the country. To be appointed to the better paying ASL instructor positions, an ASL teaching certificate is now required. Deaf publishers are selling ASL grammar books and deafness-related books to ASL students.

Research on ASL and Deaf culture is changing how the Deaf community perceives itself and its relationship with the hearing community. Deaf people, long known as a pathological group, are being recognized by researchers and professionals as a cultural group. Identity problems within the Deaf community exist, because many Deaf people are uneasy with their new identity as "normal" rather than "defective" people.

The Deaf leadership, though fragmented, is changing. ASL instructors and advocates are becoming leaders of social change. Spoken English skills are becoming less and less of a requirement of a Deaf person in a leadership position. This is a shift away from past leaders who typically had become Deaf in later childhood and who possessed English speech skills. The Deaf community now has culturally acceptable means of making language choices in interpreting situations and in the presentation of lectures. There is pride in passing on ASL to Deaf children.

The changing patterns of interaction within the Deaf community—and also between the Deaf and hearing communities—that have resulted from ASL research need to be studied. Friction may be developing between native signers (those Deaf people who have Deaf parents) and non-native signers (those Deaf people who have hearing parents and who did not learn sign in their family home). Native signers seem to possess a fluency and knowledge of ASL seldom equaled by non-native signers.

Also, some Deaf people have become militants, isolating themselves from the hearing community. As a consequence of being deprived of ASL and knowledge of ASL for most of their lives, some Deaf people are hostile toward hearing people. Other Deaf people who are members of the hearing community discover the Deaf community and learn ASL. Hearing individuals may accuse them of selling out. More and more hearing people now sign ASL, thus loosening the walls of the Deaf community. There are more opportunities for mixed settings where Deaf and hearing cultural values clash. Cross-cultural situations and changing interaction patterns should be studied.

In the future, increased metalinguistic awareness of ASL will result in a more cohesive Deaf community. Participation in politics will become more direct with the emergence of a "Deaf" lobby. ASL usage by interpreters and other hearing people will be the barometer of success of Deaf people's demand to have ASL in their daily situations. ASL as a language will continue to evolve, and its lexicon will expand. Deafened adults may learn ASL to overcome their loss of English listening skills. Experimentation with written ASL will be widespread. Most importantly, the Deaf community will have greater clout in shaping its own destiny, including the education of Deaf children.

The greatest challenge still facing the Deaf community lies in extending the knowledge gained from research on ASL into the schools, thereby fostering a bilingual, bicultural approach to the education of Deaf children—in other words, teaching ASL and English, and an appreciation of Deaf culture. With the expansion of ASL research and higher education for Deaf people, members of the Deaf community will be able to take a primary role as teachers, administrators, teacher trainers, and educational policy makers in educating their children.

The new status of Deaf people will influence language choice in parent-infant programs, as well as child-rearing practices. Parents of Deaf children, by combining forces with the Deaf community, will form a potentially powerful group.

ASL, rooted biologically and culturally in Deaf people, is a unifying force in the Deaf community. Achievements gained through the use of ASL/English interpreters have enabled the Deaf community to emerge as a vibrant and visible minority group. The biggest obstacle the Deaf community must overcome is the educational practices that fragment the Deaf community and shackle Deaf children's intellectual, academic, psychological, and cultural growth.

Presenting the Television Program, "It's My Hands' Turn to Speak"

MARIE-THÉRÈSE ABBOU

The opening show of the television program entitled "It's My Hands' Turn to Speak" in 1979 marked the premiere of a deaf person in France signing in French Sign Language (LSF) on TV. Prior to that event, there had only been a news spot for hard of hearing people, featuring a person who interpreted the news using signed French instead of LSF.

The producer of the program, Daniele Bouvet, said this about the new show:

> This television program is for all children and their parents. The fun part of the show is that it can also be shared. It is particularly meant for very young children, to whom people don't always have enough time to tell stories. The beauty of these tales told in sign language will enhance the pleasure they will derive from this show and help to develop their hunger for communication and for language, without which no one can grow up, nor ever want to read.

I was the storyteller for "It's My Hands' Turn to Speak" for five years. Following a certain amount of show time, I asked both deaf and hearing individuals—some familiar with LSF and some not—to give me their opinions. The reaction of both deaf and hearing people was positive overall.

Reactions of the Deaf Audience

When the program first began, deaf people reacted immediately and very strongly in a negative way. For them, showing their language on television was a threat. They believed that hearing people would get to know LSF and could ridicule them more easily. Also, they preferred to stay invisible to protect themselves.

Initially, that reaction made me feel very guilty. I felt that I was betraying the Deaf community, of which I was a part. But after thinking it over, I finally realized that LSF is a living language like English or Russian—languages open to the world—so why not LSF? Moreover, I was only showing sign language and not revealing anything about actual *Deaf culture*.

Deaf people came to realize, however, how well this program permitted hearing people to see and identify deaf individuals as integral human beings with their own language; it showed that deaf people were not debilitated—they could communicate. The show was broadcast not only in France, but also in such countries as Martinique, Guadeloupe, Iran, and Tunisia.

Finally, deaf people became relieved about the impact of the program and were even proud of it. It represented them and gave them a means to improve their overall situation. Isolated as they had been in the provinces and out in the country, they could now see themselves as "people who had been on television," and that gave an enormous boost to their self-esteem. After years of cultural and linguistic oppression, this was a door opening to the world.

Reactions of Hearing Individuals

The hearing audience was astonished to discover the potential of deaf people, previously considered as handicapped, but now seen to be using an undeniably beautiful language. They began to see deaf people as human beings like themselves, with only language and culture making them different.

The information legitimized by this program reassured hearing people. The deaf individual was no longer someone unknown. Suddenly, in the metro, in the street, in other public places, they were now trying to communicate with deaf individuals using mime and by pointing. They understood that if they adapted themselves, communication would be possible. What a change!

What a surprise for some parents of deaf children, from whom the existence of LSF had been hidden! They wrote to me for the cassettes, to learn where they could get lessons in LSF and to meet other deaf people. Hearing individuals also were buying cassettes or recording the program in order to play them again at social centers, or so that they could work with autistic children using a visual approach. I took note of the fact that hearing and deaf people could watch the same program, making frequent exchanges possible between these two worlds.

I also was aware of the drawbacks: Hearing professionals working with deaf children were using tapes of these stories to evaluate the spontaneous comprehension level of children in LSF, and thereby deciding whether or not they really needed it! Thus, the children were asked to watch the story and answer several questions in writing. Obviously, this kind of exercise was doomed to fail since the children had received an oralist training in which signing was prohibited. But the specialists could thereby attest to the children's lack of understanding and thus claim that LSF was not a true language.

There also was the problem of different signing from one region to the next. This meant that it often was difficult even for children who knew LSF to understand the message.

It was difficult for certain deaf children to know where they stood, psychologically. Some parents were refusing to allow their child to watch a program in which one could see "a deaf person stupidly gesticulating in all directions." We knew that some children were witnessing rejection by their own parents while realizing that they were deaf like "this character." Other deaf children, who understood the importance of LSF in communicating, were insisting upon seeing the program, and this led to major family disputes.

After the program had been on the air nine years, I felt that this experience had benefited hearing people more than deaf people. Initially, the producer and I had a common purpose: to acquaint people with LSF. After two years of work, I noticed that, in actuality, the objective for each of us had been different.

The producer wanted above all to give all children access to the pleasure inherent in a story for deaf children, using LSF as the vehicle. She also wanted the program to permit hearing people to learn signing, and thus to be able gradually to recognize LSF. She thought, too, that she would be helping children with language problems to improve their language skills and thus avoid future academic failure. Her primary audience was hearing children.

My purpose was to tell stories in sign language in a way that would permit the deaf audience access to a hearing culture and, ultimately, to teach them, through LSF, what a tale really is. I wanted, too, to provide a means for deaf children isolated in the provinces and deprived of contact with deaf adults to learn sign language. I also wanted to acquaint the hearing public with sign language, and finally, I thought the program would help deaf people become more conscious of their own language. Seeing it on television, they could reflect upon it and cease to consider themselves as handicapped; instead, they could see themselves as normal people who simply have a different language.

Technically speaking, the producer had to summarize the tales, because we only had five minutes of live showtime. She wanted the LSF translation to stay as close as possible to the French, which often prevented me from expressing my language spontaneously. I felt very strongly that the two languages were too closely linked. I wanted to be able to tell the story in LSF without following the French text word for word, but still respecting the sense of the tale.

We discussed this many times, but finally I had to go along with her preferences. My expression therefore more closely resembled signed French. I tried to elaborate upon it, using mime to make it more closely resemble LSF so it would seem less contrived. But it was always necessary for the signing to occur one to two seconds after the narrator's voice so that the young hearing audience could understand the relationship of the word to the sign. This required me to synchronize my signing with the French sentence.

I had asked to have a simple screen as a stage property upon which the animal images would be projected as I signed them, in order to provide the deaf children with a more complete understanding of the tale. This prop also would be an aid for those children who, depending upon their region, might not have learned the same signs. But I was always told that there were technical and other difficulties, and my suggestion was rejected. The worst thing for me was that these hearing people who had the decision-making power had not realized the importance of visual imagery to help deaf children assimilate the tale.

I stopped doing the program in 1984, and Philippe Galant replaced me. The same problems continued for him, with the addition of another problem: The producer wanted him to do the same mime technique again, at the same rhythm, signing the same way I had done!

What a pity! Philippe does such a beautiful rendering in LSF. Those deaf people who knew him could not understand why he started to sign the same way I did. His presentation no longer seemed natural.

All these difficulties were apparently related to the requirement of distancing oneself from each language, and only an interpreter can do this work in an objective way. Afterward, the two can be adapted to each other, while still respecting each one's unique nature. Of course, the producer considered LSF, but that wasn't enough. Distancing oneself properly seems to me to be the fundamental requirement.

In short, the deaf audience got precious little from this broadcast, except perhaps some fun. It was beneficial to specialists working with deaf children in approaching reading and written French, and also to those doing linguistic research.

The danger is that, because they aren't able to differentiate the signing used on the program from true sign language, hearing individuals will buy the tapes to learn LSF but will not actually be exposed to it.

In conclusion, I think that the solution for avoiding this kind of error would be to respect both languages deeply so that both the deaf and the hearing person can get from them what they each need. The essential thing is that they should each be able to get a lot of pleasure from the tale, detach themselves from a written text, and yet retain its meaning.

Sign Language Varieties in British Television: An Historical Perspective

BENCIE WOLL, LORNA ALLSOP, AND RACHEL SPENCE

When research into British Sign Language (BSL) first began, public settings for its use were very limited. Because there was, and still is, no written form of the language, all publications for the Deaf community are in English. Schools for deaf students had not taught classes using BSL since the beginning of the century, although covert signing between pupils in residential schools was permitted. Television programs, such as "News Review," targeted at deaf audiences, used English subtitles.

But public use of British Sign Language began to change in 1981. Following a television program in BSL and pressure from deaf people, the British Broadcasting Corporation (BBC) began "See Hear," the first magazine program in Britain with sign language and content of specific interest to a deaf audience. Since "See Hear" began, both its use of sign language and program content have evolved to meet the needs of the Deaf community better.

During the time "See Hear" has been on the BBC, the use of sign language has also evolved in other areas. The past five years have seen the introduction of Signed English in schools for deaf students and the introduction of training assessment programs in Sign Supported English and BSL. Sign language interpreter training has begun, and the British Deaf Association has introduced a campaign to gain official governmental recognition of BSL as the language of the Deaf community. A number of public settings, such as political conferences, now make BSL interpreters available. Several other national and local television programs for deaf audiences use either interpreters or signing presenters; the Queen's Christmas message is presented in a signed form; and in April 1988, the BBC launched a series teaching BSL to hearing viewers.

The rapidly expanding use of signing in public areas has probably affected BSL in two related ways: It has exposed viewers to a much wider range of signers than they might have encountered previously, and it has made people more accepting of varieties of BSL in public use. The aim of our project has been to study changes in attitudes toward BSL and changes in BSL itself in the past seven years, using data from "See Hear" and from interviews with signers to explore these two areas.

The availability of virtually a complete archive of all signing on television provides a unique opportunity for research. By providing a case study of a minority language undergoing rapid changes, this area is of interest not only to those concerned with research on sign languages, but also to those concerned with sociolinguistics in general.

Video Archive Data

Since 1981 there have been eight series of "See Hear," each consisting of between twenty and twenty-six half-hour programs, with occasional special programs of longer duration. Both hearing and deaf people, signers and non-signers, appear on the programs, which have both simultaneous interpreting between English and BSL, as well as captioning.

The project has as its overall aims:

❖ To describe changes in BSL as exemplified by the signing used on television from 1981 to the present

❖ To explore changes in attitude toward signing and varieties of signing on television

❖ To describe variations in signing and attitudes toward these variations by comparing different signers on television programs and attitudes of viewers

❖ To test the hypothesis that there have been observable and consistent changes in the past eight years on television and that these reflect changing attitudes toward BSL.

Because the project only began in January of this year, analyses are still in the preliminary stage. However, the early findings support the hypothesis that substantial changes in the signing presented on television have taken place.

Three areas have been analyzed for this project: correspondence received by the BBC about British Sign Language, communication mode, and content.

Correspondence

The BBC allowed the project access to its "See Hear" letter archives covering 1981 to 1987. We were able to make copies of those letters that commented on any linguistic aspects of the programs. Information that could identify the authors was removed, but any demographic information, such as gender, age, or city, was retained.

It must be remembered that in 1981, signers did not have a clear label for the language they used. While the term BSL had been introduced by researchers in 1977, deaf people themselves used only the term "sign" or "deaf sign."

The selected letters were sorted according to the issues addressed. These were the signing used in the program (further divided into positive and negative comments), lipreading and speech, fingerspelling, captioning, and comments on how well the presenters represented the Deaf community and its language. This paper will deal with just the first category—signing—and other categories will be dealt with in later analyses.

The sixty letters we obtained included fifty-four comments on signing, thirty-three of which were negative and twenty-four of which were positive. Some letters contained more than one reference to signing, and often there was both praise and criticism in the same letter.

The negative comments usually referred to the unintelligibility of the signs. Sometimes this was ascribed to regional dialects, other times to new or simply different signs. Some representative comments were as follows:

❖ "Some of the signs are unfamiliar, especially from one presenter who I suspect invents some of them."

❖ "I watched 'See Hear' in Northern Ireland. Belfast sign language is nearer to Scottish sign language and is different from yours."

❖ "We have found it rather difficult to understand some of the signs in the studio. I appreciate that our signs vary slightly in parts of the country, like accents in the hearing world, but I have traveled widely, and some of your signs are new to me."

The positive comments referred to the intelligibility of the signing:

❖ "I could understand what you were doing with your sign language."

❖ "It was easy to follow [that part] due to his plain signing."

❖ "We found all the presenters easy to follow."

The number of comments is too small to allow much meaningful statistical analysis, but certain trends do emerge.

Clear distinctions arise when the comments are divided into regions. Between 1981 and 1987, there was only one negative comment from the south coastal region, and seven positive comments. In the Midlands, the emphasis changed, with thirteen negative comments and only six positive. The reason for this southern preference is unclear. Coming from London, the program's signs would have a bias toward a southern dialect, and yet the central southern region, which includes London, spawned more negative than positive comments. It could be that we simply have too few letters to allow any more than a suggestion of greater satisfaction in the south than the north.

Over the years, complaints about unintelligibility declined in number. This could be because people were finding the signing more intelligible or because they were becoming resigned to it! The number of letters containing comments about language dropped off dramatically after 1982, with only ten comments for the four years from 1984 to 1987. This could perhaps indicate satisfaction with the language used, or at least indifference to the question. It is important, however, to bear in mind that signers less skilled in English may feel unhappy about writing. In the second phase of this project, we will address this problem as part of our interviews with viewers.

Communication Mode

Data related to communication mode came from the first six series, broadcast between 1981 and 1987. All programs were coded as to whether people appearing on them were deaf, hard of hearing, or hearing. The communication mode chosen by each person appearing on each program was coded by using a five-point continuum ranging from sign-only at one end to voice-only at the other. The use of this continuum does not imply that British Sign Language and English are seen as varying along a continuum.

The points on the continuum were defined as follows:

The Study of Sign Language in Society

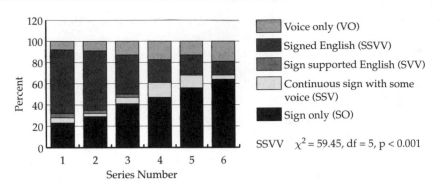

FIGURE 1: Communication mode used by deaf and hard of hearing people appearing on "See Hear."

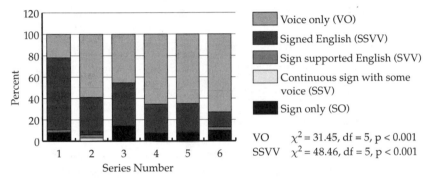

FIGURE 2: Communication mode used by hearing people appearing on "See Hear."

- ❖ SO: Sign only, no use of voice.

- ❖ SSV: Voice was used intermittently, but sign continuously.

- ❖ SSVV: This might be characterized as simultaneous communication, or Signed English—signing and speaking were given approximately equal weight and both were used continuously.

- ❖ SVV: Voice was used continuously; sign was used intermittently. This might be labeled Sign Supported English.

- ❖ VO: Voice only; no use of signing.

For the purpose of this presentation, all deaf and hard of hearing people have been analyzed as one group, with hearing people analyzed separately (see Figures 1 and 2).

The percentage of hearing people appearing on the program—about 40 percent—did not vary significantly through the first six series. The communication mode chosen by both deaf and hearing people, however, showed marked changes across this time.

A number of observations can be made from these data. First, the number of hearing people using voice-only tripled from the first series to the sixth. Second, SSVV communication declined from 68 percent in the first series to 15 percent in the sixth series. Before discussing possible reasons for these changes, we will examine the findings for the deaf people on the program.

Like the hearing group, the deaf group showed a shift away from SSVV communication, but unlike the hearing group, the shift was largely accounted for by moving toward sign-only communication.

TABLE 1: Content Categories

Content Code	Category
D	Deaf Life
H	Hearing Life
D/H	Contact between the deaf and hearing communities
M	Medical and health issues
C	Children
E/T/I	Education/Technology/Information
SD	Self-Definition—Rights-Cultural-Research-Language
D/B	Deaf-Blind
HOH	Hard of Hearing and Deafened
O	Others

A number of explanations are possible, although any explanation at this point will need to be substantiated by further analysis. Perhaps the shift from the "middle" ground for both hearing and deaf people is related to a shifting of cultural and linguistic identities. Hearing people may feel that use of signs only is culturally inappropriate, while deaf people may feel greater confidence and acceptability in using sign only. The decline in SSVV communication coincides with a time of increasing awareness of the differences between BSL and English and the impossibility of adequately combining the two. Support for both of these explanations can be found in the content analysis.

Content Analysis

The content analysis also included all programs from the first six series. Each item on a program was coded according to the ten content categories shown in Table 1.

The Deaf Life section consisted of items relating to the lives, interests, and hobbies of members of the Deaf community. The Hearing Life section consisted of items that had no connection with the Deaf community; for example, one item reported the death of a famous actor.

The Deaf-Hearing section had two types of items—either about the lives of deaf people in relation to hearing people, or vice versa. For example, one item was about a deaf actress, with the focus on her success in the hearing world.

The Medical section included items such as treatment for tinnitus and rubella vaccination. The Education, Technology, and Information section dealt with items on schools, educational courses for deaf people, telephones for deaf people, and details of how to obtain disabled persons' bus passes.

The Self-Definition section consisted of items relating to deaf people's awareness of society and community, including the rights of deaf people and their own identity, culture, and language.

The Deaf-Blind section consisted of all items in this content range including interests and hobbies, education, etc. The Hard of Hearing and Deafened People section consisted of the same range of items as found in the Deaf-Blind section.

The "Others" section was for items that could not be categorized according to the previous divisions. For example, one item was about a partially deaf man who had written a book of reminiscences about life as a gravedigger.

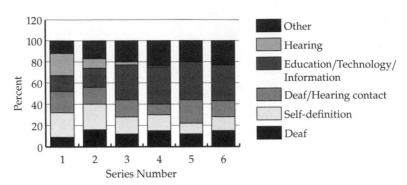

FIGURE 3: Content analysis of programs in the first six series of "See Hear."

Before looking at Figure 3, one should note that these counts are based on how many program items were in each category. It may be the case that "Deaf" topics, for example, are fewer but longer, and we will analyze this in the near future.

The changes in content emphasis over time reflected in Figure 3 appear to be associated with changes in the production and presentation team over the first six series. The presenters in the first series were a hearing son of deaf parents and a woman who had become deaf in her teens. There were no prelingually deaf people involved, either as presenters or researchers.

In the second series, one presenter was a deaf person who had been educated orally, but who had later identified with the Deaf community. The presenter of the first series had moved to the post of researcher. For the third series, eight different deaf presenters appeared. This led to complaints about lack of continuity in signing, so from the fourth series on, two new permanent presenters were used.

The change from a hearing to a deaf researcher also may have contributed to the decrease in items from the hearing culture. These changes in the research and presentation team reflect changes in the program producers' awareness of core interests for deaf people. Together with the data on communication mode, they reflect a heightened sense of deaf people as a community with a shared language and culture.

Estonian Sign Language Yesterday, Today, Tomorrow

REGINA TOOM

stonia is situated on the south coast of the Baltic Sea, and has a territory of 45,000 square kilometers. The population is 1.5 million, 60 percent of whom are indigenous Estonians. The number of deaf people is over 1,400, and 20 percent of them were born deaf. It is estimated that 10,000 people directly and continuously interact with deaf people, although the number of people who use and understand Estonian Sign Language (ESL), on at least an elementary level, is approximately 2,000.

The first purposeful investigation of ESL was a joint undertaking by Tartu University and the Estonian Union of the Deaf (EUD), who also financed the project in 1988. Currently, there is only one full-time researcher, the author of this report.

This situation is a direct consequence of the language policy that has prevailed in the Soviet Union for decades (and that was actively implemented in Estonia also). The leading incentive of the language policy is to promote the Russian language and lessen attention to the national minorities and the development of their languages. As a result, many languages of the national minorities have become extinct or are on the verge of extinction. Because the remaining languages are also threatened, the republics have been forced to amend their constitutions to defend their languages. For example, the languages of the Baltic republics of Estonia, Latvia, and Lithuania were declared languages and a law was adopted to defend them. Against this nonsupportive background it is not surprising that many linguists do not recognize sign languages at all. Unfortunately, even the central body of the deaf in Estonia, the EUD, has not agreed upon a policy to defend and develop ESL.

Despite all efforts to curtail its existence, ESL doubtlessly exists. However, researchers have not yet managed to establish exactly and reliably its history and development. Some data reveal that ESL began to be used only at the beginning of this century. But there are also data that show that the starting point of ESL may be traced to the nineteenth or possibly the eighteenth century. Although we lack reliable data about the end of the last century and about earlier periods, it appears that ESL developed in an unorganized way among the people. It is quite probable that in Estonian schools for the deaf, the first of which was established in 1866, ESL was neither taught nor allowed to be used.

A significant impact on the development of ESL is being made by the body of interpreters who use it. In Estonia there are six officially recognized interpreters employed by the EUD. All six are female, most of them being hearing children of deaf parents; their education in the use of ESL has been achieved through self-instruction. Two of them have attended short courses at the Russian Union of the Deaf in Moscow, but the training was on an elementary level and based on Russian Sign Language, which differs considerably from ESL. Although our interpreters have tried to make ESL more uniform, substantial differences are still apparent in their use of the language. Also of great importance are their levels of education. Among the six interpreters, only one has received higher education, two have a secondary (eleven years) education, two have eight years of schooling, and one has less than eight years of schooling.

The problem of interpreters' training is also important for the reason that in Estonia they do more than interpret. They are needed to assist deaf people with business management and in communicating with courts, doctors, the military, schools, employment, etc. Although interpreters are expected to fulfill the role of secretary or consultant, their varying levels of competence often result in inadequate advice or wrong interpretations, which create misunderstandings and conflicts. This situation is further aggravated because although we have six full-time interpreters, they are distributed among three regions, each one assigned to a fixed service area. A deaf person ideally can choose between the two interpreters in the region, but often he or she lacks any choice.

On the basis of our present knowledge it can be asserted that in Estonia two sign languages have been developed: Estonian Sign Language and Estonian Pidgin Sign Language. The former is a specific sign language with regularities and grammar. The majority of its users are hereditarily deaf people. At this time it cannot be determined whether Estonian Sign Language is dying out owing to the emphasis on the oral method or whether it has not yet fully developed. Estonian Pidgin Sign Language is a pidgin language based on the grammar and regularities of the sound system of the Estonian language and on the signs and manual alphabet adopted by deaf people. Estonian Pidgin Sign Language is more widespread and is used by the interpreters.

A specific linguistic environment exists in the Estonian schools for children with hearing disabilities. There is one school for hard of hearing students and another for deaf students. They both are boarding schools where the children go home on the weekends.

Among the children are descendants of deaf as well as hearing parents. Therefore, their level of preparation in sign language and their potential to use sign language in their studies are different when they enter school. Because the oral method has dominated Estonian schools, only a few of the staff know sign language even on an elementary level. For a long time the use of sign language was prohibited, even in communication with the children, although they preferred to sign among themselves. The signs used in schools differ widely from ESL signs, and they have been adopted and further developed by the children. A strong influence in the use of ESL can be attributed to deaf children of deaf parents.

Recently, there has been a surge of interest in sign language and total communication among the teachers in the schools for the deaf. Some teachers would like to learn sign language and use it to teach the Estonian language. It is our observation that their knowledge of the language and their beginning level study of ESL are not yet sufficient, but any interest in teaching deaf students must be welcomed because as we have already stated, there are two different environments in these schools—that of the sign language endorsed by the community of deaf children and that of the verbal language used by the teaching staff. Unfortunately, there is often very little contact between these environments.

Also of primary importance in our study was the analysis, collection, and registering of the signs used in Estonia. Presently, we have registered and described about 800 ESL signs, but based on research, it can be estimated that there are about 2,500–3,000 ESL signs. In 1988 we published the first dictionary of ESL, which includes 400 signs and up to 1,000 concepts. The higher number of concepts is explained by the forming of compound words and by synonymy, i.e., one sign corresponding to several Estonian words. A subsequent analysis and comparison of the vocabulary with the language environment showed that despite profound preparatory work, the opinions of the interpreters and the deaf community differed in about 10 percent of the cases.

In addition to our research and analysis, we have also popularized ESL through the support provided by Estonian television. In May 1988, the first program about the deaf and for the deaf was broadcast. The program was interpreted into ESL and a special section was devoted to ESL. Since then, a 45-minute show is broadcast once a month, part of which is devoted to beginner's training in ESL.

Because of the sharp rise in interest in ESL, we felt compelled to study problems connected with the methods of teaching it. We faced great difficulties since there is no literature on this subject in Estonia, but now we have a system of recommendations and exercises for learning Estonian Pidgin Sign Language on the elementary level. The exercises cover approximately 500 signs, and the methods are primarily meant to be used by those who work with deaf people in the enterprises of the EUD.

Earlier we expressed our regret that the central body of the Estonian deaf, the EUD, has not supported a continuous policy concerning the defense and development of ESL. The EUD membership is 1,600, two-thirds of whom are deaf. Of vital concern is the fact that in the framework of the EUD no special language requirements have been set for hearing people who are in direct contact with deaf people. The result is that many people who work in the EUD do not know ESL and can only communicate with deaf coworkers with the assistance of interpreters. Despite this policy of separateness, people who are employed in the EUD receive additional remuneration because the Soviet social policy considers deaf people as invalids. The EUD presently finances the research work on ESL, and although the contract ends this year, it is probable that the EUD will continue its financial support.

We hope that we shall succeed in continuing our research and maintaining and developing the language of the small deaf community of Estonia—ESL—for Estonia, for the deaf people of the world, and for the world culture.

An Overview of Current Sign Language Projects in Switzerland

PENNY BOYES BRAEM

Before I begin to describe current sign language projects in Switzerland, I think it is important to make two points about Switzerland in general.

The first point, which is obvious but has important consequences, is that Switzerland is a very small country. In terms of land, Switzerland is approximately the size of Vermont and New Hampshire together. The total population of all of Switzerland is about half that of New York City.

The second point to keep in mind is that, in some regards, there is no "Switzerland." The daily life and influential institutions of the natives are not Swiss but rather Swiss German or Swiss French or Swiss Italian or Swiss Romansch. The natives live separated in different regions, each of which has its own cantons—or states—its own language and culture, and surprisingly little contact with other regions.

The federal form of government encourages and maintains these subdivisions. What is called states rights in the United States is carried to an extreme in Switzerland. Except for national roads, trains, the post, and the army, almost everything in Switzerland is organized by the twentysix separate cantons. There is thus no Federal Bureau of Education, no central agency responsible for Swiss culture. Even the federal tax doesn't amount to much—the cantonal tax makes up for it!

As for international relations, Switzerland prides itself on being neutral. Although there are extensive international contacts through banks and large companies, Switzerland belongs neither to the United Nations nor to the European Community.

Deaf Populations of Switzerland

Let's look now at the situation of the deaf population in this small, subdivided country.

The following figures are only estimates, because there are no official statistics on people with disabilities for the whole of Switzerland. There are a total of 7,800 deaf people in Switzerland. This figure presumably does not include those deafened in old age, but one doesn't know for sure. Of these 7,800 deaf people, 6,000 live in the German part, 1,500 in the French part, and 300 in the Italian part.

The deaf people living in each of these areas learn different spoken languages at school—German, French, and Italian. They also have different sign languages. The sign language in the French part, for example, more closely resembles the sign language of France than it does the sign language of German Switzerland. The sign language of German Switzerland more closely resembles that of Southern Germany than it does that of French or Italian Switzerland.

The situation is even more complicated. Within each sign language area, there are sign language dialects. The sign dialect of Geneva, for example, is different from that of Neuchatel; the signs of Zurich are different from those of Bern. The dialects, not unexpectedly, seem to be based on regional schools for deaf students.

There is no uniform Swiss German sign language corresponding to the fairly standardized American Sign Language. One of the reasons for this is that in Switzerland we don't have anything equivalent to a central university for deaf students, such as Gallaudet University in the United States, that could function as a standardizing influence on sign language.

Consequences of the Situation for Sign Language Projects

What are the consequences of the situation described above for sign language projects? What are the problems facing new interpreter training programs, sign language courses, and research projects in this very small country further divided into almost autonomous language areas, with a small deaf population that is scattered throughout these regions and that has different spoken and different sign languages and dialects?

One of the first problems is that usually there are not enough deaf people living in any one canton to justify the financial outlay necessary to run such projects. Projects therefore must be developed for an entire region—for all of the cantons in German Switzerland or those of French Switzerland. Financing for such projects must then involve separate arrangements with several cantonal governments, or the projects must apply to one of the very few federal agencies, such as the agency for insurance for handicapped people.

Because of the regional nature of sign language projects, many of the people involved in the project—both hearing and deaf—must travel to a different canton where the project is taking place. This geographical problem means, in turn, that sign language or interpreter training classes can only be organized once a week or on a one-weekend-per-month basis.

Because of the different sign language dialects within a region, organizers of sign language courses and interpreter training programs must also make important decisions about which of the dialects will be used for the new video material and which illustrations will be used in the programs.

On top of these problems specific to Switzerland, there is the problem specific to sign language, which is the fact that it is still not recognized as a language by the society as a whole. Like many European countries, Switzerland still treats its deaf citizens primarily as handicapped hearing people and not as a language minority.

The vast majority of educators of deaf people in Switzerland are still trying to fulfill the aims of oral education and believe that sign language has no place in schools for deaf students. The Swiss public is generally unaware that sign language exists. Until three years ago, there were no trained sign language interpreters in Switzerland so, for example, hearing students never saw sign language in courses attended by deaf people. Only relatively recently have signs been used on television, and then primarily in the half-hour TV programs for deaf people that appear twice a month, usually at unpopular viewing times.

Despite all the obstacles to sign language I have listed, however, several promising new sign language projects have been developed in Switzerland within the last ten years. I would like to describe briefly projects in the German and French parts of Switzerland in the following areas: schools for deaf students, sign language courses, interpreter training programs, research, and theater.

Although Switzerland is made up of four regions, there are not yet any projects involving sign language in the very small Italian part. The even smaller Romansch area is too busy trying to save its spoken language from dying out to pay much attention to any sign language that might exist there.

Current Sign Language Projects in French and German Switzerland

Schools for Deaf Students

The exclusively oral education method of most schools for deaf students in Switzerland is strongly supported by the official associations of parents of deaf children. In addition, oralism is the only method taught in teacher training programs. Because teacher training programs do not accept deaf individuals, there are no deaf people working as trained teachers in Swiss schools.

There are, however, two notable exceptions to this otherwise total oral school environment: the schools for deaf students in Geneva (French) and Zurich (German).

The Geneva School for the Deaf is quite small but has for the past several years been one of the few schools in the world that has attempted to implement a real bilingual education system for deaf children—spoken and written French and French Swiss Sign Language.

Several deaf adults are employed in the school to serve as sign language role models for the children and the hearing staff. The school employs a full-time sign language interpreter for staff meetings and other functions.

In the German part, the Zurich School for the Deaf is much larger and also has begun experimenting for the past couple of years with signs. However, this school has chosen to use a form of signed German in the classroom for the purpose of helping the children learn German.

Deaf people have been involved in choosing—or in some cases inventing—and illustrating the signs to be used in this program, as well as teaching them to the hearing teaching staff. The first phase of this experiment comes to a close this year, and one can expect a written report on the effects of this system in facilitating the learning of the spoken language.

Informally, I think one can already say that the use of signed German in the Zurich school has helped to sensitize most of the school staff to the helpfulness of signing in any form. This is already a great change from the previous generally antagonistic attitude of the teachers to any form of signing. The experiment has also served as a consciousness raiser for some of the deaf adults who have been helping with the project. They have expressed increasing awareness of and appreciation for the communicative effectiveness of their own sign language as compared with the signed German system used in the school.

Sign Language Courses

All sign language courses are relatively recent in Switzerland; they began in about 1979 in the French part and in 1985 in the German part. Both areas face the same problems of teacher training and lack of sign language materials—there are not yet any sign language dictionaries in Switzerland. Throughout Switzerland, all sign language teachers are deaf, an advantage the Swiss courses have over more well-established sign language programs in other countries.

In the French part of Switzerland, sign language courses are offered in several cities. The deaf teachers of these courses have organized themselves into a teachers' association that meets about once a month to exchange information and for further training. There is no formal training program for the teachers, but many of them in French Switzerland have attended training programs for sign language teachers in France, especially those in Paris.

The curriculum for these courses is pretty much worked out separately by the teachers in the different cities. There does exist, however, a written curriculum with materials for a one-year course at the intermediate level, designed for people wanting to qualify for an interpreter training program.

The courses in German Switzerland are just now getting off the ground. They are organized by the Swiss German Deaf Association, which recruits the teachers and has set up the basic structure of the courses. The Deaf Association has also just set up a new three-year training program for sign language teachers of the German part.

So far, courses have been offered only in Zurich and Bern, although there are plans to add courses in other cities as more deaf people become interested in teaching. The advantage of having only deaf people as sign language teachers has a flip side, i.e., not all deaf people who use sign language are interested in teaching it. Recruitment of enough deaf teachers is a current problem in German Switzerland.

The series of courses offered so far begins with nonverbal communication and a theoretical introduction to the linguistics of sign language, followed by practical courses on an elementary level. Courses on more intermediate and advanced levels, which are essentially for the new interpreter training program, are being planned for the near future.

Materials and curriculum for these courses have been developed by deaf teachers in Zurich and Bern. There is also a new inter-regional project for illustrating about 3,000 Swiss German signs as source material for sign language courses throughout German Switzerland. This illustration project is complicated by the regional variations of signs.

Interpreter Training Programs

Until 1983, there were no trained sign language interpreters in all of Switzerland. Even untrained individuals—usually children of deaf parents—who used signs in informal interpreting situations were very, very rare. "Interpretation for deaf people" generally meant oral interpreting. As I have mentioned before, this has also meant that almost all forms of higher education have been closed to most deaf people, not to mention their inability to participate in a wide variety of political and cultural organizations in Switzerland.

Within the past couple years, however, this situation has begun to change, largely owing to the initiative of deaf individuals in both the French and German parts who have encouraged their deaf friends to make organized demands for sign language interpreting services.

The first pilot interpreter training program in Switzerland ran from 1983 to 1986 in the French part, in Lausanne. The regional sign language, and not a signed form of the spoken language, was used from the beginning of the training. The concept of the program drew upon the help of experienced American, English, and French sign language interpreter trainers, several of whom came to Lausanne to teach the Swiss students.

At the end of the three-year training, two forms of certificates were awarded. We decided not to base the certificates on ability to interpret in either signed French or in French Swiss Sign Language, based on the American model. Instead, certificates were given for competency in interpreting in two different kinds of situations: liaison interpreting (for individuals and small groups) and conference interpreting.

Deaf people were involved as teachers and advisors throughout this training program. A professional spoken language interpreter gave a two-year course training the oral side (spoken French) of the students' interpretation.

After the first class of students graduated, plans were made to place the program within the Department of Interpretation at the University of Geneva. Political problems have delayed this development, but we still have hopes that the training of sign language interpreters in the same school with students studying to be spoken language interpreters will be realizable.

In German Switzerland, the first group of interpreting students in a new program in Zurich completed the first three-year phase of their training just this year. The emphasis in this phase was on theory and oral interpreting. Training in sign language and sign language interpreting was very minimal and came only in the last few months.

The programs have a new director, and in the next phase there will be much more emphasis on sign language and on the involvement of deaf teachers in the training.

Research

With the topic of research we come to the matter that occupies me most. In 1983, I started the small private Center for Sign Language Research in the German part of Switzerland (Basel). I hoped to be able to look at the linguistic aspects of the local sign language quietly—quietly because it seemed at the time that no one else in Switzerland was particularly interested in the topic of sign language research.

The problem with doing sign language research in a small country where sign language projects are just beginning is that one quickly finds oneself doing more sign language advocacy than research. Since 1983, most of my time has not been spent on pure research but on helping out when asked on various sign language projects—sign language courses, interpreter training programs, and the dissemination of information to the general public on sign language in the form of lectures, articles, and interviews. It has been an immensely rich period during which I have come to know a large number of deaf people working on projects in the French and German parts of Switzerland. I have learned a lot from these friends and colleagues—including French!

My research up until now has been primarily a pilot study on dialects of Swiss German Sign Language, an experimental study of the word order in Swiss French and German sign languages, and a collection of short stories signed by deaf Swiss Germans. Current projects include a grant proposal for a general linguistic description of Swiss German Sign Language, which if funded will allow me to work with Andreas Kolb; and finishing a small pilot sign language dictionary in French Switzerland, a project in which Marie Louise Fournier is also involved.

There are several very capable colleagues in the French and German parts of Switzerland who are also involved in sign language research projects. Benno Caramore, a hearing colleague from Zurich, has just finished an interesting dissertation on the use of signs in Swiss schools for deaf students in the nineteenth century.

Theater

German Switzerland has no tradition of sign language theater. Yet one of the reasons Andreas Kolb is at this conference is owing to his interest in theater and its potential development in German Switzerland. So after about a year, you will probably be able to direct your questions on sign theater in German Switzerland to him.

French Switzerland has more of a tradition of sign theater, partly owing to the influences from France. For several years now, there has been a yearly soiree, a whole evening of sign language skits put on by young deaf people from Geneva.

Summary

To sum up this brief overview of sign language projects in Switzerland, I think in the next five years we can fully expect to see an exciting blossoming of a wide variety of sign language projects all over Switzerland. Because the hearing society continues largely to ignore if not overtly suppress sign language, this growth is stimulated and nurtured largely by the deaf community itself. With such solid native-user roots, one can hope for a long season and rich harvests.

Sign Language Research in Germany

GUDULA LIST

We are delighted that no one has objected to a group from German-speaking countries taking part in The Deaf Way. After all, it is *our* tradition, the "German Method," that has created such burdens for deaf communities. Special education for deaf people is still largely oralistic in German-speaking nations. Efforts on our part to correct this situation are long overdue, so I am glad to be able to report that interdisciplinary research on sign language is making some progress, although this progress is slow.

In this paper, I will present an overview of the educational use of sign language and sign language research in Germany at the present time.

In the area of special education, four universities in western Germany offer academic studies for teachers at schools for deaf students and others working in deaf education: Cologne, Hamburg, Heidelberg, and Munich. In the German Democratic Republic (GDR), there are a few places as well, and what I report here for western Germany seems to apply in an even more pronounced way to the GDR.

Only a few years ago, the former teacher training institutions became integrated into universities, but they still focus predominantly on traditional pedagogy. Research, when it is done at all, focuses more on the methodology and technology of teaching than on basic research on deafness. Indeed, technology and medicine, with their supply of hearing aids, are more prominent partners of special education for deaf students than are sociology and psychology of language, which certainly would be more useful for examining the appropriateness of oralistic education. Courses in sign language are part of the curriculum, although often not compulsory, and most of these courses teach signed German rather than German Sign Language. For the most part, they are by far less efficient than courses taught in some other countries.

Thus, in general, academic studies prepare future educators for a rather traditional, oralistic sort of teaching, both inside and outside the schools for deaf students. It is true that a great many teachers in training are open minded about sign language and the communication needs of the children they will teach. But this is by no means a guarantee that strategies of education within these schools will change. Many new teachers finally submit to the governing policy, and those who might be expected to resist often refuse to go into teaching at all.

Therefore, no rapid modification can be expected in schooling policy. Neither is change likely to result from within the academic discipline of special education. Like elsewhere in the world, change can only occur through two routes: The first is a growing self-confidence within the deaf community, making deaf people more assured so they can claim their rights—especially their right for interpreting. And second is an academic interest in sign language outside of special education—in linguistics, anthropology, cognitive and developmental psychology, and neuropsychology.

The linguistic and psycholinguistic debate about language universals clearly is not yet settled in Germany. In part, this has to do with facts that can be explained by sociology of language. The degree of standardization of German Sign Language, and the degree of participation and acceptance by deaf people themselves, cannot be compared with ASL usage in the United States. There are evident consequences of long-lasting suppression of sign language in Germany, and a considerable time lag in consolidation of language levels and regional performance, compared with North America.

We are fortunate to have the American scholar, Penny Boyes Braem, helping with her studies of sign language at Basel. [Editor's note: See Boyes Braem, this volume.] We also have the Center for German Sign Language in Hamburg (which, by the way, is not connected with special education for deaf students at the same university). Siegmund Prillwitz and his crew—half of whom are deaf—are working hard at this Center, although they do not receive unanimous support from the outside.

We are still behind in cataloging and describing sign language, and especially in more elaborate linguistic theory. The burden of such linguistic work, which is really in its infancy, rests almost entirely on the shoulders of the Center of German Sign Language at Hamburg. Work at the Center began in the 1970s. At first, it concentrated on fighting the prejudices about sign language and developing the first educational programs, including signs for families, early education programs, kindergartens, and schools for deaf students.

Since the mid-1980s, the Center has focused on research into German Sign Language and its potential use in bilingual education. Apart from compilation of sign dictionaries and initial stages of a grammar of German Sign Language, major emphasis is currently given to the development of new research methods. The Hamburg Notation System, an internationally applicable written computer sign language, and other programs for transcription and linguistic data-processing are being developed. [Editor's note: See Zienert, this volume.]

As part of a large-scale survey on German sign language, deaf staff members at the Center currently are conducting video surveys among deaf people of the Federal Republic of Germany. This research will later be transferred to a computer-based written form and analyzed. These are certainly plans that will keep the Center busy well into the next millennium!

Meanwhile, the movement toward greater knowledge and acceptance of deaf people and their language is supported by the public relations work of the nonprofit "Gessellschaft fur Gebardensprache und Kommunikation Gehörloser e.V." (Association for Sign Language and Communication of the Deaf). This organization was founded by members of the Center, and the two groups work closely together. The association organizes public events, issues a quarterly journal, *Das Zeichen*, and offers a series of books and videos that provide information about the situation of deaf people and sign language.

These activities do produce positive effects in the academic world and with the general public. At the same time, however, there is still a great deal of controversy. Not only is oralism still striving to survive; the undeniable diversity and code variety of sign language used by deaf Germans, as well as the often misunderstood "iconicity" and "privacy" of sign languages in general, provide arguments against sign language in a controversy that is, in essence, political.

It would be unrealistic to expect a growing self-confidence and language consciousness in deaf people, hearing relatives, and responsible individuals in associations of

deal people without further struggle. However, international communication models
from the outside—for example, reports from Gallaudet University—are gaining influence. Some deaf people are beginning to oppose their representatives who favor signed
German instead of German Sign Language. Pride and interest in the genuine language
of deaf people is growing.

For example, recently we had a remarkable evening at Cologne University when
Penny Boyes Braem gave a lecture on sign language research. A great many deaf people
were present, some of them from far away, and both the lecture and lively discussion
were interpreted. This might seem routine to you. But at Cologne University it was a
sort of peaceful revolution that produced obvious effects even on colleagues from the
area of special education who had come to participate!

Perhaps most important at present is our vital and openly expressed need for interpreters, which fortunately has received official confirmation by the European Parliament. The recognition of this need is important not only on a practical level but also for
the debate on the language status of sign languages.

It is encouraging to observe that, in discussing the interpreting problem, one federal
association of deaf people after another is abolishing the term "Gehörlosendolmetscher"
(interpreter for the deaf) in favor of the term "Gebardensprachdolmetscher" (interpreter
for sign languages). That is a most significant indication of the movement of consciousness away from the claim for social services and toward a claim for acknowledging
German Sign Language as a complete and independent language.

The issue of interpreting seems indeed to be a meeting point for the evolving self-
esteem of the deaf community and academic work on sign language in linguistics and
other humanities disciplines. Yet until now, training interpreters in Germany has been
deplorably unsystematic; in fact, a large-scale, empirically based professional curriculum does not exist. In the face of daily needs, many urgently needed programs are
being implemented. But it will be extremely important to find a solution during the
next decade that will satisfy the urgent requirements, on the one hand, while meeting
appropriate academic standards for interpreter training, on the other.

Interpreting between signed and spoken languages, already a highly demanding
profession, faces additional problems related to roles and the lack of instructors and
instructional materials. Unlike conventional interpreting, which is primarily concerned
with the two languages, sign language interpreting is mixed up with social care and
personal mediation and assistance. It is important to define the functions and roles of
interpreters, and to establish guidelines for the various aspects of this complex activity.

In order to develop this field, we need thorough analyses. Fortunately, one of the
few academic activities related to sign language in my country is a contribution relevant
to the interpreting problem. Horst Ebbinghaus and Jens Hessmann, two linguists from
the Free University of Berlin, spent two years doing field research on a project whose
results will be published this year. Analyses such as this one will be needed for the
large amount of work that lies ahead.

Hamburg also is playing a leading role in developing programs for interpreters.
But even there, efforts suffer from a lack of personnel to do the training. Up until now,
administrative and financial resources for developing adequate regional programs have
also been lacking.

Sign language research is also still sadly lacking. A multidisciplinary-based presentation of evidence about the language status of sign language in general and of German
Sign Language in particular is vitally needed. At this point, I become rather subdued;
apart from the work in Hamburg, there isn't much to report about Germany in this
respect.

Ebbinghaus and Hessmann now are engaged in a new project of basic linguistic research that concerns the involvement of articulatory movements of German oral words in German Sign Language. [Editor's note: See Ebbinghaus and Hessman, this volume.] To the best of my knowledge, some linguistic research in Hamburg and Berlin, some scattered studies on history, and research on psychology in Cologne are virtually all that exist.

So I am left with the embarrassing situation of having to conclude with a few remarks about the research that I myself hope to do at the University of Cologne. At Cologne, I teach psychology to students who study special education in the field of language disorders, such as developmental disturbances, aphasia, or stuttering. But I also teach psychology to students of special education for deaf people. My research interests have always been in cognition, neuropsychology, and psychology of language, but it has only been in the last few years that I began to concentrate on deafness.

Doing research in this area has a few modest advantages, such as the broad spectrum of scientific fields that are relevant for psychological sign language research. But it also has obvious disadvantages: My coworkers and I must learn more about deafness and deaf communication. And, most embarrassing for myself, I am at the very beginning of learning to sign.

In my teaching, which must cover a wide range of subjects, I try to include in psychology of language a respect for deaf people as a group that has its own proper language and is not language disabled. This attitude is slightly subversive, occurring as it does within the field of special eduction for disabled people.

Fortunately, psychology of language is a well developed field, at least as far as oral languages are concerned. And there are some strong arguments, hard to contradict, being made in relation to **sign language**. In particular, *primary language competence is the prerequisite for establishing internal mechanisms of secondary language abilities.* Compelling evidence comes, for example, from hearing children who are learning to read and write. In a similar way, there is no doubt that deaf students' learning is enhanced by competence in primary sign language.

Impressive knowledge exists in developmental psychology and neuro-psychology about what "primary language acquisition" means for the hearing child. On the other hand, it is evident that oral language cannot be acquired as a primary language by a deaf individual. Because reading and writing abilities in the major language are vital for deaf people—although obviously immensely difficult to acquire—and instruction in this area must be improved, the only possible line of thought for someone who is not deformed by oralistic ideology is: *We must study the nature of processes that underlie signing as a primary language* in order to determine the best educational means for teaching deaf students to read and write. In short, we need to know which internal recording processes lead from sign to script and from script to sign.

Ultimately, my research is meant to be applied in instructional settings, but it will first of all be basic research on psychological aspects of signing and therefore can contribute to the debate on the status of sign languages. To consider primary sign competence as the basis for learning other forms of language indeed raises in a decisive way, and from the angle of psychology, the question of language universals—those elements present in all natural languages.

The "split brain" studies demonstrating cortical lateralization of signing have proved to be of very limited value. In fact, I think all these studies of "hemisphericity"— the degree of functional specialization of the cerebral hemispheres of the brain—have caused more harm than good. Not only are most of them to be criticized on grounds of methodology; much more annoying is the use some people make of right hemisphere involvement in signing. This leads to a lot of infertile discussions with those who are not well informed about neuropsychology in general, let alone about the participation of the right hemisphere in oral language processing.

Although it is true that all language operation is a result of cooperation between the left and right cortex, as well as subcortical regions, it is still imperative to describe in detail those psychological processes that are indeed specific to the dominant hemisphere. Modern neuropsychology, especially the clinical branch of it, has become quite competent in this respect.

The left hemisphere seems to structure input sequentially, thus providing a framework for kinetic memory of voluntary acts. This kinetic memory is based on the interlocking of motor function with double feedback, either visual or kinesthetic (in signing) or auditory and kinesthetic (in speaking).

Speaking and hearing as well as production and decoding of sign are examples from a wider range of higher activities governed by such systematically structured and sequentially ordered principles. Some of these activities are learned through immediate manipulation of objects or through imitating the acts of others. Some, such as pantomime, become representational and do not depend on contextual feedback.

However, there seems to be an additional fact that makes language processing not only a nonmanipulative and context-free sequential activity but also unique among representational acts: the natural way kinetic memory is acquired in social contact with speaking or signing people.

For the work in my institute, this interpretation implies the need for investigation of levels of processing in signing and sign comprehension, and investigation of different feedback components in signing. So we will try to explore sign production and comprehension under various conditions.

In the long run, the results of such studies could be used to investigate coding strategies to help deaf people handle the written word. There is evidence that recoding in sign and fingerspelling plays a role in reading and writing by deaf people. But such measures usually seem to be adopted in a nondissected way, taking signs or fingerspelled complexes as whole-word equivalents without really making use of linguistic coding—that is, of analytic and synthetic operations.

I agree with colleagues working in the same field that a broad base of experience and knowledge can motivate people to learn more through books and written material, thereby improving their reading and writing. And I especially agree with those who stress the importance of language consciousness and metalinguistic knowledge. However, the ability to think about written and oral language is a secondary learning process that can only grow out of knowledge of one's proper language, which itself demands the ability to acquire and use that language.

So if one wants to facilitate deaf people's handling of the written word, one must consider not only primary sign language competence as the indispensable base for learning, but also promote reflection about morphology of sign languages. Only on this base can the comprehension of the linguistic structure of oral languages and their written forms become possible.

It is not easy to raise funds for the kind of research I have tried to describe. This is all the more true in a country where sign language does not yet possess the dignity of an academically established subject. All applications for funds have to pass through the close scrutiny of experts in an established discipline. And even considering Hamburg, there is no discipline of sign language study in Germany producing enough scholars with the required expertise in the field. Worse, we are still fighting for sign language to gain its rightful acceptance as a natural and distinct language.

In concluding, I would like to offer a hearty expression of gratitude for the support that Americans have given us through the wealth of experience and research gathered and made available to us. Within the German scene of empirical psychology, I am considered terribly heuristic in my research plans, willing to explore assumptions about sign language without a strong foundation in earlier German investigation. The work that needs to be done in Germany, in other words, depends greatly on our ability to make reference to the work Americans have already done.

The Center for German Sign Language in Hamburg: Deaf People Doing Research on Their Language with Video and Computers

HEIKO ZIENERT

Sign language research and the use of signs for teaching deaf students are relatively recent developments in Germany. Until 1975, scientific research in Germany was not in the least interested in manual signs or sign language. This attitude was quite different from the situation in America and many other countries. In Germany, sign language existed in secret within the deaf community.

In 1975 Dr. Siegmund Prillwitz, a psycholinguist at the University of Hamburg, was commissioned by the Department for Deaf Education to work on improving the oral teaching method from a linguistic point of view. For this purpose, Professor Prillwitz attended classes at the school for the deaf in Hamburg for many hours. There he was struck by the difference between the spoken language used in the lessons and the sign language used during breaks.

Prillwitz showed more and more interest in this "break" language. His interest and research resulted in a book entitled *Zum Zusammenhang von Kognition, Kommunikation und Sprache mit Bezug auf die Gehörlosenproblematik [On the Relations Between Cognition, Communication, and Language with Reference to the Problematics of the Deaf]* (Prillwitz, 1982). In this book the prejudices against deaf people and their sign language are proved through scientific reasoning to be wrong.

Until 1980 there were no real sign language interpreters in Germany. The situation was essentially a mess, in which anyone could claim to be an interpreter and offer services as such. In 1980, hearing and deaf people from Hamburg started gathering information on the practice of interpreting in other countries. As a result, a code of ethics for sign language interpreters was developed, translation techniques were taught in training programs, and the right of deaf people to choose an interpreter freely was made more widely known. The situation in Germany gradually began to change.

In 1981, Professor Prillwitz began to look for deaf individuals to work with him. I was among those who began to pay him private visits. The work consisted of comparing and contrasting the ways spoken German and sign language communicated similar concepts. In each session, Prillwitz explained to his deaf consultants the grammar used in spoken language when conveying certain thoughts, then asked us to explain how sign language grammar worked to convey similar information. Six years later, this leisure-time research, which began as a hobby, resulted in the opening of the Center for German Sign Language and Communication of the Deaf. After only a short while, the University of Hamburg became the first university in Germany to recognize sign language in its Department of German by including courses in which German Sign Language (GSL) was taught as a language in its own right, distinct from spoken German. This was the beginning of official courses in GSL, which are still being developed and are conducted by deaf lecturers.

In 1985, the first German-sponsored international congress on the subject of signs in the education and training of deaf people was held in Germany. Previous public discussions in Germany had dealt only with topics based on an oralistic philosophy, but that came to an end in 1985. About 1,000 people came streaming into Hamburg to learn something about signs, sign language, and the potential use of signs in educating deaf children.

Despite the new openness to sign language, our efforts to found an institute were not successful until the government of Hamburg provided us with a house. The Center for German Sign Language and Communication of the Deaf was opened in 1987. From an original staff of eight, the Center has grown to a staff of forty, half of them deaf.

The staff does research on the grammar of sign language, develops concepts for sign language courses, and works with computers to develop a sign writing system among many other things. Hearing and deaf people in the Center get along well with each other. The hearing staff members accept sign language and try to learn it. They consider the deaf staff members equal partners.

Our work in the area of methods and application of computer technology includes the development of and research on a formalized writing system for sign language. The first notation system in America was developed by Dr. William Stokoe in 1960. Following this tradition, we are attempting in Hamburg to develop an international notation system in order to record sign language. This system is called "HamNoSys."

Earlier sign writing systems often used combinations of letters to represent—very abstractly—the various handshapes, etc. We changed that by using new symbols that are orientated toward the iconicity (or pictorial power) of handshapes and signs. It is our goal to generate computer-animated pictures that are created on the basis of the symbols of our notation system. Users will be able to enter known information into the computer, which is programmed to lead the user toward more information either from parts of signs to complete signs and words or—moving the opposite way—from words to signs and their component parts. At the center of this process are the symbolic notations of sign parts.

A great deal of preparatory work was required for HamNoSys because a large amount of material is needed to generate a sign-writing system and pictures. First, we videotaped human models in an effort to obtain images of a full range of possible angles and positions of lower and upper arms, the upper body, and all forty relevant GSL handshapes. Our goal was to use these videotaped images as the basis for drawings that could be stored in a computer, then assembled into animated representations of signs in response to keyed-in words used as prompts. It proved to be excessively tiresome, however, for models to be recorded in all the possible angles in this way, so we switched to working with plaster figures that functioned as models, and we recorded these figures on videotape. This still was not easy. For one handshape, for instance, we recorded a vast range of levels and positions. This number is to be multiplied by the about forty relevant GSL handshapes. Needless to say, quite a lot of work is involved, but there is no way to avoid it.

The computer program, "HamNoSys Editor," may be used to generate HamNoSys symbols without prior knowledge of this system of writing signs. The user responds to questions asked by the computer by clicking appropriate answers about the known characteristics of a sign—the location, whether the sign is one-handed or two-handed, etc.—then the computer displays the HamNoSys symbols for these data. The computer then can suggest through pictures possible signs featuring those characteristics. The Editor is meant for beginners who don't know HamNoSys yet; for those people the computer will do all the work by directly showing symbols and pictures.

So far, sign language dictionaries have been static, showing photos or drawings into which various arrows are inserted in one way or another. But there is no life in that. Therefore, we are developing a program called *Hamburg Animated Dictionary of Sign Language* (HANDS). It is just the same as a dictionary, but shows animated pictures on a computer when you type a word. The entry is converted into HamNoSys by the computer, which then assembles the various body parts as individual drawings and displays them in a programmed sequence resulting in an animation of a manual sign, in essence a translation into sign language of the originally entered word. For example, you might key in the word "home," and then the sign HOME will immediately appear on the computer screen. That is how our dictionary works. At the moment it is in German Sign Language, but it will not remain confined solely to that. Later it may work internationally for any language. The user could key in words in German, English, Spanish, French, Italian, etc., and could choose between German Sign Language, American Sign Language, etc.

We gather the material for the computer dictionary in three ways:

❖ We conduct nationwide interviews with deaf people on video.

❖ We conduct sign surveys on technical terms. For example, a three-year project sponsored by the Federal Ministry will develop new methods and learning materials for the vocational advancement of deaf people in the field of computer technology.

❖ Surveys of signs for technical terms have been collected by gathering terms that deaf university students encounter in their studies and pass along to their sign language interpreters.

The Center also is conducting research on the grammar of German Sign Language. So far, research in this area has been somewhat superficial. This research is very important for sign language courses. Deaf people themselves are currently developing grammatical examples for German Sign Language that might be suitable as practice material. The first book on this subject in Germany, *Skizze der Grammatik der DGS [An Outline of the Grammar of GSL]*, was written in 1985 (Prillwitz, 1985). Our work has continued along these lines, and we have found that the contents of this unpublished manuscript have needed to be revised. We are currently working on a revised edition.

We were confronted with the question of how to do research into GSL. Should we sign ourselves and analyze our signing at the same time? Of course we couldn't do that. The deaf Center staff members are selecting deaf individuals from all over Germany whom they will then visit and interview on videotape. They will ask many questions about the life and experiences of the interviewees. We also are trying to conduct a nationwide video survey of natural sign language data. We have already completed fifty such videocassettes. Each of these recordings will later be transcribed into HamNoSys. They form the basis of our sign language research.

Sign language teaching continues to be an important part of our work. I already mentioned that the first sign language course took place at the University of Hamburg in 1981. Since then, the courses have been constantly improved. In the beginning few people took our courses, but the number of participants has increased steadily. Today we have about 300 students each semester. Five deaf individuals have been assigned to lecturing posts as sign language teachers. There are a total of eight course groups on five progressive levels.

I also mentioned that the first training program for sign language interpreters began in 1980. But back then sign language interpreting hadn't yet been recognized as a legitimate profession, so the training was in many ways a transitional solution.

It is the objective of the Center for GSL to integrate the training of sign language interpreters into a course of studies at the university and to have qualified interpreters recognized as full-fledged professionals. At the moment, a training concept is being worked out. The preparations are in full swing.

We are already busy working on the concept of a sign language course on videotape. We have two objectives in mind. First, we want to develop materials to accompany our courses in order to provide the participants with an opportunity for further private education. This is necessary because there still are places where no sign language courses are offered. Additionally, interested individuals from all parts of Germany would have the opportunity to study sign language through a kind of correspondence course.

A special group of experts is working on the topic of sign language and education. A project for preschool education involves research on the communication situation of deaf and hearing families with deaf children. Visits made to these families were recorded on videotape, and the communication between mother and child was analyzed. The results had tremendous impact, showing the great need of hearing parents for information about sign language. Arguments were further advanced, as a consequence of this study, for bilingual preschool education instead of a one-sided oralistic preschool education. The first volume of a parents' guide, *Elternbuch I; Zeig Mir Deine Sprache [Show Me Your Language]* (Prillwitz, Wisch, and Wudtke, 1991), and the scientific study accompanying this project have already been published.

A school project is closely related to the project for preschool education. The participating children are the same ones studied earlier in kindergarten, and then at school. We were particularly interested in finding out about the children's course of development with signs—whether they made better cognitive progress than the other children who are educated by oral methods. The accompanying scientific study is continuing as a long-term group study. The results of the study of the students' preschool years have now been published in the book, *Gebarden in der Vorschulischen Erziehung Gehörloser Kinder [Signs in the Pre-School Education of Deaf Children]* (Prillwitz and Wudtke, 1988). All of the literature mentioned may be obtained through the Center.

The Center is addressing the acquisition of written language and the question of bilingualism. Acquisition of written language means how children can best learn to read and, of course, write. Previously, deaf people considered written language as something that pertained to hearing people and, therefore, was not suitable for deaf children. But now pictures, signs, and writing are becoming more interrelated, and research is being done on this. The Center at the University of Hamburg aims to get rid of oralism as a teaching method for deaf children without, however, solely favoring sign language. Instead, we choose a third alternative—bilingualism—based on international experience from countries such as Sweden and Switzerland. Along these lines, an overall bilingual concept for schools for deaf students that includes concrete plans of learning units for teachers, students, and parents is currently being developed within the scope of the school project.

The Center staff is taking care of deaf children. Staff members want to tell deaf children fairy tales and stories in order to inspire them. So far, there is no material to do that. Only books are available; television programs exclusively feature spoken language, which is boring for deaf children because they cannot understand it. We started producing videos, adapted from children's books, for deaf children to watch. Deaf and hearing people worked together to convert spoken language concepts into sign language. This resulted in a video for children that was broadcast on television. In addition to fairy tale videos in GSL, we also offer videos in signed German. And now we are doing research on what kind of film will be understood better by the children, signed German or GSL.

The Association for German Sign Language and Communication of the Deaf is affiliated with the Center. The task of the Association is to provide information in key areas through public relations efforts such as events, services, and dissemination of information.

The Association publishes *Das Zeichen [The Sign]*, a quarterly journal containing important information on deaf people, education, training, interpreters, sign courses, results of research into the grammar of GSL, international news, workshops, congresses, and many other things. The journal provides a complete list of sign courses offered in various places in Germany.

Our publication series consists of literature that originated from our projects, conference proceedings, and translation of international research findings into German.

We also have a collection of videos on various subjects: seminars and events, preschool education for parents of deaf children, fairy tales, courses in GSL, television recordings, films on culture, and international videos on sign language research and history. Interested individuals can either purchase or borrow these videotapes, and anyone who does not have a video recorder may use the equipment in our Center to watch the videos. In order to be able to offer all these publications at the lowest possible price, we founded our own publishing firm, *Zentrumsverlag Signum* [Latin: the sign], which also will publish literature in English.

All of our efforts at the Center for GSL and Communication of the Deaf are meant to foster hope for a recognition of sign language and for the assertion of the rights of deaf people as a linguistic minority group in Germany. Another important milestone on the way toward these goals will be the International Congress in Hamburg in March of 1990, which will be patronized by the Federal President of our country, Mr. Richard von Weizsäcker.

References

Prillwitz, S. 1982. *Zum Zusammenhang von Kognition, Kommunikation und Sprache mit Bezug auf die Gehörlosenproblematik [On the Relations Between Cognition, Communication, and Language with Reference to the Problematics of the Deaf]*. Stuttgart: Kohlhammer.

Prillwitz, S. 1985. *Skizze der Grammatik der DGS [An Outline of the Grammar of GSL]*. Unpublished manuscript.

Prillwitz, S., Wisch, and H. Wudtke. 1991. *Elternbuch I; Zeig Mir Deine Sprache [Show Me Your Language]*. Hamburg: SIGNUM-Press.

Prillwitz, S., and H. Wudtke. 1988. *Gebärden in der Vorschulischen Erziehung Gehörloser Kinder [Signs in the Preschool Education of Deaf Children]*. Hamburg: SIGNUM-Press.

German Words in German Sign Language: Do They Tell Us Something New About Sign Languages?

HORST EBBINGHAUS AND JENS HESSMANN

I n this paper we are going to outline some of the ideas relevant to the work on German Sign Language (GSL) carried out at the Free University of Berlin and supported by the German Research Foundation. With Prof. Dr. Helmut Richter acting as our supervisor, we have been involved in sign language research since 1986. At the beginning of 1989, our team was significantly enlarged and now includes two native signers of GSL, Gunter Puttrich-Reignard and Sabine Fries. Joanna Martin, a hearing American keenly interested in sign language and the deaf world, has also joined us.

Our work is empirical in spirit, and we are concentrating on collecting and transcribing data from GSL use in natural communicative settings. Previous experience with deaf people's signing in Germany has led us to adopt a specific analytical perspective: Our goal is to describe the relationship between elements of spoken German and communication generally considered to be elements of sign language. Our empirical work has led us to believe that there are German words *in* GSL; in other words, that we should recognize spoken language elements as an integral part of a sign language.

We suspect the above claim will startle many. There is a general belief that progress for deaf people hinges on the recognition of sign languages as languages in their own right. In that context, the use deaf people make of spoken language elements tends to be regarded as a carryover from the oralistic indoctrination deaf education has inflicted on deaf people for too long. Given the history of oppression the signing community has faced, such an assumption is understandable, but we believe it is somewhat unfortunate. In our view, neither recognizing sign languages as languages in their own right nor taking an unambiguous stand in the struggle for the rights of the deaf community precludes acknowledging that there may be important relationships between signed and spoken languages that a valid description of sign language should systematically take account of.

This paper, originally presented at The Deaf Way, has been published in a slightly different form in *Current Trends in European Sign Language Research: Proceedings of the Third European Congress on Sign Language Research (International Studies on Sign Language and the Communication of the Deaf, volume 9)*, edited by Siegmund Prillwitz and Tomas Vollhaber, 1990, pp. 97–112, Hamburg, Germany: SIGNUM-Press.

Previous references to spoken language elements in natural sign language use have been scarce and somewhat apologetic. Odd-Inge Schroeder (1985) makes a strong plea for recognizing the role of mouthing in Norwegian Sign Language; as the title of his article indicates, he is well aware that such a recognition causes "a problem in phonological description." Speaking of Dutch signing, Trude Schermer (1985) remarks that "as of 1983 I would say that the existence of a pure sign language, without the occurrence of any speech, among deaf adults, is more or less a theoretical construct" (p. 288), but Schermer predicts that the role of speech in natural signing "will decrease in the future" (p. 286). This may or may not be so. Still, if sign language is to be an empirically justifiable notion, we should be wary of constructing theories that do not fit the facts of signing as it normally occurs.

By way of introducing our topic, we will brush aside theoretical questions and start with this bold assumption: Signed communication is multichannel communication and should be regarded as the result of an interaction between different types of meaningful units. In order to do justice to sign language as a *visual* means of communication we should recognize at least the following types of meaningful units:

Manual Units. As the central units of sign language, manual signs have of course received much attention, and there are many detailed analyses of the form and use of these units. In working upon sign language empirically, it is not always easy to decide whether a given movement of the hand can be regarded as a sign or not, but for the most part manual units may be considered relatively well defined.

Nonmanual Units. Again, there is nothing new about nonmanual elements such as facial expression, though just how we should conceive of their relationship to manual units and whether there are communicative uses of the body that we would not consider to be part of signing proper seems far from clear. But this is not our topic. Let us simply remark that we are not convinced that nonmanual units can be usefully reduced to formal parameters, and it will probably turn out that we need a fairly wide notion of nonmanual units that allows for all sorts of communicatively intended body behavior.

Oral Units. A language like GSL forces us to recognize another type of meaningful unit that we suggest calling oral units. By oral unit we do not mean anything you can do with your mouth. Very often, of course, this is part of nonmanual behavior or even in itself constitutes a nonmanual unit. Rather, an oral unit is a movement of the mouth and tongue that can be traced back to spoken language. An oral unit is an articulatory movement that is intended to resemble the kind of movement one ordinarily observes when a particular word is spoken. Whether or not an oral unit is accompanied by any sound is irrelevant in this context. Normally, it is not.

Recognizing oral units as part of a sign language may seem a strange idea. Nevertheless, there is a good reason for proceeding in this way, and we will try to show why mouthing should not be excluded from our inquiries into signed communication. First, we will make you familiar with the kind of data that made us start to wonder about the relationship between spoken German and GSL.

We are going to describe a piece of natural sign language use among German deaf people. A young deaf woman is engaged in a Sunday afternoon conversation with her deaf brother and a deaf friend. (In order to capture this conversation as naturally as possible on videotape, cameras were set up by a deaf member of our team and his hearing assistant, both of whom then left the scene.) The three participants had not seen each other for some time. The piece of the conversation we describe occurred about half an hour after the start of the conversation. It includes an extensive account of a trip the young woman had made to southern Germany. This segment lasts two minutes and forty seconds. The basic storyline is as follows:

The signer and another boy went to a town by car and visited a girl. After some conversation the girl suggested going to another town where she wanted to pick up her boyfriend while the signer visited another friend. So they went and separated. The girl was to pick up the signer about an hour later. Unfortunately, the signer's friend wasn't in. She kept waiting. It was late in the evening by now and cold. Finally, a friendly neighbor opened the door for her and she found the apartment on the second floor. This did not help much, because her friend wasn't in. So the signer left him a note and went down again. But after waiting outside for some time, she observed the friend's car arriving. When the friend saw her, there was a big "hello." They went up to the apartment again and woke up the friend's girlfriend, who had been sleeping all the time. The signer dutifully admired the apartment. They all sat down and talked until suddenly the bell rang and it was time to go. Outside, the girl was waiting to take the signer back to her home. So they said goodbye. The signer remembers that the friends sent greetings to her brother and the friend to whom she was signing.

The story is told with great attention to detail, as when the signer describes the friendly neighbor and compares him to other hearing people she has asked for similar favors, or when she relates how seeing her friends' shoes helped her to find out which apartment was theirs. We may assume that the signer's brother and friend fully comprehend this story. Why? For one thing, as signers of GSL they are familiar with the manual signs used here and they know certain nonmanual units and grammatical mechanisms that may be specific to GSL. But we think there is another reason: They routinely identify the words the signer is mouthing as part of her signing.

Deaf people are, of course, more or less constantly confronted with spoken language. This orientation towards spoken language is reinforced by their educations. We do not have to dwell on the fact that oralism has been particularly strong in Germany. "The German Method" was once a by-word for oralism. Being able to make use of spoken language is an obvious advantage for deaf people. Our signing example provides a good illustration of this when the signer relates how she addressed the friendly hearing neighbor. "May I come in?" she asked, and the fact that this phrase was spoken is made clear by her exaggerated way of mouthing. The signer's narrative here seems to emphasize how aspects of spoken language are useful when communicating with hearing people. Other details from the videotape, however, show that in GSL mouthing is also frequently used, even in direct communication between deaf people.

There is no established tradition of fingerspelling in GSL. This is puzzling, because many German deaf people know the international manual alphabet. They simply do not seem to make very much use of it. Again, our example illustrates this. The signer mentions two place names. Both times they are established by mouthing with little assistance from manual signals. (In one case, actually, the fingerspelled letter "n" is used.) A special technique is applied that involves an emphasis on mouthing, repetition of the word, and a brief interactive comprehension check. This approach may not be particularly elegant, but it seems to work well enough and probably prevents a more extensive use of fingerspelling.

Even though sound is inaccessible to most deaf people, the use of spoken language may not be all that unnatural for them. Of course, you may think that the linguistic conditions of the deaf minority are such that, apart from very restricted uses, the elements of spoken language do not enter sign language proper. In fact, this is what we expected ourselves but did not find to be true, at least for German deaf people. To begin with, the use of spoken language elements is startlingly pervasive. The signer in our example used 185 word tokens within two and one half minutes, which is considerable, even though in ordinary speaking there may be some 300 to 500 word tokens in the same time. You may expect that we have been trying to determine whether there are German deaf people who do not use spoken language elements in communicating with other deaf people, and whether our observations were owing to what is known as "sign language diglossia." So far, the result is negative. We are quite convinced that the conversation we have described is typical of GSL usage.

The notion of GSL as an independent language is a fairly new one. As much pride as German deaf people may have taken in the use of their manual signs, there does not seem to be any historical perception of signing as a language. In fact, the lack of awareness of sign language norms creates great problems for linguistic research. Asking a deaf person to decide whether a given utterance is correct in terms of GSL usage or not is anything but a straightforward affair. There is, on the other hand, a great deal of evidence that German deaf people regard their signing as related to spoken German. The acting president of the German Deaf Association recently disclaimed the status of German deaf people as a linguistic minority on the grounds that GSL—which he clearly distinguishes from signed German—is based upon spoken German.

We conducted a series of interviews with a number of deaf people in Germany in which we tried to press this point. There was every reason to believe that our informants considered the use of speaking as natural, even in informal and intimate interaction with other deaf people. Anecdotally, it might be added that when the film *Children of a Lesser God* was shown in Germany, some deaf people seemed to react negatively to the heroine's refusal to speak. On closer inspection, such criticism seemed to refer not so much to the character Sarah's refusal to use her voice, but to the fact that her signing was not accompanied by any mouthing!

The circumstantial evidence discussed so far should induce us to take mouthing, as displayed in the natural communication of German deaf people, seriously. The use of spoken language elements should not be neglected, and instead of searching for "pure sign," we should try to understand why mouthing is so consistently used. To us, this is a question of function: If it can be shown that the use of spoken words is functional for signed communication, this seems to provide sufficient explanation for their occurrence. In order to show in what way mouthing can become linguistically functional within signed utterances and discourse, we need to take a look at *perception* generally and *linguistic perception* in particular.

Vision does not consist simply of seeing shapes and colors, and hearing—if you can hear—does not consist simply of perceiving sounds and noises. You may see a dog jumping over a fence, a hammer lying in a tool box, or an old friend smiling at you. You may hear the dog barking, the hammer rattling against the sides of the tool box, or your friend laughing. Perceptions such as these have traditionally been conceived of as no more than a sort of imprint that occurs passively in reaction to input from the senses. Because no conscious effort is involved in perceiving the world through these senses, this view seems to be in accord with a commonly held notion of perception.

And yet, there is strong evidence that perception is not just a passive reaction. Most psychologists today seem to agree that perception involves interpretative processes: In perceiving the world we make sense of it. We use our knowledge to "read" the sensory signals available. In discussing what he calls "the vast and still largely mysterious jumps between the sensation and the perception of an object," psychologist Richard L. Gregory (1987) speaks of "intelligent leaps of the mind, which may land on error." Indeed, your perceptual assumptions may be wrong: As it turns out, it wasn't a dog, it wasn't a hammer, and it wasn't your old friend you were seeing.

One indication that perception is an intelligent activity involving "making sense" is the effect contextual information may have on how we perceive the world. Context is a key notion for devising realistic accounts of perception. Under ordinary conditions, effects of contextual information are not normally apparent. But think of a lion crossing a street in Washington, D.C.—you might well walk on thinking that you had seen a dog because that would be a frequent and much more understandable sight. Conversely, if you saw a dog in a cage in the zoo next to the elephants, you might *not* think it was a dog, because your mind would not naturally leap to that interpretation. Furthermore, you may not be able to recognize a tool unless you see it being put to appropriate use. You may not recognize acquaintances outside the context in which you met them. Indeed, you may not immediately recognize your boss when you see him on the beach instead of in the office. Active use of context seems to be of particular relevance if there is some kind of ambiguity or lack of clarity involved: If you are puzzled by what your senses tell you, you immediately start looking for contextual clues in an effort to understand.

We think it important to keep fundamental issues like these in mind when we turn to *linguistic* perception. As far as oral language is concerned, linguistic perception largely boils down to *word recognition*. Again, it seems inadequate to conceive of word recognition as a merely passive process. The difficulties encountered in devising speech recognition by machines provide evidence for just that point. If you can hear, nothing seems easier than recognizing the words someone speaks in your language. However, a foreigner with little experience in English will rely heavily on contextual clues in his effort to identify words said to him, as will a native speaker of a spoken language if he tries to understand the words of a song or listens to a radio program when the reception is blurred. The *written* word surely seems self-explanatory. But think of a handwritten letter: What seems to happen when you try to decipher an unfamiliar handwriting is that you use contextual information in order to decide upon the words used in the letter.

To us, all this points to the fact that *speechreading* as a way of perceiving spoken language is not, as it is usually seen, so fundamentally different from other forms of linguistic perception. The basic processes involved seem very similar. What *is* different is that the perceptual difficulty is greatly increased. What in listening to or reading language is the exception becomes a general condition in the case of speechreading. Anyone with experience in speechreading knows the great importance of contextual information: Familiarity with a speaker and topic, knowing what is going to happen in a given situation, and any kind of information that has a bearing on what someone might say may increase the chances of successful speechreading. This is so because contextual information provides clues for making sense of the ambiguous movements of the mouth and tongue. Contextual information, so to speak, delineates a cognitive area that has to be searched for a suitable reading of the sensory signals available. Speechreading is a highly problematic form of linguistic perception. It should be noted, though, that the reliance on contextual information it involves is not so unusual as it may seem at first glance.

Let us draw the general observations on perception and the more particular remarks on different forms of linguistic perception together in an attempt to explain the aspect of sign language use we are concerned with here. So far, we have not differentiated between the various types of context (linguistic context, situational context, expectations and assumptions of the participants, etc.), and we have been mainly concerned with sequential context—things that are given prior to the object, event, or word perceived.

Indeed, any such information can be relevant to speechreading, which is nothing but a rapid series of interpretations. But since speechreading is a form of *visual* perception, contextual information in this case may take a very specific form, and this is what we want to draw attention to. As is well known, although not always fully appreciated, the notion of *simultaneity* is central for visual perception. Different things can be seen more or less simultaneously. In one glance out of a window you may instantly recognize cars, people, trees, houses, and many other things. What we would like to point out is that in the simultaneous perception of more than one object, one of the objects perceived may provide contextual information that allows you to identify another object. The first object thus functions as a *simultaneous contextual cue* for the second object. Very general cognitive mechanisms are involved here, and yet to us this seems of immediate relevance for understanding the relationship between signs and words in signed utterances.

Let us look at a simple example:

What you see is a particular shape, a triangle. This is not quite what we intend this figure to be, however. We will therefore give you a contextual clue:

There is probably little difficulty now in seeing the shape as a tent. What you are seeing is a tree on the left and a tent on the right, and you see a tent because we have added a tree. The tree thus functions as a contextual cue for seeing the object on the right as a tent.

In the above example, a spatial relationship between the objects seems to be involved, the contextual cue of the tree prompting our minds to interpret the triangle as part of a scene. The contextual cue provided by a juxtaposed object, however, is not always spatial, or scenic. Indeed, completely different categories of objects can nevertheless provide contextual cues important for interpretation. Let us turn to another example: bk

You will probably not know what to make of this, even if you are told that this is supposed to be English. So, let us add a piece of contextual information: bk

A moment's thought may have given you the idea that what you see here has something to do with the English word "book." If this did not occur to you, the suggestion should nevertheless make sense to you. It should be fairly easy to look at these two objects and think, "Book, why not?" What we would like to suggest is that what you see here is a fairly good model for how the relationship between signs and mouthed words in signed utterances works. The object on the left can be regarded as standing for a manual sign, the object on the right, the two letters, can be seen as representing the articulatory movements you see if someone mouths a word.

In examining the implications of our model we should distinguish between two aspects: We are dealing with two separate objects perceived simultaneously that engage in a *functional* relationship and at the same time are related *semantically*.

Let us take the *functional* relationship first. We have introduced the rectangle as a contextual cue for the object on the right. What we want to say, basically, is that whenever words are mouthed in signed utterances, the accompanying sign serves as a contextual cue for the word. The addition of this contextual cue provides a systematic solution to perceptual problems encountered in speechreading. The basic reason for defining the relationship in this way is that, of the two objects, signs are more salient and far more accessible than words seen as articulatory movements. But this is not the whole story. You may ask, "How do we recognize what the rectangle is all about or, for that matter, that a certain movement of the hand is a particular sign?" Apart from any consideration of the formal properties of signs and their perception, we should notice two things:

1. The sort of simultaneous perception we are talking about is usually set within a sequential context. There may be other clues (for example, we may have been talking about the decline of literacy). There may even be further simultaneous clues from nonmanual units of signing (for example, a physical portrayal of the action of reading).
2. There may well be some reciprocity involved in the process of simultaneously perceiving a rectangle and letters, or sign and word. In this sense, the two sides may contextualize each other: The rectangle gives a clue for making sense of "bk," just as "bk" gives a clue for making sense of the rectangle. Without going into the details of this interactive process, one should note the overall effect: It is one of stability of perception. We think this is of great importance. Once you get used to the general procedure, a combination of rectangle and "bk" serves its purpose as well as a string of letters such as "b-o-o-k" does, although the two function differently. As far as signs and words are concerned, pragmatic factors may indeed make the use of spoken words redundant in certain contexts, but, all in all, both sides seem to stabilize each other in such a way that their combined use is strongly preferred.

Let us now turn to the *semantic* relationship between the two objects. It is important to note that we have been talking about functional relationships between *independent* objects. Our starting point was that we are dealing with different types of meaningful units. On the other hand, the functional relationship suggested presupposes some sort of positive semantic relationship. The combination of rectangle and "bk" makes sense because you instantly relate the rectangular shape to what a book normally looks like. In that case, a triangle or a circle would not do as a contextual cue. Similarly, for signs to contextualize words there must be some readily identifiable relationship between the meanings of the two. It is probably fair to say that in many cases of a simultaneous occurrence of sign and word, what we get is a specific and strong semantic relationship, namely one of semantic identity.

If someone makes a sign for "car," for instance, and at the same time speaks the word "car," there is no reason to assume that sign and word have different meanings. And yet, it is important to maintain that we are dealing with two separately meaningful units. The basic reason is this: Even if there is a word articulated side-by-side with a sign, the independence of the sign provides the signer with a great resource for semantic elaboration. A sign for "book" may serve as a contextual cue for the spoken word "book," but at the same time, the specific form of the sign may provide further information, for example, about the size of the book or its relative position in space. Similarly, a sign for "give" may contextualize the spoken word "give" and at the same time, via its spatial properties, provide relational information about the objects and people involved in the process of giving.

Finally, the independence of manual and oral units can also be demonstrated by pointing to the less common opposite phenomenon: Sometimes in GSL-signing it is the spoken word that provides semantic elaboration. This is illustrated in our signing example. The signer describes where she was sitting and chatting to her friends. She uses the German sign for "room," but the word she uses simultaneously is "living room." It is unlikely that she considers this piece of information to be irrelevant. Quite simply, she can rely on the fact that, under the given circumstances, those she is addressing will lipread the expression "living room" without her spelling it out in so many signs.

Under the given circumstances must be stressed: We are presupposing conditions normally given in natural signing, that is, a basic form of the word is used and the word is spoken in relative isolation from other words so that its beginning and ending can be easily identified. These conditions are not normally given in signed German, and this may account for many of the problems encountered with this form of communication. This should not obscure the fact, though, that sign language creates conditions in which the use of spoken words *can* become functional. Traditional accounts seem to be based on the idea that signs *represent* words. This simply ignores the specific conditions afforded by the visual modality: Co-occurring signs and words *interact* in their perception.

Let us summarize what we have said so far. While circumstantial evidence points to the role spoken words may play in GSL signing, closer inspection of the perceptual conditions of signed utterances reveals how signs and words interact in the process of understanding of such utterances. The use of mouthed words in a sign language may be linguistically functional because the way signs serve as contextual cues results in perceptually stable combinations of signs and words. This does *not*, on the other hand, reduce signing to some kind of "cued speech." Engaging in functional relationships with spoken words does not stop signs from leading their independent lives.

Recognizing the role of mouthed words adds another facet to understanding sign language without calling into question that it is basically a unique and powerful way of making the most of hands, arms, body, head, and face for communicative purposes. To illustrate this point, let us go back to an excerpt taken from our example of GSL conversation above. The signer has been taken up to her friend's apartment, the friend's girlfriend has been awakened, and then:

> She [the girlfriend] was very excited and got up immediately. I was shown around the rooms and admired them. Pretty rooms, very nice, but then that was enough. We sat down in the living room and were wrapped up in our signing until suddenly we were interrupted by the doorbell ringing, letting me know that I had to stop and go downstairs. I was picked up and taken home.

Figure 1 is a transcript of this passage, showing nonmanual, manual, and oral units. Two basic things may be observed in this segment of videotape: Mouthing occurs, but there is much more to this sequence of signing than just the use of words. We will take up these observations in turn.

As far as mouthing is concerned, silently articulated words are accompanied by signs that function as contextual cues. There is something very important to be noticed in the way mouthed words are used. It will not do to regard this use of German words as an attempt at speaking German. Speaking German implies using German words according to the rules of the structure of spoken or written German. No attempt at adhering to the rules of spoken or written German is made in this case. In fact, no at-

excited ————————————————————————			
(gestured) GET-UP IMMEDIATELY GET-UP GET-UP		INDEX-x PERSON-me	
up immediately up up		onto	
	impressed acknowledging ————————————		
SHOW ROOM	INDEX-x ASTONISHED GOOD ROOM GOOD PRETTY GOOD ROOM		
show room	good room good pretty nice room		
	increasingly intense	frustrated——	
FINISH ENOUGH	SIT SIT ROOM SIGN++ ———	STUCK HEAR	
enough	living-room		
——	resigned		
BELL INFORM-me	(gestured)	INDEX-me DOWN	PICK-UP-me GONE
		must down	pick-up home
affirmation			
(gestured)	(ca. 15 seconds)		

Note. Nonmanual, manual, and oral units are transcribed on separate lines. Vertical and horizontal relationships translate into temporal simultaneity and succession respectively. The top line records nonmanual behavior, using semantic labels to indicate the occurrence of a particular unit (dotted lines indicate temporal extension of a unit). Manual signs are glossed on the middle line ("-x" and "-me" indicate reference points or specific directions; "+" stands for repetition; the double gloss refers to left and right hand respectively). Spoken words that can be identified by speechreading are recorded on the bottom line.

FIGURE 1: Transcript of a signed passage.

tempt at establishing sequential relations between German words is made. In general, what we find in GSL is a very selective use of German words; certain word categories such as articles, conjunctions, and prepositions are rarely used at all. If words are used, they are normally stripped of all those morphosyntactic properties that generally serve to establish syntactic relations in German sentences. One does, in fact, occasionally find certain combinations of words that seem to resemble remnants of German syntactic units (for example, combinations of modal verb and verb, adjective and noun, and verb and noun). But often this resemblance may be coincidental. What we are trying to suggest is that the way isolated German words are used in natural signing cannot be regarded as an instance of inadequate German language use. As of yet, no grammatical rules for the use of German words within GSL utterances have been identified.

Another way of putting this is that German words are used in GSL, but what you see is not German proper. So, let us look at what else there is. Obviously, not all the signs are accompanied by mouthing. There are deictic signs indexing points in space; there are a number of conventional manual and nonmanual units that are never accompanied by spoken words; finally, there are a number of signs that may be accompanied by a word in certain contexts but are not here in this case. Further, you should note how use is being made of the possibilities of the signing space. Directional signs may be used independently of whether or not they are accompanied by words (cf. INFORM-me vs. PICK-UP-me). Actually, the interaction between German words and the specific visual mechanisms of sign language is quite subtle. The signer uses the word "auf," which one would expect to be a preposition comparable to English "on" or "onto." But in fact it is not used as part of a prepositional phrase here. Rather, it is combined with the directional sign PERSON. Rooms are being shown; the sign specifies to whom they are being shown. In GSL, the combination of the word "auf" and the accompanying directional sign seems to be used as a kind of object marker.

These observations lead to the following conclusion: German signers use German words, and insofar as these are part of sign language utterances, they should be considered as a separate type of meaningful unit. Using German words in GSL is basically a *lexical* device. As oral units, words are integrated in the sequential context established by means of the manual and nonmanual units of GSL. Syntactic relations are established by the kind of devices that have been described as grammatical mechanisms within sign language research. What we are dealing with is *not* the consequence of a spontaneous mixing of languages. Rather, GSL is a language in its own right that assimilates spoken language material for its own purposes.

In conclusion, we will outline some of the questions and implications that arise from the kind of approach taken here. First of all, we think that much more empirical work needs to be done on the interaction between manual and oral units in natural sign language use before any reliable conclusions can be reached. If our conclusion is correct, GSL provides the slots into which German words have to fit. The kind of initial observation we have made is that words are used predominantly in referential expressions, although comparatively rarely in predicate expressions. This line of inquiry seems particularly promising to us and is central to our work in Berlin.

Second, there are implications for the lexical description of GSL. Signs are commonly identified and named by German words that are supposed to give an indication of the sign's meaning. This procedure has a curious result: There are many signs with identical forms that seem to have related meanings. What seems to be the case is that one and the same sign can be combined with different—though semantically related—words. It would be preferable to specify whether each sign is normally accompanied by mouthing, and if so, indicate the range of admissible German words. One effect of systematically making use of spoken language word material seems to be that the number of manual signs current in GSL is considerably smaller than is generally supposed.

Third, some words are needed on what is often believed to be the backbone of sign language linguistics, phonemic analyses. Phonemic analyses, as provided by "sign phonology," are powerful descriptive devices, but their value seems to be limited. It is not clear whether what has been developed for manual units can be applied to nonmanual or oral units of sign language. Further, if what has been said here about the perception of sign and word is anywhere near the truth, we should be wary of interpreting descriptive theories as implicit theories of perception. All too often this appears to be done, and to us this does not seem to do justice to the complexity of perceiving sign language—or anything for that matter.

Finally, we have addressed the subject of German Sign Language because it is a language we have researched over the last three years. Whether anything that has been said can be applied to other sign languages remains to be seen. I would urge students of other sign languages, however, to pay attention not only to the way sign language makes language visible through manual and nonmanual elements, but also to how it gives meaning even to those elusive movements of the lips and tongue. Seen in this light, recognizing words in a sign language is yet another tribute to the great creativity and ingenuity of deaf people.

References

Gregory, R. L. 1987. *The Oxford Companion to the Mind.* New York: Oxford University Press. p. 599.

Schermer, T. M. 1985. "Analysis of Natural Discourse of Deaf Adults in the Netherlands: Observations on Dutch Sign Language." In *SLR '83: Proceedings of the Third International Symposium on Sign Language Research*, ed. W. Stokoe and V. Volterra. Silver Spring, MD: Linstok Press and Rome, Italy: Istituto di Psicologia. pp. 281–288.

Schroeder, Odd-Inge. 1985. "A Problem in Phonological Description." In *SLR '83: Proceedings of the Third International Symposium on Sign Language Research*, ed. W. Stokoe and V. Volterra. Silver Spring, MD: Linstok Press and Rome, Italy: Istituto di Psicologia. pp. 194–201.

Sign Language and Deaf Culture in Italy

ANNA FOLCHI

The objective of my work is to compile as comprehensive a collection as possible of Italian signs. However, I am still far from this goal because of the large number of Italian signs. Originally, my purpose was to prepare a dictionary of sign language, but it seems to me now that the planned dictionary could become, rather, an encyclopedia, which would take years of work and research. Currently, my three collaborators and I have already begun research on the first book of signs, which will be entitled *The First 400 Signs to Communicate with Italian Deaf People* (Angelini, Borgioli, Folchi, and Mastromatteo, 1991).

Compiling a book of Italian signs is very difficult, however, because Italy is a country—perhaps one of a very few—where signs may vary considerably from region to region. For our dictionary, we chose the most commonly used signs, the ones most comprehensible to people from all regions of the country.

We have been forced to eliminate many important words from our original list because the signs vary too widely. For example, signs for the days of the week, the months, and colors are different in various regions of the country. The difference in regional signs can be compared with the different dialects used by hearing people in Italy. There are too many differences among the signs used in each Italian region to be able to compile one standard dictionary for everyone. Even in the same town, the signs used by some groups of people are often different from those used by other groups. Signs may depend, for example, on the school where people have studied, or on the deaf club to which they belong.

The Signs in Different Italian Towns

I am Italian, and I live in Florence, where there are about 800 deaf people. Naturally, we have our own signs. I have compared these with the signs of other Italian towns to try to clarify how they differ from ours, and among themselves.

It may be useful to divide Italy into different areas and towns so that we may see the situation more clearly. For these areas and towns, I have information on the difference between the signs used in that area and those used in Florence, and on other defining features or peculiarities of their signs.

Northern Italy

Turin—The signs here are both somewhat similar and somewhat different from the ones we use in Florence, but we can understand them. Only the signs for MOTHER and FATHER are very different; these two signs are identical to the ones used in Trieste, although it is not clear why.

Genova—The signs are rather comprehensible to us. However, a school for deaf students in Genova taught its own particular manual alphabet.

Milan—In general, people from Florence can understand these signs. But I have also noticed that there is a group of deaf people between the ages of twenty-five and thirty who have a very unique way to communicate. For some words, they even use numbers as synonyms. Perhaps this habit originates from their school days, when they didn't want hearing adults—for example, teaching assistants who knew only signed Italian—to understand them. Another explanation could be the fact that Milan, like Turin, is a city that receives emigrants from the South, and these "signed numbers" may originate from the lottery there; for example, seventy-five equals "liar," and twenty-three equals "stupid."

Trieste—The signs are completely different and, for us, more dificult to understand than other groups of Italian signs. Maybe this is owing to the influence of the Yugoslavian or French culture.

Padua—The only residential high school for deaf students is located here. The signs used are quite mixed because the deaf students come from various locations and are not greatly influenced by local signs. Primarily they use their own signs, mixed with those used in the school, apparently without any communication problems. However, when these students return to their hometowns during holidays, they often use the signs of the school to communicate with the deaf people of their own region, perhaps to show that they can use both languages.

Central Italy

Bologna—Here almost everyone uses the signs of the Gualandi Residential School, which has its main campus in this city; but the signs used by adult deaf people seem to be more "polished."

Florence—This city, where I live, has two deaf clubs that originated from two different residential schools: Gualandi School and the National Residential School for the Deaf. These two groups of deaf people use somewhat different signs. The first group is composed of elderly people, while the second group consists of young people who have a wide knowledge of different signs.

Siena—The deaf people in this town who attended the famous Pendola Residential School there still use the signs from their school days.

Rome—The capital of Italy and a large city, Rome has three famous residential schools for deaf students and many meeting places and deaf clubs. A variety of different signs are used there. In fact, I would call Rome the "Tower of Babel." But deaf people understand each other, and they are even understood by deaf people from other towns.

Southern Italy

Naples/Palermo—People in the South, both deaf and hearing, have the habit of using many gestures; a hearing person can quite easily be mistaken for a deaf one. The deaf people from the South use signs more frequently, and they live much better than those from the North because they don't have as much difficulty communicating with the hearing people. These signs and gestures are numerous and varied, perhaps owing to the different conquests by the Spanish or the Arabs. Because these conquerors used languages other than Italian, they may have found that signs and gestures were the best means of communication, and they continue to use this means today.

The southern signs are more expressive than those from the North, and for me they are often inexplicable. There are signs that only deaf people can understand—"signs without words"—and it is impossible to translate them into corresponding words in Italian. Translating them into spoken Italian would require many words and sentences.

Sardinia—Like Sicily, Sardinia is an island, but here deaf people don't have unique signs, and the signs aren't connected to the regional culture as are other typically southern signs. Up until about the age of forty-five, most adults use the signs of the schools they attended on the Italian peninsula, in places such as Rome, Padua, and Turin.

Knowledge and Use of Signs

I would like now to examine deaf people's knowledge of signs. Our research indicates that deaf people can be divided into three groups. The first group is deaf people who know only the signs learned during their early years. These are people whose experiences and interactions with people from different regions have been limited, and they often refuse to understand different signs. Some of them are very old, and others are not quite so old. Once they finish school, they return to their own towns or small villages and keep using the same signs. They have never had the possibility of moving; they have limited friendships and acquaintances.

The second group is deaf people who know and use the signs taken from the deaf clubs they attend, perhaps forgetting those they learned in school. This group includes deaf people who are not too old, or even young people who have a broader range of experience than those from the first group. They can understand different signs used by other signers, and they even ask, "What is it?" "Why do you say so?" "Why do you do this?" when they notice a sign they don't now.

The third group is composed primarily of younger deaf people who use their own signs but know other signs different from their own. These are "modern" people, and their numbers are growing. They can communicate with each other even if they often use different signs, perhaps even without realizing that the other person is using a different sign. They are flexible and versatile.

After having distinguished these three groups, I wish now to talk about the first group in greater detail. The signs used by the older deaf people are particularly interesting, but unfortunately they are disappearing. These signs are very broad and not very refined, but they are always beautiful. Many of the signs are intimately connected to the social and cultural context of the past generation, which was very different from the present one.

Considering together the first and the second group, let us examine the school environment, particularly one residential school, Istituto Gualandi (Gualandi School), which has branches in different Italian towns. The signs used in the branches are rather similar, for the most part, because the educators of the Gualandi School—nuns and priests who don't have a fixed residence—are often transferred from one residential school to another, and they use a group of similar signs.

But there is one curious detail: The signs used by women are different from those used by men. For example, at the Gualandi Residential School in Bologna, in the period when my parents and my aunt were children (about 1930), there were two departments within the same building, divided by a wall—one for girls and one for boys. It was a religious Catholic school, and during that very rigid period, even though the nuns and priests met and communicated with each other, boys and girls never saw each other.

So even though the school was the same, "male" and "female" signs were totally different, with not even one similar sign. In spite of this difference, my father and his sister never encountered many difficulties during the summer holidays, because they exchanged their different signs.

Let us now examine two other details that concern the change of signs over time. The old signs and the new ones look completely different at first, but if we observe them more closely, we can see that some are really the same signs, with forms that have changed slightly over the years. For example, the old sign PADUA was done in a very wide and heavy way, and little by little it has become more limited and lighter, or, we might say, more fluent.

The signs also depend on the very life experiences of the people who use them, which change over time. This is also true for the culture they express. For example, the old people could talk very well about the time of war and fascism, while today young people discuss the same topics in a simplified manner. In contrast, young people talk very well about rock music or UFOs, while older deaf people talk about these topics in a much more limited way because they are indifferent to this type of modern culture.

Differences in Signs in Italy

About 80 percent of the signs in any given region of Italy are different from the signs in other areas of the country. I have noticed that, in general, the signs that are similar often refer to things that are very common. A certain sign in different regions may be made in different locations but with the same hand configuration, or the location may be the same but the hand configuration changes.

To generalize about signs in different areas, I can say that facial expression and eye position are almost the same. Movements are usually—but not always—very similar. Nouns are often the same. Some adjectives are similar, while others are different. Verbs are generally very similar, but differences can be found, depending upon the specific verb.

Concrete signs are very easy to understand, even when they are different, but abstract signs are very difficult to understand if they are different. However, sometimes we can understand them if they are accompanied by facial expressions. Numbers are similar, especially those from one to ten, but they differ from the number eleven on. However, they are usually comprehensible.

I would like to mention another peculiarity concerning the numbers of the Pendola Residential School in Siena. The elderly deaf people who attended the school—and even some young people—use the numbers in a unique way. People from other regions always sign numbers in neutral space, even if the signs are different, while the numbers of the group in Siena are made in contact with the face and the thorax.

The sign NUMBERS is more or less similar throughout Italy; the only real variation I have found is in Turin, where the sign for NUMBERS resembles the sign TO DREAM; I think this is related to the lottery game, and so to dreams.

The signs for the days of the week are generally all different, with a few exceptions: Sometimes we find the same sign for Monday, made with the hand configuration "L" for the first letter of the Italian word Monday. Something similar is also noted in the sign SUNDAY, which is made with the hand configuration D (Old dactylology), for the first letter of the Italian word. Almost all the other signs for the days of the week differ from region to region. Some signs for days of the week, which related each day to a different chore, were developed to help small children remember the days of the week in their proper order.

It is interesting to note that in Rome the sign SATURDAY is made with the hand configuration "horns" contacting the upper left side of the chest. It is thought that the use of this sign is related to the sign for JEW, because in Rome there is a large Jewish community and their Sabbath is on Saturday. In other towns, people do not normally know the meaning of this sign, which is connected to the Roman culture.

The signs for the months are very complicated and all different throughout the country, but some are comprehensible because of the particular symbology of some months. I will give you a few examples.

February is the time of carnivals. The signs for this month are different, but they are always connected to the idea of the mask. March symbolizes spring, and May is symbolic of the mother of Jesus for religious people. June is connected to the growth of wheat, or the period of final exams in school. August is connected to the sweat owing to the heat; September is the grape harvest; December is the month of Christmas—the birth of Baby Jesus or the Christmas tree.

Even for the colors, the signs are very different, except for RED, the most common color sign. Even if the orientation and the hand configuration are often different, the location used for the sign RED is always the same—around the mouth. Similar observations can be made for the sign WHITE, a symbol of purity and splendor, or for the sign BLACK, where the dark complexion of the skin or the chimney-sweep is recalled. Throughout Italy, the signs for the other colors are completely different region by region.

Sometimes even the signs that refer to the most common objects and concepts may be different. For example, almost everyone uses a similar sign for HOUSE that resembles the shape of the roof, but there are two other very particular signs. The sign used in Rome may be related to knocking at the door. The sign used in Palermo may be related to the flies that love to stay inside the house. These insects are more numerous in the southern regions, but it is important to specify that it is a very ancient sign. Perhaps, long ago, children said, "I go to the place where there are lots of flies" instead of "I'm going home."

These are just a few examples of differences in signs. In Italy there are many signs that look the same but have different meanings in different towns. To avoid misunderstanding, these signs must always be accompanied by lipreading. Some examples are CLOWN/HOMOSEXUAL (Florence and Rome); and SICK/ROME (Trieste and Rome).

In addition, the same hand configuration may represent a negative aspect in many different signs. An example is the "horns" hand configuration. Some signs that use this hand configuration and that always have a negative connotation are HORNS, DEVIL, HELL, TO QUARREL, JOKE, TEMPTATION, and SNAIL (slow). This handshape has the same negative meaning even in gestures of hearing people, as in the sign for cuckold and evil eye. The most famous hand configuration in the world is I LOVE YOU, but for us Italian people this is not good because even if there is one more finger, it is similar to the negative hand configuration for "horns."

Conclusion

To conclude, I would like to tell you that I realize the Italian situation is really chaotic, but it is wonderful, and I can assure you that I am very proud of it. However, it is a big problem for foreigners. If you really want to learn our sign language, I would advise you to stay there for ten years at least!

But don't be alarmed. You can learn to communicate quickly with the hearing people, whose gestures are all the same, from North to South.

References

Angelini, N., R. Borgioli, A. Folchi, and M. Mastromatteo. 1991. *I Primi 400 Segni (The First 400 Signs to Communicate with Italian Deaf People)*. Florence, Italy: La Nuova Italia Editrice.

Name Signs in Swedish Sign Language: Their Formation and Use

T O M A S   H E D B E R G

This is a report on a project that began while I was working on another project with a broader focus. That project, called "Documentation of Old and Regional Signs and the History of the Deaf," was financed by the Swedish National Association of the Deaf and its Department of Sign Language. The objective was to document old and regional signs by videotaping interviews with deaf senior citizens, who were asked to relate memories of their childhood, school days, working life, activities in the deaf club, and so on.

In addition to this work, I was interested in name signs and was therefore curious to see what my informants' name signs were. I also began to make notes of name signs I encountered.

Name signs are signs for the proper names of individuals. Often they are derived from certain characteristics of a person.

After a while, I noticed that there seemed to be different types of name signs. I became interested in finding out the origin of name signs, how they are created, and their use. Even later I noticed that certain types of name signs and their function change with time.

Only a few papers have been published on this subject. Nationally we have Fondelius (1916) and Österberg (1916). Internationally there is Supalla (1985).

The name signs of people of earlier generations are mainly known by elderly people. Unfortunately, these signs are gradually lost and cannot survive from generation to generation unless they are documented in some way, either by means of video recordings or with a special notation system.

The aim of this presentation is partly to account for the origin and use of name signs and partly to describe a classification system for name signs.

So far, I have documented 3,114 name signs for a total of 2,671 individuals. The difference between the number of people and the number of name signs (443) is owing to the fact that one person may have two or more variations of a name sign, or two or more completely different name signs.

Translated into English by Anna-Lena Nilsson.

How Name Signs Are Acquired

Name signs can be said to form a part of our culture. The tradition of deaf people giving name signs to each other has been used for generations, and is still in use.

In the past, when deaf children in schools for deaf students wanted to say something about a friend or teacher but did not know his or her name, they described the characteristics of that person with a sign, perhaps relating to clothing or behavior. Gradually, as the same description was repeatedly used for a person, an established sign developed.

At some schools, older pupils—"sponsors"—took care of the beginners. They told them what to do and how to do it, for example, to use their personal towels and toothbrushes, make their beds, and polish their shoes. The beginners also had to memorize their school admittance number because clothes and shoes were marked with this number. The sponsors also used to "baptize" newcomers in sign language. One little boy with a blue and white sailor suit was given the name sign BLUE/THREE-FINGERS-ON-THE-UPPER-ARM-MOVING-IN-A-V-SHAPE. In this manner, new pupils were given their name signs.

Earlier Literature

As I mentioned earlier, there is not a great deal of material published on name signs. The oldest documents on name signs are a passage in a book *Teckenspraket* (Österberg 1916),[1] and an article in the magazine *Tidning för dövstumma* (Fondelius, 1916), which is also printed in the book *Kontakt* (Nordhelm, 1972, pp. 53–55).

In his article, Gunnar Fondelius says:

> Among the deaf and dumb, given names and family names are rarely used when referring to a person who is deaf and dumb. These names would have to be fingerspelled by using the manual alphabet, which is too slow, and often they do not know the person's Christian name. So much more are the sign language names remembered. Pupils at our schools for the deaf are given a name in sign language as soon as they enter school, derived from some characteristic in their appearance, dress, manner, or something similar. This name sign is then kept for the rest of the student's life. (Fondelius, 1916)

Name Signs Today and Yesterday

It is not known how long name signs have existed. They may have existed since before the nineteenth century, because if there were many deaf members of a family, it is reasonable to believe that they used name signs for themselves, their relatives, and neighbors. My brother Ulf and I created signs for our relatives and neighbors before we entered the school for deaf students.

The oldest name signs in my collection are the signs for Stina Ryholm, Per Aron Borg, and Albert Berg. They were described to me by Frida Söderberg,[2] °ʃˆ⁴ who was born in 1898 in Ödeshög. She told me that she attended the Manilla School for the Deaf in Stockholm between 1906 and 1914. When she caught diphtheria, she was taken to

---

1 If not otherwise stated, the people mentioned are deaf.
2 Transcriptions according to Brita Bergman's "Transcription System . . ." (1982).

the sickroom on the top floor. There she met an elderly deaf woman who lived opposite the sickroom. Her name was Stina Ryholm (1822–1912).

Stina Ryholm told Frida Söderberg about her life and her memories of her school days. Her first teachers were the founder of the Manilla School for the Deaf, Per Aron Borg (1771–1839, hearing) and his son Ossian Borg (hearing). When she finished school, she was allowed to stay on and work as a nursing assistant and kitchen maid until she retired. After her retirement, she was allowed to keep her room at the school. Stina Ryholm was known among deaf people because she was one of the last pupils to attend Manhem outside of the Manilla School for the Deaf.

During our conversations, Frida Söderberg showed me the name signs of Per Aron Borg and Stina Ryholm, and also of Albert Berg (1832–1916). Berg, vice president of the local deaf club in Stockholm for many years, also was known as a marine painter.

Stina Ryholm: ⌒ ⅄⌃⋮   Per Aron Borg: ₐΩ⌃•⋮   Albert Berg: ⌒˙⌠⌃•⋮

I recently met a teacher from the Manilla School for the deaf who told me that a couple of years ago pupils had used initialized signs for their given names, or increasingly fingerspelled the whole name. This was also true for other schools for deaf students. A "D" would then represent Daniel or Daniela, something that can cause confusion and does not work well. The older types of name signs, derived from ways of dressing or with a color sign as the initial sign in a compound, seemed to be gradually disappearing. The teacher was of the opinion that it would be good if the old type of signs could be re-introduced in our culture. The same teacher later told me that initialized signs were no longer used among pupils in the first grade at the Manilla School for the Deaf. Their name signs are derived from their appearance or manner. This is good news!

How Do You Ask for a Person's Name Sign?

When you ask a member of the group of people who use sign language, WHAT NAME INDEX-f? (What's your name?) the usual reply is to fingerspell one's given name. There is almost always a follow-up question: WHAT POSS.-f SIGN? (What's your sign?). The reply then is to show one's name sign.

When you introduce yourself, you sign INDEX-c NAME (My name is . . . .) and fingerspell your given name. Then you show your name sign. The order also can be reversed.

The Etymology of Signs

Etymology is "the theory about original meanings of words, which may be quite different from the meaning that the word has today" (Nilsson, 1977).

Looking into this area, I had to find the origins of name signs. The only means I had of doing so was to ask individuals how they got their name signs. Usually, they knew exactly why they were given their name signs.

Most of the 3,114 name signs in my material have an arbitrary shape. For example, it is impossible to guess the origin of the name sign of the nurse, Signe Lagerstedt (hearing), because there is no visible connection between the shape of the sign and its original referent. Her name sign is performed like this: The flat hand with the thumb touching the palm is in contact with the forehead, is twisted fully, and then touches the forehead again. It is not possible to guess the motivation of the sign immediately, but it is imaginable that it has something to do with hairstyle or headgear, such as a lock of hair or a hat with the brim turned up. According to my information, this name sign can be derived from a lock of hair.

Classes of Name Signs

I will here present a classification of name signs. The classification system is based on the motivation of the sign form. In many cases name signs are motivated in relation to the referent. Starting from this fact, I will divide the signs into different groups, depending on the characteristics of the referent from which they are derived. Different characteristics of the referent may be focused on appearance, mannerisms, resemblance, occupation, or place of origin. They also can be based on school admittance number or name.

It is not possible to see the meaning of these name signs until you have understood their origin. The classification is based on 1,108 of the 3,114 name signs. They are the ones for which I have been given an etymological explanation by my informaants. So far I have been able to define six different classes of name signs. They are based on appearance, mannerisms, resemblance, and social groups, but also are influenced by name, initials, Swedish words, and admittance number.

I have chosen a few examples from the 1,108 name signs, which I will present later. They have been chosen because they are good, clear examples of the various classes, and also because people who are alive today gave their consent for me to use their name signs in this presentation.

The following are some of the different classes of name signs:

Appearance

This type of name sign constitutes a comparatively large part of the group I compiled. They are derived from prominent, visible characteristics of a person. There are two subgroups: one relating to physical characteristics and one relating to clothing.

Physical Characteristics. In this subgroup, signs relating to prominent physical features of the face or body are found, such as snub nose, big front teeth, or an amputated arm. Bror Dahlberg had blue eyes, which gave him the sign for BLUE, followed by shaking the index finger sideways by the right eye.

Another example is the name sign for Stina Johansson, who has a birthmark on one cheek. Her name sign is, therefore, the sign for BROWN, followed by touching the cheek with the thumb and index finger touching each other, and the rest of the fingers are closed.

Signs for hairstyle also are assigned to this subgroup. There are actually quite a few signs related to hairstyle in my material. So far I have found more than forty. I would like to mention one, referring to a teacher at the Manilla School for the deaf named Rut Brinkman (hearing). She had her hair in a bun at the nape of her neck, something that resulted in the following name sign: The flat hand is held at the nape of the neck, the turned fully around. This name sign also has come to mean "library" at the school because Rut Brinkman was in charge of the library at the Manilla School for the Deaf.

Clothing. The second subgroup consists of signs related to clothes and other items worn by the person. Items described may include glasses, headgear, crutches, hearing aid, or earrings. This subgroup of name signs is also comparatively large.

Karl Sandström, for example, had a sailor suit with a tie and received this name sign: The flat hand is moved down on the chest and at the same time the handshape changes into an "O" which is then moved back up again. The fingers are then immediately spread and the hand moved downward.

Another name sign can be derived from the fact that the person in question had a bow in her plaits. The name sign is performed like this: The index finger, middle finger, and thumb are bent toward each other and held to the right side of the neck. They are then moved forward and spread. The movement is repeated on the left side. The name sign belongs to Sonja Forsell.

Mannerisms

This class consists of name signs denoting a recurring mannerism or some other act frequently performed by the person. It is a fairly large group of signs.

A typical example of this type of sign is performed like this: The right forearm is rested on the left forearm, and both arms are moved with a swinging up-and-down movement. This name sign belongs to Anette Rosing and was derived from the fact that she used to hold her arms folded during her first years in the school for deaf students.

Signe Lampa, nursery school teacher at the Vänersborg School for the Deaf (hearing), used to stand in front of the children, who were eating at long tables, and say grace before dinner in the canteen every day. Her name sign is therefore the sign for PRAYER moved around a bit.

Another kind of name sign consists of a sign frequently used by the person in question. Kjell Hovlin has such a name sign: Both flat hands are hooked together at the web between the thumb and the index finger. This is a regional variant (from the North) of the sign AND, which he uses frequently, followed by a pause, when he is going to say something.

Resemblance

Only a few of the signs in my material have been assigned to this class, which has two subgroups.

Appearance. This subgroup of name signs focuses on how a person looks, and this, in turn, is compared with something. In other words, if a person looks like something, the sign for that thing is then used as the name sign. Ida Lundvik (hearing) was actually as small and thin as a pinkie. Her name sign is therefore the right index finger and thumb held around the left pinkie and moved up and down.

Another person was given the sign for SHEEP: The right index finger and middle finger are moved from the wrist toward the shoulder of the left arm, at the same time making cutting movements. It is the name sign of Rune Norberg, motivated by the fact that his hair looks like wool.

Manner. The second subgroup consists of signs referring to how people do something, which in turn is compared to something else. Actions may be compared to something that an animal does, for example.

The name sign of Ove Fransson is an excellent example of this: A hand held in the shape of a "C" touches the eye a couple of times. The sign means "monkey" and is an old regional sign formerly used in the province of Småland. The sign was assigned to Ove Fransson for his skill in climbing trees, just like a monkey.

Social Group

There are many signs assigned to this group, all of which have something to do with social status, and it consists of four subgroups.

Occupation. These name signs focus on the occupation of a person. So far I have found signs for a number of occupations: shoemaker, tailor, carpenter, consultant, clergyman, painter, typographer, etc. In this case they also function as name signs. August Ljungkvist was a shoemaker and was given the sign SHOEMAKER, but with the mouth pattern "August." Name signs in this group can also refer to where a person worked. Elisabeth Johansson worked at Tidaholms Tändsticksfabrik (match factory) and her name sign was therefore MATCH, with the mouth pattern "Elisabeth."

Geographic Origin. In this second subgroup, signs focus on where a person comes from—a country, a province, a city, etc. Jörgen Christensen came from Denmark. His name sign was DENMARK with the mouth pattern "Jorgen."

Family Background. The third subgroup consists of name signs related to the background of the family and its social status. The signs often refer to the occupation of a person's parents. The name sign of Per Nordheim is a good example of this. He was the son of an officer and was therefore given the name sign OFFICER.

Inherited Name Signs. In the fourth subgroup, name signs derived from kinship are found. A person can inherit the name sign of a relative, such as a sister, brother, parent, or spouse. These name signs can be said to be "inherited name signs." One good example of this is the name sign of Sigurd Åkerström. It is performed like this: The right index finger is held at the left shoulder, then moved down in a curve toward the elbow and at the same time turned slightly. This was also the name sign of his mother.

Numbers

Few of the name signs in my material fit into this classification. There are a number of name signs, used mainly in the south of Sweden, that are based on an individual's admittance number to the school for deaf students. The shape of the name sign is therefore influenced by signs for numbers. The name sign of Astrid Fejr was 923. First the sign for nine is performed—all fingers except the thumb are held downward, then moved quickly upward and the handshape changed into index finger and middle finger extended (2); the ring finger is immediately added (3). The mouth pattern is "Astrid," not the numbers in question.

Name

This class of name sign focuses on the name of a person. It is quite a large group of signs, which can be divided into four subgroups.

Signs for Names. The name signs of this subgroup are derived from a person's given name or family name. The name sign is influenced by an already existing sign for a name, providing that a sign for that particular name exists, of course. In this case one sign represents a specific name. There is, for example, a sign for the given name Ingvar: A spread hand with all fingers slightly bent touches the cheek a couple of times. Birgitta is another name that has an established sign: A bent index finger and middle finger touch the cheek a couple of times. Examples of other names in this subgroup are Anders, Erik, and Svea.

Initialized Signs. The signs of this second subgroup are also derived from a person's name, but in this case an abbreviation of the given name or family name. The signs are called initialized signs. For given names it is common to shake the handshape of the letter in the manual alphabet that corresponds to the first letter of the name. The name sign of Kerstin Olsson is a K that is shaken.

Sam Supalla mentions in his paper (1985) that initialized signs also can be performed on various parts of the body and on the face. Initialized name signs are predominant in American Sign Language, but there are only a few in Swedish Sign Language. I only have three in my material. In Sweden, initialized signs performed in the neutral space in front of the signer's body are more common.

Complete Word Similarity. This subgroup is also based on a person's name, but in this case the name sign is influenced by a Swedish word. A person named Björn (meaning bear) may receive the name sign BEAR. The name sign then looks exactly like the sign for the corresponding, homonymous common name.

Partial Word Similarity. The name signs of the fourth subgroup are also derived from a person's name, but in this case the likeness is not complete. The name sign for a person whose family name is Franklin, for example, can be derived from a similar word such as Frankrike (meaning France). Only partial word similarity accounts for these name signs.

Combinations of Name Signs

Some name signs are combinations of two classes of name signs. There are many compounded name signs of this kind. If there are two people with the same given name, different compounds may be created to avoid mix-ups. For Stig Johansson and Stig Lundahl, the initial sign of the compound is the same. STIG is signed with the index finger touching the right temple, twisted a couple of times. Then the last sign of the compound is added. In Stig Johansson's case, the sign for the name Johansson is performed: a fist with thumb and forefinger touching and extended moves in a circle by the cheek. For Stig Lundahl, his family name is sometimes fingerspelled as a second part of the compound, after the sign STIG, depending on the conversational situation.

Change of Name Signs

A person may, for various reasons, have had two or three different name signs in his or her life. Ebba Söderlund, for example, had her own name sign from her school days: ᴗN⌃ᵒᵗⵛ∩ but lost it after a time when she married Verner Söderlund. Through her marriage, she acquired a new name sign, that of her husband: ⌡J⌡⌽/ꝻⵛH�⵮ with the addition of the sign WIFE to form a compound. It is not quite clear why she lost her own name sign; one possibility is that her husband was more well known in the deaf community.

Another example is that of Christina Johansson. When she moved to Stockholm, she had to change her old name sign for a new one: ⌒Vᶴ⌃ᵒⵜᵒ because the old one was identical with the name sign for Barbro Almquist: Oᴧⵛ�163Jⵛᴧⵛ . They both work at the local deaf club in Stockholm, and it is understandable that they wanted to avoid confusion. Barbro Almquist, because she was a member longer than Christina Johansson, kept her name sign.

Change of Shape in Name Signs

After having worked with my material for a while, I noticed that some signs changed their shape with time. There were many changes in the shape of compounded name signs in particular, and from what I could see, they were exactly the same as the changes in ordinary signs.

In his report on compounded signs in Swedish Sign Language (1982), Lars Wallin mentions signs that today are one sign, but are described as compounds in O. Österberg's *Teckenspråket* (1916). What used to be two signs put together in a compound is today perceived as one sign.

According to Wallin (1982), the handshape of the articulator is changed. The shape of the articulator in the last part of the compound influences the handshape of the initial sign. This description also can be applied to name signs. One good example showing this is the name sign of Gunnar Brahns. His sign can be derived from a blue and white Navy suit. In performing his compounded name sign, the bent index finger of the sign WHITE is assimilated to the shape of the initial sign in the compound, three extended fingers (W).

According to Wallin, the initial sign in a compound may move to a position closer to that of the last part of the compound. This process, too, can be seen in my material, e.g., the older version of the name sign of Karl Flodin: The sign WHITE using the flat hand with the thumb extended, which used to be performed on the right side of the chest, has been moved to the cheek. In other words, in the compound WHITE/PALE: ⟩∧ꜣ⟂ Jꜚ the articulation is concentrated on the cheek. His name sign is motivated by pale cheeks.

As for articulation in name signs, the number of movements is often reduced. If contact is established a number of times in a row or if there is contact in a zig-zag movement, then it is often replaced by a smooth movement. This tendency resembles what Wallin has described regarding reduction in the articulation in Swedish Sign Language (1982). The name sign of Wally Lindberg can be derived from a wine-colored dress with a large white collar and big buttons on two sides. In its older form it is transcribed like this: []ꜛBBꜜꜝ⁘˙˙˙˙. The present form of this name sign no longer has the repeated contact by the chest but is performed like this: []ꜛBBꜜꜝ .

The exchange of one handshape for another also occurs. This is the case in Arthur Carsand's original name sign: ▵Lꜚ˙/ᄇVꜝ⁙ where the index finger is exchanged for a spread hand with a bent middle finger: ▵⋇ꜚ˙/ᄇ⋇ꜝ⁙ Because the middle finger is longer than the index finger, this change makes the sign easier to perform. When there is contact in a sign, it is often the middle finger that establishes such contact, something that can be seen in many signs.

Conclusion

In conclusion, I would like to say that the purpose of my research is also to spread knowledge to both deaf and hearing people about name signs and their different classes. Perhaps name signs for clothes and colors, which are disappearing as the first elements in compounds, could then come into use again. It would also be of interest to compare Swedish name signs to American name signs as well as to name signs in other sign languages with respect to classes, formation, and use.

References

Bergman, B. 1982. *Teckenspråkstranskription.* Forskning om tecken språk nr X. Stockholm: Stockholms Universitet, Institutionem för lingvistik.

Fondelius, G. 1916. "Teckenspråksnamn." *Tidning för dövstumma* nr 8 och 9, sid 36.

Nilsson, S. 1977. Språkliga termer. Bröderna Ekstrands Tryckeri AB, Lund.

Nordheim, P. 1972. *Kontakt:* Avsnittet . "Enöga fick ja av Locken." sid 53–55. (uo)

Österberg, O. 1916. *Teckenspråket.* Alfred Perssons förlag, Uppsala. (Karaktärisering-stecken sid 17 och 80).

Supalla. 1985. *The Arbitrary Name Sign System in American Sign Language.* Unpublished paper.

Wallin, L. 1982. Sammansatta tecken i svenska teckenspråket. Forskning om teckenspråk nr VIII. Stockholm: Stockholms Universitet, Institutionem för lingvistik.

Training Deaf People as British Sign Language Tutors

CLARK DENMARK

The present interest in teaching British Sign Language (BSL) can be traced back to the time when the British Deaf Association (BDA), the national organization of Deaf people in the United Kingdom, established a Communication Skills Project in 1979. One aim of the project was to produce a teaching manual for BSL tutors. A number of meetings and workshops were held during the development of the manual and after its publication, under the direction of Mrs. Dorothy Miles, the Deaf artist and leader who coordinated the project.

The manual's publication, along with sign language research projects at Moray House College, Edinburgh and the University of Bristol, and a twenty-week British Broadcasting Corporation (BBC) TV series, "See Hear," presented in sign, prompted a great demand for more information and materials on teaching sign language. The BDA began receiving an increasing number of inquiries from its Deaf members, asking how they could become sign language tutors.

In 1982 the BBC announced that it would begin broadcasting an introductory sign language series entitled "A Beginner's Guide to British Sign Language." That same year, Lilian Lawson of the BDA conducted a survey to find out what form of sign language was being taught in classes at that time. The survey showed that out of fifty-seven classes that responded, only seven claimed to be teaching BSL; the other fifty were teaching sign in relation to English. The survey also revealed that most of the teachers were predominantly hearing signers or Deaf people with English and speech. The dramatic shift toward British Sign Language that has taken place since the time of that survey is most clearly shown by the fact that many more Deaf people, people for whom BSL is their only or preferred language, are now engaged in teaching sign language.

In August 1984, after a number of unsuccessful attempts to establish a program to train Deaf people as BSL tutors, the BDA initiated the British Sign Language Training Agency (BSLTA) project in conjunction with the Department of Sociology and Social Policy at the University of Durham. The project began in January 1985. Its principal aim was to train Deaf users of BSL to become BSL tutors. Two other important goals were to develop a curriculum for teaching an introductory BSL course through which non-signing hearing and deaf people could be introduced to BSL; and through BSL classes, to contribute to the process of advancing "real" integration between Deaf and hearing

A revised version of this paper, which was originally presented at The Deaf Way, was later presented at the International Congress on Sign Language Research and Application, March 23–25, 1990, in Hamburg. That version has been printed in *Sign Language Research and Application*, edited by Siegmund Prillwitz and Tomas Vollhaber, 1990, Hamburg, Germany: SIGNUM-Press.

people by giving hearing people the opportunity to learn the visual-gestural language of the Deaf community.

Establishing the Project

The BSLTA project could have been established by the BDA within its own organization, but it was felt that it would be more appropriate to locate it within an institution of higher education. At that time, the BDA was already sponsoring work in the Department of Sociology and Social Policy at the University of Durham. A university setting, it was hoped, would enhance the status of BSL, place BSL in the context of other languages being studied and taught at the university level, and provide access to language departments engaged in second language teaching. The course could be accredited by the university, and Deaf people would have access to university certificate-level courses.

Through its university setting, the program could establish links with other universities and colleges engaged in sign language research and teaching. Finally, the establishment of the course in BSL would provide a base for developing and establishing other courses in the fields of sign language and Deaf studies.

In order to establish a training course to enable deaf users of BSL to become tutors of their own language at a foundation level, the following objectives were identified:

1. Develop a curriculum for a foundation-level BSL tutor training course.
2. Establish the course and have it taught in BSL by Deaf staff members of the project team.
3. Devise appropriate examination and assessment procedures for the course.
4. Develop a curriculum for an introductory BSL course to be taught to hearing people (and deaf and hard of hearing people unfamiliar with the language) by tutors trained on the BSL tutor training course.
5. Develop a direct experience teaching method that uses BSL as the language of instruction for the teaching of the introductory BSL course referred to above.
6. Prepare and produce course study materials, including an introductory course syllabus in BSL on videotape and in written English.

Setting up the Training Course

I will now discuss some of the practical problems we encountered in setting up and operating the training course, and how we attempted to solve them. By September 1985, the planning of the curriculum and structure of the course had reached an advanced stage. We invited a number of experienced sign language tutors—all but one of whom were Deaf—to meet with us and share their views on the proposed course curriculum and structure. After four days of discussion, a final course proposal was endorsed. The first training course was held in December 1985. Since then, a total of fifteen courses have been conducted. The project is now known as the British Sign Language Tutor Training Course (Foundation Level). The name was changed in 1987 when the course was granted certificate status by the University of Durham.

In changing the format of the course, we had to consider several factors. Residential course requirements would have to be kept to a minimum because most of the Deaf trainees would be employed and would be unable to get more than three weeks off work, or might have family responsibilities that would not allow them to be away from home for extended periods. Most employed Deaf trainees would have to use their personal leave to enable them to attend the course, or take leave without pay. The cost of the course would have to be kept to a minimum because some people would be attending at their own expense if the local education authority, Deaf club, or charities were unable to sponsor their attendance.

Most Deaf trainees would not be able to travel to and from home every day to attend the residential weeks of the course. (It was intended that students would be drawn from all parts of the United Kingdom.) In addition, their competence in English would probably be insufficient to enable them to undertake a course based on written English. Most Deaf trainees would not previously have taken any form of examination, and they would not have undertaken any form of further education since they left school.

With these considerations in mind, we adopted a format where BSL would be the language of instruction, and the course would be taught by the Deaf members of the project team. During the first two years, I was the only full-time course tutor; assistant tutors were employed for specific sessions. During 1987–1988, the Manpower Services Commission (Department of Employment) agreed to subsidize the training course, and we were able to employ two additional full-time tutors to teach eight classes. In 1988–89, this was reduced to one additional full-time tutor for two classes.

The course was organized on a residential basis. This was seen as the most appropriate format, given the constraints mentioned above. The residential part of the course enabled trainees to work together and share experiences. In the evening, trainees were able to go over work they found difficult with other trainees or the course tutors, who were usually around until late each evening.

Distance learning through videotapes compensated for the limited time available during the residential weeks of the course. It allowed issues to be addressed in-depth and gave trainees the opportunity to study the summaries of lectures and the introductory BSL syllabus at their own pace in BSL. A number of students have said the video is "like having someone from the training course in the living room to guide me along." This, in part, compensates for the major disadvantage of a national distance learning course—the lack of local tutorial support.

Each course lasted for approximately twenty-five weeks, and trainees were required to attend three residential weeks, known as "residential blocks," during this period. Each block originally lasted five days, but this time was later increased to seven days so that we could finish earlier in the evening. In the ten to twelve weeks between each residential block, trainees were required to engage in home study, using BSL videotapes that included summaries of lectures and the introductory BSL syllabus.

Ten trainees per group was seen as the ideal size. It enabled us to establish and maintain the all-important tutor/student rapport, which would have been more difficult with a larger group. It also meant that tutors could give more individual attention to trainees and not be dependent on a lecture-based format. A maximum of twelve trainees could be accepted, but that put a strain on both the trainees and tutors.

Through the combination of residential and distance learning, we were able to ensure that the course met certificate-level standards. Without the study videotapes, we would have been required to extend the residential weeks of the course, which would make attendance impossible for most trainees. The use of study videotapes enabled us to offer places to a greater number of Deaf people.

Between the second and third blocks of their course, trainees undertook a ten-week practice teaching session in their home area. The practice teaching was assessed by a member of the project team, with each trainee receiving two visits from a member of the project teaching staff. The first was a guidance visit in which a member of the staff observed the trainee teaching class. Afterwards, the staff tutor discussed with the trainee what had been observed and offered guidance if needed. The visit provided the trainee with the opportunity to discuss any concerns or matters relating to his or her teaching, the syllabus, or the placement. The trainee received a written guidance report from the staff tutor after the visit. The second visit was an assessment visit. It enabled trainees to produce a video letter in BSL, through which matters relating to their teaching practice or the course could be raised with project staff.

The final examination was conducted in BSL. A written examination would have presented a major stumbling block to the majority of trainees because BSL does not have a conventional written form. An examination in written English would be beyond the competence of most of the trainees taking the course.

Examination questions were presented in BSL on videotape. The trainee viewed the examination videotape on a TV monitor and controlled the tape with a hand-held remote control. When the trainee was ready to answer a question, he or she informed the investigator, who recorded the signed answer on videotape. Trainees were required to pass both the final examination and their teaching practice placement in order to be eligible for course certification. If they failed the examination, they were allowed to retake it, subject to the agreement of the Board of Examiners.

Videotape Syllabus

We developed a syllabus for an introductory BSL course to be taught to nonsigners by tutors trained on the course. It was based on an ASL syllabus developed by Vista College in California. We had researched various teaching curricula that were available at that time and were in the process of extending Dorothy Miles' manual for BSL tutors.

We intended to incorporate the excellent guidance contained in Baker-Shenk and Cokely's *ASL: A Teacher's Resource Text on Curriculum, Methods, and Evaluation*, or the "Green Book," as it is widely known (1980). However, when I attended the National Symposium on Sign Language Research and Teaching (NSSLRT) symposium in 1986 in Las Vegas, Nevada, I saw the most recent work in the Vista College Series *Signing Naturally* (Smith, Lentz, and Mikos, 1988), along with Rochester Institute of Technology's *Basic Sign Communication*. The *Signing Naturally* curriculum incorporated a similar approach to the one we had intended to develop in relation to the introductory BSL curriculum.

The Vista College syllabus was in the final stages of testing, and I became one of a number of field testers working in collaboration with Vista College. Because it had been tried and tested and appeared ideally suited to our requirements, we accepted Vista's offer to make use of the syllabus, and we based our introductory BSL syllabus on Vista's, translating it from ASL into BSL and making changes to reflect cultural differences.

The Vista syllabus had been developed on the basis of the latest sign language research. We found its approach very positive. It enabled us to introduce BSL to nonsigners as a second language and to use the direct experience method of teaching. In this method, the tutor uses the target language (BSL) as the language of instruction. No explanations about the language are presented in the spoken language of the students. Deaf tutors using this method are not placed at a disadvantage because of their inability to communicate with their students through spoken English. This method is also particularly appropriate for teaching an introductory BSL course, because BSL does not have a spoken form.

We found that the Vista syllabus developed positive attitudes in both the Deaf tutors and the beginners. It created greater understanding of language use in context and effectively enabled tutors to overcome the patronizing attitude that has, in the past and unfortunately still today, characterized the attitude of many hearing people toward Deaf people.

The syllabus was prepared and produced in BSL on videotape, forming part of the trainee's study tapes. A written guide to the syllabus accompanied the set of demonstration tapes, which featured the Deaf course tutors teaching the syllabus to a group of hearing beginners. A series of written English handouts was given to the students to provide background information about BSL, the Deaf community in Britain, and Deaf culture.

Use of Videotapes in Tutor Training

It was clear from the beginning that videotapes also would play a crucial role in recruiting suitably qualified members of the Deaf community to train as tutors of their own language. Many members of the Deaf community, through no fault of their own, are not comfortable in situations where they are required to work in English. The Vista College syllabus was designed for use by bilingual Deaf people. Thus, their English competence was considerably higher than that of those who have been through our training course. As already stated, our examination is conducted in sign language and recorded on videotape. Without such adaptations, our course would have been inaccessible to the great majority of Deaf trainees who have successfully completed it.

Funding

During 1985–1986, 132 people were offered places in the course, subject to payment of the course fee. Forty-five Deaf people accepted the offer. Of these, thirty-three had their course fee paid by local authorities. Other sources of sponsorship included local centers for Deaf people, the Deaf person's place of employment, and local charities.

Because of difficulties involved in obtaining funding, it was impossible to plan more than one course at a time. We were unable to confirm courses until ten people with funding had enrolled. To facilitate the courses, the BDA agreed to subsidize courses in 1985–86. It was clear, however, that it would be impossible to establish the course properly without block funding, and the BDA did not have the financial resources to do so. The process of applying to local authorities involved the individual preparation of each application. The project simply did not have the staff to continue to pursue funding in this way.

In October 1986, therefore, the BDA applied to the Manpower Services Commission (now known as the Department of Employment/Training) for funding to enable eighty Deaf people to attend the tutor training course. A grant of £153,843 was made to the BDA for this purpose. Further applications were also successful for the years 1988–1989 and 1989–1990, for twenty and thirty places respectively. These grants have enabled the project to make enormous advances. Without the grants, progress would have been slow and difficult.

Contribution of the Course to the Deaf Community

The tutor training course has given the Deaf community in Britain a great boost in confidence. It has given Deaf people a sense of pride in their own language, which in the past had often been viewed as a matter of shame. It has strengthened their sense of their own identity. If we list the Deaf people who have been through the training course and compare their situations before and after the training, the change is readily apparent, with at least twenty-five, I would estimate, gaining the opportunity for the first time to demonstrate their true potential.

The project has enhanced—both directly and indirectly—the employment and training opportunities of Deaf people who have attended the course. The training and qualification provided by the course have encouraged them to apply for jobs that previously they would not have considered. A number of advertisements have specifically invited applications from Deaf people who have attended the BSL tutor training course. About fifty have become self-employed sign language tutors. Their attitude toward hearing people has changed now that they are aware of the obvious respect in which they are held.

The fact that Deaf people are now engaged in teaching hearing people BSL will, we feel, make a major contribution to enhancing, in general, the employment opportunities of Deaf people in this country. It provides Deaf people with the opportunity to address what has been described as their greatest obstacle in obtaining employment commensurate with their abilities: the attitudes of hearing people.

Hearing people who attend BSL classes taught by trained Deaf tutors will, we believe, form a very different perception of Deaf people from that which has prevailed in the past. Such change is a necessary prerequisite to Deaf people's gaining equal opportunity for training and employment. Because the course has only been in existence for four years, we are only in a position to refer to the short-term successes. One wonders what the long-term benefits of this new-found confidence will bring.

It's Not All Roses!

The major expansion of the project in the last few years has been made possible through Department of Employment funding. The BDA has continued to contribute to the cost of the course but does not have the financial resources to fund by itself a course of this size. Recent changes in government policy, however, have led to Department of Employment funding only being available for unemployed Deaf people attending the course. The future funding of the course is a matter of grave concern to us. This financial uncertainly means that staff can only be employed on short-term contracts, and it obviously creates problems for Deaf people who wish to take the course.

A criticism that has been made of the videotaped syllabus is that it does not encourage trainees to develop their own teaching materials and approaches to teaching. It also has led a number of trainees to think that this is the only possible way to teach! We need to find more time to address these issues to ensure that trainees do not become rigid in their approach to teaching. The course provides a base; it is not in itself an end. It is but one of many possible approaches to the teaching of BSL.

The new-found confidence of some trainees has had some unforeseen consequences. Some are forever arguing or debating with other deaf people who do not share their views the pros and cons of BSL and of teaching BSL by the direct experience method. At times when they are unable to support their arguments, they reply that "Durham University says so," instead of swallowing their pride and replying, "I don't have the answer to that at the moment, but I will get back to you." A lecture entitled "Learn to Walk before you Run" has been included in the training course in an attempt to address this issue.

The reaction of the long-oppressed majority of those who make up the Deaf community—those described as "oral failures" who now realize the language that they use, BSL, is a language in its own right, distinct from English—has had serious repercussions for relationships both within and outside the community. A bitter battle is raging within the Deaf community regarding the issue of language preference and use: BSL or English.

The minority of deaf people in England who are proficient and successful in English have traditionally been considered successful by hearing society and also were viewed as superior by members of the Deaf community. These individuals are now having to "look over their shoulders" and watch as Deaf people whose strength is BSL, but not English, are beginning to gain recognition and success in a totally new context. Although this tension is not necessarily unhealthy, it has to some extent had a damaging effect on the campaign for advancing the use of sign language in both the Deaf and the wider community. We do not view the languages as alternatives: In Britain, both BSL and English (in visual form, both written and sign systems) are, or should be, the languages of the Deaf community.

Current Developments

The success of the project has contributed to a number of current developments. The project has been used as a model by other institutions interested in providing vocational training courses for Deaf people, such as the Youth Leadership training course offered jointly by the BDA and Salford Youth Service, and the "Sign Language Resource Person" training course offered by the BDA and various groups in the field of Deaf education.

An important development to which the course has contributed is the establishment of advanced diploma/master of arts courses in sign language studies at the University of Durham. The courses offer qualifications in four major areas: BSL/English interpreting, teaching BSL, applied studies, and research and theory. They represent a milestone in the long campaign to achieve recognition for BSL.

Conclusion

The BSLTA project has, we believe, achieved many positive objectives—but not without considerable difficulty. It has placed excessive demands on the time of staff members. The course itself is not perfect; there is room for improvement in a number of areas. Nevertheless, if we were asked to start again, I am sure we would have done much the same thing (but insisting on more staff to ease the workload). We hope you will agree that the opportunities the course has provided for Deaf people—and, in turn, for nonsigning hearing and deaf people—have made the project well worth undertaking.

References

Baker-Shenk, C., and D. Cokely. 1980. *American Sign Language: A Teacher's Resource Text on Curriculum, Methods, and Evaluation.* Washington, DC: Gallaudet University Press.

Smith, C., E. Lentz, and K. Mikos. 1988. *VISTA Signing Naturally; Teacher's Curriculum Guide: Level 1.* San Diego, CA: DawnSign Press.

Teaching Across Modalities: BSL for Hearing People

FRANCES ELTON

Until very recently, most sign language tutors who worked with Deaf people in a social service capacity were hearing people or Deaf people with good speech. Signs were usually taught from a word list. Sentences were based on English word order, with both Deaf and hearing tutors usually using their voices throughout the lessons.

However, when students met Deaf people outside the classroom, they usually found it very difficult to communicate with them. It was even suggested that this was because some Deaf people signed in an "ungrammatical" way! Most Deaf people, in turn, found it difficult to communicate with most of the hearing people who had attended such sign classes. As a consequence, conversations, when they did occur, were usually very limited.

Things began to change dramatically in the late 1970s when British Sign Language (BSL) research projects were established in centers of higher education, most notably at Moray House College in Edinburgh and at Bristol University. It was not until the 1980s, however, that significant numbers of Deaf people really became involved in teaching sign classes. Training courses were established in London, in Glasgow, at Bristol University, and, since 1985, at Durham University. Not all the courses that were established, however, provided training in BSL.

During the 1987–1988 broadcast season, a weekly television series entitled "British Sign Language for Beginners" was broadcast. As a consequence, the demand by hearing people for sign language classes increased. The very limited number of Deaf tutors offering BSL classes were totally unable to meet the demand.

The Durham University British Sign Language Tutor Training Course was established to address the shortage of trained Deaf BSL tutors, as described in Clark Denmark's paper. The project was sponsored by the British Deaf Association, the national representative organization of adult Deaf people in Britain. The course was taught in BSL. Deaf people did not have to be fluent in English to apply or to be offered a place in the course. The main selection criterion was the Deaf applicant's competence in BSL and potential to become a BSL tutor, for which fluency in English is not a prerequisite.

Course Principles

At Durham, we use a structured functional notational syllabus developed by Vista College, Berkeley, California, adapted to the Deaf culture of Britain and translated into BSL.

The introductory syllabus is based on the first ten units (Foundation Level) of the Vista syllabus (Smith, Lentz, and Mikos, 1988). The first five units are given to the tutors during their training course; the other five, after they have successfully completed it. For the first time, Deaf tutors are being trained to teach their own language. The course content is based on everyday usage of the language. The unit titles include 1) Exchanging Personal Information, 2) Getting Around, 3) Identifying and Describing Others, 4) Making a Request, 5) Locating and Describing Objects, 6) Sharing Family Background, 7) Offering Assistance, 8) Describing What Happened, 9) Giving Directions, and 10) Making a Suggestion.

It is also the first time that hearing (and nonsigning deaf) people have been able to learn British Sign Language as a second language, taught by Deaf tutors, using BSL as the language of instruction. For some languages, students need to be skilled in four areas of competence: listening, speaking, reading, and writing. BSL does not have a conventional written form; it is a visual-gestural language. The focus is therefore on face-to-face interaction and use of video and television. Tutors concentrate on helping students develop skill in face-to-face conversation in BSL.

Teaching BSL as a Second Language

The "progressive approach" to teaching described by Ingrams (1977) and Smith, Lentz, and Mikos (1988) changed ideas about how sign languages should be taught. General principles of this approach followed the tutor training course. First is the principle of natural language before "artificial" languages. This means exposing students to BSL before Sign Supported English or Signed English, for example. We feel students will learn other communication modes better—if they need to acquire competence in such modes of communication—if they start from an understanding of BSL, a natural visual language.

In the past BSL was "hidden" from hearing people. They were taught in a way that suggested that sign language was based on English. In our approach, teaching is done through the target language so that students learn signs as units of the new language rather than as glosses of English words. As Ingrams says, "The progress of their learning may be slow, as in learning any new language, but once the foundations are established, progress proceeds at a reasonable speed."

Because BSL is the language of the British Deaf community, we also need to give information about the community and its culture. This is done through handouts distributed during the course. Classroom teaching will not by itself develop communicative competence. Students are therefore encouraged to mix with Deaf people whenever possible.

Learning a sign language is different from learning a spoken foreign language. The students have to adjust from using their voices to using their hands, using their eyes instead of their ears, and to making greater use of facial expression and body movement. We use structured games and activities to help them adjust. These are carefully selected and used for specific purposes to solve particular problems of adjustment. Unlike Southern Europeans, the people of Northern Europe, especially the British, are famed for their "stiff upper lip," so teaching them nonmanual features and body movements, especially, is not an easy task.

A second principle of the progressive approach is comprehension before production. Before the students begin to sign, they should understand what is being signed to them in the classroom. In the past, teachers have emphasized production. Many people, including some interpreters, can sign well but have great difficulty understanding Deaf people who use BSL. We suggest that tutors of BSL introduce new vocabulary in context, giving students the opportunity to comprehend short sentences. Only after this do the students begin to make their own signs.

The lessons are structured so that areas covered in previous classes are reviewed and reinforced throughout the course in different ways. This spiraling curriculum approach, on the evidence of the students who have been through the courses, has proved successful.

Students do continue to find it difficult to move from thinking in their first language, English, to thinking in BSL. They are tested on their ability to use the grammar of their new language. This is done in a number of different ways, such as through the use of cue cards and role play. These are used to check the appropriate use of grammatical features of BSL, sign order, and fluency of signing.

The direct experience method is used to teach students BSL. This method involves instruction in the target language. The students are enabled to communicate about real things and people. When teaching new vocabulary—for example, "teacher," "student," "teach," "learn"—the tutor uses drawings to help introduce the new vocabulary in context.

At the end of each lesson, we do dialogue practice activities, which are usually described on a flip-chart. The dialogues are presented in English, the first language of the hearing students, but do not involve direct translations from written English. The students read the dialogue instructions and then the tutor demonstrates how the dialogue may be signed in BSL. The students then attempt to sign the dialogue. For example:

> SIGNER A: ASK B FOR HIS/HER NAME
> SIGNER B: GIVE NAME. ASK FOR HIS/HER NAME
> SIGNER A: GIVE NAME
> SIGNER A: ASK IF THE PERSON IS DEAF
> SIGNER B: RESPOND
> SIGNER A: ASK IF THE PERSON IS A STUDENT
> SIGNER B: RESPOND

Video

Each unit comprises a number of lessons. At the end of each unit, there are practice and review activities. These allow the tutor to assess the students' receptive and production skills. BSL dialogues, signed by Deaf people on video, are used as part of these lessons. The students watch the short dialogues, then attempt to copy how they were signed by the two signers. In this way, the students are exposed to the signing of different Deaf people and are able to improve their production skills.

There are also main dialogues on video, which are usually shown at the end of the lesson. We use a question list to test the students' receptive skills. The main dialogue is longer than the short dialogues and includes all the vocabulary taught in the unit. In between showing the short and main dialogues, students usually participate in a cue card activity in which they are asked to sign in BSL.

These activities enable us to evaluate their learning and our teaching in relation to the unit. If the students do well in these activities, we know that our teaching has been successful. If they do not, we should be able to identify why it was not successful. In later units, plays are also included. These enable us to assess the students' awareness of certain aspects of Deaf culture, such as touching and waving for attention, and the use of certain equipment, such as the minicom and flashing lights.

Duration of the Course

Because students come from all walks of life, and many have family and/or work responsibilities, the BSL classes usually take place weekly in the evenings. They are usually two hours long, with a break for coffee or tea halfway through. The foundation course is designed to take three terms to complete (seventy-two hours in all). The curriculum also can be used for concentrated full-time crash courses. The classes usually include people of different backgrounds, but whenever possible, we suggest that all should be new to signing so that they at least have that in common. This also makes it easier for the tutor to plan the course.

We have found it difficult to teach mixed groups that include students who have attended sign classes before that were not in BSL. It is very difficult to get such students to unlearn what they have learned and to sign in BSL. They tend to revert to English-based signing such as Sign Supported English or Signed English. To make teaching and learning successful, the tutors are encouraged to accept up to a maximum of ten students per class, but in many areas, local education authorities insist on a minimum class size of sixteen students, which creates problems.

Assessment

There are now two assessment bodies in the United Kingdom. The Council for the Advancement of Communication with Deaf People, based in the School of Education at Durham University, covers Northern Ireland, England, and Wales. The Scottish Association of Sign Language Interpreters covers Scotland.

When assessments began, the ones for the introductory stage were not "language based"—not based on BSL. They assessed what was described as "communication skills." The old curriculum covered particular topic areas, such as introductions, occupations, food and drink, numbers, places, weather, and holidays. Each of these lessons usually involved the introduction of a vocabulary of twenty to thirty signs. In comparison, our lessons usually involve four or five new vocabulary items, introduced in the context of BSL sentences.

Policies have now changed as to language-based assessments, and curriculum has been amended to cover subject headings similar to those listed above. Our tutor training program does not at this time include assessor training. We are considering how we might most appropriately contribute to assessor training.

The tutor training course has been running for three years. We would like to carry out a proper evaluation of the course but have not yet been able to do this owing to lack of funds. The Deaf community's reaction to the course has been very positive, in particular to the fact that the course is conducted in BSL, is taught by Deaf tutors, and enables Deaf people to train to become tutors of their own language.

The fact that the course was granted university recognition has been important in advancing recognition and acceptance of BSL in Britain. There has been great demand from hearing people for placement in courses taught by tutors who have trained at Durham.

References

Ingrams, R. M. 1977. *Principles and Procedures of Teaching Sign Languages.* Carlisle, Great Britain: Ingledown Ltd.

Smith, C., E. M. Lentz, and K. Mikos. 1988. *VISTA Signing Naturally; Teacher's Curriculum Guide: Level 1.* San Diego, CA: DawnSign Press.

Teaching Sign Language Communication and Interpretation

ASGER BERGMANN

Danish Sign Language, DSL, is my native language. I was born in Denmark to deaf parents, and my wife and our two children are also deaf. We use DSL in our everyday life. I learned American Sign Language during my one year of study at Gallaudet College in 1974–1975, but that was fifteen years ago, so I've forgotten many signs.

The purpose of my paper is to give a short presentation about the teaching of DSL as a foreign language at the college and university level of education in Denmark. We have a one-year, full-time sign language training program offered to hearing students who want to become sign language interpreters. We also have a new one-year, full-time training program for sign language interpreters. This second program is focused on exercises in interpreting from Danish to DSL and vice versa.

Background of the Training Program

As in other countries, deaf people in Denmark have fought for societal acceptance of sign language, the education of deaf people, the right of deaf people to have the same opportunities as the majority of society, development of professional and qualified interpreters, and interpreter services free of charge for all deaf people in all situations.

After many years this fight has been successful, and the need for professional interpreters is exploding in our country. In 1986 we started a two-year, full-time formal education program for sign language interpreters at the College of Trade and Business Administration in Copenhagen. This college has several training programs for foreign language interpreters: English, French, German, Spanish, etc. It is important for the education and training of sign language interpreters to be provided at the same level as training for interpreters of spoken languages.

The teaching is done in close cooperation with the Center for Total Communication in Copenhagen, and the program is financially supported by the Ministry of Education. Twenty students are admitted every year during a five-year experimental period. The only qualification for admission is a college degree, which is the same as the requirement for admission to university foreign language programs. The students who enter the program have no knowledge of sign language or deafness.

The Curriculum

The academic year is from September 1 through June 31, and there are 1,200 hours of classroom teaching required. The goals of the interpreter training program are stated as follows:

1. The students must learn to master DSL at a level where they can communicate freely with deaf people in daily conversation;
2. The students must learn about deaf history, deaf culture, and the social-psychological aspects of the lives of deaf and hard of hearing people; and
3. The students must learn about general linguistics, and the grammar and function of sign language.

Topics for the classes include general linguistics, sign language (DSL), Danish, the mouthhand system, fingerspelling, transcription, notation of signs/signwriting, bilingualism, minority cultures, sociolinguistic status of sign language, the medical and psychological views of deafness, deaf organizations (national and international), deaf history and culture, and trends in the education of deaf persons.

Eight hundred hours of coursework are focused on sign language training. The remaining four hundred hours are theory and examination. Since the students know neither deafness nor sign language when they enter the program, it is important that we introduce them to the deaf community through visits to deaf clubs, sports activities, institutions, and schools for the deaf.

Sign language is taught primarily by eight teachers who are themselves deaf. It is very intensive work with two or three teachers involved at the same time. All teachers have worked at the Center of Total Communication for several years, and most have DSL as their native language. The Center has fifteen years experience teaching sign language at different levels, as well as conducting research, developing teaching materials, and producing videos for educational purposes. However, 1986 was the first time the Center and its staff have had the opportunity to develop a real language teaching program with classroom teaching daily from 9:00 a.m. to 3:00 p.m. for nine months.

We start with a group of twenty students September 1 and finish with an examination at the end of June. The basic teaching method we use is (1) learn to understand sign language and (2) learn to produce sign language. The philosophy behind our teaching method is based on techniques for teaching a foreign language, ideas from sign language training programs in other countries, and experiences drawn from the Center's intensive sign language training program over the past sixteen years.

Sign language is used for instruction and conversation in the classroom from the very first day. If necessary, spoken Danish is used with an interpreter. Lessons with theoretical topics are given by both hearing and deaf teachers in either Danish or DSL. An extensive amount of time is devoted to exercises in the language video laboratory, and each student has his/her own video recording equipment. Students can also see a lot of videotapes of deaf adults and children telling stories in DSL. They can record their own retelling of the stories on videotape and compare their DSL to that of the deaf storyteller. It's a unique tool for independent and individual studies offering an opportunity to study the varieties of sign language used by deaf people.

During the first year, students are given an exam in four parts. They must pass all four parts to qualify for the second year interpreter training program. The exam consists of (1) a written examination on deafness, deaf history and culture, sign language and communication, and deaf organizations; (2) translation of a monologue from DSL into

Danish (includes questions on the grammar of DSL, analysis of signed Danish/simultaneous communication using elements of Danish and DSL); (3) competence in DSL (retelling of a Danish text in DSL); and (4) competence in communication (conversation in DSL about cultural, social, and linguistic topics concerning deafness).

The second year of our program, from September 1 to June 31, includes 450 hours of classroom teaching with the rest of the time spent in independent studies at the language-video laboratory or in interpreting practice. Goals of the second year are as follows:

1. The students must be fluent in both DSL and Danish;
2. The students must be able to perceive meaning given in one language and transmit it to achieve equivalent meaning in the other; and
3. The students must be able to interpret fluently.

Topics covered in the second year of the program are Danish, sign language (DSL), interpreting (process, ethics, and role), notetaking, sign-notation, speech-training, cooperation with other interpreters, concentration exercises, and psychology. At the second year level we have both hearing and deaf teachers. The teaching in DSL interpreting and ethnics is done by teachers from the Center; the teachers from the College give instruction in Danish, speech-training, and concentration. We think it is valuable that the training of sign language interpreters is done by both teachers from the Center and those from the College's foreign language interpreter training programs. This cooperation ensures high standards for our program.

During the second year students also are given a four-part examination by external examiners, both hearing and deaf, who set standards for professional qualifications. The four areas of testing are (1) simultaneous interpreting from spoken Danish into DSL, (2) simultaneous voice-interpreting from DSL into spoken Danish, (3) written examination on interpreting ethics, and (4) interpreting a dialogue.

In 1986–1987 eighteen students passed the first year examinations. In 1987–1988 seventeen passed the first-year and sixteen the second-year exams, and in 1988–1989 fifteen passed the first year and eleven, the second year exams. Since we are the only country in Europe that has set up this kind of formal education for interpreter training within the existing educational system, we have some observations and discussion to share with you.

First, is it possible for hearing students to learn DSL in only nine months? Can they communicate with deaf people fluently and at a satisfactory level? The answer is yes. The successful result of such an effort usually requires, however, that students receive intensive teaching every day; students attend class every day; students have opportunities to talk to many different deaf people; students are in a sign language environment that encourages communicative development; teachers are skilled and trained language teachers; teachers are enthusiastic about their teaching (much more so than teachers in traditional language courses); and that teaching methods and materials have been developed, evaluated, and adjusted.

The Center, which is known for its research projects, teaching, and material development, has sixteen years of experience in teaching sign langauge and has set up courses for active and experienced interpreters for many years. Those interpreters have different backgrounds from our students, and most have deaf parents. Without this experience, I don't think we could manage our present task.

Second, is it possible for a newly trained interpreter to interpret fluently after only two years? My answer to this question is *yes, but* . . . .

When a person is skilled in sign language communication, it does not mean that he/she is also automatically skilled in interpreting. An interpreter must have good abilities to concentrate, memorize, and translate. Some students become very skilled DSL-users, but have difficulties with interpreting because their knowledge about the world is limited. Curiosity and thirst for knowledge are also important to be an excellent interpreter. Our experienced interpreters want us to add to the list voice-interpreting ability, which they think is a very difficult task, but it seems many of our new interpreters manage voice-interpreting better. Why? We have found that the experienced interpreters who don't like voice-interpreting, often have weak Danish language skills. From foreign language interpreters we know that it is easier to translate from a foreign language into a native language.

Our new interpreters are skilled in Danish—since they have a higher educational background, a college degree—and their training focuses on the understanding of DSL (receptive skills). Therefore, it is not so difficult for them to translate the message into Danish, their native language, but some do have problems translating from Danish into DSL. They need more training in DSL.

Another problem we have is that students need much more interpreting practice. Therefore, we are asking the Ministry of Education for an extension of the education program by half a year or one year. Since the goal of this education is to train interpreters for basic interpreting in everyday situations, both new and experienced interpreters need further education in specialized vocabularies, court interpreting, congress and festival interpreting, interpreting from English into DSL (and vice versa), and interpreter cooperation.

This pioneer work for the Center has been very interesting; however, we want to have a broader educational training program that qualifies sign language interpreters to interpret in more situations, instead of a basic educational program.

Educational Methods for Teaching Sign Language

JOSETTE BOUCHAUVEAU

I am going to be discussing how to teach sign language to beginning students, but first I will share with you a little background about myself.

I was born profoundly deaf, and I am now an educational director and teacher of sign language for the Academy of French Sign Language (ALSF), an association created ten years ago to promote the use of French Sign Language (LSF). The ALSF is headquartered in the Paris Institute for Young Deaf Individuals. In the school courtyard there is a statue of l'Abbé de l'Epée, founder of the first free public educational institution for deaf people.

During the ALSF's years of operation, several people have influenced my teaching style, including Gil Eastman, a deaf American, and deaf Frenchmen Guy Bouchauveau (my brother) and Jean-Claude Poulain. These individuals taught me specific educational uses of C.N.V. (nonverbal communication) skills. I also worked with Bill Moody, another American, and with several deaf individuals in research on grammar and on several books related to LSF. My work organizing and teaching classes in LSF in the evenings after my regular job was a very interesting experience. After that, I worked full-time for two years with the International Visual Theatre (IVT), which is devoted to LSF education. I am also an actress with IVT. Since 1988 I have been working again with ALSF full time. Teaching methods have been changing during the past four years, and I always try to exchange ideas with other deaf teachers and learn from their successes and failures.

In my classes at ALSF, I teach beginning through advanced (nearly interpreter-level) students—adults, parents of deaf children, professionals, friends, and deaf people who do not know sign language. I also participate in LSF workshops for children.

How to Teach

The basic rule for teaching sign language to beginning students is to avoid speech, keep your mouth closed, and use only signs. I feel that an interpreter is not needed during the first days of the course. The instruction can manage to provide orientation to the students through other communication channels.

Beginning sign language students often are uneasy when they first encounter a deaf teacher, so the instructor must be pleasant when welcoming them. Drawing or showing pictures as a way of communicating is not recommended, but classroom rules and explanations for them can be expressed through written signs or posters, such as: "No Smoking," "No Talking," or (as a joke) "No Looking at Each Other's Hands," and so on.

Funny facial expressions can be added by the teacher when showing these posters—for example, "No Smoking" with a twist of the mouth.

If the classroom includes people who are preparing to become teachers of deaf students, these student teachers must get into the habit of keeping silent during their entire training. They must be interrupted when they are seen speaking aloud to deaf students, for example, in the cafeteria during breaks. They need to learn about Deaf culture and be introduced to deaf individuals from the beginning of their training.

Pictures illustrating LSF syntax are often useful tools in teaching LSF, as are videotapes and such miscellaneous instructional tools as guessing games, plays, or games of opposites.

In order to be understood, teachers must try to provide wide, clear, simple signs. The result is often very successful, but sometimes students fail to understand because they themselves are blocked.

Changing Attitudes

Hearing people are often prisoners of their bodies. Because they are often inhibited, they must be taught how to touch with their hands and use facial expressions. At the start of my sign language courses, I group students in a circle and ask them to get each other's attention by firmly touching each other in turn. Then the sign teacher can begin a demonstration of initial signs using different facial expressions, for example, when calling someone by tapping him or her on the shoulder or shaking someone's hand while saying hello. The students usually have fun doing this, and it is a good way to begin helping them learn how to be physically expressive. Following such exercises, the students are more at ease in expressing themselves through sign language.

Students also can join hands and arms, engaging in pulling and pushing exercises. This, too, helps them become more comfortable with touch. Touching people—on the shoulder or other parts of the body to get someone's attention, for example—is part of our Deaf culture. Hearing people do not like to be touched by strangers, and they have to be taught that it is acceptable within Deaf culture.

Other examples of educational methods that could be used in the classroom to encourage more expressive communication among the hearing students include using pictures of facial expressions to elicit feelings, or playing a "feelings" guessing game in which each student takes a turn making a facial expression without using signs, and the others must guess what feeling is represented. Afterwards, the hearing students feel less imprisoned by their bodies.

Teaching LSF Syntax

Students should be taught LSF syntax as soon as possible, without the use of nonverbal communication. Signed French should be avoided; it is not grammatically correct LSF! LSF syntax should be taught through demonstration, without explanation of its grammatical structure, because it is inherently grammatical. At first the exercises in LSF syntax are difficult, but as the students progress, the exercises become simpler.

In teaching LSF syntax, we can show pictures, play games, tell stories, and invent plays with different roles assigned. Students are encouraged to express themselves as much as possible using sign language with a proposed theme. Hearing individuals must learn to use their eyes and remember the signs visually.

Avoiding Spoken French

Hearing people in France think in spoken French. One of the purposes of sign language class is to try to make them think pictorially and reduce their dependency on spoken French. Total immersion in sign language, through such instructional tools as guessing games with questions and answers devised entirely in LSF, will help the students gradually lessen their dependence on spoken French and increase their visual skills.

LSF Grammar

LSF grammar is not always easily understood. Sign language students can begin to learn LSF grammar by comparing it to spoken French; thus they will see that the two languages have different structures. To teach beginners, however, grammar does not need to be explained: The students will be amply stimulated at this stage by the presentation of homonyms in sign language.

Homonyms in spoken languages are words that are spelled and pronounced alike but have different meanings. The different meanings are made understandable through contextual clues. (For example, in English the word "bear" can refer either to enduring something unpleasant or to a large animal that lives in forests.) Homonyms in sign languages are signs that have different meanings but look alike. The differences in meaning between sign language homonyms can be determined through contextual clues. Some examples in LSF, with French glosses, are shown in Figure 1. Examples such as these demonstrate that the meanings associated with a particular sign may vary and that signs, like spoken words, must be understood in context. To make this concept clearer, I sometimes ask the students, "Do we eat an interpreter?" Learning about sign language homonyms also clarifies that signs were not invented to stand for particular spoken words, but in the context of sign language itself.

At the advanced level, we approach LSF grammatical structure in more detail, showing distinctions of meaning can be clarified in sign language to differentiate similar but nevertheless significantly dissimilar concepts. Comparisons might be made, for example, between how LSF would communicate the following slightly different statements: (1) I break the glass. (2) The glass breaks. (3) The window is broken.

At the ALSF, we often work with the help of videotapes. For example, we will first view a tape showing a deaf person telling a story. If the students don't understand the story, we review it sequence by sequence to study its signs together. This way, the students discover—sometimes to their astonishment—the richness of French Sign Language.

We also videotape each student telling a story. We then look at the film together to make any necessary corrections. Some hearing people are inhibited in expressing themselves in front of a camera, but they must learn to sign in front of deaf people, so the camera is a good experience.

Feeling More at Ease

Some people have specific communication problems. These groups may include deaf people who have been isolated, parents of deaf children, or hearing individuals who have become deaf. If parents are having difficulty accepting their deaf child, I try to provide them with information about the way deaf people live, so they perhaps will see their child differently and accept his or her deafness. Often, parents are reassured simply by meeting well adjusted deaf adults who live just like everybody else.

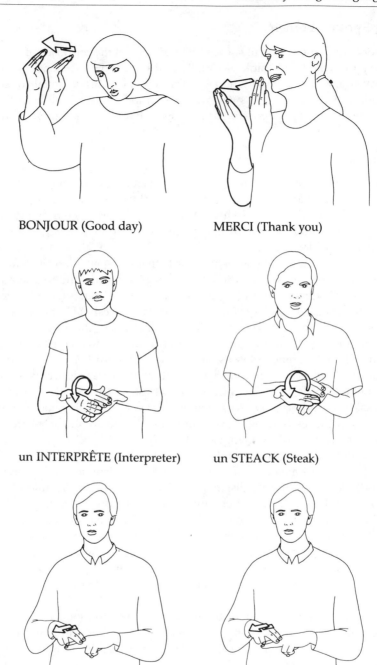

BONJOUR (Good day)   MERCI (Thank you)

un INTERPRÈTE (Interpreter)   un STEACK (Steak)

CHOCOLAT (Chocolate)   VIDE (Empty)

FIGURE 1: Examples of homonyms in French Sign Language.
Note. Illustrations are from La Langue des Signes; Tome 2; Dictionnaire Bilingue
Elementaire (pp. 37, 41, 61, 132, and 142) by B. Moody, A. Vourc'h, and M. Girod, 1986.
Paris: Ellipses. Copyright 1986 by the International Visual Theatre. Reprinted by
permission.

It is the duty of the teacher to create a pleasant atmosphere in sign language classes so that students can feel comfortable. Thanks to training in sign language, people's behavior often changes, and they become increasingly open, more expressive, and more self-confident.

Establishing Successful Relations

Teachers should try to establish successful relations among the various members in their classes. At the ALSF, the larger group is frequently divided into two, three, or four smaller parts so that the same people are not always together. This way each student can take turns working with every other student in the group. When problems with relationships occur, the teacher must intervene and not just avoid the situation.

I have had courses with twelve people in which two groups—a faster one and a slower one—were formed. In this situation, I was forced to adapt my teaching methods to match their levels. To gain the students' confidence, I grouped them in circles, then—within each circle—I conversed with the students or they conversed among themselves on a friendly basis, using signs.

Inventing Signs

Often hearing individuals want to transform the deaf sign language by inventing their own new signs. Two examples are

DIRECTOR made with the alphabet letter "D," followed by the vocabulary, or

A PERSON WHO SKIS, signed with two fingers of one hand on two fingers of the other hand.

Teachers of sign language must refuse to accept such invented signs. Students must be made to respect the configuration of LSF, which is a true language.

SERAC

SERAC's Efforts to Provide Interpreters in France

GILES VERLET

M y colleagues and I will be discussing the establishment and activities of the first interpreter training program for sign language
interpreters in France. It seems ironic that as we celebrate the
bicentennial of the death of the Abbé de l'Epée, founder of education for deaf students in France, we are only now beginning
to train sign language interpreters. Yet such is the case. France is trailing considerably
behind many other countries in matters related both to the education of deaf students
and to the resolution of communication difficulties between deaf and hearing people.

The four of us will leave discussions of France's educational problems to others
and will limit ourselves to the topic of interpreter training. But before discussing interpreting, some mention should be made of SERAC, an acronym that translates into
English as "deaf-hearing-research-action-communication." This nonprofit organization
was founded several years ago with one overall objective: to serve as an instrument
for enhancing communication between deaf and hearing people on both a sociocultural
and a professional basis.

In addition to that global objective, we seek to provide form and coherence to
numerous disorganized initiatives and plans, to work toward reversing the general tendency to trivialize the problems of deaf people, and to bring the hearing world closer to
understanding the condition of deaf people, despite the fact that so many issues tend
to keep these worlds apart.

Others before us have tried to initiate plans for interpreter training programs in
France, but they failed for several reasons. The first is financing. The French have plenty
of ideas and plans, but the French government wishes to finance only those projects
that have already been established. It is easier to generate ideas than to realize them;
that is one reason why there are many failures.

The second reason for the previous failures to establish interpreter training opportunities is that most of the plans were conceived by specialized social work personnel,
whose jobs consisted of assisting deaf people on a permanent basis. Rather than considering the competence required to be effective interpreters, their main concern centered
around the distance they should maintain with respect to their primary job and with
respect to their deaf acquaintances elsewhere.

The third reason is related to the ponderous centralization of the French culture.
The majority's standard of normalcy and conformity still guides French society. Today,

however, things are evolving, and sign language is no longer suppressed, at least not overtly.

These difficulties and failures are of interest only to the extent that they permit us to avoid repeating the same mistakes. In order to gain full recognition as a university training program similar to other linguistic training programs, the SERAC plan was based upon experience gained in other countries, both with sign languages and with spoken languages. Rather than appealing to the good will of the universities in France (which are cash-poor because they must depend solely on government funding), SERAC applied for and received government subsidies designated for the retraining of job applicants.

Further, we felt that to entrust a university with the job of determining the content and academic methodology of an interpreter training program would be to condemn the project to the planning stage forever. Instead, we ourselves created the program and have revised it as we have learned more. This has allowed our teaching methods to be more flexible and to reflect the teachers' motivation to succeed. Agnés Vourc'h will discuss the ongoing applied research that we are conducting while we provide classes.

It might seem somewhat dangerous to begin an interpreter training program without offering diplomas to its graduates, but the French university system is so designed that a diploma is only recognized if the corresponding educational program already exists. We decided to take this risk because France is sadly lacking in high quality interpreters. Our training is at a university master's level. Despite the urgent need for interpreters, the duration of the study program corresponds to four university semesters.

The program includes intensive interpreter training, but—operating on the assumption that one can only translate well what one knows well—also includes classes that cover the most common areas of intervention: medical, social, and legal matters, and interpreting situations related to education, training, and professional life. No interpreter education can afford to ignore the groups for whom its graduates will translate. Therefore, we have prepared classes which view the "deaf condition" from cultural, sociological, and psychological perspectives.

The major difficulty we face in recruiting students is that France lacks hearing people who know how to sign. This is owing primarily to historical constraints. The nineteenth-century French mass movements favoring political unity, with their consequent uprisings against regional idiosyncrasies, intensified opposition to sign language in the same way that they strengthened resistance to dialects and patois.

The lack of skilled signers also is partly owing to a nineteenth-century bourgeois society that attempted to hide disabled people—particularly deaf people, who could be concealed by teaching them to speak. Even if today's deaf people are once again starting to teach their language to hearing people, it will still be a long time before we can make up for this late start. It was, therefore, necessary to integrate with interpreter training a major and more intensive sign language study program, which Victor Abbou will discuss."

Apart from the training, which is not particularly innovative when compared with that being done in the United States, it is probably our interpreter service that offers some original features.

In the majority of countries that have them, almost all interpreting service agencies function on a liberal profession (i.e., freelance) basis. We decided to take a different approach. First of all, we believe that interpreting is a trade, and therefore should be paid on a yearly salaried basis, regardless of fluctuations in demand.

Moreover, we consider that in a deaf person's daily activities, he or she has the right to communicate and that this same right exists for the hearing person—whether he or she is a doctor, postal carrier, or bureaucrat—who comes into contact with a deaf person.

Consequently, we believe that it is the responsibility of public service agencies to integrate this dimension of communication into their program operations, and to finance interpreters. Under no circumstances should the deaf individual have to find or pay for more (or less) effective alternative methods of communication.

It was hard to convince public services to subsidize interpreters, but we managed. Using this means of financing, we have been able to provide interpreters on more than a thousand occasions in the Paris region over the last two years.

Interpreting should not, however, be limited to administrative matters. The cultural needs of deaf people are vast, and in this area, too, France is considerably behind. Dominique Hof will address this issue.

Although much still remains to be done, SERAC, through its educational program and interpreting service, is facilitating communication and, with the help of others, is striving to build between deaf and hearing people—day-by-day and stone-by-stone—a bridge that will be strong and durable.

Linguistics Applied to the Training of Interpreters

AGNÉS VOURC'H

The work group in which I participate as a linguist has two objectives. One is to provide deaf teachers of French Sign Language (LSF) with current data and a linguistic viewpoint. The other is to develop, step-by-step, an interpreter training program based upon a comprehensive grammatical overview of LSF. In planning this program, we ask questions such as: What action plan should be followed? What areas need particular in-depth study? What problems are most likely to be encountered by a future interpreter?

These various points are discussed in depth. Results are then applied using, among other means, original videotapes focusing on particular grammatical, historical, or other topics. The students "test-run" these tapes.

In addition, in my role as a linguist, I work directly with the students for about three hours every week throughout the course of their training.

People identify with their own language, and they use it without giving it much thought. But when one wishes to become an interpreter, it seems essential that one's own language should become an object of study. If one cannot examine one's own language, then it will be difficult to study another language with interpreting in mind. I seek to inculcate in my students the distancing required for them to separate themselves from their own language.

To interpret is to shift from one language to another without losing sight of the meaning of what is being interpreted, whether at the word, sentence, or discourse level. To be an LSF interpreter requires switching from an auditory image to a visual image while maintaining a mental image. This is true also in the reverse direction, translating from LSF into French.

The contribution of linguistics to the training process is to enable students to grasp more fully the contrastive structure inherent in languages in general, and then prepare them to discern the structure of a specific language.

In the area of phonology, every sign can be described in terms of handshape, location, orientation, and movement. A difference in any one of these elements is sufficient to establish the difference, or contrast, between two signs with different meanings. An example in LSF is provided by the signs TO-BE-PATIENT and WICKED, which are similar in handshape and movement, differing in location and orientation. The study of phonology can guide the interpreting student in noting the contrasting features of signs that are similar to each other.

The concept of contrast applies at the level of syntax as well. For example, comparing various combinations of nouns and verbs allows the students to see that there are different classes of verbs based on agreement rules. In French Sign Language, some verbs that are translated with the same French word change their form in LSF to agree with the noun, while other verbs do not. Students can grasp this difference in verb type by contrasting sentences such as I-BUY A-GLASS (FLOWERS, BOOK, BAG) with sentences such as I-TAKE A-GLASS (FLOWERS, BOOK, BAG). In the first example, the form of the verb is identical in each sentence, while in the second, it changes depending on the paricular noun that follows.

Linguistics also provides interpreters with access to the semantics appropriate for collaborating with a deaf teacher. Indeed, it is imperative that interpreters know how to distinguish the various semantic groups and what they represent. If, within a given language, a word has a specific meaning, it is only so because of its contrastive relationship to other words of the same paradigm, terms that represent the same reality in different ways.

In sign language, this leads to consideration of the components of a reality vastly different for deaf people than it is for hearing people. For example, would hearing people imagine that three expressions such as "meanwhile, elsewhere," "fog," and "to be vague" belong to the same semantic family? I would think not. However, such is the case in LSF: They are all from the series "I can't see what is happening."

This example reveals the bicultural aspect of interpreting, an aspect that must be studied beforehand in a theoretical context in order to be understood. If the interpreter does not know what he or she is seeking in a language, then he or she has little chance of finding it.

The speech, words, sentences, and sense of a language are expressed through discourse. Speech is the rhythm of the sentence; connections between words and phrases are pauses composing its melody and accent.

One of our activities is to provide interpreting students with the means to analyze an LSF speech on videotape, initially by sentence, then by signs. The work is hard at first because the end-of-enunciation indicators are very different in sign language.

The pause is an indicator of the end of an enunciation and, as such, it is of primary importance in understanding the message. In order to be effective, future interpreters must have a precise idea of what is happening in the pauses of their own speech, the intonation and accents. Only after understanding this can such knowledge be applied to a visual language.

The linking word is another potentially confusing phenomenon that exists in sign language as well as in oral language. Countless false interpretations have been made because a link was interpreted as a sign.

Finally, there are the melody and accent. In spoken language, the voice conveys the melody and accent. In LSF it is the facial expression and the shoulder movements, the degree of emphasis given to various motions. One of the essential problems for a person with aphasia—an impaired ability to express one's self using language—is a loss of melodiousness. This is one reason why aphasics are so difficult to understand.

To prevent future interpreters from becoming "melody aphasics" in LSF, we felt it was vital to provide them, through linguistics, with a pertinent overview of both their own language and the language they must comprehend.

Dominique Hof will discuss other activities used in the interpreter training program.

The Interpreter as Actor

DOMINIQUE HOF

What qualities are essential in order to become a good interpreter?

My predecessors have already mentioned several requirements: above all, to be an excellent user of each of the languages; to have a thorough knowledge of the various cultures one is addressing; to have the ability to distance oneself, with the help of linguistic analysis; and to attain a high comprehension level and superior mental training.

However, the interpreter is also a *communication manager* between two negotiators. As in everything else human, communication is not solely a matter of rules and skill; it is full of unspoken comment, mood, and subjectivity. For example, if an interpreter translates the sense of the words without also translating the irony and humor of the communicator, he or she is making a serious mistake that can go as far as to convey the opposite meaning. It is not the word that is translated, but the *meaning*, the *thought*.

Deaf people are very visually oriented and pick up many nonverbal messages. The interpreter, therefore, conveys much information, often unintentionally, through body language. The face has a grammatical role. The eyebrows can indicate conditionality or negation. A look can conjugate verbs or situate the narrator. The shoulders assign roles and punctuate sentences.

While it is true that mastery of these rules is vital, an interpreter with a shifty glance conveys a sense of panic to deaf people. A person signing with shrugged shoulders reveals a lack of confidence. The deaf individual receiving these impressions is placed in a position of inferiority: "My interpreter is undependable; I'm going to be lost or at a disadvantage."

What a responsibility! The interpreter must provide deaf clients with equal opportunity in any interpreting situation. To do that, the communication manager, the interpreter, must inspire two feelings in his or her clients: security and agreeability.

Security implies that the interpreter uses clarity of language and expression, maintains neutrality, and conveys the impression of mastery of the situation.

Agreeability within the exchange means that gestures are aesthetically pleasing, precise, and free of unrelated meaning, and that the interpreter presents himself well, with appropriate physical attributes (hair, clothing, and body) under control.

Communication should be lively, with the interpreter changing mood via voice or gesture, and conveying the personality differences between the contributors.

Thus, the interpreter cannot be satisfied with being merely a good technician. The interpreter is an actor and must be creative. The instrument of this creativity is the body.

In order to provide interpreting students with a well rounded education, SERAC introduced Artistic Studies as an indispensable part of the basic curriculum. Theatrical director and deaf actor Alfredo Corrado was invited to work with students on facial and bodily expressions. Rafaël Djaim, a hearing choreographer endowed with the practical, directive language of an actor who has worked with deaf people, helped students progress through gestural aesthetics, athletic work using the body, and individual and group improvisation.

My involvement in the creative training of interpreters consisted of coordinating these activities together with a deaf colleague. I also conducted an adaptation workshop for poetry and gestural song translation.

The concern reflected by all of these activities is to make interpreters aware of the multifaceted nature of language. They must become flexible enough to improvise a message termed "international" or "nonverbal" with a deaf stranger or an illiterate person; translate a museum visit or theatrical scene without involuntarily patronizing deaf people; or translate Victor Hugo, Molière, or Shakespeare into street-level sign language.

In summary, we believe that our interpreters must enjoy handling the beauty in both languages, be able to express themselves with their bodies, and convey the pleasure of communication to their clients.

Sign Language Interpreting in France
VICTOR ABBOU

In this paper, I would like to discuss my experiences, not as an interpreter, but as a consumer of interpreting services. I work in the deaf community of France and know how interpreters for deaf people have been and are being used there.

As recently as thirty years ago there were no professional interpreters in France. There were hearing people who knew sign language and helped deaf people communicate, but these people were not trained interpreters.

It was not very long ago that I first met a professional interpreter. This person explained to me what he did, and it was a great discovery for me. I thought it would be interesting to teach sign language to students interested in becoming interpreters. Later, I went on to do just that, teaching sign language to diverse groups of people: professionals, parents of deaf childern, and other interested hearing people. In the process I, too, have learned a great deal. It has been an enriching experience.

I also conducted some research on the deaf community in Paris and in the provinces, a new area of inquiry at the time. My observations led me to conclude that the quality of interpreting services for deaf people was badly in need of improvement. In spite of the popularity of sign language courses, the number of professional interpreters was not increasing. Why were people who had learned sign language not becoming interpreters? The reasons were many.

To be a quality interpreter, one must have not only excellent sign language skills, but also knowledge of the culture of deaf people. If an interpreter were not accustomed to living or working with deaf people, he or she could not relate to deaf culture or deaf people.

Because deaf people were not accustomed to working with professional interpreters, they often felt awkward and were sometimes aggressive or unpleasant in their interactions with them. Deaf people with such limited experience were not in a position to advise interpreters on how to do their jobs. In any case, deaf people should not be expected to work as unpaid interpreter trainers.

As a result, interpreters often felt afraid in interpreting situations; interaction with deaf people was often difficult. It seemed to the interpreters that deaf people were judging them without fully understanding the difficulties inherent in the interpreting situation. The interpreters often did not feel competent to handle the demands placed on them.

In many cases, however, the interpreters *were* incompetent. They had very little experience, were often clumsy, and made many mistakes. Some were not very tolerant with deaf people. Rivalries developed between those who were more skilled and those whose skills were not so fully developed. Some simply became bored and decided not to continue with their careers as interpreters. It is a pity this situation developed as it did, and the blame must be shared equally between hearing and deaf people.

For their part, many deaf people were unaware of the principles that guide interpreters in their work. For example, they did not know that there are strict principles of neutrality for sign language interpreters, just as there are for spoken language interpreters. Interpreters are responsible only to aid in communication; the deaf people thought that interpreters were there to help them in any way necessary.

Deaf people were also unaware that a spoken word could be translated with several signs, or that a sign could represent several words. The lack of this knowledge made the interpreter's task even more difficult. For example, at a popular exhibit of the paintings of Gaugin, two interpreters were employed to work simultaneously. Deaf people in the crowd recognized that the two interpretations differed slightly, and they were outraged. They expected an interpreter to be like a machine; they did not realize that each interpreter must find his or her own way of expressing the true meaning of the spoken message, or that the same meaning can be expressed using different signs. In this way, sign language interpreting is like any other kind of translating anywhere in the world. Deaf people needed to be educated in these matters. Only gradually was this problem recognized.

Another situation that presents serious problems for both deaf people and sign language interpreters occurs when the need for an interpreter is overlooked in the planning of an event. For example, often a deaf person arrives at a meeting only to find that no interpreter has been scheduled for the session. Quickly, a hearing person who has some knowledge of sign language, but no formal interpreter training, is pressed into service as an interpreter. The hearing person, who received no prior notification that this would occur, is put in an awkward position. Despite the interpreter's best efforts, the deaf person most frequently does not receive quality interpreting services. Naturally, such incidents complicate the lives of trained interpreters by undermining their status as professionals.

The task of interpreters in France is further complicated by the different levels of sign language used there. There are expert signers, oral deaf people who sign only a little, and deaf immigrants to France who have their own distinct signs. Research is being conducted on the various forms of LSF presently in use in France.

Because the role of the interpreter is still not well defined in France, there is great potential for misunderstanding. Interpreting situations can turn into arguments, and one scenario is often repeated: A doctor or policeman, for instance, not realizing the interpreter's obligation to maintain neutrality, will say something to the interpreter that he or she does not wish the deaf client to know. When the interpreter, fulfilling the responsibilities of the job, conveys the message to the client, the result can be angry feelings all around. The interpreting relationship is a delicate one, and such miscommunications are frequent.

In spite of all the difficulties, there are interpreters who have attained a very high level of skill. It is these more experienced interpreters who are called upon to interpret for conferences. However, we also must remember that less experienced interpreters will improve only if we employ them. Deaf people and interpreters need each other. It is only through the services of interpreters that we deaf people can understand what happens in the hearing community. As interpreting services have become more widely available, many things have been clarified for the deaf people of France; now they can understand much about the community that surrounds them.

Still, there are not enough professional interpreters to meet the growing demand. For this reason, we established an organization to provide qualified interpreting services to the deaf community. This began as a small effort; at first, the organization did not even have a name, and responded to only one or two requests per month. Since its informal founding, our organization has grown considerably. SERAC, as the organization has been known since 1988, now receives approximately fifty calls per month requesting the services of interpreters.

In addition to its interpreting service, which provides its employees with an annual salary, SERAC conducts sign language research, the results of which are utilized by the interpreters in their work. One topic of research has been the role of facial expressions in LSF. We are also conducting studies on methods for training new interpreters and retraining working interpreters whose skills are not up to date. The results of these efforts have been very positive.

Because we did not have enough interpreters to satisfy the demand, we decided to create a formal interpreter training program as well. This fifteen-month course of study is taught by two deaf teachers. In the spring of 1989, Bill Moody, an American interpreter of ASL and LSF, paid us a visit. He helped us organize our training program—a monumental though extremely stimulating task. He also worked directly with our students. There is still much to do in developing our program, and we continue to receive advice from Bill, with whom we have maintained a very good relationship. I believe there should be more exchanges such as this between Americans and French people, in which we might also provide training in LSF to people from overseas so that someday we might have LSF translated directly to voice and text in a variety of languages.

Meanwhile, our work continues. In September of 1989, we will begin a second fifteen-month training course. SERAC is building for the future, and our work fills us with joy. The success of our program means success for the entire deaf community.

From One to Many and from Many to One: A Comparative Analysis of ASL and the English Lexicon

JEFFREY DAVIS AND KATHY JANKOWSKI

This paper represents a study of some semantic differences between American Sign Language (ASL) and English words. An ASL sign, for example, may require several English words to capture its meaning (sometimes referred to as a multimeaning sign). An English word may also require several ASL signs to convey its meaning accurately. There may even be cases where English words do not adequately convey the meaning of an ASL sign and vice versa.

This has important implications for interpreters, who must regularly make choices about which lexical items best convey meaning from one language to another. The fact that there is not always a one-to-one correspondence between lexical items in ASL and English, or between any two languages, for that matter, also has important implications for second language learners and individuals who attempt to sign and speak English simultaneously.

Interpreters and second language learners must learn the nuances, subtleties, and range of implied meanings of words or signs in the target language. There is evidence to suggest that when one attempts to sign and speak English simultaneously, the accuracy of the message is either skewed or lost altogether.

Data are presented from our observations of various interpreting and classroom contexts to demonstrate ASL and English vocabulary that often give interpreters, teachers, and students a difficult time.

Signing and Speaking Simultaneously

The simultaneous use of spoken English and signs is typically referred to as Simultaneous Communication or SimCom. Johnson, Liddell, and Erting (1989, p. 5) refer to it as Sign Supported Speech (SSS) "in order to focus on the assumption that speech is seen as the primary signal in the conglomerate of signing and speaking."

The primary goal of SSS, as it is used in educational arenas, is to encode linguistic features of spoken English with manual signs; this is also referred to as Manually Coded English (MCE). Some signs are invented to represent visually formal features of

English, such as the copula, tense agreement, inflectional and derivative morphemes, and root morphemes of English. These systems also borrow heavily from the lexicon of ASL.

An attempt is made to create a one-to-one or literal correspondence between English words and ASL signs for the express purpose of encoding English words. That is, lexical forms are borrowed from ASL for the purpose of encoding English forms, usually without concern for preserving the meaning of the ASL sign being borrowed.

In contrast to ASL, these artificially developed systems for visually representing English have none of the characteristics of natural languages. According to Johnson et al. (1989, p. 5):

> They have been developed in large part, not through regular use by a community, but by committee; they tend to be taught rather than acquired; and what grammatical organization they have derives purely from another language. Thus, although a people using SSS are moving their hands, they are not using a sign language.

Production and representational problems associated with speaking and signing at the same time, such as omissions, deletions, or semantic skewing, are well documented in the literature (see, e.g., Marmor and Pettito, 1979). Signing while simultaneously speaking appears to be so cognitively and physically demanding that both manual and spoken components of the message are negatively affected. As Johnson et al. (1989, p. 5) describe it:

> A hearing person will typically begin to audit the speech portion of the signal and will allow the sign signal to deteriorate either by omitting signs randomly or by deleting those signs that do not fit the rhythmic pattern of English speech. At the same time, the spoken signal is typically slowed down and altered phonologically and is often characterized by excessive halting, hesitation phenomena, repetition, or other delaying tactics. In general, the less the speech signal is altered, the more the signed signal will be unintelligible. In our view it is not an exaggeration to say that the signed portion of the SSS presented in virtually all American deaf education is only partially comprehensible, even to skilled native signers.

Johnson et al. further discuss the failure of SSS as a means of representing English for the input of natural language and "as a vehicle for the transmission of curricular material."

Form, Meaning, and Function

The goal of translation, interpretation, and transliteration is first and foremost the transfer of meaning from one language to another. This is accomplished by changing the form of the first language to the form of a second language while accurately conveying the intended meaning. In other words, the forms of each language, also referred to as the "surface structures," are changed while meaning is transferred and held constant.

Highly skilled interpreters and people who are bilingual, for example, often make the transfer from one language to the other without necessarily thinking about the semantic structure overtly. They are able to make the linguistic and cultural adjustments necessary to convey meaning accurately.

In translation studies, for example, it has long been recognized that there is not a one-to-one correspondence between the forms of two different languages. While it is possible for the interpreter/translator to discover the meaning of the source language and re-express the meaning in the target language, there is ordinarily no full equivalence. Even apparent synonymy does not yield equivalence, and the interpreter/translator must often use a combination of lexical items in order to interpret accurately the meaning of a single word (Jakobson, 1959; Nida and Taber, 1969; Bassnett-McGuire, 1980; and Larson, 1984).

The interpreter/translator, then, must transcend the purely linguistic surface forms, analyze the source language text for meaning, and restructure the message into the target language. This is also true any time someone wishes to translate an English text into ASL, or vice versa.

There are many examples in the literature that demonstrate the complexities of transferring meaning between languages. Even the most simple, straightforward examples warrant careful consideration. Consider, for example, interpreting "yes" and "hello" into French, German, and Italian (data from Bassnett-McGuire, 1980, pp. 16–17). For translation of the English word "yes," standard dictionaries give

French: oui; si
German: ja
Italian: si

First, the existence of the two terms in French represent usage not found in the other languages. That is, whereas "oui" is generally used to convey affirmation, "si" is used to convey contradiction, contention, and dissent. Further, "yes" cannot always be translated with the single words "oui," "ja," or "si." French, German, and Italian frequently reduplicate affirmatives in a different way from English—for example, si, si, si; ja, ja, ja; oui, oui, oui. Bassnett-McGuire (1980, p. 17) points out that "the Italian or German translation of 'yes' by a single word can, at times, appear excessively brusque, whilst the stringing together of affirmatives in English is so hyperbolic that it often creates a comic effect."

For the translation of the English greeting "hello," dictionaries give:

French: ca va?; hallo
German: wie geht's; hallo
Italian: ola; pronto; ciao

In contrast to English, which makes no distinction between the word used for greeting someone in person and that used when answering the telephone, French, German, and Italian all do make that distinction. According to Bassnett-McGuire (1980), "pronto" in Italian and "hallo" in German function strictly as telephone greetings; French and German use rhetorical questions as greetings that would be considered formal in English, such as, "How do you do?"; and "ciao" is used in Italian as a greeting as well as in departure.

The fact that language forms as basic as affirmations and greetings have different functions and meanings according to the language context in which they are being used demonstrates the complex nature of the transfer of meaning between languages. Larson

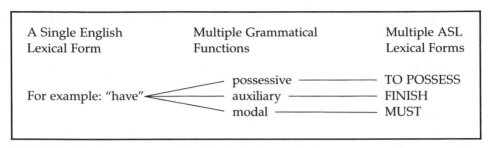

FIGURE 1: From one to many: English to ASL

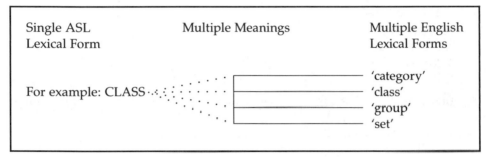

FIGURE 2: From one to many: ASL to English

(1984, p. 5) provides examples that show that the transfer of meaning "is not simply a matter of different word choices, but of different grammatical structures as well."

For example, consider the different language forms used to convey the meaning "a person, who is the speaker, possesses money": English uses "I have money;" Japanese and Latin use forms that literally say "to me there is money;" Arabic and Russian use forms that say "with me there is money;" and Aguaruna and Turkish use forms that say "my money exists" (examples from Larson, 1984, p. 5).

One of the universal characteristics of language is that one form may express a variety of meanings, or a single meaning may be expressed in a variety of forms. Hence the title of this paper: From One to Many and From Many to One. That is, a single word in one language may have several different meanings; a single meaning may be conveyed by multiple lexical items; or a word in one language will need to be translated by several words or vice versa. This is not only limited to lexical items, but is also true for phrases that may express several different meanings.

These complex configurations of form and meaning present a challenge to individuals translating or interpreting between languages. Second language learners also have a great deal of difficulty with these differences in meaning. The examples below, from ASL and English, are not intended to exhaust the possible range of meanings conveyed by words or phrases in either language, but are presented to show that these universal linguistic characteristics already discussed also apply to the ASL-English contact situation.

The first possibility is that a single lexical item in one language may express multiple grammatical functions or meanings, whereas another language may require multiple lexical items to convey multiple functions or meanings. This is illustrated in Figures 1 and 2.

The first set of examples presented below demonstrates that a single lexical item in English, with many different meanings, is conveyed by different lexical items in ASL, depending on the intended meaning. For example, in English, "have" is used in some of the following ways:

1. I have a new car. (used here as a possessive)
2a. I have been to Europe.
2b. I have not been to Europe. (used as an auxiliary in these cases)
3. I have to go now. (used in the case as a modal)

In contrast, ASL uses different lexical items to convey the above functions and meanings of "have":

1. TO-POSSESS
2a. FINISH
2b. LATE
3. MUST

Another example is that English uses one form for "call" for a variety of meanings:

1. My friends call me Bob.
2. Call me when you get home.
3. Call for help.
4. Call in the next patient.

The meaning of "call" is conveyed with different lexical items in ASL:

1. NAME
2. CALL-ON-PHONE or CALL-ON-TDD (depending on context)
3. TO-CALL-OUT-FOR (similar form for SHOUT or SCREAM)
4. TO-SUMMON

According to some accounts (e.g., the *Reader's Digest Great Encyclopedic Dictionary*) there are fifty-four meanings for the English word "run." Consider the following uses of "run":

1. They had a run in with each other.
2. Are you going to run in the marathon?
3. She had a run in her stocking.
4. Do you think she will run for president?

In ASL these meanings are expressed with different forms:

1. CONFLICT or CONFRONT-EACH-OTHER
2. TO RUN (there are different regional forms for this use of run)
3. G-CLASSIFIER "run in stocking"
4. TO-APPLY

In the set of examples listed in Table 1, a concept that may be expressed with multiple lexical items in English is conveyed by a single lexical item in ASL.

**TABLE 1. Multiple Lexical Items in English Conveyed by
Single Lexical Items in ASL**

English	ASL
brilliant; smart; intelligent; bright	SMART
beautiful; attractive; pretty; gorgeous; lovely	BEAUTIFUL
class; category; group; set	CLASS
administer; control; handle; manipulate; direct	CONTROL

These examples demonstrate that words are made up of bundles of meanings. An examination of any dictionary will reveal that words usually convey multiple meanings. As Larson (1984, p. 6) puts it: "*Meaning components* are 'packaged' into lexical items, but they are 'packaged' differently in one language than in another."

As pointed out in the beginning of this section, there is ordinarily no one-to-one correspondence of words or phrases between two different languages. Artificially developed sign systems, in which new signs are created or borrowed from the existing lexicon of ASL to encode English syntax, violate this basic principle of natural language.

Summary and Conclusions

This paper has presented examples of lexical items from ASL that do not have a one-to-one translation or correspondence to lexical items in English, and lexical items from English that also do not have a one-to-one correspondence or translation to lexical items in ASL. Sometimes an ASL sign requires more than one English word to capture its meaning, and vice versa. One cannot assume that there is always a one-to-one correspondence between words or phrases in the two languages.

This is a universal linguistic principle that applies to all natural languages in the world. There are some ASL signs and English words, for example, that have several different meanings, depending on the context of the communication event. If a signer or speaker does not know the appropriate use of the lexical item, or that the lexical item in question may have multiple meanings, then the intended meaning can be skewed or misunderstood.

The fact that there are words in both languages that have multiple meanings has important implications for individuals learning sign language as a second language and for interpreters, who interpret between both languages. The vocabulary items from both languages must be translated appropriately in order to preserve their accurate and intended meaning.

In the case of signing and speaking at the same time, in particular, the intended meaning is often lost. The research evidence suggests that, with the possible exception of a few balanced bilinguals who are skilled at speaking and signing simultaneously, most individuals cannot speak and sign simultaneously. When individuals attempt to do this, the meaning of the message in one or both of the languages is often skewed or lost altogether.

The research suggests that there has been a general failure of deaf education in the United States as reflected in the below grade-level performance of deaf children. The primary mode of communication in virtually all deaf education programs is speaking and signing simultaneously. Formal bilingual education is virtually nonexistent in this country. It is rare for ASL to be taught in any school for deaf students, and it is still prohibited in many schools.

Absence of bilingual education and monolingual attitudes mark the underachievement of other linguistic minorities. One has to wonder what negative consequences the absence of bilingual education and the long history of monolingual English education have had on the achievement of deaf people.

References

Bassnett-McGuire, Susan. 1980. *Translation Studies.* London: Methuen & Co.

Jakobson, Roman. 1959. "On Linguistic Aspects of Translation." In *On Translation*, ed. R. A. Brower. Cambridge: Harvard University Press.

Johnson, Robert E., Scott K. Liddell, and Carol J. Erting. 1989. "Unlocking the Curriculum: Principles for Achieving Access in Deaf Education." Gallaudet Research Institute Working Paper 89-3. Washington, DC: Gallaudet University.

Larson, Mildred L. 1984. *Meaning-Based Translation: A Guide to Cross-language Equivalence.* New York: University Press of America.

Marmor, Gloria, and Laura Petitto. 1979. "Simultaneous Communication in a Deaf Classroom: How Well Is English Grammar Represented?" *Sign Language Studies* 23: 99–136.

Nida, Eugene, and Charles Taber. 1969. *The Theory and Practice of Translation.* Leiden: E. J. Brill.

PART FOUR

Diversity in the Deaf Community

Editor's Introduction

The shared experience of being Deaf in a predominately hearing world—especially among those who have been deaf since birth or childhood—tends to create a bond among Deaf people in spite of national, racial, medical, or behavioral differences. Hearing people, by contrast, seldom identify so strongly with each other simply on the basis of shared experiences resulting from hearing. Nevertheless, it would be misleading to suggest that differences among Deaf people are disregarded within Deaf communities. The papers in this section—almost entirely from the United States—suggest that a range of attitudes, sometimes including an impulse to ostracize, exist within Deaf communities toward members of various Deaf minority groups.

The opening paper by Tanis Doe (Canada) provides an overview of groups that experience varying degrees and kinds of oppression within Deaf communities in general. Some readers may be surprised to find Deaf women described as perhaps the largest group oppressed by other Deaf people, in this case, because of persistent sexist attitudes that tend to give women lower status than men and make it difficult for Deaf women to achieve prominence in Deaf organizations. A paper by Sheryl Emery and Jeanette Slone (United States) describes how the discrimination experienced by black people and by deaf people in America is compounded when a person is both black and deaf. They discuss their struggle to be perceived as professional adults in an atmosphere of negative stereotypes. In his paper, Anthony Aramburo (United States) discusses the importance of recognizing and appreciating the mixed allegiances of members of the black Deaf community.

Thomas Kane (United States) discusses the subculture of gay people in America's Deaf community. In addition to providing information on the special values of Deaf gay men, Kane urges that the larger Deaf community try to overcome the prejudices toward this group that tend to be reinforced by religious groups and by American society in general. In her paper, Jean Modry (United States) points out that the main difficulty experienced by Deaf substance abusers is that the Deaf community itself does not provide sufficient rehabilitation or support programs for these people. Existing programs, she says, fail to be sensitive both to this group's substance abuse and to the linguistic and cultural factors affecting Deaf people. Modry suggests that the communication difficulties experienced by Deaf people in English-dominant treatment programs tend to reinforce the very sense of inadequacy that pushes many Deaf people into substance abuse in the first place.

Beverly Butters and Nancy Kirkendall (United States) discuss the helpful role community colleges can play in enabling rural Deaf people to get together and overcome some of their feelings of isolation and social impoverishment. Roderick MacDonald (United States) then discusses how Deaf-Blind people have managed to overcome many obstacles to develop their own separate culture. The final paper in this section, by

Bill Graham and Marymargaret Sharp-Pucci (United States), addresses the problems late-deafened individuals face in finding a place in the larger Deaf community.

It is hoped that these papers will help inform members of Deaf and hearing communities alike about the concerns and needs of various deaf minority populations. Ideally, increased understanding will help overcome prejudice and lead to greater unity among all Deaf people. Although these papers are primarily concerned with minority groups in America, it can safely be assumed that similar groups, experiencing similar degrees of isolation and misunderstanding, exist all over the world.

Multiple Minorities: Communities Within the Deaf Community

TANIS DOE

Issues of concern to the deaf community have received the attention of researchers in the areas of language, cognition, education, culture, and human behavior. While these are issues shared by all deaf people, some within the deaf community face additional issues that are often overlooked by researchers.

Deaf people constitute a numerical and cultural minority in terms of their participation within the dominant hearing culture. But minorities and minority communities exist within the deaf community itself as well. This paper will discuss the issues and experiences of the members of some of these multiple minorities and explore how they interact with both the deaf community and the hearing majority. The purpose of this paper is to begin a discussion about the issues of individuals and minorities who are oppressed within the deaf community.

Characteristics of Multiple Minorities

Being deaf is a dominant characteristic that places an individual in the category of minority. Deafness is an ascribed status that Higgins (1980) has shown to be a master status in many circumstances, often superseding other characteristics so that the person becomes identified as deaf first, both by others and by him- or herself.

Being deaf and also being black, or gay, or female, or Hispanic, or Asian, or having other disabilities, or being "different" puts an individual in a multiple minority category. People can belong by virtue of their characteristics or by choice (Barile, 1987). Deaf people who are perceived as being different (i.e., as having more than deafness as an identifying characteristic) are often placed in this category by the deaf community itself. In addition, they may be assigned the lower status that goes with this categorization (Deegan, 1982). One of the more common characteristics that can marginalize a deaf person is having a mental disability—being either mentally ill or mentally retarded. Deaf people view mental disabilities as deviant, much as hearing society does.

But the deaf community also commits a form of "social closure" when faced with deaf people of multiple minority status (Gaslin, 1971). For example, many deaf communities are not open to or welcoming of deaf people with additional disabilities, and deaf organizations have actively excluded deaf peddlers and beggars (Higgins, 1980, Chapter 4). Sometimes the majority deaf community manifests this attitude by holding meetings in locations that are physically inaccessible to people in wheelchairs, but more often it is conveyed in the attitude of deaf people that these people (those of multiple minority status) are NOT SAME—not like us. This reaction comes partly from the influence of the hearing world toward the so-called norm. Deaf people have been socialized to strive toward normality, so they can often be intolerant of atypical people (Moores, 1982; Rodda and Grove, 1988; Doe, 1988).

Marginal Communities: "Living on the Borders"

Deaf Women

Many deaf women are active participants in deaf community organizations, particularly cultural organizations and theaters. Sports groups within the deaf community tend to have activities for both men and women, and often women are included in leadership positions. Professionally, deaf women often choose to work in such fields as rehabilitation services and education of deaf students (Rosen, 1984). But generally, the deaf community does not give deaf women status or roles equal to those of deaf men. Deaf women also have been somewhat excluded from the women's movement, despite the involvement of some feminist interpreters (Chaussy, 1977). In 1974, the *Deaf American* published a special edition on deaf women in history that revealed that most of those seen as cultural heroes and leaders in North American deaf society were men. A special article was needed to set the record straight—to show that women were there, too. Unfortunately, little more was said about women, and no similar articles have been published in the *Deaf American* since that time.

Both in the family and in the community, women are marginalized by stereotypes and expectations held by the dominant culture (Dodd, 1977; Robinson, 1979). Through their education in a hearing-controlled environment, deaf students receive and internalize gender role norms that assign to men the characteristics of being aggressive, strong, stable, and autonomous, and to women the characteristics of being passive, weak, emotional, and dependent (Miller, 1986).

These stereotypes may seem familiar, because they could easily be those applied to hearing-deaf dichotomies as well: Hearing people are aggressive, strong, stable, and autonomous; deaf people are passive, weak, emotional, and dependent. Being both deaf and female compounds these stereotypes, and the deaf community itself perpetuates these distinctions (Cook and Rossett, 1975). Deaf women have been relegated primarily to the positions deemed suitable for them by the male-dominated communities (both deaf and hearing). The expectations of deaf women are similar to those of women in general—to nurture children and husband, to care for the home, and to be supportive but not in control. Women may achieve, but only in suitable occupations—nursing, teaching, secretarial work, or counseling, for example. Higher expectations, such as being the head of the family, earning a steady income, providing leadership, and maintaining control, are reserved for men—both hearing and deaf (Schein and Delk, 1974; Nash and Nash, 1981).

As deaf men started climbing the social ladder, they began to depend more heavily on women to support them by working in the home, raising the children, running the household, and often working outside the home for extra cash. But men continued to gain status at the expense of women, and social pressures often resulted in abusive families and violence against women. The expectation that deaf men are to be in control without the corresponding social supports for resolving problems has led to increased violence against deaf women, just as similar expectations have led to violence against hearing women. Many deaf women suffer from abuse and harassment from spouses, friends, or family, and they are more likely to be sexually assaulted than hearing women (Disabled Women in Canada, 1988). Unfortunately, these same women are less likely to seek help or press legal charges.

Lack of communication with hearing women, isolation from others in general, and educational and employment barriers have forced deaf women into the marginal, multiple minority category (Barile, 1987). Deaf women are more likely to associate with each other than with hearing women because of their shared experiences and easier access to each other. These women have common experiences that are valuable and deserve to be investigated in a way that will respect their lives as deaf women.

Gay and Lesbian Deaf People

One of the outstanding and beautiful aspects of deaf culture is its openness and straightforwardness. In the deaf community, people tend to say what they mean and "tell it like it is." Because signing is such a public language and because of personal perceptions, homosexual deaf people tend to be known in the deaf community as homosexuals, whether or not they want to be. Over time, gay and lesbian deaf people are identified as such by the deaf community and are placed in a marginal role by virtue of their multiple minority status (Zakarewsky, 1979).

Deaf people tend to be endogamous in terms of marriage partners. Although some marry hearing or hard of hearing people, a large number of heterosexual deaf people marry other deaf people (Shaul, 1979). Many deaf people meet their future spouses in residential schools; seeking a lifetime partner within the deaf community is a common occurrence. For gay and lesbian deaf people, however, this partner-seeking can be a very intimidating experience.

The deaf gay person has a smaller number of deaf people to consider as future partners and is often unable to look beyond to the hearing community. Despite some interaction with gay hearing people who know sign language, such as gay interpreters and gay people with deaf parents, deaf people generally have not had open access to the hearing gay or lesbian communities. Gay and lesbian deaf people often participate in their own community activities, gathering for coffee or dancing, or attending a meeting with another organization.

Recently, issues such as AIDS and child custody have brought gay deaf people to the political arena; now they are beginning to demand equal access to services and information. Generally speaking, however, deaf lesbians and gays are still marginalized by both the hearing gay community and the deaf community. They risk persecution both from their family members and the general public, where homophobia is worsened when it is combined with ignorance about deaf people.

Other Minorities Within the Deaf Community

Homosexual deaf people are to some degree an invisible minority, able to blend in with the general population of hearing or deaf people. But deaf people of color are members of ethnic minorities; they are more visible and immediately recognized as different. Deaf people of color may either be born in a white-majority country or come to one as immigrants. Central and South Americans, Asians, black people of all origins, and other ethnic minorities have one thing in common: In a white environment, they are visible. Their visibility presents a potential risk to their status. The white deaf community may not see itself as prejudiced or unwelcoming, but the structure of society is stratified on the basis of gender, class, disability, and race (Bowe, 1971). Black people in North America have fought for years for equal opportunity and reward, but still receive far less social status and access to resources than their white counterparts (Anderson and Bowe, 1972).

Discrimination

One of the predominant characteristics of hearing society is its widespread discrimination against minorities. Governments in many countries are accused of discriminating against women, children, elderly people, disabled people, gay people, people of color, and native people (Moscovitch and Drover, 1981). These situations arise from both intentional discrimination and systemic discrimination. There are many problems with society today that prevent certain groups of people from receiving the full benefit of the law based on their physical characteristics. Racism, sexism, able-ism, and all forms of prejudice are based on ignorance and the perpetuation of exploitation.

The deaf community, unfortunately, is no exception. Deaf people suffer from the same ignorance about disabled people, women, gay people, native people, and people of color; in fact, sometimes the ignorance displayed within the deaf community is worse than that of the hearing community. Because of their inadequate education and limited access to information, deaf people may hold misinformed views or opinions on a number of issues. Each person has the right to an opinion, but often this opinion is formed under misguided circumstances (Bowe, 1971; Dodd, 1977).

Racism is often present and visible in the deaf community. Ethnic minorities are treated differently there. Black, Hispanic, and immigrant deaf people tend to associate strongly with their own cultural group if they are not accepted by the general deaf community. This puts them into the multiple minority category. They are members not only of the deaf culture, but also of their own ethnic cultures, which may or may not fit with deaf culture (Anderson and Bowe, 1972).

Some of the most serious examples of this involve native peoples. Whether in Canada, the United States, or Australia, native people traditionally have been treated as possessions of the state and have not been allowed to control their own activities (Frideres, 1987). All of the problems of being a native person in a colonized society that has developed into a capitalist wage economy deaf native people must suffer twice. Not only are they removed from their reservations and homes to attend deaf schools, but they rarely encounter facilities that teach their native languages in sign language or, for that matter, even in spoken language. Native people who are deaf are deprived of their own ethnic heritage both by this communication gap and by physical removal from their homes. They are often marginalized by cultural and historical oppression in a white deaf community.

Deaf people who attain the highest positions of employment, education, and leadership tend to be white, able-bodied men. Those who face the worst social and economic problems tend to be deaf women of color and deaf people with additional disabilities. The deaf community treats multiple minorities in much the same way as deaf people are treated by the hearing majority—by discriminating against them. It is important to see how the general deaf community reacted to this type of discrimination from hearing people.

Even under oppressive circumstances, and despite a lack of education, the deaf community grew strong. Deaf people have become politically active and have achieved great things over the last century. To fight oppression and discrimination, deaf people united and became cohesive. They also became somewhat exclusive (Nash and Nash, 1981; Padden and Humphries, 1988). It was not easy to be part of the deaf community once it became well organized and established its own status. The best historical example is the exclusion of beggars from deaf associations. Deaf people did not want to be associated with peddling or begging and sought to discourage deaf people from, and punish them for, engaging in such activities (Higgins, 1980). As deaf people became more able to communicate with the hearing public, they rejected the labels "mute," "dumb," and "dummy," but at the same time marginalized deaf people who were mentally handicapped, mentally ill, or less able to communicate.

The general social advancement of deaf people has brought all deaf people a higher status, but also has created a hierarchy based on inequality—all deaf people are equal, but some deaf people are more equal than others. The structural inequalities of hearing society have been transmitted to the deaf.

Reactions

Just as deaf people were able to unite and push against the oppression of hearing society, deaf people of multiple minority status are also struggling with these issues. Black deaf organizations, deaf women's groups, and advocates for mentally disabled deaf people are beginning to demand their rights. Owing to the serious disadvantages faced by these groups, they probably will be slower in starting and progressing, but they *will* make an impact. Organizations from the mainstream society are beginning to open up to deaf people. Now deaf gays and lesbians, deaf people of color, and deaf people with other disabilities are looking to mainstream organizations for support and advocacy and are finding ways to secure these services.

The efforts of multiple minorities have not been unified or organized, primarily because of their small numbers and lack of power. The issues that affect multiple minorities are not valued or given high priority by the deaf community, which has its own agenda. But women's rights, AIDS, employment equity, and de-institutionalization are all vital social issues that do affect the deaf community and are issues that the deaf community must address. Deaf people can address the issues of marginalized deaf people by trying to be more inclusive and more open to differences.

The deaf community may well succeed in becoming the model of a tolerant culture for the rest of society. To do so, deaf people must break the bonds of oppression and stop being either oppressed or oppressors. This will allow the humanization of all people and the inclusion of minorities in all levels of social life to occur.

References

Anderson, G., and F. Bowe. December, 1972. "Racism Within the Deaf Community." *American Annals of the Deaf.*

Barile, M. 1987. "Disabled Women, Multiple Minorities." *COPOH Proceedings.*

Bowe, F. June, 1971. "Non-white Deaf Persons: Education, Psychology and Occupational Review." *American Annals of the Deaf.*

Chaussy, A. 1977. "Deaf Women and the Women's Movement." *The Deaf American* 29: 10–11.

Cook, L., and A. Rossett. June, 1975. "The Sex Role Attitudes of Deaf Adolescent Women and Their Implications for Vocational Choice." *American Annals of the Deaf.*

Deegan, M. J. 1982. "Multiple Minority Groups. A Case of Disabled Women."

"Disabled Women in Canada." July 1988. *Communiqu'elle.* [Newsletter of the Canadian Advisory Council on the Status of Women.]

Dodd, J. October, 1977. "Overcoming Occupational Stereotypes Related to Sex and Deafness." *American Annals of the Deaf.*

Doe, T. M. 1988. "Ontario Schooling and the Status of the Deaf: An Enquiry into Inequality, Status Assignment, and Educational Power." Unpublished master's thesis, Carleton University, Ottawa.

Frideres, J. 1987. "Native People and Canadian Education." In *The Political Economy of Canadian Schooling,* ed. T. Wotherspoon. Toronto: Methuen Publishing.

Gaslin, D. 1971. *Handbook of Socialization Theory and Research.* Skokie: Rand McNally.

Higgins, P. 1980. *Outsiders in a Hearing World: A Sociology of Deafness.* Beverly Hills, CA: Sage Publishing.

Miller, J. B. 1986. *Toward a New Psychology of Women.* 2d ed. Boston: Beacon Press.

Moores, D. 1982. *Educating the Deaf.* Boston: Houghton Mifflin.

Moscovitch, A., and G. Drover. 1981. *Inequality.* Toronto: University of Toronto Press.

Nash, J., and A. Nash. 1981. *Deafness in Society.* Toronto: Lexington Books.

Padden, C., and T. Humphries. 1988. *Deaf in America: Voices from a Culture.* Cambridge: Harvard University Press.

Robinson, L. 1979. "Sexuality and Deaf Culture." *Sexuality and Disability* 2 (3).

Rodda, M., and C. Grove. 1988. *Language, Cognition, and Deafness.* Englewood Cliffs: Laurence Erlbaum Publishing.

Rosen, R. 1974. "Deaf Women—We Were There Too!" *The Deaf American* 36 (3).

Schein, J., and M. Delk. 1974. *The Deaf Population of the United States.* Silver Spring, MD: National Association of the Deaf.

Shaul, S. 1979. "Deafness and Human Sexuality: A Developmental Review." *American Annals of the Deaf.*

Wotherspoon, T., ed. 1987. *The Political Economy of Canadian Schooling.* Toronto: Methuen Publishing.

Zakarewsky, G. T. 1979. "Patterns of Support Among Gay/Lesbian Deaf Persons." *Sexuality and Disability* 2 (3).

How Long Must We Wait?

SHERYL EMERY AND JEANETTE SLONE

I t is our opinion that black deaf people have not shared equally in the benefits afforded to deaf people in general. Very few black deaf people hold key positions of power, wealth, and social status. The number of black deaf students obtaining professional degrees lags far behind that of white deaf students, and the quality of education is significantly lower for black deaf students. Institutional racism in both mainstream and deaf communities contributes to these disparities. Discrimination, both subtle and overt, does still exist in the deaf community, which leans toward conservatism.

Where do black deaf people fit in? We are not included in the larger white hearing community. We are often not accepted by the white deaf community. We are often ignored and hidden in the black community. And just as the deaf community can be split into different subgroups, the black deaf community can be divided into pre-lingually deafened vs. adventitiously deafened, professional vs. grassroots, oral vs. manual, young vs. old, and male vs. female. The community can be split in many other ways, making each subgroup even smaller and possibly more isolated.

Black Culture

Among adventitiously deafened black adults, cultural identification is usually considered before one's deafness. However, prelingually deafened black people, especially those who attended schools for the deaf, identify with deafness first. They usually do not sense their black identity until they begin to search for mates and find that cross-racial dating is frowned upon.

What is black culture? It is the food we eat, the way we wear our hair, our stories and folklore, our history, songs, and games. One of the strongest components of black culture is religion. The politics of social gospel were born in the black church, and black political careers are most often born and bred in the pulpit. Black preachers are some of the most eloquent and memorable orators. During the 1984 presidential elections, Jesse Jackson was quoted frequently as stating, "I'd rather have Roosevelt in a wheelchair than Ronald Reagan on a horse."

Black spiritual singers have also played important roles, as have the songs they sing:

> Steal away, steal away, steal away to Jesus
> Steal away, steal away home
> I ain't got long to be here.

This gospel song is more than just a song; slaves once sang it to inform other slaves that someone was planning to escape. Another song, "Go Down Moses," told slaves that Harriet Tubman was leading a pack of slaves north that night.

Cultural ignorance is widespread throughout the United States, touching all races and social classes, and within the black community, too few families are paying attention to the cultural needs of their youngsters. The culture of black people is just as important as the culture of deafness.

Being Black and Deaf

Being black and deaf is like being a speck of pepper in a pile of salt. If you see a speck, you want to remove it. That is how we feel sometimes: removed from the black community, removed from the deaf community.

Society's perspective of black people is generally very negative; it is mired in myths and racism. Poverty, AIDS, unemployment, and violence exist in both black and white communities, especially those plagued by high unemployment and drugs. The media would generally have you believe that all black people are violent and none of us can be trusted. Other than the Cosbys, you rarely see a strong black family on television. The ability and strength of the black community is generally not recognized. Not all of our households are run by women, not all black men run from their responsibilities, not all black kids drop out of high school, nor do the majority of us sell dope. As a race we have had to be strong to withstand slavery and discrimination. American Indians were nearly wiped off the face of the earth, yet the Afro-American has survived despite the odds.

As educated black deaf professionals, we are sometimes separated from black people who have not pursued college degrees. Although we would like to be respected for our knowledge as professionals, most often we are seen as having knowledge only of black deaf people or deafness. We are not recognized for what we know about human behavior and the human services field.

Black deaf grassroots people and black deaf professionals must join together for survival, support, and interpersonal relationships. Without role models within each group, the culture cannot be passed from one generation to the next. When we join forces, we all benefit.

Black Interpreters

The National Association of Black Interpreters is a new movement to organize black interpreters and to expand their expertise from the pulpit to the podium. There are a number of reasons for this effort. Many interpreters from the white community will not go into a black community; they do not feel comfortable, especially at night. Nonblack interpreters often have no sense of cultural perspective or the rules of social interaction in the black deaf community. No interpreter training program that we know of includes a course for interpreters on race relations. In addition, a white interpreter at a black rally sticks out like a sore thumb.

Relationships

As previously stated, interracial dating, like intermarriage between deaf and hearing people, is still not widely accepted. Once someone asked me which would be considered more taboo—a black deaf male marrying a black hearing woman, or a black deaf male marrying a white deaf woman? We have no answer to that question. But we do answer that, despite differences of race, hearing ability, and communication choices, we all have something to learn from one another. There is a uniqueness to being black and deaf in America, and we are beginning to be recognized, to stand up and be counted.

Black Deaf Awareness Quiz

1. Name one black deaf person with a Ph.D.

2. Who are the authors of the book entitled *Black and Deaf in America: Are we that Different?*

3. Name the black deaf actor who portrayed a deaf gang member in an episode of "Beauty and the Beast." This person also was featured in a satiric video called "Hire the Handicapped."

4. (a) Who was the first Executive Director of National B.D.A.?
   (b) Name at least one founder.

5. Match the name with the vocation:
(a) Black deaf female manager at Pan American airlines	1. Byron Hampton
	2. Patricia Joyner
(b) Black deaf architect	3. Naomi Simms
(c) Black deaf model featured in major magazine ads	4. Patricia Johnson
	5. Edward Hudson
(d) Black deaf Peace Corps volunteer in Africa	6. Stedman Graham

6. Dr. Andrew Foster established how many schools and assemblies in Africa?

7. (a) How many black Queens have been named Miss Gallaudet?
   (b) Name(s) _____

8. (a) Where was the first Black Deaf Advocates Regional Conference held?
   (b) Where was the most recent Conference held?

9. Which black church in Washington, D.C. has the oldest deaf ministry?

10. The interpreting community in New York was in an uproar when which of the following black plays featured two non-RID affiliated black interpreters?
    (a) Your Arms Too Short to Box With God
    (b) Mamma I want to Sing
    (c) The Wiz

11. Gallaudet College was once segregated?
    (a) true
    (b) false

12. In 1989, there are still some segregated clubs for the deaf that do not permit blacks to join as full members.
    (a) true
    (b) false

13. Who or what was "Jim Crow"?

14. The Civil Rights Movement was sparked by:
    (a) Martin Luther King's death
    (b) Rosa Parks' refusal to give up her bus seat to a white person
    (c) Blacks attempting to enroll in white schools

15. Black hearing people used "sign language" in the underground railroad.
    (a) true
    (b) false

Answers to Black Deaf Awareness Quiz:

1. Dr. Glen Anderson
   Dr. Seth Ocloo
   Dr. Andrew Foster
   Dr. Diane Brooks (and there are others)

2. Earnest Hairston and Linwood Smith

3. Jack Burrs

4. Sheryl (Guest) Emery
   Lottie Crook, Anne Wilson, Bob Howard and many others

5. (a) Pan American manager   4. Patricia Johnson, NY
   (b) Architect   1. Byron Hampton, IN
   (c) Model   2. Patricia Joyner
   (d) Peace Corps volunteer   5. Edward Hudson

6. 31 schools and 35 assemblies

7. Only one: Carolyn McCaskill-Emerson

8. (a) Howard University, Washington, D.C.
   (b) The Ponchartrain Hotel, Detroit Michigan

9. Shiloh Baptist Church

10. (b) Mamma I Want to Sing

11. True

12. True

13. Laws that prevented blacks from participating in certain events and using certain accommodations

14. (b) Rosa Parks' refusal to give up her bus seat

15. True. Slaves invented "signs" and code words to identify passengers, conductors, and safe houses.

Sociolinguistic Aspects of the Black Deaf Community

ANTHONY J. ARAMBURO

The black deaf community can be described as a group of individuals who live in a "hearing and color-conscious society" (Anderson, 1972). They are continually striving to overcome the communication problems faced in everyday living while still having to contend with the racist attitudes that govern society. They are a group of individuals who appear to be immersed in both the black and deaf cultures.

At least three issues surface as a result of this "double immersion." One issue concerns the actual reality of a black deaf community, as distinct from both the black community and the deaf community. A second issue concerns identity: Given the immersion in both black and deaf cultures, the question is whether the individual's identity is primarily as a member of the black community, the deaf community, or the black deaf community. A third issue concerns communication patterns in black signing and white signing; casual observation reveals that black deaf individuals sign differently with white signers than they do with other black signers.

This paper summarizes a study conducted to investigate all these issues. Data presented here that relate to the issue of identity are from a survey conducted with sixty black deaf individuals. For the issue of communication patterns, videotapes were made of the conversational interaction of seven dyads controlled for race, audiological status, and signing skills.

The Black Deaf Community

As defined by Hillery (1974), a community is a general social system in which a group of people live together, share common goals, and carry out certain responsibilities to each other. Loomis (1983) states that communities strive to protect the resources that will serve to inform future generations of their cultural past. Padden (1980) distinguishes between culture and community and refers to the former as a set of learned behaviors of a group of people who have their own language, values, rules for behavior, and traditions. She goes on to point out that the membership of a deaf community is not limited to individuals who are culturally deaf, but may also include hearing and deaf people who are not culturally deaf yet still interact with culturally deaf people and see themselves as working with them in various common concerns (Padden, 1980, pp. 92–3).

A longer version of this Deaf Way presentation appeared in *The Sociolinguistics of the Deaf Community*, 1989, edited by C. Lucas, San Diego, CA: Academic Press.

Evidence of the existence of both a black community and a deaf community is presented elsewhere (e.g., Higgins, 1980, and Padden, 1980).

The first issue here concerns the reality of the black deaf community, as distinct from both the black community and the deaf community. The contention here is that a black deaf community does indeed exist and that it shares the characteristics and values of both the black community and the deaf community. In addition, it has some characteristics and values that are unique.

The black deaf community shares with the black community the obstacle of societal prejudices against black people. The unemployment rate is higher in the black community than in the white community; it is higher still among blacks in the deaf community. There are few black political leaders in the black community; they are nonexistent in the black deaf community. Both the black community and the black deaf community share a racial heritage and the struggles that blacks endured in obtaining their civil rights.

Features shared by the black deaf community and the deaf community are largely in the domain of communication. Their language, American Sign Language, is an important factor in the social life of the deaf community. Social activities such as sporting events (where the teams are made up of deaf players), deaf club activities, and deafness-related conferences and meetings attract deaf individuals because all involved can identify with the mode of communication used—ASL. Stereotypes of deaf people as dumb, uneducated, and unable to work, to name a few, affect both the general deaf community and the black deaf community. The black deaf individual, however, also must overcome the additional stereotypes that society at large places on blacks.

Characteristics and values that are unique to the black deaf community can be identified by looking at patterns of social interaction, education, and use of sign language. For example, many of the clubs where black deaf people go for social purposes cater primarily to the black deaf community. This is true in most cities (Higgins, 1980). There is also, in most cities, a meeting place where the white deaf go for their social activities. No law or rule laid down by the deaf community mandates this occurrence; it is something that simply happens. The separation of social meeting places is evidence of the existence of a black deaf community. The clubs where the black deaf meet are their places for disseminating key information about how they will carry out certain functions as a group. Club meetings, sports meetings, dances, card socials, and personal celebrations such as birthdays and anniversaries all happen at the clubhouse. Information related to jobs, problems that members are faced with, and new laws pertaining to the deaf are all available at the deaf club.

Not many black deaf individuals have the luxury of owning a telecommunication device for the deaf (TDD), so the telephone is not a viable means for relaying information. Members of the black deaf community do not all live in the same area of the city. For those who do live in close proximity, the clubhouse is the most convenient place for meeting to discuss and pass on information.

Observation of the black deaf community confirms that black deaf people usually marry other black deaf people. Judging from married couples in the black deaf community, an individual tends to marry another black deaf individual who attended the same residential school. When a black deaf individual does marry a hearing person, that hearing spouse is usually also black.

Educational patterns also provide evidence of the existence of a black deaf community. In recent years, the black and deaf communities have made significant achievements in the area of education. Blacks no longer must settle for an education that is "separate but equal" and can freely attend any school or university for which they are qualified. During the days of racial segregation, however, most elementary school programs for black deaf children were set up on campuses that accommodated an all-black student population. The programs were mediocre (Hairston and Smith, 1983) and in most cases, the administrative personnel had no expertise in the field of deaf education. Teachers in black schools for deaf students were not required to have college course work related to the education of deaf children. College programs that provided blacks with a degree in education offered no course work specifically geared to educating deaf students.

Then, as now, educational programs for the deaf did not require teachers to be versed in American Sign Language, and programs designed to teach sign language to teachers were rare. The manual alphabet was the predominant mode for teaching in many schools with black deaf students. Often entire lessons were fingerspelled. In many schools, sign language was not permitted in the classroom.

Today, black deaf children who are born to hearing parents face the same predicament as their peers in the past: Many hearing parents refuse to communicate with their children through sign language. Parents leave the burden of educating their child solely to the school system.

Black deaf children born to deaf parents have an advantage over their peers with hearing parents, because deaf parents communicate with their children through sign language. When these students go to the residential schools, they bring sign language with them. Outside the classroom, students converse using sign language. Playground activities and other nonclassroom activities permit students to develop their language and social skills. During the years when black schools were not permitted to compete with white schools in athletic activities, black students had to travel in order to compete with rival schools. During these visits, black deaf students shared their language and taught each other new signs.

Upon completing school, most black deaf students learn a trade in order to make their living, and this choice of vocational training greatly lessens the number of black deaf students entering college (Christiansen and Barnartt, 1987). It has been suggested that a correlation exists between this choice and students' inadequate English skills. Many black deaf students are graduating with a high school certificate, not a high school diploma, and the number of black deaf students entering colleges and universities is still small.

Black deaf individuals lag behind both the black and the deaf communities in terms of advancement. The black deaf person is doubly affected, insofar as being labeled black, poor, and disabled amounts to simultaneous placement in two devalued worlds (Alcocer, 1974). Blacks in general have made considerable gains, but members of the black deaf community have had a difficult time emulating their success. Deaf people in general did not participate in a movement to improve their civil rights until the 1970s, when they actively joined other organizations of disabled people in transforming their own special civil rights issues into the 1973 Rehabilitation Act (Boros and Stuckless, 1982). The black deaf community, having missed the opportunity to gain advancement alongside the black community, must now advocate for itself. Many black deaf individuals state that they have noticed no real improvements overall in the black deaf community. Being discriminated against on the basis of deafness is difficult enough to overcome, but the joint impact of handicap discrimination and ethnic discrimination compounds the hardship and increases the barriers to success.

Further evidence of the existence of a black deaf community comes from differences observed between black signing and white signing. This paper will provide evidence of how black signing differs from white signing, mainly in the area of lexical choices.

On the whole, members of the black deaf community are aware of both their black culture and their deaf culture. Much as members of the black community pass on to future generations cultural resources such as black art, black folklore, and black spirituals, members of the black deaf community pass along similar cultural resources. For example, the oral history of residential school experiences from the era when schools were segregated parallels the oral history of the black community about slavery.

Black or Deaf?

As discussed earlier, black deaf individuals are immersed in both black and deaf cultures and can be part of both cultures, so a question of identity arises. Does a black deaf individual identify primarily with the black community or with the deaf community? A survey of sixty members of the black deaf community in the Washington, D.C. area attempted to answer this question.

A majority of the participants were high school and college students attending the Model Secondary School for the Deaf (MSSD) and Gallaudet University. Older members of the Washington, D.C. black deaf community were sought to represent the adult black deaf population. Approximately one-third of the individuals interviewed lived in the Washington, D.C. area. Individuals were selected from three age groups: eighteen to twenty-five; twenty-six to thirty-five; and thirty-six and above. A representative sample of ten men and ten women from each age group was sought.

In actuality, a total of thirty-three men and twenty-seven women, with a median age of 27.1 years participated in the study. Fourteen participants (23 percent) learned sign language before age six, and forty-six participants (77 percent) learned sign language after age six. Fifty of the participants (88 percent) attended residential schools. Four of the participants (7 percent) were children of deaf parents, and fifty-six participants (93 percent) were children of hearing parents. Fifty-five participants (92 percent) described themselves as native signers of ASL.

The interviews with participants were conducted on an informal, one-on-one basis. ASL was used throughout the interviews as the primary mode of communication.

Several questions were asked of the respondents to determine their experiences of black culture and the black community in general:

- ❖ Who are some black leaders you recognize as influential in the black community?
- ❖ Where did you acquire your knowledge of black history?
- ❖ Have you ever felt you were discriminated against or treated differently not because you are deaf but because you are black?
- ❖ In terms of upward achievement, where do you see the black community headed?
- ❖ What contribution(s) do you feel black deaf people can make in bringing about racial equality?

Other questions explored deaf culture and the black deaf community:

- ❖ Do you feel there is a deaf culture existing in the deaf community?
- ❖ Who are some deaf leaders you identify with?
- ❖ What is the most significant achievement obtained by deaf people?

❖ When in school, were you taught deaf culture in class?

❖ Did you ever feel you were discriminated against or treated differently because you are deaf?

The final set of questions dealt with the respondents' feelings about being black and deaf:

❖ How does black culture and the black community differ from deaf culture and the black deaf community?

❖ What are advancements you notice that have been made by black deaf individuals?

❖ Do you feel black deaf culture is alive and strong in the black deaf community?

❖ What do you see as the most significant barrier black deaf individuals have to overcome in order to be considered equal in the black community and also in the deaf community?

❖ What do you hope to contribute to the black deaf community?

❖ Which do you identify with first, your black culture or your deaf culture?

Results

The survey provided a general answer to the question of identity. Eight participants (13 percent) said that they identify themselves as deaf before they identify as black; but fifty-two participants (87 percent) identified themselves as black first. Among those participants who identified their deafness first, the majority had deaf parents and were educated in a residential school for the deaf. They were more integrated into the deaf community than those who identified with their blackness first.

In contrast, the respondents who identified with black culture first said that they see their color as more visible than their deafness and that they want respect for their ethnicity before their deafness. One comment was typical of many of the black-identified participants: "You see I am black first. My deafness is not noticed until I speak or use my hands to communicate."

Members of this group, as expected, gave more detailed answers than the deaf-identified group to questions about black culture. The majority said that they did not learn about black culture in school. They learned about their black heritage from parents and siblings and on their own. Most could identify with present problems facing blacks, and many of the answers focused on racial discrimination.

All of the participants agreed that there is a deaf culture. When asked about prominent deaf leaders, a majority of the participants named Thomas Hopkins Gallaudet most frequently and nearly exclusively. No contemporary deaf leaders were identified as making a substantial contribution to the deaf community. Many of the participants, however, provided names from their school or local community when asked whom they felt had made a contribution to the deaf community.

All of the participants agreed that the deaf community has progressed in recent years. Achievements were noted in the areas of employment opportunity and education. All participants felt that they had been discriminated against or treated differently because of their deafness, their blackness, or both. Many of the participants also mentioned that they felt they were discriminated against or treated differently by members of the deaf community as well as by members of the general hearing community.

In many of their responses to questions about the black deaf community, participants mentioned parallels between the black community and the deaf community. Also mentioned were notable accomplishments that blacks have made since the civil rights movement began. The barrier of communication was seen as the most prevalent obstacle separating the black deaf community from the black and deaf communities.

Black deaf individuals often find themselves alienated from the dominant black culture. The participants who strongly identified with their black deaf culture also noted that differences in ways of signing exist between black deaf and white deaf individuals. They mentioned, too, the separation of black deaf clubs and white deaf clubs as an ongoing dilemma that illustrates the separateness of the two cultures.

The following excerpts from the interviews reflect the harsh realities facing members of the black deaf community:

❖ The black community in general has more opportunities for advancement than the black deaf community.

❖ Black deaf women have a much harder time succeeding than their male counterparts.

❖ The black deaf community has seen little or no progress within the last ten to fifteen years.

❖ The total number of blacks pursuing higher education has increased, while the number of black deaf individuals pursuing higher education is still comparatively low.

❖ The deaf community has made progress, but the black deaf community still lags behind.

❖ Communication is important in terms of socializing skills.

❖ Black deaf individuals' communication skills are weak when relating to the general black community.

❖ Sign language skills are an important tool in functioning in the black deaf community.

❖ Upward mobility is difficult for black deaf people to achieve without sufficient role models.

❖ We have just begun to see a focus on black culture and black history in the education setting.

❖ Much of what black deaf people learn about black culture they learn through reading they do on their own or what family members teach them. We learned nothing in the schools.

❖ Black deaf people have to identify with their blackness first because of its visibility. Deafness is invisible. You do not notice I am deaf until I begin to communicate.

Members of the black deaf community have well developed feelings and sentiments toward each other. They behave according to well defined norms of what is proper and improper in their black deaf culture. Throughout the interviews, the sense of identity and the feeling of belonging were apparent in the comments and behavior of the participants. Although the greater percentage of participants identified themselves as black first and deaf second, the black deaf community is nonetheless cohesive and highly motivated.

Communication Patterns

As discussed earlier, differences have been observed between black signing and white signing. It also has been casually observed that black deaf individuals sign differently with white signers than they do with other black signers. The second part of the study collected empirical data on sign language production in black-white interaction. These data provided evidence of code-switching by black signers.

Specifically, the conversational interaction of seven dyads was videotaped. Participants in the study were two black deaf men, both native ASL users (identified as X and Y); one black hearing man, a professional working in the deaf community; one white deaf man, a native ASL user; and one white hearing man, a professional working in research on deafness.

Table 1 presents the composition of the seven dyads set up among these five participants and the language used in each dyad by the participants. Each dyad was videotaped for approximately twenty minutes while the two participants, alone together in the taping room, engaged in casual conversation. ASL was the predominant mode of communication used when both participants were deaf (native ASL users). When either of the hearing participants was involved, the predominant mode of communication was ASL-like signing, as opposed to pure ASL.

Dyads 1, 2, 4, and 5—combinations of deaf and hearing subjects—showed evidence of code-switching. Although the predominant mode of communication in these dyads was ASL-like signing, the deaf participant in each dyad often began the conversation in ASL and then switched to incorporate more English in the signing.

Dyads 6 and 7—black deaf talking with white deaf subjects—displayed sign variation with ASL, as opposed to code-switching to ASL-like signing. ASL was used by both speakers in these dyads as their primary mode of communication.

Nonmanual features also were different between these two groups. Exaggerated body movements and facial expressions were not so prevalent when a deaf participant conversed with a hearing participant as compared to when both participants were deaf.

In setting up this project, it was hypothesized that the deaf participants would sign differently when paired with a hearing participant than when paired with each other. In light of this hypothesis, what took place in dyad 3—two black deaf participants—is significant when compared to dyads 6 and 7. ASL was used in all there dyads. Yet in dyad 3, the two black deaf participants used signs when paired together that they did not use when paired separately with the white deaf participant. Specifically, the citation forms of FLIRT, SCHOOL, and BOSS occurred in dyads 6 and 7, but black forms of these signs occurred in dyad 3. When asked about these particular forms and others not described here, the black deaf participants characterized them as older signs used by blacks, originating from the time when blacks attended segregated schools for the deaf. One of the black deaf participants explained that the forms are not used when a black person is with "a person who is not a part of that culture."

Black deaf participants interacting with each other also tended to use more exaggerated facial expressions and to use their signing space more fully than when they interacted with white deaf subjects. In contrast, the two black deaf participants, X in

TABLE 1: Composition of Conversational Dyads and Language Used

Dyad	Participants	Language
1	Black deaf$_x$-Black hearing	ASL-like signing
2	Black deaf$_y$-Black hearing	ASL-like signing
3	Black deaf$_x$-Black deaf$_y$	ASL
4	Black deaf$_x$-White hearing	ASL-like signing
5	Black deaf$_y$-White hearing	ASL-like signing
6	Black deaf$_x$-White deaf	ASL
7	Black deaf$_y$-White deaf	ASL

dyad 6 and Y in dyad 7, used less exaggerated facial expressions, fewer body movements, and a smaller signing space when conversing with the white deaf participant than when conversing with each other.

Other studies provide additional evidence of variation in ASL that is related to ethnic background (e.g., Woodward and De Santis, 1977; Woodward and Erting, 1975). Other findings of the present study suggest that the two sociolinguistic oppositions of deaf-hearing and black-white can have interlocking effects on conversation. For example, in dyad 6, the black deaf participant X is more of a passive listener when conversing with the white deaf participant than in his other conversations. Although black participant Y is far from passive in his conversation with this same white deaf participant in dyad 7, the only instances where Y interrupts in order to speak are when he is conversing with the other black deaf participant.

Summary and Conclusions

The existence of a black deaf community is in part evidenced by the survival of all-black clubs for deaf people, where members go to socialize in a setting that satisfies their communication needs. The existence of this community is reinforced by a history of segregated schooling. The lack of adequate facilities and qualified personnel needed to prepare black deaf individuals for the future is reflected not only in the high levels of unemployment and underemployment found in the black deaf community, but also in the small number of black deaf individuals who enter institutions of higher learning.

In the study described here, a survey was used to answer the question of which community black deaf individuals identify with first, the black community or the deaf community. The majority of the respondents identified first with the black community. They believe that they are seen by others as black first because, unlike skin color, their deafness only becomes visible when they communicate with ASL. The remaining respondents who identified themselves first with the deaf community are more immersed in this community than the black-identified group; they are from deaf families, grew up in residential schools, and socialize mostly within the deaf community as adults.

The language of the black deaf community is ASL. Yet variations of ASL occur when members of the black deaf community engage in conversations among themselves. The present study found that black deaf individuals commonly use signs that are unknown to outsiders. These "black signs," which developed in segregated black residential schools, are used when conversing with other black deaf people; when conversing with white deaf individuals, black deaf people use standard ASL signs. This sociolinguistic variation provides additional evidence for the existence of a black deaf community.

As an essential part of the deaf community, the black deaf community faces the challenges of securing better education, more promising employment opportunities, and social advancements similar to those already achieved by members of the black community at large. Both in drawing attention to these issues and in describing some sociolinguistic features of black deaf communication, this paper is aimed at stimulating further research on the black deaf community. It is hoped that future studies will increase our understanding of this particular minority group as well as other minorities within the deaf community at large.

References

Alcocer, A. M. 1974. *Proceedings of the Working Conference on Minority Deaf.* Center on Deafness, California State University at Northridge.

Anderson, G. B. 1972. "Vocational Rehabilitation Services and the Black Deaf." *Journal of Rehabilitation of the Deaf* 6 (2): 126–128.

Boros, A., and R. Stuckless. 1982. "The Dynamics of Social Lag Among Deaf People." In *Social Aspects of Deafness: Vol. 6. Deaf People and Social Changes,* ed. A. Boros and R. Stuckless. Washington, DC: Gallaudet University, Department of Sociology. pp. 15–45.

Christiansen, J. B., and S. N. Barnartt. 1987. "The Silent Minority: The Socioeconomic Status of Deaf People." In *Understanding Deafness Socially,* ed. P. C. Higgins and J. E. Nash. Springfield, IL: Thomas. pp. 171–196.

Hairston, E., and L. Smith. 1983. *Black and Deaf in America.* Silver Spring, MD: T.J. Publishers.

Higgins, P. C. 1980. *Outsiders in a Hearing World: A Sociology of Deafness.* Beverly Hills, CA: Sage Publications.

Hillery, G. 1974. *Communal Organizations.* Chicago: Chicago University Press.

Loomis, O. H. 1983. *Cultural Conversation: The Protection of Cultural Heritage in the United States.* Washington, DC: United States Government Printing Office.

Padden, C. 1980. "The Deaf Community and the Culture of Deaf People." In *Sign Language and the Deaf Community,* ed. C. Baker and R. Battison. Silver Spring, MD: National Association of the Deaf. pp. 89–103.

Woodward, J. C., and S. De Santis. 1977. "Two to One It Happens: Dynamic Phonology in Two Sign Languages." *Sign Language Studies* 17: 329–346.

Woodward, J. C., and C. Erting. 1975. "Synchronic Variation and Historical Change in American Sign Language." *Language Science* 37: 9–12.

Deaf Gay Men's Culture

THOMAS P. KANE

Yes, there *is* a subculture of gay people in the deaf community. I became interested in this subject after taking a course given by Dr. Barbara Kannapell while I was a student at Gallaudet University. I would like to focus this paper on the culture of deaf gay men, as this culture is more familiar to me than the subculture of deaf lesbians.

To my knowledge, there is nothing in the research literature on the subject of Deaf gay culture. There is a similar shortage of research on the cultures of deaf Blacks, deaf women, and deaf Christians. It is hoped that this paper will spark other studies of subcultures within the deaf community.

The terms "homosexual" and "gay" have different meanings, although there may be only a faint line drawn between them. "Homosexuality" is a label for sexual behavior between members of the same sex, which has existed since the beginning of mankind. History tells us that the homosexual experience was prevalent in ancient Greece, was a part of the rituals of some tribes, and was practiced in informal societies, such as those of pirates. It was the Puritan tradition that made homosexuality taboo in America. Homosexual behavior is common today in prisons and institutions. There is much research claiming that nearly every male will have at least one homosexual experience in his life, usually during puberty.

The term "gay" refers to those confirmed homosexuals who have adopted "gayness" as their lifestyle. Gay people usually live in large cities and settle in predominantly gay communities, where their lifestyle is tolerated. One major difference in values between gay men and straight men is that straight men have learned not to cry or otherwise show their feelings, while gay men believe in expressing their feelings freely. This difference often leads straight men to look down on gay men as weak.

While they consider themselves a minority, similar to Blacks and Hispanics, deaf gays differ in that they constitute a minority within a minority. For the purposes of this paper, I will use the abbreviation "DGM" for Deaf Gay Man. I emphasize that in my descriptions of DGMs, I will be speaking in generalities; I do not mean to imply that *all* DGMs are as I describe them, though I believe my observations are true of *most* DGMs much of the time.

In many respects, DGMs do not differ from the general deaf population. A DGM may have attended an institution for the deaf or a mainstream public school, be a high school dropout or a Ph.D. DGMs use all types and degrees of communication modes. There are even deaf gay men who regard themselves as "anti-deaf."

There are, however, definite differences between deaf gays and members of the deaf community in general. DGMs interact with hearing gays far more often than straight (heterosexual) deaf people interact with straight hearing people. Deaf straight people tend to socialize with and marry other deaf people; marriage to a hearing person is a rare occurrence in the straight deaf world. However, while many DGMs maintain long-term relationships with hearing gay men, relationships between deaf gay men are rare.

Members of the hearing gay community are also more aware of and sensitive to the needs of deaf people than are people in the straight world. For example, the hearing gay community usually provides sign language interpreters for its political rallies, Gay Pride Day events, national gay rights marches, etc. The "I love you" sign is well known in the gay community. The deaf straight community, by comparison, has a long way to go in educating their hearing peers about deafness.

DGMs' use of sign language differs from that of straight deaf people. DGMs often exaggerate their language in creative and humorous ways, which makes their conversations more enjoyable. Because there is a specialized vocabulary in the gay culture, DGMs have invented some signs, such as "cruise," "drag," "butch," and "one-night stand," that are unfamiliar to deaf straight people. There is also a secret code language—in sign—which offers privacy in conversation among deaf gay men. For example, "green and yellow" (gay), "golf" (gay), "basketball" (bisexual), and "softball" (straight) are signs gay deaf men use when they get together. A few years ago at a gay deaf convention in Washington, DC, I saw the audience give their different local, national, and foreign signs—forty-five in total—for "homosexual," "gay," and "lesbian."

One cultural value shared by DGMs is that of cooperating and sticking together to protect each other from narrow-minded people. It is said that when a DGM meets someone new, the first thought that comes to his mind is, "Is this person accepting and understanding or prejudiced?" The DGM knows that, to answer this question, he can check with another DGM for a "reference." This saves the time and effort of building friendship and trust with a person who ultimately would prove unaccepting. The DGM feels assurance in the knowledge that, if a new person is prejudiced, he can protect himself from being betrayed or rejected, common experiences for a DGM. If the person is OK, on the other hand, the DGM can let his hair down with comfort.

If a DGM travels to another city, he often stops at the home of another DGM. DGMs prefer gay bars to deaf clubs, and his host can lead him to bars where DGMs tend to hang out. Like moths, they are attracted to the light for socializing; they often can be found near cigarette machines or video games, where the lights are brighter and it is easier to read each others signs. Similarly, at beaches where deaf straight people get together, there is always a section off to one side for the privacy of DGMs. When a DGM introduces someone new to other DGMs at a social event, he first informs the others whether the new person is hearing or deaf, then gives his name.

DGMs do not mix easily with deaf bisexual men. DGMs consider bisexual men to be confused about which group they really belong to. Their situation is similar to that of a hard of hearing person who is unsure whether he belongs to the deaf world or the hearing world. Sometimes bisexual men consider themselves as more straight than gay, and this is a big turn-off to DGMs, similar to the situation where a hard of hearing person denies his hearing impairment to deaf people.

There is a myth that the gay world is a sad and lonely world. In my view, this is a fallacy. (I personally consider it no worse than the straight world, which has dysfunctional families, broken homes, and a high divorce rate.) Nevertheless, there is an enormous need among deaf gay youth for positive DGM role models, especially during adolescence. Some of the common conflicts experienced by young DGMs include questions of identity: Who am I? Is being gay really okay? Should I reveal my sexual identity to my parents? How can I live well in straight society? Sometimes these young men talk to counselors or psychologists to understand themselves better and to boost their self-esteem. Often, however, they leave a counseling session more confused because of the counselor or psychologist's lack of awareness of gay culture.

To address this and other problems in their communities, deaf gays have established organizations of their own. For example, there is a local organization for deaf gay people in Washington, D.C. called the *Capital Metro Rainbow Alliance*. It was founded in 1977 as an independent social club for deaf gay people, but the alliance sometimes works with hearing gay organizations as well. There are similar organizations all over the United States and Canada. There is also a national organization for deaf gay people called the *Rainbow Alliance of the Deaf*, which holds a convention in a different city every two years.

I have noticed that a DGM may call himself a "deaf gay" in the hearing gay community, whereas in the deaf community he will call himself a "gay deaf," in both cases to set himself apart from the general community. I have asked many DGMs to pick which of these so-called handicaps is more important to them—deafness or gayness. All have chosen deafness! I have also asked, "Suppose there are two candidates running for President of the United States: one who favors nondiscrimination toward gay people and one who favors equal opportunities for handicapped people. Which one would you vote for?" The response has been overwhelmingly in support of the candidate who is on the side of the handicapped. This shows that these members of the DGM community consider deafness to be a more significant issue in their lives than their sexual preference.

Still, deaf gays do experience discrimination based on their sexual orientation. In the words of Shirley Chisholm, the first Black female Representative in the United States Congress, "Discrimination is alive and well!" Discrimination is not only a matter of a person not getting a job or a promotion, it represents a prejudice that classifies a person as fitting one of those stereotypes of which society disapproves. Today this prejudice is reinforced by the church and the media.

There is no doubt that straight deaf individuals as well have experienced discrimination and are fighting for better conditions. Dr. I. King Jordan has said, "Deaf people can do anything—except hear." The same is true of deaf gay people; they are no different from anyone else except in their sexual preference.

Cultural Implications of Treating the Hearing-Impaired Substance Abuser

JEAN MODRY

The purpose of this paper, a consolidation of my experiences as a Deaf professional working with the Deaf community in the area of substance abuse, is to provide a mini crash course in the cultural implications to consider when treating the Deaf addict. It does not offer solutions, but only gives a base of understanding as to where the linguistically and culturally Deaf addict is most rooted.

It is a documented fact that Deaf people have their own culture, their own standards of behavior, and their own language. If substance-abuse professionals understand Deaf people as a culturally different group and respect that difference, the treatment they provide will be more appropriate, more beneficial, and will yield higher rates of success. As with any culture, there are individual characteristics and anomalies among linguistically and culturally Deaf Americans that defy generalization; this paper covers those aspects of Deaf culture that seem to interfere with the success of traditional addictions counseling programs. Ideas in this paper were gathered from my direct contact with case management, conversations with members of the Deaf community recovering from substance abuse, and readings in this specialized area.

Visualize this scene: A troop of English-speaking American computer technicians travel to Ethiopia where they build a huge, modern facility in the midst of arid farmland. The facility houses many advanced computer systems. These computer whizzes set up training classes that are conducted in English, expecting the Ethiopians to understand everything that they are taught in English. They also expect the Ethiopians to change their behavior and adopt the Americans' ways. For example, Ethiopians are accustomed to squatting in, what is for them, a comfortable position while doing many of their chores. Imagine their bewilderment when they are told that this is not the right way to sit. They are instructed to bend their bodies into ninety degree angles in order to accommodate their torsos to the chairs facing the computer terminals. They are expected to hold their arms straight out in front of them and cup their hands into a claw-like position. For hours at a time, they must lightly touch a flat, box-like device called a "keyboard." Wearing loin cloths, the Ethiopians shiver in their air-conditioned cubicles. Ethiopians, accustomed to working with the natural resources of their land, consider themselves productive. Now it is implied that the only way they can be productive is to stay within the small confines of a computer cubicle.

What will be the success rate of this project? Poor? Right! Why? Each respective culture perceives situations differently. The Ethiopians perceive this situation as the more powerful culture's (Americans) imposing its standards on them in a disrespectful way. Not surprisingly, the project backfires and both cultures part feeling frustrated and hostile toward each other.

It is difficult to visualize such a scene occurring in this day and age. Americans like to think that, in general, they are respectful of other cultures and would not impose their standards on them. American professionals, especially, perceive themselves as an advanced group that respects the relationship between human beings and the properties of their cultures.

It is ironic, therefore, that many professionals who work with the Deaf community do not give a second thought to plucking Deaf people from their culture and submerging them in the professionals' (hearing) culture when rendering their services. Many professionals insist on speaking English when "communicating" with linguistically and culturally Deaf people.

When two cultures do not speak the same language, miscommunication occurs, and the minority culture develops mistrust towards the majority culture. Hearing professionals from the dominant culture have a tendency to measure the world around them, and to derive conclusions, using their own set of standards. It is not uncommon for them to impose their standards on the Deaf minority and, if there is a failure or a miscommunication, to consider it a deficiency within the minority rather then a deficiency in their own approach or method.

For example, tests were conducted to measure the self-esteem of hearing people, and norms were developed. These same tests with hearing norms were then conducted within the Deaf culture, with the conclusion that Deaf people in general exhibited lower self-esteem than their hearing counterparts. What would these professionals find if they focused on measuring the levels of self-esteem solely within the Deaf community? They might find that lower self-esteem is actually the norm for Deaf people. They might find that this is not a deficiency but a human condition based in their culture.

It is very difficult for a member of a minority group to make the transition to the majority culture without a well thought-out and sufficiently long acculturation process. "Acculturation" refers to the transfer of culture from one ethnic group to another. Ideally, the acculturation process should involve professionals who are bilingual and bicultural to bridge the gap between two different cultures. With the assistance of such people, and the reliable and valid information about the majority culture they could provide, one could cross from one culture to another with more confidence. The knowledge gained of the majority culture would be more reliable and valid.

The Maryknoll Mission describes this concept clearly in a simple poem.

Go to the people
Live among them
Learn from them
Love them
Serve them
Start with what they know
and build on what they have.

It is common knowledge that the Deaf culture is not so advanced as the hearing culture in the area of substance abuse treatment. Almost all of the existing alcoholism agencies in the United States are designed by hearing people for verbal, hearing people. It has also been documented that Deaf substance abusers are often placed into treatment programs that are designed for verbal, hearing substance abusers.

When Deaf substance abusers complete in-patient programs designed for hearing people, they often relapse owing to the lack of support services in their culture. Statistics show that, of those Deaf substance abusers who underwent treatment and did not have community support services after treatment, almost 100 percent resumed their former patterns of abuse. Of what value is it to pluck a Deaf substance abuser from his culture and place him into a program designed for a verbal, hearing person, knowing that back home there are no support services? This practice creates an inevitable path to relapse.

Moreover, referring Deaf people to programs designed for hearing people tends to create a false hope in the Deaf substance abuser, his family, and the community—a hope that the Deaf addict is going to improve. But the Deaf substance abuser is not going to improve, because improvement is dependent on community support services.

In order for Deaf substance abusers to have a fighting chance at maintaining sobriety, alcoholism agencies must start with the community support systems that already exist within the Deaf culture and are utilized by Deaf people ("Start with what they know"). The Department of Rehabilitative Services (DORS), interpreter referral services, centers for independent living, Deaf clubs, and churches with Deaf parishes are support systems presently utilized by Deaf people. Alcoholism agencies can work with these support services and related resources that exist within the Deaf community ("Build on what they have"). Once alcoholism agencies have gained an in-depth understanding of the Deaf culture, they can then begin the acculturation process—the process of bridging the gap between the two cultures to ensure a better flow of knowledge and expertise from one culture to another.

Language is the locus of all cultures, and the acculturation process starts with learning the language of the minority, in this case, ASL (American Sign Language). If we do not share a common language we cannot bridge the gap between cultures.

American Sign Language and Treatment Considerations

In the Deaf culture in general, and when working with the Deaf substance abuser in particular, the key to developing trust is familiarity with the semantics and syntax of the language of Deaf people—ASL. ASL is an ideographic language; its delivery style is more pictorial and less symbolic than that of English. However, the message presented by Alcoholics Anonymous, Narcotics Anonymous, and by treatment centers is often very symbolic. With this linguistic gap, it is easy to see why communication problems arise; it is difficult to communicate a symbolic message to a culture that uses an ideographic language.

Use of visual aids is one methodology that can be used to bridge the linguistic gap. Professionals must construct a linguistic continuum for important terms used in the substance abuse treatment field, ranging from the concrete (pictures) to the symbolic (English terms). After a concept is introduced and understood in a pictorial fashion, the Deaf client can move along the continuum to the more symbolic message. In this way the Deaf substance abuser will have at least a foothold on the language used in treatment centers.

The process of introducing a new concept to the Deaf substance abuser is more complicated than introducing a new concept to the hearing substance abuser. Language and concepts that exist within the dominant culture may not be present within the minority culture, and vice versa. The Deaf substance abuser must learn the new terminology and the corresponding signs (if they exist in his repertoire), then try to derive a meaning for that word from his experiences within his own culture.

It is common to find that the Deaf substance abuser lacks the experiences needed to understand the concept being introduced. The concept of empowerment, so vital to the recovery process, provides a good example. When a hearing counselor introduces the concept of empowerment to the average hearing alcoholic, he expects that his definitions and examples will be understood, for empowerment exists abundantly within the hearing culture. Not only do Deaf people lack the language base needed to understand this concept, but behavior reflecting empowerment practically does not exist within their culture.

The empowerment process involves a change in the substance abuser's behavior and feelings of self-worth. Theoretically, the goal of the Deaf substance abuser is to take charge of his own life (become empowered) and advocate for himself. But many Deaf addicts come from environments (hearing families, educational institutions, etc.) where their experiences consisted primarily of relating and/or submitting to authority rather than exercising their own power of reasoning. Many Deaf substance abusers grow up in family environments where most things are done for them. Hearing professionals, too, have traditionally made decisions for Deaf people. Consequently, the chances of a Deaf person's experiencing personal growth through making decisions and using the power of reason have been minimized. As a result of having been treated paternalistically, the Deaf substance abuser often comes into treatment with the attitude, "I can't do it. You do it for me." These dependency behaviors on the part of Deaf substance abusers too often continue beyond their adolescent years into adulthood.

To complicate matters further, the Deaf substance abuser is isolated by communication barriers erected by the hearing culture. Many families do not attempt to learn sign language to communicate with their Deaf offspring. The Deaf substance abuser is often out of touch with his environment because he receives information hours, days, weeks, or even months after the hearing community has received it. This delayed communication process encourages the Deaf substance abuser to be reactive instead of pro-active toward situations around him.

These life experiences do not promote the habits of setting goals, pursuing these goals, and experiencing the consequences, which are necessary to the development of one's self. The point is that the Deaf substance abuser often lacks the life experiences within his culture necessary to understand the concept of empowerment, a term used often in alcoholism agencies designed by the hearing.

It is common to find hearing counselors who have tried to force a Deaf substance abuser to communicate on the counselor's terms. For instance, a counselor in an individual counseling session might ask a Deaf substance abuser, "Where are we at now with this?" If this question were interpreted word for word into sign language, the Deaf ASL user would most likely reply with a puzzled expression on his face, "in your office." The structure of the question means one thing in English, but when it is interpreted in the exact form into sign language it means something quite different.

There are other instances when it is not possible to translate the exact meaning of a spoken question into ASL. Certain abstract words used in treatment, for example, "serenity" and "higher power," are difficult to sign. Many words are impossible to communicate in such a way that they are understood in the same way by both hearing and Deaf people. It is very difficult to define many of the words used in an alcoholism agency designed for the hearing so that their meanings are understood by Deaf people, just as it is difficult to translate some ASL signs into English.

It has been observed that some professionals will shut out a Deaf substance abuser who is trying to communicate in ASL, because the professional does not understand ASL. In many instances, when using a sign language transliterator instead of a certified sign language interpreter, ASL comes across to the hearing professional as "broken English," which is not only incomprehensible, but wrongly implies a lack of communication and language skills—and therefore intelligence—on the part of the Deaf person. It has been reported that some professionals have tried to structure Deaf substance abusers' learning and communication environments to maintain control over what the Deaf substance abusers sign so the professionals could understand them. Do such situations foster the trust essential for successful treatment? No!

When a common linguistic bond, in which both cultures understand one another, is established and maintained, trust will increase between the hearing agencies and professionals and the Deaf community and Deaf substance abusers. ASL allows the Deaf substance abuser to express himself freely with much greater depth and understanding than English would allow. Ease of communication is the basis of treatment, and the key to developing a bond of trust with the Deaf substance abuser is to learn and understand the nuances of ASL. This process will ensure a healthier working relationship with fewer barriers between the two cultures.

In order to develop rapport with the Deaf client, the counselor, in addition to understanding the problems associated with communication, must have a thorough awareness of other cultural implications of deafness when providing treatment services. This leads us to a discussion of Deaf culture.

Deaf Culture and Treatment Considerations

The Deaf community is very small and closely knit, with a strong sense of conformity. Because information is transmitted primarily by word of mouth, it is difficult to update information flowing within the Deaf community. Even the media's efforts to raise public awareness of substance abuse have not had an impact on the Deaf community because the media primarily serve the hearing culture.

The Deaf community at large has a very conservative attitude about alcoholism, considering it an unacceptable behavior. Many Deaf people tend to see alcoholism and drug addiction as evidence of personal weakness and/or as a moral failing. That this antiquated view of addiction persists is a result of the communication barriers that inhibit the flow of information on current trends in addictions treatment into the Deaf culture.

Members of the Deaf community tend to see things in black and white: You have a bad habit, therefore you are a bad person. The Deaf community also has one of the most efficient "grapevine" systems that exists. Word of mouth travels quickly, and the Deaf substance abuser, fearing reprisal from the Deaf community, often will not admit his addiction and will be reluctant to seek treatment or to work through a recovery program. The tendency of the Deaf community to view addictions as sinful denies the substance abuser the emotional support needed to seek treatment, as well as the support services needed to work through an individualized sobriety plan.

The treatment process itself is also influenced by the cultural characteristics of the Deaf substance abuser. The linguistically and culturally Deaf person's identity as a Deaf person is so deeply ingrained that it often interferes with the ability to relate to other identities, for example, the identity proclaimed in the statement, "I am an alcoholic." It has been reported in informal surveys that even if the Deaf substance abuser acknowledges in an Alcoholics Anonymous (AA) meeting conducted by the hearing culture that he is an alcoholic, he is left with a feeling of something missing within himself.

AA can be seen as a subculture. All members of this subculture speak AA lingo and share the basic purpose of maintaining sobriety. There is a feeling of oneness in the group, for all the hearing participants share a basic identity as alcoholics. AA philosophy holds that one must admit he is an alcoholic first, before all else, and must maintain that focus. This is very difficult for a culturally and linguistically Deaf substance abuser to do because his foremost identity is as a Deaf person.

When a Deaf person attends an AA meeting, he often feels inferior within the predominantly hearing group. This defeats the purpose of the AA meeting, where theoretically everyone is of equal status. In Chicago, the consistency rate of linguistically and culturally Deaf alcoholics' attendance in AA meetings is extremely poor. Would the negative feelings Deaf people have about AA persist if there were AA meetings run by Deaf people for Deaf people? Deaf substance abusers usually feel helpless to change their images within the Deaf community or to incorporate new ways of thinking about an old problem; these tasks appear overwhelming. They also tend to believe that their problems are unique and most likely the result of their disability. Just imagine their awakening when they discover that they are not alone with this "disease," when they find that other people have problems just as serious as their own and that there are ways to cope with these difficulties.

There exists a group, though new and still microscopic, of recovering substance abusers within the Deaf community. Some linguistically and culturally Deaf leaders are openly facing their own addictions, and this will pave the way for other Deaf community members to follow, allowing linguistically and culturally Deaf people to begin to learn more about who they are. "I'm Deaf and an alcoholic," will become an Americanized version of the Russian "glasnost" [openness].

Once Deaf people have that foundation, they can start building the columns needed to support the bridge to and from the substance abusers in the hearing culture. With the acculturation process at work, the gap between the two cultures will be bridged, and the hearing culture, which has more expertise in the area of chemical dependency, will be better able to share its knowledge with the Deaf community.

Given the pioneering stage of this field, many issues remain unresolved—for instance, are the twelve steps of AA culturally transferrable? In spite of the controversies though, counseling approaches useful with the Deaf substance abuser have already emerged. Traditional therapeutic techniques have been combined with nontraditional approaches and adapted to the linguistically and culturally Deaf substance abuser's special needs. But this field has yet to standardize and validate examinations of the various theoretical approaches used in the provision of substance abuse treatment for Deaf people. More research is needed.

References and Suggested Reading

Boros, Alex. 1983. "Alcoholism and Deaf People." *Gallaudet Today* 13 (3): 9–11.

Chough, Steven K. 1981. "The Trust vs. Mistrust Phenomenon among Deaf Persons." *Mental Health Substance Abuse and Deafness Monograph No. 7*, pp. 17–19.

McCrone, William P. 1982. "Serving the Deaf Substance Abuser." *Journal of Psychoactive Drugs* 14 (3): 199–203.

Stokoe, William. 1978. "Sign Language vs. Spoken Language." *Sign Language Studies* 18: 69–80.

Watson, Douglas. 1981. "Substance Abuse Services for Deaf Clients: A Question of Accessibility." *Mental Health Substance Abuse and Deafness Monograph No. 7.* pp. 13–16.

Wentzel, Carol. 1985. "An Outline for Working with the Hearing Impaired in an Inpatient Abuse Treatment Program." Position paper, National Association of Alcoholism and Substance Counselors.

The Social Life of Deaf People in Rural Communities: Implications for Community Colleges

BEVERLY BUTTERS AND NANCY KIRKENDALL

Opportunities for deaf adults to interact with each other are limited or nonexistent in many rural areas of the United States. Frequently, deaf people must drive considerable distances to metropolitan areas to participate in social or cultural activities. Time, expense, road conditions, and availability of transportation often prohibit travel to the more metropolitan areas where deaf activities, captioned movies, or deaf theater may be available. As a result, the deaf adult often feels isolated in his own community.

Community colleges located in strategic areas throughout a state, including extension centers located in remote rural areas, can facilitate social interaction among deaf people. Additionally, community colleges, well known for their ability to be creative, innovative, and flexible, are an ideal vehicle for delivery of services to the isolated rural deaf population.

Centralia College is a rural community college with a student population of 3,500 located in southwestern Washington. The college has been attempting to bring isolated deaf adults together through social opportunities and deaf awareness. The college organized an advisory committee to assist in these efforts. The committee consisted of nine energetic individuals and included deaf people, parents of deaf children, a professional interpreter, and individuals employed in public school programs for deaf people. The group met regularly throughout the winter, spring, and summer of 1987 to plan how the college could best offer programs and services to deaf individuals.

In the fall of 1987, Centralia College established the Hearing Impaired Studies Program. When the college's Public Information Office announced the program through the Centralia newspaper, our telephones rang steadily for weeks. Because the response was so great, the college staff was unable to answer all questions on an individual basis, and an orientation meeting was scheduled. More than seventy-five people flocked to the initial orientation session, eager to learn about the college's new program.

The program was designed to train people as sign language interpreters and public school classroom aides. However, many of the people who enrolled in our classes wanted to learn American Sign Language in order to communicate with deaf people in the community. The first classes were so full that students had to be turned away. To accommodate the numbers of individuals interested in learning sign language, two classes were offered—one in the daytime and the other in the evening. Deaf people were encouraged to attend the classes, free of charge, to meet new people interested in the deaf community.

The college was able to showcase the new program through news releases to the local newspaper and radio stations. One newspaper reporter was so interested in this new program that she became instrumental in keeping deaf awareness in the press in southwestern Washington. When the college acquired its first TDD, she wrote a story that included pictures. For another story she traveled to the remote eastern part of Lewis County to interview a deaf man. The local newspaper has been extremely interested in supporting the college's efforts to provide these much needed services.

The new program has been a tremendous asset to Centralia College. At the end of the first quarter of sign language classes, the college's child care director called our office and asked if there was anyone interested in teaching some signs to the children. Nancy Kirkendall jumped at this opportunity. She called the director to ask if she could teach signs to the children as part of a professional development project she had applied for through the American Association of Women in Community and Junior Colleges.

A six-month sign language program, geared to the children's ages at the child care center, was developed. Once a week, Nancy taught the children—whose ages ranged from three to six—some very basic signs. Because of the children's ages and because their attention spans varied, the classes could be held for only about fifteen minutes at a time. The child care workers also sat in on these sessions and learned the signs. They would reinforce the children's use of signs during the rest of the week. For example, when the children were taught the signs for "yes" and "no," the day care workers later asked the children to answer their questions with the yes or no signs. Also, books about deaf children were read to the children so that they could understand a little about deafness and not be afraid of deaf people. Nancy's work and her subsequent report received nationwide attention, which further enhanced the college's image.

Centralia College offers a number of student-funded clubs designed to meet the special needs of its students. One, the Sign On Club, provides opportunities for deaf and hearing people to socialize and plans events to raise deaf awareness in the community. One activity sponsored by the club was the creation of T-shirts and sweatshirts imprinted with "ASL Spoken Here" in both fingerspelling and English. These shirts were sold to raise funds for the club and to raise deaf awareness.

Another activity is the Sign On Club Movie Night. Once a month, free, closed-captioned movies—ranging from pure entertainment movies, such as *Popeye*, to movies concerned with deaf awareness, such as *Deaf Like Me*—are shown at the college. The local paper regularly announces the movies in a special section that focuses on area events, and everyone in the community is invited. Deaf people from a three-county area attend these functions. Many people bring refreshments to share and stay late to socialize. Currently, the college provides the only formal opportunities in the county for deaf adults to meet.

Prior to the Hearing Impaired Studies Program, Centralia College had no adaptive equipment for deaf people. With the establishment of the program, staff at the college began to assess what equipment would be needed to assist deaf students. The first item purchased was a TDD. One of the instructors in the program was deaf, and the purchase of the TDD made this instructor much more accessible to students. Additionally, the college's quarterly newsletter carries the TDD number, enabling deaf people who live in the college's service area to inquire about programs. An amplifier was purchased for the telephone handset in the Instruction Office, making telephone communication available to the hard of hearing on campus. This equipment is available to instructors, students, and any other community member who needs to use the equipment to communicate with others.

Members of the advisory committee expressed the need for courses to be more accessible to deaf students, so a closed-captioning decoder was purchased. It is housed in the college library and enables students and other interested people to view a variety of closed-captioned videos. Available at the library are videos related to deaf education, entertainment videos, and video courses to be taken for credit. The decoder is also used for the movie night. The use of the decoder at the college has opened an avenue of education and entertainment not previously available in the community.

The Hearing Impaired Studies Program became the impetus for the development of courses on closed-captioned videotape. At the inception of the new program, Centralia College offered four closed-captioned video courses, and the college has since developed an additional four. These courses cover psychology, physics, literature, philosophy, political science, math, and economics. Any faculty member may request the use of the decoder when showing educational videos in regular classes.

The Centralia College library has the largest collection in the county of printed materials related to deaf issues, including numerous books about sign language, ranging from children's beginning sign language books to books on American Sign Language syntax and grammar. The college is pleased to have major works by such well known authors as Fant, Cokely and Baker, and Riekehof. Centralia College is a member of the Registry of Interpreters for the Deaf and the National Association of the Deaf. Information about DeafPride and other organizations is available through the college library or the Instruction Office.

Resource material is not limited to printed items. The college has purchased instructional software for the use of anyone interested in using a computer to learn sign language. Sign language games also are available for the use of students and the community.

Centralia College has become regionally recognized as a source of comprehensive information on deafness. For example, when community members need an interpreter, they call the college for a referral. Students often take advantage of interpreting situations to sharpen their skills. Community members also may contact the college when someone is needed to teach sign language, for example at a Brownie meeting or a church event. Deaf or hard of hearing people may contact the college to find out how to go about obtaining a TDD through the state Department of Social and Health Services.

As a result of the commitment of Centralia College to raising deaf awareness and providing as many services as possible to the deaf community, deaf people who live in Lewis County now feel at home in their own community.

Deaf-Blindness: An Emerging Culture?

RODERICK J. MACDONALD

ulture: the totality of socially transmitted behavior patterns, arts, beliefs, institutions, and all other products of human work and thought characteristic of a population or community at a given time (Morris, 1981).
    Recognition of the existence of a deaf culture has been an important factor in the recognition that deaf people are bona fide members of society. While no one would argue that it is a good thing to be deaf, recognition of the deaf culture encourages deaf people to accept their deafness as a fact of life and to feel pride in their accomplishments and in those of other deaf people.

But is there a separate culture of deaf-blind people? Could there be a separate community of deaf people with unique behavior patterns, skills, beliefs, and other cultural traits, i.e., a unique culture of deaf-blind people? With this paper I hope to show that the answer is yes.

To prepare this paper, I sent a questionnaire to approximately fifty individuals with intimate knowledge of deaf-blind people. Approximately half of these individuals were themselves deaf-blind. Of the approximately fifteen people who replied in time for me to use their responses in this paper, all but one felt there was, in fact, a deaf-blind culture. Some replied with a hesitant "yes," others with a surprised but no less confident affirmative. And several responded with such exuberant, even passionate, excitement that one wonders why this issue has not received much more attention.

The only respondent who felt that a culture of deaf-blind people did not exist in its own right—a sighted and hearing person who has provided volunteer services to deaf-blind people for many years—stated that her belief was based on the fact that, as a nondeaf-blind person, she felt completely comfortable and socially accepted by deaf-blind people, and that the atmosphere at gatherings of deaf-blind people was no different from that found at gatherings of other community groups.

In this paper, I will trace the emergence of deaf-blind people, through education, employment, and social union, into a modern community and culture. Deaf-blind people today are attaining new levels of individual achievement never thought possible

I wish to express my grateful thanks to Dr. McCay Vernon for his encouragement, support, and input for this paper. Dr. Vernon is one of the most outspoken advocates for improved services to deaf-blind people, a leading psychologist in the field of deaf-blindness, and a close personal friend. I would also like to express my thanks to the many people who offered the ideas, support, and criticism that have made this paper possible. In particular I would like to thank Jackie Coker, Geraldine Lawhorn, and Robert Smithdas, deaf-blind people with long histories of outstanding personal achievement, for their input and support. I would also like to acknowledge the valuable assistance provided by those who responded to my questionnaire.

only a few years ago. Of equal importance, deaf-blind people are creating a culture within the greater society that deserves to be recognized and respected as unique and different.

History of the Education of Deaf-Blind People

No one knows how many persons throughout history were both deaf and blind, for there seems to be virtually no record of a deaf-blind person until the eighteenth century. Perhaps the sole exception is found in the journal of John Winthrop, governor of the Massachusetts Bay Colony, who wrote in 1637 of meeting an elderly deaf-blind woman in the town of Ipswich. It seems clear from his description, however, that the woman had good sight and hearing for much of her life, since she was able to receive receptive communication through the printing of block letters on her palm and very likely retained understandable speech.

By the end of the eighteenth century, deaf-blind persons were known to the authorities in France, England, Scotland, and Ireland, but it is unknown which deaf-blind person was the first to receive an effective education. Perhaps the first deaf-blind person to be taught a formal language was Victorine Morriseau (1789–1832) in Paris. Her education, however, seems to have been confined exclusively to religion. This was common of the education given many disabled people at that time.

The story of James Mitchell, the deaf-blind son of a Scottish minister, born November 11, 1795, is related by the Scottish philosopher Dugald Stewart in "An Account of a Boy Born Blind and Deaf (Stewart and Smith, 1971)." Mitchell had some sight, although both his blindness and deafness were congenital. He may have been the first deaf-blind person to communicate primarily through the use of signs.

It is generally accepted that the first deaf-blind person to benefit from a formal education was Laura Dewey Bridgman. Born in Hanover, New Hampshire on December 21, 1829, Laura lost her sight and hearing, as well as her senses of taste and smell, to the ravages of a fever at the age of two years. She had learned to speak some words by this time, but soon lost this skill and never regained it. In 1837, Laura was brought to the Perkins School for the Blind, where she was taught by Dr. Samuel Gridley Howe, the first director of the Perkins School. Laura's success in becoming a well educated and well informed woman is one of the truly great landmarks in the history of education. She taught the world that deaf-blind people can learn.

Four other deaf-blind students were admitted to the school during the 1840s, although none approached the academic achievements of Laura Bridgman. She died at the Perkins School on May 24, 1889. Before her death, she met the young Helen Keller, who was brought to Perkins by Anne Sullivan. It is interesting to note that Laura taught Anne Sullivan the American one-hand manual alphabet, so in a significant way, Laura contributed to Helen Keller's education.

It is a popular belief that most deaf-blind children are educated in schools for blind students. This is probably owing to the pioneering work of the Perkins School, and to the fact that the two best known deaf-blind students in the nineteenth century—Laura Bridgman and Helen Keller—were both associated with Perkins. In fact, however, until the turn of the century, the New York Institute for the Education of the Deaf educated as many deaf-blind students as did Perkins. The first was a deaf student who had lost his eyesight three years after being admitted to the school. The New York school educated eight deaf-blind students during the nineteenth century.

By the end of the nineteenth century, other schools were taking an active role in educating deaf-blind children. As the century came to a close, sixteen deaf-blind children were enrolled in a total of nine schools, most of them institutions for deaf children.

There is little material available on the education of deaf-blind children in the early part of the twentieth century. In 1906, Willie Elizabeth Robin became the first deaf-blind female to graduate from the Perkins School, and in 1938 Winthrop Chapman became the first deaf-blind male to do so.

In the early 1930s, Perkins became the first school to have a separate department devoted to the education of deaf-blind children. Its first head was Inis B. Hall, a trained teacher of the deaf, who arrived at Perkins in 1931. Shortly thereafter, six other American schools opened departments for the education of deaf-blind children.

Helen Adams Keller (1880–1968) is easily the best known deaf-blind person of all time. In 1904, when she graduated from Radcliffe College, she was the first deaf-blind person to earn a university degree. Through her writings, public speaking, and advocacy on behalf of blind and deaf-blind people, she was the single most important factor in the development of services for deaf-blind people. Ironically, Helen Keller did much more for blind people than for deaf-blind people.

By 1967, seven other deaf-blind Americans had graduated from American colleges and universities. In 1953, Robert Smithdas became the first to earn a master's degree. Today more than 100 deaf-blind Americans have earned college degrees, more than two dozen have earned master's degrees, and approximately six have earned doctoral degrees.

Employment

There is very little material available on the subject of the employment of deaf-blind persons. It is possible that Helen Keller was the first deaf-blind person who could support herself through gainful employment. However, Helen came from a well-to-do family, and much of her work was of a volunteer nature. During her career, she was employed by the Massachusetts Commission for the Blind, conducted a lecture tour, was in a vaudeville sketch, made a motion picture, did public relations work for the American Foundation for the Blind, and wrote extensively.

Thomas Stringer (1886–1945) entered the Perkins School in 1891 from a Pennsylvania almshouse. Shortly thereafter, a fund was started to support his education. His academic accomplishments were rather modest, but he was very good with his hands and became a skilled craftsman in woodworking. After leaving Perkins in 1913, he went to live with guardians in Pennsylvania, where he earned money making vegetable crates for local farmers, his future secured by this income and by the fund that had been started for him at Perkins.

Three other former Perkins students were able to support themselves through employment in sheltered workshops in the early part of the twentieth century. Cora Adelia Crocker, born in 1885, and Marion Rostron, born in 1889, were both successfully employed as chair caners by Woolson House, a sheltered workshop in Cambridge, Massachusetts. Chester H. Roberts, born in 1898, was employed in the broom shop operated by the Massachusetts Commission for the Blind, also in Cambridge.

Stephen Cartwright (1892–1938) was educated at Carnegie Tech as an engineer. At the age of thirty-three, he lost his sight and hearing as the result of a cerebral hemorrhage caused by a skull fracture. He became a radio announcer after becoming deaf-blind.

Helen May Martin was educated at home before entering the Kansas School for the

Deaf in her late teens. She was a talented pianist who learned to read musical scores in New York Point and then memorize them. She made many concert appearances throughout the midwest during the 1920s.

Just as the Perkins School has been recognized as the leader in education of deaf-blind children, the Industrial Home for the Blind, in Brooklyn, New York, has been a leader in the rehabilitation and employment of deaf-blind adults. The Industrial Home for the Blind first gave employment to a deaf-blind man in 1925, and by 1944 there were thirteen deaf-blind persons employed at the IHB Industries. That year, IHB opened a special department to serve deaf-blind adults. This was the first such effort of a non-educational nature in the United States.

Today, deaf-blind people work in a wide variety of jobs, including computer-related positions, accounting, rehabilitation, and teaching.

Organizations of Deaf-Blind People

In the late 1930s, Francis W. Bates, a blind man with a severe hearing loss, founded the American League for the Deaf-Blind. Initially this organization was established to provide personal services to deaf-blind Americans. However, the League also enabled deaf-blind individuals to keep in touch with each other through correspondence. Shortly after Mr. Bates' death in 1948, the League became a membership organization, and its name was changed to the American League of the Deaf-Blind. The same organization is known today as the American Association of the Deaf-Blind (AADB).

The first national convention of deaf-blind persons was held in Ohio in 1975, through the pioneering efforts of Doris M. J. Callahan, then-president of the AADB, and with financial and administrative support from the Helen Keller National Center for Deaf-Blind Youths and Adults and the Cleveland Society for the Blind. With the exception of 1978, the AADB Convention has been held every year since and has grown into the largest annual gathering of deaf-blind persons in the world. In 1988, a total of 607 persons, 228 of them deaf-blind, took part in the thirteenth such convention. Fifty-nine visitors from other countries attended the 1988 convention. What is particularly noteworthy is that deaf-blind people themselves organize and manage these large conventions. This self-determination has been made possible in large part through the generous financial support of the American Foundation for the Blind.

Today, more than a dozen countries have organizations of deaf-blind people. Whether deaf-blind people should form and manage their own organizations or should belong instead to organizations for deaf people or for blind people is still a controversial issue. However, it is clear that a strong movement exists for deaf-blind people to take a leadership role in managing their own affairs, a movement that is leading rapidly to a desire among deaf-blind individuals for self-determination, self-respect, and self-fulfillment.

An Emerging Culture?

Environment plays a major role in determining one's culture and psychology. Deaf-blindness, especially when it is of early onset, alters a person's perceived environment in highly significant ways that are shared by deaf-blind people and by no other group. Thus, certain behaviors, customs, and ideas are unique to deaf-blind people and central to the thesis that a separate culture of deaf-blind people does exist. This is not to suggest that deaf-blind people do not also share much with the greater "hearing-sighted" and deaf cultures.

While the above factors contribute to the existence of a deaf-blind culture, there is one major variable that prevents this culture from developing to its fullest—the isolation of deaf-blind people from each other. Jews, Blacks, Muslims, Japanese, and other groups have cultures that are highly developed because members of these groups interact extensively and freely with each other. They often live near others of their kind, and usually share a common language that may or may not be known to the majority population.

Until fairly recently, the idea of a unique culture of deaf-blind people would not have been tenable. Few deaf-blind adults had the opportunity to socialize regularly with their peers. Social interaction, for the most part, came through correspondence, a medium hardly suitable to the establishment of a unique culture. However, from this primitive beginning the seeds were sown. Deaf-blind people were able, through correspondence, to express freely their ideas, needs, experiences, and longings, which later provided the basis for a unique cultural development.

One necessary ingredient for the existence and maintenance of any culture is the domestic union of two members of the affinity group—the custom we normally refer to as marriage. Marriages of deaf-blind people to hearing or deaf spouses were rare prior to 1950, and marriage of two deaf-blind individuals was actively discouraged by society. Early in this century, Alexander Graham Bell encouraged Helen Keller to consider the possibility of marriage, should she find a man she could love. She responded by saying that she could not imagine any man wanting to marry her; she supposed it would be like marrying a statue, because she had neither sight nor hearing. The bathos of this statement would be considered an insult by many deaf-blind people today. However, it was not until fairly recently that the marriage and parenthood of two deaf-blind adults achieved anything approaching acceptance within the community. Although there are at least thirty married deaf-blind couples in the United States today—and several new marriages occurring each year—there is still considerable prejudice against such unions on the part of relatives, professionals, and the general public.

Deaf-blind culture is, at the present time, in a relatively primitive—yet important—stage of development, because its members do not usually have opportunities for frequent social interaction with peers. Despite this obstacle, the following are identified dimensions of a culture unique to the deaf-blind community.

Touch. Deaf-blind people must touch to make any kind of meaningful social contact. Touch is also required for communication. Thus, among those who are deaf-blind, extensive touching, both between the sexes and with members of the same sex, is acceptable and universal. Tactile contact that is commonplace among deaf-blind people would result in charges of sexual harassment or assumptions of homosexuality among nondeaf-blind individuals. For example, what would the average sighted woman think if a deaf-blind man she did not know asked to feel her facial features? A similar request would not be considered unreasonable by a deaf-blind woman for whom touch is the only way of learning about one's environment. Of course, there are ample examples of deaf-blind men (and women) who make a "good thing" of this need for and acceptance of touch by going beyond what is needed for communication, but the percentage of "dirty old men" in the deaf-blind community is probably no greater than in other cultures.

The widespread use of touch in the deaf-blind community has several implications. In the general population there exists a wide range of difference in tolerance for touching. Most people in society, however, are extremely defensive about any tactile contact with another person, especially in public. Touching arouses feelings and impulses with which they feel uncomfortable. The result is that these people reject contact with those who are deaf-blind. Thus, deaf-blind people often face rejection from others, through no fault of their own, owing to the essential role of touch in their culture and to the general public's reaction to this.

Group Communication. In all cultures except that of the deaf-blind, group conversations are common. This is not true for deaf-blind people, for whom all communication is one-to-one. This changes the basic nature of human interaction. For example, at a social gathering of hearing or deaf people, it is common for one person to be talking while a group of others listens. In this way, many individuals can share ideas and information in a manner that is not an option for deafblind people. As a result, the exchange of information is much slower and less economical for deaf-blind people. In addition, the whole social structure at social gatherings is different.

Dependence on Interpreters. Unlike members of any other culture, deaf-blind people are almost entirely dependent on interpreters for interaction with the majority cultures and institutions of their society. This situation results in isolation, extensive costs, incomplete communication, and, in many cases, a hostile-dependent relationship with the interpreter. This situation is further aggravated by the fact that the vast majority of skilled interpreters have been trained to work with deaf people, and have little or no preparation for or training in the unique communication needs of those who are both deaf and blind.

Social Mores. Deaf-blindness alters the framework of social interaction. For example, at a party, if one member of a deaf-blind pair wants to dance or talk with someone else, is the other member of the deaf-blind pair just left to sit in isolation? How do deaf-blind people mingle within groups? Is it a matter of bumping into one another and introducing oneself? These problems create an entire set of new and unique social rules. For example, when dining with deaf-blind people, it is considered appropriate for each individual to begin eating whenever food has been served, whereas in other cultures polite behavior dictates that everyone wait for the host or hostess to be served before eating. Additionally, it is considered acceptable for deaf-blind people to use their fingers during meals, and as a result, deaf-blind people often prefer not to talk during meals, since their hands would also be needed for communication.

Similarly, when one wants to talk with a deaf-blind person who is reading Braille, the polite thing to do is to touch lightly the individual's hand, arm, or shoulder, and to wait until the deaf-blind person can find an appropriate stopping place before lifting his or her hands from the Braille page.

When initiating a conversation with a deaf-blind person, it is common courtesy to identify oneself, even if one is well known to the deaf-blind person. This is unnecessary in any other culture, since both sight and hearing permit ready identification of those with whom we are communicating. It is of critical social importance to deaf-blind people, however, that they know immediately with whom they are communicating, since otherwise there is the danger of saying the wrong thing to the wrong person.

Proper etiquette also prevails when visiting the home of a deaf-blind person. When visiting the home of a sighted person, the norm is to look at, but not touch, furnishings and objects in the living room. Since touch is so important to deaf-blind people, it is natural that guests should be free to touch objects in the living room. Many deaf-blind people would, in fact, be quite pleased if a visitor showed an interest in their home by doing this. Exploring one's environment is considered appropriate behavior, but one should never enter the bedroom or open closed doors or cupboards in a deaf-blind person's home without permission. Another word of caution here: One should never move objects in a deaf-blind person's home without that person's knowledge, for the deaf-blind person must control placement of belongings in order to maintain order in the home.

Games. Games and sports such as soccer, baseball, cricket, bullfighting, and horse racing are integral to most cultures. The games and sports enjoyed by deaf-blind people tend to be more sedentary, such as board games and card games. Tandem bicycle riding with a sighted person is quite popular, but spectator sports are inaccessible. However, many deaf-blind people do enjoy sporting events in the abstract, for instance by following the local football team through newspaper reports.

Class Barriers. Most cultures consist of huge numbers of people in close geographical proximity. In such cultures, class barriers are universal. These classes are created by such variables as economic conditions, education, religion, social status, or employment status.

In the small culture of deaf-blind people, there are groupings based on such factors as English language competence, fluency in native sign language, and method of communication. However, because the size of the total population is small, class distinctions, as seen in other cultures, are not nearly as significant in the deaf-blind culture.

Reduced General Knowledge. Because deaf-blindness poses such a severe obstacle to education and communication, most deaf-blind people miss out on much general information that is readily accessible to others. As a result, conversation in the deaf-blind culture often centers on social interaction, news about one another, and such basic issues as food, weather, shopping, conveniences, and aids and devices of special use to deaf-blind people.

Economics. Since deaf-blindness makes earning money significantly more difficult, the deaf-blind culture is one of minimal material wealth. Social opportunities in the community generally must be organized with the financial or organizational assistance of community agencies, because deaf-blind people themselves are often unable to afford public entertainment options, especially if they must also pay for an interpreter in order to participate in these opportunities.

Language. The theoretical issues of language and deaf-blindness are fascinating. Because deaf-blind individuals as a rule do not have an opportunity to interact as a group on a continuous basis, as deaf people have done for at least the past several centuries, they have not developed a separate tactile language. Instead, native sign languages and manual alphabets have been adapted for use by deaf-blind people.

There are interesting parallels to this. For example, for years blind people tried to read raised print letters, trying to adapt to what sighted people used. In fact, sighted professionals condemned any attempt to develop a system especially for blind people. Similarly, for centuries deaf people were forced to read lips and learn speech, thus adapting their communication to the needs of hearing people rather than to the needs of deaf people. Today, many deaf people use sign language, a method of communication that is uniquely appropriate for people who use their eyes for receptive communication.

In my opinion, deaf-blind people are gradually adapting sign language and fingerspelling to meet their own unique communication needs. Subtle changes are beginning to appear. For example, a deaf-blind person who relies on fingerspelling as a primary communication method and who is fluent in Braille may often incorporate Braille contractions into the fingerspelling if the person with whom he or she is conversing is also familiar with Braille. In addition, many people who used sign language almost exclusively as deaf people will gradually use more and more fingerspelling once they have been totally blind for a period of time.

It is my view that if deaf-blind people were allowed more opportunities to interact with each other on a continuous basis, they would gradually develop a tactile, manual language ideally suited to their needs—that is, to the sense of touch. While this tactile language would have its roots in spoken and signed languages, it would gradually develop the unique grammar and syntax typical of independent languages.

Summary

Deaf-blindness provides sociologists and others a unique opportunity to see how a culture develops from almost total nonexistence into an emerging structure with the potential for further development. Such variables as communication, opportunity for interaction, physical differences, economic differences, education, modality of language, and dependency all enter into the nature of the unique culture deaf-blind people have developed. With advances in technology, increased opportunities in education, employment, and social interaction, and with the development of leadership skills among deaf-blind people, I predict an increasingly sophisticated and rich cultural development for the deaf-blind community.

References and Suggested Reading

American Foundation for the Blind. 1976. *The Unseen Minority: A Social History of Blindness in the United States.* New York: David McCay Company.

Church, C. 1964. *A Follow-up Study: Former Deaf-Blind Pupils at Perkins School for the Blind.* Watertown, MA: no information available.

Gannon, J. 1981. *Deaf Heritage.* Silver Spring, MD: National Association of the Deaf.

Morris, W. Ed. 1981. *The American Heritage Dictionary of the English Language.* Boston: Houghton Mifflin Company. p. 321.

Salmon, P. 1970. *Out of the Shadows.* New Hyde Park, NY: National Center for Deaf-Blind Youths and Adults.

Stewart, D., and A. Smith. 1971. Essays on Philosophical Subjects. New York: Garland Publications.

Wade, W. 1904. *The Blind-Deaf.* Indianapolis, IN: Hecker Brothers.

Waterhouse, E. 1977. "Education of the Deaf-Blind in the United States of America, 1837–1967." In *State of the Art: Perspectives on Serving Deaf-Blind Children.* Sacramento, CA: Southwest Regional Center for Services to Deaf-Blind Children. pp. 5–17.

The Special Challenge of Late-Deafened Adults: Another Deaf Way

BILL GRAHAM AND MARYMARGARET SHARP-PUCCI

eaf or hearing—which?" This is a question often posed to the late-deafened individual. The answer is an enigmatic one. Physically, the deafened individual is deaf; the hearing mechanism is nonfunctional for the purposes of conversational speech, with or without hearing aids or other amplification. Culturally, this same individual is hearing; his or her language, thoughts, memories, and dreams are born of a distinctly hearing world. How one harmonizes the dissonance of these two identities is the challenge of the late-deafened adult.

The Late-Deafened Population

Definition

A variety of definitions are used to refer to individuals who have experienced a loss of hearing at a time other than at birth. "Adventitious deafness" is a generic term; it simply means the hearing loss has taken place some time after birth. It makes no distinction between hearing loss occurring at the age of twenty-four months or the age of twenty-four years.

The term "deafened" has a more specific meaning. A deafened individual is one "who at one time possessed enough hearing to learn language and oral communication through hearing, but who now suffers with a loss of hearing so severe that audition is useless for purposes of receiving oral communication" (Luey and Per-Lee, 1983).

More recently, the term "late-onset deafness" has come into being. It describes a deafness that occurs in the adult years that causes fundamental changes in the way the person lives (Association of Late Deafened Adults, 1987a). The loss may have been sudden or may have happened gradually over a period of years.

Prevalence

Exactly how large is this late-deafened population? This question cannot be answered easily. The only comprehensive study of the deaf population in the United States took place in 1974 (Schein and Delk, 1974). The data that resulted, now fifteen years old, are no longer precisely accurate, but they do provide interesting insight into the make-up of the deaf population.

If you question the general population about their image of a deaf person, they will typically describe a person who has been deaf since birth. The truth, however, is that congenitally deaf people account for only a small percentage of the overall deaf population. According to Schein and Delk (1974), 13.4 million people in the United States have a hearing loss ranging from mild to profound. Only 1.8 million of these individuals are deaf, and only 0.4 million became deaf before the age of nineteen years. This results in a staggering percentage of the deaf population falling under the category of late-deafened—approximately 78 percent, or 1.4 million people (Schein and Delk, 1974).

What has caused this significant number of people to become deaf in their adult years? Perhaps most prevalent is neurofibromatosis, a condition of tumor growth. Traumatic injury to the head contributes to the numbers, as do infectious diseases such as meningitis. Adverse drug reactions have caused their share of deafness, and aging of the hearing mechanism (presbycusis) is an important factor as well. The causes of late-onset deafness and its complications are many and varied, contributing significantly to the diversity of this population.

The Late-Deafened Challenge

The special challenges facing the late-deafened individual are many. Perhaps the most striking of these is the synthesis of two global identities: audiologically deaf and culturally hearing. The late-deafened individual has an established and distinct identification with the world. His marital, familial, societal, and vocational identities are by now securely rooted in spoken language and hearing mores, traditions, and opportunities. With the onset of deafness, spoken language no longer carries the power or place it once did, and opportunities connected with the ability to hear often cease to exist. Former identities begin to dissolve, and it is quickly realized that loss of hearing is a powerful loss of self. Developing a healthy new self is dependent in part on how well the deafened individual meets the new challenges before him.

The Challenge of Communication

The late-deafened individual has grown up in a world of free-flowing communication. In the past, communication just happened; it was not a goal for which one strived. Now, successful communication has become a system of carefully planned strategies. Communicative strategies are individual in the sense that any one person may use a number of different techniques. A gathering of late-deafened individuals may reveal a variety of communication modes, and group members often share the philosophy, "Use what works for you." While some individuals prefer to rely on oral methods, others may feel most comfortable in written communication, and still others choose to learn sign language.

It is believed that relatively few deafened adults learn sign language (Benderly, 1980). When sign language does become the method of choice, it is predominantly manually coded English that is used, not American Sign Language (ASL). While becoming truly proficient with a manually coded form of spoken English is a formidable task for many adults, entering into the world of ASL, a completely new and different language, is considered impossible by most and so attempted by few. In the end, only a fraction of the deafened population relies on sign language as its primary mode of communication. Of this percentage, the majority do not use or understand ASL structure and syntax.

There is a dual importance in finding comfort in a preferred method of communication. On a basic level, understanding what takes place in the world about you depends on successful communication. On a higher level, communication skills have the power to act as an avenue of societal or cultural acceptance. An individual's ability to use the accepted communication methods of the hearing world, such as speechreading, influences one's continued acceptance in that world. Failure in this mode leads to an intensifying sense of detachment from one's former hearing identification and from one's former life.

In the same sense, an individual's ability to communicate effectively in the deaf world (for example, through ASL) affects that person's potential for entry and acceptance into the deaf community. Failure in communication leads the deafened individual to realize that his place in society may no longer exist. Communication and the deafened person's ability to succeed at it are a key to belonging to a culture, whether that culture is deaf or hearing.

The Challenge of Culture

Deafened individuals are said to exist between two worlds, often not knowing which is their own. The hearing world views the late-deafened person as deaf. This judgment is based on physical status. The deaf world views this same person as hearing, and this judgment is based on experiential status. Deafened individuals often view themselves as neither. They are unique in that their deafness carries no identity. Luey and Per-Lee (1983) note that identity implies a bond to a definable culture, and the deafened individual often has none.

Despite all their attempts to remain in the hearing world, former hearing peers view deafened individuals differently; they now have extra needs and manifest liabilities. Marriage, family, and career are touched not only by the perceptions and expectations of others, but also by the altered perceptions of the deafened individuals themselves.

The late-deafened adult is often encouraged by professionals to initiate contacts and become involved with deaf people. The distinction between deaf and deafened is generally absent in this referral. Deafened individuals may naively believe that the deaf community can replace the hearing world from which they have become so disengaged. There are two reasons why this cultural shift does not carry a high probability of success. Most importantly, late-deafened individuals lack the communication skills (ASL) needed to interact fully with the deaf community; this in itself labels them outsiders. Second, they also lack the shared experience of growing up deaf, much as the congenitally deaf person cannot know the experience of becoming deaf. The deafened individual is simply caught between the two worlds.

Reid and Villareal (1988) have investigated the experience of existing "between" cultures. They emphasize the tremendous sense of cultural alienation that comes with the inability to identify fully with either side. The transition from hearing to deaf can be viewed along a continuum.

Hearing ———————————————— Deaf

Exactly where the deafened individual fits on this continuum depends on several factors:

❖ physical characteristics (degree of hearing loss and the presence or absence of accompanying disabilities)

❖ communication mode or modes (proficiency in manually coded English, ASL, or speechreading, and degree of comfort in using these modes)

❖ how well one functions overall in either culture (knowledge of and conformance to conventions and expectations)

❖ messages received from either culture

❖ degree of exposure to or interaction with either culture

❖ amount of positive support from members of either culture

❖ congruence of personal and cultural values (where the deafened individual wishes to belong).

This sense of "betweenness" may be best understood by reviewing the thoughts of late-deafened individuals themselves. What follows is a selection of questions and answers excerpted from "Aldanonymous," a feature column in the Association of Late Deafened Adults newsletter, *ALDA News* (1987b, 1988a, 1988b, 1989). The column poses a question to which readers may respond anonymously. All answers are printed for the general readership.

HOW HAS DEAFNESS AFFECTED YOUR FEELINGS ABOUT YOURSELF?

If I can somehow communicate, I'm fine. But when I can't communicate, I feel very sorry for myself and think I don't really belong anywhere.

Deafness has changed my way of thinking of myself and of the worlds (deaf and hearing) around me. I feel so inadequate. I feel so frustrated.

When I first lost my hearing I was very frightened and became so tense around hearing people that for several years I closed myself away from people and stopped seeing friends and didn't try to make new ones. My self-esteem was really low. I gained a lot of weight and became very shy. I hate this part because it's very painful.

WHEN WAS THE FIRST TIME YOU MET A DEAF PERSON—BEFORE OR AFTER YOU BECAME DEAF? WHAT WAS YOUR REACTION?

My first course in sign language—a class composed of fifteen hearing adults; myself, as the only deaf student; and our teacher, who was born deaf and did not speak. It was a very trying and frustrating situation as we were all ill-prepared to communicate with one another. I realized I was witnessing a prime example of the struggles between the Deaf World and the Hearing World, and I wondered, "Where do I fit in?"

Since I lost what was left of my hearing. I have met three born-deaf folks who are excellent at lipreading. I envy them. I have never met a born-deaf person who was sad, bitter, or frustrated.

HAVE YOU SPENT A LOT OF TIME WITH PEOPLE WHO ARE BORN DEAF? WHY OR WHY NOT?

No, I haven't spent much time with people who were born deaf. I generally feel uncomfortable in their presence because I don't sign as well as they do, and I don't understand the signs they throw my way. It seems worse to be with born-deaf people I don't understand than to be with hearing people I don't understand. With hearing people you expect the communication problems, but with deaf people you feel like there should be some feeling of community, and most often there isn't. That can be frustrating and painful.

I've spent a lot of time with deaf people. I'm meeting more and more. It's helping me to accept deafness. Communication is no problem—they all know I'm lousy at signing. I think they're more patient, understanding.

I never knew deaf people until I joined a deaf bowling league. These people I communicated with could read my lips and spoke slowly, adding some sign when they spoke to me one-on-one. However, I was more left out with the deaf than the hearing when they talked in a group.

DO YOU FEEL MORE COMFORTABLE IN SOCIAL SITUATIONS WITH HEARING PEOPLE OR WITH DEAF PEOPLE?

I once had an interpreter friend who objected when I referred to myself as deaf. I was instead, she insisted, a "deafened hearing person," which sounded convoluted at the time but which I now agree is true. Socially and culturally I *am* hearing—despite the fact that I can't hear. So the easiest and most re-laxed gatherings for me are composed of hearing people (or hard of hearing or late-deaf people) who can sign pidgin (English word order). That's not my bias against American Sign Language showing; I love to watch native signers conversing in ASL, but just can't understand it!

I would say that I am most comfortable in a group that is composed of hearing people of whom at least some are fluent in sign language. My closest friends are people who are or have been sign language interpreters. I find that I have more in common with hearing people and feel more comfortable socially with them—when I can understand them! To me, comfort in a social situation is determined by ease of communication, and I am most comfortable communicating in sign language. I guess it doesn't matter much if the people are deaf or hearing—just so communication is taking place!

Actually, I have never felt completely comfortable with either hearing or deaf; I always seem to be somewhere in the middle, sort of like the man without a country.

The words of deafened people mirror what research has told us. These individuals have described the experience of losing their sense of cultural identity and facing the difficulty or impossibility of entering into a new one. Individual responses, of course, range from positive to negative and usually fall somewhere in-between. In-between is that place in which the late-deafened individual is often thrust, but this need not always be the case. There is an answer to the cultural limbo of late-onset deafness. We would like to share this answer through Bill Graham's description of his own experiences.

Another Deaf Way—Bill Graham's Story

When I was in college, I gradually began to lose my hearing. I had a sensorineural hearing disorder that I apparently inherited. By the time I was twenty-five years old—about eleven years ago—I could no longer hear on the telephone. As my deafness progressed, I went through denial, frustration, anger, confusion—the usual things a person feels after suffering a serious loss. I became isolated from most of my old friends and had trouble feeling at peace in any kind of social situation.

By the early 1980s I had become so frustrated with trying to read people's lips that I decided to learn sign language. I took the entire ASL curriculum at the Chicago Hearing Society, and then headed for the nearest deaf club to meet some people who were like me—deaf people. I figured I'd make new friends and feel good about myself again. But it didn't work out that way. My first visit to the deaf club provided a stern dose of reality. I was, quite clearly, an outsider. And after several visits to the club, I wasn't sure I wanted to become an insider. I felt more confused and lost than ever.

But I didn't give up. I became involved with a group that worked to make theater accessible to deaf people. I soon had some deaf friends, and eventually I learned to sign fairly well. But every deaf person I knew communicated far more easily than I. Even worse, I didn't feel I had much in common with any of them except for deafness. I still felt isolated socially. I had both hearing and deaf friends, but I didn't seem to fit in with either.

Then, a little more than two years ago, some big excitement came into my life. I invited twelve Chicago-area people who, like myself, had become deaf as adults, to my house for a party. Only three or four of us had met before. I got names for the party from a list of late-deafened adults developed by Kathie Hering, a social services worker who is herself late-deafened.

The party was a smashing success. Although most of us were total strangers who had never so much as spoken to another late-deafened person, we found it easy to be in one another's company. There was a special feeling in the room—a feeling of belonging, of unspoken understanding, of patience with our similar communication difficulties. A week after the party, I wrote a letter to all the people on the mailing list, expressing my view that something extraordinary had occurred. The enthusiastic response to that letter led me to begin a regular newsletter, through which we consolidated a group that eventually became known as the Association of Late-Deafened Adults, or ALDA.

The ALDA newsletter quickly became a hot item, and its circulation grew. Within several months, I was in touch with late-deafened people in many parts of the country. The letters I received had recurring themes: Late-deafened adults felt socially isolated, their lives had changed markedly because of their deafness, they were excited to hear that a group for late-deafened adults had started, and they wished that they knew some late-deafened people in their area.

Most of the late-deafened people who wrote lived entirely in the hearing world. Many of them knew about Self-Help for Hard of Hearing People (SHHH), and some were members of that organization. But by and large, they felt that the focus of SHHH—on assistive listening devices and techniques—missed their needs as deaf people. Only a few letters came from late-deafened adults who socialized chiefly with people who grew up deaf. Many people sent me money so they could continue to receive the newsletter. Everyone sent good wishes and encouragement.

This great outpouring of interest and support made it clear that ALDA had touched a nerve among late-deafened people. As I gradually learned more about the deaf and hard of hearing community in the United States, it was easy to understand why. Interaction among late-deafened adults and support services for them were virtually nonexistent.

Only a handful of institutions and organizations seemed to recognize that late-deafened people are a unique population group with special needs. These widely scattered outposts of awareness included the National Technical Institute for the Deaf (NTID) in Rochester, N.Y., which conducts special education and rehabilitation programs for the late-deafened; the Deaf Counseling, Advocacy, and Rehabilitation Agency (DCARA) in San Leandro, Calif., where Edna Shipley-Conner works as a rehabilitation counselor specializing in late-deafened adults; the Adult Loss of Hearing Association (ALOHA) in Tucson, Ariz., which serves as a local support network for people who have lost hearing in their adult years; and Gallaudet University in Washington, D.C., which has a late-deafened president and programs that late-deafened people can find useful. But the focus at Gallaudet, of course, is on people who grew up deaf. Clearly, very little was being done for late-deafened Americans.

Amazed and intrigued by this situation, I continued writing newsletters and working to further ALDA's development in any way I could. Meanwhile, many other late-deafened people became actively involved in ALDA, and the group grew tremendously. Today, a little more than two years after we started ALDA with the names of twenty-five late-deafened people in the Chicago area, our group has a mailing list of more than 400 names nationwide.

A variety of activities and support services for late-deafened adults have been developed through ALDA. In the Chicago area, ALDA sponsors three weekly self-help groups for late-deafened adults. These groups give members the opportunity to share feelings and experiences related to their deafness. Also in Chicago, ALDA holds monthly social events that give late-deafened people a chance to mingle. The socials have included captioned movies, dance performances, dinners, bowling outings, and numerous parties.

Most members of ALDA, however, live outside the Chicago area. The ALDA newsletter serves as their meeting place, with several regular columns that encourage the exchange of ideas, experiences, and information. Through the newsletter and other forms of networking, ALDA has become an information and resource center for late-deafened adults. Members of ALDA have given presentations on late-deafness at seminars and conventions and serve as consultants to service providers on matters related to late-deafness. This year, the first chapter of ALDA outside the Chicago area was established in Boston. The response to it has been terrific. We expect other chapters to start soon in places such as Rochester, NY, Washington, DC, southern Illinois, and the Bay Area of California.

All of these activities have created for the first time a growing, vigorous network of late-deafened adults nationwide. For the first time, many late-deafened adults are realizing that they are not alone. Through ALDA, they are finding many other people who share their problems, feelings, experiences, and attitudes. In ALDA, late-deafened adults are finding a place where they fit.

By interacting through ALDA, late-deafened people also are finding new approaches to their problems. For example, communicating with a group of late-deafened adults poses a particularly challenging problem because the receptive skills of late-deafened people vary widely. Some late-deafened people prefer lipreading to sign language; others prefer sign; and others do so poorly at both that they may have no preference.

When ALDA began self-help groups for late-deafened people, it became essential to find a communication method that was easily understandable to everyone. We dealt with this problem by devising a simple real-time captioning system consisting of a $100 computer, a television set, and a typist. The computer is hooked up to the television, and as the typist types the conversation on the computer keyboard, the words appear on the television screen. Members of the self-help group use the captions as needed to retrieve words they ordinarily would miss. We also use this captioning system at ALDA business meetings and many other group activities.

As ALDA continues to grow, late-deafened adults will achieve greater and greater solidarity. Through interactions among themselves, late-deafened people will consolidate their ideas and develop ways of dealing with their special problems. In this way, late-deafened adults will establish their identity and culture.

The Deaf Way celebrates deaf culture as it has developed chiefly through people who grew up deaf. It celebrates a rich and remarkable way of life that developed over many years of early-deafened people interacting with one another. But the Deaf Way is not the only way of life for people who are deaf. For the vast majority of late-deafened people, the Deaf Way will always be somebody else's way. Through ALDA, late-deafened adults are finding their own way.

References

Association of Late Deafened Adults. 1987a. "Dear Friends." *ALDA News* 1 (2): 1.

Association of Late Deafened Adults. 1987b. "Aldanonymous." *ALDA News* 1 (5): 5.

Association of Late Deafened Adults. 1988a. "Aldanonymous." *ALDA News* 2 (3): 5.

Association of Late Deafened Adults. 1988b. "Aldanonymous." *ALDA News* 2 (4): 6–7.

Association of Late Deafened Adults. 1989. "Aldanonymous." *ALDA News* 3 (1): 7–8.

Benderly, B. L. 1980. *Dancing Without Music: Deafness in America*. Garden City, NY: Anchor Press/Doubleday.

Luey, H. S., and M. S. Per-Lee. 1983. *What Should I Do Now? Problems and Adaptations of the Deafened Adult*. Washington, DC: The National Academy of Gallaudet College.

Reid, C., and P. Villareal. 1988. "Between Cultures: Meeting the Needs of Individuals with Marginal Cultural Identity." Paper presented at the Conference of the American Association for Counseling and Development, Chicago, Illinois, March.

Schein, J. D., and M. T. Delk. 1974. *The Deaf Population in the United States*. Silver Spring, MD: National Association of the Deaf.

PART FIVE

Deaf clubs and sports

Editor's Introduction

One of the most popular attractions during the week of The Deaf Way Conference and Festival was a large tent set up on the Gallaudet University campus, called the "International Deaf Club." Each evening, after the intense intellectual discussions of the Conference were finished, this tent became the setting of social interaction, entertainment, and generally festive activity by Deaf Way participants. Here they could make new friends in a socially agreeable place, often extending the scope of their friendships to include Deaf people from other lands, many or most of whom used different sign languages. Participants felt encouraged during these get-togethers to search for mutually comprehensible, visually accessible communication, in spite of the diversity of geographic and linguistic origins. For Deaf participants especially, the mutual bond of a visual rather than auditory orientation to life pulled people together; they identified with each other's experiences as Deaf people from predominately hearing societies.

One tangible outcome of this week-long association was that ever since The Deaf Way, sign language instructors at Gallaudet have taught the country signs used by deaf people from those countries (signs they learned during The Deaf Way), rather than the signs (sometimes unflattering) previously used to represent those countries in American Sign Language.

In a sense, each of the papers in this section describes one or another manifestation of the urge of Deaf people (and sometimes of the hearing friends of Deaf people) to get together, to share experiences, to participate in an activity (such as a particular sport or game), and to acquire information important for survival and success—all in a highly supportive environment (like the one in the International Deaf Club) without the communication barriers usually presented by the hearing world. In spite of this important common thread, however, a careful reading of these papers reveals that the clubs and associations formed by Deaf people in different countries inevitably take different forms, and that these forms represent not only the differing wishes of various Deaf communities, but also the social philosophies and attitudes of various nations with regard to minority populations in general, and to Deaf people in particular.

Yerker Andersson's (United States) paper on the Stockholm Deaf Club, for example, describes a highly sophisticated association of Deaf groups whose functions are largely supported by the Swedish government, a government that is remarkably responsive to the special needs of minority populations. Andersson's account of a typical year's activities headquartered in the Stockholm Deaf Club's "Deaf House" includes a rich array of athletic, social, cultural, and educational events. Particularly revealing is his report that the club teaches Swedish Sign Language to hundreds of individuals annually and that club-sponsored courses in American Sign Language and English are also popular.

The portrayal by Stephanie Hall (United States) of a deaf club in Philadelphia, Pennsylvania contrasts with Andersson's Stockholm club in that instead of appearing to be an integral part of a social establishment that embraces and supports Deaf people, it is characterized as a kind of refuge or oasis, where Deaf people can escape the mis-understandings and frustrations usually presented by the hearing world. Hall portrays this club as a safe haven where Deaf people can meet potential spouses, have fun, get advice, and learn strategies from Deaf mentors for finding jobs.

The next two papers suggest that in most countries considerable financial resource-fulness is needed for Deaf clubs to become established and have an impact. Adolf Van Den Heuvel (Belgium) describes the slow evolution of the Madosa club in Antwerp, Belgium and how money was collected, bit by bit, to buy a house for club activities. He emphasizes the importance of Deaf people's staying united, in spite of differences of age and interests, in order to gain the collective power to accomplish needed goals. Similarly, the paper by Madan Vasishta and Meher Sethna (India) portrays Deaf clubs in India as organizations struggling with meager resources to bring Deaf people together to meet needs that would otherwise be overlooked. This paper suggests that cultural values in India are more often than not at cross-purposes with Deaf people's wishes.

Miren Segovia's (Basque region, Spain) paper describes the work of the Deaf Union of Guipúzcoa, a Basque association supported by "various public organizations" as well as membership fees. Although this association serves many of the social, recre-ational, cultural, and educational needs typical of other Deaf clubs, it is unusual in that it places considerable emphasis on enabling Deaf people to participate more effectively in activities with hearing people.

Although Segovia's paper emphasizes the potential value of increasing Deaf people's participation in society, the next two papers, concerning Deaf people's interest in sports, appear to make a contrasting point. The paper by Orazio Romeo (Italy) and Lisa Renery (United States) points out that although Deaf Italians' interest in sports is so intense that the sports-related aspects of Italian Sign Language are detailed and rich, Deaf teams have been less competitive since mainstreaming (beginning in 1978) led to the placement of the best deaf players on hearing teams. They indicate that good Deaf players are increasingly without signing peers and that the importance for Deaf athletes of being part of the Deaf community is being forgotten. Donalda Ammons and Margery Miller (United States) similarly point out that Deaf youths' competence in sports is too often viewed as an avenue toward full integration into activities with hearing people. The problem with this, they say, is that Deaf children may be abruptly forced into situa-tions that require lipreading, depriving them of the more natural option of participating in athletics with Deaf peers.

Bruce Gross (United States) then reports on the efforts of the World Recreation Association of the Deaf to plan and facilitate recreation and leisure activities that include both Deaf and hearing people. Gross emphasizes that for such an effort to succeed, special interpreting services may be required. The paper also appears to make the point that when such services are provided, Deaf people's recreational options expand, and the abilities of hearing and Deaf participants to enjoy their interactions with each other are increased.

The Stockholm Deaf Club: A Case Study

YERKER ANDERSSON

Compared to other disabled groups, deaf people are highly organized. In practically all the countries where educational services are available for all deaf children, deaf people have successfully formed organizations at all levels, from local to national. Their international organizations (World Federation of the Deaf, Comité International des Sports des Sourds, International Committee on Silent Chess) are among the oldest in the world. This network suggests that cooperation among deaf people is well developed.

The structure of organizations of deaf persons and deaf culture in different countries is influenced by the culture of the dominant group. As pride in local heritage and community pride are emphasized more in European countries than in the United States, local organizations are expected to be more important for deaf persons in Europe (Andersson, 1987, p. 263). The local organizations of deaf people in European cities provide a place where deaf people can share their experiences, feelings, and ideas, where people can preserve their natural language, and where deaf people can reach a political consensus.

The Nordic local organizations go further by offering adult or continuing education programs, day care services for deaf children, courses in sign language, and lectures. In some countries the local organization is also used as a center for audiological, counseling, or rehabilitation services, and several local organizations are trying to assume responsibility for interpreting services as well. From sociological and anthropological viewpoints, then, the local organization serves as an important agent in the transmission of deaf culture.

While the national and international organizations of the deaf are relatively stable and secure, local organizations of the deaf in several highly industrialized countries are facing some profound social changes.

Deaf people in most metropolitan cities now enjoy a much greater variety of activities and consequently try to create more and more specialized clubs. For example, there are recreational and sportfishing events or clubs in the United States and Europe. This kind of social change will certainly continue the preservation of sign language and the enrichment of local deaf heritage, but may weaken the political and social unity of deaf people.

The proliferation of cultural and recreational activities occurs not only among deaf people, but also among people with normal hearing. Sociologists and anthropologists agree that it is an inevitable trend in most countries around the world. Any attempt to reverse the trend would be viewed as a repression of human development or as a suppression of human freedom.

Thus, clubs for the deaf in major metropolitan areas may have to be flexible enough to meet the changing needs of deaf persons, if they want to survive. To that end, deaf clubs will need to consider several alternatives, each with its own advantages and disadvantages. The five primary alternatives are dissolution, consolidation, centralization, satelliting, and centrality.

Dissolution is an alternative most local organizations, of course, would try to avoid. But some deaf clubs in some metropolitan cities have been forced to disband owing to lack of interest.

In several European countries, several deaf clubs have successfully merged into a single organization to expand their membership and budget. This kind of consolidation is not popular, however, because it requires members of the new organization to abandon their old reference groups and develop a new one. However, consolidation does permit deaf people to expand their political and social solidarity.

Deaf clubs in large cities in North America and in a few European countries have taken a slightly different alternative to consolidation. These clubs have formed a coordinating council while permitting the clubs to retain their independence and identity. This strategy, centralization, works well as long as the individual clubs have a strong desire to cooperate among themselves.

In certain cities in the United States and in a few European countries, clubs for the deaf often use a deaf community center—often managed by a church, school, or welfare agency—as a meeting place, while retaining their separate addresses as "satellite offices." The deaf leaders of these deaf clubs have no political influence on the boards of such centers.

Deaf people in Stockholm, Sweden, have chosen a slightly different alternative, one that is unique and worth studying. Instead of developing new organizations outside their existing social clubs, they have tried to keep all their activities together within one place. This fifth alternative could be called centrality.

In sociology, the concepts of centralization and centrality do not have the same meaning. The crucial difference between centrality and centralization is the distribution of power. In centralization, the main organization develops power by limiting the number of decision- or policy-makers, expecting organizations in its network to follow the decisions of the main organization. Thus, the participation level among organizations in this network is low. In centrality, however, the main organization develops power by maintaining the flow of information among organizations in its network. The participation level in this case is high (see Boje and Whetten, 1961).

The Stockholm alternative is a good example of centrality. The social club in Stockholm shares its physical facilities and resources with several deaf organizations. All the organizations in the network have separate boards, memberships, activities, and budgets, but persons joining one or more organizations in the Stockholm network must become members of the social club if they want to participate in its activities. In effect, members can develop a high level of participation in *both* the main organization and the other organizations in the Stockholm network. This feature, called overlapping memberships, is not found in centralization.

The organizations and their network are described below.

Founded in 1868, the Stockholm deaf club—Stockholms Dövas Förening in Swedish and abbreviated as SDF—has a membership of over 1,000 persons, of whom about 150 are hearing. By agreement with the city government, the SDF rents an old, renovated three-story house—formerly a police station and now an historical landmark—popularly called the Deaf House. This building has two large meeting rooms, a snack bar (serving no alcohol), and several offices and classrooms. The house is accessible for mobility-impaired persons. Its physical space is usually adequate for daily activities and board meetings, but has often been inadequate for club meetings and lectures.

The SDF provides a place for activities designed to meet the social, emotional, and cultural needs of deaf individuals. In this way, it is similar to most local social clubs of deaf people around the world. Unlike many clubs, however, the SDF offers a regular program of lectures and adult education courses. According to its 1988 annual report, for example, the SDF arranged ten lectures, five discussion nights, and four video nights, in addition to its traditional parties. Courses in Swedish Sign Language were offered to a total of 309 participants. In cooperation with nearby continuing education schools, the SDF also organized evening courses in nine different subjects, including American Sign Language (ASL) and English, with an enrollment of 262 persons.

During the month of February alone there was a lecture and panel discussion on name signs that attracted over fifty persons. An all-deaf panel discussion "What will happen to deaf people in the year 2000?" was attended by over 150 persons. On every Tuesday morning in February, over fifty deaf pensioners met and shared their experiences over coffee and bread. One of the general meetings of the SDF held during that month was attended by over 100 members. Every Wednesday evening, deaf people visited over coffee. On other days chess and bridge players held practice sessions. Every Friday evening, the youth club had its own social meeting at the SDF.

Like many deaf clubs in Sweden and in the Federal Republic of Germany, the SDF owns and maintains a resort center outside Stockholm, with boating, swimming, and other recreational facilities and full board for up to sixty participants. The resort center has a full-time staff separate from that of the SDF. This center is required by law to be accessible to persons with disabilities. It is supervised by a foundation with a separate board elected from and by the SDF membership.

Funds for the SDF are administered by another board, again elected from and by the SDF members. This board awards small grants averaging about $6,000 per year to students, researchers, and needy persons.

Thus, the members of the SDF must elect three separate boards annually—the SDF board, the resort center board, and the financial board—in addition to selecting committees.

Although both hearing and deaf persons are eligible for membership on the SDF boards, the majority of board members have been deaf, and the present board is all deaf. The full- and part-time staff of the SDF consists of one administrator; one club consultant, who provides secretarial services and maintains relations with other organizations; one social worker; one education specialist; two clerks; one youth specialist; two janitors; one computer facilities supervisor; one or two snack bar managers; and four to six sign language teachers.

At present only the social worker, one of the janitors, and the clerks are hearing. The staff salaries are covered in part by government contributions, in agreement with unemployment agencies. Whenever there is a vacant position in the SDF, the unemployment agencies refer applicants for interviews. If the SDF accepts one of these applicants, the unemployment agency will pay a part of the salary. The SDF has the right to fire persons for unsatisfactory performance within a given period, and employees are free to resign. This system has apparently worked well.

Including the SDF, there are a total of sixteen organizations for deaf people with separate memberships and boards in Stockholm (Table 1). This proliferation is not unusual in many metropolitan areas. For example, there are over thirty deaf clubs in London or New York. What is remarkable about the organizations in Stockholm is that practically all of them have consented to maintain their offices and meet within the SDF.

TABLE 1: Organizations for Deaf People in Stockholm

Local Organization	Membership Size
Art club	124
Sportfishing club	52
Sports club	354
Bridge club	47
Retired Persons club	150
Theater group	N/A
Youth club	272
Parents of the deaf club	153
Auto club	132
Women's club	N/A
Chess club	15
Deafened Adult section	22
Folkdance group	N/A
International group	56
Four suburban sections	71
	(average number per session)

Although they share the same physical facilities with the SDF, these organizations are responsible for their own programs and expenses. They can, however, receive assistance from the SDF administrator or from the club consultant in applying for grants from local governments or foundations.

Only the sports club has a full-time executive, whose salary is also covered in part by unemployment agencies. This club has a total of fourteen sections in such activities as bowling, basketball, volleyball, soccer, and swimming. These sections each have their own boards, but their expenses and schedules are coordinated by the executive of the sports club.

The suburban sections also function as clubs and have their own boards and budgets. Each of the sections organizes lectures, parties, and other events in a rented room in its suburb. The SDF provides no financial support to the suburban sections but is obligated to assist the sections in applying for grants from local governments or foundations.

At the end of the year, all organizations and sections are required to prepare an annual report on their activities. The annual report, as a rule, lists the activities, lectures, and other events of the past year. Financial reports and a list of the officers and committees are included in the annual reports as well. Summaries of the reports from the sixteen organizations are then published in the SDF annual report, which is about forty pages thick.

Thus, each local organization or section is permitted to be autonomous and to retain its identity, but all the clubs conduct their affairs and have both social and business meetings within a building maintained by the SDF.

When activities are occurring in the Deaf House, officers of the various organizations are available for consultation. In this way, club leaders maintain a close relationship with the "grassroots" deaf person at least once a week, allowing deaf members to share with the club leaders their opinions on the actions of the national or regional organizations. In addition, deaf individuals often come to the Deaf House to discuss their concerns with the administrator, social worker, or club consultant. SDF leaders are obligated to bring these concerns, if accepted at the local meetings, to the attention of the national or regional federation of the deaf.

Another unusual feature of the SDF is its daycare service for parents of deaf children. The day care center, located next to the Deaf House, is supervised by a social service agency. The members of its staff are both deaf and hearing. On the playground, deaf children can observe deaf adults entering and leaving the SDF building, thus becoming exposed to the deaf adult world. I myself have stopped many times to chat with these deaf children on my way to the Deaf House, where I conducted my research. Their level of communication is very high and their command of Swedish Sign Language is excellent. Such a feature does not exist in deaf clubs in other countries I have visited.

About 80 percent of the SDF budget comes from both direct and indirect support from local governments. The rest comes from such sources as membership fees (3 percent), registration fees for courses (11 percent), profit from events (.7 percent), and other contributions (4 percent). Local governments in twenty-five suburbs and nearby cities support the SDF directly because deaf people are recognized as a natural and enriching part of society. Government support covers unemployment benefits, adult education programs, lectures, and social services. Every year the SDF appoints a local deaf resident to protect its interests at meetings of the government or at meetings of advisory councils in each suburb or nearby city.

In summary, the SDF serves as a central place where deaf people can be unified in their dealings with local government agencies and mass media while still permitting the creation of new activities or organizations. These deaf organizations within the SDF network are independent and have their own elections and boards yet still exert some influence on decision-making within the SDF through overlapping memberships.

The Swedish government has a policy of protecting and preserving minorities, subcultures, and other human groups. It considers only formal organizations as the legitimate representatives of the communities they serve. Thus, individuals or schools wanting to represent such communities cannot expect any direct government recognition or support but may receive grants for their projects, provided that the officially recognized organizations have no objection to the proposed projects. For example, the Swedish Federation of the Deaf—not the universities or other schools, as in the United States—receives grants directly from the government to supervise an adult education school and an interpreter training program.

Recently the Swedish Federation of the Deaf has cooperated for the first time with two other consumer organizations—one for deaf and hard of hearing people and the other for parents of deaf and hard of hearing children—in evaluating audiological services in Sweden. Previously, only service providers such as audiologists and other professionals evaluated these audiological services. In comparison, the National Association of the Deaf in the United States has no direct influence on educational policies, interpreter training programs, or Peace Corps programs for deaf people in developing countries.

In conclusion, as pluralism is now a universal trend in industrialized countries, local organizations of deaf people must be prepared to choose the most appropriate alternative to meet the current needs of their constituency. At present, there are five alternatives for local organizations of the deaf—dissolution, consolidation, centralization, satelliting, and centrality.

This case study of the Stockholm deaf club suggests that one of the alternatives—

centrality—might be appropriate for other local organizations if deaf people desire to retain their political and social consensus in pluralistic societies.

References

Andersson, Yerker. 1987. "Culture-Subculture." In *Gallaudet Encyclopedia of Deafness and Deaf People,* ed. John V. Van Cleve. Englewood, NJ: McGraw-Hill. pp. 261–264.

Boje, David M., and David A. Whetten. 1981. "Effects of Organizational Strategies and Contextual Constraints on Centrality and Attributions of Influence in Interorganizational Networks." *Administrative Science Quarterly* 26: 378–395.

Hörselvårdsutredningen. 1989. *Slutrapport* (Evaluation of audiological services in Sweden).

Stokholms Dövas Förening. 1989. "Styrelse-och Revisionsberättelse för år 1988" (Annual Report).

Silent Club: An Ethnographic Study of Folklore Among the Deaf

STEPHANIE A. HALL

In the world of Deaf Americans, the Deaf club is an important landmark. Deaf clubs exist in every major urban area in the United States. Cities where there are large populations of Deaf people may contain several clubs. These clubs provide more than just a place for Deaf people to socialize. The club is where they look for adult guidance in their youth, where they can obtain employment information and advice, where they may meet their future spouses (85 percent of deaf people marry other deaf people (Schein and Delk, 1974)), or where a Deaf stranger in town may find aid and friendship.

When I became interested in studying Deaf folklore, I chose a Deaf club in Philadelphia as a place to observe this folklore as it is used in its social context. I also wanted to understand more about Deaf clubs as social institutions created by and for Deaf people. Between 1980 and 1986 I did "participant observation" in one Philadelphia club and participated in many events in the Philadelphia Deaf community. Basing my approach on Dell Hymes' concept of ethnography of communication (Hymes, 1964, 1972, 1974), I focused on the uses of artistic communication in the setting of the club.

By agreement with the club I will use the pseudonym "Eastern Silent Club" to protect the members' privacy. Readers who know Philadelphia may be able to guess the club's real name. Please remember that the members wish to maintain their privacy.

As I worked on my study, I found it was not enough to simply go into a Deaf club and describe what people did there. I also had to contend with many misunderstandings about Deaf people and biases against Deaf culture. One professor at my university questioned whether Deaf people could be said to have a culture. Another questioned my ethics in doing the study in the first place. He wanted to know whether such a study would just promote the use of American Sign Language (ASL) instead of English among Deaf people and encourage them not to integrate into the rest of American society.

I was surprised to find biases against Deaf clubs among hearing signers as well. One interpreter I met at the Eastern Silent Club said:

> This place depresses me. You know, most of these people are illiterate. . . . It gets worse every generation. The deaf kids with hearing parents might have

A substantially revised version of this paper was published as "Door into Deaf Culture: Folklore in an American Deaf Social Club" in *Sign Language Studies*, volume 73 (Winter, 1991), pp. 421–429.

pretty good English, but then they have deaf children and so on. They just get more and more illiterate. [September 1980][1]

I should say I think most interpreters in Philadelphia would disagree with this opinion. But another Philadelphia interpreter expressed an opinion I think is more common. "The Deaf club is just a bar," she said. "I don't go to hearing bars, so why should I want to go to a Deaf bar?" [April, 1988.]

Decisions about deaf education and social services for Deaf people have often been based on such incomplete or false information about the ways Deaf Americans live their lives. Studies of sign language and the social aspects of deafness likewise have been colored by false assumptions. Both hearing and Deaf researchers need to work together to develop an accurate picture of Deaf Americans. One important way of accomplishing this is by allowing Deaf people to teach us about their culture. In this paper, therefore, I will allow the "Eastern Silent Club" members to tell you about themselves.

As a hearing friend and I were leaving the club one night, a club member in her early sixties got up and showed us to the door. She laughed at herself for doing so, signing, "Look at me. I act as though this were my home." Then she became serious, adding

> But this is like my home. You know, for Deaf people the Deaf club is like a second home. Hearing people don't have anything like that. They go home from work, put on headphones, and listen to their stereos or watch television. But Deaf people get together and socialize at their club. It's like a second home.

In the synopsis of a play called *Tales from a Clubroom*, Deaf playwrights Eugene Bergman and Bernard Bragg express a similar feeling:

> In any city, the club of the deaf is the heart of the deaf community. It is the principal meeting place and forum of the deaf. It is, in most cases, the only place where they can socialize. It is their ballroom, their bar, their motion picture house, their theatre, their coffeehouse, their community center—all rolled into one. It is a piece of their own land in exile—an oasis in the world of sound. (Bergman and Bragg, 1981, p. vii)

As these Deaf authors explain, the Deaf club is an essential part of any Deaf community. Deaf American society is made up of many small communities, usually found in urban areas near schools for Deaf people, or in places where Deaf people may find employment. These local Deaf communities are held together through a network of social organizations run by and for Deaf people, which include Deaf clubs, alumni associations, religious groups, and athletic teams.

Local communities stay in touch with one another through such national organizations as the National Association of the Deaf and the American Athletic Association of the Deaf. These organizational features of Deaf society are the outward manifestations of Deaf individuals' sense of themselves as a people. Through such organizations, Deaf people express their need for association with one another, their sense of a shared heritage (Gannon, 1980), and their shared goals for the future (Padden, 1980). The

---

[1] Dates enclosed in brackets refer to the time of a conversation or interview.

values, attitudes, and goals of Deaf Americans, together with the literary and linguistic heritage carried by sign language, comprise what is referred to as "Deaf culture" (see Carmel, 1987).

Founded in 1919, the Eastern Silent Club is one of America's oldest continuously operating Deaf clubs. The club has about five hundred members. But this does not reflect the club's true population, as only a fraction of those people who avail themselves of club services are dues-paying members. Its members range in age from eighteen to ninety. The club members display an equally wide range of economic levels, ethnic affiliations, educational backgrounds, levels of literacy, and hearing abilities. Most members are white and attended one of the schools for Deaf people in the Philadelphia area. Although membership was restricted to men until 1986, with an auxiliary organization provided for women, most club functions were open to both sexes. This separation of men's and women's clubs was once quite common in the United States.

The major language used at the club is American Sign Language. Orally trained deaf Philadelphians who do not sign do attend some social functions at the club and may be admitted as members if they show a willingness to learn signs.

One of the official functions of the Eastern Silent Club is to establish and support such athletic organizations as basketball, softball, bowling, and shuffleboard teams. The other—and, many members would say, more important—function of the club is to provide entertainment and a social gathering place for its members. The nightly recreation includes the bar, music from the jukebox, shuffleboard, and card games. Every fourth Saturday the older members play pinochle. Charitable raffles and drawings for door prizes occur on Saturdays, Pinochle nights, and on special occasions. At irregular intervals the club holds birthday parties, picnics, excursions, and camping trips. There are also yearly celebrations of major holidays.

The Eastern Silent Club facility has a large front room with a bar and a large back room for club meetings and parties. There are smaller meeting rooms downstairs and offices upstairs. A small kitchen makes it possible for the club to hold dinners or to serve snacks at parties.

Many of the activities at the Eastern Silent Club are similar to what might be found at any American social club. But the celebrations at the Deaf club also provide opportunities for the members to express their own special interests and concerns. For example, at this Philadelphia club there are six yearly masquerade events with competitions at each for best costume. Costuming is extremely popular among Deaf people, and this club provides its members with many opportunities to dress up. St. Patrick's Day, Valentine's Day, and Halloween are all celebrated with masquerade parties. In addition, the club also sponsors Western Night, Rock and Roll Night, and Pajama Night each year.

Halloween is the biggest masquerade event at the club and often draws friends and visitors from other parts of the country. It is only on Halloween that costumers try to conceal their identity with masks. Deaf costumers who wish to conceal their identities from their friends must wear gloves in addition to masks, and even change the way they walk so they won't be recognized by the way they move. "Do you know me?" they ask the large audience of party-goers not in costume, who try to guess.

Concealing oneself is considered fun in many communities and is especially fun for Deaf people, who often know each other so well. The costumes sometimes express Deaf identity, as with the woman who dressed up in a cardboard "I Love You" hand. Sometimes the costumes express a grimmer side of the Deaf experience. Many of the costumers who competed in the "monster" category, for example, dressed as doctors, blood-covered surgeons, and patients. Perhaps these monstrous doctors expressed childhood fears; many Deaf people were taken from doctor to doctor by parents looking for a cure for deafness.

When I entered the Halloween costume contest myself in 1980, I learned some lessons about Deaf culture. "Act," a friend told me. "You have to perform for the judges." Performance and characterization are as important as having a good costume. I was also surprised when those of us who didn't win were still given a small consolation prize. "That's the Deaf way!" explained my friend. "Among the Deaf everyone wins!" So, while these celebrations are for enjoyment, they also express and reinforce "the Deaf way."

The leisure activity that club members seem to enjoy most, however, is simply talking to one another. People arrive early and stay late, long after the movies and the games are over, just to sit and talk. Pinochle games often dissolve into conversation. The bar frequently becomes a forum for group discussion. The enthusiasm for conversation is unusually intense among Deaf people because, for many of them, communication is severely limited during regular daily activities. For those who cannot interact with other signers at work or at home, the Deaf club provides a crucial opportunity for obtaining information and social interaction. One of the major reasons for the existence of the club is to provide an atmosphere where sign language may be used freely. In an otherwise mixed group, sign language is the most important unifying factor.

The club works hard to teach the values and language that are important to its members. Young people entering the club may come from various educational methods. Some may sign well, others may know only a few signs, and still others may use a manually coded English system instead of the ASL common to members of the club. Older club members pay attention to younger members and try to teach them about Deaf language and history. Often strong mentor relationships develop between older and younger club members. One club member, who now has a Ph.D., explained the tradition of mentoring this way:

> There is an older man here at the Club, H-E-N-R-Y [uses name sign] Henry. . . .
> He was president of the Club a long time ago. When I was young and I first
> started socializing with Deaf people I didn't know very much, I was awkward.
> But Henry looked at me and saw potential in me, so he guided me along. I
> never became an officer of the Club or anything like that. I was a trustee for
> a while but I wasn't interested in becoming an officer. Still, I think I owe a lot
> to Henry. I think his taking an interest in me helped me to become successful
> later in life. So now I see this young man here, he's smart, he has potential, so
> I try to guide him along the way Henry guided me. [April 1985]

Often mentors use traditional stories, riddles, jokes, and sign play to teach about sign language. The riddles can show, for example, a way *not* to sign, that there are right and wrong ways of signing. Personal experience narratives also help teach about Deaf history, language, and values. A past president of the club who is a mentor to many young people told this story to a young man who came from a mainstream program:

> I remember one time in mathematics class. We had a Deaf mathematics teacher
> but he couldn't sign to us. It wasn't his fault. It was his job and he had to do
> what they told him. But one time he was trying to explain something and we
> didn't understand and we didn't understand. He explained and explained but
> the students said, "I don't understand, I don't understand." So he explained

and explained again. Still the students said, "I don't understand, I don't understand." So he went to the door of the classroom and looked up towards the office to see if anyone was watching [mimes action]. He closed the door, signed very fast, and then we understood! [March 1985]

This story contains important information about the educational history of many of the Deaf people that younger club members will associate with, about the attitudes towards signs many of them have, and about the importance of communication between Deaf people. Mentors also give advice to their pupils about life problems. The mentors may help them get jobs or council them about relationships. Most importantly, mentors help teach young people how to live their lives as Deaf people.

The Deaf club, then, is a place for entertainment, a place for the free use of sign language, and a place for the values and language of Deaf people to be taught. It has another important function: The Deaf club is an embassy. Through its association with such larger organizations as the National Association of the Deaf and the American Athletic Association of the Deaf, the local club maintains ties between the local Deaf community and other communities throughout the country. One effect of this is that members feel that what they do in their club also influences Deaf people in other locales. One of the reasons the Eastern Silent Club considered the policy change to admit women as members was because most other clubs in the country had already begun admitting women. When the club finally went through the lengthy process of rewriting its constitution to include women, it was, as far as anyone at the club knew, the last club in the United States to make this change. One of the club officers pointed this out to me:

> Today is history. Now, here, is Deaf history, because now the last all-men's Deaf club has accepted women. Now, today, we have a new Deaf tradition: Men and women are equals. I want you to write that down for your book that that happened here in Philadelphia. [April 1985]

This officer clearly feels that the Philadelphia club's policy affects all of Deaf America. Whether the effect is really large or small, it is important to understand that Deaf Americans feel this sense of connectedness, and that clubs help establish this connectedness.

The Deaf club is more than just a bar. It is a cultural institution in Deaf society that celebrates and perpetuates Deaf culture. Far from threatening Deaf education, it is a place where Deaf people educate one another. Rather than a refuge for unsuccessful Deaf people, it is a place where successful Deaf professionals may serve as mentors for younger Deaf people. And far from isolating Deaf people, the club provides connections between Deaf communities across America.

In the relaxed atmosphere of the club, embedded in the conversations, stories, celebrations, and even the rules of the club, one may find expressed the concerns, values, aesthetics, and ethics of Deaf culture. Because, as Eugene Bergman and Bernard Bragg have told us, the Deaf club is a piece of the Deaf person's "own land in exile," it is an excellent place to begin to develop an understanding of that "land."

References

Bragg, B., and E. Bergman. 1981. *Tales from a Clubroom*. Washington, DC: Gallaudet College Press.

Carmel, S. 1987. *A Study of Deaf Culture in an American Urban Deaf Community.* Ph.D. diss., American University, Department of Anthropology, Washington, DC.

Gannon, J. 1980. *Deaf Heritage: A Narrative History of Deaf America.* Silver Spring, MD: National Association of the Deaf.

Hymes, D. 1964. "Introduction: Towards Ethnographies of Communication." In *Language in Culture and Society: A Reader in Linguistics and Anthropology,* ed. D. Hymes. New York: Harper and Row. pp. 3–14.

Hymes, D. 1972. "Models of the Interaction of Language and Social Life." In *Directions in Sociolinguistics: The Ethnography of Communication,* ed. J. Gumperz and D. Hymes. New York: Holt, Rinehart, and Winston. pp. 35–71.

Hymes, D. 1974. *Foundations in Sociolinguistics.* Philadelphia: University of Pennsylvania Press.

Padden, C. 1980. "The Deaf Community and the Culture of Deaf People." In *Sign Language and the Deaf Community: Essays in Honor of William C. Stokoe,* ed. C. Baker and R. Battison. Silver Spring, MD: National Association of the Deaf. pp. 89–103.

Schein, J., and M. Delk. 1974. *The Deaf Population of the United States.* Silver Spring, MD: National Association of the Deaf.

The Origin, Development, and Working Activities of Madosa V.Z.W.

ADOLF VAN DEN HEUVEL

The history of Madosa V.Z.W. (Verenigingen zonder winstgevend doel, a non-profit organization)—the society for deaf people in Antwerp—reflects the periods of history during which it has existed. Its founding members and their successors have seen the society grow through turbulent times and change from a purely social gathering place for young people to an organization that includes athletic events and other activities of interest to a wider range of individuals. This paper will give a brief outline of the history of our organization.

The First Fifty Years

De maatschappij der doven van Antwerpen (the Society for the Deaf in Antwerp) was founded in 1894, but documents in the society's archives reveal that deaf adults in Antwerp were already active much earlier than that.

Georges de Harven, a deaf man, founded Belgium's first society for deaf people in 1859 in Antwerp. This group met in the Café du Nord at Grote Markt 20. De Harven brought back from Paris a bust of the Abbé de l'Epée, which he later donated to the society.

After a few years, J. Coremans was elected president of this society. Coremans noted that it was possible to find deaf people everywhere who use sign language as their primary means of expression, so there were many potential members for the group.

By 1893 the society, which now consisted of twenty deaf people, was called De Jonge Vrienden (The Young Friends) and met weekly. On February 4, 1894, following the request of Coremans and the other members of the group, negotiations to gain official status for the society began, and by February 11, 1894, the formal establishment of the society had become fact.

The society moved to a new location in Antwerp and elected Jan Van Achteren as the first president of the officially sanctioned society. By this time, there were twenty-three members. The goal of the society was to establish a place where deaf people could meet regularly for social activities. By 1899, a theater group of deaf people had already made its appearance on stage.

World War I began in 1914, and the society had to suspend its formal activities until 1918. However, people who had been members of the society still sought opportunities to get together for entertainment and socializing.

By 1921, the theater performances had became less successful, owing to the increasing popularity of movies. To provide another activity for its members, the sporting club was founded in 1922, and in 1924 the first international athletic games took place. Three Antwerp members, coached by a Mr. Westerhoff, the society president, entered this competition.

In 1927, the society replaced its original flag, which it had obtained in 1904. The 1927 flag is still on display in the Madosa club today, surrounded by sixteen glittering medals.

The Fifth International Congress took place in Liege in 1930, and for the first time, eight Jewish deaf people from Antwerp attended. Belgium was also celebrating its centennial of independence at this time.

By January 1931, the society's membership had declined considerably. Nevertheless, on February 8, 1931, a new section known as Tehuis (Home) was established within the club. The membership increased again as deaf people joined Tehuis, but they did not necessarily also become members of the society, because membership in a section did not require membership in the society as a whole.

In 1936, the Madosa society cofounded the National Association of the Belgian Catholic Deaf and Dumb. Three years later, the town council of Antwerp issued a certificate stating that all deaf people in the province of Antwerp were exempt from the tax on keeping a dog, an exemption that Madosa had lobbied for. Later that year, Madosa began publishing its own monthly periodical.

World War II began on May 10, 1940, and all society activities were again suspended. The dues for Tehuis were exempted for the year of 1940.

In 1941 the deaf clubs from Turnhout, Boom, and Lier joined with Madosa, and for the first time the deaf football club was the Belgian champion. But times were hard, and the next year the deaf clubs from Boom and Lier did not enroll again as members. In 1944 the club from Turnhout also resigned as a member.

The Society After Fifty Years of Existence

The society celebrated its fiftieth anniversary in 1944 with the usual banquet and celebration, but there were no great festivities because of the hard economic situation imposed by the war (which finally ended in 1945). The meetings of the society were very turbulent around this time, and a new board was chosen.

In 1946, a shuffleboard club for deaf people was founded, followed in 1947 by a tourist club. That same year the sporting club celebrated its twenty-fifth anniversary and got its own new flag. Although Tehuis had its own board, a new committee was set up for the purpose of buying a new house for that section of the society.

In 1949 Madosa had been in existence for fifty-five years, and again a new flag was designed, this time by Antoon Van Gils, a deaf artist. Edward Verheezen wrote a jubilee edition of the periodical describing the 1894–1949 period.

In those days, undoubtedly the most important event in the deaf community was the release of the movie *Johnny Belinda*. In this film, Jane Wyman magnificently played the character of Belinda, a deaf girl. This film was a tremendous success. In 1950, seven deaf people went to visit all the cinemas in town to collect money for a meeting house for Madosa. With the money they collected, Madosa was able to buy a building on Lange Lozanastraat in Antwerp in 1951.

Deaf people supplied all the labor to renovate the house. The money collected, however, was insufficient to cover all the costs of the project, so a decision was made to borrow money from the members. Arrangements were made to pay back the loans within ten years, without interest. Deaf members worked very hard to raise money, and after only seven years, all the loans were paid off.

More social clubs for deaf people were established in Antwerp during the 1950s, including a card-playing club in 1951 and a billiards club in 1956. In 1960 a club for elderly people was established, and in 1961 a collectors' club came into existence. These clubs, too, became sections within Madosa.

The sporting club separated from Madosa in 1960. This affected the organization in a negative way. Before 1960, there was very good spirit and collaboration among deaf people, but now this understanding no longer exists. Deaf people attend either the Madosa meetings or the sporting club events, but few deaf people visit both clubs. It is my hope that the activities of both groups can be united again in one building so that everyone has contact with both clubs, and that a spirit of cooperation can develop once again.

Also in 1960, Madosa received a beautiful present from one of its members: a frame with a metal reproduction of the Abbé de l'Epée and twenty-six little hands forming the letters of the manual alphabet. A family member of the Madosa member found this frame in Diest at an antique dealers' exhibition.

The photography club for deaf people in Antwerp was founded in 1975. Two years later, in 1977, deaf women became more active with the establishment of the ladies club for deaf people in Antwerp. Also in 1977, for the first time the ladies club organized a great carnival at the Madosa house. Today this is an annual event, and deaf associations come from far and wide to join our carnival party.

The Federation of Flemish Associations of the Deaf (FEVLADO) was established in 1977. The Federation originated partly from the National Association of the Belgian Catholic Deaf and Dumb, which had existed since 1936, and which unites most Flemish and Walloon deaf associations. (The Flemings and Walloons are two language groups of Belgium. The Flemings speak a dialect of Dutch, the Walloons a dialect of French.)

There are twenty-three associations for deaf people affiliated with the Federation. Through these affiliated associations, the Federation represents more than 1,600 members. Madosa has been affiliated with the Federation since its founding.

There are several important aims of the Federation:

❖ To ensure that all deaf associations continue their excellent mutual collaboration

❖ To defend the interests of deaf people

❖ To unite all different sign dialects

❖ To extend the official interpreter school set up by the Federation

❖ To organize Signed Dutch courses in Flanders.

One of the Signed Dutch courses takes place yearly at the Madosa center. One of the aims of this course is to give hearing people the opportunity to learn sign language so they can communicate fluently with deaf people. The teacher of this course is a deaf person. The first course at the Madosa center was held in 1984.

In 1986, Madosa became the owner of another building, which deaf members renovated. In this house, educational and recreational activities are held regularly, in addition to social activities such as parties, dances, and barbecues.

In 1987, a "first" occurred in the association when a woman, Maria Asselberghs, was elected president of Madosa. Her parents were also deaf, and her father had served as president of Madosa from 1951 to 1960.

Owing to the high unemployment rate in Belgium, the Ministry of Labor and Employment created special work statutes to enable unemployed people to start working in nonprofit associations. The wages of these employees are paid by the State Service for the Provision of Labor. As a result, the Federation was able to employ twenty people.

In 1987, the Federation established the Provincial Follow-up Care Service for the Deaf in Antwerp. This service is housed in the Madosa clubroom. Its aim is to provide individual guidance to all deaf and hard of hearing people on social, material, and moral levels. The board of this after-care service consists of the secretary and president of the Federation plus representatives of the four existing associations of the deaf and hard of hearing people in the province of Antwerp, including three representatives from Madosa.

Since 1987, the Madosa building also has housed the secretariat of the association of the hard of hearing. The members of this association are people who became deaf or hard of hearing later in life. The aim is to get these people out of their isolation and help them to solve their specific problems and to re-establish meaningful lives. Members of this group use lipreading instead of sign language to communicate.

In 1988, for the first time, we organized a great carnival party for the children. The aim of this party was to encourage deaf and hearing parents to communicate with each other. And at last, also in 1988, deaf people from the Flemish-speaking part of Belgium got their own text telephones (the Walloon deaf already had such devices). After many discussions, Belgian deaf people selected the "Minitel," a telephone device of French origin.

Today (1989), in addition to its bimonthly publication, the following Madosa sections still exist:

❖ De dovenspaarkas (the savings bank for deaf people)

❖ De Antwerpse Dovenkaartersclub (the cards club for deaf people in Antwerp)

❖ De Dovenbiljartclub Antwerpen (the billiards club for deaf people in Antwerp)

❖ De Doventoeristenclub Antwerpen (the tourist club for deaf people in Antwerp)

❖ Ouden van dagen (the elderly deaf club)

❖ De Dovenbakspelclub (the shuffleboard club for deaf people)

❖ De Dovendamesclub Antwerpen (the deaf women's club in Antwerp).

The clubs' associations that form Madosa are necessary for deaf people. At Madosa, deaf people can meet each other, relax together, participate in sports and recreational activities, and organize cultural events. The intention is not to separate deaf people from hearing people. But without Madosa and other organizations like it, deaf people would not have sufficient opportunities to take part in such activities owing to communication barriers.

Clubs for Deaf People in India

MADAN M. VASISHTA AND MEHER SETHNA

C lubs, associations, societies, or federations for deaf people are found in almost all large cities in India. They are a natural outgrowth of a social and linguistic minority's desire to get together. In smaller towns where there are no formal groups or clubs, deaf people still get together for various activities.

We recently conducted a survey to gather information about the social and cultural life of deaf people in India. This was the first known effort to document information about clubs and other organizations for deaf people in this country.

A survey form designed to collect preliminary data was sent to forty-eight selected clubs for deaf people. We wanted to keep the sample small and still have various types of clubs represented. Of the forty-eight questionnaires sent out, twenty-two were returned after three follow-up letters. Only nineteen were included in this analysis; three of the returned questionnaires were incomplete.

Our own experience working with deaf people and as active participants in such clubs makes us believe that the information collected is sufficiently representative to provide an accurate description of clubs for deaf people in India.

Membership in the responding clubs ranged from a low of fifteen to a high of 650. The average club had 192 members. However, a majority of these clubs have about 100 active members. Almost all club members are deaf, but often hearing people are welcome as honorary members.

The major sources of financial support for these clubs are membership fees, government grants, private donations, and advertisement revenue from program books. There are two kinds of membership fees—life and annual. Life memberships range from 50 to 300 rupees [roughly $3–18], and the annual membership fee ranges from 5 to 101 rupees. Members are not very regular in paying their dues, however, and the treasurer often has to be very persistent. Government grants are rare and are usually given for specific projects. Voluntary donations throughout the year are sometimes received, but more donations are collected through the flag week campaigns.

Almost all clubs have serious financial problems. Their limited resources force them to keep their activities to the bare minimum. Rarely does a club have its own building: most use rented or donated quarters for club activities.

Almost all the clubs are active in sports. The most popular sports are cricket and badminton (74 percent of the clubs engage in both of these activities). Soccer (63 percent) and gymnastics (42 percent) are also very popular. There appears to be very mild interest in field hockey (21 percent), a sport in which India had led the world until the last decade. Some clubs also are involved in table tennis, volleyball, and swimming.

Deaf clubs compete with each other, as well as with groups of hearing people, in cricket, badminton, and soccer. Regional sports competitions are also held to select athletes for the World Games for the Deaf. The All India Sports Council for the Deaf is planning ways to hold even more frequent organized athletic events for deaf people.

The services these clubs and associations provide vary, depending on the demand of the membership and the resources available. Helping needy members is the most common service.

Most of the clubs that responded to our survey provide family counseling, which usually involves interpreting. Club members with good oral communication skills often help clarify misunderstandings caused by lack of communication between a deaf person and his or her family.

Marriage arrangements are the second most common service provided by the clubs. In India, where most marriages are arranged, marriages between deaf and hearing people are fairly common. These are usually arranged by the parents. Deaf clubs help their deaf members find deaf marriage partners. The deaf-deaf marriage, a fairly recent phenomenon in India, is becoming very popular.

Deaf club members also help each other find suitable employment. This is a mostly informal, but highly effective, function of these clubs. Employed members recommend their friends to their employers or share information with other club members about available jobs.

More than half of the clubs that responded to the survey have adult basic education programs. Usually these are classes to help illiterate or semiliterate deaf people develop better reading and writing skills. Tutoring is provided by 37 percent of the clubs. This tutoring, usually free, is provided by hearing friends and deaf club members to help other members pass high school equivalency examinations.

Only 42 percent of the clubs have libraries or reading rooms on the premises. There are few books in these libraries. The reading rooms usually have local newspapers and popular magazines.

The clubs also provide a place for leisure activities. Board games (offered by 84 percent of the clubs surveyed) are the most common leisure time activity, followed by drama and mime performances (79 percent), group travel (74 percent), picnics (68 percent), and watching television (68 percent) and videotaped movies (42 percent). Attending movies in a cinema, once a staple activity of these clubs, is the least popular form of entertainment now, attracting only 36 percent of the clubs. The United States is not the only country where going to the movies has been replaced by watching television and videotapes.

Almost all the clubs observe major national holidays and festivals, usually with a picnic and sports meet. These family activities are heavily attended.

Most of the deaf clubs in India were established through the joint efforts of deaf and hearing people. Traditionally, the presidents of these clubs have been hearing individuals who can help get donations from other hearing organizations and also act as interpreters and spokespersons for the clubs. There now seems to be some change in this tradition. Only a little over half (53 percent) of the clubs have hearing presidents now, and only 12 percent have hearing vice presidents. The general secretary is the most important official in a club. He or she is responsible for all administrative work. Most of the clubs' officeholders are deaf people: general secretaries (88 percent), assistant secretaries (92 percent), treasurers (94 percent), and board members (83 percent). This is a refreshing change. Deaf people in India appear to be taking more active roles in the administration of their organizations.

All of these clubs have a very impressive list of future plans. Most want to have their own buildings. Deaf people in India prefer to live in proximity to other deaf people, so there is a widespread need for hostels for deaf adults. Because India has a tradition of extended families living together, it is very difficult for a deaf person to leave the family. It is, however, also very difficult to live with an extended family where, in most cases, there are no meaningful communication opportunities for the deaf member.

Most of the other plans of these clubs include providing training and job opportunities for deaf people. The state and central governments have large-scale projects in place in this area; however, unemployment and a lack of marketable skills remain major problems for deaf people in India. Therefore, the desire of these clubs to make training and employment a priority is laudable.

We limited the collection of data to these few but very important areas we have just described. We hope to have follow-up surveys to collect additional information. Such information will help these clubs learn about each other's activities and also begin some cooperative ventures.

The Deaf Union of Guipúzcoa

MIREN SEGOVIA

The purpose of this paper is to introduce the Deaf Union of Guipúzcoa, an organization that brings together a significant number of deaf people from the province of Guipúzcoa, Spain. The Deaf Union promotes cultural, recreational, and social activities and provides a gathering place for deaf people. The Union is a private, nonprofit organization belonging to its deaf members and is supported by various public institutions and through membership fees. At present, there are 160 members ranging in age from eighteen to eighty, but the organization makes its services available to all the deaf people of Guipúzcoa.

Because the Deaf Union of Guipúzcoa is governed by its deaf members, it is a place where we deaf people can participate in any type of activity we wish. It is also a place where we can get information that, owing to our deafness, we do not have access to in the outside world. Because we, as members, are responsible for the operations of the Deaf Union, it is our obligation to make it a place of reunion as well as something more: an integral center where we can develop in personal, cultural, and physical areas. All of our members are responsible for contributing their support to the effort to make the Deaf Union a center of complete service to deaf people.

In this paper, I will discuss the history, goals, and operations of our association, the characteristics of its members, and some of the ideas that make the Deaf Union of Guipúzcoa an association and institution that acknowledges the needs of all deaf people.

History of the Deaf Union of Guipúzcoa

For some time the deaf people of Guipúzcoa had felt the need for a place to get together, so they decided to meet in a bar. They later became part of a hearing association but were not comfortable there, so they went back to the bar. In 1961, with money raised from the members themselves and from hearing parents of deaf people, the group established quarters of its own. After a while, the group grew too large for this location, and the members were faced with the need to look for a larger one. In 1984, with the help of public organizations, we moved to our present location at Calle Reyes Católicos No. 14 in San Sebastian, Guipúzcoa.

Today, the Deaf Union provides facilities and services including a cafeteria, bar and catering services (staffed by members of the association), a gastronomical society, a library, an auditorium/conference room, cultural services, and videos.

Goals and Objectives

The goals of the association are to create and promote solidarity among deaf people; to foster participation in cultural, recreational, and social activities, and to encourage members to unite, both socially and in the work force, to eliminate discrimination.

One of the association's objectives is to be an open center where various activities can be planned and organized. These include activities, both within the organization and in the mainstream community, that promote communication and relationships between hearing and deaf people. Activities sponsored by the Deaf Union include recreational games and sports, mime, tapestry-making, arts and crafts, and conferences. The Deaf Union also sponsors its members' participation in sports and cultural activities in the hearing community. Members have the opportunity to suggest activities to the board of directors, which supports any type of idea or project geared toward creating links either within our community or with the hearing community.

The Deaf Union promotes the social integration of deaf people by fostering various activities outside of the association. Activities requiring special attention or services, such as conferences, cultural support classes, etc., are carried out within the association. Hearing people who show interest in the deaf community also have access to the activities and services of the association.

For direct services to our deaf members, we have a department of social assistance. This department, coordinated by a deaf woman who is a social worker, provides information and consultation on personal, family, social, and work-related problems. It also provides assistance in bureaucratic transactions and to members encountering difficulties in communication with other centers or institutions.

Owing to a lack of concern and sensitivity for deaf issues and a shortage of relevant information, society often fails to address the communication needs of deaf people. The Deaf Union is a place where members share in a larger identity and can focus their attention on these needs. This does not mean the Deaf Union is not receptive to the hearing world; in 1987, our old statutes were modified to allow hearing people to become members, with opportunities equal to those of deaf members. Naturally, we limit the number of hearing members in order not to sidetrack the objectives of the association.

A goal of the Deaf Union is to prepare deaf people to cope and develop in both the deaf world and the hearing world and to break through the withdrawal and mistrust the handicap imposes on us. To achieve this goal, the association has established a number of objectives:

❖ To give the required attention and time to persons affected by hearing loss

❖ To help them establish trust and confidence in themselves

❖ To maintain as many sources of information as possible

❖ To counteract the idealization of hearing people

❖ To work against the belief that deaf people are not capable of participating in certain activities because they are deaf and

❖ To work for equal opportunity in every area—academic, vocational, social, etc.

We believe that the present disposition of our members is favorable to achieving all the objectives mentioned above. When all these issues are addressed by the deaf and hearing communities, the problems that deaf people experience today will vanish.

Conclusions

Since I became president of the Deaf Union in 1987, I have thought that we should establish contacts with people outside the organization, participate in congresses and festivals, and collaborate with other groups. Because the Deaf Union was very traditional in its activities, we were neither widely known nor sought out by those who did know of us. I did not like that at all.

Many members of the Deaf Union have been marginalized by the hearing society, have not had the opportunity to be educated or to feel the support of their families, and have not had satisfying relationships with hearing people. These people need more contact with the outside world to open their minds to our social reality.

Opening the Deaf Union to the outside world was not an easy job. Some of the members thought these changes meant that we wanted to cut ourselves off from deaf people to blend in with the hearing. But, with patience, I made them see reality. I realized that I would not be able to change the organization from top to bottom immediately. It can be done, but only gradually.

It is my dream that the day will arrive when deaf people and hearing people will be able to understand each other and work together.

The Role of "Silent Sports" in Italian Deaf Culture

ORAZIO ROMEO AND LISA J. RENERY

During her first weeks as an intern at the Mason Perkins Fund in Rome, Lisa Renery was struck by her new Deaf acquaintances' constant references to sports. Having played on soccer teams with Deaf companions, I was enthusiastic when she expressed interest in conducting a study on Italian Deaf people's involvement in sports. Because we both hoped to bring a slice of Italian Deaf life to The Deaf Way, we decided that a popular topic such as sports would offer a glimpse at the "way" of Deaf people in Italy.

We conducted structured interviews with more than thirty men and women from all over Italy to help us assess the value of organized sports in the Deaf community. Our questions dealt with the signs used to name and describe sports activities, attitudes and perceptions about Deaf sports, and the relative popularity of Deaf sports today as compared with past years.

Beginning with the question of language, it is important to mention that Italy is a country with many sign language dialects. Signs as basic as MOTHER and FATHER are often different from one region to another. We wanted to learn whether the same would hold true for sports signs. Although most of the people we interviewed expressed their doubts that sports signs would be any less subject to variation than other signs, our data revealed the opposite to be true. We observed that if sports signs differed at all, they often differed in handshape alone. The more important sports—soccer, track and field, skiing, and tennis—showed very little regional variation. Signs of less popular activities—horse racing, ice and roller skating, and cycle racing—showed one or more variants while still differing only in handshape and movement.

How is it that sports signs are all so similar in a country with so many regional variations? It is possible that the active nature and physical orientation of sports make uniformity of signs more likely. In addition, the fact that organized sports offer Deaf athletes the opportunity to travel contributes to the adoption of signs from one region to another and even to the blending of signs from different regions.

Every culture produces linguistic terms according to its needs. The number and richness of these terms reflect the importance of a particular activity or institution in that culture. The emotional and social worth of sports in the Italian Deaf community is reflected in elaborate sets of signs—particularly in soccer, the most popular Italian sport. Soccer has an extensive list of signs to describe the plays and maneuvers, rules, equipment, positions, and calls of the game. From my own experience on the soccer team at Gallaudet—which I attended on a Mason Perkins scholarship—I know that in the United States, where soccer is not so popular, the repertory of soccer terms is smaller and less detailed. However, Deaf people in the United States make up for this in their football signs, which are numerous and rich in detail. Cultures do indeed create signs for activities that are important to them.

To learn about the origins of sports in Italy, we examined various Deaf publications, both past and present. In the history of Italian Deaf sports, there are two particularly important figures. The first, Emidio Pacenza, is considered to have been the founding father of organized sports for Deaf people in Italy. In Milan in 1923 he made the acquaintance of the secretary general of the National Sports Association of the Deaf in Belgium. It was from him that Pacenza learned with surprise that nearly every European nation other than Italy had its own Deaf sports association.

The following year at the World Games for the Deaf in Paris, Roberto DeMarchis, the second great figure in Italian Deaf sports, became the first athlete to represent Italy at the games. DeMarchis took the initiative to enter the games independently and came back with gold medals in the 100 and 1500 meter free-style swimming events.

This was impetus enough for sports enthusiast Pacenza. He realized that the time was ripe for a Deaf sports organization in Italy. In 1925, armed with a great deal of passion and energy, he founded in Milan and Genoa the first Deaf sports associations in Italy. In 1929 Pacenza became director of the Silent Sports Commission of Italy, which in 1953 became the Federation of Silent Sports of Italy (FSSI).

For Pacenza and his cofounders, organized sports provided not only a channel for athletic recreation for Deaf people, but a way to extend their cultural and social horizons. They envisioned the Deaf community enjoying sports activity because it would allow them to come together with other Deaf people from all over Italy and abroad, and give them a sense of solidarity.

They also hoped the FSSI would offer Deaf people a means of overcoming what they themselves perceived as inequality between themselves and their hearing peers. For the first time, Deaf people would be able to use sports to assert their equality. In 1930 one writer for a Deaf publication described the presence of sports as a "ray of sunshine" in the Deaf person's cloud-filled sky.

Does this same exuberance for Deaf sports in Italy exist today? Have Pacenza's aspirations for the Deaf community been realized? Does participation in sports indeed promote a sense of Deaf community and solidarity?

The answers are both positive and negative. Our informants fell into three groups. About half of all the people we interviewed admitted that what they appreciate most about sports is the social and cultural satisfaction that playing with their Deaf peers can give them. Quite a few in this first group said they would never have participated in organized sports had there not been a Deaf team to join; they would not have considered playing with a hearing team. The social interaction that Deaf sports made available to them was as important as, if not more important than, the activity itself.

While some referred to sports as a way to make new friends, others mentioned it as a means of maintaining old ties. Because there are almost no TDDs in private homes and no organized telephone relay services to help Deaf people in Italy contact each other, travel is really the only way to maintain long-distance friendships. Sports represents one way of mobilizing the Italian Deaf community.

The second group was made up of those who play for both Deaf and hearing teams. These individuals also said they enjoyed Deaf sports for the social benefits mentioned above. When looking for serious competition, however, they played on hearing teams.

This attitude toward organized Deaf sports was shared by members of the third group, who bypassed Deaf teams to play exclusively on hearing ones. Of the three groups, only members of this last group shared a truly negative image of Deaf sports. Playing with hearing people gave them access to better facilities, more demanding coaches, and a higher degree of challenge and discipline. Not surprisingly, the one strong dissatisfaction expressed by these athletes concerned communication difficulties they experienced with their hearing teammates. Although communication was clear and unencumbered while they were engaged in the game, they had little success in tearing down the barriers that went up off the playing field.

Why are Deaf teams traditionally less well prepared than hearing ones? What factors keep Deaf teams from flourishing as it was hoped they would? According to many of the people we interviewed, the small size of the Deaf community in comparison with the hearing community is the biggest factor. Coaches of Deaf teams are unable to be really selective in their choice of players. Any and all able-bodied young Deaf people are begged to fill the ranks of the team. Players from one sport are even "borrowed" by another during the first sport's off season.

Consequently, coaches are restricted from exercising the appropriate amount of discipline for fear of alienating any less-than-committed players. While in hearing sports it is considered a good thing to discourage players who are not sufficiently dedicated or skilled, many Deaf teams cannot afford to be so strict. Consequently, it is also likely that ineffective coaches will go on to produce ineffective coaches for future teams, and another generation of Deaf players in search of discipline and expert coaching will seek out hearing teams.

On occasion, when there are not enough Deaf players in one community, players may be "bought" by another community. That is, a player is asked to move to a new town and receives a monthly stipend to cover the costs of travel, room, and board. Another way to compensate for the smaller size of the Deaf community is to take hearing players onto Deaf teams. Often a Deaf team's roster will be more than half filled with hearing members. Although Deaf teams do not necessarily want to resort to recruiting hearing members, it is often necessary to keep the team alive.

Another effect of the small size of the Deaf community is that Deaf teams are less well funded than hearing teams, which contributes to their comparatively poorer standards of play. Because amateur hearing teams have a larger pool of participants, they are better known and have more sources of funding for their activities, such as support from local sponsors. Deaf teams, however, rely more on community events sponsored by local Deaf clubs, such as parties and lotteries, as well as the often insufficient contributions from regional or national associations for Deaf people. Because of the less competitive nature of Deaf teams, it is far less feasible for them to charge admission to sporting events, as hearing teams often do. Unfortunately, the very players whom Deaf teams could use to draw in admissions are drawn themselves to hearing teams.

It can be predicted that, if the downward trend in participation continues, Deaf teams will need to resort increasingly to measures such as taking on hearing members When we asked informants about that trend and inquired about the possible reasons behind it, fingers pointed to a seemingly unrelated event in the field of Deaf education. In 1978 the Italian government passed a law that resulted in the mainstreaming of a majority of Deaf children into hearing schools. Because far fewer Deaf children are attending residential institutions, many such schools have been forced to close down or have been taken over by predominantly hearing classes.

The results of this law have already been shown to be quite devastating. One single deaf or hard of hearing child is placed in a class, or even an entire school, with no deaf or hard of hearing companion. Because the regular teachers are not trained in Deaf education, "special" teachers are assigned to the classrooms. These assistants also know little about Deaf children and have been exposed to as little manual communication as the children themselves. The fact that this generation is no longer being exposed to sign language, which had traditionally been passed on from child to child, threatens grave consequences, not only for the children themselves, but for the Deaf community in general.

The implications are certainly worthy of note: The deaf or hard of hearing child, now isolated from his or her peers, is not only deprived of sign language, but also of membership in a Deaf community. Deprived of the language and of their rightful sense of belonging to the Deaf community, these mainstreamed children are, not surprisingly, taking less interest in Deaf sports. By the same token, sports associations that previously recruited members from residential schools are finding it more difficult to find players to fill their teams. Sports teams are now composed less of younger players and more of players in their thirties, who would have stopped playing the game earlier had there been the usual turnover of players.

Fortunately, there promises to be some light at the end of the tunnel. Because of the deficiencies of mainstreaming, a small but tireless group of educators is pushing not only for manual communication schools, but for bilingualism—that is, Italian and Italian Sign Language in the classroom—as well as special classes for Deaf children in hearing schools. Even if the Deaf child does not grow up in a residential school environment, the child should have linguistic contact with Deaf peers to make him or her feel part of the community. With this sense of belonging to the community, new generations of Deaf children should once again be able to engage in community activities, such as sports, with greater ease.

The FSSI will soon be working under the National Olympic Committee of Italy to direct more funds to Deaf sports. The Committee has never before included Deaf people in its sponsorship of sports for people with disabilities. It is hoped and even anticipated that this new source of funding will create a more competitive sports environment for Deaf teams, with better facilities, coaches, and equipment. In this way Deaf teams will not only draw back their own athletes lost to hearing sports, but also attract new members who might not previously have had access to information about Deaf sports.

Sports, Deafness, and the Family

DONALDA K. AMMONS
AND MARGERY S. MILLER

S ports play an important role in the lives of deaf people. We participate in athletic activities for a variety of reasons: for health and fitness,
for recreation, for social interaction, and for the pursuit of excellence
in sports through training and competition. But limited information
about the sports opportunities for deaf individuals and certain perspectives about deafness held by individual families and society at large may create
obstacles that limit a deaf youth's access to the benefits derived from involvement in
sports.

If children with a variety of physical differences (so-called disabilities) were lined
up—children with cerebral palsy or muscular dystrophy, children who use wheelchairs
or crutches, and children who are deaf—one's first reaction would be that the deaf child
does not belong in the group. That is, when it comes to participation in sports, there
appears to be no "handicap" in being deaf. In fact, the United States Olympic Committee's Committee on Sports for the Disabled often has heated arguments concerning
the allotment of funds to training programs for deaf youth or to the American Athletic
Association of the Deaf (AAAD), because some of the committee members view deaf
people as able-bodied persons.

Many deaf people would agree with this description. Yet, if there is no difference
between the bodies of deaf and hearing athletes, why is it that deaf athletes, for the
most part, are not performing at the same level as hearing athletes? Their bodies are the
same. Their minds are the same. Their desire to achieve and to excel is the same. But
their achievement is not the same.

As is usually the case when we talk about any issue relating to deafness, the communication differences and the hearing world's seeming indifference to the communication
needs of deaf individuals are at the root of the problem. For years, many families of deaf
children have selected a hearing standard of communication as the measuring stick of
success for their children. If the child can communicate through speech and speechreading, then the child is a success. If, however, the child must rely on signs, thus limiting
the number of potential communication partners in the hearing world, then the child is
a failure. Often parents feel that they too have failed.

It is often taken as a symbol of success that a deaf child can successfully blend
in with a group of hearing children. Through their child's participation, without using
sign language, in a mainstreamed sports environment, some parents hope to prove to
themselves and to the world that their child is capable. The question is, capable of what?

Their child may be capable of blending in, of not appearing different on the outside, of not looking deaf, of not creating any problems for the coach. But is that enough?

Parental attitudes have long been known to exert a powerful influence on children. If parents believe a child is going to be successful, the child believes the same thing. Yet most parents have a false sense of what constitutes success. They believe mere participation is success, and that "not letting the disability get you down" should be the theme. "Not letting the disability get you down" usually translates into hiding the fact that the deaf child is different by pretending that hearing children and deaf children communicate the same way. However, real success can occur when parents acknowledge and strive to accommodate the communication differences their deaf child experiences. Then, parents can truly believe that their children can function competently.

We feel that it is all right for deaf children to look deaf and to be different without being viewed as a deficient copy of a hearing child. It is our belief that efforts to conceal the communication differences inherent in being a deaf child and to encourage deaf children to participate in the world of sports as if their deafness did not exist are the very reasons why deaf children have been denied appropriate and comprehensive training and competitive opportunities for years.

We will now briefly describe some simple yet critically important guidelines for deaf children to gain the maximum benefit from participating in sports. These guidelines are for deaf youth, their parents, and advocates of deaf youth all over the world. The suggestions are divided into those that pertain to mainstream athletic activities and those specific to sports opportunities exclusively for deaf youth.

Mainstream Sports Programs for Deaf Youth

If parents and their deaf children decide to include mainstream athletic activities as all or part of the child's involvement in sports, we suggest that the following guidelines be considered.

First, parents should let the decision to be involved in this kind of sports activity be made by the child, once they feel that he or she is ready to make this decision. If a child is too young to decide about mainstream sports and parents make this decision, they should be sure that the child is comfortable about it and not under any stress or pressure. If the child appears to be unhappy and confused, the situation may become a negative experience rather than a positive one.

No matter how young the child, even as young as preschool, if he or she uses sign language at home and/or in school, parents should request that a sign language interpreter be present during all practices and athletic events. Although some people believe that very young deaf children are not ready to use an interpreter in an educational setting, an interpreter who is experienced in working with very young children can make the necessary adjustments and provide the deaf child with the same communication that hearing children receive.

Contrary to what many parents believe, deaf children will learn to feel most comfortable in mainstream athletic situations when they have *full* access to what is being communicated and do not have to pretend they are hearing or struggle to understand through lipreading. Remember that one of the important benefits of participation in sports is their recreational and leisure value. Deaf children do not need yet another lesson in lipreading when they are trying to learn about sports for the purpose of enjoyment or future competition. Their efforts should be on the field, on the court, in the pool, on the track, or wherever the events take place. Their efforts should also be in the mind, trying to make the smartest play. But their efforts should not revolve around trying to figure out what the coach said or who is talking at any given moment.

If possible, parents should teach the deaf child's teammates a few signs that relate to the sport so they can have some direct communication with the child. Parents should state their desire to do this to the coach and have a time set aside for a mini sign-lesson. Having a coach who can sign fluently would be the ideal situation for a deaf child in a mainstream sports setting, but experience has taught us that there are very few people meeting this requirement who are not already involved in "deaf only" sports programs. A deaf coach who is interested in working with hearing and deaf athletes could be a solution to the communication problem experienced by deaf children in mainstream settings. Through the use of an interpreter, hearing children could overcome their "handicap"—that of not understanding sign language!

Sports Activities Specifically for Deaf Athletes

With more and more deaf children attending mainstream educational programs in their hometowns, an entire generation of deaf children is being denied opportunities to participate fully in athletic events with other deaf children and with deaf coaches (or hearing coaches who are fluent signers). They are being denied experiences that are richly rewarding from the perspectives of fitness, competition, recreation, and social interaction. They are denied access to these programs owing partly to a lack of awareness on the part of mainstream educational programs and partly to the limited contact between local school districts and residential schools for the deaf. This separation arises from the competition for deaf students and the vast philosophical differences between "separate" and "blended" approaches to educating deaf students.

The secret of sports programs for deaf youth remains just that—a secret—owing partly to a lack of information provided to mainstream educational programs and partly to the lack of consistent and persistent contact between parents' groups and individual parents and organizations such as the AAAD.

The AAAD must become more responsive to the needs of young deaf athletes, who are the hope of tomorrow. Without strong training programs for deaf children, we will be continually trying to "catch up" with hearing athletes.

Training programs specifically for deaf athletes typically start when children are much older than is appropriate. We do not provide enough training programs on local and state levels for deaf children, and we do not have a formal system for identifying all of the deaf children in mainstream settings who might be interested in and benefit from these programs. We must make every effort, therefore, to develop numerous training programs for young deaf children and older deaf athletes. We must inform parents and educators about the enormous benefits to deaf children of developing skills and competing with other deaf children when they choose to do so. And we must train deaf coaches to provide the best possible programs for our deaf youth.

It is our obligation, our duty, and our privilege to inform parents and educators about the positive and richly rewarding opportunities available to deaf children and youth in athletic programs specifically designed for and by deaf individuals.

Mainstreaming—A New Concept for Recreation and Leisure in the Deaf Community

BRUCE GROSS

I n 1984 a new concept was given form with the establishment of the Southern California Recreation Association of the Deaf (SCRAD). SCRAD was founded on the concept that the deaf community could expand its horizons by taking part in general activities of the hearing community, while receiving specialized services as needed for full participation and understanding in such activities. In 1986, the organization's success enabled it to look to the future, and the World Recreation Association of the Deaf (WRAD) was born.

The most common experiences in the deaf community until this time were activities—such as parties, card games, and other small and medium-sized group events—with only deaf participants. The purposes of WRAD were to take the deaf participants out of the restrictive recreational and leisure activities of the past, to enlarge the scope of recreational, social, and other leisure activities in the deaf community, to educate the deaf community on issues of general community interest, and to educate the hearing community on the needs of the deaf with the goal of full participation by deaf people in the community at large.

The idea of mainstreaming for recreation and leisure activities started as an experiment in the bicultural integration of deaf and hearing communities. Since the deaf community was not experienced with mainstream activities in the hearing community at large, the project plan was to integrate deaf people slowly into the recreational and leisure activities available within the hearing community. Because the project started in a geographical area where many secondary school- and college-age deaf students live, these student groups formed the base for the project. It was felt that many older deaf people would join the activities once they were made aware of the opportunities. This, indeed, proved to be the case.

Another important aspect of this project was to integrate as many different subcultures of the deaf community as possible. Many members of the target population were from countries other than the United States.

The initial project plan involved activities geared to the recreational and social needs of the target population. Our first event was a racquetball party at a club. The club provided access to its jacuzzi, sauna, and steam facilities, board games, racquetball equipment, and refreshments. This event proved very popular because none of the local deaf clubs was able to provide such a wide range of activities.

The next activity was a deaf skiing day at a local resort, with a deaf ski instructor provided. Other activities included bicycling trips around the region on general bicycle routes. These events have continued and have formed the basis of the group's activities by providing knowledge of possibilities for recreation and leisure activities of which members of the deaf community had not been aware.

Another purpose of the group is to provide information to the deaf community about recreational and about employment options and opportunities deaf people may not have thought were available to them. In 1985 the group established a lecture series with the goal of expanding the intellectual horizons of its members. Our deaf speakers have included a person who hiked across a large portion of the United States, a dancer, a diver, an airplane builder/pilot, a doctor, a veterinarian, a physical therapist, people who have held administrative positions in colleges and high schools, and others who have achieved prominence in television and finance. We have attempted to show that, although there are numerous difficulties facing deaf people, with persistence and determination one can succeed as a professional in many areas formerly thought to be restricted to hearing people.

Many deaf people in the community feel shy or reluctant to participate in the activities of the hearing world, owing to real or imagined difficulties in communication and interpersonal relations. By holding group events for deaf people in the hearing world, WRAD has succeeded in helping them overcome such fears. WRAD tours to local cultural attractions are conducted as group activities, with interpreters provided for access to information, but differ in no other way from the experiences enjoyed by the hearing community.

WRAD events at local amusement parks have been very successful, with attendance at one recent function totalling more than 1,500, including deaf people, their families, and friends. Interpreters, both volunteer and paid, have assisted at these events, and deaf participants are assured that, should any emergency arise, there is an interpreter available. In addition, the participants have the advantage of lower group rates for admission and use of the facilities. In all other aspects, however, the deaf participants enjoy the park and its attractions in the same manner as hearing participants, without undue restrictions.

WRAD now has chapters on both the west and east coasts. To ensure that the group's foremost consideration remains the needs and welfare of the deaf community, the bylaws of each chapter, and those of the master organization, stipulate that the president and first vice-president must be deaf or hard of hearing. The second vice-president, however, must be a hearing person. This integration of the hearing and deaf cultures has been an educational experience for the participants on our governing Boards of Directors; our deaf board members have achieved greater understanding of the operations of government—knowledge that had not been readily available to the deaf community.

The planning of these events has been a successful educational experience as well. The Boards of Directors have gained experience in contractual matters, interaction with the representatives of community recreational and leisure centers, bargaining and negotiation, expressing the needs of the deaf participants, and in arranging for the satisfaction of those needs, which include the provision of interpreters well in advance of an event. In addition, the hearing owners and operators of local facilities used for the group events have gained knowledge and awareness of the needs of the deaf community. WRAD has received many letters from the hearing owners and operators of local recreational facilities and amusement parks, expressing their appreciation for the knowledge and information gained from WRAD during the planning of events at their facilities. In many cases these facilities have now made permanent accommodations for deaf participants as a result of the guidance and encouragement of WRAD.

Our experiment has achieved more than we had planned for it; our goal of integrating the deaf person into the mainstream of available general activities, with support services when necessary, has been highly successful. The individual participating in such events enjoys a positive psychological outlook on the community at large. The general community is now considered a place full of opportunities for personal benefit. This is in contrast to the outlook of the past, in which the community was seen as a barrier to personal fulfillment.

Our participants from countries other than the United States have enjoyed the activities and have benefitted greatly from the intercultural interaction between themselves and the general community of deaf persons born in the United States. In our geographical region, people from other countries and other races have traditionally segregated themselves into separate clubs and organizations.

A special cultural success has been the introduction of deaf participants into the hearing world, with its great diversity, its opportunities, and most especially its manners, philosophy, and norms. For a deaf person raised within the closed deaf environment, it is often difficult to understand the hearing world, and therefore to participate in it. WRAD has attempted to provide its deaf participants with social and societal integration and knowledge about the general culture of the hearing community.

After only four years we have seen a greater willingness on the part of the deaf participants to foster wider contacts and relationships in the hearing and deaf communities. In that time span, WRAD's membership has grown from twelve to over 1,000 people. And the idea is still growing: WRAD now has four official chapters, and more are starting at this time. We have received invitations to speak to groups throughout the United States as well as inquiries about our project from as far away as Nigeria and the Orient.

For too long now the deaf community has encountered, from both the hearing and deaf worlds, a message of "You can't." There has been very little of the information on the general society that allows deaf people to prove "I can." WRAD teaches the social and societal skills needed by each individual for personal growth, in a supportive, fun, and enjoyable manner. The more involved a person wishes to be with the project, the more skills and information he or she will gain. Participants are able to interact with the group at their own levels, and as they gain personal independence and interpersonal skills, many may advance to higher levels of responsibility in the organization.

We take pride in the fact that all of our events—and all of our successes—result from the efforts of individual volunteers from the deaf and hearing communities in the spirit of bicultural understanding and mutual respect for the abilities of the individual participants. At the same time, the organization recognizes the special communication needs of the deaf community within the hearing world, and maintains a philosophy of making special services available when necessary. We have discovered that the mainstreaming of the deaf community into the culture of the hearing does not dilute the deaf culture, but rather expands opportunities for deaf people and provides education to hearing people about the beauty and joy of deaf culture.

PART SIX

The Deaf Child in the Family

Editor's Introduction

pproximately 90 percent of deaf children worldwide are born into hearing households to parents who initially have no knowledge of sign language or of what it may mean to be deaf. Members of the medical community, whom hearing parents tend to regard as authorities on deafness, are more often than not unable to give parents positive advice concerning the possibilities for their deaf child, except in the area of hearing amplification. The likelihood that deaf children—isolated from people proficient in sign language—may experience linguistic, social, and emotional impoverishment during a crucial developmental period is high. This is especially true in countries where Deaf communities do not exist or are difficult to find, and information concerning deaf children's need for visually accessible language input is generally unavailable.

Most of the papers in this section represent the views of parents who have achieved (often after a considerable struggle) an understanding of deaf children's ability to flourish in an environment that makes full use of their visual acuity and intellectual capacity. Some readers, however, may find it instructive to read the last paper (by Assumpta Naniwe) first. That paper's depiction of parents' levels of understanding and attitudes toward deafness in Burundi (as of 1989) is saddening, as are the apparent consequences for deaf children growing up in such circumstances. Nevertheless, conditions in Burundi at the time of The Deaf Way were not radically unlike conditions facing deaf children in many nations around the world.

The paper by Roberta Thomas (United States) (one portion of a three-part presentation) expresses the view that hearing parents must learn to allow deaf children "to be deaf." Thomas states that once she accepted her child's difference, she benefited in many ways, learning about a culture and language she had never known about before and discovering that her deaf child could be "a source of pride and joy." Michael Tillander (Finland) then describes the difficulties hearing parents face as they struggle to accept their child's deafness, to learn sign language themselves, and to ensure that their child gains adequate access to Deaf culture. He stresses the importance of parents banding together for mutual support in these efforts.

Ritva Bergmann (Denmark) presents the point of view of a Deaf parent of a Deaf child. Like the previous two presenters, she expresses the conviction that deaf children need to become bilingual, learning the majority language through reading and writing and sign language as a first language. Although she expresses joy at the realization that her Deaf children felt none of the shame about deafness she had experienced as a child, she also expresses concern over her children's difficulty accepting and dealing positively with hearing people. In the following paper by Jean-François Mercurio (France), we are given a glimpse into what many consider to be the ideal situation for a deaf child: to be brought up in a Deaf household in which the parents sign fluently and are comfortable with being Deaf. Mercurio emphasizes that his daughter Sophie, growing up under such circumstances, learned sign language on a schedule matching hearing children's acquisition of spoken language. Furthermore, he points out, she benefited from her parents' complete acceptance of her deafness and never experienced the kind of implicit or explicit rejection that, in Mercurio's view, may lead to serious emotional problems.

A paper by Myriam de Luján (Venezuela) describes a systematic effort in Venezuela to identify deaf infants early and provide a high degree of support for both infants and parents to learn sign language and interact with Deaf people. De Luján describes the young Deaf adults who teach mothers and infants sign language in Venezuela's Center for Infant Development as "pioneers in a revolution of hope." The marginalization of deaf children described in the final paper by Assumpte Naniwe (Burundi), contrasts vividly with this hopeful picture.

Bringing Up Our Children to Be Bilingual and Bicultural: A Three-Part Presentation

ROBERTA THOMAS

My son Jesse, who is thirteen and deaf, asked me last week what I knew about deafness before he was born. "Nothing," I said. "You invented deafness!" Deaf children in hearing families invent deafness for their families.

In this paper I will consider the question of bringing up deaf children bilingually and biculturally. If we truly celebrate deafness, I cannot imagine any families, hearing or deaf, bringing up deaf children any other way.

A good deal has been written about the grief that hearing parents experience when they discover that their child is deaf. Much of this "grief," however, is a result of the way that society views deaf people. The severe stigma of deafness, its low incidence, and early medical intervention in deaf children's education all collaborate to intensify this grief and make it very difficult for hearing parents to see that their deaf child is first and foremost a child who, in the words of I. King Jordan, the deaf president of Gallaudet University, "can do anything but hear."

We hear it said that parents must be given "options." I wonder how new parents of deaf children can make intelligent choices when they don't yet understand the complex issues related to language acquisition, when they are unaware that there is a moral component to choices that involve communication and the right of deaf children to be deaf. Reflecting the norms of most hearing cultures, parents reflect the views of the professionals with whom they interact, and many professionals "pathologize" deafness. The challenge in overcoming this prejudice is enormous for parents because we have no models who are not hearing.

I knew just what kind of mother I would be when I had children—a perfect one. I would make none of the mistakes my mother made. My children would grow up surrounded by love, the sunshine of approval. They would be joyously happy *and a credit to me!* But Jesse wasn't what I had in mind at the baby shower. I need to add that neither are my other children, who have had the audacity to grow up exactly as they saw fit despite my fond dreams at their cradles.

But at the same time, it surely seemed as though this small person shattered my dreams and was more than I could handle. I didn't know how to be the perfect mother for a deaf child. "God," I thought, "You made a big mistake. You dropped that child at the *wrong house.* You know that super mother on the next street? The one who makes cookies for all the bake sales? Now, that mother can 'do deaf.' *I can't do deaf.*"

We were fortunate. Our family was helped to recover from the initial shock of having a deaf child by many people, deaf and hearing, who made it possible for us to look at our child, not as an afflicted human being, but as a human being who was deaf. Deaf people helped us understand that once we began communicating with our child, he would indeed grow normally, acquire language, be educated, and become a member of the hearing community, the deaf community, and the world.

Having Jesse taught me that there are many ways of being human: a black way, a white way, a male way, a female way, a deaf way, a hearing way—and that all of these ways are human. Equality doesn't mean that all human beings must be the same. Equality means that we must respect differences between human beings. Deafness is a difference; it need not be a deficit. Once parents understand this, they can make the imaginative leap of understanding that will make it possible for them to let their child be deaf and at the same time make him or her a member of the family and the larger culture.

Jesse signed to me the other day, "I use a quiet language; you use a noisy one. That is the difference between deaf and hearing people." We began to learn that quiet language, and Jesse became a member of our family. I discovered that just because I did not know his voice, it did not mean that I didn't know him. We hearing people see our voices as an expression of our being, and we have a hard time letting go of that deep feeling.

When Jesse was two and three, he chatted away in sign language at a great rate. He was adorable. Like any verbal hearing child, he said (signed) absolutely everything that came into his head. He never shut up. When my friends, his grandparents, uncles, and aunts came to visit, they mostly didn't understand him, and a lot of life is lost in translation. In fact, they looked at Jesse as afflicted. Yes, everyone thought he was cute, but his deafness was viewed as a tragedy.

I used to dread visitors: They left me depressed and uncertain. No one meant any harm, but it was upsetting that the burning questions were always about speech and lipreading. Over and over, I would explain that a child cannot acquire a spoken language with ears that can't hear. Over and over, I would explain that to Jesse, English on the mouth looked little different from Chinese; that no two-year-old knows a lot of English; that no one can lipread a language he/she doesn't know; that only 30 percent of English is visible on the mouth anyway. Today, ten years later, I am still explaining.

We lived near Philadelphia. Two deaf women—Lillian Hoshauer and April Nelson —ran the Deaf Hearing Communication Center (DHCC), and we went there to learn how to sign. We learned a lot more than sign, however. DHCC nurtured us and changed us and helped us recognize that we could successfully bring up our child bilingually and biculturally, once we were able to allow Jesse to be deaf and to understand deafness as another culture and not an affliction.

Jesse loved Tuesday nights at DHCC, and so did I. There was always a social hour before class. He would race into the room and start chattering at someone. He would sign, "My mother told me that if you take medicine out of the cabinet and eat it, then you will DIE!" He would look grim. And a lovely deaf grandmother would pick him up and kiss him and hug him and tell him in sign that he was adorable. And she would take him over to a group of her friends and say, "Jesse, tell them about the medicine." And while she looked on, with pride and pleasure, Jesse would tell his story again, and they would hug him and smile and laugh and talk with him. I was convinced that Jesse was the most wonderful child in America, and so was he.

DHCC gave Jesse critical and essential pride in himself. It was the family that hearing parents with deaf children don't have—that extended family of relatives and friends to admire and adore your child, to reassure you and make you both feel confident and capable and proud.

At DHCC deafness was *not* a tragedy or an affliction; it was normal. Jesse was an ordinary darling little boy, and I was an ordinary doting mother. I learned to respect deaf culture and the deaf community as a rich and essential part of my son's life. Through DHCC, I learned to see deafness simply as another way of being human. I don't think that hearing parents can ever develop that perspective without the help of deaf people.

The stigma of deafness in our culture is overwhelming. The idea that *deaf* and *normal* can be compatible is an alien one because the model for normal is *hearing*. Parents rush to oral programs that promise speech, that promise to make their children as close to "hearing" as possible. Sign language, which makes deafness so boldly visible, is rejected. Parents don't understand the difference between speech and language, or that one can *know* English or French or Danish without *speaking* it. We somehow believe that our native language magically exists inside our deaf children, waiting to be miraculously unleashed by a speech therapist.

Historically, education of deaf children has focused on the medical model of deafness as a sickness or "pathology" and hearing as normal. The pathologizing of deafness inevitably has led to an education devoted to *annihilating* rather than *accommodating* the difference of deafness. From the point of view of the hearing world, this is called "overcoming" deafness.

Our language reflects these attitudes. Our children are *communication disordered.* They are *diagnosed* at *speech* and *hearing* centers—precisely what our children can't do well or at all. Other children have teachers; ours have *therapists* or *pathologists.* Until I had a deaf child, I thought pathologists cut up cadavers!

Alice Walker, a black American writer, has written that black children in America grow up believing that their blackness is something wrong with them. Deaf children often grow up with the same terrible message. She tells about her five-year-old daughter's kindergarten teacher in a small southern town—a great, warm, grandmotherly black woman. Walker said she was glad that her black daughter could look into her black teacher's eyes and see her history and glimpse her destiny. Deaf children are most often denied this reassurance.

If a child is an "afflicted" creature who needs to be "cured," then a hearing parent can't really feel comfortable as a parent. In a world where deafness is a deficit and not a difference, hearing parents lose their power. But if deafness is a difference, then we can bring up and educate children who use, primarily, a "quiet" language instead of a "noisy" one. We can be ordinary parents if our children are ordinary children. We can replace the hearing model for success with a deaf model for success. We can bring up our children bilingually and biculturally.

If a child is first and foremost a child, then we should look to educating a whole child and stop confusing speech clinics with educational programs. We can insist that our children are provided exactly the same education as that available to their hearing peers, but in sign. We can make sure that they have the reassurance of deaf adults and deaf culture in their lives, to give them pride, a sense of destiny, and the knowledge that their deafness is not something wrong with them.

One hears a lot about parents being partners with the educational system. Anyone who has been in any relationship for more than five minutes knows that there can be no partnership without equality. Parents can have an equal role in education when they are no longer disempowered. Parents are empowered when they allow and encourage their deaf children to be nurtured by two cultures—deaf and hearing.

It is a great relief when we parents realize that our deaf children are merely differ-ent, not deficient. This is not to say that it isn't an issue for hearing parents to recognize that their deaf children belong to a minority group to which they themselves don't be-long. But that is not a tragedy. All of our children leave the nest and become who they are. If we allow our deaf children to be deaf and nurture them as deaf human beings, not as imperfect hearing ones, then they can take a proper role in the deaf and hearing worlds, and we can take our proper role as their proud parents.

Those who find bilingualism and biculturalism unacceptable say that the world is hearing and therefore our children must be ready for the world. That is the battle cry of oralism. The fact is, one can function fine as a deaf person in a hearing world, or a black person in a white world; no one should have to "pass" to be acceptable. It is a fallacy that one can only function in the hearing world if one is like hearing people.

By the same token, to encourage a separatist view of deaf culture is equally dimin-ishing to our children. It is extremism to suggest to deaf individuals that they must choose between the deaf world and the hearing world. I urge Jesse to choose both the deaf and hearing worlds because I wish to fill his spirit and not fill him with the poison of self-deprecation that is oralism or the despair at the hearing world that is separatism.

We should struggle against any forces in the hearing or deaf world that suggest to Jesse or any other deaf person that deaf culture and language are inferior, inadequate, and not a proper nourishment for his soul. We should also point to all the literature that demonstrates the educational benefit of American Sign Language and deaf culture.

We should struggle equally against any forces in the deaf or hearing world that suggest to any deaf person that loving to read, for example, or having hearing parents, or participating in hearing culture is less than truly "deaf." Nor can we ignore the fact that the hearing world is the world that pays salaries, and that empowerment of deaf people in that world is critical for their well being. Surely we can avoid exchanging one intolerance for another.

My son Jesse will be part of hearing American culture because he is American and because he is literate. His deaf identity, pride, self-respect, and a key part of his edu-cation as a human being will come in large measure from deaf culture. Jesse's minority status does not make him either less human or less normal, nor does it restrict his participation in either the deaf world or the hearing world.

Jesse wrote a speech about his goals in life:

> It is hard for me to decide goals in life because I am deaf. Let me elaborate a little. You see, it's an imperfect world. Most, if not all people in minority groups (deaf, black, disabled, etc.) will agree, perhaps especially to that. What I am saying is that there is a phenomenon that exists in the world. This phenomenon I'm talking about starts with a big, horrid "D"—discrimination. There are still a lot of people whose faces show sympathy at the word "deaf" and gasp at the thought of the world devoid of hearing. Those people think, "My God, deaf people *can't hear*, there must be something terrible astray with them!" So they don't respect deaf people and think they are inferior. A lot of deaf people and kids (especially if they don't know other deaf adults) feel that it is bad to be deaf. I feel that I am proud to be me: *deaf*.
>
> I don't think there should be such a thing as "overcoming" deafness be-cause I think deaf people should try to succeed as deaf people. When the phrase "overcoming deafness" is used, I feel that must mean becoming more hearing, which is absolutely ridiculous. Don't you think a person should be what he is? I am deaf; I will succeed as a deaf person.

We parents have a long, hard struggle in learning about deafness and bringing up our deaf children. We have a lot of overcoming to do ourselves. The struggle goes on.

There also are benefits to raising a deaf child. I have learned about a culture and language that I knew nothing about before. I have made friends among deaf and hearing people whom I otherwise would never have known. Jesse also has given me another very special gift. From Jesse, I found that, in fact, I *could* bring up a deaf child and that this child, like my other children, could be a profound source of pride and joy to me.

Jesse told me that he was a wonderful role model for me; he doesn't realize how incredibly right he is. Jesse has been my greatest teacher about deafness, the world, and myself.

Having a deaf child changes one's life. When we are willing to allow that child to be deaf, the changes are no longer painful and dreadful: They become, instead, the opportunity for our imaginations and our spirits to grow. For that, I am indebted to my deaf son, Jesse, and all the deaf children and adults with whom he shares his destiny as a bicultural, bilingual, deaf human being.

MICHAEL TILLANDER

*H*ow do parents in Finland bring up deaf children to be bilingual and bicultural? Regardless of where one lives, three important issues must be addressed: Parents of deaf children must accept their child's deafness, learn sign language, and provide the deaf child access to both cultures. Is this easier or more difficult in a country that is constitutionally bilingual? It is certainly easier for parents who are themselves bilingual, but the educational system has not really taken advantage of this situation.

Acceptance of Deafness

All over the world, parents are being told they must accept their child's deafness. This is easy to say, but hard to implement. Moreover, the phrase has many different meanings. Parents who really accept deafness, learn sign language, and acquaint themselves with Deaf culture usually are a disappointment to the medical profession. While some doctors understand the importance of sign language, others feel their first duty is to use the residual hearing of their "patients." This ideological controversy affects parents in different ways. Some parents become apathetic, which is unfortunate, while others rebel against the establishment. Some people benefit from being rebels: Their efforts to get things done in spite of the system provide fuel for further efforts. For others however, the result may be an unproductive bitterness.

While it is very difficult to guide the acceptance process and thus ensure a positive result, we parents of deaf children have one approach that usually helps: We work together on our problems. The potential for cooperation between parents is seldom used fully. Parents are segregated in the name of medical confidentiality, or perhaps because the medical profession fears that if parents unite, they might undermine its authority.

Another hindrance to the process of acceptance is the everlasting need to explain deafness and the special needs of the deaf child. In a sparsely populated country such as Finland, deafness is a rare occurrence. Officials in the medical, social, and educational services seldom have much knowledge of deafness. Parents must provide this information, a duty that is very stressful to many of us. Again, the local or national association of parents can help enormously.

Learning Sign Language

Learning sign language is also something easier said than done. Sign will be the deaf child's first language, but how can parents provide a normal signing environment for the child when they don't know sign themselves and there is no time to learn it? What is the use of early diagnosis if months or years are wasted before parents and siblings can even start learning sign? In Finland parents of deaf children are entitled to 100 hours of instruction at home, and also to courses in sign language. This looks fine on paper, but parents first must convince themselves that they need it, convince a hearing professional that society should pay for it, and then find a competent teacher near their home.

Even when parents manage to get instruction in sign, there remains the old controversy: Should parents speak when signing or not? Determining the extent of hearing loss in small children is a difficult task. The audiogram will not give a reliable indication of a child's ability to understand language. Hearing professionals therefore want to have it both ways and advise parents to speak when signing. They feel it is important not to preclude the use of speech and residual hearing by over-reliance on sign. Unfortunately, nobody speaks out for sign language or the rights of Deaf people to their own language. As a result many parents feel they ought to use both modes—speaking and signing at the same time—rather than the native sign language.

Here we run into another problem. There is no formalized "Signed Finnish," as there are signed systems of English. If one wants to sign and speak simultaneously, the result will be a Pidgin Sign Finnish. A few hearing people may succeed in doing this, but the majority will succeed only in breaking most grammatical rules of both languages. The profession of teaching sign is still in its infancy. All available resources must be used in developing educational materials, dictionaries, and teaching methods, and in training deaf and hearing sign language teachers. We cannot afford to develop a formalized Signed Finnish.

In spite of all these difficulties, a lot of progress has been made since the early 1970s, when parents first were allowed to attend courses in signing. This progress would not have been possible without close cooperation between parents and Deaf people on all levels—personal, local, and national.

Providing Access to Two Cultures

This requirement is probably less difficult to fulfill than the others. Culture and language are inseparable in many respects. It is a hearing parent's duty to provide the deaf child access to the "mainstream" culture. Some planning is required; most people do not realize how much culture is aurally oriented until they have a deaf child. Interpreters may be available for some activities, but parents must take care of transportation themselves, as they would for a hearing child.

Television will probably be an important medium for the deaf child. In Finland most films not in Finnish have captions in Finnish and Swedish. News, sports, domestic films, and children's programs are usually not captioned. A special decoding device for optional captioning is available; the service covers one Finnish film a week, important sports events, and news pages. There are also some signed programs for children, religious services, and a weekly news broadcast, but parents of deaf children still have to do a lot of interpreting of TV programs.

To provide access to Deaf culture, parents need help from Deaf people. A lack of contact with Deaf people may make deaf children believe either that they will become hearing when they grow up, or that they will cease to exist. Parents who have personal friends who are Deaf are lucky, especially if the friends also have deaf children. Parents also can visit the local Deaf club; arrangements can be made by sign teachers or the local society of parents of deaf children. Deaf children should become members of Deaf clubs as early as possible; parents sometimes can join also. As members, parents get a lot of information, and children can attend local and national events.

The Finnish Association of the Deaf provides an important information service through its monthly, signed news bulletin on videocassette. This is available free of charge to households with deaf members. The bulletin contains material for different age brackets. Usually a folk tale or fairy story is included. Finnish parents use such stories in bringing up their hearing children; it is a common way to transfer moral values. Parents of deaf children may not realize that their children, too, need to share this kind of cultural heritage. Parents sometimes may feel (perhaps rightly) that their signing skill is insufficient to tell stories. Native signing ability is necessary to render a fairy tale intelligible to young deaf children.

Bilingualism in Education

Education is the most important service society provides for children, and it is especially important for deaf children. Education of deaf people in Finland began in the 1840s and went through the usual dark age of oralism. Present legislation, passed in 1983, mentions sign language as an auxiliary language and as a possible method for educating deaf people. According to the present nationwide curriculum, adopted in 1987, bilingualism is one goal of deaf education. The Finnish Association of the Deaf and the parents' association are lobbying for a higher legal status for sign language.

These efforts, however, probably will not reap the desired results until orally trained teachers retire, the education program for teachers of deaf people is revised, and Deaf teachers of deaf people start working in our schools. The legislation that required teachers to have "normal" hearing and sight has been repealed, and the first class of Deaf teachers should start studying this fall. A program for educating Deaf assistant teachers is being planned, and one for training Deaf classroom assistants will start this fall.

A Special Case of Bilingualism

Finland is constitutionally a bilingual country. Most Finns speak Finnish, and the Swedish-speaking minority must learn Finnish as a second language. This situation is analogous to that of Deaf people: They too must learn Finnish from scratch, as a foreign language. One might suppose that teachers of Deaf people could use the existing expertise to teach Finnish as a second language. Sadly, this is not the case. Teachers of Deaf people receive no instruction in teaching Finnish as a second language and consequently reject the foreign-language approach entirely.

On the personal level, there are some advantages to living in a bilingual country. Parents who are bilingual themselves accept the bilingualism of Deaf people more easily. A bilingual background is also a benefit when parents must help their deaf child acquire the spoken language of the hearing majority.

Research into spoken-language bilingualism shows that true bilingualism is not achieved by mixing two languages indiscriminately. This approach often results in "semilingualism" and even illiteracy. We must work for a general recognition of sign as a true, distinct language—the primary language of Deaf people—and for the acceptance and implementation of an important corollary: that the spoken national language must be taught as a second language, using methods appropriate to foreign language teaching.

RITVA BERGMANN

I was born in Finland. My parents are deaf, and Finnish Sign Language is my native language. I moved to Denmark eighteen years ago and married a Dane. My husband and I are deaf, and we use Danish Sign Language in our everyday life. We have two deaf children, twelve and ten years of age. Since the birth of our children, our goal in bringing them up has been that they become bilingual and bicultural. Our children are deaf and will obviously be members of the deaf community, but at the same time they must learn to associate with hearing people in order to be integrated in the hearing community—the Danish culture. Both children are in a school for deaf children.

Recently, when our son was playing with his computer, he wrote "The Law of the Deaf." I was surprised and thought it was very interesting, so I asked him for a copy of "The Law."

The Law of the Deaf

1. All teachers at schools for deaf must use sign language before employment.
2. Text-telephone deluxe for all deaf people and without *any discussion.*
3. Selective subjects except for math, English (as a foreign language), sign language, and the class-session.
4. Sign language as a subject in all schools.
5. All hearing people must use sign language—if not—they are to be sentenced to death.

6. Computers for all deaf students in the classrooms.
7. Technical aids free of charge to every deaf—and that is flat!
8. The Danish Parliament must consist of 50 percent deaf members.
9. The Danish Broadcasting should broadcast twenty-five minutes news in sign language and five minutes in Danish! *Every day!*
10. Deaf-film Video should transmit twenty-five minutes news in the Danish Broadcasting.
11. Deaf people should be employed as consultants in the Danish Broadcasting.
12. Zero percent tax for deaf people.
13. No gaping from hearing people!
14. No homework for deaf children!
15. No speech training for deaf children!
16. Interpreters free of charge for all deaf people.
17. Jobs for all deaf people—and that's flat!
18. Education free of charge for all deaf people.
19. Grammatical exercises forbidden.
20. Ninety-nine percent tax for all hearing people.
21. Deaf people can get everything they want.
22. This law must be obeyed and must be valid for every citizen.

Approved by the Deaf Autonomy the 7th of February, 1989
a twelve-year-old boy

The question is, have we succeeded in our goal of raising bicultural children? Of course, he wrote in Danish. I have translated it into English, but I can tell you that his Danish is very good. His reading and writing skills in Danish are equal to those of hearing children of the same age, and he is fluent in Danish Sign Language too. Therefore, there is no doubt that our son is bilingual.

But is he bicultural?

He lives in two cultures: deaf culture and hearing culture. To me, it is important to have a good attitude toward both cultures. You must accept and respect two cultures if you want to be considered a bicultural person. Our boy has deaf awareness. He is proud of his sign language. He is happy to be a member of the deaf community and does not consider himself a handicapped person.

When I was a little girl, I always felt it was bad to be deaf. My deaf parents were sorry about my deafness. I always tried to behave like a hearing person and was happy when hearing people did not realize that I was deaf. In many situations, I felt I was oppressed. During my study year at Gallaudet University, I revolted. Today deaf pride and deaf awareness matter a great deal to me. I do not want to see my children suffering from the same feelings about deafness I once had.

So, on the one hand, it is really nice to see that our son considers himself a normal boy who just happens to be deaf and to have sign language as his native language. He does not feel oppressed. He is proud of himself. That is wonderful! But on the other hand, I am worried about his attitude toward hearing people. I do not want reverse discrimination—hearing people oppressed by deaf people. I want equality for both deaf and hearing people. We must respect each other.

Why did our son write "The Law of the Deaf"? Was it by chance? Was it only for fun? Is it really what he feels about being deaf in a hearing-majority culture? Or was it because he is at the age of puberty? I don't know. I have not yet analyzed it, but I think that "The Law of the Deaf" is food for thought.

When we moved to Copenhagen three years ago, our deaf daughter tried to make new friends in the neighborhood. She was seven years old at the time, and there were several hearing children living on our street. To communicate with them, our daughter tried to use total communication: She talked, signed, gestured, and drew.

One day she invited a new hearing girlfriend to our house. Our daughter showed her girlfriend around. She pointed to her bedroom and said without signing, "bedroom." I knew that she could not pronounce the word correctly, but her girlfriend nodded. She understood what our daughter meant. Our daughter continued showing the other rooms and talked and talked. When she had finished, she turned to me and said, "Gosh, it's hard to talk!"

Later we noticed that her girlfriend had learned many signs. It was interesting to see how the two girls communicated with each other. The hearing girl was, of course, fascinated by sign language, but after a short time their friendship stopped.

Now our daughter thinks that hearing people are boring. She prefers to associate with deaf people. She is very outgoing and loves to be with people—but only with deaf people. Sometimes she plays with hearing children, but those children have deaf parents or siblings.

My husband and I have both hearing and deaf friends, but I admit that most of our hearing friends can sign. I know that many deaf people want hearing friends, but such friendships require that both hearing and deaf can communicate with each other smoothly and freely or have a common language—sign language.

Sign Language Acquisition Among Deaf Children with Deaf Parents

JEAN-FRANÇOIS MERCURIO

*I*n this paper, I wish to discuss the psycholinguistic development of deaf children with deaf parents, how they build their language—sign language, of course—from birth to age three. I will attempt to illustrate my points with photographs taken from a videotape of my deaf daughter Sophie learning sign language at home. These images may help make my point more clearly than if I simply try to explain things from a theoretical point of view. The first part of the videotape was made when Sophie was fourteen months old, communicating with her mother. At that time, she was just starting to walk and she was also just starting to communicate with sign language.

The beginning of the videotape shows Sophie and her mother looking at pictures of herself on the wall. At one point, after she recognizes that the pictures are of herself, she communicates this recognition by pointing to herself (Figure 1). This is a simple but important part of a deaf child's gradual development of sign language.

The picture on the left of Figure 2 shows my daughter formulating a sign that would not likely be understood out of the context of our immediate family. You see, the adults in our family were at that time producing a made-up family sign for "dog" that is exactly the reverse of Sophie's sign. As is shown in the picture on the right, when I produce the sign, the back of my hand touches my chin and my fingers open and close as if in imitation of a dog barking. When Sophie makes the sign in the videotape, however, she imitates what she sees when looking at her parents' hand—not as we actually do it, but *as she sees it*—with the back of her hand facing away and the fingers opening and closing toward her face. The picture in the bottom center, by the way, shows the conventional sign for DOG used in adult discourse by users of French Sign Language.

When I first noticed how Sophie was producing the family sign DOG, I worried about what appeared to me to be a serious disorientation of Sophie's fingers when signing. I thought, "This is terrible; she cannot communicate correctly in sign language." I talked to hearing friends and asked them if their hearing children at fourteen months of age spoke perfect French. They told me, "No. Children at fourteen months of age are just starting to talk. They are beginning to build their language. Hearing children at

---

Illustrations are from *La Langue des Signes; Tome 2; Dictionnaire Bilingue Elementaire* (p. 152) by B. Moody, A. Vourc'h, and M. Girod, 1986. Paris: Ellipses. Copyright 1986 by the International Visual Theatre. Reprinted by permission.

FIGURE 1: Sophie identifying herself as subject of picture.

*Sophie sees dog, then
produces family sign with
reversed palm orientation.*

*Jean Mercurio demonstrating
correct Mercurio family sign
for DOG.*

*DOG in French Sign
Language (LSF)*

FIGURE 2: Home signs and LSF sign for DOG.

Sophie signs DOG.   *Sophie shows dog's location (outside).*

FIGURE 3: Examples of successful communication.

this stage articulate words incorrectly before they learn the correct way. The bad sign language of a deaf child is the same as the bad spoken language of a fourteen-month-old hearing child. Be patient! Your child will learn to do the signs correctly after a while."

The pictures in Figure 3 suggest how successful communication through signs—even when the signs are clumsily produced—can and should be positively reinforced by parents. You have already seen Sophie signing DOG. The situation was that Sophie's mother had carried her to the kitchen window. After signing DOG, Sophie pointed through the window. Her mother—having seen Sophie say that the dog was outside—went to get the dog and bring it into the house. So Sophie was able to say something in sign language and thereby elicit an appropriate response. There was an immediate action after she produced a sign.

Reinforcement through appropriate response by an adult is very important for the successful building of sign language in a deaf child. Language is best built by connecting it to the fulfillment of the needs and requests of the child. This is fundamental. I am not going to discuss all the controversies regarding the morality or immorality of various educational approaches. I am only showing how sign language is built with a deaf child and how it is best done through actions reinforced by appropriate reactions.

The left image in Figure 4 shows Sophie reproducing wrongly the sign CAT. She puts her index finger close to her nose, showing that she is aware of the location of the beginning of the sign, but she does not produce the rest of the sign as it is done in French Sign Language. Nevertheless, this is typical of how deaf infants begin to learn sign language. They notice correctly some aspect of the sign and produce that aspect, but not the entire sign as they will later on. The correct way to sign CAT in French Sign Language is shown on the right side of Figure 4.

One day, Sophie's mother asked Sophie, "Where is the cat book?" Although Sophie did not produce the sign accurately, she clearly understood the sign as her mother produced it, because she immediately went to look for the book in which a cat appears as a character. She received a message and acted appropriately in response. The sense of mastery that accompanied this newfound ability could be seen in Sophie's happy expression as she carried the book to her mother. One way of looking at this event is that mastery of language is helping to build Sophie's personality and *vice versa*.

Another example of Sophie's attempts at making signs can be seen in Figure 5. After Sophie watched her mother sign BOAT, she responded with the same sign not made as well. Elsewhere on the videotape, Sophie is shown beginning to make her first sentence, which was, "The dog is sitting." In several other instances, she appears to

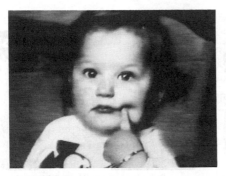

Sophie's sign for CAT (left), shows an awareness of the location of the beginning of the sign.

CAT in French Sign Language (LSF)

FIGURE 4: Sophie's sign and LSF sign for CAT.

FIGURE 5: Sophie signs BOAT in her own way.

be using two or more signs to begin to build sentences. She still does not make them well, but she clearly demonstrates in these efforts that she is understanding much of the meaning being communicated by her mother's signing.

When a child—deaf or hearing—begins to walk, he or she starts clumsily, walking correctly only after much trial and error. Similarly, no child knows from the outset how to dress himself or herself correctly. Very young children button their clothes slowly and laboriously. After a while, however, they start to get the hang of it. We could add to these skills others, such as those involved in personal hygiene and manners while eating. The process of learning those skills, too, begins with a clumsy stage that leads in time to mastery. Language development—spoken or signed—follows a similar evolution.

A family's communication during mealtimes sometimes includes examples of trial-and-error language use that can be rewarding to study. I have found many interesting exchanges, for instance, in the videotaped interactions between my fourteen-month-old daughter Sophie and her mother on such occasions. In one sequence, Sophie seems to be waiting impatiently for her food. She signs, "I am hungry," with facial expressions and body language that suggest, "This is taking too long!" She also shows with her finger that she wants something to drink, but she does it with her index finger instead of with her thumb, which would be the correct way in LSF. In what follows, some significant interactions occur that I have attempted to analyze.

The mother gives Sophie a bottle of milk she has heated, but Sophie is clearly not pleased. She tearfully attempts to sign, "It is too hot," but her mother, not understanding, signs, "Don't cry. Stop crying!" Sophie attempts to explain, "It is *hot!*" Her signing is clumsy, however, and her mother still does not seem to understand. Mother asks Sophie to calm down and stop crying. The girl responds, again, "It is hot!" Now the mother appears to understand what Sophie is saying, but when she touches the bottle she disagrees. She signs, "No, you are crazy."

Intrigued by this new sign, "CRAZY," Sophie repeats it, but instead of doing it in the correct LSF position, around the temple, she does it on the cheek. She repeatedly signs, "You are crazy," in this incorrect way. Her mother, understanding that Sophie is learning the sign, signs "CRAZY" again to Sophie, very clearly putting her finger in the right place on her head so Sophie can see. Sophie then repeats the sign more correctly and—having gotten engrossed in this learning process—becomes calm, forgetting her complaint about the milk.

After studying this type of learning situation in deaf families, I was fascinated when I discovered that the same sort of learning process occurs among hearing children with hearing parents. Vocabulary-building appears to happen in the same way, whether the vocabulary consists of signs or spoken words. For both spoken and signed language acquisition, of course, much more is involved than just vocabulary: Emotion, facial expression, rhythm, and other prosodic features are also critical aspects. The abundance of such features in sign language, in fact, demonstrates the richness of the language.

Unfortunately, most deaf children are denied the many benefits of this crucial early stage of sign language development. We know that deaf children who do not have this possibility of communication at an early age often experience psychological disorders later on that make the problem of being deaf much more serious than it needs to be. These psychological disorders are almost always owing to the child's inability to communicate pain, suffering, or his or her wishes through signs. In fact, early access to sign language would prevent almost all of the difficulties confronting the child, allowing him or her to develop in a completely normal way.

Whenever a deaf child in a signing environment asks for something, as in the videotape I've been discussing in which Sophie asks to see the dog more closely, or asks for food, etc., the mother or father can always respond to such requests. These responses enable children not only to develop themselves personally, but also to build their language while fulfilling their needs. Children who do not have access to this early communication frequently face difficulties later on—often only one or two years later—because all the normal, slow psycholinguistic evolution we've been describing is blocked from the outset.

Anyone reading this paper can play an important role by bringing it or its ideas to the attention of a hearing parent with a deaf child. These parents need to understand that if they and their deaf child learn sign language—beginning very early—many difficulties and psychological disorders can be avoided. This is a fundamental point of my paper.

As for my daughter Sophie, by the time she was videotaped at two years of age, many changes were evident in her signing. Looking at the videotape, I can see that her signs are done well on a sign-by-sign basis and she clearly knows how to make sentences. Her sentences at age two are much more elaborate and better structured than those she was producing at the age of fourteen months. She knows how to indicate, for example, the space where a chair is around a table. In fact, the sophistication of her sentence-building suggests that—from a psycholinguistic perspective—a huge evolution occurred between the ages of fourteen and twenty-four months.

In my family, my wife is deaf, I am deaf, and my daughter is deaf. We all communicate with sign language. At home, Sophie is in a complete sign language environment. At one point, in the videotape made when she was two, I tell her that I am going with her to look for one of her friends to bring to our home to play with her. Sophie understands completely—with no problem whatsoever. At other points in the videotape, I can be seen urging Sophie to eat with correct manners or to go to bed at a certain time. She obviously understands me, because in both cases she endeavors with clearly articulated signs to negotiate compromises concerning my demands. When I remain firm, however, she finally accepts. My point is that clear communication is so taken for granted in these sequences that it hardly seems to be the issue. In my view, that is as it should be.

In case you are wondering, Sophie is presently attending kindergarten at a "bilingual" school in Poitiers. Since we chose to use sign language in our family, so that my little girl could learn to use sign language correctly, I did not want her to begin her education in a completely oral school, which is still the type of schooling most deaf children receive in France. Within the setting of a bilingual school, I was confident that her sign language would not only be used to great educational advantage, but would also steadily improve through contact with deaf teachers and other signing deaf children.

Although much more could obviously be said concerning the important subject of deaf children's development from birth to age two, my main point is simply that if these children are helped to develop sign language as their first language, and if fluency and clarity in sign language are well established early in deaf children's lives, and if the educational setting the children eventually go to takes full advantage of this facility with sign language, then we can expect the children to develop in a completely normal, healthy way.

A strong grasp of sign language is what enables deaf people to learn about their world and pursue their goals with confidence. It is like the bar that standing passengers on a bus must cling to lest they fall.

The Early Intervention Program for Deaf Children: A Bilingual Experience

MYRIAM A. DE LUJÁN

The Center for Infant Development (CDI) in Mérida, Venezuela is a unit of the Ministry of Education that serves high risk children from birth to three years of age. We operate under the Integral Assistance for the Deaf Child Program and have been working to implement a better model for educating young children with hearing loss. In the specific area of deafness, we attempt to detect the problem as early as possible. Our program is divided into five areas: detection, education, family, community, and research.

Detection

CDI is located near the hospital of the Universidad de Los Andes (University of the Andes—ULA) and therefore has easy access to the services of that hospital. We have close ties with the hospital's Neonatology Service, and we lecture and conduct seminars for hospital personnel on detection of prelingual deafness. We also provide seminars at the Graduate School of Pediatrics as part of their Social Pediatrics classes.

Because the pediatricians have such a high level of awareness and understanding of the importance of auditory function to the child's development, we receive immediate language therapy referrals from them when there is any suspicion of auditory immaturity or deficit. The mothers are then instructed in how to do an observation and follow-up plan of auditory function. This plan includes keeping precise information about situations in which auditory stimulus is presented: the baby's state (quietly awake, restless, engaged in play, sleeping, etc.), the response the baby makes to the stimulus (blinking, changing or stopping activity, changing breathing rhythm, finding or looking for the sound source), and the speed of the response. Once responses to these questions have been completed, we meet with the parents to analyze the results. After a re-evaluation at the institution, if necessary, the child may be referred to another institution for audiological evaluation and possible hearing aid prescription. It is very important for the early detection team to verify the results of audiological evaluations by using corresponding results obtained at the clinic.

Because accompanying disorders may be noted in the first year of a deaf child's life, especially if the deafness is a consequence of rubella during the mother's first trimester of pregnancy, our pediatricians monitor the deaf child's physical, affective, and cognitive development.

Once an auditory disorder is verified, the child is enrolled in our program to start the educational process.

Education

The Venezuelan Ministry of Education has stated that deaf children should have effective access to their own language as early as possible. To achieve this objective we provide the child—and, in the best of cases, the nursing infant—with an environment filled with accessible language. The primary and unchangeable objective of the CDI program is the creation of a linguistic frame to establish the language needed for socialization and learning. We do not consider language as an end in itself, but rather as a means to reach the highest levels of abstraction and conceptualization. This is an opportunity that, up to now, we have denied the deaf child. As I will describe, we have employed strategies of great social relevance to carry out our objective.

Deaf youth have been a central element in the program, and they are incorporated into our interdisciplinary team in the same way as any new team member. They receive orientation in the areas of child development and psychology, and are rotated through the different work areas in the institution, performing administrative duties and participating in clinical and study meetings with the rest of the personnel.

Integrating deaf youth into the professional team has not been an easy task. Although we have a mature team that has been together for several years, the inclusion of new members who are also speakers of another language (as are deaf youth) has imposed certain necessary changes: providing workshops on sign language for personnel, providing interpreters at clinical and study meetings, spending time with new members to collaborate on their academic pursuits, and presenting information in a form accessible to team members with limited academic experience.

We are deeply proud of what we have achieved with this approach. We have had the good fortune to have on the team two young people with a strong desire to succeed, an admirable capacity for work, and an understanding that they are collaborating in a sociological process that will have positive effects on the development and evolution of their deaf community. They see themselves as pioneers in a "revolution of hope."

We have employed these young deaf people as facilitators for hearing parents of deaf children. Some people worry about including a third party when the relationship of the parents with their baby is just beginning, but we do not see the deaf youths as "interpreters" between the parents and the baby. We defend at all costs the preservation of authenticity in the mother-child relationship, and we believe that no one can achieve a more effective level of communication with a baby than his or her mother, even if the mother speaks a language different from the one that will become the baby's natural language. We are gratified by the results of studies we have conducted on the effect of how babies receive the first meaningful contacts from the mother. We found that it is very important for mothers to give their children enough signs and gestures at the pre-linguistic stage, and we facilitate that process by providing opportunities for mothers to learn certain fixed forms of Venezuelan Sign Language (LSV) from their deaf "monitors."

Our greatest achievement has been to earn a level of credibility for a communicative approach that leads parents to more effective "talking" with their babies at an early age. What remains then is for the parents to learn the lexicon, syntax and pragmatic use of LSV. This comes later and reflects the individual level of dedication, linguistic ability and degree of consciousness of each parent.

We were touched by Carol Erting's article, "Sign Language and Communication Between Adults and Children" (1980). We fully share her view of deaf people as "masters of language, positive models, authorities in sign language" in the classroom. However, after reading the conclusions of her work, we were surprised to learn that Total Communication is still used in the education of deaf students in the United States. Dr. Erting's article was the basis of an important change in the role of the young deaf workers in our program. Hearing people now work as *assistants* in our work room because of our limited skill in the use of LSV.

When we speak of "frame" in linguistics, we find that comparing data about language is easier when there are greater numbers of language-users around our little apprentices. The children attend the program in groups, and the age of enrollment is whatever the child's age happens to be at the time the hearing loss is detected. The groups are also attended by hearing mothers, brothers, and sisters, as well as by hearing children who "speak" LSV. A psychologist, a language therapist, and an educational psychologist—all of whom know LSV—attend the groups on a rotating schedule. Frequently other young deaf people attend also.

The work room has become a meeting place where communication between adults and children using a common language—LSV—prevails. Until March 1989, the children attended the group twice a week in two-hour sessions, but after a visit last month from Dr. Robert E. Johnson of the Department of Linguistics at Gallaudet University, we developed a nursery model. Now the children attend all morning daily and are cared for by the two deaf youths, a mother, and some of the professionals previously mentioned. The change in schedule was based on Dr. Johnson's observation that, by attending only twice a week, the children did not have a real possibility of incorporating the linguistic frame. The last day of each week is dedicated to sharing with the parents in an LSV workshop, and to reviewing the vocabulary emphasized during the week.

Once a week the deaf youth visit the children's homes to facilitate interaction between the parents and a representative of the deaf community which, sooner or later, their children will enter to some degree. Social workers also visit the homes to evaluate the socioeconomic situation of every household and the lexical priorities of each family.

Regarding educational activities, we support a constructivist theory of child development. We believe that children should be active subjects—or builders—of their own learning, and the knowledge of interest to us is LSV. We encourage all opportunities for children to be exposed to the language, while respecting the developmental stage of the learner. For instance, at the sensory-motor stage we emphasize all the typical behaviors that occur in early interaction between mother and child, especially "simulated anger," periods of sustained interaction, expressions of "surprise laughing," eye contact, body games, repetitive imitation, and manual gestures from our own culture that can be translated into LSV.

At the pre-operative stage, we encourage the acquisition of pre-concepts and center vocabulary on areas of interest to the child—family, animals, food, toys, vehicles, etc.— not only in the workroom but also outside, with real objects. Field trips to the zoo, the park, the airport, the bus terminal, the market, etc., provide vivid experiences of great value to the cognitive and linguistic development of the child.

Family Assistance

The CDI works within the framework of a "School for Parents," which considers parents as cotherapists at all times. Parents who have a deaf child need early and accurate information in a form appropriate to the parent's level of cultural and emotional understanding. It is disrespectful to forget that parents are grieving the fact that they have given birth to a deaf child, and the psychological support needed during this time cannot be postponed. Providing reliable information about their situation is the only way to gain the cooperation of parents. With that cooperation we can help them help their children toward lives full of learning and social satisfaction. Therefore, the assistance team must contribute in this effort to help the parents, using language appropriate to the situation, and must especially involve deaf facilitators as role models of healthy, intelligent adults with proper social skills: people who are able "to love and to work."

Community Information

CDI maintains a permanent collection of media information including publications from the Ministry of Education and the ULA; press articles; television interviews; and videotapes on sign language, education, early assistance to the deaf, and "singing with signs" choirs. A recent workshop, "Production of TV Programs by the Deaf for the Deaf," was conducted under the direction of Professor Jane Norman of Gallaudet University. This was the first program prepared through an agreement between ULA Television and Andina Television of Mérida to be broadcast nationwide.

Research

Because of the population we serve, we at CDI have an important opportunity to do research and have conducted several research projects.

Detection

In the area of early detection, our pediatricians conducted studies on the biological background of the population of children served in our program. Those studies are published by the Division of Special Education, which updates them with newly enrolled children. In addition, because we have observed differences in motor coordination and certain balance reactions between deaf and hearing children, we are conducting a comparative study in the area of physical therapy.

Emotional Development

Three years ago we presented the findings of a study, based on a sample of twenty-five cases, entitled "Relationship of the Mother to the Child with an Auditory Loss."

Linguistics

CDI is the site for a study, financed by the Center of Scientific and Humanistic Development of the ULA, entitled "Linguistic Study of the Venezuelan Sign Language." We also have undertaken as a top priority a research project entitled "The Acquisition of LSV by Deaf Children Younger Than Three Years Old." The principal investigator of this project will present her findings in a thesis for her master's degree in Linguistics from ULA under Professor Lourdes Pietrosemoli.

Early language acquisition is a subject of great interest to us, and one to which we are especially dedicated. CDI conducted a descriptive study of the semantic aspects of LSV that uses psychogenetic theory to explain how the acquisition of first meanings occurs through the collection of undifferentiated expressions of signs and gestures. It describes the forms of LSV acquired during the pre-linguistic stage using some of the criteria established by Dr. Virginia Volterra (Volterra and Erting, 1994).

Regarding the linguistic stage of language development, we endorse the studies of such authorities as Tervort, Verbeck, Bellugi, Klima, Meadow, Feidman, Edmonson, Caseill, Massoni, Osella, Bouvet, Prinz, Supalla, McIntire, Boyes Braem, and Erting (whose influence has been the basis for our adoption of better teaching methods).

With regard to the acquisition of LSV syntax and lexicon, the results of our work with deaf children have paralleled the results of some of the research we have read. However, with our most recently enrolled group we have observed results better than those of recent studies.

We have also focused on presenting a detailed parallel between the spoken-language development of hearing children and the LSV development of deaf children ages birth to three years, dividing this comparison into semantic, pragmatic, phonological, and syntactic areas. This also serves as a didactic resource for training our personnel. In the area of phonology, we have a special interest in adopting the analytical model described by Johnson.

The Bilingual Experience

Until now we have discussed how to create favorable conditions to give deaf children access to a natural language, but the title of our presentation refers to "A Bilingual Experience." This reflects our interest in conceptualizing the oral language of Venezuela—Spanish—as a second language for deaf children. To do so we must refer to another research project, entitled "Acquisition of the Written Language without the Mediation of Oral Language." This research, financed by the Organization of American States and the Ministry of Education of Venezuela, is in progress at two schools—one in Caracas and the other in Mérida (Myriam de Velez and Ofella Tancredi de Corredor)—under my coordination and that of Professor Carlos Sanchez. The project is directed by Dr. Sanchez, who also wrote the Proposal of Integral Assistance for the Deaf Child.

Thanks to advances we have made from that research, we now theorize that text should be considered a means of access to the spoken language. Other authors who have arrived at the same conclusion are Johnson, Liddell, and Erting (1989) in "Unlocking the Curriculum."

Following the ideal of a spontaneous building of written language, we try with our young children to achieve only an approximation of the written language that hearing people speak. We have observed productions at the first levels of drawing and writing described by Ferreiro (1982), and we have seen a search for parallels between the written form of the language and the spoken form, as well as between the written form and the manual alphabet.

Speech training is not provided by the CDI. We know that, outside the CDI, the deaf child will be exposed to speech most of the time. At the Center there are people who speak to each other all the time, and the children can see that they use a different form of communication. Sometimes hearing people address the children through speech, and we have observed the deaf children attempting to code-switch in order to address hearing people. In the group we also have two hearing children of bilingual deaf parents. We are monitoring them from a linguistic viewpoint, hoping to obtain data that will help us understand second-language development.

For now our major effort and our absolute commitment are devoted to LSV—working to gain for it the status it deserves and to make it available to deaf children, who will make it their own.

References

Erting, C. 1980. "Sign Language and Communication Between Adults and Children." In *Sign Language and the Deaf Community*, ed. C. Baker-Shenk and R. Battison. Silver Spring, MD: National Association of the Deaf.

Ferreiro, E. 1982. *Literacy Before Schooling*. Exeter, NH: Heinemann Educational Books.

Johnson, R. E., S. K. Liddell, and C. J. Erting. 1989. "Unlocking the Curriculum: Principles for Achieving Access in Deaf Education." Gallaudet Research Institute Working/Occasional Paper Series, No. 89-3. Washington, DC: Gallaudet Research Institute.

Volterra, V., and C. J. Erting, eds. 1994. *From Gesture to Language in Hearing and Deaf Children*. Washington, DC: Gallaudet University Press.

The Deaf Child in Burundi Society

ASSUMPTA NANIWE

Located in the heart of Africa, Burundi is bordered on the north by Rwanda, on the south and east by Tanzania, and on the west by Zaire. Its surface area is about 10,745 square miles [27,834 square kilometers]. According to statistics provided by the Burundi Department of the Census (1986), the population of Burundi is approximately 4,782,407, with a density of about 445 inhabitants per square mile.

Burundi is a country of high plateaus broken up into narrow, extended hills, each bearing its own name. Family groups occupy these hills; there are no villages per se, just residents dispersed about the hills. This way of life constitutes a major inconvenience for deaf people, who live solitary lives within their families. They do not have many opportunities to meet each other, which does not encourage the birth and expansion of a deaf community within Burundi.

The society of Burundi considers deafness as a handicap reflecting the will of an all-powerful Supreme Being who gives, takes, and directs the life of each person. This fatalistic belief can cause resignation and inertia in parents seeking solutions appropriate for children with specific deafness-related problems. Following an active search for a therapeutic solution, usually made at the time the deafness is discovered, there often comes a period of total detachment from the deaf child. No education is considered for this child, who is not "like the others." Parents resign themselves to seeing the child as "the handicapped one," who will be materially supported by his family but who will not benefit from education appropriate to his disability.

Deaf education is not yet organized on a national level in Burundi. However, there are now two small schools, recently created by missionary organizations, that serve deaf children. Like any new organization, these schools are still determining their objectives. They are confronted by many problems, notably that of choosing an educational method appropriate for these deaf children to help them achieve adequate education and to facilitate their integration into their society.

The purpose of this paper is to present a selection of statements gathered in a survey designed to explore the status of deaf persons growing up in Burundi. One hundred and twenty people—sixty parents of deaf children and sixty parents without deaf children—were individually interviewed for approximately an hour each. These interviews, though carried out using a rather detailed and systematic interview format to permit coverage of diverse aspects of the subject's life, were flexible enough that each parent could make his or her own contribution about the proposed subjects with considerable autonomy. The value of this procedure—letting the parents speak their own minds—

is that it permits a record of what is most strongly felt and most immediately recalled, and provides a glimpse into what a deaf person's life is really like in Burundi society.

The most important hypothesis held at the beginning of this project was that deaf people grow up on the margin of society, even though, in this community-based society, there is no way to live a solitary life. Indeed, though the deaf child lives in the heart of his or her family, communication barriers prevent the deaf child from being considered a member of society and from participating in community activities. *Because of this fact, the deaf person is condemned to live a life of abandonment and isolation even in the midst of others.*

The testimony of the parents seems to confirm this hypothesis. The following statements illustrate the ways in which some parents described the situations experienced by their deaf children.

The father of a deaf sixteen-year-old boy said:

> Everywhere in this area, they call him "Nyamuragi," or "the deaf one." All deaf people are called that. You know, a deaf-mute receives no social recognition aside from his peers, his brothers, his sisters, and his parents. You see, I realize that even his cousins make fun of him when I'm out of sight. As for strangers . . . [at this point in the interview, the father was silent a moment] . . . tramps pursue him in the street, screaming at him. Some even throw stones at him. But those who do truly have no heart, no education. You know, an educated child would not do that. He would have pity for another who is deprived.

The mother of a thirty-three-year-old woman commented:

> When people see a deaf person walking in the street, they have the impression that he is a well person, someone like everybody else. But . . . [again a silence occurs] . . . he is a brainless person, because you have to feed him, nourish him, dress him. In fact, you have to do everything for him.

When the interviewer asked this mother if she meant that "a deaf person is unintelligent," the mother replied:

> Alas, yes. Do you think that I consider my daughter to be like other children, a child who can't be depended upon, who expects to get everything from others? [The silence returns again; this time there is a real block.] Now she's thirty years old. Other daughters of her age already have three, four, and even five children. And her, what is she? Always dragging next to me, she never married, she will never be able to. But you know, it's not that she wouldn't want it. What, have I not tried to keep her from running after men? [This affirmation is punctuated by embarrassed laughter.] Because you know, men only think of having a good time, and no one will think of marrying her, so you understand that "Nyamuragi" doesn't know what it means to have children by an unknown father, and I'm the one who must think of it in her place. [Later another member of this family commented that the mother of this deaf girl had already forced her to have three abortions against her daughter's will.]

When asked whether she had thought of explaining to her daughter these things about life, the mother replied:

How can you communicate with someone who can't speak? Tell me how I can explain all that to someone who doesn't seem to be living in this world? It's already hard with normal people, those with a tongue like ours, to whom one can say, "This isn't good, this is very bad, this is great," and who manage despite everything to do foolish things. And, with a person without hearing, without intelligence . . . [another silence] . . . . When she was still small, it wasn't so bad. She was, in fact, a very reserved child, never leaving the house. She did the little household tasks I showed her. In fact, she was a timid child. I think it was particularly after she reached six or seven years old, I don't remember, that she began to play with the others and they made fun of her. Overnight I never saw her look happy again. She didn't want to play again with the other children; she stayed with me. And since I realize that many children are wicked with deaf people, I prefer that she stays with me.

These statements mirror the marginalization of deaf children as they mature within Burundi society. They are not valued, they are the "guinea pigs" for the other children, and they cause many difficulties for their parents. This lack of esteem toward deaf people is apparent in the very name given to the deaf person. In the Burundi language, a deaf person is designated by the term "ikiragi" in the singular, and "ibiragi" in the plural. These are terms linked with notions of muteness and stupidity, and all deaf people carry the common name of "Nyamuragi." Despite the fact that deaf children are given names by their families as are their hearing brothers and sisters, these names are abandoned as soon as the deafness is discovered, and the deaf children are henceforth called "Nyamuragi," even by their parents.

The mother of a deaf ten-year-old girl said, "My daughter's name is 'Spes' but you know, from the moment we knew she was deaf, she's been called 'Nyamuragi' or 'the deaf one.' She doesn't use her own name any more." When asked why she wasn't called by her real name, the child's mother replied, "I don't know, that's how it's done, deaf people have a single name. In fact, that's what hurts the parents of a child suffering from this handicap, because they are very aware that others don't like the child and will make fun of him."

This lack of respect toward deaf people appears at various stages of the deaf person's life. As a child, he may be able to play with other children at first, but they later scorn him and behave in such a way that he will gradually have to avoid their company. The mother of an eight-year-old deaf child said:

I have to admit that she only plays with people she knows well. When she sees someone that she doesn't know she prefers to leave, then comes over beside me. She doesn't like people to notice she is like that and when she tries to speak and strange sounds come out, those who don't know her start to look startled, show curiosity or frankly ridicule her. Then "Nyamuragi" doesn't like that and she returns to the house, crying.

As an adult, it is difficult for deaf people to achieve the same status in Burundi society as hearing people, to take on the roles generally filled by those of their age and sex. For example, some deaf boys have been able, with the help of their families, to marry and establish a home, but it is especially hard, if not impossible, for a deaf woman to marry. This was emphasized by almost all the parents, especially those with deaf daughters. The mother of a deaf twenty-five-year-old woman stated, for example,

"What pains me is that it's a daughter. Otherwise, if the child is deaf, he's a child like the others . . . . It is more serious because it is a deaf daughter and that she can't get married."

Another mother of a ten-year-old deaf girl also stressed this problem: "I see no future for her, since in any case she will never have a husband." A silence occurs before she asks, "Have you ever seen men marry handicapped women?"

In Burundi society, then, a deaf person, treated like an inferior being in all aspects of life, does not enjoy the same social treatment as others. Some parents do not expect much from their deaf children, even going so far as to isolate them from their brothers and sisters. In short, these deaf children are the "living dead."

Although some parents do recognize the intelligence of their deaf children, they encounter a communication problem they consider insurmountable. One father of a six-year-old boy stated, "Mine is an intelligent child, who understands many things but can't express them." Another parent, however, put it this way: "If the deaf were intelligent, they would speak like everybody else does." Obviously, the popular perception is that language is linked to thought, and without language, communication is impossible.

It should be pointed out that in traditional Burundi society, speech plays a vital role in everyday life. The education of deaf children in Burundi is all the more complicated because instruction is transmitted through an oral tradition. During evening meetings of all family members, adults convey the various lessons considered indispensable to the children's healthy development. Thus proverbs, short stories, guessing games, and songs are sources of knowledge for the hearing child, for whom they are readily accessible. Unfortunately, however, this knowledge is inaccessible to the deaf child, who is unable to participate in family leisure activities owing to the hearing loss.

The father of a sixteen-year-old boy emphasized this problem:

> You know, I wanted him to learn things—to know what is good, what is evil. I can teach many things to the other children, particularly in the evening when everyone is back home and the chores are done for the day. But he—he goes off to sleep. Why does he stay in the dark without listening to what we are saying?

Some families in the study were able to devise a simple code, usually limited to naming material things, which did not permit complete communication but allowed minimal conversation. The father of a seven-year-old deaf boy stated:

> It is true that he has signs to designate one thing or another, not much but at least it's that. But it's only to represent the objects that he can see. It's impossible for him to describe something that happened outside the house. For example, when he goes out to play and he fights with his little companions, he comes back crying and he can show us that someone hit him, he knows who did it, he takes us by the hand to show us who struck him because he doesn't know his name. But for his own friends, his brothers, his mother and myself, he has invented signs to represent each member of the family. We have all learned them. But that's not much. With so little, you can't say a lot.

When the interviewer indicated that these manual codes might represent "a kind of language," the father replied, "What language, since he doesn't know how to articulate? Forget it, I know that my child can't speak and never will."

Another parent of a thirty-year-old deaf woman commented on the subject of communication between the family and the deaf child this way:

> Since we have been living with each other, we understand each other a little better thanks to certain signs. For example, to signify that the other daughters are married . . . [at this point, the mother indicates a gesture that the daughter uses—a mother nursing her baby] . . . . She uses similar small signs with me that I understand and her brothers and sisters do too. For example, as her father has a beard, to speak of him she makes the sign of a beard. Because of that, even if she has trouble saying what she is thinking, those around her can sometimes guess what she means. We have no conversations with her because it's impossible with a deaf person.

The mother of a twenty-five-year-old woman told the interviewer, "We have signs that we use to mean this or that. One day I may discover an object and want to tell my daughter to take it. I think about it, and I find a corresponding sign. And from that moment, we refer to it that way. She also invents signs that both of us learn, but we can't say much."

While communication is complex but possible for a few families, many parents confess their total inability to communicate with their deaf children. The father of an 11-year-old boy told us, "What language can I speak with him? Even if I shout, he looks at me and laughs. I know he understands nothing."

The mother of a ten-year-old girl admitted, "What pains me is that she can't tell you what she's thinking. For example, when she is sick, it is up to me, her mother, to guess what's wrong. She cries, shows that her head or her stomach hurts, touching only the spot where it hurts, so I can guess that something is wrong."

This inability to communicate and interact with those around them often influences the behavior of these deaf children. They are generally described by family members as quicktempered, aggressive, and brutal. Their companions try to keep them in line, while those who know them less well prefer to avoid them. According to the mother of a thirteen-year-old boy, "If he has something on his mind, he does it. If not, he throws temper tantrums that everybody in this family dreads. It fact, he is known around here as a big bully, and I'm sure that no one would dare touch him for fear of being beaten up."

The father of a sixteen-year-old deaf boy admitted,

> When Pierre is very angry, when it gets difficult, everyone is fed up. But we try to console him and calm him down. You don't know the anger of deaf-mutes—it's frightening! If they are truly angered, they can grab pickaxes, machetes . . . [here, the father stops, pensive] . . . . You know, the deaf are not intelligent. They always do what they want to and don't understand the consequences of their acts.

Despite the negative image of the deaf child that dominates the statements of these parents, some do recognize certain qualities that facilitate the relationship of the deaf child with his or her environment. The deaf child is usually thought to be a good worker, even if the child's availability for work often depends on his or her mood. Deaf children can be a major source of labor in an environment where the assistance of every family member represents an indispensable contribution towards the family's survival.

The mother of a twenty-year-old woman said:

> She's a hard-working child who has always been beside me. I have many children, as you can see, and my deaf daughter has helped me to take care of them. I assure you, she's very precious to me. Now that she has grown up, I am like a queen in my own house—she does the kitchen duties, she's the one who sweeps, who brings back water. When I'm not home, she does the cooking. I have no reason to worry because I know she will handle everything.

These diverse statements reflect the various ways in which deaf persons are perceived in the Burundi society. It is obvious that the parents of deaf children feel that these children cause many problems for their families. The family suffers, on the one hand, because their child is different from others and will never totally belong in society or benefit from the same social consideration as other members in the community and, on the other hand, because they do not know how to assist the child. During one interview the mother of a ten-year-old daughter clearly expressed the helplessness parents feel over their child's deafness: "If only people existed who could tell us how to care for this child! I have heard of this kind of children's school but I can't imagine what they could teach them."

Fortunately, this negative image of the deaf child is less deep-rooted in families with deaf children who are attending school. These parents notice many changes in the behavior of their children. The father of a fifteen-year-old boy observed:

> When he had been to school, we noticed many differences. He is no longer very sad, he doesn't often have excessive anger, although even now we try not to aggravate him. I think he knows many things now and when he's with his schoolmates, he acts like a different child. They have their own special signs that they have learned at school. Sometimes he teaches me these signs but I forget quickly . . . [the father laughs at this particular place in his story]. Fortunately, his brothers and sisters know them a little, so they can talk to each other and tell stories. Sometimes I hear them burst out laughing and when I go to look, it's "Nyamuragi" (the deaf-mute) who is making them laugh.

Another parent had similar comments:

> He's been going to school for three years now and since then I have the impression that he has learned many things. Don't ask me what, because I'm illiterate. I understand nothing of all their writings but I have noticed a very big change in what he is doing. He has learned to read, count, and speak with signs. I don't understand the signs but when he is with his schoolmates, they have the same language, using their eyes, their arms, their mouths. It's very funny, but no one else understands it. In fact, it's the only time I ever see Vincent radiant because he can joke around with his friends, tell things, while with us, with his little brothers and sisters, the only noises you hear are the slaps!

From the interviews with these parents of deaf children, several conclusions can be drawn. Burundi society itself contributes to the exclusion of the deaf population from normal social relationships, either directly—through such discriminatory practices as ridicule, stoning, and denying deaf people responsibilities and even the right to marry and lead a normal social life—or indirectly, through the inadequacy or absence of social integration measures.

Although in some cases a rudimentary communication code is employed between the various family members, in most cases there is no way for the deaf child to communicate with society. He is therefore condemned to experience his own "silent world," isolated among others in an environment incapable of adapting itself to his deafness.

In order for deaf people to be assimilated into the Burundi society, therefore, various potential solutions must be explored. First, the Burundi society must recognize that deafness does not necessarily represent ignorance or deviant behavior. There is no cause-and-effect connection linking deafness and intelligence. It is because the deaf child is denied access to education appropriate to his environment that his knowledge is inadequate and his behavior becomes inappropriate.

Second, the education of young deaf persons must be part of a global educational policy in Burundi, addressing both the deaf individual and Burundi society as a whole.

Third, families with deaf children should understand the need for the deaf child to meet other deaf persons. They have to break with the tradition that encourages the family to hide their handicapped children and isolate them from others.

Only through the education and development of a deaf community that is conscious of its potential will the problems confronting deaf individuals growing up in Burundi society be resolved. This is especially true regarding the challenge of changing the perceptions held about deaf people. Only when these perceptions have been changed can deaf people be recognized as full and contributing members of the Burundi community.

PART SEVEN

Education

Editor's Introduction

When it was decided by vote among the 164 delegates at the International Congress of Milan in 1880 that sign language should be universally suppressed in deaf education programs, only one deaf delegate—James Denison, Principal of Kendall School at Gallaudet College—was in attendance. Denison was one of only six delegates who voted for the continued use of sign language (Van Cleve and Crouch, 1989). As was implied by Gallaudet University's president, I. King Jordan, in his keynote address, The Deaf Way was seen by many participants as an opportunity to reassert a Deaf perspective and to begin to restore to Deaf people some of the power lost more than a century earlier in Milan. Several of the papers in this section consequently express views that, at the time of The Deaf Way, were widely at variance with the policies and practices of the vast majority of deaf education programs around the world. Other papers demonstrate that acceptance of the premise that sign language should be used in classrooms is only a step—though an extremely important one—toward solving the many problems that face educators of deaf students.

The first three papers argue that there is need for radical change in deaf education programs in the United States. Sam Supalla (United States) states that full access to the subjects taught in school can only be achieved by deaf students if they are given ample opportunity early in life to acquire a natural sign language and if teachers are enabled to use this language effectively to teach the students. Robert E. Johnson, Scott Liddell, and Carol Erting (United States) then present an overview of their paper "Unlocking the Curriculum." They argue that deaf education in the United States is failing to teach deaf students competently because teachers' communication modes tend to be based on spoken rather than signed language, even when (as in most total communication programs) signs are added to the spoken message. Janie Simmons (United States) contends that deaf education programs need to be reconceived as serving a unique minority cultural group and that the majority culture's language (in its written form) should be taught as the students' second language by teachers fluent in the children's first (signed) language.

Britta Hansen (Denmark) reports on how linguistic research in the two decades prior to The Deaf Way had ultimately led deaf education in Denmark toward a bilingual approach. As of 1989, Hansen indicates, teachers and parents were taking intensive courses in Danish Sign Language, by then generally regarded in Denmark as deaf children's first language and the primary language of classroom instruction. Danish was being taught primarily through reading and writing. Christina Edenas explains in the following paper that Sweden went through a similar process of research modifying practice, except that its government went so far as to declare Swedish Sign Language (SSL) deaf children's official first language, making knowledge of this language a requirement for teachers in deaf education programs. Edenas then discusses her method of using detailed analyses of videotapes as a means of improving educators' ability to comprehend and produce SSL in the classroom.

In the next paper, Kathleena Whitesell (United States) describes how Glenda Zmijewski (United States), a deaf kindergarten teacher, employs a broad repertoire of signing skills as she discusses a story with deaf children. This paper, combined with the following one by Susan Mather (United States) on visual signals used to regulate class discussions, moves beyond abstract linguistic questions to concerns about effective strategies for managing groups of deaf children and about advantages Deaf teachers may bring to the task of educating these children. A paper by Vicki Hanson and Carol Padden (United States) explains how interactive videodisc technology can provide a technological answer to questions about how to enable deaf children to become truly bilingual—that is, fluent in both a natural sign language and in the written form of the majority culture's language.

A paper by Ildi Batory (Denmark) describes how psychodrama helped deaf secondary students in Denmark increase their sense of positive options in situations that generally led to feelings of isolation and alienation—an important learning experience seldom made a part of deaf students' curriculum. In the next paper, Randolph Mowry (United States) discusses how the placement of deaf students in mainstream or residential settings may have a profound impact on these students' social networks and perceptions of identity, outcomes that need to be carefully considered by those involved in making placement decisions.

Douglas Bahl (United States) raises the subject of the importance for deaf students that Deaf Studies be included as part of their curriculum. He states that deaf students need to learn in school about the accomplishments of Deaf people and the rich heritage of Deaf culture to which they can aspire to contribute. Bahl emphasizes that Deaf studies should be taught primarily by Deaf adults who can act as role models for deaf children. The final paper in this section, by Linda Warby and Michael Clancy (Australia), makes the important point that deaf people's need for information and a sense of cultural identity does not end when they become adults. The paper reports on the efforts of Australia's Adult Education Centre to create videos that will provide Australia's diverse deaf population with information about that continent's valuable Deaf heritage.

References

Van Cleve, J. V., and B. A. Crouch. 1989. *A Place of Their Own: Creating the Deaf Community in America*. Washington, DC: Gallaudet University Press. pp. 109–110.

Equality in Educational Opportunities: The Deaf Version

SAMUEL SUPALLA

Language is an essential ingredient of education. When children arrive in school, they generally have mastered the spoken language used by their particular linguistic community. The language the child brings to the classroom is usually the same as that of the teacher. These two conditions of basic language competence and use of common language, prerequisites for an effective learning environment, are presumed to apply to most children in the United States. For children coming from linguistic-minority homes, only the first assumption may be true, however, and children who are deaf may not even be competent in *any* language. Even if they are fluent in American Sign Language (ASL), their teachers probably are not. Thus, neither of these prerequisites is being met for most deaf children.

The right of deaf children to have access to a language they can acquire and master (e.g., ASL) is an issue that policymakers have never adequately addressed. This right is further obscured by the Individuals with Disabilities Education Act (IDEA; formerly titled the Education for All Handicapped Children Act, or P.L. 94–142), which is typically interpreted as fostering mainstreaming in regular hearing public schools for many deaf children, while totally disregarding their unique linguistic needs. The intent of this law is to provide handicapped children with appropriate education within the least restrictive environment. The bottom line is that desegregation in education for children with disabilities means equality in educational opportunity, just as it did for African-Americans in earlier decades. Evidence shows that this is not necessarily true for deaf children. The Commission on Education of the Deaf (COED) Report (1988) concluded that the emphasis on mainstreaming encouraged by IDEA has been more detrimental than beneficial for many deaf children.

"Barriers" and "least restrictive environments" need to be interpreted differently for deaf people than for members of other groups with disabilities. For deaf people, the barrier is communicative as well as physical in origin. The impact of modality on the development and use of language must also be considered, however. Deaf children are generally unable to learn spoken languages, such as English, naturally. ASL, on the other hand, is a fully accessible language in terms of learnability and use. With two languages in mind, should deaf children then be provided bilingual education? If so, they might be placed under the protection of the Bilingual Education Act, with other

After this paper was presented at The Deaf Way, it was updated with new citations for publication in *A Free Hand: Enfranchising the Education of Deaf Children*, 1992 (Silver Spring, MD: T.J. Publishers, Inc.). The editors of this volume have chosen to present here the revised version, with references that postdate The Deaf Way.

linguistic minority children. Would this Act effectively meet the educational needs of deaf children? This is another question we need to address.

These two questions are complex, and one implies the other. As previously pointed out, deaf children entering school frequently do not have ASL as a native language, or *any* language for that matter. Thus, many of them need to learn two languages instead of one—two languages that differ in modalities. Are these differences significant enough to disallow any formal link between bilingual education and education of deaf children? That remains to be seen.

The Existing Situation: A Policy Analysis

Deaf children require qualitatively different services than hearing children who, handicapped or not, generally begin school with well-developed competence in spoken English. This competence makes that language utilizable as the medium of their instruction and for the development of reading and writing skills. Deaf children, on the other hand, often lack skill in English when beginning school (Moores and Kluwin, 1986). Their patterns of English language learning resemble those of children learning English as a second language (Quigley and Paul, 1984).

More importantly, there are indications that ASL promotes the learning of English as a second language for deaf children in a way similar to the way that bilingual situations promote learning for hearing linguistic minority children. In the case of deaf children, the need to develop a "mother tongue" (e.g., ASL) is stressed in order to facilitate the learning of a second language (e.g., English) within the context of bilingualism (Johnson, Liddell, and Erting, 1989). In short, their educational situation shares more common features with linguistic minority children than with children with physical or mental handicaps.

Residential Schools: Language Acquisition and Maintenance

Residential schools for the deaf are more than just schools in which many deaf children enroll. These schools have a special role in fostering and maintaining the language of the Deaf community. ASL is maintained and transmitted to succeeding deaf generations primarily because most deaf adults marry other deaf persons (Rainer, Altshuter, and Kallman, 1963). A small percentage of these marriages produce deaf children. For such a child born in a family of deaf parents, ASL is likely to become the native language (Quigley and Paul, 1984).

Upon enrollment in a residential school, this child then becomes the linguistic and cultural model for deaf peers from hearing families. Deaf children born to hearing parents make up the majority of the total deaf child population (Quigley and Kretschmer, 1982). These children acquire ASL naturally through immersion with native ASL-signing children, usually through informal exposure on the playgrounds or in the dormitories of residential schools (Padden and Humphries, 1988). Upon school completion, they then assimilate into the Deaf community, which is unified by the language (Meadow, 1972; Stokes and Menyuk, 1975), and the cycle repeats itself.

Johnson and Erting (1989) argue that ASL has become a powerful instrument essential for both ethnicity and socialization processes of deaf children. The residential school system has apparently provided a congenial environment for developing both processes, with a concentration of deaf children in sufficient numbers to facilitate and maintain the processes as described above for generations. Although ASL may play a crucial role in the lives of deaf children, this does not necessarily mean that such signed language is widely promoted by educational policy, however. In fact, ASL has been severely oppressed as a language throughout much of the history of deaf education (Lane, 1980). This oppression is largely attributed to serious misconceptions about ASL as a language (Markowicz, 1980) and about bilingualism in general.

Consequences of Prevailing Educational Policies

Educational policies disregarding ASL have had damaging consequences. For example, without ASL, deaf children do not have full linguistic access to subject matter taught in the classroom (Johnson et al., 1989). It is true that ASL has been successfully transmitted from child to child, but this unique language learning and maintenance among deaf children takes place in the dormitory and playground, not in the classroom. Moreover, deaf children may achieve native or native-like competence in ASL, but such competence is not tapped for instructional purposes or in learning English as a second language. Finally, deaf children who are born to hearing parents are not exposed to ASL until they enter residential school, which often happens after the "critical period" for native language acquisition has been passed (Newport, 1990; Newport and T. Supalla, under revision). Many deaf children thus lose the opportunity to acquire ASL as a first language.

With the advent of mainstreaming for deaf children, one distressing fact is that more and more of them are being denied access to ASL altogether (S. Supalla, 1986). While it may not have been the intent of IDEA, the nature of placement has apparently made the language situation of deaf children worse. Residential schools have experienced drastic drops in enrollment and face threats of closure. While deaf parents tend to view these schools as the locus of Deaf culture and object strongly to dictates as to where they should place their children (Meadow, 1975), hearing parents usually have a completely different perception and are in favor of mainstreaming for school placement. Consequently, a rising number of deaf children have been mainstreamed, without contact with deaf peers with deaf parents. Even more distressing is the fact that these children are often exposed to Manually Coded English (MCE) as their sole linguistic input.

MCE is made up of a number of artificial English-based sign systems developed during the early 1970s as mainstreaming became more popular. During the same period, it had become more widely recognized that purely oral approaches had drawbacks, and signing tended to be used more in the classroom. However, the idea that ASL could have a potentially positive role in the education of deaf children continued to be rejected. It was hoped that deaf children could acquire English naturally through MCE, just as they can acquire ASL naturally: There are studies showing dramatic results of deaf children acquiring and using ASL as a native language (Newport and Meier, 1986).

However, according to S. Supalla (1990; 1991), MCE is not a natural language, nor should it be treated as one. Deaf children are reported to experience great difficulty in acquiring MCE. More importantly, these children have resorted to changing MCE into a more efficient system approaching the structures of natural signed languages. Thus, new signed systems have evolved that do not follow ASL structure. This may be a threat to ASL as the signed language of deaf people in the United States. Since language is what holds a community together, it can also be a threat to the cohesiveness of the Deaf community as a whole.

Toward Constructive Legislative Action

The Commission on Education of the Deaf (COED) Report has criticized the whole-sale application of mainstreaming for deaf children and recommended that attention must be given to their linguistic needs, along with other factors, when considering school placement. Residential school settings are not ideal either, however. While they may be considered the locus of ASL and Deaf culture, most do not have policies sensitive to the educational needs of deaf children. More importantly, it appears that there is no legal protection of the right of deaf children to acquire or use ASL, as compared with the linguistic rights of other linguistic minority children protected under the Bilingual Education Act (BEA). We need legislation that effectively addresses the specific needs of deaf children, i.e., either a modification of a law already in existence or a new one. The Deaf community recently began its own version of the civil rights movement with the 1988 student protest at Gallaudet University. The present debate involves what strategy should be undertaken for equality in educational opportunities: the Deaf version.

Presently, there is a law in existence relating to deaf education known as the Education of the Deaf Act (EDA). This Act does not concern itself with what actions should be undertaken to meet the linguistic needs of deaf children. Its primary focus is providing federal (financial) assistance to Gallaudet University, Kendall Demonstration Elementary School for the Deaf, the Model Secondary School for the Deaf and the National Technical Institute for the Deaf. Since the EDA does not contribute much to other areas of deaf education, some people feel that the educational needs of deaf children would be best supported under the Bilingual Education Act. BEA's philosophy, goals and justifications are appealing, particularly the idea that equality of educational opportunity does not necessarily mean equality of treatment, as well as the idea that linguistic minority students are denied a meaningful education if they are instructed only in English (*Lau v. Nichols*, 1874). As a matter of fact, the COED Report has recommended that deaf children be considered for coverage under the BEA. Yet, as with IDEA, wholesale application of the Act to deaf education would be dangerous for several reasons.

First, it must be understood that the goals of bilingual education are of secondary importance when considered within the context of desegregation, which for several decades has been a major goal in public education in the United States (Applewhite, 1979). If linguistic minority students are to be taught in their native language, they must be segregated from majority language students. According to the *Keyes v. School District No. 1, Denver* decision, the role of bilingual education is defined as being subordinate to a plan for school desegregation. Bilingual education in the United States thus follows a transitional model. This transition period is specified as five years. By that time, linguistic minority children should be able to function in the majority language and will no longer be covered by the Act.

Deaf children have been excluded from coverage by the BEA because their language learning problems are presumed to be caused by a medical pathology rather than as the result of being a part of a linguistic and cultural minority group. Reagan (1985) presents compelling evidence supporting the contention that deaf people do indeed constitute a linguistic and cultural minority group. Further, Rutherford (1988) describes the impact of hearing loss in shaping the linguistic and cultural experience of deaf people. If this is true, then there is a strong link between the disability itself (e.g., hearing loss), and the linguistic/cultural minority status of deaf people. The question remains whether this recognition means that the BEA is applicable to them. There are several reasons why it may not be applicable.

For one thing, to be covered by the Act, children must both have limited English proficiency *and* possess a native language other than English. According to BEA, a "native language" for a child with limited English proficiency is the language that child uses. If the child has so little language that the native language cannot be determined, then the language used by the parents would determine eligibility. Bear in mind that, while deaf children may be limited in English proficiency, most of them do not possess ASL as a native language either, nor do their parents use ASL at home. These children probably will learn ASL later in life, but with the rise of mainstreaming and the decline of residential school enrollment, this may not happen until they leave school and become assimilated into the Deaf community. It may therefore be that deaf children will not meet the criteria for being included, even if their linguistic minority status is recognized.

Even more important is whether it is possible for the Act to meet the particular educational needs of deaf children. Since hearing children acquire at least one language at home, if that language is not English, then they can benefit from a bilingual education program at school. In other words, they experience an appropriate linguistic environment both at home and at school. For most deaf children, the opposite is true since their linguistic environment does not normally include opportunities to learn language naturally, be it at home or at school.

Thus, English cannot be regarded as a "natural" language for deaf children. Owing to sensory deprivation, they cannot learn it in the natural way (e.g., through hearing it spoken). They must instead rely on its written form, which is a much less effective way of learning a language. The same is true of deaf children learning English orally: They must be formally taught. ASL, on the other hand, is fully accessible to them (with no formal instruction required) and can be thus described as their natural language. Successfully learning English through reading depends heavily on their having learned ASL first. More importantly, Liben (1978) may be correct in stating that establishing a strong language base is the most important factor in deaf children's educational development. Accordingly, the appropriate linguistic environment for deaf children, whether at home or at school, would involve the use of ASL, or some other natural signed language.

It is important to realize that the BEA is transitional in nature, with a limit on the amount of time allowed for the transition to the majority language to take place. This is obviously not realistic for deaf children. For example, deaf children of deaf parents who use ASL at home may be eligible according to the criteria of the BEA, but these children can only use ASL in the classroom up to five years. Then, how are they expected to make the transition from ASL to English? The same is true for deaf children of hearing parents who might learn and use ASL at home. Although it would be possible to make a transition to another natural signed language (e.g., Danish Sign Language), this is not the case for transition from a signed language to a spoken language. For deaf children, English is not capable of functioning as the primary language of instruction. Therefore, the notion of bilingual education for deaf children needs to be redefined. ASL would need to be the primary language of instruction throughout their school years. Thus, the BEA is not completely applicable to the deaf educational scene. Is it possible for the Act to be altered to the extent that it can serve deaf children effectively? This is highly questionable.

For one thing, changes would be needed that are specific to deaf children as a group, and these changes would not be applicable to the population at large. Suppose the Act were modified to the extent that it directed programs to introduce deaf children to ASL as their native language when they were very young. This would not coincide with the original intent of the BEA, which was not to create more bilinguals but to accommodate the needs of those in existence.

Additionally, the reason that BEA mandates a transitional model of bilingual educa-tion is that the ultimate objective is desegregation of linguistic minority group members. While this may be a reasonable goal for hearing children, it is not for deaf children since attempts to mainstream them in public schools have proved to be disastrous. However, if the BEA were to direct that deaf children use ASL throughout their school years, this would be defeating the purpose of the Act, as originally construed.

While it is clearly not appropriate to have deaf education covered by the present Bilingual Education Act, this does not mean that we cannot apply a bilingual education model to meet deaf educational concerns. An ideal model would guarantee the right of deaf children to ASL, and it would involve both the school and the home. English could be introduced as a second language through its written form, and the language of instruction would remain exclusively ASL. Were the unique circumstances surrounding deafness made clear to the American public, it might become more tolerant with the notion of introducing and fostering ASL as the native language of deaf children.

The essential point here is that deaf children do not have any choice between ASL and English. Only ASL, or another signed language, can be considered a natural lan-guage for them. This is not a matter of choice; it is a matter of access. The notion of denying deaf children access to a language they can learn easily and naturally is a powerful one that raises questions both morally and legally.

Promotion-Oriented Language Rights: A Possible Solution

According to Macias (1979), federal law does not guarantee language choice or lan-guage rights explicitly. However, two types of language rights are recognized: tolerance-oriented and promotion-oriented. Tolerance-oriented language rights involve the right to freedom from discrimination based on language, and the right to have such language. One reason the "maintenance" model of bilingual education has been rejected in the United States is that linguistic minority groups generally tend to move from their mi-nority language toward the majority language after two or three generations. Thus, the transitional model is considered more appropriate, providing linguistic minority chil-dren with the right to use their native language educationally only until they master English.

Promotion-oriented language rights, on the other hand, regulate the manner in which public institutions may use and cultivate the languages and cultures of minori-ties. In order to claim promotive language rights, a linguistic minority group must first establish that the language in question has a proven maintenance of at least three generations. In the United States, there are linguistic minority groups that meet this criterion (e.g., residents of Puerto Rico and Native Americans).

Despite the type of language rights involved, no person should be denied access to a mother tongue. Without access, in the words of Macias (1979), "the heart of the right to use one's own language is offered as sacrifice at the legal altar of formal equality" (p. 48). Deaf children's being denied access to ASL may be a gross violation of their right to equal treatment under the law. ASL, which has endured in the Deaf community for almost two centuries, is the natural, native language of deaf Americans. Consequently, the Deaf community surely should be entitled to promotive language rights status.

Deaf children need to experience a full linguistic environment for equal educational opportunities to be realized. Adequate educational development is expected to follow. Deaf children must have a language that works for them in terms of learnability and use; if they do, they will experience an education similar to that of hearing children.

Yet, even if ASL were to be recognized and promoted as the language of instruction for all deaf children, we would still face the problem that bilingual education implies segregation, which contradicts prevailing educational policy in the United States. Recall that bilingual education for hearing children is supposed to be only compensatory, and thus, transitory in nature. In the case of deaf children, the transitional bilingual education model would obviously not work.

Moreover, the residential school setting may provide the appropriate linguistic environment for deaf children. A serious case of segregation prevails here, and this may require a form of reverse mainstreaming to offset the possible legal consequences. For example, the residential schools that traditionally serve deaf students would have to be open to hearing students as well. These hearing students would have the right to their signed language, and many of those making this choice would likely be children of deaf parents. The distinction between attending the residential schools for the deaf and regular schools would be based on the language and modality used for instruction (e.g., ASL vs. English). One positive outcome could be that larger numbers of students would attend "ASL schools," thus prompting the establishment of satellite schools (e.g., day schools) in close proximity to deaf children's homes.

Bilingual Education for Deaf Students: Perspectives for the Future

Bilingual approaches that use ASL as the primary language of instruction are now being used in programs designed specifically for deaf students. The degree of commitment to ASL in these programs varies, ranging from the establishment of a pilot class (Strong, 1988) to a schoolwide language policy (i.e., Indiana School for the Deaf). Interestingly enough, the role of natural signed languages has recently been receiving more attention in other countries also. In one case, it has resulted in the creation of an official signed language: In Sweden, promotive language rights are being given to the Deaf community, and Swedish Sign Language is recognized as the official signed language, along with spoken Swedish as the official spoken language (Davies, 1991). If we were to follow the Swedish example, it might help solve a remaining problem that has not yet been satisfactorily addressed.

Most deaf children are born to nonsigning hearing parents. If deaf children were to have promotive language rights, the state would be entitled to guarantee their access to ASL. This would involve federal legislation creating incentives for the state and local agencies to set up parent/infant programs similar to those occurring in Sweden (Davies, 1991). The parents would then be able to acquire some proficiency in ASL in these programs and could interact with deaf adults while learning ASL from them. They could also learn about Deaf culture and the realities of deafness. Deaf children of hearing parents refusing to learn and use ASL would be protected in the same way as are children who suffer from parental neglect or child abuse.

Since none of the existing laws (EDA, BEA, and IDEA) adequately meets the educational needs of deaf children, new legislation may be called for. Since deaf children are part of a linguistic minority group owing to their hearing loss, an overlap exists between their disabled status and their minority group status. This places them in an entirely different category from hearing children who are disabled, or hearing children who are members of a linguistic minority group. The fact that the natural mode of communication for deaf children is in a different modality points to striking differences in needs to be fulfilled. The unique relationship between ASL and English must be noted, with English identified as the "nonprimary" language for instructional use. Language access must be guaranteed for children with nonsigning hearing parents before they enroll in school by finding ways of giving them opportunities to acquire ASL. We need to move toward educational policies that promote true equality of educational opportunities: *The Deaf Version.*

This movement would need to undergo stages similar to those the bilingual education movement has undergone. The first step would be court litigation focusing on the legal status of present educational policies for deaf children. The court would have to decide whether denial of access to ASL constituted a denial of the right of deaf children to full participation in education, and thus equal opportunity to learn. If this were established, a case could be made against such discriminatory practices. If the court were to recognize the essential role of natural signed languages in the educational development of deaf children and conclude that programs not using ASL were denying deaf children meaningful educational opportunities, then these programs would be in conflict with prevailing legislation stipulating every child's right to an equal education.

Complying with the law would inevitably result in substantial changes in existing policies in programs for the deaf across the nation. Further state and federal legislation might follow, involving any measures required to help implement programs providing full access to ASL for deaf children (e.g., ASL intervention programs). At the federal level, the Education of the Deaf Act could be targeted for amendments reflecting the shift in focus for education of the deaf. It is hoped that these changes will help us meet the vital prerequisites for providing language access and educational advancement for deaf children. In the end, the notion of equality in educational opportunities finally may be achieved.

References

Applewhite, S. 1979. "The Legal Dialect of Bilingual Education." In *Bilingual Education and Public Policy in the United States,* ed. R. Padilla. Ypsilanti, MI: Eastern Michigan University Department of Foreign Language and Bilingual Studies. pp. 3–15.

Bowe, F., ed. 1988. *Toward Equality; Education of the Deaf.* Final Report of the United States Congress Commission on Education of the Deaf. Washington, DC: United States Government Printing Office.

Davies, S. 1991. "The Transition Toward Bilingual Education of Deaf Children in Sweden and Denmark: Perspectives on Language." *Sign Language Studies* 71: 169–195.

Johnson, R., and C. Erting. 1989. "Ethnicity and Socialization in a Classroom for Deaf Children." In *The Sociolinguistics of the Deaf Community,* ed. C. Lucas. San Diego: Academic Press. pp. 41–83.

Johnson, R., S. Liddell, and C. Erting. 1989. "Unlocking the Curriculum: Principles for Achieving Access in Deaf Education." Gallaudet Research Institute Working Paper, 89–3. Washington, DC: Gallaudet Research Institute.

Lane, H. 1980. "Historical: A Chronology of the Oppression of Sign Language in France and the United States." In *Recent Perspectives on American Sign Language,* ed. H. Lane and F. Grosjean. Hillsdale, NJ: Lawrence Erlbaum. pp. 119–161.

Liben, L. 1979. "The Development of Deaf Children: An Overview of Issues." In *Deaf Children: Developmental Perspectives,* ed. L. Liben. New York: Academic Press. pp. 3–20.

Macias, R. 1979. "Choice of Language as a Human Right: Public Policy Implications in the United States." In *Bilingual Education and Public Policy in the United States*, ed. R. Padilla. Ypsilanti, MI: Eastern Michigan University Department of Foreign Languages and Bilingual Studies. pp. 39–51.

Markowicz, H. 1980. "Myths about American Sign Language." In *Recent Perspectives on American Sign Language*, ed. H. Lane and F. Grosjean. Hillsdale, NJ: Lawrence Erlbaum. pp. 1–6.

Meadow, K. 1972. "Sociolinguistics, Sign Language, and the Deaf Subculture." In *Psycholinguistics and Total Communication: The State of the Art*, ed. T. O'Rourke. Silver Spring, MD: National Association of the Deaf.

Moores, D., and T. Kluwin. 1986. "Issues in School Placement." In *Deaf Children in America*, ed. A. Schildroth and M. Karchmer. San Diego: College-Hill Press. pp. 105–124.

Newport, E. 1990. "Constraints on Learning Studies in the Acquisition of American Sign Language." *Papers and Reports on Child Language Development* 23: 1–22.

Newport, E., and R. Meier 1986. "The Acquisition of American Sign Language." In *The Cross-Linguistic Study of Language Acquisition*, ed. D. I. Slobin. Hillsdale, NJ: Lawrence Erlbaum. pp. 861–938.

Newport, E., and T. Supalla. "Critical Period Effects in the Acquisition of a Primary Language: The Influence of Maturational State on the Acquisition of Complex Morphology in American Sign Language." Manuscript under revision.

Padden, C., and T. Humphries. 1986. *Deaf in America: Voices from a Culture*. Cambridge: Harvard University Press.

Paul, P. 1987. "A Perspective on Using American Sign Language to Teach English as a Second Language." *Teaching English to Deaf and Second-Language Students* 5 (3): 10–16.

Quigley, S., and R. Kretschmer. 1982. *The Education of Deaf Children*. Baltimore, MD: University Park Press.

Quigley, S., and P. Paul. 1984. *Language and Deafness*. San Diego: College-Hill Press.

Rainer, J., K. Altshuler, and F. Kallman. 1963. *Family and Mental Health Problems in a Deaf Population*. New York: Columbia University Press.

Reagan, T. 1985. "The Deaf as a Linguistic Minority: Educational Considerations." *Harvard Educational Review* 55: 265–277.

Rutherford, S. 1988. "The Culture of American Deaf People." *Sign Language Studies*. 58: 129–148.

Supalla, S. 1986. "Manually Coded English: The Modality Question in Signed Language Development." Unpublished master's thesis, University of Illinois, Urbana-Champaign.

Supalla, S. 1990. "Segmentation of Manually Coded English: Problems in the Mapping of English in the Visual/Gestural Mode." Unpublished diss., University of Illinois, Urbana-Champaign.

Supalla, S. 1991. "Manually Coded English: The Modality Question in Signed Language Development." In *Theoretical Issues in Sign Language Research*, ed. P. Siple and S. Fischer. Chicago: University of Chicago Press. 2 (Psychology): 85–109.

A Brief Overview of "Unlocking the Curriculum"

ROBERT E. JOHNSON, SCOTT K. LIDDELL,
AND CAROL J. ERTING

This presentation will include a summary of a long paper published by the Gallaudet Research Institute earlier this year, called "Unlocking the Curriculum: Principles for Achieving Access in Deaf Education" (Johnson, Liddell, and Erting, 1989). We would like to begin, however, with a brief description of certain events that led us to produce this paper.

First, we've all regarded deaf education as a closed system. Parents of deaf children, deaf people themselves, and professionals in linguistics and psychology have written about the inadequacies of deaf education, but have been relatively powerless in terms of having any real influence. Then, almost exactly sixteen months ago, deaf people rose up and took control of Gallaudet University, the premier deaf institution in the world. This event by itself raised expectations that the system might be subject to change.

Second, we've seen natural sign languages become the language of the classroom in several foreign countries. Some examples are Sweden, Denmark, and Venezuela. Although years of linguistic research conducted at Gallaudet would support the adoption of such language policies in the United States, it appears that the United States has been falling behind other countries in modifying policy and practice to address the implications of such research.

During the past year, a fortunate chain of circumstances brought the three of us in contact with officials of a state board of education comprised of people in a position to establish a model program who seemed receptive to ideas about American Sign Language (ASL). We proposed to them establishing a model program that would begin with children who will be born in the next year or so and would continue for ten years. After discussing these issues with officials of the State Department of Education, they asked us to submit a written proposal. Although the Department of Education decided against embarking on a program of this scope, writing that proposal led more or less directly to the paper we now will summarize—a paper that has generated considerable discussion.

The education of deaf students in the United States is not as it should be. Recent studies (e.g., Allen, 1986) have found that patterns of low achievement have persisted more than a decade after the beginning of Total Communication programs. Not only that, in each year of school deaf students fall further and further behind in reading and mathematics achievement. We've seen the results of an entire generation of deaf students going through the system. Comparisons of assessment data gathered over many years suggest that neither Total Communication nor mainstreaming—two movements widely believed to have improved deaf students' access to quality education—have significantly improved these averages. We propose that there are primarily two reasons for the failure of the system: the first, lack of linguistic access to curricular content; the second, a cycle of low expectations.

It is our view that a higher rate of success could be attained if there were changes in the way deaf children are educated—changes that acknowledge these children's need for early competence in a visually accessible, "natural" language (such as ASL) and for classroom instruction that uses that language to ensure deaf students' access to curricular material.

Many studies have shown (Brasel, 1975; Meadow, 1967; Stevenson, 1964; Stuckless and Birch, 1966; Vernon and Koh, 1970) that the less than 10 percent of deaf students who have deaf parents already tend to achieve at higher levels in all areas (including English) than do deaf children with hearing parents. The reason for these higher achievement levels is probably that most deaf children with deaf parents have access from birth to a natural sign language, thus giving them a strong language base during a critical developmental stage. We define a sign language such as ASL as "natural" because it evolved through use over a long period of time, has its own unique grammar and syntax, and was not artificially designed in an effort to represent a spoken language such as English. Through family interaction, deaf children of deaf parents generally receive early linguistic, intellectual, and social-emotional stimulation in a natural sign language that enables them to arrive at school ready to learn, with a large fund of information about the world.

Deaf children with deaf parents tend to outperform their deaf peers in spite of, rather than because of, America's educational system. None of the communication policies generally maintained by schools—including oral approaches, simultaneous communication, manually encoded English, or Cued Speech—enables teachers either to understand fully children who use ASL or to use ASL themselves for instructional purposes.

Although deaf children with deaf parents are thereby placed at a distinct disadvantage in school in comparison with most hearing children (who are taught in their native language), they are nevertheless far better prepared socially, linguistically, and intellectually for existing school programs than the ninety-plus percent of deaf children with two hearing parents. That majority of deaf students generally arrive in school with severely circumscribed funds of information about the world and poorly developed language skills in *both* spoken English and sign language.

Traditional communication practices used to teach deaf children in the United States fail to educate deaf children because they are based on spoken English, a language deaf children cannot hear. Total Communication did not start out this way, but it has come to mean simultaneous communication ("SimCom"). Because it calls for teachers to sign, it has come to stand as a symbol of opposition to oralism and as such has enjoyed substantial support from the adult deaf population. But what is simultaneous communication? It's signing and talking at the same time. This description, however, is misleading, because the two messages are not equal.

Hearing teachers using simultaneous communication tend to monitor their own speech and present sequences of signs perceived by deaf students as bits of sentences with no obvious grammatical organization. We define all simultaneous communication systems as "Sign Supported Speech" (SSS), because speech generally predominates in this form of discourse. The effort to speak and sign at the same time often contributes to a breakdown in the intelligibility of the signed message, making it fail to represent English, ASL, or any language.

We have analyzed a segment of a videotape of a preschool teacher communicating with a four-year-old deaf child using SSS. In this brief sample, the teacher consistently misarticulates signs, a problem compounded by the fact that her misarticulations often result in signs that actually mean something else, for example, DEVIL and HORSE for RABBIT, CAN'T for CAN, and FREEZE for WANT. But more problematic is the incongruity of her signs with her spoken English. It is clear that her signing is not in any sense an exact representation of English speech. Many English words are not represented by signs, and there is no consistent pattern to what is eliminated. The end result is signed sentences that are mostly incomprehensible, often contradictory to the intended meaning, and largely incomplete.

The fact is that there is no conclusive evidence that deaf students actually learn English grammar from observing a manual representation of that language, even when teachers are much more proficient at articulating signs and presenting signed representations of all aspects of a spoken communication than the teacher described above. One researcher conducted a study (Supalla, 1986) of the signing of deaf students who had been in a signed English environment for several years without any intervening influence from users of ASL. He found that each child in this "ideal" signed English setting formed an idiosyncratic grammar, containing innovations quite unlike English. This study clearly suggests that it is unrealistic to expect that exposure to signed English will lead naturally to the acquisition of competent English grammar, either spoken or signed.

The widely held belief of parents and educators that deaf children should be addressed in spoken and/or signed English in their early years and introduced to ASL much later (if at all) is the reverse of what is needed to ensure these children's optimal intellectual development, including the development of their facility in reading and writing in English. Numerous studies by developmental psychologists indicate that a child's first language can and should be learned in the first few years of life, and linguistic studies show that the visual accessibility of a natural sign language such as ASL makes that language the logical first language of deaf children in the United States.

Early acquisition of ASL may also be important to our goal of teaching English to deaf children. Research on bilingualism suggests that children and second language learners need a foundation in one natural language before attempting to learn a second language. One linguistics study (Paulston, 1977) states "that mother tongue development facilitates the learning of the second language, and there are serious implications that without such development neither language may be learned well, resulting in semilingualism" (p. 93).

The report of the recent Commission on Education of the Deaf (1988) states that ASL is a "full-fledged native minority language to which all of the provisions of the Bilingual Education Act should apply" (p. 9). Since most deaf children have hearing parents, radical changes in early intervention programs and ways of advising and assisting parents of deaf children will clearly need to be adopted before teachers will be able to assume that most deaf students entering school are fluent users of ASL, ready to be instructed in that language. We agree fully with the Commission's statement that "too seldom recognized is the need for a deaf child to have other deaf children as part of his or her peer group, and to be exposed to deaf adults" (p. 9). As we will mention in our recommendations later on, one way to help deaf children of hearing parents learn ASL would be through the employment of deaf daycare providers.

If we are correct in concluding that educational content could be taught to deaf children as effectively in ASL as it is or can be to hearing children in English, then it must follow that training programs in deaf education need to be radically changed. At present, however, in most such programs it is rare to have a course about deaf people interacting with each other, a course that teaches about the role of ASL in the ordinary development of deaf children, or even a course that teaches a future teacher to understand or produce ASL. In fact, virtually all such programs teach only some system for Sign Supported Speech, usually requiring only two or three such classes.

We would contend that speech-centered deaf education is perpetuated, in part, by the widespread belief that low academic achievement is an inevitable consequence of deafness and that the present system, which does not require that teachers learn or use ASL, is as effective as any that can be devised. The system has been able to convince its own members and the general public that the failure of speech-centered deaf education, which *includes* Total Communication programs, has been the fault of the students rather than of the system or the practices of the people in it.

It is our belief that if deaf children were introduced to ASL early and if teachers became proficient at using ASL to teach deaf students, the students' average achievement levels would very likely rise significantly.

The Guiding Principles of a Model Program for Educating Deaf Children

We now will describe a proposed model program that, if developed, could help demonstrate the results of a system of deaf education that would use ASL for classroom instruction and that would teach English as a separate, second language through reading and writing. This program would extend from daycare and preschool components through high school. We readily admit that the implementation of such a program would be a very difficult task, and we do not expect that such a program will quickly or easily alleviate the ills of deaf education, or that it will make the process simple or noncontroversial. If there is one lesson that arises from the history of deaf education, it is that solutions to problems are quite complex. We do believe, however, that our proposed model will achieve much more acceptable results than any of the options currently being employed in the United States.

We will not describe here all the details of our proposed model, but we hope to establish an educational program with the following components:

❖ A Family Support Program will provide educational and emotional support for the families of deaf children and will encourage parents to accept their deaf child as a capable person whose first linguistic task must be to learn a language other than that of the parents in order to succeed.

❖ A Family-Infant-Toddler Program will develop ASL skills in deaf infants and toddlers. It will develop signing and interaction skills among their parents and siblings as well.

❖ Beginning in a Preschool-Kindergarten Program, deaf and hearing teachers, each of whom will be bilingual in ASL and English, will teach the children.

❖ Grades one through twelve will have as their goal to enable deaf students to learn exactly the same curricular content as their hearing peers do, using special techniques and materials to teach English literacy.

The model will feature a child development center, a program for developing special materials and resources, and strong administrative and research components.

The following twelve "guiding principles" suggest the model's underlying philosophy:

1. Deaf children will learn if given access to the things we want them to learn.
2. The first language of deaf children should be a natural sign language (ASL).
3. The acquisition of a natural sign language should begin as early as possible in order to take advantage of critical period effects.
4. The best models for natural sign language acquisition, the development of a social identity, and the enhancement of self-esteem for deaf children are deaf signers who use the language proficiently.
5. The natural sign language acquired by a deaf child provides the best access to educational content.
6. Sign language and spoken language are not the same and must be kept separate both in use and in the curriculum.
7. The learning of a spoken language (English) for a deaf person is a process of learning a second language through literacy (reading and writing).
8. Speech should not be employed as the primary vehicle for the learning of a spoken language for deaf children.
9. The development of speech-related skills must be accomplished through a program that has available a variety of approaches, each designed for a specific combination of etiology and severity of hearing loss.
10. Deaf children are not seen as "defective models" of normally hearing children.
11. There is nothing wrong with being deaf (an observation also made in the report of the Commission on Education of the Deaf).
12. The "Least Restrictive Environment" for deaf children is one in which they may acquire a natural sign language and through that language achieve access to a spoken language and the content of the school curriculum.

References

Allen, T. E. 1986. "Patterns of Academic Achievement among Hearing Impaired Students: 1974–1983." In *Deaf Children in America,* ed. Arthur N. Schildroth and Michael A. Karchmer. San Diego: College-Hill Press. pp. 161–206.

Brasel, K. 1975. "The Influence of Early Language and Communication in Environments on the Development of Language in Deaf Children." Unpublished doctoral dissertation, University of Illinois, Urbana-Champaign.

Commission on Education of the Deaf. 1988. *Toward Equality: A Report to the President and the Congress of the United States.* Washington, DC: United States Government Printing Office.

Johnson, R. E., S. K. Liddell, and C. J. Erting. 1989. "Unlocking the Curriculum: Principles for Achieving Access in Deaf Education." Gallaudet Research Institute Working/Occasional Paper Series, No. 89-3. Washington, DC: Gallaudet Research Institute.

Meadow, K. 1967. "The Effect of Early Manual Communication and Family Climate on the Deaf Child's Environment." Unpublished doctoral dissertation, University of California, Berkeley.

Paulston, C. B. 1977. "Research." In *Bilingual Education: Current Perspectives*. 2 (Linguistics): 87–151. Washington, DC: Center for Applied Linguistics.

Stevenson, E. 1964. "A Study of the Educational Achievement of Deaf Children and Deaf Parents." *California News* 80 (4): 143.

Stuckless, E., and J. Birch. 1966. "The Influence of Early Manual Communication on the Linguistic Development of Deaf Children." *American Annals of the Deaf* 111 (4): 425–460, 499–504.

Supalla, S. 1986. "Manually Coded English: The Modality Question in Signed Language Development." Unpublished master's thesis, University of Illinois, Urbana-Champaign.

Vernon, M., and S. Koe. 1970. "Effects of Manual Communication on Deaf Children's Educational Achievement, Linguistic Competence, Oral Skills, and Psychological Development." *American Annals of the Deaf* 115 (5): 527–536.

The Language Arts curriculum in Programs for Deaf children

JANIE SIMMONS

Research on American Sign Language and the deaf community establishes the fact that the majority of deaf adults and deaf children of deaf community members share their own language and culture (Stokoe, 1978; Baker and Cokely, 1980; Wilbur, 1988). Deaf children of hearing parents also have gained access to the deaf community at some point in their lives, primarily through residential schools (Padden and Humphries, 1988).

Nevertheless, the notion that deaf children are indeed linguistically and culturally unique in ways comparable to hearing minority children is still met with a great deal of resistance in educational circles (Lane, 1984; Reagan, 1985).

Theoretical and pedagogical models in deaf education are derived largely from pathological views of deafness—views that define deaf children as "hearing-handicapped" rather than as members of a culturally and linguistically unique group. Furthermore, traditional explanations for the persistent failure of deaf children to achieve on par with their hearing peers focus on the deficiency of hearing impairment itself—a state internal to the deaf child.

Therefore, these models reinforce the view that the inadequacy of deaf children's overall academic development can be attributed to the fact of deafness itself. They do not take into account inappropriate teaching philosophies and methods, or other historical and social factors. Consequently, the pathological model poses a serious threat to the development of new approaches to teaching deaf children.

A number of researchers have challenged the more traditional views of deafness (Vernon and Makowsky, 1969; Charrow and Wilbur, 1975; Baker and Battison, 1980; Woodward, 1982; Lane, 1984; Reagan, 1988; Padden and Humphries, 1988). Their work has helped legitimize the efforts of deaf individuals throughout the last century who have opposed the pathological model and declared their language and culture as fit for human purposes as any oral language and culture. Still, very little socially based research has been undertaken in the field of deaf education.

In this paper I will briefly outline a broad set of recommendations drawn from research on hearing, minority populations. I believe these recommendations hold promise for the development of a more theoretically sound and culturally appropriate language arts curriculum in programs for deaf children.

Socially Based Approaches and Recommendations

Socially based perspectives stress the contextual, socially produced nature of meaning—its negotiation by speakers in context over time. All deaf children, simply by being born into the human community, are social beings and makers of meaning. They have personal and cultural histories that bear upon their experience of growing up as deaf individuals in families—both hearing and deaf—from various linguistic, ethnic, class, and cultural backgrounds.

The majority of deaf children in the United States enter school with little or no exposure to native American Sign Language (ASL) users. Therefore, socially based approaches suggest the need, at the very least, to use, validate, and expand upon whatever communication methods these young children do use to make meaning and act upon their surroundings.

At most, these approaches stress the need to create completely accessible linguistic and educational environments for all deaf children. Thus, it is necessary to consider the ways in which the majority of deaf children—those with hearing parents—achieve communication through practical strategies more dependent on extralinguistic context and the negotiation of shared meanings than on language (Gee, 1986a). This communication style does not lend itself easily to the task of becoming literate in yet another language—English.

Young deaf children of hearing parents do communicate with their parents, siblings, and other deaf peers, even though their command of a formal language system is not so developed as that of mainstream and hearing minority children. Nevertheless, the essential questions that need to be addressed by researchers and practitioners are basically the same: How do these children make meanings? What discourse styles and strategies do they use? How did they acquire these practices? Are they truly lacking in communication? And finally, what needs to be done to improve their communication skills and academic development?

These questions remain unanswered (and usually unasked) as the child begins school. There, the child is required to learn the English language, relatively unencountered up until then and difficult to access given the hearing impairment.

I will now suggest five very broad recommendations based on theoretical and pedagogical approaches, which have either proven successful or promise to be successful in the education of hearing minority children.

1. Exploit the full range of purposes for which language is used in any given speech community (Michaels, 1981; Heath, 1983). Research from within the field of deaf education has indicated strongly that methods representing the English language manually are difficult for deaf children to perceive and process (Supalla, 1986). Manually Coded English is the method most widely used in programs for deaf children nationwide (Moores, 1987). The question has been raised as to whether the structure of a spoken language can actually be incorporated into a sign medium (Supalla, 1986).

In addition, research has shown that deaf children, even those with limited exposure to native signers, create their own linguistic structures. These structures more closely resemble those found in native sign languages than the adult models that children are exposed to in their classrooms (Gee and Goodhart, 1985). This finding has been evidenced in at least two studies (Gee and Goodhart, 1985; Supalla, 1986). It is related to earlier work that sought to explain the emergence of sign systems—"home signs"—developed by deaf children even when peer interaction and adult signing models are severely restricted (Goldin-Meadow and Feldman, 1975).

The educational implications of these research efforts raise serious questions for educators. A major question is whether any of the methods currently used is adequate to serve the full range of purposes for which the English language is normally used, both in and out of school, and on which acquisition depends. Researchers need to shift the focus away from the deficiency of deafness toward the nature of spoken, written, and signed languages and the acquisitional processes relevant to each.

2. *Attempt to give equal value to many forms of discourse in the classroom as complementary ways of communicating, thinking, and acting* (Hymes, 1981; Wells, 1986). The almost exclusive focus on English language literacy in programs for deaf children is but another example of schooling that overemphasizes literacy in a majority language at the expense of other forms of discourse (Wells, 1986). Mainstream children come to school already relatively competent in the spoken language required of them in school, while minority children are deficient in this area (Scollon and Scollon, 1981; Michaels, 1981; Heath, 1983; Gee, 1987a). Wells (1986) recommends that schools evaluate the quality of teaching that takes place and reconsider the narrowly placed value on literacy as the only way to learn in the primary curriculum.

Deaf children must be allowed to communicate by whatever means they have at their disposal and most certainly should be reinforced in their use of signed languages such as ASL, which are recognizable to linguists as being as complex and effective as any other natural language (Gee, 1983; Wilbur, 1988).

3. *Treat the acquisition of literacy similarly to the acquisition of a second language* (Gee, 1987b). Similar to many minority children, deaf children of both hearing and deaf parents tend not to have experienced meaning-making through reading and writing activities begun at home with their parents. Because the majority of their parents do not use ASL, they also have not experienced the ASL storytelling and other forms of narrative expression common in deaf families and within the deaf community (Padden and Humphries, 1988).

For deaf children of deaf parents, literacy acquisition is a two-step process. In their primary language socialization, deaf children of deaf parents learn to understand and participate in narrative experiences, which involve the sustained expression of ideas through the use of symbolic language. Experience with English language literacy thus requires a second step—familiarity with the particular forms and functions of English language use.

For deaf children of hearing parents, literacy acquisition involves a three-step process. First, these children must acquire a formal language system—ASL—for face-to-face communication. Then more literate forms of ASL, followed by English language literacy, can be introduced.

How might literate forms of ASL be introduced into the language arts curriculum? Videotaping in the classroom can provide meaningful, functional experiences for children in "literate" language use. In this way, videotaping can be made analogous to reading and writing. Young deaf children should be given opportunities to "read" and "write" tapes in much the same way as hearing children learn to read and write written stories. They also can critique their own and other's narratives, and compare them across genres and even across languages, once they have acquired sufficient competencies in English.

Research by Gee (1987a, 1986a), Michaels (1981), Heath (1983) and Wells (1986) warns against focusing merely on the language of instruction in the curriculum. That strategy will not in itself ensure the kind of success deaf children deserve. Deaf children, like minority hearing children, must also acquire the mainstream discourse strategies and styles that embody middleclass, school-based literacy practices. These styles value explicitness and social detachment over meanings expressed through face-to-face interactions (Gee, 1986a).

Given the environments in which deaf children acquire their primary language systems, including ASL, practice with "literate" language use is limited. The problem for educators, then, is to produce an environment more conducive to the acquisition of mainstream discourse practices, including school-based literacy, while also valuing other forms of discourse and cultural expression (Wells, 1986; Heath, 1983).

4. *Emphasize guided peer interaction and learning, and exploit the resources of the community as well* (Heath, 1983; Wells, 1986). Teachers of deaf children need to emphasize one-to-one and small group learning situations where interactions can be similar to those of mothers with their normally developing hearing children. In this way, participants can arrive at mutual understanding in a supportive environment (Wells, 1986).

More accomplished deaf peers and deaf adult community members are essential to this process. For example, many deaf adults are skilled at communicating with deaf children from a wide variety of linguistic and social backgrounds. Such individuals are best equipped to communicate with and further develop the linguistic and academic potential of deaf children.

5. *Consider fully the social context of literacy and schooling for any dominated minority group* (Trueba, 1987; Cummins, 1986; Ogbu and Matute-Bianchi, 1986). Do deaf children resist acquiring the language and social norms of hearing society, which has historically sought to suppress the young child's natural desire to communicate in a visual/manual mode? The notion of a "discourse" as an ideological and theoretical concept (Gee, 1987a) may be useful as a starting point in seeking to answer this question. Gee defines a discourse as "a socially accepted association among ways of using language, of thinking, and of acting that can be used to identify oneself as a member of a socially meaningful group or social network" (Gee, 1987a).

Conclusions

In the context of deaf education, it is necessary to get back to the most essential questions: What is language? What is literacy? How are language and literacy acquired and developed? And, what kinds of language and literacy socialization provide optimal support for deaf children? The implications drawn from the hearing minority literature provide recommendations for a variety of theoretical and pedagogical approaches in the education of deaf children.

This research also suggests the need to reconsider the practice of mainstreaming because it segregates deaf children from each other and from their community, thereby limiting their social, linguistic, and overall development. The refusal to consider the implications of viewing deaf children as different rather than as deficient have been profound for deaf education. Deaf children of hearing parents, particularly, cannot participate fully in a completely accessible linguistic community and culture unless they are schooled with other deaf peers and adult role models.

Many deaf community members themselves are very active in deaf pride movements, lobbying efforts, and other local, state, and international activities to promote equal rights and opportunities for deaf individuals. Teachers of deaf students also must become advocates for children and families. They must make these struggles visible to deaf children in order to enhance deaf children's self-esteem and encourage the development of leadership skills.

The current focus on education, linguistics, psychology, and anthropology in reformulating our understanding of language and literacy development goes hand-in-hand with reformulations of deafness. This kind of change promises to lead to a more profound understanding of the problems deaf children face in developing reading, writing, and communication skills. This focus also can be used to direct the energies of researchers and practitioners—together with the deaf community—toward the development of a more theoretically sound and culturally appropriate language arts curriculum for deaf children.

While there is no proof these alternate conceptions and methods of teaching language and literacy to deaf children will be successful, evidence abounds for the failure of present approaches. Processes of language acquisition and development are universal for all children, hearing and deaf, regardless of language modality. At the same time, the fact of deafness offers both constraints—in terms of speech—and limitless possibilities for language development.

These possibilities deserve recognition, renewed research efforts, and a commitment to design model educational environments that benefit those deaf children whose use of language is radically different from that of their hearing parents and teachers.

References

Baker, C., and R. Battison. 1980. *Sign Language and the Deaf Community: Essays in Honor of William C. Stokoe*. Silver Spring, MD: National Association of the Deaf.

Baker, C., and D. Cokely. 1980. *American Sign Language: A Teacher's Resource Text on Language and Culture*. Silver Spring, MD: T.J. Publishers, Inc.

Charrow, V., and R. Wilbur. 1975. "The Deaf Child as a Linguistic Minority." *Theory into Practice* 14 (5): 353–359.

Cummins, J. 1986. "Empowering Minority Students: A Framework for Intervention." *Harvard Education Review* 56 (1): 18–35.

Gee, J. P. 1986. "Orality and Literacy: From the Savage Mind to Ways with Words." *TESOL Quarterly* 20: 719–746.

Gee, J. P. 1987a. "What is Literacy?" Paper presented at the Mailman Foundation Conference on Families and Literacy. Harvard Graduate School of Education, Cambridge, MA, March 6–7.

Gee, J. P. 1987b. "Dracula, The Vampire Lestat, and TESOL." Paper presented at the Plenary Session of the Fall MATSOL Conference, Medford, MA, to appear in *TESOL Quarterly*.

Gee, J. P., and W. Goodhart. 1985. "Nativization, Linguistic Theory, and Deaf Language Acquisition." *Sign Language Studies* 49: 291–342.

Goldin-Meadow, S., and H. Feldman. 1975. "The Creation of a Communication System: A Study of Deaf Children of Hearing Parents." *American Annals of the Deaf* 3 (5): 510–522.

Heath, S. B. 1983. *Ways with Words: Language, Life and Work in Communities and Classrooms*. Cambridge, England: Cambridge University Press.

Hymes, D. 1981. *"In Vain I Tried to Tell You": Essays in Native American Ethnopoetics*. Philadelphia: University of Pennsylvania Press.

Lane, H. 1984. *When the Mind Hears: A History of the Deaf.* New York: Random House.

Michaels, S. 1981. " 'Sharing Time': Children's Narrative Styles at Home and at School." *Anthropology and Education Quarterly* 18 (4).

Moores, D. 1987. *Educating the Deaf: Psychology, Principles, and Practices.* 3d ed. Boston: Houghton Mifflin Company.

Ogbu, J., and M. E. Matute-Bianchi. 1986. "Understanding Socio-cultural Factors: Knowledge, Identity, and School Adjustment." In *Beyond Language: Social and Cultural Factors in Schooling Language Minority Students.* Sacramento, CA: Bilingual Education Office. pp. 73–142.

Padden, C., and T. Humphries. 1988. *Deaf in America: Voices from a Culture.* Cambridge: Harvard University Press.

Reagan, T. in press. "Multiculturalism and the Deaf: An Educational Manifesto." *Journal of Research and Development in Education* 21 (2).

Reagan, T. 1985. "The Deaf as a Linguistic Minority." *HER* 55 (3).

Scollon, R., and S. B. K. Scollon. 1981. *Narrative, Literacy and Face in Interethnic Communication.* Norwood, NJ: Ablex Publishing Corporation.

Stokoe, W. 1978. *Sign Language Structure.* A revised edition from 1960 monograph. Silver Spring, MD: Linstok Press.

Supalla, S. 1986. "Manually Coded English: The Modality Question in Signed Language Development." Unpublished master's thesis, Graduate College of the University of Illinois at Urbana-Champaign.

Trueba, H. T. 1987. *Success or Failure? Learning and the Language Minority Student.* Cambridge: Newbury House Publishers.

Vernon, M., and B. Makowsky. 1969. "Deafness and Minority Group Dynamics." *The Deaf American* 21 (11): 3–6.

Wells, G. 1986. *The Meaning Makers: Children Learning Language and Using Language to Learn.* Portsmouth: Heinemann Press.

Wilbur, R. 1987. *American Sign Language: Linguistic and Applied Dimensions.* 2d ed. Boston: Little, Brown, and Company.

Woodward, J. 1982. *How You Gonna Get to Heaven If You Can't Talk With Jesus: On Depathologizing Deafness.* Silver Spring, MD: T.J. Publishers, Inc.

Trends in the Progress Toward Bilingual Education for Deaf Children in Denmark

BRITTA HANSEN

The linguistic situation in the Danish deaf community is very complex. Although in recent years deaf people have defined themselves as a linguistic minority, with Danish Sign Language (DSL) as their primary language and Danish as their second language, no deaf person actually masters the spoken language fluently. The bilingualism we find in the deaf community will always be different from the bilingualism we may find among hearing people, owing to deaf people's inevitable handicap of not being able to hear, lipread, or even speak the majority culture's language with a great degree of fluency.

So, however idealistic we might be when setting up the goals for the bilingual education of deaf children, we will—in order to respect the identity of any deaf person—also have to modify our expectations and teaching methods when it comes to teaching deaf children a second language that was developed for a sense they do not have.

Our definition of a bilingual deaf adult must, therefore, exclude the requirement of being able to speak a language. We call deaf people bilingual if they are fluent signers of DSL and able to read and write the Danish language. Bilingual deaf persons will be able to use whichever language they feel most comfortable with. When they converse with deaf friends or hearing people who know DSL, they will use this language. When they converse with hearing people, they might write Danish on paper, speak and listen through an interpreter, or use speech if it is intelligible. When communicating with hearing people who speak and sign at the same time, they might choose to use a pidgin form of DSL, which is very different from the native DSL, but more intelligible to the hearing person because this pidgin form relies heavily upon the Danish spoken language. So most deaf people function linguistically on a continuum ranging from the use of pure DSL, through use of pidgin forms that are mixtures of DSL and Danish, to the use of Danish spoken or written language.

When it comes to using the Danish language in both its spoken and written forms, however, most deaf adults have severe problems. Research by the British psychologist R. Conrad (1979) showed that 30 percent of the deaf fifteen- and sixteen-year-olds who

---

A revised version of this paper, which was originally presented at The Deaf Way, was later presented at the International Congress on Sign Language Research and Application, March 23–25, 1990, in Hamburg. That version has been printed in *Sign Language Research and Application*, edited by Siegmund Prillwitz and Tomas Vollhaber, 1990, Hamburg, Germany: SIGNUM-Press.

left school were illiterate, and less than 10 percent could read at an appropriate age level. Their lipreading abilities were equally unsatisfactory, and only one-fourth of all students had speech that could be understood by their own teachers.

We have also seen these alarming results in Denmark during the years when classroom teaching was carried out using mainly the monolingual approach.

Teachers have struggled, but they have never been able to teach the average deaf child the language of the majority to anything near a level satisfactory for daily communication with hearing people. As a result, deaf people have not acquired the social, cognitive, and academic skills to become fully integrated members of society. They have been excluded and isolated, their potential neglected, because the educational system has focused primarily on their disability and not on their strengths. They have become stigmatized as individuals and as a group.

From Total Communication to Bilingualism

In the late 1960s, changes started occurring within the education of deaf students in Denmark. Total Communication, or the Simultaneous Method, using Danish spoken language supported by visual means such as signs, fingerspelling, and the mouth-hand system (a phonetic aid to help lipreading and articulation) was introduced in some of the early intervention programs and most of the schools for deaf students. It soon became *the* method of teaching deaf children language, as well as social and academic skills. Parents and teachers generally claimed that their communication with the deaf children improved tremendously. Suddenly through visual means, deaf children were able to take part in conversations—and they were able to communicate their questions, emotions, and needs through an individually created linguistic system.

However, although the communication between deaf children and their surrounding hearing community improved drastically, their Danish skills did not improve to the same extent—and they continued to communicate among themselves and with deaf adults in a sign system completely different from the one the hearing parents and teachers used, a system the teachers and parents could not understand.

In the early 1970s, the Center for Total Communication started conducting research into deaf children's mutual signed communication and the sign language used by deaf adults. Our results showed that this visual system of gestures was actually a language in its own right with phonological, morphological, and syntactic rules. As a result of our research, we published dictionaries, teaching tapes, and books. We set up intensive week-long and weekend courses to introduce DSL to teachers and parents. Also, we were asked by teachers of deaf students to evaluate what they actually did while communicating through the simultaneous use of spoken language and signs. Our findings questioned the whole concept of teaching deaf children through a monolingual approach, even if this approach now included the addition of signs and other visual clues.

We taped the teachers' signed and spoken communication, and later presented the tapes to them without sound—just as it must have been for the deaf children. More often than not they could not fully understand their own simultaneous communication when the sound was turned off. They realized that although they believed that they were conveying the Danish language to the children using a sign for every word and some grammatical signals to convey grammatical patterns such as inflection, time, and plurality, they never did this consistently. Producing a sign takes longer than producing a spoken word so, to keep up the normal speed of speech, they omitted signs and pertinent grammatical visual clues.

The children did not get a visual version of Danish; instead, they got a very inconsistent linguistic input, where quite often they understood neither the signs nor the spoken words. They tended to become "half lingual," mixing the two languages in order to communicate, but they had no idea where one language ended and the other began.

During the past ten years, the recognition of these problems, combined with our new knowledge and acceptance of DSL as a minority language, has enabled parents and teachers to become increasingly aware of the potential of DSL for enhancing deaf children's development of cognitive, linguistic, social, and academic skills.

The First Experimental Bilingual Approach—1982

The first experimental class to attempt a bilingual approach was established in Copenhagen in 1982 with seven deaf and two hard of hearing six-year-old children. It was the parents who promoted the idea of bilingualism, wanting their children to have DSL as their first language, or "mother tongue," and Danish as their second language, or "their first foreign language." They wanted the two languages used separately, but with equal status in the classroom. The school agreed, and four teachers committed themselves to the experiment, two of them skilled but not native DSL signers, one a deaf native signer, and one skilled in the use of Simultaneous Communication but wanting to learn and use DSL.

The Center for Total Communication was involved in the experiment in several ways. We set up courses in DSL for the teachers and parents, we evaluated the children's and the teachers' sign language usage and development, and we helped produce teaching tapes in DSL.

What Kind of Communication Did the Children Use when the Project Started in 1982?

Two of the children had parents who signed DSL, and they mastered DSL in a way comparable to hearing children of the same age using spoken Danish. Both of them code-switched to Signed Danish if necessary when communicating with hearing adults or with some of their deaf friends who knew only this way of communicating. Most of the other children communicated by means of spoken Danish supported by signs, a simultaneous approach that had been their main means of communication with their hearing parents. A few did not know Danish at all, so they could not communicate very well using a simultaneous approach; furthermore, they did not sign DSL at an age-appropriate level. They communicated mainly through a very basic way of signing, using pantomime supplemented with a few Danish words.

Although most of the parents recognized that they communicated with their child using Simultaneous Communication, they all wanted DSL to be the primary language in the classroom and in teaching, because they understood that deaf adults who felt at ease with their visual language chose DSL as their main means of communication. The parents therefore concluded that using DSL in the classroom would support their children's educational, social, and cognitive development.

How Did the Teachers Cope with the Use of DSL?

The group of hearing teachers had been involved or interested in Danish Sign Language research. They knew that, for them, it was a "foreign" language, so they planned to get DSL support from a deaf teaching assistant, as well as from the children themselves, especially those who had parents who signed DSL. In the teaching situations they worked at using Danish and DSL separately in order to make the children aware of the differences in usage and function between the two languages. They tried consciously to assign the same status to the two languages and acknowledge when the children expressed themselves using DSL creatively and precisely.

Not being native signers, they asked for evaluations of their own DSL signing skills through videotapes of their signing that they presented to the Center for Total Communication. These evaluations resulted in some teaching of DSL to the teachers, but more importantly, they resulted in the teachers' total acceptance of not being able to be "adult models of DSL." Ever since, the project has had deaf adults involved in the teaching and production of teaching tapes.

How Did the Parents Cope with This New Approach?

Although they had agreed to the same ideology, the parents were not a homogenous group. Several parents continued using Simultaneous Communication at home because it was the easiest and most functional means of communicating within a hearing family. But others slowly changed their style of communication into more DSL-like signing. They took courses in DSL developed especially for them as a group by the Center for Total Communication. Because their signing skills were very different, we used videotapes of their own children's signing during the courses, which proved to be a very beneficial approach. Studying the spontaneous signing of their own child proved to be very motivating in furthering their own understanding of DSL.

The parents began to organize special group events, such as camping trips, and engaged deaf adults as assistants. They also arranged activities where their deaf children could meet other age groups of deaf children and adults.

Was It a Bilingual Education Situation?

The parents wanted their children to be bilingual, using DSL as their primary language but also mastering written and spoken Danish. However, the children's linguistic capacities in DSL, spoken Danish, and Signed Danish were different. In order to develop DSL as the children's primary and common language, most of the teaching time at the beginning of the project was devoted to the acceptance, usage, and learning of this language.

The parents were impatient and wanted it all to happen at the same time. They wanted more teaching of spoken and written Danish. Through meetings, the language problems in the educational process were discussed and explained, and a consensus was reached: "We trust that the DSL-approach will give our children the best opportunity to also learn Danish, and we must accept that it takes some time for the group of children to develop DSL skills at a reasonably equal level."

The program started out primarily concentrating on DSL as the target language, shifting slowly during the first two years into a more bilingual approach, with Danish as an equally important part of the teaching curriculum. The group changed only slightly during the first few years. One of the hard of hearing children left the group after the first year because her parents, who were deaf themselves, found that she could function adequately in a hearing school thanks to the support of deaf adult resources at home. This child was successfully integrated until 1988, spending most of her leisure time with the other deaf children and deaf adults. She is now back in the group because she and her parents found that at her present age she will benefit more from the bilingual program.

How Did the Children Communicate in DSL?

Seven of the nine children did not communicate in DSL when they started school. Some preferred to communicate through Signed Danish or spoken Danish. Clearly, the children who quickly developed or already knew DSL became the most popular "storytellers" or communicators in general, whereas the children who spoke Danish had problems being "listened to" by the other children. On the other hand, the teachers found it difficult not to react faster and more spontaneously to the Danish-speaking children, simply because at the beginning of the process they understood them better. As they say themselves in the reports they have published, sound is very powerful for hearing people.

There has been continuous and dramatic progress in the children's general ability to communicate since they started the program. Today DSL has become the primary language of all the children, and it is used as the common means of communication when they are together and when specific topics are being taught or discussed in the classroom. Still, an interesting pattern has been noticed. During their leisure time, the children who from the start mastered Danish rather well tended to stick together, and the children who signed fluently still tended to be the storytellers.

When they communicate with their parents, all the children whose parents cannot sign DSL code-switch. The parents have not felt any rejection from their children owing to their lack of DSL-signing skills.

Evaluations of the Children's Sign Language

The teachers have asked the Center to evaluate the children's sign language development. The first time we received videotapes with the children's retelling of cartoons, we found that two of the children communicated in DSL at an age-appropriate level, but that the rest had problems coping with the grammar of DSL and with an appropriate sign vocabulary. Most of the children either spoke Danish supported by signs in a way that was too communicatively restricted to catch the receiver's interest, whether deaf or hearing, or they communicated in a loose pantomime type of signing that was far below their age level.

The last time we evaluated their DSL skills—at that time the children were eight to nine years old—a radical change had occurred. Seven of the children now signed DSL fluently, and only one—although her DSL skills had improved tremendously—still did not sign at an age-appropriate level. All of the children showed an increase in vocabulary and could tell a story without searching for signs. They were also able to show that they knew the grammar of DSL to such a degree that deaf adults could follow their communication. We have diagnosed some grammatical patterns that seem to be difficult for most of the children at this level, such as the use of proforms, the more complicated patterns of movements, the use of facial expressions and body movements to modulate signs, and the use of topicalization.

Methodological Problems in the Evaluation of Children's Sign Lnguage

Most deaf children have hearing parents, and that means they tend to switch to a mixture of Danish and sign whenever they are placed in a situation with hearing teachers and researchers. Also very few researchers and teachers have the native feeling and understanding of DSL that will allow them to understand the variety and spontaneous subtlety we see in the children's language. Furthermore, the linguistic description of DSL vocabulary and grammar is still under way. And, finally, we have no model of the stages of sign language acquisition. How did we cope with these problems, and what did we learn?

The Material

The first attempts to evaluate the children's sign language were based on their retelling of cartoons to a teacher. Because most of the children's signing at that time was rather primitive, we did not find serious methodological problems in using cartoons as an input. We discussed the performance of each child with the teachers, trying to find points where we thought that the children could benefit from conscious support. For example, one child used one hand configuration for almost all signs; several others performed the retelling through pantomime rather than DSL; and others tried to retell it all in Danish.

When we got videotapes two years later, when the children were eight- and nine-year olds, we realized that there was a serious problem in analyzing their language from their retelling of an animated film. They told the story to a deaf assistant teacher with whom they were used to communicating. That meant that they did not code-switch to a "hearing" kind of signing. Their sign language performance, though, was far below what we knew they had mastered in daily conversation.

Therefore, we recognized that what we saw was not how the children had actually mastered DSL, but how they signed in this specific evaluation situation. At this older age level, for example, retelling a narrative did not motivate them.

Several of the children did not use simultaneous messages, that is, they did not use facial expressions and body movements as modulators for signs. One did not use gaze, pointing, or body movements to represent the protagonists of the story, but said "monkey says," "fireman says," and so on. He used a continual backward-forward movement that completely destroyed the normal rhythm of a monologue in DSL. Most of the children had problems developing the flow of the story. They did not use movements and holds to mark dramatically important events or changes from one setting or situation to another.

Seeing this, we realized that it is difficult to use the retelling of animated films to evaluate children's productive language skills. Most of the children's performances were very different from their ordinary communication and at a much lower level both linguistically and communicatively. Some of them did not take the care to give the story a rhythmic flow, while others had problems remembering the story, and still others played with the situation.

We then realized that placing eight- or nine-year-old children—hearing or deaf—in a situation where communication was restricted to retelling a story they had not chosen themselves did not motivate them to perform DSL at the level of their actual skills.

After we informed the teachers of this, they gave us tapes in which the children spontaneously told about their summer vacations. Analyzing those tapes—which was a much harder task for us—taught us that most of the children's problems with DSL in the retelling situation disappeared when they were put in a situation where they wanted to communicate their experiences to their peers. Then they performed linguistically at an age-appropriate level, except for the one child who seemed to have problems with DSL as well as Danish.

We could only make this evaluation because the staff of the Center includes people with knowledge of linguistics and language acquisition as well as knowledge and native understanding of DSL. Without a researcher who was a native signer, and without her insights into sign language and the children's daily communication, we would not have been able to do the evaluation at a professional level.

Hearing linguists and educational researchers usually do not know sign language well enough to understand what is actually being said by the children when they communicate spontaneously. Instead, they tend to set up "situations suitable for research," where the children must perform within a structured situation that does not bring out their actual linguistic and communicative competence. I see this as one of the very severe problems in the evaluation of deaf children's sign language development.

The Teaching of Danish as the Second Language

The first year of teaching, as mentioned above, concentrated on communication in DSL. In the second year, Danish was introduced as the children's first foreign language. Some of the children had excellent skills in Danish owing to early reading programs and/or some residual hearing. Others had no Danish skills at all. Therefore, they were split into groups for learning Danish.

Danish was taught using spoken language, written texts, speech correction, articulation exercises, speech/lipreading, fingerspelling, the Danish mouth-hand system, and training in intonation and speech rhythm. For example, sentences were written on the blackboard. The children read them aloud and then tried to translate the sentences into DSL. The translation did not concentrate on the transliteration of individual words, because those words gain their meaning from the way they are actually connected in the sentence. Instead, the translation was conceptual. This is the only way in which the teacher could know if the children had actually grasped the whole meaning. The grammar was then taught through DSL, because this was the language the children most easily understood. The sentences were then repeated during the following days in natural communication, using spoken Danish.

After the difficult sentences had been explained, the children tried to read a whole story on their own. The teacher then asked them questions in Danish about the story and expected them to answer in Danish—either spoken only or supplemented with fingerspelling, mouth-hand system, and individual signs.

If the children did not understand the questions in Danish, the teacher reformulated the question in Danish and finally translated the question into DSL, if necessary. Also the teacher explained the meanings of the words the children did not fully understand.

The children sometimes chose to play a game. They all put their hands below the table, and then they communicated with each other in spoken language. They enjoyed this very much, and they became very creative in setting up communicative issues and situations they could handle successfully.

Danish used as a language separate from DSL was also supported by use of the

Phonic Ear system. It was only turned on in the Danish lessons to make the children aware of the different modes in which the two languages are conveyed.

Today the classroom is a "normal" classroom where topics are taught in the children's native language, as well as a laboratory for acquiring skills in Danish. The children constantly ask, "What is this in Danish?" and they force the teachers to conduct more and more of the teaching in Danish supported by signs or other visual means.

Articulated speech is now one of the aims of several of the children. They want to be able to speak, but they will not feel inferior as human beings if the teachers tell the children their pronunciation is neither correct nor intelligible.

Results of the Bilingual Approach

The children's reading skills have improved tremendously compared to what we used to see in the education of deaf students generally. Whereas 10 to 15 percent of deaf children used to learn to read for meaning, we now see 55 percent of them being able to do this at the age of twelve. That means that 55 percent read Danish at an age-appropriate level.

Twenty-two percent can read at a transitional stage, where they search for the meaning of individual words, idioms, and certain grammatical structures. This group is expected to develop their reading skills to an age-appropriate level before leaving school. The remaining 23 percent read as signal readers: They tend to grasp one word out of several and through that try to understand the whole message. Before the bilingual approach, more than 56 percent of the deaf children left school as signal readers. This radical improvement in the children's reading skills is one very important result of the bilingual teaching program.

Also, the students' lipreading skills have improved, simply because they now know so much more of the Danish language. However, their spoken language skills have not improved so radically owing to the very different problems involved in the production of sounds the deaf child cannot hear or control.

What is even more important is the children's development of cognitive, social, and academic skills. They can communicate about the world and control their own daily lives through linguistic means, which include discussions of what is right and wrong, and why. They have the power to influence what is going to happen to them. They can argue and understand an argument, sometimes to an extent that is as subtle and irritating as it is with hearing children, provoking adults into new areas of explanation and thinking.

They are not ashamed of using DSL openly, and neither are their parents. They are proud of what they can do with their language and also very curious about what hearing people can do with theirs. Some of them recently wrote a letter of complaint to the Danish television network saying that DSL should be used in the programs for deaf people instead of simultaneous spoken and signed language. They can diagnose when a person is not skilled in DSL and relies on pidgin variations, and they discuss among themselves whether this person is "okay" or "not okay."

They know about some of the differences between spoken Danish and written Danish, and they accept their situation as deaf people in a hearing society. They are the first group of deaf children actually to question the way they are approached by hearing people, while, at the same time, accepting that they are different.

Consequences of the Bilingual Experiments in the Early 1980s

Since the first experimental group so clearly proved that a bilingual approach was generally more successful than any other teaching ideology we have tried in Denmark, a radical change has taken place. The bilingual approach is now accepted by the Ministry of Education, by schools for deaf students, and by the parents' association.

Most parents of deaf children start learning DSL when their child is diagnosed as deaf. Not all of them become equally skilled in this language, but they accept DSL as their child's "mother tongue." Therefore, the parents try to compensate for their lack of fluency in DSL by giving the preschool child opportunities to be with other deaf children and adults. The teachers are struggling to become proficient users of Danish Sign Language and the children benefit from this positive attitude, which clearly can be measured in their sign language competence when entering school. Today deaf children, on the average, enter school with the same grasp of language as hearing children.

At the time of the first bilingual experiment, our linguistic analysis revealed that within the first years, students reached linguistic and cognitive skills appropriate to their age. Today, we see deaf children entering school with still better cognitive and linguistic skills.

We have realized that we still do not fully know what "age-appropriate sign language competence" is, because deaf children seemingly acquire an increasingly higher level of skills owing to the improved linguistic input they get from their surroundings.

The Latest Project: DSL as a Topic in the Education of Deaf Students

The latest project in which the Center is involved is concerned with how to teach sign language as a topic in the educational curriculum for deaf children—a topic equivalent in status to Danish, geography, or physics. We have set up a twenty-four-week teaching program for a group of seven-year-old deaf children. The teacher, a deaf kindergarten teacher, has been working for three years with sign language research and teaching at the Center for Total Communication.

The program includes an analysis of the children's sign language competence based on two video recordings in which they retell a film and another in which they spontaneously tell stories to their peers in the group. This analysis is presented to the teachers in order to make them aware of the children's standards of signing. Parents have the opportunity to discuss the evaluation as well. Furthermore, a teacher training program is included, in which the teachers have their signing evaluated, followed up by some sign language teaching sessions.

The children enjoy this sign language teaching, which is mainly storytelling, games, "grammatical" exercises, or topics for discussion such as, "What can hearing people hear?" all done in DSL.

This approach is also experimentally included in some other teaching programs. One of the problems, though, is that the hearing teachers do not have sufficient training in DSL and, therefore, have to depend on a limited number of video recordings of deaf people telling stories. An important issue for the coming years is to establish a higher standard of DSL for teachers as well as for students within the schools for deaf students.

References and Suggested Reading

Conrad, R. 1979. *The Deaf Schoolchild: Language and Cognitive Function*. London: Harper and Row.

Hansen, B. 1986. "Døves Tosprogethed." *Skolepsykologi* 4: 396–409.

Hansen, B. 1987. "Sign Language and Bilingualism." In *Sign and School*, ed. J. Kyle. Philadelphia: Multilingual Matters Ltd.

Kjær Sørensen, R., and B. Hansen. 1976. *The Sign Language of Deaf Children in Denmark*. København: Døves Center for Total Kommunikation.

Kjær Sørensen, R., W. Lewis, H. Lütz, and J. Sønnichsen. 1983. *To-sproget Døveundervisning*. Copenhagen: Københavns Kommunale Skolevæsen.

Kjær Sørensen, R., W. Lewis, H. Lütz, and T. Ravn. 1984. *To-sproget Døveundervisning*. 2. Copenhagen: Københavns Kommunale Skolevæsen.

Kjær Sørensen, R., W. Lewis, H. Lütz, and T. Ravn. 1988. *To-sproget Døveundervisning*. 3. Copenhagen: Københavns Kommunale Skolevæsen.

Vestberg Rasmussen, P. 1983. *Undervisning af Hørehæmmede Børn*. Aalborg: Døveskolernes Materialelaboratorium.

Improving Sign Language Skills of Hearing Teachers: A Swedish Experiment

CHRISTINA EDENAS

Throughout much of this century, a central question debated internationally has been the place of sign language in schools for deaf people. We would like to think we're winning the battle for more instructional use of sign language. If we look at the situation globally, many, if not most, schools for the deaf now use some sort of signing in the classroom. And in some countries more skilled deaf signers are now finding professional roles in deaf classrooms, as teachers, counselors, and trainers.

But most of today's teachers are hearing, and many of them lack sufficient fluency in sign language. This is a simple demographic reality. So one of the central questions of deaf education for the next twenty to thirty years will be: How do we improve the sign language communication skills of hearing teachers?

Attacking the problem at its source, sign language training during teacher training is certainly part of the answer. On-the-job training by being paired with a skilled deaf signer is certainly another. But where these alternatives are lacking, or cannot be implemented, the standard answer is continuing education classes in sign language. By "continuing education in sign language" I mean formal classroom training in sign language, taught by deaf students or former students either in the hours immediately after work or in the evenings.

Although there have been great advances recently in the quality of sign language textbooks, as well as in the linguistic and pedagogic techniques that can be employed in the classroom, these methods of improving sign language skills are limited. Could we be missing something? Are there any alternative methods?

Goals of a Study

In 1988, the Swedish Board of Education (a national organization) solicited proposals on the topic of methods to improve teachers' sign language skills. I subsequently conducted a six-month pilot study of the subject. My objectives were as follows:

❖ To evaluate individual teachers' needs for improvement in both sign language skills and communication skills.

The author of this paper wishes to thank Robbin Battison for his invaluable assistance in the paper's preparation.

❖ To examine how these skills (or lack of them) affect classroom management and instructional techniques.

❖ To record classroom instruction and interaction on videotape for the above purposes.

❖ To explore the potential value of individual communication tutorials for sign language analysis, counseling, and instruction.

Setting

Because the setting for this study differs from those in most other countries, let's begin with some facts about Sweden as a country. Sweden has a population of about 8.6 million people, roughly 8,000 of whom are deaf. Of these 8,000, approximately 550 are students between the ages of seven and sixteen These students are all subject to a national school system with special language policies I will describe in a moment.

The school in which I work, the Manilla School in Stockholm, was founded in 1809. It was formerly a residential school, but students now travel daily to school from as far away as seventy-five miles (120 kilometers).

Classrooms are most often handled by a team of two teachers, either coteachers or a teacher plus an assistant. The teacher-student ratio is about one to five in an average class. Unlike what is done in many other countries, teachers in Sweden usually work with the same group of students for several years. But specialized teachers do teach such subjects as art or physical education to students of a variety of ages.

Deaf adults do not form a large presence at the school. Although all 120 students are deaf, only ten of the fifty-five teachers are. (This total includes part-time, as well as full-time teachers.) Of the five administrators, none is deaf, and of twenty-one support staff, only six are deaf.

Education and Communication: National Policy and Practice

The educational system in Sweden is national, and standards and practices are determined and enforced centrally. All schools for the deaf fall under this system; there are no private schools for the deaf.

In 1982, a new national curriculum mandated bilingual education as a key element in deaf education. "Bilingual" education does not mean simultaneous signing and speaking, but systematic exposure to both Swedish Sign Language (SSL) and Swedish (signed, written, and spoken). Another element of this national curriculum is that all deaf students, regardless of country of origin or family circumstances, are deemed to have SSL as their first language.

As indicated earlier, beyond the sign language offered in basic teacher training, continuing education in sign language has only been offered in a single format—group classes. This format, however, has two disadvantages. First, there is naturally a broad range of signing ability among the various teachers taking a given sign language class. Second, the appropriateness and effectiveness of such instruction is limited when, as in the case of Sweden, there are no regular observations or evaluations of teachers' classroom techniques or communication skills. No explicit connection is made in the sign language classes between teachers' communication difficulties on the job and their needs for sign language instruction. Furthermore, of the seven schools for the deaf in Sweden, only two have a full-time sign language instructor.

Another problematical fact is that members of most school communities in Sweden have only infrequent exposure to professional interpreters at the school. The government-run interpreter coordination offices prioritize the placement of interpreters in social service, legal, and medical settings—not in school settings. It is not uncommon for teachers and administrators to double as interpreters during staff meetings, parent conferences, and public presentations with visitors, despite the psychological burden, the potential conflicts of interest, and the lack of professional training as interpreters.

Finally, we must consider that the ultimate goal of evaluation is to give feedback and to improve performance. In its extreme form, sign language evaluation may detect a teacher who cannot communicate effectively enough in sign language to perform his or her duties. However, there is no legal way in Sweden to remove an incompetent teacher.

Data Gathering and Discussion Methods

All participants in this study were guaranteed anonymity, which means that only group data are reported. When specific examples are cited later in the results section, identifying details are always obscured.

The eight participants in this pilot study were all volunteers, who received no special compensation for their cooperation. Their range of teaching experience was from five to fifteen years, and they currently work about twenty-four to twenty-nine classroom hours per week. Their students ranged in age from nine to seventeen.

Each participant was subject to fifteen to twenty minutes of videotaping in his or her classroom, either weekly or biweekly. At a later session, I sat with each participant for joint viewing and discussion. Including both the videotaping and discussion sessions, there were a total of three to six sessions per individual participant. Overall, I spent 190 hours videotaping, discussing, and tutoring during this pilot project.

In cooperative, exploratory sessions with the teachers, we developed a "main method" and several variants to help the teachers improve sign language skills, according to their own expressed improvement goals. We focussed on qualitative, not quantitative data.

The main method was for the tutor to view the tapes alone and make notes, looking for things to praise because they are hard to do, as well as items to correct or question. The next step of this approach was for the participant to view the tapes with the tutor, then discuss both the praiseworthy and problematical items.

One variant method was designed to improve teachers' comprehension of student signing. Students were videotaped under two distinct conditions. In one session, students were asked to give informal presentations, adjusting their signing as they normally would to adapt to the teacher's signing. In another session, the students were videotaped while signing to each other in a group, using whatever slang or language level they would naturally use in a discussion among deaf peers, without the constraint of worrying about a teacher's ability to understand. Then the tutor and teacher view the tapes repeatedly, endeavoring to understand the students and to formulate questions about signing not understood. Finally, the tutor and teacher meet with the students to clarify items not understood on the tapes.

Another variant method was designed to focus more on teachers' expressive skills in sign language. Teachers were videotaped in a rehearsal of a lecture. The tutor and teacher then together critiqued the videotape. Later, the actual lecture was videotaped, and this tape also was viewed and discussed by both the tutor and the teacher.

Results

Results from these exercises and discussions were grouped into the following distinct categories: attitudes, use of voice, body posture, facial expressions, hand dominance, extralinguistic communication, and sign articulation and grammar.

Attitudes

These teachers had surprisingly low confidence in their signing abilities. In many cases, this project represented the first time they had viewed themselves on videotape, signing in their own classrooms. A typical reaction was initial embarrassment, followed by interest.

All of the participating teachers expressed a strong desire to improve their communication abilities. They felt the students weren't understanding them. They also felt they had limited opportunities to improve their skills. Participants noted that they had no problems in conversations with individual students (in which the students presumably adjusted their language), but they did seem to be afraid of long, open-ended group discussions. They said they would get "lost in the discussion;" they were afraid of losing control in their classrooms.

When I looked at the videotapes, I could see that the participants seemed to structure their classes in the following manner: a lecture, followed by a brief discussion, followed by a student work session. This structure clearly served, in part at least, to minimize the risk of longer discussions.

Use of Voice

As I stated earlier, the national policy embodied in our curriculum does not call for simultaneous communication, but bilingualism. In the Swedish context, this means systematic and comparative use of 1) Swedish Sign Language and 2) Signed, written, and spoken Swedish. Bilingualism does *not* mean speaking and signing simultaneously.

In light of the above policy, many teachers in this study tended to use their voice excessively, particularly those who worked with a hearing coteacher or assistant. Among other things, this simultaneous speaking and signing led to signing in Swedish word order rather than to signing that matched the morphology and syntax of Swedish Sign Language. This practice also led to the deletion of individual signs needed for visual comprehension, but omitted because the teacher had vocalized a word instead. Furthermore, emotions were being put into the voice, not into the signs and facial expressions where they belong.

Body Posture

I can offer two examples of how body posture affected communicative performance and effectiveness in this study.

One teacher characteristically led her class while sitting at a table. During our discussions, she complained of back strain and upper arm strain. Simply pointing out that she signed while leaning her arms on the table led to a more relaxed signing posture.

In several other cases, I counseled teachers who sit to limit that position to five minutes—not for their sakes but for their students' sake. It was my judgment that they were losing the attention of their students in some cases because it is simply monotonous and tiring to look at a signer who doesn't move.

Facial Expressions

I counseled several of the participants on correct use of facial expressions, and in several cases worked intensively with participants who seemed to have stereotyped facial expressions while signing. This kind of topic is hard to bring up with people you work with. Viewing the videotapes repeatedly, they eventually learned to recognize their own behavior and to modulate their facial expressions more appropriately.

Hand Dominance

In one of the most remarkable encounters I had, I noticed on the videotapes that one of the teachers seemed to have no dominant hand when she signed. Sometimes she signed like a righthander, and occasionally like a left-hander. She also reported that some signs were "hard to produce."

She was in fact left-handed, but it seems that ten years ago, her first sign language teacher had convinced her to sign as a right-handed person. In counseling her, I just said, "Feel free to use your left hand. Left-handed people do, you know." She began immediately to change her behavior and seemed relieved by this discovery that we made together, during our first session. She was excited by this revelation, which seemed to strengthen her self-confidence. If only every behavior were so easy to change!

Extralinguistic Communication

This category included all gestural and corporal behaviors that were communicative, but did not involve formal signing abilities. One example would be the methods teachers used to get their students' attention. Many waved their hands, rather ineffectually, at each of their students in turn. I taught them a technique of making a brief, sharp, waving movement, followed by a pause, which tends to synchronize the students' behavior in directing eye-gaze towards the teacher. This approach not only required less physical effort, it was also easy to learn and quickly gave the teachers a more appropriately authoritative appearance.

Sign Articulation and Grammar

When you think of improving sign language and communication skills, you perhaps think of improving the production of individual signs, choosing the right sign, or getting the grammar right for a particular communication situation. Such an approach, however, was not the focus of this study. Although some such adjustments were suggested, my main effort was to point out the principles underlying certain kinds of errors, so that teachers could proceed on their own to find ways to make further adjustments.

For example, several of the teachers who were otherwise capable and fluent signers did not seem aware that they were signing in Swedish word order until I pointed this out to them. Also, I learned from discussing the videotapes with the teachers that in cases where individual signs had been learned incorrectly, they were often taken into the classroom setting and never corrected. Although several of the teachers said that they had expected their students to correct their signs, it was quite obvious from well-established errors and faulty productions that the children (especially the very young children) did not correct the mistaken signs, but simply adapted to them. The teachers, in turn, became blind to their own mistakes. Although the teachers needed to learn how to produce many signs correctly, my role was primarily to diagnose the source of the problem and suggest ways the teachers could acquire reliable feedback outside of the classroom.

Recommendations to School Administrators

❖ Team-teaching assignments should take into account how coteachers will influence each other's communication development.

❖ A role should be created for "Sign Language Communication Consultants" in today's schools for the deaf. These individuals should be skilled signers (deaf or hearing) with advanced linguistic knowledge, classroom experience, and personalities suited to evaluating and training peer teachers.

Recommendations for Sign Language Teaching

❖ Strive to ensure that students' first impressions of sign language are valid. It is hard to change later.

❖ Stress the importance of integrating appropriate facial expressions and body posture with signs.

❖ Give teachers practice communicating with the age group they are actually working with; don't limit their sign language instruction to the signing of deaf adults.

Recommendations for Sign Language Research

❖ Investigate sign language use in the complete context of its use, rather than in isolation.

❖ Investigate causes and possible remedies for nonfluency in practical settings.

❖ Investigate the physical and psychological relationships among communication skills, working conditions, and job stress. After all, signing is hard work!

A Deaf Teacher and a Hearing Researcher Collaborating: From ASL to English in a Kindergarten Classroom

KATHLEENA M. WHITESELL, AND GLENDA ZMIJEWSKI

I t is Tuesday, a warm spring day in North Carolina. Mrs. Zmijewski (Mrs. Z), a deaf kindergarten teacher, her aide, and her five six-year-old deaf students have welcomed me into their kindergarten class for the week so I can study how the teacher communicates with the children.

They have just spent their morning in "playroom choices," with each child working with a variety of developmental learning materials, followed by "snack time," a period in which conversation is encouraged and initiated by both students and teacher. This conversation time is quite a feat, because this is the first year the class has been together. All of the children are prelingually deaf and have severe to profound hearing losses. They all sign to varying degrees; none has parents or family members who are fluent signers, and none has intelligible speech. Moreover, one little boy has only been in the class a few weeks and has been described as having severe behavior disorders.

Mrs. Z tells her students to gather their chairs in a semicircle around the screen in the front of the room. With all five chairs at arm's length from the teacher's chair and touching on each side, Mrs. Z motions and tells the aide to "go ahead." The filmstrip title "Susie, The Little Blue Coupe," and the subtitle "adapted from the Walt Disney motion picture of the same title," appear on the screen.

Mrs. Z begins speaking and signing/fingerspelling simultaneously: "S-U-S-I-E (gives name sign) the little blue C-O-U-P-E (car)." We share this signed and spoken rendition with you because the focus of this study became Mrs. Z's code-switching during the seventeen-minute segment of "Susie, The Little Blue Coupe" as she shared it with her students.

While examining the deaf teacher's code-switching communicative behavior, the following questions are addressed:

❖ Who should study sign language?

❖ What is the role of the deaf teacher-researcher in linguistic analysis?

❖ How and where should such research be carried out?

❖ Why is there a need for such research?

❖ What is the nature of one deaf teacher's code-switching behavior as she shares stories with her students?

This presentation describes the verbal and nonverbal components of the code-switching behavior of this deaf teacher with her kindergarten students during story-telling time. It is based upon naturalistic descriptive data obtained from videotape analysis. How this teacher makes transitions between English or English-like communication and ASL or ASL-like communication, and the seeming functions surrounding the code-switching behavior, are described.

It is important to note that the initial focus of our research was far more general: to look at Mrs. Z's classroom communication with her students during the course of a typical school week. Time and space do not permit us to share how we arrived at this particular focus from 150 pages of field notes, six hours and forty-eight minutes of videotape records, and twenty-one major activities. Suffice it to say that after working with several layers of data, we decided to microanalyze one week of Mrs. Z's storytelling time with her students.

How we sifted through all these data also must be left for another forum, but as we worked with the data, it became increasingly obvious that the teacher engaged her students during story time. She meaningfully communicated stories to them in a group setting, despite their various communication and literacy levels.

The storytelling events also were of interest because code-switching was occurring, which we felt might have some effect on the smooth flow of communication. Finally, because the benefits of storytelling have been widely documented, and it is a classroom event that cuts across all grade levels, we were eager to see how that was actually accomplished by at least one skillful communicator in a school setting with a group of deaf kindergartners.

We believe that such research should be conducted by a native signer and a person knowledgeable in communication, child language learning, and literacy learning. In this situation, the deaf teacher and the hearing researcher appeared to be sufficiently knowledgeable. We also met the criteria that such research should be done in as natural an environment as possible, one in which teacher and researcher have a trusting relationship. The only other needs were video equipment and the time and interest to engage in the tedious task of linguistic analysis of such records.

It was intriguing that once into the story, "Susie, The Little Blue Coupe," Mrs. Z seemed to be committed to giving her students access to the English written code by initially signing the English text and reading it as it appeared—in English. Then, when she felt some part of that English was not understood or needed clarification, she would code-switch into English-like, ASL-like, or ASL communication to define, reword, question, link, mark direct discourse, or intensify what she had just read in English. She did so fluidly, with no apparent breakdown in communication.

Looking at the sixty-one departures from the English text of the filmstrip, we began to see patterns in the code-switching. The departures were located where one might expect: They most frequently occurred at the end of a frame (thirty-five times or 57 percent); less frequently in the middle (sixteen times—26 percent), and least frequently at the beginning (ten times—17 percent). Five of those at the beginning were to mark the fact that a character was talking. The other five departures at the beginning were either to "intensify" or to "link" (provide inferencing). Patterns also could be seen in many of the forms used. For example, all departures to ask a question were done in English or English-like form. Marking discourse was predominantly English-like, while all intensifying was done using ASL or ASL-like forms.

What can we say qualitatively about the code-switching? We will try to answer that question by giving you a flavor of code-switching done to define a word or phrase, because that was the main reason for departing and thus code-switching. We will look at examples across the code-switching continuum from English-like, ASL-like, and ASL, both in the middle and at the end of the story.

Overall, departing from the story to give a definition occurred more times than departing for any other reason (twenty-five out of sixty-one times, or 42 percent of the departures). Such defining occurred thirteen times within frames and twelve times at the end of frames. The form generally used to accomplish the defining was ASL or ASL-like communication, followed by English-like communication.

English-Like Code Used to Define (Nine Overall)

Mrs. Z defined "owner" in frame 26, which read: "But her owner* decided he needed a new car."

She said and signed the first part (to the *) and then:

> Said: "the man who owned Susie"
> Signed: MAN WHO O-W-N-E-D S (name sign)

Another example of defining using an English-like code can be seen in defining "miracle" in frame 53, which read:

> Frame: It was like a miracle.
> Said: It was like a miracle same as magic.
> Signed (Off screen): SAMEMAGIC (nodding in the affirmative the entire time)

There were also three cases of departing to define using English-like coding that had to do with figurative language. That is, "fast company" in the sentence "She found herself in pretty fast company;" "look over" in "He looked Susie over very carefully;" and "big wheels" in "She met all the big wheels." One example is indicative of the others: the teacher defined "big wheels" in frame 13, which read:

> Frame: She met all the big wheels.
> Said: She met all the big wheels.
> Signed: S-H-E MEET ALL—
>   Nonverbal + superlative +
> Said: important car
> Signed: IMPORTANT CAR

Mrs. Z's other English-like definitions were similar to the ones described above. She signed and fingerspelled in English word order, generally she signed and spoke simultaneously, yet often with more words spoken than were signed.

ASL-Like Coding Used to Define (Six Overall)

This generally involved some voicing, which often began after the sign was articulated. Also, nonverbal movements such as facial expression were more pronounced than they were in the above English-like defining. Gaze was also important here.

ASL-like defining can be seen in frame 21 for "fading":

> Frame: Her color was fading
> Said: Now her color was fading.
> Signed: NOW HER COLOR WAS FADE
>   (no voice)
>   tongue protruding
>   gaze on signing hands

Then she:

> Said: Look dull
> Signed: LOOK-ED D-U-L-L

Additional examples of Mrs. Z's ASL-like defining indicated that she made substantially more use of space and used classifiers from time to time, two commonly used components of ASL not generally seen in more English-like signing. These characteristics were seen in defining "stripped her fenders" (frame 50) and in "shackled her down and hopped her up" (frame 51). We will look at the last one.

Once again, after providing the English-like rendition of the text, Mrs. Z departed after "up;" with no voice she gestured jacking up the car and then pointed and said, "up" as she gazed up as though looking at the imaginary car she had just jacked up in her signing space. While still looking up, she said and signed "FIX." From the "FIX" sign, her right index finger jutted down and, moving her eyes to that gesture/sign she said, "put her down." Last, she signed "FIX" but did not voice it, and then signed and voiced "WORK AROUND THE CAR"—gazing at those signs and then fleetingly at her students before looking back at the screen again. Most of the ASL-like signing was also done gazing at the signed objects in their signing space, with proportionately less time gazing at the students.

ASL Signing Used to Define (Ten Overall)

We will look at three examples of using ASL to define: "Suddenly lost control" (frame 41); "left out in the cold" (frame 31); and "oil ran dry" (frame 36).

After signing the English text, "as Susie sped through the streets she suddenly lost control," Mrs. Z proceeded to switch into ASL to define "lost control." Widening her eyes, sticking out her tongue, and shifting her upper torso from side to side as she looked down the imaginary street upon which her right classifier was swerving, one could readily envision Susie losing control.

In similar ASL fashion, with bent shaking "three" classifier handshapes (almost resembling the "hurt" sign), pursed lips, and eyes gazing at her sign, Mrs. Z leaned forward and rounded her shoulders over her shaking hands, brows furrowed, as she defined "left out in the cold."

Yet another ASL definition occurred when, eyes widened, she momentarily gazed at the neutral signing space above her students' heads, then closed her eyes and abruptly opened them again, flinging her mouth wide open as she simultaneously signed "scared" with not a word to be heard, to define "her oil ran dry."

Conclusion

Any implications are tentative at best in light of the early stages of this analysis. However, perhaps the most important finding to the researcher was that an engaging teacher who happened to be deaf, who was a skilled communicator, and who was committed to teaching English and making that written form accessible to her somewhat linguistically limited deaf kindergarten students, could do so by code-switching.

Moreover, there were patterns to her code-switching, and she accomplished such transitions into and out of the English text with relative ease in an activity that truly seemed to be jointly constructed by both her and her students.

What seemed most important to the teacher was the fact that she, too, could be seen as a researcher in an activity that proved to be far more complex and multifaceted than it was initially perceived to be.

Several additional points seem to make this research important:

1. It sheds some light on the "how" of storytelling with deaf children in a school setting, information not even widely available on hearing children, as indicated by Cochran-Smith (1984) and Martinez and Teale (1988). It also indicates a strong need for additional studies.

2. It demonstrates to us how stimulating and empowering collaborative research can be as well as how needed it is, perhaps especially among deaf and hearing people when studying signing (Bissex, 1986; Erting, 1988; Goswami and Stillman, 1987; Graves, 1981, 1983; Harste, 1988; Heath, 1983; Heath and Thomas, 1984, among others).

3. It lends some credence to the idea that clear communication may not be a matter of how inadequately English is being rendered (Marmor and Pettito, 1979; Swisher and Thompson, 1985), or that signing is done with an inconsistent fit between what is signed and what is spoken (Allen and Woodward, 1987), or even that deaf teachers are very likely providing their students with inconsistent English signing patterns (Allen and Woodward, 1987). Rather, when one's signing is examined in the communication context in which it is used, at least in this one situation, departures from either purely English or ASL are patterned and demonstrate competence, not deviance.

4. It causes us to wonder if the teacher's deafness was a driving factor in her successful code-switching while storytelling, as one might infer from the work of Erting (1988), or if that is only part of the picture and a hearing teacher might be equally effective.

5. It also causes speculation as to whether the vast majority of teachers of deaf students might be dealing with a continuum of signing that needs to be more closely examined in light of what we currently know about child language learning and literacy. It would be helpful similarly to study teachers designated as "skillful communicators" and "not very skillful communicators" in the classroom and to see how their code-switching is related to their position on language as well as their manual skills.

In summary, forms of communication such as signing—on any part of the continuum we have described—are only part of the picture; those forms must be studied within the context of the *purpose* and the *content* teachers are trying to share. This pilot study has shown that it was most beneficial to consider a teacher's signing behavior as the vehicle for successfully engaging her students while interpreting a filmstrip story to them, and that such behavior is very important, although not the only factor, in a successful storytelling experience.

References

Allen, T., and J. Woodward. 1987. "Teacher Characteristics and the Degree to which Teachers Incorporate Features of English in Their Sign Communication with Hearing-Impaired Students." *American Annals of the Deaf* 131 (2): 61–67.

Bissex, G. 1986. "What Is a Teacher-Researcher?" *Language Arts* 63 (6): 482–484.

Cochran-Smith, M. 1984. *The Making of a Reader.* Norwood, NJ: Ablex.

Erting, C. 1988. "Acquiring Linguistic and Social Identity: Interactions of Deaf Children with a Hearing Teacher and a Deaf Adult." In *Language, Learning and Deafness,* ed. M. Strong. Cambridge: Cambridge University Press.

Goswami, D., and P. Stillman. 1987. *Reclaiming the Classroom: Teacher Research as an Agency for Change.* Portsmouth, NH: Heinemann.

Graves, D. 1981. "Research Update: Where Have All the Teachers Gone?" *Language Arts* 58 (4): 492–497.

Graves, D. 1983. *Writing: Teachers and Children at Work.* Portsmouth, NH: Heinemann.

Harste, J. 1988. "Tomorrow's Readers Today: Becoming a Profession of Collaborative Learners." In *Dialogues in Literacy Research: Thirty-Seventh Yearbook of the National Reading Conference,* ed. J. Readence, R. Baldwin, J. Konopak, and P. O'Keefe. Chicago: The National Reading Conference, Inc. pp. 3–13.

Heath, S. B. 1983. *Ways with Words: Language, Life and Work in Communities and Classrooms.* New York: Cambridge University Press.

Heath, S., with C. Thomas. 1984. "The Achievement of Preschool Literacy for Mother and Child." In *Awakening to Literacy,* ed. H. Goelman, A. Oberg, and F. Smith. Portsmouth, NH: Heinemann. pp. 51–72.

Marmor, G., and L. Petitto. 1979. "Simultaneous Communication in the Classroom: How Well Is English Grammar Represented?" *Sign Language Studies* 23: 99–136.

Martinez, M., and W. Teale. 1988. "Reading in a Kindergarten Classroom Library." *The Reading Teacher* 41: 568–572.

Swisher, V., and M. Thompson. 1985. "Mothers Learning Simultaneous Communication: The Dimensions of the Task." *American Annals of the Deaf* 130: 212–217.

Classroom Turn-Taking Mechanism: Effective Strategies for Using Eye Gaze as a Regulator

SUSAN M. MATHER

I t is well documented that the turn-taking strategies used in classrooms are different from those used in other conversational settings. Mehan (1979) points out that in classroom discussions the "current speaker selects next speaker," almost exclusively. The teacher, as the current speaker, selects a student as the next speaker, but when the student finishes, the turn to speak automatically returns to the teacher. This turn-taking strategy differs from that in everyday conversation, in which the speaker self-selects and the next speaker "takes the floor" at the end of a turn.

There are certain turn-taking signals, known as regulators, that are regularly used in conversation. In spoken English conversations the regulators include body motion, sociocentric sequences ("but-um," "or something," "you know"), a drop in paralinguistic pitch or intensity, paralinguistic drawl, intonation, and other cues.

Regulators also are used in signed discourse. Baker (1977) implies that turn-taking strategies used in signed conversation differ from those used in spoken conversation because a deaf person cannot initiate signing until the other person is looking at him or her. A person cannot "say" something and be "heard" if the other person is not watching. This constraint makes eye gaze one of the most powerful regulators in sign language, because it absolutely determines when a speaker can sign. Baker also observes that those who are not aware of or do not employ eye gaze rules in signed conversation often will experience difficulty in having "smooth" exchanges, or confusion about taking turns to sign. She mentions two kinds of eye gaze: positive eye gaze at a specified addressee (+gaze), and negative (no) eye gaze at the addressee (−gaze).

The question-answer format is one of the most prevalent methods of turn-taking in American classrooms. One signals a question by using intonation in spoken language; however, this is different for signed discourse.

The predominant nonmanual signals for "yes/no" questions are raised brows, widely opened eyes, head forward/downward, and positive eye gaze; the nonmanual signals for "wh" questions are contracted brows and positive eye gaze with no predication for head position. A teacher who fails to use these signals when asking a question

Another version of this paper was published in *Sign Language Studies*, volume 54, Spring, 1987, pp. 11–29.

and then fails to get an answer may think that the student does not know the answer and proceed to supply it. Or the teacher who does not recognize these signals may not recognize a student's sentence as a question and may replay inappropriately.

General observations of classroom performance among deaf students indicate that these students respond more often to teacher-initiated questions in a deaf teacher's classroom than in a hearing teacher's classroom.

Even hearing teachers in an elementary school for deaf children have told me that, of two teachers who seem to be equally competent in signing, the one who is a native signer reads a story "better" than the one who acquires signing as a second language. The hearing teachers feel that the deaf teacher "has something" that they do not have. They also reported that in the native signer's class, students responded to questions better than in the non-native signer's class.

The "something" these teachers were referring to probably has to do, in part at least, with the ability to use eye gaze and grammatical markers effectively and consistently as regulators in group activities.

As will be seen in the transcribed records of story reading, the turn-taking mechanism is much smoother in the classroom of the native signer, whose name is David, than for the class of the non-native signer, Helen. There were more interruptions and disruptions, and more wrong answers and non-responses to the teacher's questions in Helen's class than in David's.

Background

The data for this study were collected in classrooms for deaf children in a large city in the eastern United States. David is a deaf native signer. He prefers to use signs without voice because he believes it is important that he and his students understand each other fully. His five students, who have hearing parents, came to the school in the fall, and the videotape was made in May, so these students had been learning sign language for only eight months at the time of this study.

Helen is a hearing person, a native English speaker and a skilled signer. She learned her sign language skills during a one-year training in manual communication. At the time of the study, she had been signing for seven years, and used voice and sign simultaneously. Her students were four preschool deaf children of deaf parents, all four years of age and in their second year in the preschool program. They were native American Sign Language (ASL) users, able to switch between ASL with deaf people and a variety of signing closer to English with hearing people or those who did not understand ASL.

The teachers made different use of eye gaze and nonmanual signals in various situations. This difference appears responsible, at least in part, for the striking differences in communication found throughout the videotape. I will discuss the teacher's use of eye gaze in six different areas.

During preliminary observations, I found two major types of eye gaze used by the native signer as regulators: individual gaze (I-Gaze) and group-indicating gaze (G-Gaze).

Individual Gaze (I-Gaze)

I-Gaze requires mutual eye contact between the speaker and an individual addressee. This gaze is held until the speaker finishes or receives a reply from the addressee. When a teacher uses I-Gaze while signing to a student who is seated next to another, both students know that the question is directed to the former. If the teacher wants to speak to a particular student in a group, the teacher must use I-Gaze with that student to signal everyone in the group that only that particular student is being addressed. If a teacher does not use I-Gaze, the students in the group would be at a loss to know who is the target of the questioning.

Group-Indicating Gaze (G-Gaze)

The second type of eye gaze observed is a group-indicating gaze (G-Gaze). This may be used in a group as small as two individuals, in addition to the speaker. Its purpose is to tell the group that the speaker is treating the group as a unit and not signaling out an individual. G-Gaze must appear to be evenly directed toward all members of the group and must move constantly around the group without pausing. It typically takes the form of a smooth arc-like gaze from one side of the group to the other. This gaze—not I-Gaze—is invariably used by the teacher who is a native signer. If the teacher intends to address the group but instead uses I-Gaze, one student would assume the addressee role and the others would assume that they were "off the hook" for the time being, or until the gaze was directed at them.

One incident illustrates the difficulty that can be caused by not using appropriate gaze. A teacher who is not a native signer signed to the students in a classroom that they did not know the story—directing I-Gaze at one particular student. This student replied defensively, saying that he did know the story. The teacher responded that she knew that *he* knew the story. Thus, the student singled out by the inappropriate I-Gaze felt called upon to defend himself against a false accusation that the teacher had not intended to make specifically to this student. It is difficult to imagine what degree of credibility the other students attached to this exchange.

Initiating a Story Reading Session

Before David initiated a story reading, he waited until his students were ready. He employed several initiating techniques, such as waiting with arms down, waving one or both hands in the students' field of vision, touching a student individually, or asking the students if they are ready for the reading. To indicate that he or she was paying attention, each student responded with I-Gaze and nodding. David often acknowledged this by nodding in return, double-checking visually that the student was still focused. After getting the attention of all, he would pause for a while to be sure that everyone's attention was held before he started his narration.

Unlike David, even though she did check with a student or get one of her students' attention, Helen failed to check with all the students to make sure that they were paying attention before beginning a story reading. Failure to do so probably accounts for the interruptions and delays in Helen's story reading.

Asking a Question

In the videotaped sessions, David always asked questions of the group first. Then, if there were no response, he would ask a particular student. Helen often asked a particular student to answer a question first, rather than the group. Whether a teacher should ask the group or one member first is not in question here, and it is not clear whether this difference in teacher strategy had an impact on classroom interaction. It should be noted, however, that throughout the entire story reading session, Helen asked only nine questions, and only two were answered by students. David, on the other hand, asked forty-one questions, and all of them were answered by the students themselves.

This appears to suggest that the turn-taking strategies used by the teachers do make an important difference in the positive responses of the students. More study would be needed to determine whether teacher variables, other than eye gaze and nonmanual question signals, are responsible for differences in student response.

As mentioned earlier, David did not use voice and signs simultaneously. This may explain his greater use of nonmanual signals in asking questions.

Helen stated that she would sometimes use voice without signing but would normally sign and use voice simultaneously. This may explain her failure to use appropriate nonmanual signals. It appears that her vocal intonation patterns indicated questions, but the students could not hear them and were not likely to see a question in Helen's simultaneous utterance if it had no appropriate nonmanual indications. Our study suggests that when asking questions of students who cannot hear, a teacher will get best results by using appropriate nonmanual, grammatical signals, not by relying solely on vocal intonation for conveying the linguistic or paralinguistic information needed to signal questions.

Using a Book

During the entire course of the videotaping, I observed that Helen's students frequently asked to see the pictures once more, sometimes even trying to take the book from her lap. All of these incidents followed her showing of the book by raising it a little from her lap and putting it down again with the pictures facing the class. Whether the pictures facing the students creates a distraction for them is unclear. Although David used the same book, there is no instance on videotape of a student asking to see it again. David's technique for using the book included showing it around slowly, with G-Gaze, until each of the students looked at the picture while leaning forward to see it and then leaned back, indicating that he or she was finished. David then put the book back on his lap with the pictures facing him, not the student.

The technique Helen used was appropriate for hearing kids, because they have the privilege of seeing and listening to storytelling at the same time. Deaf children, however, have to look at the picture first, then "listen" to the story—or vice versa.

Handling a Distraction or Interruption

Because Helen did not get the class's attention before beginning story reading, distractions and interruptions from her students occurred throughout her narrative session. During these distractions, Helen did not maintain I-Gaze at the student addressed, but shifted her gaze to the interrupting student. David did just the opposite. He maintained I-Gaze with the student to whom he asked the question whenever possible; without shifting his gaze from the addressee, he used his hands to quiet the distraction-causing student. There was one incident in which he had to break contact because of a distraction. In this case he signaled to the intended addressee to hold on before he shifted his I-Gaze to the distracting student.

Suggested Techniques

The observed behavior and the discussion above, experience as a teacher, and interactions with native signers all suggest the following techniques for using eye gaze in classrooms:

1. Initiating a story reading (and other class activity) may be done effectively in one or more of these ways: (a) waiting with arms down (away from the signing position); (b) waving one or both hands in the students' fields of vision; (c) touching a student individually; (d) asking the students if they are ready for the reading. To indicate that he or she is attending to the teacher, each student responds with I-Gaze and nodding. The teacher should acknowledge by nodding in return, double-checking visually that the student is still focused. After getting the attention of all, the teacher should pause for a while to be sure that the attention of all is held; only then should the teacher initiate the reading proper.

2. I-Gaze should be used to establish and maintain mutual eye gaze with a specific student, thus clearly indicating to that one and to the others in the class who is the intended addressee of a question.

3. G-Gaze is essential if the question is addressed to two or more students as potential answerers. This gaze needs to be smoothly and evenly directed to all in the group, allowing each about the same length in eye focus. The gaze of the teacher should not shift abruptly from one member of the group to another.

4. In asking a question (whether in signing alone or signing and speaking), the teacher should use appropriate nonmanual signals of grammatical form and intention, i.e., signals that the utterance is a question and that it is directed either to a specific individual or to anyone in the group who wishes to respond. After asking a question of the group—with G-Gaze of course—the teacher should pause until one or more students indicate desire to answer. Selecting the answerer, the teacher should establish I-Gaze with that one, hold it during the answer, and acknowledge by (a) signing YES or RIGHT or (b) pointing and nodding, meaning "Yes, you are right." If the teacher wants to ask a particular student to answer a question, the teacher should use I-Gaze and the nonmanual signs appropriate to the question type (see above and Baker-Shenk, 1985). I-Gaze must be maintained until the student finishes answering, or in the case of a distraction or interruption, until the student addressed has been told to hold on.

5. Showing a book or a picture to the group, the teacher should show it slowly around, using G-Gaze and allowing enough (and equal) time for each one to see it (and time for them to indicate by body shift or other signal that they have seen it).

6. Dealing with an interruption or distraction calls for more complex strategy. If one or more students create a distraction during story reading, the teacher can (a) ignore it by maintaining eye gaze with the current addressee, (b) maintain eye gaze with the current addressee while using one or both hands to touch, or sign STOP or QUIET to the offending student, or (c) shift I-Gaze directly to the offender *after* telling the intended addressee to "hold" or "wait a minute."

Conclusion

This study shows that using eye gaze and nonmanual grammatical markers are the two effective turn-taking mechanisms in a classroom of deaf students. It also suggests that in order to regulate turn taking effectively, the teacher must use two different kinds of eye gaze and also send appropriate nonmanual signals so that addressees will know whether the utterance is a question or not. Whatever the language level of the deaf students, the teacher needs to be sensitive to the effects of eye gaze and nonmanual behaviors and the students' comprehension of the message.

Other factors that have not yet been examined may influence the difference in turn-taking techniques between the two classes studied. These may include changes in body motion or signing, relationships between the use of nonmanual signals and vocal intonation, use or non-use of voice while signing, and English-like or ASL-like signing. Further studies on turn-taking mechanisms are needed in other group activities such as lectures, group discussion, or a class or meeting with only one deaf participant, and by interpreters and teachers in mainstreaming programs. Such studies could help determine which teacher or interpreter performances will ensure the most effective participation by deaf and hard of hearing students.

References

Baker, C. 1977. "Regulators and Turn-taking in American Sign Language." In *On the Other Hand*, ed. Friedman. New York: Academic Press. pp. 215–236.

Mehan, H. 1979. *Learning Lessons.* Cambridge: Harvard University Press.

The Use of Interactive Videodisc Technology for Bilingual Instruction in American Sign Language and English

VICKI L. HANSON AND CAROL A. PADDEN

e will report here on an interactive videodisc system, called "HandsOn," that uses a bilingual approach toward teaching English to elementary-aged deaf students.

Given that many deaf children are competent in American Sign Language (ASL), we sought to use this language competence as a part of their education about English. Although there have been advocates for the greater use of ASL in the eduction of deaf children (Barnum, 1984; Johnson, Liddell, and Erting, 1989; Kannapell, 1974; Strong, 1980), few concrete proposals have been made for how to use ASL and English together for language instruction. With "HandsOn," we explore various possibilities for their joint use.

For this experimental project, we have created videodiscs containing stories signed in ASL. Under computer control, both the ASL video and English text can be presented on the same computer screen simultaneously. The children are able to go back and forth between ASL and written English versions of the same stories.

"HandsOn" has been in use at one residential school for deaf children since January 1988, and more recently has started being used at a second residential school. It continues to undergo modifications based on user feedback and ideas for new possibilities of presenting the two languages. We here describe "HandsOn" as it currently exists, report on students' and teachers' reactions to it, and discuss results of early evaluations.

Equipment

"HandsOn" runs on an IBM InfoWindow ™ system. The hardware components of this system are an InfoWindow display monitor, an IBM personal computer, and a videodisc player. This InfoWindow system allows computer output to be overlaid on video,

We wish to thank the staff and students of the elementary school at the California School for the Deaf-Fremont and the New York School for the Deaf who have been participating with us in this work. We are grateful for their suggestions about improvements and their patience in this experimental effort.

enabling both ASL video and English text to be presented on one monitor. This system also makes available touch screen technology, enabling students to indicate their responses simply by touching the computer screen.

The videodiscs we use are ones we have developed specifically for "HandsOn." Each disc contains several stories signed in ASL. Videodiscs have so far been created on the topics of children's literature, science, American social studies, conservation, and how things work. Stories on these discs are appropriate for elementary-age children and range from a narration of "Goldilocks and the Three Bears," to presentations on plants and dinosaurs, to information about Martin Luther King Jr., to discussions of endangered species and the environment, to explanations of how magnets and computers work.

Software

The system we describe here is fully interactive. In designing "HandsOn," we were guided by the principle that students, rather than being presented with a pre-programmed instructional sequence, should have various options available to them. As a result, students using "HandsOn" make their own choices about which story and which activity option to use at each point in time.

Students begin by selecting a story from a menu. Following this, they select an activity from a menu of activity options. Having selected a story and activity, students continue to make choices within each activity.

For example, while being presented a written text of a story during the "read a story" option, students have the choice of seeing the ASL version of any sentence on the screen, of moving forward or backward in the English text, or of exiting the "read" option and returning to the menu from which they may choose one of the other activity options. "HandsOn" thus provides for student-directed exploration in learning English. In this respect, it differs quite dramatically from traditional computer drill and practice instruction.

A goal in this project is to explore ways that ASL and English can be used together in a bilingual instructional approach. We have sought to develop activities that go beyond simple word/sign translations. Instead, we are developing tasks that require students to interact with English and ASL in a story context, with translations between the two languages occurring at the sentence level. For example, in one component of the program, the students "caption" ASL stories in English.

Our initial evaluations of "HandsOn" dealt with making the system easily usable by students and teachers without outside intervention. This required observations of students' usage of the system and discussions with teachers.

Based on this feedback, "HandsOn" has undergone several changes since we began (see Hanson and Padden, 1988, 1989, 1990). The system is now quite easy to use. Students quickly figure out they can explore the capabilities of the program simply by touching the different "touch boxes" on the screen. The most complicated activity option, "caption a story," has ASL instructions included on the videodisc.

We also have evaluated a variety of activity options that include both reading and writing tasks. Based on feedback from students and teachers, we have added, deleted, and revised these options. The six activity options we have explored are as follows:

1. *Read a story*, in which students read English text and can request the ASL version of an English sentence by touching that sentence on the computer screen.

2. *Vocabulary,* in which students are shown a list of vocabulary words from the story and can get an ASL definition of any one of these items by touching that English word on the screen.

3. *Answer questions about a story,* in which students are asked questions, in English, about the stories and must respond by using the keyboard to type their answers (in English). When students need help understanding the question, they can touch the question on the screen to get the ASL version. When students need help with an answer, they can scan the English text or scan the ASL video. Signed feedback about answers is provided.

4. *Write a story,* in which students write an English summary of one of the stories. This option was difficult to use within the constraints of students' keyboarding skills and class schedules. The "caption a story" option was introduced to replace it.

5. *Caption a story,* in which students write English captions for segments of the ASL version of stories. The ASL segments can then be played back with the students' English captions overlaid on the ASL, creating an effect that appears much like a closed-captioned TV show or movie. In addition, students can get a printout of their captions.

6. *Watch a story,* in which students watch one of the stories signed in ASL. The students can touch the computer screen to get the English version of the ASL sentence currently being signed.

Student Population

The target population for "HandsOn" is elementary-aged deaf children who are fluent in the use of ASL. We assume some basic reading ability on the part of the user. This basic reading ability requires that students be able to read the activity options names and the labels on the touch buttons (e.g., "read a story," "answer questions," "see signs").

Despite our early targeting toward the upper elementary school grades, however, we found that teachers of the younger students, even kindergartners, were interested in using the program. For now, these youngest students use only the "watch" option. Given the interest expressed by the teachers of these younger children, we would hope to be able to develop a range of tasks that could be used even by these younger children.

More recently, "HandsOn" has been used by high school students. We note, however, that not all the stories we have developed are appropriate to these older students' interests. The "HandsOn" software itself, however, is appropriate for these older students.

Evaluation of "HandsOn"

Students enjoy using "HandsOn." They enjoy seeing the signing on the computer screen, and they like the interaction afforded by the program. They are very quick to understand how to use the system. "HandsOn" is effectively used by students working singly or in pairs. When working in pairs, the students interact constantly. They discuss which story and which activity option to select, and often debate about which student gets to touch the screen or to type. They also constructively interact by helping each other with vocabulary when reading, and with all aspects of writing and answering questions.

Importantly, we also have received enthusiastic feedback from teachers. Particularly relevant was one story told to us by a teacher about one student, fluent in ASL, who, despite being in upper elementary school, had never made much progress in learning to read English. The teacher reported working with this student on the "read a story" option, repeatedly demonstrating to the student how to go back and forth between the English and ASL versions of a story. At one point, the student suddenly pointed to an English word on the computer screen and spontaneously made the sign for that word. According to the teacher, this was the first time the student had really understood the connection between the two languages.

This "read a story" option has been a very effective component of "HandsOn." We can see students, such as in the above example, learning much from this component. The "answer questions" option also has been very popular with students. They are excited about the interaction with the computer and by the signed feedback when they answer a question. "Caption a story" is a relatively new component of "HandsOn" and thus has been tried less than the other activity options.

We have recently completed a preliminary evaluation of "HandsOn" using reading comprehension as our measure. Our experimental design controlled for possible reading improvements unrelated to the use of "HandsOn." To accomplish this goal, each participating student served as his/her own control by twice reading a test story and answering a set of questions about it—once with a paper and pencil version of the story and questions, and once with the "HandsOn" version of the story and questions. To control for order effects, some of these students did the "HandsOn" version first, while others did the "HandsOn" version second.

Our comprehension measure was the percentage of correct answers to the set of questions, which were directed at understanding the content of the story. To date, we have analyzed the results for three classes of upper elementary school students. We found that these students were significantly better at answering the comprehension questions using the "HandsOn" version of the test than answering questions in the paper and pencil version of the test. These results suggest that such a system for language instruction can benefit deaf children.

Summary

In sum, this project explores the use of a computerized bilingual ASL/English instructional approach for teaching written English to deaf children. "HandsOn" is still under development. From a technical standpoint, the project is feasible. From the enthusiastic reactions of students and teachers and from the positive results of our early study, we are encouraged about the potential of this technology for use with deaf students.

References

Barnum, M. 1984. "In Support of Bilingual/Bicultural Education for Deaf Children." *American Annals of the Deaf* 129: 404–408.

Hanson, V. L., and C. A. Padden. 1988. "The Use of Videodisc Interactive Technology for Bilingual Instruction in American Sign Language and English." *The Quarterly Newsletter of the Laboratory of Comparative Human Cognition* 10: 92–95.

Hanson, V. L., and C. A. Padden. 1989. "The Use of Interactive Video for Bilingual ASL/English Instruction of Deaf Children." *American Annals of the Deaf* 134: 209–213.

Hanson, V. L., and C. A. Padden. 1990. "Bilingual ASL/English Instruction of Deaf Children." In *Cognition, Education and Multimedia: Exploring Ideas in High-Technology,* ed. D. Nix and R. Spiro. Hillsdale, NJ: Erlbaum. pp. 49–63.

Johnson, R. E., S. K. Liddell, and C. J. Erting. 1989. "Unlocking the Curriculum: Principles for Achieving Access in Deaf Education." Gallaudet Research Institute Working Paper 89–3, Gallaudet University, Washington, DC.

Kannapell, B. June, 1974. "Bilingualism: A New Direction in the Education of the Deaf." *The Deaf American* 26: 9–15.

Strong, M. 1988. "A Bilingual Approach to the Education of Young Deaf Children: ASL and English." In *Language Learning and Deafness,* ed. M. Strong. Cambridge: The Cambridge University Press. pp. 113–129.

Effectiveness of Psychodrama and Sociodrama Among Young Deaf and Hard of Hearing Secondary School Students at Nyborgskolen, Denmark

ILDI BATORY

Psychodrama promises to be an effective technique to use with deaf and hard of hearing clients. This paper describes a study that I undertook with a group of young deaf and hard of hearing secondary students at Nyborgskolen, Denmark involving psychodrama as a method of psychotherapy. It was the first time any form of group therapy had been used with a deaf population in Denmark.

The hypothesis of this study is that following psychodrama, there would be a decrease of the individual student's social isolation in the classroom, and the development of a better self-image and increased self-esteem. The effectiveness of the psychodrama would be measured through the use of psychological tests.

Psychodrama is an action therapy method devised by Jacob L. Moreno in Vienna in 1922. It involves group dynamics, role playing, and analysis of social systems to help facilitate behavior changes, reorganize thinking patterns, and develop new perceptions (Buchanan, 1984).

The client's tool in psychodrama is the *stage*, a living space where fantasy and reality meet. The *protagonist* is the central character of the psychodrama session. The *auxiliary ego* or *egos* are people within the group selected by the protagonist. They allow the protagonist to explore his or her life drama with actual or imagined situations. The objective of the procedure is to allow the protagonist to develop control over his or her life.

Through providing support for and identifying with the protagonist, the *audience* or *group* may also benefit by gaining more awareness of their own feelings (Batory, 1987). The leader of the group, the *director*, guides the experiences of protagonist and the group and also facilitates interaction among group members.

As an effective treatment for use with deaf clients, psychodrama was first described by Clayton and Robinson (1971), followed by Stein (1976), Swink (1979), and Vernon (1979). In psychodrama, deaf clients may express their feelings through gestures, body movements, facial expressions, verbal expressions, sign language and/or spoken language, mime, and fingerspelling.

Some research related to psychodrama and deafness exists, such as that discussed in the article, "Role Playing and Spontaneity in Teaching Social Skills to Deaf Adolescents" (Stein, 1976). Stein's study showed six deficient social skills of deaf adolescents: "limited role repertoire, concrete thought as opposed to the development of abstract thought, limited information about the culture, isolation, rigid code of behavior, and dependence." Stein showed in her study that those social skills improved through role playing and spontaneity training.

In her study, Barrett analyzed the effects of "Self-Image and Social Adjustment Change in Deaf Adolescents Participating in a Social Living Class" (1985). The social living class is psychodrama carried out in the classroom. This model was developed by the psychodrama section at St. Elizabeths Hospital in Washington, D.C.

Barrett concluded that the "psychodramatic techniques and social living class had aided the children in preparing for more successful and satisfying interactions with the world by offering the opportunity, through psychodrama, to create and manipulate the world as they experienced it" (p. 10). The social living class also has been conducted with deaf adolescents (Bond, 1980), and it was stated that deaf children are able to develop alternative roles dealing with social issues outside of the classroom and to increase spontaneity.

Subjects and Methods

My research study was conducted with students at Nyborgskolen, the only secondary school for deaf students in Denmark. The students ranged in ages from seventeen to twenty-one. The research design was a two-group pre- and post-test arrangement by Palle Vestberg Rasmussen, Associate Professor at the Royal School of Educational Studies. Subjects were divided into two groups of nine students each.

Pre-tests were administered to both Group A, the experimental group, and B, the control group. Following the pre-tests, Group A participated in ten psychodrama sessions of ninety minutes each, over a five-week period. Both groups were then administered post-tests.

Upon completion of the post-tests, Group B participated in psychodrama sessions of the same number, time, and duration. Post-tests were administered to both groups once again at the end of this second experimental period.

This project provided an opportunity for the first use of the Danish version of the Meadow/Kendall Social-Emotional Assessment Inventory—the Social-Emotional Funktion (SEF) by Meadow/Dyssegaard. The SEF, based on a sample of 410 students in Denmark, is a teacher's report inventory, consisting of fifty-eight items, for measuring observable behavior in three categories: social adjustment, self-esteem, and emotional adjustment.

Other cognitive tests given to the students were the performance tests from the Wechsler Adult Intelligence Scale, the Raven Intelligence Test, reading tests, and the Sociometric Picture Choice Test.

The SEF test was administered by the head of the project, Lars von der Lieth, Professor of Clinical Psychology at the Audiologopedic Centre. One or two teachers from each class also participated. The psychodrama and sociodrama classes were directed by the psychodrama therapist, who is deaf herself and fluent in Danish Sign Language.

Results

The hypothesis of the project was that consistent student participation in classroom psychodrama and sociodrama sessions would result in a decrease of individual social isolation. The students would also be given a basis for developing a positive self-image and increased self-esteem.

Additionally, the hypothesis stated that no change would be seen in the above areas with the control group until they eventually participated in classroom psychodrama and sociodrama sessions.

Although final analysis of the data from the SEF and the cognitive testing are not complete at this time, I will mention three tendencies that show improvement: socio-metric picture arrangement, the teacher's comments after the experiment, and my own subjective impressions as the therapist in the experiment.

The sociometric picture arrangement indicated significant positive changes among the students following their participation in the psychodrama and sociodrama sessions.

The most striking results of the students' experiences in the psychodrama and sociodrama program have been related through subjective verbal reports from the classroom teachers. *Without exception,* they have observed significant positive changes in the students who attended the program on a regular basis. Students who had previously been socially isolated in the classroom experienced increased acceptance and respect from their peers.

The teachers expressed disappointment in the short duration of the total program. The period of the psychodrama *was* very short, perhaps too short to show measurable effects in the teacher's inventory. This is something we will better understand when the data analysis is complete. However, in research one must compromise, and the permitted duration was limited.

The teachers also expressed a desire to learn about the techniques that were used. They felt that an ongoing program of this nature would be extremely beneficial to the students. It was also felt that implementing similar programs earlier in students' educational experience would better prepare them to deal with personal and social issues such as deaf vs. hearing, communication, power, and social norms of behavior.

Conclusion

Participation in classroom psychodrama and sociodrama provided students with an opportunity to look at themselves, re-enact old roles, and change, modify, and develop new roles as desired. They were able to use their peers in the class to provide feedback and assume various roles to help resolve conflicts.

In summary, psychodrama and sociodrama in the classroom helped the students experience more successful interactions with their environment, attain a better acceptance of themselves, and discover opportunities to re-create and manipulate the world as they experienced it.

Because this study prompted the first use of group therapy with deaf people in Denmark, further data analyses of this study and future studies with other groups will be necessary in order to verify the effectiveness of psychodrama and sociodrama with deaf students, their families, and professionals working within the field of deafness.

References

Batory, I. 1987. *The Effectiveness of Psychodrama: An Action Method for a Group of Schizophrenics, Deaf Patients.* Unpublished manuscript, University of Copenhagen.

Barrett, E. M. 1985. "Self-Image and Social Adjustment Change in Deaf Adolescents Participating in a Social Living Class." *Journal of Group Psychotherapy, Psychodrama and Sociometry* 39 (1): 3–11.

Buchanan, D. R. 1984. "Psychodrama." In *The Psychosocial Therapies: Part II of the Psychiatric Therapies,* ed. T. B. Karasu. Washington, DC: The American Psychiatric Association.

Bond, S. 1980. *Social Living with Deaf Adolescents: An Exploratory Study.* Unpublished manuscript.

Clayton, L., and L. Robinson. 1971. "Psychodrama with Deaf People." *American Annals of the Deaf* 116: 415–419.

Moreno, J. L. 1964. *Psychodrama.* Vol. I. New York: Beacon House.

Stein, M. 1976. *Role Playing and Spontaneity in Teaching Social Skills to Deaf Adolescents.* Unpublished manuscript, Psychodrama Department at St. Elizabeths Hospital, Washington, DC.

Swink, D. F. 1979. *Therapists and Therapies with Deaf People: The Need for Specialized Training, Attitude Exploration, and Novel Approaches.* Paper presented at the ninth Southeast Regional Institute on Education and Rehabilitation of the Deaf.

Vernon, M. Fall, 1978. "Deafness and Mental Health: Some Theoretical Views." *Gallaudet Today* 9 (1): 9–13.

What Deaf High School Seniors Tell Us About Their Social Networks

RANDOLPH L. MOWRY

The uniqueness of the Deaf community has been attributed to its close-knit and supportive nature (Becker, 1980; Jacobs, 1974; Padden and Humphries, 1988; and Padden, 1980). The community functions as any cultural group, providing a focus, a sense of identity, and ways for interpreting the world (Padden and Humphries, 1988).

Many deaf people are not born into Deaf families; therefore, the community is the mechanism through which deaf people learn about Deaf culture. With the increased federal commitment in the United States to mainstreaming during the 1970s (which continues today), many Deaf adults are concerned about the integration of deaf youth into the Deaf community (Becker, 1980; Padden and Humphries, 1988).

In the past, the residential school was the place where students who were not born to Deaf parents learned about Deaf culture. Now the educational background of deaf students can vary tremendously. Individuals can start out in either a mainstream or a residential program and can switch back and forth between the two. The student may be in a residential program but be mainstreamed for several classes. The student may be the only deaf student in a mainstream program or be in a program with only a few other Deaf students. It is infrequent that a deaf student has one continuous educational placement.

Very little documentation exists about who Deaf students include in their social networks. A social network can be defined as a set of people connected by a set of interpersonal ties (Wellman, 1981), i.e., any person with whom an individual has a social relationship, professionally (e.g., with a counselor or lawyer) or informally (e.g., friend or sibling). It is presumed that deaf students in residential programs have networks that are weighted in favor of deaf people: They are in a setting that has many deaf students and some Deaf adults. The situation for mainstreamed students is very different. These students are surrounded primarily by hearing peers and possibly a few deaf students. Deaf adults are rarely present.

This study was not designed to identify every member of each student's social network, but to determine a particular segment of the full social network. Deaf high school

The research from which this paper was derived was supported in part by grant #GOO86C3501 from the National Institute on Disability and Rehabilitation Research, Department of Education.

seniors were asked to identify the particular people to whom they turn for emotional or practical assistance, or companionship—to identify who they use as "supporters."

Method

Respondents

Respondents were all Deaf high school seniors from the class of 1988 attending residential and mainstreamed programs in five midwestern and southwestern states. Total sample size was 115 students (seventy-seven residential, thirty-eight mainstreamed). The sample was predominantly white (76 percent); however, the percentages are close to national figures for race distribution. Males were overrepresented (62 percent). There were no race or gender differences between the residential and mainstreamed groups.

Data Collection

Data were collected using a questionnaire specifically designed for the study. The questionnaire required students to list up to four people they used for "help, advice, and friendship." For each listed supporter, the students indicated the relationship (e.g., mother, friend), hearing status, and gender. In addition, the students rated each supporter on sign language competency. Finally, the students rated the degree to which particular supportive actions were available to them. Students also reported their membership in various Deaf consumer and social organizations.

Supportive actions were categorized into four groups. The first group was *belonging;* items in this group indicated feelings of being valued and a part of a group. The second supportive action category indicated *tangible support,* such as loans of money or assistance with everyday tasks. The third category represented *emotional assistance;* items in this category indicated support when the person was feeling sad, lonely, or wanted to discuss worries. The final category reflected *problem assistance*—support with particular problem areas such as school, boyfriends or girlfriends, and family.

Results

Structural Features of the Networks

Supporters listed by the students were categorized into six groups: parents, siblings, extended family, friends, teachers, and others (Figure 1). Friends were the most frequently cited supporter by both residential and mainstreamed students, followed by parents.

The primary difference that can be seen in the types of supporters relates to two categories—siblings and teachers. Residential students cited siblings with a greater frequency than did the mainstreamed students. Conversely, teachers were more frequently indicated as supporters by mainstreamed students than by residential students.

Given the categories of supporters, it is not surprising that the network is predominantly composed of hearing people; family members of deaf students are mostly hearing, as are teachers. As Figure 2 indicates, only a small percentage of mainstreamed students had predominantly Deaf networks; residential students also had a low percentage of deaf supporters, but considerably higher than the mainstreamed students.

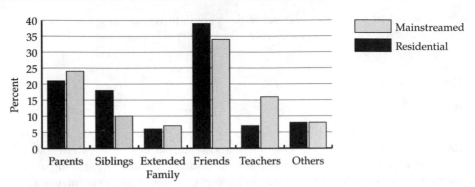

FIGURE 1: Categories of supporters listed by students.

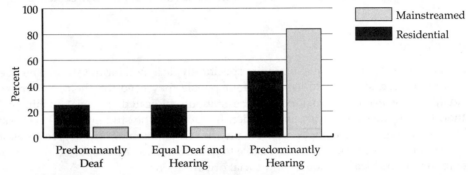

FIGURE 2: Hearing status of students' support network.

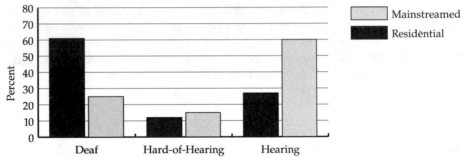

FIGURE 3: Hearing status of friends.

The one category where hearing status of supporters did vary by educational placement was friends; the hearing status of friends was dependent on where the student
attended school. Students at residential schools listed a majority of deaf friends, whereas
students in mainstream programs cited hearing friends. However, students in both
educational settings did cite both hearing and deaf friends (Figure 3).

Sign Language Competence of Supporters

All of the residential students and 73 percent of the mainstreamed students used sign
language as part of their communication system. Forty-four percent of the residential
students supplemented signing with speech; 68 percent of mainstreamed students used
speech as a supplement.

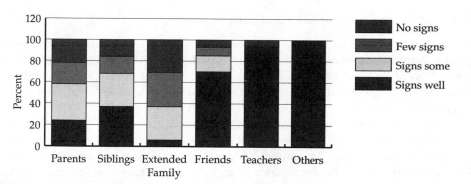

FIGURE 4: **Sign language skills of residential students' supporters.**

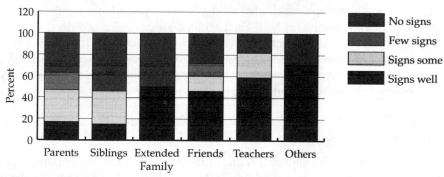

FIGURE 5: **Sign language skills of mainstreamed students' supporters.**

The students rated each listed supporter's sign language skill on a four-point scale: signs well, signs some, only knows a few signs, and does not sign. Even though sign language was an important component of the students' communication systems, supporters often did not possess this skill. Students in residential programs were more likely to cite supporters who "signed well" or "signed some": more than half of the parents (58 percent) and siblings (69 percent) signed well or some (Figure 4). For mainstreamed students the percentages for the same categories were 48 percent for parents and 46 percent for siblings (Figure 5). Of particular interest were the signing abilities of friends. For residential students, 72 percent of the friends signed well, with an additional 16 percent signing some. Mainstreamed students indicated that 48 percent of their friends signed well and 13 percent signed some. A sizeable portion (28 percent) of the mainstreamed students' friends knew no sign language (see Figures 4 and 5).

Sources of Supportive Actions

As shown above, the students listed several different categories of people they used for social support. Were particular categories of supporters used to provide particular types of support? For both groups of students, friends were the most frequent source of three supportive actions—belonging, emotional assistance, and problem assistance. Parents were the most frequent source of tangible support.

There was one major difference in support sources related to educational placement. For students in mainstream programs, parents formed a secondary level of support for belonging, emotional assistance, and problem assistance. In the case of residential students, friends and siblings provided a secondary source for tangible support.

Participation in Deaf Consumer and Social Groups

Students were asked to indicate their membership in the following Deaf consumer groups: National Association of the Deaf (NAD), Junior NAD (Jr. NAD), and their state association of the Deaf (ST-AD). The students also indicated their membership in the following social groups: a local Deaf club, an athletic group of the Deaf, and a church group of the Deaf.

In general, student membership in these consumer or social groups was small. Considering consumer groups, residential students were most likely to be a member of the Jr. NAD (34 percent). In contrast, 16 percent of the mainstreamed students were members of Jr. NAD. The discrepancy in membership between residential and mainstreamed students also was substantial for the NAD (12 percent vs. 0 percent) and for ST-AD (18 percent vs. 5 percent).

Regarding social groups, residential students displayed a higher membership rate than mainstreamed students for both Deaf athletic groups (47 percent vs. 14 percent) and churches with other Deaf members (40 percent vs. 22 percent). The exception to the higher membership rates for residential students was in involvement with local Deaf clubs. Approximately equal percentages of residential and mainstreamed students were members of Deaf clubs (21 percent and 22 percent respectively).

Implications

This study illustrates some similarities and differences in the social networks of deaf high school students in residential and mainstream settings. The two groups surveyed were very similar in the composition of their networks: Proportions of friends and family members were similar. Both groups included a high number of hearing people, both with and without sign language skills. Both groups tended to favor friends as their primary source of supportive actions—for feeling wanted, for emotional comfort and help, and for specific assistance with problems.

Nevertheless, there were differences between residential and mainstreamed students. Residential students, by virtue of their setting, included significantly more deaf friends in their networks than did the mainstreamed students. Residential students also had more involvement with Deaf organizations for social and consumer activities. Mainstreamed students, even though friends constituted the primary source of supportive actions, reported a strong secondary level of support from parents; this source of support was not so well developed for residential students.

What do these results mean for the Deaf community and Deaf culture in the United States? One implication is that the Deaf community is changing as a result of federal educational policy that emphasizes mainstreaming. Previous writing describing the Deaf community has emphasized peer relationships as the cornerstone of the community: The peer group is the primary socialization unit and the primary source of interaction (Becker, 1987). The peer group is also the source of Deaf identity, critical to self-worth (Becker, 1987; Padden and Humphries, 1988). In the past, the residential school was the hub for the development of the Deaf peer group.

Today, however, the educational placement of Deaf students is complicated. Of the 115 students in this study, only 26 percent started in a residential program and remained there for their entire education. The remaining students experienced placements in mainstreamed programs, often switching to and from residential programs. This circumstance is not conducive to forming a Deaf identity; the peer group is too frequently disrupted.

In addition, 30 percent of the deaf students attended mainstream programs almost exclusively from elementary school onward. These students have had little exposure to deaf people—peers or adults. As the results demonstrated, the mainstreamed students' peer network (friends) was heavily weighted toward hearing people. Their adult network was almost entirely hearing. The opportunity to form a Deaf identity that is more than a recognition of audiological differences was limited.

For many hearing people, the critical problem is that the Deaf person does not hear. Therefore, speech production and speech reading are critical for success and to be considered "normal." Only to the extent that the student can master these skills can he or she develop a positive identity, but not necessarily a Deaf identity.

As indicated earlier, the networks of both residential and mainstreamed students involved significant numbers of hearing people. These people were considered important sources for various kinds of support—in particular, emotional and problem assistance. This inclusion of hearing people as sources of assistance for emotional comfort and problem-solving reflects a change for the Deaf community. Many of these hearing people were family members, particularly parents; it is natural and expected that family members are important in an adolescent's life. However, the role of deaf supporters in the student's life outside the family was limited, especially for the mainstreamed student.

The residential students in the study had access to a deaf peer group. As the results suggested, these peers were important sources of various supportive actions. Presumably these peers would pass on the collective cultural knowledge and solutions for dealing with everyday problems. In addition, residential students had contact with more Deaf adult role models; 28 percent of the nonfamilial adults cited as supporters were Deaf.

The mainstreamed students, on the other hand, had very limited access to a Deaf peer group. Very few of their friends were Deaf; in fact, many mainstreamed students attended programs in which they were the only Deaf person or one of a very few. The chance to learn about the strategies Deaf people have evolved for handling common problems was restricted. The students' contact with Deaf adult role models also was limited; only 7 percent of the nonfamilial adult supporters were Deaf.

Increasingly, it is recognized that deafness has meaning beyond the audiological concerns (Higgins, 1988; Padden and Humphries, 1988). Through both their interaction with other Deaf people and through their participation in society as a whole, Deaf people have created a "way-of-being-human." This way-of-being-human is what Padden and Humphries (1988) call "historically created lives" (p. 111). To access this "Deaf Way," deaf youth need to have exposure to it.

Current educational policies do not take into account the important role of the Deaf community and culture in enhancing deaf people's lives. This neglect is a disservice to deaf students, whose options may be restricted, because they will be less able to cope with the world. As Padden and Humphries (1988) state: "When deaf children are denied connections with Deaf people . . . they lose access to a history of solutions created for them by other people like themselves" (p. 120).

Mainstream programs have a responsibility beyond the academic preparation of deaf students. Just as the school has a responsibility for maintaining an environment that promotes the emotional well-being and growth of its hearing students, the school with a mainstream program has the same responsibility for its deaf students. For the deaf student, well-being and growth involve an understanding of his or her deafness and its impact on living in a hearing world. This understanding is facilitated by access to a deaf peer group and adult Deaf role models.

A brief story may demonstrate this point. This author was told of a mainstreamed deaf student in the southern United States. Academically she was an exceptional student. During her senior year her grades plummeted; she was close to being unable to graduate. Concerned teachers and other staff, all hearing, were at a loss to explain what was happening. Finally the girl revealed her fear—she thought that she would die after graduation from high school. Why? She had never met a Deaf adult!

This story represents an extreme incident, but nonetheless illustrates how isolating a small mainstream program can be. This girl's understanding and acceptance of her deafness was distorted. Lacking contact with Deaf people, she did not know that she had a place in the world beyond high school. The story illustrates the importance of deaf students having access to other Deaf peers and role models.

Mainstream programs that include Deaf adults as administrators, teachers, counselors, and aides have moved towards providing a more positive social environment for the deaf student. It is still necessary, however, that the number of deaf students in any one mainstreamed program be reasonably large so that deaf students can develop a deaf peer group and thereby enhance their understanding of deafness. As the results indicated, having a deaf peer group does not mean disregard for hearing people; deaf students in residential programs included a significant percentage of hearing friends in their peer groups.

Residential schools frequently include information about Deaf culture in their educational programs. Mainstream programs also could do this. Schools often have black awareness programs and black history classes, and invite black speakers to talk with the students. Such practices could be adopted in mainstream programs and would benefit both deaf and hearing students, just as black awareness programs benefit everyone.

It is not only the responsibility of the school to encourage positive development: The family also should play a role. Earlier it was noted that the family was an important source of support, especially for mainstreamed students. Hearing family members can share the responsibility for the development of a Deaf identity in the student. The family can make sure the student has access to Deaf adults and peers in the community, and can participate with the student in activities sponsored by local Deaf organizations. There could be deafness-related literature, such as the *Deaf American*, the *NAD Broadcaster*, and *Tales from a Clubroom* (Bragg and Bergman, 1981) in the home. The technology that improves accessibility for deaf people, such as TDDs, decoders, and flashing alarms, also should be available. The family should learn to use sign language. The family that follows these examples shows the deaf child that being deaf is all right; it starts the process of forming a positive Deaf identity.

In conclusion, the students in this study described a part of their social networks. Even though the networks were similar, certain differences indicated that deaf students in mainstream programs may not have equal access to the unique cultural heritage of the Deaf community. Ultimately this reduced access may contribute to more limited options, instead of increased options, for the deaf student.

Mainstream programs can counteract this situation by purposefully including more Deaf awareness activities and hiring Deaf staff to the benefit of all students. Families can help, too, by ensuring that their deaf child has access to Deaf people, activities, and materials.

References

Becker, G. 1980. *Growing Old in Silence*. Berkeley, CA: University of California Press.

Becker, G. 1987. "Lifelong Socialization and Adaptive Behavior of Deaf People." In *Understanding Deafness Socially*, ed. P. C. Higgins and J. E. Nash. Springfield, IL: Charles C. Thomas.

Bragg, B., and E. Bergman. 1981. *Tales from a Clubroom*. Washington, DC: Gallaudet College Press.

Higgins, P. C. 1988. "Introduction." In *Understanding Deafness Socially*, ed. P. C. Higgins and J. E. Nash. Springfield, IL: Charles C. Thomas.

Jacobs, L. M. 1974. *A Deaf Adult Speaks Out*. Washington, DC: Gallaudet College Press.

Padden, C. 1980. "The Deaf Community and the Culture of Deaf People." In *Sign Language and the Deaf Community: Essays in Honor of William C. Stokoe*, ed. C. Baker and R. Battison. Silver Spring, MD: National Association of the Deaf.

Padden, C., and T. Humphries. 1988. *Deaf in America: Voices from a Culture*. Cambridge: Harvard University Press.

Wellman, B. 1981. "Applying Network Analyses to the Study of Support." In *Social Networks and Social Support*, ed. B. H. Gottlieb. London: Sage.

A Deaf Studies Curriculum for High School Teachers

DOUGLAS D. BAHL

Why is it imperative that schools for deaf students throughout the world offer a separate deaf studies curriculum today? We have always been able to preserve our deaf culture through the years, and many famous deaf folklore stories have been passed down through the generations.

It is known that American Sign Language (ASL) has been accepted as a legitimate, separate language from English. Our rich deaf heritage has been accepted as well. Deaf awareness programs have brought many positive responses from hearing people all over the world, and an increasing number of hearing people are taking sign language classes in order to communicate effectively with deaf people.

Nevertheless, a deaf studies curriculum is needed for a number of reasons. Today, black high school students are granted increasing opportunities to enjoy their rich cultural heritage by pursuing expanded knowledge in Afro-American studies. With the changing trend of public school curricula toward offering a variety of minority studies, deaf students also should have access to accurate information about their deaf cultural differences or similarities.

Because of their increasing involvement in many affairs, owing partly to the Gallaudet University protest for a deaf president in 1988, deaf people are becoming more visible in exercising their rights. More and more are getting into administration and serving on various committees dealing with deafness. Dr. I. King Jordan has become the first deaf president of Gallaudet University. Dr. Robert Davila was appointed Assistant Secretary in the Office of Special Education and Rehabilitation Services by President George Bush.

In view of the deaf civil rights movements, it is much more imperative that deaf studies courses be initiated in high schools in order to inspire deaf students to become proud, confident, competent first-class citizens in our society. Such courses will enable them to understand the implications of their deafness and how to maintain or develop a healthy perspective. In other words, to paraphrase Dr. Jordan, these students should see themselves as whole human beings who can do anything that hearing people can, except hear.

Today a growing number of high schools are offering courses in the area of deaf studies. Some schools for deaf students probably do not include deaf studies owing to the lack of textbooks on deaf culture designed for deaf youth. Developing a syllabus and materials for a course in deaf studies would require a great many hours of preparation.

Not only do more schools and colleges need to offer deaf perspectives in their programs, they also need to consider both the quality and focus of concern. Do we pay enough attention to courses that should be added to teacher training programs? In the past, more emphasis was placed on speech and auditory training in these programs. For example, when I was a graduate student, I was required to take the course, "Teaching Speech to Deaf Children," while other hearing classmates were not required to take sign language classes in order to become certified teachers of deaf students. Deaf studies should be considered an important asset to the teacher training curriculum.

Attitudes toward deaf people and their sign language are often acquired at an early age, and these attitudes are frequently both stereotyped and prejudiced. Deaf children are too easily seen as problems by their hearing teachers and other staff members who lack understanding of and respect for both ASL and deaf culture.

A climate of prejudice will often result in the underachievement of deaf children, who may often be confused about which language they are using. Many hearing teachers with deaf education teaching certificates cannot sign as well as their students, and even more disturbing is the fact that they often cannot even understand their students. These students may eventually model their sign language after whoever has taught them, which could result in idiosyncratic use of language with diminished utility for communication.

One important concept here is that every deaf student has the right to an early language environment in which American Sign Language is used. Acquiring a language base as soon as possible also will allow cognitive structures to develop and mature. With proficiency in ASL, a logical systematic transition to written English can be more readily accomplished.

At most residential schools, deaf students often learn ASL and become familiar with deaf culture in the dormitories, away from the formal classroom. They are introduced to the social life of deaf students in an informal dormitory environment, where they experience a strong bond of communication during their school years. This knowledge and sense of belonging is transferred through the deaf children of deaf parents who have graduated from the same school, or from the deaf staff members. With this system, many deaf graduates still feel at times that their language is inferior because they have not learned in classrooms that theirs is a proper and unique language.

Because the number of deaf teachers is currently small, the deaf studies curriculum needs to supplement the lack of exposure our students have to deaf culture. Through deaf studies, deaf people can be invited to classes, teach mini-courses, and serve as role models. This contact with deaf adults from various walks of life would be the best vehicle for preparing students for their future roles as deaf adults. They can see how the deaf presenters accept their deafness and how they express their feelings about being deaf with other deaf people.

This precious involvement with the deaf community can eventually lead to a smooth transition from school into a community where the students will already have good contacts with their mentors and role models. This, in turn, will serve to make the deaf studies courses a better learning environment for deaf students.

Obviously the time has come for us seriously to consider implementation of deaf studies in all schools and programs for deaf students. In 1978 we implemented a course called Deaf Awareness at the Minnesota State Academy for the Deaf (MSAD). It was offered as an elective course for juniors and seniors on a semester basis. The topics included various communication methods, understanding hearing loss, and the deaf community. This course is now known as Deaf Studies and is currently offered as a required course for every high school student.

When I decided to incorporate deaf heritage into the deaf awareness course, the question arose in my mind, "Why don't we have deaf studies?" Back in 1976, when I was in my first year of teaching American history at MSAD, many of my students asked me why deaf people did not appear in history textbooks. They wanted me to discuss famous deaf people. I was very much surprised and touched by their request.

This prompted me to look up the local historical materials related to deafness in our school library. Eventually I found the materials and developed my deaf heritage unit in conjunction with the American history curriculum. I presented biographies of famous deaf people from Minnesota as well as other parts of this country. I noticed that the students became more motivated, asked more questions, and more often took the initiative to communicate.

On a personal level, I have been involved in deaf historical research and continue to share this information with my classes. The task of collecting information is both time-consuming and expensive, but it is vital to the development of the present deaf studies curriculum at MSAD. Because no textbooks on deaf studies are available, reading materials have been gathered from a wide variety of sources. I have revised the curriculum several times owing to new information I continue to find on deaf culture and the many new interesting publications regarding deafness. I also needed to add some more units to the present curriculum.

The Aims and General Objectives of Deaf Studies

In developing the deaf studies curriculum, I have attempted to provide three significant areas of focus: knowledge, attitudes, and skills. A key concept in this curriculum is that reciprocal relationships exist between each area of focus. Knowledge affects attitudes; attitudes in turn affect knowledge; both affect skills, and so on. These three areas cannot appropriately be thought of as occupying separate domains, each distinct from the other.

Figure 1 proposes distinctions between three separate levels of knowledge, and between three main themes. The three levels of knowledge—description, analysis, and evaluation—merge with each other and affect each other but can be kept separate for the sake of clarity. The three major themes—deaf culture, interdependent relationships, and conflict—are inevitably arbitrary, but at least they have a common-sense appeal and can be used as a basis for syllabus planning.

Knowledge of Deaf Culture

1. *Description*—Deaf students will be able to perceive and describe the main ways in which their deaf culture is similar to and different from hearing society.
2. *Analysis*—Deaf students will compare and contrast physical, communication, and social aspects of the two cultures.
3. *Evaluation*—Deaf students will respond with personal views and judgments on the advantages and disadvantages of membership in the deaf and the hearing society.

Knowledge of Interdependent Relationships

1. *Description*—Deaf students will be able to perceive and describe the main ways in which events and trends in the deaf community can affect and be affected by events and trends in hearing society.

FIGURE 1: The general objectives of Deaf Studies.

2. *Analysis*—Deaf students will analyze this relationship with respect to the concepts of rights, equality, and due process of law. They will cite examples from their own and other cultures.
3. *Evaluation*—Deaf students will respond with personal views and judgments on controversial issues and theories related to societal relationships.

Knowledge of Conflict

1. *Description*—Deaf students will be able to describe some of the main cultural conflicts of today and to identify examples of cultural conflict in their personal experience or from personal observation.
2. *Analysis*—Deaf students will understand objective conflicts of interest, misunderstanding, stereotypes, prejudice, oppression, discrimination, and other related areas.
3. *Evaluation*—Deaf students will respond with personal views and judgments regarding the causes and mechanisms of conflict.

Attitudes

1. *Self-respect*—Deaf students will have a sense of their own worth as individuals, confidence in their own ability to understand complex issues and solve problems, and pride in their own particular social, cultural, and family backgrounds.
2. *Curiosity*—Deaf students will be motivated to find out more about issues related to living in the deaf community and the hearing community, particularly those issues that directly affect their own lives.
3. *Open-mindedness*—Deaf students will approach issues with a critical but open

mind and will be ready to change and/or add to their ideas and commitments as they learn more.

4. *Appreciation of deaf culture and other cultures*—Deaf students will be ready to accept and appreciate the values of deaf culture as well as other cultures in our community and other communities.

5. *Justice*—Deaf students will understand and value democratic principles and processes at local, national, and international levels.

6. *Commitment*—Deaf students will be ready to commit themselves to the creation and maintenance of a more just social order through active membership in particular organizations.

Skills

1. *Enquiry*—Deaf students will be able to find and record information about deaf studies from books, photographs, newspapers, and audio-visual materials and will be able to interview deaf people to gain a better understanding of society in general through the experiences of others.

2. *Expression*—Deaf students will be able to explore and express their ideas and feelings using a variety of communication methods and also participate in independent projects such as ASL storytelling and poetry, written prose, discussion, and pictorial expressions of various kinds.

3. *Reasoning*—Deaf students will be able to compare and contrast, generalize, hypothesize, form conclusions, and explain and justify their views with sound reason and evidence.

4. *Empathy*—Deaf students will be able to empathize with the feelings and perspectives of other people in situations different from their own deaf culture.

5. *Social skills*—Deaf students will be able to express their views, wishes, and feelings clearly in various situations through their relationships with each other or through group discussions with members of the deaf community and other minority groups, and to understand accurately the words and behavior of others.

6. *Political skills*—Deaf students will be able to join with others to influence decision-making concerning the education they are currently receiving; issues at various levels within their own deaf community; and in local, national, and international affairs.

The aims of an effective deaf studies program are ambitious and present a tremendous challenge. The teachers' attitude affects the success of teaching deaf studies. The teacher must always keep in mind the goals that have been set for the deaf studies curriculum and work toward the end product of deaf students who have developed respect for themselves and others and who have the ambition to use their abilities to the fullest extent.

The deaf studies classroom teacher, in my opinion, should be a member of the deaf social group and should also be a participant in significant activities in the deaf community. His or her role should not be limited to being a social studies teacher and a member of the Parent-Teachers Association. Rather, the deaf studies teacher also should participate actively in community service activities, because in this way the teacher will gain invaluable insights that will increase his or her effectiveness in teaching deaf studies.

Deaf studies can be a rich and vibrant offering that will motivate and inspire deaf students. Its implementation in schools and programs for deaf students are long overdue. High schools must include deaf studies curricula so that every deaf student's curiosity about what it is like to be a deaf adult in both the hearing and deaf worlds will be greatly accelerated.

All deaf students should be offered the opportunity to know and understand their own heritage and culture. With this knowledge, they will be empowered with the sense of identity, confidence, and security they will need to meet life's challenges and be successful and productive citizens.

Adult Education in the Deaf Community: The Australian Deaf Heritage

LINDA WARBY AND MICHAEL CLANCY

The deaf and hard of hearing community includes a wide diversity of individuals with varying communication styles. Within this community is the Deaf culture, those people who communicate with sign language. Why the capital "D" for Deaf?

Using "Deaf" as a proper noun is an important part of the identity of Deaf people, for whom the term "disabled" fits uncomfortably. If you have a group of deaf people communicating fluently in sign, and one hearing person, who is not, then who is disabled? It depends on your perspective.

For Deaf people, the issue is clear. Belonging to "The Deaf Community" and using sign language lie at the very core of a Deaf person's identity. So while deafness is a description of a condition, "Deaf" is viewed as the name of a cultural group (like the British, the French, etc.).

Members of the Deaf community have common interests, concerns, and needs. A number of these are addressed in community adult education. The Adult Education Centre for Deaf and Hearing Impaired Persons in Sydney, Australia, provides a range of courses that promote the development of individuals and the community. These include reading and writing, computer skills, assertiveness training, stress management, Deaf studies, and lobbying skills.

However, community adult education is not limited to a standard range of short courses offered regularly to a large population. Deaf people in Australia are a small, dispersed population, many of whom share negative experiences of education and are reluctant to venture near a classroom. Nevertheless, any analysis of the condition of Australian Deaf people indicates that many are undereducated, have low literacy levels, and have poor access to information. As individuals and as a community, they have lacked many of the tools that provide the basis for self-determination.

An important role of adult education within a community is to use the educational model to work with the positive community-building activities of that community. An additional goal of this Adult Education Centre (AEC) is the production of educational resources. The AEC has demonstrated that there is a market for materials such as sign language videos.

So how does an educational center support the promotion and collection of Deaf history and culture, and at the same time produce educational resources?

The New South Wales Association of the Deaf is the umbrella organization of Deaf clubs in New South Wales. They are concerned with promoting many of the issues and concerns of Deaf people, including Deaf rights and culture.

The Adult Education Centre and the New South Wales Association of the Deaf have negotiated an agreement to work jointly on a project that will record and preserve Deaf culture, produce an important educational resource, and at the same time lead to important learning outcomes for those involved in the project.

Working together, both of these organizations have undertaken the Bicentennial Collection of Deaf History on video—an oral history told in sign language. This history is composed of stories told in a visual language that does not convert easily to written English. Videotape has been used to record the life experiences of senior Deaf people. In this way, both organizations are working together to produce a cultural treasure that will grow in significance with the passing years.

The Adult Education Centre has provided the organizational structure for this production. The AEC's role has involved facilitating meetings, setting priorities, developing the budget, and supporting applications for grants. The AEC also provided video production information, negotiated with the production house, and provided the function of executive producer.

The AEC's role has also included a training component—training interviewers, providing information, introducing an oral history consultant, reviewing pilot programs, and training in making editing decisions. Involvement in a project such as this is a real hands-on learning experience, as real and as relevant as classroom learning.

In addition, the AEC provided the important financial investment in the project. While we are seeking funds from other sources, the AEC is underwriting the project. If there is no funding, the AEC will sell the videos at a price that would recover this investment.

The New South Wales Association of the Deaf provided the link with the Deaf community. Deaf leaders were involved in areas such as planning the project, selecting the interviewees, providing the interviewers, briefing the interviewees, and organizing timetable details. They reviewed the videotapes and made editing decisions. They will be interpreting the sign language into an English script. At the same time they are learning about interviewing, oral history recording, video production, and project coordination. These are important skills in a community that requires video skills if it is to record its language and culture.

The team has successfully completed ten half-hour interviews and has made many of the required editing decisions. They are about to record another ten interviews. These will be compiled, and a voice interpretation will be placed on the soundtrack. A written script will be produced to go with each video.

By the middle of 1989, we expect to have completed a project that will provide a resource of special value to Deaf education and sign language instruction and research. It will be sold throughout Australia and New Zealand.

At the same time, the Deaf community has acquired a historical record of great significance. With the advance of technology, the collection will in time be transferred to a laser disk, which will provide a permanent record of the use of sign language in 1988 and insights into the lives of deaf people in the middle and early twentieth century. This collection has been aptly given the name, "Heritage in Our Hands."

PART EIGHT

Deaf/Hearing Interaction

Editor's Introduction

Interactions between Deaf and hearing people tend all too often to be marred by superficiality, misunderstanding, and prejudice. The statistical rarity of profound, childhood deafness (occurring in fewer than one in a thousand people) no doubt helps to perpetuate this problem. Unless family members are deaf or deafness is related to professional concerns, hearing people seldom feel motivated to learn sign language or to try to understand Deaf culture. Unfortunately, even the hearing parents and educators of deaf children—who have much at stake in deaf children's development—are often more interested in helping these children speak and behave as much as possible like hearing children than in learning to take full advantage of the children's propensity for sign language and thirst for visually accessible knowledge.

In light of the above, it is understandable that many of the papers in this section express frustration and anger over the failure of hearing people to recognize and make appropriate use of Deaf people's strengths. Some express the view that Deaf people must find more effective ways to bring their needs and capabilities to the attention of a predominately hearing world. The Deaf Way Conference itself was one forum in which such an effort was undertaken; the publication of this volume is yet another.

Ritva Bergmann (Denmark), a Deaf mother of Deaf children, recalls in the first of these papers being advised by hearing counselors always to speak when she signed, a practice that forced her to abandon the natural patterns of Danish Sign Language. Bergmann reports that she eventually rebelled against this mandate, much to the delight of her own children and her deaf daycare charges, who appreciated this expression of acceptance and celebration of being Deaf.

The next three papers describe a range of problems experienced by Deaf people growing up or working with hearing people in France. At the time of The Deaf Way (and presently) oralism still prevailed in French deaf education programs, in spite of the existence of a few experimental bilingual education classes and programs. Rachid Mimoun describes how deaf children brought up in oral home and school environments tend to be deprived of the subtle and detailed flow of information everyone needs to adjust behavior to match social expectations and opportunities. Mimoun rejects the tendency to blame deaf children for failing to learn, saying that hearing parents and educators, refusing to learn and use sign language with deaf children, have "not adapted to the situation."

Pascal Smith (France) describes his experience as the only Deaf teacher in a deaf education program. Although the children Smith taught (signing without voice) thrived in his presence, and although their parents appreciated his value to their children (and themselves), Smith felt threatened by the school's hearing (and oral) educators, who made little effort to communicate with him, who were reluctant to acknowledge the significance of his contribution, and who regarded his advice as impertinent. Daniel Abbou (France) then describes a similar teaching experience in which he became increasingly disillusioned with the "pipe dream" of integration, noting that hearing teachers generally avoided him, possibly out of fear of being shown to be unable to communicate effectively with a Deaf, nonspeaking adult.

In her paper, Lourdes Pietrosemoli (Venezuela) analyzes some seldom-mentioned consequences of oral educational policies in which the integration of deaf people into hearing society is held up as the primary goal. Pietrosemoli shows through various Venezuelan examples that there are limits to the extent to which Deaf and hearing people can expect fully to understand each other if the hearing people are unfamiliar with Deaf culture and sign language as it is used by Deaf people. She implies that a realistic acceptance of these limitations might be wiser than clinging to illusory expectations.

Leo Jacobs (United States) points out that in the United States Deaf people generally strive for a balance between full social lives within their "own society" and interactions with hearing people in which respect for Deaf people's separate language and culture is requested. Jacobs maintains that although hearing Americans' attitudes toward Deaf people have improved in recent years, it is still common for hearing people to approach Deaf Americans in an unconsciously patronizing manner. In the following paper, Robert Sanderson (United States) demonstrates the importance to Deaf individuals of having sufficient numbers of service providers (such as rehabilitation counselors) who are experienced in interacting with Deaf clients. Sanderson implies that service providers who are offering information and advice rather than mere technical assistance are of little value to Deaf clients unless they understand sign language.

In the next paper, Liisa Kauppinen (Finland) points out that if Deaf people are passive and fail to clarify their needs and demand their rights, hearing people will ignore them (providing either no education or oral education) or will try to change them surgically (through cochlear implants) into hearing people. Kauppinen urges Deaf people to break their dependency on hearing people and unite behind a global demand for education through sign language. "If we who are Deaf don't learn to govern our own lives," Kauppinen says, "others will decide things for us."

Alan Jones (South Africa) describes a variety of initiatives undertaken by the South African National Council for the Deaf (SANC) to bring the needs and capabilities of Deaf people to the attention of hearing South Africans, most of whom have no idea how to communicate with Deaf people. J. S. David's (Sri Lanka) description of conditions in Sri Lanka illustrates how misinformation about deafness can tragically affect deaf children's lives—years often being wasted while hearing parents futilely await the spontaneous emergence of speech in these children.

Valerie Moon (Australia) describes numerous steps being taken in Australia to overcome hearing people's ignorance of deafness and to make library and other services more accessible and appealing to Deaf Australians. Moon's paper points out that Deaf people can sometimes find reliable allies in the hearing world, with whom they can work cooperatively to improve conditions for the Deaf community.

In this section's final paper, Ann Billington-Bahl (United States) discusses the potential benefits to Deaf Americans of a surge of interest among hearing people in learning sign language and interacting more effectively with Deaf people. Billington-Bahl attributes much of this interest to the impact of such films as *Children of a Lesser God* and to the Deaf President Now movement of 1988.

Experiences of a Deaf Mother and Preschool Teacher

RITVA BERGMANN

In Denmark, all families with deaf children are entitled to parent guidance from the schools for the deaf, the audiology centers and the Children's Clinic in Copenhagen. Most parents of deaf children are hearing, and all parent counselors are also hearing. There are no deaf parent counselors in our country— yet.

I experienced parent guidance twelve years ago. Perhaps you will wonder if it is necessary to give parent guidance to deaf parents of deaf children: Deaf people know everything about deafness. We know what it is like to be deaf. We master sign language, and we don't have any communication problems. You can compare deaf parents and their deaf children with hearing parents and their hearing children; neither group needs support or parent guidance, because their children are normal. But is this always true? No—you cannot say for certain.

We must remember that hearing parents normally have excellent sources of information on childbearing and children—contacts with people, workshops and courses, prenatal classes, TV, radio, books, and so on—that may not be available to deaf parents.

Our hearing parent counselor felt that it was unnecessary to guide us, not only because we are deaf, but also because we are teachers. As teachers, we often give hearing parents guidance and information about deafness, so what could a parent counselor tell us that we didn't already know? But we were new parents, and just as many other parents, we had thousands of questions. We were uncertain of what to do. There is a big difference between being a professional and being a parent.

We needed to talk with professionals, but unfortunately we became the professionals in this situation instead of being the parents. We had to guide our child's daycare center. We gave the teaching assistant sign language lessons and information about how to stimulate language development. We did it for free, because we wanted our child to be happy and able to communicate with someone in sign language. We gave and gave, but what about ourselves? We really needed guidance, but we got none.

Since most deaf children have hearing parents, the parent guidance program was developed and designed for hearing parents who know nothing about deafness and sign language. The parent counselors have programs of standard questions to ask during visits with hearing families with deaf children. These questions might include: Can your child hear when you are vacuum-cleaning? Does your child use his or her voice? Does your child benefit from his or her hearing aid? How on earth can we—deaf parents— answer such questions?

The parent counselor suggested that I borrow different musical instruments so our deaf child would experience different sounds, learn to differentiate them, benefit more from his hearing aid, and so on. Well, I thought, now we must have music in our deaf home. Now we must be like other families. No normal family life without music!

Through this kind of parent guidance, we deaf parents would come to feel that we are not good enough. Maybe we are good examples of the failure of the education of the deaf. Our children should not be as we were. They must learn to speak better, to read and write better, to have more knowledge, to be more integrated in the hearing community, and so on.

One day my husband proudly told our parent counselor that our daughter, at the age of almost nine months, had signed BATH. She asked, "Can your daughter pronounce the word 'bath?'" My husband became frustrated, because it was more important to her that our daughter be able to speak.

When I proudly said that our child, at the age of twenty months, had mastered 170 different signs, the counselor asked me, "How many words can your child pronounce?" I also became frustrated with the fact that she was more interested in words than in signs.

The parent counselor showed a picture of a dog and to check if our son could sign DOG. But our son, at the age of two, had known what a dog was for several months. He was now very interested in knowing the different breeds of dogs, and of course he signed POODLE. The counselor didn't know the sign for poodle and said, "No, it's not BATH; It's DOG." (The sign POODLE is similar to BATH.) She told me that I had to work with my son every day because it was important for him to have concepts.

At three, our son had well developed sign language. His language level was equal to the spoken language level of a hearing child of the same age. Another parent counselor wanted to know how many signs our son had mastered. I pointed out the he had normal language development. He not only used single signs, but he also signed sentences. It seemed that she didn't realize that our son had mastered a language—maybe because many books and articles were talking about numbers of signs rather than about signed sentences.

When a parent counselor visits a hearing family with a deaf child, she says, "Please remember to use signs when you are talking with your child." Suddenly the hearing family feels a big change in their everyday communication. Now they must use a mode of communication that is strange to them. It is difficult to talk in this new way. New problems arise for the family.

We had the same experience with our first deaf child. Our parent counselor said to us, "Please remember to use voice when you are talking with your child." Suddenly communication became odd to us; we had always used Danish Sign Language without voice in our deaf families. Out with Danish Sign Language! Now we should use another mode of communication—signed Danish with voice. Our deaf grandparents should also use their voices while talking with their deaf grandchild.

We started to use signed Danish with voice, but we wondered if we were doing the right thing. On the one hand, we wanted to use our native language—sign language—but on the other hand, we wanted our boy to learn to talk. If we only used sign language, would it mean that we weren't giving him a chance to learn to talk? We were divided on that question, but when we had our second baby two-and-a-half years later, we knew that we should use sign language without voice. Since then we have felt that we are doing the right thing.

What about creating a program specifically for deaf parents of deaf children? We do not have the same problems and needs as hearing parents. I am sure that deaf parents of deaf children would be happy to have deaf people as their parent counselors, but we have none in Denmark. I believe that in Sweden there are three parent counselors who are deaf, and that they are doing very well. They work with both deaf and hearing parents. I think it is a good idea to have both deaf and hearing parent counselors. They can cooperate, complement each other, and share their knowledge and experience.

As a preschool teacher, I had some experiences in guiding hearing parents of deaf children. The hearing parents told me that there was a big difference between hearing and deaf teachers. They told me that they often had bad feelings about not forcing their deaf children to use voice or a hearing aid at home. I was always the first person to say "Let your child decide whether he or she wants to use voice and hearing aids or not."

I worked as a preschool teacher for eight years. In the beginning, I used Total Communication while communicating with and teaching deaf kids; this meant that I signed and talked at the same time. The school had only two deaf teachers at the time, my husband and me, but I noticed that my deaf students had a hard time discerning which of their teachers were deaf and which hearing, because all of us were signing and talking simultaneously. I felt I was putting on a show for the deaf kids, a show that I was hearing. So one day I made a resolution: I stopped signing and talking at the same time. I began to use Danish Sign Language, which my family and friends have always used in everyday communication.

What happened? The deaf kids became happier, and they understood me much more easily than before. Now it is clear to them that I am *deaf*, not a poor copy of a hearing person. From that day on, the deaf kids could better identify with me.

Of course, in other situations I talked—when shopping, for example. It was a good experience for the children to see how I managed to communicate with hearing people. Sometimes they could understand me. Sometimes I had to use paper and pencil because they could not.

In Denmark, we are developing a new philosophy in the education of the deaf. We are working toward bilingualism. Deaf children become bilingual by having Danish Sign Language and Danish as two equal languages. Bilingualism in the education of the deaf also means that children have Danish Sign Language as their first language. They will learn Danish later, as their second language. It will be taught as a foreign language.

The goals of sign language as a subject in the curriculum are that deaf students

❖ Become aware that their sign language *is* a language

❖ Know the grammar and morphology of Danish Sign Language

❖ Be able to compare Danish Sign Language with Danish and vice versa

❖ Know about deaf culture through Danish Sign Language as we know Danish culture through Danish

❖ Know about the history of the deaf and

❖ Be able to enjoy telling stories in Danish Sign Language.

❖ By giving the same status to these two separate languages, Danish Sign Language and Danish, we try to make deaf kids bilingual and bicultural.

It is not simple. There is still a long way to go.

The Deaf Community: Why This Difficult Relationship with the Hearing?

RACHID MIMOUN

It is obvious that hearing adults usually communicate easily and are completely at home in society, while deaf individuals have many problems integrating. This creates impediments in relations between deaf and hearing persons. I think that in order to explain these impediments, one must look to the respective childhoods of deaf and hearing people.

Within the culture of the hearing, being able to hear is critical. Hearing people establish their social world and become a part of that world on the basis of a hearing norm. Deaf children develop differently. They base their behavior on their own perception of things.

When attending class at a very early age, hearing children already possess a language, an oral language, the hearing language, acquired through language immersion. This process permits them to conceptualize and understand what is being said around them and to express themselves through cries, which gradually develop into speech.

Such children have a totally valuable and fertile auditory life. To cite an example, when a child drops a bottle on the ground, an adult can intervene, explaining: "You must be careful of bottles, they can break," etc. Thus, there is an explanatory dimension for the hearing child through spoken language, which is deeply significant.

For deaf individuals, it is a different story. When they are small, deaf children are totally deprived of any language. (Of course, I am referring to those deaf children lacking exposure to French Sign Language—LSF.) Deaf children understand nothing of the conversations between two hearing persons. They play alone and, as they do not have full access to an auditory language, are unable to comprehend the language around them. If a deaf child should drop a bottle on the ground, hearing adults may scold the child, but they cannot explain to the child why a bottle should not be dropped.

This specific example shows just how precious language can be for social integration and for understanding one's own life. Without language, deaf children cannot be rendered responsible by means of explanation, as hearing children can. Hearing children can say, "Ah, yes. That's right; they told me this and that." They are able to grasp the consequences and are thus rendered responsible for their actions. Deaf children are not; they are left to their own devices. They inhabit a nonsensical world. They do not progress.

Here is another example: When a teacher introduces a subject to a hearing student, the student usually answers, "Thank you," knowing that in society, one offers thanks for such things. The deaf child, on the other hand, will offer no thanks. The teacher must intervene to tell the deaf child, "Thank me; you have to do it," without giving any explanations. The deaf child experiences this intervention as humiliating. He or she is unable to understand why these social rules were established, has no way of knowing that they are a standard for all of society.

There is also the issue of facial expression. Very often a hearing child who forgets to say "thank you" is looked at irritatedly by a hearing adult. The hearing child will make the connection with the situation that has just occurred—forgetting to say "thank you." The deaf child, however, will simply suspect that the adult is wicked. Such failures to communicate often lead to behavior problems in deaf adolescents.

Hearing children, after one or two awkward incidents or errors, manage to right things again. Because they have been immersed in the language, in explanations, they can foresee the consequences of their actions. For deaf children, the opposite occurs; they don't correct their misunderstandings. Quite the contrary—their behavior problems become more and more serious, to the point in the relationship where the hearing adult will be forced to punish the deaf child to make the child realize that he or she has committed an error.

Not until they are sixteen or seventeen years old do deaf adolescents begin to understand that breaking things is wasteful, while a ten-year-old hearing child will have already grasped the idea. These differences, and the potential estrangement and conflict that can develop between deaf and hearing people, become noticeable around the age of eighteen, at adulthood.

In my opinion, the problems in relations between deaf and hearing individuals are attributable to the schools. Many things are lacking in the education of deaf children, which does not allow them to become whole, self-sufficient human beings in society. Hearing children, on the other hand, learn the social rules that permit them to belong. Of course, there may be some obstacles for hearing adults as well, but it is safe to say that 70 percent of deaf adults have not grasped the rules of a primarily hearing society. Having received an education in a system in which they were able to understand everything, adult hearing persons are prepared to take part in life, to respect the law, to respect the rules. Deaf children have no idea of a what a law is, because their hearing teachers, ignorant of sign language, were unable to communicate that information.

When one is hearing and cannot communicate with deaf people, it is difficult to understand the way deaf people think and thus to respond to their needs. Deaf children end up with a somewhat unrealistic conception of their environment because their teachers are unable to answer their questions with subtlety or detail. Instead of saying that it is deaf children who have behavioral problems, perhaps one must reverse the issue and say that it is the hearing instructor who has not adapted to the situation.

Later, as adults, hearing persons continue to acquire learning because they have an appropriate foundation to do so. But deaf children experience their coming of age—that is to say, their eighteenth birthday—as a holiday. They no longer wish to be submissive, as they have had to be during their formative years. The only way they have to reject their education is to contact hearing persons as little as possible and to regroup among deaf people who can answer their questions. The problem is that they are asking these questions at the age of twenty, when they could have asked them much earlier if they had been in contact with people who knew their language.

In deaf culture, explanations are given in the traditional LSF manner, meaning that the older individuals explain to the younger ones what life is like according to their own experience. Deaf adults get this information at twenty years of age, while hearing children get it much earlier, through their teachers and in their social lives. That is why deaf adults of twenty cannot achieve total social integration—which brings us to the current problems between deaf and hearing people.

Often a deaf child will interrupt a conversation between two hearing adults. Why? Because the child does not know the rules about participating in a conversation. The reaction of the hearing people is very often violently to rebuff the deaf child, who fails to understand why he or she is not being allowed to contribute. I believe this experience of being forbidden to communicate removes all desire on the child's part to contact hearing persons again. In a hearing family with a deaf child, the family, which should provide the ideal place for communication, fails to meet its responsibility. Hearing children having problems relating to their teachers can talk about it with their parents and request explanations from them; there is always the option of falling back on the family if school isn't going well. Hearing children can master the social rules either with family or at school, while deaf children are denied this possibility. Their deadlock occurs both at school and at home.

The communication rules of hearing people are unlike those of deaf people. For example, a deaf individual will get someone's attention by tapping on his or her shoulder, which is neither admissible nor tolerated among hearing people. Hearing rules about conversation function on an exclusively verbal level, while for deaf persons, they operate on the physical and visual levels. Thus, in most deaf/hearing interactions, the deaf person must read the lips of the hearing person, and the hearing person may become uncomfortable, feeling that the deaf person is staring at him or her. However, this behavior is in fact a cultural norm for deaf people, who must concentrate intently to interpret hearing people's facial expressions.

The apprenticeship of participation, as it relates to the hearing world, has never been explained to deaf children. The deaf child cannot understand how to interject himself or herself into a conversation, but if the child had already lived in a world of language—a language such as LSF, for example—he or she could understand what taking one's turn means. People could explain the conversational rules for both deaf and hearing worlds.

Hearing teachers are often not aware of all of their students' problems. They impute the troubles of deaf children to behavioral difficulties, without really being aware of the consequences or the causes of this behavior. A hearing adult dealing with a hearing child can have complete awareness of the child's problems because, through language, the adult can grasp all the subtleties of the child's behavior—a hesitation in the voice, a sad tone. A deaf child interacting with a hearing teacher cannot benefit from this kind of relationship. Deaf children thus find themselves left on their own, unable to express their troubles and frustrations. In their own defense, hearing teachers can cite national educational problems and institutional limitations and say that they cannot change their behavior; they are committed to the recommended educational methods.

In 1987, following several years of experience with a bilingual class, I observed that the deaf children in this class had the same understanding of society, the same comprehension of their world, as hearing children of the same age. Because the deaf children relate to me—a deaf adult—I can make myself available to them. I establish communication almost on all fours, so that I will be at eye level and able to help them follow what I tell them. My language is as precise as possible, so that the children can thoroughly understand what is being said. In the example of the dropped bottle, I can tell them why a bottle falls and why they should not let it fall. I can also teach them, through language, to envisage their own future. These children are ready to plan what they will be as adults.

Deaf children do not initially express themselves in a perfect way; they are rather awkward at first. Yet deaf adults are absolutely able to understand them, because they use the same language. Just as a hearing child babbles at first, and the mother knows what the child is saying, gradually deaf children acquire their own language and manage to communicate with as many people as possible. As a deaf adult, I can understand the prattle and awkward expressions of deaf children and respond to their questions. The deaf children in bilingual classes now will have no behavioral difficulties when they are twenty, of that I am sure.

One day I saw a deaf child push a hearing child on the playground. He quickly returned to apologize to the hearing child, something that never occurred with deaf children receiving an oralist education. Moreover, when I am signing with another deaf adult in LSF, my students know at what moment to interrupt. They can, through the vehicle of their deaf environment, identify with the rules of a particular society. I think that at eighteen they will be able to integrate themselves into hearing society and understand the rules by which they will have to abide.

At the present time, deaf adults communicating with each other in the street cannot stand to have a hearing person watch them, and they are aggressive about it. But I am convinced that when the children in my class now reach the age of twenty, they will not be ashamed of their language. They will be proud of it and share it with hearing people.

I have asked myself many questions about the way in which deaf people have learned to become a part of society. Today they learn this outside of school, when they reach adulthood. In the bilingual education we are establishing, however, deaf children are being prepared to become social beings at a very early age. This, as far as I am concerned, is the result that can be achieved for deaf children through bilingual education. I hope that the people in government responsible for setting educational policy will soon realize what a difference bilingual education can make.

We also should remember, however, that the family has a crucial role to play in explaining things to the deaf child. Family members too should be able to communicate in LSF in order to provide the child with the same advantages as a hearing child, who can count as much on his or her family as on the school.

I believe we must consider the complexity of hearing people's relationships with deaf children and the way that hearing people express themselves with deaf children, and avoid transferring the problems of communication to the child. Hearing adults should understand and be cognizant of how the deaf children with whom they interact may perceive them.

A Professional Deaf Educator in Spite of the System

PASCAL SMITH

Many special schools for deaf students in France are now seeking deaf teachers because the deaf population is starting to mobilize in defense of their language and their rights. Parents of deaf children are also waking up and demanding the use of signing in the schools, which are obliged to adapt to the trend. Large city schools have no trouble locating deaf individuals to recruit for these positions because deaf communities are fairly widespread there. In the particular average-size mountain region town that made me an offer, however, locating an education specialist proved to be more difficult.

The school sent requests throughout France, especially to schools for young deaf persons. As I was unemployed at the time, I considered their offer very attractive, especially because as a child I had dreamed of becoming a teacher—a dream that my own instructors felt was unrealistic. After a visit to the school, meetings, and discussions, I found myself hired and suddenly thrust into a very difficult position.

With my parents and sisters who are deaf, I had lived until that time nearly exclusively in a deaf community, meeting hearing persons only occasionally when necessary. Now here I was, submerged full-time in an unknown hearing world, and, further, without any professional experience.

No deaf person in France can receive a diploma to work with children. Our speech education does not permit us to reach a level high enough for such an achievement. Throughout my school years, I had been repeatedly told that anything even slightly intellectual was too hard for me. My belief in my potential had been suppressed, and naturally I was worried to find myself in a post of responsibility.

My First Encounter with the Children and their Parents

Then I met the children, a group between six and nine years of age. Initially I was struck by the poverty of their language, and I was obliged to regress in my communications to meet them on their level. For their part, the children, who only occasionally had had the opportunity of meeting adult deaf people, were delighted that a deaf person should come there to stay, just for their sake. They looked at me wide-eyed, just as I no doubt looked at them. We were equally eager to get to know each other and communicate, but we were not at ease.

What made it truly difficult was that hearing people were always observing us. We needed some time to forget their presence and feel at home with each other. I was even more uncomfortable than the children under the eyes of these hearing observers. They were hearing individuals, yes, but—even worse—they were professionals watching and evaluating me. Almost all novices have had similar feelings, but for a deaf novice, what anguish to experience this from hearing people to whom one feels inferior!

The hearing group was not much more relaxed than I was. I commanded enough respect for them to feel they had to sign with me, but they were self-conscious about their own lack of ability in signing and hesitated to communicate.

As for the parents, they remained silent during an introductory meeting. It was doubtless my presence that made them react so intensely. For six years or more, they had been asking themselves questions about their child's future. Then suddenly they were confronted with a young deaf adult, the image of what their child might become.

My Experience in the Town

At first I was happy enough about being hired. But this feeling gave way very quickly to anxiety. I soon felt lost amidst these hearing people. By nature, I'm a great gabber, used to talking a blue streak, but I now found myself completely isolated. The school administrators had been in a hurry to hire a deaf person, and now they were very proud to show me off to everyone. However, in their haste, they had forgotten about the interpreting problem.

Of course, I quickly became acquainted with the town's deaf population. But there too my enthusiasm was soon dampened. Coming from a large city, I was used to meeting a lot of deaf people easily. In a mountain town, however, communication is more difficult, and inhabitants are slightly isolated within their region. I found myself with self-absorbed deaf individuals whose social life was very limited—people who were not used to taking responsibilities and had few cultural, political, or social skills, or little knowledge.

These deaf people signed, of course, but their language level was a reflection of their lives—simple and routine. They often mixed signing and speech together. In fact, the deaf person who signs and uses speech is considered educated, intelligent. Those not using speech are viewed as ignorant, even simple-minded.

I became known as "the mute one" because I signed without speech, and because I did so, people thought of me as someone who would probably have a lot of trouble taking care of himself.

My Life at the School

The children had already used some signing before I came, but they did not attach a lot of importance to it. Speech was emphasized. As a result of our meetings and exchanges, they gradually began to feel they could truly express themselves with their hands, that this was simple to do and to understand, and thus that signing had real value as a communication tool. A new sense of identity gradually developed as we worked together. Happy to be like this adult whom they were getting to know, the children began to accept the fact that they were deaf. Relationships among the children themselves became closer as they also developed relationships with me. Although they had good, sharing, affectionate relationships with hearing individuals, they could not trust them absolutely. In fact, if a hearing adult explained something to them, they would come to me for confirmation.

My Work with the Hearing Team

The professionals at the school had given much thought to hiring a deaf individual. They realized the need to include French Sign Language (LSF) and wanted a bilingual project as part of their program. Yet they could not bring themselves to consider me a full-fledged member of their team, a totally responsible professional. They perceived me as an "advisor," with no more status than that. They had hired a deaf person to prevent children unable to reach an acceptable speech level from failing, but they considered me fairly useless with children already able to speak. In other words, they were proceeding with their work as usual, thinking of me as an auxiliary tool to shore up their failures.

With no experience in the field, I hoped and expected to work with totally competent and knowledgeable professionals. Over time I was able to observe them at work—how they taught the children, what they taught—and I began to think of other ways to teach that seemed more appropriate to me. Gradually I began to intercede to explain my point of view and offer my observations. At first, my suggestions were welcomed, and instructors modified some elements of their teaching methods. But after a while, they began to feel that I was meddling a little too much in their affairs.

This was a delicate situation that made me most uncomfortable. As a modest young beginner, I was giving advice to educated, competent people. My confidence grew, however, with encounters, dialogues, and discussions. Eventually I came to feel that, even when my ideas were being questioned, I was correct in my objections to their methods. And that is when the war began. I was trying to understand their viewpoint, their methodology, and I knew that the weight of tradition was on their side. They had the power of "know-how." All I had was brand-new glimmerings of ideas about a better way of teaching. I must have seemed somewhat expendable.

It is not easy for a deaf individual to establish his place in the sun, to achieve status. For example, he works in a class with a hearing person who has well defined credentials and who is professionally known. If the children improve, the hearing person may take credit for the success and the deaf person's contribution may remain unacknowledged.

Professional hearing individuals cannot seem to fathom what the deaf culture is, its distinctive identity. They cannot comprehend who a deaf child really is and don't understand his or her uniqueness. In part because of these misunderstandings, they are always trying to make the deaf child more like the hearing child.

The Parents' View of the Deaf Person on the Team

What the parents see is a deaf person signing, without speech. They never get beyond that. Yet it is essential to provide them with the model of a deaf adult so that they can imagine what their child will become.

I am perceived two different ways by parents, depending upon whether or not their child is already speaking. Parents whose children have not yet reached the oral level are the most relieved to view this "acceptable" picture. When the first LSF courses were held, all the parents turned out. Gradually, the parents of the "speaking" deaf children deserted, never to return, while the other parents continued to attend classes.

It was easier for me to establish relationships with parents than with the professionals. Consider, for example, the parents of a young deaf girl who lived far away from the school but nevertheless made the journey to attend LSF classes. They told me afterwards that they were very anxious about what they would learn. They wanted to know what it means to be a deaf person; they had no valid or even hopeful idea. When they met me, they were comforted to find that I was a completely normal, ordinary person. For them, that meant that their daughter could turn out to be a normal adult.

As the days passed, thanks to our encounters, our meetings, the LSF courses, and my occasional home visits, the parents began to assign great importance to my position, especially because they could observe their children changing and progressing very rapidly. All of them told me that their children had improved tremendously following my arrival and that all of their children adored me. Naturally, though, as they were all hearing persons and had dreamed of having a hearing child, they had been shocked by their child's deafness and had held on to the hope of seeing them speak as they could. The parents truly welcomed LSF and gave their full confidence to the deaf individual teaching it. Yet they remained obedient to the professional hearing team, who knew what words to use to influence them and who, above all, possessed the "know-how." Of course, they had no idea what was really going on between team members.

My Thoughts after Teaching in a Special School

The position of a deaf individual wishing to work in a special school for deaf students in France is not an easy one. In fact, the problems are enormous. Initially, there is the difference in culture and languages. In addition, the bilingual objectives of such schools are in no way clear.

Hearing individuals continue emphasizing oral French communication; written French is awarded second place, and LSF, barely deemed a language, is considered instead an auxiliary tool. Personally, I placed LSF at the top of my list and written French in second place. Then oral instruction could follow depending upon parental preferences. In practice, my biggest problem was the absence of an interpreter.

The children notably improved, despite the retention of traditional methods. As for the parents, they are now demanding LSF and, on observing their children's development, are forging their own philosophies. They managed to learn just about as much as they want to know on their children's behalf, but they are up against the power of the "know-how" team.

The local deaf community only reinforces the problem. If professionals and parents were surrounded by active deaf people defending and asserting their rights, they would have to take their views into account. But a docile, reserved deaf adult population, deprived of autonomy, only provides the professionals with a negative image of what to expect from the children, whom they regard as "poor handicapped children."

Despite the children's progress, the situation as a whole was difficult for me to endure. Team problems were so basic that I felt as though I were a puppet in the professionals' hands. My own experience has made me think of the dozens of deaf people hired by special schools. They face the same problems as I did: no interpreters, and manipulation caused by inexperience.

Since the deaf population began to wake up and create bilingual classes and assert their rights, the schools have been forced to take some action. In order to save themselves the embarrassment of missing out on the trend, they have hired deaf people to "try out" LSF. Inherent in this kind of manipulation is a great danger for the future and a grave risk for us deaf people. If all the schools meet with failure in this experiment, the blame will be placed on deaf people and LSF. Other deaf persons working toward a true bilingualism will also be told that their effort is worthless because the assertion of failure will be applied across the board to all methods utilizing LSF, and, therefore, to bilingualism as well.

True, the hiring of a deaf person by a school is desirable, both for the children and for the deaf individual. But be warned that any failure that may result will be blamed upon the deaf person.

Hearing–Deaf Relations

DANIEL ABBOU

I would like to discuss, from a personal point of view, the relationships that can be cultivated between the world of the deaf and the world of the hearing.

I started out as a carpenter. I made various kinds of furniture and tables. Many deaf people like me have worked in manual trades, as painters, dressmakers, or printers. It was personally meaningful to me to be a workman and to be able to create a product. I could see the result of my work; thus I was worth something. There was something positive in me, and that belief helped give me confidence. Other deaf people have also experienced this satisfaction and confidence.

I did notice that when hearing people first met me—a deaf individual—they seemed ill at ease. They also seemed to have some preconceptions about deaf people, and were quite surprised by my professional abilities. But the fact that I was able to compare an object that I had created with those of my hearing co-workers allowed us to establish an exchange based on work.

I then realized two things: First, both deaf and hearing people need to allow a certain time to pass in establishing true communication in which the deaf individual can be acknowledged as a person. This is what I call the delay factor. This communication can occur despite language problems. Second, some kind of third-party intermediary element is needed in order to establish contact; this could be an object or an action of some kind.

Later, I observed a similar process—the different feelings deaf people inspire, the delay factor, and the need for some intermediary element—in my other contacts with hearing individuals. For example, I participated in sports such as football and tennis outside of school, and hearing people would ask me, "Really, you play football? Where? You mean you play it with hearing people?" I got thousands of questions about my leisure activities.

I resented hearing people's curiosity about me. I felt I was their equal in sports. I knew that I could adapt to any situation or individual. Unlike deaf people educated in the oral method, I was able to engage in social exchanges. Speech-oriented deaf people have difficulty getting to know either deaf *or* hearing people, because they are never comfortable with the delay necessary for their communication method to work.

After working as a carpenter, I was hired by a special school for deaf children to participate in an oralist project held in a bilingual class setting. This was an outstanding opportunity for me, considering how hard it is to get a job at such a school without a diploma.

I thought that I could assist the hearing specialists while working with the children. My experience as a teacher of French Sign Language (LSF) at the International Visual Theater had taught me that I could provide effective support regarding this particular language. However, as the sole deaf person in this large hearing group, I was soon completely beyond my depth.

What a pipe dream it is to speak of integrating deaf children with hearing children when a group of hearing professionals can't even accept a deaf adult on their team! The lack of recognition of the deaf individual in this kind of school seemed very serious to me. Had I been hired only so that the deaf children could identify with me? At the same time, I asked myself a lot of questions about these deaf children and their future.

Many things about the school bothered me. I kept seeing hearing people coming toward me with eyes as big as saucers, probably thinking, "What's with this deaf person? What is he here for?" I also was asking myself what was going on. In my carpentry workshop, everything went smoothly; elsewhere, I felt tense.

There were, however, several hearing people who knew a little LSF, particularly the person working with me in the bilingual class. The situation in this class was bilingual because there was a deaf instructor presenting LSF and a hearing instructor presenting written and spoken French.

We knew what limitations we had encountered in respect to our class and could imagine what other classes had to confront. Nevertheless, I had to go see what was occurring in the other classes and exchange and test my ideas with my hearing colleagues. This was very difficult to do, and I had to make a big effort to be flexible and diplomatic. I was always the one who took the first step, telling myself, "I must enter the world of hearing people, since it is difficult for them to enter mine."

I really tried for a very long time, and sincerely, but in vain. The moment I tackled an instructional problem with my hearing colleagues, a conflict would arise owing to the hearing individual's preconceptions about a deaf person who uses LSF. Moreover, my lack of training and the fact that I had no diploma were handicaps in this kind of work. (In contrast, deaf professionals with diplomas get immediate recognition.) Little by little, I found myself imprisoned inside this bilingual class, isolated from the other classes.

I had less and less communication with hearing people, and their attitude shocked me more than once. I feel that both hearing and deaf people should try to make an effort to establish communication, but at the school there was a group of hearing people who refused to approach me. Why was that? Were they so afraid of my desire to appear a deaf person, which is what I am? Was it so hard for them to accept my uniqueness as a deaf individual? Were they afraid to find themselves handicapped in front of children who were beginning to express themselves in LSF better than they could?

Finally, after five years of worsening conflict, I resigned. I felt bitter and disillusioned; my hopes for a successful bilingual project for this school were dashed. I took it as a personal failure.

Now I had to start all over again at zero and try to detach myself from my former experience. I got a job working in a bilingual center for children ages birth to six. At first, people judged me—whether speaking or signing—as a deaf person, but I felt that the situation could progress and that people could change. My administrative status was different, too; before, I had been a teacher, now I was an actual LSF instructor. My language was being taken seriously.

With time, I saw that this new experience was a positive one for me. I was meeting with various team members face-to-face, including the director and psychologist. I wanted them to regard me as an authentically deaf individual.

What interested me was working with the parents. Initially, they needed me to speak to them about my life as a deaf person. Gradually, owing to my relationship with their children, they began to recognize me as a professional. Because I didn't speak, the parents realized it was possible to communicate by means other than speech.

But actually, the parents' confidence was based more on the fact that they observed communication between deaf and hearing instructors than on their contact with a deaf adult. At this center, we instructors were aware of the mutual benefits we derived from our professional communications; we all listened to each other.

Following my experience at the center, I wanted to broaden my knowledge of other people with different backgrounds. It was for this reason that I joined Rainbow House, a center created by Françoise Dolto. It welcomes deaf children and their deaf parents, but also hearing children up to six years old. It was at Rainbow House that I found my true vocation.

Every hearing team member had participated in psychoanalysis; unfortunately, at the present time in France there are no deaf or truly bilingual psychoanalysts for deaf people. The role of psychoanalysis seems essential to me because it provides a means to approach the problem of the deaf in general, evaluate them in depth, improve the relationships between deaf and hearing parents, and create a communication network between deaf or hearing parents and specialists.

Hearing individuals who enter Rainbow Hose know in advance that they will be meeting deaf people, so I don't feel that I am considered a strange person. This is also the only professional relationship in which I do not feel that I am competing with hearing people. I have nothing to teach or to prove; I am there as a person just like the other team members.

A direct encounter between deaf people and hearing parents does not always go smoothly, but it is easier when children who want to know each other are present to act as intermediaries. Usually the children address the adults there without making a distinction between hearing and deaf people. When the parents realize that their child is communicating with an individual they know to be deaf, they are usually ready to communicate with that person also. The reverse is also true: When parents agree to meet with me, there is no problem thereafter with their children.

At Rainbow House, we noticed that many of the mothers who come there speak a foreign language. It is as if they sense that this is a place where language differences do not constitute a major obstacle to the creation of friendly bonds, where what matters is the welcome given to a human being.

Conclusion

In my contacts with people who are not deaf, I have always been able to adapt myself while maintaining my identity as a deaf person. I have observed that communication is always possible—with the exception of my experience at the special school, where my presence as a deaf individual irritated my hearing colleagues and exacerbated their frustration in trying to communicate with deaf children.

I have noted how often hearing people have preconceived, often negative, images about deaf people, and that it is necessary to allow some time together to dispel these images. Each of the two worlds—deaf and hearing—has its unique visual or auditory culture, and the possibility of total immersion in both cultures is limited.

There is a saying that seems to sum up my whole experience: "After a difficult trek through the jungle, advancing arduously in fitful starts, I have finally come upon a clearing . . . ."

Sign Terminology for Sex and Death in Venezuelan Deaf and Hearing Cultures: A Preliminary Study of Pragmatic Interference

LOURDES PIETROSEMOLI

The following dialogue actually occurred in a formal situation between a deaf woman (A) and a hearing woman (B) in Venezuela:

A: "Are you married?"
B: "No."
A: "You must have lovers, then."

It is pragmatically ill-formed in light of Venezuelan culture and, I dare say, in light of most mainstream western cultures. For the second statement of person A to be appropriate, A and B should have known each other for a considerable length of time, in which case A would already know the marital status of B. On the other hand, if A and B do not know each other well, as shown by the first question, then the subject of lovers is inappropriate.

Exchanges analogous to the one described above are common between deaf and hearing people in Venezuelan culture and usually result in pragmatic interferences. These conflicts in the functional use of the language have several results. Hearing people often consider deaf people to be naive, rude, or inappropriately direct. Deaf people, on the other hand, contend that hearing people usually misinterpret and misunderstand the signs they use, even when the deaf person explains their real meaning. Hearing people are sometimes shocked by the discourse of deaf people, even when both groups use spoken Spanish, as in the example cited above.

In this paper, I will examine linguistic factors that contribute to the communicative interference responsible for the above views. To this end, I will examine the use of lexicon and expressions related to the subjects of sex and death. The misuse of language in these areas usually leads to situations in which cultural norms are violated, while the appropriate use of language in these areas is an important part of being a native speaker of a language.

Another reason for examining the areas of sex and death is that the transmission of expressions related to these subjects has two main sources: The nonmarked expressions are usually acquired at home with the rest of the lexicon; the more marked ones, considered uncivil or vulgar, are acquired through the peer group at school, in the streets, or wherever conversations take place. This double source of acquisition has interesting implications in this study.

Misinterpretation of Signs

The so-called misinterpretation of signs is, in our view, related to two facts. First is the rank assigned by hearing people to the signs they use to talk about specific subjects, along with the incorporation (through borrowing) of some troublesome signs used by hearing people into the Venezuelan Sign Language (LSV) lexicon.

Second is the similarity between some of the structural aspects of common signs in LSV and the structural aspects of signs used by hearing people to talk about taboo themes.

The Rank of Signs in the Hearing Culture

A simple test was designed to find out how hearing people ranked the use of signs in specific situations. Subjects were given the following lists of equivalent expressions (each including five words or phrases and one sign commonly used by hearing people). They were asked to assign each expression a rank on a scale of increasing/decreasing politeness and to construct sentences using the expressions.

List 1: Expressions Related to Death
1. fallecer (perish)
2. estirar la pata (kick the bucket)
3. sign commonly used by hearing people to make reference to death (may function as a verb or a noun)
4. pasar a mejor vida (pass away)
5. morir (die)
6. expirar (expire)

List 2: Expressions Related to Sex
1. hacer el amor (make love)
2. tener relaciones sexuales (have sex)
3. copular (copulate)
4. sign commonly used by hearing people with roughly the same meaning
5. coger (fuck)
6. cohabitar (cohabit)

The evaluation of hearing people was as expected. One of the terms in each list (#5 in List 1 and #2 in List 2) qualified as the unmarked term, with a wide range of uses. Three of the terms qualified as markedly polite, and the slang and signed terms were placed at the extreme low end of the scale. The most polite and least polite terms have a narrower pragmatic distribution (i.e., a narrower range of uses). The results are represented in Figures 1 and 2.

The sentence-building test gave the same results as the ordering task. One detail worth mentioning is that the nouns chosen as subjects (in the case of the intransitive

```
    1   6   4   5     3 or 2
+   _____|___   −
              politeness
```

FIGURE 1: Expressions related to death.

```
    6   3   1   2     5 or 4
+   _____|___   −
              politeness
```

FIGURE 2: Expressions related to sex.

verbs) and objects (in the case of transitive verbs) of the slang and signed verbs usually referred to animals or low-class people.

Indiscriminate Borrowing

Deaf people's responses were quite different. Because both deaf and hearing people in general share the same values and views about sex and death, there is also a proliferation of signs to talk about these subjects in LSV. However, based on this study—according to what has been reported by the informants and our own observations—it appears that the LSV lexicon is not organized on a vertical scale of politeness; one sign is as good as another to talk about death or sex. The difference in use is more related to geographical dialect or personal preference. (One may argue that deaf Venezuelan persons are not usually involved in the same kind of social situations as hearing persons. As a consequence, their linguistic exchanges would require a different set of pragmatic rules. This is a point well worth researching in the future.)

Furthermore, the fact that "hearing signs" are structured the same way as LSV signs—signs that can be described as discrete sequences of features—makes all signs, both LSV signs and signs used by hearing people, intrinsically alike as linguistically arbitrary symbols in the mind of the deaf user. This facilitates the indiscriminate borrowing of signs from the hearing world. Though deaf people usually think they look more "hearing-like" if they use signs from the hearing culture, such borrowed signs are often considered highly uncivil by hearing people themselves. For example, two of the signs commonly used by hearing people with the meaning of "sexual intercourse" and "death/die" have been incorporated into LSV lexicon with the same status and distributional range as the more genuine signs of the deaf culture. (It is worth noting that genuine LSV signs used to refer to this topic are less understandable to hearing persons. Their use, therefore, would cause less interference.)

Structural Similarities

There are some structural similarities between the features of some common signs in LSV and the features of signs used in the hearing culture to refer to taboo themes. Below are six pairs of signs usually reported by deaf Venezuelans as troublesome when used or explained to hearing people. The signs marked "a" are common signs in Venezuelan Sign Language. The ones marked "b" are signs widely used in Venezuelan hearing culture (HC).

1a. PARTY (LSV): One- or two-handed sign. Y handshape. Two sequences of move (M) and hold (H) to equal (MHMH). Hands facing each other at shoulder height. The ulnar sides of the hands are toward the front vertical plane. The thumbs point to the back vertical plane of signer.

1b. "Sexual Intercourse" (HC): One-handed sign. Y handshape. Nonspecified sequences of MH. The ulnar side of hand faces the horizontal plane, and the thumb points upward.

2a. GOING HOME (LSV): Two-handed sign. MH sequence. The weak hand in slightly curved B handshape with opposed thumb and the back side parallel to horizontal plane. The strong hand has a B handshape with unopposed thumb, and its ulnar part is oriented to the horizontal plane. It traces a diagonal movement in front of the signer's chest until its ulnar part touches the weak hand placed at the same height.

2b. "Fuck you" (HC): Two-handed sign. MH sequence. The weak hand in curved B handshape with the fingers facing the tip of the thumb. The strong hand has a D handshape with its ulnar side oriented to the horizontal plane. It traces a diagonal movement in front of the signer's chest toward the weak hand placed at the same height.

3a. LAS TAPIAS (the name of a place) (LSV): Two-handed sign. MH sequence. The weak hand in a B handshape, thumb opposed. Palm facing the horizontal plane. The strong hand has all but middle finger closed. The palm faces the horizontal plane. It approaches the weak hand until the base of the strong hand touches the back of the weak hand.

3b. "Fuck you" (HC): One-handed sign. Same handshape as strong hand in 3a. The back side of the hand faces the vertical plane of the signer or the tip of the middle finger faces the object of the verb.

4a. "T" (LSV): The sign that corresponds to the letter "T" in the manual alphabet. This is a hold.

4b. "Fuck you" (HC): T handshape. It is usually a MH.

5a. SURE and ALWAYS (LSV): One-handed sign. D handshape with tips of thumb and index in contact (MH and MHMH respectively). Ulnar part of hand facing the horizontal plane.

5b. "Queer" (as an insult); "Anus" (HC): One-handed sign. D handshape with tips of thumb and index in contact. It can be either a H, a MH, or a sequence of MHMH.

6a. MILLIONAIRE (LSV): Two-handed sign. A HMH sequence. The weak hand in B handshape. Unopposed thumb. The ulnar part of hand makes contact with the inside part of the angle between right forearm and arm. The strong hand has a B handshape with unopposed thumb. Its back faces the horizontal plane during the first hold. At the end, it faces the vertical plane.

6b. "Fuck you" (HC): This sign has basically the same structure as 6a, but the strong hand has an S handshape.

The rough similarities and differences between the articulatory features of these signs are represented in Table 1.

It is worth mentioning that recently, linguistic change has been introduced by deaf users to modify the signs for LAS TAPIAS, "T," and MILLIONAIRE. The changes represent an effort to eliminate the features that make these signs similar to the "fuck you" signs used by hearing people. In the case of LAS TAPIAS, the handshape of the strong hand has been changed from a fist with an extended middle finger to a D handshape. In the case of "T," the handshape has changed from a fist to a handshape with three fingers extended, which results in a variant of the letter "F," but with the ulnar side of the

TABLE 1: Similarities and Differences Between Articulatory Features of Selected Signs

LSV	HC	Similarities	Differences
1a	1b	Movement features, point of contact	Facing, orientation
2a	2b	Movement features	Facing, orientation, point of contact
3a	3b	Movement features	Facing, orientation, Point of contact
4a	4b	Facing, orientation, point of contact	Movement features
5a	5b	Point of contact	Movement features, facing, orientation
6a	6b	Movement features, facing, orientation	Point of contact

index in contact with the thumb's fingernail. In the last case, MILLIONAIRE, the entire sign has changed, producing two homonymous terms: MILLIONAIRE and BLOOD.

Misinterpretation of Spoken Language

The dialogue at the opening of this paper took place between a deaf woman and a hearing woman immediately after they had been introduced to each other in a rather formal situation. The deaf woman is married to a hearing man. She has completed grammar school (the highest educational status achieved by the average deaf person in Venezuela), is a professional dancer, and is very prominent in her deaf community. Audiologically, she is considered hard of hearing rather than completely deaf. She enjoys social exchanges with hearing people because, in her view, "if deaf people communicate only among themselves, they do not know what is going on in the world." She communicated basically through spoken Spanish with a good level of vocal proficiency, although in the presence of hearing people, she is seldom reluctant to use LSV. She considers herself a good Spanish speaker and is against the use of LSV in schools as a means of instruction. Nevertheless, she is the protagonist of a dialogue that immediately—without her noticing—disqualifies her as an efficient speaker of Spanish (in linguistic terms) and as a courteous person (in social terms).

Her case is by no means atypical or isolated. It is, rather, a common situation for deaf people raised in the oralist tradition. Oralism, either in its overt form or under the name of Total Communication, is the most common approach to deaf education in Venezuela.

Before interpreting the information presented thus far, I will recapitulate some of the important points:

1. Hearing people react negatively toward some signs used to talk about specific matters in common situations.
2. Deaf Venezuelans generally do not perceive the difference in the use of signs taken from the hearing world and the use of their own signs, especially if both sets of signs refer to the same things in the outside world.
3. Hearing people's signs (real signs, not paralinguistic movements) refer mostly to taboo subjects: sex, death, money, digestive functions, etc.; hence the misinterpretation of normal LSV signs that share some features with these hearing signs.

4. Deaf people have introduced some changes to make these signs more acceptable in their social exchanges with hearing people.
5. Spoken Spanish has a proliferation of terms and expressions related to taboo subjects. It is an important part of the Spanish language acquisition process to match the use of each item with specific, appropriate situations.
6. Deaf Venezuelan people usually show little or no mastery of some of the basic pragmatic rules of spoken Spanish.

The facts above summarize the current situation of deaf Venezuelan people in their daily attempts at social integration into the mainstream culture. They also show that deaf and hearing Venezuelan groups have lived thus far in parallel worlds, with little or no interaction between them except for the occasional contact provided by the educational system.

The indiscriminate borrowing of "forbidden" signs on the part of deaf people and the misinterpretation of common LSV signs on the part of hearing people prove that the integration of these two groups is still in a very early stage. (I also must mention that the status of LSV as a legitimate linguistic system has only recently been recognized. The concept of using LSV as a means of transmitting knowledge is also quite new and not widely accepted.)

The sociolinguistic interference produced by the use of signs is related to the early attempts of deaf people to reaffirm their identity as DEAF and not as "second-class speakers" or "semi-speakers." They also show how little contact the groups have had after all these years of deaf education and attempts at integration through the oralist approach.

The interference in the case of the deaf woman using spoken Spanish is both more puzzling and more revealing. Deaf Venezuelans over the age of eighteen have had spoken Spanish as the only model of language acquisition throughout their oralist education. As I mentioned earlier, mastering the use of specific vocabulary in specific situations is part of being a native speaker of a language. I also have mentioned that the lexicon examined here and its corresponding use has two main sources for acquisition. One is the family, through daily linguistic interaction: In the normal acquisition of language, the home environment provides the more stable, dictionary-type, less marked terms to make reference to taboo subjects. The peer group usually provides the child with another set of terms and expressions to make reference to the same subjects in other contexts. Part of the socialization process through language is learning when, where, and how to use these terms.

In the case of deaf people over the age of eighteen in Venezuela, neither the family nor the school environment has provided information about basic linguistic pragmatics. On the one hand, deaf children do not get this information at home because most of them have hearing parents and, as a consequence, linguistic interaction at home is usually very limited. But they do not acquire this basic information at school, either. The peer group can inform a newcomer about the use of sign language, but they probably share the same level of ignorance about the use of spoken language in the hearing world.

To summarize, the misunderstandings between deaf and hearing people produced by the use of signs are typical of first-contact situations between a visual culture and a hearing culture. As such, they play an important role in the process of integration of deaf individuals into mainstream society. Deaf people in Venezuela are still trying to find a place in the world as DEAF individuals with a legitimate means of communication.

The misinterpretation of speech, however, is evidence of a different kind of problem—the cultural isolation that is characteristic of deaf Venezuelan people educated in the oralist tradition. It shows that the current oralist approach to deaf education has failed to accomplish its main goal, the formation of proficient speakers of Spanish.

The example chosen for this paper provides evidence that the approach toward deaf education of the last two or three decades has not presented deaf children with an accessible or coherent model for language acquisition. This fact has important implications for the future life of these deaf individuals. In the best case—that is, if some kind of signing were permitted in school—the child had some model for sign language acquisition and went through a socialization process within his or her peer group. This socialization enabled the child to function as a competent member of the deaf community.

In the worst case—a strict oralist education—the deaf individual did not acquire LSV or spoken Spanish, but left school with the false assumption that he or she could function in the hearing world as a speaker of Spanish. As a consequence, the individual would not know the basic linguistic rules necessary to be accepted by the hearing culture. The results show that, in the specific case examined, the desire to be a part of the hearing culture does not alone qualify one as a competent member of that culture. To know the rules is just as important.

Unconscious Discrimination

LEO M. JACOBS

eafness and the communication disability associated with it have placed deaf people in a minority group within a majority population of people who hear and speak. The disability has given us our own language, which has also spawned a separate community and culture. We have survived and enjoyed full lives within our own society. We are able to interact to some degree with the general community in order to have our needs served, whether they be familial, social, recreational, or related to employment or health. However, because we do have problems communicating with hearing people, there is a long history of prejudice and discrimination against us by the hearing majority.

Over the two hundred years of American history, that prejudice and discrimination have been slowly replaced by greater understanding and appreciation of the rationale for a separate language and culture. I believe that I can safely say that the conditions for deaf citizens in America are much better and more advanced than those in other parts of the world. Yet we have not achieved the full understanding on the part of the hearing majority that would bring treatment of deaf citizens to full equity with that of other citizens. We are still faced with some misconceptions and mistreatment.

The Gallaudet University protest last year (1988), which met with incredible coverage by the world's media and resulted in a deaf president for the university, was responsible for a great advancement in public understanding and sympathy for the language and culture of the deaf. One would think that public prejudice and discrimination have almost disappeared for the American deaf community, as evidenced by the rapid opening of new opportunities and increased upward mobility for deaf people.

I assure you that prejudice and discrimination, although much diminished, have not completely disappeared. They have, rather, gone underground, into the subconscious of many hearing people who would probably strenuously deny having any prejudice at all!

I do not accuse the whole hearing population of practicing this bias: Those who have had very little or no contact with deaf citizens probably have the least bias. I suggest that when hearing people become involved with deafness for the wrong reasons and with unhealthy attitudes toward deaf people, their prejudice becomes more pronounced in direct proportion to the amount of time they spend in contact with the deaf population as well as the closeness of the contact.

Perhaps the most common problem between deaf and hearing people is the practice of a double standard. Hearing people who would probably be well mannered, open minded, conciliatory, and generally pleasant with other hearing people undergo a subtle change in their conduct when they are with deaf individuals. Then they are likely to be more paternalistic, overbearing, reproving, and impatient. It is sad to relate that we also find this double standard among some deaf persons toward their own people! This is more apparent among deaf persons who have achieved positions of leadership or other distinguished roles in the deaf community, and who have distanced themselves from those in lesser roles and become impatient with the deaf "person on the street."

The attitude described above is usually unconscious and unrecognized by the offenders. I would like to suggest that before you begin communication with a deaf person, you should pause and review what is on the tip of your tongue. Would you express yourself exactly the same way with a hearing person? If you are convinced that the answer is yes, then you can proceed with a clear conscience. I am quite sure, however, that many times the answer would be no. If so, you should give yourself a mental shake and try to perceive the other person as you would a hearing person. Then the correct words will probably automatically come to the lips (or rather, the hands!). I am certain that unconscious offenders will improve with this kind of self-monitoring and eventually express themselves in the same manner to both hearing and deaf people.

When hearing people who are ignorant of the ramifications of deafness encounter our disability, they are most likely to regard it as a pathology, something to be fixed or cured. This attitude entails an emphasis on therapy and/or prostheses. Therefore, when small children are found to be deaf, they are immediately fitted with hearing aids and given oral rehabilitation therapy. No thought is given to the great need of these little tykes for communication that is truly effortless and that provides them access to the great world of concepts and, later on, to the school curriculum.

Instead of being exposed to input from their environment, as children with normal hearing are, the deaf and hard of hearing kids are given sounds they cannot hear and moving lips they cannot read. Their ignorance and bewilderment continue beyond the normal threshold of understanding and reasoning.

This blocking of development and access to knowledge is another aspect of unconscious discrimination against deaf people by a hearing public that is unaware of the real need of deaf children to learn about their environment and how to cope with it.

This is evident when one compares the deaf children of hearing parents with the deaf children of deaf parents, who have had no communication problems since they were born. These fortunate young ones are, for the most part, earlier and better able to cope with life.

The "crab theory" is a popular metaphor that pertains to minority group dynamics. It holds that individuals in less successfully integrated minority groups have not learned to work together to overcome individual differences or to achieve mutual political goals that would lead to advancement in the general community. These people are more inclined to snipe at each other and criticize their leaders, thus promoting further disunity among their ranks. They behave like crabs in a pot, which tend to pull down those who have crawled over the others toward the top. Hence, the crab theory.

The crab theory is especially relevant to minority groups that have not achieved successful integration into the majority culture, such as blacks, Chicanos, people from Third World countries, etc. On the other hand, Jews, Chinese, Japanese, etc., may be said to have achieved success in assimilation into the culture of the majority; these latter groups are accorded more acceptance by the majority group.

In view of the usual patterns in the deaf community, the above-stated principle seems to apply to it as well. This is another example of unconscious discrimination, this time from within our own group. Recent events, however, seem to show that we are learning to pull together to achieve our political goals. Apparently, we are pulling away from the crab theory and achieving a higher status in the general community.

In an article in *TV Digest* by Malcolm-Jamal Warner (1988), the actor who plays Theo in the "Cosby Show" discusses racism as it applies to him. He writes that although racism seems to be disappearing, it is still evident in many ways. While his fan mail demonstrates, for the most part, no overt racism—and downplays color in discussing common issues such as boy-girl relationships, teen-age problems, etc.—Warner has experienced many cases of covert prejudice. His comments and experiences can very easily be transferred from the black issue to that of deafness.

A kid writing to Malcolm apologizing for being white or, on the other hand, a kid saying he's black and "down" with him, can easily be pictured as a hearing child writing to a deaf celebrity and apologizing for the fact that he can hear or saying that he can sign very well and, for this reason, they should be great friends.

Malcolm wrote that it is not possible to grow up black without a great awareness of black history—of injustices done to black people, of prejudices that still exist today, of the civil rights movement, of apartheid. Doesn't this sound familiar? Shades of Gallaudet, Clerc, the Gallaudet protest, and the subtle prejudice that we still meet occasionally. The only difference seems to be that we do not have apartheid by decree—although there were a few historical attempts at colonizing us!

In his article, Malcolm spoke of dating a girl who was part white and part Asian. She was a model, and Malcolm thought of bringing her on the set as an extra. He discussed her enthusiastically with his buddies. When he brought her on the set, his friends asked him why he hadn't said that she was not black. I can almost picture a deaf actor doing the same with a current love interest who is hearing and being asked the same question: Why hadn't he mentioned she was hearing?

As an actor, Malcolm has experienced stereotyping of blacks by whites. He has heard them say that the Huxtables are not a typical black family. I can almost envision the same reaction should there be a sitcom in which a family whose members are all deaf acts like a normal hearing family. The hearing audience would have expected them to play stereotyped roles as naive or ignorant people, people making animal-like sounds, psychopaths or wide-eyed victims.

To reiterate, I believe that we will continue to meet with unconscious prejudice as long as public stereotyping of deaf individuals continues.

Public attitudes toward deafness vary by extreme degrees. In my travels overseas I have met with attitudes that varied from extreme rudeness to cloying pity. The more advanced and educated a country is, the less prejudice and the fewer misconceptions exist.

However, bias toward deaf people still exists all over the world, even in the most enlightened countries. We may never achieve Utopia, but the road to it would include greater exposure to deafness through education, constant political action, increased contacts with the hearing community, and good press. These activities will have a greater effect if they are led by the deaf community. This, of course, is not meant to downplay the great accomplishments for the deaf community achieved by our many hearing friends, but rather to suggest that the impression upon unenlightened hearing people would be greater if the efforts were made by deaf people themselves.

References

Warner, M. 1988. *TV Guide*, September, 4–7.

The Impact of Rehabilitation Philosophies on the Deaf Client

ROBERT G. SANDERSON

ew governmental laws have had more impact upon the rehabilitation of deaf adults in the United States than the Rehabilitation Act of 1973 and its amendments. Prior to the enactment of this public law, deaf people seeking assistance for job training or further education beyond high school were at the mercy of widely varying state policies, funding, and personnel.

Within a short time after the implementation of the Act, disabled people throughout the country began receiving more consistent services as states developed their programs as a result of federal rules and regulations tied to funding. Although rehabilitation has been around since 1920 under various names in the government bureaucracy, such as the Office of Vocational Rehabilitation, the Rehabilitation Services Administration (RSA) brought together and integrated comprehensive, uniform services in a nationwide system.

In the early 1960s, just prior to the benchmark Act, a series of RSA-sponsored workshops focused attention on a disability that had been largely ignored—deafness. It was brought out that few services were available to deaf people, compared with those offered to other disabled people. Further, there was virtually a total lack of professionals competent to work with deaf people.

Without going into a detailed history, the workshops gave the states a shove, and the Rehabilitation Act of 1973 provided the means to implement expanded services. To meet the demand, a new breed of professionals came on the scene: rehabilitation counselors for the deaf (RCDs) and state coordinators for the deaf.

As they sought identity as a profession, certain conflicts arose: Without a long history of development, specialized education, and a specific area of activity differing from that of social work, which was already well established, where did they fit into the scheme of the helping professions? Were they merely social workers with added responsibilities? Or were they rehabilitation workers with added social work responsibilities? Or were they merely job hunters for disabled people? Or perhaps psychological counselors? Or all of the above? And what kind of an education would a rehabilitation counselor for the deaf need to carry out the functions and responsibilities cited in the law?

Duties cited in the law included processing intake applications, conducting preliminary diagnostic studies, and formulating comprehensive evaluations of individuals' disabilities from medical work-ups. Referral sources had to be consulted to develop appraisals of individuals' work habits. The rehabilitation counselor then had to develop written rehabilitation programs for each client. Other duties included job development and placement, counseling throughout all of these processes, monitoring of progress in either education or work, caseload management (paperwork!), and budget management. All of the above had to be managed while meeting supervisory expectations and administrative rules, regulations, and production (the numbers game).

Training

How does an educational program train rehabilitation counselors, both general and specialized, to deal with cases such as the following true case?

The Case of the Frozen Dog

Counselor X was on a visit to a female client at her home. The house was a filthy mess, the two young children were dressed in dirty, food-stained clothing, the sink was piled high with unwashed dishes, and dried dog droppings littered the floor of the kitchen. The little black dog that had always greeted the counselor on previous visits was not in the house.

Upon asking the client where the dog was, she said it was in the freezer.

The freezer?!

Yes. She lifted the top of the small freezer and, sure enough, there in the corner, among a few packages of food, was the little black dog, well frozen.

After mastering his consternation, the counselor asked, "How come?"

Well, the children were heartbroken when the dog was killed by a car, the client told him, so she decided to freeze the dog and take it out once in a while so the kids could pet it.

Now I have some questions for you. Is there an authority who says freezing a dog for such purposes is just not done? Does the rehabilitation counselor step in here and give the client some social understanding or training? When does the counselor's own cultural background impinge on decisions? How did his philosophical or psychological training prepare him?

Then, too, what kind of an education would be needed to cope with the letter of the law, "serving first those with the most severe handicaps so that they may prepare for and engage in gainful employment" (PL 93-112, Sec. 2 [1]). A wide range of disabling conditions come under this section: mobility conditions, blindness, deafness, heart conditions, mental problems, retardation, speech problems, cerebral palsy, Morgan's disease—indeed, a litany of problems that might well be read from a medical text, or *Gray's Anatomy*.

The universities were caught unprepared during the early years. It seemed that the word "rehabilitation" represented a new concept, although the idea and art of helping certain disabled individuals regain functions was around for a long time in hospitals and medical clinics. Yet it was only a short ten years ago I examined a university curriculum that was supposed to aim at the education of candidates for rehabilitation counseling positions; I discovered that the emphasis was on theory, psychology, and educational psychology, with very little on the nitty-gritty of daily casework faced by counselors. There was next to nothing on dealing with deafness, although the problem of communication was described briefly. The "psychology of disability" in one course attempted to teach a few things about many disabilities, with very little depth in any.

I am happy to report that changes have been made, and there are more university programs focusing on rehabilitation and dealing intelligently with this eighty-year-old profession. But I am *not* happy with a certain philosophical trend I see occurring at state, regional, and federal levels: less specialization and more generalized caseloads.

Special Units vs. General Caseloads

During the late 1960s and 1970s the push was to set up special units to deal with unique disabilities, such as mental retardation, blindness, and deafness. A remarkable unit of Services to the Adult Deaf was developed in Utah under the Division of Rehabilitation Services, Utah State Board of Education, and this became a model for other states. Very soon a "Model State Plan for Serving a Deaf Population" was developed by the Rehabilitation Services Administration in cooperation with professionals from several universities and line coordinators and counselors from the field.

Word from around the field of rehabilitation of deaf people is that the special units were slowly phased out, although rehabilitation counselors for deaf people were retained to serve deaf people within district offices. The state coordinators for the deaf, responsible for training and consultation, and in some cases direct supervision of the RCDs, were phased out, transferred, or given other responsibilities. The RCDs were left with no professional interaction with others working in the field of deafness, no one with greater training or expertise to look up to for advice. RCDs were thus functioning in a vacuum.

Does this have an impact on the deaf client? Indeed it does. Deaf people with special needs, some of which can be quite expensive, come in each day to see the RCD. In turn, the RCD must struggle with a supervisor who likely has little or no understanding of deafness in order to get approval of the budget for the individually written rehabilitation program, or for the program itself. Everything must be justified in writing and documented, and the case folder must be in order. Time passes while all of this is going on—frequently too much time—and the client may lose interest and confidence in rehabilitation. Believe me, it does happen.

The line rehabilitation counselor with a general caseload is expected to deal with any and all disabilities referred, regardless of his or her aptitude, skills, or desires to deal with special groups. My hang-up, of course, is deafness, and I wish it to be known that I am not alone in having hangups: Every counselor, general or special, has them in abundance, along with supervisors, coordinators, specialists, and administrators.

It is my contention that a general counselor who is not able to use American Sign Language or Pidgin Sign English effectively is severely handicapped in trying to communicate with and help a deaf person who does. Interpreters, bless them, are frequently-used alternatives for direct communication between counselor and client—and it is unfortunate that all too frequently the interpreter is thrust into the counselor's role as a result. The question then arises whether the deaf client is getting the best possible service from the counselor.

Allow me to digress for a moment. I have another case to share with you. Again, it's true. It happened.

The Case of the Threat to Kill

> Counselor Z learned through one of his deaf friends that one of his deaf clients
> was telling other deaf people that his wife was going to divorce him because
> she was in love with the counselor. So he was going to kill the counselor.

A brash, bravado threat? Well, maybe, and maybe not. Threats to kill are serious
business and should never be ignored or taken lightly, especially not when the client
was an unpredictable paranoid.

I have some questions for you. How do you go about determining the validity of
the threat—was it true or just a rumor? If true, what steps should be taken to defuse
the crisis? What did the professor at the university say about such things (in theory)?
What would a generalist supervisor advise his counselor to do?

It is very likely that the general counselor has no knowledge whatever, or only the
most superficial understanding, of the culture from which a deaf client comes. Quoting PL 93-112 again, Section 7, (4)b: "The term evaluation of rehabilitation potential
means, as appropriate in each case . . . a diagnostic study consisting of a comprehensive
evaluation of pertinent medical, psychological, vocational, educational, cultural, social,
and environmental factors which bear on the individual's handicap to employment and
rehabilitation potential."

This legal requirement puts a tremendous burden upon a counselor who has a
general caseload and who is faced with a large number of clients. That counselor will
invariably take the easiest way out in order to meet production expectations of the
supervisor and administrator. Clearly, the easiest way out will be for the counselor to
work with those who are easiest to communicate with and who take the least amount
of time. The deaf person is not exactly ignored, but the counselor may not give prompt
and appropriate services. The case may drag on and on until the deaf person decides it's
not worth the time to return to rehab. There are other techniques; sometimes the wise
counselor will look for a colleague who has "had more luck with deaf people" and ask
to transfer the case.

I do not wish to be completely negative toward general counselors; I have high respect for many of my former colleagues who did some great work with disabled people.
I have met some great general counselors who were generalists by decree, not because
they wanted to be. Some were able to communicate well with deaf people, but those
were rare birds indeed, and they were scattered thinly throughout the states.

I also know some rehabilitation counselors who state flatly that they do not want
any deaf people in their caseloads simply because of their inability to understand them
or communicate with them at a meaningful level. Apart from sign communication, such
counselors quickly learned that with deaf people the written word also was difficult to
understand.

I believe that the generalist philosophy in rehabilitation does a disservice to deaf
clients. The full potential of deaf people is not realized when administrators review the
low output or production of specialized deaf caseloads and high cost and decide that
the *agency* would be better served by merging deaf clients into general caseloads.

It is usually a policy that a state is divided into regions and districts. Supervisors
preside over such districts, and counselors are assigned to specific areas and are expected to work with whatever disability crosses the district office threshold. The reality
is that deaf people are scattered throughout an urban area, and they will gravitate to a
counselor they like, regardless of district lines.

Similarly, a counselor who works closely with deaf people should not be strictly limited to a particular district. Strict district lines are artificial barriers to good services to deaf clients. After all, rehabilitation is in business to serve those who need help, not to serve those who are protecting turf.

But what of the direct impact the generalist philosophy may have on the deaf client? Consider how difficult it will be for a nonspeaking deaf person with poor reading and writing skills—but a quite normal mentality and physique—to express to the nonsigning general counselor his or her expectations, hopes, desires, and interests for employment or further education. What will this deaf person think when the counselor, seeking a quick closure, suggests a janitorial job in a local church, or a dishwashing job in the Super Dooper Cafe, or any number of similar menial jobs, rather than undertaking a lengthy evaluation to determine latent potential?

Many deaf people who have difficulty with the English language—but not their own American Sign Language—have turned out to be superior computer operators, programmers, cabinet craftsmen, mechanics, draftsmen, statisticians, electronics specialists, and artists, among other occupations. The deaf community is compact; everyone knows almost everyone else—where they work, who they marry, where they live, and even their bowling scores. What will be the impression of rehab that the deaf applicant takes home? The credibility of the rehabilitation profession as well as the counselor is on the line. Word gets around the deaf community very quickly that a particular counselor is just trying to place deaf people in "low, poor paying jobs."

Are you ready for another true case?

The Case of the Call for Help

Counselor Y greeted the female schizophrenic client in his office and asked her to be seated for a moment while he went into the outer office to get her case file from his secretary.

He returned in no more than one minute to find her with her skirt up, panties down around her ankles, squatting in the corner and urinating on his carpet.

I have some questions for you. How does a male counselor deal with this situation right now? Does he declare her nonfeasible and close her case and sigh with relief? Does he stand and watch and wait for her to finish? Does he quickly thumb through his case service manual to find the proper procedure for dealing with unexpected crises? Or does he ring up his supervisor, who told him to stick to job training and forget social work, and ask for immediate advice?

Because many deaf people have educational and social deficits, whether they graduate from residential schools for deaf students or public high schools, the rehabilitation counselor rapidly discovers that traditional approaches are not efficient or effective. He may find that he is thrust into a father confessor role one minute, a sex counselor the next, a banking consultant, a marriage counselor, a psychologist—and the supervisor enters the scene to tell him to stick to job training and placement and to get more closures than last year before the end of this fiscal year. Leave the social work to social workers!

Those who work in the field of deafness know well that for many years there were not, and still are not, enough social workers with communicative skills to serve deaf people. During the 1960s and 1970s, for example, there were fewer than a dozen hearing and deaf social workers in the entire United States capable of serving deaf people. Hence, by default those rehabilitation men and women, RCDs, had to fill these gaps in serving deaf people *before* a rehabilitation plan could be successful.

It is with pleasure I note that in the past few years Gallaudet University, the National Technical Institute for the Deaf, and the Rochester Institute of Technology have begun producing graduate students in social work. And one day, I hope, some of them will end up in my state.

Given that certain counselors may be competent in communicating with their deaf clients, other factors enter the relationships. The counselor's orientation and preferred approach will certainly have an effect upon the client. Does the counselor use an eclectic method? Does he or she use a currently popular psychological system, such as that espoused by Carl Rogers (unconditional acceptance), Williamsen's reality-oriented approach, or Thorne's scientific approach?

These and other approaches to counseling were designed or developed for hearing people, not for deaf people, because all of them depend upon full and easy communication. Then, too, J. D. Bozarth (*Models and Functions of Counseling for Applied Settings and Rehabilitation Workers*, July 1972, University of Arkansas) states, "Regardless of the emotional needs of some of his clients, the rehabilitation counselor is *not* primarily a psychotherapist, nor is he in a position (at least in the majority of offices) to offer any long-range therapeutic help to his clientele. He lacks the training, time, privacy, physical facilities, and administrative authority to provide therapeutic help." Obviously Bozarth has never had a deaf caseload!

Time and again, the RCD has found that he or she is the major, if not the only, local resource for remedying some of the multiple deficits presented by some deaf clients before they can be successfully placed in gainful employment.

Regardless of administrative or supervisory decree, the RCD will use certain basic approaches that are part of his or her own personality and philosophical bent, and which are necessary to secure the desired results. Apart from the counselor's skill in communicating in sign language, other competencies enter into the relationship:

❖ general knowledge of deafness and its effect on the individual's personality

❖ general knowledge of other disabilities

❖ career guidance skills

❖ job market knowledge

❖ education and social background of client

❖ counselor's work experience

❖ knowledge of state, local, and national resources for education and technical training for deaf people

❖ knowledge of state and federal rehabilitation regulations

❖ knowledge of individual written rehabilitation program requirements

❖ knowledge of agency paperwork requirements

❖ adherence to standards of ethics and confidentiality, especially with respect to the deaf community

❖ ability to interpret the vocational rehabilitation process for deaf clients

❖ understanding of medical terminology with respect to deafness—audiology, audiograms, ear pathology, and medical reports

❖ ability to use and understand aptitude, personality, and psychological tests with deaf clients

❖ knowledge about the value systems of different cultures (ethnic differences)

❖ knowledge of socioeconomic variables and their effects on clients

❖ knowledge of the impact of multiple disabilities on the deaf person in areas such as self-image

❖ counselor's awareness of his or her own value systems

❖ counselor's awareness of the effect of parental influences, desires, education, and philosophy of communication on the family

These competencies (if the counselor is lucky enough to have them all) add up to a very special, sensitive, understanding, accepting person: an RCD, a Rehabilitation Counselor for the Deaf.

A final word on the impact of administrative and supervisory philosophy on deaf clients as well as the counselors who serve them: Production is always a source of frustration for counselors on the line. It takes considerably more time to work with deaf people than it does for those who have hearing. Why is this so?

Communication per se is slower. Sign language and fingerspelling are not so quick as the spoken word; the eye is not so quick as the ear.

Comprehension must be confirmed and reconfirmed. Educational levels are involved. Words and phrases must be adjusted to the deaf person's understanding; many deaf people, though possessing normal intelligence, function at a fourth-grade reading/writing level in English.

Telephone/TDD (telecommunications device for deaf people) use takes five or six times as long. The average deaf person not only does not know how to type, but also does not know how to express himself or herself in writing.

Illiteracy in English, combined with excellent verbal skills in American Sign Language, challenge understanding by the counselor.

Multiple disabilities in addition to deafness may be present. An example is the person who has cerebral palsy or uncontrollable hands and arms, who understands signs but cannot use them. Patience and time are required to achieve even simple understanding.

And how does the counselor go about training such people for gainful employment and then finding jobs for them? How does the counselor persuade reluctant employers to give them a chance? Time, my friends, I repeat with as much emphasis as I can. *It takes much, much longer to rehabilitate deaf people than hearing people of whatever disability.*

Promoting the Interests of Deaf People

LIISA KAUPPINEN

What should we deaf people as a group know and do to ensure equality of opportunity for ourselves, to cope with the difficulties we encounter daily in a predominately hearing world, and to make optimal use of our abilities in our chosen work?

First, we must know and remember our history, and look to it as a source of strength. Second, we must make our identity increasingly clear by discovering and maximizing our own special abilities. Third, we must enhance our consciousness, knowledge of our situation, and determination to assume responsibility and take needed action.

Deaf people are fortunate today to be protected by such national and international human rights agreements as the United Nations Declaration on the Rights of Children, various agreements on the right of all human beings to an education, and rights granted in some nations concerning deaf people's use of their own language and the furtherance of their economic independence. In spite of these gains, however, many laws and norms—both written and unwritten—continue to oppress deaf people.

For example, the majority of deaf people in the world—nearly 80 percent—are still deprived of any education at all. Furthermore, of the deaf people who receive an education, only 1 percent have the right to receive it in any form of sign language. In other words, 99 percent of the deaf people in the world today who receive an education do so through an oral teaching method.

The majority of deaf people of the world are still unwanted. Instead of working to change their attitudes toward deaf people and striving to make the environment more suitable for deaf individuals—more visually accessible, for instance—hearing people still tend to fight against deafness. Medical science continues to try to find ways of retrieving the sense of hearing; people continue to insist on the use of the one channel—hearing—which does not work with deaf people. The prevailing view is that deafness is a disease, a serious defect, a disability.

Deaf people as a group, however, do not see themselves as defective or disabled. They do not think there is anything wrong with them, something lacking in their personalities. Deaf people as a group know they are whole and sound, and not disabled. Consequently, there is constant friction between these two viewpoints, resulting from the lack of understanding.

Deaf people have problems in their relations with people who are not deaf (or people who are not deaf have problems in their relations with the deaf), but deaf people do not experience these problems as a disability.

Deaf people must assume full responsibility for everything that concerns them. They can't just continue complaining about injustice; rather, they must act and work to re-educate people, starting with the people who first diagnose deafness in a child. It is important to focus on the training of doctors, psychologists, and others who give first-hand information to the parents of a deaf child. For example, a professional who would describe any deaf child as "speech impaired" is simply not the right person to be giving information to parents.

We must assume more responsibility for everything that concerns the first years of a deaf child's life—mental development, the learning of language, social skills—and we must help the child to learn about our history and development, and to learn ways of dealing with society. This can be accomplished by supporting the families of deaf children and making the living environments of deaf children more stimulating.

We need to find ways to teach survival strategies to deaf people of different age groups. Deaf people must learn more ways of coping with day-to-day and long-term difficulties, efforts that could be facilitated through training programs. Deaf people need to be encouraged to gain control of their own lives and not think of themselves as living in the custody of society. The habit of dependency must be broken, and one of the best ways of accomplishing this is through education. Education alone can give deaf people of all ages the ability to compete in society.

The basic criticism deaf people level against the way deaf children are most commonly educated is the same all over the world. The method most commonly used for teaching deaf children is painfully difficult to understand. This method, in which the use of sign language is completely or almost completely forbidden, has been called oralism. Various adaptations of sign language intended to make it more like spoken language have not made the situation any easier.

The controversy between oral and sign methods has often been fruitless and has frequently led to misunderstandings. The most common misconception is that deaf people are against speech and want to use sign language only because they are lazy. Another delusion is that sign language isolates deaf people from society. In spite of deaf people's assertions, supported by research findings, hearing people still apparently find it difficult to believe and understand that the use of sign language raises the level of teaching for deaf students. With the optimal use of sign language, deaf people have unlimited possibilities and are able to develop themselves as fully as any other person able to learn in his or her own language.

Even today, most of the teaching offered to deaf children fails badly. Most deaf students leave school hardly able to read or write. In the "Old World," Europe, which has the longest tradition of deaf education, many old schools for deaf people have closed. Following the reforming winds of the 1960s, deaf students have been integrated into regular classrooms with hearing children. This integration is good for some groups of the handicapped, but not for deaf people.

In regular classrooms, no one can communicate with deaf children, and deaf students are therefore completely isolated. The whole situation has the opposite of the intended effect, and the deaf child fails to learn sign language, to say nothing of the subject matter being taught. As a consequence, many deaf people now have serious problems with language, in addition to social and psychological problems.

Hearing people are now trying to find solutions to these problems by turning to such technological panaceas as cochlear implants. Many parents have been persuaded that these devices will help their children manage normally in society, the same illusion as that created by the invention of the hearing aid. Believe it or not, many deaf children have been punished for not hearing when they have their hearing aid in their ear. Those individuals who do benefit from hearing aids have been held up as models for deaf children. (*He* can hear, so why can't *you?*)

Since the 1960s, people have been talking about "progress" through better hearing aids and through more integration with hearing children. But has this really been progress? What is progress? We deaf people think that real progress has taken place where sign language in its true form has been put into use. Progress of this kind has released the resources of deaf people and made them conscious of themselves and their situation in this world. As long as deaf people have no possibility of deciding what kind of teaching we need, and as long as we are outsiders in everything else that concerns us, we have no hope of gaining equality and asserting our value as human beings. If we don't start breaking the power structure, there will be no progress.

What kind of a change do we need, how will it be done, and who will help whom? "If you carry water to a well, it will not stay there long," says a Finnish proverb. To help deaf people in a patronizing way is to carry water to a well. That is not the best way for us to begin making progress. We deaf people must take the initiative through self-development. We must cultivate awareness of political, social, cultural, and economic relationships and their effect on our position. First comes knowledge, then knowing how to act, then acting.

Much factual knowledge now becomes outdated in three to five years. We can't keep all the information we need in our heads anymore; it has to be stored in computers. We deaf people must learn to understand this change. We must learn to work along with it and make it serve us. If we who are deaf don't learn to govern our own lives, others will decide things for us. We may have to progress through many stages of development rather quickly to catch up with others and begin truly to manage our own affairs in this world.

We must begin to have a global perspective in all our activism. The concept of promoting deaf activism, still new, is not a consensus view in many countries, and so our efforts all too frequently fail to affect the general culture. We need strong and stable forms of activism, the courage to look for ways—even nonconventional ways—of accomplishing needed change, and a constant view of the global nature of our efforts. We deaf people must strengthen our international ties and establish a strong cooperative basis for eventually assuming full responsibility for all our affairs. We need highly educated people, deaf scholars and scientists who can help us solve the problems of education on both national and international levels, study the life circumstances of deaf people in both industrial and developing countries, and become more aware of existing laws and norms (both explicit and implicit) so we can act in an informed manner against injustices.

In addition, we must define many things, create a basis for a philosophy of equality, think of what it means to be deaf, and consider the following questions:

1. Is a deaf person handicapped, and if so, where, when, and in what situations?
2. What is our attitude toward human beings in general, and how does this compare to our attitude toward deaf people?
3. What would constitute equality between deaf people and hearing people?
4. What is the appropriate role of cultural activity among deaf people as it relates to their community, their language, and their history?
5. What are the best political and other channels of influence, and strategies for needed change?
6. How and to what extent should deaf organizations join forces internationally with other handicapped groups to achieve common goals?

7. And what, more precisely, are the rights of all handicapped people in relation to the human rights agenda asserted by the United Nations?

One of the conclusions reached by a conference of Nobel Prize winners in 1988 was that "the wealth of humankind is in its variety. This variety must be protected in all of its manifestations." The most difficult of the current problems of humankind are universal and interdependent. We who are deaf are part of the universe. There have always been deaf people, and there always will be. It is our duty to work for our own benefit and for the common benefit of all people.

Deaf Awareness Programs in South Africa

ALAN JONES

In 1863 the first school for deaf students in South Africa was opened in Cape Town. Legislation concerning special schools, including schools for deaf students, was adopted by Parliament in 1928. From then on, the government has continued to recognize that special schools for the handicapped need to be subsidized and given special consideration.

Over the years, there has been a subtle shift among educators of disabled children from placing emphasis on the disability itself to focusing on the child, who happens to have a disability. This attitude personalizes the problem and emphasizes the ability of the person rather than the disability. There was a realization that handicapped people are individuals in their own right and do not all act or react in the same way.

In South Africa there are no private schools. All schools for the deaf are heavily subsidized by the government, which is in a position to supply the most advanced equipment. As you all know, that alone does not guarantee the best eduction, because the quality of the teachers and the methods used often outweigh the need for advanced equipment. In this regard, I am extremely grateful that a majority of schools for deaf students—even those formerly wedded to oralism—are now using Total Communication as the preferred method.

A new spirit is emerging among our local deaf people, and they are being given more say in their own affairs. Deaf people are now serving on the Executive Committee of the National Council for the Deaf, and other disability groups are now merging and integrating in order to give more weight to their concerns. A survey of some half a million people conducted by the South African National Council for the Deaf (SANC) showed that a staggering 86 percent of South Africans had no understanding of the causes or problems of deafness. Generally, they had no idea how to communicate with deaf or hard of hearing people, who number about one and a half million in our country alone.

In 1987, the South African National Council for the Deaf included for the first time a large number of deaf people on its Executive Committee. Previously, except in rare instances, deaf people had only been appointed to subordinate committees.

Strategic Planning

The dynamic director of the SANC, Mrs. Henna Opperman, organized a strategic planning session last year that involved a three-day meeting at a country retreat, away from the bustle of the city. We just talked "deaf-deaf-deaf," with no telephones or TTYs and no interruptions. It was think, talk, and plan. The key phrase of the session was "If you do not know where you are going, how will you know when you get there?"

The planning session inspired us to introduce a deaf awareness program using several means, such as television, radio, and newspapers—an expensive task, because advertising does not come cheaply today. We became more united in our purpose and developed a sense of loyalty to each other and to our cause. I seemed to get a new aim and enthusiasm, as indeed we all did. We were inspired to go out and use our God-given talents to gain understanding for deaf people and to help them develop their potential.

Here are some of the components of our deaf awareness program:

❖ *Deaf Achiever's Award:* This annual award receives wide publicity.

❖ *Television:* We are sponsoring an eighteen-part television series, which will air during peak times each evening of the week. Deaf people also will appear and make their views known.

❖ *Posters:* A deaf executive was given the opportunity of judging slides to be made into posters for nationwide publicity.

❖ *Silent Messenger:* This magazine, the only monthly magazine published for deaf people, has a growing number of subscribers.

❖ *Leadership Courses:* These courses are designed to help deaf people develop their talents.

Sign Language

After the planning session, I tackled my own assignments with renewed energy. My efforts include continuing to teach my sign language courses, as I have done for many years. This year the class was the largest I ever had. It opened with more than ninety people from all races and from many walks of life. All passed the test at the end of the twelve-week course. There is a lack of hearing people able to act as interpreters, and these courses have produced some people who are gifted in that area.

I have spent many years working closely with Black and Indian schools for the deaf and teaching sign language to teachers and social workers among all racial groups. Because of language and cultural differences, people from various racial groups attend separate schools.

Some of my other activities include addressing meetings, talking to school children, and being deeply involved in helping the Human Sciences Research Council in its gigantic task of preparing and publishing a new sign language dictionary for use in South Africa. When you realize that this dictionary will have to encompass no less than seven completely different languages, you will know why I refer to the task as gigantic.

Visualizing Sound

I had been wondering for some time what we could do for Deafness Awareness Week in September last year (1988). After much thought, I decided to promote the idea of visualizing sound by having a photographic competition. Without the help of the Natal Association of the Deaf, and the expert advice of a Durban photographer, Teresa Woodcock, the enterprise would not have been the success it was. It was publicized widely, and we managed to obtain the services of some of the country's best photographers to judge the entries.

The brochure for the competition noted that deaf people hear with their eyes, and it asked for photographs that illustrate as imaginatively as possible sounds that a deaf person would not be able to hear, such as an alarm clock, a siren, waves crashing on the beach, a kettle boiling, or a dog barking. A cash prize was offered, and the several hundred photos that were entered in the contest were on display during Deafness Awareness Week.

The competition gave deaf people unprecedented publicity. Deaf people discovered, to their surprise, that many things that they thought were silent actually produced sound. And hearing people suddenly realized just how little deaf people knew about sound and how much—even more than they had imagined—deaf people were missing by not being able to hear.

And what wonderful ideas were portrayed in those photographs! Deaf schools said the competition stimulated development of language in the classroom and renewed interest in photography. Others said it helped pupils to develop inquiring minds. Response from the public was extremely positive. I hope in the future to help organize a grand competition on a national scale and, who knows, even on an international scale.

Fundraising as Public Awareness

In South Africa, all schools for the deaf supplement their funds by having street collections. We deaf people accept this method of fundraising as a duty. We have activities such as garage sales and flea markets to support our local deaf associations and clubs. At the national level, the SANC obtains sponsorship for subsidizing the purchase of TTYs, computers, and other devices to assist deaf people.

We are well aware of the needs of poorer people in the deaf community, and we collect and distribute food parcels and clothing to them. The special needs of the aged deaf are also one of our concerns. In addition, we try to help the professional social workers by finding employment for deaf people of all races.

Registry of the Deaf

Another enormous task in this country is to try to create and maintain a registry of all deaf people. This must be done because there are so many deaf people in our rural areas who are seldom reached until it is too late for them to be given a proper education.

Black Deaf South Africans

There are huge cultural differences between Black and White South Africans that must be bridged. For example, a Black father usually wants his child to live with him under his own roof. It is hard to explain to him that his child must go to a boarding school. Also, many Black people prefer to rely on witch doctors rather than on modern medicine.

We must—and do—respect their traditions. But at the same time, we must encourage them to listen to sound advice about the need for early special training. Many such parents have brought their deaf children to schools only to be shocked to find that valuable time has been tragically wasted. I am sure many of you know of similar situations, even in the United States. The United States is clearly a world leader in deaf education and, quite honestly, I believe we are literally hundreds of years behind.

Deaf Awareness 1989

Looking to the future, we are planning a sign language marathon to be held during Deafness Awareness Week in 1989. It will coincide with the Diamond Jubilee of the South African National Council for the Deaf. It is hoped that the first prize will be a diamond, to be presented to the person who signs continuously for the longest period of time. We hope to have sponsors to support each competitor, and so generate funds for future development of schools and societies.

Deaf Awareness Program: A Suggestion

J. S. DAVID

As the title indicates, this paper is a suggestion. My intention is not to list the prevailing misconceptions and misunderstandings about deafness, deaf people, and sign language. Rather, it is to promote a line of thinking and action that may lead people to undertake meaningful and effective programs. I am sure there are many well-meaning, able, and efficient people who can give form and direction to my suggestion.

As the head of the only Tamil school for the deaf in Sri Lanka for the past fifteen years, I have been troubled by the fact that deaf children are first brought to school long after the admission age of five. Some parents have even brought children who are in their teens. Of the 138 children admitted during the past five years, the average age of admission has been 8.4 years. The ages of the children admitted in these five years range from five to thirteen. Only five children have received any counseling before the age of five.

In my capacity as principal, I have interviewed and counseled parents of deaf students for the past ten years. I have found that the reason parents do not enroll their deaf children in school early is not so much their lack of awareness of existing facilities as it is their misconceptions about deafness and the influence of the society around them. Also, when many parents finally do bring their child to be admitted to school, it is more because they are unable to control the child at home—owing to the communication gap—than for education. They tell me that their child is "getting angry too quickly and is not obedient." It is at that stage they begin to search for an institution that will "take care" of their child.

In many countries, the society at large has no useful knowledge about deafness or its effects. But, initially, it is members of society who influence the thinking and actions of the parents of deaf children. In countries such as Sri Lanka, where there is an extended family system and close village ties, the influence of society is especially strong. Elders, relatives, neighbors, and friends tell parents that their deaf child will never speak if he or she is sent to a school for deaf students; instead, the child will begin to use signs.

People do not understand the relationship between speech and hearing. Even educated people do not think about this connection. They have no need to. One of the comments they make is, "The deaf are usually also dumb, aren't they?" I have heard even qualified medical practitioners make this comment. Many visitors to my school have shown surprise that the deaf students are able to utter words. On the other hand, people think that if deaf children can utter a few words at home, then they need not go to the school for deaf students because they have the ability to speak.

People do not know that sign language is accepted around the world as a true language or that it is the natural language of deaf people. They are unaware that many deaf people who use sign language have a high level of education and functioning.

Society's obsession with speech ability and its negative attitude toward sign language have resulted in second-class citizen status for deaf people. The preoccupation with speech as the only vehicle for acquiring language and knowledge is a denial of the distinctive culture and natural language of deaf people. It is also a denial of the potential of deaf people, which results in the denial of opportunity for deaf people, which in turn results in the rejection of deaf people as persons.

In our part of the globe, astrologers play a very important part in decision making. If a child has not begun to say a few words by the age of two, the parents consult an astrologer; it is almost a rule. The astrologer looks at the planetary positions at the time of the child's birth. Invariably, he consoles the parents by telling them that the child is going through an unfavorable influence of the planets and that the child will acquire the ability to speak by age eight, nine, or ten, with a favorable change of the planetary positions. Also, the parents are asked to take various religious vows to appease the gods so the planetary changes will have the desired effect.

Parents experience feelings of guilt, believing that the gods have punished them with a deaf child. So they begin the process of appeasing the gods, hoping for a cure. They wait for the predicted age, when the favorable influence of the stars will allow their child to speak. Later, dejected, they realize their child's condition is not going to change. (Let me say here that it is not my intention to question astrology or discredit astrologers. I am aware that only those whose predictions have not come true have come to me.)

Many parents also have reported to me that medical personnel have advised them that their child would speak when he or she reaches maturity and have prescribed long-term treatments. This reinforces parents' hope for a cure, so they wait and carry out the prescribed treatment. I am aware that patients would stay only with those doctors who treat them and not with those who tell them that the problem is beyond medical science. But how will parents know that medical science has its limitations? How will they know that many have traveled this path before and found that deafness is permanent? How will they know that success in life can be achieved in spite of deafness?

I believe it is fear of the unknown that is the cause of this negative attitude toward deaf people in my society. It is not out of place here to relate my own experience with deaf people. My first acquaintance with a deaf person was in my village in the beautiful tea gardens in the hills of Sri Lanka. There was one deaf person, who was known as "dumb" and who was made fun of by everybody. He never went to school. He was a laborer. At that time I was in secondary school. I felt sorry for him but gave him no more thought than that.

My second acquaintance with a deaf person occurred when I was a teacher. I sat on the jury for a murder trial in which the only eyewitness was a deaf person with no formal education. The process of interpretation was long and tiresome. I couldn't believe he could communicate properly; I thought he was not intelligent enough. My attitude was to discount his testimony. He said, "I saw the murder; I shouted." I thought he could not have made a noise because he was "dumb." I asked him to demonstrate his shout in the courtroom, and he did.

My third acquaintance was when I accepted the position of principal at the school for the deaf. I accepted this position purely through my desire to help the "helpless" in society. I did not even know the connection between speech and hearing. Initially I accepted the position with a "caring" attitude. Now my attitude is different. I can't understand why people should think so negatively about deaf people. People like to tell me that I am doing a great service; I like to tell them, "I am doing a job, for which I am being paid."

How can we reach society at large to make them aware of deafness, deaf people, deaf culture and sign language? I believe that hearing adults are too busy living their own lives to give any serious thought to all the publicity about deaf people, unless they have a direct and immediate application for the information. Also, adult attitudes that are already established are difficult to change. A visit to a school for deaf students may evoke sympathy and wonder. But they may just end up thanking God they are not deaf and putting it out of their minds.

I think it will be more effective if we reach hearing children. We must influence children in a forceful manner so that knowledge about deafness and deaf people will have a bearing on their own achievements. It should be part of the lessons they must learn. When we reach the children, we will also reach the adults, because the children will discuss what they learn with adults, or at least they will speak out when they encounter adult behavior that conflicts with their own attitudes, developed at school.

In Sri Lanka, the social studies syllabus (or the humanities syllabus at the secondary school level) contains information about the culture, language, and habits of ethnic groups within the country and different races in other countries. Schools sometimes organize an "international day," when the children depict the dress, food, culture, and language of various ethnic groups. This lesson is intended to develop an appreciation and acceptance of differences. But somehow they have given no thought to a different cultural group living close to them and among them. Could we not reach the children around the globe with information about deafness?

They ought to be told that a person with a handicap need not remain a handicapped person. They need to be told that a person with a handicap has a birthright to a full life and that society has the responsibility to provide that opportunity. In the Tamil language, there is a saying: "Ilamiayit kalvi silaiyil eluthuhu." It means, "Education while young remains like carvings on stone." One of the aims of education is to prepare people for living in harmony with the rest of society. They must learn about deafness and the deaf people who are part of this society.

It is not my intention to spell out the lesson plan or lessons, or even to suggest at what levels information about deaf people must be introduced; that will require much more thought. But the preparation of materials should leave room for individual choice regarding the method of communication used—from manualism to Total Communication to pure oralism. Maybe we will have more people join the debate, which in itself is not bad at all.

I will say that the subject of deafness and deaf people should be taught under a broad heading: "Understanding people who are different." It is my dream that, under this heading, the next generation will learn about the different cultures in their own country and the world, one of which is deaf culture.

When we promote the concept of a separate deaf culture, we also must take adequate steps to ensure that the culture is understood and accepted. What better way can we find than to begin the process with children in their formative years, whose attitudes are yet in the making.

One way to reach children would be to write children's stories with deaf characters. Such stories would bring out the positive sides of deaf people and also show how negative attitudes affect deaf people and those around them. The children's stories I have read so far seem only to reinforce negative attitudes. They depict deaf people as beggars and as people always giving wrong answers.

I remember a story that I read in my younger days. A blind man carrying an earthen pot along a village road at night is carrying a lamp. People laugh at him and say, "You are blind—of what use is the lamp to you?" He replies, "I am carrying the lamp for you, so that in the dark you may not knock against me and break this pot." This story certainly enhanced the image of the blind in my mind.

I am very much aware that the world is not yet fully ready to give minority groups their rights or to coexist with those who have less power. Man is eager to grab for himself and not to share. Man is trying to climb the ladder of progress by trampling on the shoulders of others, rather than pulling them along with him. If only we learn to care and share, then the progress of everyone may be slower, but it will be surer and more lasting. If we do not, we will continue to witness the violence and destruction we see in this world today.

Sharing Experiences: Deafness Awareness Programs in Australia

VALERIE MOON

I would like to open with a quotation from an anthology compiled by Brian Grant entitled *The Quiet Ear: Deafness in Literature* (1987): "The special duty of the deaf is, in the first place, to spare other people as much fatigue as possible" (from the autobiography of Harriet Martineau, 1802–1876).

Many people today, both deaf and hearing, still share this belief. The fact that this is usually an *unconscious* belief makes it even more troubling. Let me tell you a story to illustrate this.

Last year the State Library of New South Wales, where I work, hosted a Deafness Expo in the library as part of Deafness Awareness Week. During this very successful day, one of our deaf helpers, Kevin, was approached by one of the library's regular patrons. Kevin was deep in conversation with another visitor when the patron approached him from behind and asked him a question. Completely unaware that he was being addressed, Kevin continued with his conversation. The library patron became very angry and abusive.

At this point I stepped in, asked him what his problem was, and pointed out that Kevin was deaf. The library patron went into a great tirade about how Kevin should wear "those things in his ears." Through gritted teeth, I asked him why he thought Kevin should wear uncomfortable—and, in Kevin's case, totally useless—hearing aids. He replied, "So that we [hearing people] will know that he is deaf." I still wonder about the effect this had on Kevin's young sons, who were standing nearby.

Some of the deafness awareness programs I will describe are aimed at changing attitudes like those displayed by our library client.

Some Background

John Day and Alice Hagemeyer visited Australia eighteen months ago to speak at the first Australian conference on library services for deaf and hard of hearing people. They gave us a wonderful gift: They shared with us their thoughts and their experiences. In the tradition of giftgiving, I hope, through this paper, to give something back.

John highlighted the problems that can be encountered when an English-speaking American and an English-speaking Australian attempt to communicate. This subject arose because I had written to John and asked him to talk to our Australian audience about "library services for tertiary students." Because the word "tertiary" was so familiar to me, it didn't occur to me to use a term more familiar to people in the United States to describe college and university students. As a linguist and a librarian, John, of course, worked out what I was talking about and delivered a terrific paper on the needs of deaf students.

The question of language and communication is fundamental to an understanding of the deaf community. Terminology can be a sensitive issue. Sometimes it is sensitive because of cultural difference. For instance, in Australia the expression "the disabled" is frowned upon and the expression "the handicapped" is considered absolutely unacceptable. (From my reading I assume that both these terms are quite acceptable in the United States.)

In place of these terms, we use the phrase "people with disabilities"—emphasizing the person first and the disability second. Another example that springs to mind is the use of the terms "mentally retarded" or "mentally handicapped," which also are seen frequently in American literature. In Australia, these terms are so disliked that many librarians would hesitate to buy a book that referred to the mentally retarded or mentally handicapped. I use these examples to demonstrate my point about cultural differences.

The other interesting aspect relating to the use of language is that we tend to adapt our terminology depending upon who we are talking to and where we happen to be. For instance, in this paper I will be using the terms "deaf community," "people with hearing difficulties," and "deaf and hearing impaired" almost interchangeably to describe everyone who is affected by deafness or hearing loss. In other settings I would take much greater care to use the term "deaf community" to refer only to the signing community. I would do this in deference to the views of the audience.

From a sermon on the use of language, I would like now to move to a geography and social history lesson by making some comparisons between the United States and Australia. I hope this will help you see my paper in context.

First, the United States and Australia are very similar in physical size—Australia is around 3 million square miles, while the United States is around 3.6 million square miles. We also have similar histories—for example, both countries started as colonial outposts; we have each relied on immigration to build our present populations and, therefore, today have multicultural communities with English as their main language; we have both relied on industry and agriculture for our (sometimes precarious) economic development; and we both appear to be developing a greater awareness of the needs of the deaf community. So you can see that we appear to have a lot of things in common.

The area where we differ most is in the size of our populations. The population of Australia is just over 16 million people, while the population of the United States is 240 million—sixteen times larger than Australia's!

It is estimated that 15 percent of our 16 million people have some form of disability and that more than 1 million people in Australia have some form of hearing impairment. Of these, approximately 40,000 have either been born deaf or have acquired a hearing loss early enough in childhood to require specialized educational services.

The most recent figures available indicate that about 7,000 prelingually deaf Australians are fluent in sign language and use it as their preferred medium of communication. Australian Sign Language (Auslan) is recognized as a language in its own right, although in our very multicultural society it is still one of the smaller language groups.

Australia is divided into six states (each with its own government and laws) and two territories. When talking about library services, I will be referring primarily to services in the state of New South Wales (NSW), where we have a non-centralized system.

By that I mean that the State Library of New South Wales has no direct control over the eighty-one major public libraries and 300 branch libraries in that state. Public libraries in NSW depend almost entirely upon their local governments for funding. The level of this funding varies considerably.

For many years the State Library of New South Wales has provided a "support and leadership" role for libraries in the state. My role as special needs consultant in charge of library services for people with disabilities is an example of how we try to provide support and leadership. In this position I am responsible for providing *support* through a consulting service and through a "support collection" of special-format materials (e.g., large-print books, talking books, captioned videos, high interest/low vocabulary materials, and tape-and-text materials); and *leadership* through the provision of staff training programs, information services, involvement in policy issues (across a very broad spectrum), and awareness raising.

When I began in this position less than five years ago, I had very little knowledge of the library needs of people with hearing difficulties; I also knew very little about the deaf community itself. Like many other people, my main experience of deafness had been limited to mild frustrations with a grandmother who couldn't hear what I was saying when I spoke to her very loudly within inches of her ear, but who could hear me whisper something I didn't want her to hear from fifty feet away!

I decided that I should consult someone who had been associated with the field of deafness for many years. I went, therefore, to the headquarters of the Deaf Society of New South Wales and talked with a man who had been involved with the society for more than thirty years. I asked him, "What can libraries do for deaf people?" He replied, with some puzzlement, "Nothing—deaf people don't use libraries." At first I was crushed by this response; then, after a lot of thought, I decided to treat it as a challenge! Some of the library programs I am going to describe were—and still are—a response to that challenge.

In hindsight, I am convinced that this challenge came at exactly the right time, a time of great change in the Australian deaf community. In many ways the past few years have been like a roller coaster ride: There have been ups and downs but also, at all times, a clearly directed momentum. That momentum is toward recognition of the deaf community as a distinct and valued cultural group with all the rights that this recognition implies. I am often thankful that we Australian librarians jumped on the roller coaster at the right time.

I will tell you a little about some specific deafness awareness programs involving libraries. Then I will describe some general community education/awareness-raising programs in which libraries have participated.

"Opening Doors for Closed Ears"

In March 1988 the State Library of New South Wales hosted a major conference on library services for deaf and hard of hearing people entitled "Opening Doors for Closed Ears." The aims of this conference were to raise librarians' awareness of the library and information needs of people who are deaf or hard of hearing, to raise the awareness of people from the deaf community of the resources and services available through libraries, and to act as a catalyst for the development of library services.

Planning for this conference began after I visited libraries and other agencies in the United States and Canada as part of a Churchill Fellowship study tour. I first thought of holding such a conference during my visit with Alice Hagemeyer at the District of

Columbia Public Library. I have never asked Alice whether she actually believed me when I said to her, "I'm going back to Australia to plan a conference, and I'd love for you to be a guest speaker," but both she and John did come to Australia, and the rest, as the saying goes, is history!

Most of the major activities that have occurred in our libraries since that time have arisen from the recommendations of that conference. Below is a summary of those recommendations and the actions taken in response to them:

1. Every library should purchase a TTY (telephone device for the deaf).

   Action: The State Library of NSW has purchased eight TTYs—two for use in the library and six for loan. Many public libraries and some university libraries in NSW now have TTYs. Similar actions are being taken in other states.

2. Every library should set up at least one service area equipped with an assistive listening device.

   Action: The State Library of NSW and several major public libraries have installed such equipment.

3. Every library should include awareness of hearing impairment in its staff training program, and every effort should be made to promote library services to the deaf community.

   Action: This is an ongoing commitment. Aspects are described below.

4. Library staff should be encouraged to develop basic sign language skills and other appropriate communication skills.

   Action: Introductory sign classes are held during work hours at the State Library at regular intervals. Staff are encouraged to go on to higher levels of study on their own time. Other programs are described below.

5. A committee should be formed to investigate the development of an information-sharing mechanism similar to *The Red Notebook* (Hagemeyer, 1989).

   Action: This is still the subject of discussion by a committee of people from the deaf community.

6. All libraries should examine their collections to ensure that they include information reflecting the various viewpoints on issues of importance to the deaf community.

   Action: This action is in progress.

7. All libraries should establish captioned video collections.

   Action: Discussed in detail below.

8. All libraries should actively participate in and promote the "Hearing Help Scheme."

   Action: Discussed in detail below.

9. A signed storytelling program should be developed for public libraries and schools.

   Action: This program is being developed currently. It will be a major statewide activity during the Year of the Reader and the International Year of Literacy in 1990.

10. Support should be sought to assist a delegation of people from Australia to participate in the international Deaf Way Conference and Festival.

Action: A number of people were able to attend.

I would like to expand on a couple of these programs.

Establishment of Captioned Video Collections (Recommendation 7)

In Australia we use "closed captions" (which require a decoder to access the captions) on our television programs and "open captions" (which require no special equipment) on our videos. Captioned videos, therefore, are a special-format material; collections of these materials are separate from the standard, uncaptioned video collections.

The Australian Caption Centre, the only captioning agency in Australia, launched its captioned video library project as part of the Opening Doors conference. Late in 1988 the State Library of NSW allocated grants of more than $20,000 each to three major public libraries in NSW to establish collections of these videos in their libraries. As part of this grant, the libraries were required to install TTYs and to carry out staff training and awareness-raising programs.

Collections of varying sizes also have been established in a number of other public libraries. Many of these libraries have held very successful launches of their other services for the deaf community, thus alerting deaf people to the availability of these services. The State Library of NSW also has established a collection of captioned videos as part of the support collection of special-format materials for people with disabilities.

Participation in Deafness Awareness Week Programs (Recommendation 3)

Each year in August, the Australian Deafness Council holds a Deafness Awareness Week. This is always an excellent time for libraries to focus on materials and services for the deaf community. The State Library of NSW has for many years supported these activities by distributing posters, book lists, programs, and other awareness-raising materials to libraries throughout the state. In the last two years, we have had a much closer involvement in this event.

Last year at the official opening of Deafness Awareness Week, a Deafness Expo was held at the State Library. The occasion was considerably enlivened when the guest of honor, the Minister for Education, was the victim of a very rowdy and emotional demonstration by deaf students who were protesting against the introduction of student fees. As you can imagine, this attracted a good deal of media attention. We are still not sure, however, if that was quite the sort of awareness raising we intended!

The Deafness Expo involved a full day of workshops, displays, theater performances, and talks dealing with all aspects of deafness. Following the success of this program, another Deafness Expo will be held in the State Library this September, again as part of Deafness Awareness Week. The Deafness Expo is aimed at both deaf and hearing people. For many deaf people, this is their first introduction to a library. Many become regular users of services they had not realized were available to them.

I will move on now to describe some community projects in which libraries have become involved.

Participation in the Hearing Help Scheme (Recommendation 8)

The Hearing Help Scheme was developed by Better Hearing Australia. Libraries throughout Australia are participating in this scheme, which involves placing a Hearing Help reception-desk card in all community facilities—theaters, restaurants, banks, business offices, clubs, and, of course, libraries—in order to facilitate communication for people who are deaf and hard of hearing.

The scheme uses the "ear" symbol that has been adopted officially by organizations for deaf people throughout the world. The aim is to have this symbol displayed wherever people with hearing difficulties can be assured of receiving the hearing help they need. For instance, it can be used to indicate that there are assistive listening devices available, or it can be used to indicate that staff are sensitive to the communication needs of people with hearing difficulties.

A package of materials has been developed to facilitate communication and raise awareness of the communication needs of people with hearing difficulties. This package includes:

❖ A Hearing Help card, which is carried by the individual and produced to alert service providers to the needs of the client. On the back of the card are four simple tips for improving communication.

❖ A reception-desk card. This is a free-standing card to be placed permanently on service desks or counters to indicate the willingness of the staff to assist people with hearing difficulties.

❖ A selection of posters and a window sticker aimed at promoting the Hearing Help scheme.

ACCESS 2000

A more recent development is the ACCESS 2000 project. This program, which is modeled on a Canadian program of the same name, has been developed by the Australian Deafness Council. ACCESS 2000 has two major thrusts—staff training and the promotion of assistive listening devices. The project involves the use of a video entitled "I'll Talk to You if You'll Talk to Me," which teaches some of the techniques that can facilitate interaction with clients who have different forms of hearing difficulty. Again, the ear symbol is used to signify that staff in a particular setting are trained to communicate with these clients.

We have used this program very effectively as the basis for staff training and awareness programs in public libraries. It provides an excellent starting point for discussion of the various aspects of deafness and the ways in which communication can be facilitated.

Conclusion

Most of the programs I have described aim to raise the awareness of both hearing and deaf people. Most have been developed in consultation with people from the deaf community. Each of these programs has contributed to a better understanding of the ways in which libraries can offer meaningful services for the deaf community.

Although we believe we can see very positive results, we also recognize that we have a long way to go. The biggest challenge is in changing attitudes such as those displayed by the library patron who felt it was the duty of the deaf person to wear hearing aids to make life easier for hearing people—the same attitude as that expressed in my opening quote.

Having brought myself back to my starting point, I would like to conclude by dipping again into Brian Grant's anthology for a quotation that touches on a number of relevant issues, including that of attitudes:

> The troubles of the deaf are not, primarily, to be solved by money and good works. Of course it is nice when a hard-of-hearing group gets a minibus to tootle it around the countryside, and deaf children's schools need money for equipment and teachers. *But . . . [it is] the attitude of hearing people that is the core of the problem. If people included them in, deafness would be a bearable disability. . . .* So send no money, knit no blankets, get up no church bazaars. *Just talk to them. That'll do it* (Katharine Whitehorn—from the *Observer 21*, November 1971).

References

Grant, Brian. Ed. 1987. *The Quiet Ear: Deafness in Literature.* London: Andre Deutsch.

Hagemeyer, A. Ed. 1989—Updated biannually. *The Red Notebook.* Silver Spring, MD: Library for Deaf Action.

ASL Is Finally Accepted as a Foreign Language in High Schools!

ANN BILLINGTON-BAHL

High schools and universities throughout the United States are now beginning to incorporate for-credit courses in American Sign Language into their foreign language curricula. Why is this happening now instead of years ago?

American Sign Language (ASL) is at least 200 years old and is one of the most commonly used languages in the country. Only during the past twenty years, however, have linguists officially "discovered" ASL as a true language with its own grammatical rules, which are very different from those of English. This is a major breakthrough for deaf people all over the country.

How will the students who are taking German or Spanish classes in high school keep up their skills in the years to come? One way is to travel to other countries and experience the cultures there. Those who are taking American Sign Language, however, have a great opportunity to use it right where they are.

As a result of the movie *Children of a Lesser God* and the Gallaudet protest for a deaf president, more sign language classes are forming than ever before, and enrollments are overflowing. With media exposure, American Sign Language is becoming much more visible. At least once a day you can observe American Sign Language on a TV program or a commercial. Children as young as one to three years old are learning sign language by watching *Sesame Street* every day.

It is time for colleges, universities, and high schools to accept and incorporate American Sign Language into their foreign language curricula. Doing so will greatly help overcome ignorance of the language and culture of deaf people, while at the same time enriching the education of college and high school students. It can also help keep deaf culture alive at a time when so many deaf students are mainstreamed into public schools. If hearing students learn more about our culture and are sensitive to the needs of deaf people, then deaf students will have higher self-esteem and not feel pressured to conform to the hearing culture.

Students who are learning American Sign Language are our future doctors, nurses, interpreters, teachers, and parents and siblings of deaf children. If we plant the seeds of good attitude, respect, and advocacy for American Sign Language and deaf culture in their hearts while they are young, our future should look brighter. If they become professionals in deafness, they can become our allies instead of our oppressors.

I have been asked many times why I let hearing students learn our private language and rob us of our superior knowledge of it. My answer is that it is the same as having them learn any other language. I feel it is very important to instill good attitudes in these young people so they will be easier to work with in the future. Young people learn so much more quickly.

I foresee a growth in the use of American Sign Language in the years to come because of a more widespread understanding of deafness than existed in the past. Several states (California, Michigan, and Minnesota) have already passed laws recognizing American Sign Language as the language of deaf people and have allowed high school students to take American Sign Language for credit to meet foreign language requirements. Maine and Texas passed resolutions identifying American Sign Language as a foreign language. Iowa recently approved a bill to grant foreign language credit for university courses in ASL. Legislation to accept ASL as the language of deaf people also was passed in Manitoba, Canada.

In June 1986, as a result of efforts by the Legislative Coalition for the Hearing-Impaired, the Minnesota State Board of Education adopted a motion to recognize ASL as fulfilling "modern-classical language requirements." This issue had been triggered two years earlier by a deaf student at the University of Minnesota who asked the university to accept his proficiency in sign language as fulfillment of the foreign language requirement. This deaf student argued that he was already fluent in two languages—ASL and English—and should not be required to learn a third.

At first his petition was denied. The Scholastic Standing Committee ruled that sign language did not meet three requirements for a language: research potential, a national culture, and syntax. Of course, the deaf student appealed this decision. The university later reversed its position and has begun formulating a curriculum proposal. The University of Minnesota will begin offering ASL as a foreign language in 1990. It is presently searching for a qualified teacher.

St. Thomas University, also in Minnesota, now accepts the study of ASL in fulfillment of its foreign language requirement. The problem now is to change the attitudes of teachers and professionals so they too will accept American Sign Language.

Many other universities are presently offering ASL as an elective course in various departments. I have been teaching ASL at Mankato State University for the past five years. The course had already been listed in the Rehabilitative Counseling Department for several years before I started teaching there. My supervisor understands the need to transfer this course into the Foreign Language Department. The problem now is budget cuts, which are affecting every department; I sense a resistance on the part of the administration to add a new curriculum. We are continuing to work on this, so it is possible that the ASL course will be transferred within the next few years.

The fact that many states have already passed laws accepting ASL does not mean things will change immediately. The next step for some of us is to educate professionals to accept ASL as a separate language from English. I strongly believe that with our united work, we can push more states to pass laws recognizing ASL as a true language in its own right, and to add ASL to the curricula of their high schools and universities.

Faribault Senior High School is the only public school in the state of Minnesota to offer American Sign Language as a foreign language, along with Spanish and German. Three years ago, it was offered as an elective course on a trial basis. The fact that this course was already being offered at the high school when the law recognizing ASL was passed indicates how much the administration supported the idea. I still cannot believe how easy it was to get it started. This school year (1988–89) is the first year the course is being offered for credit to fulfill the foreign language requirement for college admission.

When ASL was first offered, as an elective, the course was funded by the Minnesota State Academy for the Deaf (MSAD) through a contract with the Faribault Public Schools. Owing to its success the first year, the Faribault Board of Education agreed to have the Faribault School District #656 fund the course for the remainder of its existence. During both semesters of the first year, only a beginning course was offered. The program has since been expanded to include an advanced course, offered during the second semester. We are planning to offer a full one- or two-year course within the next two years.

The advantage of having the ASL course at Faribault Senior High School is that MSAD is located right in Faribault. Some of the MSAD deaf students, from kindergarten students to high school seniors, are mainstreamed into the Faribault public school system. The deaf students take anywhere from three to six classes a day at the public schools. They accept this as a challenge that helps them to gain experience being in a different culture.

Being exposed to deaf students and interpreters in their classrooms has sparked an interest among the hearing students in learning our unique language. They really want to communicate and become friends with the deaf students. Through the mainstreaming of some deaf students, the hearing students have gained a great opportunity to interact with the deaf community.

The ASL course requires students to pay close attention to, and participate in, deaf cultural exchanges. When in class, students are required to wear earplugs that reduce the sound of voices to the point where they cannot be heard, even as whispers. This practice seems to be quite effective, although there are times when some students are not so cooperative as we'd like them to be.

In each of my classes, I have a deaf student from MSAD as a student assistant. This is a positive asset to the class. The students have an exposure to different signing styles, as well as the chance to observe natural communication exchanges between two deaf people. It is also an opportunity for the deaf assistant to learn about his or her language. Many of the assistants have transferred to MSAD from public schools where they were taught signed English. They earn one-half credit for their work experience. The duties of an assistant are as follows:

- ❖ recording students' attendance in the record book and on the attendance sheet
- ❖ handling visual aid equipment
- ❖ helping the teacher with practice sessions
- ❖ helping check answers on some tests
- ❖ watching all students to be sure they use correct signs, correcting them if necessary
- ❖ participating in some class activities
- ❖ sharing some stories for receptive practice
- ❖ running some errands for the teacher if necessary
- ❖ being willing to accept corrections or suggestions from the teacher whenever necessary.

I really benefit from their assistance as much as they benefit from our class.

Curriculum and Objectives

What curriculum do we use? What are the objectives of the ASL courses at Faribault Senior High School? I will try to share with you what we are doing at Faribault Senior High School and what we hope to accomplish within the next few years.

The ASL courses offered are for half a credit each. Classes meet for one hour each day for one full semester. The following course descriptions and objectives are listed in the students' books:

> **American Sign Language I** (Grades 10, 11, 12). Credit: 1/2 credit. Course objectives:

❖ To demonstrate the ability to communicate on a basic level using American Sign Language and fingerspelling, both receptively and expressively.

❖ To recognize that American Sign Language is a true language, with a grammar and syntax different from those of English.

❖ To increase awareness and knowledge of deafness and the deaf community.

❖ To become familiar with communication devices and techniques used by deaf people.

❖ To gain confidence in meeting and communicating with deaf people.

> Course description: This course is for students who are as serious about learning American Sign Language as they would be any other language. The course is an introduction to the basics of American Sign Language and fingerspelling, with emphasis on both receptive and expressive skills. Students will not only learn signs, but work on grammatical features, using facial expression, classifiers, spatialization, and directionality through drills, games, activities, and projects. Students will also learn about deafness and the deaf community through films, guest speakers, readings, and visits to the Minnesota State Academy for the Deaf. Field experiences at the Academy will provide students opportunities to use their signing skills in a natural context.

> **American Sign Language II** (Grades 10, 11, 12). Credit: 1/2 credit. Prerequisite: Must have taken American Sign Language I and passed with a minimum score of 80 percent, or with permission from the instructor.

> Course description: This course emphasizes the spontaneous interactive use of everyday American Sign Language. The students will expand their introductory comprehension skills, production skills, and conversational constraints. Special emphasis is placed on acquiring additional functional grammatical structures and information related to everyday experiences of Deaf Americans. A project will be done at the end of the semester. Students will have a chance to interview a deaf person. At least 1/2 hour of practice outside of class each day is required.

These course descriptions will probably be revised again later this year [1989].

What approach do we use to teach hearing students our language? Since I began teaching sign language in 1975, I have tried different approaches. I was never satisfied with any one of them until I started using the Direct Method, which was an improvement over previous approaches. After seeing a demonstration of the new Vista Curriculum (Lentz, Mikos, and Smith, 1989), however, I became very excited. This functional-notation approach is the most appropriate because it emphasizes interpersonal and cross-cultural communication, which is the most natural way to acquire language. What students learn in class applies to their real-life situations. The students can bring a videotape home each day to practice, which helps improve their receptive skills.

For the past nine years, I have used *A Basic Course in American Sign Language* (Humphries, Padden, and O'Rourke, 1980) and "the green book," *ASL: A Student Text, Units 1–18* (Baker-Shenk and Cokely, 1980). When I was asked to teach at Faribault Senior High School, the school administration had already ordered *Basic Sign Communication* by the National Technical Institute for the Deaf. Because MSAD is using this curriculum, they felt it might help to have the same one at Faribault Senior High.

I supplement this curriculum with other ASL materials, including videotapes of deaf people signing in ASL, which really help. This coming fall we will finally be able to use the new Vista Curriculum. I have heard rave reviews from other sign language teachers who are currently using this curriculum, and have already ordered it for my classes at both the university and the high school.

We are presently working on establishing a sign language club at the high school. Because we are offering only two levels of courses, a club would give students a greater opportunity to keep up their skills in preparation for college. One possible activity for students in the club would be to put on a variety show with the deaf students during an assembly. This club would promote deaf awareness on campus as well as in the community. We are planning to have either a silent evening or weekend, where no voice will be allowed at all! This would be the students' total immersion into deaf culture.

Environment is a crucial part of learning language and culture. The one disadvantage I am experiencing right now is that the school is so overcrowded I do not have my own room and must use another teacher's room while he or she has a prep hour. I would like to have more freedom to change the room I teach in to fit the culture, as they do in German and Spanish classes. It is my long-range plan to find a permanent classroom where video equipment would always be available. It may be possible in the near future to have the class transfer to MSAD, where the students would experience a change of culture. I am sure that with the wonderful administration we have, this could become a reality.

Last fall I became a member of the high school's foreign language committee. We met together to evaluate the needs and priorities for the Modern World Language curriculum. From that meeting I can see how ASL teachers' needs may be different from those of spoken foreign language teachers, because their courses are speech- and hearing-based, whereas ours are visually based.

There is a great need for teachers of ASL to meet together and share concerns and ideas about teaching ASL to hearing high school students. I know that such teaching will become widespread throughout the country, and we can work together to help those who are starting new classes and to encourage other qualified deaf teachers to teach those classes. This is a very exciting new adventure!

References

Baker-Shenk, C., and D. Cokely. 1980. *American Sign Language: A Student Text, Units 1–9* and *American Sign Language: A Student Text, Units 10–18*. Silver Spring, MD: T.J. Publishers, Inc.

Humphries, T., C. Padden, and T. O'Rourke. 1980. *A Basic Course in American Sign Language.* Silver Spring, MD: T.J. Publishers, Inc.

Lentz, E., K. Mikos, and C. Smith. 1989. *Signing Naturally Student Workbook and Video-texts, Level 1.* San Diego, CA: DawnSign Press.

The importance of hands and eyes to deaf people was repeatedly emphasized during the conference and festival (see following page).

The Deaf Way Festival included a wide array of dramatic performances by deaf theater groups from many nations (see following pages).

Painting by Jaén Arrabal

A high level of artistic accomplishment by deaf artists and craftspeople was on display at The Deaf Way (see facing and following pages).

Painting by Chuck Baird

PART NINE

Deaf People and the Arts

Editor's Introduction

When he became Gallaudet University's first deaf president in 1988, I. King Jordan said, "Deaf people can do anything—except hear!" These words continue to be invoked all over the world as a challenge to negative assumptions about deaf people's abilities. In many areas of human endeavor—such as in the arts—only ignorance of Deaf people's accomplishments could account for the persistence of such negative beliefs. In the performing and visual arts, especially, it should be abundantly clear from the wealth of work already accomplished that Deaf artists' capabilities and potential are unlimited.

Those capabilities were particularly evident during The Deaf Way Conference and Festival. In the evenings during that week, plays were brilliantly performed by Deaf theatrical groups from many nations. There were excellent offerings in mime, dance, and comedy, as well as many displays of paintings and crafts of high artistic merit. Had it been universally witnessed, the Deaf art presented at The Deaf Way would in itself have put to rest any assumptions about Deaf people's inferiority.

The papers in this section not only provide further testimony concerning Deaf artists' hard-won achievements around the world, but also demonstrate that the task facing Deaf artists involves many issues that defy simple solutions. Doug Alker (England), discusses problems related to the negative images of Deaf people projected by producers of films and television shows in England. Alker suggests that the Deaf community in England needs to take a more active role in clarifying its true identity and shattering the old stereotypes. The problem, Alker states, is that many Deaf people in England need first to overcome their own doubts about their capabilities, doubts which have resulted, in part, from the negative images they've internalized from the media and other sources since childhood.

Gunilla Wågström-Lundqvist (Sweden) points out in her paper that although Deaf artists in Sweden have become full participants in Swedish culture and even "world culture," the creation of Deaf theater or Deaf art—which by definition would differentiate Deaf from hearing culture—has been slow to develop in Sweden. It appears that Deaf artists face an interesting difficulty in attempting to formulate and express a unique Deaf vision in a society in which they have so clearly benefited from the many accommodations made to their communication and socialization needs.

Ann Silver (United States) then discusses a topic related to the one examined by Doug Alker: the powerful effects of the images of Deaf people projected by films produced in Hollywood. Because these images often constitute hearing people's first exposure to Deaf people, Silver states, they tend to condition hearing people's attitudes, and therefore influence Deaf people's "fate." For these reasons, Silver feels, it is important that Deaf people themselves become engaged, not only in acting, but also in writing, directing, producing, and consulting, whenever images of Deaf people are to be presented in films.

In the following panel discussion led by Phyllis Frelich Steinberg (United States), seven successful Deaf Americans from the film, theater, and television industries discuss a variety of topics. (In addition to Frelich Steinberg, the panel included Linda Bove, Julianna Fjeld, Marlee Matlin, Howie Seago, Terrylene, and Ed Waterstreet.) Each panelist tells of his or her individual struggle to succeed in a fast-paced business in which Deaf people must persuasively sell their skills—more often than not to producers and directors who know no sign language and are ignorant of Deaf culture. The panelists generally agree that the American Deaf community should insist that Deaf roles be acted by Deaf, not hearing actors.

The next two papers examine issues related to the theatrical offerings of Deaf theater groups in Australia and the United States, two countries of similar size on opposite sides of the earth. Both papers describe the difficulties Deaf companies face in trying to create drama satisfying to Deaf and hearing audiences alike. Carol-lee Aquiline (Australia) points out that performances that appeal greatly to Deaf spectators, but not to hearing spectators, may need to be modified—not only because hearing audiences are necessary for a company's economic survival, but also because Deaf artists generally wish to enlarge (not shrink) the scope of their art's power to communicate. Don Bangs (United States) then points out—in the course of his analysis of three American Deaf theatrical groups—that when a company chooses to alter the natural qualities of sign language to make it synchronize more perfectly with voicing (provided for hearing audiences), Deaf spectators may feel less than complete satisfaction with the results. Bangs' and Aquiline's discussions suggest that there are no simple solutions to such problems, but they agree that the process of creating theater for both Deaf and hearing people is invariably exciting and worthwhile. Bangs adds that Deaf theater groups "must make sure that theater performances can be enjoyed by Deaf audiences. They deserve access to the unique theatrical experience their culture and language have made possible."

In the next paper Gregorio Jaen Arrabal (Spain) tells his own story—the story of a gifted Deaf painter whose talents were fortunately discovered and nurtured by some remarkable teachers. Arrabal emphasizes that his long journey toward a fulfilling life as an artist was made possible largely because his parents believed in his talent and unfailingly supported his efforts to excel, often making considerable sacrifices on his behalf. The final paper by Betty Miller (United States), also concerned with visual arts, represents the efforts of a group of Deaf American artists to conceptualize what might constitute Deaf visual art that would distinguish it from the work of hearing artists. It is clear from this paper and all the papers in this section that Deaf artists must struggle both to create their vision and to make their vision be seen.

Misconceptions of Deaf Culture in the Media and the Arts

DOUG ALKER

What do we mean by "deaf culture"? I will go along with the American researcher Simon J. Carmel and define it as the whole lifestyle of a special group. The life of a deaf person is obviously different from that of a hearing person in the respect that deaf people depend on visual stimuli and have a common visual language. These facts lead to practices and customs that are unique to the deaf community, such as using flashing lights as doorbells, using text-telephones, getting the attention of another person by waving one's hands, etc.

The subject "media and the arts" covers a very wide range. This paper will focus attention on the press, television, and the theater in England.

In the media, deaf people are generally seen as defective, pathetic people, second-class members of society in need of rectification. Hardly any sign language is shown in the media, and there are rarely any interviews of deaf people. The "Does he take sugar?" syndrome prevails. For example, when nineteen British tourists, seventeen of whom were deaf, were injured in a terrorist attack in Greece, not one of the deaf victims was consulted for his or her experience of the bomb blast. One journalist from an English national newspaper approached the tour guide for her comments. Another evidently felt it was more reliable to interview a ten-year-old hearing child and ask for her interpretation of the panic the deaf tourists experienced.

The British theater is no better. Many so-called deaf theater performances are actively based on the hearing concept of what deaf people can do; they were not developed from the deaf experience, and they do not portray deaf characters or deaf culture. Such works are based on the medical model of deafness, with attention on overcoming disability rather than promoting the abilities of deaf people. Where is the culture, pride, identity, language, and community of deaf people?

The importance of the media goes beyond publicity and awareness; it involves the question of public attitudes toward deaf people. Attitudes are widely recognized as the main deterrent to successful interactions in society. Attitudes also determine the treatment an individual receives, which will then influence the personality development of that individual. Research has shown that inaccurate, stereotyped, and negative portrayals of deaf people create negative attitudes in individuals, which are then projected on all those who are deaf. The results of such negative attitudes toward deaf people are devastating.

Such attitudes are usually communicated by society through avoidance, anxiety, overprotectiveness, pity, segregation, alienation, and rejection. The results for deaf people are feelings of embarrassment, self-pity, self-consciousness, dependence, apathy, and lack of motivation, as well as lowered self-image and stunted vocational development.

Interaction between deaf people and people who are not deaf is one of the most effective ways of modifying negative public attitudes, and two qualities inherent in successful interactions are recognition and respect. To alter the attitudes of society successfully, it is important to encourage respect and recognition in interaction. Because the primary source of information is the mass media, it is obvious that the negative images of deaf people projected by the media must be modified if deaf people are to achieve equal status in society.

Analysis of available material yields six key issues relating to media misconceptions of deafness:

❖ marginalization of deaf people in the mainstream media

❖ focus on the medical model of deafness

❖ stereotyping of deaf people

❖ lack of attention to deaf rights issues

❖ use of language demeaning to deaf people, and

❖ failure to consult deaf adults on deaf issues.

Deaf people and deaf issues, generally excluded from mainstream programs, are almost invisible in the media image of British society. What we see is a classic example of the "ghetto versus mainstream" conflict experienced by other minority groups in British society. Instead of portraying people's differences, the media culture marginalizes deaf people by confining positive images of deaf people to special programs for the deaf only. The effect of this marginalization is the representation of deaf people as abnormal and not part of mainstream society.

When deaf people are featured, the media are highly selective in the images they choose to present to the public. Generally, they portray deaf people only as pairs of nonfunctioning ears, at the expense of any other aspect of their lives. They tend to concentrate on medical operations, fund-raising, and legal awards to people who suddenly become deaf, presenting selective images based on the medical model of deaf people as subnormal.

The effect of the media's focus on the medical model has been to obscure linguistic issues related to deafness and the fact that deaf people have rights—to access to sign language and to equal opportunities in education, training, and employment—which they are often denied. Far from relating such information, the media reinforce discrimination in society by burying these issues of access under an avalanche of negative stereotypes.

Deaf people achieving professional employment as fashion models, nurses, etc., are stereotyped as one-in-a-million heroes, as if we shouldn't expect the mass of ordinary deaf people to have such aspirations because they are deaf. At the opposite end of the spectrum lies the stereotype of deaf people as helpless, diffident people "trapped in a world of silence." If the media honestly felt that, for instance, a deaf woman becoming a fashion model were so newsworthy, why could they not have asked why she was the first deaf person ever to be given the opportunity? Why could they not question the negative attitudes of the colleges and fashion agencies and ask why no deaf person had this opportunity before?

Stereotypes underlie most media images of deaf people, and must be changed. The statement, "despite being profoundly deaf, John Brown got a job as a cook," places the blame for the struggle on the individual's deafness rather than on the system that handicaps deaf people. The statement should be rephrased, "despite having difficulties with employers' attitudes, John Brown got a job as a cook." This places the blame more fairly, on the disabling society that deaf people struggle against.

Another example of the media's ignoring the deaf rights aspect of a story is that of a deaf man portrayed by a local paper as the "brave hero who broke the sound barrier" in earning his Heavy Goods Vehicle driver's license. Actually, he had broken through the ridiculous medical regulations that unnecessarily bar many deaf people from driving trucks. Similarly, a three-year-old deaf child was portrayed as being "trapped in a world of silence," whereas, in reality, she was trapped by the refusal of local authorities to provide a Phonic Ear amplification system and sign language in her education.

The language used by the media may not seem an obvious source of discrimination, but it often reinforces public prejudices toward deaf people. Newspaper headlines proclaiming "Thatcher Deaf to Pleas" or "USA and Russia in Dialogue of the Deaf" tend to associate deafness with obstinacy and noncommunication. Outdated terms like "deaf and dumb" create associations with mental handicap, while the terms "hearing impaired" and "nonhearing" both medicalize deafness and deny deaf people their basic identity in the same way that South Africa denies basic rights to black people by classifying them as "nonwhites."

Media reports on deaf issues rarely consult deaf adults. Media journalists and producers tend to consult politicians, social workers, doctors, charities, and even the hearing children of deaf parents in order to find out what deaf people think or what they want from society. This creates the risk of misrepresenting the views of deaf people and denies deaf people their right to a voice in the media.

Why do these misconceptions exist, and what can be done to rectify them? Before we actually take the media to task, we must recognize that they are only partly at fault. Deaf people and deaf organizations themselves bear some responsibility.

Deaf people must look at themselves and their own attitudes. Consider, for example, a hypothetical newspaper headline: "Deaf Man Batters Child." Deaf people might react to such a headline in a variety of ways. Those who identify themselves as "deaf" might react as a black person would to the word "black"; their reaction would depend on the content of the headline and whether it contained negative implications about deaf people. Others might react negatively to the mere use of the word "deaf," preferring to be identified as hearing impaired or hard of hearing. It is no wonder the media are confused.

Deaf people must sort themselves out, and hiding behind the label "hearing impaired" will not help; either we are deaf or we are not. We either have a separate identity or we do not. When this matter is settled, the media will know at least where we stand, and, hopefully, we will be able to react accordingly.

We also must consider the attitudes of organizations of and for deaf people. Some regard deaf people as their flock. Others have long-established reputations for patronization. Teachers' organizations, having long regarded deaf children as limited, have lower expectations of them than of hearing children. Some organizations of the deaf give awards to deaf achievers. At a recent Young Deaf Achievers competition, only two of the ten finalists could sign. The winner could not sign and spoke when interviewed by the media. So much for the promotion of deaf culture! If such organizations are paternalistic and patronizing, regarding deaf people as handicapped, we should not be surprised if the media respond in a similar manner.

We cannot presume that society accepts the concept of deaf people as a linguistic minority group with its own separate culture; even "oral" deaf people refuse to accept this concept, and many "grassroots" deaf people are unaware of the issue. We must translate our culture into something more tangible and promote it, wear it on our sleeves as black people do theirs. The media will then become more aware and, possibly, respond appropriately.

As for the deaf theater, many of the plays and performances are based on hearing people's experiences and try to fit deaf people into them—like the chimpanzee's tea party, where apes imitate the actions and habits of the human race. Where are the plays and performances based on the deaf experience? Where are the productions based on the use of sign language? We see hardly any. If this pseudo-deaf theater is all there is to see, it is not surprising that the media conceive of deaf people as defective medical models struggling to be like "normal" hearing people. We have the responsibility of encouraging more deaf playwrights and promoting productions of their plays.

After sorting out these issues for ourselves, we can take on the media with confidence and pursue such goals as

❖ involvement of deaf people in mainstream television roles, as well as in interviews, crowd scenes, and quiz shows

❖ guidelines for the use of language, use of interpreters, and other relevant issues, and

❖ presentation of deaf theater productions through mainstream media channels as cultural events in their own right.

There are, in fact, already some examples of good media practice, but they have occurred only as occasional flashes. What is needed is for this sort of thing to occur on a regular basis.

In conclusion, correction of the media's conception of deaf culture and the consequent development of positive attitudes toward deafness by society are vital, but let us first get our own house in order, sort ourselves out, and make our identity clear. Let organizations for and of the deaf and professionals in the field of deafness ensure that their attitudes toward deafness are positive. Let us be aware of our culture and wear it with pride. Then, in dealing with the media's misconceptions of deaf culture we will all be able to move with unity, strength, and conviction.

The Challenge to Deaf People in the Arts Today

GUNILLA WÅGSTRÖM-LUNDQVIST

The quality of life for deaf people around the world differs, depending on their country's attitudes toward deaf people and its level of political, economic, social, and cultural development. In the twentieth century, Swedish people are striving for equality and fair participation in the culture of their society. In the spring of 1974, the Swedish Parliament established cultural-political goals that indicate that cultural policy will be shaped with more regard for the experiences of disadvantaged groups, such as handicapped people.

At present there are still many barriers to access to the arts. For example, people might think that providing a hearing loop in a theater would allow deaf people to follow the performance, but a loop can help only people who are hard of hearing.

In 1976, deaf people and handicapped people (we deaf people do not consider ourselves handicapped, but as an ethnic minority with our own language and culture) made our own cultural proposal, "Culture for Everyone," in which we demanded that everyone have an equal right to access to the arts. As a result, in 1977 the Silent Theater (Tyst Teater), the only theater for the deaf in Sweden, was officially recognized and became affiliated with the National Theater, thus becoming a professional theater group. We also got television programs in sign language for both children and adults.

These developments have motivated us to seek our roots and the sources of stories and traditions about deaf people. We discussed among ourselves our own awareness and self-knowledge, our possibilities and rights in society, and our relationships to each other and to hearing people.

The Silent Theater and sign language TV programs have helped to make sign language popular and accessible to the general public. The increasing use of sign language in news and educational programs proves the acceptance of sign language as a way of communicating among deaf people. However, we have experienced problems with the efforts of hearing people to make TV programs for deaf people.

Hearing people

❖ do not understand deaf culture or sign language, with all its possibilities of expression;

❖ cannot adjust a production process that was created for hearing people;

❖ cannot detach themselves from their associations to pictures as hearing people;

❖ cannot translate into spoken language what deaf people communicate visually; and

❖ find it easy to make deaf people communicate on hearing people's terms.

We often hear that deaf children enjoy the TV programs made for them by hearing people, but children are not able to evaluate critically what they watch. Moreover, deaf children have no other programs for comparison, and few or no opportunities to process their thoughts and experiences of the programs they have seen.

Movies and TV

Once, when I was making a program for children, I worked with a photographer who had, up to that time, never met deaf people. I carefully prepared him on how a taping with deaf children would proceed. During the first taping, with some eight-year-old school children, the photographer just stood there and did not understand anything. He could not follow the deaf children taking turns while signing. I had to give him a signal when he should follow with the camera, but that didn't work out either. It took him quite a while to learn that the taping had to be done in the way that one would film a silent movie.

The tradition of watching films is different among deaf people than among hearing people. Hearing people live in a world where experiences are attached to sounds. In a movie, speech and sound often give hints on how to interpret what one sees. Deaf people experience movies in a different way: Having no support from sound, we can experience only the pictures.

Sign language is built on vision, containing elements that resemble "movie language" with its wide-angle shots, close-ups, panning, and so on. We should be aware of these features of sign language and use them when we make movies. In this way, we can develop a tradition of making movies that fit deaf people and allow deaf people to feel that the programs reflect a part of themselves.

Today, however, there may be more interest in making television programs *about* deaf people than *for* deaf people. Consider, for example, sign language programs for hearing people: These might not help deaf people, because they can create strange attitudes about deafness. Deaf people need TV programs made specifically for them in order to become more knowledgeable. They can then encounter society in the right way and avoid misunderstandings.

What purpose will making our own programs have for deaf people, as participants and as an audience? Participants will be inspired to invest in future work that will create new career possibilities. The deaf audience will gain a stronger sense of identity and learn to understand the programs and process their experiences more easily.

Theater

The Silent Theater began as an amateur group in 1970 with the purpose of being a visual theater. Hearing people thought it was unique to express one's self in body language, and we were more expressive than hearing people in that regard. We who acted, though, as well as the deaf audience, felt something lacking in this mode of expression; we felt very limited. Hearing people got the impression that visual theater suited us well because we were mute. This impression was false; we had merely been suppressing our sign language on stage. When the Silent Theater became affiliated with the National Theater in 1977, it had to adjust to both deaf and hearing audiences in order to survive financially. As a result, deaf people are still waiting for their own theater—a deaf theater.

In 1980, Ms. Lolo Danielsson and I collaborated on the Nordic deaf culture and Theater Project, in which we interviewed theater groups in Scandinavia. The results showed that groups with deaf leaders could discuss in depth how plays were to be performed and how sign language could be presented on stage. These discussions were on an artistic and cultural level. In contrast, theater groups that had hearing leaders, or in which the majority of the actors were hearing, discussed mostly day to day problems. The work of none of these groups was firmly established; the deaf members did not have enough knowledge of themselves as deaf people, of deaf culture, of their environment, or of their relationships to other people. They had a hard time generating and developing their own ideas. Many of them felt hemmed in and insecure. They felt that they needed more knowledge and education, and that it was the theater that could help them to develop personally.

A lot of effort is required of deaf people themselves to find their own approaches to art. Analysis, point of view, intuition, and personal experience are needed. One must also know deaf traditions, values, and language to provide the deaf audience with a feeling of intensity and a need to see more deaf theater. These elements will also give hearing audiences insight and understanding of deaf people. It is easy to create sign language theater: There are innumerable manuscripts that can be translated into sign language, and it can be nice to watch familiar plays. It is much harder, though, to find deaf manuscripts and make deaf theater from that source.

There are also questions about art. Should art come before deafness? Many deaf actors identify as deaf first and actors second. I think the two tie together, because we are discussing *deaf* culture and *deaf* theater. The important thing with art in deaf culture is to achieve continuity in artistic creation and an organization to develop and promote the work of culture.

The Deaf Artist

It is not easy to be an artist today. People have less respect for a professional artist than for an ordinary house painter. People think that artists are having fun when they are working; they do not consider art to be work. This is a common misconception of the artist's working conditions.

The artist's experience and background are often the motifs of his or her work. What about the deaf artist? Is it possible for other deaf people to recognize themselves in the motifs of his or her work? Very often deaf artists are influenced by the art world of the hearing. Hearing schools teach technique but know nothing of the art history of the deaf. Where can the deaf artist get inspiration in order not to be misunderstood as an artist?

There are difficulties in translating deaf culture into practice in the arts. One source of difficulty can be found in our childhoods and in the schools for the deaf.

We adult deaf people grew up with little cultural stimulation. In most cases our parents were hearing, with very little knowledge of sign language. The culture they gave us was on their terms. They had no natural way to tell stories or fairy tales, to sing songs or recite nursery rhymes to us.

Our schools were strongly oralist. People were afraid that sign language would interfere with our development of speech, which was regarded as very important. Education concentrated on speech, and we received very little knowledge about society.

In the past, there was very little contact between deaf adults and deaf children. The deaf clubs had no contact with the schools. Children were not members of the deaf clubs and did not participate in activities there. Neither could deaf children participate in the hearing culture, because it was and is based on hearing and speech.

The current situation is different. Swedish schools for the deaf are now bilingual. Many teachers of the deaf understand the importance of this and engage themselves in learning more sign language. The teachers sign better today, and there are more and more deaf staff and faculty. The deaf schools offer more of a signing environment, where deaf students have opportunities for natural communication with teachers and other personnel. We are now trying to incorporate the arts into the new curriculum.

Deaf clubs now work more closely with the schools, and recreational centers are often located close to deaf clubs to encourage contact with deaf adults. This socialization gives deaf children a sense of self and eases their way toward developing an identity as a deaf adult.

Deaf Cultural Workers in Sweden

I estimate that there are twenty deaf cultural workers in Sweden (twelve amateurs and eight professionals). I will call them "producers." These twenty producers provide culture to about 9,000 deaf people, whom I will call "consumers." I am sure that the ratio of producers to consumers is similar in other countries.

How can eight professional producers satisfy all 9,000 deaf people with thirty television programs, eight publications, and two plays each year without a contact network for developing deaf arts and culture?

We who belong to the producer group are the same deaf people who went through the old school for the deaf, where we received no natural cultural stimulation. We have been forced to fight in order to work in the arts. We need support, encouragement, and above all, stimulation. Job opportunities in the arts can be infrequent and strung out in small pieces.

Because consumers often do not share the same experiences that have shaped us as producers, it is difficult to orient them to our work. What knowledge do we deaf adults have to give to deaf children growing up with bilingualism as a fact of life—we who went to school under the old model, when oralism was dominant?

Because we have no deaf role models, we must cut ourselves loose from the hearing and seek new roads. We shall not look for new trails in the forest, but walk straight through the forest, discover our opportunities, and develop them.

How Can We Develop Deaf Art and Culture?

We in the international deaf arts community should act together to

❖ sponsor exchange programs between countries in the form of guest performances;

❖ arrange exhibits, courses, seminars, and book fairs;

❖ publish bulletins about the deaf cultural world;

❖ create a contact network for professional groups, such as artists, actors, and producers;

❖ compile a directory of organizations working in deaf arts education, such as drama schools and dance schools; and

❖ create an inventory and archive of deaf manuscripts, books, television programs,
films, etc.

These actions might lead to the creation of new professions with more jobs, contracts, projects, and performances.

Conclusion

Like Martin Luther King, Jr., I also have a dream: that we who work in the arts will join together in a world community of culture, where great exchanges take place. I envision the establishment of an international cultural center that will have connections to all countries and promote cultural activities all over the world. In this way, we will increase the number of deaf producers and achieve a balance with hearing producers. Deaf children and youth will have the opportunity to enter the world of the arts in a natural way, and deaf people will be better able to cope with living and participating in both Deaf and hearing cultures.

How Does Hollywood See Us, and How Do We See Hollywood?

ANN SILVER

How does Hollywood see us, and how do we see Hollywood?

The international deaf community has recently undergone great political and cultural changes. Nineteen eighty-eight was an historic year in the struggle for deaf rights, thanks to the spectacular Gallaudet uprising, which finally brought deaf awareness into the public consciousness worldwide.

The film and television industries, however, remain largely ignorant of this progress. The American deaf community has had some success in winning respect, but this success is still not enough.

What are the important issues that need to be addressed in the film and TV culture? Does Hollywood present a fair and accurate picture of deaf people? How do we deal with "deafism" (discrimination against deaf people)? How do films and TV shows affect deaf children? Can Hollywood afford to give up old deaf stereotypes? How do we safeguard and enhance the integrity and dignity of, and respect for, our culture and language?

I do not have all the answers to these questions—you must ultimately answer them for yourselves—but I will provide a variety of viewpoints, facts, and ideas that may help you in reaching conclusions.

Hollywood's Impact on the General Public

Motion pictures and television are vital forms of communication, powerful media capable of evoking emotions, shaping ideas, and affecting attitudes and behaviors. The media—entertainment, news, and information—influence the way millions of deaf and hearing viewers live and think.

The deaf world had very little cultural influence upon the public until the 1960s and 1970s. During these decades, a popular demand for sign language classes began to grow, the National Theater of the Deaf was founded, American Sign Language (ASL) was recognized as a language, the I Love You sign was revived, the advent of closed-captioning created a recognized deaf consumer audience, and the number of scripts with deaf themes, as well as the number of deaf actors, increased significantly.

Copyright 1989. All rights reserved by author.

These milestones put deaf people and deaf culture on the national map, but they were not enough to convince Hollywood to recognize or accept deaf people as a genuine cultural minority.

Attitudes and Behaviors

The absence of deaf culture and deaf people from the media has an effect on the attitudes of hearing people, who must learn about deafness from teachers, friends, parents, neighbors, and newspaper stories, and whose early patterns of perception usually persist into adulthood.

"Deaf and dumb" and "deaf-mute" are terms from long ago which meant "deaf and speechless" but which, over the years, have taken on negative meanings. Hollywood perpetuates such demeaning labels and inaccurate images about us because of the slapdash research on deafness conducted by writers, producers, casting people, and directors.

Film and TV images usually portray deaf people either as having perfect speech and lipreading skills (even when not facing the speaker) or as being perfectly mute and able only to point at things. What the audience sees on TV or in films about deaf people is what it comes to expect of real deaf people. Situations where hearing people actually meet us are almost always embarrassing, awkward, or confusing because of the stereotypes they expect. Thus, we feel self-defeated and helpless.

If we had gotten Hollywood on the right track—depicting real deaf people—ninety years ago, deaf people might have had a different fate. Therefore, changing Hollywood's present attitude is major goal. Although we cannot expect to change Hollywood overnight, we all can take every opportunity to persuade, educate, and advise.

Global Exchange of Deaf Media

International exchanges of deaf-related film, TV, and video offer hearing and deaf people valuable cross-cultural insights into the international deaf experience. The exchange is like cultural vitamins, making our people strong by giving them a sense of deaf pride and identity. After all, we are the producers, consumers, and promoters of our own deaf culture.

When I visited Japan in 1986, I brought along some American videotapes. I showed my Japanese deaf friends the TV movie drama "Love is Never Silent." Their enthusiastic response prompted a Japanese TV station to televise that movie nationwide—twice.

Films, TV shows, and videos shown in international film festivals and competitions, conferences, and informal cultural exchanges can have a wide impact on cultural understanding. We have ample deaf-related film and TV materials, as well as deaf films created by deaf filmmakers, that bring greater awareness of deafness. Why not have an international deaf film festival?

Discrimination Against Deaf Actors

The frustrations of deaf actors from around the world—their struggles and rejections—have not changed significantly through the years. In Japan, for instance, there are many community-based deaf theater groups all over the country, yet Japanese deaf actors are forbidden to play deaf roles on TV, in films, or on the stage.

Here in the United States, Hollywood tends to think that deaf actors should act only in films and TV shows about deaf people, yet the industry often deprives the deaf actor of even these roles. While "blackface" acting is a thing of the past, Hollywood still allows hearing actors to play deaf roles. For example, Gene Wilder portrays a deaf character in the film *See No Evil, Hear No Evil*. Each time a role such as this goes to a hearing actor, we are culturally raped.

Studios and networks sometimes ask for crash-courses on deaf culture, sign language, deaf mannerisms, and the "deaf style" of acting with no intention of hiring deaf actors for the deaf roles. Why do deaf people, as well as hearing sign language instructors and interpreters, prostitute themselves by providing such services?

Obviously, these people find money more important than principle. The people who refuse this work and stand up for the deaf against job thievery deserve our respect and gratitude.

Celebrating Our Cultural Achievements

Long before the Gallaudet protest became a catalyst for changing deaf society and for exerting our influence on hearing society, deaf actors had a number of notable successes in Hollywood. The fact that there is a dynamic community of deaf actors, in spite of years of obstacles, is good reason to celebrate.

Deaf actors have appeared in major roles in such films as *And Your Name is Jonah*, *A Summer to Remember*, *Love Is Never Silent*, *Have You Tried Talking to Patty?*, *Children of a Lesser God*, and *Bridge to Silence*. Deaf actors have appeared in episodes of the TV series *Cagney and Lacey*, *The Equalizer*, *Beauty and the Beast*, and *Star Trek: The Next Generation*. These successes are a sign of increasing deaf awareness and acceptance, a belated acknowledgment that may be attributed to a change within the hearing public.

It is time we acknowledge people among us who were willing to express dissatisfaction or anger with Hollywood's ongoing system of abuse. Those who starred in the above films, as well as other deaf actors and those deaf people behind the cameras, have been pioneers in correcting the deaf image. Let us pay tribute to them, for they are our real-life heroes.

Role Models

The young deaf viewer's identification with deaf characters in films or on TV is very important because these images and portrayals can influence attitudes and behaviors.

A young deaf child who watches a deaf character on TV and later finds out that the deaf role was actually played by a hearing actor could feel ambivalence about his or her own identity as a deaf person. He or she may grow up with a belief that hearing actors speak, sign, and act better than deaf actors.

Patty Duke, who played Helen Keller in *The Miracle Worker*, was my first screen idol and also my first role model (who else?). All along I thought Patty Duke was deaf-blind in real life. Imagine how long it took me to find out the truth.

In order to prevent such betrayal and distrust, we should become positive role models to both deaf and hearing children, but to deaf children in particular. We must give children the opportunity to experience and build self-awareness and self-acceptance. Our kids need inspiration, and they need guidance to know what is and is not culturally correct.

The best place to fight Hollywood deafism is in our deaf schools. If we give our children understanding and appreciation of our rich culture and sign language, the students will gain a deaf heritage and become more creative, more aware, and more assertive global deaf citizens.

Anyone who carefully avoids uncomfortable situations or does not publicly come to the aid of our cause is definitely in the wrong industry. Who cares how many trophies, medals, or prizes one has earned, or how much fame and fortune? Those who succeed owe it to the deaf community to reach back and help others. As the ranks of deaf actors, writers, consultants, and producers grow, so grow our support and our influence in Hollywood.

Employment Opportunities Behind the Cameras

It would be a mistake to downplay the importance of writing, directing, producing, and consulting—fields in which deaf people have not achieved eminence. Hollywood is still shockingly backward in hiring, training, and promoting deaf people. This lack of progress in employment is inexcusable. If we want to point Hollywood in the right direction, we will have to develop, write, and sell scripts that include deaf characters. With more opportunities, film concepts can be broadened to include stories by deaf people and about deaf culture.

Reruns of the Past

Lately, vintage movies and early TV shows have become popular among both young and old fans. As if reincarnated, they have appeared in art theaters, on videotapes, and as reruns on television. This comes as wonderful news to those of us who were deprived of the pleasure of these classic movies and TV shows during our childhoods, long before the advent of closed-captioning. Unfortunately, many of these recycled films and TV segments contain deaf-related myths, distorted images, demeaning labels, and hearing actors playing deaf characters.

Ethics

We have every right to be concerned about the content of every script and about the kind of message produced by the Hollywood hacks who write about us. We also have the right to monitor the development and production of deaf-related works, to ensure script accuracy, positive portrayals, proper sign language sightlines, protection of deaf roles, appropriate casting procedures, and so forth.

Because ASL and deaf acting are cultural phenomena still new to the entertainment industry, there are currently no established standards, policies, or ethical criteria to guide the industry. To help deal with problems of discrimination, insensitivity, and ignorance, we must work with TV networks and film studios and their respective unions to reinforce our equal rights and full participation.

What Hollywood needs is ethical sensitivity, not paternalism.

Political Activism

If you think that deaf protest activities against Hollywood began only ten or fifteen years ago, you are mistaken. A newspaper item was printed in the *Wisconsin Times for the Deaf* in 1911, which read in part: "Deaf mutes are protesting against actors using sign language or inventing signs in moving picture exhibitions in imitation of a deaf mute as it is foul and profane."

More recently, collective lobbying and networking have led to a number of protest actions: the National Association of the Deaf protest against CBS for its refusal to use closed-captions; demonstrations against a movie-house for showing MGM's *Voices*, which did not use a deaf actress; and the national letter-writing campaign against CBS for hiring a hearing actress for a deaf role in "The Equalizer."

The lack of an organizational base, though, can prevent us from making a bigger impact on Hollywood. A media liaison is essential in helping bridge the gap between Hollywood and the deaf community. Like black, feminist, gay, and religious coalition groups, we need people to monitor actions that affect the deaf community. I understand that American deaf actors are now forming such a group.

One of our goals must be to increase awareness of the industry's unfair practices. Whenever we see exploitation or abuse, we must act quickly. Because Hollywood is a revolving-door industry where everything happens fast, we must have a greater readiness to intervene when matters of conflict arise. We also must encourage professional sign language teaching and interpreting groups to join us in dissuading people from participating in deaf-related ventures that refuse employment to deaf people.

Conclusion

Dialogue between deaf and hearing people is absolutely necessary if we are to work together on an equal basis. With common sense, cooperation, and understanding, we can break down the barriers that stand in our way. As deaf people, let us use our culture, our sign language, our heritage, and our creative arts to "Gallaudet-ize" the Hollywoods of the world.

Hollywood Through Deaf Eyes: A Panel Discussion

PHYLLIS FRELICH, Moderator

I would like to introduce six people who, through their work and art, have helped make important changes in America's entertainment industry on behalf of all deaf people. First, we have Linda Bove—well known for her many years on the children's television show, *Sesame Street*. Next is Julianna Fjeld, best known as coexecutive producer of the Emmy Award-winning television film, *Love Is Never Silent*. Marlee Matlin is the winner of an Academy Award for her portrayal of Sarah Norman in the film version of *Children of a Lesser God*. Howie Seago is known for his much-publicized title role in the play *Ajax* at La Jolla Playhouse in California and at the Kennedy Center in Washington, D.C. Ed Waterstreet has added to a distinguished acting and directing career his portrayal of Abel Ryder in "Love is Never Silent." And Terrylene, who is also with us, has made significant contributions as an actress in the television series *Beauty and the Beast*.

When I was a student at Gallaudet, there was no degree offered in theater. A career for a deaf person in theater was unheard of. I was lost. My friends told me that a degree in Library Science would be the best choice for a deaf woman because then I could follow my deaf husband anywhere he got a job. I could work in the town library. Well, I graduated with my degree in Library Science but didn't have a husband to follow.

Fortunately for me, David Hays, the founder and artistic director of the National Theatre of the Deaf (NTD), saw me in 1967 in a Gallaudet University production and asked me to become one of the founding members of the company. That was really a ground-breaking event for many of us. NTD was where we learned our craft. We studied acting, directing, designing, dancing, fencing, and the range of movement training from classical mime to Tai Chi to tumbling.

Because of my training at NTD, I was able to go out and try my luck in the bigger world. That was not easy. There were many smiling, nodding faces. For a while I thought that maybe the only place for a deaf actor to work was NTD. My big break came when I met Mark Medoff in 1978. I was able to help him develop a new play, *Children of a Lesser God*, from scratch. The rest is history. The success of that play and then the movie version is something most people are already aware of.

But, in spite of the many awards and the recognition we received during the two wonderful years the play was on Broadway, I was without work for the two years after the play closed. Why was that? Artistic achievement for, by, about, or with deaf performers is still not common. I mean, for those who smiled and nodded to use us on

---

The following text is a slightly edited transcript of a signed, videotaped panel discussion, with audience participation, that occurred during The Deaf Way.

any project at all is truly rare. I understood that many of the difficulties we face as deaf persons and aspiring performers are the same as those encountered by members of any minority group. People are naturally uncomfortable about something new.

When you link that discomfort with most people's natural shyness about communication difficulties, you can begin to imagine what's involved in convincing most producers to use deaf actors. They're afraid of not being able to communicate, of losing time and money, or whatever. Also, they're worried about what will sell. After all, in their eyes, like it or not, we're disabled. In fact, deaf actors are grouped under "disabled" in our unions. It doesn't matter that we say we are a cultural minority because we feel we are separated from the majority by language, not physical disability.

Fortunately, in looking at past successful projects involving deaf actors and actresses, it is clear that authenticity sells. We are generally better than anyone at playing our own roles. After being in this business for more than twenty years, however, I see that I can't be just an actress, waiting for scripts to come to me. I have to sell ideas. I have to try to write. I have to become a politician, fighting for the rights of deaf performers.

Nevertheless, when I look back at my own lifetime, I can see how things have really changed for the better in the United States. There are many more of us in the film and television media playing different roles. And sign language is everywhere. Especially since the founding of NTD, with its expertise in portraying the beauty of the language in the theater medium, sign language is now taught in virtually every college and university. Gallaudet University now offers a degree in Theater, and what's more, NTD is not the only place where deaf actors can now work. I believe things will continue to improve.

LINDA BOVE: I am in agreement with Phyllis' description of the overall situation for deaf performers in America. As for myself, I intend to focus on the story of my involvement with the children's television show, *Sesame Street*.

I was first placed on *Sesame Street* fourteen years ago rather abruptly, when I was a young actress. I was a guest artist for the first two years because, at that time, I was still a member of the National Theatre of the Deaf. My work on the show and at NTD gave me the motivation to try to become a full-time actress. Those first few years on *Sesame Street* I could see problems in the way writers who didn't know much about deaf people tried to write me into the show, but I didn't know what to do about them.

Several years later, I decided to leave NTD so I could work full time on *Sesame Street*. Before I knew it, I was involved not just as an actress. I found that there were a variety of things I could do about those problems. First, I could advise the writers about problems in the scripts that should be changed. Years later, I found that I could also solve problems by functioning as a kind of director. I learned to instruct the directors on how to film me so that all the signs could be clearly seen. I had to work with the camera man to show the space needed to make sure signs were not cut out of the frame.

I also took on the role of advocate. When the producers were looking for an actor to play the part of my father several years ago, for example, they brought in a hearing actor to play this deaf character—thinking it would be okay. I had to say that it would be better to have a deaf person play a deaf role. I felt obliged to become an advocate, although I never intended to be one and, at first, didn't want this additional duty. I wanted to focus on being an actress—a person, an actress, and deaf. I now think, however, that taking on this added responsibility helped me become a better person and a better actress because it gave me a wider range of experiences over the years. It was very rewarding and it gave me a new perspective on the industry as a whole.

Over the years on the show I found that I had more and more say in the scripts. The writers tended to stay on the show for a long time too. I became comfortable in approaching them directly to suggest ideas, rather than communicating through a third party. Every year I tried to get as many of the writers as possible to meet with me. The meetings were nice, but I noticed that many of the writers were hesitant. As Phyllis said, they didn't want to show their ignorance. It was owing to lack of exposure to deaf people; I don't blame them. But I saw many stares across the room in the meetings.

I thought, "This isn't working. I'm not satisfied." So, I came up with the idea of talking with the writers via the telephone. I thought it would be a good idea to hire an interpreter to come over to my house every other week to interpret the calls. The producers supported the idea and provided funding for the interpreter's time and service. Then I talked with the writers—one at a time—in their homes, and that seemed to make it easier for them. They felt more comfortable talking. They felt they could ask silly, stupid questions. And I really enjoyed answering them, brainstorming new ideas. We continued this during the summer months.

When I came back to work in the fall and read the scripts, I found that my character was more fleshed out. The writers finally understood that they should write me as a person first, then look at the extra elements I bring to the show: sign language and the everyday life things for deaf people. For example, they didn't know how I wake up in the morning or how a deaf person would know when a baby is crying. That's the type of information they needed to ask.

Maybe you're wondering how I work on set. Of course, there is an interpreter there with me every time I go to work from morning until evening. But because everyone has gotten used to having me around, the interpreter has become "invisible." When I talk with someone, that individual looks at me, and the interpreter is there in the background, and it all works out fine. The actors have learned how to use the interpreter properly and the crew also is used to working with the interpreter around.

I feel very fortunate and grateful that I've been able to stay with *Sesame Street* for fourteen years. I hope there are many more years to come, and that there will be many other deaf people on the show in the future.

JULIANNA FJELD: I've been an actress for twenty years and a producer for five years. That second career began in 1985 when I became a coexecutive producer—with Marian Rees & Associates and the NBC Hallmark Hall of Fame—of Joanne Greenberg's book *In This Sign* in the form of the television film, *Love Is Never Silent*. We won two Emmy awards: one for the director, Joseph Sargent, and one for the three producers, Marian Rees, Dorothea Petrie, and myself for the "Best Picture in 1986." Because of those experiences, I'd like to share how I began my work as a producer.

First, I want to quote John Schuchman, author of *Hollywood Speaks*, about people behind the camera: "The ultimate breakthrough in the way deaf people are portrayed in film will be when more deaf people move behind the camera and do the producing, directing, writing, and technical advisement." That has been done, and the best example is *Love Is Never Silent*. That really was the beginning.

I recall that when I decided in 1977 to move to Los Angeles from New York to make a tremendous jump into that foreign city, Hollywood, Hollywood looked at me and Gregg Brooks as if we were from Mars. It was as if, in the eyes of hearing people, we were wearing antennae and were in the Hollywood Zoo. The truth is that this experience was very painful for my soul, and I decided to get away from that "Hollywood Zoo" feeling by becoming a producer.

My training to produce began in a theater called the Mark Taper Forum in Los Angeles. There I had three years of providing "visual workshops" with the Taper people. The staff at the Taper Forum, for example, allowed Joseph Castronovo and me to introduce new ways of having interpreted performances with interpreters on stage. After a few years of this mind-blowing method, deaf theater patrons started to request theater *about* the deaf experience. The Taper Forum had been looking for just such plays when Mark Medoff brought the Taper a script, *Children of a Lesser God.* And the rest is history—the results were explosive.

After *Children of a Lesser God* went to Broadway, I started to look for different areas outside the Taper Forum. I was ready to get *Love Is Never Silent* off the ground. The experiences I had at the Taper Forum gave me the tools I needed to approach the entertainment industry with new confidence. I didn't become a producer overnight. It took ten years.

I was recently talking with Gregg Brooks, who shared my "Hollywood Zoo" experience, about the flood of young deaf actors now in Hollywood. Gregg, who works at Paramount Studios, said, "There are two deaf groups in show business. The first are the pioneers—those who had the vision to come west. The second group consists of the settlers who are following." I am truly grateful to have settlers now helping me with my projects, as I help them with their projects. Yes, we are helping each other in order to erase that terrible word, "novelty." Now, deaf people in different areas of show business can be part of the entertainment mainstream, and deaf and hearing people increasingly can work together.

MARLEE MATLIN: I'd like to summarize for you how I got involved in theater. I began when I was seven years old in Chicago, Illinois at the Chicago Theater of the Deaf for Children. I performed with that children's company in schools and clubs and learned a lot about acting from that experience. I continued acting until I entered high school, when I decided I wanted to play, not work. At that time, even though my goal was to become a film actress, I didn't really believe that deaf people could become film actors and actresses. I now know that I was wrong.

After high school, I attended a community college in Illinois. I was studying to become a cop. It didn't work out, obviously. I thought about acting again. A friend of mine told me about an audition for *Children of a Lesser God.* I replied, "Oh, no. I'm not interested in acting again, and *Children of a Lesser God* is a famous play. I couldn't do that." She said, "You should try." So, I did. And I got the role of Lydia, a secondary role in *Children.* And I worked on the play and truly enjoyed it.

Then one day I heard that Paramount was going to make a film version of *Children.* The thought of it frightened me, so I avoided it. Later, I heard that a casting agent would be coming to the theater to look for people to be in the film. In a day or two, the cast was brought to the office of the agent to audition for various roles in *Children.* I did my thing, not very enthusiastically. I just did it. I thought, "Well, it's an experience. Why not?"

What happened was that Paramount saw me "in the background," whatever that means, and wanted to see me audition for the role of Sarah. That really freaked me out. I said fine, I'd try. I auditioned two or three more times. I went to New York. That was my first trip to New York and it was all so new to me. I auditioned for the director. I worked with my eventual costar, William Hurt. I got the role about a month later. That's an experience I'll never forget. We shot the film. I won the Oscar. I moved to New York and then California. I've been in California for almost two years now.

I'd like to explain the work I'm doing now and how I get work. I don't wait for anyone to approach me with work. I approach the various studios—big studios and small ones. I talk with the people who are creating the scripts. I come up with ideas for scripts and I get help from people who approach me with ideas. We collaborate on ideas and then take them to studios and the scriptwriters. Right now I have about seven or eight projects in the works.

Sometimes people come to me with finished scripts. The first question I ask is, "Would you be willing to make this hearing role a deaf role?" Sometimes people are shocked by that question. They hadn't thought of that. They expect me to play a hearing role and talk and be just like a hearing actress. I tell them, "No. I can't do that." Then, I tell them what I want.

On the other hand, I recently made a television film for CBS called *Bridge to Silence*. I spoke in that film, as many of you know. That was difficult for me, even though I've spoken all my life. I attended public schools; I have a hearing family and have always been able to speak well—well enough to be understood. So, I am willing to accept a speaking role if it is appropriate for me and I feel comfortable in the role.

Shifting to another topic, besides my acting career, I'm now working with NCI, the National Captioning Institute. As a deaf person, I believe that all television programs, all films and videos that are sold, and all classic films should be closed captioned, because all of us watch TV and films and have the same interests as everyone else. I've written letters to 250 to 300 people in the entertainment industry. Almost everyone has responded favorably. When I get all the names together I'll set up a benefit to raise money to pay for closed captioning everything.

HOWIE SEAGO: Of all the skills needed by deaf people wishing to act on stage or work in Hollywood on films, I think one of the most important is good language skills in English. You must be fluent in writing and reading English. Other communication skills are important too, but you have to know how to communicate with hearing people. I don't mean speech. You can communicate through writing back and forth, and you should know how to use an interpreter—whether that be a friend who is interpreting or a professional interpreter. When you are skilled at working with an interpreter, people are impressed.

Hearing people are not going to be patient, however, while you tell them your dreams of becoming a deaf star. Many people have approached me and said, "I want to be like Marlee," and I respond, "Oh, can you read and write well?" When they answer "so-so" I tell them "so-so" is not good enough. You have to be a *great* writer and *avid* reader. The bottom line is you have to go to school and study hard to gain those skills. Hearing people are not going to wait while you struggle to communicate. In the film industry time is money. For someone to waste his or her time on you is to waste his or her money. That just doesn't happen. And when the director tells you what is wanted for the part, you have to take that information in and be ready to perform.

We deaf people must have good writing skills so that we can express our ideas ourselves. For example, when Julianna read *In This Sign* and was moved by it, she needed to have the skills to transform the concept of the book into the script for *Love Is Never Silent*. She needed to write clearly to convey her ideas to others and bring her project to life.

We need more people like Julianna to produce and direct, so join us in this battle. Actors and actresses are important, but we need some deaf brains *behind* the cameras as well. We need deaf writers. You all have wonderful ideas, humorous tales of your experiences growing up deaf and being with hearing people. We could gather those stories and create many marvelous productions—*many!* You have the ideas. Who could tell our story better than deaf people? I'm tired of hearing people taking advantage of us, using our stories and becoming rich. I want to see more people like *us* producing and taking charge! You've got to have the guts, the heart, and the tenacity to roll up your sleeves and work to make a production really happen.

I have a good example. One day, my wife and I were sitting at home watching *Star Trek* on TV. My wife gave me a nudge and said, "Why don't you do an episode on *Star Trek*? A deaf character could easily fit into that show. Think of the different creative ways you could communicate. You could use a machine." And she was right. There was an idea. As I sat there like a bump on a log, watching the program, *she* came up with this idea.

So that got me thinking, and I wrote down several possibilities for an episode and ways voicing could be provided for my role. One of the ideas I came up with was to have gloves that I would wear with a built-in voice box. Another idea was that several people could voice for me. (In one play I once saw, the voice came from a portrait of a man on the wall. An actor was in the portrait voicing for the deaf actor.) Well, the producers were astonished. They had never thought of many of these possibilities before. They picked the idea of having three characters voice for me.

After I had submitted that idea, I left to work on another project. When I got the call that *Star Trek* wanted me to perform on an episode, I was amazed. In the story, two groups were on the verge of war and my character was the one to negotiate peace between them. My initial understanding was that as I signed, any of the three voicers could speak for me. I thought everything looked good.

But soon I found out that they expected me to wear a band across my forehead and that this apparatus supposedly allowed my thoughts to be communicated to the three voicers. Well, to me this seemed like a hearing aid on the forehead. It also seemed a bit dog-like to be wearing a collar. That didn't sit well with me. Then they suggested that the band across my forehead would fall off and break during the story and that I would have to find a way to communicate with the three voicers. That struck me as something similar to a hearing aid breaking. In the story they came up with, the band broke, and through modern science I gained the ability to speak overnight! The problem was solved by learning speech!

Well, my heart sank when I saw that. I told them I didn't want that story. I grew up deaf in an oral school, struggling to learn to speak—getting smacked in the head when I didn't say it right. I could not go along with this story. I told my agent to turn it down, and that caused quite a stir because the offer had been made. But I insisted. I treasure sign—love it. My heart would not let me accept such a role. I thought of the deaf children who would watch that program and see me gain speech to solve the problem. I could just imagine their teachers, parents, and relatives pointing to me and saying, "See, *he* learned to speak. Be like *him*." I put my foot down and said, "No!"

My agent reluctantly told the producer that I couldn't accept the story and asked if it could be changed. Well, the producer accepted my position and changed the story to accommodate my beliefs. My agent was flabbergasted, and when he told me, I couldn't believe it either. My wife had the same reaction. So I agreed to do it, and we started filming. There were many small problems with the script that needed to be changed— and they were. We ironed the problems out along the way and made the picture—much to my relief.

As I see it, it's time for hearing oppression of deaf people to end and for deaf talent to rise. The way to get more deaf people into top positions in the entertainment industry is to start nurturing the children now. Encourage them to become involved in learning English, acting, set design and construction, painting, and let their minds expand. We must do it!

Terrylene: Ever since I was a little girl, I played actor. Even though others said, "Cute little girl, your dreams are bigger than reality," I made up my mind to act.

I sneaked into the bathroom, stood in front of the mirror, and started creating, escaping into a world where anything is possible.

I am an actor. I have no choice. I must create. Acting and my life are inseparable. I also write poetry. My need for a creative outlet has helped me solve many of the problems in life that we all share.

I also write short stories, songs, and plays. Technically, I'm not that good of a writer. Thank goodness, people don't always want technique. Sometimes they want gut feelings, blood, sweat and tears. By blood, I don't mean as in warfare or combat, I mean the truth flowing from your heart. That is what I do well. I give you my heart. Sometimes it's hard because if I give you my heart, you might not understand it. You might even break it. But all artists have this struggle. It's the price we pay for honesty.

Here I am, standing in front of the mirror, creating with my hands. Then, a loud deaf knock scares me back to reality.

Today the cycle of reality is the same—only tougher. Hollywood is not the glamour life we would like to believe. People don't say, "Cute" anymore. They say: "You're deaf. What's your story line? Can you use your voice a little bit? Interpreters are expensive. You're talented, but oh, this might be difficult."

We cannot blame Hollywood. Most hearing people have no idea how to communicate in the deaf world. Since Hollywood is a business and business people work to make money, they see deaf actors as a risk. We walk to the doors of theater, film, and TV and knock. From inside they say, "Who's there?" We knock again and they yell back, "Who's there?" We can't hear them and they can't see us. There's no exchange and the communication falls apart.

Together, we can and will offer new dimensions to the performing arts. We have tremendous gifts to offer people: our language, culture, and experiences—our ability to express our knowledge and visual sensitivity, still unknown to the audio world. We must be leaders. We must use our creativity to teach the hearing our truth.

It is amazing that as we approach the 1990s there has been only one creative work large enough to qualify for a Tony and an Oscar. But this work had deafness as its primary topic. We need to go beyond that if we want to succeed. We must create roles where we are people first. We must act them with elegance and beauty so hearing people will begin to learn to hear with their eyes.

I see a future with more of us working. We need deaf writers, directors, and producers to move faster into the future Hollywood, to the day when we have a deaf show on prime time TV, for instance. But we can't do it if we let others do it for us.

If my presence here today accomplishes anything, I hope it is to spark some interest, provide a little encouragement. You not only *can* do it, you *must* do it. We need you. We need all of us to join hands, and together build the future.

Ed Waterstreet: I feel I can relate to each of the heartfelt stories presented so far concerning the challenges of this business, but let me just say this: Be patient. I've been learning how to be an actor for twenty years. I'm still learning how to be an actor. You must be patient.

Now I'm directing. Occasionally that means directing hearing productions. For the first time, a deaf person is directing hearing productions. How did that happen? First, I started giving workshops for hearing actors and they began to feel comfortable with me. Then, from time to time I gave technical advice to hearing members of the entertainment business. On the strength of those experiences, it seemed natural enough for me to move on to directing a small production. When the production company found they were comfortable with me, they asked me to direct a larger production—a musical. Can you imagine that? Me? Directing a musical? I brought in an interpreter/assistant director who also served as my ears. We worked very closely together, understanding each other's overlapping roles. It took me six years and much patience to reach that point.

An example of that patience was clear when I was working on "Love is Never Silent" five years ago. On the first day of shooting the hearing crew was uncomfortable with us. I could understand that. We had been shooting all morning and, when it came time for lunch, a huge spread was laid out on the table. I gestured to the stage manager that Phyllis and I would like to eat. Well, the stage manager had a concerned expression on his face. He waved his hands and shook his head and said, "Wait, wait!"

Phyllis and I stood there wondering what the problem could be. The stage manager ran off down the hall. Meanwhile, the rest of the crew was digging into their noontime meal while Phyllis and I looked on hungrily. We wanted to eat but thought maybe we were needed for more shooting. So we waited and waited. Finally, the stage manager returned with an interpreter in tow. When the two of them got up to us the stage manager spoke and the interpreter signed, "Please, eat."

I gestured to the stage manager that it was not necessary for him to run down the hall and get the interpreter to communicate a message like that. I showed him how to sign "Eat—this way." He mimicked my signs with a great smile. After five weeks, communication was no problem. So the point is—be patient.

PHYLLIS FRELICH: I want to thank all of the presenters and raise some questions they may volunteer to answer. First, is it okay for a hearing person to play a deaf role? Would anyone like to answer that? We all know that Dustin Hoffman played an autistic savant in *Rain Man* and Larry Drake played a learning disabled character on *L.A. Law*. Is it the same when a hearing person plays our roles? Where do we draw the line? What is acting?

LINDA BOVE: That question comes up often in the entertainment business. There are those who would say, "There's nothing wrong with that." What I've tried to say is that we are recognized as a minority with its own culture, with its own language, American Sign Language, and several other features that make us a minority. So I contrast us to other groups like developmentally disabled people. Do they have group identification? Do they have their own culture? Do they have their own language? We have those things, and we are strong because of them. And we can therefore fight against hearing actors' taking deaf roles. Even if a hearing actor is self-trained, you can tell that they are not deaf. Being deaf is not a part of them. Our culture, language, and history are obvious. We grew up with them. So, that's a big problem.

PHYLLIS FRELICH: We all know that Meryl Streep is a great actress. She's played many roles requiring different languages. Do you think she could play a deaf role?

HOWIE SEAGO: No. I don't think it's right for a hearing person to play a deaf actor's role. It's wrong, because we have a distinct language and culture. Speaking strictly as an actor, I wish all actors—hearing and deaf—had the artistic freedom to play any role they choose. Maybe some day roles will be plentiful, and we can all choose any role we want. But as a deaf person, I say, "No!" It's not right for a hearing person to play a deaf role. It's not fair. Things are not equal now. There are many more roles available for hearing actors than deaf actors.

MARLEE MATLIN: Yesterday, a hearing actress came up to me and said she had something to confess. She told me which state she came from and that in her state she had played Sarah Norman in *Children of a Lesser God*. She said she didn't know what to do. She asked if I was mad at her. I said I didn't know, and at that moment I honestly couldn't respond. But she made me think about the concept that actors, whether they be hearing or deaf, are actors. Artists play whatever role they are able to. That's the concept. But somehow in the cases we're discussing, I don't know how to respond. Maybe some of you can help me figure out how to respond to that concept.

JULIANNA FJELD: Speaking as a producer, I understand how actors feel. I used to be an actor out there fighting, and I felt I had very little power. As a producer, I have much more power and can get things done faster. As a producer, I know which actors I need to pull in for productions. So what I suggest is that those of you who are producers, join us! That way we will have greater power in getting deaf actors. Another thing: As a producer, I look for the big name actors. I've gone to Linda, Phyllis, and the others. For the money, I want actors and names that people will recognize. Let's say I want an actor to take on a mentally retarded role, like Dustin Hoffman did in *Rain Man*. But suppose I want a deaf person. I hope that some day I'll be able to put out a call for that type of role and have many names to choose from. Right now there are very few of us. Ten years ago, there was no one in the business. We were all hungry and pounding on doors. Things have progressed over the past ten years and ten years from now we may have deaf producers and deaf actors working together to have the power to forge ahead.

TERRYLENE: Because I'm an actress myself, I want to be able to play any role. When a character is developed, who decides that the role is necessarily a speaking role? Who makes that decision? We just assume because the majority of people are hearing that the character is hearing. Right now we need those deaf roles to show our work. We need deaf characters. That's our only opportunity to break through. Later, when hearing people allow us to play their roles, that's when we can allow them to play our roles.

PHYLLIS FRELICH: How do we fight against the stereotyped roles offered to us? And do we have some influence in making changes in the characters?

JULIANNA FJELD: Years ago I would meet deaf people who were very angry. I wouldn't want to work with them. I want to work with deaf people who have an inner strength and peace. Those are the people I want to work with and encourage. I used to be one of those angry people. And when something was wrong with a character in a script, I let that anger show to try to make changes. But what happened was that people didn't want to work with me. I had to work to let the positive, warm side of me show when trying to make changes in a character. I found people much more receptive and changes did happen. So it's that friendliness, that strength that works, not anger.

ED WATERSTREET: We were talking about stereotypes. Four years ago I got a job on a soap opera called "The Judge." I looked at the script and saw that my character was the janitor. I thought this could have been the same role created for a deaf person twenty years ago. I suggested that the deaf character might have a more prestigious position. At first, the writer balked. I asked that the writer and producer think about it. They asked for my help with ideas, so I made several suggestions. I suggested perhaps an engineer, or a similar position. The next day, it was changed. So we don't have to accept every role as written. We can find a way to make changes. That's what happened to me.

PHYLLIS FRELICH: Is it frustrating for you to use sign language and work with directors who don't sign? How do you deal with that?

MARLEE MATLIN: My experience working on *Children* was that I met with the director and the first question I asked her was, "Do you know sign language? Are you ready to work with a deaf company?" The director was moved and immediately started taking a sign class. She did not become a fluent signer but was able to communicate the technical aspects of directing. Sometimes the director worked with an interpreter as well. But that director, Randa Haynes, preferred to communicate one-on-one with the actors. Most of the time there was an interpreter available. I think it's important for directors to learn sign, not so much to sign fluently, but to have a rapport with the actors. Another director I worked with did not learn to sign and depended on the interpreters. I think we need to send out the message that directors—and crews—working with deaf actors need to learn sign language, because communication is what's most important.

JULIANNA FJELD: With *Love Is Never Silent* I worked with the same people for four years, working with an interpreter. They were really frightened about working with this deaf group, and it took us four years to eliminate that barrier and proceed. We worked with an interpreter. When we selected a director, we picked someone who knows deaf culture. He didn't know sign language. He's from Italy and used his hands to communicate. He was open to anything. Using an interpreter, it was easy for the director to communicate with Phyllis and Ed. As time went on, everything worked out just fine. You can pick a director who is open, as we did, or one who is closed. If your director is closed, good luck.

LINDA BOVE: I'd like to share an experience with you from *Sesame Street*. The problem I had was we have three directors who work in rotation. I find working with each of them to be interesting. One director prefers to work through an interpreter. And I accept that. He has said that he'd like to learn sign language. Often hearing people will say that they'd like to learn to sign but they never get around to it. They may not be able to learn to sign, so I just accept that in them. It takes patience. Then there is one director who likes to talk directly to me and I encourage that. The interpreter knows to back off at that point and let us work it out. We've been working together for four years, so I know what I'm doing. I know what he wants—what he's looking for. Luckily, in my situation, I had an extended time to work with the directors. But in a job that takes five weeks, you do the best you can. We've had the same crew for a long time and the crew has picked up signs. But it was not until last spring that the producers said that they think it's time that we set up a class for the producers, directors, and anyone else on staff so they can learn enough sign to communicate for the fall season. I hope that works. It's never too late.

TERRYLENE: For *Beauty and the Beast*, the director and I met and were talking about the scripts. The director asked me—through an interpreter—if I was depressed that he didn't sign. I responded that that was silly. I don't expect the world to know sign language. But I do expect that you will take the time and be willing to sit down and let me explain deaf culture so you can be aware and sensitive. If you don't know sign, that's okay, as long as you try to be sensitive and pay attention to technical advice from the actors who are deaf.

PHYLLIS FRELICH: I want to thank all of the panelists. If individuals in the audience would like to do something to support greater involvement by deaf people in the performing arts, I suggest you write letters to the television networks proposing different ways deaf people can and should be involved in productions. Remember, a letter is assumed to represent 5,000 voices. That means there are 4,999 others who think the same as you but are too lazy to write. If each of you wrote, producers would assume that many thousands of people feel as you do, and they would be moved to hire more deaf people.

Theater of the Deaf in Australia

CAROL-LEE AQUILINE

The Deaf Way is an exciting opportunity for Deaf theater in Australia to come up from "down under" and share with a large number of Deaf colleagues from around the world what is happening with us. I am sure that only a very small number of people realize that this year—1989—the professional Theatre of the Deaf in Australia celebrates its tenth anniversary. We have been very much the hidden company of the Deaf theater world—mainly because of the distance and expense for anyone from Australia to contact the "outside world." The Deaf Way has provided that first all-out contact. Although the main focus of my paper will be the Australian Theatre of the Deaf, I would also like to take the opportunity to throw in a few snippets here and there about the amateur companies across Australia.

I think it is important to give a little background on the development of Deaf theater in Australia. I have seen old photographs and films of what were called concerts. Unlike concerts in America, a concert in Australia is not necessarily musical, but can be comprised of skits, poetry, dance and music—what in America is usually called a variety show. These records of Deaf concerts from the 1930s and 1940s show pretty young ladies in filmy white dresses mostly performing dance, with some poetry and songs. Many of the songs had a religious theme. Although I am sure that their work and that of performers in the 1950s and 1960s was quite lovely to watch, it was not until the early 1970s that serious thought was given to the formation of a Deaf theater group.

Australia's one professional Deaf theater company had its beginnings under the guidance of what was then called the Adult Deaf Society of New South Wales. This group provided an opportunity for local members of the Deaf community to perform in and view theatrical productions. Similar groups were started in the cities of Adelaide, Melbourne, and Brisbane, and, although the Melbourne group has now folded, the other two amateur companies remain active.

Following a tour of Australia by the National Theatre of the Deaf in 1974, the Australian Elizabethan Theatre Trust began a long-term commitment to develop a professional theater of the Deaf in Australia and hired a hearing director to work with the New South Wales (NSW) group. The early years were spent taking classes in mime, acting, dance, and mask, followed by performances in major Sydney theaters of *King Lear*, *Of Rogues and Clowns*, and *Five Flights to Freedom*. In 1979, with backing from the Australia Council's Theatre Board and the Australian Elizabethan Theatre Trust, the Australian Theatre of the Deaf was launched as a fully professional theater company.

By 1986, the company had developed sixteen original productions for school children, with performances in Tasmania, Melbourne, South Australia, the Australian Capital Territory, plus regional centers and towns throughout NSW. Recently, the company expanded this touring record to include Victoria and Queensland, with the goal of eventually touring all the Australian states. The company has also appeared on local and national television and before His Royal Highness the Prince of Wales. Founding member Nola Colefax has been awarded the Order of Australia medal. More recent productions of the company include *The Winter's Tale, The Threepenny Opera, Man Equals Man, Waiting for Godot, Sganarelle,* and *The Lady of Larkspur Lotion.*

Since 1979, the company has undergone many changes. I am the fifth artistic director, and of course, with each new artistic director come new ideas and vision for the company. It is interesting to note that we seem to have come full circle, in the sense that the first artistic director aimed for as visual a style as possible, with minimal reliance on the spoken word. This philosophy evolved under the second and third artistic directors to mean more sign language, backed up by spoken dialogue. The company's current aim is to find as visual a style as possible that can be understood by everyone in the audience with minimal aid from either sign language or voice.

There are many companies and individual performers in Australia today who claim to present visual theater. For some, this means mime, as it often did for our company in its early stages of development. For some, it is abstract images presented with concrete sounds or words to provide meaning. For others, visual theater means puppetry, dance, acrobatics, or any combination of these things. This variety of meaning has presented the problem for our company to more clearly define just what this much-used term means to us and why our brand of visual theater is unique. We are no longer able to sit back and just present ourselves in Australian Sign Language with spoken English dialogue back-up, trusting that people will accept that as visual enough. Not only is the competition too intense nowadays, but it seems that our audience is no longer satisfied with simple sign language theater. And, actually, neither is the company.

We do not want to be a mime company, nor do we want to become a puppetry, dance, movement, or acrobatics company like any other. We want a unique style of performance based on the expressive skills of our Deaf artists. In 1989, the company continues a process of exploration begun in 1988—a process we envision eventually leading us to defining our style more clearly. The exploration process includes work that stems from sign language—i.e., visual vernacular and sign mime—and work that will explore and develop the company's skills in movement and physical expression, as well as in visual clarity. We aim to create a theater style and practice built on and developed from the particular ability and vision of the Deaf actor, which has its roots in Deaf experience and the perception of the world through the eyes of Deaf people.

This does not necessarily mean we must do plays about deafness, but we do aim to develop the "Deaf sensibility" in terms of the writing, acting, devising, and directing of the company's work. This Deaf sensibility is what we have that no other theater company in Australia has. As Deaf people, we have an advantage in that we know what it means to live in a completely visual world. Our challenge is to find a way to present this clearly and vividly and with meaning, to present theater of excellence that enlightens, empowers, and entertains its audience. Hearing audiences depend heavily on sound, but we aim to make the visual impact so strong that sound becomes unimportant or secondary.

A major step in this direction was taken in 1988, when a company of three Deaf actors and I developed a play called *Five Steps Beyond.* This play was aimed at a high school audience, and any sound in the play was used not to give meaning to what was happening visually, but rather to give hearing ears something to focus on.

The Deaf community responded overwhelmingly in support of the play, declaring it one of the best, if not *the* best production the company had done. The hearing community was not so enthusiastic. Although most of the hearing high schools responded favorably to having something so visual performed for the students, hearing professionals in the theater industry stated that, for them, the production lacked clarity. It was definitely a learning experience for all involved, one that helped the Theatre of the Deaf establish ground rules as to which direction the company needed to move in to produce a form of theater that could communicate to, as well as excite, both Deaf and hearing audiences.

It is also important to mention the sort of work other Deaf theater groups in Australia are doing. The most active of the amateur groups is the Queensland Theatre of the Deaf, based in Brisbane. In a sense, it may be more accurate to call this group semi-professional, as its members are paid for some of the work they do. For example, at the recent World Expo '88 in Brisbane, the group was commissioned to do short mime pieces at the Australian Pavilion. Most of the Queensland Theatre's productions are mime, and most of these are held at the Queensland Deaf Society for the Deaf community to enjoy. This company is run by Deaf people, although they sometimes bring in hearing theater professionals to teach classes, guest direct, or write.

In Adelaide there is an amateur company called the Gestures Theatre of the Deaf. Formed around 1985, it is run by hearing people who thought that the Deaf community in South Australia was missing something by not having their own theater company. As far as I know, they have done only one or two performances, and their style is to use sign language with voice back-up. Again, I believe that most of their performances are held at the Deaf society in Adelaide for the Deaf community there.

Another new company in NSW is called The Visionaries, and I am one of the three members of this troupe. The Visionaries began at a Deaf sports event in Australia in 1987, when the Theatre of the Deaf was invited to perform but could not because of other commitments. Since that performance, The Visionaries have been invited to perform at numerous other Deaf functions, filling a need in the Deaf community to have a quality company as an alternative to the Australian Theatre of the Deaf. The Visionaries are also more of a semiprofessional group, as the three actors, all of whom are deaf, are theater professionals who are paid for the work they do. The group performs a mixture of sign language theater, song-signing, and sign mime for a predominantly Deaf audience, although it hopes to do more general public work in the future.

Australia is a big country, yet there are only these three small companies, in addition to the professional company, to provide theater from a Deaf perspective. Part of the reason for this lack of Deaf theater groups is the general lack of awareness in hearing Australian society about deafness and Deaf people. When people hear the name "Theatre of the Deaf," they assume the performance will be in sign language, only for Deaf people, and not understandable to them. So they do not make an effort to come and see the performance.

Although our company has done a bit to change this view, we still have to fight the fact that Deaf people are still very much a silent and hidden minority in a larger society. It is only in the past few years that Deaf culture is emerging as a strong, valid, and important subdivision of the larger Australian culture. For example, the first Australian Sign Language (Auslan) dictionary just came out this past February (1989). For our company, this lack of awareness about deafness poses a special problem: Should we retain the name "Theatre of the Deaf"? Although we are very strong on Deaf pride, in the past couple of years we have begun to think that we need to find a new name for the company, and perhaps use "Theatre of the Deaf" only as a subtitle. A new name, linked to the style we are exploring, might bring more people to see the company's work. This, in turn, might help expand Deaf theater across Australia.

A second major problem restricting the expansion of Deaf theater is that of finding Deaf people interested in theater and acting, even as just a hobby. When I first arrived in Australia, membership in the amateur companies was strong, and there were always people interested in working for the professional company. In the past few years, however, this interest has declined sharply. Most Deaf people in Australia today are more interested in sports. As I mentioned before, the amateur company in Melbourne closed down, as did an amateur company in NSW, owing to lack of interest.

Deaf people in Australia do not have the same exposure to theater as Deaf people in the United States, and for many the idea of actually getting paid for theater work is still incomprehensible. I have lost count of the number of times I have been asked what I do for a living and, after replying that I work with the Theatre of the Deaf, gotten the response, "Yes, I know, but what do you do for full-time work?" The situation is slowly improving, as we have more and more commercial plays interpreted into sign language and as the Theatre of the Deaf gains more and more recognition. But there is still the need to educate young Deaf people about theater as an entertainment medium and as a possible professional path.

To try to spread interest and skill, every year in January—our summer time—the Theatre of the Deaf has a two-week summer school that is open to Deaf and hearing people eighteen years of age and older. This past January it became more of a youth summer school, as most of the applicants were fourteen or fifteen years old.

Apart from performances and summer schools, we also hold regularly scheduled workshops in the schools, for other theater companies, and in community venues. These workshops primarily focus on encouraging people to communicate nonverbally, to use their faces, bodies, and hands more. For the company, these workshops are another good way to spread awareness about Deaf people and about our theater work.

Together with a Deaf man, I led a week-long drama workshop in a high school with Deaf students, attended by Deaf students from five other high schools as well. This workshop, held last December [1988], was the first time any sort of drama training had been made available to these Deaf children, and I am pleased to say it was a huge success. We hope it will be offered again this year and every year. A big dream of mine is for the company to establish some sort of Deaf drama outreach program, where we would do residencies in schools or other facilities to lead workshops and perform for Deaf children and adults. Through this sort of exposure and subtle education about theater, we hope, the number of Deaf people interested in theater will rise again.

Another plus for Deaf theater in Australia is that more and more commercial theater productions are being interpreted into Auslan. Interpreted theater began only in 1984, when *Children of a Lesser God* was interpreted into Auslan from ASL. Now both Sydney and Melbourne have at least five shows interpreted regularly each year. In Sydney these shows are a mixture of dramas, comedies, and musicals. In Melbourne, for some reason, they are all musicals!

These interpreted performances are a benefit to Deaf theater in two ways: Once again they bring an awareness to the general theater public about sign language, and often this leads people to discover the Theatre of the Deaf when they inquire about the interpreted performances; secondly, there is more opportunity for the Deaf community to see theater and enjoy it. Thus Deaf people are slowly becoming more interested in and appreciative of theater, and this fosters interest in seeing what the Theatre of the Deaf is doing. We hope this greater understanding of theater will lead to a resurgence of interest in bringing theater back to life.

Deaf theater in Australia, ten years old on a professional level and even older as an amateur venue, nevertheless remains young and experimental. We are finding there are no easy answers—we must educate our audience to enjoy a visual style, and we must explore and define what a visual style is for us as a company. In the past few years, a lot of exciting work has been happening, and more and more interest has been shown in the company. I recently discussed our company's explorations with a hearing director who said, "What your ideas and visions are about is not just the Theatre of the Deaf—in doing all of this and making it work, you are making a strong statement about good theater in general. For me, this exploration is thrilling; it is what theater is all about."

What Is a Deaf Performing Arts Experience?

DON BANGS

According to Patrick Graybill (1985), the 1970s ushered in a "Golden Age" of sign language performing arts. Over the past fifteen years, American critics of the performing arts have awarded their highest honors to theater, television, and film programs in sign language. In 1977, the National Theatre of the Deaf received a Special Tony Award. *Children of a Lesser God* won three 1980 Tony Awards: Best Non-Musical Play, Best Actor, and Best Actress. (The Best Actress award went to Phyllis Frelich, the first Deaf person to receive this award.) In 1986, *Love Is Never Silent*, a Hallmark Hall of Fame special developed by Deaf coexecutive producer Julianna Fjeld, received a national Emmy Award. (More than twenty regional Emmys have been awarded for sign language productions over the past fifteen years (Bangs, 1986).) Marlee Matlin became the first Deaf person to win an Academy Award, receiving a 1987 Oscar for her starring role in the film version of *Children of a Lesser God.* She was the third person to win such an award for a role using sign language.

The 1970s also introduced the "Age of Access" for disabled people, as they persuaded Congress to enact such landmark legislation as Section 504, which mandates that all programs receiving funding from the federal government must be accessible to disabled people. Deaf people have become much more assertive about their rights in recent years, thanks to the 1988 Deaf President Now movement at Gallaudet University.

The Golden Age and the Age of Access have created dilemmas for many theater, film, and television production companies. How can Deaf culture and sign language be incorporated into the theatrical event to meet the needs of Deaf spectators? And what about hearing spectators? How can the promise of performing arts in sign language theater be realized for people who are unfamiliar with Deaf culture? And, finally, can both audiences be satisfied with the same performance? To discuss these dilemmas, I will focus primarily on theater productions, although my points about theater can also be applied to television and film.

Many theater companies have attempted to meet the needs of Deaf patrons by providing sign language interpreters, usually at one side of the proscenium, during special performances. But is this really a theater experience for Deaf audiences? Can Deaf spectators who try to follow the signs of an interpreter in one location while viewing a theatrical production somewhere else really receive a theatrical experience comparable to that of their hearing counterparts?

Over the past 100 years, a number of special theaters in America have presented theater works in sign language supplemented by voice narration. These theaters have included the Gallaudet University Theater, the National Theatre of the Deaf, the National

Technical Institute for the Deaf, the Fairmount Theatre of the Deaf, Chalb Productions, and many other regional theater programs. Despite their efforts, these theaters have had to struggle to engage the Deaf audiences in the performance onstage.

When Deaf audiences do not respond well to a particular sign language theater production, it is tempting to excuse the situation by saying that the Deaf audience was not sophisticated enough to understand the performance. However, Greek tragedies were staged before audiences with little education, and Shakespeare wrote his plays for people with less than a third grade reading level. These works endure today as classics of the theater. Before we write off Deaf viewers as unsophisticated, we should take a closer look at what happens when a Deaf person views a sign language production.

Complicating our efforts to understand the experience of Deaf audience members is the fact that we may find a hearing viewer with a completely different perspective on sign language and deafness seated in the same theater. Unsophisticated hearing audience members may see sign language as mime, gesture, or some other nonverbal medium. They may be amazed that people with hearing losses can perform "in spite of their handicap." In contrast, Deaf audience members may be very proud of their language and of their fellow Deaf people performing on stage. The reactions of Deaf and hearing spectators to sign language performances by Deaf actors will obviously be different.

Defining the Theater Experience

After more than 100 years of theater activity involving Deaf people and sign language, there is still very little information about the audience's perspective of the theater experience. In 1973, Dorothy Miles and Lou Fant wrote a monograph in which they describe two forms of theater. One, "sign language theater," appeals primarily to Deaf audiences; the other, Deaf theater, to a mixture of hearing and Deaf theater patrons. In sign language theater:

> [t]he production is based on the text of a play by a hearing author, translated into sign language. It is performed by two casts, a signing cast in prominent position and a less-noticeable voicing cast. The work does not deal with deafness or situations involving deaf characters.

In Deaf theater:

> [t]he work is based on situations unique to Deaf people and is generally performed in a realistic or naturalistic style. Often, the performance is presented solely in sign language, without voice narration. The theme or motif of the work involves issues of concern to Deaf people or conflicts between Deaf and hearing people. (pp. 18–23)

With advances in theater productions, there have been several other forms of theater added to these two major categories. The first are cross-cultural plays, such as *Children of a Lesser God* and *The Signal Season of Dummy Hoy*. The second type are performances focusing on the creative nature of sign language, such as *Circus of Signs*, a work by the Fairmount Theater of the Deaf that uses a circus format to demonstrate the many artistic possibilities of sign language. The third group comprises hybrid works—hearing plays adapted into works about Deaf culture—such as *The Touch* by Hughes Memorial Theater. There are also works in which one character signs and everyone else speaks, such as Peter Sellars' production of *Ajax*, featuring Deaf actor Howie Seago, and the Berkeley Repertory Theater's *Good Person of Szechuan*, with Freda Norman.

Miles and Fant, and several other sign language theater critics, have suggested that certain forms of theater work best with Deaf audiences:

> [S]ign language productions have depended heavily on skits, songs mimicry and melodrama . . . broad farce or heavy suspense thrillers. . . . An audience which has been exposed mainly to unsophisticated material performed by untrained actors and relating almost exclusively to a "foreign" culture is unlikely to develop a taste for serious theater. (Miles and Fant, 1975, p. 26)

However, two plays that have been successful with Deaf audiences are *The Gin Game* (a Theatre in Sign production), in which two characters do nothing but chat and play cards, and *The Glass Menagerie* (a SignRise production), which is primarily a psychological play rather than one of physical action. So we must take a closer look at what happens when a Deaf or hearing person sits down in the theater to watch a play. There are many things to consider!

Bernard Beckerman (1970, p. 131) suggests, for example, that the experience of a theater-goer is influenced by both the on-stage event and the background circumstances of the audience. *The Diary of Anne Frank* tells the story of an ordinary Jewish family, but because we are aware that the Gestapo lie in wait outside the attic setting to drag the Frank family off to the gas chambers, we are touched and terrified by the experience.

The theater event and the backgrounds of the audience members can either harmonize or clash. For example, hearing theater patrons may see a National Theatre of the Deaf performance of *The Heart Is a Lonely Hunter* and feel sympathy for the lonely and isolated Deaf protagonist, John Singer. They may believe that losing one's hearing is a tragic situation. A Deaf audience, in contrast, will respond to John Singer with exasperation, wondering why he doesn't move to a big city and develop his own social circle at the Deaf club instead of wasting his time visiting a Deaf mental patient with whom he has nothing in common, and trying to lipread the sorrowful tales of his hearing "friends," who don't even bother to learn how to communicate with him in sign language. Many Deaf theater works, especially those dealing with Deaf culture issues, produce different reactions in Deaf and hearing audiences because of the differing world views of these groups.

Another way that the audience and the performance connect is through the creation of an imaginary world within the minds of the audience members. In *The Theatrical Event*, David Cole states that the relationship between the actor and the audience is like that between a medicine man, or shaman, and his community. The shaman has the power to depart from the physical world, make contact with the spirit world, and bring this world back to the community. In the same way, the actor departs from a world of platforms, flats, and fake furniture to make contact with the imaginary world of the play and brings this imaginary world back to the audience. Cole suggests that the mystery, excitement, and tension felt by the shaman's community is much like that of the theater audience as they make contact with the imaginary world of the actors.

How is this related to sign language theater? To what imaginary world can a Deaf actor transport his audiences? If a script is based on Deaf culture and performed by Deaf actors before audiences of Deaf people, the actors, depending on their abilities, can bring back an imaginary world that is familiar to the audience. However, if the imaginary world is based on hearing culture, or if the performer interacts with the imaginary world and the audience in ways conflicting with Deaf culture, then the task becomes more difficult, perhaps impossible. Hearing audiences present an even greater challenge, because the Deaf actor is not only from a different culture but uses a strange and unfamiliar medium of communication that is accessible to the audience only through the voicing actors. So, a sign language production has quite a challenge in arousing the imaginations of either Deaf or hearing audiences.

It also must arouse the audience's emotions. T. J. Scheff, in *Catharsis in Ritual, Healing and Drama*, has described how the emotional catharsis of the audience—their laughter and tears—comes from a release of emotions they have repressed in the past. But this emotional release cannot happen unless audience members identify with what is happening on stage. They must feel emotionally attached to the characters in a performance, and they must also have the appropriate emotional distance from the performance. If they are too close, the emotional response will be overwhelming, but if they are too distant the catharsis will not take place (1979). Obviously, in a sign language production, many things can interfere with this balance, such as bad acting, poor translation, unclear concepts, and other production flaws.

A theater director who wishes to involve the imaginations and emotions of Deaf and hearing audiences, despite their different backgrounds, faces quite a challenge. For hearing theater patrons, a theater production with strong Deaf cultural elements may be so different from their own experience that they "tune out." For Deaf audiences, on the other hand, a sign language production that is made more "hearing" may prevent the audience from becoming involved emotionally and imaginatively in the performance.

A Study of Three Theaters

To understand better the relationship of Deaf and hearing audiences with the on-stage performance, I conducted a study of three theaters that have played a prominent role in the golden age of sign language theater: the National Theatre of the Deaf, founded in 1966, which has geared its productions primarily for hearing audiences; the Fairmount Theatre of the Deaf, founded in 1975, which has attempted to meet the needs of both Deaf and hearing audiences in the greater metropolitan Cleveland area; and the Department of Performing Arts at the National Technical Institute of the Deaf, founded in 1968, which has served primarily the needs of the Deaf student and local community populations of a major postsecondary education program in Rochester, New York.

My research involved a review of primary documents and videotapes, and interviews with leading Deaf artists from each theater: Linda Bove and Ed Waterstreet from NTD; Brian and Jackie Kilpatrick from the Fairmount Theatre of the Deaf; and Patrick Graybill from the NTID Department of Performing Arts.

I also analyzed how each theater dealt with four aspects of sign language theater that seem to influence the effectiveness of the audience-performance relationship: (1) themes used to develop original theater works, and the types or genres of hearing works adapted into sign language productions; (2) sign language styles displayed in performance; (3) elements of Deaf culture featured in various theater productions; and (4) use of the theater space and other production considerations.

The Evolution of the Three Theaters

As pioneers in Deaf theater, the National Theatre of the Deaf, the Department of Performing Arts at NTID, and the Fairmount Theater of the Deaf had to do more than create outstanding productions; they also had to educate and sensitize their audiences. Their challenge was twofold: to expand and deepen perceptions of Deaf audiences about the nature of Deaf theater, and to expose hearing audiences to Deaf performing artists to show that sign language was a valid form of theatrical expression. In the beginning hearing audiences could not imagine such a possibility:

> Question: —Theater of the Death? . . .
> Answer: —No, no, Deaf, DEAF!
> Silence. (Hays, 1969, p. 7.)

The founders of each of the three theater companies reflected the audience focus of that theater. The hearing founder of NTD, David Hays, tailored his productions primarily toward hearing audiences. The hearing and Deaf cofounders of the Fairmount Theatre of the Deaf, Charles St. Clair and Brian Kilpatrick, chose to focus on both Deaf and hearing audiences simultaneously. Deaf professor Robert Panara, who persuaded the students at the National Technical Institute of the Deaf to establish a drama club, had no doubt from the beginning that their audiences would be primarily deaf.

The success of these companies suggests that the founders combined a rare talent for the theater with an intimate knowledge of their audiences. Perhaps one requirement for an effective theater program is that the director be a member of the potential audience for that theater or, at least, be sensitive to and aware of the needs of that audience.

The premiere production of each theater company used the same format—a theatrical collage of adapted and improvised short works. The collage for NTD included Saroyan's light-hearted *The Man with his Heart in the Highlands,* the stylized Japanese tragedy *Tale of Kasane,* a collection of poems, *Tyger, Tyger!* and *Other Burnings,* and the Puccini opera *Gianni Schicchi.* The intent was to expose hearing and Deaf audiences to the art of sign language in a variety of theatrical forms.

Fairmount Theater of the Deaf's production of *My Eyes Are My Ears* presented vignettes from the lives of Deaf people to deepen understanding of Deaf issues for both hearing and Deaf audiences. The NTID Drama Club collage mixed short theater genres familiar to Deaf student audiences and introduced new forms, such as Haiku poetry.

As these theater companies continued to produce sign language theater works, each developed a unique theatrical style that reflected the needs of its particular audience. Performances by the National Theatre of the Deaf combined signed renditions with beautifully choreographed movement and on-stage voice narration, elevating sign language theater to an art form. The Fairmount Theater of the Deaf concerned itself more with issues faced by Deaf people in their relationship with hearing people. This was an effective strategy for engaging both Deaf and hearing audiences. While FTD also used performance techniques to display the beauty and power of sign language, as in the musical *Alice in Deafinity,* it usually combined realistic situations with rhetorical speeches to illustrate life as a Deaf person in a hearing world. The theater program at NTID, more concerned with Deaf audiences, tended to stage productions that featured traditional Deaf cultural works or that imitated hearing theater with a unique Deaf twist.

The efforts of the three theater groups to engage their target audiences met with varying levels of success. The National Theatre of the Deaf was able to convince skeptical hearing audiences that Deaf people could perform professional quality work, transforming near-empty houses at the beginning of their first tour into sold-out, enthusiastic houses by the end of the tour and for all tours thereafter. The reactions of Deaf audiences were much more mixed and, according to Deaf reviewers, Deaf audiences preferred works that were simple and understandable rather than highly sophisticated and abstract. They also preferred humorous rather than serious works, and full-length rather than piecemeal works. These were preferences NTD found difficult to satisfy.

Performances by the Fairmount Theatre of the Deaf also were greeted with positive reactions from hearing audiences and critics, although patronizing attitudes were more prevalent because many of their original works featured Deaf people as victims. FTD performances were also well received among Deaf audiences, who were drawn in by the strong plot lines and engaging Deaf and hearing characters.

Performances of the NTID Drama Club were well attended and enthusiastically applauded by Deaf audiences, who identified strongly with the on-stage action and cultural motifs of the performances. Hearing patrons, most of whom had some familiarity with sign language and Deaf culture, were also engaged by their performances.

Once the three theaters had established themselves with their respective audiences, each began to experiment and expand its own concept of sign language theater. The area of experimentation was different for each theater: NTD created new works developed from original material or adapted from various sources; FTD experimented with a variety of nonmusical plays written for the hearing theater; and the Theatre program at NTID developed original and conventional works following the patterns of both NTD and FTD.

Considerations of Theme and Genre

Because of differences in audience focus, the repertoires of the National Theatre of the Deaf, the theater program at NTID, and the Fairmount Theatre of the Deaf have varied. However, Deaf and hearing audience responses to the works of these three theaters have shown some strong similarities.

According to David Hays, NTD has tended to choose plays that "we can make our own," rather than simple translations of hearing plays into sign language. Their thirty-four theater works from 1967–1987 included eleven adaptations of myths, legends, and fairy tales. Two forms predominated: the "hero" tale and the spoof. They also produced seven works of poetry or lyric prose; seven works of a stylized nature, such as farce, opera, or Japanese theater; seven contemporary plays; and two original works about deafness.

At NTID the emphasis has been on exposing Deaf student audiences to a variety of theatrical genres, including Deaf cultural forms. Thus, early NTID Drama Club productions included a mix of skits, songs interpreted into sign language, poetry renditions, and one-act plays. The forty-three productions staged later by the Educational and Experimental Theatre and the Department of Performing Arts have included thirteen musical plays, ten contemporary works, nine works by Shakespeare and other classic dramatists, nine works with an epic structure or based on fairy tales or works of popular literature, and two original works about deafness.

Because of their deaf-hearing, cross-cultural focus and their mission to educate the hearing public about the world of Deaf people, the Fairmount Theatre of the Deaf has created many more original works. Twelve, or almost half of the total repertoire of twenty-seven works, have been original. Among these originals, five deal with Deaf issues, and two demonstrate the artistry of sign language or mime. The remaining five are more conventional hearing plays that closely resemble the fifteen translated plays produced by FTD. Among the twenty original and translated works based on hearing culture, there are six farces or melodramas, five contemporary plays, four works based on epics or fairy tales, three musical or verse plays, and two theater classics.

The hearing patrons of NTD, NTID Theatre, and FTD have favored a narrow range of theatrical forms that includes renditions of musical plays; works of poetry or lyric prose; epic stories based on myth, legend, and folklore; reinterpretations and spoofs of fairy tales and popular literary forms; works with a high degree of stylization, such as farce and melodrama; and sign language versions of theater classics. It is not surprising that many of these theatrical genres can reduce the distance between hearing audiences unfamiliar with sign language and Deaf culture and the on-stage signed performances of Deaf actors. Poetry and music, for example, literally strike a chord with hearing spectators, making them more receptive to sign language imagery. Epics, myths, and fairy tales may be appropriate forms for the seemingly primitive and magical nature of signing, and the combination can entrance hearing audiences into an archetypal and child-like fantasy world. Similarly, the perceived "pictures in the air" can be effectively matched to stylized genres such as farce and melodrama. Finally, theater classics, and works of literature will be familiar to the audience but also fascinating when staged in a fresh and innovative form.

Unfortunately, this mix of the familiar and the fantastic does not always work with Deaf audiences. Musical plays, works of poetry, and lyric prose do not resonate well with Deaf spectators. Many Deaf people have an aversion to poetry caused by insufficient or culturally oppressive exposure to literature in schools for the deaf. Furthermore, because many of these sign language performances are artistic illustrations of English poetry and song rather than poetic renditions in their own right, Deaf audiences often find them difficult to follow. Epics, myths, and fairy tales, as well as farce and melodrama, can effectively engage Deaf audiences because of their emphasis on basic plots, physical action, and bold characterizations. However, the impact on Deaf audiences is different because, unlike their hearing counterparts, they perceive sign language as a uniquely visual medium of communication rather than magical pictures in the air. Finally, theater and literary classics may have a diminished effect on Deaf audiences because the works are less familiar to them. Most classics, however, are based on universal themes that resonate with all audiences regardless of their familiarity with the work. For example, two different sign language productions of *The Glass Menagerie* have been successful with both hearing audiences familiar with this classic and with Deaf people, who identify with the universal themes it presents.

One theater genre that has been effective in engaging Deaf audiences has been that of contemporary realism, especially as seen in well-translated plays performed by skilled actors. The realistic nuances of these performance seem more transparent to Deaf spectators and reflect their own day-to-day experiences. Even works such as *The Gin Game*, which has virtually no physical action, have earned standing ovations from Deaf spectators. By contrast, these same works have been less successful with hearing audiences because the realistic portrayal of a rather unfamiliar on-stage world creates for them a greater degree of distance from the performance.

Works based on the culture of Deaf people have also generated different responses from Deaf and hearing audiences, although the reactions have been positive for the most part. Several themes have predominated in these original works, most of which have been drawn from the personal lives of the Deaf performers: (1) the problem of communication between Deaf and hearing people; (2) the important role of schools for the

Deaf in teaching sign language and Deaf culture, and the oppressive attitudes toward Deaf people maintained in these same schools; (3) the need to treat Deaf people with dignity, and (4) the marvelous beauty and artistry of American Sign Language.

Obviously, the efforts of the Deaf minority to overcome the oppressive hearing majority and to create positive self-esteem is a struggle with which both Deaf and hearing audiences can identify, even if they do so from differing perspectives. At the same time, these works turn the tables on hearing audiences; now it is the hearing spectator who is unaware of cultural aspects of the play. This is one reason why Deaf audiences consistently give standing ovations for *My Third Eye,* while hearing audiences enjoy it more as an educational experience than an entertainment.

The Sign Language Styles Displayed in Performance

To develop an effective translation, both the artistry of sign language and its communicative function must be considered. The former aspect carries more weight with hearing audiences, as they rely on the voiced narration while enjoying the visual imagery of artistic signs. By contrast, Deaf audiences are more concerned with the clarity of the sign language translation, because they cannot hear the voiced narration. These conflicting audience needs have challenged each theater to search for a sign language translation that works with both Deaf and hearing audiences.

NTD, with its hearing audience focus, has gone farthest in its development of the artistry of sign language. By modifying the handshape, location, movement, and orientation of signs, and by using special mimetic signs called classifiers, NTD performers have created a visually striking effect that engages hearing audiences—especially in the performance of poetry or lyric prose. At the same time, the NTD translations have attempted to keep signed and voiced narrations as close to each other in sequence as possible, so hearing audiences experience a coherent and highly saturated visual and auditory experience.

Unfortunately, for a variety of reasons, this artistic emphasis has not been effective with Deaf audiences. The grammatical structure of NTD's signed renditions is different from that of American Sign Language, and this poses comprehension problems for Deaf audiences. Also, the increased number of signs in NTD's special translations requires a faster pace of signing to keep up with the voice narration. Finally, the artistic signs themselves are sometimes confusing to Deaf audiences. Works that have been most effective, such as *On the Harmfulness of Tobacco* and *The Gin Game,* were developed with less emphasis on the artistry of sign language and more on its communicative function.

NTID, sensitive to the needs of its student audience, has been less inclined to exaggerate the artistic nature of sign language. It has also been blessed with two very skilled translators, Robert Panara and Patrick Graybill, who have wisely focused on the communicative aspects of translation. Through the work of Brian Kilpatrick and Andrew Diskant, and my own work, FTD has created a balanced form of theatrical sign language that is artistically pleasing for hearing audiences, yet comprehensible to Deaf theatergoers.

Deaf Cultural Elements Within a Performance

As a reflection of their different audiences, the different theaters have varied in their Deaf cultural emphasis. NTD and FTD, which must consider hearing audience needs, have muted this emphasis, while the NTID theatre, which caters to a Deaf student audience, has at times emphasized Deaf culture.

All three theaters, however, have followed certain rules based on Deaf cultural models. One of the more obvious rules is that actors must maintain eye contact when communicating with each other on stage. This cultural convention contrasts with the freedom of hearing actors to look anywhere while speaking to another character and can sometimes distance the hearing audience from the on-stage action. The energy communicated between Deaf actors, however, more than makes up for this problem. Interestingly, NTD breaks the "fourth wall" convention and allows signing actors to speak directly to the audience to reduce the psychological distance. Sometimes the eye-contact rule also may be broken. For example, at the trial of Mr. Zero in NTID's *The Adding Machine*, Zero addressed the audience with his back to the jury so that they could not see his signs; this was quite acceptable to NTID's audiences. In FTD's *Dracula*, as Jonathan wrote letters to his beloved, another actor signed his thoughts while standing behind him. This device was later used in NTD's *The Heart is a Lonely Hunter*.

Another convention usually observed by the three companies is the avoidance of using Deaf actors to portray hearing characters or hearing actors to portray Deaf characters. For example, a cultural convention would be violated if a Deaf performer picked up a phone and signed the dialogue. NTD solved this problem in its production of *All the Way Home* by having the hearing character Rufus interpret a phone call to his Deaf parents. In both the FTD and the NTID versions of *The Odd Couple*, ringing doorbells and telephones were indicated by flashing lights, and phone conversations used special devices for the deaf. Any time a theater has deviated from this convention, there has been confusion for both Deaf and hearing audiences as, for example, in NTD's *The Heart is a Lonely Hunter*, in which Deaf actors portrayed both hearing and Deaf characters.

Despite the cultural questions that arose in the situations above, none of the theaters was willing to tamper with the basic script to clarify Deaf or hearing aspects of the characters and their situations. They chose instead to use unobtrusive staging techniques and sign language nuances to make the point that a character was either hearing or deaf.

Deaf culture sometimes affects the inner lives of some of the performers, even in plays without a Deaf cultural aspect. For example, when Patrick Graybill performed as the henpecked lecturer in *On the Harmfulness of Tobacco*, and as Weller Martin in *The Gin Game*, he based his characters on Deaf people from his past. Ed Waterstreet, on the other hand, has been less inclined to create a Deaf inner life if the role did not call for it; however, he interviewed several Deaf people to create the Deaf character of Abel in "Love is Never Silent."

All three theaters have strongly supported the efforts of Deaf professionals to portray Deaf character roles, and the many protests and letters to Hollywood have had a positive influence on employment opportunities for Deaf actors.

Theater Space and Production Considerations

Theater productions in sign language have had to observe a few staging precautions unique to this medium. A primary requirement has been effective performance space. Because it is a touring theater, NTD has not had the luxury of performing in specially designed theaters. However, it has avoided arena and thrust stages and tailored its performances to proscenium theaters of varied sizes. NTID Theatre has been blessed with a medium-sized theater uniquely designed for Deaf patrons, with sharply raked audi-

760   Deaf People and the Arts

THE
DEAF
WAY
🌿

ence seating, an extended apron, and various technological devices for Deaf performers and patrons. FTD has performed in two houses. One is a small, eight-seat theater with sharply raked seating and intimately placed performance space. The second is a larger theater with shallower rake but better sight lines and a raised stage. These spaces have proven quite accommodating for sign language performances.

Sets, props, and costumes have been designed both for their aesthetic effect and to facilitate the unique visual communication that takes place in this type of theater. Even though settings have varied, from the sparse designs of NTD's David Hays to the technologically complex arrangements at NTID, their design has also maintained a subdued effect so that signs may be read. Props have been simplified and kept to a minimum, especially at NTD, so they will not impede the signing. In designing costumes, care has also been taken to see that, at least for the upper body, the design does not distract from the signed renditions. In blocking the performers, communicative and aesthetic functions must be kept in balance by creating imaginative stage pictures without interfering with the comprehension of the sign language performances.

One of the most challenging aspects of staging is the integration of signing performers and voicing performers. Adopting a practice initiated by the National Theatre of the Deaf, all three theaters have incorporated the voicing actors into the performance, either by making them subsidiary characters—such as servants, window washers, catatonic patients in a mental hospital, or guests in a hotel lobby—or by creating stylized approaches, such as Bunraku narrators or neutrally dressed background performers. The theaters have taken precautions to ensure that the placement of the voice actors does not distract the audience, but Deaf theatergoers have not been particularly enthusiastic about the extra players on stage. By contrast, hearing audiences have enjoyed the integrated visual and auditory effects of these performances. At NTID and FTD, some productions have returned to the older idea of placing voice actors off-stage. Patrick Graybill has found this especially necessary in situations where an illusion of intimacy is required. He feels that audiences would not believe an intimate conversation between two people if it were voice narrated by, for example, a window-washer observing them from outside the window.

Conclusion: The Deaf Theater Experience

At the outset, we noted that two different audiences, with contrasting word views, attend sign language theater productions. Many hearing patrons feel sympathy toward the Deaf characters, whom they hope will be able to overcome the suffering caused by the handicap of deafness. They also are impressed with sign language, which they view as a sort of picture language or mime. In contrast, Deaf audiences do not consider themselves handicapped, are not anxious to become hearing people, and are quite proud of their cultural heritage and of American Sign Language, which they view as a language like any other.

How, then, can sign language theaters develop works that will engage these two different audiences? Interestingly, some theaters for the Deaf in Europe, according to a recent article in *The Drama Review*, have solved the problem by eliminating voice narrators entirely and forcing hearing audiences to enter the world of Deaf people through the experience of silence (Cohen, 1989, pp. 68–78). Such an extreme solution does not seem feasible for sign language theaters in America, especially because financial and critical support often comes from hearing people. Perhaps what is needed, instead, is for a sign language theater to define its audience carefully and use a collaboration of Deaf and hearing theater artists to develop productions to meet the needs of this particular audience.

There is one final word of caution about defining a theater's audience: As much as possible, we must make sure that theater performances can be enjoyed by Deaf audiences. They deserve access to the unique theatrical experience their culture and language have made possible.

References

Bangs, D. 1986. "Television and Motion Pictures and Deaf People." *Gallaudet Encyclopedia of Deaf People and Deafness,* ed. John V. Van Cleve. 2: 212–219. New York: McGraw Hill.

Beckerman, Bernard. 1970. *Dynamics of Drama.* New York: Alfred A. Knopf.

Cohen, Hilary. Spring, 1989. "Theatre by and for the Deaf." *The Drama Review.*

Graybill, Patrick. May 23, 1985. "Keynote Speech at Deaf Awareness Month 'Celebration.'" University of California at Berkeley.

Hays, David. January/February, 1969. "We've Come of Age." *Theatre Crafts.*

Miles, Dorothy, and Louie J. Fant, Jr. ca. 1975. *Sign Language Theatre and Deaf Theatre: New Definitions and Directions.* Unpublished monograph.

Scheff, T. J. 1979. *Catharsis in Healing, Ritual, and Drama.* Berkeley: University of California Press.

Deaf People in the Arts: One Man's Struggles and Accomplishments

GREGORIO JESUS JAÉN ARRABAL

I was born hearing. At the age of two I came down with the measles—according to doctors, one of the most frequent causes of deafness. My parents say that this illness did not appear to affect me greatly, but after some time they noticed that I had become distracted and that my vocabulary had stopped growing. In the first years of life, children acquire new words daily; in time, this permits them to hold conversations. I, however, continued to use only the few words I had learned before getting sick.

I have the great fortune of having marvelous parents. When they realized that I was deaf, their world crumbled around them, but they fought to get the best care for me. They began a long pilgrimage from doctor to doctor and clinic to clinic. At times they received conflicting diagnoses, but finally several doctors concurred that my deafness was not curable. I still had some hearing in my left ear, and fighting to keep it was my only option. Many tears and much pain found their way into my parents' home. I was then their only son, and they had placed in me all their hopes and dreams, which they now were forced to abandon. They were left with no alternative but to accept the circumstances and look for the best school for me.

The Spanish American Speech Institute specialized in working with deaf students, following the oral method. Along with general education, its principal objective was that we learn to speak like hearing people. Therefore, communication through signs and mime was strictly prohibited. But whenever we could, we students broke that rule, which seemed absurd to us. It was more comfortable to communicate through gestures than through the spoken word, which obligated us to read lips. In spite of this preference, I did become a fairly skilled lipreader, probably owing in part to my residual hearing.

Owing to the lack of subsidies available at that time, the Institute—"the school," as we called it—was expensive for my father, whose salary as a bank employee was not very high. My parents sacrificed themselves to the point of lacking basic necessities so that I might have an education and a chance to make a life for myself. More than half of my father's salary went toward my tuition, month after month, year after year.

Nevertheless, I was a happy child—happy in my ignorance. Even though my parents told me to apply myself and take advantage of my time at school, I did not have a clear notion of what money was or of the high price my parents were paying so that I could have a solid cultural education. The years of my elementary and secondary education at the school were marvelous, unforgettable years, and the friendships that developed among my classmates have continued through the years.

I was fourteen years old and still attending the Spanish American Speech Institute when the first painting contest for deaf children was organized by the Fundación General Mediterránea and *Proas* magazine. Encouraged by my parents, I entered in the children's category. All of the schools for deaf students in Spain sent works from their students, and several hundred pictures were entered. Try to imagine my joy upon winning the *first prize* in a contest on the national level! The prize was a camera, some toys, and a plaque. I was filled with happiness, and my parents and brother felt real satisfaction.

Naturally, when the exhibition of the selected paintings opened, my parents went to see it. They looked the paintings over again and again, and finally they arrived at the conclusion that some of the paintings on display were better than mine. So they approached the president of the selection committee, Señor Juan de Contreras y López de Ayala, the Marquis of Lozoya. The Marquis was a kind man, an eminent art critic, historian, and connoisseur of paintings of all time periods. They asked him why the committee had given me first prize, because they had seen other paintings in the exhibition that they believed were painted better than mine. According to my father, the Marquis answered with a smile:

> Pardon me—not better painted. Better drawn, yes, but this is a painting contest, not a drawing contest. Your son has an innate sense of color. He plays with colors; he mixes them with the know-how of a professional in order to obtain a tone, a precise shade. He works with the texture he wants until he gets it, and that can be appreciated by analyzing each of his lines. There are many works that are better drawn than your son's, but none is better painted.

> I will give you some advice. If he likes painting, which I believe he does, the best thing you can do is to take him to a school for painting so that he may perfect the undeniable qualities that he has, so that he can learn the why behind many of the things found in a painting, and so that when he is old enough, he can go to the School of Fine Arts. If he works, he can reach a positive mark.

The words of the Marquis filled my parents with enthusiasm, and they prepared to make the new sacrifice of paying for a painting school for me. Going to the painting academy in addition to my normal class schedule at the Spanish American Speech Institute would require sacrifice on my part also, for I would have to give up my spare time. My parents made me aware of the conversation they had with the Marquis. The idea of going to a painting academy was attractive to me, not so much because I liked painting, but because I would be able to go to a new and different place. But learning to paint also was my dream, so without hesitating I merrily responded "yes," that I wanted to learn to paint. Now, after having painted an infinite number of paintings and having studied with the best painters—the masters—I realize that one must always continue to learn, that one can never master all there is about this job or this art (whichever term you prefer).

And so I enrolled in the Decorative Arts School of Madrid, and there my first problems began. I was the only deaf person in my class. Groups of friends had already formed, and I did not know anyone. The students spoke quickly, with their backs to me, and many of them were quite a bit older than I was, so it was hard to relate to them. Even though I was not particularly bashful at that time, I did not talk to anyone because

I did not know the meanings of many words. As if that were not enough, the instructor assigned to me had a giant moustache that covered his lips! Plus, being used to teaching young hearing people, he did not pay the least bit of attention to me. He spoke very fast, with his back turned to me, so I had difficulty grasping his explanations.

I was disappointed in my new school. Far removed from the world of my family and from my old school, I was so tormented by this first real contact with the hearing world that I began to fear attending classes. When I could stand it no longer, I told my parents how I felt.

Fortunately, at about that time the First Congress of the Deaf of Spain was to meet. As always, my parents encouraged me to enter some work in its art contest. I painted another painting in a hurry and, without much hope, entered it in the Congress' art show. To my surprise, I won the first prize in Young People's Painting.

Once again my hopes were renewed, and I was prepared to struggle against all the problems and inconveniences again—though later on, there were more of these than I ever could have foreseen! My parents talked with the headmaster of the Decorative Arts School. They explained my situation and told him that the instructor had ignored my deafness even though he had been informed about it at the beginning of classes. As a result of this meeting, I was transferred to another class.

My new instructor, Señor Francisco Soto Mesa, was a young man with great knowledge of painting and a special gift for teaching. Upon being informed of my hearing problem, he concerned himself with showing me attention, so I felt secure that he would attend to any questions I might have. He took me under his protective guidance, and everything became much easier for me.

I was quite shy by then and—as is common with deaf people—I also struggled with language limitations. I did not ask many questions because I was afraid that I didn't know how. Therefore, when I went home, I carried in my head an unending list of questions to ask my father—about words that the instructor had told us, taking for granted that we knew the meanings, or words that my classmates had used. Naturally, my father was not always willing to answer my questions, but even after explaining a word to me, he always made me look up that word in the dictionary.

At this time, a professional photography course to be held in the Center for Image Studies was offered, and a few scholarships were made available to students of the Spanish American Speech Institute. Almost all of the students at the Institute who were old enough to qualify applied for the scholarships, and I was among the recipients. This course in professional photography helped me quite a bit—I learned many concepts closely related to painting, such as focusing, colors, monochromes, shadows, and backlighting. My parents encouraged me and once again made sacrifices, this time to buy me a camera and all the accessories worthy of a professional photographer.

Because all of the students in the photography course were deaf, the instructor had to adapt his teaching for us. The greatest inconvenience we encountered was during darkroom practice; we had to develop our own photographs, but could not see the teacher's instructions once we were in the darkroom. He was forced to give us the instructions before we went into the room. Finishing these studies required quite a bit of work and dedication from all of us. During this time, I entered the first photography contest for deaf people in Spain and received Honorable Mention from the sponsor, the Kodak Company.

As I neared the end of my basic studies, I had to think about a job that would provide some income. My family and I decided that I would take some classes in hole-punching, a profession with great employment possibilities in Spain. After I finished my hole-punching classes, my father met with the manager of a business that had positions open. The manager told my father that I could work there without pay until I gained speed in my work, then they would pay me a salary.

A short time after I began working, I told my father that I was working at the same level as the rest of the workers and that he could speak with the boss about starting my salary. The manager, however, did not hold to his agreement. He believed that he could continue to exploit me by claiming my work was not as fast as that of the paid employees. He told my father that he still wasn't able to trust me with a job requiring responsibility, although for some time I had been doing my job well enough to satisfy the departmental boss (who had also tried to convince the manager to pay me). This dispute ended when I was told I would have to work the night shift; my father told the manager that the exploitation of his son had gone far enough and that I would work for his company no longer.

Unfortunately, this was not an isolated incident. Even today, there are many scoundrels, disguised as benefactors, who exploit deaf people and get rich from their work. In Spain, these exploiters take advantage of the financial credits that the government gives them to help deaf and disabled people. Because the government does not thoroughly investigate these businesses, the owners are allowed to grow rich while their deaf employees live in poverty, unable even to think of the future without shivers of anguish. In my opinion, the governments of the world should pay more attention to the circumstances of deaf people and try to prevent their being exploited in this manner. I believe that deaf people work with more dedication than those who hear. They are also irreplaceable in some jobs because noises don't affect them and they are therefore better able to focus on their work.

These first encounters with the hearing world depressed me quite a bit, but my parents, with their love and affection, tried to help. They did all they could to enroll me in the School of Fine Arts, but this was not possible. I enrolled instead at the Madrid School of Arts and Crafts, where I began my studies with two years of classes in painting and artistic drawing. Later I studied graphic design and illustration because I believed that courses in these areas would provide me with more options for future employment and because the subject matter was closely related to painting and would help me achieve my goal of becoming a painter.

I can still remember my first day at the Madrid School of Arts and Crafts. There were boys and girls everywhere. The halls overflowed with people coming and going, but it seemed to me that they didn't know where they were going. The little I heard was a constant buzzing. Seventy to eighty students packed themselves into a small classroom, with hardly any space to move around. The instructor—perhaps worried because of the excessive number of young people pressed together in the room—gave us a cool and impersonal greeting. He called the roll, and when we answered, he looked at us over his glasses in a vague way, without looking directly at anyone in particular. When the class began, he spoke rapidly, as if he were in a hurry to finish. Some students begged him to speak more slowly, and I breathed easier then, because I realized that I was not the only person who had not understood anything he had said. The instructor slowed his pace a little, but if it had not been for some classmates who later loaned me their notes, it would have been impossible for me to finish that first course. Later, with experience, I began to choose the best place to sit in the classroom, where I could see the instructor's mouth.

How often I longed for my years in the Spanish American Speech Institute! There we were all friends. The teachers understood us with little effort, and we understood them. We treated our teachers with the familiarity that years of living together bring and trusted them as friends. But my general studies were now over, and I had no option other than to adjust myself to a new and less accommodating environment.

At the Madrid School of Arts and Crafts I was exposed to many new words, more technical and more difficult to understand, and I had to study harder to pass all the courses. Some concepts were difficult to decipher, and at times I was totally confused. The immeasurable help of my classmates enabled me to overcome my difficulties with the theories, and I returned the favor by sharing with them my knowledge of color, a knowledge based on intuition.

The history of art course was truly torture for me. The instructor would turn out the lights and show slides, continuing his lecture in the dark. Because I could not see his face, I was limited to watching the slides very carefully and writing down whatever most caught my attention. However, this did not always correspond to the instructor's explanation. Afterwards, I compared my notes with those of my classmates. On some occasions, I did not turn in work because I had not heard the assignment. After this happened several times, my friends began to tell me about the required assignments.

I had several different instructors during my course of study at the School of Arts and Crafts. Some spoke with clear voices and looked at us when they spoke, while others conducted class on the blackboard and spoke with their backs turned to the class as they made their diagrams. Ironically, an instructor whom my hearing classmates complained about because she spoke too softly was easy for me to understand because she pronounced words very clearly and spoke slowly.

I thought that when I finished my course of studies in graphic design and illustration I would have no difficulty in finding a job; within weeks I would begin to earn money and would no longer depend on my parents for financial support. But that was a dream. In reality, my search for a job was a long road full of obstacles.

I applied for work everywhere I could think of, but it was not possible to get a job related to my artistic training. I visited print shops, advertising agencies, the publishing offices of newspapers and magazines—any place where I saw the possibility of working. The answer to my request for work was almost always either, "The position has been filled" or, "We want somebody with experience." I began trying to guess which of those phrases would be used to reject me and I rarely guessed wrong.

When I returned home my parents always had a word of encouragement to lift my spirits. "Don't worry," they would say, "wait until next time." Their support soothed my sorrow. I will never grow tired of saying that I could always count on my family— my parents and my brother. They have helped me with everything, encouraging me to carry on, never to weaken. Their courage and hope have allowed me to overcome all of the difficulties that I have encountered in my lifetime.

Painting helped me relax. I would go down to the study to paint, and on many occasions someone had to call me to come up to eat. Whatever I had painted in the morning, I would usually undo in the afternoon or vice versa.

I visited all of the museums in Madrid, and whenever I had the opportunity, I would go out to the provinces to see other museums. I spent entire days attending exhibitions and visiting galleries. I offered my works to several galleries, but because I did not have a "name," the gallery owners were not interested. I began to suspect that they rejected my work not only because I was unknown but because I was deaf, that they believed that my being deaf would harm the reputation of their galleries. I saw the whispering, the sidelong glances, and for some time I was bitter about this. My desperation increased, and my personality began to turn sour.

About this time I met and became good friends with Lin Shiau Yun, a Chinese painter who lived in Madrid, and whose work had been shown in several exhibitions. Lin advised me to change my style, noting that there were many figurative and impressionist painters who drew very well, but not many who had mastered color and made it pleasing to the eye. Following Lin's advice, I began to conceive my paintings in abstract form, thinking I would be more successful in this style. I set to work, painting an infinite number of pictures on stiff paper, canvases, boards, —anything that could be painted on passed by my easel. I did not like everything I painted, so I would re-do my works— paint over them, do new sketches, harmonize the colors. I compared my new works with my old ones to assess my progress and saw that I was succeeding; the paintings I constructed in my head were coming out onto canvas as I had envisioned them.

Toward the end of 1985, Lin proposed that I go to China with him. He believed that acupuncture could help me recover some if not all of my hearing, so he wanted me to be examined by Chinese doctors. I told him that his idea sounded fabulous to me, but that I had to think about it before making a decision.

Lin left Spain in January and took some of my paintings with him. Soon, he wrote to tell me that his contacts in Hong Kong liked my work and wanted me to paint more. He encouraged me to come in May, and this time I agreed.

Before I left, I spent several weeks in a constant state of painting fever, creating paintings to sell to defray the huge expense of going to China. I imagined that this trip, my first trip outside Spain, would be my launch to fame, that from then on the entire world would know me. I painted three or four paintings at once, painted over old paintings, made variations on themes. After preparing some seventy paintings, I packed my paintings and my suitcases and struck out into the unknown with no defense but my hope and my faith in God. I did not know a word of either English or Chinese, but I felt sure that with a little bit of luck everything would go well.

I had never travelled so many hours by plane. When I arrived in Hong Kong, twenty-eight hours after leaving Madrid, I didn't know if it was day or night. Lin was waiting for me at the airport as promised, and when I saw him I breathed a little easier. We stayed in Hong Kong for a few days at the home of a friend of his, who bought a few of my paintings. I sold the rest at a gallery.

In Hong Kong, everything was new to me, from the food to the way of life, and for that reason I was anxious to see everything and not miss anything. We explored Hong Kong from top to bottom, then went to Shanghai, where I met Lin's family and visited his doctor friend.

After examining me, the doctor said that if I had visited him when I was still a child, he would have been able to produce better results. Now, because so many years had gone by since my illness, the bones in my ears had solidified too much. However, although it was not very probable that I would recover much of my hearing, he did perform some acupuncture treatments on me.

Lin and I also visited Peking and other cities in China, as well as Macao and Taiwan. Taiwan's capital, Taipei, was a place I liked very much; here we did not limit ourselves to the city and its monuments, but also took time to see the museums, galleries, and exhibition halls, and to comment on the works of art we had seen.

Even more important to me than the places we visited was meeting and seeing the works of several outstanding painters, including Manmelin Huaji, painter and designer of the official seals of China; Lin Danzhai, a marvelous painter of Chinese history; and Lin's former instructor, Zhu QuiShan, who was at that time ninety-eight years old.

It was a delight to see how agile Zhu was in spite of his age, and to feel his charm as he looked at me with his sparkling and happy eyes. We spent days studying with Zhu, contrasting his diverse styles and learning from them. I studied his techniques, his attention to detail, the changes he made to the colors he used, the planning of his canvases. It was an unforgettable experience, made possible by the patience of my good friend, Lin, who translated for me, speaking broken Spanish and repeating to me again and again anything that I could not understand—which was quite a bit.

After three months, I left China for Spain, stopping on my way in London to visit the city and its museums. When I telephoned my parents in Madrid to let them know of my plans, I found that I could hear my mother's voice perfectly! It seems that, through the acupuncture treatments, I had recovered much of the hearing in one ear. My parents were overjoyed, but the sad reality is that I later lost this hearing as well.

As I have said, I do not know either English or Chinese. This fact, along with my hearing loss and the shyness I must overcome every time I speak with a new person, has made my life a constant struggle. Not only is it depressing to be unable to communicate with the people one knows, but the lack of understanding on the part of hearing people, and the superior attitude they sometimes adopt, are more harmful to deaf people than even the most painful corporal punishment. The situation can make one want to give up.

Still, I have overcome and carried on with a smile on my face. When I see my deaf friends underestimating themselves or feeling ashamed to speak with a hearing person or someone they don't know, I recommend that they forget about their problem, that they be themselves, that they speak slowly and try to make themselves understood. We must forget our deficiencies in order to integrate ourselves into the hearing world in which we must live. We cannot mold society to fit our needs; we must mold ourselves to adapt to our environment.

Upon my return from London, I had to plan my future, which I saw as very dark. I was not willing to run once again from place to place looking for a job related to my training; I would accept any job, as long as I earned enough to buy painting materials and cover my expenses. Still, I had difficulty finding work. People and governments deny that they discriminate against the handicapped, but they mistake discrimination for compassion. They feel sorry for us, but they take advantage of us at the first opportunity. There is no relationship between what they say and what they do.

For example, at one of my latest exhibitions, a reporter and critic from a very important magazine asked me about the prizes I had won. Upon hearing me tell the reporter that I had won them in contests for deaf people, the director of the gallery said to her, "You have no need to even mention that Gregorio is deaf; nobody cares about that . . . ." The following day, my father visited the reporter at the publishing office of the magazine. They both commented on the director's statement, and his implication that my deafness was a negative influence on my paintings—as if I painted by ear, and for that reason, my paintings might be viewed as inferior to those of a hearing person. Perhaps the gallery director forgot that one of the greatest painters of all time was Francisco de Goya y Lucientes, who became deaf at the age of forty-two. Goya painted some of his most extraordinary works after he became deaf, and died at the age of eighty-two, having spent almost half of his life as a deaf artist.

My own accomplishments as an artist have come slowly but surely. I have participated in a total of twenty-two exhibitions, fourteen collective and eight individual, and the art critics have treated me very well. I would like to share with you some of their reviews:

> There is happiness in the color which intensified the forms, setting the flat areas in motion. His soft pastel colors are his favorite as well as black, white, rose, purple, and red. There is a search for his line of style, an interest in the

spectator liking his painting, through brief, singular brush strokes which make his personal style . . . . (Begoña Delgado, in *Visión Tres* magazine.)

It is not informative painting; these are spaces where the lack of definition recreates itself until it makes up bodies of thought with its abstract forms and always expressive colors. There are no concrete figures in Jaén Arrabal's works—figurations, yes, because the artist feels the pulse of his intention and manifests spatial concepts which overflow with light and are reflected in the soul like a mirror. For that reason, there is poetic and emotional content . . . . (José Pérez-Guerra Sánchez, critic and director of *El Punto de las Artes* magazine.)

Two important museums are owners of my work: the Cuenca Province Museum and the Picasso de Buitrago del Lozoya Museum in the province of Madrid. This is enough, I feel, to demonstrate my accomplishments as an artist. This year (1989), if nothing happens to prevent it, I will have eight individual exhibitions and four or five collective ones.

I hope my story has been of value. I also hope you do not see in me a winner: I still have a long road to travel before reaching that status. Nevertheless, you may see in my story that, whether hearing or deaf, one can triumph only if he is willing to struggle, work, and study, with his sights set on a goal and without weakening for even an instant. And it is especially important for one to know that there is a family willing to help him.

De'VIA (Deaf View/Image Art)

BETTY G. MILLER

In 1971, I began expressing my Deaf experiences through paintings and drawings. Since that time, an increasing number of other Deaf visual artists have also begun to create work based on their own Deaf experiences. These artists have often discussed whether or not there is such a thing as "Deaf Art" as a separate genre or school of thought. Although formal workshops were held from time to time to discuss this concept, all were short in duration, and none reached any formal conclusions.

A little over a month before The Deaf Way Conference and Festival, I facilitated a four-day workshop at Gallaudet University focusing on the question, "What is Deaf Art?" Paul Johnston was the cofacilitator. The artists who attended discussed in depth their experiences as Deaf artists, debated common elements to be found in Deaf Art, and developed both a visual and a written manifesto.

With perceptions that are based mainly on the visual and tactile, it would seem natural for Deaf people to express their reactions, including thoughts and feelings, through visual and tactile channels. In the daily lives of most Deaf people, this expression occurs through Sign Language and gesture. In the lives of Deaf artists, however, all the resources of visual communication available to, and learned through, the hearing arts world are also incorporated into their individual artistic expression.

However, to date, no agreement has been reached by Deaf artists on what, if any, influence their deafness has had on their art work, or what influence their art work has had on the Deaf community. Are Deaf artists simply "hearing artists" who can't hear? Or are they part of a cultural minority that is reflected in some way in their art work? Are they Deaf people who aspire to the same goals and objectives as all artists, but who communicate in their own language and from their own unique cultural perspectives?

Some Deaf artists feel that visual art can be a "way of life" among Deaf people and a part of Deaf culture in the same manner that music is a way of life among the hearing society. Visual art can enlighten Deaf and hearing observers by presenting experiences reflective of a Deaf person's world view. This, in turn, can strengthen a Deaf observer's sense of identity within the Deaf culture.

Although Deaf culture has existed for at least the past hundred years, it has only been in the last twenty-five years that Deaf culture has been brought to the attention

Prior to The Deaf Way Conference and Festival, nine Deaf artists gathered at Gallaudet University May 25–28, 1989 for a workshop entitled "Expression: American Deaf Art." The purpose of the workshop was to explore issues related to Deaf Visual Art, which includes painting, sculpture, printmaking, collage, photography, and fiber arts. The participating artists were Betty G. Miller, Ed.D., painter; Paul Johnston, Ph.D., sculptor; Deborah M. Sonnenstrahl, Ph.D., art historian; Chuck Baird, painter; Guy Wonder, sculptor; Alex Wilhite, painter; Sandi InchesVasnick, fiber artist; Nancy Creighton, fiber artist; and Lai-Yok Ho, video artist (who videotaped the four-day workshop). This paper, presented by Betty G. Miller at The Deaf Way, describes the workshop process and the resulting Manifesto.

of society as a whole. This is especially true since the Deaf President Now movement and the media coverage surrounding that event. Deaf people's attitudes are changing profoundly. Deaf artists, educators, and community leaders are demanding new opportunities for self-development and definition within our American society. They are insisting that their contribution can be made only by being themselves, not by attempting to be faded carbon copies of hearing people.

But is there such a thing as Deaf Art? The works of emerging Deaf artists seem to show evidence of experiences that represent facets in the lives and expressions of the millions of Deaf individuals who live in the United States. Many characteristics seem to be born out of a common Deaf experience, whether this be growing up in a world of muffled, indistinct sounds or one that involves communicating with visual rather than auditory symbols. And finally, there are the political and cultural visual statements that are expressed in the works of certain Deaf artists. These characteristics need to be explored and examined.

The workshop, held May 25–28, 1989, provided the opportunity to explore many of these questions. The Deaf artists who participated in the event addressed Deaf culture's influence on their own work, and the influences their work has had on Deaf culture, with a view towards examining the need for the classification and study of Deaf Art as a distinct and separate genre. One of the results of the workshop was the development of a term to identify a specific genre of Deaf Art: De'VIA, which stands for DeafView/ Image Art. This name, De'VIA, evolved out of discussion on the relative merits of an English or an ASL name. The final name, though a combination of the two, has the natural flow of ASL as the predominant consideration.

Another product of the workshop was the development of a De'VIA Manifesto, which is printed in its entirety on p. 772.

MANIFESTO

De'VIA represents Deaf artists and perceptions based on their Deaf experiences. It uses formal art elements with the intention of expressing innate cultural or physical Deaf experience. These experiences may include Deaf metaphors, Deaf perspectives, and Deaf insight in relationship with the environment (both the natural world and Deaf cultural environment), spiritual life, and everyday life.

De'VIA can be identified by formal elements such as Deaf artists' possible tendency to use contrasting colors and values, intense colors, contrasting textures. It may also most often include a centralized focus, with exaggeration or emphasis on hands and on facial features, especially eyes, mouths, and ears. Currently, Deaf artists tend to work in human scale with these exaggerations, and not exaggerate the space around these elements.

There is a difference between Deaf artists and De'VIA. Deaf artists are those who use art in any form, media, or subject matter, and who are held to the same artistic standards as other artists. De'VIA is created when the artists intend to express their Deaf experiences through visual art. De'VIA may also be created by deafened or hearing artists, if the intention is to create work that is born of their *Deaf* experience (a possible example would be art by a hearing child of Deaf parents). It is clearly possible for Deaf artists not to work in the area of De'VIA.

While applied and decorative arts may also use the qualities of De'VIA (high contrast, centralized focus, exaggeration of specific features), this manifesto is specifically written to cover the traditional fields of visual fine arts (painting, sculpture, drawing, photography, printmaking) as well as alternative media when used as fine art, such as fiber arts, ceramics, neon, and collage.

[signed]　　Paul Johnston, Alex Wilhite, Betty G. Miller, Sandi Inches, Guy Wonder, Chuck Baird, Deborah M. Sonnenstrahl, Nancy Creighton, and Lai-Yok Ho.

PART TEN

Deaf People and Human Rights Issues

Editor's Introduction

The concept of human rights tends to be invoked when the laws and practices of a particular society fail to protect certain individuals or groups from harmful or unjust treatment by their fellow citizens. The human rights violations most frequently experienced by deaf people include language deprivation, educational impoverishment, and various forms of cultural and social oppression. Ironically, these violations may often be inflicted by individuals who believe they are serving deaf people's best interests. As Mary Malzkuhn (United States) puts it in her paper in this section, an attitude of "benevolent paternalism" underlies many hearing professionals' efforts to suppress tendencies—toward the use of sign language, for instance—that bring attention to Deaf people's differences from hearing people. The papers in this section collectively suggest that such efforts in reality prevent Deaf people from developing their linguistic capabilities, their educational potential, their cultural identities, and their attainment of fulfilling roles in society. As Harlan Lane (United States) suggests in his paper, only a pluralistic society, willing to accept and nurture differences, can hope to realize all of those aims for its Deaf, as well as its hearing, citizens.

The opening paper, by Hurst Hannum (United States), indicates that blatant human rights violations in World Wars I and II led to acceptance among most countries of the need for a global articulation and defense of human rights. The United Nations (U.N.) has assumed this role through declarations of principles that can in some cases be backed up by force. Hannum says that many U.N. declarations implicitly support the rights of Deaf people to maintain and enjoy their own language and culture. He suggests, however, that because of vested interests, combined with ignorance of Deaf people's concerns and issues, it will be necessary for Deaf communities to take the lead in asserting their linguistic, cultural, or political rights. Hannum cites the Deaf President Now movement [discussed by a panel in this section] as one successful instance of such self-assertion. He says information from The Deaf Way, similarly, may serve to convey the concerns and rights of Deaf people to an otherwise ignorant world.

Although Malzkuhn, in the next paper, agrees with the necessity of Deaf people's assertion of their rights, she suggests that where society has failed to educate deaf people, and where illiteracy and low self-esteem have resulted, intervention through international organizations may be required. Mamadou Barry (Guinea and United Nations) similarly suggests in his paper that governments could play a significant role in enlightening societies about Deaf people's needs and rights and that the United Nations (at which he is an officer) would ideally help to coordinate such efforts on an international level. Barry's paper affirms Deaf people's right to be regarded as a linguistic minority population deserving to be taught in their native sign language and given access to interpreters. Malzkuhn points out that although the oppression experienced in many developing nations is often shocking, more subtle, but also insidious, forms of oppression occur in highly developed nations as well, where sign languages are in many instances overlooked or suppressed.

The next seven papers provide accounts of individual countries or regions in which oppressive conditions prevailed at the time of The Deaf Way. It should be emphasized that these accounts, representative of conditions typical of many nations, are not being singled out as unusual. Stephen Dhalee's (Bangladesh) paper about Bangladesh, for instance, creates a picture that in its essentials is continually reenacted in country after country. The majority of deaf people in Bangladesh, Dhalee reports, are uneducated, unemployed, and isolated from the rest of society. A nearly universal acceptance of oralist and integrationist ideas by hearing people in Bangladesh—however well intentioned—in effect prevents Deaf people from gaining access to information, from participating fully in society, or from producing leaders able to assert effectively Deaf people's right to be different.

The above description of deaf people's plight in Bangladesh could apply almost word-for-word to Vanetta Lampropoulou's description of conditions in Greece, Marius Rock Titus' account of French-speaking Africa, Alberto Paliza Farfan's portrayal of Peru, Aggrey Sawuka's view of "developing" countries, Celina Hutzler's paper on Brazil, and Miguel Santillán and Alfredo Toro's description of conditions in Ecuador. The papers on Peru, Brazil, and Ecuador do offer some encouragement in that they describe a range of efforts by Deaf people to organize and struggle to overcome some of these oppressive conditions. Other countries represented in the first section of this book could easily join the ranks presented here, along with many others not represented at The Deaf Way Conference.

The remaining papers in this section discuss a variety of ways through which Deaf people, either individually or collectively, can aspire to overcome oppressive conditions. Joseph Collins (England), for example, describes a project undertaken by Deaf people in England to make public information more accessible to the Deaf community through videotaped expositions in British Sign Language. A group presentation by Mary Malzkuhn, Jerry Covell, Greg Hlibok, and Bridgetta Bourne-Firl (United States) then reviews the dramatic week in which Deaf Americans successfully demanded that Gallaudet University (the world's only liberal arts university with an undergraduate program exclusively for deaf people) have its first deaf president.

Harlan Lane (United States) takes the step in his paper of celebrating deafness and suggesting that Deaf culture should be widely studied and taught. He indicates that greater knowledge of Deaf people's past and present achievements will strengthen Deaf students' aspirations and enhance hearing educators' understanding and expectations. Roger Carver and Tanis Doe (Canada) review the demeaning effects of centuries of oppression by hearing educators and suggest that many hearing people now in positions of authority over Deaf people's lives may need to step aside so that Deaf people can assume leadership in the definition, celebration, and transmission of Deaf culture.

Gerald Bateman (United States) points out that many areas of Deaf people's lives could be improved if the Deaf community would take fuller advantage of political mechanisms for insisting on needed changes. Bateman emphasizes the importance of agitating for change that will put more Deaf leaders in teaching positions and other positions in which they can act as role models for Deaf people. Kevin Nolan (United States) then describes his own dramatic journey into politics, during which he learned that many of the obstacles facing deaf people can be overcome through a combination of patience and perseverance.

Human Rights and the Deaf

HURST HANNUM

Human rights" is a term that has become increasingly familiar in recent years, and it is invoked by individuals and groups throughout the world living under all political and economic systems. Yet most legally binding international human rights norms (and this is the fairly narrow definition that I will employ in this paper) are little more than two decades old. This relatively short history explains some of the limitations that activists find frustrating as they attempt to implement international human rights standards. Nevertheless, progress has been made in raising people's awareness that they do have universally recognized rights. That this progress was achieved in such a short time justifies a modest optimism that human rights will become an increasingly powerful concept in years to come.

Before the creation of the United Nations (U.N.) in 1945, a country's treatment of its own citizens was essentially beyond the reach of international law. There were only two exceptions: 1) a state had to afford a certain minimum standard of justice to foreigners within its jurisdiction (on the theory that an injury to a foreigner is an indirect injury to the country of which that individual is a citizen) and, 2) a state might have had certain limited rights to intervene in another state where there were truly egregious human rights violations, such as massacres or pogroms. Even these latter rights, however, were rarely asserted, and the wall of state sovereignty effectively prevented outside assistance to injured individuals or groups.

There were a few chinks in the armor of sovereignty during the era of the League of Nations. There existed some treaty-based protections for minorities, though the demise of the League of Nations meant the end of these special regimes. The International Labor Organization, which has had an admirable record in protecting the human rights of workers, was founded in 1919. Also in the early twentieth century, there were widely ratified international conventions that dealt with the laws of war and the abolition of slavery.

With these few exceptions, individual rights were not a matter of international concern until the mid-twentieth century. Though the world did recognize and condemn the atrocities committed by Germany and Japan during the Second World War, those of the Allies, such as the fire-bombing of Dresden and the internment of Japanese Americans, were conveniently forgotten.

One of the fundamental purposes of the newly created United Nations, in addition to preserving peace, was "to reaffirm faith in fundamental human rights;" in 1948, the U.N. General Assembly unanimously adopted the Universal Declaration of Human Rights, as well as the Convention against Genocide.

At the time of its adoption, the Universal Declaration was merely a recommendation, "a common standard of achievement for all peoples and all nations," but it became the foundation upon which dozens of human rights treaties and mechanisms have been based. Today there are conventions, declarations, and other international instruments concerned with human rights in general and with many specific areas of concern, such as apartheid, slavery, refugees, torture, workers' rights, and racial, religious, and sex discrimination.

While many of these treaties have been widely ratified (although, I must add regretfully, most have not been ratified by the United States), their implementation depends in large part on the good faith of the states that have accepted them. While one should not underestimate the power of world public opinion or diplomatic pressure, there is no international police force to mandate compliance.

Nevertheless, international human rights norms do provide a standard that international and domestic advocacy groups can use to lobby for improvements in human rights. The increasing awareness of international human rights is at least in part responsible for such recent events as the democracy movements in Eastern Europe, the Soviet Union, and China; the overthrow of dictatorships from Haiti to the Philippines; and the growing awareness of individuals around the world of their rights to a more equitable economic and physical environment. The growth of human rights monitoring groups during the past decade has been phenomenal. Amnesty International, perhaps the best-known nongovernmental human rights organization, was awarded the Nobel Prize for Peace in 1977.

This is the historical context in which the human rights of deaf people should be understood. In addition to promoting its own special interests, the deaf community should became a part of this larger human rights lobby. Implementing international prohibitions against racial and religious discrimination and torture, guaranteeing fair trials, and ending hunger and homelessness are causes that need support, and the role of the deaf community is as vital in resolving these larger issues as that of any other group.

Nevertheless, the more urgent question is whether international human rights can help to counteract the discrimination and ignorance deaf people have encountered throughout history. Are there international "deaf rights" that can be asserted against governments, employers, or the administrators of universities?

As mentioned earlier, international law has occasionally protected the rights of minorities, particularly religious and linguistic minorities. As European borders changed in the late nineteenth century and in the post-World War I period, special minority rights were included in the treaties that created new states, and these rights were imposed upon the war's losers.

These protections were important. They generally included nondiscrimination, the right to use one's own language, the right to establish private schools, and the right to preserve one's culture. Language was often the feature used to define a minority group, and constitutional recognition as a linguistic minority could imply certain regional political rights as well as offer cultural protection.

Today, it is increasingly widely recognized that the deaf community can be described as a linguistic minority, and that native signed languages are linguistically equivalent to spoken languages. This recognition is probably significant in political and social terms, but it does not automatically lead to firm conclusions about the extent of minority rights that a deaf community might enjoy.

Historically, those minorities—linguistic and others—that have acquired special political status have been geographically concentrated or distinct from the majority society. Indeed, minority rights are often recognized only in particular regions of a country: They do not necessarily apply to an individual minority member wherever he or she happens to be. Thus, even if the deaf community can be considered a "linguistic minority" in the classic sense of that term (and I believe that it can), the full implications of that status—particularly when members of the minority are dispersed throughout society—remain unclear.

Nonetheless, members of the deaf community surely have the right to respect for their language and their culture, as do other minority communities. Some countries (such as Norway and Sweden) have recognized government's positive obligation to promote and preserve minority cultures when they are threatened, in addition to its more passive obligation not to destroy minority cultures or force minority group members to adopt the culture of the dominant society. When a state recognizes such affirmative obligations, deaf demands for improved education, social services, employment opportunities, and other conditions essential to developing deaf culture should be received with greater understanding and support.

There has been some international attention devoted to defining the rights of "disabled persons." Although deaf people have an obvious disability—impairment of hearing—they probably do not fall within this international definition, and many deaf people rightly consider that they should not be labeled "disabled." Nevertheless, one should be aware of the Declaration on the Rights of Disabled Persons, adopted by the U.N. General Assembly in 1975, which states that disabled persons have the same fundamental rights as all other citizens. They have the right to treatment and education "which will enable them to develop their capabilities to the maximum." The declaration also provides that the "special needs [of disabled persons are to be] taken into consideration at all stages of economic and social planning." At a minimum, deaf people too should have their needs taken into account and should be able to develop their capabilities to the maximum.

Another international human right relevant to the deaf community is the right to education. According to the International Covenant on Economic, Social and Cultural Rights (that has been ratified by over ninety countries, again excluding the United States), education is to be "directed to the full development of the human personality and the sense of its dignity, and shall strengthen the respect for human rights and fundamental freedoms . . . [Education] shall enable all persons to participate effectively in a free society . . . ." Deaf people are as entitled to an education that will enable them "to participate effectively" in society as are hearing people; quality education for deaf people is a right, not a privilege.

The right to participate in the political and economic life of a society is fundamental to any concept of deaf rights—or, indeed, the rights of any minority. The right of participation is distinct from the right to maintain and promote culture or language. It involves access to the political and economic power available in the larger society, physical access to means of communication, and other benefits of society that hearing people take for granted.

Full participation of deaf people in the larger hearing society is possible because, to quote what seems to have become the motto of the deaf community, "Deaf people can do everything except hear." However, this observation needs elaboration. "Doing everything" requires a willingness to act. Participation is an equation: On one side there must be a nondiscriminatory society that is open to participation, while on the other side, there must be an individual who wants to participate in that society.

To a great extent, international human rights norms respond to only the first half of the equation, guaranteeing the possibility of full expression of deaf community culture and removing social and legal barriers that might prevent individual deaf persons from realizing their full potential.

There is no internationally recognized "right" of a deaf person to be a doctor, law-yer, or teacher; each individual simply has the right not to be discriminated against in pursuit of those goals. Similarly, there is no "right" for students at Gallaudet to have a deaf president. The deaf community does have the right—and in this case, the ability—to acquire sufficient political power to make a deaf president a reality.

As these last few observations suggest, it is important to distinguish between the limited collection of international rights outlined above—rights to nondiscrimination, language, culture, education, and even participation—and the broader social and politi-cal demands of the deaf community. However, both the assertion of rights and demands for political and economic power require activism. Of course, the deaf community should ask lawyers, politicians, and others in the hearing community to support its efforts, but success can be founded only on the initiatives of the deaf community itself.

In conclusion, we should remember that most human rights—for example, the rights to be free from torture and imprisonment, or to have sufficient food and shelter—are of equal concern to the deaf and hearing communities. In addition, deaf people have the right to be equal and effective participants in society, and society has an obligation to make that participation possible. But at this stage of the deaf community's political awareness (an awareness that has evidently increased considerably since March, 1988), the most important right of the deaf community may be its right to define itself, to enjoy its own culture and to recognize and appreciate its own values.

A recent magazine article described the events at Gallaudet in March, 1988 as "an exercise in self-determination" by the students and faculty. The Deaf Way is a continua-tion of that exercise, and I appreciate having had the opportunity to participate, in a very small way, in this event.

The Human Rights of the Deaf

MARY CLAVEAU MALZKUHN

My first personal encounter with human rights issues occurred at a residential school when I was ten or eleven years old. After being told that my dormitory mates and I could not go to a movie because we went "too often" (every Saturday certainly did not seem too often to *us*), I was sufficiently provoked to lead a strike at the school. This sense of outrage over injustices of any kind has remained with me all these years, an attitude that may help explain why I have always been such a staunch supporter of human rights causes.

I would trace my intellectual interest in human rights to my coursework under Richard Pierre Claude at the University of Maryland. Claude not only teaches Constitutional Law and the historical development of the human rights concept, but also acts as a strong advocate of many human rights issues. Upon becoming my advisor, mentor, and friend (not necessarily in that order), Richard inspired in me an intense interest in and commitment to various human rights causes. I have continued to work in this area, looking primarily at the relationship between human rights and the concerns of Deaf people worldwide.

What are human rights? Maurice Cranston (1973) writes that this label was coined in the twentieth century to refer to what people in other centuries have called "natural rights" or the "rights of man." Although definitions of this term are frequently ambiguous, I believe we can safely say that human rights are those we have simply because we are humans, whether or not specific governments have encoded them into the national or local legal system. There is no simple way to anticipate which human problems can best be resolved by invoking the human rights concept. The United States Supreme Court, however, has frequently referred to human rights in justifying its decisions, particularly when no specific precedent could be found in either the United States Constitution or in subsequent court rulings. Examples would be decisions regarding the right to use birth control and the right of people of different races to marry.

Another example of a court decision based on the concept of human rights comes from Israel. In 1962, Adolph Eichmann, a leading figure in the Nazi's efforts to exterminate Jews during World War II, was tried in Israel for his crimes. Holder has summarized this case as follows:

> At the time he committed his atrocities, there was no state of Israel and consequently no Israeli law. There is a principle of criminal law in all parts of the civilized world that a man should not be tried for something not specifically prohibited by a statute in force at the time he did it. In the Eichmann case, however, there was a consensus among legal experts that natural law and civilized

behavior prohibit the extermination of millions of people, and so Eichmann was tried, convicted, and executed under natural law. (1990)

Where did the notion of human rights come from? Thomas Jefferson, in writing the Declaration of Independence, borrowed the term "inalienable rights" from the seventeenth century English philosopher, John Locke. The roots of this philosophy go back to ancient times. It probably began at least as early as when Aristotle first expounded the concept of "absolute justice." Aristotle believed that natural law arose from man's ability to reason and, hence, to determine what justice should mean and to help bring it about (Sahakin, 1968, p. 76).

In the thirteenth century, St. Thomas Aquinas modified Aristotle's concept by adding the concept that God, rather than simply man's reason, is the source of this natural law. Aquinas defined natural law as part of the divine will of God, which could be discovered through man's use of the natural power of reason. Aquinas also believed that natural law ideally plays a role in the establishment of governments to meet the needs of mankind. If the state makes laws that contravene human rights, these laws must fall (Sahakin, 1968, p. 104).

John Locke agreed with Aquinas about natural law, but he was not so certain that God was its source. To Locke, natural law meant that men, because of their humanity, have certain inalienable rights that should not be taken away by the state or other men. Locke's view was that government should exist only by the consent of the governed. His "Social Contract" theory (Sahakin, 1968, pp. 154–155) holds that government's main purpose is to preserve the life, liberty, and property of citizens. It should have no power except that which is used for the good of the people. The basic human rights of citizens, in other words, should limit the power of the ruler, who has no right to deny or override those rights. Locke's conclusion is this: If the government breaks the trust of the people who established it or if it interferes with the liberty of its citizens, the citizens have the right to rebel and make a new contract under which they may govern themselves.

My focus today is on the human rights of Deaf people and how they are being dealt with, ignored, or overridden in various parts of the world. In my view, Deaf people's human rights are being continually violated all over the globe, sometimes in subtle ways, but often in ways that are quite flagrant.

The most common subtle form of human rights violation for all disabled groups has been identified as "benevolent paternalism." Michael Palumbo (1982, p. 3) writes that paternalism is the prevailing attitude of most societies toward disabled groups. He mentions in his book, *Human Rights: Meaning and History* (1982, p. 110), the case of a blind person who was found to have been negligent in an accident simply because he left home by himself. "The public policy," Palumbo says, "is one of benevolent paternalism, protecting handicapped people so as to allow them to live in seclusion with as little pain as possible" (1982, p. 110). Implicit in this statement is the view that benevolent paternalism also serves to prevent disabled people from being a disturbance to society.

Society had and still has this tendency to "protect" those it deems unable to fend for themselves. For Deaf people, the manifestations of benevolent paternalism are so pervasive and subtle that its negative effects may generally go unrecognized both by those who administer it and those who are affected by it. One way to determine how benevolent paternalism affects Deaf people is to consider the extent to which Deaf people in any given school, state, or nation are consulted concerning policies or even asked to help administer programs affecting Deaf people. If the answer is that Deaf adults are seldom if ever consulted concerning such matters as the communication policies adhered to by schools, then benevolent paternalism may be the ruling force. Hearing people, in such cases, assume that they and they alone know what is best for Deaf people. A well-known example would be the international decision made in Milan in 1880 to institute oral Deaf education programs because these were regarded by certain hearing authorities as what Deaf children truly needed. Deaf people have bitterly protested this decision ever since, even though everyone involved insisted that they were only thinking of what was best for us.

The global situation for Deaf people would be bad enough if benevolent paternalism were the only form of human rights violation they had to contend with. Unfortunately, however, Deaf people in many countries must contend with human rights violations that threaten even their most basic human needs and rights. Abraham Maslow, a social scientist, proposed the following five-level hierarchy of human needs. These needs are met to varying degrees in various societies, depending in part on the level of care a society has for its people:

> Level I: *Physiological*. The basic need here is for food, clothing, and shelter, all necessary for survival. According to Maslow, once this need is satisfied people begin to think about the next step.

> Level II: *Safety and Security*. This need involves the establishment of adequate forces to ensure protection and stability in the environment. When this need is met the next step is considered.

> Level III. *Social*. This refers to needs for belonging, sharing, and association, all of which must be accomplished before one can reach the next level. It should go without saying that communication needs are central to fulfilling social needs and that Deaf people often encounter serious obstacles at this level.

> Level IV. *Ego*. The needs of achieving, developing self-confidence, winning recognition, and asserting one's independence come next. Here we find the realm of education, and for Deaf people, all the difficulties associated with either educational systems that fail to meet their communication needs or— even worse—the complete lack of any educational system suited to their special needs.

> Level V. *Self-Fulfillment*. The highest level need, which becomes important after ego needs are satisfied, is the desire to express one's full potential as a thinking, loving, spiritual human being. Of course, many Deaf people have reached this level, and most are capable of it, but all too many are limited by society's failure to consider self-fulfillment a real possibility for Deaf people, or to help lay a foundation for their self-fulfillment. (Maslow, 1954)

I am sorry to say that, if we use Maslow's hierarchy or practically any measure of society's recognition and nurturance of human rights, Deaf people's rights are seriously jeopardized, one way or another, all over the world. As one who is very interested in Deaf people's situations on a global scale, I am fortunate indeed to work at Gallaudet, whose 228 foreign students present a veritable gold mine of data from the international scene. Some of these students have complaints (those who are willing to speak up), even though these students are obviously fortunate to have been prepared for Gallaudet and to have been allowed by their home country to come here.

One of my former students came to me to find out how his government could be persuaded to make better laws for disabled people in Singapore in general and for Deaf people in particular. Although he felt grateful that he had been allowed to come to Gallaudet, he suspected that his government had made a one-time exception for him. He was concerned that he would not be able to get a well-paying job when he returned to his own country after completing his education. He stated that the human rights of Deaf people in Singapore were receiving token, rather than serious, recognition.

This student and his Deaf countrymen, however, are undoubtedly much more fortunate than the Deaf people of certain other nations. There are no Deaf students at Gallaudet from some Spanish-speaking countries. The Deaf people in many of these countries are considered to have very few rights of any kind. Dr. Donalda Ammons of Gallaudet's Foreign Language Department (the department's only Deaf member) agreed to share what she knows about such countries. Ammons travels extensively and during the summers has taken her Spanish classes to places where only Spanish is spoken.

Ammons has found that Deaf people in Central and South America are less than second class citizens. Their families, for the most part, are Catholic and the parents generally see their child's deafness as a punishment by God. Well-to-do parents in these countries send their Deaf children to private schools where oralism is the method of teaching. Other Deaf children's schooling, if there *is* any, is provided by missionaries. Nuns are the primary teachers. The nuns do not use sign language, only speech, because these schools subscribe to oralism also. The Deaf children learn handcrafts: sewing for the girls and mechanics for the boys. Many of these children have in essence been abandoned at these schools and may never see their parents again.

It must be remembered that there are not very many big cities in either Central and South America. Most Deaf children, therefore, live in rural areas. Poor families often do not send their Deaf children to schools at all but use them to support the hearing members of the family, often by being objects of sympathy to lure people into patronizing the parents' stores. Deaf children are often abandoned on the streets.

What becomes of Deaf people as they grow up in these countries? They become bootblacks, beggars, and vendors of such items as chewing gum. Illiteracy among the total Deaf population, not surprisingly, is around 80 percent. Those with some hearing fare much better (just as the one-eyed man is the king in the land of the blind). Many Deaf women do not work. Those who do are often employed as domestics. Deaf men often work as mechanics, laborers, and money counters in banks. Ammons finds that they are highly skilled in mimicry—they tend to parrot everything that is said to them—but their leadership skills are nil. Deaf people in these countries appear not to marry other deaf people. When they date, their hearing siblings usually act as their chaperones. Hearing women help their Deaf husbands succeed, and this leaves Deaf women with nothing (yet another significant example of human rights deprivation among Deaf people).

In these countries, there are no sign language dictionaries that might help Deaf people learn or maintain formal signs. Deaf people there often use bastardized signs that serve as the dialect of any given district from which they come. In some countries, they do socialize at Deaf clubs, which are important as places where Deaf people help each other acquire a sense of normalcy, at least among themselves. Many communicate with each other by using the oral skills they learned in schools. Others are best able to communicate their thoughts through painting. Technology is twenty to thirty years behind that in the United States, so they have never even seen TDDs, which may be just as well, since their illiteracy would impede their ability to use such devices.

Deprivations of the kinds I have just described must be addressed. Efforts must be made to assure that Deaf people all over the world receive the education they deserve. Deaf people need to have their sense of self-worth restored. Where in Maslow's hierarchy do the Deaf people of these and other nations fit? Are any of their human rights being met? Are some being met, but significant others overlooked, ignored, or suppressed?

The United Nations Universal Declaration of Human Rights recognizes that all members of the human family have an inherent dignity and inalienable rights to justice and peace. It states that disregard and contempt for human rights have resulted in barbarous acts that have outraged the conscience of mankind. An awareness of this tendency has apparently not touched the collective conscience of the hearing population in South and Central America, however, which for the most part continues to treat Deaf people shabbily. Such treatment, nevertheless, should shock the consciences of all Deaf people fortunate enough to have benefitted from their society's recognition of their inherent dignity and inalienable human rights.

Article 1 of the Declaration of Human Rights states that all human beings are born free and equal in dignity and rights. Article 5 promises that no one shall be subjected to cruel, inhuman, or degrading treatment or punishment. Article 26 promotes the right to education. What can be done to secure these rights for Deaf people in Third World countries? Mr. Hannum posed the question of whether or not a declaration of international human rights can help counteract the discrimination and ignorance Deaf people have contended with throughout history. My answer is certain: It must be done!

When I went to the Palermo, Sicily convention of the World Federation of the Deaf (WFD), I presented a paper on the human rights of Deaf people, but there has been no follow-up on this. Perhaps we should convince the WFD to act as a mediator or emissary between deprived Deaf people and the governments of countries in which they live. A Declaration of Deaf People's Human Rights should be created that can be used to help compel needed changes by governments, employers, and school administrators. Schools for the Deaf in Third World countries simply must incorporate sign language along with speech and speech reading. Dictionaries of sign language in these countries are also a must to maintain a strong bond among Deaf people as well as to support their claims to the status of a linguistic minority and to improve communication with the hearing society.

Because deafness is an invisible handicap and because of the communication barrier that results from deafness, there are many who have no conception of Deaf people's capabilities. Surely something could be done to help establish that Deaf people are a linguistic minority group, fully deserving the special considerations appropriate for such a group. I learned from Dr. Ammons, however, that in many nations a seemingly insurmountable communication barrier is placed routinely between Deaf children and the surrounding society. American Deaf people are now able to say that we can do anything but hear. It is about time that Deaf people of all nations be allowed to say the same thing.

Sixteen months ago, after an announcement that Gallaudet's Board of Trustees had chosen a hearing woman with no signing skills to be the seventh president of the University—even though there were two other qualified candidates who were Deaf—Deaf students staged a protest that quickly was joined by the whole Deaf community of the United States. That memorable time has been immortalized by Jack R. Gannon as *The Week the World Heard Gallaudet* (1989). On March 13, 1988, Gallaudet chose the first Deaf president in its 124 years of existence. At that time Gallaudet also named its first Deaf chairman of the board. These decisions in themselves show how the takeover of the campus brought about beneficial change.

In the year and more since those events, what has Gallaudet University shown the world? In spite of the assurances of the ousted Chairman of the Board that a Deaf person would find it impossible to establish and maintain open communication and a solid relationship with Congress, Gallaudet's first Deaf president, I. King Jordan, has fulfilled his role very well indeed. But what about education for deaf people? I am deeply concerned that because of rampant mainstreaming, future generations will lose the cohesiveness that unites schools for the Deaf with their graduates when the welfare of these schools is threatened. And what about the future leaders of Deaf people? Will they fight for Deaf people's rights? I fear they will not. I worry that Deaf people will become increasingly individualistic and care less about the plight of others. The changes we hoped for have not really materialized as yet. Will they ever?

Enrollment at Gallaudet last fall showed a rather high number of mainstreamed students who were inspired by the protest to come to Gallaudet. Will this trend continue? Has the protest of 1988 succeeded in changing the attitudes of society? To an extent, I would say. But an important question remains: How much has the world really listened to the unmet needs of Deaf children of all nations? Will the week the world heard Gallaudet University be remembered as an educational spur and challenge for Deaf people all over the world, in much the same manner that the ill-famed Milan Manifesto was, but this time as a positive rather than negative influence?

All over the United States there have been attempts to close down one school for the Deaf after the other, as legislators and special education "experts" seek to show us what is best for us. It is time that, once and for all, we stamp out this benevolent paternalism that threatens to place us in shackles once again.

References

Cranston, M. 1973. *What Are Human Rights?* New York: Taplinger Publishing Co., Inc.

Gannon, J. R. 1989. *The Week the World Heard Gallaudet.* Washington, DC: Gallaudet University Press.

Holder, A. R. 1987. *The Meaning of the Constitution.* New York: Barron's Educational Series, Inc.

Maslow, A. 1954. *Motivation and Personality.* New York: Harper and Row. (Also see Ewing, D. 1972. *Freedom Inside the Organization: Bringing Civil Liberties to the Workplace.* New York: McGraw-Hill. pp. 47–48.)

Palumbo, M. 1982. *Human Rights: Meaning and History.* Malabar, FL: R. E. Krieger Publishing Co.

Sahakin, W. S. 1968. *History of Philosophy.* New York: Barnes and Noble.

Deafness and the Political Agenda

MAMADOU BARRY

The United Nations Centre for Social Development and Humanitarian Affairs in Vienna, Austria, host of the secretariat for the 1981 International Year of Disabled Persons, is currently designated as the "nucleus and brain-trust" for social policy and social development within the United Nations. The Centre actively seeks social policy options and strategies for social change—essential ingredients for further socioeconomic progress and improvement in the quality of life for the people of our member countries. We have undertaken these activities jointly with our social partners, universities such as Gallaudet.

The Centre also monitors and promotes awareness of and support for internationally developed strategies for integrating all social groups, including people with disabilities, into the mainstream of society. The Centre for Social Development and Humanitarian Affairs is the focal point within the United Nations for all issues related to disability, including monitoring and evaluating the implementation of the World Programme of Action concerning disabled people. The main focus of our work is initiating, developing, and monitoring efforts to provide equal opportunities for disabled people.

The midterm review of the United Nations Decade of Disabled Persons, undertaken in 1987, has revealed little progress in this area, especially in the least developed countries, where people with disabilities are additionally disadvantaged by economic and social conditions. Despite significant advances in techniques for teaching and training people with disabilities, and important and innovative developments in the field of special education, progress has been limited primarily to a few countries and to a few urban centers in others. There is great variation in the quality of special education: Some countries provide a high level of education for disabled people, while others offer virtually nothing.

In most countries, education for deaf people is hampered by communication barriers. Because most developing countries have not yet overcome these barriers, many deaf people are cut off from education, and thus from further personal and vocational development.

During the midterm review, it was acknowledged that insufficient attention had been paid to people with communication disabilities. It was therefore recommended that special attention be given to the rights of deaf and severely hard of hearing people: that they should be recognized as a linguistic minority, that they have the right to have their native sign languages accepted as official first languages to be used in communication and instruction, and that they have the right to access to sign language interpreters.

Gallaudet University has done excellent work in implementing these recommendations. In fact, Gallaudet started long before the International Year of Disabled Persons or the proclamation of the Decade of Disabled Persons. We should also note the many commendable efforts undertaken in several countries to improve the quality of life enjoyed by deaf and hard of hearing people and to develop and use their potentials and talents.

In our advocacy of equal opportunities for deaf people in education, development, and integration in socioeconomic life, we should concentrate our efforts in three basic areas: political and social action, the sharing of innovative approaches between countries, and cooperation among countries in setting goals for improving conditions for their deaf citizens.

The ultimate responsibility for remedying the conditions that lead to disability and for dealing with the consequences of disability rests with government. Governments should take the lead in awakening the consciousness of their publics regarding the gains to be derived from including disabled people in every area of social, economic, and political life. It is the responsibility of governments to take into account the needs and concerns of deaf persons in overall planning. We have already seen, in some countries, the appointment of disabled people, especially visually impaired and physically disabled people, to decision-making posts as high as that of cabinet minister (though to my knowledge no deaf person has been appointed to such a high-level position).

It should be recognized, however, that disabled people are the best advocates of social change and public awareness of stereotypes and prejudices in society. If experience serves as a guide, the right of people with disabilities to participate in society will be achieved primarily through persistent political and social action.

How can deaf or hard of hearing people themselves promote awareness of their rights within the framework of the United Nations Decade of Disabled Persons? We must first recognize the importance of strengthening organizations of deaf and hard of hearing people. The growth, strength, and development of such organizations are the conditions *sine qua non* for any real progress in the field of deafness. Let us jointly support the initiatives and actions of those organizations able to identify needs, suggest suitable and effective solutions, and provide services complementary to those provided by governments.

There is wide variation in the level of socioeconomic development among countries and, therefore, in the programs they offer to deaf people. We must work to improve the exchange of information and experiences among countries. Innovative and successful approaches should be widely disseminated and shared. It is the intention of the United Nations to develop its capacity to act as a clearinghouse, which may become a powerful tool for building solidarity among countries of North, South, East, and West, and for supporting the efforts of countries with scarce resources.

What concrete actions would be required to improve the living conditions of deaf people? How can we assist developing countries in setting up and developing a strong organizational base for deaf people on a national level?

Progress in reaching the goals of the World Programme of Action can be achieved more quickly, efficiently, and economically if close cooperation and a unified approach are maintained at all levels among governments, agencies and bodies of the United Nations, nongovernmental organizations, and universities. The United Nations is ready to take on this challenge and to participate in this partnership in order to promote the advancement of people who are deaf or hard of hearing.

Discrimination Against Deaf People in Bangladesh

STEPHEN P. DHALEE

The purpose of this paper is to reveal the poor conditions suffered by the deaf people in my country, Bangladesh. In most countries, deaf people are deprived of their political rights and consigned to a subhuman existence. This is especially true for the deaf people of Bangladesh, where deaf people are uneducated, unemployed, and isolated from the rest of society. Most deaf people in Bangladesh live in poverty, and even those few who are financially secure suffer a great many problems.

Before we examine the plight of deaf people in Bangladesh, however, let us consider the general issue of rights. In my opinion, the term "rights" refers to those things essential to living a normal and healthy life. There are social, political, cultural and economic rights; the United Nations has defined a set of fundamental human rights.

The rights of deaf people are nothing more than the same rights that apply to all other people. The problem for deaf people is that, like other classes of handicapped people, they require special arrangements in order to enjoy these rights.

In the developing countries, deaf people are often uneducated, unskilled, and deprived of almost all their social, economic, cultural and political rights. In these countries, it is not generally accepted that deaf people constitute a separate social and cultural group, and the trend in many countries is to try to assimilate deaf people with the hearing majority. While hearing people readily admit the special needs of those with other disabilities—for instance, the necessity of wheelchairs for those with physical disabilities and of braille for blind people—they hesitate to recognize the necessity of sign language for deaf people.

This situation is not unique to the developing world; even in advanced countries like the United States and Great Britain, where they receive education and training, deaf people often do not get the opportunities they deserve.

As a result of the lack of deaf leaders, deaf people are dependent upon the sympathy of the hearing majority. The United Nations Decade of Disabled Persons has provided us with an occasion to make the general public aware of the needs of handicapped people and also with an opportunity for handicapped people themselves to unite to secure their rights. But who do we see on the stage? It is hearing people who organize the meetings and conferences and prepare the proposals for projects to rehabilitate deaf people. Their endeavors are praiseworthy—and we need their help and cooperation—but hearing people tend to be egocentric in their approach to the problems of deaf people.

If one is to help a person, one must know that person well. One must live closely with him to learn about his abilities and disabilities and to find ways of developing his latent talents. One must not force one's own ideas upon that person, but rather must try to provide the necessary environment for his development. In the efforts of hearing people to help deaf people, however, we see the opposite approach.

Many of us know what it means to be a member of a minority group, to see one's language and culture neglected, to be compelled to accept the language, culture, and arts of the majority group. Though considered outsiders in their own lands and deprived of many social and political rights, minority group members nevertheless may struggle to secure those rights. In Bangladesh, the struggle is made especially difficult by those who advocate the use of oral methods to teach deaf children.

Oralists favor integrating deaf people with the hearing, where deaf people feel lost. The oralists are working hard to sway public opinion in favor of their own ideas and to prevent deaf people from organizing to oppose them. There is already support for oralism in Bangladesh, where deafness is mistakenly thought of as a minor, curable defect. In a society where almost all deaf people are uneducated or undereducated and thus incapable of deciding what is best for them, the activities of such people are very dangerous.

Unemployment is a serious problem for deaf people of Bangladesh. There are no laws or high-powered committees to protect deaf people's right to employment. As a result, there are many deaf young men who have some sort of manual training but still must wait many years for employment. The salary paid to deaf people is so low that even those who find a job are forced to depend on their families for support. I myself have experienced the frustration of remaining unemployed for long years and of being discriminated against in my salary. These and other problems have caused many deaf people to leave Bangladesh.

The general public in Bangladesh, including most parents of deaf children, is ignorant about deaf people and the problems of deafness. In fact, very few hearing people even think about deaf people. This ignorance has dire consequences for deaf people. Deaf girls, for example, live in utter loneliness, shut inside their homes with no opportunities for recreation or social contact. More than one young deaf woman has committed suicide after her hearing parents refused to allow her to marry a deaf man. Such events are not uncommon.

The spiritual condition of deaf people in my country is hopeless. Most of them are indifferent to religion. Some of them are addicted to drugs. In the Christian community in Bangladesh there are a fairly large number of deaf people, but the church is unwilling to work among them or to train priests in sign language so that they might lead special worship services for deaf people. I proposed a rehabilitation project that would use the total communication system with underprivileged and abandoned deaf children, but neither the church nor any voluntary organization would agree to fund the project.

The education of deaf children in Bangladesh is in great need of improvement. Those who live in Dhalee City and some of the larger towns get the benefit of education and rehabilitation. However, there is a serious lack of qualified teachers and educational materials. There have been instances of mistreatment of deaf students and other misconduct by the employees of the government schools. The country has no adequate teacher training program, and no scholarships are available for teacher training abroad.

Another major problem for education is the lack of a well-developed sign language. Though there are signs for common everyday conversations, there are no signs for many words, and no one has yet felt the need to develop such signs.

The present academic and technical training facilities, if accompanied by a well-trained teaching staff, could produce rich fruits, but nearly 70 percent of the deaf population lives in villages, and therefore receives no education at all. We need several residential schools to serve the rural areas of the country. These schools must be free, because the poor population cannot bear the cost and because some parents are unwilling to spend much money on their deaf children. I have proposed such an educational and rehabilitative center for deaf people, but the authorities consider the project too ambitious and have refused to fund it.

I call upon the attendees of The Deaf Way Conference and the authorities at Gallaudet University to give their attention to the plight of deaf people in Bangladesh and to extend their support and cooperation to the Bangladesh National Federation of the Deaf, the central organization of the country's deaf population. As the joint secretary of the Federation, I have informed a newly elected committee about the multifaceted problems that deaf people in Bangladesh face, but strong international support for our efforts will undoubtedly hasten the deliverance of the deaf people of Bangladesh.

The Vocational Distribution of Deaf People in Greece

VENETTA LAMPROPOULOU

*I*n this paper, I will summarize data collected in a study of deaf people in Greece: their educational background, job searching procedures, types of employment, salary scales, problems on the job, unemployment rates, and other demographic characteristics.

In the study, a random sample of 300 deaf individuals was drawn from the membership lists of deaf organizations in the cities of Athens, Patras, and Thessaloniki, and the town of Serres. These 300 deaf people were then asked to complete a questionnaire about their vocational status.

Of the 300, 148 agreed to respond to the questionnaire. Some of the nonparticipants expressed fear of losing their jobs if they were to answer the questionnaire. The data collected from the 148 respondents were analyzed, and means, variance, and distributions of the major variables such as educational background, types of employment, and job-selection procedures were calculated.

The study resulted in several major findings.

Characteristics of Respondents

❖ Most of the people who participated in this study were males (71 percent males, 29 percent females) and most were married (64.5 percent married, 33.3 percent single, and 2 percent divorced). The divorce rate in this sample was very low.

❖ The ages of the respondents ranged from less than twenty years old to more than sixty. The age group with the largest representation (30 percent) was that of people between thirty and forty years of age. Most of the respondents identified themselves as deaf (90.4 percent). Only 9.6 percent identified themselves as hard of hearing.

Educational Status

❖ Forty-nine percent of the respondents reported completing less than two years of schooling. For 26.8 percent of respondents, the highest grade completed was in elementary school; for 8.7 percent, in junior high or high school. Eight percent had attended an institution of higher education.

❖ Most of the respondents had received their elementary and secondary education at special schools for deaf students (92.1 percent), while only 7.8 percent had gone to hearing schools.

Vocational Status

❖ Most of the respondents (79.7 percent) were employed, with the remainder being either unemployed or retired. The mean time of unemployment was three years. The majority of employed respondents (83.7 percent) held permanent jobs, and 66.6 percent were working under contracts (as opposed to being paid an hourly wage).

❖ Forty-four percent of respondents worked in private business or small shops, 19.8 percent worked in factories, 16.1 percent were in civil service, and 12.5 percent were self-employed, mostly in the fields of printing and graphic arts.

❖ A slight majority of employed respondents (53 percent) received very low salaries—under 60,000 drachmas per month ($1.00 = 170 drachmas). Twenty-nine percent received between 60,000 to 80,000 drachmas per month, and 11 percent received between 80,000 to 100,000. A small number (6 percent) reported salaries of more than 100,000 drachmas, and 1.7 percent reported more than 200,000 drachmas. In Greece, 200,000 drachmas is considered an adequate salary.

❖ Because the vocational rehabilitation services in Greece are very limited, most deaf people find employment through friends or relatives. In this study, 77 percent of the employed respondents had found jobs through friends and relatives; only 12 percent had found work through government agencies and/ or schools.

❖ Majorities of employed respondents indicated that they had good relationships with their hearing colleagues (54.1 percent) and with their supervisors (60.4 percent). Respondents also indicated that most of the problems that they faced in their jobs were related to communication difficulties and the prejudices of hearing people, who, they reported, treated them as second-class citizens.

❖ On-the-job problems, according to the respondents, occurred because they lacked sufficient training. They also felt that in order to improve their job situations, they needed better education, more help in training, and greater sensitivity to their needs on the part of hearing people.

Implications

The major findings of this study indicate that deaf people in Greece are poorly equipped for vocational placement and development. Most of them are illiterate or have very limited education. Most are unskilled and have no previous job training. In Greece, few provisions are made for job placement or any kind of on-the-job assistance; most deaf people find jobs through friends and relatives and work in factories and small shops in jobs requiring only manual skills. A number of deaf people have their own printing or graphic arts businesses, and some are employed in the civil service. A small number of deaf people who have graduated from college hold professional positions.

As expected, because of the low salaries deaf people receive, their financial situation as a group is not good; their standard of living is lower than that of the majority of people in Greece.

The greatest problems facing deaf people are difficulties in communication, prejudice against deaf people in the hearing population, and the poor availability of vocational training.

More positively, this study finds that deaf people in Greece, when employed, seem to enjoy stable positions and good relations with their employers. They adapt well and make great efforts to overcome problems on the job. In my opinion, with better education, more training, and greater acceptance from hearing people, more deaf people in Greece could become responsible, productive citizens.

References

Government Paper. 1981. *The Vocational Rehabilitation Act*, 80/31.3.1981. Athens.

Government Paper. 1985. *The Educational and Vocational Training of the Handicapped Act*, 167/30.9.85 AT. Athens.

Lazanas, V. 1984. "The Vocational Rehabilitation of the Deaf." In *Problems of the Deaf.* Athens.

The Oppression of Deaf People as Cultural Minorities in Developing Countries

AGGREY A. SAWUKA

The oppression of deaf people and the suppression of sign language and deaf culture by the governments of developing countries began under colonialism in the nineteenth century. Colonial governments adopted oralism after the 1880 International Congress of Teachers of the Deaf in Milan, where a majority of the delegates voted in favor of the oral method for teaching deaf students. History shows that, even after independence, deaf people have been the least known and least cared for among handicapped people. Most associations of deaf people in developing countries were founded recently in comparison with those of other groups of handicapped people.

The economies of most developing countries are based on agriculture, and the economic difficulties created by low world-market prices for agricultural products have an indirect influence on associations of deaf people by limiting their countries' ability to subsidize their activities. This is a well-known problem caused by external forces. To understand the oppression of deaf people in developing countries, however, it is equally important to consider problems that are internal to these countries. The subject of this paper will be the forms of oppression that arise from internal problems in developing countries.

For the purposes of this paper, our concept of oppression will include any action that interferes with deaf people learning and using their sign languages just as freely as the members of many hearing subcultures are allowed to use their spoken languages—all in the interest of better understanding their environment. We will not consider oppression as an outright evil on the part of people who are not deaf, but will instead focus on oppression as a symptom of problems we will seek to diagnose. We deaf people must show the world that we are experts on the subject of our selves, otherwise we will never succeed in our struggle to improve our lives.

General Culture

In some developing countries traditional cultures direct the mother of a newborn baby to stay for a certain period of time with an elder woman, who assists the new mother and imparts her knowledge of life and motherhood. Where such traditions are observed, deafness is detected very early, even in rural areas, though hard of hearing children may not be so easily detected.

In developing countries, deaf and hard of hearing people make up between 0.5 percent and 1 percent of the total population. Approximately 10 to 15 percent of these people are deaf, and the incidence of deafness may increase as standards of living in these countries deteriorate. Most hearing people in developing countries know that deaf people usually use signs and have their own subculture within the multitude of cultures of hearing people. Unfortunately, the majority of hearing people are unaware of the crucial role played by sign language and deaf culture in the physical and mental development of deaf people. This lack of awareness is manifest in the varieties of oppression affecting deaf people.

Oppression of Children

Human beings begin to develop their mental, vocal, and linguistic abilities during infancy. But while the linguistic development of the hearing infant is stimulated by sound, that of the deaf infant is stimulated by body movements. In developing countries, neither parents, doctors, social workers, nor other professionals know the importance of this phenomenon. Professionals continue to give parents of deaf children only the hope that their children might be rehabilitated and integrated with hearing people.

As they grow, and as interaction with hearing children becomes more difficult, deaf children experience increasing distress; the dynamic spirit of life is smothered in them. Hearing children are more sympathetic to physical handicaps they can see than to deafness, which they cannot. So the deaf child becomes a caricature, the butt of jokes, someone to be teased. This kind of oppression is innocent: Because of their tender age and the lack of information about deafness, young hearing children are unable to understand the plight of their deaf playmates.

Oppression Through Ignorance

In developing countries today, most school-age children go to school. The primary school entrance age is between six and eight years, even in schools for deaf people. When they first arrive at school, deaf children are typically overjoyed to meet other deaf children with whom they can communicate. However, the linguistic and cultural oppression of the oral school environment is detrimental to their intellectual growth. The slowing of their development is masked by the behavioral changes associated with enculturation into the oral system, but it is interaction with other deaf children that accounts for any further progress they might make. Group interaction counteracts, though only in part, the deprivation of the oral school setting.

Unfortunately, parents' ignorance about deafness often leads them to join with the oppressors of deaf people. The parental role is strong during the school years, but more often than not parents support the policies of the school personnel rather than their own children.

Institutional Oppression

Institutional oppression is the most open kind of oppression in many developing countries. It begins with the politicization of the general policies of education for the benefit of national unity. Deaf students in particular are oppressed by schools that do not allow the use of sign language. In many countries there are few if any specific policies for education of deaf people allowing the use of natural sign languages. Most schools opt for either oralism or total communication.

In many countries, the government agencies responsible for the education of deaf students provide only a primary school education. One reason for the scarcity of secondary school programs for deaf people is that most developing countries use more than one language in their educational systems. Of course, it is difficult for deaf people to perform well under oralism when more than one spoken language is used, and few deaf students advance to secondary level work.

In the developing countries, it is common for a hearing child to learn his or her second language before the age of twelve. The fact that many deaf children in developing countries have not yet been exposed to *any* adult language model at that age may permanently hinder their language development. Because the suppression of sign language through institutional regulations and oral methods deprives them of linguistic stimulation, deaf people also have lagged in their development of skills in the spoken and written language of the hearing society and, thus, in their intellectual development. It is impossible for deaf people to learn the spoken language of the society at large before learning their first language—sign language.

Mainstream and total communication settings—where lipreading, speaking, and reading and writing are measured as if they were true indicators of the intelligence of deaf people—are in conflict with deaf cultural values. This is why many deaf people grow up without much interest in school. Integration remains the major aim of rehabilitation, especially in postprimary school vocational training, but such environments contribute to oppression both inside and outside of the schools.

Oppression Through Self-Denial

In many developing countries, deaf people who use signs are given derogatory names, such as "dumb," and "mute," and are considered mentally defective. During childhood and adolescence, deaf children are encouraged to look down on their schoolmates who do not learn lipreading and speech. In one study, when deaf children were interviewed by a hearing researcher they denied their knowledge of sign language and deaf culture for fear of being thought inferior. When interviewed by a deaf researcher, however, the children felt free to express themselves in sign language.

Oppression Through Sex Bias

Because most deaf students in developing countries reach puberty while they are still in primary school (which they often do not complete until the age of seventeen), there is a problem regarding sex education for these students. Unfortunately, the basic strategy used by schools to avoid pregnancies among these students is not to provide sex education, but to inculcate fear and mistrust of both sexual activity and frank discussions of sexual facts, problems, and values.

Whatever advantage this strategy may have in the short run, it tends to mark sex as a taboo subject for a lifetime. In most cases, female deaf adults are the group most affected; their resulting ignorance of sexual matters leaves them vulnerable to unwanted pregnancies, false promises of marriage, and so on. About 80 percent of deaf females who complete school have children but no husbands and continue to live with their parents. The strategy to avoid even discussing sex also adversely affects projects geared toward assisting adult deaf women in many developing countries. Many projects fail owing to deaf women's discomfort with the open discussions upon which the success of such projects depends.

Intrainstitutional Oppression

The majority of schools for deaf people are owned and operated by religious bodies and voluntary organizations that compel their administrators to evaluate teachers according to the value orientations of the owners. In such a situation, teachers who are sympathetic to deaf people tend to avoid open remarks in support of the deaf struggle. Most prefer to remain silent rather than risk conflict with their superiors.

These teachers (most of whom are trained in special education) often discover after gaining some experience in schools for deaf people that they are ill trained to deal with the fundamental problems of deafness. I interviewed a group of teachers of deaf people about their training. Taken as a whole, 65 percent of the teachers believed that they had been ill trained, while 35 percent believed that they had been well trained. Younger teachers (those between the ages of twenty-one and forty) were more likely to consider themselves ill trained (85 percent), while older teachers (between forty-one and sixty) were more likely to consider themselves well trained (55 percent).

According to the above figures, it is clear that age plays a major role in resisting or accepting sign language. Any new emphasis on sign language in the classroom would require retraining of teachers; older teachers fear losing their jobs because their schools might find it uneconomical to retrain them. They also believe it would be difficult for them to meet new sign language requirements. As a result, older teachers use their influential positions to curtail any relationships with institutions sympathetic to the plight of deaf people who are thus willing to use sign language.

Another form of intrainstitutional oppression can be seen when teachers attempt to change their schools' curriculum requirements in order to compensate for their own inadequate training. In most such cases, curriculum developers accept the request of the teacher. But when parents raise concerns about their deaf child's progress in school, the school's response is often to blame the child rather than the faults in the curriculum or consider the difficulties deaf people face in interaction with the hearing society.

National associations of deaf people also have been affected by intrainstitutional oppression, especially in the area of leadership. During the formative stages of the national level associations, teachers and social workers typically played a very prominent role in running the affairs of these organizations. The deaf leaders served more as figureheads than as representatives of the deaf members.

Later, when deaf adults with considerable knowledge and education joined the associations, the quality of leadership improved. The new, more able deaf leaders often discovered evidence of mismanagement by their predecessors, and when they began to educate their fellow members, they found that these people were nervous around them; the less educated deaf association members felt inferior to their more educated leaders. When this phenomenon of mistrust and negative attitudes was investigated, it became clear that the teachers and social workers who worked with the associations had created this artificial conflict with the aim of dividing the deaf community in order to control deaf people more easily.

In developing countries, the hearing professionals working with deaf people have fostered a dependency syndrome that sustains the professionals in their role as a vital link between the deaf and hearing worlds. In most cases their efforts have regrettably succeeded. If this practice is allowed to continue, and if deaf people with superior knowledge and technical competence in any field continue to be regarded as threats by their fellow members, associations of deaf people will lack the cooperation and solidarity necessary to lobby for change in their societies.

Interinstitutional Oppression

Despite financial constraints, the governments of most developing countries provide some meager subsidies to facilitate the formation of national associations of deaf people and the development of grass-roots organizations at the district or county level. In the process, however, hearing teachers and social workers have infiltrated the management of these associations, which they influence to suit their own purposes. It is owing to this outside influence that many associations of deaf people tend to avoid relations with institutions of higher learning, such as their local universities, which might be inclined to cooperate in studies of sign language.

In most developing countries, deaf people are under the jurisdiction of the ministry concerned with education when they are in primary school and under the ministry concerned with social welfare during and after their postprimary school vocational training, whether they are employed or not. Each ministry acts independently and without input from the national deaf associations, and there is no interministerial coordination to avoid duplication of work. Moreover, because ministries of social welfare and ministries of education often have conflicting views of the role of deaf associations, the associations are unlikely to influence successfully educational and communication practices affecting all deaf children if they rely too much on either ministry.

Recommendations

1. When the majority in a society believe that deaf people are mentally defective, authorities should re-examine their policies, curricula, etc. in relation to deaf people and take stock of the problems arising from their failure to recognize sign language and deaf culture and to provide a better future for deaf people.
2. Deaf associations that have not yet formed committees for the parents of deaf children should do so. There is no easier or better education for parents of deaf children than to participate in the deaf associations.
3. Schools for deaf people are not so subject to outside pressure as schools for people who are not deaf, not because they are specialized, but because they are not publicly known. If the public is made aware of the operations of deaf schools, it will exert an influence to improve them.
4. The international community should not be led to believe that there are no educated deaf people in developing countries. To do so is to deny the existence of many well-educated, postlingually deaf people.
5. The deaf association should invite institutions of higher learning to assist them in carrying out sign language research.
6. To counter resistance against sign language and deaf culture, deaf people in developing countries should work to build a common understanding of their environment, which is very similar throughout the developing world.
7. Deaf people should not allow themselves to be divided into categories based on level of education or age at onset of hearing loss. These distinctions should not be the basis for social classes. Deaf culture reflects one single identity.

8. Universities and other institutions of higher learning in developed countries should assist in recommending and providing sign language materials to universities in developing countries.

9. Institutions concerned with deaf people should be changed to allow deaf people more control in the affairs that affect them.

Conclusion

Societies are usually comprised of many communities that overlap each other to some degree. In the developing countries, the deaf community is thought of as a school community or an institutional community and not as a social community. In these countries, consequently, deaf people are oppressed by being denied their sign language and their culture. As we remind ourselves that deaf history is a history of oppression, let us work to build a future that is free of oppression.

Better Education for Deaf People in French-Speaking Africa

MARIUS ROCK TITUS

There are approximately 140,000 deaf people and 1,800,000 hard of hearing people of all ages in French-speaking Africa, which includes such countries as Benin, Burkina Faso, Burundi, Cameroon, the Central African Republic, Chad, Congo, Gabon, Guinea, Ivory Coast, Mali, Mauritania, Niger, Rwanda, Senegal, Togo, and Zaire, to name a few. As one of the few representatives of French-speaking Africa at The Deaf Way conference, I present this paper on behalf of the deaf community in these countries.

We stand poised at a critical juncture. The Deaf Way conference takes place during the United Nations Decade of the Disabled Person, which has already witnessed the accession of a deaf person to the presidency of Gallaudet University. The chairman of the Board of Trustees of this important institution, Mr. Philip Bravin, is also deaf. The powerful nonviolent revolution in the history of deaf people that occurred in March, 1988 has sent a challenging message to the world that, to quote President I. King Jordan, "deaf people can do anything but hear." This message was sent in English and in American Sign Language. Is it being heard and understood in the French-speaking communities of Africa?

I believe we all must take the responsibility to ensure that this message is constructed in the minds of everyone who is concerned about development in French-speaking Africa. I write now as one of the construction workers.

In the words of Mary Hatwood Futrell, "the mission of education must now and forever be defined by the needs of children." These needs are greater in French-speaking Africa than anywhere else, and the gap between promises and performance is widening immensely owing to a number of factors: political instability, lack of freedom, lack of respect for human rights, the ever-present poverty in Africa, the lack of deaf awareness, and the deliberate rejection of deaf people, who are too often classified as invalids, second-class citizens destined to be beggars, or people possessed by demons.

There are many needs related to the education of deaf people in French-speaking Africa—needs ranging from programs of teacher training, linguistic research, and books, especially sign language books specific to the deaf community of French-speaking Africa. In French-speaking Africa, governments have full control over education and anything related to it. Any innovation that does not agree with the government's ideology is not tolerated. Yet, often the innovators are more knowledgeable about deaf education than are the local authorities.

That I am able to communicate with my hands today and that I am able to be in the United States for higher education I owe in part to one such innovator, the late Dr. Andrew Foster. I am the first deaf student from French-speaking Africa to graduate from Gallaudet University. I attribute this privilege to an act of God—because Dr. Foster believed it was God who sent him to Africa to promote deaf education. He came to do what France, the master colonizer, should have done but did not. He came to do what local governments and educators should have done but did not.

As the first black deaf American to graduate from Gallaudet University in 1956, Dr. Foster saw clearly the needs of deaf people in Africa. He founded the Christian Mission for Deaf Africans—now known as the Christian Mission for the Deaf—and traveled throughout Africa establishing and helping establish schools for deaf students. Sometimes it took him years of persistent effort to convince local governments and educators of the need for such schools and to obtain permission to set them up. Dr. Foster began his work in Ghana and Nigeria—English-speaking countries—soon after graduating ·from Gallaudet, and gradually his work spread through some twenty-one African countries. By the time of his death in a plane crash on December 3, 1987, he had participated in the establishment of thirty-one schools.

Unfortunately, Dr. Foster did not begin working in French-speaking Africa until 1974, when he obtained permission to establish the first school for deaf students in Ivory Coast. The following year, Dr. Foster launched a massive campaign to open schools for deaf students in ten other French-speaking countries where previously none had existed.

In 1976, he started a special four-week summer course for new French-speaking teachers of deaf students. This course, in which I was instrumental, produced a workforce of teachers that enabled him to open schools in Togo and Chad in 1976 and in Benin, Senegal, and the Central African Republic in 1977. As the summer courses continued, Dr. Foster expanded his work to other countries where schools for deaf students had never existed, such as Burkina Faso in 1980 and Gabon in 1981, followed by Burundi and Zaire. Politics and religion prevented him from opening schools in some countries, such as Mali, Mauritania, Niger, and Guinea. However, Dr. Foster was still able, at no charge, to train teachers of deaf students in some of these countries. Between 1976 and 1985, he trained approximately 110 teachers of deaf students. By the time of his death, that number is believed to have reached 130.

All of Dr. Foster's work was paid for with American dollars collected from individuals and church organizations. I recently received a letter from Dr. Foster's widow in Africa, where she was visiting schools he had established. Mrs. Foster mentioned that many of these schools still need American funding to remain open. Their needs range from instructional materials to school facilities, not to mention teachers' salaries, which too often have been paid months late. According to Mrs. Foster, at some schools, teachers' salaries are paid from America by the Christian Mission for the Deaf. Because many deaf children are found in rural areas, transportation to and from school is difficult if not lacking. Under such conditions, it is almost unthinkable to establish a large residential school, even in the capital city of a country.

I first met Dr. Foster in June, 1977, during my first year of medical school at the University of Benin in West Africa. He pointed out that I was wasting my time and money as the only deaf person among 3,000 students at the university. Frustrated by the lack of support services and my inability to cope with the communication system at the university, I accepted Dr. Foster's advice to become an educator of deaf students. Now, that dream has become a reality, and I am a budding educator of deaf students. I plan to continue the work that Dr. Foster started. As a black deaf American, he left an example for us to follow, whether or not we are deaf, black, or American; our race, hearing status, and nationality are less important than our capability, willingness, and sacrifice.

No part of our planet will know prosperity and peace until every part of our planet knows prosperity and peace, and in this respect, French-speaking Africa is a forgotten area; it is at the bottom of the list when it comes to the development of educational opportunities for deaf people. Dr. Foster started his work in an English-speaking country, Ghana, but died thirty-one years later in a French-speaking country, Rwanda, while on his way to establish new schools in the region. This is a clear indication that much is still left to be done in French-speaking Africa.

I must congratulate Dr. Harlan Lane, who has had the vision to assist deaf people in French-speaking Africa, beginning in Burundi. His work is a step forward in our efforts to bring French-speaking Africa in line with English-speaking Africa, where deaf education is more advanced.

As we approach the twenty-first century, my conviction is that the key to our future is saving not the African gorilla or the African elephant, but our own children. Too much American money is raised to save the African elephant, while the deaf children of French-speaking Africa are dying of malnutrition in the darkness of ignorance. We must also stop valuing weapons more than the lives of African deaf children. Their future is not in an army base packed with missiles, but in their minds, which are full of potential. To deprive these children of education and training is to commit an act of violence—I would say even an act of terrorism.

As Adolfo Perez Esquivel of Argentina has remarked, "Usually we speak of violence only when it has reached an extreme. But it is also violence when children are dying of malnutrition, when unions are not free, when housing is scarce and health care inadequate"—and, more importantly, when education is lacking or inadequate. We need to stop this violence.

According to research by the Center for Advanced Study of International Development at Michigan State University, world population will grow by another billion people during the 1990s. This is not good news, of course; no nation can achieve its social and economic goals with extremely high population growth. Chances are, however, that something *can* be done.

It is an undeniable fact that Africa in general, and French-speaking Africa in particular, are becoming poorer and poorer. Yet, as evidenced by a report of the United States House of Representatives Task Force on Foreign Assistance, aid to this most distressed continent is always at the lowest level. In the limited assistance sent to French-speaking Africa, education itself has received less and less consideration. The gap between assistance for education and assistance for food is very wide. Those committed to the development of the Third World believe that Africa needs bread, and indeed Africa does. But give me bread, and I will eat today and tomorrow. Then I will continue to beg for bread, and you may—or may not—continue to give it to me. If I find no bread in the next few days, weeks, or months, I cannot feed myself, and I will die. Instead, teach me how to bake and help me—by equipping me to start baking—and I will eat bread and feed others for years and years. That is what should happen but does not. It can happen only if a revolution in attitudes occurs.

To address the problems facing deaf people in French-speaking Africa I offer the following suggestions:

1. Every concerned American should write letters asking members of Congress to support legislation encouraging adequate funding of education.

2. Capable individuals, regardless of national origin, should help French-speaking Africa get loans and grants for educational projects and programs.

3. The World Federation of the Deaf should mobilize and assist researchers who will concentrate their energies on French-speaking Africa to determine the nature of the problem and come up with ways to improve the situation. I do not suggest that Americans have the ability to sweep in with the solutions to all of our problems, but they do have the ability to help. One possible approach is to encourage deaf people and people with interest and experience in deaf education to serve as Peace Corps volunteers and missionaries in French-speaking Africa. This would surely become an important means of attacking a number of basic constraints to the development of deaf education in French-speaking Africa.

4. Gallaudet University was once an American school, but individuals from other countries, such as Laurent Clerc and the Abbé de l'Epée, are partly responsible for its existence. Today it is more of an international school, and with its present status as the mother-school of deaf people all around the world, Gallaudet should assist—via the International Center on Deafness—in the launching of special academic programs and a campaign to promote awareness of deafness and related issues in French-speaking Africa.

5. Gallaudet—in conjunction with agencies such as the United Nations, the World Bank, the World Health Organization, UNICEF, UNESCO, and concerned African governments—should bring government officials and educators from French-speaking African countries to the United States yearly or biannually to enable them to learn what deaf people can do. This knowledge might foster a revolution in attitudes toward deaf people and their needs.

6. Gallaudet should start regular one-year training courses for French-speaking African teachers and interpreters who do not qualify for admission to the University. In addition, linguistic research could be conducted with the goal of standardizing a sign language for the deaf people of French-speaking Africa.

7. Gallaudet should give special attention to qualified prospective degree-program students from French-speaking Africa by giving them a full tuition waiver or free room and board if they do not have a full scholarship. This will help defray college costs that are becoming astronomical.

8. Nongovernmental organizations should be encouraged to make innovative contributions to the education of deaf people, especially in French-speaking Africa.

9. Enterprises with commercial interests in French-speaking Africa, such as the Shell Oil Company, represent a stable resource base and should be encouraged to support deaf education in the countries where they operate.

10. Individuals, families, and churches should consider sponsoring or adopting deaf children from French-speaking Africa. This process may take the form of either bringing the child to the United States to live, or paying for the child's school supplies and school lunch while the child remains in Africa.

11. The World Federation of the Deaf should create and propose to the United Nations legislation to defend the human rights and improve the living standards of deaf people worldwide. This legislation should be written in terminology specific to deafness, and should not include references to "disability" or "handicap."

In conclusion, if the American dollar bill can be inscribed, "In God We Trust," let us not leave God out of our own struggle. We shall surely succeed.

The Problem of the Peruvian Deaf Person

ALBERTO PALIZA FARFAN

I am assembling here condensations of a number of my thoughts already presented more elaborately in various Peruvian journals and books, concerning the long and ongoing history of the use, neglect, and abuse of the Sign Language of Peru (LSP). Since the advent of my incurable deafness, at the age of twelve, my mind and my life have become closely bound to my deaf friends, my wife (deaf since birth), and the entire Peruvian deaf community. All of my work has been developed in response to what I have perceived as an urgent mandate from the deaf community in Peru. This community's heritage has been transmitted from generation to generation of deaf people through LSP.

Centuries of hearing people's discussions about the problems of Peruvian deaf people—filled with evasive talk about administrative, legal, or religious mechanisms for maintaining government- or church-centered guardianship over this "disabled group"—have hidden or distorted the true source of the problems. All of this talk has been fruitless. It apparently remains for a critic from the deaf community to uncover the real problems, which can clearly be seen in many aspects of Peru's history.

The current problems of Peruvian deaf people are rooted in stereotypes dating back as far as the 1500s. Ordinances in the colonial era, from 1544 to 1815, when Peru was subject to Spanish rule, all describe "deaf mute" individuals as among "the disabled" and give no indication of any substantive recognition of the value of sign language. In the Republican era, from 1825 to the present, deaf people have at least benefited from the dissolution of Spanish rule to the extent that the right to self-expression in sign language has had a slightly better chance to become recognized. Nevertheless, one can find in articles of civil code from earlier in this period such statements as: "Deaf mutes are unfit to marry." Similarly, Peru's Supreme Health Decrees still state that "The deaf are forbidden to drive automobiles."

We of the Peruvian deaf community maintain that any attempt to resolve Peruvian deaf people's problems with administrative measures, with theoretical proposals, with teaching methods created by hearing people—all with the ostensible goal of assimilating deaf people into hearing society—constitutes a superficial endeavor designed to ensure that the supremacy of hearing people over deaf people will persist. Unfortunately, we deaf people currently find ourselves in the situation of being compelled by laws and ordinances into an essentially powerless integration—largely against our will—into an exclusively hearing environment. The specialist, the otorhinologist, the sociologist, the lawyer—all end up conspiring to become our "hearing administrators," inflicting their decisions paternalistically upon deaf people, whether or not we want their help.

Hearing administrators have for centuries based all their actions on the theoretical premise that deaf people are inferior. The result has been either that deaf people
were warehoused on a mere subsistence level with the mentally retarded in specialized
centers throughout the republic or at other times they were mixed in with the hearing
from an early age—without proper support in schools, sanatariums, and religious clois-
ters. What successes deaf Peruvians have accomplished, they have managed in spite
of, rather than because of, the institutions created for them by hearing administrators.
Increasing numbers of deaf people in recent times have managed—through their own
determination and mutual support—to assimilate admirably into the culture and technology of the hearing society. This group's dynamic and creative efforts, in fact, have
contributed to the consciousness of deaf people's real problems, which turn out not at
all to be what hearing administrators have implied they were.

It is increasingly clear that the centuries-old denigration of the Peruvian deaf person has been little more than a cheap invention of petty lawyers codifying the superior
attitudes of hearing administrative boards. Appealing to lofty moral judgments based
on an old repertoire of nationalist ideas, these hearing administrators have persisted
in viewing deaf people as failing to meet the high standards of Peruvian hearing civilization. From this perspective, the deaf community is seen as a laggard ethnic group,
its children badly in need of constant training in integration and socialization skills.
Those of us who have come to see these standards for what they are must seek international support from human rights organizations in the United States and Europe that
denounce such oppressive views.

The deaf community of Peru, through its own national organization formed in 1960,
represents above all the hope of eventually overcoming this oppression, although it has
proven most efficacious in serving to defend the deaf community's views through the
appointment of outspoken representatives, an orientation that certainly owes much to
the idealism of Juan B. Marroquin, Spanish deaf leader. Unfortunately, this organization's bold hopes of overcoming an oppressive system have not been totally realized.
In fact, our humanitarian preaching has neither detained nor embarrassed the hearing
administration in Peru, nor has it been able to improve that administration's methods.
Many deaf Peruvians, I am sorry to report, no longer have faith that the struggle against
such an administration will ever succeed. These deaf people, weary of struggling, often
prefer the sense of solidarity and strength gained from allowing their hands to be bound
by the reigning psychological oppression and siding with those who oppose allowing
deaf people to have the freedom of their own opinions.

One small voice on behalf of reason and morality, with regard to deaf people, was
provided by religious activists (including some Spanish deaf clergy) over the centuries.
These groups, however, never proved to have sufficient dedication to achieve anything
more than establish occasional protection ordinances for deaf people. Although adherence to these ordinances was officially ordered, they never had a substantial impact on
the lot of deaf people in Peru. In fact, in Catholic boarding schools where deaf children
should have benefited, they clearly did not. The supposedly religious people obliged to
care for them paid no attention to deaf children's real problems or to the heritage of the
deaf community. Although these children were sometimes allowed to learn and practice signs, if they did not agree to pursue speech training, they were regarded by friars
as intractable. In general, the Catholic Church, to which three-fourths of the Peruvian
nation belongs, dismissed deaf people's language and culture as an impertinence.

Today, the hope for an ecclesiastic solution to deaf people's problems has been
proved historically to be the most unrealistic hope of all. Those who represent this
hope—and there are some—are not even concerned like their distant relatives, the

Spanish deaf clergy, with obtaining a new declaration of freedom for deaf people. Once groups of these people become sufficiently organized, they tend to send a hearing missionary to serve as a mediator to secure whatever services they request. They fail to insist that the social work of the Catholic Church simply cannot be carried out in the context of an integrationist order, because such an order in itself completely fails to recognize the real problems of deaf people. It strikes me as a great pity that this is the case, for there is certainly much useful social service deaf people could do within the context of the Catholic Church if the Church were not blind to deaf people's needs. But since it apparently is blind to those needs, I can only ask, what resources does the Church have to move forward in this area?

The adventist missions have moved ahead of the Catholic clergy in responding to deaf people's needs in that they allow deaf individuals the freedom to become self-appointed leaders, whose assemblies allow deaf people the right to express their individual opinions according to the dictates of their consciences.

To say that deaf Peruvians have an educational problem is, of course, true, but in itself, such an observation misses the real point or the real problem. So long as school administrators and teachers have an integrationist, oralist philosophy, there will continue to be social and, indeed, economic factors impeding deaf people's educations. No innovative, didactic technique introduced into schools ruled by such a philosophy can possibly help. The fact is that schools at great expense drag out deaf students' educations past the age of twenty-two, simply because the teachers—unable to reach the students orally—never arrive at a sense that the students are yet prepared for the outside world. Within this system, the hearing, oralist educators are hopelessly doomed to disassociate themselves from understanding the real problems and needs of the deaf community.

The most elementary, progressive concept would be to change things through free communication, introducing sign language into classroom instruction. From a practical standpoint, deaf students' educations could then be briefer and cheaper. From an educational standpoint, deaf students at last would be able truly to learn. When this truth is understood, the solving formula will finally have been discovered for deaf schools. Wherever this formula would be used, deaf children from the earliest age would benefit educationally and would feel an unprecedented sense of confidence and security.

But of course, such a formula is not presently being used or even sought in Peru, since educators are apparently content to remain aloof from any concern for the real needs of the deaf community. In fact, there does not presently exist even the vaguest suggestion that any group of educators feels the slightest responsibility for deaf people's problems in Peru. And yet, I would propose that the neglect of Peruvian Sign Language (LSP) by educators and others—including some deaf people themselves—is the primary problem of Peru's deaf community.

Those of us in Peru's deaf community who have been studying and working to define the "deaf Peruvian's problem" wish to state that our perspective differs in an important way from the humanitarian and social perspective that has been articulated as part of the apostolic work of the missionaries by whom a pro-deaf campaign has been supported. Our study tends to establish the nature of the problem fundamentally and specifically in the *communication* that exists or does not exist among deaf people and between deaf people and hearing people.

We found ourselves rebelling particularly against the reflexive and defensive tendencies of the oral deaf or deaf people who separate themselves from the deaf community—those who allow themselves very little or no interest in learning LSP. We also found ourselves rebelling against hearing individuals with an apparent allergy to even *thinking* about LSP, whose tendency is to reduce deaf people's problems to administrative, pedagogic, ethnic, or moral dimensions in order to cloak the real problem at all costs: the deficient use of sign language between the deaf person and his interlocutor. The most absurd of the charges made against us is that we have been excessively emotional in our advocacy for the increased use of LSP. In fact, we have generally assumed a very objective attitude. At the outset of our efforts, not satisfied with merely asserting deaf people's rights in the realms of education, culture, progress, and love, we categorically asserted above all those our right to LSP through the espousal of the philosophy of total communication. The relationship between the currently wide diversity in form of LSP and the widespread prohibitions against its use is clearly evident. But those of us involved in this work in the deaf community have no interest in trying to tamper with or attenuate LSP in order to make it fit into some simplified rendering. On the contrary, we insist that the language be accepted unequivocally in its unadulterated form.

The most serious problem presently facing LSP is the generally accepted *de facto* application of pure oralism throughout Peru, a philosophy that has historically had no other purpose than to eradicate LSP and hence to make the situation of the deaf person truly pathetic. Pure oralism, imported to Peru during its 150 years as a republic, has tended to block real professional concern about the genuine problems of the deaf person. All of the so-called Republican administrations have preserved this pure oralist position, copied and imported, whose simplistic principles have often moved educators to take up brutal practices. Today, there is not a single deaf person in Peru who would say that he or she has never been mistreated in order to force him or her to intone an audible voice. In fact, Peruvian deaf education has followed the ancient Spanish adage, which goes, "With blood the voice comes out."

As a logical consequence of its oralist position, Peru has squelched the free development of LSP. The majority of deaf people end up secluding themselves within some narrow sector of the deaf community without full awareness of what is being done linguistically by deaf people throughout Peru. Without official or educational support, they look for private ways of coping with their silent existence, and they end up expressing themselves manually to a few other deaf people—and sometimes to hearing people—in defiance of and opposition to oralism. Unfortunately, the resulting mimicry of limited numbers of deaf people limits the range of their expressive capabilities in sign language—one of the consequences of the general complacency toward and oppression of deaf people in Peru. The result is that every deaf Peruvian appears to have his or her own peculiar way of communicating with his hands. Now, as has been noted by hearing people who are presently trying to decipher the structure of LSP, this suppressed development of LSP serves ironically to prolong deaf people's forced integration into hearing society. The lack of development of LSP, though caused by oralists' oppressive tactics, unfortunately adds to the view that LSP is inferior to Peru's spoken language.

And yet, LSP is the heart of the culture of Peru's deaf community. In this, both widely used signing conventions and signing developed in relative reclusion must be embraced. LSP certainly needs to grow, to develop its full linguistic potential, yet it is critical that both widely and more rarely used expressions be affirmed during this process. One ought not recklessly to change conventions that have their roots in the natural expression of deaf people. The consequence of ignoring this principle, inevitably, would be to push deaf people and sign language once again into a primarily isolated existence, the opposite of the needed and intended development.

Putting LSP into action by paying heed to every natural variation, of course, does not lend itself to unarguable formulations. The problem of deaf people's having been isolated for centuries among a few deaf and many hearing people will appear in all its magnitude. This is the price of our having lived for so long under the rule of men acting on the false plane of integrationist facts and ideas! Nevertheless, any effort to change LSP quickly would be in vain. Such an effort, for example, would likely result in negative reactions if it seemed to favor only forms of LSP used by leaders or groups presumed to have dominance within the deaf community.

In my view, each deaf Peruvian has the right and responsibility—in the context of his or her institution—to help the professionals and future specialists by giving them a knowledge of LSP and, thereby, of deafness. I think that the time to teach the philosophy of total communication in Peru is long overdue, and I consider the importance of using unadulterated LSP to be so fundamentally unquestionable and concrete that it gives a peculiar character to our LSP. In my view, the survival of the Peruvian deaf community and of LSP depends on the willingness and determination of Peruvian deaf people to assert their identity as part of this community and to make use of LSP in daily life. Those who doubt the wisdom of this suggestion should take a look at the North American experience and progress there toward a more liberal philosophy and practice over the last twenty years.

In the 1960s in Spain a nostalgic movement began with the goals of reclaiming signs of Spanish origin and of promoting the use of conventional Spanish Sign Language among Spanish deaf people. A problem arose thereafter in Peru as a result of efforts to evoke among deaf Peruvians a sense of connectedness to this movement and to the Spanish deaf community. Deaf Peruvians in reality felt a degree of linguistic disconnectedness from Spanish deaf people. Although much of LSP can be traced to Spanish Sign Language, much of the signing in Peru's deaf community arose naturally among deaf people whose necessary isolation offered limited opportunities for learning signs of Spanish origin. Although the influence of visiting deaf Spaniards has indeed been felt, the novelty of their "conventionalism" has generally been at odds with Peruvian "regionalism." LSP may have been deepened somewhat as a result of this Spanish movement, but in general the natural distinctiveness of LSP tends to predominate.

In my view, the most appropriate way of regarding LSP is to see it as a varying blend of conventional and reclusive signing. It is quite possible for a deaf Peruvian to negotiate daily life and discuss personal matters of all sorts using primarily regional or folkloric signs. Although this signing has the disadvantage of being quite heterogeneous in form around the country, the influence of deaf Spanish and Latin American visitors—each bringing his or her suggestions for conventional reform—does not really solve the problem. Deaf people of varying backgrounds in Peru are often, frankly, compelled to guess at the interpretation of another's signing. The real reason for this situation, I believe, is that institutions for deaf people assume no interest in or responsibility for sign language, which therefore tends to be consistently used only by small groups of deaf people who live together. For a reasonably consistent, national form of LSP to evolve, there would need to be some sort of official recognition of the importance of and need for a national sign language.

In general, the subordination and suppression of LSP is the worst problem facing deaf people in Peru. Deaf individuals of necessity live in a visual world, and their way of seeing the world inevitably is translated by their hands into their liberation. It is important for hearing people to try to appreciate deaf people's unique sensibilities and capabilities. In Peru today at least 45 percent of professional deaf people regard LSP as their primary language for communication. These individuals are working together in an effort to enrich the Peruvian deaf community's awareness and use of sign language, promoting the open use of signing not only for improved communication among deaf people, but also for improved understanding of deaf people by hearing society.

The tradition of a visual language, passed from hand to hand among deaf people, is the spirit and nourishing mother of the deaf community, attracting and entertaining large numbers of deaf people, appeasing them and urging them to avoid the impulse to rebel, encouraging them to actively participate in functions promoted by the deaf community, and providing individual deaf people with the means of expressing their own identities. Particularly among the profoundly deaf, there is clearly a deaf community with its own language, culture, history, and set of traditions that persists in carving out its own social niche. This reality cannot be denied, even though this community developed historically under the oppressive philosophy of pure oralism.

So what is to be done concerning the question of LSP in our time? In many parts of Peru, the existence of a nationalistic feeling tends to drown out the aspirations of those favoring the increased recognition and use of LSP. In one sense, it is strange that nationalism would have this effect, since it is not, in Peru, a movement or trend strong enough to be backed up with a real program; rather, it is merely the empty expression of a kind of nationwide despondency or feeling of dissatisfaction. One problem may have been that although the claims of those favoring more recognition of LSP are impressive in a general sense, the arguments for LSP need to be articulated in greater detail to be truly persuasive. Also, the question of LSP needs to be presented in new terms that leave aside the foreign influences of the nineteenth century.

It seems to me that the following proposals might help orient us as we pursue a detailed examination of the subject of LSP:

1. Controversy between different institutions serving deaf people is unnecessary and anachronistic. For example, the controversy between conservative and liberal fanatics over which signs should prevail (i.e., conventional versus regional) must be abandoned. The point that must be insisted upon is that the freedom of individual deaf Peruvians to use LSP, in whatever form is natural to them, must not be restricted. The new generation is not concerned with old battles over stubbornness, formality, and administrative mechanisms. What matters to them is a serious investigation of the structure of LSP in all its variety.

2. Historically, leaders in Peru's deaf community have not used the tactics most likely to serve the community's better interests. For example, third party interlocutors have often been used to promote their views. Today, personal persuasion of more deaf Peruvians to become interested in sign language is more likely to be successful and beneficial.

3. Deaf Peruvians who are especially dexterous and fluent in LSP, possibly (in some cases) as a result of foreign influence, may be justifiably sought out for their potential leadership of Peru's deaf community. Leaders with these qualities are certainly needed both to exert authority over other deaf people and to deal with authority figures outside the deaf community. Also, such leaders might recruit the services of other deaf individuals able to express their reasoning manually.

4. One of the problems affecting the lack of social organization in Peru's deaf community is certainly its administration. The solution, however, is not in administration, per se. Nor is it in the free use of signing. Our social organization and the cultural value of LSP need to be integrally reviewed and transformed.

5. It is difficult to define and demarcate in Peru which communities of deaf people have existed historically as such. Some still show the artificial influence of tendencies dating back to Spanish oralistic rule; consequently, these do not have a tradition, nor a reality genuinely emanating from the deaf people themselves and the history of the deaf community.

As various leaders battle each other over which form of LSP should prevail, there is a danger, in my opinion that many deaf individuals—sparsely distributed in remote areas of Peru—will be overlooked. Leaders In Peru's effort to define and develop LSP ought to take care to include these individual's views and preferences in their efforts. Otherwise, they may commit crimes similar to those perpetrated by oralists in the name of social conviction concerning solutions to the problems of Peru's deaf people and deaf community.

Are Deaf Children "Allowed" Signing?

CELINA RIBEIRO HUTZLER

A gente vai contra a corrente
até não poder resistir
na volta do barco é que sente
o quanto deixou de cumprir
Chico Buarque, *Roda Viva*[1]

In Recife (population 2 million), the capital of the state of Pernambuco in northeast Brazil, two very different worlds coexist: that of the Deaf community, in which Deaf people use Brazilian Sign Language (LIBRAS); and that of the parents, teachers, and therapists of "hearing impaired"[2] children, who try to teach these children to speak. These two worlds are now coming into contact.

There is a strong stigma attached to the use of sign language (Goffman, 1982), which cannot be ignored.[3] For the parents of hearing impaired children, as well as educators and therapists, the use of sign language can be considered as a "crossing over" to another world—the world of *difference with equality*. The emphasis on equality here indicates a full acceptance of deafness that is very difficult for the ethnocentric Hearing community. The purpose of this paper is to describe the efforts of one institution to assist parents, teachers, and therapists in "crossing over" to an acceptance of deafness and sign language. I have collected four types of data for this study: field notes from participant-observation; semistructured and unstructured interviews of parents and educators; questionnaires; and notes from workshops with deaf adults.

Similar stories have been told before in other places and in other languages. Many researchers (Bouvet, 1980; Johnson and Erting, 1989; Erting, 1985, 1978) emphasize that the very essence of Deaf identity is the acceptance and use of sign language—the mother language of Deaf people. Deaf ethnicity is built in Deaf communities, having among its main traits the preference for signing.

Acceptance of Deaf people requires respect for their language and a greater visibility for Deaf people and the Deaf community. Deaf people in Brazil have been largely invisible, partly owing to a general distrust of community and minority movements on the part of Brazilian authorities. This tendency was exacerbated by the military coup

---

1 "We go against the stream / until we can't resist / when the boat returns / we feel how much has not been done."
2 The dichotomy of "hearing impaired" versus "Deaf" is of symbolic importance in this discussion.
3 Among my informants is a Deaf couple with a four-year-old hearing daughter. Both parents are fluent in LIBRAS but have a poor command of Portuguese. The daughter is being raised by her grandmother because the parents fear that signing at home will adversely affect her development of speech.

of 1964. Only after the re-democratization of Brazilian society in the 1980s did Deaf movements and Deaf associations emerge.

The ethnocentricity of the Hearing community also contributes to the invisibility of the Deaf community. Parents, teachers, and therapists of Deaf children have internalized this ethnocentricity so strongly that they often refuse to see their children as "deaf." The children are "hearing impaired"—waiting to speak. The ability to speak and read lips will allow them to become full-fledged members of society; it will make them human (see Sapir, 1949).

In the typical view, the use of sign language is abnormal, almost nonhuman behavior. This view is not unique to Brazil, as the specialized literature shows exhaustively, but neither is it universal (Wegrocki, 1962). In her research on the Urubu-Kaapor tribe, Lucinda Brito (1987) found that the use of sign language by deaf members, accepted by the tribe as a whole, does not preclude full participation in community life.

Recent defenses of sign language have relied on two main arguments: that sign language is a legitimate language and is thus "cultural;" and that acquisition of sign language does not block the development of speech and so does not block "normalization." These two points have played a strategic role in the current process of pedagogical change in Brazil and have been crucial to the acceptance of the Total Communication philosophy there.

However, in Brazil Total Communication is considered less as an opportunity for deaf children to choose the means of communication that suits them best than as a step toward their development of speech (the accepted "normal" behavior). Except for a few linguists (Brito among them), most advocates of Total Communication emphasize that signing provides access to information that makes it easier for deaf children to learn the vernacular language (i.e. Portuguese, the majority language of Brazil). Total Communication, thus, has been more readily accepted than any purely gesturalist pedagogy for deaf children.[4] Because Total Communication is considered only as a step toward "oralization," there has been no concern about the destructive effects of bi-modal communication on Brazilian Sign Language.

In selecting a school setting for their deaf children, parents in Recife can choose from among a regular private school, two special private schools for the deaf, and special classes in public schools. The choice, however, is more limited than it seems. Few private schools accept handicapped children, and those that do are not prepared to give these children academic support. My research on the performance of deaf children in regular classes in the private school system shows a direct relationship between speech ability and school success; only the few children who have a satisfactory command of spoken Portuguese do well in these schools. The great majority of deaf students in regular private schools experience repeated failure.

Neither are the private schools for deaf children satisfactory. The D. Bosco School (not its real name) will serve as an example. This school was founded in 1952 and is supported by a Catholic group and through public and private grants. In the past, its administration was so authoritarian that deaf adults who attended the school as children—now members of the Pernambuco Association of the Deaf (Associação de Surdos de Pernambuco, or ASSPE)—give terrible accounts of their experiences there.

In a recent interview, the current president of the school said that "in the beginning we adopted a pure oralist method . . . but this was not a successful psychological

---

4 One cannot consider Total Communication as a gesturalist pedagogy; it is a compromise between oralism and gesturalism. Our field work in Brazil shows a paradox: The schools that have adopted Total Communication claim to combine speech and signing, but few of their teachers know LIBRAS or any other sign language.

experience. The pedagogy was changed to combine speech and signing" (Phaelante, 1987, pp. 18–19). My personal observations at the school indicate that signing is allowed in informal settings, but that speech, with signing only as an adjunct, is used in the classrooms. The school does not teach sign language, so it is passed down from child to child.

The school president's personality has kept her apart from both the handicapped movements and the professionals working in other schools and clinics. In this regard, she has not helped to improve the image or visibility of sign language; in the local area, signing is seen as something that the "poor kids" of the D. Bosco school, unable to speak, must use to communicate. Nonetheless, the school plays an important role in the preservation of sign language by providing a place for the transmission of sign language between students. The school also publishes a magazine containing information about sign language and Total Communication.

A second private school for deaf children was recently opened. It is operated by the Evangelical Church for the benefit of poor children and has adopted Total Communication. Unfortunately, no one has studied conditions at this school yet.

According to Brazilian law, special education in the public school system is the responsibility of the individual states. Nevertheless, because the states depend heavily on federal funds, the Federal Board of Education (Ministério da Educação) has a powerful influence on the schools. The Board maintains an oralist philosophy, and until 1987, all special classes for deaf students in the state of Pernambuco (there is no special school for deaf children in the public school system there) were taught using the oral method. Owing to the influence of the new Director of Special Education, however, the public schools of Pernambuco plan a gradual shift to the Total Communication philosophy.

In addition to school programs for deaf children, there are clinics and rehabilitation centers in Recife that specialize in oral training. One such institution (which I will refer to as "the Center"), the focus of this paper, was founded thirteen years ago by a group of parents and therapists. The Center used the Verbo-Tonal[5] method, a pure (or fanatical) form of oralism that was seen by both parents and therapists as *the* most modern method, the only method capable of teaching the hearing impaired to talk. Today the Center has an enrollment of about 130 patients between the ages of one and sixteen. The Center's work consists entirely of rehabilitation; its patients are expected to receive a mainstream education elsewhere, preferably in the private school system (Hutzler, 1986). The Center is highly regarded even by its critics (who emphasize its "elitist" characteristics). Its highly qualified staff has a real concern for the quality of the therapy and research conducted at the Center and for the democratization of the Center's services.

Until two years ago, the staff of the Center refused to consider any method but oralism. They did not use the word "deaf" and only seldom used the term "hearing impaired." Their belief in oralism was so strong that they never considered the ratio between the number of patients who succeeded in developing speech and the number who did not. Of course, some children had great success in learning to speak, and they were made the showpieces of the institution. Failures were blamed on a lack of effort on the part of the child, the family, or the therapist. The staff, waiting for a child to learn to speak, often extended the period of therapy again and again, never considering that the method itself was to blame for the lack of success.

My research and that of others (Godinho, 1982) shows that most parents never

5 The Verbo-Tonal method was developed by Dr. P. Guberina at the University of Zagreb, Yugoslavia. It is a well-known oral method, based on linguistic and psychological principles of language development, that emphasizes aural rehabilitation using advanced electronic equipment.

really accept their deaf children as being "deaf." The parents of the children at the Center supported the views of the staff, whose belief in oralism only reaffirmed the parents' dreams that their children would speak someday. Naturally, the children were not taught to sign, and neither parents nor staff dared to allow the children to come into contact with the Deaf community for fear that they might be "polluted" with sign language.

The turning point in this situation occurred at the First Meeting of the Hearing Impaired, held by the Handicapped Council of Pernambuco (Conselho Estadual de Apoio às Pessoas Portadoras de Deficiência) and the then-new Pernambuco Association of the Deaf (Associação de Surdos de Pernambuco, or ASSPE) in September 1986. This meeting brought together representatives of public and private schools and clinics, students, and professionals, but its primary purpose was to give voice to the experiences and concerns of Deaf people.

Among the Deaf people who attended the 1986 meeting, 83 percent claimed to be fluent in sign language. An equal percentage belonged to the ASSPE. Sixty percent of the Deaf attendees and 66 percent of the ASSPE members present were former students at the D. Bosco School. Almost all of these former students (93 percent) said they were fluent in Brazilian Sign Language. These data (collected using a questionnaire distributed to forty-six Deaf adults attending the meeting) suggest the importance of the school for deaf children in building Deaf identity and confirm the relationship between Deaf identity and sign language (Johnson and Erting, 1989; Erting, 1985, 1978; Denton, 1986, 1984, 1971; Hutzler, 1988). Such schools serve as a place where sign language is learned, and Deaf culture is transmitted.[6]

The Deaf people present at the 1986 meeting had an acute perception of the importance of a Deaf association, as their comments[7] illustrate.

> The deaf child learns how to sign at school. But the family is not able to sign and they cannot communicate.
>
> It is necessary that the Deaf of Recife know more about the ASSPE. It is a good thing for the Deaf to have a place to get together, although some deaf do not want to get together with other deaf.
>
> It is very difficult for a deaf child to understand the teacher in oralist schools. The teacher speaks and speaks and the deaf does not understand. The teacher must learn sign language to teach the deaf.
>
> To speak is good, but to speak is the difficulty of the deaf.
>
> A few were more radical in their opinions: "To speak is not important for the Deaf."

The representatives of the Center present at the meeting were surprised; they had never dealt with the opinions of Deaf people about deafness and deaf education. They had not dealt with Deaf adults able to express their thoughts and feelings. They brought the information they gained back to the Center, began to discuss with other staff members the advantages of sign language, and searched the literature for additional infor-

---

6 Some of my hearing informants who are critical of the D. Bosco school disagree with this interpretation. When asked where they learned sign language, many Deaf informants answered, "I just learned." I interpret such answers to mean that the informants learned sign language through informal peer interactions, which they did not identify as learning situations.

7 These comments are taken from the author's notes from the workshops "The Family and the Deaf" and "The School and the Deaf."

mation supporting the use of sign language in therapeutic settings. These discussions about sign language led to a philosophical split at the Center: Part of the staff insisted on the exclusive practice of oralism and moved its operations to another building. Although the remaining faction was not in total agreement, after less than a year they came to a decision: Deaf children at the Center would be allowed to sign.

The first reactions were negative. The parents had chosen to place their children at the Center so they would learn to talk. "She can stay here twenty years more," said the mother of one teenage girl, "but my child will learn to *speak*." (Her daughter had been in speech therapy for over four years and could not talk "yet.") "No! My child will not speak like a monkey," said another mother, who found sign language unacceptable because, to her, it resembled the behavior of animals. Another parent threatened, "If the other kids start signing, I will take my child out of this place." At a parents' meeting held after the staff's announcement of the change, no more than a few supported the idea that signing could be good for deaf children.[8]

But the process had been started and could not be stopped. As the staff continued to learn about sign language (in the Total Communication version), the Center offered its first sign language class, with a Deaf teacher. This year [1989], two more classes are being offered, and the Center plans to adopt Total Communication with some of its rehabilitation groups in 1990. A private school that traditionally enrolls deaf students has agreed to open a Total Communication class for students from the Center. Special materials for teaching sign language are to be produced. These are dramatic developments, but the process of "crossing over" has been slow and painful.

The changes at the Center influenced the Pernambuco public schools' recent decision to implement Total Communication in its special classes for deaf students. This transition has also been difficult. The teachers as a group do not reject signing, but they have yet to learn sign language, and there are no qualified sign language teachers in Recife. (The members of the ASSPE know how to sign but not how to teach sign language; the sign language classes the Association has offered since 1986 are characterized more by good will than by pedagogical expertise.) There are still very few schools and clinics in Brazil with experience in Total Communication and, with the exception of the Escola Concórdia de Porto Alegre (Hoemann, 1983), such institutions are scattered and isolated (Abreu, 1987). We still have a long way to go.

On this journey, this crossing over, only the Deaf community is truly qualified to lead. Deaf people are the natural choice as sign language teachers, because only they can convey the richness of sign language. Only Deaf people can fight for its legitimacy. The Deaf community clearly established its position in favor of Total Communication at the First Brazilian Congress of the Deaf in Campinas, São Paulo in October 1988. But the Deaf community cannot accomplish all of its goals alone. Because Hearing people hold the power in society, Deaf people must make alliances with the Hearing community.

Since 1985, I have conducted research on the Deaf community of Recife. In these four years, my personal views about Deaf people and deaf education have changed; I think that I have been able to cross over. Deaf people have been the compass for this personal passage, and the data of my field research indicate that they are serving as the compass in a huge crossover now taking place in the educational system. In order to read one's direction, however, one must see the compass: The invisibility of the Deaf community must be overcome. This will require Deaf people to fight for their civil rights and establish alliances with other civil rights and community movements. It will require

---

8 Parents' comments are taken from the author's field notes.

alliances with those people who feel for and empathize with Deaf people—those who are able to accept *difference with equality*.

References

Abreu, A. C. 1987. "Relatório das Visitas às Escolas e Associações de Surdos no Mês de Outubro." *Nordeste Silencioso* 3 (18): 20–22.

Bouvet, D. 1980. *L'Enfant Sourd: Un Être de Langage*. Genève: University de Genève.

Brito, L. F. 1987. "Socialização, Linguagem e Cognição em Surdos." *Nordeste Silencioso* 3 (18): 13–14.

Denton, D. 1971. *Educational Crises*. Frederick, MD: Maryland School for the Deaf.

Denton, D. 1986. *More than a School*. Frederick, MD: Maryland School for the Deaf.

Denton, D. 1984. *A Culture Celebrates*. Frederick, MD: Maryland School for the Deaf.

Erting, C. 1985. "Linguistic Variation in a School for Deaf Children." In *Proceedings of the Third International Symposium on Sign Language Research*, ed. W. Stokoe and V. Volterra. Silver Spring, MD: Linstok Press.

Erting, C. 1978. "Language Policy and Deaf Ethnicity in the United States." *Sign Language Studies* 19: 139–152.

Godinho, E. 1982. *Surdez e Significado Social*. São Paulo: Cortez.

Goffman, E. 1982. *Estigma, Notas sobre a Manipulação da Identidade Deteriorada*, trad. M. B. Nunes. Rio de Janeiro: Zahar.

Hoemann, H. W. 1983. *Linguagem de Sinais do Brasil*. Porto Alegre: Centro Educacional para Deficientes Auditivos.

Hutzler, C. R. 1988. "Surdez, Linguagem, Etnia e Luta." In *Sem Nordeste, o Que Há de Novo?* Natal: Nordeste Graf. pp. 125–134.

Hutzler, C. R. 1986. "Reabilitação de Deficientes Auditivos: Articulação Famílias e Profissionais." In *Sistemas de Cura, as Alternativas do Povo*. Recife: UFPE/MA. pp. 201–216.

Johnson, R., and C. Erting. 1989. "Ethnicity and Socialization in a Classroom for Deaf Children." In *The Sociolinguistics of the Deaf Community*, ed. C. Lucas. San Diego: Academic Press. pp. 41–83.

Phaelante, V. 1987. "Instituto Domingos Sávio—35 Anos." *Nordeste Silencioso* 3 (17): 18–19.

Sapir, E. 1949. "The Unconscious Patterning of Behavior in Society." In *Selected Writings of Edward Sapir in Language, Culture, and Personality*, ed. D. Mandelbaum. Berkeley: University of California Press.

Wegrocki, H. J. 1962. "A Critique of Cultural and Statistical Concepts of Abnormality." In *Personality in Nature, Society, and Culture*, ed. C. Kluckhohn. New York: Alfred Knopf. pp. 691–701.

The Mano a Mano Project

MIGUEL SANTILLÁN AND ALFREDO TORO

The Mano a Mano (Hand to Hand) Project is a development program for deaf people in Ecuador carried out by the Fray Luis Ponce de León Society of Deaf Adults. The ultimate goals of this project are to preserve the values of Ecuadorian deaf adults, improve their standard of living, and make their abilities and capacities known to the hearing community. The purpose of this paper is to describe the ideas, goals, and objectives of the Mano a Mano Project as they were developed in 1982, to report on the program's activities, achievements, and obstacles, and to present a final evaluation of the project's work. Before discussing the Mano a Mano Project, however, we will provide some background information on deaf people in Ecuador and the Fray Luis Ponce de León Society of Deaf Adults and its activities.

Deaf People in Ecuador

Deafness is a communication disorder that pervades all aspects of a deaf person's life, and the difficulties it creates can be even greater when the disorder is not immediately detected. Deafness and other similar language disorders represent the second largest group of disabilities in Ecuador. Mental retardation, blindness, and physical handicaps of lesser degrees represent the largest group. In Latin America, as well as in other developing countries around the world, there is a natural tendency to associate "mute" people with mentally and emotionally underdeveloped people.

The three clearly marked geographical and cultural zones of Ecuador have hindered access to and exchange of information and ideas among the deaf people of the country. Because of this geographical isolation, it is natural to find different signs used from city to city and from one region to another. However, something that is not natural, and that has delayed deaf people in unifying, is the suppression of sign language in daily life and in the classroom.

The methods used in the Ecuadorian schools to educate all deaf students are based on the principles of oralism. These methods require mastery of both the spoken language and lipreading, very specialized and demanding skills one cannot acquire without first having the ability to communicate and comprehend the meaning of things.

The ability to organize ideas, to understand others' ideas, and to participate fully in a society depends on the ability to communicate and use the language of that society. In this regard, language and culture are inseparable. Language is the vehicle for the transmission of culture from one person to another, generation after generation; it is impossible to learn about culture without language. The suppression of sign language in Ecuador has deprived the country's deaf people of access to the Spanish language and to the culture shared by their hearing fellow citizens. The lack of communication between deaf children and hearing parents creates numerous problems for both. Without the necessary access to language, deaf children are unable to establish the natural bond with parents, the community, and society in general. The deaf are left oppressed and in a cultural state of limbo.

This situation reflects two different social attitudes prevalent in Ecuador. First, if a person's language—in this case, sign language—is not accepted, then the person is not accepted. Second, if it is believed that a person does not have a language—as is believed of deaf people who use sign language—in the eyes of society that person is incomplete and inferior. The recognition of sign language as a valid means of communication and its use at home and in the classroom would eliminate a great deal of the cultural colonialism that affects the majority of Ecuador's deaf people.

To understand a culture, one must develop certain skills, including reading. The average reading level of an Ecuadorian deaf person who has completed the typical nine years of study and obtained an Elementary Education Certificate is similar to that of a hearing third-grader. This in no way reflects the deaf student's intelligence but is the result of oral education, which has prohibited or ignored the use of sign language as an educational tool.

Reading involves a process of using one's knowledge about our surroundings to understand printed words. Deaf individuals who are isolated from the surrounding culture will never be able to master reading completely because they do not possess all the knowledge shared by the culture and represented in the printed words. This, of course, limits their expressive communication as well as their ability to receive and understand information.

Furthermore, it is undeniable that a person's individuality lies in his or her language. Language defines the characteristics of nations and is an absolute prerequisite for a group trying to gain recognition as a legitimate entity. Throughout the years it has been demonstrated that language and history are the first two needs of Man. Loss of this history and language—or worse, their repression—is the final conquest of an aggressor. It is a chain on the soul that enslaves nations.

The Fray Luis Ponce de León Society of Deaf Adults

To overcome the linguistic and cultural oppression that inhibits both the deaf people of Ecuador and the society in which they live, change is necessary. To help facilitate this change, the Fray Luis Ponce de León Society of Deaf Adults was formed on December 5, 1975. It became a corporation on July 31, 1978. The goal of the Society is to be of social, cultural, recreational, educational, and economic benefit to its members through mutual cooperative effort:

❖ Social, regarding both the relationships among people with disabilities and their efforts to secure state-supported services

❖ Cultural, in the sense that the arts and sciences constitute the rational cultivation of new generations

❖ Recreational, in the sense that physical education and sports are practiced by deaf people at both the national and international levels

❖ Educational—The Society will offer courses geared toward improving the various activities of deaf people

❖ Economic—The Society hopes to establish a vocational school to ensure that people with hearing loss can benefit from rehabilitation, increased work opportunities, and advancement at factories and other workplaces that hire deaf people.

With the limited resources the Society itself could generate—through the donations of its members and, finally, a subsidy from the Ministry of Social Welfare in Ecuador—the Society has developed a number of informal programs. The following programs have been offered at various times, depending on the Society's resources at any given point:

❖ Literacy courses for deaf adults who do not know how to read

❖ Hairdressing and tailoring courses, directed especially toward deaf women as training for future work

❖ Locksmithing and industrial mechanics courses, directed toward deaf adults also with the goal of job placement

❖ Sports programs, primarily soccer, intended mainly for deaf men

❖ Social and cultural programs, including festivals, celebrations, beauty pageants, small discussion groups, and assemblies.

As is common for any organization with the goal of fighting for the human rights of deaf people, there have been obstacles, but the lessons we have learned from our mistakes have left clear paths for the future. The constant struggle of deaf people—who after many years, ended up joining groups and working for their own common welfare—has lessened the danger that the deaf community will die out and gives deaf people the courage to continue working for the advancement of their community.

The Mano a Mano Project

In 1982, after two years of initial investigation and preparation, the Fray Luis Ponce de León Society established the Mano a Mano Project, with the main goals of bettering the standard of living for thousands of deaf citizens and assuring the maintenance of their language and culture. Four major objectives of the Mano a Mano Project were to assess the extent of deafness in Ecuador, to code and preserve Ecuadorian Sign Language, to expand the vocational opportunities open to deaf people, and to train deaf leaders.

Among the planned results of the Mano a Mano Project were the production of a dictionary/textbook of sign language (including an explanation of manual communication and discussions of the basis of the language and its use in education) and the establishment of manual communication and sign language courses to promote the recognition and use of manual communication and signs. It was hoped that, as recognition of sign language grew, more and more people would attend sign language classes.

To stimulate interest in linguistic research on sign language and to make known the need for properly trained interpreters for deaf people, presentations and lectures at the university level were planned. A group of hearing people skilled in the art of manual communication would be organized to train professional interpreters. The Mano a Mano Project would offer classes for adults in the deaf community concentrating on refining their basic language skills, expanding their experiential bases, and broadening their vocational horizons.

In general, the project would pave the way for deaf people so that when they felt able to do so by themselves, they could form their own national organization.

Assessment

The statistics available in Ecuador reflect only the number of deaf and hard of hearing individuals who are enrolled in special schools. The alarming reality, however, is that many deaf individuals never go to school or are taken out of school to work such unskilled jobs as looking after parked cars. Because a census of the deaf people living in Ecuador was beyond our means, the Mano a Mano Project began with the identification of groups of deaf people and research into their needs. The first step in this process was to find deaf communities and define their potentials.

A deaf community is a group of people who live in a specific area, who have shared goals and, in one way or another, work to meet these goals. A deaf community may include people who are not deaf but who actively defend the goals of the community and work with deaf people to reach those goals. Deaf communities are usually described in pathological terms that focus on the etiologies of hearing loss and how these impediments affect the behavior of deaf people. It should be clarified that deaf people form their own communities to meet their basic needs, just as people in any other culture do.

When one analyzes any given culture, one must consider the values that are shared by that culture. Deaf communities serve the very important purpose of socialization. Through social activities, deaf people make important contacts with other deaf individuals. Just like their hearing counterparts, they enjoy talking to others who share their beliefs, attitudes, and experiences.

Sign Language and Communication

One of the aims of the project was to improve the communication skills of deaf people. Before the beginning of the project, deaf people did not pay much attention to their communication system and hearing people did not consider the value of that system as a means to improve the education offered to deaf students. From the outset, we in the Mano a Mano Project believed that the availability of a basic text/dictionary of sign language for the use of deaf people in Ecuador would inspire their development of basic language skills in the schools.

The average teacher of deaf students in Ecuador does not socialize with his or her students after work. Typically, this is owing to the inability of both parties to communicate with each other; the deaf people cannot communicate well orally, and those who can hear are not able to communicate manually. Because it is easier for hearing people to become fluent in sign language than for deaf people to become fluent in oral communication, we thought it desirable to increase the number of hearing people who can sign; in this way, the global linguistic environment would be enriched. With the creation of a supportive linguistic environment, even more people would learn sign language. The experiences, feelings, frustrations, and ideals of deaf people could be translated into the words and concepts of Spanish. This would help deaf people define their roles in the world as well as understand the roles and actions of others.

A sign language text for parents, teachers, and deaf people would also facilitate communication and the exchange of ideas both within and between geographical regions. The coding and preservation of Ecuadorian Sign Language in book form was, thus, one of the main objectives of this project.

The ability to control one's environment is directly related to the control of one's language. If that control is exercised from outside the community, its members are subjected to external influences and develop a sense of impotence. If it comes from within and is generated by the community itself, community members feel a sense of power and control over their own destiny.

In order to study a language, one must understand the people who use it. For this reason, we chose deaf individuals to be the first researchers; they know their language better than any hearing person does. Deaf people participated in the research of their own language and in the preparation of the book *Sign Language: A Basic Guide about Special Means of Communication*, which was published by the Fray Luis Ponce de León Society as part of the Mano a Mano Project. Deaf people modeled for the photographs of the 250 signs that appeared in the book. The photos were taken by deaf people in Quito. Descriptions of the signs were written by deaf people in Quito and Guayaquil, and supplementary drawings were made in Guayaquil. Deaf people also participated in the later stages of the publication of the book of signs, reviewing the rough draft of the text, photocopying, doing layout, printing, and preparing a distribution plan.

The book includes a resource guide that provides information about the history of the book's preparation, explanations about deafness, myths and truths about deafness, and the history of manual communication in Ecuador and around the world. It also includes an explanation of the linguistic aspects of signs used in Ecuador and a comparison of regional signs, a discussion of teaching methods for use with deaf students, a national directory of schools and rehabilitation centers for deaf people, and a message from deaf adults to the parents of deaf children.

About a dozen deaf people participated in an eight-day workshop at the Society on the use of the resource guide and the linguistic and syntactic aspects of the sign language of Ecuador. Meetings also were held with deaf people from Guayaquil to discuss the objectives of the book of signs.

Through the Mano a Mano Project, deaf people have been trained to work as sign language teachers, and sign language classes have been offered to hearing people, teachers, parents, and the general public. Special sign classes were developed to train Peace Corps volunteers who work with deaf people in different regions of the country. Illiterate deaf people have been trained in sign language, with the goal of using the communication system to provide training in reading, writing, and mathematics.

Results of the project's work in the area of communication also can be seen outside the Society of Deaf Adults. Almost all of the schools for deaf students in the country now recognize and use sign language and the manual alphabet. The majority of the teachers at these schools have received some kind of training in manual communication. Almost all the deaf children in schools for deaf students communicate among themselves by using sign language and the manual alphabet.

Through programs established by the Mano a Mano Project, many parents have received information and training in the use of formal systems of manual communication, and the general public has seen sign language used in formal settings, both directly—through television and public meetings—and indirectly—on the street, on the buses, in restaurants, and at the deaf theater. Sign language interpreters have been used for public meetings and ceremonies, leadership workshops, displays, total communication courses, and the Channel 4 news. As a result of all these developments, deaf people have become motivated to learn more about their language by participating in the programs of the Society for Deaf Adults.

Artistic and Vocational Training

Other aims of the Mano a Mano Project were to improve the formal and informal education and expand the employment prospects of members of the Society, and to improve
the image of deaf people in the mind of the hearing public.

The project established workshops—in black and white photography, audiovisuals,
serigraphy (silk-screening), and theater—which have helped expand vocational opportunities for deaf people. With skills acquired in these workshops, deaf people have put
on photography exhibitions and produced instructional audiovisual materials in the
areas of psychology, art, and accounting. Workshop participants also have produced
promotional videotapes for the deaf theater, developed a seminar on art and disabled
people, developed instructional materials for use in the literacy program (including two
units on cash management and basic accounting, and graphic materials for teaching
basic sign language), and participated in research on sign language conducted through
Bristol University in England.

An art seminar resulted in the development of a small business that produces
promotional photographs and photographs for ID cards. A small business to produce
stamped T-shirts is being developed.

The Mano a Mano Project has also provided opportunities for creative development.
Deaf people have begun to learn photography and to make videotapes of parties, social
events, and sports activities held in the deaf community. Basic studies of serigraphic
techniques and design of patterns for T-shirts were some other artistic endeavors. A
fine arts exhibition was held in the House of Ecuadorian Culture, with proceeds from
the sale of art works going to the deaf artists.

In November 1983, deaf people from the Society of Deaf Adults established a theater
school, where students receive instruction on movement, body control, and pantomime.
Members of the first graduating class went on to establish a theater company, which
gave its first public performance in November 1984. The Central Bank has sponsored
the deaf theater and paid stipends to its members.

The deaf theater has created opportunities for deaf participants to receive both
formal and informal training. Deaf people have joined the Theater Workers Association and members of the theater have conducted workshops and performances for deaf
people in the provinces. Through the deaf theater, deaf people have been trained in
areas such as mask production, dance, and bodily expression. Classes in drawing,
plastic art, and mask production were offered to the members of the theater in 1983.

All of the activities of the deaf community that have come before the public eye—
photography, the deaf theater, sign language courses, serigraphy, and the promotion of
the book of signs—have contributed to the creation of a new image of deaf people.

Leadership Training

To ensure their future, deaf people must unite and develop the abilities and self-
sufficiency that will allow them to maintain control over their own lives and to be seen
by the hearing community as worthy of respect and self-determination. We in the Mano
a Mano program saw the lack of serious organizations for deaf people in the country as
the consequence of a lack of leadership skills in the deaf community. Once these skills
were learned and leadership was established, it would be possible to organize local and
national groups.

Our leadership training programs were aimed not only at bettering the mental
health of the individuals involved, but also at creating a sense of power in the world,

both individually and collectively. The Mano a Mano leadership training program began in June 1983, with the specific aim of strengthening deaf people's skills in the areas of organization, leadership, and economic self-sufficiency. Technical assistance was provided by Gallaudet University and through the Inter-American Foundation. The program of the Mano a Mano Project was divided into three areas: the value of leadership, developing organizational skills, and stages of organizational participation.

The first leadership development workshop included participants from groups in Quito, Cuenca, and Guayaquil. Members of the Society for Deaf Adults visited and held mini-workshops for the deaf people of Ambato, Riobamba, Guayaquil, Manta, and Portoviejo and helped form a branch of the Society in Ambato. In Riobamba they assisted in the formation of the Chimborazo Center for Deaf Adults. They participated in a leadership training course in Guayaquil in 1983 and in an accounting workshop there in 1985.

Members of the Society for Deaf Adults have also participated in events sponsored by other organizations. The former president of the Society participated in a workshop on marketing organized by the Peace Corps. Deaf people were presenters at a 1985 seminar organized by the Peace Corps for teachers of deaf students and participated in several joint social activities, including the sale of calendars at the North American and British Ladies Bazaar in 1983, the sale of food and T-shirts at the United States Embassy picnic in 1984–1985, and the sale of products at an exhibition of disabled people in 1985.

One goal of this program is the integration of deaf people in the mainstream of the hearing community through programs of civic awareness to promote, create, or increase new work opportunities for deaf people. Based on the sociolinguistic principle of the acceptance of a people through the acceptance of their language, the first step toward increased community awareness is to offer the public the opportunity to learn about the deaf community by learning sign language. The Fray Luis Ponce de León Society of Deaf Adults had begun to work in this area, but its work was limited owing to lack of a textbook. Efforts undertaken through the Mano a Mano Project to produce such a text should greatly facilitate the acceptance of sign language

Current Work of the Mano a Mano Project

Funding for Mano a Mano was to have concluded on December 31, 1988. However, in November 1988, the Fray Luis Ponce de León Society of Deaf Adults proposed to the Interamerican Foundation that it extend funding to allow Mano a Mano to send a delegation to The Deaf Way Conference and Festival. This proposal stressed the importance that the Mano a Mano Project has had for the Ecuadorian deaf community, the importance of the artistic expressions of our deaf brothers and sisters—who in some cases were rescued through the activities of the project—and the need to make our experiences known to similar communities in other countries.

The answer we received from the Interamerican Foundation was positive. It was agreed that we would participate in both The Deaf Way Conference and in the arts festival, specifically in the areas of mime and dance. The expiration date of the Mano a Mano Project was postponed to September 30, 1989.

The Inter-American Foundation's representative, Kris Krueger, informed us that the Foundation would finance all the operations and management expenses as well as half of the transportation costs to The Deaf Way. To finance the other half of the airfare, we obtained support from government and private entities. Mimes and dance professionals were chosen to take charge of the technical training of our artists, and we held meetings with the people who had worked with the Mano a Mano Project to prepare this final report, which we presented at The Deaf Way.

We continue to meet with representatives of Comunidec, the organization head-quartered in Quito that is responsible for overseeing the implementation of the Mano a Mano program, and with representatives of the Interamerican Foundation.

Project Needs

Although funding for the Mano a Mano Project has ended, many of the workshops and enterprises begun under its aegis continue, as does the need for further support and training of the participants involved in them.

In the area of technical training, the photographers need further instruction in advanced black and white techniques, in using photography in the production of stories and other teaching materials, and in photographic techniques that communicate social and political subjects. They also need help in establishing for-profit ventures such as producing children's school pictures, supplying promotional pictures for other institutions, or making identification card pictures.

Those involved in the planned T-shirt business require formal training in the techniques of serigraphy, including selection of materials, design, integration of photography, production, and marketing. Such training also could enhance the stamped T-shirt workshop.

Deaf people need formal training in the use of video equipment, including techniques of producing and editing videos about sign language, deafness, and the history of deaf education as told by elderly deaf people.

Continuing support is needed for the deaf theater group, including use of the body, ways of incorporating dance in the theater, and training in different schools of thought about technique. We hope to develop more workshops in the areas of puppetry, dance, masks, and music, and to stage performances at deaf schools and for the general public. We believe that the deaf theater should be used as a means of promoting the situation of deaf people within the hearing society and promoting organization and solidarity among deaf people.

In addition, the people involved in all these projects need training in business management: feasibility studies, marketing, and accounting systems. Follow-up is needed in the areas of organization, management, and leadership promotion.

The Society of Deaf Adults Today

The Fray Luis Ponce de León Society of Deaf Adults, which has carried out the Mano a Mano Project, is experiencing needs of its own. Owing to changes in its administration, the Society is facing serious problems at the management level. As a consequence, the organization is fragmented, and the participation of deaf people in daily activities within the Society has decreased. Consistent and firm management directed toward the achievement of specific, concrete objectives is needed. Moreover, the membership of the organization must be increased, and its actions must be strengthened.

The new board of the Society, which includes the authors of this paper, has an opportunity to give the project and the Society new order and direction and possesses the necessary experience to do so.

Membership can be increased by offering more services for deaf people and more activities of interest to deaf people such as the following:

❖ Literacy program (The Society, with the support of the government's Office of Literacy, should reinstate the informal classes that constituted the literacy program.)

❖ Lectures and programs for deaf people in the areas of sports, culture, business, and higher education

❖ Activities and classes for women, including talks about home economics, cooking, sewing, and carpentry

❖ Support for the use of sign language, the manual alphabet, reading, and writing throughout all of the Society's activities.

The Society must also increase its activities directed toward the hearing community by

❖ Providing support to parents and information about deafness from the point of view of deaf people

❖ Promoting sign language by offering classes for hearing teachers, parents, and the general public

❖ Training hearing people to work as interpreters for deaf people at schools and universities, special courses, public meetings, and when needed in legal, medical, and personal matters

❖ Promoting the interaction of deaf children and youth with deaf adults through services and activities directed toward the schools for deaf students

❖ Promoting the organization of a census to locate deaf people in both cities and the more isolated parts of the country—such efforts should be coordinated with the appropriate public institutions.

Conclusion

As a result of the programs developed under the Mano a Mano Project, changes have occurred in deaf individuals and in the Society for Deaf Adults as a whole. Members of the Society and its Board are using managerial practices that, as recently as three years ago, they didn't even know existed. A deaf person is now in charge of accounting, and accounting classes are taught by a deaf person. Three years ago the Society had no system to control the distribution of materials and equipment; now there is an inventory system. A deaf person is now in charge of accounting, and a deaf person teaches the accounting classes. Society meetings are now better organized, with an agenda and a moderator, and administrative terms and concepts are used regularly.

Today members of the Society of Deaf Adults are able to discuss many matters related to deaf education, communication, organization and training of deaf people, integration of hearing people in the deaf community, human rights, and the needs of deaf people. Three years ago curiosity about those subjects did not exist. Perhaps the major success of the project up to now was never even considered as an original goal: The minds and hearts of deaf people have been stimulated to consider their conditions and their potentials.

Deaf People's Civil Rights to Information

JOSEPH COLLINS

The London Deaf Video Project (LDVP) was established four years ago in 1985. At that time, the Greater London Council (GLC) was running a campaign to inform ethnic minority groups about the welfare benefits to which they were entitled. Leaflets were published in minority languages such as Hindi, and there were posters and advertisements all over London from which hearing people could get full information.

However, because the average reading age of a profoundly deaf person leaving school is eight and a half years—functionally illiterate—much of the printed information was not getting through to the London deaf community. Deaf people did not fully understand the written information and therefore were not claiming the benefits to which they were entitled from the Department of Health or other social service agencies.

It occurred to the British Deaf Association (BDA) and Paddy Ladd, a deaf man with experience working in television, that the GLC should be translating English information about welfare benefits and other social services into British Sign Language (BSL) for the deaf community. The BDA and Ladd argued that if the GLC were translating information into minority languages in leaflet form, it should produce visual information in British Sign Language on video also. They recommended further that the GLC provide videotape recorders to London deaf clubs to make it possible for deaf people to view the tapes.

Both Ladd and the BDA had some experience in the world of video, and their arguments convinced the GLC, which granted the money to set up the London Deaf Video Project in November, 1985.

The LDVP team, which includes four people (three deaf and one hearing), arrived at work in 1985 to find a bare room. They needed to start from scratch, and many questions needed to be answered: How many videos should they make? How would they contact deaf people? Did the deaf clubs have video machines? The team arranged an open meeting, which was attended by twenty-four deaf people from fifteen London clubs. Together, they made a list of twenty-seven subjects on which they thought information should be made available in BSL on video.

The team was pleased with the open meeting, but twenty-seven topics! They needed to prioritize them. They decided that AIDS was the most important subject to bring to the awareness of the deaf community. They produced fifty copies of this video. Within a few weeks they had run out of copies, so they produced another batch. The deaf community now had access to the same information about AIDS as the hearing world.

Unfortunately, in April, 1986, after the video project was in operation only a few months, the Greater London Council was abolished, and the project had to close down until further funding could be found. The London Boroughs Grants Unit agreed to fund the project, which reopened in June 1986, and continues to cover most of its costs.

To date, the LDVP has produced videos on AIDS, smoking, the legal rights of gays and lesbians, starting a business, welfare benefits, solicitors, planning for retirement, fundraising, and the black deaf community. Excerpts from some of these videos have been shown on television. A support unit for deaf AIDS sufferers was set up as a result of the AIDS video. The videos have opened up areas of information that previously were inaccessible to deaf people.

That is the history of the project, but what now? What are our plans for the future?

Recently, the LDVP team has met with the representatives of public service providers such as the police, fire brigades, gas companies, electric companies, and insurance companies. Many of them provide informational videos for hearing people, but nothing that deaf people could understand. We have been advising them about adding BSL interpreters to their existing videos, which can be done at an approximate cost of £800 per video. If our negotiations with these public service providers are successful, the deaf community will gain access to a lot more information.

The LDVP has also used deaf narrators to add BSL to a video without using an interpreter. We did this in our "Do It Yourself" youth video. Deaf people found the deaf narrator more fascinating than a hearing interpreter, and the narration was truer to the deaf culture than an interpreter's signing would have been.

In advising public service providers about BSL videos, we find ourselves also teaching about deaf awareness, interpreters, and the use of Minicoms (TTYs), and so on. Making deaf people aware of the public services available to them is not enough if, when they approach the companies and agencies providing these services, they find no one who understands their needs or is able to communicate with them.

The LDVP team has met with the personnel of other video projects, deaf and hearing, to share advice and friendly criticism and to encourage growth and improvement. In this way, we have helped producers of videos for hearing people become more aware of the needs of deaf people.

Recently we had a one-day trial video workshop for deaf people. It went well, in part because it was led by a deaf tutor instead of a hearing tutor with an interpreter. Participants were able to share ideas on camera shots and scripts freely. The workshop gave them a better understanding of video, encouraged a greater interest in media work, and we hope, motivated them to take other television and video courses.

We choose our video presenters from among the members of the grass-roots deaf community, hoping to encourage them to go into television and video work. Some really do have hidden talent, and we try to bring this out to provide them with experience for the future.

This September we will add another deaf person to our staff to serve as an outreach worker. This person will encourage the use of BSL information videos in deaf clubs, schools, and libraries. We feel it is important for our project to improve its links with the deaf clubs in this way. Because deaf clubs are slow to answer letters and, of course, do not use the telephone, the outreach worker will communicate with their members face-to-face in BSL. The outreach worker also will encourage schools and libraries to stock BSL videos for deaf people in their areas. We hope that, as a result, schools and libraries will exhibit greater awareness of the deaf community and deaf culture in London and Britain. This work looks promising, and we hope it will be successful.

We also have plans for a video roadshow, to be held in September [1989] in London, which will raise awareness among both deaf and hearing people of the video project and the use of the medium. We are always trying to improve ways of influencing grass-roots deaf people, but our tight budget is a problem.

The LDVP studios are nothing like the film studios of Hollywood. We have struggled to acquire the necessary equipment and so far have only one camera, several video recorders, and lights. We rent editing equipment when necessary, but hope to acquire more editing equipment of our own.

The LDVP is still climbing the mountain. Our work will be complete only when the local and central governments realize their responsibility to pay for the production of BSL information videos to provide deaf people with the same access to information as hearing people.

Meanwhile, we continue to make contacts and spread the word. There was a successful deaf video festival in Bulgaria last year. It would be nice to hold a similar festival in England sometime in the future. As a result of the Bulgarian festival, we have made good connections with other European deaf video projects, with whom we exchange videoletters to share ideas. It is wonderful to be able to use sign language rather than written English: With video there is no problem communicating.

The European Commission Regional Secretariat of the World Federation of the Deaf has backed the use of video for disseminating information to the deaf community. In a motion put before the European Parliament, the secretariat urged the member states to ensure that all relevant government circulars on welfare benefits, health, and employment be produced using sign language on video for the use of the deaf community. If this motion is passed, all government public information by law be must be translated into sign language on video for deaf people. This really would be the peak of the mountain!

In Britain we have a long way to go—but we have made a start. What about your country? What are you and your national deaf association doing to make public information accessible to your deaf community? Do you already have a deaf video project similar to ours? LDVP would like to hear about it. Or would you like to set up a video project but you're not sure how to begin? Let us know, and maybe we can help.

So come on, get those cameras out and start the film rolling! Let's get the information out to the deaf people who need it.

Deaf President Now

MARY C. MALZKUHN, JERRY COVELL, GREG HLIBOK, AND BRIDGETTA BOURNE-FIRL

I n March of 1988, Gallaudet University became the focus of worldwide attention as students and alumni closed the campus for seven dramatic days to
protest the appointment of a hearing person as president of the University. The
protest—which became known by the chant repeated throughout the week,
"Deaf President Now!"—was lauded for the nonviolence, organization, and
effectiveness of its actions, and for the justice and timeliness of its cause.

In its 124-year history, Gallaudet University had been served by six presidents, all
of them hearing. As the Gallaudet Board of Trustees considered candidates to replace
the outgoing president, support grew in the University and the deaf community for the
appointment of a deaf person. Indeed, because a number of qualified deaf people were
among the final candidates, many expected that Gallaudet would soon have its first deaf
president.

When the Board of Trustees, composed predominantly of hearing people, passed
over two highly qualified deaf academics with many years of experience in deaf education in favor of a hearing university administrator who had only limited contact with
deaf people and sign language, the University community was shocked and outraged.

The student leaders of the Deaf President Now protest, with the help of Gallaudet alumni, leaders of the deaf community, and members of the Gallaudet faculty and
staff, channeled that shock and outrage into a peaceful protest that not only won the
appointment of Gallaudet's first deaf president and the establishment of a deaf majority
on the Board of Trustees, but also succeeded in changing the way millions of people
around the world, both hearing and deaf, think about the capabilities and potential of
deaf people.

At a Deaf Way symposium chaired by Mary C. Malzkuhn, three of the four student
leaders of the Deaf President Now (DPN) council, Jerry Covell, Bridgetta Bourne-Firl,
and Greg Hlibok, gave their impressions of the events of that momentous week.

MARY MALZKUHN: I am very pleased to be introducing three of my former students
today. I am proud of the role they and Tim Rarus, another former student of mine who
could not be with us today, played in the Deaf President Now (DPN) protest in March
1988. The first speaker I will introduce is Jerry Covell. During many of the interviews
he has had since DPN, Jerry puzzled me when he claimed that I was somehow behind
the protest. I was puzzled because I didn't really get very involved during the protest
itself. I didn't have tenure yet and was working on my dissertation to get that out of
the way. Finally, I went to Jerry and asked, "Why do you keep saying I was behind the
protest?" He said that in my class I was always focusing on specific legal cases, particularly those involving constitutional law. When I did this with regard to laws concerning

human rights and minorities, I would always ask, "Well, what about the deaf?" Jerry said he hated that question, but eventually it really hit him that human rights issues have direct relevance to deaf people. Who would have guessed then, though, the impact this understanding would soon have on his and other people's actions during the DPN protest?

JERRY COVELL: I'm very happy to be here today, and I'm happy that you could be here to share our experiences as we reflect on that time—after sixteen months, we can say "reflect."

When our former president, Dr. Lee, decided to resign his position to work for the company of one of the members of the Board of Trustees,[1] we students had never really thought about having a deaf president. Though there was some talk among ourselves, we didn't seriously consider the possibility until December 1987 or January 1988. At that time, a group called "The Ducks" was formed. This was a group of seven or eight men, most from Gallaudet or formerly from Gallaudet, who were all strong leaders in the deaf community.[2] They decided that it was important, in fact key, to get the students involved in having a deaf president. So in January they started planning for a rally the following March, March 1st. They asked students to participate, and I agreed.

I can recall going to the cafeteria to talk to the students, saying that we must have a deaf president. The students said that a deaf person could not be president of the University because the president has to use the phone and deal with Congress. If Gallaudet were to survive, they said, we must have a hearing president: There was no way a deaf person could be president of Gallaudet if the University were to continue. When I saw that I thought, "can't . . . ," and I wondered. And of course I felt hurt because I thought a deaf person could do the job. So I continued to go to the cafeteria.

By the way, the reason I went to the cafeteria was that it is the best place on campus to reach a large number of students. The academic buildings are too spread out. The cafeteria is the one place where I could talk to most of the student body. It's the place to share information and ideas. For weeks I talked, and there was a promotion stressing the importance of having a deaf president.

Then the rally drew near. The Board of Trustees was considering six candidates for the position of president, three hearing and three deaf. We were ecstatic—three deaf people had made the final cut. So let's say there were ten hearing applicants and five deaf applicants, and the list was narrowed down to three deaf and three hearing finalists. It showed that deaf people could make it that far. It meant we could do more.

The last week of February, the Board of Trustees announced that there were three finalists for the position, and surprisingly, two of them were deaf.[3] So we all felt fairly sure that there would be a deaf president for the University. It would happen. We were all very sure that we couldn't lose.

Then came March 1, the day of the rally.[4] Everyone turned out, students, faculty,

---

1 Dr. Jerry C. Lee, Gallaudet University president from 1984 to 1987, resigned the presidency to take a position with a company owned by the family of Gallaudet University Board of Trustees Chair Jane Bassett Spilman.

2 In his book *The Week the World Heard Gallaudet* (1989, Washington, DC: Gallaudet University Press), Jack R. Gannon identifies the members of this group as Paul Singleton, Jeff Rosen, Fred Weiner, Mike O'Donnell, Jamie Tucker, and Steve Hlibok.

3 The three finalists were Dr. I. King Jordan, Dean of the College of Arts and Sciences at Gallaudet, Dr. Harvey J. Corson, Superintendent of the Louisiana School for the Deaf, and Dr. Elisabeth Ann Zinser, Vice Chancellor of the University of North Carolina at Greensboro. Drs. Jordan and Corson are deaf; Dr. Zinser, hearing.

4 The rally, organized by the group of alumni Covell refers to as "The Ducks" and held at the Gallaudet football field, drew a crowd estimated at 1,500—500 more than the organizers expected. The theme of the rally was "The Time is Now!" Speakers at the March 1 rally included Gary Olsen, executive director of the National Association of the Deaf; Yerker Andersson, president of the World Federation of the Deaf; Roslyn Rosen, dean of Gallaudet's

and staff. No one was in a teaching mood that day. All came to see what would be said. Speakers from all over the country stressed the importance of having a deaf president. One presenter—I can't remember who it was—said, "This is Gallaudet, a school for deaf people, the only one in the world. Yet in the buildings here the public phones are not accessible to deaf people. You have to go to an office and plead to borrow one— and hope that it's not broken—and search around to find a TTY you can use. That's outrageous! If we had a deaf president, he would make sure that all the phones in the buildings were accessible to deaf people."

I'll always remember that day. We had high hopes. We felt positive we would win.

Then on Sunday, March 6th, the shock came. The Board of Trustees announced that Dr. Elisabeth Ann Zinser, a hearing person, had been selected as president of the University. The news came in the form of a press release that read, "Gallaudet University is proud to announce the appointment of the first woman president in the history of the University."

[On the evening of Sunday, March 6, a crowd of Gallaudet students, staff, and alumni had gathered at the campus expecting a formal announcement by the board. They were angered both by the board's choice of a hearing president and the fact that the choice was made public through a press release and not in an address to the university community.]

Now I'll be honest with you. I've got nothing against women. I think highly of women. But Jesus! Why not a deaf president instead of a woman president? We asked for a deaf president; we never asked for a woman. To make things worse, she was hearing. That was it! We really blew up. The crowd went wild and marched to the Mayflower Hotel, where the Board of Trustees was staying. As soon as we read that paper, we hit the streets.

[The crowd of Gallaudet students and their supporters that poured out of the campus and onto Florida Avenue that night did not have a permit to demonstrate. District of Columbia police, however, unable to communicate effectively with the demonstrators, chose to provide an escort to the hotel, blocking off traffic along the way. The crowd gathered at the entrance to the hotel, demanding an explanation. Board of Trustees Chair Spilman eventually consented to meet with the protesters' three representatives, SBG President Greg Hlibok, Past SBG President Tim Rarus, and Jeff Rosen, an attorney and Gallaudet alumnus.]

The Board was having a leisurely dinner when they were suddenly interrupted by a crowd of students, complete with police cars and flashing lights. They were scared, and I think that was when they first realized we were angry. We told them that they had betrayed us. We had worked, we had held a rally, we had collected petitions and letters of support from congressmen and presidential candidates. Yet they would dare to ignore our request—one of the most simple and logical of requests—they would dare to ignore it? And they thought we would accept their decision? *No!*

Our representatives demanded that Mrs. Spilman come down and speak to the crowd, and she agreed, though she didn't appreciate the fact that we had interrupted her meal. People have always bowed down to her. By the time she came down, we had already waited for two or three hours, and many of us had left for the White House to protest there. We screamed and yelled outside the White House gate, hoping to wake the president. After a while, we decided to march to the Capitol, but the Capitol Police were lined up and would not let us pass. Finally, we went back to Gallaudet.

College for Continuing Education; B. J. Wood, commissioner of the Massachusetts Commission for the Deaf and the Hard of Hearing; and representatives of the students, staff, and faculty of Gallaudet University. The featured speaker of the event was Jack Levesque, executive director of the Deaf Counseling, Advocacy and Referral Agency of California.

Can you imagine what that night was like? We had marched from Gallaudet all the way downtown to the Mayflower Hotel, then to the White House, then to the Capitol, and finally back to Gallaudet. It was good exercise for all of us, and a way to use that energy. I didn't even feel it; I was so intent on having a deaf president. That was all I could think of.

When we got back to campus, we started talking about what we needed to do to close the University. We set up committees of people who would handle closing the gates and moving cars to block the entrances. When morning came, we had succeeded; campus was closed. Even Gallaudet Security was nowhere to be found. The best part was when the faculty arrived at campus Monday morning and found that school was closed. They hastily parked their cars in the neighborhood and joined the protest. There were some who felt that what we were doing was wrong and went back home, but many felt the same way we did and joined the effort, even though their illegally parked cars were being towed away.

We wanted a meeting with the board, and we had established four demands:

1. The hearing person selected as president must leave. (That was Dr. Zinser. We signed it "sinner" because "Zinser" sounds like "sinner." It was awful, but that's the way we signed it. Anyway, she must go, and she must be replaced by a deaf person.)
2. Mrs. Spilman must resign from the Board of Trustees.
3. The board must have a majority of deaf members.
4. There must be no reprisals or reprimands against any of the students, faculty, staff, or anyone in the Gallaudet community involved in the protest.

[The Board of Trustees had agreed to meet that day, Monday, with representatives of the students and then to hold an informational session for the campus community at the Gallaudet field house. A delegation of two faculty members, two staff members, and ten students met with the board. After several hours of discussion and negotiation, the board decided to reject all four of the protesters' demands.

At the meeting in the field house, Mrs. Spilman addressed the crowd, but before she could finish her statement, Dr. Harvey Goodstein, a math professor and a member of the delegation, announced that the board had refused the students' demands and encouraged the crowd to walk out.]

When we met with the trustees, we saw that they hadn't listened. Chairperson Spilman got up and said that the board had already reached a decision and that Dr. Zinser was overqualified for the position. At this point she was interrupted, and there was general chaos in the room. We knew her answer was no. The room went wild with noise. Mrs. Spilman stood in front of all of us and said, "I can't hear you." Someone pulled the fire alarm. Lights were flashing and the siren was blaring in the gym. The crowd of people revolted in a rage and marched out of the gym and out onto the street. Again we marched to the White House and the Capitol, angry to the point that we weren't thinking straight. We finally marched back to the University.

When we got back to campus, we decided that the school must remain closed. There was confusion; there was no clear chain of command. The DPN protest involved the faculty, staff, students, alumni, and the deaf community. We didn't know who was in charge. We talked and talked, and it was tough. We kept the school closed and worked until we had established the DPN Council.

The president of the student body, Greg Hlibok, was at the top of the organizational structure. There were three officers under him: Tim, Bridgetta, and me. Each of us headed a committee. Everyone was involved in sharing ideas. By then it was Tuesday, and the school was still closed.

There were rumors floating about that the police might try to ram the gate. We had also heard that Dr. Zinser might be brought in by helicopter, so people were on their guard, searching the sky for intruders. We were ready to lie on the ground to prevent any helicopter from landing. Each car that came in was searched; we asked to look in the trunks to make sure that Dr. Zinser did not try to sneak in to take control of the University. We did not want her to set foot on campus.

On Tuesday there were many threats saying we did not have the authority to do what we were doing. We were on guard at each entrance to the campus. We decided that we needed the Gallaudet buses to block the gates. Students used their cars to push the buses into place at the entrances. Later we were able to get hold of the keys and drove the buses into place. To make it more difficult for anyone to move the buses, we flattened the tires. They couldn't be moved. We had secured the campus, and that was a great feeling.

Many of the faculty and staff had joined our effort. They voted to support the protest and the students.[5] The deaf community supported us. Deaf schools voiced their support. People all over the world supported the effort. We were strong and felt the board had no choice but to give up. But they didn't. They stubbornly hung in there, and so did we.

[On Wednesday, March 9, SBG President Greg Hlibok appeared with Gallaudet President Zinser and actress Marlee Matlin on ABC's "Nightline."]

Around midnight on Thursday, we received the news that Dr. Zinser had resigned her position. She said that the school should be left to deaf people now. Remember, a president without support cannot succeed. She said that rather than hurt Gallaudet she would resign.

The students celebrated, calling everyone together by pulling the fire alarms. We all went to the gym to find out what had happened and if it was true that Dr. Zinser had resigned.

[On Friday, March 11, there was another march from the Gallaudet campus to the U.S. Capitol, this one organized by the National Association of the Deaf.]

You might think that one of our demands was met at this point, but we actually still had 3½ demands left. The first demand was that Dr. Zinser must resign *and* be replaced by a deaf president. She had resigned, but there was no deaf president. So half of that demand was still left. The next morning, when between 3,000 and 5,000 of us marched on the Capitol, we chanted "3½!, 3½!" Some of Gallaudet's neighbors walked with us or joined in the chorus by blowing their car horns as they drove by, in a gesture of solidarity. We kept the message of "3½!" going and rallied at the Capitol with much fanfare before dispersing to meet with the senators from our states. It was a good day; the sun was out and it was beautiful. It was exciting.

On Saturday, we held "Board Busters" day. We served "board burgers" and enjoyed a picnic.

[Meanwhile, the campus remained closed as students, supporters, and members of the press awaited further word from the Board of Trustees. The DPN council continued to meet twice a day.

On the evening of Sunday, March 13, SBG President Greg Hlibok was summoned to receive a TTY call from Trustee Philip Bravin. Bravin announced that the Board of Trustees had chosen

---

5 On Wednesday, March 9, the Gallaudet faculty voted 147 to 5 in support of the students' demands.

Dr. I. King Jordan as the next president of Gallaudet and that Jane Bassett Spilman had resigned from the board. The trustees would choose a task force to appoint new members of a reconstituted, majority-deaf board, of which Bravin himself would be the new chair. No action would be taken against anyone involved in the protest.]

On Sunday, it was all over. We heard that the board was going to make an announcement. The rest, as you know, is history.

BRIDGETTA BOURNE-FIRL: I would first of all like to comment on something Mary Malzkuhn mentioned earlier. It is true that in her government class, we were always talking about civil rights issues as they related to black people and other minority groups. Mary was always asking that question about human rights and deaf people. Why is it, she would say, that these other groups are always mentioned in discussions about civil rights, but never deaf people? We heard this over and over, as if a nail were being driven into our heads. Finally, we decided we should protest so we would get good grades in Mary's class.

I would like to emphasize that the DPN protest succeeded because of all the different skills people brought to it. People brought their own talents to our efforts that week, and no person was considered any better than another. For example, when we needed to move the buses to block the gates, a student from NYC who was skilled at hot-wiring used his talents to help. He looked like someone who might belong to a gang—rough looking, with shaggy hair—but he had a contribution to make. Everyone used his or her skills to make the protest successful. I would like to talk about the skills that got me involved with the protest.

I remember that first Sunday night of the protest, when everyone was in the street after they announced that a hearing woman had been made president of the University. That was a real blow. We had such expectations, and they were not met. I personally had thought that the Board of Trustees would listen to us. They had received so many letters from individuals, organizations, and politicians.

I had felt so sure they would follow our wishes and select a deaf person to be president that I stayed in my room that night to study (it was getting close to exam time). But my conscience was nagging at me. I went to the gym—that's where the Board was to make their announcement—but it was empty. I asked where everyone was and I was told they were in the street. So I rushed down to the street to find deaf people sitting in the middle of it, blocking traffic. Florida Avenue is a major road with fast-moving traffic, but that night it was filled with angry deaf people.

When I got there someone handed me a paper. The first line read, "First Woman President of Gallaudet University." I looked at it in shock. I'm a woman and I support women, but I looked at the mass of deaf people in the street and thought, "I support women *but wait*—I support deaf people first." I threw down the paper and joined the crowd. I was angry because I had thought the Board of Trustees would listen to us. When they didn't it was a shock. For a long time the quiet requests and demands of deaf people have been ignored. This time we clearly said that we wanted a deaf person to lead this university—and they *still* ignored us. We couldn't believe that! Furious, we marched to the Mayflower hotel, shouting and ranting.

When we got there three men from the group of protesters went up to talk with Jane Spilman. The angry crowd was downstairs, restless. I was watching all the men doing the talking, giving orders. There were other women there, but none was in charge, and that bothered me.

Then a good friend, Paul Singleton, asked, "who here knows how to cheerlead?" I was a cheerleader! I was a cheerleader for my high school basketball and football teams and for my first two years at Gallaudet. I know people think that cheerleading is frivolous, but I have always thought of it as a sport. I grabbed that opportunity to get up and lead a cheer, "Spilman Out!" From that point, the crowd expected me to continue running the show. That night I held to that role and, as a result, I became one of the student leaders. So cheerleading was the skill that got me involved in the protest.

Being at The Deaf Way conference is really a thrill. I just arrived from traveling in Europe, and I'm feeling a little jet lagged—I'm sure many of you are feeling that way too—but since I've been here this morning and seen that our message is out there, I know that we *will* have a better future. That's certain.

Often when we have a great experience and are inspired by what we have learned, we want to bring it home and share it. When people back home who didn't share our experience don't understand our enthusiasm, it can be frustrating. We go back to our jobs and back to business as usual, and we can experience a let-down. Don't let that happen. Carry the inspiration home. Work to share it, and we will support you all the way. We wish you the best of luck as you fight to get what you want in your home countries.

GREG HLIBOK: The months of February and March 1988 were the most hectic time of my life. In February, I was running for the office of SBG president. I was also in the probationary period of joining a fraternity, and there were several fraternity rules I had to follow. It was a very exciting time, but I never dreamed of what would happen to me the very next month.

The day I finished my probationary period with the fraternity I participated in the first meeting of a group of deaf leaders. At that meeting, we planned a March 1 rally to impress upon the Board of Trustees that we meant business—that we wanted a deaf president. At that time many students, faculty, and staff members were talking about having a deaf president. We were optimistic that a deaf person would be selected. Because two out of the three finalists were deaf, we felt that we had a 66 percent chance to have a deaf president.

On February 29th, I was inaugurated as president of the SBG. The next day was the rally. My first speech as president was during that rally. It was all new to me, and I was just getting my feet wet. After that, I was in a whirlwind of activity.

There had been a lot of discussion in February, but we never really talked about plans for a protest. We never planned for a protest—we planned the protest while it was happening. We planned everything at the last minute, but it worked perfectly. It was wonderful.

I'll never forget those moments. I wouldn't trade those times for anything. I really must thank every deaf individual for giving us the sheer numbers we needed. And it was their support and spirit that gave us the inspiration we needed. The fact that so many deaf people were behind us gave us confidence to do what we wanted to do, to get our way.

Deaf people were the key to our success. The protest never would have happened if it were run by hearing people—never. It worked because we are deaf. Deaf people have a special bond. Bridgetta Bourne and I recently toured Europe. In Europe, when we'd see a deaf person there was an instant link between us. Hearing people don't have that kind of connection.

On the first day of the protest, when we found out that Dr. Zinser had been appointed, we marched in fury to the hotel where the board was staying. We took control of the street. The police tried to stop us by talking to us through bull horns, but we couldn't hear them, so we just kept going. When they figured out that we were deaf, they left us alone. If we had been hearing, the police could have used the fact that we ignored them as an argument to arrest us. Because we were deaf, they let us go.

Another factor that contributed to the success of the DPN protest was the attention of the media—I call them Ted Koppell and Company. The media were our best friends; there is no question about it. The media carried our message to the world. In China there were articles in the newspaper. In Europe there were articles in the newspaper. News of the protest spread throughout the world. The media's response to our protest was like a chemical reaction. They were drawn to our story, and they fed on it. The first march was Sunday. By Monday the media people were running after us. There were radio, press, and TV reporters at the campus. I remember it very well. During the first few days, the staff and students were eager to talk with them when they approached us for interviews. During the last few days, we actually avoided them, avoided those questions—especially me. I set up a schedule of times when I could be interviewed.

The reporters enjoyed their time with us. When the week was over, some of them were so happy for us that they cried along with us. Even though they were supposed to be neutral, many said is was one of the best experiences of their lives. They truly lived with us for that week and became our best friends. I must commend the media people.

I'd like to share one experience from "Nightline." I had done many interviews during the week, but I strongly believe that a turning point in our protest was the Wednesday night program of "Nightline," which has an international audience.

Before the show, I was very nervous. I met Ted Koppell, and we talked for a few minutes about the interview. During that thirty-minute interview, Dr. Zinser was hit over and over with various viewpoints. Marlee Matlin made statements. I made statements. Ted Koppell made a closing statement. Dr. Zinser was pummeled with attacks. We really wore her out. I must give special thanks to Ted Koppell. At the end of his program, he usually presents his reaction to the discussion. At the end of our session, he told Dr. Zinser that she appeared to be acting as a puppet of the Board of Trustees. She was really crushed by that statement. She left the studio immediately afterward. We celebrated; we knew Koppell's remark was significant. Millions of viewers in America and around the world had seen that moment. We were thrilled. Within the next twenty-four hours Dr. Zinser resigned, canceled the interviews she was scheduled to give, and disappeared from public view. She stayed home and talked with her lawyers. After that, the students' enthusiasm really took off, and I want to thank the media for making that happen. Thanks to Koppell and Company.

After the Gallaudet Protest was over, many organizations—*many*—called the SBG office asking for guidelines on how to run a successful protest. They wanted textbooks. They wanted speakers to talk about the protest. I had to tell them honestly: If you're hearing, it's going to be more difficult. You know that quote "Deaf people can do anything, except hear." We turned it around and said, "Hearing people can do anything except be deaf." If you're deaf, a protest will be easier.

DPN was a first in history. The protest actually brought Gallaudet to a halt for that week. I've never heard of any student protest that actually paralyzed a university for a week. But we did it. We paralyzed Gallaudet—took complete control of the campus. It was really a wonderful experience, quite a thrill. We told the police what to do on campus. We controlled everything. It all worked so beautifully because it was done in a nonviolent way. We succeeded because we were able to make a positive impression on the world.

The DPN protest was successful, and the results can be summed up in three Rs:

1. Recognition—We got a lot of recognition around the world. People now recognize the needs of the deaf community.
2. Respect—There is now greater respect for deaf people's needs.
3. Responsibility—And that belongs to all of us. We deaf people have the responsibility to control our own destinies. We are the ones who run our own lives!

I'm pleased to be here to talk about what happened during the DPN protest, but I don't want you to think we're just focusing on the past. This story—this past—is a tool we can use to fight in the future. We will be united. There will always be a cause. There will always be room for improvement. The deaf community will look at us, learn from us, and use our experience as a tool for the future.

Deaf Studies Before and After the Revolution

HARLAN LANE

We are gathered here from all parts of the globe to celebrate deafness; to celebrate the Deaf way. The French title of this meeting says it clearly: Vivre la surdité! Long live deafness.

What is there to celebrate? The flourishing of Deaf arts. The thriving field of Deaf history. The burgeoning study of sign languages. The growing awareness of Deaf culture. The courage of our young Deaf leaders. And mounting hearing acceptance of the Deaf difference. Vivre la différence! Vivre la surdité.

There are those who say, "You cannot 'celebrate' deafness—you can only regret it." Let them come here and learn. There are those who measure deafness only in terms of loss, not in terms of gain. Let them come here and learn. Here they will find art, not audiograms; language, not laryngology; culture and communication. Let them come here and learn. There are those who say, "It's a hearing world." Let them come here and see that it's a Deaf world, too.

Deaf people have an inalienable right to be different. The acceptance of this right will grow only as our knowledge of the Deaf way grows and spreads. Knowledge of the Deaf way is called, collectively, Deaf studies. Deaf studies includes the Deaf arts—dance, design, film and TV, narrative, painting, poetry, theater. It includes Deaf history, contemporary and past; government, law and Deaf people; the examination of Deaf education—its conduct and its consequences; sign languages—their analysis, instruction, and interpretation; and systematic reflection on Deaf culture—from church to sports, from family studies to the workplace. Deaf studies is all this and much more.

To embrace Deaf studies is to celebrate, study, teach, and learn the rainbow of our existence. Its premise is pluralism. It is incompatible with paternalism. The Deaf Frenchman who founded education of Deaf children in America, Laurent Clerc, understood this well. "Every creature," Clerc wrote, "every work of God, is admirably made. We vary in our forms and functions, in our hearts and minds. We can only thank God for the rich diversity of His creation" (Lane, 1986).

Some readers will recognize my intellectual debt to Albert Memmi, Frantz Fanon, Paolo Freire, and Sally Tomlinson. I am grateful to Professor Tony Smith of Tufts University and to Charlotte Baker-Shenk of Western Maryland University for guiding me to these sources and discussing their thoughts with me. Franklin Philip provided some useful observations on the women's movement, and he and William Isham criticized the first draft of this address. I would also like to acknowledge helpful exchanges with Susan Rutherford (University of California, Berkeley), Penny Boyes Braem (Forschungzentrum für Gebärdensprache, Basel), and Sherman Wilcox (University of New Mexico). The 1985 *Report of the Task Force on Deaf Studies* of the Gallaudet University Deafness-Related Concerns Council, Barbara Kannapell, Chairperson, was a valuable resource.

Deaf studies programs in our schools and universities contribute to scholarship and improve the lives of Deaf and hearing people, but Deaf studies exists with or without formal acceptance by hearing institutions. There were no Deaf studies programs when, in the late 1700s, the first deaf author—Pierre Desloges—published his study of French Sign Language and the Paris Deaf community. There were no Deaf studies programs when, nearly a century later, Ferdinand Berthier wrote biographies of Deaf and hearing educators and essays on law and deaf people, nor when, in this century, the American National Association of the Deaf created films of great sign language orators, a heritage for generations to come. There were no programs, but there was important, insightful scholarship in Deaf studies, nevertheless.

The overriding goal of Deaf studies is to understand better the lives of Deaf people so as to improve their lot, just as the goal of women's studies is to understand and improve the lot of women, and the goal of Black studies is to understand and improve the lot of Black people. These and similar disciplines seek to redress a wrong, namely, the oppression of a minority; they are unlike the social sciences because they are explicitly aimed at improving the lives of the group concerned. Deaf studies, like Black studies, is a revolutionary discipline because it seeks to redistribute power through knowledge and reform.

Each of these fields draws on the social sciences and humanities but has its own issues and theories. The intellectual leaders of the women's movement, for example, recognize that women's rights are not simply satisfied by identical treatment with men. Thus, new mothers may need more time off from work than new fathers. When should women be treated the same as men and when different? Black thinkers in America commonly assert that we must redress past wrongs to Black people by now discriminating in their favor. But sometimes benefits work against you in the long run. Does the welfare money the government gives unwed Black mothers make them dependent, discourage them from building careers, and prolong their oppression? Questions like these lie at the heart of Women's studies and Black studies.

What are the central issues in *Deaf* studies? Since the field aims to redress a wrong, namely, the oppression of a minority, it follows that the principles of repression in general, and of oppression of Deaf people in particular, are at the very core of the field. Moreover, wherever you investigate Deaf studies you will find evidence of oppression. If you study language, you will find here a language minority whose people are prohibited from using their language in many walks of life. If you study education, you will find a system that perpetuates a working underclass. If you study history, you will learn about the timeless yearning of Deaf people for a place of their own, and how hearing people stole the rightful place of Deaf adults in the lives of Deaf children. Here are some of the general principles of oppression whose application to Deaf people needs to be examined further by Deaf studies.

Oppression is alienating. The oppressor is on a balance scale with the oppressed; if his level is high economically, socially, or in power, it is only because the other's is low. He may insist on the extreme deficiencies of the oppressed, or on his own distinguished abilities, or both. The oppressor becomes increasingly distanced from the oppressed. Is there indeed alienation between Deaf people and the hearing people who play a role in their lives? Does it arise in part because hearing people insist on their own merits and on the failings of Deaf children and adults? How could the balance be redistributed in favor of Deaf people? Deaf studies is centrally concerned with questions such as these about oppression and alienation.

Oppression is also self-justifying. The purpose of the fantastic devaluation of the oppressed is the overvaluation of the oppressor, and therefore the justification of the oppressor's role. The oppressors seem to say, "The oppressed is less than we are, and, in contrast, we are more than he—why else are we in authority?" Accordingly, Deaf studies needs to examine whether the hearing professions serving Deaf people seek to justify their roles by affirming the *dis*-abilities of Deaf people and, if so, to consider why these professions are concerned with justifying themselves.

Oppression is self-disguising. It aims to hold on to power by hiding its usurpation of power. In an act of mystification, it locates the source of the oppression in the oppressed. The oppressor seems to reason, "Either the oppressed are backward precisely because they are receiving my help, which is unthinkable, or they are backward because they cannot profit from it." The oppressor's belief in the native inferiority of the oppressed supports the entire system. Deaf studies needs to identify the ways in which hearing people disguise their self-interest with regard to Deaf people, and the field needs to demystify their claims.

Oppression is self-fulfilling. By according the oppressed less freedom, less dignity, less power to shape their lives, oppression creates a downtrodden class that seems incapable of wisely managing freedom.

Oppression is self-contradictory. The oppressor wants to recast the oppressed in the image of the oppressor. In the extreme, he wants them to disappear; they are an embarrassment and worse. Yet the oppressor cannot survive without the oppressed; they are necessary to his professional existence.

Oppression is the enemy of true history and true social science. The false history the oppressor writes is not the history of the people he plunders but the history of his own people as regards all they have skimmed off and violated. The social science the oppressor conducts begins with conclusions and ends with clumsy demonstrations.

Oppression is self-selecting. Why has the oppressor chosen to spend his life dealing with the oppressed? If his own kind are so superior, why not stay among them? But the oppressor is a god among the oppressed.

Oppression is self-deluding. The oppressor seeks awards, diplomas, and medals, not only to impress the oppressed but also to reassure himself. His defense is the value of his culture, which he imposes on the oppressed. The more this imposition fails, the more desperate become his embrace of it and his measures to enforce it.

Oppression corrupts the oppressed. Each oppressed society has a pyramid of tyranny. The oppressed who joins the ranks of the oppressors is often worse than the oppressors themselves; he shows haughty disdain for his brothers, for he is aping his masters. When the system is challenged, he defends it aggressively. In the end, he adopts the values of the oppressors, the very values that decree he is less than they are. Such leaders will sit around a felt-covered table with the oppressor and debate the agenda. Isn't it a good sign, they say, that we have been invited to sit down? They will be satisfied by a statement of position and a call for further study. Most of the oppressed are illiterate, but they are the subject of a huge body of literature. The leaders are out of touch with the people who urgently need a better job and better education for their children.

Oppression is structural, not individual. It is a matter of relations between social groups, not a matter of individual decision. A person may chose not to be involved with the oppressed, but once he accepts that involvement he cannot refuse its conditions, which predate his birth and will probably outlast his life. There are no good and bad members of the oppressing class—only those who accept their reality as oppressors and a few who do not. One of these few, a renegade, may struggle for a more equal distribution of power, but the privileges he denounces are those he enjoys. And the oppressors are furious with him. His actions question the validity of theirs. He can take further steps to enter the class of the oppressed, but he is not one of them and does not really want to be—they are different people.

What then can people of good will do? If you are in the oppressing majority, you can become informed and share that information—you can help women or Blacks or Deaf people understand the nature and means of their oppression. If you are in the oppressed minority, you have a special responsibility not only to learn and teach but also to act on behalf of reform. The strength of the oppressed is in their collectivity. Virtually everyone will be cast down or virtually everyone will rise up. Therefore, you must rise up and help your brothers and sisters rise up. The oppressed are capable of improving their lot. In America, the women's suffrage movement, the civil rights movement, the Gallaudet Revolution prove this. Therefore, oppressed people share in the responsibility for their own oppression.

Of all the issues Deaf studies treats, none illustrates better the operation of oppression, and none is more vital to Deaf people themselves than Deaf education. The hearing people in charge of special education are in a position to mystify others—that is, to mask social reality—on behalf of their own interests. For example, teachers of Deaf people continually make judgments about the capabilities of the pupils they teach, judgments often based on social rather than educational criteria. Hearing teachers label as multiply-handicapped an incredible one-third of all deaf children in America. Most of these children, condemned to vegetate for ten years in an environment in which learning is not possible for them, are said to have a so-called learning disorder. Black Deaf children and signing Deaf children are, in addition, promiscuously labeled as emotionally disturbed (Wolff and Harkins, 1986; Lane, 1988). This is a mystification of the role of the teacher and the school in the failure of education. Most of these children come from the laboring classes, and the education they receive ensures that they will stay in the laboring classes.

All over the world, powerful social groups are categorizing and classifying weaker social groups and treating them unequally. The rationalizations differ, but benevolent humanitarianism is a common one. This explanation denies and masks the vested interests of hearing teachers, administrators, and other professionals. For example, it is not benevolent humanitarianism that has largely excluded Deaf people from the profession of teaching Deaf people; it is, instead, economic self-interest.

Before the Gallaudet Revolution, it was possible for the field of Deaf studies to accept uncritically the explanations that people with power gave for their actions. Many thought about Deaf education without making allowance for conflict. The field of Deaf studies considered the special needs of Deaf children in special education but failed to consider the needs and interests of the teachers and others with power who have shaped Deaf education into the form it now has.

Then came the Gallaudet Revolution, laying bare the conflicts among various interests in Deaf education. It was Deaf studies that made the Gallaudet Revolution possible, for outrage requires a standard of just treatment. Once Deaf leaders came to understand, thanks to Deaf studies, that they were members of a linguistic and cultural minority in America, they saw hearing paternalism no longer as benevolent concern for their welfare but as blatant and intolerable discrimination against them. Now, after the Gallaudet Revolution, pre-revolutionary oppressed forms of thinking are no longer possible. Deaf studies knows now that it must examine critically the roles assigned to teachers, parents, pupils, and professionals. Pupils are associated in Deaf education with negative attributes: incapacity, inability, and powerlessness. Parents are viewed as incompetent. Teachers are trained only to combat the supposed special limitations of the pupils, as the system perceives them, and not actually to instruct in academic subjects. Teachers and professionals tend to come from socially dominant groups. Professionals are outside and above the working-class clientele that accepts the mystique of their superior abilities and rational decisions.

In short, the field of Deaf studies in America has grown up and lost its taste for fairy tales. It now knows that a first priority is to acquire a wider social, historical, and political perspective on Deaf education.

Who Should Study Deaf Studies?

Deaf leaders are crucial consumers of Deaf studies, for they must provide the intellectual leadership of the Deaf minority. They must draw up the agenda for reform, and they must carry it out. They will do this more intelligently and successfully if their knowledge spans the whole spectrum of Deaf studies and if, with that knowledge, they have analyzed and refined the great issues of oppression that face their minority. Shall Deaf people grasp the banner of "handicapped," with all the short-term benefits it brings, or will they find that banner masks the unique language and culture of Deaf people? Shall Deaf people strive for more success on hearing terms—better English literacy, wider acceptance in the job market—or shall they seek also to change those terms by working for better sign language literacy and developing Deaf markets? Shall Deaf leaders aim to rally all the community in behalf of a few clearly stated reforms, or shall they recognize the enormous diversity of Deaf people by qualifying their goals—at the risk of qualified progress?

Deaf scholars are not only consumers of Deaf studies but are also among its producers—and this is vital. Whether the subject is Deaf culture, Deaf language, or Deaf arts, the Deaf scholar brings a unique insight, intuition, and creative imagination to the process of discovery, theorizing, and dissemination. Few would take seriously the pronouncements of a group of male scholars about the behavior of women, or descriptions by a group of exclusively white scholars about the lives of Blacks. Why is it then that our scientific journals have accepted as gospel the most irresponsible and insulting claims about Deaf people, made by hearing people without Deaf collaboration?

The present shortage of Deaf scholars is a very great limitation on the field of Deaf studies. Deaf people, like Black people, are hampered in their efforts to describe and overcome their oppression by the oppressive nature of the education they receive. If all Deaf college students had the opportunity to learn about the history, social and linguistic structures, and arts of their nation's Deaf community, the field of Deaf studies would win the commitment of more Deaf scholars. It would leap forward, and so would efforts to improve the lives of Deaf people.

But Deaf college students and Deaf adults in general will find it rewarding to pursue Deaf studies for some more personal reasons. In learning through Deaf history about the lives of Deaf people before them, they can imagine more possible lives for themselves. In learning about Deaf society, Deaf education, and Deaf culture, they can better equip themselves to be advocates for Deaf people. In seeing their personal struggles projected onto the screen of the Deaf arts, they can better understand what is unique to them and what in their struggle they share with millions of other Deaf people. And they can laugh and cry and rage and applaud as timeless Deaf themes touch them deeply. It is no simple matter, however, to bring Deaf studies to most Deaf adults. For reasons that lie at the heart of this field, the schools failed them pitifully when they were young—and they know it. They know that hearing people set the agenda of instruction. They know that hearing people tried to teach them in a hearing way and with a spoken language.

They will not soon forget the pain of being led blindfolded through a dense thicket of English along a path not of their own choosing. This problem is worthy of the deepest thought of Deaf leaders—how can we bring the enjoyment and liberation of Deaf studies to Deaf adults?

However great the need for Deaf adults to pursue Deaf studies, the need is even greater for the Deaf child and his or her parents. Rural Deaf children in some countries live far apart with no schools to bring them together and into contact with Deaf adults. In other countries, Deaf children are actively discouraged from contact with each other and with Deaf adults and are flung pell-mell into local hearing schools. These children may be harmed seriously in their linguistic, psychological, and educational development. Magazines, books, films, theater, and other means of bringing Deaf studies to Deaf children could make a vital difference in their lives.

The laws of the United States, as the laws of many other countries, recognize that "a primary means by which a child learns is through the use of the child's native language and cultural heritage" (see Lane, 1988). The courts have ordered schools with children not fluent in English to educate them using their fluent language, to hire teachers from their minority group, and to include bicultural education in the school day. (The Code of Federal Regulations further defines "native language" as primary language: 500.4 34 C.F.R. Ch. 5, 7.) Schools with many Hispanic American students, for example, use Spanish with children not fluent in English, have Hispanic-American teachers, and teach Hispanic studies. These rights were won through great struggle.

Most Deaf children in the world have as their primary language the sign language of their country. Where national laws provide for bilingual education, children who use sign language should receive equal treatment under the law—instruction using their language, Deaf teachers, and Deaf studies. Even countries that refuse to provide bilingual education, however, should provide it for this language minority, for the national oral language can never serve Deaf children in place of their manual language, and their parents' hearing culture can never serve in place of Deaf culture. In the few, progressive countries where Deaf studies is a necessary part of the education of Deaf children, those children find in the schools a reaffirmation of their identity, a sense of psychological well being, and an environment conducive to learning.

What does Deaf studies have to offer to the parents of a Deaf child? Communication. Insight. Empathy. Acceptance. Respect. The love of their child. That's all.

Another audience for Deaf studies is people in the professions serving Deaf people —teachers, interpreters, counselors, psychologists, and so on. Consider the teacher's need for a knowledge of Deaf studies. Here, according to a considerable body of research, is what is required for a successful program of educating children from a language minority (adopted from Skutnabb-Kangas, 1988):

1. The language goal in the classroom is bilingualism and not the dominance of the national language.
2. The social goal is positive for the group and not to keep it subordinate.
3. Parents and children can choose among educational programs that use the minority or majority language.
4. Teachers are bilingual and well trained.
5. Bilingual materials are available.
6. The cultural content of the materials is appropriate for the students.
7. The teacher has high expectations, but the students have high self-confidence; they know they have a fair chance of succeeding.

8. Teachers encourage the students' development in their primary language, including its art forms.
9. There is enough relevant and demanding subject matter in class to promote general knowledge and therefore proficiency in all languages.
10. Teachers encourage the students to learn the national language and to use it in accord with their abilities.
11. The students can practice the national language in peer groups.
12. The students are exposed to native users of the national language in linguistically demanding formal situations.

Ignorance of Deaf studies by teachers and teacher-trainers is one important reason that the education we deliver to children who use sign language rarely meets any of these twelve requirements.

Deaf studies is for Deaf people—be they leaders, scholars, self-advocates, or students of all ages. Deaf studies is for hearing adults—parents and professional people. But the largest potential audience for Deaf studies is hearing students pursuing a liberal education in high school and especially college. The universities have nurtured women's studies and Black studies, and they must nurture Deaf studies. After all, the accumulation of knowledge is largely carried out in the universities. What Deaf studies has to offer the average hearing student is one way of acquiring the most important knowledge of all in a liberal education—an awareness of one's own cultural assumptions.

Most people are not aware of the cultural premises that guide their lives; they are ethnocentric and naturally so, for social life would be impossible if every action required reflection. People have an unconscious mental model of their culture that makes most of their choices for them, leaving them free to grapple with the remaining choices. Their ideas about wealth, family, sexuality, and disability, for example, all seem more or less given and appropriate. They know abstractly and vaguely that other people live in other ways; but they do not know the premises that lie beneath those differences, and they cannot make the empathic leap and see the world from another vantage point. Not seeing that there is a range of choices of how to live, they do not realize that they have made such choices themselves. And because they do not realize they have made choices, in fact they have not, because to choose is an act of conscious volition. The fundamental choices have been made for them—by their parents and, most of all, by historical inevitability.

For such people, the study of another culture can be a revelation; it can liberate and empower them by helping them to imagine other premises and other ways of life. Liberated by cultural perspective, these fortunate people are more able to fashion their own lives and to "connect" with the lives of others. These are the masses of people who should study Deaf studies. Ordinary hearing people all over the world are now enriching their lives by learning sign languages. International bodies like the European Parliament and UNESCO proclaim the importance of this cultural discovery. Now an important challenge before the field of Deaf studies is to develop an enriched body of knowledge about Deaf culture and arts and to disseminate it to hearing people at large as well as to Deaf people of all ages and their hearing friends and relations.

What is Deaf studies? It is the discipline devoted to understanding the lives of Deaf people so as to improve their lot. Who should study Deaf studies? Deaf leaders, scholars, and members of the Deaf community; Deaf children and their parents; professional people serving Deaf people; and hearing people who wish to understand themselves or Deaf people better.

References

Lane, H. 1986. *When the Mind Hears: A History of the Deaf*. New York: Random House. p. 3.

Lane, H. 1988. "Is There a 'Psychology of the Deaf' "? *Exceptional Children* 55: 7–19.

Lane, H. 1988. Quoting from 20 U.S.C.S. 3222. In "Educating the American Sign Language Speaking Minority of the United States." *Sign Language Studies* 59: 221–230.

Skutnabb-Kangas, T. 1988. "Multilingualism and the Education of Minority Children." In *Minority Education*, ed. T. Skutnabb-Kangas and J. Cummins. Philadelphia: Multilingual Matters. pp. 9–44.

Wolff, A. B., and J. E. Harkins. 1986. "Multihandicapped Students." In *Deaf Children in America*, ed. A. N. Schildroth and M. A. Karchmer. San Diego, CA: College-Hill. pp. 55–82.

Rehabilitation or Oppression? Options for the Humanization of the Deaf

ROGER J. CARVER AND TANIS M. DOE

It has been at least thirty years since the Thalidomide controversy first came into the public consciousness. During the late 1950s and early 1960s, thousands of infants with deformed or missing limbs were born to mothers who had taken the tranquilizer Thalidomide during the early stages of their pregnancies. These children have grown into adults with their own opinions of the "rehabilitation" process they went through during their early years.

There appears to be a general resentment among them over efforts to "mask" their missing limbs and functions. The perception by the medical profession and by their parents was that these children were "missing" limbs and, therefore, these limbs should be replaced. They failed to realize that the children were perfectly content in using their feet and toes to perform the functions of hands and fingers. The only time they felt handicapped or disabled was when they were fitted with artificial limbs or reminded by others of their "difference."

Many of them were fitted with prostheses at an early age, and there is near unanimity among them now that these artificial limbs interfered with their ability to function, making them uncomfortable and unhappy. Many of them reacted badly to their artificial limbs and eventually chose to go without them. Most of them now express a desire to be left alone and allowed to use their remaining natural abilities to develop their own ways of coping. This is the observation of one Thalidomide victim, Len Seaby, in reference to his prostheses:

> I never really adapted to them. . . . [A]s soon as I got home back with my friends, I just threw them off. Besides, they restricted my mobility. It was much easier to adapt my own physical body than it was to work through these artificial tools. (Canada House of Commons, 1981, p. 118)

Many of these people consider artificial limbs a denial of reality and a way of appeasing the sensibilities of society. The sight of a person using his or her feet to take on the functions of hands can be upsetting to some people; artificial limbs make them look less different. This raises a question: For whose benefit were the "rehabilitation" and prostheses designed—the user or the beholder?

This paper has also appeared in the *Canadian Journal of the Deaf*, 3 (3), 1989, pp. 87–99.

It is language, in short, which makes us in the truest sense human. (T. Waldron, 1987, p. 81)

The case of Thalidomide children raises the question of whether current rehabilitative practices in the field of deafness are of more benefit to the deaf children/adults or to their parents and the professionals who work with deaf people. Such practices consist of speech therapy, auditory training, and the use of prostheses such as hearing aids and cochlear implants. Since the Thalidomide children expressed their unhappiness and discontent with prostheses, it may be that such rehabilitative practices were oppressive. Do such practices as aural habilitation constitute for deaf people a form of oppression?

There have been numerous references in the literature to deaf people as oppressed people (Abberley, 1987; Baker-Shenk, 1985; Carver, 1987; Doe, 1988; Kyle and Pullen, 1988; Lane, 1986). Deaf children and adults have been victimized by systemic, though not necessarily intentional, oppression. This oppression takes the form of collective discrimination against deaf people based primarily on their lack of hearing and lack of power. Discrimination in employment, education and social interaction with a predominantly hearing society is reflected in the low status of deaf people.

The life of a deaf person is filled with intervention by hearing people, from identification of hearing loss to maturity. This paper will discuss two systemic means of oppression of deaf people. One is the system of so-called rehabilitation of deaf people, beginning primarily in early childhood and extending through vocational rehabilitation. The other is the separation of deaf people from the means of control over their lives—the political oppression of deaf people.

Beginning with the premise that deaf people have been oppressed sets the task at determining how this process has occurred and how it continues. We will not attempt to substantiate the claim of oppression; the lower social status, lower incomes, and overall limitations imposed on deaf people by society are self-evident. The question is this: How does this oppression occur? There can not be simply a direct relationship between hearing loss and status, because the biological mechanisms of hearing do not control society.

The Deficit Model

The orientation of the literature and research in the field of deafness has been toward *deficits* in the functioning of deaf people (Abberley, 1987; Carver, 1989; Kyle and Pullen, 1988). There appears to be a lack of focus on the *assets* that predict academic success. Webster (1988) notes that teachers working under the deficit model "tend to assume that the learning difficulties experienced by the child, lie *within* the child" (p. 4, author's italics). He notes that the deficit model "encourages teachers to exacerbate a child's handicap by attributing every problem which arises to the child's disability" (p. 4). He suggests that it may be more effective to modify the learning situation than to modify the child. Kyle and Pullen (1988) are more specific:

> This model has the assumption that *differences in physical, sensory or mental capabilities necessarily produce a defective member of society.* Such a situation then requires remediation or treatment. Indeed, *not to treat*, given the knowledge of difference offends against an implied "Hippocratic oath" shared by all members of our enlightened society. A diagnosis of deafness then requires the action which firstly looks for a cure and then indicates a long term remediation, further

rehabilitation and eventually care. It is difficult within society to contemplate not taking action when someone is discovered not to hear, but deaf people are beginning to report to us their unease with this type of response to diagnosis and with their subsequent educational treatment. (p. 50, authors' italics)

Given the emphasis on the deficit in the hearing function, professionals will attempt to rehabilitate the very young deaf child, who may actually have little or no need for rehabilitation in the first place. In a sense, this rehabilitation actually may be aimed more at the child's parents and the society, who probably feel the "loss" more than the deaf child does.

Oppression and the Effects of Power

In a traditional class analysis, the existence of a lower class or working class is beneficial to those holding power (Porter, 1965; Schecter, 1977; Weber, 1968). It is not simply a function of society to have stratification on the basis of status, but stratification is essential to the accumulation of capital by those in power. Control and power in society are held for the most part by upper class hearing men. These include businessmen, politicians, senior bureaucrats, and professionals. Although there are some women and, to a much lesser degree, deaf people in these positions, power is primarily in the hands of hearing men.

Given that power rests with a small minority of people who are not deaf, the oppression that results from the treatment of deaf people must be traced to those in positions of influence. Deaf people, with few exceptions, have been victims and not actors in this process. Schlesinger aptly describes powerlessness as "an individual's perception of self as not having the cognitive competence, psychological skills, instrumental resources, and/or environmental support systems needed to successfully influence his or her environment" (1986, p. 4).

Rehabilitative and Pedagogical Oppression

The formal education system is a very powerful tool in the reproduction of the social system, with all of its inequalities and imperfections (Collins, 1971; Bowles and Gintis, 1976; Brown, 1987). Education as a social process, however, does not begin in kindergarten or end with university or postsecondary studies. Education, or access to education, becomes possible at the earliest age and ends with death. In the philosophical school of John Dewey, education is its own goal; living is learning, and to cease to learn is to die (Dewey, 1902). For deaf people too, education is a life-long experience, but for them it is also oppressive.

Parents have control over the deaf child from the moment of birth. In 90 percent of the cases, the parents are hearing, with little or no prior experience with deafness (Moores, 1982). The parents, to a certain extent, are also victims; their dependence on the expertise of professionals for the successful rearing of their deaf children puts them at risk of exploitation. This parental vulnerability is one reason those in power are so successful at oppressing deaf people.

The deaf child, powerless at this stage, is put under the authority of a variety of professionals such as physicians, specialists, audiologists, speech pathologists, early childhood educators and psychologists. While most hearing children also experience interaction with professionals, the majority of hearing children share the same language as these professionals. The rehabilitation process can be mutually satisfying if both parties participate.

The difficulties of Spanish- or French-speaking children being treated by English-speaking professionals are considerable, but these minority-language children share their language and culture with their families. Deaf children share their language and culture with neither the professionals nor their hearing parents. The critical time for learning language passes so quickly that, before long, the deaf child is delayed in language of any kind. The fortunate few deaf children born to deaf parents know the difference acceptance, communication, and natural development make.

One of the basic elements of oppression identified by Freire is *prescription:*

> Every prescription represents the imposition of one man's choice upon another, transforming the consciousness of the man prescribed to into one that conforms with the prescriber's consciousness. Thus the behavior of the oppressed is a prescribed behavior, following as it does the guidelines of the oppressor. (1972, p. 31)

In this light, the transformation of the deaf child into a "hearing" person through the above intervention processes can be described as such a prescription process imposed by the hearing upon deaf people. It also explains the century of emphasis on speech and auditory training in education of deaf people. The International Congresses on Education of the Deaf, despite their nominal focus on education, have concentrated predominantly on the topics of speech and auditory training (Brill, 1984). It is not surprising that the central theme of the most recent Congress, held in Manchester, England in 1985, was "not the failure of deaf education but the promise of cochlear implants, as if the profession believed that the only hope for deaf education was to provide it miraculously with hearing children" (Abberley, 1987, p. 9). It is indeed as Lane says: "Schools were transformed into speech clinics" (1984, p. 398).

Language is a key issue in identifying the process of oppression. Language has been given the valued status of distinguishing humans from other animals. It has also held communities together and divided countries for cultural reasons (Wotherspoon, 1987). For deaf people, language is perhaps the central issue in oppression. Woodward and Allen (1987), in a study of ASL use among 1,888 teachers of deaf people in the United States, produce some disturbing findings: 1) Only 140 (2 percent) claimed to use ASL; 2) Of the 140, only twenty-five may be using it; and 3) Of the twenty-five, only six probably are using it. The investigators conclude, "Many teachers still do not know the difference between ASL and English, nor do they tend to use ASL as their primary method of classroom communication" (p. 9). Considering the historical hostility of the educational system toward ASL (Erting, 1978; Lane, 1984), it is not surprising that illiteracy and educational failure are common in deaf education. As Paul (1973) says, "The deaf person who is truly bilingual and who knows both Ameslan and English is rarely encouraged to be equally proud of both" (p. 41).

Equally disconcerting is a study by Woodward, Allen, and Schildroth (1988) of teacher role models in elementary school programs for deaf and hard of hearing children. It shows that the proportion of hearing teachers is 88.9 percent in special school programs for deaf people and 95.6 percent in local school programs. It is cause for concern that so few teachers in local school programs are deaf when the trend toward more local programs is on the rise. As the authors suggest, the vast majority of hearing teachers in such elementary programs "serve as role models of cultural values" (p. 190).

In this light, that fact that the language and culture of deaf people are not being made accessible to deaf children while the dominant hearing language and culture are being imposed represents a basic form of oppression.

Freire has developed a model of a form of oppression that is based on pedagogy and language (1972). This pedagogy exists not only in the classroom but also in the relations between any learner and teacher. Language includes not only literacy and the use of language, but also knowledge that is based in language (written materials). A teacher, in this context, is any person who attempts to transfer his or her knowledge to a person perceived to be without knowledge (Freire, 1972, 1973). Knowledge is traditionally based in language, and without some form of conversational or written language, access to this knowledge is limited.

This is referred to as the "banking" concept of education; the teacher deposits information into the student (Freire, 1973). Freire has associated this approach with the oppressors' belief that the oppressed represents "the pathology of a healthy society" (1972, p. 60). Because deafness is considered a pathological state by the hearing society, it is not surprising that education and rehabilitation of deaf people have largely followed this model. Freire criticizes this approach as oppressive because it implies that the learner has nothing of value and needs to be filled with ideas by the teacher. He cites as an example illiterate Brazilian peasants who are taught as if they knew nothing. By being filled with information from the teachers, they are shaped to meet the needs of the social system. They are given just enough information to be useful but not enough to be independent and possibly critical (Freire, 1985).

This model is applicable to the historical situation of deaf people. Deaf children have been treated as if they had no ability to learn on their own. Specific efforts have been made to teach them English or another dominant spoken language. Efforts to teach deaf people spoken and written language have often taken precedence over the teaching of knowledge (Furth, 1966; Rodda and Grove, 1987). The knowledge that is taught is provided selectively. Deaf people are receivers of information that is created and controlled by the hearing system. The use of language and the limitations of knowledge are oppressive to deaf people, yet they are to some extent beneficial to the greater social structure. Wotherspoon explains:

> At a more general level the school system ensured that all members of society, whatever their occupational destiny, had sufficiently internalized the norms and values which legitimatized the existing distribution of jobs and rewards as natural, and hence more or less fair. (1987, p. 46)

Hearing people have reasonable motives in teaching language to deaf children. They expect that without it deaf children would be difficult to control and difficult to train. Parents who speak and hear have a natural desire for their deaf children to be like them. Audiologists and speech pathologists are motivated by their own professional interests, as well as the belief in the normality and superiority of speech and hearing, to "help" deaf people learn to listen and talk as a way to improve the quality of their lives. Educators from preschool to secondary levels want deaf children to have English or some language so they can be taught; deaf children with a language base, preferably one as similar as possible to the dominant one, will be open to deposits from educators.

What is the content of this deposit? In the vast majority of school systems, deaf students are limited to vocational programs and, at most, a few academic programs in the liberal arts (Schein and Delk, 1974; Moores, 1982). Students are actually trained and prepared for lives as subordinates in society (Doe, 1988). They are expected to follow the rules, obey the instructors, and learn what they are taught (Evans and Falk, 1986). This system is successful at producing a deaf person ready for subordination. Deaf people are treated in a way that assigns not only a lower occupational status and income but also a marginal role in society.

Hearing professionals and policy makers have vested interests in the marginal role of deaf people. It is much easier to train deaf people for roles in manual labor, where their skills are useful and transferable, than to prepare them for careers in law and business, which require a high degree of literacy, and where they will need the services of interpreters and telephone relays. Society wants deaf people to participate, but only in assigned and somewhat stereotypical roles (Jacobs, 1974; Schein and Delk, 1974).

Although the effective protest of the Gallaudet students in 1988 broke a long tradition of passivity in the deaf community, the collective political power of deaf people is still not very great. Deaf people have participated continuously in efforts to change the systems of rehabilitation, education, and employment and have made important contributions in all these areas. But, while some have been recognized for their contributions, more often their efforts to make themselves heard have been ignored or denigrated. Programs have been implemented, but only in a piecemeal fashion. In fact, a number of deaf professionals have been unwitting tools in the oppression of deaf people by maintaining the dependency of deaf people (Baker-Shenk, 1985).

Cultural Action and Humanization

Freire (1972, 1973) calls for cultural action to humanize and liberate the oppressed. He suggests that the oppressed must achieve a critical consciousness that will allow them to know what they learn. Freire also argues that this process cannot be successfully implemented by the oppressors: The oppressed themselves must become conscious of their oppression and learn liberation. This implies that deaf people must have access to information that will explain their marginalization and allow them to participate in knowledge. The exclusion of deaf people from real input and control in the systems that treat deaf people must be stopped. Deaf people must have meaningful participation in and control over their own language and culture.

For this to happen, a radical change in the status quo is required. Hearing professionals, and even some deaf persons, may have to give up their positions of power to allow the humanization of deaf people through true learning and literacy. As Freire points out, the oppressor cannot generate this liberation process; the initiative has to come from the oppressed. The only way for the oppressor to contribute to this process is to enter into a true solidarity with the oppressed. This happens when the oppressor ceases to regard the oppressed as objects and begins to regard them as "persons who have been unjustly dealt with, deprived of their voice, cheated in the sale of their labor—when he stops making pious, sentimental, and individualistic gestures and risks an act of love" (Freire, 1972, p. 35).

Waldron's observation on language as a humanizing feature, cited earlier in this paper, serves here as a fitting conclusion. Deaf people are human beings in every sense; they all share the same desire to participate in the affairs of humanity. Not to be denied, deaf people have devised their own ways to cope with and make sense of their world on their way to full and equal participation. They can achieve this goal more quickly by using their own language as a primary tool, developing it to its fullest potential, and by taking control of the so-called intervention and rehabilitation processes that shape their crucial formative years. The struggle of deaf people throughout the world to preserve and restore sign language should be perceived as an effort to regain their humanity. Only when deaf people have regained their humanity can their hearing oppressors recover their own.

References

Abberley, P. 1987. "The Concept of Oppression and the Development of a Social Theory of Disability." *Disability, Handicap and Society* 2 (1): 5–19.

Baker-Shenk, C. 1985. *Characteristics of Oppressing and Oppressed People: Their Effect on the Interpreting Context*. Paper presented at the National Convention of the Registry of Interpreters of the Deaf, San Diego.

Bowles, S., and H. Gintis. 1976. *Schooling in Capitalist America*. New York: Basic Books.

Brill, R. 1984. *International Congresses on Education of the Deaf: An Analytical History, 1878–1980*. Washington, DC: Gallaudet College Press.

Brown, R. 1987. "Opportunities and Challenges." Presentation to the National Forum on Post-Secondary Education. Saskatoon: Forum Secretariat.

Canada House of Commons. 1981. *Obstacles*. Report of the Special Committee on the Disabled and the Handicapped. Ottawa: Minister of Supply and Services Canada.

Carver, R. 1987. "An Oppressive Silence." *Canadian Journal of the Deaf/La Revue Sourds du Canada* 1: 26–44.

Carver, R. 1989. "Illiteracy of the Deaf: A Genuine Educational Puzzle or an Instrument of Oppression? A Critical Review." Unpublished master's thesis, University of Alberta, Edmonton.

Collins, R. 1971. "Functional and Conflict Theories of Educational Stratification." *American Sociological Review* 36: 1002–1019.

Dewey, J. 1902. *The Child and the Curriculum*. Chicago: University of Chicago Press.

Doe, T. M. 1988. "Ontario Schooling and the Status of the Deaf: An Enquiry into Inequality, Status Assignment, and Educational Power." Unpublished master's thesis, Carleton University, Ottawa.

Erting, C. 1978. "Language Policy and Deaf Ethnicity in the United States." *Sign Language Studies* 19: 139–152.

Evans, D., and W. Falk. 1986. *Learning to Be Deaf*. Beverly Hills: Sage Publications.

Freire, P. 1972. *Pedagogy of the Oppressed*. New York: Herder and Herder.

Freire, P. 1973. *Education for Critical Consciousness*. New York: Continuum.

Freire, P. 1985. *Politics of Education: Power, Culture and Liberation*. South Hadley, MA: Bergin and Garvey Publishers.

Furth, H. 1966a. *Thinking Without Language*. New York: The Free Press.

Jacobs, L. 1974. *A Deaf Adult Speaks Out*. Washington, DC: Gallaudet College Press.

Kyle, J., and G. Pullen. 1988. "Cultures in Contact: Deaf and Hearing People." *Disability, Handicap, and Society* 3 (1): 49–61.

Lane, H. 1984. *When the Mind Hears: A History of the Deaf*. New York: Random House.

Lane, H. 1986. "Taking Education into Your Own Hands: A Keynote Address." In *Life and Work in the 21st Century: The Deaf Person of Tomorrow: Proceedings of the 1986 NAD Forum*. Silver Spring, MD: National Association of the Deaf.

Moores, D. 1982. *Educating the Deaf: Psychology, Principles and Practices*. Boston, MA: Houghton Mifflin.

Paul, M. E. 1973. "Education as Communication: Questions for Educators of Deaf Persons." In *Deafpride Papers: Perspectives and Options*. Washington, DC: Deafpride.

Porter, J. 1965. *The Vertical Mosaic: An Analysis of Social Class and Power in Canada*. Toronto: University of Toronto Press.

Rodda, M., and C. Grove. 1987. *Language, Cognition and Deafness*. Hillsdale, NJ: Lawrence Erlbaum Associates.

Schecter, S. 1977. "Capitalism, Class and Educational Reform in Canada." In *The Canadian State: Political Economy and Power*, ed. L. Panitch. Toronto: University of Toronto Press.

Schein, J., and M. Delk. 1974. *The Deaf Population of the United States*. Silver Spring, MD: National Association of the Deaf.

Schlesinger, H. S. 1986. "Effect of Powerlessness on Dialogue and Development: Disability, Poverty and the Human Condition." In *Psychosocial Interventions with Sensorially Disabled Persons*, ed. K. Heller. New York: Grune and Stratton.

Waldron, T. 1987. *Principles of Language and Mind*. London: Routledge, Kegan and Paul.

Weber, M. 1968. *Economy and Society*. New York: Free Press.

Webster, A. 1988. "Deafness and Learning to Read 1: Theoretical and Research Issues." *The Journal of the British Association of Teachers of the Deaf* 12 (4): 77–83.

Woodward, J., and T. Allen. 1987. "Classroom Use of ASL by Teachers." *Sign Language Studies* 54: 1–10.

Wotherspoon, T., ed. 1987. *The Political Economy of Canadian Schooling*. Toronto: Methuen.

Political Activism in the Deaf Community: An Exploratory Study of Deaf Leaders in Rochester, New York

GERALD C. BATEMAN, JR.

I n this report, I will summarize the results of a study that examined the insights, perceptions, and experiences of a selected group of deaf and hard of hearing adults who are leaders in the deaf community of Rochester, New York. Rochester is an excellent community in which to conduct this kind of research. There are approximately 50,000 deaf and hard of hearing people in the area, one of the highest per capita populations of deaf and hard of hearing people in the United States. Two major educational institutions and numerous organizations of deaf and hard of hearing people have served the educational, social, and civic needs of the community's citizens for many years. These institutions and organizations also foster the development of social and political networks among their members, a necessary element of political activism.

The major goal of this study was to determine the factors that have helped or hindered these deaf and hard of hearing leaders in becoming politically active and to obtain their perceptions of the forces that have shaped the political activism of other deaf people in the Rochester area.

The informant group consisted of deaf people who were currently in leadership roles in a variety of local organizations of deaf people. The qualitative research approach of open-ended, intensive interviews was used to generate findings.

Ten issues were investigated: (1) deaf adults' understanding of what political activism is, (2) their self-perceived barriers to political activism, (3) the impact of families on the development of political activism, (4) the impact of schools on the development of political activism, (5) communication concerns in political activism, (6) the deaf leaders' experiences in political activism, (7) their attitude toward working with other deaf people, as well as hearing people, to achieve political goals, (8) their self-perceived political and social concerns, as well as accomplishments, in the deaf community, (9) the impact of captioned news programs on deaf people's sense of political awareness and activism, and (10) the roles of organizations of deaf and hard of hearing people in political activism.

The leaders expressed their views on what political activism means and how important it had been for them. One of the recurring themes was that political activism is a process of making changes to improve the lives of the members of the deaf and hard of hearing community to overcome the inequities in services and in the treatment of deaf people by hearing people. Many of the leaders reported feeling that they had to become spokespeople and activists to convince hearing people, especially legislators, that services for deaf and hard of hearing individuals have not been adequate and need to be upgraded. As one leader stated, "All [deaf] people are recognized as people." Therefore, everyone has the right to equal access to the services provided to the general community.

The leaders acknowledged the fact that within the deaf community there are two sides or factions regarding the issue of political activism. One leader said:

> I see two threads to political activism in the deaf community. One is the deaf-related issues . . . more captions on TV, TTY relay service, in other words, telephone accessibility, tax exemptions for what we spend, what it cost us for being deaf, what we have to pay for doorbell lights, TTY, decoders and all the things we have to pay for, we're looking for tax exemptions. Now there are deaf people that are politically active in pursuing those issues. Now that other part is the world issues . . . social issues like gay rights, abortion, against nuclear arms, education, education for our children, those are the broader issues.

Several leaders expressed concerns that the members of their organizations or communities focus their attention only on deafness-related issues while usually disregarding issues that affect the hearing and deaf communities as a whole. The attitude seems to be one of "let the hearing people take care of that for us."

Ironically, even when deafness-related issues or projects needed to be resolved, the leaders found themselves working alone or with very few deaf people. Deaf people also have the attitude that the leaders "can do the work for us." The feeling of political disenfranchisement and the lack of political involvement among many of the deaf people were major problems for the leaders. Regardless of these pervasive attitudes, the leaders have continued their efforts because, as one said, "If I didn't do something myself, nothing was going to happen." Another leader made a statement that reflected the sentiments of several of the others:

> The reason I wanted to participate was because I just wanted to see things happen. I wanted to get involved so the next generation could benefit from that and enjoy the work that we did now. I think up until now we have struggled and have been very frustrated and I just want to see future generations enjoy and reap the benefits or our work now and have a better life.

The leaders' responses to interview questions indicated that several attitudinal, as well as societal, barriers have hindered the development of political activism among many of the deaf people in Rochester. Specifically, some of the barriers involved include a lack of understanding about what political activism and the political process are; apathy; a sense of disenfranchisement; dependency; a sense of isolation; and a lack of a strong sense of what a community should be.

Several of the leaders perceived that many deaf people do not fully understand what politics or political activism is and how they could make it work for them. They found that the word "politics" is "the most misunderstood word among deaf people . . .

because they do not have political experience or power yet, they're not able to define it."
When they do attempt to define the term, they tend to define it in a simplistic manner,
such as "politics means writing bills and having them passed by Congress."

At the same time, many deaf people feel that politics belongs to the "upper crust,
well-educated" deaf people as well as to hearing people. As one leader stated,

> Deaf people feel that politics is way, way up the scale, that other deaf people
> who might be involved in politics must mean they are very, very intelligent and
> way above me and I see many, many deaf people who feel it's such a fancy . . .
> such a high falutin' thing to be involved in politics that they don't want to be
> involved in it themselves.

In addition, several of the leaders reported believing that the "hands-off" attitude
toward political involvement came from the frustrations of dealing with hearing people,
because "hearing people were always taking advantage of deaf people and deaf people
just sort of accepted their lot and whatever was meted out to them." The leaders felt
powerless to change these feelings of dependency. There were strong feelings that hearing teachers and families and the lack of deaf role models have had tremendous impact
on encouraging the development of these attitudes of apathy and dependency.

Resistance to change and an attitude of complacency were other barriers deaf
leaders have had to deal with within the deaf community. There have been fears in the
deaf community that if the leaders try to bring in new ideas or changes to the community, deaf people might lose what they already have, such as Social Security Income
and possibly their jobs. "Don't create a stir" and "Don't rock the boat" are common
comments made by deaf people regarding their leaders' efforts at change. Leaders who
try to make suggestions for change are often labeled "troublemakers." These kinds of
attitudes have made gaining cooperation and support from the members of the deaf
community a struggle for the leaders.

The feeling of isolation has had a tremendous impact on the development of political activism in the deaf community. The majority of deaf adults in Rochester work in
situations where there are very few deaf coworkers or none at all. Thus, they do not
have the same benefits of sharing information and ideas as do their hearing coworkers.
Opportunities for information-sharing exchanges do not occur for deaf employees until
the end of the workday, when they can meet other deaf people at the club or at meetings. As a result, deaf organizations that were formed for political or civic purposes
tend to be more like social organizations. As one leader said, "Deaf people join these
organizations for social purposes." Instead of discussing issues and concerns at these
meetings, the people tend to exchange news and gossip.

As the leaders discussed their feelings and perceptions about the "social roles" in
organizations, they also expressed their concerns about the lack of cohesiveness within
the deaf community. Like any community, the deaf community in Rochester is made up
of many different kinds of people. Deafness, according to these leaders, has not been
enough to bind the people together. For example, a recently deafened leader experienced rejection from the community because she was considered "hard of hearing,"
regardless of the severity of her hearing loss. The same is true for many other hard of
hearing people who have tried to participate in the deaf community's political and social
activities. One's level of educational attainment is also a cause of division among deaf
people. The more educated a deaf person becomes, the more he or she may experience
rejection by the general deaf community, where many of the members do not have a

college education. There is also division among such deaf minorities as deaf blacks, deaf hispanics, and deaf gays.

Working with deaf people was a challenge to the leaders because of the attitudinal barriers they have had to overcome. Another source of considerable frustration reported by the leaders was working with hearing people on political issues and concerns, but the deaf leaders have realized that working with hearing people is a necessity in order to achieve needed goals and changes. The issues with which the deaf community has had to deal are basically a reflection of minority/majority group interactions. Because the deaf community tends to be small in comparison to the hearing community, the deaf leaders reported believing "that their wishes and concerns are often ignored by the hearing legislators." To overcome the problems of inequality, conformity, and oppression posed by the hearing community, some of the leaders said that they had to become "ambassadors" of the deaf community and educate the hearing community about deaf culture and the needs of deaf people. But, as one leader put it, "Deaf people who are involved in politics are going three or four times the extra mile" to educate the public: The Gallaudet University student protest did much to educate the public about the capabilities, needs, and concerns of deaf people.

Having deaf role models was an extremely important issue to all the leaders interviewed in this study. Having a deaf role model helped each of them become involved in political activities. Through the role models, they saw that being politically active could make a difference in their lives and in the lives of others in the community. For example,

> I think that in the community in which I lived, we just happened to have many . . . exceptional people. . . . I wanted to be like them, and they taught me to think differently. They taught me to take different approach to things than what I normally would have [if I] had not been exposed to them.

There was a feeling among the leaders that deaf youngsters and young adults are not being exposed to deaf role models early enough in their lives. In discussing the importance of exposure to deaf role models at an early age, the issue of having more deaf teachers surfaced. Several of these leaders reported having deaf teachers at some point during their academic years. As one said, "The best teachers I had were deaf teachers." The leaders found that although there are fine hearing teachers of deaf students, they did not have the in-depth understanding of deaf culture and were not role models for young deaf students to emulate. The general consensus was that the presence of deaf teachers has positive effects on deaf students, and many more deaf teachers are needed in the profession.

These leaders saw themselves as role models as well as teachers or mentors to the members of the deaf community. Their activities show other deaf people how the political process works and how to become part of that process. Members of the deaf community have also depended upon these leaders to explain current social and political issues to them. Some of the leaders felt that there is a great need for a national-level deaf role model or leader.

> We really need someone like Martin Luther King to shake us up, and we don't have anybody like that. . . . We need these role models in higher levels of government. We need them in actually any level—government or private sector. By having these role models, it will serve to educate other people just by their own example.

There was a very strong feeling among the leaders that parents play a very important role in developing their children's sense of political activism. According to them, the basic issue is the level of communication within the families. In other words, having deaf or hearing parents is not the important issue; the important issue is how well the parents communicate with their deaf children. The leaders shared experiences of "dinner-time conversations" when political topics were discussed, and they felt that they had been included in those discussions. They also talked about the times their parents brought them to meetings at the deaf club or other organizations, as well as to the polling place to watch their parents vote. Through their parents and other family members, these leaders developed healthy attitudes toward the political process.

According to these deaf leaders, educational experiences played a very significant role in their becoming politically active. They felt that, through education, deaf people can overcome ignorance and misunderstanding of the political process, become more aware of political and social issues, and develop problem-solving skills and the ability to access the political system to meet their needs. As one leader said,

> I think education is probably the most important part of [political activism]. Without that education you probably would not be aware of things that are happening in the world. You would be isolating yourself from things, and the more educated you are the better you can look at an issue and know how you can approach people about it. Really there is no limit to the value of education.

Although the leaders discussed the value of education in political activism, they also expressed their concerns about the lack of a strong civics or citizenship education curriculum in both residential and mainstream educational programs. They reported feeling that many of the teachers only scratched the surface in their civics courses and did not emphasize the fact that "politics is an important thing for them [the students] and that it's part of their lives."

During discussions on prior educational experiences, several of the leaders commented that patronizing attitudes prevalent in residential and mainstreamed schools were a real problem. They felt that teachers of deaf students, especially hearing teachers, tend to pity the deaf students, to do things for them, and to be condescending toward them, with students becoming passive and submissive as a result.

The leaders also felt that deaf students are not encouraged to be "independent and free thinkers." "Deaf students are afraid of criticism. We do have the right to express ourselves, our feelings, our opinions, but we are afraid to." "Can't" seems to be a catchword according to some of the leaders, as in "I can't do this, I can't do that, and they were told that and they believed it." These kinds of attitudes are often carried over into adulthood, a process that has serious impact on the development of independence and assertiveness, which are important elements in political activism.

Discussion among the deaf leaders interviewed for this study also focused on communication concerns, such as frustrations experienced in finding qualified interpreters for meetings. The lack of qualified interpreters has had a negative impact on the deaf community as it has isolated deaf people from the political process. Deaf people have felt that decisions have been made in the community by hearing people without their input or support. Along with the "hassle" of trying to find an interpreter for meetings, there is also the issue of payment. The cost of hiring interpreters, in addition to the listening and signalling devices deaf people have to purchase for day-to-day living, adds to the financial burden deaf people face. Some feel they should not have the extra financial burden of paying for their own interpreters so they can attend meetings they have the right to attend as citizens or representatives of the community or organization.

Communication was a significant concern among the leaders, and they considered this to be a major barrier for many deaf people. Hearing people need to be educated about the communication needs of deaf people, but, as one leader said, "We can't force them all [hearing people] to learn sign language." Deaf people need to become more assertive and let the public know what their needs are. The communication channels between deaf and hearing people need to be improved.

Captioning of television programs, including news reports, has played an important role in encouraging the growth of political activism in the deaf community, according to the views of the deaf leaders. It has done much to improve deaf people's sense of political awareness and knowledge of the issues. Captioning has also helped change deaf people's attitudes regarding such political actions as voting, by increasing their interest and understanding of the process and issues involved. Those leaders who have children also reported that captioning had helped improve their children's reading skills.

While they praised the benefits of captioning, however, the deaf leaders also expressed their concern about some negative impacts it has had on the deaf community and organizations. As one leader said,

> When there weren't any captions on TV, people tended to go to the clubs that would have movies captioned and then everybody would talk about politics and talk about the movie or whatever and had big discussions. Now with the new technology that's in place by captioning, people don't go to the clubs anymore . . . . The membership has dwindled. Where are the political discussions now?

So, captioning is a mixed blessing. Similar comments were made about the impact of TTYs and TDDs. They are extremely helpful, but they have also decreased the need for deaf people to gather at a club or home to share information or discuss issues.

Thus, the level of political activism in the deaf community has increased in recent years thanks to better educational standards and the increased use of captioned news and television programs that improve deaf people's knowledge and understanding of political and social issues and the political process. Yet there are barriers still to be overcome. The hearing community still needs to be further educated and made more sensitive to the needs of deaf people. More qualified deaf teachers are needed in the schools to serve as role models for deaf and hard of hearing students. More qualified interpreters are needed so more deaf people can attend town and school meetings and political functions.

Patronizing attitudes in schools and in the community have to be eliminated. One way to accomplish this is by educating people about patronizing behaviors. Organizations of deaf people need to find ways to improve networking among themselves so they can work as one unit, sharing information and concerns. All too often, organizations of the deaf function independently of each other. Increased political activism by members of the deaf community can do much to improve the political, social, and economic lives of deaf people.

Don't Stand There—Run!

KEVIN J. NOLAN

After reading the Preamble to the Constitution of the United States —you know how it goes: "*We the people* of the United States in order to form a more perfect union, establish justice, insure domestic tranquility, provide for the common defence, promote the general welfare, and secure the blessings of liberty to ourselves . . . ."—I have asked myself countless times, "Why can't a hearing impaired person like me serve the citizens and take part in the government?" This question was on my mind for a long time.

As we know, politics is a hectic way of life and yet it is an essential part of our government. Unfortunately, few deaf people become interested and get involved in politics. It is a fact that in the last few years, more and more deaf people are beginning to get involved, but not to the point of holding a public office.

What made me decide to run for local office? I have had a passion for politics ever since the Kennedy era, and also I wanted to feel the impact of meeting people. As a citizen, I have always wanted to serve the people, but I was hesitant about running for public office, because I was concerned about the voters' reaction to my deafness. I was also new to politics, a comparative unknown in my community with only a small circle of friends. I had been a resident of Northampton, Massachusetts (population 35,000) for only six years. I had concerns about my first run for city council in a ward once represented by Calvin Coolidge. My opponent was well liked and had a reputation for integrity. He had been in office for twenty years.

I refused to mention my plans to anyone but my family owing to my experiences in the past. For example, when I mentioned my goal to friends, they tended to say, "Oh, that's an impossible task," or "You can't do this." Owing to lack of support, I almost lost my hope and self-confidence.

During the previous two years I had served in an appointed position on a committee to advise the mayor of Northampton on the handicapped. Through this experience I gained confidence and knew I wanted to serve.

But was I ready to run? I had to make an assessment and ask myself some hard questions:

❖ Would I be willing to accept the sense of isolation and loneliness that candidates and office holders sometimes feel?

❖ Would I have the time to run for and hold public office?

❖ Could I accept the anger and criticism of voters when I made a decision that was contrary to their opinions?

❖ Would I be able to function with all kinds of people?

❖ Would I be able to accept attacks by the media?

❖ Would I be able to control my emotions?

❖ Would the voters accept me and treat me as a person?

❖ Would they be willing to communicate with me despite my handicap?

❖ Would I accept the negative reactions of the voters?

❖ Could I promote myself?

❖ Did my candidacy have broad-based support?

❖ Would I have enough stamina?

❖ Would I have the support and cooperation of my family?

At the same time, I was thinking about the advice I have given to my students during my years of teaching and counseling. I kept telling them not to let their disability stop them from reaching their goals. I'd say, "Try it; do it. I will respect you no matter whether you succeed or fail." Finally, after considering every facet of the situation, I took my own advice. I knew that if I didn't try, I would regret it for the rest of my life. Beside this, my family provided the encouragement I needed. I said to myself, "Don't stand there—run!"

I announced my candidacy on July 11th, my youngest son Keith's birthday, in the very same classroom at the Clarke School where I received my first training back in September 1950. My campaign slogan was, "It's time for a change and it's time for new thinking on the issues that confront the city."

Originally, my supporters and I thought I might lose the first time around. We would learn from this first time and set our sights on the next election. But as the months passed and more people learned about my campaign, the mood shifted. "Forget about the next time," I thought. "Focus on *this* time." A winning attitude began to filter through my growing campaign camp. As my campaign picked up speed, I began to attract considerable attention. Key people, including the mayor, several city council members, and the state representative, gave me their support.

My son Kevin Jr. proved a valuable asset. He had been a paperboy for a couple of years. He knew the area and knew the people. I made a lot of important contacts through him.

When it came to campaigning, I decided to knock on doors to convince the voters that I had the capacity to serve them well despite my deafness. With the unfailing support of my family, I knocked on doors in all kinds of weather, talked with residents about a number of issues, and gave new ideas for old problems. One thing that's interesting is that people never asked me about my handicap. Fortunately, they looked at me as a person. And once more I took advantage of my good communication skills, which made my campaign possible.

Some voters were unwilling to talk to me. I have no idea whether they were disinterested in politics, whether they didn't have the patience to listen, or whether they were uncomfortable communicating with me. All my life, I have always been prepared for both the bad and the good. One of the strengths that helped me during the campaign was my fine sense of humor, which immediately put people at ease.

The students in my school also were involved with my campaign. I knew their participation would be a great educational experience for them. Many voters said that these young students had made a big impact on them; they really admired the students' performance. The students saw the importance of my running and benefitted from their work. A very important aspect of my campaign was to give deaf children the chance to see deaf adults succeeding in something very important and worthwhile.

Probably one of the major factors of my winning was a debate between my opponent and me. It gave me the opportunity to convince voters that I had the capacity to answer their questions.

On election day, the voting was very close. It was hard at first to say who was winning, and I paced the floor as if I were awaiting the birth of a baby. I won the election by seven votes, but the incumbent requested a recount. I earned three extra votes from that.

I give the voters of Northampton credit. They should be proud of themselves. They were good models for other voters in our country because they showed their willingness to accept my deafness and to look at deaf people as individuals with talents and abilities that can make our country stronger.

Running for public office wasn't an easy task, but it was worthwhile. One thing my campaign taught me was the essential characteristics of a successful candidate: You need large doses of tolerance, patience, humor, open-mindedness, and persistence.

I wanted to be a good example for the deaf community, to show other deaf people that they, too, can knock down the barricades that have kept them out of politics; to show them that they can be leaders in the hearing society.

Afterword

Global Perspectives on The Deaf Way

MICHAEL A. KARCHMER

Almost exactly a year ago, I had the honor of making a presentation to the Association of Canadian Educators of the Hearing Impaired meeting in St. John's, Newfoundland. I gave my presentation the curious title, "Woodstock, Poland, and The Deaf Way." I used the presentation to talk about The Deaf Way, which had only happened a month before. I tried to describe The Deaf Way for those who hadn't been there, to reflect on its meaning, and to place it in some kind of context. In trying to describe the context of The Deaf Way, I expressed the thesis (now obvious) that the years 1988 and 1989 would be seen as pivotal years in this century, both in the world at large and in the world of deafness. Further, what was happening in the world of deaf people had to be seen in the context of what was happening in the world at large. Also, it seemed to me that the events of 1988 and 1989 could be compared in importance to events twenty years before in 1968 and 1969.

I won't repeat my entire discussion of a year ago, but I *will* repeat the thought that in some important ways, The Deaf Way can be compared to Woodstock. For those of you who don't know or don't remember, Woodstock, New York, was the site of a week-long rock festival in 1969 that attracted upwards of 500,000 people. Whatever did or did not actually happen at Woodstock, the event came to symbolize the spirit of an entire generation of young people living in challenging times. In an important sense, I think that The Deaf Way was the deaf Woodstock because it was the positive expression of deaf and hearing people coming together with a sense of shared community—discovering depth and diversity and finding strength in this diversity. The Deaf Way had a serious side, but above all it was a celebration of the creative potential of deaf people expressed in cultures around the world.

The last three years have been momentous times for the world. When I gave my talk a year ago in Newfoundland, Poland had just held its first open elections in forty years, and events instigated by a democracy movement were unfolding in China. Of course, I did not predict the crumbling of the Berlin Wall, the reunification of Germany, the incredible changes in Eastern Europe and in the Soviet Union, and the rapid thaw in East-West relations. Throughout the world, people are striving for self-determination, for greater control over their own lives, for freedom to find their identities within specific cultural contexts.

This presentation, given in August 1990 to the International Congress on the Education of the Deaf (in Rochester, N.Y.), reflects on the relationship of The Deaf Way to other momentous events occurring in the still unfolding era of political and social upheaval that began in the late 1980s.

In the world of deafness, 1988 and 1989 were equally landmark years. In 1988, the Gallaudet protest leading to the selection of Gallaudet's first deaf president was the catalyst that sparked many changes. As in the world at large, deaf people started to take new pride in their identity and began to seek more control over their own lives and to demand fuller access to the benefits of society.

Just as the Gallaudet student-inspired protests were clearly the catalyst for change, I think that, in the future, The Deaf Way will be seen as a related and almost equally important event.

Why do I say this? Because it pointed the way to new possibilities, reinforced new attitudes, and explored the vitality of the deaf experience worldwide.

Let me expand briefly on the uniqueness of this event and why it represented a marked departure from past professional gatherings. First, The Deaf Way was not trying to fix anything about deaf people. Its purpose was to bring people together to understand and explore the language, culture, and history of deaf people through the conference and to *experience* these things by means of the festival. The Deaf Way was not about disability—it was about ability; it was about the creative energies of deaf people expressed in their own cultures.

The Deaf Way was a professional event, to be sure, but one with a difference. First and foremost, it was designed to meet the requirements of people whose primary mode of experiencing the world is through vision. We have been told about accessibility at The Deaf Way. The point is that accessibility had a clear meaning: Accessibility was not thought of as providing deaf people access to what the hearing world was saying. Rather, it was providing equal access to all participants.

If there was a problem with access at The Deaf Way, it was in accommodating hearing people who were accustomed to depending on their ears alone. A hearing participant wrote us after The Deaf Way to complain mildly that the informational needs of deaf people were catered to more than those of hearing people. In this regard, the organizers of The Deaf Way may be guilty as charged and proud of it.

One of the important aspects of The Deaf Way is that it provided increased visibility for deaf communities throughout the world. For example, performing groups from several countries obtained support to attend The Deaf Way from their own countries' governments. Some of this support came from governments that had never before acknowledged the existence of their deaf communities.

When people left The Deaf Way, there was a "glow." In a short week, so much had been learned, experienced, and accomplished by all who attended. For many people, the glow lingers.

This was expressed well by a deaf person who wrote us to say, "So many people left feeling very positive. When we left, we were very proud to be deaf and The Deaf Way reaffirmed it again and again."

The question for us now is how to translate this glow into a force that benefits deaf people around the world.

More Than Memories: The Deaf Way Sparks Worldwide Change for Deaf People

LYNNE MCCONNELL

Two years ago this summer, more than 6,000 people from eighty-one countries gathered in Washington, D.C., for The Deaf Way Conference and Festival, a first-of-its-kind event. They came together to share information about their language, culture, and history through both scholarly presentations and artistic expression. During the week-long occasion, participants attended presentations of more than 500 scholarly papers in meeting rooms and auditoriums in the Omni Shoreham Hotel in downtown Washington. Each evening, artistic events were performed on Gallaudet University's Kendall Green campus, including plays, storytelling, dancing, song signing, and a variety of other activities that focused on deaf people, their sign languages, and their cultures. The week-long, milestone event took more than two years to plan, with 300 people working to make it a reality, and cost about $1,500,000. Major sponsors for The Deaf Way were Ronald McDonald Children's Charities and AT&T. Substantial support was also received from the National Endowment for the Arts, the Coca-Cola Foundation, and the Mid-Atlantic Coca-Cola Bottling Company.

Just days after The Deaf Way Conference and Festival ended, its staff organizers began receiving letters of praise. In letter after letter, deaf people described the event as the happiest time of their lives and spoke of memories they would cherish forever.

But today, The Deaf Way has become much more than memories. It continues to make an impact on the lives of deaf people throughout the world. In many countries, deaf people have new communication systems, a new network of deaf friends, and an awareness that, as deaf people, they have the potential to attain levels of education, employment, and artistic expression equal to that attained by hearing people.

"The Deaf Way was sort of an outstanding exclamation point in terms of reaffirming the 'can do' attitude or positive contributions that deaf people and deaf groups can make for themselves," says Eli Savanick, director of the International Center on Deafness (ICD). "A remarkable number of places, people, and groups created very organized reporting procedures. People didn't just have a good time. People literally went back and reported on this. We've seen it in pictures in magazines, in the number of people asking for materials, and in the letters we get here."

This article, from the Summer 1991 issue of the periodical Gallaudet Today, *reports on some of the long-range effects The Deaf Way had on participants.*

The event had an effect on the Gallaudet community as well, says Jean Lindquist, coordinator of special projects with the Division of Development and formerly assistant coordinator for The Deaf Way. "The campus was united in making The Deaf Way succeed, and virtually every department was involved in the conference and festival," she says. "Students, faculty, staff, and alumni put in downright heroic efforts to make our international guests feel welcome."

The final product, says Lindquist, was a state-of-the-art event that was as accessible as possible to all participants, and one that set a new standard of accessibility for international meetings of deaf people.

The Deaf Way also helped introduce both technology and interpreters to some countries. "For most deaf Brazilians, the first time they ever saw a TDD was at The Deaf Way," says Renato Sindicic, who last May became the first student from that country to graduate from Gallaudet. "I told them, 'Buy it. It is important for you.'" Sindicic's friends were skeptical. It took some persuasion, but finally they bought TDDs. One friend, Roberto Pascucci, bought TDDs for himself, his parents, his wife's mother, and his sister. A few days after The Deaf Way, Pascucci told Sindicic that the people who bought TDDs were using them daily in Brazil. "[Pascucci's] very proud to show the other staff at the bank where he works how to use the TDD, and that he can get along without an interpreter," says Sindicic. "For the first time, he can have a private phone conversation with his wife or daughter. Now he's developing a directory of all the deaf TDD users in Brazil. I think he has about eighty names."

If it were not for The Deaf Way, says Sindicic, deaf people in Brazil would not have interpreters, either, or the limited captioning and interpreting they now have on television. Some deaf Brazilians are even trying to start a newsletter for the deaf community in Brazil. They also have increased their interaction with deaf people in Uruguay, Argentina, and Chile.

During the three years before The Deaf Way that Sindicic studied at Gallaudet University, no one from Brazil visited the campus, he says. Since The Deaf Way, however, Sindicic has given campus tours to many visiting Brazilians. "When I asked them how they know about Gallaudet, they say, 'We heard about The Deaf Way.'"

Diane Lopez came to The Deaf Way from Costa Rica, where she is coordinator of a group of instructors who teach Costa Rican Sign Language. This group, called LESCO, is sponsored by Gallaudet's international center in Costa Rica, located at the University of Costa Rica in San José. LESCO also receives funds from the Council on Rehabilitation in Costa Rica.

A deaf teacher of deaf children, Lopez presented her research on Costa Rican Sign Language at The Deaf Way and stayed on as an intern at the ICD for six months. "I got a lot of good ideas of what deaf children can do, and I was able to implement them at home," she says. "Before coming to The Deaf Way, I didn't realize how limited my scope was. The Deaf Way really expanded my vision of what deaf people can do."

Lopez showed her videotapes of the event to parents of deaf children in Costa Rica to demonstrate that deaf people can do anything, she says. She also convinced the Children's International Summer Vision program, which sponsors international children's camps, to include deaf children in their recreational and educational activities. Initially, she took four deaf children from Costa Rica to a camp in Canada. Lopez is planning an international camp in Costa Rica in December [1991]. Next year [1992], she will take a group of Costa Rican deaf children to a camp in France, and she is considering holding a second camp in Costa Rica. She is also trying to set up a branch of the World Recreation Association of the Deaf [see paper by Gross in Part Five of this volume] in her country and working with its national legislature to change the law that bans deaf people from driving cars.

"In Costa Rica and in many smaller countries, a few deaf people shoulder the responsibility for the whole deaf community," says Savanick. As one of only two people in Costa Rica who have university degrees, Lopez is one of these leaders. She teaches children all day, and at night she teaches sign language to parents and works on programs and activities for the deaf community.

"Often, those people burn out," says Savanick. "One very important thing The Deaf Way did was to re-light their fires."

Deaf people in France also seem to be moving toward achieving a better place for themselves, according to Rev. Brien McCarthy, Catholic chaplain at Gallaudet University's Northwest Campus and at The American University. Because of The Deaf Way, he says, they have seen how deaf people in the United States have acquired certain rights related to interpreters, both in terms of the certification process and in their right to require certain agencies to provide interpreters for them. "[French deaf people] now are looking for a way of implementing those same sorts of processes and making the government responsive to the needs of deaf people," McCarthy says.

McCarthy has been associated with deaf people in France since 1969, but his contacts there and the frequency of his trips have increased greatly since The Deaf Way, to five trips in less than two years. He also more frequently hosts groups of French deaf students coming to the United States.

In France, "There is definitely a feeling of solidarity with American deaf people that wasn't there before," says McCarthy. One French group videotaped extensive portions of The Deaf Way and then broadcast it on Saturday morning television in France. In October and in April of this year, McCarthy helped coordinate American visits for groups of deaf French students, teachers, and clergy. "All of these trips grew out of the experiences French people had at The Deaf Way," he says. French and American deaf people also took a ski trip together, which was based on relationships formed at The Deaf Way. In addition, a group of French educators of deaf people toured the Model Secondary School for the Deaf last fall in direct response to information from students who attended The Deaf Way.

When members of the National Federation of the Deaf in France asked the Fondation Franco-Americaine in Paris to help them go to The Deaf Way, the foundation subsidized their trip. In addition, its executive director, Michel Jaoul, became so interested in issues that concern deaf people that the foundation in Paris joined with the French-American Foundation in New York to set up a colloquium in Paris in October 1991. The purpose of the colloquium " 'Deaf People in Society: Education and Access' is to exchange ideas on a variety of topics related to deaf people in society and to lay groundwork for future collaboration between the two foundations," says Dr. Carol Erting, former program cochairwoman for The Deaf Way and director of Gallaudet Research Institute's Culture and Communication Studies Program. Each topic will have both French and American presenters. Both Erting and Harry Markowicz, an assistant professor of English at Gallaudet, are on the advisory board for the colloquium.

According to Michiko Tsuchiya of Japan, a Deaf Way Conference presenter [see paper in Part One of this volume], the more than sixty deaf Japanese people who attended The Deaf Way published a full report on the event for the deaf community in Japan. Those who attended were impressed that interpreting was provided in a number of sign languages, she says. "Last year, I witnessed that different ways of interpreting were introduced at a meeting for hard of hearing people—that is, Japanese Sign Language and Signing Exact Japanese. It was apparently inspired by The Deaf Way, because some of the Deaf Way participants coordinated the meeting."

Many Deaf Way participants also observed the advanced research into American Sign Language in the United States and felt that they must study Japanese Sign Language and get it recognized as a true language, says Tsuchiya. Last summer [in 1990], an almost national scale debate on improving the education of deaf students in Japan included support for using sign language for classroom instruction. "It was pointed out in some way that it is necessary to establish the deaf identity and deaf culture," she says, "because the majority of deaf people have not been aware of them. The Deaf Way has more or less indirectly affected these events in the past year."

The Deaf Way also made a lasting impression on Dr. Dilip Deshmukh of the Deaf School and Institute of Speech and Hearing in Ichalkaranji, India. Almost one year after the event, he wrote, "After The Deaf Way, I realized that sign language plays a vital role in the education, development, and rehabilitation of deaf people. However, in my country, the method of education is still strongly oral. I am trying my level best to convince [educators in my country] of the importance of sign language."

To that end, Deshmukh has written articles for Indian publications about The Deaf Way and the importance of sign language in the education and lives of deaf people. He has also given presentations at a number of meetings, including the International Conference of the Indian Association of Physical Medicine and Rehabilitation held in January 1991, and has started using Indian Sign Language at the Deaf School and Institute of Speech and Hearing in Ichalkaranji.

Deshmukh also is planning a collaborative project with the National Institute on Deafness and Other Communication Disorders [at the National Institutes of Health in Bethesda, Maryland, U.S.]. "We could do this only because I attended The Deaf Way," he says. He will continue his efforts "until deaf people in my country will be able to enjoy life like The Deaf Way."

This recognition of sign language, sparked and reinforced by The Deaf Way, involves even more than communication and education. Thirty-eight deaf theater groups offered to present their shows at the eleventh World Congress of the World Federation of the Deaf in Tokyo this summer [1991]. "In the past, the number of applying theaters of the deaf usually was somewhere from five to eight," says Dr. Yerker Andersson, president of the World Federation of the Deaf and a professor of sociology at Gallaudet. "Deaf people have now recognized the artistic potentialities of their sign language, which probably was a result of The Deaf Way."

The Rev. Brien McCarthy, too, witnessed this when he visited deaf theater groups in France and Singapore. The talk always went back to The Deaf Way, he says. The actors spoke of the vast exchange of ideas at The Deaf Way and their renewed confidence in their potential to create good theater productions.

Gallaudet University's History Department took interest expressed at The Deaf Way and developed the First International Conference on Deaf History, which was held at Gallaudet June 20 through 22, 1991. Among the countries represented at the conference were France, Germany, Italy, Russia, Spain, Iceland, Belgium, the Netherlands, Canada, Puerto Rico, and the United States.

Several countries that were represented at The Deaf Way have held their own national versions of the event. Among these were Canada and Australia. The Canadian Cultural Society of the Deaf presented Gallaudet University an award last February for its role in The Deaf Way.

Like the artistry produced by the deaf individuals and groups it inspired, much of the impact of The Deaf Way is visual. It is TDDs in countries where no one had them before; it is people who, rather than huddle together to hide their signs, now sign freely on the streets; it is the interpreters present at singing concerts for the first time.

But much more of the impact of The Deaf Way is subtle, with changes emerging without fanfare. The change can be seen in reports that a few staunch oralists in France, Italy, and India have modified their views on sign language. It can be found in a new strength and firmness in people's signs and more frequent and larger gatherings of deaf people. The impact is felt in the expressive signs describing what people saw at The Deaf Way, and in discussions about what they can do to make their country recognize the rights and needs of its deaf citizens. As Michiko Tsuchiya says, "The international event has revealed to us that there is nothing wrong with being deaf; rather, we have immense power in our own right and limitless potential for self-realization."

contributors

DANIEL ABBOU has for many years taught deaf students in bilingual education programs in France. He has also been involved in activities aimed at increasing hearing people's knowledge and appreciation of sign language, bilingual education, and deaf identity. He teaches at the Centre d'Expérimental Bilingue pour Enfants Sourds and is a communication specialist at the Centre d'Aide du Travail Jean Moulins.

MARIE-THÉRÈSE ABBOU was born deaf to a deaf family. Beginning in 1979, she was the first deaf professional to work in the first bilingual class for deaf students in France. She has taught French Sign Language (LSF) and nonverbal communication to hearing parents and professionals. She has participated in linguistic research on LSF and on language development among deaf children. Abbou is currently teaching deaf students in a bilingual program in Argenteuil.

VICTOR ABBOU taught French Sign Language (LSF) for seven years at the University of Paris and was an actor with the International Visual Theatre in Paris for eight years. Since the time of The Deaf Way, Mr. Abbou has been a full-time LSF instructor of student interpreters at SERAC (Sourds Entendents Recherche Action Communication).

ANTONIO CAMPOS DE ABREU, who is deaf, is a teacher of LIBRAS (Brazilian Sign Language) and has been involved for a number of years in deaf community work in his native Brazil. At the time of The Deaf Way, he was vice president of the National Federation for Education and Integration of the Deaf.

MARY JOYCELYN ADDO is a teacher of deaf students and a sign language interpreter. At the time of The Deaf Way, she was a national interpreter for the Ghana National Association of the Deaf.

ZAID ABDULLA AL-MUSLAT, who holds a doctorate in education, was General Secretary of the Department of Special Education in the Saudi Arabian Ministry of Education at the time of The Deaf Way. Today, he continues to hold this position.

DOUG ALKER was born in England and educated there in schools for the deaf that used both oral and manual systems of communication. He received a bachelor of science degree from London University and was employed for more than twenty years as a chemist with Imperial Chemical Industries. For two years he worked as a researcher for the BBC television program "See-Hear," a weekly program of news for British deaf audiences. He has been active in deaf theater and in organizations for deaf people on the local, regional, and national levels. At the time of The Deaf Way, Alker was Director of Community Services for the Royal National Institute for the Deaf in London. Alker is currently director of quality and development at the Royal National Institute for Deaf People in London.

LORNA ALLSOP, born deaf to a deaf family, has worked in television and video production for deaf viewers. British Sign Language is her first language. At the time of The Deaf Way she was conducting research at The Centre for Deaf Studies at the University of Bristol. She is currently studying lexical and grammatical features of International Sign as a research associate at the Centre.

DONALDA K. AMMONS, who is deaf, was chair of the United States team to the

World Games for the Deaf and Director of the Foreign Studies Program at Gallaudet University at the time of The Deaf Way.

YERKER ANDERSSON is serving his third term as president of the World Federation of the Deaf and is a Professor of Sociology at Gallaudet University. At the time of The Deaf Way, he had recently conducted a survey of national federations of the deaf in selected European countries. He also studied the local organizations of the deaf in Stockholm, Copenhagen, Amsterdam, Glasgow, Turnhout, Frankfurt, Prague, and Warsaw, which serve as focal points in the deaf community. His paper is based on that research, which was supported by the World Institute on Disability.

CAROL-LEE AQUILINE worked for four years as an actor with the National Theatre of the Deaf (NTD) before moving to Australia in 1982 to work as a guest actor and workshop leader with the Australian Theatre of the Deaf. She has directed and performed in numerous theater, television, and film productions. At the time of her presentation at The Deaf Way, she was artistic director of the Australian Theatre of the Deaf. She is currently manager of the National Advocacy Service of the Australian Association of the Deaf and continues to work in the theater, film, and television as both an actor and director.

ANTHONY J. ARAMBURO holds a Master's in American Sign Language Linguistics from Gallaudet University and has conducted research on sign language variation in the black deaf community. At the time of The Deaf Way, Mr. Aramburo was employed by the state of Louisiana as a rehabilitation specialist working with deaf students.

KATHLEEN SHAVER ARNOS, at the time of The Deaf Way, was director of the Genetic Services Center at Gallaudet University, a position she continues to hold. A unit of Gallaudet Research Institute, the Center provides genetic evaluation and counseling services to deaf people and their families.

GREGORIO JESUS JAÉN ARRABAL was born in Madrid and became deaf at the age of two. After studying in the Decorative Arts School in Madrid, he entered the Arts and Crafts School of Madrid, where he studied graphic design and illustration. His paintings have been exhibited in New York, Hong Kong, Madrid, and Seville. His presentation at The Deaf Way focused on his personal experiences as a deaf artist.

SACKEUS P. ASHIPALA, PROFELIUS DANIEL, MARIUS N. HAIKALI, NANGOLO ISRAEL, FESTUS T. LINUS, and HENOCK H. NIILENGE (all Deaf Namibians), plus their two hearing teachers, RAUNA N. HASHIYANAH and TIMONY F. HAIDUWAH, came to the United States from Africa to analyze and develop a dictionary of Namibian Sign Language (NSL), largely in anticipation of the independence of Namibia from South Africa, which indeed occurred in December 1989. (As of the publication date of this volume, Namibia has continued to be an independent country, and the NSL dictionary has been completed.) RUTH MORGAN is a South African who holds an M.A. in Linguistics from Gallaudet University. At the time of The Deaf Way, she had spent a year at the International Center on Deafness at Gallaudet working with the group.

DOUGLAS D. BAHL became profoundly deaf at the age of two. He graduated from Gallaudet University in 1974 and continued his education at the University of Minnesota. At the time of The Deaf Way, he was teaching high school courses (Deaf Studies, Journalism, Drama, English, and Social Studies) at the Minnesota State Academy for the Deaf (MSAD) in Faribault, where he was founder and president of the MSAD school museum. He also served on the Faribault Heritage Preservation Commission.

DON BANGS has written, produced, and directed numerous television and theater productions. At the time of The Deaf Way, he was Executive Director of Signrise Cultural Arts, a deaf performing arts organization in the San Francisco Bay area, and a Ph.D. candidate in Dramatic Art at the University of California at Berkeley. Since that time, he has completed his doctorate, occupied the Powrie V. Doctor Chair of Deaf Studies at Gallaudet University, and has been director of Gallaudet's Department of Television, Film, and Photography.

MAMADOU BARRY, a former member of the Parliament of Guinea, was a member of the United Nations Secretariat of the International Year of Disabled Persons. At the time of The Deaf Way, Mr. Barry was Officer-in-Charge at the Disabled Persons Unit of the United Nations Centre for Social Development and Humanitarian Affairs in Vienna. This Centre was later relocated in New York, where Mr. Barry is still Officer-in-Charge of the Disabled Persons unit.

ILDI BATORY was a second-generation deaf woman. A native of Hungary who later became a Danish citizen, Batory held a Ph.D. in Clinical Psychology from the University of Copenhagen. At the time of the conference, she was a member of the executive board for Danish film and video and chair of a deaf parents' organization. Several months after presenting at The Deaf Way, Ildi Batory died in an automobile accident.

GERALD BATEMAN, who is deaf, taught at the Rochester School for the Deaf for twelve years before becoming an instructional developer and assistant professor at the National Technical Institute for the Deaf (NTID) in 1985. At the time of The Deaf Way, in addition to his work at NTID, Dr. Bateman was an Ed.D. candidate at the University of Rochester, where he was also an adjunct faculty member in the UR/NTID Joint Educational Specialist Program. Dr. Bateman, who received his doctorate in 1990, is currently an associate professor and senior instructional developer at NTID.

ORLANDO BENALCÁZAR is a deaf leader from Quito, Ecuador. At the time of The Deaf Way, Benalcázar was president of the Silent Association of Ecuador (Asociacion Silenciosa Ecuatoriana).

BRITA BERGMAN is a professor in the Department of Sign Language, Linguistics Institute, University of Stockholm, Sweden. She is well known internationally as one of the pioneers of sign language research. Dr. Bergman is committed to deaf community-based research, and her work is carried out in partnership with members of the Swedish deaf community. For eight years, she was a member of the Communication Commission, Sign Language Section, of the World Federation of the Deaf, and has served on the editorial board of the International Journal of Sign Linguistics.

ASGER BERGMANN was born deaf to deaf parents. He was trained as a teacher in his native Denmark and later attended Gallaudet College. At the time of The Deaf Way, Bergmann was president of the Danish Association of the Deaf and president of the Commission on Interpreting of the World Federation of the Deaf. He was also a teaching consultant at The Center for Total Communication in Copenhagen.

RITVA BERGMANN was born deaf of deaf parents in Finland. She moved to Denmark as an adult and, in 1978, became the first deaf preschool teacher in that country. At the time of The Deaf Way, she was a teacher, a member of the World Federation of the Deaf Commission on Sign Language, and president of the Danish Association of the Deaf Commission on Sign Language. Ms. Bergman continues to teach Danish Sign Language at the Center for Total Communication in Copenhagen.

M. J. BIENVENU received a Bachelor of Arts in English and a Master's in Linguistics from Gallaudet University. She has extensive experience as an instructor in American Sign Language (ASL), has made numerous presentations on American Deaf culture and the linguistics of ASL, and has served as a sign model for instructional materials in ASL. She holds comprehensive certification from the Sign Instructors Guidance Network and a Reverse Skills certificate from the Registry of Interpreters for the Deaf (RID). She has served as chair of the Deaf Caucus of the RID and as regional representative of the Conference of Interpreter Trainers. At the time of The Deaf Way, Ms. Bienvenu was codirector of The Bicultural Center in Riverdale, Maryland, a position she continues to hold.

ANN BILLINGTON-BAHL, who was born deaf, is a graduate of Gallaudet University. At the time of The Deaf Way, she was an American Sign Language teacher at Faribault Senior High School in Faribault, Minnesota and at Mankato State University.

GUY BOUCHAUVEAU—deaf from birth—entertains and enlightens both deaf and hearing audiences. His presentations have played an important role in enhancing hearing people's awareness and appreciation of nonverbal communication and deaf culture. From the time of The Deaf Way to the present, Bouchauveau has worked at the Museum of Science and Industry in Paris, teaching deaf students and giving signed lecture tours to deaf and hearing adult visitors. He is currently second vice president of the French National Federation of the Deaf.

JOSETTE BOUCHAUVEAU was born profoundly deaf. She has both taught and done research on French Sign Language, and she has acted with the International Visual Theatre. At the time of The Deaf Way, she was Educational Director at the Academy of French Sign Language in Paris, a position she continues to hold.

BRIDGETTA BOURNE-FIRL attended the Maryland School for the Deaf and graduated from Gallaudet with a B.A. in Government in 1989. Bourne-Firl received a master's degree in administration and supervision from Gallaudet University in 1990 and has become coordinator of the Professional and Community Training Program at Gallaudet's National Academy.

PENNY BOYES BRAEM was born and educated in the United States and holds a Ph.D. in Psycholinguistics from the University of California. Dr. Boyes Braem taught in United States deaf education programs and conducted research on American Sign Language before moving to Basel, Switzerland in 1974. Formerly director of the Sign Language Interpreter Training Program in Lausanne, Switzerland, at the time of The Deaf Way she was director of the Center for Sign Language Research in Basel, a position she continues to hold.

ROBERT BUCHANAN was a Ph.D. candidate in American History at the University of Wisconsin, Madison, at the time of The Deaf Way. His doctoral dissertation focuses on the activities of deaf industrial workers and activists from the 1880s to the present. His paper evolved from research he conducted at the Gallaudet University Archives in the summer of 1988.

BEVERLY BUTTERS developed the Hearing-Impaired Studies Program at Centralia College in Centralia, Washington, where, at the time of The Deaf Way, she served as Associate Dean for Continuing Education.

FRANK CACCAMISE served as senior research associate and director of the Technical Signs Project at NTID at the time of The Deaf Way. He is codeveloper (with William Newell) of the Sign Communication Proficiency Interview, an assessment procedure used at a number of schools and institutions serving deaf people.

MIREILLE CAISSY received a Bachelor's in Special Education for children with learning disabilities from the University of Montreal in 1983. She served as vice president of the Quebec Center for Hearing Impairment, taught French to deaf students for four years, and helped organize interpreting services for deaf students attending postsecondary educational programs. Ms. Caissy received a Master's in Communication from the University of Quebec in Montreal in 1993.

ANA REGINA E SOUZA CAMPELLO, who is deaf herself, has worked for years on issues of concern to the deaf communities of Brazil. A teacher of LIBRAS (Brazilian Sign Language), Ms. Campello was President of the National Federation for the Education and Integration of the Deaf in Rio de Janeiro, Brazil at the time of The Deaf Way.

BREDA CARTY became progressively deaf beginning at the age of four. Born in Australia, she holds an M.A. in Education from Gallaudet University and has taught at the Learning Center for Deaf Children in Framingham, Massachusetts and the Victorian School for Deaf Children in Melbourne, Australia. At the time of The Deaf Way, Ms. Carty was a research associate with the Deafness Resources Project of the Brisbane College of Advanced Education, Brisbane, Australia. She is currently a research fellow at Griffith University in Brisbane, Australia.

ROGER CARVER, a graduate of Gallaudet University, holds an M.Ed. in Educational Psychology. At the time of The Deaf Way, Mr. Carver was editor of the Canadian Journal of the Deaf and coordinator of the Western Canadian Centre of Specialization in Deafness at the University of Alberta. Mr. Carver is currently Director of Programs and Services at the Deaf Children's Society of British Columbia in Vancouver.

JAMES CHIEN-MIN CHAO, deaf since the age of three, was engaged in graduate study at Gallaudet University at the time of The Deaf Way. He has subsequently completed his degree and is now the standing director of the Chinese National Association of the Deaf in the Republic of China. Responsible for training sign language instructors, he is the author of the book *Taiwan Natural Sign Language* and is conducting research on sign language and deaf education.

JOHN B. CHRISTIANSEN received his M.A. from the University of Wisconsin, Milwaukee and his Ph.D. from the University of California, Riverside. He has authored or coauthored a number of papers on issues related to deafness, such as the socioeconomic status of deaf people and the 1988 Deaf President Now protest, and was associate editor of the *Gallaudet Encyclopedia of Deaf People and Deafness*. Currently a professor of sociology at Gallaudet University, Dr. Christiansen had been a member of the Gallaudet faculty for twelve years at the time of The Deaf Way.

MICHAEL CLANCY was Director of the Adult Education Centre for Deaf and Hearing Impaired Persons (AEC) in Sydney, Australia at the time of The Deaf Way. He also was a coordinator of the Collection of Deaf History project, working within the terms of a cooperative agreement between the AEC and the New South Wales Association of the Deaf.

LARRY COLEMAN holds a Ph.D. in Communication. At the time of The Deaf Way, he was an associate professor in the School of Communication at Gallaudet University and project officer and administrator for the Annenberg/CPB Project of the Corporation for Public Broadcasting. Dr. Colemam has had extensive experience in the areas of storytelling, humor, and folklore.

JOSEPH COLLINS is a cofounder of Deaf Owl Films, a company that produces short TV films for deaf viewers. At the time of The Deaf Way, Mr. Collins was acting coordinator of the London Deaf Video Project and a volunteer committee member of the British Deaf Association Southern Regional Council.

MARIANNE COLLINS-AHLGREN was a doctoral candidate at the Victoria Uni-

versity of Wellington, New Zealand at the time of her presentation at The Deaf
Way. Her dissertation analyzed New Zealand Sign Language. During the past thirty
years, she has been interested in the language development of deaf children in the
United States, Singapore, South Africa, and Thailand and in the sign languages of
the deaf communities in these countries.

SERENA CORAZZA is from Trieste, Italy. She is the deaf child of deaf parents and
has been active in the Italian deaf community. A sign language researcher with
a focus on describing the linguistic structure of Italian Sign Language (LIS), she
spent the 1987–1988 academic year at Gallaudet University on a scholarship from
the Mason-Perkins Fund (a scholarship fund administered through the Fulbright
Commission). While there, she conducted two research projects on the structure
of LIS. She presented her research on classifier predicates in LIS at the conference
Theoretical Issues in Sign Language Research II in May of 1988.

JERRY COVELL attended the Maryland School for the Deaf and graduated from
Gallaudet with a B.A. in American Government in 1988. Covell is currently the
executive director of the Missouri Commission for the Deaf.

BARRY CROUCH is a contributor to the *Gallaudet Encyclopedia of Deaf People and Deafness*[1] and coauthor, with John V. Van Cleve, of *A Place of Their Own: Creating the Deaf
Community in America*.[2] At the time of The Deaf Way, he was a professor of history
at Gallaudet University, a position he continues to hold.

JEAN DAVIA was a law student and served as Director General of the Association of
Deaf Adults at the time of The Deaf Way. He was also involved in sporting events
and associations for deaf people. Mr. DaVia is currently working at a residence for
deaf students in Ottawa, Ontario.

J. S. DAVID holds an M.Ed. from Smith College. At the time of The Deaf Way, he
was the principal of the Nuffield School in Kaitadi, Sri Lanka, the only school for
deaf students and blind students in that country. He was also working on a signed
system of the Tamil language and a sign language dictionary.

JEFFREY DAVIS has worked as a counselor, interpreter, interpreter educator, and
researcher in the deaf community. At the time of The Deaf Way, he was a Ph.D. candidate in Educational Linguistics at the University of New Mexico and was teaching
in the Master's Degree program in interpreting at Gallaudet University. Dr. Davis
is currently teaching and conducting research at the University of Arizona.

CLARK DENMARK was working in the Deaf Studies Research Unit in the Department of Sociology and Social Policy at the University of Durham, England, at the
time of The Deaf Way. He is currently Director of Studies, Centre for Deaf Studies,
University of Bristol.

PATRICK DEVLIEGER is an anthropologist from Belgium who has studied attitudes toward disability in sub-Saharan Africa. At the time of The Deaf Way, he
was associate expert in special education with the UNESCO Sub-Regional Project
for Special Education in Eastern Africa. Mr. Devlieger is currently pursuing his
doctorate in anthropology at the University of Illinois, Champaign-Urbana.

STEPHEN DHALEE became deaf at the age of thirteen. A translator of Christian
literature and a teacher of deaf students, he has written a number of articles on

---

1 J. V. Van Cleve, ed., *Gallaudet Encyclopedia of Deaf People and Deafness* (New York: McGraw-Hill Book Company,
   Inc., 1987).
2 J. V. Van Cleve and B. A. Crouch, *A Place of Their Own; Creating the Deaf Community in America* (Washington, DC:
   Gallaudet University Press, 1989).

deafness. Mr. Dhalee is a member of the Dhaka Association of the Deaf and the Bangladesh National Federation of the Deaf.

TRUDE DIMMEL was general secretary of the Austrian Society for the Deaf, a position she continues to hold, at the time of The Deaf Way. Ms. Dimmel's husband, Peter Dimmel, is a well-known deaf sculptor. The Dimmels live in Lenz, Austria.

TANIS DOE is a deaf researcher in social policy and welfare. At the time of The Deaf Way, she held an M.S.W. in Policy and Administration and was a Ph.D. candidate in Educational Foundations at the University of Alberta, Canada. Dr. Doe was recently awarded her doctorate.

CATHERINE (KATY) DOWNS was a genetic associate with the Genetic Services Center at Gallaudet University at the time of The Deaf Way. Ms. Downs now resides in East Lansing, Michigan and holds certification from both the American Board of Medical Genetics and the National Registry of Interpreters for the Deaf. She continues to conduct research on the attitudes of Deaf adults toward genetic counseling.

HORST EBBINGHAUS and JENS HESSMANN, at the time of The Deaf Way, had completed a study of sign language interpreting in Berlin and were studying the relationship between German Sign Language and spoken German. They continue to conduct research on German Sign Language at the Free University of Berlin.

CHRISTINA EDENAS is a hearing educator born to deaf parents. She has worked as a teacher, interpreter, curriculum developer, and administrator in deaf education programs in Sweden. Ms. Edenas holds an M.A. in Deaf Education from Gallaudet University.

FRANCES ELTON was a course tutor in the University of Durham British Sign Language (BSL) Tutor Training Course. At the time of The Deaf Way, she was affiliated with the Deaf Studies Research Unit in the Department of Sociology and Social Policy at the University of Durham. Elton is currently a research fellow in sign language studies at the university and is the director of the BSL Tutor Training Course.

SHERYL EMERY became deaf from spinal meningitis at the age of fourteen. She is a graduate of Gallaudet University and holds an M.A. in Deafness Rehabilitation from New York University. She served as the first national executive director of the National Black Deaf Advocates, as a member of Michigan's State Mental Health Advisory Council for the Hearing Impaired, and on the staffs of United States Senators Dole and Richman. At the time of The Deaf Way, Ms. Emery was a rehabilitation counselor with the State of Michigan.

CAROL J. ERTING played important roles in conceiving and planning The Deaf Way Conference and Festival and in the creation of this volume. She holds a Ph.D. in cultural anthropology from The American University and an M.A. in Deaf Education from Northwestern University. Her research includes analyses of discourse among teachers, parents, and deaf children and cross-cultural research on deaf education. Since 1988, she has been director of the Culture and Communication Studies Program in the Gallaudet Research Institute at Gallaudet University.

ALBERTO PALIZA FARFAN, who became deaf at the age of twelve, has worked for many years for deaf associations in Lima, Arequipa, Huancayo, and Cusco, Peru. He is currently employed by the Department of Public Education in Cusco, where he is also director of the Christian Center for the Deaf. Paliza Farfan has been honored for his work as a sign language teacher in Peru.

JAMES J. FERNANDES is a former Chair of the Department of Communication Arts at Gallaudet University. At the time of The Deaf Way, he was a professor on the Gallaudet faculty and Director of the Gallaudet University Regional Center at Kapiolani Community College in Honolulu, Hawaii, positions he continues to hold. Dr. Fernandes holds a Ph.D. in Speech Communication from the University of Michigan.

CATHERINE (KITTY) FISCHER, at the time of The Deaf Way, was supervisor of the Learning Resources Center at the Model Secondary School for the Deaf in Washington, D.C., a position she continues to hold. She received her B.A. in Library Science and her M.S. in Educational Technology from Gallaudet University. One of her favorite pastimes is conducting genealogical research.

ANNA FOLCHI lives in Monza, Italy. At the time of The Deaf Way, she had spent a number of years studying Italian Sign Language and Deaf culture. She was affiliated with both the National Organization of the Deaf (Ente Nazionale Sordomuti) and the National Research Council (Consiglio Nazionale delle Ricerche). Currently, she teaches sign language, conducts workshops on Deaf culture, and continues her research on the history and culture of Deaf Italians.

YOLANDA RODRÍGUEZ FRATICELLI was born in Puerto Rico to a family with a history of deafness. She attended oral deaf schools and hearing schools in the United States, Germany, and Puerto Rico. At the time of The Deaf Way, she was employed with the Puerto Rico Department of Public Instruction teaching deaf children at the Rafael Hernandez School, and was working toward a master's degree at the University of Puerto Rico.

PHYLLIS FRELICH is well known for her portrayals of Sarah Norman in the original stage version of Children of a Lesser God and Janice Ryder in the television film "Love is Never Silent."

CARMEN VELÁSQUEZ GARCIÁ was president of the Association of the Deaf in Guayaquil, Ecuador at the time of The Deaf Way. She was also a member of the National Federation of the Deaf in Ecuador.

NELSON GARCIÁ was president of the Deaf Adult Society, "Fray Luis Ponce de León," at the time of The Deaf Way.

MERV GARRETSON was the coordinator of The Deaf Way Conference and Festival during the week-long event's final, sixteen-month planning and implementation phase. Born to a cattle ranching family in northern Wyoming, he became totally deaf from spinal meningitis at the age of five. He attended the Colorado School for the Deaf, Gallaudet College, the University of Wyoming, and the University of Maryland. Classroom teacher, school principal, university professor, and administrator, he has been active in local, state, national, and international organizations of the deaf over the last half century.

BARBARA GERNER DE GARCIA was a doctoral student at Boston University, conducting research on Dominican Sign Language and working to develop and implement a program for Spanish-using deaf children in the Boston public schools. Since The Deaf Way, Dr. Gerner de Garcia has completed her doctorate and is currently assistant professor in the Department of Educational Foundations and Research at Gallaudet University.

BILL GRAHAM became deaf as an adult. He is a cofounder of the Association of Late Deafened Adults (ALDA). At the time of The Deaf Way, Mr. Graham was Life Sciences Editor for The World Book Encyclopedia, where he also taught courses in sign language.

BRUCE GROSS is a deaf teacher of deaf high school students and the founder and president of the World Recreation Association of the Deaf. He received a B.A. from

Gallaudet University and M.A.s in Special Education and in Administration and Supervision from California State University at Northridge.

ANWAR SHAMSHUDIN KHAWAJI HAJI is a hearing businessman who volunteers his time to help improve the life of deaf people in Pakistan. At the time of The Deaf Way, Shamshudin was Vice President of the Ismailia Organization of the Deaf, Karachi, Pakistan. He graduated from the University of Karachi in 1972.

EDWARD T. HALL is an anthropologist, author, and lecturer. He received his Ph.D. in Anthropology from Columbia University in 1942, and has written and lectured extensively on the subjects of culture and communication. He is a partner in Edward T. Hall Associates, a consulting firm specializing in intercultural communication. Dr. Hall is currently working on the second volume of his book *An Anthropology of Everyday Life*.

STEPHANIE A. HALL had recently completed her Ph.D. through the Department of Folklore and Folklife at the University of Pennsylvania at the time of The Deaf Way, and she was an archivist at the American Folklife Center of the Library of Congress, where she continues to work. The material presented in her paper is based on research conducted for her dissertation, an ethnographic study of folklore in a Philadelphia, Pennsylvania deaf social club.

HURST HANNUM is a scholar and attorney with extensive experience in the areas of human rights and international law and the author of several books on international human rights. At the time of The Deaf Way, Mr. Hannum was a Jennings Randolph Peace Fellow with the United States Institute of Peace, associate professor at the Fletcher School of Law and Diplomacy at Tufts University, and adjunct professor at the American University College of Law.

BRITTA HANSEN has worked as a psychiatric social worker with deaf clients and as director of the Center for Total Communication in Copenhagen. She has conducted research on Danish Sign Language and has developed sign language training programs for teachers, parents, and interpreters.

VICKI HANSON holds a Ph.D. in Cognitive Psychology from the University of Oregon. At the time of The Deaf Way, she was a member of the research staff of the Exploratory Education Systems Group in the Research Division of IBM, a position she continues to hold. Dr. Hanson's current work involves developing multimedia educational materials.

HÉLÈNE HÉBERT, who holds a Bachelor's in Education, taught deaf children at the elementary school level and also taught adult literacy for three years. She served as president of the Quebec Cultural Society of the Deaf from 1986 to 1988 and was responsible for a project that compiled a dictionary of LSQ. Ms. Hébert is currently teaching deaf students in a special class at a high school called Polyvalente LucienPage.

TOMAS HEDBERG, who was born deaf, has a bachelor's degree in Swedish Sign Language and Swedish as a second language from the University of Stockholm. At the time of The Deaf Way, he was working for the Department of Sign Language in the University of Stockholm's Institute of Linguistics. His research was also supported by the Swedish National Association of the Deaf.

ULF HEDBERG, a native of Sweden, has been deaf since birth. A former teacher, Hedberg holds an M.A. in Archives from Sweden. When he presented his paper at The Deaf Way, he was an archivist at the Gallaudet University Archives, a position he continues to hold.

GREG HLIBOK attended the Lexington School for the Deaf. He became president of the Gallaudet Student Body Government (SBG) on March 1, 1988, the very day of the first rally in support of a deaf president. Within days, he found himself at the head of the largest student movement in Gallaudet's history. At the time of The Deaf Way, Hlibok was completing a B.A. in Government at Gallaudet. Hlibok is now a fourth-year law student at Hofstra University in New York.

DOMINIQUE HOF was trained as a speech therapist. She was a coauthor of the first volume of the dictionary of French Sign Language (LSF) published in 1983 by the International Visual Theatre. (B. Moody, A. Vourc'h, D. Hof, and M. Girod, *La Langue des Signes;* Tome 1; Paris: Ellipses, 1983). She helped establish the Centre d'Education Bilingue pour Enfants Sourds. Hof helped create *Vu,* a magazine about visual-gestural communication. She cofounded SERAC (Sourds Entendents Recherche Action Communication), where she directs interpreter and cultural programs.

CELINA RIBEIRO HUTZLER, the hearing mother of a deaf child, was an associate professor of anthropology at the Federal University of Pernambuco in Brazil at the time of The Deaf Way. She has conducted research involving deaf children and adults. In 1989, she was engaged in planning the first public school for deaf students in the state of Pernambuco.

LEO JACOBS was born in San Francisco and attended the California School for the Deaf in Berkeley. He received B.A. and M.A. degrees from Gallaudet College (now Gallaudet University) and was the first holder of the Powrie V. Doctor Chair in Deaf Studies there. Mr. Jacobs is the author of *A Deaf Adult Speaks Out.*

KATHY JANKOWSKI, a graduate of Gallaudet University, holds a Ph.D. in Public Communication from the University of Maryland. She has worked as a counselor at the Louisiana School for the Deaf, as a program director for Deafpride, Inc., and as a sign communication specialist at the National Technical Institute for the Deaf in Rochester, New York. At the time of The Deaf Way, Dr. Jankowski taught in the School of Communication at Gallaudet. Currently, she is superintendent of the Central North Carolina School for the Deaf.

ROBERT E. JOHNSON is an anthropologist and linguist interested in the study of sign languages and their place in deaf communities. He holds a B.A. in Psychology from Stanford University and a Ph.D. in Anthropology from Washington State University. At the time of The Deaf Way, Dr. Johnson was chair of the Department of Linguistics and Interpreting at Gallaudet University. He is currently head of the linguistics division of that department.

ALAN JONES was born in South Africa and attended St. Vincent's School for the Deaf there. At the time of The Deaf Way, he was a computer programmer/systems analyst with the University of Durban and a teacher of sign language. Mr. Jones was also a member of the Natal Association of the Deaf and the Executive Committee of the South African National Council for the Deaf.

I. KING JORDAN gained international recognition in March 1988 when he became Gallaudet University's eighth president, the institution's first deaf president in its then 124-year history. A former faculty member in Gallaudet's Department of Psychology, with a Ph.D. in Psychology from the University of Tennessee, Jordan had already become—by the time of The Deaf Way—a very public figure, a spokesperson for the Deaf community, and a symbol of deaf people's potential.

RAGHAV BIR JOSHI was born in Nepal in 1963 and attended the school for the deaf in Kathmandu. After studying at the Multipurpose Training Centre for the Deaf in New Delhi, India, he returned to Nepal and started a business in photography and video rentals. He has served on the executive committee of the Kathmandu Association of the Deaf since its establishment in 1980 and at the time of The Deaf Way held the position of vice president.

THOMAS KANE was born and grew up in New York City, where he experienced a variety of educational settings: a Catholic school for deaf students, an oral school, a hearing school, and a residential school for deaf students. He graduated from Gallaudet University in 1986 with a B.A. in Communication Arts. At the time of The Deaf Way, he was a member of the Capital Metro Rainbow Alliance, a Washington, D.C. area organization of gay and lesbian deaf people. Subsequent to The Deaf Way, Mr. Kane, who has served as historian of the Rainbow Alliance, was honored for his fifteen years of service to that organization.

BARBARA KANNAPELL, born deaf to Deaf parents, is a sociologist and consultant on Deaf culture and bilingual education who has conducted workshops in the United States and abroad. Dr. Kannapell has had a long association with Gallaudet University as a research assistant and linguistics specialist. She served as chairperson of the President's Council on Deafness and is also cofounder of Deafpride, Inc., a community-based organization in Washington, D.C. that advocates for the rights of Deaf people and their families. At the time of The Deaf Way, Dr. Kannapell was president of Deafpride, Inc.

ALEXIS KARACOSTAS is a psychiatrist who has been working with deaf clients since 1989. He organized the Bicentennial Exhibition, "La Pouvoir des Signes," held in Paris in 1990. The author of many papers concerning deaf history, deaf education, and the relationship of medical ethics to deaf people, Karacostas is president of the Association GESTES (Groupe d'Etudes Spécialisé Thérapies et Surdités).

MICHAEL A. KARCHMER has been Dean of Graduate Studies and Research at Gallaudet University since 1988. He played an important role in the promotion, planning, and implementation of The Deaf Way and was instrumental in making the creation of this volume possible.

LIISA KAUPPINEN is well known for her work in support of equal rights for deaf people, recognition of sign languages, and bilingualism. At the time of The Deaf Way, she was Executive Director of the Finnish Association of the Deaf and General Secretary of the World Federation of the Deaf.

JANE F. KELLEHER, who has been deaf since birth, holds a Ph.D. in Comparative Literature from the University of Iowa. At the time of The Deaf Way, she was Coordinator of the Sign Language Interpreter Training Program at the University of Hawaii. She had formerly served as Director of the American Sign Language and Interpreting programs at Northeastern University and as Chair of the Department of Sign Communication at Gallaudet University. In January 1990 Dr. Kelleher was appointed Director of the Statewide Center For Students with Hearing and Visual Impairments, becoming the first deaf woman in the United States to head a school for deaf students.

NANCY KIRKENDALL was Program Assistant to the Associate Dean for Continuing Education at Centralia College at the time of The Deaf Way.

PADDY LADD, a deaf activist, is a cofounder of the National Union of the Deaf, an advocacy group in London, England. He is also a cofounder of the London Deaf Video Project and has directed and produced deaf television programs. He has been employed in deaf social and community work and has been a constant advocate of reform in deaf education. In 1992–1993, Ladd held the Powrie Doctor Chair of Deaf Studies at Gallaudet University. He is currently pursuing his doctorate at the University of Bristol in England.

VENETTA LAMPROPOULOU was born in Greece and received her higher education in the United States. She taught for eight years at the Lexington School for the
Deaf in Jackson Heights, New York. At the time of The Deaf Way she was director
of the National Institute for the Deaf in Athens, Greece and a lecturer in special
education at the University of Patras. Dr. Lampropoulou holds a Ph.D. in Deafness
Rehabilitation from New York University.

HARLAN LANE is the author of countless articles and several books related to deafness, including *When the Mind Hears, The Wild Boy of Aveyron,* and *The Mask of Be-
nevolence.* A former Powrie V. Doctor Chair of Deaf Studies at Gallaudet University,
at the time of The Deaf Way Dr. Lane was a professor of psychology at Northeastern University, where he currently holds the position of Distinguished University
Professor.

ARTHUR LeBLANC was a board member of the Office of Handicapped Persons of
Quebec, the Quebec Center of Hearing Impairment, the Canadian Counsel of Hearing Impairment, and the Committee for Interpreting Services (under the Secretary
of State of Canada) at the time of The Deaf Way. He was also editor of *Voir Dire* (the
French Deaf Review). From the time of The Deaf Way, Mr. LeBlanc has worked for
the newspaper *La Presse* in addition to his work on *Voir Dire* and for a number of
deaf associations.

SCOTT K. LIDDELL holds an M.A. and Ph.D. in Linguistics from the University
of California at San Diego. His work in American Sign Language syntax, segmental
description of ASL signs, and morphological processes in ASL has led to a long-
standing interest in linguistic issues in deaf education. He is currently chairperson
of Gallaudet's Department of Linguistics and Interpreting.

GUDULA LIST is Professor of Psychology at Cologne University. At the time of
The Deaf Way, her main areas of study were neuropsychology, psycholinguistics,
developmental language disorders, and deafness. It should be noted that the conference occurred two years prior to the unification of East and West Germany; hence
the "German Democratic Republic" alluded to in the third paragraph was soon to
be reunited with its western neighbor.

GÜNTHER LIST, an author and researcher, holds a Ph.D. in history. At the time
of The Deaf Way, he was preparing a project, later carried out at the Humboldt
Universität, on the history of German and French oralism entitled The Deaf Person
and His "Educability." Dr. List is currently writing a book on the same subject.

KAREN LLOYD was born in Australia and became deaf at the age of eight. In the
summer of 1989, she was senior librarian with the State Library of New South
Wales and the editor of *Sound Off,* a magazine publishing the works of deaf writers.
She has devoted much of her career to encouraging deaf people to enrich existing
literature to include stories (in writing and on videotape) by deaf people.

CEIL LUCAS holds a Ph.D. in Sociolinguistics from Georgetown University. She is a
professor in the Department of Linguistics and Interpreting at Gallaudet University,
where she has taught and conducted research since 1983. Dr. Lucas is the editor of
the book *The Sociolinguistics of the Deaf Community* (New York: Academic Press, 1989)
and has coauthored (with Clayton Valli) the book *Language Contact in the American
Deaf Community* (New York: Academic Press, 1992).

MYRIAM A. DE LUJÁN was a language therapist who had worked for twelve
years in special education programs for deaf children in Venezuela. At the time
of The Deaf Way, she was working toward a master's degree in Linguistics at the
University of the Andes, where she was investigating the acquisition of literacy in
deaf children through exposure to visual rather than oral language.

RODERICK J. MACDONALD, who is deaf-blind, was president of the American Association of the Deaf-Blind, Inc., a Silver Spring, Maryland-based organization, at the time of The Deaf Way.

MARY MALZKUHN received her B.A. and M.A. from Gallaudet University in American Studies and her Ph.D. from the University of Maryland in Public Law and American Government. At the time of The Deaf Way, she taught in the Department of Government at Gallaudet and served on the University's Judiciary Board. Dr. Malzkuhn is currently chair of Gallaudet's Department of Government and serves as a human rights expert for the World Federation of the Deaf.

SUSAN M. MATHER was a full-time researcher at the Gallaudet Research Institute (GRI) in its Center for Studies in Education and Human Development at the time of her presentation at The Deaf Way. She has published articles in *Sign Language Studies* and *The Sociolinguistics of the Deaf Community* (edited by C. Lucas). She now has a Ph.D. in Sociolinguistics from Georgetown University, Washington, D.C., and is conducting research in the GRI's Culture and Communication Studies Program.

LYNNE MCCONNELL has been a writer in Gallaudet's Department of Publications and Production since 1987. Her article appeared in the Summer 1991 issue of *Gallaudet Today* two years after The Deaf Way Conference and Festival.

JEAN-FRANÇOIS MERCURIO was Director of the Bilingual Education Program for Deaf Students at a public school in Poitiers, France at the time of The Deaf Way. He taught French Sign Language (LSF) and French within the bilingual education program. He taught sign language to parents as well as to children. He died in 1990.

BETTY G. MILLER was born in Chicago of deaf parents. She is well known for her visual representations of the deaf experience. She taught art at Gallaudet University for eighteen years and was artist in residence at the Model Secondary School for the Deaf in Washington, D.C., in 1986. At the time of The Deaf Way, she was working as both a professional artist and as an alcohol and drug abuse counselor. Dr. Miller is currently coordinator of projects of The Second Chance program at Deafpride, Inc., working with deaf people in recovery from alcohol and drug abuse in the Washington, D.C., area. She continues to work as a deaf artist.

MARGERY S. MILLER, former coordinator of the Family Life Program at the National Academy at Gallaudet, was the interim director of the National Academy at the time of The Deaf Way. She subsequently served as Director of the Counseling and Development Center at Gallaudet's School of Preparatory Studies. Dr. Miller is currently an associate professor in the Department of Psychology at Gallaudet.

RACHID MIMOUN, who is deaf, was a French Sign Language (LSF) instructor in a bilingual class in Châlon-sur-Saône, France, at the time of The Deaf Way. In addition, he taught LSF to hearing adults and trained deaf adults to teach LSF. Since 1982 Mr. Mimoun had been active in efforts to gain recognition for LSF, participating in several deaf associations in France and in international conferences on deafness, bilingualism, and sign language research. He is currently teaching at l'Ecole de la Malgrange in Nancy, France. He is first vice president of the French National Federation of the Deaf.

MARILYN MITCHELL has been a teacher, interpreter, actress, writer, and editor, working at schools for deaf students, a vocational technical institute, and NTID, where she was an Assistant Professor in the Department of Support Services Education at the time of the conference.

JEAN MODRY, who is deaf, has been a teacher of deaf students and is a trained addictions counselor. Her professional experiences include one-on-one counseling, group sessions, and conducting substance abuse education and prevention seminars. Modry is currently an associate executive director of the Chicago Hearing Society.

VALERIE MOON was special needs consultant with the State Library of New South Wales, Australia at the time of The Deaf Way. She was responsible for establishing library services for people with disabilities within the State Library and encouraging the development of these services in the ninety-seven public library systems of the state of New South Wales. Ms. Moon is currently manager of the Public Libraries Branch of the State Library of New South Wales.

RANDOLPH MOWRY is a researcher in the areas of social support for deaf persons, social networks in the deaf community, and linking of formal and informal networks to provide appropriate services for deaf people. He holds a Ph.D. in Community Psychology. In the summer of 1989, he was an assistant research professor with the University of Arkansas Research and Training Center on Deafness and Hearing Impairment, where he is still employed.

ASSUMPTA NANIWE was pursuing a doctorate at the Université Libre de Bruxelles, Brussels, Belgium at the time of The Deaf Way. Her dissertation focuses on the situation of deaf infants in Burundi and on necessary steps to improve the integration of deaf children into Burundi society. Naniwe is the hearing mother of a deaf child. She is currently an associate professor at the University of Burundi and the head of an organization promoting the education and welfare of deaf children in Burundi.

KEVIN NOLAN attended the Clarke School for the Deaf, the National Technical Institute for the Deaf (NTID), and Western Maryland College. He has taught at the Maryland School for the Deaf, the Beverly School, NTID, the Clarke School, and the Sunshine Cottage School. Nolan was the first person born deaf to be elected to the city council of Northampton, Massachussetts. Mr. Nolan is currently a guidance counselor at the Clarke School for the Deaf, cocurator of the Clarke Museum, and a member of the National Association of the Deaf's National Commission on Equal Educational Opportunities for Deaf Children.

JOSEPHINE O'LEARY is the deaf founder of the Art and Cultural Society for the Deaf in Dublin, Ireland. She also founded the *Irish Deaf Journal*. At the time of The Deaf Way, she was a researcher and presenter for "Sign of the Times," a television program for deaf people in Ireland.

CAROL O'REILLY was a member of the Board of Directors of the Australian Association of the Deaf and honorary secretary of the Queensland Association of the Deaf at the time of The Deaf Way.

DOLORES OGLIA was research coordinator at the National Technical Institute for the Deaf (NTID) at the time of The Deaf Way. She has coproduced instructional videotapes and coauthored sign manuals in a variety of technical and specialized areas.

EMMANUEL OJILE was born in Nigeria and became deaf at the age of seventeen. He attended Gallaudet University, receiving an M.A. in Developmental Psychology. At the time of The Deaf Way, he was on leave from his position as Assistant Professor of Special Education at the University of Jos, Nigeria, to complete a Ph.D. in Educational Psychology at the University of Alberta, Canada. After receiving his doctorate, he returned to the University of Jos, where he is a senior lecturer in special education.

ALEXANDER D. OKYERE was born in 1940. He lost his hearing in 1965. He taught deaf Ghanaian students from 1966 to 1979, at which time he enrolled at Gallaudet University in Washington, D.C. He received a B.A. in Economics from Gallaudet in 1982 and an M.Ed. from Western Maryland College in 1983. After returning to Ghana, he led a revival of the nearly defunct Ghana National Association of the Deaf and worked to mobilize parents and educators of deaf children to create greater awareness of the plight of the Ghanaian deaf people. At the time of The Deaf Way, Mr. Okyere taught Economics and English at the Secondary/Technical School for the Deaf in Mampong-Akwapim, Ghana.

VALDEKO PAAVEL graduated from Tallinn Pedagogical Institute in 1982 as a teacher of manual training and drawing. After teaching in a vocational school for eight years, he joined the Department of Sociology at Tartu University in 1986 as a scientist. In 1987 Mr. Paavel graduated from Tartu University as a psychologist. At the time of The Deaf Way, he was employed in the Laboratory of Sociology of Delinquent Behavior, studying the history, social composition, system of education, culture, and language of the Estonian deaf population. At that time, Estonia was a republic of the Soviet Union. In 1991, it became an independent country.

CAROL PADDEN received a Ph.D. in Linguistics from the University of California, San Diego (UCSD). She is coauthor, with her husband Tom Humphries, of *Deaf in America: Voices from a Culture* (1988). At the time of her presentation, she was Associate Professor in the Department of Communication at UCSD, where she continues to serve on the faculty. Dr. Padden's research interests include language learning and literacy in young deaf children.

JAROSLAV PAUL, at the time of The Deaf Way, served as the first secretary of the Union of the Disabled, Prague, Czechoslovakia. In 1993, Czechoslovakia was formally divided into two separate countries, the Czech Republic and the Slovak Republic.

LOURDES PIETROSEMOLI is a Venezuelan linguist. At the time of The Deaf Way, she was coordinator of the Postgraduate Program in Linguistics at the University of the Andes and was conducting research on Venezuelan Sign Language.

PAOLA PINNA is a member of Studio Informazione Lingua Italiana dei Segni (SILIS), a group of deaf and hearing researchers based in Rome. At the time of The Deaf Way, she was collaborating on an experiment in bilingual education at the State Residential School of the Deaf in Via Nomentana.

SUSAN PLANN holds a doctorate in Romance Linguistics and has published articles on Spanish syntax. At the time of The Deaf Way, she was an associate professor of Spanish and Portuguese at the University of California, Los Angeles (a position she continues to hold) and was working on a history of deaf people in Spain.

ANNE T. QUARTARARO is a historian specializing in modern French history and European social history. At the time of The Deaf Way, she was an Associate Professor of History at the United States Naval Academy, Annapolis, Maryland, where she continues her research on the social history of the French deaf community.

LAURA PAGLIARI RAMPELLI, who had been a teacher at the Via Nomentana school, was employed at the Istituto di Psicologia of the Consiglio Nazionalle delle Ricerche (Italian National Research Council) at the time of The Deaf Way. Laura Rampelli died in October 1991.

LISA RENERY worked for the Mason Perkins Fund as an intern at the time of The Deaf Way.

ORAZIO ROMEO, who is deaf, attended Gallaudet University from 1986 to 1987 on a scholarship from the Mason Perkins Fund (administered through the Fulbright Commission). In the summer of 1989 he was a research assistant with the Mason Perkins Fund in Rome.

PAOLO ROSSINI is an Italian Sign Language instructor. He followed in the footsteps of his father and grandfather in attending the Via Nomentana school. Mr. Rossini is also a member of SILIS.

ROBERT G. SANDERSON graduated from Gallaudet College in 1941 and later earned an Ed.D. from Brigham Young University. He spent twenty years with the Center for the Deaf in Utah as a rehabilitation counselor, coordinator, and director. A past president of the National Association of the Deaf, Dr. Sanderson was, at the time of the conference, a member of the Gallaudet University Board of Trustees and Chairman of the Board of the National Fraternal Society of the Deaf.

MIGUEL SANTILLÁN was first vice president of the provisional board of the first Deaf Assembly of Ecuador. At the time of The Deaf Way, he was assistant to the Fray Luis Ponce de León Society for Deaf Adults and provisional president of the National Federation of the Deaf of Ecuador.

AGGREY SAWUKA was born in northern Tanzania. In 1986 he became the first deaf student to attend the University of Dar-es-Salaam. In 1987 he was elected Chairman of the Tanzania Association of the Deaf.

MIREN SEGOVIA, profoundly deaf since the age of three, was president of the Unión de Sordos de Guipúzcoa (Deaf Union of Guipúzcoa) in the Basque region of Spain at the time of The Deaf Way.

MEHER SETHNA, also from India, received an M.A. in counseling from Gallaudet in 1984. Since then, she has worked as a counselor, interpreter, researcher, and advocate for deaf people in her native city, Bombay. At the time of The Deaf Way, she was a research associate at the Jung National Institute on Deafness, Bombay.

MARYMARGARET SHARP-PUCCI became deaf after a head injury. At the time of the conference, she was a faculty member in the Department of Communicative Disorders at Northern Illinois University and Project Director at the Rehabilitation Services Administration Institute on Deafness. She is now associate director of administrative affairs at the Shock Trauma Institute, Loyola University Medical Center.

ANN SILVER is an author, journalist, and film/television analyst affiliated with "Silent News." She holds a B.A. in Commercial Art from Gallaudet University and an M.A. in Graphics Media from New York University. She has exhibited her work in the United States, France, Sweden, and Japan, and has made television appearances on ABC's "World News Tonight," PBS's "Deaf Mosaic," the Swedish Educational Broadcasting Corporation, and NHK, the Japanese Broadcasting Corporation. Ms. Silver is a recipient of the Gallaudet University Outstanding Alumnus of the Year award (1978), a Japan-United States Friendship Commission Fellowship, and the New York Society of the Deaf's Cultural Arts Leadership Award. Ms. Silver is currently Art Scholar-in-Residence at the Washington State Arts Commission in Seattle, Washington.

JANIE SIMMONS was a doctoral candidate at the Graduate School of Education, Harvard University, at the time of The Deaf Way. Ms. Simmons is currently completing her dissertation on the social construction of AIDS in the Puerto Rican community of Roxbury, Massachusetts.

ROBERT SIMMONS was born deaf. He attended St. Vincent's School for the Deaf in Johannesburg, South Africa. He holds a Ph.D. in Neuroanatomy and at the time of The Deaf Way was an assistant professor and senior lecturer in the Department of Anatomy and Human Biology, University of the Witwatersrand, Johannesburg. A member of the Executive Committee of the South African Council for the Deaf, Dr. Simmons was also working with the Human Scientific Research Council on Sign

Language Development. He is now director of the Witwatersrand Sign Language School in Johannesburg.

JEANETTE SLONE became deaf as a child. She holds a B.A. in Social Work from Gallaudet and has worked as an educational advisor and case advocate. At the time of the conference, Ms. Slone served as project coordinator for a parenting program serving deaf clients.

PASCAL SMITH was born deaf to deaf parents in 1966. He has two deaf sisters. He went to a residential school for the deaf, then worked for a while as a plumber. Later, he became an "educateur" (a vocation similar to that of a dormitory counselor) at a residential school. At the time of The Deaf Way, he was an instructor at a bilingual class at Chalon-sur-Saône. He also taught French Sign Language (LSF).

RACHEL SPENCE is currently working as a lecturer in Deaf Studies at The Centre for Deaf Studies at the University of Bristol. Her main focus of interest is in BSL linguistics. Her research for her Ph.D. dissertation is on the role of fingerspelling in BSL.

LYNN STIRLING received her B.A. in American Studies from Gallaudet and her M.Ed. in Deafness from Western Maryland College. She taught preschool-age children at the Kendall Demonstration Elementary School for nine years. At the time of The Deaf Way, she was a teacher of social studies at the Model Secondary School for the Deaf in Washington, D.C., where she continues to teach today.

WILLIAM STOKOE, professor emeritus of Gallaudet University, holds a Ph.D. in English from Cornell University and was Chair of the English Department at Gallaudet College when he began his ground-breaking research on American Sign Language. In 1960, he published the first linguistic study of any sign language, *Sign Language Structure*, in which he identified American Sign Language as a complete language with a structure independent of a spoken language. In 1965, with Dorothy Casterline and Carl Croneberg, he published *A Dictionary of American Sign Language*. Through these and other works he virtually created the field of sign language linguistics. He has edited the professional journal, *Sign Language Studies*, since 1972.

RACHEL STONE received a B.A. in Art History from Gallaudet University and an M.Ed. in Deaf Education from Western Maryland College. She taught preschool-age children at the Kendall Demonstration Elementary School in Washington, D.C. for seven years. A program cochair of The Deaf Way, Ms. Stone became assistant superintendent at the Indiana School for the Deaf in 1990. She is currently pursuing a doctorate in Special Education Administration at Gallaudet University.

SAMUEL SUPALLA is deaf from a deaf family. His research ranges from theoretical aspects of signed language development to language planning and policy issues. He has done extensive research on manually coded English and its impact on language development of deaf children. At the time of The Deaf Way, he was a doctoral candidate at the University of Illinois at Urbana-Champaign, majoring in Educational Policy Studies. He is currently director of Sign Language Studies in the Division of Special Education and Rehabilitation at the University of Arizona in Tucson.

TED SUPALLA is a second-generation deaf person. At the time of The Deaf Way, he was Assistant Professor of Linguistics in the Department of Foreign Languages, Literatures, and Linguistics at the University of Rochester. Dr. Supalla is currently an Associate Professor of Linguistics at the University of Rochester.

ADOLPHE SURURU was Minister of Education for the Republic of Burundi, with offices at Buyenzi College in Bujumbura, Burundi, at the time of The Deaf Way.

KAMPOL SUWANARAT began his studies in an experimental school for deaf people in Thailand that later became the first formal school for deaf people in that country. A graduate of the Poh Chang Commercial Art College in Bangkok, Mr. Suwanarat taught art in the School for the Deaf for fifteen years. He has served as Chairman of the Center for Alumni of Schools for the Deaf and as a member of the governing board of the Council of Disabled Persons in Thailand. At the time of The Deaf Way, he had served as the General Manager of the National Association of the Deaf in Thailand (NADT) since its creation in 1984. Mr. Suwanarat is a recipient of the annual National Award for Outstanding Disabled Citizen in Thailand.

ROBERTA THOMAS has long been active in United States organizations of parents of deaf children. She founded the Action Alliance of Parents of Deaf Children in Philadelphia and developed and directed Project Hope, a home intervention program through which deaf adults and parents of deaf children offer help to other parents of deaf children. At the time of The Deaf Way, she was executive director of the American Society of Deaf Children. She is currently director of alumni and parent relations at Beaver College in Glenside, Pennsylvania.

MICHAEL TILLANDER is the hearing parent of a deaf child. At the time of The Deaf Way, he was an active member of a Finnish association of parents of deaf children.

MARIUS ROCK TITUS, one of nine deaf members in a family of thirteen, was born in Benin. He was the first deaf student from French-speaking Africa to graduate from Gallaudet University. Mr. Titus holds an M.S. from Gallaudet in Instructional Design and has trained teachers of deaf students in seventeen African countries. At the time of The Deaf Way, he was coordinator of the United Nations/Namibia Leadership Training Program at the International Center on Deafness at Gallaudet. Mr. Titus is currently an instructor in the Department of Mathematics and Computer Science and a lecturer in the Department of Foreign Languages and Literatures at Gallaudet University.

REGINA TOOM was trained as a teacher of deaf students and at the time of The Deaf Way, she worked as an interpreter for the Estonian Union of the Deaf and was conducting research on Estonian Sign Language in the Department of Sociology at Tartu University. At the time of The Deaf Way, Estonia was a republic of the Soviet Union; in 1991, it became an independent country.

ALFREDO TORO, former president of the Fray Luis Ponce de León Society, was treasurer of the Pre-Confederation of Organizations of Persons with Disabilities in Ecuador and coordinator of the Mano a Mano Project. He is currently vice president of the National Federation of the Deaf of Ecuador (FENASEC).

BERNARD TRUFFAUT publishes a journal concerning deaf history: *Les Cahiers de l'Histoire des Sourds*. He has taught at a school for deaf students in Orléans, France and has worked in job retraining programs for unemployed deaf adults. Currently, he conducts workshops in schools for deaf students, sensitizing young deaf people to deaf history. Truffaut is the adjutant general secretary of the French National Federation of the Deaf.

MICHIKO TSUCHIYA is a native of Tokyo, Japan. She graduated from the School for the Deaf in Ichikawa-shi, which is affiliated with the University of Tsukuba, and received a B.A. from Gallaudet College in 1969. Since the time of The Deaf Way, she has been an assistant for the Association of Educational Research for the Deaf at the School for the Deaf at the University of Tsukuba.

JAMES TUCKER, a 1981 Gallaudet graduate, was Director of Admissions at Gallaudet at the time of The Deaf Way. He was an instructor in the English Department at Gallaudet from 1985 to 1989 and taught at the California School for the Deaf—Fremont from 1983 to 1985. From 1981 to 1982 he worked as an ASL researcher in the Salk Institute for Biological Studies in La Jolla, California. He is now superintendent of the Maryland School for the Deaf.

CLAYTON VALLI has a Ph.D. in Linguistics and American Sign Language (ASL) Poetics from Union Institute. Since obtaining his Master's in Linguistics from Gallaudet University's Department of Linguistics and Interpreting, he has taught and conducted research on ASL and ASL poetry at Gallaudet. Dr. Valli has coauthored (with Ceil Lucas) the book *Linguistics of American Sign Language* (Washington, DC: Gallaudet University Press, 1992).

ADOLF VAN DEN HEUVEL was born deaf of deaf parents and is fluent in Flemish Sign Language as well as Spanish Sign Language. At the time of The Deaf Way, he was a member of Madosa, the deaf club of Antwerp, Belgium.

MADAN VASISHTA, a native of India who became deaf at the age of eleven, came to the United States in 1967 to attend Gallaudet College. He received B.S., M.A., and Ph.D. degrees from Gallaudet and taught at the Kendall Demonstration Elementary School, which is on the Gallaudet campus. At the time of The Deaf Way, he was associate principal at the Texas School for the Deaf. Later he became superintendent of the Eastern North Carolina School for the Deaf.

GILES VERLET taught English Literature at The Catholic University in Paris and was Dean of the Modern Language Faculty at Essec Business School before becoming president of a large interpreting service for foreign workers and their families in France. He was a cofounder of SERAC (Sourds Entendents Recherche Action Communication) in 1987 and is its current president.

VIRGINIA VOLTERRA is the author of many publications on language and deafness. At the time of The Deaf Way, she was a senior researcher at the Istituto di Psicologia in Rome, Italy, a position she continues to hold.

AGNÉS VOURC'H trained as a speech therapist and linguist; she has worked with deaf children since 1973. With the International Visual Theatre she helped create a dictionary of French Sign Language (LSF) in 1983 and 1986. (B. Moody, A. Vourc'h, D. Hof, and M. Girod, *La Langue des Signes*; Tomes 1 and 2; Paris: Ellipses, 1983 and 1986). Since 1979 she has taught general linguistics to deaf professionals and to student interpreters at SERAC (Sourds Entendents Recherche Action Communication). She is currently the director of a school for deaf students in Paris, called CELEM.

GUNILLA WÅGSTRÖM-LUNDQVIST attended the Brigitta School for the Deaf in Örebro, Sweden and the Blockhusudden High School for the Deaf in Stockholm. She received a degree in textile art and design from the National College of Art, Craft, and Design in Stockholm. She later studied production at the Drama Institute in Stockholm and anthropology, literature, and sign language at the University of Stockholm. From 1970 to 1977, she was a member of the Silent Theater (except for the period 1974–1975, when she was with the National Theatre of the Deaf in Connecticut). At the time she delivered her plenary presentation at The Deaf Way, she had worked as a television producer at the Swedish Educational Broadcast Company for five years. She is still working with the Swedish Educational Broadcast Company.

LARS WALLIN is the first deaf Ph.D. candidate in the Department of Sign Language, Linguistics Institute, University of Stockholm. His linguistic research on Swedish Sign Language is highly respected by sign language researchers throughout the world. In 1987, he was invited to give a plenary address to the X World Congress of the World Federation of the Deaf in Helsinki, Finland, and in 1988 he presented one of the keynote addresses at the International Conference on Theoretical Issues in Sign Language Research in Washington, D.C. He is a member of the board of the International Sign Linguistics Association and an active member of the Swedish deaf community, on both the local and national level.

LINDA WARBY, a member of the New South Wales Association of the Deaf, was born deaf of deaf parents. She was a residential worker at the North Rocks School for the Deaf and Blind and later taught sign language classes for deaf adults. At the time of The Deaf Way, Ms. Warby was a coordinator and principal interviewer of Australia's Bicentennial Collection of Deaf History.

KATHLEENA WHITESELL is an experienced teacher, administrator, and interpreter. At the time of The Deaf Way, she was Assistant Professor and Coordinator of the Teacher Education Program at Lenoir-Rhyne College and doctoral candidate at the University of Cincinnati. Dr. Whitesell has completed her doctorate and is still employed at Lenoir-Rhyne College

JONNA WIDELL was born in Denmark, a hearing child in a deaf family. She holds the Danish equivalent of a Ph.D. in Sociology and has been active for years in the deaf community as a teacher, interpreter, and lecturer. Since The Deaf Way, Dr. Widell has published a number of articles on deafness in Scandinavia. She recently produced a bilingual (Danish Sign Language and Danish) package of print and video instructional materials on the subject of Danish deaf culture.

BENCIE WOLL is a linguist who pioneered research on British Sign Language (BSL). For many years Director of The Centre for Deaf Studies at the University of Bristol, she is currently running Bristol's Access for Deaf students initiative. Her current research includes studies on sign language acquisition in children of deaf families and work with Lorna Allsop on International Sign.

GLENDA ZMIJEWSKI is a graduate of the North Carolina School for the Deaf and holds both a B.A. and an M.A. from Gallaudet University. Ms. Zmijewski has taught manual communication and ASL at community colleges and lectured on communication issues and on the history of deaf education. She is currently teaching at the Indiana School for the Deaf.

HEIKO ZIENERT became deaf at an early age. He continues to be employed at the Center for German Sign Language and Communication of the Deaf, Hamburg, as a researcher, a teacher of sign language and interpreting, and a lecturer on German Sign Language.

ABRAHAM ZWIEBEL, who was born and educated in Israel, is a psychologist who works with deaf and hard of hearing people. From 1983 to 1985 he was International Visiting Scholar at the Gallaudet Research Institute, Gallaudet University. At the time of The Deaf Way, Dr. Zwiebel was head of the Special Education Program at Bar Ilan University in Ramat Gan, Israel. Dr. Zwiebel is currently a visiting professor at the Ontario Institute for Studies in Education in Toronto.

Index

Page numbers in italics indicate illustrations; *t* indicates a table